D A

A B

ALGEBRA 2

and Trigonometry

ALGEBRA 2
and Trigonometry

John Benson
Evanston Township High School
Evanston, Illinois

Sara Dodge
Evanston Township High School
Evanston, Illinois

Walter Dodge
New Trier High School
Winnetka, Illinois

Charles Hamberg
Illinois Mathematics and
Science Academy
Aurora, Illinois

George Milauskas
Illinois Mathematics and
Science Academy
Aurora, Illinois

Richard Rukin
Evanston Township High School
Evanston, Illinois

 MᴇL McDougal, Littell & Company

Evanston, Illinois
New York   Dallas   Sacramento   Columbia, SC

Reviewers

Agnes B. Bailey
Sacramento High School, Retired
Sacramento, California

Judy Bush
Countryside High School
Clearwater, Florida

Dr. Jean Reddy-Clement
State Mathematics Supervisor
Louisiana Department of Education
Baton Rouge, Louisiana

Carol Forman
Catoctin Senior High School
Thurmont, Maryland

Dr. Terry Parks
Director of Mathematics, K-12
Shawnee Mission School District
Shawnee Mission, Kansas

We would like to thank the many teachers and students that field tested this book over an entire school year, 1989-1990. Their suggestions, comments, and criticisms helped to shape a final product we are proud to publish.

ISBN 0-8123-5868-6

Copyright © 1991 by McDougal, Littell & Company
Box 1667, Evanston, Illinois 60204

92 93 94/15 14 13 12 11 10 9 8 7 6 5 4

CONTENTS

Benjamin Banneker

Black Heritage USA 15c

HANDBOOK 726

A Letter to Students

Welcome to second-year algebra! As high school teachers, we find mathematics enjoyable, challenging, useful, and exciting. We have written this book in the hope that you will share these feelings.

In first-year algebra, you learned a great deal. For many students, a review of these ideas is necessary before new, more challenging topics can be mastered. We have tried to incorporate review into the presentation of new material so that you can review and extend your earlier learning as quickly as possible. You will therefore spend the year learning, reviewing, and retaining what you learn.

In Chapter 1, you will encounter a classic problem and approach it in a variety of ways. Problem solving is a process rather than an answer. We all learn by trying to solve problems. We can solve some problems quickly. Others take time, several tries, and often some frustration. We learn from what we try, and we learn from our mistakes.

We have written this book for you. We want you to be able to read it and use it as a reference. When you work independently, read the text. Look up information. Use the examples and the sample problems. Ask questions. Share questions and ideas with your teacher. Talk to your classmates. Mathematics can help you learn how to learn. We hope your experience this year learning mathematics will be rewarding and exciting.

Let us tell you about some parts of the book.

Part One: Introduction

explains concepts and skills. Examples show these ideas in practice.

Part Two: Sample Problems

applies the information from Part One. The sample problems, along with the examples, are models you can refer to when you solve the Exercises and Problems sections.

Part Three: Exercises and Problems

is where you practice and really learn the concepts and skills of algebra. This is where you learn to be a problem solver, one of the most important tasks you have this year. We have tried to make these exercises and problems worthwhile. In each section you will find problems that

▲ *practice the ideas in today's lesson*

▲ *review the ideas from yesterday's lesson, last week's lesson, and last month's lesson and apply these ideas to the current topic*

▲ *introduce ideas you will learn tomorrow or next week or even later*

Thus, you will learn concepts over days, weeks, and months so that by the end of the year, all these different concepts that seemed puzzling when you first saw them will be firmly integrated in your understanding. To give you an idea of how problem sets combine practicing, reviewing, and introducing concepts, we have labeled the problems in Section 2.4.

At the end of each chapter, you will find:

CHAPTER SUMMARY *of ideas, vocabulary, and skills*
REVIEW PROBLEMS
CHAPTER TEST

In addition to the sixteen chapters of the book, there are two components you will find useful.

SHORT SUBJECTS

These topics can be a review for many students, as in the case of Exponents and Factoring, or enrichment, as in the case of Mathematical Induction.

HANDBOOK

This section is included as a quick reference for topics that are treated in many Algebra 1 courses.

Good luck. We wish you well and hope that by the end of this year you will share some of our excitement about mathematics.

John Benson   Charles L. Hamberg

Sara H. Dodge   George Milauskas

Walter Dodge   Richard Rukin

CHAPTER

1 PROBLEM SOLVING

Can you identify the complex patterns in this textile from ancient Peru (c. A.D. 800)?

INTRODUCTION TO PROBLEM SOLVING

Our society depends more and more on mathematics—in the sciences, in medicine, in business, in government, in the military, in city planning, in transportation. In fact, it is hard to find a field in which mathematical skills and ideas are not important. This book will help you expand your knowledge of mathematics and develop your problem-solving ability.

Five main themes are emphasized throughout this book.

I. Functions
II. Graphing and Modeling
III. Applications
IV. Problem Solving
V. Communicating Mathematics

You will find that a scientific calculator is an important tool for carrying out complex calculations. You will also see some ways in which computers and graphing calculators can make your work more interesting, efficient, and productive.

The Handshake Problem

Solving any problem involves both a *process* and an *answer*. The process—the way you approach the problem and the method you use to find an answer—can be the most interesting and important part of a solution. We encourage you to try solving problems in a variety of ways. By experimenting with different approaches, you can learn a great deal of mathematics.

Now let's look at a problem.

The Handshake Problem

Professor Hill had 25 students in her first-period class. On the first day of class, she asked them to shake hands and introduce themselves to one another. When they were finished, she asked the students, "How many handshakes have just been exchanged?"

In this chapter, your mission will be to explore a number of ways of solving Professor Hill's problem. Along the way, you will apply the techniques you discover to other sorts of problems. You will also discover that it is important to be able to explain why a solution works.

A Way of Solving the Problem

One way to solve Professor Hill's handshake problem is to ask a group of 25 people to shake hands, keeping a record of the number of handshakes. Keeping track of the handshakes, however, can be difficult unless we develop an organized procedure. The following are three of the possible ways of organizing the handshakes.

Method 1

Person 1 can shake hands with each of the others, for a total of 24 handshakes. Then person 2 can shake hands with each of the remaining 23 people, person 3 can shake with each of the remaining 22, and so on. There will be $24 + 23 + 22 + \ldots + 4 + 3 + 2 + 1$, or 300, handshakes in all.

Method 2

Person 2 (P_2) shakes with person 1 (P_1).	1 handshake
P_3 shakes with P_2 and then P_1.	$1 + 2$ more = 3 shakes
P_4 shakes with P_3, then P_2, then P_1.	$3 + 3$ more = 6 shakes
P_5 shakes with $P_4, P_3, P_2,$ and P_1	$6 + 4$ more = 10 shakes
P_6 shakes with $P_5, P_4, P_3, P_2,$ and P_1.	$10 + 5$ more = 15 shakes

.
.
.

P_{25} shakes with P_{24} through P_1. $276 + 24$ more = 300 shakes

Again, the total is 300 handshakes.

Method 3

We can choose any convenient kind of symbol and set up a *model* of the handshakes. At the right is a model in which the 25 letters A, B, C, . . . , Y are used to represent the 25 students. In the model, each handshake is indicated by a pair of letters. Again, the result is 300.

By using an orderly pattern, we can be sure that we have counted the handshakes without missing any.

```
AB   BC   . . .   VW   WX   XY
AC   BD   . . .   VX   WY
AD   BE   . . .   VY
AE   BF   . . .
AF   BG   . . .
AG   BH   . . .
 .    .
 .    .
 .    .
AX   BY
AY
```

$24 + 23 + \ldots + 3 + 2 + 1$
= 300 handshakes in all

Problem Set

1 John must go to court to explain what happened in an accident involving his car and a car driven by Rodney Hott. How might John re-create the events for the judge, showing what led to the accident?

2 A new design for a shopping center was developed by Archie Teck. What could he do to help a possible backer understand his idea?

3 There are eight high schools in the Skyway Athletic Conference. How many games must be scheduled for each school's team to play every other conference team

    a One time?   **b** Two times?   **c** n times?

4 In a classroom, a row of four seats is to be occupied by four students—Ann, Bob, Carlos, and Dai. Use a model to decide

    a In how many ways the four students can be seated in the four seats

    b In how many of these arrangements Carlos will be in the first seat

5 A large square is to be covered with smaller, 1-inch squares in a variety of colors. When the larger square is covered, no row, column, or main diagonal may contain squares of the same color.

    a How many distinct arrangements are possible if the large square is 3 by 3 inches and three of the small squares are red, three are white, and three are blue?

    b Find a possible arrangement if the large square is 4 by 4 inches and there are four red, four white, four blue, and four green 1-inch squares.

6 Copy the diagram shown.

    a How many dots are in the 10-by-10 graph?

    b Remove a main diagonal. How many dots are in the remaining diagram?

    c How many dots are in the lower triangular portion of the new diagram?

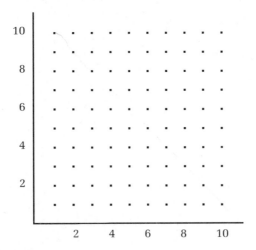

GRAPHIC SOLUTIONS

Objective

After studying this section, you will be familiar with

■ Using a graph to model a problem

Part One: Introduction

Graphing is a powerful method of organizing information. The handshake problem can be modeled by a graph in which each ordered pair (x, y) represents a handshake between person x and person y. For example, the ordered pair (6, 5) represents a handshake between person 6 and person 5.

In Professor Hill's class of 25 students, the value of x and the value of y can range from 1 to 25. There are 625 (that is, $25 \cdot 25$) points on the graph.

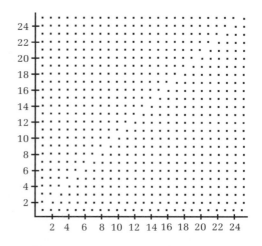

The model is not yet correct. Ordered pairs in which $x = y$, such as (1, 1), must be eliminated, since no one shakes his or her own hand. When these points are removed, there are $625 - 25$, or 600, points left.

Since the ordered pairs (6, 5) and (5, 6) represent the same handshake, we do not need both points. By eliminating all such duplicates, we divide the number of points in half.

There are 300 points left, so there is a total of 300 handshakes. Compare this graph with the model for Method 3 in the preceding section.

Now consider the following problem.

Paul's Pizza Parlor offers a choice of two styles of pizza—thick and thin crust—and four toppings, one topping per pizza—mushroom, sausage, onions, and green peppers. How many different pizzas can be ordered?

To solve this problem, we can use a graphing technique known as a *tree diagram.* By counting the number of branches at the end of the tree, we can conclude that there are eight choices.

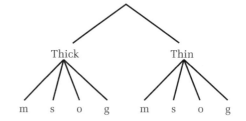

Part Two: Sample Problem

Problem

The path of a rumor can be found by recording who tells the rumor to whom. Suppose that Alice and Greg always tell each other. Bill always tells Doug and Alice. Carol always tells Fran and Greg. Helen and Doug always tell each other. Greg always tells Doug. Helen always tells Carol.

In order to spread a rumor completely, who should be told first? Who will be the last to know?

Solution

In this case we will use a *directed graph,* also known as a *digraph.* Arrows show the directions in which information flows. Notice that Fran receives but does not pass on information and that Bill passes on information but does not receive it from any other member of the group. Therefore, the only way to ensure that Bill will hear the rumor is to tell him. By following the arrows, we can verify that the rumor will eventually reach all the others in the group. Fran will be the last to know.

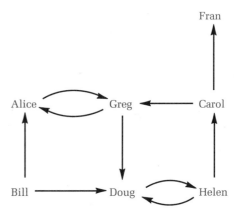

Part Three: Exercises and Problems

1 Paul owes Quincy, Ruth, and Sara $1 each. Ruth owes Quincy and Paul $2 each. Sara owes Ruth and Tom $3 each. Tom owes Ruth $4.

   a Draw a digraph and label each arrow with the amount of money owed.

   b If each person starts with $10, pays all that he or she owes, and receives all that is owed to him or her, how much money will each have?

2 By graphing ordered pairs, develop a general formula for the number of handshakes exchanged by any number n of people.

3 The Travelers planned to travel from their home in Madison, Wisconsin, to Las Vegas, Nevada. Terry Traveler researched several routes, shown in the diagram. The time estimates (in hours) are taken from a road atlas.

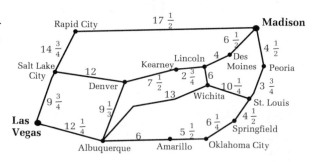

  a Which is the fastest route from Madison to Las Vegas?
  b What is the estimated travel time for that route?
  c Suppose the Travelers decide to visit relatives in Denver on the way. What is the fastest route to Las Vegas via Denver?

4 Rae Sponsibal is in charge of staffing the refreshment stand for school sporting events. There will be ten such events, and Rae has a staff of five workers. She needs two persons to run the stand at each event, and she wants each person to work the same number of events. Create a working schedule for the five people.

5 A digraph is shown. A path can be identified by listing, in order, the points it passes through—thus, p_4p_3, $p_1p_2p_1$, and $p_1p_2p_5p_3$ are three possible paths.

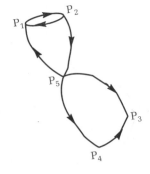

  a Find the shortest path from p_1 to p_4.
  b Is there a path that passes through all five points? If so, find it. If not, explain why not.
  c Is there a path that passes through all five points and then returns to the starting point? If so, what is it? If not, explain why not.

6 Four jobs need to be done, and four workers are available. The chart shows how long each worker takes to complete each job. If each job is to be assigned to a different worker, how should the jobs be assigned so that the total number of working hours is minimized?

	Job 1	Job 2	Job 3	Job 4
Joel	3 hr	4 hr	2 hr	3 hr
Noel	4 hr	2 hr	3 hr	2 hr
Zoel	3 hr	3 hr	2 hr	2 hr
Roel	1 hr	3 hr	2 hr	3 hr

GEOMETRIC MODELING

Objective

After studying this section, you will be familiar with
- Using geometric models in the solutions of problems

Part One: Introduction

In order to find the solution to a problem, we often relate the problem to a model. In Section 1.2, we used graphing to model problems. A geometric diagram is another useful type of model.

For Professor Hill's problem, imagine that the 25 people are 25 points on a circle and think of each handshake as a chord of the circle. Twenty-four chords end at each of the 25 points, so the number of chords might seem to be 25(24), or 600. However, since each chord has 2 endpoints, we have counted each chord twice. The number of chords is really $\frac{1}{2}(24 \cdot 25)$, or 300.

Another geometric model of the handshake problem is a polygon with 25 vertices connected by diagonals. The vertices represent the people. Each of the sides and each diagonal of the polygon represents a handshake.

To use this model, we apply a formula from geometry—the number of diagonals in a polygon with n sides is equal to $\frac{n(n-3)}{2}$. Therefore,

Total number
of segments
(handshakes) = number of diagonals + number of sides

$$= \frac{n(n-3)}{2} + n$$

$$= \frac{n^2 - 3n + 2n}{2}$$

$$= \frac{n^2 - n}{2}$$

In our problem $n = 25$, so the number of handshakes is $\frac{25^2 - 25}{2}$, or 300.

Part Two: Sample Problem

Problem   Can a person walk across each of the seven bridges shown in the diagram without crossing over any bridge twice? (This is a famous eighteenth-century problem concerning seven bridges in the city of Königsberg, East Prussia, now Kaliningrad, U.S.S.R.)

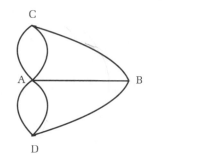

Solution   We can create a geometric model known as a **network**. Each segment represents a bridge, and each lettered point represents a land region. The problem is to trace the entire network without lifting your pencil from the page and without tracing any segment twice. By starting at each point in turn and trying possible paths, you will find that this is impossible.

Part Three: Exercises and Problems

1 Find the number of diagonals in a polygon with 25 sides.

2 Another general solution to the handshake problem is suggested by the diagrams. (A general solution is one that will work with any number of handshakes.) Use the diagrams to develop a general formula for the number of handshakes.

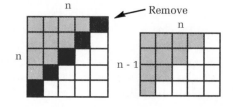

3 Six people are divided into two three-person teams for a singles tennis tournament.

  a How many games must be played for each of the people to play each of the others?
  b Suppose each person on the first team is married to a person on the second team. How many games will be played if spouses may not play each other?
  c How many games will be played if members of the same team may not play each other?

4 Four numbers are placed in squares. The sum of the numbers in the first row is 6. The sum of the numbers in the second row is 12. The sum of the first column is 10, and the sum in the second column is 8. What might the four numbers be?

5 See whether you can draw each of the networks shown without lifting your pencil from the paper. You must not go over any of the segments more than once or miss any segment. Try to think of a strategy that you can use to draw such diagrams. Three of these cannot be drawn. Why not? How might you tell just by looking at the network whether it can be completely traced? (Hint: Try counting the segments that meet at each point of intersection. Where must a successful path begin?)

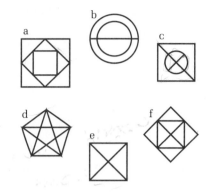

6 Ten baseball teams are in a play-off. How many games will they play if

  a Each team plays every other team once?
  b Each team plays every other team twice?

7 In the network shown, arrows indicate the directions of travel from point to point. List the number of ways in which it is possible to go from A to each indicated point.

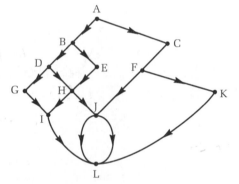

a B	**b** D	**c** E
d G	**e** H	**f** I
g C	**h** F	**i** J
j K	**k** L	

8 a Show how to place 8 checkers on an 8-by-8 checkerboard so that each row, column, and main diagonal contains exactly 1 checker.
  b Show how to place 16 checkers on a checkerboard so that exactly 2 checkers will be in each row, column, and main diagonal.

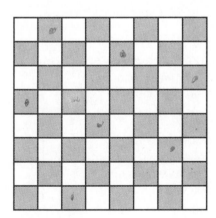

1.4 FINDING A PATTERN

$$\text{Sigma} \quad \sum_{k=5}^{35}(k-4)$$

Objectives

After studying this section, you will be familiar with
- How examining simpler cases can lead to a solution of a problem
- How a computer can be used to simulate a problem

Part One: Introduction

Looking at Simpler Cases

When a problem involves a complicated situation, as the handshake problem does, a common problem-solving strategy is to look at simpler cases, find a pattern, and then apply that pattern to solving the original problem.

Let's look at the handshake problem for two, three, four, or more people.

With two people, there is one handshake.
Adding a third person adds two handshakes.
Adding a fourth person adds three handshakes.
If a fifth person is added, there will be four more handshakes.
If a sixth person is added, there will be five more handshakes.

.
.
.

If an nth person is added, there will be $n - 1$ more handshakes.

Thus, for n people,

Total handshakes = $1 + 2 + 3 + 4 + \ldots + (n - 1)$

We can write this sum more briefly in *sigma notation* (so called because the Greek letter sigma, Σ, is used to stand for "sum"):

$$\sum_{k=2}^{n}(k - 1)$$

This expression means "the sum of all the numbers represented by $k - 1$ when k is each whole number from 2 to n inclusively." It is a general expression for the number of handshakes exchanged by any number of people.

For Professor Hill's 25 students the number of handshakes is

$$\sum_{k=2}^{25} (k-1)$$

$$= (2-1) + (3-1) + (4-1) + (5-1) + \ldots + (25-1)$$

$$= 1 + 2 + 3 + 4 + \ldots + 24$$

$$= 300$$

Computer Simulation

Many of our solutions of Professor Hill's problem have involved repetitious work. This sort of work is just right for a computer. A computer can carry out a large number of operations in a very short time and can generate a large set of data so that patterns can be observed and analyzed.

By itself, a computer does not know how to solve problems. We need to develop a step-by-step process, called an *algorithm*, that the computer can use to solve the problem we give it. The computer can then repeat the process as many times as we want for whatever input we choose.

The BASIC program that follows uses the system that we called Method 1 (see page 4). If you have access to a computer, enter the program and run it for N = 6, N = 25, and N = 50. (Before running it for the 50-person problem, delete line 70 so that time is not spent waiting for the computer to print every handshake.)

```
 10 REM ----------------THE HANDSHAKE PROBLEM----------------
 11 REM N = Number of people shaking hands
 12 REM P1 = First person involved in handshake
 13 REM P2 = Second person involved in handshake
 14 REM NS = Total number of handshakes exchanged by all people
 15 REM ------------------------------------------------------------
 20 PRINT "Enter the number of people shaking hands==>";
 30 INPUT " ", N
 40 LET NS = 0
 50 FOR P1 =1 to N - 1
 60 FOR P2 = P1 + 1 TO N
 70 PRINT P1; "-- shakes hands with --"; P2
 80 LET NS = NS + 1
 90 NEXT P2
100 NEXT P1
120 PRINT "The total number of handshakes is: "; NS
130 END
```

How is the algorithm used in this program similar to the sigma-notation expression for the general handshake problem?

Part Two: Sample Problem

Problem   Find the value of $\displaystyle\sum_{k=1}^{100}(2k-1)$.

Solution   Adding 100 numbers would take a long time. Let's look at some simpler cases and try to find a pattern.

$$\sum_{k=1}^{1}(2k-1) = (2\cdot 1 - 1) = 1$$

$$\sum_{k=1}^{2}(2k-1) = (2\cdot 1 - 1) + (2\cdot 2 - 1) = 4$$

$$\sum_{k=1}^{3}(2k-1) = (2\cdot 1 - 1) + (2\cdot 2 - 1) + (2\cdot 3 - 1) = 9$$

$$\sum_{k=1}^{4}(2k-1) = (2\cdot 1 - 1) + (2\cdot 2 - 1) + (2\cdot 3 - 1) + (2\cdot 4 - 1) = 16$$

Notice that each value is a perfect square—the first is 1^2, the second is 2^2, and so forth. We might conclude that the answer to the original problem is 100^2, or 10,000. At this point, we are only making a reasonable guess. Later in this book, you will learn how to prove that the guess is in fact correct.

Part Three: Exercises and Problems

1 Find the next two numbers in each sequence and tell what pattern you used to find them.

a 1, 3, 5, 7, 9, 11, . . .
b 1, 4, 7, 10, 13, 16, . . .
c 0, 3, 8, 15, 24, 35, 48, 63, 80, . . .
d 1, 2, 4, 7, 11, 16, 22, . . .
e 1, 2, 4, 8, 16, 32, 64, 128, . . .
f 1, 1, 2, 3, 5, 8, 13, 21, 34, 55, . . .

2 Find the first five terms in each sequence described.

a The first term is 7. Each term is 3 less than twice the previous term.
b The nth term is equal to $2 \cdot 2^{n+3}$.

3 In any group of 367 people you will find at least 2 people with the same birthday. Explain why this is true.

4 Find each sum.   **a** $\displaystyle\sum_{k=3}^{11}(2k-5)$ **b** $\displaystyle\sum_{k=1}^{6}k^2$

5 Big Foot has ten pairs of socks in his drawer. Each pair is a different color. The socks are not paired, and the light bulb in the room is out. How many socks does Mr. Foot need to pull out of the drawer to be sure that at least two of the socks match?

6 Find the next two rows in the following pattern.

```
          1
        1   1
      1   2   1
    1   3   3   1
  1   4   6   4   1
1   5  10  10   5   1
```

7 The set {1, 3, 6, 10, 15, 21, 28, 36, 45, 55, 66, . . .} is called the set of *triangular numbers.*

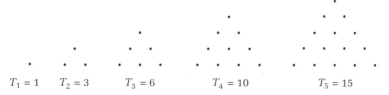

$T_1 = 1$ $T_2 = 3$ $T_3 = 6$ $T_4 = 10$ $T_5 = 15$

a Find the sums $T_1 + T_2$, $T_2 + T_3$, $T_3 + T_4$, and $T_4 + T_5$ and look for a pattern.

b Make a list and a diagram of the first five *square numbers.*

8 In algebra, the equation $x = x + 1$ has no solutions. The BASIC program in this section has the line

```
80 LET NS = NS + 1
```

What does line 80 do? How is the meaning of this statement different from that of the algebraic equation?

9 A fiddlestick factory opened in January 1987. The graph shows the relationship between monthly profits and the number of sticks produced. Use the graph to answer the following.

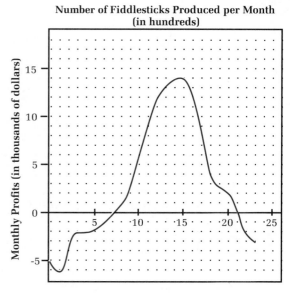

Number of Fiddlesticks Produced per Month (in hundreds)

a What are the profits when 900 sticks are produced?

b How many sticks must be produced for the profit to be $12,000?

c What are the profits when 400 sticks are produced? What does this result mean and how might you account for it?

d How many sticks must be produced in order for the factory to break even?

e How many must be produced in order for the profits to exceed $6,000?

f Why might the profits begin to decline at some point and become negative when more than 1600 fiddlesticks are produced?

g If you were the manager of the factory, how many sticks would you produce? Why?

A RECURSIVE SOLUTION

Objective

After studying this section, you will be familiar with
- Using a recursive pattern to solve a problem

Part One: Introduction

What happens to the total number of handshakes whenever a new person is added to the group?

When a person enters a room containing ten people who have already exchanged handshakes, he or she must shake hands with each of the ten people, increasing the total number of handshakes by ten. Therefore, using H_n to represent the number of handshakes exchanged by n people, we can say that $H_{11} = H_{10} + 10$. In the same way,

$$H_{10} = H_9 + 9$$
$$H_9 = H_8 + 8$$
$$H_8 = H_7 + 7$$
$$H_7 = H_6 + 6$$
.
.
.

We know that for two people there is only one handshake. Using this information and reversing the pattern, we can calculate the number of handshakes exchanged by any larger group of people.

$$H_2 = 1$$
$$H_3 = H_2 + 2 = 3$$
$$H_4 = H_3 + 3 = 6$$
$$H_5 = H_4 + 4 = 10$$
.
.
.

$$H_n = H_{n-1} + (n - 1)$$

A process of this sort, in which each result depends on the preceding result, is called **recursive.** We can use a recursive technique to solve a problem whenever we can see a definite relationship between successive results in a series of operations.

The following Pascal program simulates the recursive solution of the handshake problem. If you have access to Pascal, enter the program on a computer and run it for $N = 6$, $N = 25$, and $N = 50$.

```
{====================The Handshake Problem====================}

{Recursive solution in Pascal
 The number of handshakes for N people is equal to the
 number of handshakes for the Nth person plus the number
 of handshakes for all the rest of the N − 1 people.}

{=============================================================}

  Program SolveHandshakes;
   Var NumberPeople { Number of people shaking hands }
   TotalShakes: Integer; { Total number of handshakes }

   Function NumberHandshakes (NthPerson: Integer) : Integer;
     Var Person: Integer; { Person shaking hands with Nth person }
   Begin { Function NumberHandshakes }
     If NthPerson = 1 Then NumberHandshakes := 0
     Else begin { Nontrivial Case }
       For Person := 1 To NthPerson − 1 Do
       Writeln (NthPerson:5; ' --shakes hands with--',Person:5);
       NumberHandshakes := (NthPerson − 1) +
                   NumberHandshakes(NthPerson − 1)
     End { Nontrivial Case }
   End; { Function NumberHandshakes }

{-------------------------------------------------------------}

  Begin { Main Program }
   Write ('Enter the number of people ==> ');
   Readln (NumberPeople);
   Writeln;
   TotalShakes := NumberHandshakes(NumberPeople);
   Writeln;
   Writeln ('The total number of handshakes is', TotalShakes : 5)
  End. { Main Program }
```

Compare the algorithm used in this program with Method 2 of organizing handshakes, described on page 4.

Part Two: Sample Problem

Problem   Write a recursive formula that can be used to find the nth term of the sequence 1, 3, 4, 7, 11, 18, . . . , n.

Solution   Notice that, except for the first two numbers, each number in the sequence is the sum of the two preceding numbers. If T_n represents the nth term of the sequence and we know that $T_1 = 1$ and $T_2 = 3$, we can use the formula $T_n = T_{n-1} + T_{n-2}$ to find any subsequent term. (This sequence is known as the Lucas sequence and is related in interesting ways to the famous Fibonacci sequence, 1, 1, 2, 3, 5, 8, 13, . . .)

Part Three: Exercises and Problems

1 Draw a coordinate grid at least 36 squares high. Label the lower left-hand corner with the coordinates (0, 0). Put a dot there.
Move right 1 and up 1 and put a dot there.
Move right 1 and up 3 and put a dot there.
Move right 1 and up 5 and put a dot there.
Move right 1 and up 7 and put a dot there.
Move right 1 and up 9 and put a dot there.

  a Write the height y of the nth dot in summation notation.
  b Label each dot with its coordinates and observe another pattern. Write an equation that describes the relationship between x and y in each ordered pair (x, y).
  c Write a recursive formula that expresses the sum of the coordinates of the nth dot (S_n) in terms of the sum of the preceding dot's coordinates (S_{n-1}).

2 Explain how you would find all the whole-number divisors of a given positive integer. (You are creating an algorithm.)

3 Create an algorithm to find how many whole-number divisors any given positive integer has.

4 Create an algorithm to find $1 \cdot 2 \cdot 3 \cdot 4 \cdot 5 \cdot \ldots \cdot n$ recursively. (This product, symbolized $n!$, is called n factorial.)

5 The diagram represents the production lines at a toy factory.

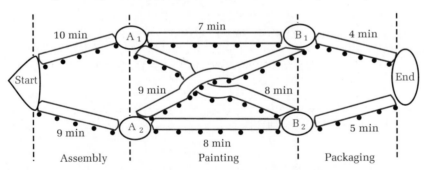

Assembly takes place on two lines. Painting is done on four lines, and packaging is done on two lines. The time it takes for a toy to pass down each line is shown.

  a What is the shortest time from start to finish?
  b If line A_1B_1 is shut down, what is the shortest time from start to finish?
  c The parts for 100 toys are fed into the starting position at a rate of 1 toy per second. At each split in the line, half the toys go one direction, and half go the other. How long does it take until the last toy comes out at the end?
  d Suppose that from the start, 40% of the toys go to A_1, and from A_1, 45% go to B_1. From A_2, 30% go to B_1. What percentage of the toys reach the end by way of B_1?

1.6 DEMONSTRATIONS

Objective

After studying this section, you will be familiar with

- Some ways in which mathematical ideas are communicated

Part One: Introduction

In mathematics, we must demonstrate the mathematical thinking behind our answers. The type of demonstration depends on the situation, but the clarity of the explanation is always as important as correct mathematics.

Many kinds of formal demonstrations are used in mathematics, including two-column proofs, paragraph proofs, indirect proofs, graphical proofs, and analytic proofs. Most mathematical communication, however, takes place in a more informal way.

In this book we use a variety of informal proofs as well as some formal proofs. We will always give enough information to explain our thinking but will not always include every step. As you proceed in your study of mathematics, you will develop a sense of how much detail is necessary in a given situation. For now, work on communicating your thinking in clear, informal style.

Example Show that $n(n + 3) + 2 = (n + 1)(n + 2)$.

To show that the two expressions are equivalent, we can perform the indicated operations and simplify the results.

Left Side
$$= n(n + 3) + 2$$
$$= n^2 + 3n + 2$$

Right Side
$$= (n + 1)(n + 2)$$
$$= n^2 + 2n + n + 2$$
$$= n^2 + 3n + 2$$

Since each side is equal to the same expression, the sides must be equal. For a fuller explanation, we would state what algebraic property was used in each step.

Problem 1   *Prove that if* $x > 0$, *then* $(1 + x)^2 > 1$.

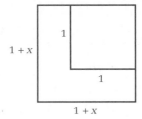

Solution   We can use a geometric model. Each side of the large square has a length of $1 + x$. The length of each side of the small square is 1. The large square has an area of $(1 + x)^2$. The small square has an area of 1. The large square is the small square plus more area, so $(1 + x)^2 > 1$.

Problem 2   *Each indicated product of three consecutive integers is divisible by* 6. *Will this be true for any three consecutive integers?*

$$1(2)(3) = 6 \qquad\qquad 4(5)(6) = 120$$
$$2(3)(4) = 24 \qquad\qquad 13(14)(15) = 2730$$
$$3(4)(5) = 60$$

Solution   We could try calculating all products we can think of, but we couldn't be sure that *every* such product is divisible by 6. Instead, we examine some general characteristics of the numbers in any sequence of three.

Every alternate integer is even, so in every set of three consecutive integers, at least one must be divisible by 2. Every third integer is a multiple of 3, so one of the three consecutive integers must have a factor of 3. Every sixth integer has a factor of 2 and 3. Since the product will always have a factor of 2 and a factor of 3, it will always have a factor of 6. Here is another way of stating the proof:

One of the numbers will be a multiple of 2, so we can call it $2k$.
One of the numbers will be a multiple of 3, so we can call it $3h$.
The third number can be called m.
The product will be $(2k)(3h)(m) = 6(khm)$, a multiple of 6.

Part Three: Exercises and Problems

1 a Define *even number.*

   b Why would "Every other number is an even number" be an incomplete definition of *even number?*

2 Find all the numbers for which

   a The product of the number and itself is 9

   b The sum of the number and itself is 9

   c The sum of the number and itself is the same as the product of the number and itself

3 For any integer n, how would you describe each number?

   a $2n$ **b** $2n + 1$ **c** $2n - 1$ **d** $|n|$

4 Explain why the opposite of a negative number is a positive number.

5 Show that when 7 points are labeled on a circle, 21 possible chords are determined.

6 How many three-digit lock combinations can be created if each digit is one of the numbers from 0 through 7? How many of these combinations are possible if no two of the digits can be the same?

7 Solve each equation.

a $3^x = 81$ **b** $\dfrac{x}{3} = 81$ **c** $3x = 81$ **d** $x^2 = 81$

8 Explain in paragraph form why the product of any two even numbers is a multiple of 4.

9 If 50% of the cars entering each fork in the road system take the northern route, what percentage of the cars that enter the system will exit at B?

10 If Mimi has 77 marbles and Sam has 31 marbles, how many marbles should Mimi give Sam so that each will have the same number of marbles? Explain how you found the answer.

11 Explain why the sum of any two negative numbers is negative.

12 Identify the pattern to find the missing numbers.

$(3, 5) \rightarrow 2$ $(6, 1) \rightarrow 5$
$(8, 11) \rightarrow 3$ $(8, 12) \rightarrow ?$
$(2, 7) \rightarrow 5$ $(7, 7) \rightarrow ?$
$(12, 9) \rightarrow 3$ $(15, 9) \rightarrow ?$

13 Simplify $\displaystyle\sum_{x=1}^{6}(x + y) - \sum_{x=1}^{6}(x + 3)$.

14 Suppose that a polygon is formed by connecting *lattice points* (points with integer coordinates) on a graph. Find a formula that expresses the area of the polygon as a function of I, the number of lattice points inside the polygon, and S, the number of lattice points on the polygon. Two examples are shown.

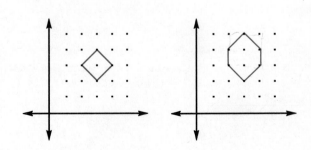

2 THE LANGUAGE OF ALGEBRA

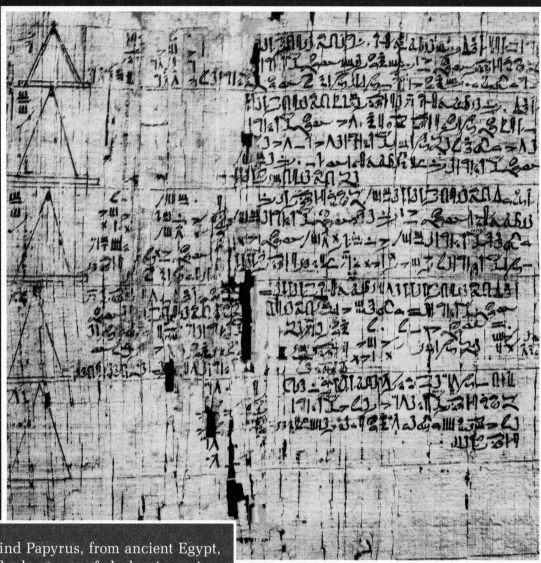

The Rhind Papyrus, from ancient Egypt, used the language of algebra in posing eighty-five word problems.

THE LANGUAGE OF EXPRESSIONS

Objectives

After studying this section, you will be able to

- Add expressions and recognize equivalent expressions
- Use the Distributive Property of Multiplication over Addition
- Calculate absolute values
- Follow the standard algebraic order of operations

Part One: Introduction

Working with Expressions

An **expression** is a mathematical phrase consisting of a number, a variable, or numbers and/or variables connected by operations.

These are expressions:

$$3x^2 - 2 + 4xy \qquad x$$

$$\frac{3x + 4}{9 - 2x} \qquad lwh \qquad |4 - 9|$$

These are not expressions:

$$9x - 5 = 6$$

$$x > 3$$

The general rule for adding expressions is that only **like terms** may be combined. **Like terms** consist of exactly the same variables raised to the same powers.

To simplify the sum, group and combine the like terms

$$(4x + 54y + 9) + (2y + x^2 + x - 9)$$
$$= x^2 + (4x + x) + (54y + 2y) + (9 - 9)$$
$$= x^2 + 5x + 56y$$

The original sum and its simplified form are **equivalent expressions,** since they have the same value for all values of x and y.

In the diagram, the area can be represented as the length times the width, $x(x + 4)$, or as the sum of the two smaller rectangles, $x^2 + 4x$. Since the two expressions represent the same area, they must be equivalent.

The Distributive Property of Multiplication over Addition

The statement $x(x + 4) = x^2 + 4x$ illustrates an important property. To find the product $x(x + 4)$, we **distribute** the x over $x + 4$. We are allowed to do so by the Distributive Property of Multiplication over Addition.

The Distributive Property of Multiplication over Addition

If *a*, *b*, and *c* are real numbers, then $a(b + c) = ab + ac$ and $(b + c)a = ba + ca$.

This property can also show how expressions are subtracted. Remember that two numbers with a sum of zero—like 9 and -9, $-\frac{3}{4}$ and $\frac{3}{4}$, and x and $-x$ are known as **opposites**, or **additive inverses**, and that subtraction is defined as the inverse of addition.

 If a and b are real numbers, $a - b = a + (-b)$.

We subtract an expression by adding its opposite. An opposite can be found by distributing -1 over each term of the expression.

Example   *Simplify* $2(6x^2 - 5x + 9) - (3x^2 + 2x - 4)$.

$$2(6x^2 - 5x + 9) - (3x^2 + 2x - 4)$$

Distribute and
add the opposite $= (12x^2 - 10x + 18) + (-3x^2 - 2x + 4)$
Group like terms $= (12x^2 - 3x^2) + (-10x - 2x) + (18 + 4)$
Combine like terms $= 9x^2 - 12x + 22$

Absolute Value

Mathematicians often need to refer to the numerical value of an expression without regard to its sign. This is the expression's *absolute value*.

> *The absolute value of a real number a, written $|a|$, is equal to a if a is positive or zero or to $-a$ if a is negative.*

$$|a| = \begin{cases} a \text{ when } a \geq 0 \\ -a \text{ when } a < 0 \end{cases}$$

Since $-a$ is positive when $a < 0$, an absolute value will always be a nonnegative number.

$|6| = 6$ $\left|-\frac{3}{5}\right| = \frac{3}{5}$ $|0| = 0$

Order of Operations

You may recall the standard algebraic order of operations.

Order of Operations in an Expression

1. Evaluate all expressions within grouping symbols.

2. Evaluate all powers and roots.

3. Perform all multiplications and divisions from left to right.

4. Perform all additions and subtractions from left to right.

Example   *Perform the indicated operations.*
$$-3 + 4 \cdot (2 + 7)^2 \div 2 - 5\sqrt{6 + 3}$$

	$-3 + 4 \cdot (2 + 7)^2 \div 2 - 5\sqrt{6 + 3}$
Evaluate grouped expressions	$= -3 + 4 \cdot 9^2 \div 2 - 5\sqrt{9}$
Evaluate powers and roots	$= -3 + 4 \cdot 81 \div 2 - 5 \cdot 3$
Multiply and divide	$= -3 + 162 - 15$
Add and subtract	$= 144$

Most scientific calculators use the standard algebraic order of operations. The operations in the preceding example can be performed on a calculator by entering

3 ± + 4 × (2 + 7) x^2 ÷ 2 − 5 × (6 + 3) √ =

Part Two: Sample Problems

Problem 1   *Express the total area of rectangle ABCD.*

Solution   We could use a formula for the total area of the rectangle.

Area = length · width
     = $(x + 4)(x + 3)$

We could also express the total area as the sum of the areas of the four smaller rectangles.

Area = $x^2 + 4x + 3x + 12$
     = $x^2 + 7x + 12$

Since the expressions $(x + 4)(x + 3)$ and $x^2 + 7x + 12$ express the same area, they are equivalent expressions.

Problem 2   Let $y = 4x^2 + (3x)^2$. Make a table showing the values of y when the values of x are $\{-2, -1, 0, 1, 2, 3\}$.

Solution   First, we simplify the expression on the right-hand side of the equation.

$$y = 4x^2 + (3x)^2$$
$$= 4x^2 + 9x^2$$
$$= 13x^2$$

Now we can substitute the given values for x in the expression $13x^2$ to find the corresponding values of y.

x	−2	−1	0	1	2	3
y	52	13	0	13	52	117

Problem 3   Perform the indicated operations.

$$5 + 2 \cdot 4^2 + |-3 + (-2)| + \frac{\sqrt{9 + 16} - (-3)^2}{2}$$

Solution   We follow the standard algebraic order of operations.

$$5 + 2 \cdot 4^2 + |-3 + (-2)| + \frac{\sqrt{9 + 16} - (-3)^2}{2}$$

$$= 5 + 2 \cdot 16 + |-5| + \frac{\sqrt{25} - 9}{2}$$

$$= 5 + 32 + 5 + \frac{-4}{2}$$

$$= 42 - 2$$

$$= 40$$

Part Three: Exercises and Problems

Warm-up Exercises

In problems 1 and 2, simplify each expression.

1 $(x + 3) + (x + 5)$

2 $(x + 5) - (x + 6)$

In problems 3 and 4, use the distributive property to rewrite each expression.

3 $3(2x + 7)$

4 $ax + ay$

5 a Write two algebraic expressions to describe the total area of the figure.
   b Draw an area diagram to illustrate the expression $x(4 + 2x)$. Then find a second algebraic expression that describes the same area.

In problems 6–11, perform the indicated operations.

6 $5 + 3^2 - (4 - 3 \cdot 7)$ **7** $(5 \cdot 2)^2 - 5 \cdot 2^2$ **8** $\sqrt{3^2 + 4^2}$

9 $|8 - 19|$ **10** $|-17 + 9|$ **11** $|-17| + |9|$

Problem Set

In problems 12–14, use the Distributive Property of Multiplication over Addition to rewrite each expression. Then combine like terms.

12 $4(8 - 3x)$ **13** $-3(5 - 7x) - 4x$ **14** $8x - (5x + 6)$

15 Express the total area of the figure in at least two different ways.

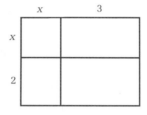

16 a Use a calculator to find the result of the following key sequence.

$$9\ \boxed{+}\ 3\ \boxed{\times}\ 6\ \boxed{\pm}\ \boxed{-}\ 8\ \boxed{=}$$

b Write an algebraic sentence that represents the calculation in part **a.**

17 Let $x = 3$.

  a Evaluate $4x + 9$.
  b Evaluate $7x - 4$.
  c Evaluate $8x - 3$.
  d Is $x = 3$ a solution of $4x + 9 = 7x - 4$?
  e Is $x = 3$ a solution of $4x + 9 = 8x - 3$?

In problems 18–20, simplify each expression.

18 $5x + 3y + 2(3y - x)$
19 $8x + 5y - (x - y)$
20 $3x \cdot 2x + 5x \cdot x - 4x \cdot 3 + 6 \cdot 2x^2$

21 Write an algebraic expression for each quantity.

  a Length AB
  b Five less than twice a number n
  c Four times the sum of a number x and 7

22 Write each expression in simplest form.

  a $x + x + x + x + x$ **b** $x \cdot x \cdot x \cdot x \cdot x \cdot x$

In problems 23–25, perform the indicated operations.

23 $3|4 - 12| + (-3)^3$

24 $3(4 - 12) + |-3|^2$

25 $\big| -21 - |-12| \big|$

In problems 26 and 27, evaluate each sum.

26 $\displaystyle\sum_{n=3}^{7}(4n + 5)$

27 $\displaystyle\sum_{n=1}^{4} 2^n$

28 Copy and complete the table of values for $y = -5(x - 2) + 1$.

x	-4	-2	6	3	-6
y					

29 The total area of the figure is equal to $(x + 6)(x + 15)$.

   a What are the areas of the small rectangles and the square?

   b Write another expression to describe the total area of the figure.

30 Write an expression for the seating capacity of a school auditorium that contains r rows with 22 seats in each and 12 rows with s seats in each.

31 Evaluate each expression to the nearest hundredth for $x = 0.84$.

   a $[(x + 5)x + 6]x + 7$

   b $x^3 + 5x^2 + 6x + 7$

In problems 32–34, evaluate each expression for $(x_1, y_1) = (2, 3)$ and $(x_2, y_2) = (8, 11)$.

32 $\dfrac{y_2 - y_1}{x_2 - x_1}$

33 $\dfrac{x_1 + x_2}{2}$

34 $\dfrac{y_1 + y_2}{2}$

In problems 35 and 36, simplify each expression.

35 $(3x^2 + 9x - 12) - (3x - x^3 + 5x^2)$

36 $(3x^2 + 2y^2 + 4x + 8y) + (x^2 - y^2)$

37 Explain, in paragraph form, why the product of any two consecutive natural numbers is even.

38 Is the sum of any two consecutive integers even? Explain your answer.

39 Let $x = 7$.

   a Evaluate $3x + 9$.

   b Evaluate $5x - 2$.

   c Evaluate $6x - 15$.

   d Is $x = 7$ a solution of $3x + 9 > 5x - 2$?

   e Is $x = 7$ a solution of $3x + 9 \geq 6x - 15$?

   f Is $x = 7$ a solution of $6x - 15 < 5x - 2$?

40 Perform the indicated operations.

$$11^2 - |2(-15)| - \sqrt{\frac{4^2}{2} + 7 \cdot 8} + 3$$

41 Let x = 9.
- **a** Evaluate $(x + 4)^2$.
- **b** Evaluate $x^2 + 4^2$.
- **c** Evaluate $x^2 + 8x + 16$.
- **d** Which of the expressions in parts **a–c** are equivalent?

42 Evaluate $\displaystyle\sum_{x=3}^{5}(2 + 3x)$.

43 Express the total volume of the box in at least two different ways.

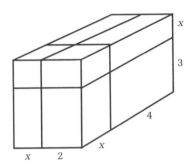

THE MATHEMATICS OF MANAGING MONEY
For Rodney Brown, the bottom line is the bottom line

"Mathematics is not only essential to my work, it *is* my work," says Chicago-based Rodney Brown, a Certified Public Accountant. What Mr. Brown does is painstaking and would try most people's patience. Making a long story short, he says: "I use formulas and do a tremendous number of calculations to make sure that a balance sheet adds up correctly." It is essential for businesses or individuals to know how much money they have, how much they have spent and on what, and how much they owe. An accountant goes through all a client's financial transactions and provides that information in a clear and organized manner.

One type of interesting problem Mr. Brown might solve for his clients is that of finding the real value of an investment they have made or are thinking of making. For example, if a client earns 8.9%-per-year interest on an investment of $15,000, the dollar value of the interest is $1335. "They may in fact earn that much money, but the real value of what they receive is considerably less after taxes and inflation," Mr. Brown says. If tax on earnings is 28% and inflation is 6.7%, then the real value of the earnings is (0.089 − 0.067) · $15,000 − (0.28 · $1335). The result is −$43.80!

Mr. Brown graduated with a bachelor's degree in accounting from the University of Illinois at Chicago. "Using mathematics forces you to think logically and clearly," he says.

SOLVING EQUATIONS

Objectives

After studying this section, you will be able to
- Recognize equivalent equations
- Solve equations by using properties of equality
- Express solutions of equations as ordered pairs

Part One: Introduction

Equivalent Equations

Equations with the same solution(s) are called ***equivalent equations.*** For example, $x + 6 = 17$, $x + 8 = 19$, and $x = 11$ are equivalent equations because all have the same solution, 11.

Some Properties Used in Solving Equations

To solve an equation, we use this general procedure.

> ***Write a series of equivalent equations until you arrive at an equivalent equation of the following form:***
> ***variable = number***

Algebraic properties are the rules that tell us what we can and cannot do. The following properties apply to all real numbers a, b, and c.

Addition and Subtraction Properties of Equality

If $a = b$, then $a + c = b + c$ and $a - c = b - c$.

We can add the same quantity to, or subtract the same quantity from, each side of an equation and the resulting equation is equivalent to the original equation.

Multiplication and Division Properties of Equality

If $a = b$, then $ac = bc$ and (if $c \neq 0$) $\frac{a}{c} = \frac{b}{c}$.

We can multiply or divide each side of an equation by the same numerical quantity (provided that the quantity is not zero) and the resulting equation is equivalent to the original equation.

Zero Product Property

If $a \cdot b = 0$, then $a = 0$ or $b = 0$.

If the product of two or more numbers is zero, at least one of the numbers must be zero.

Solving Linear Equations

To solve an equation means to find all values of the variable that make the equation a true statement. We apply the properties as we work through a solution.

Example *Solve the equation $3x - 7 = 2x + 4$.*

$$3x - 7 = 2x + 4$$

Subtract 2x from each side

$$\underline{- 2x \qquad\qquad - 2x}$$

$$x - 7 = \qquad 4$$

Add 7 to each side

$$\underline{+ 7 \qquad\qquad + 7}$$

$$x \quad = \qquad 11$$

Check

To check our work, we substitute the value 11 for the variable x in the original equation and see whether the expressions on the left side and the right side have the same value.

Left Side	Right Side
$3x - 7$	$= 2x + 4$
$= 3(11) - 7$	$= 2(11) + 4$
$= 26$	$= 26$

When $x = 11$, the sides are equal, so the answer checks.

Ordered Pairs

Although frequently listed in a table, solutions of an equation in two variables, such as x and y, are also often shown as ***ordered pairs*** (x, y), with x as the first number of each pair and y as the second number.

Example

Consider the equation $y = 2(10 - x)$.

a Make a table of values for the equation, containing the values $x = -3$, $y = 11$, $x = 0$, $y = 0$, $y = 6$, and $x = \frac{1}{2}$.

x	-3	4.5	0	10	7	$\frac{1}{2}$
y	26	11	20	0	6	19

b Write the solutions in the table as ordered pairs.

$(-3, 26)$, $(4.5, 11)$, $(0, 20)$, $(10, 0)$, $(7, 6)$, $\left(\frac{1}{2}, 19\right)$

c Is $(6, 8)$ a solution of the equation?

We substitute 6 and 8 for x and y in the equation.

$$y = 2(10 - x)$$
$$8 = 2(10 - 6)$$
$$8 = 2(4)$$
$$8 = 8$$

Since the equation makes a true statement when $(x, y) = (6, 8)$, this ordered pair is a solution of the equation.

In Section 2.4, you will see that ordered pairs can be used to plot a graph that represents an equation.

Part Two: Sample Problems

Problem 1

Two runners live 33 miles apart. Jim Schuh runs 8 miles per hour, and Swett Shurt runs 6 miles per hour. If Swett starts running toward Jim's house and Jim starts running toward Swett's house 2 hours later, how long will Jim have been running when they meet?

Solution

Let t = the number of hours Jim runs.
Then $t + 2$ = the number of hours Swett runs.
The distance run by Jim is $8t$, and that run by Swett is $6(t + 2)$.
Since the total distance is 33 miles,

$$8t + 6(t + 2) = 33$$
$$8t + 6t + 12 = 33$$
$$14t + 12 = 33$$
$$14t = 21$$
$$t = 1.5$$

Jim will have been running for 1.5 hours, or 1 hour 30 minutes.

Check
If Jim runs for 1.5 hours at 8 miles per hour, he will run $8 \cdot 1.5$, or 12, miles. If Swett runs for 3.5 hours at 6 miles per hour, he will run $6 \cdot 3.5$, or 21, miles. Since $12 + 21 = 33$, the answer checks.

Problem 2   The area of rectangle A is equal to the area of rectangle B. Find the dimensions of each rectangle.

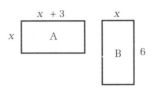

Solution   The area of rectangle A is $x(x + 3)$ and the area of rectangle B is $6x$.
Since the areas are equal, $x(x + 3) = 6x$
use the Distributive Property
of Multiplication over Addition $x^2 + 3x = 6x$

Regroup $x^2 - 3x = 0$

Use the distributive property
in reverse $x(x - 3) = 0$

Zero Product Property $x = 0 \text{ or } x - 3 = 0$

                                       $x = 0 \text{ or } x = 3$

The length of a side of a rectangle cannot be zero, so each rectangle measures 3 by 6.

Check
The area of rectangle A is $3 \cdot 6$, or 18, and the area of rectangle B is $6 \cdot 3$, or 18. The areas are equal, so the answer checks.

Part Three: Exercises and Problems

Warm-up Exercises

1 Consider the equation $6(x + 4) = 24$. Which of the steps below would be a useful first step in solving the equation?
  a Distribute the 6 on the left side.
  b Divide each side by 6.
  c Subtract 4 from each side.

2 Use the Zero Product Property to solve $z(z - 4) = 0$ for z.

3 Refer to the figure.
  a Write a formula for the perimeter P of the figure.
  b Find x if $P = 64$.

4 Is $z = 36$ a solution of $\sqrt{z} + 30 = z$?

5 Is $(x, y) = (-2, 3)$ a solution of $5y + 6x = 3$?

6 Divide both sides of $5(2x - 7) = 40$ by 5 and solve for x.

7 Copy and complete the table of values for $x = y - 4$.

x				0	5
y	0	-3	5		

8 An empty bushel weighs about 1.2 pounds, and an apple weighs about 0.7 pound.

    a What is the approximate weight of 7 apples?

    b Write an expression for the weight of *n* apples.

    c What is the approximate weight of a bushel containing 50 apples?

    d Write a formula for the weight *W* of a bushel containing *n* apples.

9 The numbers between -3 and 5 have been shaded on the number line.

    a Is $\sqrt{30}$ shaded?   **b** Is $\sqrt{22}$ shaded?   **c** Is $-\sqrt{22}$ shaded?

    d Is $-\frac{18}{5}$ shaded?   **e** Is $\frac{14}{3}$ shaded?   **f** Is -3 shaded?

Problem Set

In problems 10 and 11, solve each equation.

10 $5(3x + 2) = -50$

11 $\dfrac{3x + 6}{4} = 9$

12 Let $y = 8x + 5$.

    a Find x if $y = 2$.

    b Find x if $y = 2x - 3$.

    c Find the value of x for which $y = -31$.

13 **a** Arrange the numbers 4, -2, 3, and -7 in order from smallest to largest.

    b Multiply each number in part **a** by -1 and list the results in order from smallest to largest.

    c What effect did multiplying by -1 have on the order?

14 Billie's bank contains nickels, dimes, and quarters.

    a If Billie has eight nickels, five dimes, and seven quarters, what is the total value of the coins in the bank?

    b Suppose Billie has *n* nickels, *d* dimes, and *q* quarters. Write a formula that can be used to find *V*, the total value of the coins.

15 The graph shows the relationship between a firm's profit *P* and the number *n* of widgets it produces.

    a Find the profit if 200 widgets are produced.

    b How many widgets must be produced for a profit of $6000?

    c What happens if no widgets are produced?

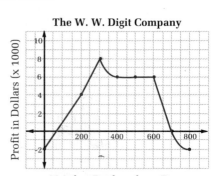

The W. W. Digit Company

Profit in Dollars (x 1000)

Number Produced per Day

16 If $w = 2x + y$, what is
   a The value of w for which $(-3, 4)$ is a solution of the equation?
   b The value of x for which $w = 8$ and $(x, 5)$ is a solution of the equation?

17 Two matrices are equal only if each pair of corresponding entries is equal. In the matrix equation below, for example, w is equal to 7. Find the values of x, y, and z.

$$\begin{bmatrix} x + 6 & 3y \\ w & 8 \end{bmatrix} = \begin{bmatrix} 10 & -24 \\ 7 & \sqrt{z} \end{bmatrix}$$

18 Consider the equation $3x - 5y = 48$.
   a If $x = 0$, what is y?   **b** If $y = 0$, what is x?

19 The perimeter of the rectangle is 62 centimeters. Find the area of the rectangle. (Hint: First find the value of x.)

$2x + 3$

$x - 5$

20 How many diagonals does a pentagon have?

21 How many diagonals does a hexagon have?

22 Write an expression for the sum of five consecutive integers if the smallest of the integers is $x + 1$.

23 Two hot-air balloons are flying over a field. The height h, in feet, of the first balloon t seconds from now can be found with the formula $h(t) = 50 + 34t$. The height g, in feet, of the second balloon t seconds from now can be found with the formula $g(t) = 400 - 16t$.
   a In how many seconds will the balloons be at the same height?
   b How high will they be at that time?

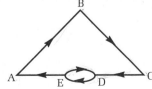

24 Solve $3x + 9y = 12z$ for x.

25 Solve $2x - 3y = 10y - 6x$ for y.

26 Solve $x + 2y = 3z$ for y.

27 At what point must you start in order to trace the entire digraph exactly once without lifting your pencil? Explain your reasoning.

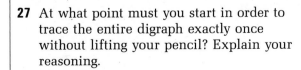

Problem Set, *continued*

In problems 28–30, solve each equation for y.

28 $y(y - 3) = 0$ **29** $(y + 3)(2y - 10) = 0$ **30** $(y - 4)^2 = 0$

31 Suppose that $y = x^2$.
   a Find the value of y for which $x = 3$ and that for which $x = -3$.
   b Find all values of x for which $y = 16$.

32 Find the values of x that satisfy each equation.
   a $|x| = 13$ **b** $|x| + 3 = 13$ **c** $|x + 3| = 13$

33 Express a in terms of x.

In problems 34–36, evaluate each expression for (x, y) = (3, −8).

34 $3(x - y) + 2x^2$ **35** $2|y - x| + 3 + 2x$ **36** $(y - x) - |x - y|$

37 If $y = 9 - 4x$ and $z = 6x - 11$, for what value of x is $y = z$?

38 Perform the indicated operations.
   a $12 - 4 \cdot 3 + 2 \cdot 3^2$ **b** $(12 - 4)3 + (2 \cdot 3)^2$
   c $12 - 4(3 + 2 \cdot 3)^2$ **d** $12 - 4|3 + 2| \cdot 3^2$

In problems 39–44, solve each equation for x and simplify each expression.

39 $10 - (6 - 3x) = 2(x + 5)$ **40** $x(2x - 4) + 3x = x(5 + 2x) + 6$

41 $\left[\frac{2}{3}(x - 3) + 7\right] \cdot 6x + 2$ **42** $2(3 - x) - 3(4 - x) = 4(5 - x)$

43 $3x = a + 2b$ **44** $a(bc + ac - ab) + b(ab + bc - ac)$

45 a Copy and complete the table of values for the equation $y = \frac{1}{2}x - 3$.

x	−6	−4	0	2	8	12
y						

   b Plot the six points on a coordinate system and connect them.
      What do you see?
   c Is the point (34, 14) on the graph of $y = \frac{1}{2}x - 3$?

46 Refer to the figure.
   a. Write an expression for the surface
      area of the box.
   b Find x if the surface area is 261.

12

6

x

36   Chapter 2   The Language of Algebra

47 Explain, in paragraph form, why the product of two odd numbers is an odd number.

48 Refer to the diagram.
   a Find the coordinates of point R.
   b Find the lengths of $\overline{PR}$ and $\overline{RQ}$.
   c Find the area of $\triangle PQR$.
   d Use the Pythagorean Theorem to find the length of $\overline{PQ}$.

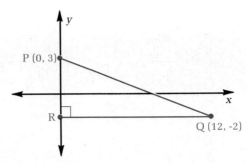

49 Two sailboats 400 meters apart are sailing toward each other. One is moving at a rate of 10 meters per second, and the other is moving at a rate of 15 meters per second.
   a In how many seconds will the boats pass each other?
   b In how many seconds will the boats be 400 meters apart again?

In problems 50–52, simplify each expression.

50 $5a \cdot 3a + 5 \cdot 3 \cdot a^2 + 5 \cdot (3a)^2 + 3(5a)^2 + (3 \cdot 5a)^2$

51 $-2x^2 + (-3)^3x^2 - 4x^2 + x^2$

52 $(3x^2 + 2x + 4) - (4 - 2x + 3x^2)$

53 If $s = 5x - 7$ and $t = x + 10$, for what value of x is $s = 2t - 4$?

54 Make a table of values for the equation $y = 3(x + 2) - 5(x - 3) + 4(x - 4)$, using the integers from -5 to 5 for values of x.

55 Find BC if $AB = x^2 + 3x - 5$ and $AC = 6 + 2x + 4x^2$.

56 Refer to the diagram.
   a Find the midpoint of $\overline{PQ}$.
   b Find the two trisection points of $\overline{PQ}$.
   c Find the three points that divide $\overline{PQ}$ into four equal parts.

57 Simplify $52(773p + 851w) - 26(851w + 773p)$.

SOLVING INEQUALITIES

Objectives

After studying this section, you will be able to
- Apply properties of inequality
- Solve linear inequalities in one variable
- Graph solutions of inequalities on the number line

Part One: Introduction

Properties of Inequality

In the preceding section, you saw that an equation states that two expressions are equal. If the values of two expressions are not equal, we can write an *inequality* using the symbol $\leq$, $\geq$, $\neq$, $>$, or $<$.

The following properties, which apply to all real numbers a, b, and c, are useful in the solution of inequalities.

Addition and Subtraction Properties of Inequality	
If $a > b$, then $a + c > b + c$ and $a - c > b - c$.	We can add the same quantity to, or subtract the same quantity from, each side of an inequality.

Multiplication and Division Properties of Inequality	
If $a > b$ and $c > 0$, then $ac > bc$ and $\frac{a}{c} > \frac{b}{c}$.	We can multiply or divide each side of an inequality by the same positive number.
If $a > b$ and $c < 0$, then $ac < bc$ and $\frac{a}{c} < \frac{b}{c}$.	When we multiply or divide each side of an inequality by a negative number, the order of the inequality is reversed.

Solving an Inequality

To solve an inequality means to find all values of the variable or variables that make the inequality a true statement. The steps we use are similar to those we use in solving equations.

Example   *Find all values of* x *for which* 9 − 2x < 17.

$$9 - 2x < 17$$

Subtract 9 from each side

$$\begin{array}{r} 9 - 2x < 17 \\ -9 \quad\quad -9 \\ \hline -2x < 8 \end{array}$$

Divide each side by −2
(remembering that division by a
negative number reverses the order)

$$\frac{-2x}{-2} > \frac{8}{-2}$$

$$x > -4$$

To check a solution of an inequality, we follow the same procedure as in checking solutions of equations.

Graphing Solutions on the Number Line

Often, a number line is used to show the solutions of linear inequalities.

Example   *For each inequality, use a number line to represent the possible values
of the variable.*

a x > 3

Because x is *greater
than* 3, the dot at 3 is
open to show that 3 is
not among the
solutions.

b y ≤ 4

Because y is *less than
or equal to* 4, the dot at
4 is solid to show that
4 is among the
solutions.

c z ≠ −3

Because z can be *any
number except* −3, all
the points on the line,
except that at −3,
represent solutions.

3

4

-3

Part Two: Sample Problems

Problem 1   *Solve* −2 < 3x − 5 < 8 *for x and graph the solution on a number line.*

Solution   The compound inequality −2 < 3x − 5 < 8 means

$$-2 < 3x - 5 \text{ and } 3x - 5 < 8$$

To solve for x, we solve each inequality and combine the solutions
in a new compound inequality.

$$\begin{array}{ccc} -2 < 3x - 5 & \text{and} & 3x - 5 < 8 \\ 3 < 3x & & 3x < 13 \\ 1 < x & & x < \dfrac{13}{3} \end{array}$$

The solution is $1 < x < \dfrac{13}{3}$. We

graph this solution by representing
the *intersection* of the graphs of the
two parts of the inequality.

1                    $\frac{13}{3}$

Problem 2   Aunt Tenna's TV Repair Service charges $45.00 for a visit and $33.75 per hour for labor and parts. Tenna estimates that a given repair job will take at least 2.5 hours but no more than 4.5 hours. What is the possible range of the bill?

Solution   If C = the total charge for a service call and t = the number of hours the call takes, $C = 45 + 33.75t$. In this case, $2.5 \leq t \leq 4.5$, so

$$C \geq 45 + 33.75(2.5) \quad \text{and} \quad C \leq 45 + 33.75(4.5)$$
$$\geq 45 + 84.375 \qquad\qquad\qquad \leq 45 + 151.875$$
$$\geq 129.375 \qquad\qquad\qquad\quad \leq 196.875$$

The bill will be at least $129.38 but no more than $196.88.

Problem 3   Find all possible values of P, the rectangle's perimeter.

Solution
$$P = 2(x - 5) + 2(13 - 2x)$$
$$= 2x - 10 + 26 - 4x$$
$$= 16 - 2x$$

The length of each side must be positive, so

$$x - 5 > 0 \quad \text{and} \quad 13 - 2x > 0$$
$$x > 5 \qquad\qquad\qquad -2x > -13$$
$$x < \frac{13}{2}$$

Since $5 < x < \dfrac{13}{2}$,

$$P < 16 - 2(5) \quad \text{and} \quad P > 16 - 2\left(\frac{13}{2}\right)$$
$$< 6 \qquad\qquad\qquad\qquad > 3$$

The perimeter, therefore, is between 3 and 6.

Part Three: Exercises and Problems

Warm-up Exercises

1 In which of the following inequalities will the inequality sign be reversed when the inequality is solved for x?

   a $x - 2 < -8$ **b** $x + 2 < -8$ **c** $-2x < 8$

   d $-2x < -8$ **e** $2x < -8$

2 Graph $x \neq -5$ on a number line.

3 Graph $-1 \leq x < 6$ on a number line.

4 Solve $14 < 6x - 7$ and graph the solution on a number line.

5 For each verbal description, write a corresponding algebraic statement.

  a The sum of y and 10 is less than the product of 3 and y.
  b The product of 5 and the square of n is not equal to 20.
  c One-fifth less than the square root of x is greater than or equal to the square root of 3.
  d The product of 2, π, and r is between 6 and 8.

6 Describe the result of each operation.

  a Multiplying both sides of $-6 < -3$ by 2
  b Multiplying both sides of $-6 < -3$ by -2

7 Describe the result of each operation.

  a Dividing both sides of $15 \geq 9$ by -3
  b Adding -5 to both sides of $15 \geq 9$

8 Write an inequality that describes the shaded area. Solve the inequality for x.

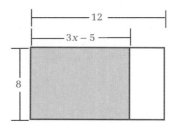

9 What must be true of the values of y if 5 times y is greater than 3?

10 Explain why the square of any integral multiple of 3 is divisible by 9.

Problem Set

In problems 11–16, solve each inequality and graph the solution on a number line.

11 $12x + 27 > 3$
12 $-7y + 15 \geq 50$
13 $4(3 - z) < 40$
14 $-3(2w + 1) \geq 15$
15 $10 \geq 3x - 11$
16 $1.5y_2 + 9.2 \leq 6.8$

In problems 17–20, express each graph as an inequality.

17

-3 -2 -1 0 1 2 3

18
-4 -3 -2 -1 0 1 2 3 4

19
-7 -6 -5 -4 -3 -2 -1 0

20
-7 -6 -5 -4 -3 -2 -1 0

21 Imagine that a new student asks you how to solve the inequality $9 - 3x \leq 5x + 11$. If the student will have no information except what you give, what will you tell the student?

Problem Set, *continued*

22 Tracey went for a long walk at a rate of 2 miles per hour. Three hours later, her brother Richard rode after her on a tandem bike at a rate of 7 miles per hour.
   a How long did it take Richard to meet Tracey?
   b How far had she walked when they met?
   c How long would it take for them to ride back on the bike, traveling at 4 miles per hour?

23 Refer to the diagram.
   a Write an inequality that represents the diagram.
   b Solve the inequality for x.

24 Make a table of values for each equation. Then graph the equation.
   a $y = 2x + 5$ **b** $y = -2$

25 Find the possible values of the perimeter of the rectangle shown.

26 Determine whether $(x, y) = (5, -2)$ is a solution of each equation.
   a $3x + y = 13$ **b** $y = 2x - 10$ **c** $y = \frac{1}{5}x - 3$

27 Solve the matrix equation for (x, y).

$$4\begin{bmatrix} x \\ y \end{bmatrix} + \begin{bmatrix} 7 \\ 2 \end{bmatrix} = \begin{bmatrix} -1 \\ 0 \end{bmatrix}$$

In problems 28–32, find each product.
28 $x^2 \cdot x^5$ **29** $3x(4x)^2$ **30** $5x^5 \cdot 5x^5$
31 $-4x(3x^2 - 7x - 5)$ **32** $x^2(3x^5 - 2x)$

33 The prices at Pavarotti's Pizzas are increasing by 15%. Rewrite the price list to reflect this change.

	Small	Medium	Large
Thin crust	6.50	7.50	8.50
Thick crust	7.50	8.50	9.50

34 For what value of k is $(5, -3)$ a solution of $4x - 3y = k$?

In problems 35–38, simplify each expression and solve each equation.
35 $2x(x + 3) + (3x)^2 + (4x)^2$ **36** $0.45x - 8 = 3.2x + 0.5$
37 $15x^4y^2 - (3x^3y)(4xy)$ **38** $5x^3 - 6x^2y - 2x^2(x - 3y)$

39 If all moves must be downward, how many different paths are there from A to B?

40 Phil A. Telist is thinking of buying 20 stamps for his collection. Some of the stamps he wants cost $0.90 each; the rest cost $1.40 each. The total price of all 20 stamps is $22.00.

    a Using x to represent the number of stamps that cost $0.90, write an expression for the number of stamps that cost $1.40.
    b Write an equation expressing the total price of the stamps as the sum of the prices of each kind.
    c Solve the equation to find how many of each kind of stamp there are.

41 If $d = \sqrt{x^2 + y^2}$ and $(x, y) = (-5, 12)$, what is the value of d?

In problems 42–45, solve each equation.

42 $10 - x = 2(x + 17)$ **43** $(x + 3)(2x - 9) = 0$

44 $9(3y + 12) = 0$ **45** $8x_3 - 9 = 3x_3 + 22$

In problems 46–51, solve each inequality and graph the solution on a number line.

46 $\dfrac{4}{3} + 5y > 2$ **47** $4.3(1.2 - 0.25x) \le -26.66$

48 $11 < \dfrac{2x + 3}{5} \le 13$ **49** $-\frac{1}{2}(n - 5) < 0$ or $\frac{1}{2}n + 1 < \frac{7}{2}$

50 $|z - 5.5| \ge 9$ **51** $3 - |y| > 1.6$

52 If the perimeter of the rectangle is at least 62 centimeters, what are the possible values of its area?

In problems 53–55, solve each inequality and graph the solution set on a number line.

53 $9x + 3 > 15x - 9$ **54** $8x - 7 \le 10x - 15$ **55** $-9(x - 3) > -18$

56 Use the table of values to write an equation expressing the values of y in terms of the values of x.

x	0	1	2	3	4	5
y	1	2	4	8	16	32

Problem Set, *continued*

57 Copy the following matrix and supply the missing data.

	At Bats	Hits	Batting Average (Hits ÷ At Bats)
Stan	26	8	?
Mickey	40	?	.300
Ted	?	12	.364

58 Find the values of a, b, and c that satisfy the equation
$3ax^2 + (b + 5)x + c - 7 = 12x^2 - 6x - 9$.

In problems 59–63, solve each equation and simplify each expression.

59 $(z - 3)(3z + 1)(5z - 8) = 0$

60 $-3|x - y| \div (6y^2 - 18xy) \cdot (2y)^2$

61 $\sqrt{y} + 5 = 6 - 2\sqrt{y}$

 62 $x - 2(x - 3) = \sqrt{533}$

63 $-8^2 - \left(\dfrac{x}{2}\right)^2 - \dfrac{1}{4}x - 64 - \dfrac{x^2 - x}{4}$

64 Consider the equation $x = \dfrac{-b + \sqrt{b^2 - 4ac}}{2a}$. What is the value of x if

a $a = 3$, $b = 1$, and $c = 4$?   **b** $a = -2$, $b = -5$, and $c = 3$?   **c** $a = 2$, $b = 4$, and $c = 1$?

65 a Write an equation relating x and y such that the solutions
include $(-2, 7)$, $(-1, 4)$, $(0, 1)$, $(1, -2)$, $(2, -5)$, and $(3, -8)$.

b Draw a graph that represents the equation you wrote in part **a**.

 66 M is the midpoint of $\overline{AB}$. N is the midpoint of $\overline{BC}$.

a Find the coordinates of points M
and N.

b Find length MN.

c Find length AC.

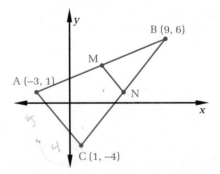

67 A cube with edges 3 inches long is painted on the outside, then
cut into smaller cubes as shown. If one of these cubes is chosen
at random, what is the probability that it

a Has exactly three painted faces?

b Has exactly one painted face?

c Has exactly four painted faces?

d Has no painted faces?

2.4 | INTRODUCTION TO GRAPHING

Height

Distance

Objectives

After studying this section, you will be able to
- Graph an equation on the Cartesian coordinate system
- Use the midpoint and distance formulas
- Understand function notation

Part One: Introduction

The Graph of an Equation

One of the most important ways to communicate mathematics is to use a graph, since graphs picture what symbols describe.

The graph of $y = \frac{x^2 + 1}{x - 2}$, generated on a graphics calculator, helps us learn about the equation. Where is the y-intercept? How many x-intercepts can we find? What are the possible values of y? What pattern, if any, does the equation describe?

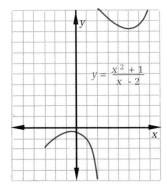

First, let's review some basic terms.

In earlier coursework, you learned about the Cartesian (or rectangular) coordinate system.

The **x-axis** and the **y-axis** intersect at right angles, dividing the plane into four regions called **quadrants,** numbered I, II, III, and IV as shown.

The point of intersection of the axes is called the **origin.** The coordinates of the origin are (0, 0).

The first coordinate of an ordered pair is called the **x-coordinate,** or the **abscissa.** The second coordinate is the **y-coordinate,** or **ordinate.**

In the diagram on the preceding page, we marked three points with their coordinates, (2, 11), (−6, −13), and (0, 5). The point (2, 11) is in Quadrant I, (−6, −13) is in Quadrant III, and (0, 5) is on an axis, not in any quadrant.

To graph an equation means to indicate all points that solve the equation.

Example   *Graph the equation y = 2x + 5.*

We make a table of values.

x	−3	−2	−1	0	1	2	3
y	−1	1	3	5	7	9	11

When we plot these points, they appear to lie on a line. To complete the graph, we connect the points, using arrows to indicate that the line continues in both directions.

The graph of y = 2x + 5 crosses the y-axis at (0, 5). The point (0, 5) is called the **y-intercept** of the graph.

The Midpoint and Distance Formulas

You may remember the formulas used to find the midpoint of a line segment and the length of a line segment.

Example   *Find the midpoint of the line segment with endpoints (−6, 4) and (−11, −10).*

To find the coordinates of the midpoint of a segment, we find the averages of the corresponding coordinates of the endpoints.

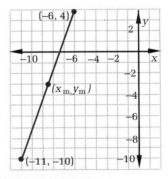

$$x_m = \frac{-6 + (-11)}{2} = -8.5$$

$$y_m = \frac{4 + (-10)}{2} = -3$$

The midpoint is $(x_m, y_m) = (-8.5, -3)$.

The Midpoint Formula

If a segment has endpoints (x_1, y_1) and (x_2, y_2), then the coordinates of its midpoint (x_m, y_m) are equal to $\left(\frac{x_1 + x_2}{2}, \frac{y_1 + y_2}{2}\right)$.

Example   *Find the length of the segment with endpoints* $(-4, 7)$ *and* $(2, -1)$.

This length is the distance between the two endpoints. We can use the distance formula, which is based on the Pythagorean Theorem. In the figure, when point C is identified at $(-4, -1)$, a right triangle is formed.

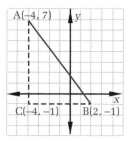

The Distance Formula

The distance d between any two points (x_1, y_1) and (x_2, y_2) in the coordinate plane is given by $d = \sqrt{(x_2 - x_1)^2 + (y_2 - y_1)^2}$.

Now we can find d in two ways.

Pythagorean Theorem

$d = \sqrt{6^2 + 8^2}$

$= \sqrt{36 + 64}$

$= \sqrt{100}$

$= 10$

Distance Formula

$d = \sqrt{[2 - (-4)]^2 + (-1 - 7)^2}$

$= \sqrt{6^2 + (-8)^2}$

$= \sqrt{100}$

$= 10$

Function Notation

The concept of a **function** is a key element in the language of algebra and will be fully developed in a later chapter. At this time we will introduce the idea, as well as function notation.

The formula $A = \pi r^2$ expresses the rule for finding the area of a circle A when the radius r is known. To put this in **function notation** we write

$A(r) = \pi r^2$

This equation makes three statements: The area A is a function of the radius r.

The radius r is the **input** variable.

$A(r)$ is the **output** value.

A function is a rule for finding one output value from an input. $A(r) = \pi r^2$ expresses the rule "the function A of r equals π times r squared."

Example   *If* $f(x) = 3x + 5$, *what are* $f(4)$ *and* $f(-7)$?

$f(4)$ is the output value when the input variable x is 4.

$f(4) = 3(4) + 5$

$= 12 + 5$

$= 17$

$f(-7)$ is the output value when the input variable x is -7.

$f(-7) = 3(-7) + 5$

$= -21 + 5$

$= -16$

Part Two: Sample Problem

Problem   *Refer to the graph of a function g.*
  a *Find g(−2).*
  b *For what value of x is g(x) = 7?*

Solution   **a** Along the horizontal axis, x repre-
      sents the input value. Along the
      vertical axis, g(x) represents the
      output value. The graph shows
      that when x is −2, the output
      g(−2) is 5.
   b According to the graph, g(x) = 7
      when x = −3.

Part Three: Exercises and Problems

As explained in the "Letter to Students," the problems in this set
have been labeled for you.

Warm-up Exercises

Practice   **1** Refer to the rectangle.
   a Find the coordinates of point C.
   b Find the area of RECT.

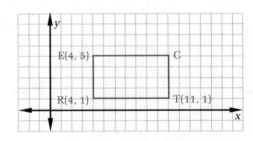

Review   **2** Copy and complete the table of values for $y = 3x - 4$.

x	−2	−1			2
y	−10		−4	−1	

Practice   **3** Find g(0) if $g(x) = 34x - 17$.

Practice   **4** Find the length of the line segment with endpoints (7, 15) and (3, 12).

Practice   **5** Match each labeled point on the graph with its description.
   a x-intercept
   b y-intercept
   c (x, y)
   d x-coordinate
   e y-coordinate

Practice   **6** Find the distance between the points (7, 15) and (13, 7).

Problem Set

Practice

7 Consider the graph of function Q.
  a Find $Q(4)$.
  b Find $Q(-1)$.
  c Find $Q(3)$.
  d For what values of x is $Q(x) = 3$?

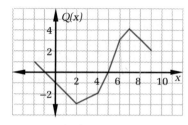

Practice

8 Refer to the diagram.
  a Find the length of $\overline{AB}$.
  b Find the midpoint of $\overline{AB}$.

Review

9 If $y = 3x^2 + kx$, for what value of k is $(x, y) = (-2, 16)$?

Review

10 If $\angle P$ is acute, what are the possible values of x?

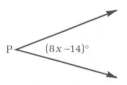

Practice

11 Let $h(x) = 3x - 6$. If the input values x are chosen from $\{-9, 0, 4, 15\}$, what is the set of output values $h(x)$?

Review

12 If $x^2 + x > 6x - 5$, determine whether
  a $x = 2$ is a solution   **b** $x = 3$ is a solution
  c $x = 4$ is a solution   **d** $x = 5$ is a solution

In problems 13–15, solve for x.

Review

13 $Q + 7x = F$ **14** $(P + Q)x = R + T$ **15** $ax + bx = c$

Review

16 The perimeter of the rectangle is 6x.
  a Use the information given in the diagram to write an equation for the perimeter.
  b Solve the equation for x.
  c Find the numerical values of the length and width of the rectangle.
  d Find the numerical value of the perimeter.

Review

17 What fractional part of AD is BC?

Problem Set, *continued*

Review
Introduce

18 The following matrix contains statistics of the Great Lakers' five starters in a recent game against Frostbite Falls.

	Field Goals	3-Point Field Goals	Free Throws Made	Free Throws Attempted
Rhea Bounder	1	1	1	3
"Magic" Johansson	10	1	5	8
Leia Upp	6	0	8	10
Zetta Zchott	4	2	4	4
Gardenia Close	2	0	3	5

a What percentage of the starters made at least one 3-point field goal?
b What percentage of the starters made at least half of their free throws?
c How many points were scored by the five starters?
d What percentage of those points were scored by the two guards, "Magic" and Zetta?

Practice
Review

19 Points A and B on a number line have coordinates of −2 and 3 respectively. Find each of the following.
a The coordinate of the reflection of A over the zero point
b The coordinate of the reflection of A over B

Practice
Introduce

20 For each table of values, write an equation that expresses the relationship between the x and y values.

a

y	0	1	2	3	4	5
x	10	9	8	7	6	5

b

x	2	3	4	$\frac{3}{8}$	$\frac{5}{12}$	$\frac{1}{10}$
y	$\frac{1}{2}$	$\frac{1}{3}$	$\frac{1}{4}$	$\frac{8}{3}$	$\frac{12}{5}$	10

Practice

21 Refer to the diagram.
a Find the coordinates of point C.
b Find AC and BC.
c Find AB.

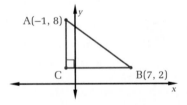

Practice

22 Find the perimeter of a parallelogram PQRS with vertices P(3, 26), Q(10, 2), R(16, 2), and S(9, 26).

Practice

23 If one endpoint of a segment is (4, 3) and the segment's midpoint is (9, 11), what is the other endpoint?

24 Write the inequalities that describe the shaded region and find the coordinates of the four vertices of the rectangle.

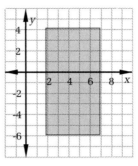

25 Solve $\displaystyle\sum_{n=1}^{3}(x + n) = 36$ for x.

26 A staircase will be built in a stairwell that is 150 inches long and 96 inches high.

  a If each step is to be 6 inches high, how many steps will be built?

  b How deep will each step be?

  c What will be the ratio of each step's height to its depth?

27 Refer to the graph.

  a For what values of x is $h(x) = 0$?

  b For what values of x is $h(x) < 0$?

  c What is the range of possible values of $h(x)$?

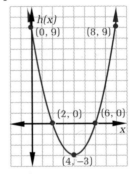

28 Pim owes Sam $5. Sam owes Bom $7. Bom owes Pim $9. What is the minimum amount of money that the people can exchange to discharge all debts? Explain.

29 Find the area of the rectangle and find the coordinates of the point where the diagonals $\overline{ET}$ and $\overline{RC}$ intersect.

30 Find the units digit of each number by analyzing the pattern of the simpler cases $2^1, 2^2, 2^3, 2^4, 2^5, \ldots$

  a 2^{36} **b** 2^{42}

MATRICES

Objectives

After studying this section, you will be able to
- Multiply a matrix by a scalar and solve matrix equations
- Add matrices
- Multiply matrices

Part One: Introduction

Matrix Definitions and Scalar Multiplication

In business, sports, science, and mathematics, it is often convenient to organize data in tables called *matrices*. A *matrix* is a rectangular arrangement of data, usually enclosed in brackets.

$$A = \begin{array}{c} \\ \\ \end{array} \begin{array}{ccc} \textbf{Column 1} & \textbf{Column 2} & \textbf{Column 3} \\ \left[\begin{array}{ccc} 3 & -4 & 18.2 \\ -1 & 11 & -36 \end{array}\right] & & \begin{array}{c} \textbf{Row 1} \\ \textbf{Row 2} \end{array} \end{array}$$

This matrix contains two horizontal rows and three vertical columns and is called a 2 × 3 (read "two by three") matrix.

Two matrices are equal if they have the same dimensions and all corresponding terms are equal. For instance, if

$$\begin{bmatrix} 3x & -4y + 2 \\ -15 & 98.6 \end{bmatrix} = \begin{bmatrix} 15 & 38 \\ -z^2 + 1 & t \end{bmatrix}$$

we can conclude that the following four statements are true.

$$3x = 15 \qquad -4y + 2 = 38 \qquad -15 = -z^2 + 1 \qquad 98.6 = t$$

Finally, to multiply a matrix by a number, we multiply each element by that number. This is called *scalar multiplication*.

Example   *Multiply* $-5x \begin{bmatrix} 3 & x \\ -4x & 1 \end{bmatrix}$.

$$-5x \begin{bmatrix} 3 & x \\ -4x & 1 \end{bmatrix} = \begin{bmatrix} -5x(3) & -5x(x) \\ -5x(-4x) & -5x(1) \end{bmatrix} = \begin{bmatrix} -15x & -5x^2 \\ 20x^2 & -5x \end{bmatrix}$$

Matrix Addition

If two matrices have the same dimensions, we can add them by adding the corresponding terms.

$$\begin{bmatrix} 12 & -3 & 9.3 \\ -6 & 14 & -2 \end{bmatrix} + \begin{bmatrix} 6.5 & 3 & 4.5 \\ -9 & 26 & 2.2 \end{bmatrix} = \begin{bmatrix} 18.5 & 0 & 13.8 \\ -15 & 40 & 0.2 \end{bmatrix}$$

Example   *Add* $\begin{bmatrix} 2 & 5 \\ x^2 - 1 & x \end{bmatrix} + \begin{bmatrix} 7 & -4 \\ 2x + 2 & 4 \end{bmatrix}.$

$$\begin{bmatrix} 2 & 5 \\ x^2 - 1 & x \end{bmatrix} + \begin{bmatrix} 7 & -4 \\ 2x + 2 & 4 \end{bmatrix} = \begin{bmatrix} 9 & 1 \\ x^2 + 2x + 1 & x + 4 \end{bmatrix}$$

Matrix Multiplication

To multiply two matrices, we multiply the elements in each *row* of the first matrix by the corresponding elements in each *column* of the second matrix and add the products.

Example   *Determine* $A \cdot B$ *for* $A = \begin{bmatrix} 2 & 5 \\ 4 & 3 \end{bmatrix}$ *and* $B = \begin{bmatrix} -7 & 9 & 0 \\ 4 & 6 & -11 \end{bmatrix}.$

Let us proceed one step at a time. We begin by multiplying the first row by the first column.

$$\begin{bmatrix} 2 & 5 \\ & \end{bmatrix} \begin{bmatrix} -7 & & \\ 4 & & \end{bmatrix} = \begin{bmatrix} 2(-7) + 5(4) & - & - \\ - & - & - \end{bmatrix}$$

$$= \begin{bmatrix} 6 & - & - \\ - & - & - \end{bmatrix}$$

We multiply the second row by the first column.

$$\begin{bmatrix} & \\ 4 & 3 \end{bmatrix} \begin{bmatrix} -7 & & \\ 4 & & \end{bmatrix} = \begin{bmatrix} 6 & - & - \\ 4(-7) + 3(4) & - & - \end{bmatrix}$$

$$= \begin{bmatrix} 6 & - & - \\ -16 & - & - \end{bmatrix}$$

We multiply the first row by the second column.

$$\begin{bmatrix} 2 & 5 \\ & \end{bmatrix} \begin{bmatrix} & 9 & \\ & 6 & \end{bmatrix} = \begin{bmatrix} 6 & 2(9) + 5(6) & - \\ -16 & - & - \end{bmatrix}$$

$$= \begin{bmatrix} 6 & 48 & - \\ -16 & - & - \end{bmatrix}$$

We continue in this way until all the elements of the product have been calculated.

$$\begin{bmatrix} 2 & 5 \\ 4 & 3 \end{bmatrix} \begin{bmatrix} -7 & 9 & 0 \\ 4 & 6 & -11 \end{bmatrix} = \begin{bmatrix} 6 & 48 & 2(0) + 5(-11) \\ -16 & 4(9) + 3(6) & 4(0) + 3(-11) \end{bmatrix}$$

$$= \begin{bmatrix} 6 & 48 & -55 \\ -16 & 54 & -33 \end{bmatrix}$$

Notice that since we multiply row elements by column elements, the number of elements in each row of the first matrix must equal the number of elements in each column of the second matrix. Because matrices A and B meet this condition, we were able to find the product A · B, but because each of B's rows has three elements and each column of A has only two elements, the product B · A cannot be determined.

In general, the product of an $m \times n$ and an $n \times p$ matrix will be an $m \times p$ matrix.

Part Two: Sample Problems

Problem 1   If $A = \begin{bmatrix} 2 & -1 & 3 \\ -5 & 11 & 7.5 \end{bmatrix}$ and $B = \begin{bmatrix} 4 & 5 & -3.2 \\ 0 & -9 & 1 \end{bmatrix}$, what is $4A + 2B$?

Solution $4A + 2B = 4\begin{bmatrix} 2 & -1 & 3 \\ -5 & 11 & 7.5 \end{bmatrix} + 2\begin{bmatrix} 4 & 5 & -3.2 \\ 0 & -9 & 1 \end{bmatrix}$

$$= \begin{bmatrix} 8 & -4 & 12 \\ -20 & 44 & 30 \end{bmatrix} + \begin{bmatrix} 8 & 10 & -6.4 \\ 0 & -18 & 2 \end{bmatrix}$$

$$= \begin{bmatrix} 16 & 6 & 5.6 \\ -20 & 26 & 32 \end{bmatrix}$$

Problem 2   *The first matrix shows batting statistics of three players for the first six weeks of the season. The second matrix shows the players' statistics for the seventh week.*

	At Bats	Hits
Tom	140	45
Rick	98	33
Harry	87	18

	At Bats	Hits
Tom	15	2
Rick	6	2
Harry	9	1

a *What are the three players' statistics for the seven weeks?*

b *What are the players' batting averages after the seven weeks?*

c *If Tom is to be a .300 hitter for a total of 210 at bats during the season, how many of his remaining 55 at bats must be hits?*

Solution   **a** To find the total statistics, we add the matrices.

$$\begin{bmatrix} 140 & 45 \\ 98 & 33 \\ 87 & 18 \end{bmatrix} + \begin{bmatrix} 15 & 2 \\ 6 & 2 \\ 9 & 1 \end{bmatrix} = \begin{bmatrix} 140+15 & 45+2 \\ 98+6 & 33+2 \\ 87+9 & 18+1 \end{bmatrix} = \begin{bmatrix} 155 & 47 \\ 104 & 35 \\ 96 & 19 \end{bmatrix} \begin{matrix} \textbf{Tom} \\ \textbf{Rick} \\ \textbf{Harry} \end{matrix}$$

with column headers **At Bats** and **Hits**

b A batting average is found by dividing hits by at bats.

Tom's average $= \dfrac{47}{155} \approx .303$

Rick's average $= \dfrac{35}{104} \approx .337$

Harry's average $= \dfrac{19}{96} \approx .198$

c If Tom is to have an average of .300, his total number x of hits divided by his 210 at bats must equal .300.

$$\dfrac{x}{210} = .300$$
$$x = 63$$

Since Tom already has 47 hits, he needs 63 − 47, or 16, more hits.

Part Three: Exercises and Problems

Warm-up Exercises

In problems 1–3, use the following matrices.

$$A = \begin{bmatrix} 3 & 2 \\ -3 & -1 \\ -2 & 1 \end{bmatrix} \qquad B = \begin{bmatrix} -5 & 4 \\ 6 & -3 \\ -6 & 2 \end{bmatrix}$$

1 Find A + B.   **2** Find −4B.   **3** Find A − B.

4 If $\begin{bmatrix} x_1 & y_1 \\ x_2 & y_2 \end{bmatrix} = \begin{bmatrix} -3 & 2 \\ -4 & -9 \end{bmatrix}$ and $m = \dfrac{y_2 - y_1}{x_2 - x_1}$, what is the value of m?

In problems 5 and 6, find each product.

5 $\begin{bmatrix} 3 & -7 \end{bmatrix}\begin{bmatrix} 2 \\ -3 \end{bmatrix}$

6 $\begin{bmatrix} -3 & -1 \\ 5 & -2 \end{bmatrix}\begin{bmatrix} 5 \\ -2 \end{bmatrix}$

7 Consider the 2 × 3 matrix $A = \begin{bmatrix} 2 & 3 & -1 \\ -5 & 0 & 4 \end{bmatrix}$.

  a Matrices of what dimensions can be added to A?
  b If we can multiply A · B, what must be true of matrix B?
  c If we can multiply C · A, what must be true of matrix C?

8 Multiply the matrices to find George's and Gracie's total pay for the week.

	Regular Hours	Overtime Hours		Hourly Wages	
George	40	12	·	5.75	Regular
Gracie	40	7		8.00	Overtime

Problem Set

In problems 9–14, use the following matrices.

$$P = \begin{bmatrix} 4 & 3 \\ -2 & 0 \\ -1 & 2 \end{bmatrix} \quad Q = \begin{bmatrix} -4 & 5 \\ 7 & -2 \\ -5 & 3 \end{bmatrix} \quad R = \begin{bmatrix} -2 & 4 \\ 3 & 1 \end{bmatrix}$$

9 Find $3P - 2Q$.

10 Find $P \cdot R$.

11 Find $Q \cdot R$.

12 Find $R \cdot P$.

13 Can the product $P \cdot Q$ be found? Explain.

14 Can P and R be added? Explain.

15 What are the values of a and b if $\begin{bmatrix} a & 5 \\ -2 & 3b \end{bmatrix} = \begin{bmatrix} -14 & 5 \\ -2 & 22 \end{bmatrix}$?

16 The following matrices show the numbers of miles driven in a year by each member of a family and the cost per mile of driving each of the family's cars (including gas, insurance, license fees, etc.).

	Miles Driven		Cost per Mile
	Car 1	Car 2	(dollars)
Mother	4537	2358	
Father	6547	3475	Car 1 [0.18]
Child 1	1579	1298	Car 2 [0.29]
Child 2	3543	1579	

a What is the cost of each person's driving?

b What is the total cost of the family's driving?

c How much would the family have saved if child 1 had always driven car 1?

17 Find each product.

a $\begin{bmatrix} 5 & -8 \\ 2 & 6 \end{bmatrix}\begin{bmatrix} -3 & 4 \\ 7 & 9 \end{bmatrix}$

b $\begin{bmatrix} 5 & -8 \\ 2 & 6 \end{bmatrix}\begin{bmatrix} 7 & 9 \\ -3 & 4 \end{bmatrix}$

c $\begin{bmatrix} 5 & -8 \\ 2 & 6 \end{bmatrix}\begin{bmatrix} 4 & -3 \\ 9 & 7 \end{bmatrix}$

18 a Find each product.

i $\begin{bmatrix} 1 & 0 \\ 0 & 1 \end{bmatrix}\begin{bmatrix} 3 & 2 \\ -1 & 4 \end{bmatrix}$

ii $\begin{bmatrix} 1 & 0 \\ 0 & 1 \end{bmatrix}\begin{bmatrix} 7 & 9 \\ -4 & 11 \end{bmatrix}$

iii $\begin{bmatrix} 1 & 0 \\ 0 & 1 \end{bmatrix}\begin{bmatrix} a & b \\ c & d \end{bmatrix}$

b The matrix $I = \begin{bmatrix} 1 & 0 \\ 0 & 1 \end{bmatrix}$ is called an *identity matrix*. If B is a 2×2 matrix, what is $I \cdot B$?

19 The matrix shows the wages of several employees. What scalar multiplier should be used to produce a product matrix representing the employees' wages after a 15% pay raise?

$$\begin{bmatrix} 115 & 425 \\ 150 & 175 \\ 135 & 249 \\ 146 & 476 \end{bmatrix}$$

20 a Use the left-hand diagram to find an expression equivalent to $(x + 7)^2$.

b Copy the right-hand diagram and supply the missing measurements. What product does this diagram represent?

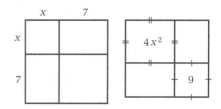

21 What are the possible values of the area of a circle if the measure of its radius is between 4 and 10?

22 The reflection of the point $(-1, 3)$ over the x-axis is $(-1, -3)$, and its reflection over the y-axis is $(1, 3)$. What is the reflection of the point $(5, -7)$ over the x-axis?

23 If you flip a fair coin, what is the probability it will land showing heads?

24 Solve each equation. Round your answers to the nearest tenth.

a $\sqrt{x} = 11.36$ **b** $x^2 = 11.36$

c $2x = 11.36$ **d** $\dfrac{x}{2} = 11.36$

25 The following matrices show the annual salaries paid to the four categories of employees (A, B, C, and D) at Wally's Widget Company and the number of employees in each category.

	Salary (dollars)				Number of Employees			
	A	**B**	**C**	**D**	**A**	**B**	**C**	**D**
3 years experience	26,000	28,000	32,000	39,000	5	3	1	2
4 years experience	29,500	35,000	37,000	41,000	0	6	4	3
5 years experience	37,000	40,000	42,000	45,000	9	2	1	5
6 years experience	42,000	45,000	48,000	49,000	16	3	0	2

a What is the total annual amount paid to the employees by Wally's?

b Suppose that a pay raise of 6% for all employees is put into effect. Write the new salary matrix.

c How much additional money will Wally's pay in salaries each year after the 6% pay raise?

26 Let $(x_1, y_1) = (3, 5)$ and $(x_2, y_2) = (-1, 4)$. Evaluate each expression.

a $\dfrac{y_2 - y_1}{x_2 - x_1}$ **b** $\dfrac{y_1 - y_2}{x_1 - x_2}$

27 Evaluate the following for $f(x) = \dfrac{9x - 63}{x^2 - 9}$.

a $f(7)$ **b** $f(3)$ **c** $f(-3)$

28 What fractional part of the graph of $-19 \le x \le 5$ is the segment represented by $-17 \le x \le -2$?

Problem Set, *continued*

29 Find the perimeter of the trapezoid shown.

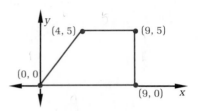

30 If $x^2 + 3x - 10 = 0$,

   a Is $x = 2$ a solution?   **b** Is $x = 5$ a solution?
   c Is $x = -2$ a solution?   **d** Is $x = -5$ a solution?

31 A warehouse has orders to ship refrigerators to stores A, B, C, and D. The refrigerators come in three styles—I, II, and III. The following matrix shows the number of refrigerators to be shipped to each store.

$$
\begin{array}{c} \\ \text{I} \\ \text{II} \\ \text{III} \end{array}
\begin{array}{cccc}
\textbf{A} & \textbf{B} & \textbf{C} & \textbf{D} \\
\left[\begin{array}{cccc} 1 & 0 & 3 & 8 \\ 6 & 2 & 1 & 1 \\ 7 & 4 & 2 & 1 \end{array}\right]
\end{array}
$$

If it costs \$40 to ship a refrigerator to store A, \$10 to ship one to store B, and \$20 to ship one to either store C or store D, what is

   a The total cost of shipping for each style of refrigerator?
   b The total cost of shipping all the refrigerators?

32 Igor takes a number, adds 5, then multiplies the sum by 2. Rogi takes a number, divides by 2, then subtracts 5 from the quotient. If you gave a number to Igor and gave his result to Rogi, what result would Rogi find?

33 Copy the following matrix, supplying the missing data.

$$
\begin{array}{l}
\textbf{Number of nickels} \\
\textbf{Number of dimes} \\
\textbf{Number of quarters} \\
\textbf{Total value (cents)}
\end{array}
\left[\begin{array}{ccccc}
3 & & 7 & x & x \\
8 & 2 & & 3x & x+2 \\
2 & 6 & 3 & 2x & 2x \\
& 200 & 150 & &
\end{array}\right]
$$

34 The shaded region represents the inter-section of which of the following inequalities?

   a $-4 \le x \le 3$
   b $-4 \le y \le 3$
   c $x > 7$
   d $x \le 7$
   e $x < 7$

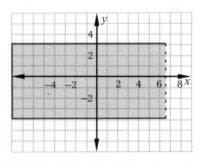

In problems 35 and 36, find the ordered pair (x, y) that satisfies both equations simultaneously.

35 $\begin{cases} x + y = 32 \\ y = x - 4 \end{cases}$

36 $\begin{cases} x + y = 13 \\ x - y = 7 \end{cases}$

In problems 37–39, let y = 10x − 35 and z = 1 − 2x.

37 Find all values of x for which $y > 0$.

38 Find all values of x for which $z \leq 17$.

39 Find all values of x for which $y \leq z$.

40 Write an equation that relates the values of x and y given in the table.

x	3	5	7	9
y	−4	−2	0	2

41 **a** Plot on a number line the values of x for which $|x - 3| = 2$.
   b Plot on a number line the values of x for which $|x - 5| = 1$.
   c Look for a pattern in parts **a** and **b**. Then sketch a number line showing the solutions of $|x - 10| = 3$.
   d Draw a diagram representing the values of x for which $|x - 7| = k$.

42 A pizza parlor offers five toppings that can be added to a basic cheese pizza.
   a How many one-topping pizzas are available?
   b How many two-topping pizzas are available?
   c How many three-topping pizzas are available?
   d How many four-topping pizzas are available?
   e How many five-topping pizzas are available?

43 Using the following matrices, calculate $C \cdot D$ and $D \cdot C$. Is matrix multiplication commutative?

$$C = \begin{bmatrix} 1 & -2 \\ 6 & 5 \end{bmatrix} \qquad D = \begin{bmatrix} 3 & 7 \\ 8 & -4 \end{bmatrix}$$

PROBABILITY

Objective

After studying this section, you will be able to
- Calculate probabilities

Part One: Introduction

In our everyday lives, we cannot always know what will happen when we make decisions. Often, however, the *chances* of events can be determined, thus allowing us to make better-informed decisions. To determine such chances, we use *probability.*

You will find probability useful in a variety of everyday situations. In addition, by setting up and solving probability problems, you will develop the kind of organized thinking that can be applied in all mathematical studies. Many probability problems are analyzed by means of the following two-part procedure.

Basic Steps for Probability Problems

1. **Find all possible outcomes in an organized manner. This process is called *exhaustive listing*.**

2. **Determine which of the possibilities yield the specified result. We will call these winners.**

Probability is calculated according to the formula

$$\text{Probability} = \frac{\text{number of winners}}{\text{number of possibilities}}$$

Part Two: Sample Problems

Problem 1

If one of the points (x, y) is randomly chosen, *what is the probability that its coordinates satisfy the inequality* $3x + 4y > 15$?

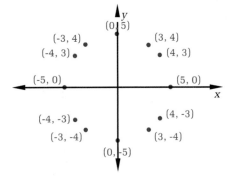

Solution

We check each possibility.

(x, y)	3x + 4y	3x + 4y > 15?
(5, 0)	3(5) + 4(0) = 15	No
(4, 3)	3(4) + 4(3) = 24	Yes
(3, 4)	3(3) + 4(4) = 25	Yes
(0, 5)	3(0) + 4(5) = 20	Yes
(−3, 4)	3(−3) + 4(4) = 7	No
(−4, 3)	3(−4) + 4(3) = 0	No
(−5, 0)	3(−5) + 4(0) = −15	No
(−4, −3)	3(−4) + 4(−3) = −24	No
(−3, −4)	3(−3) + 4(−4) = −25	No
(0, −5)	3(0) + 4(−5) = −20	No
(3, −4)	3(3) + 4(−4) = −7	No
(4, −3)	3(4) + 4(−3) = 0	No

There are 3 winners out of 12 possibilities. The probability is $\frac{3}{12}$, or $\frac{1}{4}$.

Problem 2

If three of the five figures shown are selected at random, what is the probability that all three will have perimeters greater than 28?

Solution

First, we find each perimeter.

Perimeter of figure A = 8 · 4 = 32
Perimeter of figure B = 5 · 5 = 25
Perimeter of figure C = 4 · 8 = 32
Perimeter of figure D = 10 · 3 = 30
Perimeter of figure E = 8 + 4 + 5 + 3 + 2 + 3 + 1 + 4 = 30

Three of the figures are to be selected, so we list all possible threesomes and put a box around each winner—that is, every threesome in which each figure's perimeter is greater than 28. It is important to write the list in an orderly, logical way.

ABC   [ACD]   [ADE]   BCD   BDE   [CDE]
ABD   [ACE]   BCE
ABE

The probability is $\frac{4}{10}$, or .4. (Note the similarity between this procedure and some of the approaches we used in solving the handshake problem in Chapter 1.)

Problem 3   *A point within the large rectangle is chosen at random. Find the probability that the point is in the shaded rectangle.*

Solution   The entire rectangle has an area of 10(14), or 140. The shaded rectangle has an area of 3(4), or 12. The probability is $\frac{12}{140}$, or ≈.0857.

Part Three: Exercises and Problems

Warm-up Exercises

1 The probability of a given event's occurring must be between what two numbers?

2 Give an example of a situation in which you would have to estimate the probability of a particular event.

3 A point is chosen at random from within the large rectangle.

   a What is the probability that the point is in region A? In region B? In region C? In region D?

   b What is the sum of the probabilities you found in part **a**?

4 If three of the five points shown are chosen at random, what is the probability that they are vertices of a triangle?

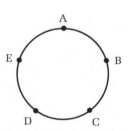

Problem Set

5 For the function $f(x) = \frac{1}{2}x - 5$, an input x is chosen at random from $\{2, 4, 6, 8, 10, 12, 14, 16\}$. What is the probability that $f(x) \leq 0$?

6 A point is chosen at random on $\overline{PQ}$.

  a If the point's coordinate is n, what is the probability that $0 \leq n \leq 14$?
  b What is the probability that the point is within 5 units of the point with coordinate 3?

7 A pancake house has five different syrups. How many different combinations of two different syrups can you use on your pancakes?

8 An engine turns a shaft 120 times per minute. Write a function n to describe the shaft's number of revolutions after t minutes.

9 Determine whether $(x, y) = (2, -5)$ is a solution of each equation.

  a $x + y = 7$ **b** $2x - y = 9$ **c** $3x - y = 11$

10 If a number is chosen at random from $\{-6, -4, -2, 0, 2, 4, 6\}$, what is the probability that it is a solution of at least one of the following equations?

  $x^2 + 8x + 12 = 0$ $x^2 = 16$ $-3x + 6 = 0$

11 Evaluate each expression for $(x_1, y_1) = (3, 5)$, $(x_2, y_2) = (5, -1)$, and $(x_3, y_3) = (6, -4)$.

  a $\dfrac{y_2 - y_1}{x_2 - x_1}$ **b** $\dfrac{y_3 - y_1}{x_3 - x_1}$ **c** $\dfrac{y_3 - y_2}{x_3 - x_2}$

12 Redd and Budd decide to race, with Redd giving Budd a 100-yard head start. Redd runs at 8 yards per second, and Budd runs at 6 yards per second. In how many seconds will Redd catch Budd?

13 Is $(x, y) = (4, 6)$ a solution of both $3x - y = 6$ and $y = 2x - 1$?

In problems 14 and 15, solve for (x, y).

14 $\begin{bmatrix} 3 & x \\ y & 2 \end{bmatrix} \begin{bmatrix} 5 \\ 6 \end{bmatrix} = \begin{bmatrix} -3 \\ -10 \end{bmatrix}$

15 $\begin{bmatrix} 4 & 0 \\ 2 & 3 \end{bmatrix} \begin{bmatrix} x \\ y \end{bmatrix} = \begin{bmatrix} -12 \\ 15 \end{bmatrix}$

Problem Set, *continued*

16 Graph each equation on the same coordinate system. What do you observe?

    a $y = 1x - 5$ **b** $y = 2x - 5$ **c** $y = 3x - 5$

17 Find matrix A.

$$3A - \begin{bmatrix} -4 & 7 & 0 \\ 2 & -6 & 5 \end{bmatrix} = \begin{bmatrix} 10 & 2 & 15 \\ 19 & 0 & -32 \end{bmatrix}$$

18 The *determinant* of a 2×2 matrix is a number such that

if $M = \begin{bmatrix} a & b \\ c & d \end{bmatrix}$, then det $M = ad - bc$.

    a Find det $\begin{bmatrix} -4 & 3 \\ 2 & 6 \end{bmatrix}$.

    b Find det $\begin{bmatrix} 3 & 2 \\ -4 & 5 \end{bmatrix}$.

    c Find det $\begin{bmatrix} 1 & 0 \\ 0 & 1 \end{bmatrix}$.

19 Suppose that $y = 3x^2 - x$ and $z = x^2 + 4$. If x is chosen at random from $\{-2, -1, 0, 1, 2, 3\}$, what is the probability that $y \le z$?

In problems 20–22, assume that *a* and *b* are chosen at random from {1, 2, 3, 4, 5, 6} and that *a* and *b* can be equal.

20 What is the probability that $a + b = 7$?

21 What is the probability that $a + b$ is even?

22 What is the probability that $a \cdot b$ is even?

23 Consider the matrix equation

$$\begin{bmatrix} 2 & 3 \\ 1 & -2 \end{bmatrix} \cdot A = \begin{bmatrix} -1 \\ 10 \end{bmatrix}.$$

    a What are the dimensions of matrix A?
    b Find matrix A.

CHAPTER SUMMARY

CONCEPTS AND PROCEDURES

After studying this chapter, you should be able to
- Add expressions and recognize equivalent expressions (2.1)
- Use the Distributive Property of Multiplication over Addition (2.1)
- Calculate absolute values (2.1)
- Follow the standard algebraic order of operations (2.1)
- Recognize equivalent equations (2.2)
- Solve equations by using properties of equality (2.2)
- Express solutions of equations as ordered pairs (2.2)
- Apply properties of inequality (2.3)
- Solve linear inequalities in one variable (2.3)
- Graph solutions of inequalities on the number line (2.3)
- Graph an equation on the Cartesian coordinate system (2.4)
- Use the midpoint and distance formulas (2.4)
- Understand function notation (2.4)
- Multiply a matrix by a scalar and solve matrix equations (2.5)
- Add and multiply matrices (2.5)
- Calculate probabilities (2.6)

VOCABULARY

abscissa (2.4)
absolute value (2.1)
additive inverse (2.1)
distribute (2.1)
equation (2.2)
equivalent expressions (2.1)
exhaustive listing (2.6)
expression (2.1)
function (2.4)
function notation (2.4)

inequality (2.3)
input (2.4)
intercept (2.4)
like terms (2.1)
linear equation (2.2)
matrix (2.5)
opposite (2.1)
ordered pair (2.2)
ordinate (2.4)

origin (2.4)
output (2.4)
probability (2.6)
quadrant (2.4)
scalar multiplication (2.5)
x-axis (2.4)
x-coordinate (2.4)
y-axis (2.4)
y-coordinate (2.4)

PROPERTIES

Addition and Subtraction Properties of Equality (2.2)
Addition and Subtraction Properties of Inequality (2.3)
Distributive Property of Multiplication over Addition (2.1)
Multiplication and Division Properties of Equality (2.2)
Multiplication and Division Properties of Inequality (2.3)
Zero Product Property (2.2)

REVIEW PROBLEMS

In problems 1–4, simplify each expression and solve each equation.

1 $(3x^2 + xy - y^2) + (5x^2 - 6xy - y^2)$

2 $-3x - 5 = -x - 9$

3 $\frac{1}{2}x + \frac{1}{3}x = 2$

4 $x^2 - y^2 + 2x^2 - 3y^2$

5 Refer to the diagram.

    a How many triangles can be drawn if {A, B, C, D, E} is the set of possible vertices?

    b If one of these triangles is chosen at random, what is the probability that point A is one of its vertices?

    c What is the probability that point A is not a vertex of the triangle chosen in part **b**?

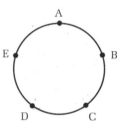

In problems 6–8, solve for x and graph the solution on a number line.

6 $19 - 8x = 67$

7 $19 - 8x > 67$

8 $-3 \le 2x + 7 \le 15$

9 Solve the matrix equation for x, y, and z.

$$\begin{bmatrix} 3x & x + 4 \\ 6 & 8 - z \end{bmatrix} = \begin{bmatrix} 2y & 12 \\ 6 & 5y \end{bmatrix}$$

In problems 10–13, simplify each expression.

10 $(x^2 - 9) - x(x + 3) + 3(x - 3)$

11 $(x + 2)x + (x + 2)3$

12 $x^2(x + 2) + 3x(x + 2) - 5(x + 2)$

13 $x^2(x - 3) + 3x(x - 3) + 9(x - 3)$

In problems 14–16, write an equation to represent each verbal description.

14 The value of y, which is eight less than five times a number n

15 The area of a rectangle with a length that is seven units greater than the width

16 The length of the hypotenuse c of a right triangle having legs with lengths a and b

17 A penny is dropped into the square box shown. What is the probability that it will land on the circular plate?

14 in.

18 Evaluate each expression for $(x, y, z) = (2, 4, -6)$.

a $\dfrac{1}{x} + \dfrac{1}{y} + \dfrac{1}{z}$

b $\dfrac{1}{x + y + z}$

19 A train leaves Transylvania Station at 8:00 A.M. and travels eastward at a rate of 25 miles per hour. Two hours later another train leaves the station, traveling westward at a rate of 35 miles per hour.

a How far apart will the trains be at 1:00 P.M?

b At what time will the trains be the same distance from the station?

c At what time will the trains be 370 miles apart?

20 Let $z = 2x + 4y + 7$. Copy the following matrix, supplying the missing values.

$$\begin{array}{c} x \\ y \\ z \end{array} \begin{bmatrix} 3 & 5 & ? & -1 \\ ? & -4 & 2 & -3 \\ 1 & ? & 15 & ? \end{bmatrix}$$

21 Simplify $-(4.2)^3 - \left(3.7 - \dfrac{12.4}{6.8 - 3.0}\right)$.

22 If $18x + 5y = 12x - 18$ and $y = 4$, what is the value of x?

23 If $10x - 18 = 3x + 5w$ and $w = -2$, what is the value of x?

24 Find each value for $f(w) = |3w - w^2|$.

a $f(7)$

b $f(-7)$

c $f(0)$

25 Let $y = x^2 + 6x + 48$ and $z = x^2 - 6x$.

a Find the value of x for which $y = z$.

b Write a simplified expression for the sum $y + z$ in terms of x.

26 The base pay for a 40-hour work week is $340. Each hour of overtime work pays $15. Copy the following matrix, supplying the missing elements.

Hours of overtime	Overtime pay	Total pay			

$$\begin{array}{l} \textbf{Hours of overtime} \\ \textbf{Overtime pay} \\ \textbf{Total pay} \end{array} \begin{bmatrix} 6 & 8 & ? & ? \\ 90 & ? & 60 & ? \\ 430 & ? & ? & 490 \end{bmatrix}$$

In problems 27–30, graph the values of x on a number line.

27 $x > 6$ or $x \leq -2$

28 $(x - 5)(x + 3) \neq 0$

29 $8 - 4x < 2(x - 8)$

30 $3 \leq x \leq 7$

In problems 31 and 32, perform the indicated operations.

31 $2 + [(6^2 - 16^2)3 + 51] + (-20)^2 + 55$

32 $\sqrt{|-13 - 27| - 15} + 10 - \dfrac{5(6)^2}{12}$

33 At Van Buren High School, a group of students were asked about the numbers of TV sets in their homes. The results are shown in the following chart.

Number of TV Sets	Frequency
0	5
1	25
2	50
3 or more	20

a What is the estimated probability that a randomly selected Van Buren student's family has no TV?

b What is the estimated probability that a randomly selected Van Buren student's family has at least three TV's?

c What is the estimated probability that a randomly selected Van Buren student's family has two or more TV's?

d Van Buren has a student population of 900. Predict the number of students in the school whose families do not own a TV.

e Why might predictions based on this sample be inaccurate? Explain your answer.

34 Mai Tagg, an appliance repairwoman, charges $44 for a house call plus $15 per half-hour for labor. Parts cost extra.

a Write a formula that can be used to find the total bill B for a repair call that takes h hours and requires parts costing p dollars.

b If a repair call took $3\frac{1}{2}$ hours and the total bill was $196, what was the charge for parts?

In problems 35–40, solve each equation.

35 $4.2w + w + 4.3 = 8.1 + 4.2w - 3.8$

36 $-7(4 - x) = 28$

37 $7.2y - 37.6 = 98.4 + 4.5y - 60.8$

38 $x(2x - 3) = 0$

39 $4x - 2(3x - 7) = 12$

40 $x^2 - 5.3x = 0$

41 Refer to the graph.

a Find the pay earned for 3 hours of overtime.

b Estimate the total pay for a week in which $4\frac{1}{2}$ hours of overtime were worked.

CHAPTER TEST

1 Graph each equation on the same coordinate system. What do you observe?

    a $y = 2x - 3$ **b** $y = 2x - 1$ **c** $y = 2x$ **d** $y = 2x + 2$

2 Find each value for $f(x) = 6x - 2$ and $g(x) = x + 4$.

    a $f(3)$ **b** $g(16)$ **c** $g(f(3))$

3 The average of 5, x, 10, and 13 is at least 9. Find x.

4 What values of x and y satisfy *both* of the following equations.

$$\begin{cases} 3x + 2y = 8 \\ y = 6 - x \end{cases}$$

5 Let $3x + 5y = 42$.

    a Find y if x = 6.   **b** Find x if y = 3.

6 If $5x + 4 \leq 15$ and $3 - x < 4$, what are the possible values of x? Graph them on a number line.

In problems 7–9, find the coordinates of A if M is the midpoint of $\overline{AB}$.

    7 M(2, 3); B(7, 4)   **8** M(−5, 1); B(3, −1)   **9** M(a, b); B(a + m, b − n)

In problems 10–13, solve each equation or inequality and simplify each expression.

10 $4x(x + 12)(x - 5) = 0$

11 $4x(x + 12) - (x - 5)$

12 $\dfrac{x - 5}{6} + \dfrac{1}{3}$

13 $-3(x + 2) > 48$

14 For what values of x is $|x| > x$ a true statement?

15 Perform the indicated operations.

$$\left| \frac{(-5 + 1.5)(17 - 9)}{(-11 + 9)^2} \right| + 3 \cdot 13 - 5 \div 2$$

Exponents and Radicals

Laws of Exponents

In earlier mathematics courses you worked with exponents in a variety of ways. As you review the laws of exponents, remember what exponents represent. In the expression a^n, a is the **base,** and n is the **exponent.** The exponent indicates how many times the base is used as a factor, as the following examples show.

$$3^4 = 3 \cdot 3 \cdot 3 \cdot 3 \qquad x^5 = x \cdot x \cdot x \cdot x \cdot x \qquad (xy)^3 = (xy)(xy)(xy)$$

The Product Rule

If a is a real number and m and n are integers, then $a^m \cdot a^n = a^{m+n}$.

Example

$$3^3 \cdot 3^2 = (3 \cdot 3 \cdot 3)(3 \cdot 3) = 3 \cdot 3 \cdot 3 \cdot 3 \cdot 3 = 3^5, \text{ or } 3^3 \cdot 3^2 = 3^{3+2} = 3^5$$

The Power Rule

If a is a real number and m and n are integers, then $(a^m)^n = a^{mn}$.

Example

$$(5^3)^5 = 5^3 \cdot 5^3 \cdot 5^3 \cdot 5^3 \cdot 5^3 = 5^{3+3+3+3+3} = 5^{15}, \text{ or } (5^3)^5 = 5^{3 \cdot 5} = 5^{15}$$

The Quotient Rule

If a is a real number and m and n are integers, then $\dfrac{a^m}{a^n} = a^{m-n}$.

Example

$$\frac{3^5}{3^2} = \frac{3 \cdot 3 \cdot 3 \cdot 3 \cdot 3}{3 \cdot 3} = \frac{3 \cdot 3}{3 \cdot 3} \cdot 3 \cdot 3 \cdot 3 = 1 \cdot 3^3 = 3^3, \text{ or } \frac{3^5}{3^2} = 3^{5-2} = 3^3$$

You may or may not have worked with negative exponents. The following definition explains what a negative exponent represents.

> *If a is a real number, $a \neq 0$, and n is an integer, then $a^{-n} = \dfrac{1}{a^n}$.*

Example

$$\frac{5^2}{5^3} = \frac{5 \cdot 5}{5 \cdot 5 \cdot 5} = 1 \cdot \frac{1}{5} = \frac{1}{5}, \text{ or } \frac{5^2}{5^3} = 5^{2-3} = 5^{-1}$$

The Product Rule, the Power Rule, and the Quotient Rule apply to expressions with negative exponents as well as those with positive exponents.

The Distributive Property of Exponentiation over Multiplication

If x and y are real numbers and n is an integer, then $x^n \cdot y^n = (x \cdot y)^n$.

Example

$$6^5 \cdot 2^5 = (6 \cdot 2)^5 = 12^5$$

The Distributive Property of Exponentiation over Division

If x and y are real numbers, $y \neq 0$, and n is an integer, then $\dfrac{x^n}{y^n} = \left(\dfrac{x}{y}\right)^n$.

Example

$$\frac{6^5}{2^5} = \left(\frac{6}{2}\right)^5 = 3^5$$

There is one more definition we need for our work with exponents.

 If a is a real number and $a \neq 0$, then $a^0 = 1$.

You can see why a number raised to the power 0 is equal to 1 by considering that according to the Quotient Rule $\frac{5^3}{5^3} = 5^{3-3} = 5^0$ and that arithmetically $\frac{5^3}{5^3} = \frac{125}{125} = 1$. The definition specifies that $a \neq 0$ because if a were 0, two definitions would be in conflict. On the one hand, we have defined a^0 as 1; on the other, you know that $0^n = 0$. To avoid this inconsistency, we agree that 0^0 is undefined.

Interpreting Radical Expressions

Since the calculator and the computer have become widely used tools, radical expressions are used less frequently by mathematicians. Still, you will see radical symbolism in your studies, so we will look at some properties of radicals. You may recall that if n is a positive integer and $y^n = x$, then $\sqrt[n]{x} = y$ (with the restriction that if n is even, x and y must be positive). This inverse relationship between powers and roots leads us to the following definition.

 If x is a real number and n is a positive integer, then $\left(\sqrt[n]{x}\right)^n = x$ whenever $\sqrt[n]{x}$ is defined.

Examples

$$\left(\sqrt[3]{-27}\right)^3 = -27 \qquad \left(\sqrt[4]{16}\right)^4 = 16$$

An expression such as $\left(\sqrt[4]{-16}\right)^4$, however, is undefined in the real-number system, since even roots of negative numbers are not defined.

The value we assign to an expression of the form $\sqrt[n]{x^n}$ depends on whether n is even or odd.

> ➤ **If x is a real number and n is a positive integer, $\sqrt[n]{x^n} = |x|$ if n is even, or $\sqrt[n]{x^n} = x$ if n is odd.**

Examples

$$\sqrt{(-2)^2} = \sqrt{4} = 2 \qquad \sqrt[3]{(-4)^3} = \sqrt[3]{-64} = -4$$

Since the radical symbol is most often used in connection with square roots, we will examine some of the properties that allow us to perform operations involving square roots.

> ➤ **If x and y are nonnegative real numbers, then $\sqrt{x}\sqrt{y} = \sqrt{xy}, \dfrac{\sqrt{x}}{\sqrt{y}} = \sqrt{\dfrac{x}{y}}$ (where $y \neq 0$), and $\sqrt{x}\sqrt{x} = x$.**

You might notice that the first two properties are restatements of the distributive properties of exponents in terms of radicals and that the last is a special case of the inverse relationship between powers and roots.

Sample Problems

Problem 1   Evaluate $5^4 \cdot \dfrac{5^3}{5^9}$.

Solution   Evaluating the expression will be easier if we simplify it first.

$$5^4 \cdot \frac{5^3}{5^9}$$

$$= 5^{4+3-9}$$

$$= 5^{-2}$$

$$= \frac{1}{5^2}$$

$$= \frac{1}{25}$$

Problem 2   Simplify $\dfrac{3x^5}{(2x^3)^{-1}} \cdot \dfrac{(x^{-4})^2}{x^2}$.

Solution   Notice that after we apply the Power Rule, it makes no difference which of the other rules we apply first.

Method 1	Method 2
$\dfrac{3x^5}{(2x^3)^{-1}} \cdot \dfrac{(x^{-4})^2}{x^2}$	$\dfrac{3x^5}{(2x^3)^{-1}} \cdot \dfrac{(x^{-4})^2}{x^2}$
Power Rule $= \dfrac{3x^5}{2^{-1}x^{-3}} \cdot \dfrac{x^{-8}}{x^2}$	Power Rule $= \dfrac{3x^5}{2^{-1}x^{-3}} \cdot \dfrac{x^{-8}}{x^2}$

$$\text{Product Rule} \quad = \frac{3x^{-3}}{2^{-1}x^{-1}} \qquad\qquad \text{Quotient Rule} = 6x^8x^{-10}$$

$$\text{Quotient Rule} = 6x^{-2} \qquad\qquad \text{Product Rule} \quad = 6x^{-2}$$

We could also write the answer in the form $\frac{6}{x^2}$.

Problem 3 Write $\sqrt{252}$ in *standard radical form*—that is, the form $a\sqrt{b}$, where *b is an integer having no perfect-square factors.*

Solution We need to find perfect-square factors of 252 and use a distributive property. Notice that the order in which we take out perfect-square factors is not important as long as we don't miss any.

Method 1	**Method 2**	**Method 3**
$\sqrt{252}$	$\sqrt{252}$	$\sqrt{252}$
$= \sqrt{9}\sqrt{28}$	$= \sqrt{4}\sqrt{63}$	$= \sqrt{36}\sqrt{7}$
$= 3\sqrt{4}\sqrt{7}$	$= 2\sqrt{9}\sqrt{7}$	$= 6\sqrt{7}$
$= 6\sqrt{7}$	$= 6\sqrt{7}$	

Problem 4 *Simplify* $\sqrt{18} + \sqrt{27} + \dfrac{\sqrt{36}}{\sqrt{18}} + \sqrt{50}.$

Solution
$$\sqrt{18} + \sqrt{27} + \frac{\sqrt{36}}{\sqrt{18}} + \sqrt{50}$$

Distributive properties $\quad = \sqrt{9}\sqrt{2} + \sqrt{9}\sqrt{3} + \sqrt{\dfrac{36}{18}} + \sqrt{25}\sqrt{2}$

Simplify terms $\quad = 3\sqrt{2} + 3\sqrt{3} + \sqrt{2} + 5\sqrt{2}$

Combine like terms $\quad = 9\sqrt{2} + 3\sqrt{3}$

Problem 5 *Multiply* $2 + \sqrt{7}$ *by* $2 - \sqrt{7}$ *and simplify your answer.*

Solution
$$\left(2 + \sqrt{7}\right)\left(2 - \sqrt{7}\right)$$
$$= 2^2 - 2\sqrt{7} + 2\sqrt{7} - \left(\sqrt{7}\right)^2$$
$$= 2^2 - \left(\sqrt{7}\right)^2$$
$$= 4 - 7$$
$$= -3$$

Notice that the answer is a rational number. Expressions of the form $a + b\sqrt{c}$ and $a - b\sqrt{c}$ will always have a rational product if a, b, and c are rational. Such expressions are called *conjugates.*

Problem 6 *Rationalize the numerator of $\frac{2 + \sqrt{5}}{3 - \sqrt{6}}$ (that is, rewrite the expression so that no radical appears in the numerator).*

Solution Multiply numerator and denominator by conjugate of numerator

$$\frac{2 + \sqrt{5}}{3 - \sqrt{6}}$$

$$= \frac{2 + \sqrt{5}}{3 - \sqrt{6}} \cdot \frac{2 - \sqrt{5}}{2 - \sqrt{5}}$$

$$= \frac{2^2 - 2\sqrt{5} + 2\sqrt{5} - (\sqrt{5})^2}{6 - 3\sqrt{5} - 2\sqrt{6} + \sqrt{30}}$$

$$= \frac{-1}{6 - 3\sqrt{5} - 2\sqrt{6} + \sqrt{30}}$$

A similar process can be used to rationalize a denominator.

Problem Set

In problems 1 and 2, simplify each expression.

1 $(2b^3)^3 \cdot 3(b^{-4})^2$

2 $\frac{12w^{-4}}{8w^8} \cdot \frac{15w^{12}}{(-6w)^2}$

In problems 3–5, indicate whether each statement is True or False (if $x \neq 0$).

3 $x^{2a} = (x^a)^2$

4 $x^a \cdot x^b = x^{ab}$

5 $\frac{x^a}{x^a} = x^1$

6 Evaluate.

a $(5^2)^3$ **b** $(5^3)^2$ **c** 5^5 **d** $(5^{2.5})^2$

7 Find the values of x and y that satisfy both of the following equations.

$$\begin{cases} 2^{2x-y} = 2^3 \\ 3^{x+y} = 3^{12} \end{cases}$$

In problems 8–10, indicate whether each statement is True or False.

8 $\left(\frac{3}{5}\right)^{-4} = \left(\frac{5}{3}\right)^4$

9 $\left(\frac{1}{3} + \frac{1}{5}\right)^{-1} = 3 + 5$

10 $\frac{1}{a + b} = \frac{1}{a} + \frac{1}{b}$

11 How many segments of length x^5 can be made from the segment shown?

$$x^{10} + 3x^7 - 2x^5$$

12 Make a table of values for each of the following equations, then sketch the equation's graph.

a $y = \sqrt{x}$ **b** $y = 2^x$

13 Find an expression for the sum of the volumes of the cube and the box.

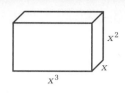

14 Evaluate each expression.

a 6^{-2} **b** $(3^{-2} + 1)^{-1}$ **c** $\left(\frac{1}{2} + \frac{1}{3}\right)^{-1}$ **d** $(2^{-1} - 3^{-1})^{-1}$

In problems 15 and 16, rewrite each expression without parentheses, using only negative exponents.

15 $\left(\dfrac{x^{-3}y^2}{w^{-4}}\right)^5$

16 $\left(\dfrac{x^{-4}y^{-3}}{w^4}\right)^5$

17 Write an expression, in simplified form, for the area of the trapezoid.

18 If $x = 9$, $y = 4$, and $n = 3$, what are the values of $(x + y)^n$ and $x^n + y^n$? Is it true that $(x + y)^n = x^n + y^n$?

19 Simplify $x \cdot x^2 + 2y \cdot 4y^2$.

20 Find the ratio of the volume of the small box to that of the large box.

21 Study the example $16^{\frac{1}{4}} = (2^4)^{\frac{1}{4}} = 2^{\frac{4}{4}} = 2^1 = 2$.
Use this method to evaluate each expression.

a $32^{\frac{1}{5}}$ **b** $64^{\frac{1}{3}}$ **c** $8^{\frac{2}{3}}$ **d** $125^{\frac{4}{3}}$

22 On a certain planet, there exists a number i such that $i^2 = -1$.
Find the value of each expression.

a i^4 **b** i^{-2} **c** $i^6 + i^8 + i^{10} + i^{12}$

23 Use the diagram to find an expression for length s in terms of x.

Area $= 2x^{-3} - 4x^{-2} + 6x^{-1}$ $2x^{-3}$

24 Solve $5 = 5^x = 5^{\frac{1}{3} \cdot y} = (5^z)^{\frac{1}{3}} = w^{\frac{1}{3}}$ for w, x, y, and z.

25 Evaluate $\dfrac{(xy^2)^{18}}{(x^2y)^{19}} \cdot \left(\dfrac{x^4}{y^4}\right)^5$ for $(x, y) = (5.2, -2)$.

26 Match each of the following sets of ordered pairs with the corresponding graph.

a (1, 2), (2, 4), (4, 16), (0, 1) **b** (0, 0), (1, 1), (−2, 2), (−1, 1)

c $\left(4, \frac{1}{2}\right), \left(\frac{1}{4}, 2\right), (1, 1), \left(16, \frac{1}{4}\right)$ **d** (0, 0), $\left(\frac{1}{4}, \frac{1}{2}\right)$, (1, 1), (4, 2)

i   **ii**   **iii**   **iv**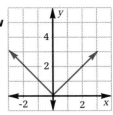

In problems 27–29, rewrite each expression without parentheses, using only positive exponents.

27 $\left(\dfrac{x^{-6}}{y^{-4}}\right)^5$ **28** $\left(\dfrac{x^3}{x^{-2}}\right)^{-5}$ **29** $(x^{-3}y^4)^{-5}$

30 Rationalize the numerator of $\dfrac{\sqrt{5} - \sqrt{3}}{2}$.

In problems 31–33, simplify each expression.

31 $\dfrac{-20xy^3z^2}{24x^4y^2z}$ **32** $x^2(x^2 - x + 2) - x^3(x - 1)$ **33** $(-xy)^4(-x^2y^2)^2$

34 Refer to the figure.

a What is the area of the figure?
b What is the sum of the areas of regions I and II?
c For what value(s) of x is $(x + 4)^2 = x^2 + 4^2$?

In problems 35–38, simplify each expression.

35 $\dfrac{xy}{x^2y + xy}$ **36** $\dfrac{10x^3 + 20x^2}{15x^4 + 30x^3}$ **37** $\dfrac{(3x^2y)^4 \cdot (5x)^3}{(15x^4y^5)^3}$ **38** $\dfrac{(xy^5)^{18}}{(xy)^{17}}$

39 Find the ordered pair (x, y) that satisfies both of the following equations.

$$\begin{cases} 4^{x+y} = 8^{10} \\ 5^{x-2y} = \dfrac{1}{5^{12}} \end{cases}$$

In problems 40–43, indicate whether each statement is True or False.

40 If $x < 0$, then $x^n < 0$. **41** If $x > 0$, then $x^{-n} > 0$.

42 $(-2.5)^2 < 2.5^2$ **43** $\left(\dfrac{1}{2}\right)^{-5} < \left(\dfrac{1}{2}\right)^{-4}$

44 Solve each of the following equations for x.

a $\sqrt{x} = 7$ **b** $\sqrt{x} = -2$

In problems 45–48, rationalize the denominator of each fraction. Write your answers in standard radical form.

45 $\dfrac{10}{\sqrt{5}}$

46 $\dfrac{\sqrt{30}}{\sqrt{5}}$

47 $\dfrac{\sqrt{20}}{\sqrt{8}}$

48 $\dfrac{2}{\sqrt{2}}$

49 Find the length of the hypotenuse of each triangle.

a

b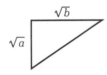

In problems 50–52, evaluate each expression.

50 $\sqrt{5}\sqrt{20}$

51 $\dfrac{\sqrt{5}}{\sqrt{20}}$

52 $\dfrac{\sqrt{2}\sqrt{14}}{\sqrt{7}}$

53 Rationalize the denominator of $\dfrac{2 + \sqrt{5}}{3 + \sqrt{5}}$, then rationalize the numerator of the resulting expression.

54 Match each equation with its graph.

a $y = \dfrac{1}{\sqrt{x}}$

b $y = \sqrt{x^2}$

c $y = \sqrt{x}$

d $y = 2^x$

i

ii

iii

iv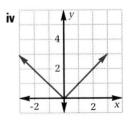

55 Simplify $5\sqrt[3]{16} - \sqrt[3]{54} + 2\sqrt[3]{128}$.

56 Find the ordered pair (x, y) that satisfies the following equations simultaneously.

$$\begin{cases} \sqrt{x} + \sqrt{y} = 2 \\ \sqrt{x} - \sqrt{y} = 1 \end{cases}$$

57 Refer to the cube.
  a Determine the length of $\overline{AB}$.
  b Determine the length of $\overline{BC}$.

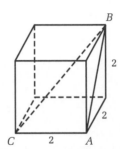

58 Solve $\left(\sqrt{2n} + 3\right)\left(\sqrt{2n} - 3\right) = 3n - 10$ for n.

LINEAR RELATIONSHIPS

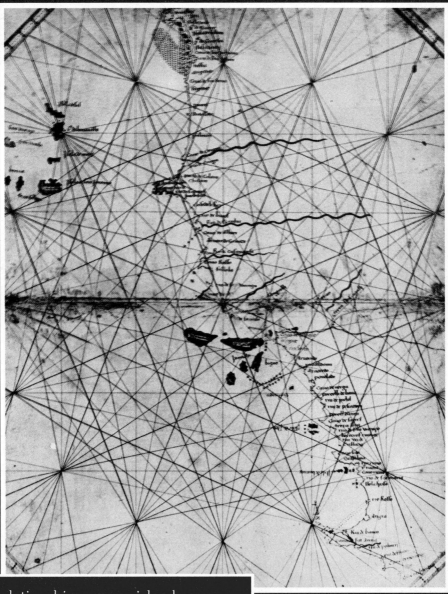

L inear relationships among islands are represented in this antique marine chart showing the West African coast.

GRAPHING LINEAR EQUATIONS

Objectives

After studying this section, you will be able to
- Determine the slope of a line
- Use the point-slope equation of a line
- Use the slope-intercept equation of a line
- Use the general equation of a line
- Use slope to determine whether two lines are perpendicular or parallel

Part One: Introduction

Slope

Slope, an important concept in graphing equations, is a rate of change from point to point on a line. There are several ways of finding and describing slope. We can choose whatever form is appropriate to a given situation.

1 We can express slope as a *rate of change*.

> **Slope is the change in y when the change in x is 1.**

Slope $= \dfrac{\text{change in } y}{1}$

2 We also use the following relationship to find slope.

> **Slope $= \dfrac{\text{change in } y}{\text{change in } x}$**

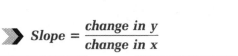

3 If we know the coordinates of two or more points on a line, we can use the slope formula.

The Slope Formula

The slope m of a line containing points (x_1, y_1) and (x_2, y_2) is given by the formula

$$m = \frac{y_2 - y_1}{x_2 - x_1}$$

Example   *Find the slope of the line containing points $(4, 7)$ and $(-5, 2)$.*

Use slope formula
$$m = \frac{y_2 - y_1}{x_2 - x_1}$$
$$= \frac{7 - 2}{4 - (-5)}$$
$$= \frac{5}{9}$$

We can classify lines by their slopes.

Lines that ascend from left to right have *positive* slope.	Lines that descend from left to right have *negative* slope.	Horizontal lines have zero slope.	Vertical lines have *undefined* slope.

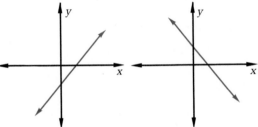

Point-Slope Equation of a Line

If we have a given point, such as $(2, 1)$, and a given slope, such as $\frac{2}{3}$, we can draw a unique line.

    In general, if (x_1, y_1) is on a line with slope m, we can write an equation of all points (x, y) on the line by using the slope formula and some algebra. The slope formula tells us that for every $(x, y) \neq (x_1, y_1)$ on the line,

$$\frac{y - y_1}{x - x_1} = m$$

Multiply $y - y_1 = m(x - x_1)$

The Point-Slope Equation of a Line

If a line has slope m and contains point (x_1, y_1), then all points (x, y) on the line satisfy the equation $y - y_1 = m(x - x_1)$.

Example   *Write an equation of the line that has a slope of $\frac{15}{17}$ and passes through*
$\left(\frac{3}{5}, -\frac{7}{11}\right)$.

We use the point-slope form.

$$y + \frac{7}{11} = \frac{15}{17}\left(x - \frac{3}{5}\right)$$

Slope-Intercept Equation of a Line

The following form of equation is useful with graphing calculators
and computer graphing programs. It also allows us to describe a line
with function notation, $f(x) = mx + b$.

The Slope-Intercept Equation of a Line

A line with equation $y = mx + b$ has slope m and y-intercept b.

Example   *Draw the graph of $f(x) = \frac{2}{3}x - 4$.*

The slope is $\frac{2}{3}$. The y-intercept is -4.
From the y-intercept $(0, -4)$, we
move three units right and two units
up. We repeat this move to find additional points and connect the
points with a line.

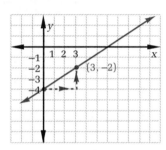

General Linear Equation of a Line

The form $ax + by = c$ is called the general form of a linear
equation. This form can be used to describe any line, including one
with undefined slope, such as the graph of $x = 5$.

Example   *Graph $2x - 5y = 15$.*

We find the x- and y-intercepts. At
the x-intercept, $y = 0$.

$$2x - 5(0) = 15$$
$$2x = 15$$
$$x = \frac{15}{2} = 7.5$$

At the y-intercept, $x = 0$.

$$2(0) - 5y = 15$$
$$-5y = 15$$
$$y = -3$$

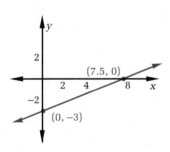

We then connect the two intercepts
with a straight line.

Parallel and Perpendicular Lines

Slope can help us determine whether two lines are parallel or perpendicular.

Example   *Find the slopes of the parallel lines ℓ and m shown.*

$$\text{Slope of line } \ell = \frac{9 - 5}{2 - 0} = 2$$

$$\text{Slope of line } m = \frac{6 - (-4)}{3 - (-2)} = 2$$

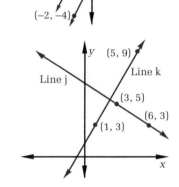

In general, nonvertical lines are parallel only if they have the same slope and different y-intercepts.

Example   *Find the slopes of the perpendicular lines j and k shown.*

$$\text{Slope of line } j = \frac{3 - 5}{6 - 3} = \frac{-2}{3}$$

$$\text{Slope of line } k = \frac{9 - 3}{5 - 1} = \frac{6}{4} = \frac{3}{2}$$

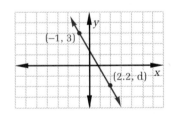

Notice that the product of the slopes, $\frac{-2}{3} \cdot \frac{3}{2}$, is equal to -1.

In general, two nonvertical lines are perpendicular only if the product of their slopes is -1. In other words, the slopes of perpendicular lines are opposite reciprocals.

Example   *Lines ℓ and m are perpendicular. Line ℓ has a slope of $-\frac{2}{7}$. Find the slope of line m.*

Lines ℓ and m are perpendicular, so their slopes are opposite reciprocals. Since the slope of line ℓ is $-\frac{2}{7}$, the slope of line m is $\frac{7}{2}$.

Part Two: Sample Problems

Problem 1   *The given line has a slope of -1.4.
Find the value of d.*

Solution   We can use the slope formula or the point-slope form.

Method 1

$$m = \frac{y_2 - y_1}{x_2 - x_1}$$

$$-1.4 = \frac{d - 3}{2.2 + 1}$$

$$-1.4 = \frac{d - 3}{3.2}$$

$$-4.48 = d - 3$$

$$-1.48 = d$$

Method 2

We use $(-1, 3)$ for (x, y) and $(2.2, d)$ for (x_1, y_1).

$$y - y_1 = m(x - x_1)$$
$$3 - d = -1.4(-1 - 2.2)$$
$$3 - d = 4.48$$
$$-d = 1.48$$
$$d = -1.48$$

Look again at the graph. The y-coordinate of (2.2, *d*) seems to be close to −1.5, so the answer is reasonable.

Problem 2   *A company plans to spend $15,000 on new computers. Each JCN PC costs $1100. A Bartlett PC costs $1800 but is faster and easier to use. What combinations of the two brands can the company buy?*

Solution   We let x = the number of JCN computers and y = the number of Bartlett computers. The equation $1100x + 1800y = 15{,}000$ indicates how many of each computer can be bought for $15,000. This equation describes a line.

$$x\text{-intercept} = \frac{15{,}000}{1100} \approx 13.6$$

$$y\text{-intercept} = \frac{15{,}000}{1800} \approx 8.3$$

Only whole numbers of computers can be bought, so the company can consider only points with integer coordinates on or below the line. The point (2, 7) is one possibility.

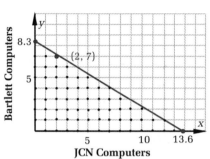

Part Three: Exercises and Problems

Warm-up Exercises

1 A line passes through the point (2, 5) and has a slope of $\frac{1}{2}$. Write the coordinates of at least three other points on the line.

2 For what values of k will the graph of $y = kx + 3$ be a descending line?

In problems 3 and 4, determine the slope of the line containing the given points.

3 (5, 2) and (−7, 8)   **4** (2, 5) and (8, −7)

5 The points shown form a line with slope $\frac{2}{3}$. Find a, b, and c.

In problems 6–10, graph each equation.

6 $3x - 5y = 30$ **7** $y = 2$ **8** $x = 5$
9 $y = 3x - 2$ **10** $y + 2 = -3(x - 3)$

11 If four of the six points shown are chosen at random, what is the probability that they are the vertices of a rectangle?

12 For what value of k are the graphs of $f(x) = -2x + 6$ and $g(x) = kx + 1$

    a Parallel?   **b** Perpendicular?

Problem Set

13 List the lines shown in order of the magnitude of their slopes, from smallest to largest.

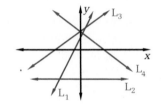

14 If the midpoint of a line segment is (0, 0) and one endpoint has coordinates (4, 7), what are the coordinates of the other endpoint?

15 Draw the line that passes through (3, 6) and (3, 11). Find its slope.

16 Determine whether each of the following algebraic statements is True or False.

    a $x^2 \cdot x^5 = x^{10}$ **b** $x^2 \cdot x^5 = x^7$ **c** $\sqrt{x^2 + y^2} = x + y$
    d $\sqrt{(x + y)^2} = x + y$ **e** $\sqrt{(x + y)^2} = |x + y|$

17 Find the slope of the line shown.

18 Jerry, an aerobic-exercise teacher, tells Pat to determine his ideal exercise heart rate, R, by subtracting his age, A, from 220 and finding a percentage of the result, corresponding to his fitness level—60% (beginner), 70% (average), or 80% (competitor).

    a Write R as a function of A for each fitness level.
    b If Pat is 23 and in average shape, what is his ideal rate?
    c If Lana is a competitive athlete with a rate R of 142, how old is she?

19 An equation is selected at random from the list below. What is the probability that its graph is an ascending line?

$y = 2x - 7$ $y = -4x + 5$ $x - 2y = 6$ $y = 7x + 4$ $y = 3$

20 Write an equation to represent each of the following lines. Then draw the line on a coordinate system.

a Slope $-\frac{2}{3}$, y-intercept 4

b Slope $\frac{3}{5}$, passes through $(-1, 2)$

21 If $(x, y) = (9, -5)$, which of the following is a true statement?

a $10x + 15y = 12$ **b** $10x + 15y > 12$ **c** $10x + 15y < 12$

22 Kathy sells popcorn to raise money for the school French club. A small box sells for $0.30, and a large box sells for $0.50.

a How much money will Kathy collect if she sells 12 small boxes and 15 large boxes?

b Write an expression for the total amount of money that Kathy would collect if she sold x small boxes of popcorn and 3 more large boxes than small boxes.

c If Kathy sold 3 more large boxes than small boxes and collected $25.50, how many boxes of popcorn did Kathy sell all together?

23 The first matrix shows the cost of clothing in three shops. The second shows the items that Sue, Sara, and Kai are shopping for.

	Scarf	Gloves	Socks
Le Chic	17.50	15.00	3.50
Le Pen	20.50	13.50	4.75
Bon Ton	22.25	9.75	5.25

A

	Sue	Sara	Kai
Scarf	2	3	1
Gloves	1	2	3
Socks	4	4	5

B

a Multiply the cost matrix by the quantity matrix.

b How much would Sue save by shopping at Le Pen rather than Bon Ton?

c Who would spend most at Bon Ton?

In problems 24 and 25, write an equation for each line described.

24 Passes through $(3, 1)$ and $(-7, 5)$

25 Slope 0, passes through $(-5, 0)$

26 In the diagram, $\overline{AD}$ is perpendicular to $\overline{BC}$. Find the value of k.

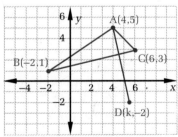

27 If a car can travel 38 miles on 2.4 gallons of gas, how many miles could the car travel on 6 gallons of gas?

Problem Set, *continued*

28 Box-seat tickets at Wiggly Field cost $16. General-admission tickets cost $10. One night the sales of both types of tickets totaled $232,672.

    a Write an equation for the possible combinations of box-seat tickets B and general-admission tickets G sold.

    b Graph the equation you wrote in part **a.**

    c Explain why it is not possible that exactly 5015 box seats were sold. Name some other impossible situations.

29 Consider the points A, B, C, D, E, and F in the diagram. Which of the points satisfy each equation or inequality?

    a $y = x - 3$

    b $y > x - 3$

    c $y < x - 3$

30 The table shows the value (in dollars) of a car after x years.

x	0	1	2	3	4	5
Value	12,600	11,100	9600	8100	6600	5100

    a What does the slope of the line described by these data mean in terms of the value of the car?

    b Using the table and common sense, predict the value of the car after ten years.

31 Let $\frac{x}{7} + \frac{y}{4} = 1$.

    a Find the value of y if x = 0.   **b** Find the value of x if y = 0.

32 If one of the following points is chosen at random, what is the probability that it lies on both the graph of $y - 1 = -2(x + 2)$ and the graph of $x - 2y = 2$?

    (0, 1)   (−1, −1)   (−0.8, −1.4)   (−1.5, 0)

33 Let $h(x) = 3x - 10$. Find all the values of a for which $h(a) + h(a + 1) = h(a + 2)$.

34 Find matrix A.

$$A + \begin{bmatrix} 2 & -3 & 7 \\ -5 & 6 & 5 \end{bmatrix} = \begin{bmatrix} 1 & 0 & -9 \\ -4 & 9 & 8 \end{bmatrix}$$

35 The graphs of $f(x) = ax + b$ and $g(x) = bx - a$ are perpendicular lines.

    a Find $f(0) \cdot g(0)$.

    b If $\frac{g(1)}{f(0)} = 5$ and a > 0, what is the value of a?

3.2 | SYSTEMS OF LINEAR EQUATIONS

Objectives

After studying this section, you will be able to
- Solve systems of linear equations by graphing
- Solve systems of linear equations algebraically

Part One: Introduction

Systems of Equations

The ordered pairs (6, 0), (0, 4), (−3, 6), and (3, 2) are some of the solutions of the equation $2x + 3y = 12$. The ordered pairs (2.5, 0), (0, −10), (1, −6), (3, 2), and (2, −2) are solutions of the equation $4x − y = 10$. Only one ordered pair satisfies both equations simultaneously. That pair, (3, 2), is the solution of the **system of linear equations** that consists of the two equations

$$\begin{cases} 2x + 3y = 12 \\ 4x - y = 10 \end{cases}$$

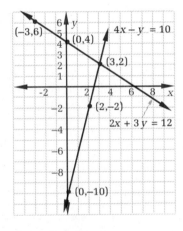

To solve a system means to find all ordered pairs (x, y) that simultaneously make all of the equations in the system true statements. A system may be referred to as a set of **simultaneous equations** with simultaneous solutions.

Solving Systems by Graphing

One way of solving a system is to graph the two equations on the same set of axes, as shown in the preceding diagram. The lines meet at a point—(3, 2)—that satisfies both equations. To check this solution, we can replace x with 3 in each equation and see whether y = 2.

$$2(3) + 3y = 12$$
$$6 + 3y = 12$$
$$3y = 6$$
$$y = 2$$

$$4(3) - y = 10$$
$$12 - y = 10$$
$$12 - 10 = y$$
$$2 = y$$

The pair (3, 2) checks as the solution of the system.

Solving Systems Algebraically

Graphing is not always the best way to solve a system. Often when we graph a system, we can only estimate the coordinates of the point of intersection. There are two algebraic methods we can use to determine the *exact* solution of a system.

If we can easily represent one variable in terms of the others, *substitution* is an appropriate method.

Example   *Solve the following system.*

$$\begin{cases} 4x + 6y = 26 \\ y = 2x + 1 \end{cases}$$

The second equation is already solved for y. We can use the value $2x + 1$ as a replacement for y in the first equation and solve for x.

$$4x + 6y = 26$$
$$4x + 6(2x + 1) = 26$$
$$4x + 12x + 6 = 26$$
$$16x + 6 = 26$$
$$16x = 20$$
$$x = 1.25$$

Now we can substitute 1.25 for x in either equation and solve for y. The second equation is the more convenient.

$$y = 2x + 1$$
$$= 2(1.25) + 1$$
$$= 3.5$$

The solution is $(x, y) = (1.25, 3.5)$. Since we used the second equation in our solution, we check the answer in the first equation.

Left Side	**Right Side**
$4x + 6y$	$= 26$
$= 4 \cdot 1.25 + 6 \cdot 3.5$	
$= 26$	

The sides are equal, so (1.25, 3.5) checks.

When both equations in a system are in general linear form, it is often easiest to use the ***multiplication-addition method***.

Example   *Solve the following system.*

$$\begin{cases} 4x - y = 17 \\ 2x + 3y = 19 \end{cases}$$

We multiply the first equation by 3 and add the equations.

$$\begin{aligned} 12x - 3y &= 51 \\ 2x + 3y &= 19 \end{aligned}$$

Add $$\begin{aligned} 14x &= 70 \\ x &= 5 \end{aligned}$$

Now we substitute 5 for x in one of the equations and solve for y.

$$2x + 3y = 19$$
$$2(5) + 3y = 19$$
$$10 + 3y = 19$$
$$3y = 9$$
$$y = 3$$

The solution is $(x, y) = (5, 3)$. To check, substitute 5 for x and 3 for y in the first equation and see whether a true statement results.

Summary

To solve a system of equations, find all ordered pairs (x, y) that satisfy both equations. Both the substitution method and the multiplication-addition method use the same basic strategy.
1. Eliminate one variable to create a single-variable equation.
2. Solve the single-variable equation.
3. Substitute the value of the variable in one of the original equations to find the value of the other variable.
4. Check your answer in the remaining equation.

Part Two: Sample Problems

Problem 1 Find the point where the graphs of $3x + 4y = -11$ and $5x - 6y = 45$ intersect.

Solution In this case, the most efficient way to determine the point of intersection is to solve a system by the multiplication-addition method.

Multiply first equation by 3	$9x + 12y = -33$
Multiply second equation by 2	$10x - 12y = 90$
Add	$19x = 57$
	$x = 3$

Substitute in first equation	$3(3) + 4y = -11$
	$4y = -20$
	$y = -5$

We check the solution $(3, -5)$ in the second equation.

Left Side	Right Side
$5x - 6y$	$= 45$
$= 5(3) - 6(-5)$	
$= 45$	

The sides are equal, so the answer checks. The lines intersect at $(3, -5)$.

Problem 2   *P. Nutt wants to sell 35 pounds of mixed nuts for $3.05 per pound. Nutt has cashews selling for $3.25 per pound and peanuts selling for $2.80 per pound. How many pounds of each type of nut should he use in the mixture?*

Solution   Let c = the number of pounds of cashews in the mixture and p = the number of pounds of peanuts. The total number of pounds is 35, so $c + p = 35$. The total value of the mixture is $3.05 \cdot 35$, so $3.25c + 2.80p = 3.05(35)$. We therefore have the system

$$\begin{cases} 3.25c + 2.8p = 106.75 \\ c + p = 35 \end{cases}$$

We can rewrite the second equation as $c = 35 - p$ and substitute for c in the first.

$$3.25c + 2.8p = 106.75$$
$$3.25(35 - p) + 2.8p = 106.75$$
$$113.75 - 3.25p + 2.8p = 106.75$$
$$-0.45p = -7$$
$$p \approx 15.6$$

Substitute 15.6 for p
in second equation. $c + 15.6 \approx 35$
$$c \approx 19.4$$

P. Nutt should use about 19.4 pounds of cashews and about 15.6 pounds of peanuts.

Part Three: Exercises and Problems

Warm-up Exercises

1 Explain why $(4, -5)$ is or is not a solution of the following system.
$$\begin{cases} y = 3x - 17 \\ 2x + y = 3 \end{cases}$$

2 Use the diagrams to solve for (x, y).

3 Of the possible methods—graphing, substitution, guess and check, and multiplication-addition—which would you choose to solve each of the given systems? Explain your choice.

a $\begin{cases} x + y = 18 \\ xy = 81 \end{cases}$ b $\begin{cases} y = 2x - 4 \\ 2x + y = 16 \end{cases}$

c $\begin{cases} w + v = 10 \\ 3.45w + 22.75v = 28.9 \end{cases}$ d $\begin{cases} y = 3x + 1 \\ y - 2 = 4(x + 1) \end{cases}$

In problems 4–6, find the point of intersection of the graphs of each pair of equations.

4 $2x - y = 6$ and $y = 2$
5 $y = 2x + 5$ and $y = -3x + 5$
6 $3x + y = 12$ and $x + y = 8$

7 Refer to the graphs of $x - 2y = 4$ and $7x + 2y = 8$.

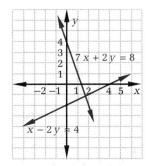

a Approximately where do the lines intersect?

b Use an algebraic method to find the exact point of intersection.

Problem Set

8 Use the diagram to solve for x and y.

9 Solve each system for (x, y).

a $\begin{cases} 3x + y = 22 \\ 2x - y = 13 \end{cases}$ **b** $\begin{cases} y = 3x - 13 \\ 3x + y = 17 \end{cases}$

c $\begin{cases} 7x - 2y = -6 \\ 5x + 2y = 12 \end{cases}$ **d** $\begin{cases} 3x + 2y = 2 \\ 2x + y = 3 \end{cases}$

10 A two-egg breakfast with hash browns and toast costs $1.85. A one-egg breakfast with hash browns and toast is $1.35. How much is charged for hash browns and toast?

11 Find x and y if the perimeter of rectangle A is 26 and the perimeter of rectangle B is 24.

12 A committee of three people is to be selected from a group of three women and two men. If the committee will be selected randomly, what is the probability that it will consist of two women and one man?

13 If $f(x) = 3x + 4$ and $g(x) = 3x - 1$, for what value of x is $f(x) = g(x)$?

14 The matrix below shows the values of four stocks on September 1 and October 1. Copy the matrix, supplying the missing information.

Stock	Value per Share, 9/1	Value per Share, 10/1	Change in Value per Share from 9/1 to 10/1
Flyer Shoes	35.50	38.25	?
JAMB	67.75	71.50	?
Cruiser Bikes	81.00	73.75	?
Vector Shirt	?	46.50	−3.25

Problem Set, *continued*

15 Alex earns \$4.75 per hour plus 1% commission on his total sales.

  a Write an equation that describes Alex's wages as a function of number of hours worked h and total sales s.

  b If Alex works eight hours a day, how much merchandise must he sell to earn at least \$60 a day?

16 Determine the value of a for which the line passing through $(6, -4)$ and $(2, a)$ has a slope of 12.

In problems 17 and 18, solve each system for (x, y).

17 $\begin{cases} y = 4x - 5 \\ y = \frac{1}{2}x + 2 \end{cases}$
 18 $\begin{cases} 3x + 2y = 7 \\ 2x - 5y = 12 \end{cases}$

In problems 19–23, multiply.

19 $x^2 \cdot x^5$ **20** $3x(4x)^2$ **21** $5x^5 \cdot 5x^5$ **22** $-4x(3x^2 - 7x - 5)$ **23** $x^2(3x^5 - 2x)$

In problems 24 and 25, solve each system for (x, y).

24 $\begin{cases} 3x - 5y = 11 \\ 8x + 10y = 6 \end{cases}$
 25 $\begin{cases} x + 3y = 32 \\ y = 2x - 1 \end{cases}$

26 Graph the line that represents the equation $y = 2x - 5$ and name a point *not* on the line. Does the point solve any of the following?

  a $y = 2x - 5$ **b** $y > 2x - 5$ **c** $y < 2x - 5$

27 If three hot dogs cost \$7.53, what do you predict to be the cost of eight hot dogs?

28 Graph the following equations on the same coordinate system.

  a $y = |x|$ **b** $y = |x| + 2$
  c $y = |x + 2|$ **d** $x = |y|$

29 If the two equations $x + y = 10$ and $y = mx + 5$ are graphed on the same coordinate plane and if m is randomly chosen from $\left\{ -2, -\frac{3}{2}, -1, -\frac{1}{2}, 0, \frac{1}{2}, 1, \frac{3}{2}, 2 \right\}$, what is the probability that the two lines will intersect in the first quadrant?

30 Find the value of k for which the slope of the line through $(-2, k)$ and $(5, 3k - 4)$ is 8.

31 Solve the matrix equation for w, x, y, and z.

$$\begin{bmatrix} 2x & x + y \\ z & y - z \end{bmatrix} = \begin{bmatrix} x + 8 & 15 \\ 7 - y & w \end{bmatrix}$$

32 If $x + 2y = 12$ and $3x - 7y = 16$, what is the value of $4x - 5y$?

33 If two points are selected at random from the following list, what is the probability that the line connecting them will be perpendicular to a line with slope $\frac{2}{3}$?

(2, 8)   (4, 5)   (8, −1)   (12, −7)

34 A Mion car costs $12,895 and gets 32 miles per gallon of gasoline. A Toyord car costs $10,550 and gets 26 miles per gallon of gasoline. Gasoline costs $1.16 per gallon.

a For each car, write an equation describing the cost of buying the car and driving it for x miles.

b How many miles would owners of the cars need to drive before the cost of buying and driving the cars would be the same?

c After how many miles of driving is the difference in the cost of buying and driving the cars $500?

CAREER PROFILE

LINEAR RELATIONSHIPS AND TART CHERRIES
Amy Iezzoni brings mathematics to the orchard

In order to grow improved varieties of plants, crops, and trees, plant breeders select and combine characteristics of existing varieties. Amy Iezzoni, an associate professor of horticulture at Michigan State University in East Lansing, is working to help breed new types of tart cherries—the kind used in pies. She is seeking alternatives to the 400-year-old Montmorency cherry, the only sour cherry grown in the United States.

"The Montmorency cherry tree is susceptible to numerous diseases and insects. And it would be better to have a series of cherry varieties that ripen at different times and that may bloom later in the spring and hence be less likely to get frosted than Montmorency," explains Dr. Iezzoni.

Dr. Iezzoni has been breeding tart cherries using pollen and seeds that she has collected from all over eastern Europe, the region that she says is the tart cherry's "center of origin and diversity." Her travels have taken her to Yugoslavia, Bulgaria, Hungary, Romania (to the Carpathian Mountains), Poland, and Sweden. "I also got seeds and pollen through the mail from the Soviet Union. Then we grew all these seedlings in East Lansing."

Using matrices, plotting the characteristics of trees bred from different seeds and pollen, and identifying equations that fit her data, Dr. Iezzoni has found that the trees growing across eastern Europe exhibit a range of characteristics that developed as the trees adapted to a range of environments.

Dr. Iezzoni has a bachelor's degree from North Carolina State University and a doctorate from the University of Wisconsin at Madison.

GRAPHING INEQUALITIES

Objectives

After studying this section, you will be able to
- Graph linear inequalities
- Find the union and the intersection of sets defined by inequalities

Part One: Introduction

Graphing Linear Inequalities

The graph of a linear equation is a set of points that form a straight line. The graph of a linear inequality is a set of points that form a region. The boundary of the region described by a linear inequality is the line found by graphing the inequality as if it were an equation.

We can graph linear inequalities quite accurately by using a ***boundary-value algorithm.***

1 Graph the boundary equation.
2 Test a point in each region.
3 Shade the appropriate region.

Example   *Graph $y > 3x + 5$.*

We use a dashed boundary line $y = 3x + 5$ to show that the points on the boundary line, such as (0, 5), are not part of the graph of the inequality.

Next we test a point in each of the two regions formed by the boundary line. The values (0, 10) in the left-hand region make the inequality a true statement; the values (0, 0) in the right-hand region do not.

If one point in a region represents a solution of the inequality, all points in the region do. We therefore shade the entire region to the left of the boundary line.

Union and Intersection

Since a graph is a set of points, we can consider more than one graph at a time by using the concepts **union** (∪) and **intersection** (∩) from the language and notation of sets. These operations are defined for sets A and B as follows:

A ∪ B = {all elements in set A or in set B or in both sets}
A ∩ B = {all elements in set A and in set B}

To define a set in terms of specific conditions, we use a colon to mean "such that." For example, {x:x > 0} is read "the set of all numbers x such that x is greater than zero."

Example Let R = {x:x < 5} and S = {x:x ≥ 3}.

a Find R ∪ S.

The single variable tells us to use a one-dimensional graph, a number line. A set that began "{(x, y):" would require a two-dimensional graph.

The union is the set of all real numbers—in set notation, {x:x ∈ ℛ}, read "the set of all numbers x such that x is an element of the real numbers."

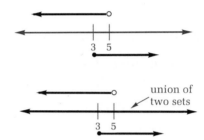
union of two sets

b Find R ∩ S.

The intersection is the set of reals between 3 and 5, including 3 but not 5. In set notation we write {x:3 ≤ x < 5}, read "the set of all numbers x such that x is greater than or equal to 3 and less than 5."

intersection of two sets

Part Two: Sample Problem

Problem Let A = {(x, y): y ≤ x + 3} and B = {(x, y): y > −2x − 3}. Graph A ∪ B and A ∩ B.

Solution Since two variables are involved, we must use two-dimensional graphs.

A ∪ B, the union, consists of all points that belong to at least one of the sets. Notice the boundary lines.

A ∩ B, the intersection, consists of points that belong to both of the sets. Again, study the boundary lines.

Part Three: Exercises and Problems

Warm-up Exercises

1 Graph $y \geq -3x + 4$.

In problems 2 and 3, sketch the graph of each set.

2 $\{(x, y){:}y < 5\}$ **3** $\{x{:}x \geq -12\}$

4 Sketch the graph of $2x + 3y \geq 12$. Is the point $(4, 7)$ on this graph?

5 Let $A = \{2, 4, 6, 8, 13, 14, 15\}$, $B = \{2, 6, 7, 9, 12, 14, 15, 17\}$, and $C = \{4, 7, 8, 9, 12, 13, 17\}$.

  a Find $A \cup B$.   **b** Find $A \cap B$.
  c Find $A \cap (B \cup C)$.   **d** Find $(A \cap B) \cup (A \cap C)$.

6 Consider the positive integers between 0 and 100. Write a simple form of each intersection.

  a {multiples of 3} $\cap$ {multiples of 2}
  b {multiples of 5} $\cap$ {multiples of 3}
  c {multiples of 6} $\cap$ {multiples of 4}

7 Graph $\dfrac{x}{4} + \dfrac{y}{5} \leq 1$.

8 Write an inequality to describe the shaded region.

Problem Set

9 Sketch the graph of $\{(x, y){:}x - 3 < 5\}$.

10 Let $A = \{(x, y){:}y < 2x + 3\}$ and $B = \{(x, y){:}y < 4x + 3\}$. Sketch the graph of $A \cap B$.

11 Draw the line that passes through $(3, 5)$ and has a slope of $\frac{2}{3}$.

  a Shade the region below the line.
  b Write an inequality to describe the shaded region.

12 Two perpendicular lines intersect at $(0.5, 7.5)$. Neither line is horizontal. Write equations of the lines.

13 Refer to the graph. Estimate the coordinates of the point where the lines intersect; then find the exact coordinates of the point.

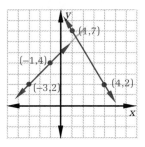

14 Find the area of the rectangle shown for each of the following values of x.

    a x = 7
    b x = −2
    c x = −6
    d What values of x make sense in this problem?

15 Let S = {(x, y):y > x} and N = {(x, y):y < −x}. If a point is selected at random from the following set, what is the probability that it is an element of S ∩ N?

{(5, 0), (5, 5), (0, 5), (−5, 5), (−5, 0), (−5, −5), (0, −5), (5, −5)}

16 The diagram shows the numbers of All-Star Games won by the American and National Leagues in the years from 1933 through 1989.

    a In which decade did the National League win the most games?
    b In which decade did the American League win the most games?
    c Which league dominated the years 1933–1949?
    d Which league dominated the years 1950–1989?

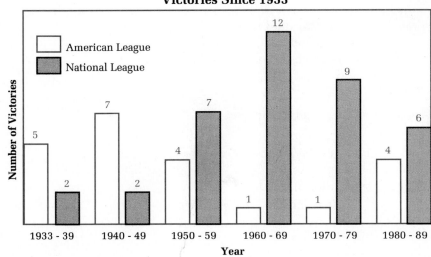

All-Star Game Victories Since 1933

Problem Set, *continued*

17 Tom mows lawns and whitewashes fences during his summer vacation. He is paid $12 for each lawn mowed and $17 for each fence painted. Last month Tom did 105 jobs and made a total of $1410. How many of each type of job did he do?

18 Evaluate each expression.

a $\displaystyle\sum_{n=2}^{6} n$

b $\displaystyle\sum_{n=2}^{6} 5n$

19 Sketch the graph of $\{(x, y) : x \geq |y|\}$.

20 Graph $-y < -x$.

21 The lines shown are perpendicular. Describe the shaded region algebraically.

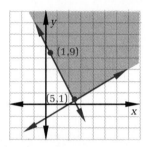

22 A linear graph contains the points $(3, -5)$ and $(7, 12)$.

a If $(a, 4)$ is also a point on this graph, what is the value of a?
b If $(-7, b)$ is also a point on this graph, what is the value of b?

23 Lonnie won a contest in which the prize was up to $85.00 worth of compact discs and audio tapes. Compact discs cost $12.95, tapes cost $7.95, and Lonnie must buy at least four items.

a Write two inequalities to describe her options.
b Graph the inequalities.
c What are the choices Lonnie could make?
d What combination of CD's and tapes should Lonnie choose if she wants to spend as much as possible of the $85.00?

In problems 24–26, draw the graph of each set.

24 $\{(x, y) : x \geq 2y + 1\}$ **25** $\{(x, y) : y \geq x^2\}$

26 $\{(x, y) : y \leq x + 3 \text{ and } 0 \leq x \leq 4\} \cap \{(x, y) : y \geq -x + 7 \text{ and } 2 \leq x \leq 6\}$

27 Solve the following system for m and b.
$$\begin{cases} 2 = 5m + b \\ 14 = 8m + b \end{cases}$$

28 Find k_1 and k_2 so that the graphs of $y = 2x + k_1$ and $y = 7x + k_2$ intersect at $(4, -3)$.

29 A number is chosen at random from $\{-5, -3, -1, 1, 3, 5\}$. What is the probability that the number cannot be used as a value of x in the function $g(x) = \frac{x + 3}{(x + 5)(x - 1)}$?

30 Graph $y - 5 \leq 2(x + 5)$.

31 In the diagram, $\triangle ABC \sim \triangle DEF$. Find the values of x and y.

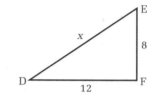

32 If $(2, -6)$ and $(-4, -12)$ are points on the graph of $y = ax^2 + b$, what are the values of a and b?

33 Graph $|y| + |x| = 4$.

34 Copy and complete the table of values for the function $f(x) = |x + 10| + |10 - x|$.

x	−20	−10	−6	0	1	8	10	12	20	50
$f(x)$										

35 Consider the sequence $2(1) + 5, 2(2) + 5, 2(3) + 5, \ldots$
  a Find the value of the thirteenth term.
  b Write an expression that represents the nth term.

36 A point is chosen at random in the square with vertices $(0, 0)$, $(0, 15)$, $(15, 15)$, and $(15, 0)$. What is the probability that the coordinates of the point satisfy the inequality $x + y \leq 10$?

37 According to the triangle-inequality property, the sum of any two sides of a triangle must be greater than the third side of the triangle.
  a Use the diagram of $\triangle ABC$ to write three inequalities based on the triangle-inequality property.
  b Graph the region that satisfies all three inequalities.

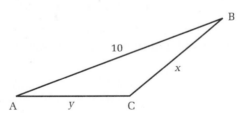

FUNCTIONS AND DIRECT VARIATION

Objectives

After studying this section, you will be able to
- Write equations that represent linear functions
- Find restrictions on the domain of a function caused by real-world constraints
- Recognize direct variation
- Express direct variation as a proportion

Part One: Introduction

Linear Functions

The following table represents Jon's earnings for a five-week period, where x = his total sales for a week and $f(x)$ = his pay for the week.

x	1000	1250	700	900	1600
$f(x)$	190	200	178	186	214

The quotient [change in $f(x)$] ÷ (change in x) represents the weekly rate of change in earnings compared to sales.

$$\frac{10}{250} = 0.04 \qquad \frac{-22}{-550} = 0.04 \qquad \frac{8}{200} = 0.04 \qquad \frac{28}{700} = 0.04$$

Because this quotient is constant, the data are *linearly related*. It is therefore possible to describe the data with a *linear function* of the following form.

$$f(x) = mx + b$$

Remember that slope, m, is a rate of change, so $m = 0.04$. To find the value of b, we substitute any pair of values in the table for x and $f(x)$.

$$f(x) = 0.04x + b$$
$$190 = 0.04(1000) + b$$
$$150 = b$$

Thus a linear function describing Jon's pay, $f(x)$, as a function of his sales, x, is $f(x) = 0.04x + 150$.

Domain

We have not yet discussed what inputs make sense in a function. Mathematically, we can calculate Jon's earnings for $x = -200$ as follows.

$$f(-200) = 0.04(-200) + 150$$
$$= 142$$

But what does this result mean? A negative value for Jon's sales does not make sense. To be sure that our results are meaningful, we need to think about what a problem's answer means in terms of the problem. (In this case, since the input is an amount of money, x not only must be nonnegative but must represent a whole number of cents.)

The function f therefore has a restricted *domain*, or set of inputs, for which its output, $f(x)$, has real-world meaning. The full definition of the function includes its domain.

$$f(x) = 0.04x + 150, \text{ where } x \geq 0 \text{ and } 100x \text{ is a whole number}$$

Domain, and the corresponding set of outputs, *range*, will be discussed again in Chapter 5.

Direct Variation

There is an important relationship between the perimeter P of a square and the length s of each side. If we double the length of the side, we double the perimeter. If we divide the length of the side by 3, the perimeter is divided by 3. We can represent the relationship between perimeter and side length with the function $P(x) = 4s$ and say that P is *directly proportional* to s. In this case, 4 is called the *constant of variation* or the *constant of proportionality*.

As you have seen, a linear relationship between $f(x)$ and x is expressed by a function of the form $f(x) = mx + b$. If $b = 0$, however, the function has the form $f(x) = mx$ and we can say that $f(x)$ varies directly as x or $f(x)$ is directly proportional to x. The slope m is the constant of variation.

Example   *The data below are linearly related. Determine whether they represent a direct variation—that is, whether $h(x)$ varies directly as x. If so, find the constant of variation.*

x	4	−7	12
$h(x)$	−24	42	−72

Because $h(x)$ is linearly related to x, $h(x) = mx + b$.

Compute the slope $$m = \frac{42 - (-24)}{-7 - 4}$$
$$= -6$$

Substitute to find b $$h(x) = -6x + b$$
$$-24 = -6(4) + b$$
$$0 = b$$

Since $b = 0$, $h(x)$ varies directly as x. The constant of variation is −6.

Example   To change a temperature from degrees Celsius C to degrees Fahrenheit F, we use the formula $F = \frac{9}{5}C + 32$. Is this an example of direct variation?

No. The formula is a function of the form $f(x) = mx + b$, but $b \neq 0$, so F does not vary directly as C.

Proportion

A useful way of expressing direct variation is by means of a *proportion*. A *proportion* is an expression of the form $\frac{a}{b} = \frac{c}{d}$, where a, b, c, and d are real numbers, $b \neq 0$, and $d \neq 0$. If (x_1, y_1) and (x_2, y_2) both satisfy a direct variation $y = mx$, then $y_1 = mx_1$ and $y_2 = mx_2$. Thus, $\frac{y_1}{x_1} = m$ and $\frac{y_2}{x_2} = m$, so $\frac{y_1}{x_1} = \frac{y_2}{x_2}$, which is a proportion.

Example   If x varies directly as y and if x = 14 when y = 15, what is the value of y when x = 7?

Since x and y vary directly, we can set up a proportion.

$$\frac{y \text{ value}}{\text{corresponding x value}} = \frac{y \text{ value}}{\text{corresponding x value}}$$

$$\frac{15}{14} = \frac{y}{7}$$

$$7(15) = 14y$$

$$7.5 = y$$

When x = 7, therefore, y = 7.5.

Part Two: Sample Problem

Problem   The number of gallons of gasoline a car uses is directly proportional to the number of miles driven. John's car uses 11.5 gallons to go 200 miles. How many gallons does it need to go 300 miles?

Solution   Let g = the number of gallons used to go 300 miles. We set up a proportion between miles and gallons.

$$\frac{\text{gallons used}}{\text{miles traveled}} = \frac{\text{gallons used}}{\text{miles traveled}}$$

$$\frac{11.5}{200} = \frac{g}{300}$$

$$17.25 = g$$

It takes $17\frac{1}{4}$ gallons to go 300 miles.

Part Three: Exercises and Problems

Warm-up Exercises

1 Katy gets paid $5 to baby-sit for 2 hours. How much should she be paid if she baby-sits for $3\frac{1}{2}$ hours?

2 Are the values in the table linearly related?

x	3	4	5	6
y	17	21	25	29

3 The values in the following table are linearly related. Does g(x) vary directly as x?

x	8	−5	0
g(x)	−32	20	0

4 If 18 cans of juice cost $7.80, how much do 60 cans cost?

5 Explain how to determine whether linearly related data represent a direct variation.

In problems 6 and 7, solve for x.

6 $\dfrac{x}{3} = \dfrac{10}{7}$

7 $\dfrac{2x - 4}{7x + 3} = \dfrac{4}{5}$

8 If y varies directly as x and if y = 30 when x = 10, what is the constant of proportionality?

Problem Set

9 Are the values in the table linearly related?

x	−5	−3	0	2	4
y	5	3	0	−2	−4

10 If Amy can type $6\frac{1}{4}$ pages in $1\frac{1}{4}$ hours, how many pages can she type in $3\frac{1}{2}$ hours?

In problems 11 and 12, solve each system.

11 $\begin{cases} 5n + 10d = 320 \\ 10n + 5d = 535 \end{cases}$

12 $\begin{cases} x + \frac{1}{2}y = 12 \\ 5x - \frac{1}{2}y = 18 \end{cases}$

In problems 13 and 14, evaluate each expression for y = 4 and x = −5.

13 $3 + 2x^2 - \dfrac{4y}{8}$

14 $x(3 + y) - y(3 + x)$

Problem Set, *continued*

15 Copy the multiplication chart shown, supplying the missing exponential expressions.

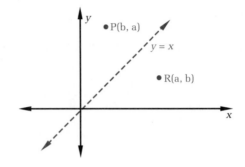

	2^5	2^8	?
?	?	2^8	?
2^2	?	?	2^{13}

16 Explain why line PR must be perpendicular to the line represented by $y = x$.

17 Does $-x$ always represent a negative value? Explain your answer in paragraph form.

In problems 18 and 19, solve each system for *m* and *b*.

18 $\begin{cases} 22.0 = 31.5m + b \\ 758.6 = 1107.8m + 31.5b \end{cases}$
$\qquad$
19 $\begin{cases} 63 = 9m + b \\ 24 = -4m + b \end{cases}$

In problems 20–22, determine which elements of $\{-20, -14, -9, -4, 0, 4, 9, 20\}$ are solutions of the equation or inequality.

20 $|x + 8| = 12$
$\qquad$
21 $x^2 = 36 - 5x$
$\qquad$
22 $x + 30 > 0$

23 The following chart relates the number of miles a compact car is driven to the number of gallons of gas used.

Miles	520	410.3	277.4	471.1
Gallons	18	14.2	9.6	16.3

a Show that the numbers of miles and gallons are directly related.
b Calculate the constant of proportionality.
c What does the constant of proportionality represent in this problem?

24 For what values of *a* and *b* are the values in the table linearly related?

x	65	83	a	111
h(x)	30	39	62	b

25 Pat has $3.85 in 25 coins, all of which are quarters and nickels. How many of each type of coin does Pat have?

26 Graph $x^2 + y^2 = 9$ and $x + y = 3$ on the same coordinate system, then determine the area of the smaller of the two closed regions formed by the graphs.

27 Refer to the diagram. Solve for (x, y).

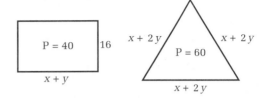

In problems 28–31, graph each set.

28 $\{(x, y):x < 2\}$ **29** $\{x:x < 2\}$ **30** $\{(x, y):y \geq -3\}$ **31** $\{y:y \geq 0\}$

32 Let $A = \{(x, y):|x| \leq 10\}$ and $B = \{(x, y):|y| \leq 6\}$.
  a Sketch the graph of $A \cap B$.
  b Find the area of the graph of $A \cap B$.

33 If you give Skip an odd number, he triples it and adds 1. If you give him an even number, he divides it by 2.
  a What will Skip give back if you give him 17?
  b What will Skip give back if you give him 52?
  c Continue the process, giving Skip his own results to work on at least 13 more times. What happens?

34 Which of the following are linearly related?
  a Circumference and radius of a circle
  b Area and radius of a circle
  c Perimeter and side of a square
  d Area and side of a square
  e Distance traveled and time spent traveling, if speed is constant

35 In the diagram, $\triangle ABE$ is similar to $\triangle CDE$.
  a Find the length of $\overline{AE}$.
  b Find the length of $\overline{AC}$.

36 Find the value of k for which the point $(0, 8)$ lies on the graph of $2x + ky = 24$.

37 If $f(x) = mx + b$ and if $f(2) = 12$ and $f(-3) = -7$, what are the values of m and b?

38 Ma Jones sells Colombian coffee at \$3.50 per pound and Bolivian coffee at \$4.39 per pound. How much of each type of coffee should Ma put in a blend that will sell for \$4 per pound if she wants 200 pounds of blended coffee?

Problem Set, *continued*

39 If $f(x)$ is linearly related to x and $f(x + 4) - f(x) = 32$, what is the slope of the graph of f?

40 Use the population curves shown to determine which animal is prey and which animal is predator. Explain your reasoning, using paragraph form.

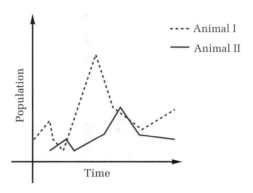

41 In trigonometry, two different measures of angles are used, degrees and radians, with 180 degrees being equivalent to π radians.

  a How many radians are equivalent to 60 degrees?
  b How many degrees are equivalent to 1.58 radians?
  c Are radians and degrees directly proportional?

42 The outputs of function h are linearly related to the inputs x. If $h(5) = 17$ and $h(8) = 29$, what is $h(x)$?

43 Write a linear function f such that $f(4) = 16$ and $f(-2) = 10$.

44 Write a system of inequalities whose solutions include all of the points shown and whose boundary lines pass through the origin.

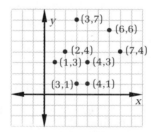

45 A gas bill is based on the number of therms used plus a fixed monthly charge. The following chart gives gas-bill information for the months of March, April, and May.

Month	Therms Used	Cost of Therms	Fixed Charge
March	457.58	175.71	7.50
April	245.63	94.32	7.50
May	132.47	50.87	7.50

  a Find the cost per therm.
  b Write a formula that can be used to find the total bill B for T therms.
  c Use this formula to find the bill for using 842.34 therms.

3.5 | FITTING A LINE TO DATA

Objectives

After studying this section, you will be able to
- Fit a line to data by estimation
- Fit a line to data by the least-squares method

Part One: Introduction

Estimating a Fitted Line

In a chemistry experiment, Bea Kerr collected the data shown in the table. When she graphed the corresponding points, the points were not collinear, but they did suggest a linear pattern. Bea used a ruler to draw a line that seemed to pass through the middle of the points.

Temperature of solvent (°C)	15	20	25	27	36	40	43	47
Powder dissolved (g)	15	13	17	21	23	26	30	31

The line Bea drew is called a ***fitted line.*** Writing an equation that represents a fitted line is easier than writing an equation that accurately describes all the data. The equation of the fitted line can be used to make predictions.

Example   *Using the fitted line that Bea drew, predict the amount of powder that would dissolve if the temperature of the solvent were 60°C.*

We use the graph to estimáte the coordinates of two points on the line, (15, 13) and (45, 28).

$$\text{Slope} = \frac{28 - 13}{45 - 15} = 0.5$$

Letting T = temperature and P = amount of powder dissolved, we use the point-slope form to write an equation that approximates the relationship between the powder dissolved and the temperature of the solvent.

$$P - 13 = 0.5(T - 15)$$

Set $T = 60$ and solve for P

$$P - 13 = 0.5(60 - 15)$$
$$P = 0.5(45) + 13$$
$$P = 22.5 + 13$$
$$P = 35.5$$

Thus, at 60°C the solvent will dissolve about 36 grams.

Fitting Lines by the Method of Least Squares

When there are many data points, graphing the points and fitting a line by estimation is not convenient. Most statisticians use an algebraic method, called the **method of least squares.** When people refer to a **regression line** or a **line of best fit**, they are referring to a line found by the least-squares method.

The line of best fit has an equation of the form $y = mx + b$. The values of m and b are determined by calculating four averages—the x average, the y average, the x^2 average, and the xy average. The constants m and b will satisfy the two equations $y = mx + b$ and $xy = mx^2 + bx$.

Example

Use the method of least squares to find an equation of the line of best fit for Bea Kerr's data. Use that equation to predict the amount of powder that would dissolve in solvent at 60°C.

We let $x =$ temperature and $y =$ amount of powder dissolved and set up a table for the four averages.

									Average (to tenths)
x	15	20	25	27	35	40	43	47	31.5
y	15	13	17	21	23	26	30	31	22.0
x^2	225	400	625	729	1225	1600	1849	2209	1107.8
xy	225	260	425	567	805	1040	1290	1457	758.6

We use the equations $y = mx + b$ and $xy = mx^2 + bx$, replacing x, y, xy, and x^2 with the averages in the table to get a system in m and b.

$$\begin{cases} 22.0 = 31.5m + b \\ 758.6 = 1107.8m + 31.5b \end{cases}$$

When we solve this system with the aid of a calculator or computer, we find that $m \approx 0.57$ and $b \approx 4.1$. An equation of the line of best fit is therefore $y = 0.57x + 4.1$. Using this equation, we set x equal to 60 and solve for y.

$$y = 0.57x + 4.1$$
$$= 0.57(60) + 4.1$$
$$= 38.3$$

We predict that at 60°C the solvent will dissolve about 38 grams of powder.

Statisticians usually use a computer or a calculator that has statistics functions to calculate regression lines. To see whether your calculator can determine a line of best fit, check your calculator manual.

Note that the fitted-line method and the least-squares method predict slightly different amounts of dissolved powder at 60°C. Which method is best? In general, the least-squares method will give the line that most accurately represents the known data. Predictions for untested data values, however, are guesses no matter which technique is used.

Part Two: Sample Problem

Problem

Use the data shown in the table to predict the average temperature in September (month 9).

Month	1	2	3	4	5	6	7	8
Average temperature (°F)	12	22	19	39	51	75	81	83

Solution

The data show a fairly consistent increase in temperature each month, but from our experience we know that the weather usually cools off after August. We could still make a guess, but it would be inappropriate to fit a line using either of the methods described in this section.

Part Three: Exercises and Problems

Warm-up Exercises

1 Write an equation of the line containing the points $(-4.2, 12)$ and $(9.9, 4)$.

2 In the graph, a line has been drawn to fit the data.

   a Choose two points on the line.
   b Determine the slope of the line.
   c Write an equation of the line.

3 Use the values in the table to compute
   a The x average
   b The y average
   c The x^2 average
   d The xy average

x	10	15	20	25	30	35	40
y	−3	5	6	11	14	18	24

4 Solve the following system for m and b. Round your answers to the nearest tenth.

$$\begin{cases} 11 = 25m + b \\ 350 = 668m + 25b \end{cases}$$

Problem Set

The following program will compute a line of best fit by the least-squares method. If you have access to a computer, you may wish to use this program as you work through the problem set.

```
10  REM This program calculates a best-fit line
20  REM by the least-squares method
30  PRINT "Enter the number of data points.==> ";: INPUT N
40  DIM X(N),Y(N)
50  FOR I = 1 TO N
60  PRINT "Enter X(";I;").==> ";: INPUT X(I)
70  PRINT "Enter Y(";I;").==> ";: INPUT Y(I)
80  NEXT I
90  X = 0: Y = 0: X^2 = 0: XY = 0
100 FOR I = 1 TO N
110 X = X + X(I): Y = Y + Y(I): X^2 = X^2 + X(I)^2: XY = XY + X(I) * Y(I)
120 NEXT I
130 X = X/N: Y = Y/N: X^2 = X^2/N: XY = XY/N
140 M = (XY - X * Y)/(X^2 - X * X)
150 B = Y - M * X
160 PRINT "The line of best fit is: ";
170 PRINT "Y = ";M;"X + ";B
180 END
```

5 In a lab experiment, a spring was stretched by various weights. The masses of the weights and the numbers of centimeters the spring stretched are shown in the following table.

Kilograms	1	2	3	4	5	6
Centimeters	1.3	2.5	3.7	5.0	6.4	7.7

a Graph the data and draw a line that approximately fits the data.

b Use the line to approximate how far the spring will be stretched by a weight having a mass of 10 kilograms.

6 Will earns $5.50 per hour as a short-order cook.
   a Write an equation that describes Will's earnings e for h hours.
   b Is e linearly related to h?
   c Does e vary directly as h?

In problems 7 and 8, find an equation of the line of best fit for each set of data.

7

x	1	2	3	4	5	6	7	8
y	12,500	11,000	9350	8225	6550	4750	3425	1788

8

x	100	450	975	1325	1750	2100
y	2620	12,125	23,590	34,720	46,240	53,975

9 Suppose that $f(b)$ is directly proportional to b and $f(7) = 38.4$.
   a Find the constant of proportionality.
   b Find $f(22)$.

10 Which elements of $\left\{(4, 3), (-3, 4), \left(0, \frac{10}{3}\right), (5, 0), (0, -5)\right\}$ are solutions of the following system?

$$\begin{cases} x^2 + y^2 = 25 \\ 2x + 3y = 10 \end{cases}$$

11 Find an equation of the line of best fit for the values in the following table.

x	4	12	9	18	35	100	78
y	31	54	49	74	133	340	270

12 Sketch the graph of $y < -\frac{1}{2}x$.

13 The following table shows temperatures inside a refrigerator during a 10-hour period.

					A.M./P.M.					
Time	8	9	10	11	12	1	2	3	4	5
Temperature (°F)	35	37	39	40	39	36	38	39	37	35

   a Why isn't the temperature constant? (Give two reasons.)
   b Estimate the slope of the line that fits the data.
   c Calculate the line of best fit by the method of least squares.
   d On a hot day, the refrigerator is left open for ten minutes, and then the temperature is measured. If these data are included in the table, what will be the effect on the line of best fit? Should the data be included?

14 Refer to the diagram. If B is the midpoint of $\overline{AC}$, what are the values of x and y?

A(−6,11)

B(−2,8)

C(x,y)

15 The expression $\sqrt{x-7}$ has a real value when $x - 7$ is positive or equals zero. For what values of x is $x - 7 \geq 0$?

16 Which of the following tables represent direct variations?

a

x	−2	0	4
y	6	0	−12

c

x	−1	0	1
y	−1	2	5

b

x	6	$\frac{1}{2}$
y	12	1

d

x	1	0
y	9	−3

17 The roads in Circleton are all either circles or portions of north-south or east-west radii.

  a How long is the shortest path from A to B?

  b How long is the longest path from A to B if no road is traveled more than once?

Town of Circleton
(Distances in km)

18 Suppose that $f(x) = 3x$ when $x > 0$ and that $f(x) = x + 1$ when $x \leq 0$. Evaluate each of the following.

  a $f(4)$ **b** $f(-2)$ **c** $f(0)$

19 One bottle of Kook Cola costs $0.80. A package of six bottles costs $3.00. What is the least possible cost of ten bottles?

20 For the data shown,

x	0	2	4	6	8	10
y	3	4	6	8	9	11

  a Find x_1, the average of the first three values of x

  b Find y_1, the average of the first three values of y

  c Find (x_2, y_2), the averages of the last three values of x and y

  d Write an equation of the line connecting the points (x_1, y_1) and (x_2, y_2) (This method of determining a fitted line is called the *method of group averages.*)

In problems 21–26, graph each equation.

21 $y = x$ **22** $y = x^2$ **23** $y = 2x$

24 $y = 2x^2$ **25** $y = \sqrt{x}$ **26** $y = \sqrt{x - 4}$

In problems 27–30, find the values of a that satisfy the equations.

27 $\dfrac{a}{4} = \dfrac{4}{a}$ **28** $\dfrac{3a + 2}{7} = \dfrac{12}{5}$

29 $\dfrac{3(a - 2) + 5}{6} = \dfrac{7(a - 1)}{2}$ **30** $\dfrac{3}{a + 2} = \dfrac{6}{2a + 4}$

31 a What is the total area of the shaded regions in the diagram?

    b If a point inside the large square is selected at random, what is the probability that it is inside a shaded region? (Express your answer in terms of x.)

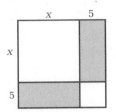

32 The distance a car travels in one revolution of the tires is directly proportional to the diameter of the tires. Lee's car travels about 88 inches in one revolution of 28-inch-diameter tires.

    a What is the constant of proportionality?

    b A truck tire is 48 inches in diameter. How far does the truck travel in one revolution of the tires?

33 In function h, $h(x)$ is linearly related to x. Write a formula for function h if $h(5) = 17$ and $h(8) = 29$.

34 Draw the graph of $-y > 2x + 1$. Then find the area of the closed region formed by the coordinate axes and the graph's boundary line.

35 a The boundary lines of the shaded region shown are parallel. Write a system of inequalities to describe the shaded region.

    b Find the area of the portion of the shaded region that lies in Quadrant II.

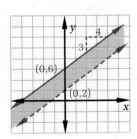

COMPOUND FUNCTIONS

Objectives

After studying this section, you will be able to
- Recognize compound functions
- Graph compound functions
- Recognize the absolute-value function as a compound function

Part One: Introduction

Compound Functions

At Sal's Stationery Store, the cost of a notebook is $1.85. However, if you buy more than five notebooks, the cost of each is $1.75. We can write the following *compound function* for the cost C(n) of n notebooks.

$$C(n) = \begin{cases} 1.85n \text{ if } n \leq 5 \\ 1.75n \text{ if } n > 5 \end{cases}$$

If $n \leq 5$, we use the first rule. If $n > 5$, we use the second rule. Thus, the prices of three notebooks and six notebooks can be calculated as follows.

$$C(3) = 1.85(3) = 5.55$$
$$C(6) = 1.75(6) = 10.50$$

Any function with different rules for different inputs is a compound function. Compound functions are said to have *split domains*.

Graphs of Compound Functions

How do we graph compound functions? Let's look at another example.

$$f(x) = \begin{cases} -x - 4 \text{ if } x < -3 \\ 2x + 5 \text{ if } x \geq -3 \end{cases}$$

To graph $y = f(x)$, we first graph the two equations $y = -x - 4$ and $y = 2x + 5$. Since x is restricted to certain values in each equation, we use only the portions of the graphs in the specified domains.

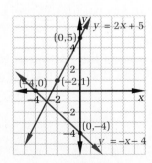

In the graph of $y = -x - 4$, we keep the part of the line to the left of $x = -3$. In the graph of $y = 2x + 5$, we keep the part of the line to the right of and including $x = -3$. The resulting V-shaped graph represents the compound function.

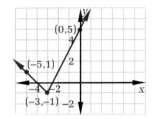

More About Absolute Value

On a number line, the distance from the origin to the point representing a number a is equivalent to the absolute value of a. Formally, absolute value is defined by means of a compound function.

> **If a is a real number, then $|a| = \begin{cases} a \text{ if } a \geq 0. \\ -a \text{ if } a < 0. \end{cases}$**

The number line at the right shows that $|-4| = 4$ and $|13.7| = 13.7$. We can also use absolute value to find the distance between any two points on the number line—if the coordinate of one point is a and the coordinate of the other is b, the distance between the points is $|a - b|$.

Some important properties of absolute value are given in the following table.

Absolute-Value Properties		
If a and b are real numbers,		
$\lvert a \rvert = \lvert -a \rvert$	$\lvert a - b \rvert = \lvert b - a \rvert$	$\lvert ab \rvert = \lvert a \rvert \lvert b \rvert$
$\lvert a + b \rvert \leq \lvert a \rvert + \lvert b \rvert$	$\lvert a \rvert \geq 0$	$\lvert a \rvert^2 = a^2$

Example *Explain why $|x| = |-x|$.*

Absolute value means distance from 0. The numbers x and $-x$ are on opposite sides of 0 but are the same distance from 0.

Example *Graph $y = |x|$.*

According to the compound-function definition of absolute value, this equation means that $y = x$ if $x \geq 0$ and that $y = -x$ if $x < 0$. We therefore graph $y = x$ and $y = -x$ and use only the part of each line that contains the specified x values. The result is the V-shaped graph shown at the right.

Part Two: Sample Problems

Problem 1   *Solve* $|x - 2| = 6$ *for x.*

Solution   The absolute value of an expression is 6 when the expression is equal to either 6 or −6.

$$|x - 2| = 6$$
$$x - 2 = 6 \text{ or } x - 2 = -6$$
$$x = 8 \qquad\qquad x = -4$$

Problem 2   *Graph each set.*

a $\{x{:}|x - 2| = 6\}$ **b** $\{(x, y){:}|x - 2| = 6\}$

Solution   **a** We graph $\{x{:}|x - 2| = 6\}$ on a number line. From Sample Problem 1, we know that the solution set consists of two points, 8 and −4.

b We graph the set of ordered pairs $\{(x, y){:}|x - 2| = 6\}$ on a coordinate plane. The graph is the set of all points (x, y) such that $x = 8$ or $x = -4$. The graph consists of the two vertical lines shown.

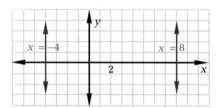

Part Three: Exercises and Problems

Warm-up Exercises

In problems 1–4, use the following compound function.

$$g(x) = \begin{cases} -x + 12 \text{ if } x < 8 \\ \tfrac{1}{2}x - 2 \text{ if } x \geq 8 \end{cases}$$

1 Find $g(-2)$.
3 Find $g(8)$.

2 Find $g(10)$.
4 Which is greater, $g(7.9)$ or $g(8.1)$?

5 Draw the graph of $y = f(x)$ for the following function f.

$$f(x) = \begin{cases} 1 \text{ if } x > 0 \\ 0 \text{ if } x = 0 \\ -1 \text{ if } x < 0 \end{cases}$$

In problems 6–9, use the following compound function.

$$h(x) = \begin{cases} x + 2 \text{ if } x \leq 4 \\ 6 \text{ if } x > 4 \end{cases}$$

6 Draw the graph of $y = h(x)$.
8 Find $h(4)$.

7 Find $h(0)$.
9 Find $h(10)$.

In problems 10–12, solve for *w*.

10 $|w + 10| = 17$

11 $|5 - w| = 15$

12 $|w - 5| = 15$

13 Tickets for a show cost $2.75 each if fewer than 25 are purchased and $2.40 each if 25 or more are purchased.

  a Write a compound function *c* for the total cost of x tickets.
  b Find $c(10)$, $c(24)$, and $c(25)$.
  c What does your answer to part **b** tell you about buying 25 tickets?

Problem Set

In problems 14–19, use the following compound function.

$$f(x) = \begin{cases} 2x \text{ if } 0 < x \le 10 \\ 20 - \frac{1}{2}x \text{ if } 10 < x < 40 \end{cases}$$

14 Find $f(-4)$.

15 Find $f(0)$.

16 Find $f(6)$.

17 Find $f(10)$.

18 Find $f(30)$.

19 Find $f(50)$.

20 Graph each of the following sets.

  a $\{x : |x + 3| = 7\}$
  b $\{(x, y) : |x + 3| = 7\}$

21 Graph each of the following equations.

  a $y = x$
  b $y = -x$
  c $y = |x|$

22 Graph each equation on the coordinate plane.

  a $|x + 5| = 9$
  b $y = x + 5$
  c $y = |x + 5|$

In problems 23 and 24, solve for x.

23 $|x + 3| = 9$

24 $4|x - 7| + 2|x - 7| = 12$

25 Express the area of the shaded region in terms of x and y.

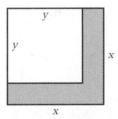

26 Calculators cost $17.95 each if 1–10 are purchased, $15.95 each if 11–200 are purchased, and $14.50 each if more than 200 are purchased.

  a Write a compound function *c* for the cost of x calculators.
  b Find $c(7)$, $c(52)$, and $c(345)$.
  c For what purchase ranges would you spend less money by buying more calculators?

Problem Set, *continued*

27 The following table shows the tolls charged at exits that are various distances from the eastern end of a tollway.

Exit number	1	2	3	4	5	6	7
Miles from east end	25	60	84	130	155	180	210
Toll (dollars)	1.25	3.75	4.00	6.00	7.25	8.50	9.75

a Graph the data, fit a line by estimation, and write an equation of the line.
b Use the method of least squares to determine an equation of the line of best fit.
c A new tollway exit is to be built 100 miles from the east end. What should the toll at that exit be?
d The tollway is being extended to the west. The toll for the entire trip from the east end to the new west end is to be $10.75. Estimate the length of the extended tollway.

28 Write a formula for a linear function g such that g(4) = 24 and g(10) = 60.

29 The graph of a linear function f is perpendicular to the graph of $g(x) = \frac{2}{3}x - 4$. If $f(6) = 14$, what is function f?

30 If $f(x)$ varies directly as x and $f(3) = 14$, for what value of x_1 is $f(x_1) = 35$?

31 Evaluate each of the following expressions for (x, y) = (5, 2). Which of the expressions are equivalent?

a $(x - y)^2$ **b** $x^2 - y^2$ **c** $x^2 - 2xy + y^2$ **d** $(x + y)(x - y)$

32 In the diagram, x is a number such that $2 \leq x \leq 5$.

a Write a function f for the ratio AC:CB.
b Find $f(4)$.

33 Let $g(x) = \sqrt{x + 5}$. Evaluate each of the following.

a g(4) **b** g(−5) **c** g(−9)

In problems 34–36, solve for p.

34 $|2p + 10| = |-15|$ **35** $-5 = 3 - |12 - 3p|$ **36** $2041 = |16p + 775|$

37 Graph the following compound function.
$$f(x) = \begin{cases} x + 1 \text{ if } x \geq 2 \\ 3 \text{ if } -2 < x < 2 \\ x + 4 \text{ if } x \leq -2 \end{cases}$$

38 Refer to the figure.

  a Write a function to describe the area A of the trapezoid.
  b Is the area of the trapezoid linearly related to x?

39 If $f(x) = |x - 4|$ and x is randomly chosen from $\{1, 2, 3, 4, 5, 6, 7, 8\}$, what is the probability that $f(x) \geq 2$?

40 Sketch the graph of each equation.
  a $y \geq |x - 3|$ **b** $y \geq |x + 3|$ **c** $y \geq |x| + 3$ **d** $y \geq |x| - 3$

41 Let $g(x) = x^2 - x$ and $h(x) = g(x) + 5$.
  a Find $g(2)$.   **b** Find $h(2)$.

42 Use a system of inequalities to describe the shaded region.

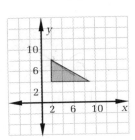

43 Which of the following statements are true?
  a $\sqrt{x^2} = |x|$ **b** $\sqrt{x^2} = x$ **c** $\sqrt{x^2} = \begin{cases} x \text{ if } x \geq 0 \\ -x \text{ if } x < 0 \end{cases}$

44 Determine which of the given ordered pairs (x, y) satisfy the following matrix equation.
$$\begin{bmatrix} 0 & 1 \\ 1 & 1 \end{bmatrix} \begin{bmatrix} x^2 \\ y^2 \end{bmatrix} = \begin{bmatrix} 16 \\ 25 \end{bmatrix}$$
  a $(3, 4)$ **b** $(-3, 4)$ **c** $(-3, -4)$
  d $(3, -4)$ **e** $(4, -3)$ **f** $(4, 3)$

In problems 45–53, determine the set of numbers that make each equation or inequality a true statement.

45 $|x| \geq x$ **46** $\frac{|x|}{x} = 1$ **47** $|x^2| = x^2$

48 $|x| \cdot x = x^2$ **49** $(\sqrt{x})^2 = |x|$ **50** $\sqrt{x^2} = x$

51 $|x| - |y| = |x - y|$ **52** $|x + y| = |x| + |y|$ **53** $(\sqrt{x^2})^2 = x^2$

In problems 54–57, write each absolute-value function as a compound function.

54 $f(x) = |x + 3|$ **55** $g(x) = 2|x - 4|$

56 $h(x) = |x - 2| + 4$ **57** $R(x) = -|x + 3|$

Problem Set, *continued*

In problems 58–61, write each compound function as an absolute-value function.

58 $f(x) = \begin{cases} x \text{ if } x \geq 0 \\ -x \text{ if } x < 0 \end{cases}$

59 $g(x) = \begin{cases} x - 2 \text{ if } x \geq 2 \\ 2 - x \text{ if } x < 2 \end{cases}$

60 $L(x) = \begin{cases} 2x + 4 \text{ if } x \geq -2 \\ -2x - 4 \text{ if } x < -2 \end{cases}$

61 $R(x) = \begin{cases} -x + 3 \text{ if } x \geq 3 \\ x - 3 \text{ if } x < 3 \end{cases}$

62 Prove that $-|a| \leq a \leq |a|$ for any real number a.

MATHEMATICAL EXCURSION

LINEAR PROGRAMMING
Organizing mathematical decision making

Some of the problems most commonly solved on computers involve linear programming, a method of formulating a problem entirely in terms of linear equations and inequalities.

For example, you could use linear programming in planning a daily diet that would give you the greatest nutritional value with the fewest calories and that would include a wide variety of foods you enjoy. Problems to which linear programming is applied always have many variables subject to defined constraints, with quantities to be minimized or maximized.

Long-distance telephone companies use linear programming in routing calls. Linear programming helps these carriers achieve the most economical use of such equipment as long-distance land lines, repeat amplifiers, and satellite terminals. In fact, a researcher for one long-distance carrier recently developed a method of linear programming that is several times faster than the existing simplex method.

What quantity do you think a long-distance company wants to minimize? What are the variables and constraints in its problem? Think of some other situations in which linear programming could be used to solve a problem.

For more information on linear programming, see the Short Subject that begins on page 466.

CHAPTER SUMMARY

CONCEPTS AND PROCEDURES

After studying this chapter, you should be able to

- Determine the slope of a line (3.1)
- Use the point-slope, slope-intercept, and general equations of a line (3.1)
- Use slope to determine whether two lines are perpendicular or parallel (3.1)
- Solve systems of linear equations graphically and algebraically (3.2)
- Graph linear inequalities (3.3)
- Find the union and the intersection of sets defined by inequalities (3.3)
- Write equations that represent linear functions (3.4)
- Find restrictions on the domain of a function caused by real-world constraints (3.4)
- Recognize direct variation (3.4)
- Express direct variation as a proportion (3.4)
- Fit a line to data by estimation and by the least-squares method (3.5)
- Recognize compound functions (3.6)
- Graph compound functions (3.6)
- Recognize the absolute-value function as a compound function (3.6)

VOCABULARY

boundary-value algorithm (3.3)
compound function (3.6)
constant of proportionality (3.4)
constant of variation (3.4)
direct variation (3.4)
directly proportional (3.4)
domain (3.4)
fitted line (3.5)
intersection (3.3)
line of best fit (3.5)
linear function (3.4)

method of least squares (3.5)
multiplication-addition method (3.2)
proportion (3.4)
range (3.4)
regression line (3.5)
simultaneous equations (3.2)
slope (3.1)
split domain (3.6)
substitution (3.2)
system of linear equations (3.2)
union (3.3)

REVIEW PROBLEMS

1 Copy and complete the table of values for $y = -3x + 8$, then graph the equation on a coordinate plane.

x	-3	-2	-1	0	1	2	3	4
y								

2 a Write, in point-slope form, an equation of a line.
b Write, in slope-intercept form, an equation of a line parallel to the first line.
c Write, in general linear form, an equation of a line perpendicular to the two parallel lines.

In problems 3–6, solve for x.

3 $2.7|x - 4.5| = 13.5$

4 $-4|x + 7| = 24$

5 $|x + 5.7| - 2.3 = 14.7$

6 $\sqrt{2}|3x - 7| = 54.9$

7 Refer to the data in the following table.

x	5	10	12	15	20	25	30	32	35	40
y	80	85	5	20	45	70	20	95	29	10

a Write an equation of the line of best fit for the data.
b Graph the ordered pairs in the table and the equation you wrote in part **a** on the same coordinate system.
c Write a paragraph describing what you found in part **b**. What do you think about the original data?

8 Let $y - 2 = 3(x - 5)$.
a Find the value of k if the point $(5, k)$ is on the graph of the equation.
b Graph the equation.

9 Graph $y = x - 3$ and $3x - 5y = 15$ on the same coordinate plane. Approximately where do the graphs intersect?

10 Bolivian coffee sells for \$4.59 per pound, and Colombian coffee sells for \$5.95 per pound. How many pounds of each coffee should be mixed to produce 4000 pounds of a mixture that will sell for \$5.10 per pound?

11 Sketch each of the described lines.

    a Passes through the origin and is parallel to the graph of
$y = 3x - 2$

    b Passes through (5, −1) and is perpendicular to the graph of
$y = \frac{2}{3}x + 4$

    c Has an x-intercept that is 4 greater than its y-intercept, with
the sum of the intercepts being 14

12 The following chart shows toll data for the Indiana Toll Road.

Exit	Mile Marker	Cost
Gary (Westport)	0	—
Portage	9	0.30
Valparaiso	19	0.65
Michigan City	27	0.95
La Porte	37	1.30
Mishawaka	64	2.25
Elkhart	80	2.80
Middlebury	95	3.80
Howe	108	3.80
Fremont	132	4.65
Eastport	157	5.50

    a Make a graph showing the relationship between distance and
cost, using Gary as a starting point.

    b Are these data approximately linearly related?

    c What is the cost per mile?

    d Write an equation relating cost to miles driven.

    e A new exit is being constructed at mile marker 122. What toll
should be charged at that exit?

13 One kite is 200 feet off the ground and is rising at a rate of 6 feet
per second. A second kite is 100 feet off the ground and is rising
at a rate of 9 feet per second.

    a Write expressions that represent the heights of the kites t
seconds from now.

    b How high will each kite be in 24 seconds?

    c When will the kites be at exactly the same height?

14 Refer to the diagram.

    a Find the value of a for which $\overline{AB} = 15$.

    b Write the equation of $\overline{AB}$ in general
linear form.

    c Find the slope of $\overline{CD}$ if $\overline{CD}$ is perpen-
dicular to $\overline{AB}$.

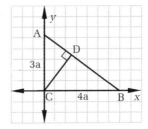

In problems 15–18, graph each set.

15 $\{(x, y): y \geq |x| + 2\}$

16 $\{x: -5 < x\}$

17 $\{(x, y): x > -3\}$

18 $\{(x, y): y \geq |x + 2|\}$

Review Problems, *continued*

19 Find the area of the triangle formed by the graphs of $y = 2$, $y = -4x + 18$, and $y = 2x + 18$.

20 Find the x- and y-intercepts of $Ax + By = C$, where $A \neq 0$ and $B \neq 0$.

21 The following table shows the cumulative numbers of photocopies that had been made by an office's machine at the end of eight consecutive months, beginning with June 1987.

Month	1	2	3	4	5	6	7	8
Copies	80,452	125,454	172,975	211,426	255,221	302,853	342,598	387,256

a Write an equation of the line of best fit for the data.
b What was the average number of copies produced per month?
c A copier needs a major overhaul every million copies. How many months after the beginning of the cumulative record should the office's machine have been overhauled?
d During what month, do you think, was the copier first used?

22 Suppose that $y = 5x$, $z = 9 - x$, and $t = 12 - 3x$. If $y + 2z = t$, what is the value of x?

23 The intersection of the graphs of $y = 7x + 4$ and $y = 2x - 1$ is the midpoint of a segment with one endpoint at $(-5, 2)$. What is the other endpoint?

24 Can absolute value be distributed over addition—that is, is $|x + y| = |x| + |y|$? Explain your answer.

25 A sheet of plywood measuring 4 feet by 8 feet is to be cut into equal numbers of 4-foot-by-2-inch strips and 4-foot-by-3-inch strips. What is the maximum number of strips that can be cut from the sheet?

26 Consider the following compound function.
$$f(x) = \begin{cases} x - 5 \text{ if } x \geq 2 \\ -4x + 5 \text{ if } x < 2 \end{cases}$$
Sketch the graph of $\{(x, f(x)):f(x) > x\}$.

27 Lia Bility opened an insurance agency in 1982. Her agency's profits for the first six years of operation are shown.

Year	1982	1983	1984	1985	1986	1987
Profit (dollars)	19,600	23,100	27,100	30,400	33,800	37,400

a Use the least-squares method to write a linear equation that approximates the data.
b Use your equation to predict the agency's profit in 1990.

CHAPTER TEST

1 Draw the line represented by each of the following descriptions.

  a $y = \frac{3}{2}x - 2$

  b Slope $-\frac{3}{4}$, contains the point $(1, -1)$

2 Refer to the diagram. Write an equation to represent each of the following.

  a A line parallel to $\overline{AB}$

  b A line perpendicular to $\overline{BC}$ at the point $(2, 1)$

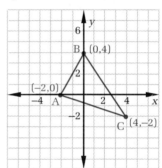

In problems 3 and 4, solve each system.

3 $\begin{cases} 4T + TC = 26 \\ 4T - TC = 14 \end{cases}$

4 $\begin{cases} y = 4x - 1 \\ 3x - 2y = 10 \end{cases}$

5 Write an equation of the line of best fit for the data in the following table.

x	10	35	60	90	145	170	210	250
y	0.35	1.25	2.10	3.25	5.10	6.00	7.40	8.75

6 If S varies directly as T and if $S = 45$ when $T = 18$, what is the value of S for each of the following values of T?

  a 6   **b** 24   **c** 42   **d** 54

7 a Graph the region defined by the inequalities $y \le -\frac{1}{2}x + 8$, $x \ge 0$, and $y \ge 0$.

  b Graph the region defined by the inequalities $y \le -\frac{1}{2}x + 16$, $x \ge 0$, and $y \ge 0$.

  c What is the ratio of the area of the region described in part **a** to the area of the region described in part **b**?

QUADRATIC FUNCTIONS

The parabola-like forms in *Bush Tucker Dreaming at Wingellina* open outward in the four cardinal directions.

4.1 | WHAT ARE QUADRATICS?

Objectives

After studying this section you will be able to
- Recognize quadratic expressions and equations
- Multiply to form quadratics

Part One: Introduction

Setting the Stage

A farmer has 75 feet of fencing with which to enclose a garden. He plans to use an existing wall and wants to have a garden with the greatest possible area. If the plot is as shown, what should the garden's dimensions be?

The area of the garden can be found with the following equation.

$$A = lw$$
$$= (75 - 2x)x$$
$$= 75x - 2x^2$$

This equation, $A = 75x - 2x^2$, is a **quadratic equation.** To find the maximum possible area, the farmer must solve the equation.

Quadratic Expressions

Quadratic expressions are polynomials of degree two. (If the terms *polynomial* and *degree* are unfamiliar to you, consult the review of these topics in the Handbook.) The following are examples of quadratic expressions.

$$w^2 \qquad x^2 + y^2 \qquad bh \qquad (x + 2)(x + 3) \qquad x^2 + 5x + 6$$

The expressions $(x + 2)(x + 3)$ and $x^2 + 5x + 6$ are equivalent. The expression $(x + 2)(x + 3)$ is in *factored* form, and the expression $x^2 + 5x + 6$ is in *expanded* form.

These are not quadratic expressions:

$$3x + y \qquad \pi d \qquad (x + 1)(x + 2)(x + 3) \qquad x^3 + 6x^2 + 11x + 6$$

The expressions $3x + y$ and πd are linear expressions. The expressions $(x + 1)(x + 2)(x + 3)$ and $x^3 + 6x^2 + 11x + 6$ are equivalent cubic expressions.

Quadratic Equations

An equation that contains at least one quadratic term and no term of a higher degree is a *quadratic equation*. Here are some examples:

$$y = x^2 + 5x + 6 \qquad x^2 + y^2 = 36 \qquad xy = 6 \qquad A = 5x + 2x^2$$

Quadratic equations are frequently used in solving area, projectile-motion, and locus problems.

Example   *Write an equation that represents a circle with its center at the origin and a radius of 5 inches.*

All the points (x, y) of the circle are 5 units from the origin, $(0, 0)$. We can use the distance formula.

$$d = \sqrt{(x_1 - x_2)^2 + (y_1 - y_2)^2}$$
$$5 = \sqrt{(x - 0)^2 + (y - 0)^2}$$
$$5 = \sqrt{x^2 + y^2}$$

Square both sides $25 = x^2 + y^2$

An equation of a circle with its center at the origin and a radius of 5 inches is $25 = x^2 + y^2$.

Multiplying to Form Quadratics

Quadratic equations are often used to represent area problems because area involves two dimensions. In the farmer's problem, the area of the garden was expressed as the product of the length and the width of a rectangle, $A = 75x - 2x^2$. Even if the farmer's garden were semicircular, its area would still be represented by a quadratic, $A = \frac{1}{2}\pi r^2$ (see Sample Problem 3). You will frequently encounter quadratics in situations where two linear expressions are multiplied.

Example   *Multiply $(x + 3)(2x - 5)$.*

$$(x + 3)(2x - 5) = 2x^2 - 5x + 6x - 15$$
$$= 2x^2 + x - 15$$

Certain products of binomials deserve careful study.

Example   *Write each expression in expanded form.*

a $(4x + 9)(4x - 9)$

$$(4x + 9)(4x - 9) = 16x^2 - 36x + 36x - 81$$
$$= 16x^2 - 81$$

This product is the difference of two perfect-square terms; it has no linear term.

b $(5x + 4)^2$

$$(5x + 4)^2 = (5x + 4)(5x + 4)$$
$$= 25x^2 + 20x + 20x + 16$$
$$= 25x^2 + 40x + 16$$

In the expansion of the square of a binomial, the first and last terms are perfect squares, and the middle term is twice the product of the terms of the binomial.

> **Sum and Difference of the Same Terms**
> $(a + b)(a - b) = a^2 - b^2$

> **Square of a Binomial**
> $(a + b)^2 = a^2 + 2ab + b^2$
> $(a - b)^2 = a^2 - 2ab + b^2$

Part Two: Sample Problems

Problem 1   Find an expression for the area of the rectangle shown.

Solution   The area of a rectangle is equal to the product of its length and its width. In this case, $A = (3x - 7)(3x + 7)$, or $A = 9x^2 - 49$.

Problem 2   Write a quadratic equation stating that the square and the rectangle have the same area.

Solution   Since the area of the rectangle is equal to the area of the square,

$$lw = (\text{side})^2$$
$$2x(x - 1) = (x + 3)^2$$

Multiply $2x^2 - 2x = x^2 + 6x + 9$

Combine like terms $x^2 - 8x = 9$

Problem 3   Find the area of a semicircular garden bounded by 75 feet of fencing and a garden wall.

Solution   The length of the fence is one-half the circumference of a circle.

$$75 = \frac{1}{2}(2\pi r)$$
$$75 = \pi r$$
$$\frac{75}{\pi} = r$$

Now we can find the area of the garden.

$$A = \frac{1}{2}(\pi r^2)$$
$$= \frac{1}{2}\pi\left(\frac{75}{\pi}\right)^2$$
$$= \frac{75^2}{2\pi} \approx 895 \text{ ft}^2$$

The area of the garden is about 895 square feet.

Section 4.1   What Are Quadratics?   **129**

Part Three: Exercises and Problems

Warm-up Exercises

1 Match each polynomial with its description.

a $\sqrt{3}x^2 - 2x$
b $10 - 3x$
c $2\pi r$
d $5x^3 - x^2 + 11x + 2$
e $3x^2 + xy + 3y$

i Linear expression
ii Quadratic expression
iii Cubic expression

2 Multiply.

a $(2x + 3)(2x - 3)$ **b** $(2x + 3)(3x - 2)$ **c** $(3x + 2)(3x - 2)$

3 Multiply.

a $(3y + 4)^2$ **b** $(4x_1 - 3)^2$

4 Write an expression for the area of the rectangle. For what values of x will the base have a positive length?

$9x + 2$

$2x + 5$

5 Each side of a square has a length of $4x + 7$. Write an expression for the area of the square.

6 Find the following products. Then explain the relationship between your answers to parts **a** and **b**.

a $(3x + 1)^2$ **b** 31^2

Problem Set

7 Which of the following are quadratic equations?

a $3 - 5x + x^2 = 0$
b $(6x - 2)(x + 3) = 0$
c $x(x + 1)(x + 2) = 0$
d $5 - 3x + x^2 = x^3$
e $xy + x^2 = 5x + y$

8 Write an expression for the area of the rectangle.

9 Let $(a, b) = (-2, 5)$.

a Evaluate $(a + b)^2$.
b Evaluate $a^2 + b^2$.
c Evaluate $a^2 + 2ab + b^2$.
d Which two expressions are equivalent?

10 Indicate whether each statement is True or False.

a $(x + 5)(x + 3) = x^2 + 15x + 8$ **b** $(x + 5)(x - 3) = x^2 + 2x - 15$
c $(x - 5)(x - 3) = x^2 - 8x - 15$ **d** $(x - 5)(x + 3) = x^2 - 15x - 15$

In problems 11–14, solve for the variable.

11 $9y - 2 - 2y + 135 = 0$ **12** $18w + 3 - w - 6 = -12w + 38.2$
13 $3(\text{Fred}) + 9 = 12(\text{Fred}) - 11$ **14** $6.5y_3 = 12y_3 - 25 + 4.1y_3$

15 Expand each expression.

a $(5x - 3)(5x + 3)$ **b** $(6x + 5)(6x + 5)$
c $(4y^3 + 6x)(4y^3 - 6x)$ **d** $(9a - b)^2$
e $(x - 1)(x + 1)(x^2 + 1)$

16 Simplify each expression.

a $\dfrac{x^4 \cdot x^5}{x^{12}}$ **b** $\dfrac{x^{-3}y^5z^{12}}{x^4y^{-2}z^{11}}$

17 Write an equation for a circle with its center at $(0, 0)$ and a radius of 4.

18 The area of the semicircular region is 16π. Find the figure's perimeter.

19 A mail-order firm's shipping charge is based on the weight of the item to be shipped and the distance it is to be shipped.

Distance (miles)	1–100	101–400	401–900	901–1500	>1500
Cost per pound	$0.43	$0.65	$0.85	$1.10	$1.50

a Find the charge for shipping a 12-pound package 750 miles.
b Find the charge for shipping a 7.5-pound package 340 miles.
c Find the charge for shipping a 15-pound package 1240 miles.
d If the shipping charge for a package is $12, what are the possible values of its weight and the shipping distance?

20 Solve each system for x and y.

a $\begin{cases} 2x + 3y = -4 \\ 4x - 5y = 8 \end{cases}$

b

Problem Set, *continued*

21 Solve each equation for x.

  a $(3x - 9)(x + 4) = 0$ **b** $6x^3(15x - 5) = 0$

  c $9(x^2 - 9)(x + 5) = 0$ **d** $(x^2 + 4)(x - 3) = 0$

22 If $(a + 4)x^2 + bx + 10 = 5x^2 + (2b - 7)x + c$, what are the values of a, b, and c?

23 Use a calculator to evaluate $\sqrt{x - 7}$, substituting the values {9, 8, 7, 6, 5} for x. Explain your results.

24 Write an equation expressing the distance d traveled by a car moving at 60 miles per hour as a function of the time t the car travels. Is this function linear?

25 a Graph $|x| < 5$ on a number line.

  b Graph $|x| < 5$ on a rectangular coordinate system.

26 Students in a chemistry class at Tech High determined the number N of grams of a certain salt that would dissolve in 150 grams of water at various Celsius temperatures C. Use their data to estimate the value of N at 60°C.

C	10	18	30	34	44	52
N	30	41	64	68	83	99

27 Write an equation for a circle with its center at $(-2, 5)$ and a radius of 6.

28 Write an expression for the area of the shaded region.

29 Find the values of b and $b + 3$ for which the ordered pairs are linearly related.

30 Solve for w_1.

  a $|w_1 - 4| = 5$ **b** $|-3w_1| w_1 = 12$

31 a For what values of a and b is $|a + b| < |a| + |b|$?

  b For what values of a and b is $|a + b| = |a| + |b|$?

32 Use a computer or a graphing calculator to graph the following equations.

   a $y = x^2$ **b** $y = x^2 + 3$ **c** $y = (x + 3)^2$

33 Graph the line segment represented by $y = 5 - 2x$ and $1 \leq y \leq 7$.

34 Write an equation stating that the rectangle and the square have

   a Equal areas
   b Equal perimeters

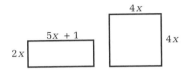

35 The sum of the first n natural numbers is equal to $\frac{n(n + 1)}{2}$.

   a If the sum of the first n natural numbers is 5050, what is the value of n?
   b Find n if the average of the first n natural numbers is 2500.

36 The accounting department at Widgets, Inc., reported the following data on the cost c (in dollars) of producing x gidgets.

x	0	100	200	300	400
c	700	2600	4500	6500	8350

   a Use the method of least squares to find an equation of the line of best fit.
   b Use your answer to part **a** to estimate the cost of producing 800 gidgets.
   c It is not reasonable to assume that your formula will be an accurate predictor of the production cost for any number of gidgets. Why not?

37 Find the missing value.

$$\begin{bmatrix} x & 4 \\ 2 & y \end{bmatrix}^2 = \begin{bmatrix} 72 & -24 \\ -12 & ? \end{bmatrix}$$

38 Find the value of x for which 60% of the area of the square is in the shaded region.

39 Refer to the graph.

   a Write an expression for $d(x)$, the distance from (0, 0) to $(x, f(x))$.
   b For what value of x is $d(x)$ a minimum?
   c What is the minimum value of $d(x)$?

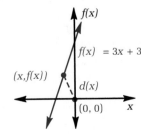

40 Graph the following functions on the same set of axes.

    a $f(x) = 2x(2x)$
    b $g(x) = (2x + 3)(2x - 3)$

41 If ten or fewer pieces of software are purchased, the cost of each piece of software is $95. If more than ten pieces of software are purchased, the cost per piece is reduced by $0.50 for each piece of software over ten.

    a Write a compound function C for the cost of x pieces of software.
    b Draw the graph of the cost function.
    c For what number of pieces of software is the total cost the greatest?
    d Is it cheaper to buy 100 pieces of software or 125 pieces of software?

HISTORICAL SNAPSHOT

ALGEBRAIC SHORTHAND

Syncopated algebra: the beginning of a standard notation system

Can you imagine algebra problems presented in words rather than symbols? That was originally how algebra problems were written and solved.

Diophantus (c. A.D. 255), considered by some to be the father of algebra, first proposed a system of algebraic notation in his treatise *Arithmetica*. His system of "syncopated algebra" was derived by dropping letters from words to form mathematical abbreviations.

Diophantus used abbreviations for powers of numbers, relationships, and operations. He replaced unknown numbers with letters and used notations for some exponents. A sample of his notation system, with English equivalents, is shown in the chart above.

Here is the English equivalent of an expression Diophantus wrote using his notation:

    PP2 C3 x 5 M P4 U6

Idea Represented	Diophantus	English Equivalent
Unknown Number	ς	x
Square (Power)	Δ^{γ}	P
Cube	κ^{γ}	C
Fourth (Square, Square)	$\Delta^{\gamma}\Delta$	PP
Fifth (Square, Cube)	$\Delta\,\kappa^{\gamma}$	PC
Sixth (Cube, Cube)	$\kappa^{\gamma}\kappa$	CC
Minus	↑	M
Unit	μ	U

Written in the symbolic notation we use today, the equation reads

$$2x^4 + 3x^3 + 5x - 4x^2 - 6, \text{ or}$$
$$2x^4 + 3x^3 - 4x^2 + 5x - 6$$

Use syncopated algebra to write equations for your classmates to solve. Remember that for Diophantus, this form of notation was state of the art!

FACTORING QUADRATICS

$$2x^2 \quad + \quad 3x \quad + \quad 1 \qquad x + 1$$

$$2x + 1$$

Objectives

After studying this section, you will be able to
- Remove common factors from expressions
- Factor trinomial products of linear binomials
- Factor special products

Part One: Introduction

Common Factors

In Section 4.1, you saw how two linear factors can be multiplied to form a quadratic expression. Mathematicians frequently reverse this process, starting with a product and trying to find the factors. **Factoring** is the inverse of multiplying.

Example   *Find factors of* $9x^3 + 45x^2 + 54x$.

The terms have a **common factor** of $9x$, which we can factor out by applying the Distributive Property of Multiplication over Addition in reverse.

$$9x^3 + 45x^2 + 54x = 9x(x^2) + 9x(5x) + 9x(6)$$
$$= 9x(x^2 + 5x + 6)$$

Factoring Trinomials

In the preceding example, we found two factors of $9x^3 + 45x^2 + 54x$. We may not, however, have *completely* factored the expression. Let's see whether the trinomial factor can itself be factored.

Example   *Factor, if possible,* $x^2 + 5x + 6$.

The terms have no common factor. If the expression can be factored, it must be a product of binomials, $(x + \triangle)(x + \square)$, where $\triangle$ and $\square$ are numbers having a product of 6. The only possibilities are 1 and 6 or 2 and 3. (We could consider -1 and -6 or -2 and -3, but for these pairs, the coefficient of the linear term would be negative.) Since $6 + 1 = 7$ and $2 + 3 = 5$ and since the coefficient of the linear term is 5, we use 2 and 3.

$$x^2 + 5x + 6 = (x + 2)(x + 3)$$

An area diagram is another way of representing the multiplication of two binomials. In the figure shown, the area of the large rectangle is equivalent to the sum of the areas of the four smaller rectangles.

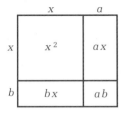

$$(x + b)(x + a) = x^2 + ax + bx + ab$$
$$= x^2 + (a + b)x + ab$$

In the preceding example, $a + b = 5$ and $ab = 6$, so the numbers 2 and 3 are the correct constant terms in the binomial factors.

Special Quadratics

The special forms of multiplication presented in Section 4.1 suggest special forms of factoring.

Example   *Factor the quadratic $81x^2 - 16$.*

This is a difference of two squares.

$$81x^2 - 16 = (9x)^2 - 4^2$$
$$= (9x + 4)(9x - 4)$$

It is useful to know that the factors of a difference of two squares are always the sum and the difference of the square roots of its terms.

The pattern that you have used to square a binomial,

$$(a + b)^2 = a^2 + 2ab + b^2$$

can be used in reverse to factor perfect-square trinomials.

Example   *Factor the quadratic $4x^2 + 12x + 9$.*

We can use an area diagram to illustrate our solution.

$$4x^2 + 12x + 9 = (2x)^2 + 2(2x)(3) + 3^2$$
$$= (2x + 3)^2$$

Part Two: Sample Problems

Problem 1   *Factor the quadratic $3x^2 - 48$.*

Solution   Since the terms have a common factor of 3, we will remove this factor first.

$$3x^2 - 48 = 3(x^2 - 16)$$

Now $x^2 - 16$ can be factored as a difference of two squares.

$$3(x^2 - 16) = 3(x + 4)(x - 4)$$

Problem 2   *Factor the quadratic* $x^2 - 10x - 24$.

Solution   Since the constant term, -24, is negative, we need to express it as the product of one positive and one negative factor. Let's look at possible factors of 24 and their differences.

Factors	Difference
24 and 1	23
12 and 2	10
8 and 3	5
6 and 4	2

The coefficient of the linear term is -10, so we use 2 and -12.

$$x^2 - 10x - 24 = (x - 12)(x + 2)$$

Note If the middle term of the trinomial had been $+10x$, the signs in the binomial factors would have been reversed.

$$x^2 + 10x - 24 = (x + 12)(x - 2)$$

Problem 3   *Factor the quadratic* $2x^2 - 5x - 12$.

Solution   There is no common factor. The coefficient of the quadratic term is 2, so the binomial factors will be of the form

$$(2x + \triangle)(x + \square)$$

The pair of factors of -12 might be -1 and 12, 1 and -12, -2 and 6, 2 and -6, -3 and 4, or 3 and -4. We could try each pair, but we can use logic and what we know about binomial factors to find the correct one. We need numbers that will give us a sum of -5 (the coefficient of the linear term) when one of them is added to the product of the other and 2 (the coefficient of the quadratic term).

$$2 \cdot 3 + (-4) = 2 \;\; \text{No}$$
$$2 \cdot (-4) + 3 = -5 \;\; \text{Yes}$$

Therefore, the factored form of $2x^2 - 5x - 12$ is $(2x + 3)(x - 4)$. We can check this result by multiplying.

$$(2x + 3)(x - 4) = 2x^2 - 8x + 3x - 12$$
$$= 2x^2 - 5x - 12$$

Part Three: Exercises and Problems

Warm-up Exercises

1 Match each quadratic expression with the method or methods you would use to factor it completely.

a $4x^2 + 64$ i Removing a common factor

b $4x^2 - 64$ ii Trinomial factoring

c $x^2 - 26x + 25$ iii Difference-of-squares factoring

d $4x^2 - 81$ iv Perfect-square-trinomial factoring

e $16x^2 - 20x - 6$

f $x^2 - 10x + 25$

In problems 2–4, factor each expression.

2 $x^2 + 7x + 12$ **3** $x^2 + 14x + 49$ **4** $8x^2 - 10x - 3$

5 Write an expression for the length of a side of the square shown.

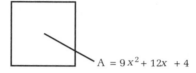

$A = 9x^2 + 12x + 4$

In problems 6–8, factor each expression completely.

6 $5x^2 - 30x + 45$ **7** $2x^2 + 4x - 6$ **8** $x^4 - y^4$

9 Express the area of the shaded region as a product of linear factors.

Problem Set

In problems 10–12, factor out the common factor.

10 $12y^3 + 16y^2 + 8y$ **11** $21y^2 + 28$ **12** $4x^3 + 7x$

13 a Copy the area diagram shown, supplying the missing terms.
   b Use the diagram to find two expressions for the area of the large rectangle.

14 Indicate whether each statement is True or False.
   a $(3x + 5)(2x - 4) = 6x^2 - 14x - 20$
   b $(3x + 5)(2x + 4) = 6x^2 + 14x + 20$

15 The price of a shirt is $11.93, and the sales-tax rate is 6.5%. How much sales tax must a purchaser of the shirt pay? What will the total cost of the shirt be?

16 a Use a calculator to find the decimal equivalents of $\frac{1}{9}, \frac{2}{9}, \frac{3}{9}$, and $\frac{4}{9}$.
   b Predict the decimal equivalents of $\frac{7}{9}, \frac{8}{9}$, and $\frac{9}{9}$.

In problems 17–19, find the largest perfect-square factor of each term.

17 144   **18** $200x^3$ **19** $32x^6$

20 Let $f(x) = (2x - 3)(2x + 3)$. What are the constant, linear, and quadratic terms of function f?

In problems 21–23, simplify each expression.

21 $(3x)^2 - 3x^2$ **22** $5x \cdot 3x - 15x^2$ **23** $8x - (5x + 6)$

24 Expand each product.

  a $(a + b)(c + d)$ **b** $(x + 2)(y - 3)$

25 **a** Write an equation that expresses the perimeter P of the rectangle as a function of x and y.

  b What is the value of P if $(x, y) = (5, 2)$?

$2y + 3$

$3x - 7$

26 **a** Copy and complete the table of values for $y = 6x^2 + x - 3$.

x	-4	-3	-2	-1	0	1	2	3	4
y									

  b Sketch the graph of $y = 6x^2 + x - 3$.

27 Solve the following matrix equation for w, x, y, and z.

$$\begin{bmatrix} |x - 3| & 14 \\ -12z & |w| + 4 \end{bmatrix} = \begin{bmatrix} 7 & 2|y + 5| \\ -|2| & 7 \end{bmatrix}$$

In problems 28–30, factor each expression completely.

28 $49w^2 - 196$ **29** $196x^2 + 49w^2$ **30** $196x^2 + 42xw + 49w^2$

31 Use a computer or a graphing calculator to graph each equation.

  a $y = x^2$ **b** $y = -x^2$ **c** $y = 3x^2$ **d** $y = -3x^2$

32 **a** Expand $(a - b)^3$.

  b Expand $(a - b)(a^2 + 2ab + b^2)$.

  c Expand $(a - b)(a^2 - 2ab + b^2)$.

  d Which two expressions are equivalent? Explain.

33 **a** Find the x-intercepts of the graph shown.

  b Solve $f(x) = 0$ for x.

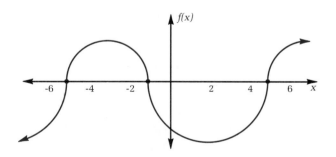

34 Factor each expression.

  a $[f(x)]^2 - [g(x)]^2$ **b** $(x + 3)^2 - 16$ **c** $x^2 + 6x - 7$

Problem Set, *continued*

35 a Explain why any even number can be written in the form 2k, where k is an integer.
b Explain why the sum of any two even numbers is even.

36 A point in square ABCD is selected at random. Find the probability that the point is in the shaded region.

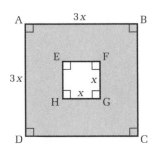

37 a Solve $x^2 = 9$ for x.   **b** Solve $y^2 = 9$ for y.
   c Solve $(x - 3)^2 = 9$ for $(x - 3)$.   **d** Solve $|x| = 3$ for x.

38 The equation of the axis of symmetry of the graph shown is $x = 66.7$. Is $f(66)$ or $f(67)$ greater in value? Explain your answer.

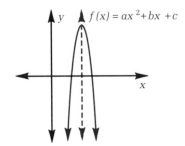

39 A rectangular rose garden's length is twice its width. The garden is surrounded by a 3-foot-wide walkway having a total area of 99 square feet. Find the dimensions of the rose garden.

40 Graph each set.
   a $\{(x, y):y = |x + 2|\}$ **b** $\{(x, y):4 = |x + 2|\}$
   c $\{x:4 = |x + 2|\}$ **d** $\{x:4 = x + 2\}$
   e $\{(x, y):4 = x + 2\}$

41 Factor each expression completely.
   a $x^4 - x^2$ **b** $x^4 - y^2$ **c** $x^4y^4 - y^4$

42 If $g(x) = x^2 + 2x + 1$ and $g(x) - f(x) = x^2$, what is $f(x)$?

43 Both Orville's plane and Wilbur's plane fly 140 miles per hour when there is no wind. Orville flew from Kitty to Hawk in 8 hours with a 10-mile-per-hour head wind. Wilbur flew the same route in 8 hours 40 minutes with a 20-mile-per-hour head wind. What is the distance from Kitty to Hawk?

44 Refer to the following table of values.

x	0	2	4	6	8	10
y	3	4	6	8	9	11

a Find x_1, the average of the first three values of x.
b Find y_1, the average of the first three values of y.
c Find (x_2, y_2), the averages of the last three values of x and y.
d Write an equation of the line connecting the points (x_1, y_1) and (x_2, y_2). (This method of finding a fitted line is known as the *method of group averages*.)

45 Factor $x^4 + 6x^2 + 9 - y^2$.

46 **a** Write a function A to represent the area of rectangle ABCD.
b What is the domain of function A?
c For what value of x is the area of ABCD half the area of the original square?

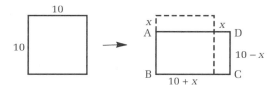

47 Solve the following equation for x.

$(x - 1)8x^2 + (x - 1)(-2x) + (-3)(x - 1) = 0$

48 Solve the following system for (x, y).

$$\begin{cases} 3^{x+y} = 27 \\ 3^{x-y} = \frac{1}{3} \end{cases}$$

49 Consider the following compound function.

$$f(x) = \begin{cases} 1 - x \text{ if } 1 \le x < 2 \text{ or } 3 \le x \le 4 \\ x \text{ if } 0 \le x < 1 \text{ or } 2 \le x < 3 \end{cases}$$

a Find $f\left(\frac{1}{2}\right)$, $f(2.5)$, $f(3.5)$, and $f(4.5)$.
b Graph $y = f(x)$.

50 If the ratio of the area of rectangle ABCF to the area of rectangle CDEF is 3:1, what is the value of x?

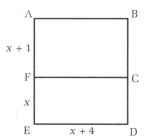

51 Sketch a graph showing all the values of (x, y) for which $(x - y)^2 > (x + y)^2$.

GRAPHING QUADRATIC FUNCTIONS

Objectives

After studying this section, you will be able to
- Recognize quadratic functions and their graphs
- Relate characteristics of a quadratic function to characteristics of its graph
- Find the real zeros of quadratic functions

Part One: Introduction

Graphing Quadratic Functions

You are familiar with the graphs of functions of the form $f(x) = mx + b$. Such functions are called linear functions because their graphs are lines. In this section, you will be introduced to **quadratic functions** and their graphs.

A **quadratic function** is a function that can be written in the form $f(x) = ax^2 + bx + c$, where a, b, and c are real numbers and $a \neq 0$. Let's construct a table of values for the simple quadratic function $f(x) = x^2$ and then plot the corresponding points.

x	-5	-4	-3	-2	-1	0	1	2	3	4
$f(x)$	25	16	9	4	1	0	1	4	9	16

The graph of this function is a ∪-shaped curve called a **parabola**.

Notice that the parabola opens upward and that the point (0, 0) is lower than any other point on the graph. This point is the parabola's **vertex.** It represents the minimum value of the function. When a parabola opens downward, its vertex represents the maximum value of the function.

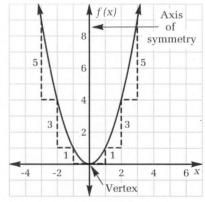

Let's look at the pattern of the values in the table. Notice that as the x values increase and decrease by 1 to the right and the left of the vertex, the values of $f(x)$ change in the pattern 1, 3, 5, 7, . . .

The line that divides the parabola into two halves that are mirror images of each other is called the graph's **axis of symmetry.** The axis of symmetry of this parabola has the equation $x = 0$.

More About Parabolas

As you have seen, determining the slope and the y-intercept of a linear function allows us to make a quick sketch of the function's graph. In the same way, when we want to sketch the graph of a quadratic function, we can rewrite the function in a form that gives us important information about its graph.

Example   *Graph the quadratic function* $f(x) = x^2 + 6x + 9$.

We begin by writing the function in factored form.

$$f(x) = x^2 + 6x + 9$$
$$= x^2 + 2(x)(3) + 3^2$$
$$= (x + 3)^2$$

By examining the squared binomial, we see that $x + 3 = 0$ when $x = -3$, so we choose values of x to the left and the right of -3.

x	−6	−5	−4	−3	−2	−1	0
f(x)	9	4	1	0	1	4	9

The point $(-3, 0)$ is the vertex of the parabola, and the axis of symmetry is $x = -3$. The values of $f(x)$ increase in the pattern 1, 3, 5, 7, . . .

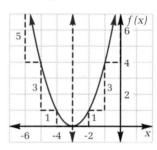

Example   *Graph* $f(x) = x^2 + 10x + 29$.

We need to rewrite the quadratic expression so that it contains a perfect-square trinomial.

$$f(x) = x^2 + 10x + 29$$
$$= x^2 + 10x + 25 + 4$$
$$= (x + 5)^2 + 4$$

Since $x + 5 = 0$ when $x = -5$, we choose values to the left and the right of -5.

x	−8	−7	−6	−5	−4	−3	−2
f(x)	13	8	5	4	5	8	13

When we plot the points, we see that the parabola's vertex is $(-5, 4)$ and its axis of symmetry is $x = -5$. Once again, the values of $f(x)$ change in the pattern 1, 3, 5, 7, . . .

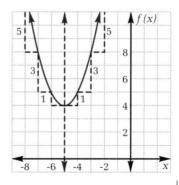

A quadratic function written in the form $f(x) = a(x - h)^2 + k$ is said to be written in **vertex form**, since the ordered pair (h, k) identifies the vertex of the function's graph. When a is positive, the parabola opens upward; when a is negative, the parabola opens downward. As the values of x change by 1 to the left and the right of the vertex, the values of $f(x)$ change in the pattern $1a$, $3a$, $5a$, $7a$, . . .

Zeros of Quadratic Functions

Now let's study the x-intercepts of the graph of a quadratic function and see how they are related to a corresponding quadratic equation.

Let's find the x-intercepts of $f(x) = 3\left(x - \frac{1}{3}\right)^2 - \frac{4}{3}$. We can see that the parabola opens upward and $\left(\frac{1}{3}, -\frac{4}{3}\right)$ is the vertex (the minimum point). As the values of x change by 1 to the left and the right of the vertex, the values of $f(x)$ will increase in the pattern $3(1)$, $3(3)$, $3(5)$, . . .

Examining the graph, we find that the x-intercepts are $(1, 0)$ and $\left(-\frac{1}{3}, 0\right)$—that is, the function is equal to zero when $x = 1$ and $x = -\frac{1}{3}$. These values of x are called the **real zeros** of the function and correspond to the real **roots** (solutions) of the equation $f(x) = 0$.

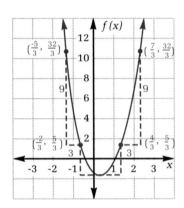

Part Two: Sample Problems

Problem 1   *Find the real zeros of the function* $h(x) = x^2 - 10x + 25$.

Solution   We first rewrite the function in vertex form so that we can identify the vertex and the pattern of change in the values of $h(x)$.

$$h(x) = x^2 - 10x + 25$$
$$= (x - 5)^2$$

The vertex of this parabola is $(5, 0)$, and the axis of symmetry is $x = 5$. The values of $h(x)$ change in the pattern 1, 3, 5, . . . The graph intersects the x-axis at only one point, $(5, 0)$. Therefore, 5 is the only zero of the function.

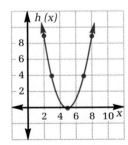

Problem 2 Graph $f(x) = -\frac{1}{2}x^2$.

Solution We can rewrite the function in vertex form as $f(x) = -\frac{1}{2}(x + 0)^2 + 0$. The vertex is $(0, 0)$, and the axis of symmetry is $x = 0$. The values of $f(x)$ will change in the pattern $-\frac{1}{2}(1)$, $-\frac{1}{2}(3)$, $-\frac{1}{2}(5)$, ... to the left and the right of the vertex. The parabola opens downward. Using all this information, we can sketch a graph without constructing a table of values.

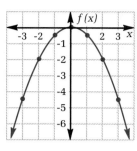

Problem 3 *Solve the garden problem presented at the beginning of Section 4.1.*

Solution We want to find the dimensions that will produce a garden with the maximum area. The function expressing the area of the garden is $f(x) = 75x - 2x^2$.

Let's solve the problem by determining the characteristics of the function's graph. First, let's find the function's zeros by letting $f(x) = 0$ and using the Zero Product Property.

$$f(x) = 75x - 2x^2$$
$$0 = x(75 - 2x)$$
$$x = 0 \text{ or } 75 - 2x = 0$$
$$x = 37.5$$

Thus, the x-intercepts of the function's graph are 0 and 37.5.

Since parabolas are symmetrical, the x-coordinate of the parabola's vertex will be midway between the two intercepts. The x-coordinate of the vertex is therefore $\frac{0 + 37.5}{2}$, or 18.75. The vertex represents the maximum value of the function, so the garden's area will be greatest when $x = 18.75$—that is, when the garden is 18.75 feet wide and $75 - 2(18.75)$, or 37.5, feet long. The maximum area is $18.75(37.5)$, or 703.125, square feet.

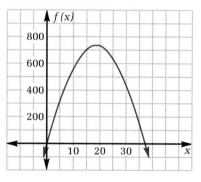

Part Three: Exercises and Problems

Warm-up Exercises

1 For what values of k does the equation $x^2 + kx + 9 = 0$ have exactly one real root?

In problems 2 and 3, write an equation in the form $y = a(x - h)^2 + k$ (vertex form) for each parabola.

2

3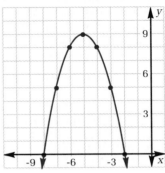

Problem Set

4 Sketch the graph of each equation.

   a $y = x^2$ **b** $y = x^2 + 4$ **c** $y = (x - 4)^2$ **d** $y = 4x^2$

5 For what values of a and b is $x^2 + ax + 9 = (x + b)^2$?

6 Match each of the following equations with its graph.

   a $y = 2(x + 3)^2$ **b** $y = (x - 2)^2$ **c** $y = -x^2$ **d** $y = x^2 - 2$

i   **ii**   **iii**   **iv**

7 Find the real zeros of the function $g(x) = x^2 + 14x + 49$.

In problems 8–10, solve for x.

8 $(2x - 6)(x + 3) = 0$ **9** $(x + 1)(x^2 - 4) = 0$ **10** $(3x - 5)(3x + 5) = 0$

In problems 11 and 12, graph each pair of equations on the same coordinate system.

11 $y = x^2 - 2$ and $y = -x^2 - 2$ **12** $y = 3x^2$ and $y = -3x^2$

In problems 13–18, simplify each expression and solve each equation.

13 $3x - 6x = 12 - 18$ **14** $-2y + 3x - 4(2x - 3y)$

15 $4.5w - 3.2y + 6w - 9.3y$ **16** $8x - (3x + 7)$

17 $2.7x - 3.2x = 14.6 - 3$ **18** $3(x + 5) + 2(4x - 3)$

19 Refer to the graph. For what value(s) of x is each statement true?

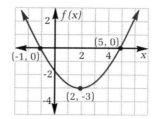

  a $f(x) = 0$
  b $f(x) < 0$
  c $f(x)$ is a minimum.

20 Gem knows that she has used at least 65 paper clips from her box of 500 but cannot remember the exact number she has used. Write an algebraic sentence describing the number of paper clips left in the box.

21 Let $a = 2$, $b = 7$, and $c = -15$.

  a Evaluate $\dfrac{-b + \sqrt{b^2 - 4ac}}{2a}$.
        b Evaluate $\dfrac{-b - \sqrt{b^2 - 4ac}}{2a}$.

  c Substitute your answers to parts **a** and **b** for x in $2x^2 + 7x - 15 = 0$. Are these values solutions of the equation?

22 Express the area of the large parallelo-gram in at least two different ways.

23 Graph $y = 2(x + 5)^2 - 3$.

24 Find the real zeros of the function $h(x) = x^2 + x - 6$.

In problems 25–28, identify each statement as True or False.

25 $(2x)^2 - (3y)^2 = (2x + 3y)(2x - 3y)$

26 $x - y = \left(\sqrt{x} + \sqrt{y}\right)\left(\sqrt{x} - \sqrt{y}\right)$, where $x > 0$ and $y > 0$

27 $x^2 - y^2 = (x - y)(x - y)$

28 $x^2 - 2xy + y^2 = (x - y)(x - y)$

29 Solve each equation for x.

  a $(x - 4)(x + 7) = 0$
        b $x^2 + 3x - 28 = 0$

30 If one of the numbers in $\{-4, -3, -2.5, -2, -1, 0, 1, 2, 2.5, 3, 4\}$ is selected at random, what is the probability that it is a solution of the equation $(y - 3)(y + 4)(2y - 5) = 0$?

31 The quadratic function $h(t) = 4t^2 - 24t + 36$ gives the height $h(t)$, in feet above the ground, of a sparrow at time t, in seconds.

  a Factor $4t^2 - 24t + 36$.
  b How far above the ground is the sparrow initially (at $t = 0$)?
  c When is the sparrow on the ground?
  d When is the sparrow again at its initial height?

32 a Write an expression for the length of a side of square ABCD if the area of the shaded region is $4x^2 - 4xy$ and $x > y$.

b Find AE.

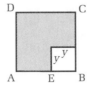

33 a Sketch a graph showing the ordered pairs (x, y) for which $xy = 0$.

b Explain your result in part **a**.

34 Solve each equation for b.

a $13 = |5 - 3b|$ **b** $|3 - b| = |b - 3|$ **c** $|b + 3| = |b - 3|$

35 A point (x, y) inside the rectangle is chosen at random. What is the probability that $x + y < 10$?

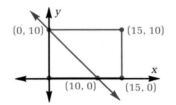

36 a Expand $(x + a)(x^2 - ax + a^2)$.   **b** Factor $x^3 + 27$.

In problems 37 and 38, factor each expression completely.

37 $2x^2 + 13x + 15$ **38** $3y(x^2 - 5x) + 6(x^2 - 5x)$

39 The surface area of a cube varies as the square of the edge of the cube.

a Write an equation expressing the surface area A as a function of the edge e if $A = 96$ when $e = 4$.

b For what value of e will the numerical value of the area be 18 times the numerical value of the length of the edge?

40 Consider two numbers a and b such that $a = b$.

$$a = b$$

Multiply both sides by a $a^2 = ab$

Subtract b^2 from both sides $a^2 - b^2 = ab - b^2$

Factor $(a + b)(a - b) = b(a - b)$

Divide both sides by $a - b$ $a + b = b$

Substitute b for a $b + b = b$

Add $2b = b$

Divide both sides by b $2 = 1$

What is wrong with this "proof" that $2 = 1$?

4.4 SOLVING QUADRATIC EQUATIONS

Objectives

After studying this section, you will be able to
- Solve quadratic equations by factoring
- Solve quadratic equations by using the quadratic formula
- Recognize when factoring can be used to solve a quadratic equation

Part One: Introduction

Solving Quadratics by Factoring

In this section, we will find the zeros of quadratic functions algebraically, by setting the quadratic function equal to zero, factoring, and then using the Zero Product Property.

Example Find the zeros of $f(x) = 2x^2 - 5x - 12$.

$$f(x) = 2x^2 - 5x - 12$$

Set $f(x) = 0$ $0 = 2x^2 - 5x - 12$

Factor $0 = (2x + 3)(x - 4)$

Zero Product Property $2x + 3 = 0$ or $x - 4 = 0$

$2x = -3$ $x = 4$

$x = -1.5$

Remember, the real zeros of a quadratic function f correspond to the x-intercepts of its graph and the real roots of $f(x) = 0$.

Example *For what values of x are the areas of the rectangle and the square equal?*

In Sample Problem 2 of Section 4.1, we found that the values of x must satisfy the equation $x^2 - 8x = 9$.

$$x^2 - 8x = 9$$

Rewrite the equation so
that one side is 0 $x^2 - 8x - 9 = 0$

Factor $(x - 9)(x + 1) = 0$

Zero Product Property $x - 9 = 0$ or $x + 1 = 0$

$x = 9$ $x = -1$

These values of x satisfy the equation, but do they both satisfy the conditions of the problem? If x = 9, the rectangle measures 18 by 8 and has an area of 144, and the square measures 12 by 12 and has an area of 144. If x = −1, however, the rectangle becomes an impossible figure with sides having negative lengths. Therefore, x = 9 is the only solution.

Solving Quadratics with the Quadratic Formula

If the quadratic polynomial in an equation of the form $ax^2 + bx + c = 0$ cannot be factored, we can solve the equation by using the *quadratic formula.*

The Quadratic Formula

If $ax^2 + bx + c = 0$ and $a \neq 0$, then

$$x = \frac{-b \pm \sqrt{b^2 - 4ac}}{2a}$$

A proof of the quadratic formula is presented in the next section. For now, let's see how it can be used.

Example   *Solve $2x^2 - 6x - 13 = 0$.*

The expression $2x^2 - 6x - 13$ is not factorable over the integers, so we will use the quadratic formula. The equation is already in the form $ax^2 + bx + c = 0$, with $a = 2$, $b = -6$, and $c = -13$.

$$x = \frac{-b \pm \sqrt{b^2 - 4ac}}{2a}$$

$$= \frac{-(-6) \pm \sqrt{(-6)^2 - 4(2)(-13)}}{2(2)}$$

$$= \frac{6 \pm \sqrt{36 + 104}}{4}$$

$$= \frac{6 \pm \sqrt{140}}{4}$$

Thus, $x \approx 4.46$ or $x \approx -1.46$.

When to Use Factoring

Factoring is often the quickest way to solve a quadratic equation, but it doesn't always work. How can you tell when to use the quadratic formula to solve such equations and when to factor?

The way to see whether a quadratic trinomial can be factored is to evaluate the *discriminant*—the expression, $b^2 - 4ac$, that is under the radical sign in the quadratic formula. Let's calculate the discriminant for some equations in which the quadratic trinomial can be factored.

Equation	Discriminant
$2x^2 - 5x - 12 = 0$	$(-5)^2 - 4(2)(-12) = 121$, or 11^2
$4x^2 - 12x + 9 = 0$	$(-12)^2 - 4(4)(9) = 0$
$-16t^2 + 96t = 0$	$96^2 - 4(-16)(0) = 96^2$

Now let's look at some equations containing expressions that cannot be factored.

Equation	Discriminant
$2x^2 - 6x - 13 = 0$	$(-6)^2 - 4(2)(-13) = 140$
$x^2 - 6x + 13 = 0$	$(-6)^2 - 4(1)(13) = -16$
$x^2 + 7x + 14 = 0$	$7^2 - 4(1)(14) = -7$

Whenever the value of the discriminant is a perfect square, the equation can be solved by factoring. If it is not a perfect square, you have already evaluated part of the quadratic formula and can quickly finish the solution. (When the value of the discriminant is negative, as in the last two instances above, the equation has no real solutions.)

Part Two: Sample Problems

Problem 1   *Which of the following equations can be solved by factoring?*

   a $2x^2 - 5x - 14 = 0$ **b** $4x^2 + 36x + 81 = 0$
   c $3y^2 - 8y - 16 = 0$ **d** $2w^2 + 5w + 4 = 0$

Solution

Equation	Discriminant	Factorable?
a $2x^2 - 5x - 14 = 0$	$(-5)^2 - 4(2)(-14) = 137$	No
b $4x^2 + 36x + 81 = 0$	$36^2 - 4(4)(81) = 0$	Yes
c $3y^2 - 8y - 16 = 0$	$(-8)^2 - 4(3)(-16) = 256$, or 16^2	Yes
d $2w^2 + 5w + 4 = 0$	$5^2 - 4(2)(4) = -7$	No

Equations **b** and **c** can be solved by factoring.

Problem 2   *Solve $x^2 = 16$ for x.*

Solution

Method 1

$$x^2 = 16$$

$$x^2 - 16 = 0$$

Factor $(x + 4)(x - 4) = 0$

$$x + 4 = 0 \text{ or } x - 4 = 0$$

$$x = -4 \qquad x = 4$$

Method 2

$$x^2 = 16$$

Take the square root of each side $\sqrt{x^2} = \sqrt{16}$

Remember, $\sqrt{x^2} = |x|$ $|x| = 4$

$$x = 4 \text{ or } x = -4$$

Problem 3 A rectangle's length is 4 inches greater than its width. Its area is 360 square inches. Find the dimensions of the rectangle.

Solution If we let w represent the width of the rectangle, then $w + 4$ represents the length of the rectangle.

$$w(w + 4) = 360$$
$$w^2 + 4w = 360$$
$$w^2 + 4w - 360 = 0$$

The value of the discriminant is $4^2 - 4(1)(-360)$, or 1456, so the quadratic trinomial cannot be factored.

$$w = \frac{-4 + \sqrt{1456}}{2} \text{ or } w = \frac{-4 - \sqrt{1456}}{2}$$

Since the value of w must be positive, we reject the second solution.

$$w = \frac{-4 + \sqrt{1456}}{2} \approx \frac{-4 + 38.16}{2} \approx 17.08$$

$$w + 4 \approx 21.08$$

The rectangle measures about 17.08 inches by 21.08 inches.

Part Three: Exercises and Problems

Warm-up Exercises

1 Let $(a, b, c) = (3, 5, -2)$.

    a Evaluate $\dfrac{-b + \sqrt{b^2 - 4ac}}{2a}$.

    b Evaluate $\dfrac{-b - \sqrt{b^2 - 4ac}}{2a}$.

2 Solve each equation.

    a $2x^2 - 6x = 0$

    b $9y^2 - 36 = 0$

    c $4z^2 + 16z = 0$

3 Solve each equation.

    a $x^2 - 9x + 20 = 0$

    b $y^2 + 6y - 16 = 0$

    c $2z^2 + 5z - 3 = 0$

Problem Set

In problems 4–6, solve for x.

4 $x^2 - 6x + 5 = 0$

5 $4x^2 - 5x - 6 = 0$

6 $6x^2 + 11x + 3 = 0$

7 For what values of x are ℓ_1 and ℓ_2 parallel?

8 Find the real zeros of $g(x) = x^2 - 5x - 6$.

9 Graph the following equations on the same coordinate system.

a $y = (x - 3)^2 + 4$ **b** $x = (y - 3)^2 + 4$

10 Graph $f(x) = x^2 - 9x + 18$ and find the x-intercepts of the function.

11 Solve for y.

a $(2y - 3)(y + 1)(3y) = 0$ **b** $(y - 2)(2y - 2)(3y - 2) = 0$ **c** $(2y + 1)(2y - 1)(3y) = 0$

In problems 12–14, solve for x.

12 $2x - 6 = 0$ **13** $2x^2 - 5x - 3 = 0$ **14** $x^2 + 3x + 4 = 0$

15 If $y = x^2 - 3x - 6$, what is the value of x when $y = -2$?

16 The square of an integer is equal to the product of the integer and 7. Find the integer.

17 The length of $\overline{AB}$ is less than 60. What are the possible values of x?

18 The slopes of eight lines are $\frac{1}{2}$, $-\frac{2}{5}$, 2, -2, -0.4, 0.5, 2.5, and $-\frac{1}{2}$. If two of the lines are selected at random, what is the probability

a That the lines are parallel?
b That the lines are perpendicular?

19 Consider the equation $(x + 7)^2 - 5(x + 7) - 14 = 0$.

a Substitute z for $x + 7$ and solve for z.
b Use your answer to part **a** to solve the original equation for x.

In problems 20 and 21, factor each expression completely.

20 $x^2 - 9y^2$ **21** $x^2 - 6xy + 9y^2$

22 If $\triangle AEF \sim \triangle BCD$, what is the length of $\overline{AE}$?

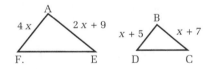

23 Solve $2\sqrt{5}x^2 + 3\sqrt{5}x = 0$ for x.

24 When there is no wind, Amelia flies her plane from Oklahoma City to San Francisco in exactly 4 hours, at an average speed of 325 miles per hour. If she were flying into a 25-mile-per-hour head wind, how long would the trip take?

25 Write a quadratic equation whose solutions are $x = -3$ and $x = 7.5$.

26 Suppose that $y \geq 7$. Solve $4x + 11 \geq 3y$ for x and graph the solution on a number line.

Problem Set, *continued*

27 Hazel bought eight pounds of cashews and four pounds of macadamia nuts for $72.48. Filbert bought three pounds of cashews and five pounds of macadamia nuts for $60.29. What is the price per pound of each type of nut?

28 Solve $[f(x)]^2 + 5[f(x)] - 14 = 0$ for $f(x)$.

29 The height $h(t)$, in feet above the ground, of a ball thrown into the air from the top of a building is given by the function $h(t) = -16(t - 2)^2 + 264$, where t is the number of seconds the ball has been in the air.

   a Sketch a graph of function h for $0 \le t \le 10$.
   b From what height was the ball thrown?
   c What height does the ball reach?
   d When does the ball strike the ground?
   e For what values of t does the function have meaning?

30 Solve for x to find
   a The length of $\overline{AC}$
   b The area of the rectangle

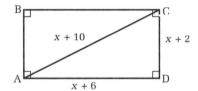

31 Copy and complete the table of values for $f(x) = \sqrt{3 - x}$.

x	−1	0	1	2	3	4	5
y							

32 The width and the length of a rectangle are in the ratio 3:4. If both the length and the width were decreased by 15 centimeters, the rectangle's area would be 252 square centimeters. Find the dimensions of the rectangle.

33 If $f(2) = 7$ and $f(5) = 16$, is $f(x)$ directly proportional to x?

34 **a** Copy the graph shown and draw a line that approximately fits the data.
   b Use the method of least squares to determine an equation of the line of best fit.

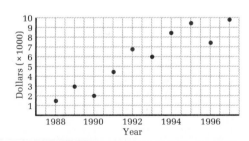

In problems 35 and 36, solve each equation for x.

35 $2(x - 3)^2 - 9(x - 3) - 5 = 0$ **36** $2(3x + 4) - 4x(3x + 4) = 0$

37 Solve each equation for x.

a $|x|^2 - 5|x| = 0$ **b** $|x|^2 - 7|x| - 8 = 0$

38 Refer to the diagram. Draw a graph showing the possible values of (x, y).

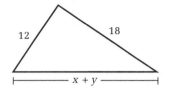

In problems 39–42, factor each expression completely.

39 $9x^2 - 27xy$ **40** $9x^2 + 24xy + 16y^2$

41 $wx + wy + zx + zy$ **42** $xy + 8x - 2y - 16$

43 Sky's airplane is at an altitude of 5000 feet and rising at a rate of 475 feet per minute. Penny's airplane is at 30,000 feet and descending at a rate of 650 feet per minute. When will the planes be at the same altitude?

44 a Copy and complete the following steps to solve for x.

$$x^2 + (a + b)x + ab = 0$$
$$x^2 + ax + bx + ab = 0$$
$$x(x + a) + b(x + a) = 0$$

b Solve $x^2 + (2c + 3d)x + 6cd = 0$ for x.
c Solve $x^2 + (3 + a)x + 3a = 0$ for x.

45 Suppose that $y = 12$ when $x = 6$ and that y varies directly as x.

a Write an equation expressing y as a function of x.
b Graph the function you wrote in part **a** for $\{y : y \leq 12\}$.

46 Routes 30 and 66 are perpendicular. On Route 30, ten miles from the intersection of the roads, is a car traveling toward the intersection at 35 miles per hour. At the same moment, a car traveling on Route 66 is passing through the intersection at 45 miles per hour.

a Assuming that the speeds of the cars remain constant, write an equation expressing the square of the distance d, in miles, between the cars as a function of time t, in hours.
b What is the minimum value of the square of the distance between the cars?
c When is this minimum value reached?
d What is the closest to each other the cars get?

47 If $x > 0$, what happens to the value of $\frac{1}{x}$ as the value of x

a Increases?
b Decreases?

Problem Set, *continued*

48 The length of a diagonal of a rectangular box is 10. The box's total surface area is 224. Find the sum of the lengths of all the edges. (Hint: What is $[x + y + z]^2$?)

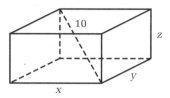

49 Given that $f(y) = y^2$, rewrite $\dfrac{f(x + h) - f(x)}{h}$ in simplest form.

50 Find the measure of minor arc CP of the circle shown.

COMPLETING THE SQUARE

Objectives

After studying this section, you will be able to

- Use the method of completing the square to determine the maximum or minimum value of a quadratic function
- Solve quadratic equations by completing the square
- Prove the quadratic formula

Part One: Introduction

Rewriting a Function in Vertex Form

As you have seen, the maximum or minimum value of a quadratic function corresponds to the y-coordinate of the vertex of the function's graph.

Consider the function $f(x) = x^2 + 12x + 23$. What is the minimum value of f? It is not easy to identify the minimum or maximum of a function in this form. If, however, the equation were in vertex form, $f(x) = a(x - h)^2 + k$, we would know that the minimum is k.

By using a process called **completing the square,** we can rewrite a quadratic function of the form $f(x) = ax^2 + bx + c$ in the form $f(x) = a(x - h)^2 + k$.

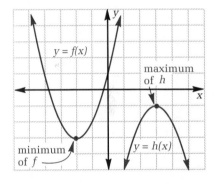

Example *Write $f(x) = x^2 + 12x + 23$ in vertex form, and find the minimum value of the function.*

We want to rewrite the quadratic expression so that it contains a trinomial of the form $x^2 + 2ax + a^2$—the square of a binomial $x + a$. To do so, we add to the first two terms the square of half the linear coefficient. Then, so that we do not change the value of the expression, we must subtract the same value.

$$f(x) = x^2 + 12x + 23$$

Rewrite, leaving space to
add and subtract a quantity
$$= (x^2 + 12x + \underline{}) - \underline{} + 23$$

Complete the square by adding
and subtracting $\left(\frac{1}{2} \cdot 12\right)^2$
$$= (x^2 + 12x + 36) - 36 + 23$$

Factor the perfect-square trinomial
and add the constants
$$= (x + 6)^2 - 13$$

The minimum value of the function can now be identified—it is -13.

Solving Equations by Completing the Square

We can also use the process of completing the square to solve a quadratic equation.

Example   *Solve the equation $x^2 - 14x - 5 = 0$ by completing the square.*

$$x^2 - 14x - 5 = 0$$

Isolate the constant term

$$x^2 - 14x = 5$$

Add $\left[\frac{1}{2}(-14)\right]^2$ to each side

(completing the square on the left)

$$x^2 - 14x + 49 = 5 + 49$$

Factor and add

$$(x - 7)^2 = 54$$

Take the square root of each side

$$|x - 7| = \sqrt{54}$$
$$|x - 7| = 3\sqrt{6}$$

$$x - 7 = 3\sqrt{6} \quad \text{or } x - 7 = -3\sqrt{6}$$
$$x = 7 + 3\sqrt{6} \qquad x = 7 - 3\sqrt{6}$$

Note   In solving an equation, you add the same quantity to both sides to complete a square. When completing the square in a quadratic function, you must add and subtract the same quantity. The two methods are related but not identical.

Deriving the Quadratic Formula

In the preceding section, we presented the quadratic formula and asked you to use it without proof. Now we will show you how the quadratic formula can be derived.

$$ax^2 + bx + c = 0$$

Divide each side by a

$$x^2 + \frac{b}{a}x + \frac{c}{a} = 0$$

Add $-\frac{c}{a}$ to each side

$$x^2 + \frac{b}{a}x = -\frac{c}{a}$$

Add $\left(\frac{b}{2a}\right)^2$ to each side

$$x^2 + \frac{b}{a}x + \left(\frac{b}{2a}\right)^2 = -\frac{c}{a} + \left(\frac{b}{2a}\right)^2$$

Factor the trinomial

$$\left(x + \frac{b}{2a}\right)^2 = -\frac{c}{a} + \frac{b^2}{4a^2}$$

On the right side, find a common denominator and add

$$\left(x + \frac{b}{2a}\right)^2 = \frac{b^2 - 4ac}{4a^2}$$

Take the square root of each side

$$x + \frac{b}{2a} = \pm\frac{\sqrt{b^2 - 4ac}}{2a}$$

Add $-\frac{b}{2a}$ to each side

$$x = \frac{-b \pm \sqrt{b^2 - 4ac}}{2a}$$

As you study this proof of the quadratic formula, you will recognize that the formula is nothing more than the solution of the equation $ax^2 + bx + c = 0$ by completing the square.

Part Two: Sample Problems

Problem 1   *Sketch the graph of $g(x) = 2x^2 - 16x + 21$.*

Solution   Identifying the characteristics of the graph will be easier if we rewrite the function in vertex form.

$$g(x) = 2x^2 - 16x + 21$$

Factor 2 out of the first two terms, leaving room to complete the square
Complete the square (Note that here we are adding and subtracting 32, not 16.)

$$= 2(x^2 - 8x + \underline{\quad}) - \underline{\quad} + 21$$
$$= 2(x^2 - 8x + 16) - 32 + 21$$
$$= 2(x - 4)^2 - 11$$

The vertex is $(4, -11)$. The graph opens upward, and the values of $g(x)$ change in the pattern $2(1)$, $2(3)$, $2(5)$, . . .

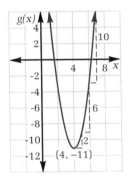

Problem 2   *Find the maximum rectangular area that can be enclosed by an existing wall and 75 feet of fencing. What will the dimensions of the enclosure be?*

Solution   This is the farmer's problem with which we began this chapter and which we solved in Section 4.3, Sample Problem 2. This time, we will solve it by completing the square.

$$A = x(75 - 2x)$$
$$= -2x^2 + 75x$$

Factor out -2

$$= -2\left(x^2 - \frac{75}{2}x\right)$$

Complete the square

$$= -2\left[x^2 - \frac{75}{2}x + \left(-\frac{75}{4}\right)^2\right] - (-2)\left(-\frac{75}{4}\right)^2$$

$$= -2\left(x - \frac{75}{4}\right)^2 + \frac{5625}{8}$$

The maximum area is $\frac{5625}{8}$, or 703.125, square feet. This area is obtained when the enclosure's width (x) is $\frac{75}{4}$, or 18.75, feet and its length is $75 - 2\left(\frac{75}{4}\right)$, or 37.5, feet.

Part Three: Exercises and Problems

Warm-up Exercises

1 What constant term is needed to complete each perfect-square trinomial?

a $x^2 + 8x + \underline{\ ?\ }$ **b** $x^2 - 6x + \underline{\ ?\ }$ **c** $x^2 + 9x + \underline{\ ?\ }$

d $4x^2 + 8x + \underline{\ ?\ }$ **e** $4x^2 + 9x + \underline{\ ?\ }$

2 What linear term is needed to complete each perfect-square trinomial?

a $x^2 + \underline{\ ?\ } + 9$ **b** $y^2 - \underline{\ ?\ } + 64$

c $y^4 + \underline{\ ?\ } + 16x^2$ **d** $x^2 + \underline{\ ?\ } + 30.25$

3 The expression $x^2 + 8x$ can be represented geometrically as shown. Find the area of the region that would complete the square.

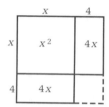

4 Find the coordinates of the vertex of each equation's graph.

a $y = (x - 3)^2 + 4$ **b** $y = (2x + 1)^2 + 5$

c $y = x^2 + 6x + 15$ **d** $y = x^2 - 10x + 5$

5 Solve each equation by completing the square.

a $x^2 + 10x = 11$ **b** $x^2 - 14x = 15$

c $x^2 + 6x = 5$ **d** $x^2 - 50x = -625$

6 Find the minimum value of each function.

a $f(x) = x^2 + 12x + 50$ **b** $g(x) = x^2 - 6x + 3$

Problem Set

In problems 7–11, rewrite each polynomial in the form $a(x - h)^2 + k$.

7 $x^2 - 8x + 45$ **8** $x^2 + 10x + 11$

9 $2x^2 + 100x + 50$ **10** $x^2 + 7x + 4$

11 $x^2 - 50x - 22$

In problems 12–15, sketch the graph of each equation.

12 $y = (x - 3)^2 + 4$ **13** $y = (2x - 1)^2 - 3$

14 $y = x^2 + 6x + 12$ **15** $y = x^2 - 14x + 45$

16 Solve each equation for y.

a $y^2 = 4y - 4$ **b** $y^2 = 9y + 36$

17 Given that $\ell_1 \parallel \ell_2$, solve for x and find $m\angle 1$.

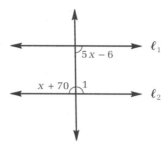

18 Write a quadratic equation whose roots are 2 and −5.

19 a Write a function for $A(x)$, the area of rectangle A.
  b Write a function for $B(x)$, the area of rectangle B.
  c Find the value(s) of x for which the areas are equal.

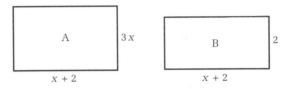

In problems 20 and 21, find the values of k for which the expressions are perfect-square trinomials.

20 $x^2 + 8x + k$

21 $x^2 + kx + 25$

22 Use the diagram to solve for (x, y, z).

23 Given the two functions $f(x) = x + 5$ and $g(x) = x - 5$, evaluate each of the following.

  a $f(7)$ **b** $g[f(7)]$ **c** $g(a)$ **d** $f[g(a)]$

24 The perimeter of the figure shown is 20. For what values of x and y will the figure have the greatest possible area?

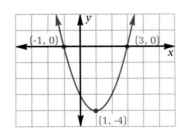

25 Solve $2x^2 - (x + 1)(x + 2) = 8$ for x.

26 Write an equation of the parabola in the form $y = ax^2 + bx + c$.

Problem Set, *continued*

27 For what value(s) of k does $f(x) = x^2 + kx + 16$ have exactly one real zero?

28 Write an equation to describe the graph shown.

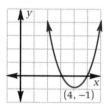

$(4, -1)$

29 Consider the equation $(12x)^2 - 6(12x) - 7 = 0$.

   a Substitute z for 12x and solve for z.

   b Use your answer to part **a** to solve the original equation for x.

30 a Write a function for $d(x)$, the vertical distance between the two curves.

   b For what value of x is $d(x)$ a minimum?

   c What is the minimum value of $d(x)$?

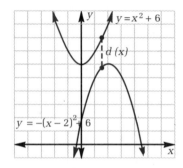

$y = x^2 + 6$

$d(x)$

$y = -(x - 2)^2 + 6$

In problems 31 and 32, use the quadratic formula to find the roots of each equation.

31 $x^2 - 3x + 1 = 0$ **32** $3x^2 + 1 = 8x$

33 An archer shoots an arrow. Its heights (in inches) at three times (in seconds) are given in the table.

Time (t)	3	5	8
Distance above ground (s)	326	350	146

0 1 2 3 4 5 6 7 8 9
Time (sec.)

   a If the arrow's path satisfies an equation of the form $s = -16t^2 + bt + c$, what are the values of b and c?

   b What is the maximum height of the arrow?

   c How far above the ground was the arrow when it was released (at $t = 0$)?

34 Write, in the form $ax^2 + bx + c = 0$, a quadratic equation whose roots are

   a −5 and 7   **b** $\frac{1}{2}$ and 4

35 Solve the following system for (x, y).

$$\begin{cases} [4 \ -2]\begin{bmatrix} x \\ y \end{bmatrix} = [15] \\ [x \ \ y]\begin{bmatrix} 3 \\ 4 \end{bmatrix} = [3] \end{cases}$$

36 Solve each equation for y.

    a $9y - y^3 = 0$ **b** $(y - 1)(y + 2) + (y - 1)(2y + 7) = 0$ **c** $32 - 2y^2 = 0$

37 Different sizes of staples are used to hold together different numbers of sheets of paper. A $\frac{1}{4}$-inch staple can hold about 30 sheets, a $\frac{3}{8}$-inch staple can hold about 70 sheets, and a $\frac{1}{2}$-inch staple can hold about 100 sheets. Estimate the number of sheets a $\frac{5}{8}$-inch staple might hold?

38 If the area of the trapezoid is 30, what is the value of x?

In problems 39 and 40, solve for x.

39 $2^{x^2-5x} = 2^6$ **40** $2^{x^2+5x} = \frac{1}{16}$

41 If $f(x) = \frac{9x + 4}{x^2 + 2x - 5}$, what are the restrictions on the value of x?

42 Find the coordinate of x if the sum of its distance from 6 and the square of its distance from 3 is a minimum. What is the minimum sum?

 43 a Find the coordinates of the vertex of the graph of $y = 4x^2 + 17x - 12$.

    b Find the coordinates of the vertex of the graph of $y = ax^2 + bx + c$.

44 Find the value(s) of k for which the graph of $y = kx$ intersects the graph of $y = x^2 + 25$ in only one point.

45 Consider the set $A_x = \{n_1, n_2, \ldots, n_x\}$. Write a function for $f(x)$, the number of subsets of A_x.

46 The difference between two numbers is 12, and the product of the numbers is 50. Find the sum of the squares of the numbers. (Hint: Start by finding $[x - y]^2$.)

APPLICATIONS OF QUADRATIC FUNCTIONS

Objectives

After studying this section, you will be able to
- Analyze and solve problems involving maximum and minimum values
- Analyze and solve projectile-motion problems

Part One: Introduction

Maximums and Minimums

Problems in business and in the physical and social sciences can often be solved by mathematical modeling. Whenever a problem can be modeled by a quadratic function, for example, we can find the maximum or minimum value of the function, and thus the best or worst outcome of the problem situation.

Example   *Andy wants the greatest possible harvest from his apple orchard. The orchard contains 220 dwarf trees per acre now, and Andy harvests, on the average, 1300 apples per tree. Because his trees are planted in rows of* 10, *he adds or removes trees only in groups of* 10. *Andy's research has shown that for every additional* 10 *trees he plants per acre, the average yield per tree in the orchard will decrease by* 50 *apples. How many trees per acre should the orchard contain to produce the maximum harvest?*

Since Andy plants trees in multiples of 10, we will let x represent the number of groups of 10 trees he adds to each acre of the orchard. The number of trees on an acre will therefore be 220 + 10x, and the average yield per tree will be 1300 − 50x apples.

$$\text{Total yield per acre} = (\text{number of trees})(\text{apples per tree})$$
$$= (220 + 10x)(1300 - 50x)$$
$$= 286{,}000 + 2000x - 500x^2$$
$$= -500(x^2 - 4x) + 286{,}000$$

Complete the square
$$= -500(x^2 - 4x + 4) + 286{,}000 + 2000$$
$$= -500(x - 2)^2 + 288{,}000$$

The maximum harvest, 288,000 apples per acre, occurs when $x = 2$. Andy should therefore plant 20 more trees per acre, so that the orchard contains 240 trees per acre. (If the value of x at the vertex had been negative, Andy would have needed to remove trees to obtain the maximum harvest.)

Projectile Motion

The term *projectile motion* refers to the motion of an object acted on only by the force of gravity. This is one of the many physical situations that can be modeled by quadratic functions. In this case, the height $h(t)$ of a projectile at any time t can be found with the quadratic function

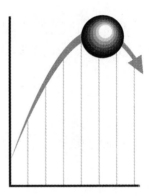

$$h(t) = -\frac{1}{2}gt^2 + v_0t + h_0$$

where g is the acceleration due to gravity, v_0 is the initial upward velocity of the object (the velocity at time zero), and h_0 is the initial height of the object. On earth, the value of g is approximately 9.8 meters per second per second (9.8 m/sec^2), or 32 feet per second per second (32 ft/sec^2).

Example   *A soccer ball resting on the ground is kicked with an initial upward velocity of 48 feet per second.*

a *Write a function for h(t), the height in feet of the ball at time t.*

We know that the problem can be modeled by a function of the form $h(t) = -\frac{1}{2}gt^2 + v_0t + h_0$. The initial height, h_0, is 0, and the initial velocity, v_0, is 48 feet per second. Since this velocity is stated in feet per second, we use 32 feet per second per second for g.

$$h(t) = -\frac{1}{2}gt^2 + v_0t + h_0$$
$$= -\frac{1}{2}(32)t^2 + 48t + 0$$
$$= -16t^2 + 48t$$

b *How many seconds after being kicked will the ball hit the ground?*

When the ball hits the ground, its height will be 0, so we set $h(t)$ equal to 0 and solve for t.

$$0 = -16t^2 + 48t$$
$$0 = -16t(t - 3)$$
$$t = 0 \text{ or } t = 3$$

The ball is on the ground at time zero (when it is kicked) and will return to the ground 3 seconds later.

c *What is the greatest height the ball will reach?*

The maximum height of the ball is the value of the function at the vertex of its graph. We can use either of two methods to determine this value.

Method 1: Completing the Square

$$h(t) = -16t^2 + 48t$$
$$= -16(t^2 - 3t)$$
$$= -16\left[t^2 - 3t + \left(\frac{3}{2}\right)^2\right] - (-16)\left(\frac{3}{2}\right)^2$$
$$= -16\left(t - \frac{3}{2}\right)^2 + 36$$

The ball will reach a maximum height of 36 feet, 1.5 seconds after being kicked.

Method 2: Symmetry of the Graph

A parabolic graph of the function can also be used to find the maximum height. In part **b,** we found that the solution of the quadratic equation $0 = -16t^2 + 48t$ is $t = 0$ or $t = 3$. Thus, the t intercepts of the parabola are 0 and 3. We know that a parabola is symmetrical about its vertex, so the function's value will be at a maximum when t is midway between 0 and 3—that is, when $t = 1.5$.

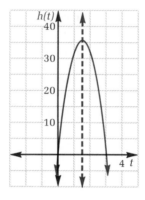

$$h(t) = -16t^2 + 48t$$
$$= -16(1.5)^2 + 48(1.5)$$
$$= -16(2.25) + 72$$
$$= 36$$

Again, the maximum height is 36 feet.

Part Two: Sample Problems

Problem 1

The graphs of $y = x^2 + 8$ and $y = 2x$ are shown. Let $d(x)$ be the vertical distance between the graphs.

a *Write a function for $d(x)$.*

b *For what values of x is the vertical distance 10?*

c *For what value of x is the vertical distance a minimum?*

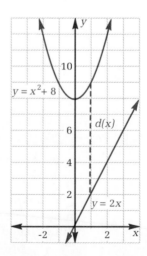

Solution

a For any value of x, the vertical distance between the graphs will be the difference between the corresponding y values.

$$d(x) = (x^2 + 8) - 2x$$
$$= x^2 - 2x + 8$$

b To find the value of x for which $d(x)$ is 10, we substitute 10 for $d(x)$ and solve the equation.

$$d(x) = x^2 - 2x + 8$$
$$10 = x^2 - 2x + 8$$
$$0 = x^2 - 2x - 2$$

By the quadratic formula,

$$x = \frac{2 \pm \sqrt{4 + 8}}{2}$$
$$= \frac{2 \pm 2\sqrt{3}}{2}$$

The distance between the graphs is 10 when x is approximately 2.73 or -0.73.

c Since $d(x)$ is a quadratic function, the distance will be a minimum at the vertex of its graph.

$$\boldsymbol{d(x) = x^2 - 2x + 8}$$

Complete the square $\qquad = (x^2 - 2x + 1) + 8 - 1$
$$= (x - 1)^2 + 7$$

The vertex is at $(1, 7)$. The minimum distance of 7 is reached when $x = 1$.

Problem 2

In 1981, there were 1000 fish in Ekal Lake. The fish population of the lake peaked at 8000 in 1986. If the number of fish varied according to a quadratic function of the form $p(x) = a(x - h)^2 + k$, where x is the number of years after 1981, what are the values of a, h, and k? When were there 6000 fish in the lake?

Solution

The maximum population of 8000 was reached 5 years after 1981. The vertex of the parabola is therefore $(5, 8000)$, so $h = 5$ and $k = 8000$.

$$p(x) = a(x - h)^2 + k$$
$$= a(x - 5)^2 + 8000$$

In 1981, when the value of x was 0, there were 1000 fish, so we can substitute 1000 for $p(x)$ and 0 for x and solve for a.

$$p(x) = a(x - 5)^2 + 8000$$
$$1000 = a(-5)^2 + 8000$$
$$-7000 = 25a$$
$$-280 = a$$

Thus, our function is $p(x) = -280(x - 5)^2 + 8000$. To find out when there were 6000 fish, we let $p(x) = 6000$ and solve for x.

$$6000 = -280(x - 5)^2 + 8000$$

$$\frac{-2000}{-280} = (x - 5)^2$$

$$(x - 5)^2 \approx 7.1429$$

$$|x - 5| \approx 2.6726$$

$$x \approx 7.6726 \text{ or } x \approx 2.3274$$

There were 6000 fish after about $2\frac{1}{3}$ years and again after about $7\frac{2}{3}$ years—that is, sometime in 1983 and sometime in 1988.

Part Three: Exercises and Problems

Warm-up Exercises

In problems 1–4, use the projectile-motion function to determine the initial upward velocity (v_0) and the initial height (h_0) of the object.

1 $h(t) = -\frac{1}{2}(32)t^2 + 45t$
2 $h(t) = -\frac{1}{2}(9.8)t^2 + 32t + 2$

3 $h(t) = -4.9t^2 + 25t + 0.5$
4 $h(t) = -16t^2 + 31t$

5 Each of the following functions describes the motion of an object acted on by the force of gravity. Find the greatest height reached by each object. (Hint: Complete the square.)

a $h(t) = -16t^2 + 64t + 100$
b $h(t) = -4.9t^2 + 19.11t + 5$

6 A Star-Go-Stop store charges \$2 for a one-day rental of a video cassette. On the average, 200 cassettes are rented from the store each day. If a survey indicates that the store's rentals will decrease by an average of 5 per day for each 10-cent increase in rental charge, what should the store charge to maximize its income?

Problem Set

7 The Epic Toothpick Company can produce up to 700 cases of toothpicks per day. The company's profit P, in thousands of dollars, is given by the formula $P = (x - 3)^2 + 5$, where x represents the number of hundreds of cases produced. What is the maximum profit the company can make in a single day?

8 a Write a function for $A(x)$, the area of the rectangle shown.
b For what values of x does this function have meaning?
c Find the area of the rectangle when $x = 10$.
d For what values of x is the area greater than 75?

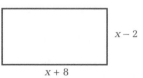

$x - 2$

$x + 8$

9 Jacob is standing at the edge of a 3000-foot-deep canyon. He kicks a ball into the air with an initial upward velocity of 32 feet per second.

   a When will the ball return to the height from which it was kicked?

   b What is the greatest height above the canyon's edge the ball will reach?

   c When will the ball hit the floor of the canyon?

10 What is the set of two-digit numbers in which the sum of the units digit and the tens digit is less than 4?

11 A rectangular plot ABCD is to be created by dividing and fencing a garden as shown. If 100 feet of fencing is used, what is the maximum area of ABCD?

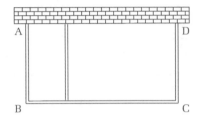

12 a Find the x-intercepts of the graph of the function
$f(x) = x^2 - 7x + 10$.

   b For what value of x will the value of $f(x)$ be a minimum?

13 Isis sells lemon ices at her lemonade stand. She charges $1.20 per ice and sells an average of 50 per day. If she could sell 1 more ice each day for each 2 cents she decreased the price, at what price should Isis sell her ices to maximize her income from them?

14 Jesse dives into a pool from the 3-meter springboard, with an initial upward velocity of 2.94 meters per second.

   a Write a function that describes Jesse's vertical motion.

   b What is Jesse's maximum height above the water?

   c After how many seconds does Jesse hit the water?

15 Solve $0.043x + 0.172x - 11.342 = 0.623x + 7.52$ for x.

16 Solve each of the following equations for x.

   a $|x| = 9$ **b** $x^2 = 81$

17 Refer to the diagram of triangle ABC.

   a Solve for x, leaving your answer in simplified radical form.

   b Between what two consecutive integers is the radical term of your answer to part **a**?

   c Use your answer to part **b** to estimate the length of $\overline{CB}$.

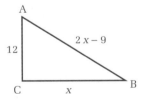

Problem Set, *continued*

In problems 18–20, solve for the variable.

18 $2x(x - 5) = 0$ **19** $2b(b - 3) + 5(b - 3) = 0$ **20** $4w^2 - 3w = 1$

21 Find the value(s) of x for which $\angle PQR$ is a right angle.

22 A water-skier jumps from a 6-foot-high ski jump with an initial upward velocity of 18 feet per second.

a When will the skier reach her greatest height above the water?

b When will the skier reach the height of the jump again?

c When will the skier land on the water?

23 A number increased by 20% of itself exceeds 80. Find the numbers.

24 Graph $y = f(x) = x^2 - 6x - 16$ and $y = g(x) = f(2x)$ on the same coordinate plane. What are the x-intercepts of the graphs of f and g?

25 Find the value(s) of x for which AC is the geometric mean of CB and AB. (You may recall that the geometric mean of two numbers a and b is $\pm\sqrt{ab}$.)

26 A model rocket is fired into the air. After 0.83 seconds, when its fuel is completely consumed, the rocket is 123 meters above the ground, traveling at a rate of 110.25 meters per second.

a When is the rocket 500 meters above the ground?

b What is the greatest height reached by the rocket?

c How much time elapses between the rocket's launch and its return to earth?

27 An isosceles trapezoid has sides as shown.

a Write an equation expressing the area A of the trapezoid as a function of x.

b Use a graphing calculator or a computer spreadsheet program to find the approximate value of A_m, the maximum area of the trapezoid.

DATA DISPLAYS

4.7

Objectives

After studying this section, you will be able to
- Read and interpret typical data displays
- Construct and interpret stem-and-leaf plots
- Construct and interpret box-and-whisker plots

Common Data Displays

The United States is rapidly becoming an "information society." In the future, much of the information on which you will base important decisions will consist of numerical data. It will be essential for you to be able to read, interpret, and work with this information.

Numerical data may be displayed in many ways. The displays that follow are typical of the types seen in newspapers, magazines, and computer-produced reports. Study each until you understand the information it contains.

Horizontal Bar Graph

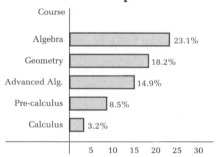

Percent of students in Apollo High School enrolled in college-preparatory math classes –1989

Vertical Bar Graph

Frequency Polygon

Production of coal by SLAGG mines

Circle (Pie) Graph

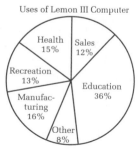

Uses of Lemon III Computer

Section 4.7   Data Displays   **171**

Chart

Production cost of a service manual for a 1990 Special Motors engine

Number of copies	Number of pages			
	48	64	80	96
10,000	2.60	3.00	3.30	3.20
8,000	2.80	3.15	3.40	3.35
6,000	3.05	3.40	3.65	3.75
4,000	3.35	3.75	3.95	4.15

Pictograph

Number of garages built by Slapmup Construction Co.

1986	🏠 🏠 🏠 🏠
1987	🏠 🏠 🏠
1988	🏠 🏠 🏠 🏠 🏠 🏠
1989	🏠 🏠 🏠 🏠 🏠

🏠 = 10 garages

More elaborate data displays can be generated by using computer graphics. We call such displays *artistic graphs*.

Rentals of Video Cassettes in Thousands

U-Rent-M Video Store

Stem-and-Leaf Plots

The following data represent the daily numbers of patients treated at the Mercy Hospital emergency room during August 1989.

16, 25, 31, 18, 16, 14, 37, 15, 26, 22, 30, 45, 34, 56, 27, 31, 19, 27, 46, 25, 33, 42, 19, 29, 34, 44, 28, 34, 26, 31, 20

We can organize these data in a *stem-and-leaf plot*.

To draw a stem-and-leaf plot, we identify the low number of patients treated, 14, and the high number of patients treated, 56. We use the tens digits as the *stems* of the plot. The stems are listed vertically with a line drawn to the right.

Stems	
1	
2	
3	
4	
5	

We now enter each data value. The first number, 16, has a tens digit of 1. Its units digit, 6, becomes a *leaf*. We put the leaf 6 to the right of the stem 1. The second number, 25, has a tens digit of 2 and a units digit of 5. We put the leaf 5 to the right of the stem 2. We continue through all the data, producing the plot shown below.

Stems	Leaves
1	6
2	5
3	
4	
5	

Stems	Leaves								
1	6	8	6	4	5	9	9		
2	5	6	2	7	7	5	9	8	6	0
3	1	7	0	4	1	3	4	4	1
4	5	6	2	4					
5	6								

We now rearrange each row of leaves in order from smallest to largest. Beneath the plot, we give a *legend* to explain the meaning of the data.

Stems	Leaves								
1	4	5	6	6	8	9	9		
2	0	2	5	5	6	6	7	7	8	9
3	0	1	1	1	3	4	4	4	7
4	2	4	5	6					
5	6								

4 | 2 indicates that 42 patients were treated one day in August 1989

A stem-and-leaf plot can easily be converted into a bar graph.

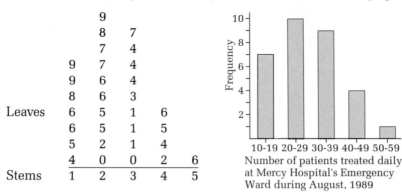

	9				
	8	7			
	7	4			
	9	7	4		
	9	6	4		
	8	6	3		
Leaves	6	5	1	6	
	6	5	1	5	
	5	2	1	4	
	4	0	0	2	6
Stems	1	2	3	4	5

Number of patients treated daily at Mercy Hospital's Emergency Ward during August, 1989

Box-and-Whisker Plots

The following data are the scores of 19 golfers finishing 18 holes in the Metro Open, arranged in ascending order.

63, 64, 66, 67, 67, 68, 68, 68, 69, 70, 71, 71, 71, 72, 73, 75, 76, 76, 78

The low score is 63, and the high score is 78. These are called the *outlier scores* of the data. The score 70 is called the *median* of the data, since it is the middle score of the set of data.

Now consider the nine scores below 70. Their median (the fifth score) is 67. Of the nine scores above 70, the median score is 73. We will use the two outliers (63 and 78), the median of the entire data (70), and the medians of the two halves (67 and 73) to draw a *box-and-whisker plot* of the golf scores.

We draw a number line, labeling the endpoints 63 and 78 and indicating the points that correspond to the values 67, 70, and 73.

The values 67, 70, and 73 are used as boundaries of the plot's boxes. The segments to the left and right of the boxes are the whiskers. We observe that the box-and-whisker plot is divided into four sections (two whiskers and two boxes). Included within each section is one-fourth (25%) of the data. Each of the numbers 67, 70, and 73, which divide the data into the four sections, is called a *quartile*. The number 67 is designated Q_1, the number 70 (the median) is designated Q_2, and the number 73 is designated Q_3.

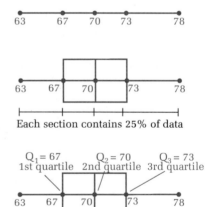

Sample Problem

Problem   *The following data represent the numbers of words typed per minute on a typing test by 10 candidates for an executive secretarial job. Draw a box-and-whisker plot of the data.*

52, 64, 77, 81, 90, 94, 99, 100, 102, 124

Solution   The smallest and largest values are 52 and 124. These are the outlier values. The median in this case is the arithmetic mean of the two middle values, 90 and 94, so the median (Q_2) is 92. The median of the values below 92 (Q_1) is 77. The median of the values above 92 (Q_3) is 100.

Using the outliers and Q_1, Q_2, and Q_3, we draw the plot.

Problem Set

1 Jordan Michaels scored the following numbers of points in the first 30 games of the 1989–1990 basketball season.

37, 33, 41, 21, 29, 31, 39, 30, 22, 30, 18, 53, 32, 36, 32,
29, 23, 41, 34, 37, 40, 27, 33, 35, 21, 19, 20, 54, 29, 35

a Display this data in a stem-and-leaf plot.
b Summarize the data by means of a box-and-whisker plot.

2 The table below shows the records of the Apollo High School baseball team from 1980 through 1989.

	Wins	Losses	
1980	16	13	55.2
1981	17	12	58.6
1982	23	8	74.2
1983	14	15	48.3
1984	19	10	65.5
1985	17	12	58.6
1986	22	7	75.9
1987	15	14	51.7
1988	13	16	44.8
1989	18	13	58.1

$$\frac{174}{10} = 17.4$$

-10.7

6.7

$$\frac{6}{17}$$
$$\frac{9}{153}$$

174

a On the same set of axes, draw frequency polygons to represent the number of wins per year and the number of losses per year.
b Find the average number of wins per year.
c In what year did the team win the greatest percentage of the games played?
d By how much does the team's average number of wins per year exceed their average number of losses per year?

$-28\overline{)-140}$

3 Determine whether each of the following statements is True or False.

a $\sqrt{36} = \sqrt{4}\sqrt{9}$
c $\sqrt{10} = \sqrt{5}\sqrt{2}$

b $\sqrt{36} = \sqrt{16} + \sqrt{20}$
d $\sqrt{10} = \sqrt{4} + \sqrt{6}$

4 The stem-and-leaf plot below represents the numbers of radar-detector units sold per week at TV Hut during a 15-week period.

```
3 | 1   1   7
2 | 0   2   3   5   6   9
1 | 3   5   7   7
0 | 8   9
```

2 | 3 indicates 23 radar-detector units sold during a week

a What was the greatest number of units sold during a week?
b What was the least number of units sold during a week?
c How many units were sold during the ninth week?
d In how many weeks were more than 20 units sold?

5 There are 17 elements in set A and 10 elements in set B. If A ∪ B contains 21 elements, what is the value of x?

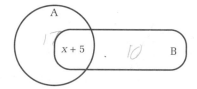

6 The box-and-whisker plot represents the scores of 85 students on a 90-item multiple-choice history exam.

a What were the high and low scores on the exam?
b By how much does the highest score exceed the lowest score?
c The middle 50% of the scores are between what two numbers?
d What scores are below Q_3?
e What is the average of the students' scores on the exam?

7 Solve the following system for (x, y).
$$\begin{cases} 2^{x+3y} = 2^{17} \\ 2^{9x-y} = 2^{13} \end{cases}$$

8 Analyze a newspaper or magazine advertisement in which numerical data are used to convince the reader to buy the advertised product. Discuss whether the advertisement offers a convincing argument.

9 The numbers of acres of corn planted in Sweetcorn County during a six-year period is shown by the frequency polygon.

a By what percentage did the acreage planted in corn increase from 1984 to 1989?
b By what percentage did the acreage planted in corn decrease from 1985 to 1986?
c The 1988 crop produced about 90 bushels of corn per acre. How much corn was produced in Sweetcorn County that year?

10 Graph the following two equations on the same coordinate system.

    a $y = 4x^2 + 2$ **b** $y = 4x + 2$

11 **a** Write an expression for the area of the shaded region.

    b What is the area of region I?

    c Write two equivalent expressions for the area of ABCD.

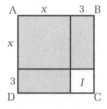

12 Mr. Matt Hematics made a stem-and-leaf plot of his pupils' scores on a test.

```
9 | 1  4  7  7  8
8 | 3  5  8  8  8  9
7 | 0  1  2  5  6  6  6  6  6  8
6 | 2  5
5 | 0  2  9  9
4 |
3 | 7
2 | 3
```

8 | 3 means a score of 83 on the test

    a What were the highest and lowest scores?

    b A grade of C was given for a score in the 68–76 range. How many students received a C?

    c What score occurred the greatest number of times? (This value is called the *mode* of the data.)

    d Jeff scored 65 points. How many students scored fewer?

    e How many students took the test?

    f Who received the highest score?

13 **a** What is the probability that a randomly selected two-digit number is a multiple of 7?

    b What is the probability that a randomly selected two-digit number is even and a multiple of 3?

14 The radius of a large spherical balloon is 4 feet and is increasing at a rate of 2.5 feet per minute.

    a When will the balloon's surface area be 400 square feet?

    b When the balloon is fully inflated, its radius is 14.8 feet. What is the surface area of the fully inflated balloon?

CHAPTER SUMMARY

CONCEPTS AND PROCEDURES

After studying this chapter, you should be able to
- Recognize quadratic expressions and equations (4.1)
- Multiply to form quadratics (4.1)
- Remove common factors from expressions (4.2)
- Factor trinomial products of linear binomials (4.2)
- Factor special products (4.2)
- Recognize quadratic functions and their graphs (4.3)
- Relate characteristics of a quadratic function to characteristics of its graph (4.3)
- Find the real zeros of quadratic functions (4.3)
- Solve quadratic equations by factoring (4.4)
- Solve quadratic equations by using the quadratic formula (4.4)
- Recognize when factoring can be used to solve a quadratic equation (4.4)
- Use the method of completing the square to determine the maximum or minimum value of a quadratic function (4.5)
- Solve quadratic equations by completing the square (4.5)
- Prove the quadratic formula (4.5)
- Analyze and solve problems involving maximum and minimum values (4.6)
- Analyze and solve projectile-motion problems (4.6)
- Read and interpret typical data displays (4.7)
- Construct and interpret stem-and-leaf plots (4.7)
- Construct and interpret box-and-whisker plots (4.7)

VOCABULARY

artistic graph (4.7)
axis of symmetry (4.3)
box-and-whisker plot (4.7)
chart (4.7)
circle graph (4.7)
common factor (4.2)
completing the square (4.5)
discriminant (4.4)
factoring (4.2)
frequency polygon (4.7)

horizontal bar graph (4.7)
leaf (4.7)
legend (4.7)
median (4.7)
outlier score (4.7)
parabola (4.3)
pictograph (4.7)
quadratic equation (4.1)
quadratic expression (4.1)
quadratic formula (4.4)

quadratic function (4.3)
quartile (4.7)
real zero (4.3)
root (4.3)
stem (4.7)
stem-and-leaf plot (4.7)
vertex (4.3)
vertex form (4.3)
vertical bar graph (4.7)

REVIEW PROBLEMS

In problems 1–6, expand each expression.

1 $3x(2x^2 - 4x)$

2 $(2x - y)(4x + 3y)$

3 $(6y + z)(6y - z)$

4 $(6x - 4)(x + 5)$

5 $(3x - 5)^2$

6 $(x + 1)(x - 1)(x - 1)$

In problems 7–9, solve for the variable by taking the square root of each side.

7 $x^2 = 100$

8 $(y - 2)^2 = 49$

9 $(2z - 1)^2 = 25$

10 Write an equation of the parabola shown.

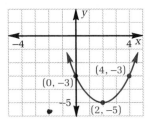

11 Graph the inequality $y \geq -4x - 10$. If a point is selected at random from $\{(-3, -2), (-1, -4), (2, 3), (5, -30), (0, -8),$ $(2, -30), (3, -30), (8, -30)\}$, what is the probability that it represents a solution of the inequality?

In problems 12–14, use the Zero Product Property to solve each equation.

12 $(x + 1)(x - 3) = 0$

13 $(x + 4)(x - 4) = 0$

14 $(2x + 1)(x + 3) = 0$

15 a Write an equation expressing the area A of the triangle as a function of x.

b What is the domain of the function you wrote in part **a**?

c Find the area of the triangle if the base is three times the height.

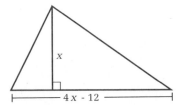

16 In a certain cubic polynomial the constant term is 5, the coefficient in the linear term is 7, and the coefficient in the quadratic term is twice the exponent in that term. The coefficient in the cubic term is the sum of the other two coefficients and the constant. Find the polynomial.

In problems 17–22, factor each expression completely.

17 $6y^2 - 5y + 1$

18 $3x^2 - 5x$

19 $6x^2 + 13x + 6$

20 $4y^3 - 12y^2$

21 $z^2 - 17z + 72$

22 $6x^3 - 12x^2 + 6x$

23 In 1988, there were 427 fires in Dawson City. The causes of the fires, as determined by the city's fire department, are shown in the graph.

   a How many fires were caused by arson?

   b How many fires were due to heating equipment?

   c How many fires were due to electrical problems?

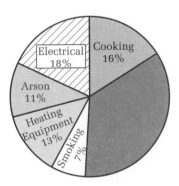

In problems 24–27, solve for x.

24 $x^2 + 10x = 24$

25 $x^2 - 8x = 5$

26 $2x^2 - 10x - 31 = 0$

27 $3x^2 + 18x - 2 = 0$

28 The diagrams show the numbers of angles smaller than 180° formed by lines that intersect at a single point. When n lines intersect at a point, they form $2n(n - 1)$ such angles.

   a How many angles smaller than 180° are formed by five lines intersecting at a point? By six lines? By seven lines?

   b How many lines intersect to form 3444 angles smaller than 180°?

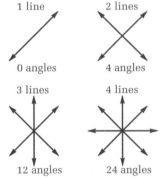

29 A dolphin's vertical movement is described by the function $h(t) = -4(t - 3)^2$, where $h(t)$ is the dolphin's height, in feet, relative to the surface of the water at time t, in seconds.

   a How far below the surface is the dolphin when $t = 0$?

   b When does the dolphin reach the surface?

   c When is the dolphin at a depth of 100 feet?

   d Graph the dolphin's height as a function of time.

30 If $y > 13$, for what values of x is $3x - 2 \geq y$? Graph your solution on a number line.

31 Expand $\left(x + \frac{1}{x}\right)^3$.

32 According to a newspaper graphic, the six most popular high-school sports among girls in 1987–1988 had the following numbers of participants (in thousands).

Basketball	392
Track & field (outdoor)	327
Vollyball	293
Softball	248
Cross-country	105
Soccer	103

    a If 1,181,000 girls participated in these six sports and no girl participated in more than two of them, how many girls participated in only one of them?

    b If 1,181,000 girls participated in these sports, what percentage of the girls participated in basketball? In softball? In cross-country?

In problems 33–35, solve for x.

33 $(x + 2)(x - 3) = x^2 - 11$ **34** $x^4 - 13x^2 + 36 = 0$

35 $(x + 1)(2x) + (x^2 + 3) = (2x + 3)(2x - 3) + 9$

36 Graph the equations $y = x^2$ and $y = x - 4$ on the same coordinate system. List the real points of intersection.

37 The tank shown is filled with water. A solid glass cube with edge x is then placed in the tank.

    a Write an equation expressing the volume V of the water remaining in the tank as a function of x.

    b What is the domain of the function you wrote in part **a**?

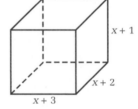

38 **a** Write a function for $A(x)$, the area of the rectangle shown.

    b For what value of x is $A(x)$ a maximum?

    c What is the maximum area of the rectangle?

In problems 39 and 40, factor each expression.

39 $(x + 1)^2 - y^2$ **40** $x^4 - 2x^2 + 1$

41 The trees in a cherry orchard bear an average of 204 pounds of fruit each when there are 90 trees per acre. For each additional tree planted per acre, the average yield per tree decreases by 2 pounds. What number of trees per acre would produce the maximum harvest?

42 Rewrite $\sum_{n=1}^{4} nx^{n-1}$ as a polynomial expression.

CHAPTER TEST

1 Determine whether each statement is True or False.

   a $x^2 + 9x + 18 = (x + 3)(x + 6)$ **b** $x^2 - 9x - 18 = (x - 3)(x + 6)$

   c $16x^2 - 9y^2 = (4x + 3y)(4x - 3y)$ **d** $x^2 + y^2 = (x + y)(x + y)$

2 Write an expression for the area of the largest rectangle in the diagram.

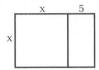

3 Solve each equation for x.

   a $3x^2 + 10x - 8 = 0$ **b** $2x^2 - 3x - 4 = 0$

4 If $f(x) = x^2 + 8x + 5$, what is the minimum value of $f(x)$?

5 Find the real zeros of the function $g(x) = 2x^2 - 5x - 3$.

6 Write an expression for the length of the side of the square shown.

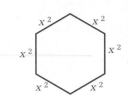

$A = 16x^2 + 24x + 9$

7 Graph each of the following equations on the same coordinate system.

   a $y = x^2$ **b** $y = (x + 3)^2$ **c** $y = (x + 3)^2 + 5$

8 For what value(s) of x are the perimeters of the figures equal?

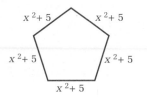

9 The geyser Old Faithful spouts water into the air up to 185 feet. If it takes 0.5 seconds for the water to reach a height of 185 feet, what is the upward velocity of the water?

10 Solve by completing the square.

   a $x^2 - 8x = 20$ **b** $y^2 + 5y = \frac{75}{4}$

11 Simplify each expression and solve each equation.

   a $6z^2 - 4z - 5 = 2(3z^2 - z) - (5z - 3)$

   b $(6z^2 - 4z - 5) + 2(3z^2 - z) - (5z - 3)$

   c $(6z^2 - 4z - 5) - 2(3z^2 - z) = 5z - 3$

5 FUNCTIONS

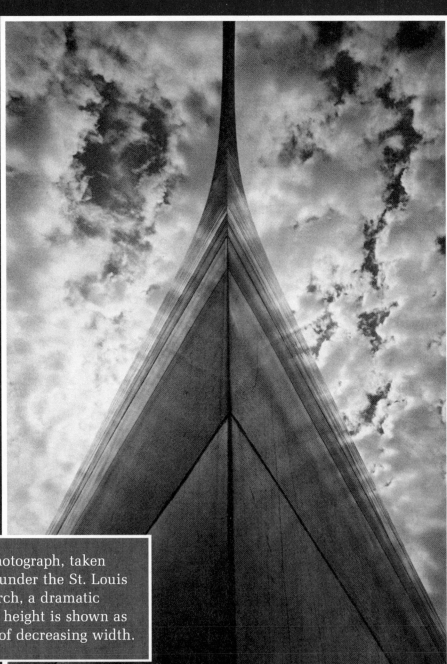

In this photograph, taken directly under the St. Louis Gateway Arch, a dramatic increase in height is shown as a function of decreasing width.

RELATIONS AND FUNCTIONS

Objectives

After studying this section, you will be able to
- Represent relations
- Recognize functions

Part One: Introduction

Relations

Peter has written a computer program that lists the factors of positive integers. When he inputs 1, the program outputs 1. When he inputs 2, the program outputs 1 and 2. When he inputs 8, the program outputs 1, 2, 4, and 8. In short, for each number Peter inputs, the program produces a set of outputs *related* to the input. This **relation** can be expressed as a set of ordered pairs of the form (input, output).

 A relation is a set of ordered pairs.

Relations can be represented in a variety of ways. Here are some of the ways of representing Peter's relation for the input values 1, 2, and 8.

Method 1: Ordered Pairs

(1, 1), (2, 1), (2, 2), (8, 1)
   (8, 2), (8, 4), (8, 8)

Method 2: Table

Number	1	2	2	8	8	8	8
Factor	1	1	2	1	2	4	8

Method 3: Mapping Diagram

Method 4: Graph

Method 5: Input-Output Diagram

Input: 1   2   8

has a
factor of

Output: 1   2   4   8

Method 6: Formula

In this case, we cannot write a formula, but we can express the rule governing the relation in set notation:

$$\{(x, y): x \in \{1, 2, 8\} \text{ and } y \text{ is a factor of } x\}$$

Notice that in a relation an input may be paired with more than one output.

Functions

A function is a special type of relation. To get a notion of how functions differ from other relations, consider a familiar function machine—a scientific calculator. Each time you use a calculator to find the square root of 13, for example, you get the same result. It is this consistency of output that distinguishes functions from relations that are not functions.

> ▶ *A function is a relation that pairs each input with exactly one output.*

The *domain* of a function is the set of all inputs for which the function produces a meaningful output. The *range* of a function is the set of all the function's meaningful outputs.

Thus, a function can be said to have three parts—an input, a rule, and an output. The rule pairs an input with its unique output. Each input is an element of the function's domain. The outputs that the rule generates make up the function's range.

Example

Does the following input set and rule define a function?
Input set: $\{-2, -1, 0, 1, 2\}$
Rule: "Has an absolute value of"

The mapping diagram shows the result of applying the rule "has an absolute value of" to the elements of $\{-2, -1, 0, 1, 2\}$. Since each input is mapped to exactly one output, the relation defined by the given information is a function.

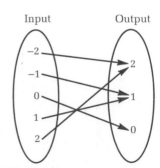

Part Two: Sample Problems

Problem 1   *Consider the relation defined by the equation $x^2 + y^2 = 25$. Is y a function of x? Is x a function of y?*

Solution   The graph of $x^2 + y^2 = 25$ is a circle with its center at the origin and a radius of 5. When $x = 3$, the value of y is 4 or -4. Since a single input value (x) produces two different output values (y), y is not a function of x. Similarly, when $y = 3$, the value of x is 4 or -4. Since a single input value (y) produces two different output values (x), x is not a function of y.

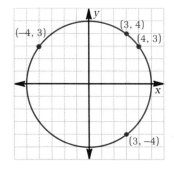

Problem 2   *Represent the function $f(x) = x^2$ for the inputs $\{-2, -1, 0, 1, 2\}$.*

Solution   The methods used to represent functions are the same as those used to represent other relations.

Method 1: Ordered Pairs

$(-2, 4), (-1, 1), (0, 0),$
$(1, 1), (2, 4)$

Method 2: Table

x	-2	-1	0	1	2
$f(x)$	4	1	0	1	4

Method 3: Mapping Diagram

Method 4: Graph

Method 5: Input-Output Diagram

Method 6: Formula

$f(x) = x^2, x \in \{-2, -1, 0, 1, 2\}$

Notice that no input is paired with more than one output.

Part Three: Exercises and Problems

Warm-up Exercises

1 Represent the relation shown in the mapping diagram in each of the following ways.

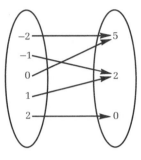

  a A set of ordered pairs
  b A table
  c A graph
  d An input-output diagram

2 Which of the following sets of ordered pairs represent functions?

  a $\{(-2, 3), (-3, 4), (-2, 5)\}$ **b** $\{(3, -2), (4, -2), (-2, 5)\}$
  c $\{(1, -1), (0, 0), (-1, 1)\}$ **d** $\{(-1, 1), (0, 0), (1, 1)\}$
  e $\{(1, -1), (0, 0), (1, 1)\}$

3 If $a = |b|$, is a a function of b? Is b a function of a?

4 Examine the mapping diagram of a function f.

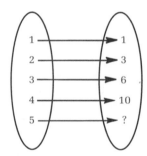

  a Predict the output for an input of 5.
  b What formula did you use to make your prediction?

5 The graph shown represents a relation in which y is a function of x.

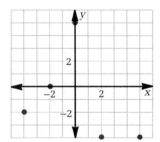

  a What is the function's domain?
  b What is the function's range?
  c Represent the function as a set of ordered pairs.

6 Let $f(x) = x^2$ and $g(x) = \sqrt{x}$.

  a Find $f(4)$.   **b** Find $g(16)$.   **c** Find $g(9)$.   **d** Find $f(3)$.

Problem Set

In problems 7 and 8, indicate whether the mapping diagram represents a relation, a function, or both.

7

8
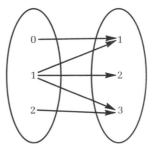

9 Represent the function $f(x) = |x - 2|$ for the inputs $\{-2, 0, 2, 4, 6\}$ in each of the following forms.

   a A set of ordered pairs   **b** A table
   c A mapping diagram   **d** A graph
   e An input-output diagram

10 The graph represents the equation $y = g(x)$, where $g(x)$ is a function.

   a Find $g(1)$.
   b Find $g(2)$.
   c Solve $g(x) = 1$ for x.
   d Solve $g(x) = -1$ for x.
   e What is the domain of function g?
   f What is the range of function g?

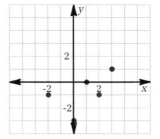

11 Is it possible for a function to have more elements in its range than in its domain? Explain your answer.

12 a Find the area of the rectangle if $x = 5$.
    b Find the area of the rectangle if $x = 0$.
    c What are the possible values of x?

$3x + 5$

$x - 2$

13 Solve $9(2x - 3) < 3x + 3$ for x and graph the solution set on a number line.

Problem Set, *continued*

14 Find the factorial key, $\boxed{x!}$, on a scientific calculator. Try applying the factorial function to a variety of inputs x. What is the greatest input value for which the calculator can evaluate a factorial?

15 An algebra class experimented with flipping a set of five coins to see how many of the five would come up heads. The graph shows the results of a number of trials of the experiment.

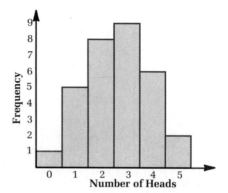

a How many times did three coins come up heads?

b How many times did all five coins come up heads?

c What is the total number of trials represented by the graph?

16 A certain photocopier can make 80 copies per minute.

a Write a function C to represent the number of copies produced in q minutes.

b Find C(3.5).

17 Indicate whether each statement is True or False.

a $\sqrt{8} = \sqrt{4}\sqrt{2}$ **b** $\sqrt{16} = \sqrt{-4}\sqrt{-4}$

18 The formula used to convert degrees Fahrenheit (F) to degrees Celsius (C) is $C = \frac{5}{9}(F - 32)$. For what values of F is C < 20?

19 Draw a mapping diagram that represents the function described by the following four statements.

  i The domain is $\{-3, 0, 5.1, 122, \pi, \sqrt{3}, 1000\}$.

  ii If the input is even, the output is 0.

 iii If the input is odd, the output is 1.

  iv If the input is not an integer, the output is -1.

20 **a** Write a function A to describe the area of the shaded region.

    b For what values of x does function A have meaning?

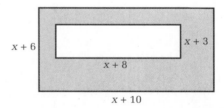

21 Consider a function p such that p(Reagan) = 1980, p(Bush) = 1988, p(Lincoln) = 1860, and p(Truman) = 1948.

a What do you think the rule for function p is?

b Find p(Kennedy) and p(Cleveland).

In problems 22–24, each table represents a relation. For each relation, indicate whether y is a function of x and whether x is a function of y.

22
x	-3	-1	1	3	5
y	27	-1	1	27	125

23
x	9	4	1	0	1	4	9
y	-3	-2	-1	0	1	2	3

24
x	-2	-1	0	1	2	3
y	2	1	0	-1	-2	-3

25 If the graph of $y = x$ is the perpendicular bisector of $\overline{AB}$, what are the coordinates of point B?

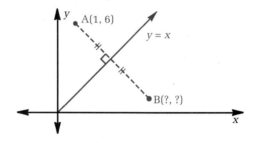

In problems 26–29, solve for x.

26 $x^2 - 8x + 15 = 0$

27 $2x^2 - 3x - 12 = 0$

28 $(2^x)^2 - 12(2^x) + 32 = 0$

29 $x^3 - (x - 3)^3 = 27$

30 a Write a function M to describe the arithmetic mean (the average) of 15, 20, 30, 55, and x.
  b Graph the equation $y = M(x)$.
  c For what value of x is the arithmetic mean 0?
  d For what value of x is the arithmetic mean 30?

31 Consider the graphs of $y = 2x^2 + 5$ and $y = x^2$.

  a Write a function d to describe the vertical distance between the two curves.
  b For what value(s) of x is $d(x) = 30$?

32 Find the key for the tangent function, tan , on a calculator. Try entering 20 tan to find tan 20, then "undo" the function by pressing INV tan

  a Find tan 45.
  b Find tan 75.
  c If tan $x = 2$, what is the value of x?

5.2 MORE ABOUT FUNCTIONS

Objectives

After studying this section, you will be able to
- Identify restrictions on the domain of a function
- Interpret composite functions
- Recognize inverse functions

Part One: Introduction

Restrictions on the Domain of a Function

Consider the function $f(x) = \frac{3}{x}$. Try to evaluate $f(0)$ with a calculator.
You should get an error display, since division by zero is undefined.
Because $f(0)$ is undefined, zero is not an element of the domain of
function f.

Since the domain of a function includes only the input values
for which the function produces a meaningful output, we frequently
need to specify that certain values are excluded from the domain.
The following chart shows some functions, along with the domain
and the range of each.

Function	Restrictions	Domain	Range
$h(y) = 4(y+3)$	None	$\{y : y \in \mathcal{R}\}$	$\{h(y) : h(y) \in \mathcal{R}\}$
$f(x) = \dfrac{16}{x-2}$	Input cannot be 2	$\{x : x \neq 2\}$	$\{f(x) : f(x) \neq 0\}$
$g(z) = \sqrt{z}$	Input must be nonnegative	$\{z : z \geq 0\}$	$\{g(z) : g(z) \geq 0\}$

In some cases, the domain of a function is restricted because of
the nature of the problem we are using it to solve. For example, if a
function's inputs represent numbers of passengers on various DC-10
airliners, the domain must be limited to nonnegative integers less
than or equal to the maximum seating capacity of the plane.

Composition of Functions

If we evaluate the function $g(x) = \sqrt{9x}$ for the input value 4, we find
that $g(4) = \sqrt{9(4)} = \sqrt{36} = 6$. There is, however, another way of
thinking about this process. We can think of function g as a
composite of two functions, $f(x) = 9x$ and $h(x) = \sqrt{x}$. We can
evaluate $g(4)$ by using the output of $f(4)$ as the input of function h.

$$f(x) = 9x \qquad\qquad\qquad h(x) = \sqrt{x}$$

$$f(4) = 9(4) \qquad\qquad\qquad h(36) = \sqrt{36}$$

$$= 36 \qquad\qquad\qquad\qquad = 6$$

Whenever we use the output of one function as the input of another function, we are creating a **composition of functions.** In this case, we say that g(x) is equivalent to $h[f(x)]$ or $h \circ f(x)$. Both of these expressions are read "h of f of x."

Example   Let $f(x) = x + 1$ and $g(x) = 2x + 3$. Find $f[g(-4)]$.

Method 1

We write a simplified expression for $f[g(x)]$, then evaluate the expression for $x = -4$.

$$f[g(x)] = f(2x + 3)$$

$$= (2x + 3) + 1$$

$$= 2x + 4$$

$$f[g(-4)] = 2(-4) + 4$$

$$= -4$$

Method 2

We evaluate $g(-4)$, then use the result as the input of f.

$$g(-4) = 2(-4) + 3$$

$$= -8 + 3$$

$$= -5$$

$$f(-5) = -5 + 1$$

$$= -4$$

Inverses

If $f(x) = 5x$ and $g(x) = \frac{x}{5}$, we can find $f[g(x)]$ and $g[f(x)]$ as follows.

$$f[g(x)] = f\!\left(\frac{x}{5}\right) \qquad\qquad\qquad g[f(x)] = g(5x)$$

$$= 5\!\left(\frac{x}{5}\right) \qquad\qquad\qquad\qquad = \frac{5x}{5}$$

$$= x \qquad\qquad\qquad\qquad\qquad = x$$

The output of each composite is the same as the input for any input value that is in the domains of both functions. Because of this relationship, functions f and g are said to be **inverses** of each other.

⟫ **If $f[g(x)] = g[f(x)] = x$ for all values of x in the domains of f and g, then f and g are inverse functions.**

A notation for the inverse of a function f is INVf. In the case of $f(x) = 5x$ and $g(x) = \frac{x}{5}$, we can say that $INVf(x) = \frac{x}{5}$ and that $INVg(x) = 5x$.

Part Two: Sample Problems

Problem 1   Find the domain of each function.
a $s(n) = \sqrt{2n + 3}$
b $A(x, y) = (3x - 5)(y + 10)$, *the formula for the area of the rectangle shown*

$3x - 5$

$y + 10$

Solution   **a** In the real-number system, the operation of taking a square root is defined only for nonnegative inputs.

$$2n + 3 \geq 0$$

$$2n \geq -3$$

$$n \geq -\frac{3}{2}$$

The domain is $\left\{ n{:}n \geq -\frac{3}{2} \right\}$.

b The length and the width of a rectangle must be positive.

$$3x - 5 > 0 \qquad\qquad\qquad y + 10 > 0$$

$$3x > 5 \qquad\qquad\qquad\quad y > -10$$

$$x > \frac{5}{3}$$

The domain is $\left\{ (x, y){:}x > \frac{5}{3} \text{ and } y > -10 \right\}$.

Problem 2   Let $f(x) = x + 2$ and $g(x) = x^2$. Find the value(s) of x for which $f[g(x)] = g[f(x)]$.

Solution   First we write simplified expressions for $f[g(x)]$ and $g[f(x)]$.

$$f[g(x)] = f(x^2) \qquad\qquad\qquad g[f(x)] = g(x + 2)$$

$$= x^2 + 2 \qquad\qquad\qquad\qquad = (x + 2)^2$$

$$\qquad\qquad\qquad\qquad\qquad = x^2 + 4x + 4$$

Now we set the composites equal to each other and solve for x.

$$f[g(x)] = g[f(x)]$$

$$x^2 + 2 = x^2 + 4x + 4$$

$$-2 = 4x$$

$$-\frac{1}{2} = x$$

The composites $f[g(x)]$ and $g[f(x)]$ are equal only when $x = -\frac{1}{2}$.

Problem 3   Let $h(x) = \sqrt{x + 7}$ and $g(x) = x^2 - 7$. Determine whether h and g are inverse functions.

Solution   If h and g are inverse functions, $h[g(x)]$ will equal x and $g[h(x)]$ will equal x for all the values of x for which h and g are defined.

$$h[g(x)] = h(x^2 - 7) \qquad\qquad g[h(x)] = g(\sqrt{x + 7})$$
$$= \sqrt{(x^2 - 7) + 7} \qquad\qquad = (\sqrt{x + 7})^2 - 7$$
$$= \sqrt{x^2} \qquad\qquad\qquad = (x + 7) - 7$$
$$= |x| \qquad\qquad\qquad\quad = x$$

Since $h[g(x)] \neq x$ when $x < 0$, h and g are not inverse functions. (In the next section, you will discover that we *can* call h and g inverse functions if we specify a restriction in the domain of g.)

Part Three: Exercises and Problems

Warm-up Exercises

1 Determine the domain and the range of each of the following functions.

a $f(x) = 3 + 5\sqrt{x}$

b $g(x) = \frac{x - 3}{5 + x}$

c $S(n) = 180(n - 2)$, the formula for the sum of the measures of the angles of an n-sided polygon

d $h(y) = \frac{2y^2}{y^2 + 5y + 6}$

2 Refer to the input-output diagram of the composite $g \circ f$.

a What is the output for an input of -2?

b Write a simplified expression for $g \circ f(x)$.

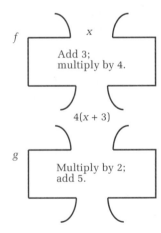

3 Let $h(x) = 3x + 2$ and $j(x) = x^2$.

a Find $h[j(4)]$.   **b** Find $j[h(4)]$.

c Is composition of functions commutative?

4 If function h is the inverse of function g, what is the value of each composite?

a $h \circ g(7)$ **b** $g \circ h(7)$ **c** $h[g(9)]$
d $g[h(9)]$ **e** $h[g(x)]$

5 Explain why $f(x) = 3x + 2$ and $g(x) = \frac{1}{3}x - \frac{2}{3}$ are inverse functions.

6 Let $f(x) = 2x + 1$ and $g(x) = x^2 - 2$.

a Evaluate $f(3)$ and $g(3)$.
b Compute $f(3) \cdot g(3)$ and $g(3) \cdot f(3)$.
c Compute $f \circ g(3)$ and $g \circ f(3)$.
d Explain why the expressions in part **b** are equivalent but those in part **c** are not.

Problem Set

7 Let $f(x) = x^2 + 4$ and $g(x) = \sqrt{x - 4}$.

a What are the restrictions on the domain of f?
b What are the restrictions on the domain of g?
c Write a simplified expression for $f[g(x)]$. What is the domain of $f \circ g$?
d Write a simplified expression for $g[f(x)]$. What is the domain of $g \circ f$?
e Find $f[g(5)]$ and $g[f(5)]$.
f Find $f[g(-4)]$ and $g[f(-4)]$.

8 Refer to the mapping diagrams.

a Find $g[f(3)]$.
b What is the domain of $g[f(x)]$?
c What is the range of $g[f(x)]$?

9 If $g(x) = 3x + 2$ and $r(x) = 2 - 5x$, what are $g \circ r(y)$ and $r \circ g(y)$?

10 For what real values of x is $\sqrt{2x + 10}$ not defined over the real numbers?

11 Let $s(x) = x^2$ and $t(x) = \sqrt{x}$.

a Find $s[t(4)]$ and $t[s(4)]$.
b Find $t[s(-9)]$ and $s[t(-9)]$.
c Are s and t inverse functions?

12 The area of the rectangle shown is 36. Find the value of x.

6

$x^2 + 5x$

13 If $f(x) = 2x + 5$ and $g(x) = 2x - 5$, are f and g inverses? Explain your answer.

14 If $f(x) = 5x + 3$ and $g(x) = x^2 - 3$, for what value(s) of x is $f(x) = g(x)$?

15 Is the relation represented by the mapping diagram a function?

a

b

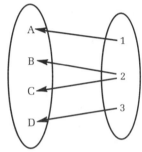

16 If $A(x) = x^2 + 5$ and $B(x) = x - 2$, for what value(s) of x is $A[B(x)] = B[A(x)]$?

17 The "greatest-integer" function of x, symbolized $[x]$, outputs the greatest integer that is less than or equal to x—for example, $[5.2] = 5$, $[-1.3] = -2$, and $[7] = 7$. Evaluate each of the following expressions.

a $[11.4]$ **b** $[0]$ **c** $[-8.3]$

d $[-5.9]$ **e** $[\pi]$ **f** $[-\sqrt{2}]$

g $\left[\dfrac{77}{3}\right]$ **h** $[x + 1] - [x]$

18 If $p(x) = x^2 + 8$ and $q(x) = 2x$, for what value(s) of x is $p[q(x)] = q[p(x)]$?

19 a Write a function m describing the measure of $\angle ABC$ in terms of x.
 b What are the restrictions on the domain of function m?
 c How does the measure of $\angle ABC$ change as the value of x increases from 2 to 5?
 d How does the measure of $\angle DBC$ change as the value of x increases from 2 to 5?

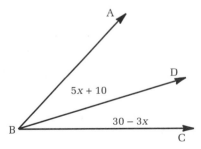

Problem Set, *continued*

20 Explain why $g(x) = x^2$ and $h(y) = y^2$ represent the same function.

21 Let $f(x) = x^2 + 1$ and $g(x) = \sqrt{x - 1}$.
  a Find $f[g(8)]$. **b** Find $g[f(8)]$.
  c Are f and g inverse functions?

22 Let $f(x) = \frac{1}{x - 2}$, where $x \neq 2$, and $g(x) = \frac{1 + 2x}{x}$, where $x \neq 0$.
  a Find $f[g(4)]$ and $g[f(4)]$.
  b Are f and g inverse functions?

23 Suppose that function s is the inverse of function r and that $r(5) = 11$.
  a Find $r \circ s(5)$. **b** Find $s \circ r(5)$. **c** Find $s(11)$.

24 Suppose that $F(A, B) = A + B$ and $G(A, B) = A \cdot B$ are functions for which the inputs A and B are matrices.
  a Find $F\left(\begin{bmatrix} 3 & 7 \\ 5 & 9 \end{bmatrix}, \begin{bmatrix} 8 & 11 \\ 20 & 17 \end{bmatrix}\right)$.
  b Find $G\left(\begin{bmatrix} 2 & 3 \\ 1 & -4 \end{bmatrix}, \begin{bmatrix} 5 & -6 \\ -3 & 8 \end{bmatrix}\right)$.
  c What is the domain of F?
  d What is the domain of G?

25 The total cost of x hamburgers priced at $1.39 each is given by the formula $C(x) = 1.39x$. The sales tax charged on a purchase of y dollars, at a tax rate of 7 percent, is given by the formula $T(y) = 0.07y$.
  a If $h(x) = T(C(x))$, what is the formula that represents function h?
  b What does the output of h represent?

26 Let $f(x) = \frac{x}{x^2 - 9}$ and $g(x) = \frac{1}{x}$.
  a Write a simplified expression for $g \circ f(x)$. What is the domain of $g \circ f$?
  b Write a simplified expression for $f \circ g(x)$. What is the domain of $f \circ g$?

27 Let $f(x) = \frac{x}{x - 1}$.
  a Find $f[f(2)]$. **b** Find $f[f(3)]$.
  c Find $f[f(-5)]$. **d** Find $f[f(1)]$.
  e What is INVf?

28 Suppose that $f(n) = 4 + f(n - 1)$ and that $f(1) = 12$.
   a Find $f(2)$.   **b** Find $f(3)$.   **c** Find $f(4)$.

29 If $P(x)$ represents the perimeter of the triangle shown, what are the domain and the range of function P?

30 If two of the functions listed below are selected at random, what is the probability that they are inverses?

$$f(x) = 2x \qquad g(x) = x + x \qquad h(x) = \frac{1}{2}x \qquad k(x) = x - 2$$

$$r(x) = \frac{x}{2} \qquad s(x) = x - x \qquad t(x) = \frac{1}{2x}$$

31 Suppose that the inputs of a function represent the numbers of sides of various polygons and that the outputs of the function represent the numbers of the polygons' diagonals.
   a Write a formula for the function.
   b What is the function's domain?
   c What is the function's range?

32 Below is part of a chart used to calculate sales tax in Yoknapatawpha County.

Amount	Tax
1–19¢	1¢
20–39¢	2¢
40–59¢	3¢
60–79¢	4¢
80–99¢	5¢

Write a function T that can be used to find the amount of sales tax charged on any purchase price p, in cents. (Hint: Use the greatest-integer notation described in problem 17.)

33 A rocket is fired upward. After 3 seconds, its fuel runs out. At that instant, it is 1550 feet above the ground and has an upward velocity of 2800 feet per second.
   a What is the rocket's maximum height?
   b How many seconds (from the time of its launch) does it take for the rocket to reach its maximum height?
   c What is the total time from the rocket's launch until it strikes the ground?

INVERSE FUNCTIONS

Objectives

After studying this section, you will be able to
- Find the inverse of a given function
- Recognize the relationship between the graphs of a function and its inverse

Part One: Introduction

Finding Inverses

In the preceding section, you learned to recognize when two functions are inverses of each other. The next step is to be able to find the inverse of a given function.

One way of finding a function's inverse is to think of the function as a process involving a sequence of steps and then to reverse this process. The function $f(x) = 3x + 5$, for example, tells us to multiply the input by 3, then add 5; so INVf must consist of the inverses of these operations performed in reverse order—that is, subtracting 5, then dividing by 3.

$$f(x) = 3x + 5 \qquad \text{INV}f(x) = \frac{x-5}{3}$$

Now consider the input-output diagram for two inverse functions, f and INVf. If an input a in function f produces an output b, then inputting b in INVf must result in an output of a. In other words, if the point with coordinates (a, b) is on the graph of f, then the point (b, a) must be on the graph of INVf.

This relationship suggests another way of finding the inverse of a function; we can interchange the input and output variables in a corresponding equation and then solve the new equation for the output variable.

Example   *If* $f(x) = 9 - 2x$, *what is* INVf?

We rewrite the function as the equation $y = 9 - 2x$. Interchanging x and y in the equation produces $x = 9 - 2y$, which we solve for y.

$$x = 9 - 2y$$

$$2y = 9 - x$$

$$y = \frac{9 - x}{2}$$

Thus, INV$f(x) = \dfrac{9 - x}{2}$.

In a number of cases, a given function does not have an inverse function unless we restrict its domain. Suppose, for example, that $g(x) = x^2$. If we interchange the variables in the equation $y = x^2$ and solve for y, we obtain $y = \pm\sqrt{x}$, in which y is not a function of x. If, however, we restrict the domain of g to $\{x : x \geq 0\}$, we can say that $g(x) = x^2$ and INV$g(x) = \sqrt{x}$.

Graphing Inverse Functions

Let's plot some points (a, b) that are on the graph of $y = 2x + 1$ and then plot the corresponding points of the form (b, a).

(a, b)	(b, a)
$(-3, -5)$	$(-5, -3)$
$(-2, -3)$	$(-3, -2)$
$(-1, -1)$	$(-1, -1)$
$(0, 1)$	$(1, 0)$
$(1, 3)$	$(3, 1)$
$(2, 5)$	$(5, 2)$

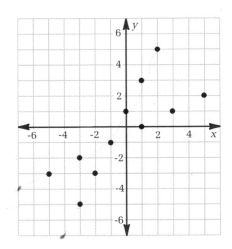

Notice that the pairs of points form a symmetrical arrangement. Now let's look at the graphs of several functions and the corresponding inverse functions.

$y = f(x) = 5x$ and
$y = \mathrm{INV}f(x) = \frac{x}{5}$

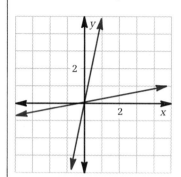

$y = f(x) = \sqrt{x}$ and
$y = \mathrm{INV}f(x) = x^2$
for domain $\{x: x \geq 0\}$

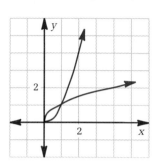

$y = f(x) = 2x + 5$ and
$y = \mathrm{INV}f(x) = \frac{x-5}{2}$

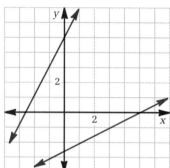

It appears that in each case the graphs of the function and its inverse are symmetric about the line $y = x$ (the line that diagonally bisects Quadrants I and III). Since this line divides the coordinate plane in such a way that the graphs of a function and its inverse are "mirror images" of each other, we say that the two graphs are *reflections* of each other over the line $y = x$.

Part Two: Sample Problems

Problem 1   Let $g(x) = x^2 + 3$, with a domain of $\{x: x \geq 0\}$, and $h(x) = \sqrt{x - 3}$, with a domain of $\{x: x \geq 3\}$.

a Are g and h inverse functions? Why or why not?
b What is the range of g? What is the range of h? What is significant about the domains and ranges of these functions?
c Graph g, h, and $h \circ g$ on the same coordinate system. What is significant about the graphs?

Solution   **a** Functions g and h are inverses, since $g[h(x)] = h[g(x)] = x$ for all values of x in the functions' domains.
b The range of g is $\{g(x): g(x) \geq 3\}$, and the range of h is $\{h(x): h(x) \geq 0\}$. Because the functions are inverses, the values in the range of g form the domain of h, and the values in the range of h form the domain of g.
c The graphs of $y = g(x)$ and $y = h(x)$ are reflections of each other over the graph of $y = h[g(x)]$, which is equivalent to $y = x$ for the values in the restricted domain.

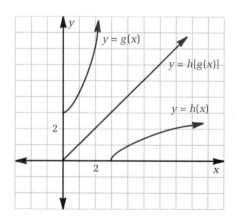

Problem 2   Let $f(x) = 2x + 4$. Find INVf and graph both functions on the same coordinate system.

Solution

Method 1
Since f involves multiplying by 2, then adding 4, INVf will involve subtracting 4, then dividing by 2.

$$INVf(x) = \frac{x - 4}{2}$$

Method 2
Exchanging x and y in the equation $y = 2x + 4$ produces $x = 2y + 4$, which we solve for y.

$$x = 2y + 4$$

$$x - 4 = 2y$$

$$\frac{x - 4}{2} = y$$

$$INVf(x) = \frac{x - 4}{2}$$

Since f and INVf are linear functions, we can find a few points on the graph of $y = f(x)$, find the reflections of these points over the line $y = x$, and connect each set of points with a straight line.

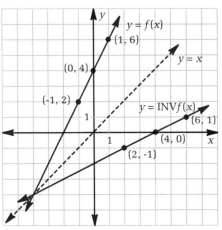

Part Three: Exercises and Problems

Warm-up Exercises

1 The points (0, 1), (2, 4), (4, 16), and (5, 25) are on the graph of a function.

  a List four points on the graph of the function's inverse.
  b Graph all eight points, along with the equation $y = x$, on a coordinate system.
  c How do the two sets of points relate to the graph of $y = x$?

In problems 2–7, find the inverse of each function.

2 $f(x) = 10x$

3 $g(x) = x - 6$

4 $h(x) = 6x + 3$

5 $p(x) = x^2 - 1$, where $x \geq 0$

6 $q(x) = \sqrt{x - 1}$, where $x \geq 1$

7 $r(x) = \dfrac{1}{2x}$, where $x \neq 0$

8 The graph represents a function G, with inputs x and outputs y.

  a What are the domain and the range of G?

  b Find the coordinates of the points representing INVG.

  c What are the domain and the range of INVG?

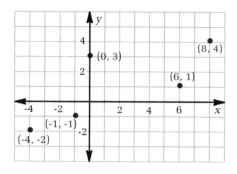

9 a Graph y = g(x) = −x² + 5. On the same coordinate system, sketch the reflection of the graph over the line y = x.

  b Does the reflection represent a function?

  c Is there a function INVg? If so, what is it?

Problem Set

10 Consider the input-output diagram.

  a If the output is 17, what was the input?

  b If the output is 133, what was the input?

  c If the output is n, what was the input?

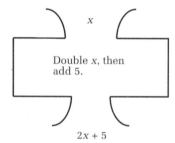

11 If a function h can be represented by {(3, 7), (4, 4), (5, 1), (6, −2), (7, 0)}, how can INVh be represented?

12 Let f(x) = −2x + 8 and g(x) = −½x + 4.

  a Graph the two functions and the line y = x on the same coordinate system.

  b Find f[g(6)] and g[f(−10)].

  c Show that f[g(x)] = x.

  d Are f and g inverses?

13 Copy and complete the table of values for two inverse functions, f and g.

x	0	1	2	3	4	5	
f(x)	5	3				4	8
g(x)	2	4	3				8

14 If $\text{INV}f(x) = 12 - \frac{1}{2}x$, what is function f?

15 The graphs of five functions are shown. If two of the graphs are selected at random, what is the probability that they represent inverse functions?

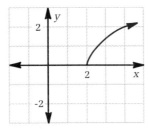

16 If $f(5) = 14$ and $f(2 \cdot 5) = 3[f(5)]$, what is the value of $f(10)$?

17 Let $f(x) = x^2$, with a domain of $\{x : 1 < x < 10\}$.

   a What is the range of f?
   b If $g(x) = \text{INV}f(x)$, what is function g?
   c What are the domain and the range of g?
   d Could you have identified the domain and the range of the inverse of f without actually finding g? If so, how?

18 The equation $S = 180(n - 2)$ represents a function that outputs the sum of the angles of a polygon when the number of the polygon's sides is input.

   a What would the inverse of the function do?
   b Write an equation corresponding to the inverse function.
   c What is the domain of the inverse function?

19 The letters a and b can be arranged in only two ways, as ab or as ba. In how many ways can the three letters a, b, and c be arranged?

20 If $f(x) = x^2$ and the domain of f is restricted to $\{x : x \le 0\}$, what is $\text{INV}f$?

21 Sketch the reflection of each of the following graphs over the line
y = x and indicate whether the reflection represents a function.

a b c d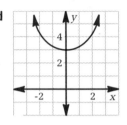

22 a Graph y = h(x) = (x − 3)² + 4. On the same coordinate system,
sketch the reflection of the graph over the line y = x.
b Does the reflection represent a function?
c Is there a function INVh? If so, what is it?

23 For each function f, find INVf. Specify restrictions on the domain
of f if necessary.
a f(x) = 3x + 4
b f(x) = $\frac{9}{x}$
c f(x) = $\frac{3}{4} - \frac{1}{2}x$
d f(x) = (x + 3)²

24 The area of the rectangle is 104 square
centimeters. Find the lengths of its sides.

x - 2

x + 7

25 If g(x) = $-\frac{2}{3}$(x + 5), what is INVg?

26 The function A(x) = x² outputs the area of a square with side
length x. The function D(x) doubles its input.

a Is A ∘ D equal to D ∘ A?
b What is the geometric meaning of A[D(x)]?
c What is the geometric meaning of D[A(x)]?

27 Let R(x) = $\frac{1}{x}$ and O(x) = −x.

a Is R its own inverse?
b Is O its own inverse?
c Find some other functions that are their own inverses.

28 Graph each of the following functions, then reflect the graph over
the line y = x and indicate whether the result represents a function.
a f(x) = 2x − 6
b g(x) = 2x² − 3
c h(x) = |x − 2|
d j(x) = 2ˣ

In problems 29–31, find the equation of each graph's axis of symmetry.

29

30

31

32 Ralph's Pretty Good Pizza offers five pizza toppings and lets customers choose any two toppings for the price of one. How many different pairs of toppings can customers select?

33 On a calculator with a $\boxed{10^x}$ key, enter 2.5 $\boxed{10^x}$. With the result still displayed, press the $\boxed{\log}$ key. Repeat this sequence for the inputs 9.2, 4.96, and −10.5. What can you conclude about the 10^x and log functions?

34 Suppose that the sales tax, $T(x)$, charged on a purchase of x dollars is given by the function $T(x) = 0.07x$.
a What is the inverse of T?
b What does the output of INVT represent?

35 Determine the equation of the line of best fit for the data points (2, 7), (5, 10), (7, 14), and (10, 16).

36 Two 2 × 2 matrices are called *inverse matrices* if their product is $\begin{bmatrix} 1 & 0 \\ 0 & 1 \end{bmatrix}$. If two of the following matrices are selected at random, what is the probability that they are inverses?

$$\begin{bmatrix} 2 & 0 \\ 0 & 2 \end{bmatrix} \qquad \begin{bmatrix} 1 & 2 \\ 2 & 5 \end{bmatrix} \qquad \begin{bmatrix} 0.5 & 0 \\ 0 & 0.5 \end{bmatrix} \qquad \begin{bmatrix} 1 & 2 \\ -2 & 5 \end{bmatrix} \qquad \begin{bmatrix} 5 & -2 \\ -2 & 1 \end{bmatrix}$$

37 Write a formula that represents the inverse of a quadratic function of the form $f(x) = a(x - h)^2 + k$, where the domain of f is restricted to $\{x : x \geq h\}$.

38 Let $f\left(\begin{bmatrix} a & b \\ c & d \end{bmatrix} \right) = 2 \begin{bmatrix} a & b \\ c & d \end{bmatrix} + 4 \begin{bmatrix} 1 & 0 \\ 0 & 1 \end{bmatrix}$.

a Find $f\left(\begin{bmatrix} 3 & 5 \\ 2 & -1 \end{bmatrix} \right)$.

b Find INVf.

c Show that $f \circ \text{INV}f\left(\begin{bmatrix} a & b \\ c & d \end{bmatrix} \right) = \begin{bmatrix} a & b \\ c & d \end{bmatrix}$.

OPERATIONS ON FUNCTIONS

Objectives

After studying this section, you will be able to
- Perform operations on the outputs of functions
- Perform operations on the inputs of functions

Part One: Introduction

Operations on Outputs

The solution to a problem frequently involves more than merely evaluating a function. Sometimes we must perform a mathematical operation on the input before evaluating the function; in other cases, we must perform an operation on the function's output.

In this section, we will explore operations on functions. The functions we will deal with will have numerical inputs and outputs so that we can see patterns more easily. Because these functions represent numbers, we will be able to apply the rules of numbers to the outputs—for example, $3[f(x)] + 5[f(x)] = 8[f(x)]$, and $2[f(x)] \cdot 4[f(x)] = 8[f(x)]^2$. Here are some more examples of operations on outputs.

Example   Let $f(x) = x^2 + 2x + 1$. Write an expression for $3[f(x)]$.

$$3[f(x)] = 3(x^2 + 2x + 1)$$
$$= 3x^2 + 6x + 3$$

Example   If $5[h(x)] = x + h(x)$, what is $h(x)$?

Remember that we consider $h(x)$ to represent a number.

$$5[h(x)] = x + h(x)$$

Subtract $h(x)$ from each side $$5[h(x)] - h(x) = x$$

$$4[h(x)] = x$$

Divide each side by 4 $$h(x) = \frac{x}{4}$$

Example   Let $g(x) = x^2 - x$. Evaluate $5[g(3)] - [g(3)]^2$.

We first evaluate $g(3)$.

$g(x) = x^2 - x$

$g(3) = 3^2 - 3$

    $= 6$

Now we substitute 6 for $g(3)$ in $5[g(3)] - [g(3)]^2$.

    $5[g(3)] - [g(3)]^2$

$= 5(6) - 6^2$

$= -6$

Operations on Inputs

There are some important differences between operating on an input of a function and operating on an output. In most cases, when operating on an input, we must know what the function represents before we do any work. Here are some examples.

Example   Let $f(x) = x^2 + 2x + 1$. Write an expression for $f(3x)$.

$f(3x) = (3x)^2 + 2(3x) + 1$

    $= 9x^2 + 6x + 1$

Notice that $f(3x)$ indicates a different operation from $3[f(x)]$, which was found in a previous example. The expression $f(3x)$ indicates that the input of function f is tripled, whereas $3[f(x)]$ represents a tripling of the function's output.

Example   If $g(x) = x^2$, what is $g(w - 5) - g(w^3)$?

$g(w - 5) - g(w^3) = (w - 5)^2 - (w^3)^2$

           $= w^2 - 10w + 25 - w^6$

Example   Let $f(x) = 3x + 1$. Is $f(a + b)$ equal to $f(a) + f(b)$?

Let's try evaluating $f(a + b)$ and $f(a) + f(b)$ for $a = 4$ and $b = 5$.

$f(x) = 3x + 1$ $f(x) = 3x + 1$

$f(a + b) = 3(4 + 5) + 1$ $f(a) + f(b) = f(4) + f(5)$

        $= 3(9) + 1$ $= [3(4) + 1] + [3(5) + 1]$

        $= 28$ $= 13 + 16$

                                                $= 29$

In this case, $f(a + b) \neq f(a) + f(b)$. This example shows that, as a rule, a function cannot be distributed over addition.

Part Two: Sample Problems

Problem 1   Let $f(x) = x^3 + x^2 - 6$. *If* $x = 5$, *what are the values of* $4[f(x)]$ *and* $f(4x)$?

Solution   The expression $4[f(x)]$ indicates an operation on output, and the expression $f(4x)$ indicates an operation on input.

$$4[f(5)] = 4(5^3 + 5^2 - 6) \qquad\qquad f(4 \cdot 5) = f(20)$$
$$= 4(125 + 25 - 6) \qquad\qquad\quad = 20^3 + 20^2 - 6$$
$$= 4 \cdot 144 \qquad\qquad\qquad\qquad = 8000 + 400 - 6$$
$$= 576 \qquad\qquad\qquad\qquad = 8394$$

Notice that $4[f(x)] \neq f(4x)$ if $x = 5$.

Problem 2   *If* $f(x) = x^2 + 2x + 3$, *what are the values of* x *for which* $f(2x) = 2[f(x)]$?

Solution $$f(2x) = 2[f(x)]$$

$$(2x)^2 + 2(2x) + 3 = 2(x^2 + 2x + 3)$$

$$4x^2 + 4x + 3 = 2x^2 + 4x + 6$$

$$2x^2 = 3$$

$$x^2 = \frac{3}{2}$$

$$x = \pm\sqrt{\frac{3}{2}}$$

$$\approx \pm 1.225$$

Problem 3   *A function* f *has the property that for all real values of* x, $f(3x) = 3[f(x)]$. *Find* $f(0)$.

Solution   We are told that $f(3x) = 3[f(x)]$ for all real inputs, so we can write the equation $f(0) = 3[f(0)]$ and solve it for $f(0)$. (Remember that $f(0)$ represents a number.)

$$f(0) = 3[f(0)]$$

Subtract $f(0)$ from each side $$0 = 3[f(0)] - f(0)$$

$$0 = 2[f(0)]$$

Divide each side by 2 $$0 = f(0)$$

Part Three: Exercises and Problems

Warm-up Exercises

1 Solve $3 \cdot f(x) + 2 = x + 2 \cdot f(x)$ for $f(x)$.

2 Solve $8 \cdot g(x) = 6x - 7 \cdot g(x)$ for $g(x)$.

3 Let $f(x) = x - 7$ and $g(x) = \sqrt{x}$. Evaluate each of the following expressions.

   a $f(3) + g(3)$ **b** $f(3) \cdot g(3)$ **c** $\dfrac{f(3)}{g(3)}$

   d $f[g(3)]$ **e** $4[f(3)] + 7[g(3)]^2$

4 **a** Write a function for $A_r(x)$, the area of the rectangle.
   b Write a formula for $A_t(x)$, the area of the triangle.
   c Let $A(x) = A_r(x) + A_t(x)$. What is the significance of function A?
   d Find $A(20)$.

5 Let $f(x) = 3x - 4$. Simplify each expression.

   a $3 \cdot f(x) + 6$ **b** $[f(x)]^2 - 7$
   c $[f(x) - 2][3 \cdot f(x) + 4]$ **d** $f[f(x)]$
   e $4[f(x)]^2 - 10[f(x)]$

6 If $f(x) = 2x - 8$, what is the value of w for which $f(w - 3) = 0$?

7 The diagram shows the graphs of $y = f(x)$ and $y = g(x)$. Sketch the graph of $y = f(x) + g(x)$.

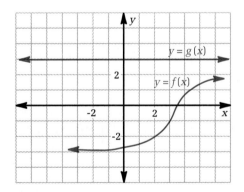

8 If $h(x) = x^2$, is $3[h(x)]$ or $h(3x)$ greater?

Problem Set

9 Let $f(x) = \sqrt{x - 5}$. Simplify each expression.

   a $f(3x)$ **b** $f(x + 5)$ **c** $f(x^2)$
   d $f(2x - 1)$ **e** $f[f(x)]$

Problem Set, *continued*

10 If $f(x) + 3 \cdot f(x) = 8[x + f(x)]$, what is $f(x)$?

11 The function $A(x) = x^2$ represents the area of the square shown. Draw an area diagram to represent each of the following expressions.

   a $3[A(x)]$
   b $A(2x)$
   c $A(x + 2)$

12 a Copy and complete the table for $f(x) = x^2 + 2x + 1$.

x	−4	−3	−2	−1	0	1	2	3	4
f(x)									
f(x − 1)									
f(x + 1)									

   b Use the table you generated in part **a** to graph $y = f(x)$, $y = f(x - 1)$, and $y = f(x + 1)$ on the same coordinate system.

13 If $f(x) = x^2 - 7$ and $f[g(x)] = x^6 - 7$, what is $g(x)$?

14 Let $f(x) = x + 2$ and $g(x) = -x + 2$. Graph f, g, and $f + g$ on the same coordinate system.

15 For what values of x are the y-coordinates of the graph shown less than zero?

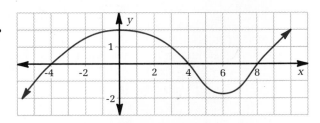

16 Basso the Clown has four different-sized tires on his miniature car. How many different ways are there for him to put the tires on the car?

17 The function $A(x, y) = xy$ outputs the area of a rectangle with side lengths x and y. Draw an area diagram to represent each of the following expressions.

   a $A(3x, y)$ **b** $A(x, 3y)$
   c $A(3x, 3y)$ **d** $3[A(x, y)]$

18 Let $f(x) = x + 1$ and $g(x) = 3$. Graph each of the following on the same coordinate system.

   a $y = f(x)$ **b** $y = g(x)$ **c** $y = f(x) + g(x)$ **d** $y = f(x) - g(x)$

19 Which of the following statements describes the sequence, 1, 3, 5, 7, 9, 11, . . . ?

    a $f(1) = 1$ and $f(2) = 3$ **b** $f(n) = f(n - 1) + 2$

    c $f(1) = 1$ and $f(n + 1) = f(n) + 2$

20 The diagram shows the graphs of $y = g(x)$ and $y = h(x)$. Sketch the graph of $y = g(x) + h(x)$.

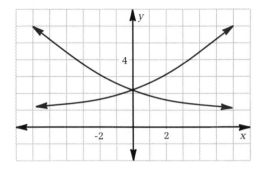

21 Let $h(x) = x^2 - 4$ and $g(x) = x - 7$.

    a If $3[Q(x)] = h(x) - g(x)$, what is $Q(x)$?

    b If $h(x) \cdot R(x) = h[g(x)]$, what is $R(x)$?

    c Find $h[g(x)]$.

    d Find $g[h(x)]$.

22 The diagram shows the graphs of $y = f(x)$ and $y = g(x)$, where $f(x) = x^2$.

    a Write a formula for function g.

    b Sketch the graph of $y = f(x) + g(x)$.

    c Write an expression for $f(x) + g(x)$.

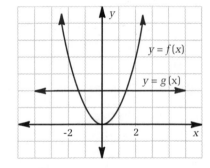

23 The function $V(x) = x^3$ outputs the volume of a cube with edge x. Draw a diagram to represent each of the following expressions.

    a $3[V(x)]$

    b $V(3x)$

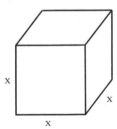

24 Suppose that $h(x + 1) = h(x) + h(x - 1)$ and that $h(0) = 3$ and $h(1) = 12$.

    a Find $h(2)$.   **b** Find $h(3)$.   **c** Find $h(4)$.

25 If $f(x) = \sqrt{x + 4}$ and $f[g(x)] = |x - 2|$, what is $g(x)$?

26 Let $w(x) = 3x - 1$ and $x = 5$. Find $w(x^2) - [w(x)]^2$.

27 Suppose that $f(xy) = f(x) + f(y)$ and that $f(2) = 0.3010$ and $f(3) = 0.4771$.

    a Find $f(6)$.   **b** Find $f(12)$.   **c** Find $f(9)$.   **d** Find $f(18)$.

28 If $g(x) = x^3$, is $g(2x)$ or $2 \cdot g(x)$ greater?

29 Alfredo's calculator was run over by a truck, so that only the keys for the digits 1, 3, 5, and 7 work now.

    a How many four-digit numbers can Alfredo enter on his calculator if he does not repeat digits?

    b How many four-digit numbers can he enter if digits can be repeated?

    c How many four-digit numbers can he enter in which at least one digit is repeated?

30 The diagram shows the graph of $y = \tan x$ for the domain $\{x: -180 \le x \le 180\}$. Sketch the reflection of this graph over the line $y = x$. Does the reflection represent a function of x?

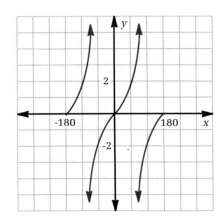

31 Function h has the following three properties.

    i $5[h(x)] = h(x) + \dfrac{x^2}{h(x)}$

    ii $h(x) > 0$

    iii The domain of function h is $\{x: x > 0\}$.

    a Find $h(x)$.   **b** Graph $y = h(x)$.

32 Consider the following compound functions.

$$f(x) = \begin{cases} x^2 \text{ if } -4 < x < 1 \\ 5 \text{ if } x = 1 \\ \sqrt{x} \text{ if } x > 1 \end{cases} \qquad g(x) = \begin{cases} 10 \text{ if } x < 4 \\ 0 \text{ if } x = 4 \\ -3 \text{ if } x > 4 \end{cases}$$

    a Find $f[g(x)]$.

    b Sketch the graph of $f \circ g$.

    c What are the domain and the range of $f \circ g$?

DISCRETE FUNCTIONS

Objectives

After studying this section, you will be able to
- Use the factorial function
- Use the permutation function
- Use the combination function

Part One: Introduction

The Factorial Function

Any function whose domain is a set of numbers that can be listed, such as the set of integers, is called a *discrete function*. In this section, we will look at three discrete functions.

First, let's look at the *factorial* function.

 The factorial function F is defined by the formula

$$F(n) = n(n-1)(n-2)(n-3) \ldots (2)(1)$$

where n is a nonnegative integer.

An exclamation point (!), is used to symbolize the word *factorial*, so another way to express $F(n)$ is $n!$, read "n factorial." By definition, $0! = 1$ and $1! = 1$.

Example   *Compute 6!.*

$6! = 6 \cdot 5 \cdot 4 \cdot 3 \cdot 2 \cdot 1$

$\quad = 720$

Example   *The rock group B4 recorded 8 songs to be released on a compact disc. In how many different ways can the songs be arranged on the disc?*

There are 8 choices for the first song. For each possible first song, there are 7 choices left for the second song. For each of the $8 \cdot 7$ ways to choose the first 2 songs, there are 6 ways to choose the third, and so on. The number of ways all 8 songs can be arranged on the disc is $8 \cdot 7 \cdot 6 \cdot 5 \cdot 4 \cdot 3 \cdot 2 \cdot 1 = 8! = 40,320$.

In general, $n!$ represents the number of ways n items can be arranged. Becoming familiar with the factorial key on a scientific calculator will save you effort and time.

The Permutation Function

Suppose that B4's recording company recorded 19 of the group's songs during a concert tour but decided to put only 8 of them on a compact disc. How many different arrangements of 8 songs can be made from the 19 songs that were recorded?

There are 19 choices for the first song, 18 for the next, and so on until 8 songs have been selected. The number of possible arrangements is therefore $19 \cdot 18 \cdot 17 \cdot 16 \cdot \ldots \cdot 12$, or 3,047,466,240. Note that

$$19 \cdot 18 \cdot 17 \cdot 16 \cdot 15 \cdot 14 \cdot 13 \cdot 12$$

$$= \frac{19 \cdot 18 \cdot 17 \cdot 16 \cdot 15 \cdot 14 \cdot 13 \cdot 12 \cdot 11 \cdot 10 \cdot 9 \cdot 8 \cdot 7 \cdot 6 \cdot 5 \cdot 4 \cdot 3 \cdot 2 \cdot 1}{11 \cdot 10 \cdot 9 \cdot 8 \cdot 7 \cdot 6 \cdot 5 \cdot 4 \cdot 3 \cdot 2 \cdot 1}$$

$$= \frac{19!}{11!}$$

$$= \frac{19!}{(19 - 8)!}$$

This suggests a formula for the **permutation** function.

> **The permutation function P is defined by the formula**
>
> $$P(n, r) = \frac{n!}{(n - r)!}$$

In general, $P(n, r)$ represents the number of ways that n objects can be *permuted*, or arranged, into groups of r objects. The domain of the permutation function is the set of *pairs* of nonnegative integers (n, r) such that $n \geq r$.

The Combination Function

B4's manager insisted that the group be allowed to select which 8 songs would be on the compact disc, though the recording company could decide how they would be arranged. In how many ways can the group choose 8 songs from the 19 without regard to their order?

This is an application of the **combination** function C, where $C(n, r)$ is the number of sets of r objects that can be chosen from n objects. To compute $C(19, 8)$, let's take a closer look at the permutation function P.

$P(19, 8)$ = total number of ways 19 songs can be arranged into groups of 8

$$= \left(\begin{array}{c} \text{number of ways 8 songs can} \\ \text{be chosen from a group of 19} \end{array} \right) \left(\begin{array}{c} \text{number of ways 8 songs} \\ \text{can be arranged} \end{array} \right)$$

The first factor is $C(19, 8)$, the number we want. The second factor equals 8!. Therefore,

$$P(19, 8) = C(19, 8) \cdot 8!$$

$$C(19, 8) = \frac{P(19, 8)}{8!}$$

$$= \frac{19!}{(19 - 8)!8!} = 75{,}582$$

There are 75,582 ways in which the group can choose 8 songs from the 19.

> **The combination function C is defined by the formula**
>
> $$C(n, r) = \frac{n!}{(n - r)!r!}$$

Part Two: Sample Problems

Problem 1   *Ms. Paskal's algebra class has 29 students and 29 desks. For the sake of variety, students change the seating arrangement each day. How many days must pass before they need to repeat a seating arrangement?*

Solution   The problem asks for the number of ways in which 29 students can be arranged, so we use the factorial function. Since 29! days is $\approx 8.84 \times 10^{30}$ days, or about 2.42×10^{28} years, they will never repeat a seating arrangement.

Problem 2   *Ms. Paskal gives 200 extra points to the 4 students who arrive first to class. How many days might she have to give out extra points if*

   a *The same 4 students cannot receive extra points twice?*
   b *The same 4 students can receive extra points more than once as long as they enter in a different order each time?*

Solution   **a** The problem is to determine how many sets of 4 students can be chosen, in any order, from a class of 29. We use the combination function.

$$C(29, 4) = \frac{29!}{25!4!} = 23{,}751$$

Ms. Paskal might have to give extra points for 23,751 days.

   b Since order is important, we use the permutation function.

$$P(29, 4) = \frac{29!}{25!} = 29 \cdot 28 \cdot 27 \cdot 26 = 570{,}024$$

Ms. Paskal might have to give extra points for 570,024 days.

In each case, Ms. Paskal could have to give out extra points for the rest of her career.

Part Three: Exercises and Problems

Warm-up Exercises

In problems 1–4, evaluate each expression.

1 5! **2** 10! **3** 15! **4** 45!

5 Harry Temmert, the morning DJ on XWTR radio, has 12 songs to play between 7 and 8 A.M. In how many different orders can Harry play these songs?

6 There are 107 competitors in a 10-kilometer race. A first prize, a second prize, and a third prize are awarded.

  a How many different groups of three people can win prizes?
  b How many different arrangements of winners of the first, second, and third prizes are there?

7 Let P be the permutation function and C be the combination function.

  a Evaluate P(7, 2).   **b** Evaluate C(7, 2).
  c Evaluate P(15, 6).   **d** Evaluate C(15, 6).
  e What conjecture might you make on the basis of your results in parts **a–d**?

8 How many different license plates are possible if each plate contains a group of six letters and/or digits?

9 If a license plate must have two letters followed by four digits, how many different license plates are possible?

Problem Set

10 Evaluate each expression.

  a $\dfrac{9!}{8!}$ **b** $\dfrac{97!}{96!}$ **c** $\dfrac{(n+1)!}{n!}$

11 Martino's Pizza offers a special pizza with 4 toppings. There are 11 toppings available to choose from. Guido decides to order a different 4-topping pizza each day.

  a Does order matter when selecting toppings for a pizza?
  b How many days can Guido go without repeating?

12 Seven points are selected on a circle.

  a How many triangles have three of these points as vertices?
  b How many quadrilaterals have four of these points as vertices?

In problems 13–16, evaluate the combination function for each pair of inputs.

13 $C(5, 4)$ **14** $C(8, 7)$ **15** $C(12, 11)$ **16** $C(51, 50)$

17 What pattern do you see in problems 13–16?

18 Find the smallest value of x for which $P(10, x) > 1000$.

19 Find the mean (average) of the elements of $\{-5, -3, -1, 11, 17, 29\}$.

In problems 20–22, let $P_2(x)$ represent the probability of a roll of x when two dice are rolled. Find each probability.

20 $P_2(7)$

21 $P_2(12)$

22 $P_2(13)$

23 a Evaluate $C(6, 2)$ and $C(6, 4)$.
   b Evaluate $C(6, 1)$ and $C(6, 5)$.
   c Evaluate $C(8, 2)$ and $C(8, 6)$.
   d Evaluate $C(8, 3)$ and $C(8, 5)$.
   e Describe any patterns you see.

24 Give the range of $f(x) = 3x^2 - 2$ for each domain.
   a $\{-2, -1, 0, 1, 2\}$ **b** $\{x: -2 \leq x \leq 2\}$

25 If $f(x) = x + 5$ and $g(y) = y - 5$, what is $3[f(4)] - 4[g(3)]$?

26 a If $f(x) = \frac{2}{3}x - 6$, what is INVf?
   b Graph $y = f(x)$ and $y = $ INV$f(x)$ on the same coordinate system.
   c What is the point of intersection of the two graphs?

27 Copy and complete the pattern of factorials. If the pattern were to continue, what would 0! be? What would $(-1)!$ be?

28 Find the smallest positive integer n for which $\frac{7!}{n}$ is not an integer.

29 If $f(x) = x!$, does f have an inverse function?

30 Use the factorial, permutation, or combination function to solve the handshake problem presented in Section 1.1. Then explain why your choice of function is appropriate.

31 Find the greatest positive integer n for which $\frac{10!}{2^n}$ is an integer.

32 If $C(9, 3) = C(9, x)$ and $x \neq 3$, what is the value of x?

33 Solve $29 \cdot 5! + 13 \cdot 5! = k!$ for k.

34 Solve $[f(x)]^2 - 12[f(x)] + 32 = 0$ for $f(x)$.

35 Consider a 50-sided polygon.
   a How many vertices does it have?
   b How many diagonals does it have?
   c If two diagonals are drawn at random, what is the probability that they have a common endpoint?

36 The graph shows postage costs for first-class mailings in Mathamerica.

   a What is the cost of mailing a 2.5-ounce package?
   b What is the cost of mailing a 1-ounce package?
   c What input values w, in ounces, give an output of $1.00?
   d Find the possible outputs if $0.8 < w < 2.3$.

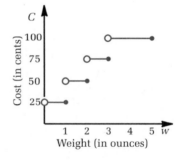

37 Let $f(x) = x!$ and $g(x) = \frac{f(x)}{x}$, where $x > 0$.
   a Find $g(3)$, $g(4)$, $g(5)$, and $g(6)$.
   b Use factorial notation to write a simple expression for $g(x)$.

38 The following table shows enrollments in mathematics classes at Parker High School.

Year	1960	1965	1970	1975	1980	1985
Enrollment	787	815	849	930	952	911

   a Graph the data and draw a fitted line.
   b Use the method of least squares to write an equation of the line of best fit.

39 Function f is defined by two rules: $f(1) = 5$ and $f(n) = 2 \cdot f(n - 1)$.
   a Evaluate $f(2)$.   **b** Evaluate $f(4)$.

40 $S(a)$ is a function whose input is an angle measure, as shown in the diagram. The output is the y-coordinate of point P, where one side of the angle intersects the square. Find each of the following.

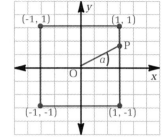

a $S(45)$
b $S(0)$
c $S(30)$
d $S(60)$
e $S(90)$

41 Show that $C(n - 1, k - 1) + C(n - 1, k) = C(n, k)$.

FUNCTIONS MAKE LIFE SIMPLER
Predictable outcomes in common experiences

If you have ever paid to take a taxi, ride on public transportation, or take a bus, train, or plane trip, you have used a function. If you can imagine having to negotiate your fare for a given trip, then you may be able to appreciate how functions simplify life.

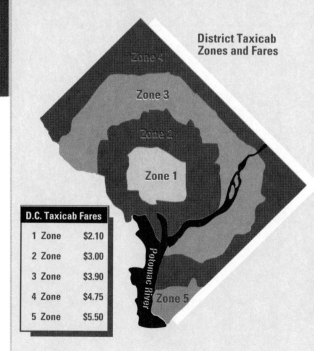

District Taxicab Zones and Fares

D.C. Taxicab Fares	
1 Zone	$2.10
2 Zone	$3.00
3 Zone	$3.90
4 Zone	$4.75
5 Zone	$5.50

In certain cities, for example, the distance you ride on a bus or subway determines how much you pay for the trip. There is usually a table or chart of zones showing the fares for travel between zones. That there is a given fare for a given distance seems obvious: what arrangement could be simpler? It *is* simple because there is a "fare function"; that is, fare is a function of distance.

Suppose the fare structure were not a function. Then there might be more than one fare for some or all distances. How could that be? In one scenario, the driver or ticket agent might bargain with each passenger for the fare that passenger would pay. In that case, there might be two or more different values for the same trip.

Another example of how we use relations that are functions occurs whenever we practice at a game of skill. A basketball player uses the knowledge that the height of the ball at a given point after a shot is taken is a function of force and direction. Only because the ball's height is a function can a player, through practice, strive for perfection. If the ball's path were not a function, it would never be possible to predict the effect of taking a shot, no matter how perfectly it was executed.

RECURSIVELY DEFINED FUNCTIONS

Objectives

After studying this section, you will be able to
- Interpret recursive definitions of functions
- Relate recursive definitions to equivalent closed-form definitions

Part One: Introduction

Recursive Definitions

Count the rays and angles in each diagram below.

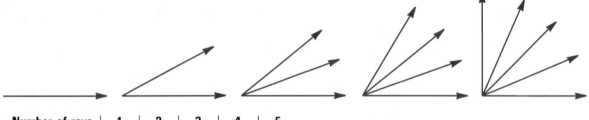

Number of rays	1	2	3	4	5
Number of angles	0	1	3	6	10

We can identify a pattern in the sequence of the inputs (the numbers of rays) and the outputs (the numbers of angles). Each time an input n is increased by 1, the corresponding output increases by n. If we express the relationship between inputs and outputs in function notation, we can represent the pattern in the following way.

$$f(1) = 0$$
$$f(2) = f(1) + 1 = 0 + 1 = 1$$
$$f(3) = f(2) + 2 = 1 + 2 = 3$$
$$f(4) = f(3) + 3 = 3 + 3 = 6$$
$$f(5) = f(4) + 4 = 6 + 4 = 10$$
$$\vdots$$
$$f(n + 1) = f(n) + n$$

A more concise way of expressing the pattern is

$f(1) = 0$

$f(n + 1) = f(n) + n$ for all positive integers $n \geq 1$

This two-part statement is called a ***recursive definition*** of function f. Every recursive definition specifies a beginning value—in this case, $f(1) = 0$—and a way to calculate each successive output in terms of the preceding output or outputs—in this case, $f(n + 1) = f(n) + n$. Most of the functions you have worked with up to now have been represented in ***closed form***. A closed-form formula, such as $f(x) = x^2 + 1$, $g(x) = 2x + 3$, or $h(x) = 8$, shows the relationship between each input and its corresponding output. A recursive definition, on the other hand, shows how each output value is related to one or more previous output values. For this reason, it may be difficult to evaluate a recursively defined function for a particular input value; but representing a function recursively is often the best way of clarifying a numerical pattern. Many functions with discrete domains can, in fact, be represented in both closed and recursive forms.

Exploring Recursively Defined Functions

We can often find interesting relationships between recursively defined functions and functions that can be expressed in closed form.

Example   *Express the following recursively defined function in closed form.*

$f(0) = 4$

$f(n + 1) = f(n) + 3$

Let's evaluate the function for successive inputs and graph the corresponding ordered pairs.

$f(0) = 4$

$f(1) = f(0) + 3 = 4 + 3 = 7$

$f(2) = f(1) + 3 = 7 + 3 = 10$

$f(3) = f(2) + 3 = 10 + 3 = 13$

$f(4) = f(3) + 3 = 13 + 3 = 16$

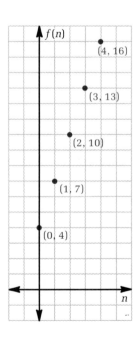

It seems that the points all lie on a line having a slope of 3—that is, a line representing a function of the form $f(x) = 3x + b$. Since we know that $f(0) = 4$, we can write the equation $4 = 3(0) + b$, or $b = 4$. We can therefore express f by means of the closed-form formula

$f(x) = 3x + 4$, where x is a nonnegative integer

Example   *Express the following recursively defined function in closed form.*

$$g(0) = 4$$

$$g(n + 1) = 3[g(n)]$$

Again, let's generate a few outputs.

$$g(0) = 4$$

$$g(1) = 3[g(0)] = 3(4) = 12$$

$$g(2) = 3[g(1)] = 3(3)(4) = 3(12) = 36$$

$$g(3) = 3[g(2)] = 3(3^2)(4) = 3(36) = 108$$

This pattern seems to involve multiplying successive powers of 3 by 4, so that a corresponding closed-form formula would be $g(x) = 4(3^x)$, where x is a nonnegative integer. We can test whether this formula in fact represents the function by using both it and the recursive definition to calculate $g(4)$.

Closed Form	**Recursive Form**
$g(x) = 4(3^x)$	$g(n + 1) = 3[g(n)]$
$g(4) = 4(3^4)$	$g(4) = 3[g(3)]$
$= 4(81)$	$= 3(108)$
$= 324$	$= 324$

The closed-form formula does seem to represent the function.

Part Two: Sample Problems

Problem 1   *Find the first eight outputs of the following recursively defined function.*

$$f(1) = 1$$

$$f(2) = 1$$

$$f(n + 1) = f(n) + f(n - 1), \text{ where } n \geq 2$$

Solution
$$f(1) = 1$$

$$f(2) = 1$$

$$f(3) = 1 + 1 = 2$$

$$f(4) = 2 + 1 = 3$$

$$f(5) = 3 + 2 = 5$$

$$f(6) = 5 + 3 = 8$$

$$f(7) = 8 + 5 = 13$$

$$f(8) = 13 + 8 = 21$$

The values generated by this function are the ***Fibonacci numbers*** a famous sequence that has many interesting properties. You will surely encounter them again.

Problem 2   *Identify the pattern of outputs of the following function.*

$$f(0) = 1$$

$$f(n + 1) = \frac{1}{1 + f(n)}$$

Solution $f(0) = 1$

$$f(1) = \frac{1}{1 + f(0)} = \frac{1}{1 + 1} = \frac{1}{2}$$

$$f(2) = \frac{1}{1 + f(1)} = \frac{1}{1 + \frac{1}{2}} = \frac{1}{\frac{3}{2}} = \frac{2}{3}$$

$$f(3) = \frac{1}{1 + f(2)} = \frac{1}{1 + \frac{2}{3}} = \frac{1}{\frac{5}{3}} = \frac{3}{5}$$

$$f(4) = \frac{1}{1 + f(3)} = \frac{1}{1 + \frac{3}{5}} = \frac{1}{\frac{8}{5}} = \frac{5}{8}$$

This pattern is not easy to identify, nor can we easily write a corresponding closed-form formula. The pattern is, however, a very interesting one. The numerators and the denominators of the successive outputs are successive Fibonacci numbers. Fibonacci numbers occur in surprising places.

Problem 3   *Is the closed-form formula corresponding to the following function linear or quadratic?*

$$f(0) = 3$$
$$f(n + 1) = f(n) + 2n$$

Solution   One way to identify the degree of a function is to examine the pattern of the differences between successive outputs. If these differences, called ***first differences,*** are constant, the function is linear; if the differences between the first differences (the ***second differences***) are constant, the function is quadratic.

n	0	1	2	3	4	5	6
$f(n)$	3	3	5	9	15	23	33

First differences: 0   2   4   6   8   10

Second differences: 2   2   2   2   2

Since the second differences are the same, this recursively defined function has a quadratic closed-form formula. (In this case, the formula is $f(x) = x^2 - x + 3$, where x is a nonnegative integer.)

Part Three: Exercises and Problems

Warm-up Exercises

1 Let $f(1) = 10$ and $f(n + 1) = 4 \cdot f(n)$. Find $f(2)$, $f(3)$, and $f(4)$.

2 Copy and complete the table for the quadratic function $f(x) = x^2 + 3x + 1$ and find the first and second differences.

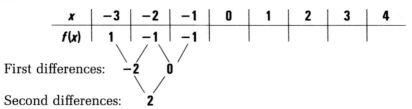

x	-3	-2	-1	0	1	2	3	4
$f(x)$	1	-1	-1					

First differences: -2 0

Second differences: 2

3 Consider the following recursively defined function.

$f(0) = 5$
$f(n) = f(n - 1) + 3$

Make a table of the first six values of $f(n)$. Is the closed-form formula corresponding to f linear or quadratic or neither?

In problems 4 and 5, define f by $f(1) = 1$ and $f(n + 1) = (n + 1) \cdot f(n)$.

4 Find $f(2)$, $f(3)$, $f(4)$, and $f(5)$.
5 Express f in closed form.

Problem Set

6 If $f(1) = 12$ and $f(n) = 2n + f(n - 1)$, what are $f(2)$, $f(3)$, $f(4)$, and $f(10)$?

7 Copy and complete the table for a quadratic function f.

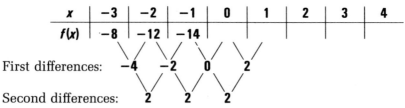

x	-3	-2	-1	0	1	2	3	4
$f(x)$	-8	-12	-14					

First differences: -4 -2 0   2

Second differences: 2   2   2

8 Refer to the six points A through F.

a How many segments can be drawn having two of these points as endpoints?
b How many triangles can be drawn having three of these points as vertices?

9 Let $F(1) = -1$ and $F(n + 1) = -1 \cdot F(n)$.

   a Find $F(2)$, $F(3)$, and $F(4)$.
   b Find $F(k)$ if k is odd.
   c Find $F(k)$ if k is even.
   d Write a closed-form formula for F.

10 Refer to the graph of function f.

   a What is the domain of f?
   b What is the range of f?

 11 If $f(1) = 0$ and $f(n + 1) = \frac{f(n) + 36}{2}$, what is $f(8)$?

12 If $\frac{n!}{(n - 2)!} = 132$, what is the value of n?

13 Let $3 \cdot f(x) + 8x = 5 \cdot f(x) - 2$. Find an expression for $f(x)$.

14 Consider the following recursively defined function.

$$h(1) = \begin{bmatrix} -1 & 0 \\ 0 & 1 \end{bmatrix}$$
$$h(n + 1) = h(n) \cdot \begin{bmatrix} 1 & 0 \\ 0 & -1 \end{bmatrix}$$

   Find $h(2)$, $h(3)$, $h(4)$, $h(5)$, and $h(6)$.

 15 There are 64 squares on a chessboard.

   a In how many ways can 3 pawns occupy different squares on the chessboard?
   b In how many ways can a king, a queen, and a rook occupy different squares on the chessboard?

16 Let $F(1) = 6$ and $F(n + 1) = F(n) + n + 1$.

   a Find $F(2)$, $F(3)$, $F(4)$, and $F(5)$.
   b Is the closed-form formula corresponding to F linear or quadratic?

Problem Set, *continued*

In problems 17 and 18, solve each system.

17 $\begin{cases} 4x - 2y = -13 \\ 2x + 2y = -5 \end{cases}$

18 $\begin{cases} y = -\frac{5}{3}x + 6 \\ 4y + x = 4 \end{cases}$

19 Sketch the graphs of $y = x^2 - x - 2$ and $y = x - 1$ on the same set of axes.

   a Approximately where do the graphs intersect?
   b Substitute $x - 1$ for y in the first equation and solve for x.

20 Let $f(0) = -9$ and $f(n) = f(n - 1) + 4$.

   a Find the slope and the y-intercept of the linear function corresponding to f.
   b Write a recursive definition of $g(x) = 3x + 10$, where x is a nonnegative integer.

21 Let $F(0) = -4$ and $F(n) = 6 + F(n - 1)$.

   a Construct a table of the first six values of $F(n)$.
   b Find the first differences of $F(n)$.
   c Write a closed-form formula for F.

22 How many six-digit license-plate numbers can be created from the digits 1, 2, 3, 4, 5, 6, 7, 8, and 9 if

   a Digits can be repeated?
   b No digit can be repeated?

23 Consider the following recursively defined function.

$F(1) = 4$
$F(2) = 6$
$F(n) = n \cdot F(n - 1) + F(n - 2)$

Construct a table of the first six values of $F(n)$.

24 Little Bo Peep counted her sheep to go to sleep. Each night she had to count 12 more sheep than the previous night before she could sleep. If 22 sheep made Peep sleep the first night, how many sheep did she count in a week?

25 Use the table to write a recursive definition of F.

n	1	2	3	4	5	6
$F(n)$	12	40	124	376	1132	3400

26 Suppose that

$F(1) = 4$
$F(n) = 4 + g(n)$, where $n \geq 1$
$g(n) = 2 \cdot g(n - 1)$

Copy and complete the following table.

n	1	2	3	4	5	6
$F(n)$						
$g(n)$						

27 Consider the following compound function.

$$F(n) = \begin{cases} 1 \text{ if } n = 1 \\ F(n - 1) + n \text{ if } n \text{ is odd and } n > 1 \\ F(n - 1) - n \text{ if } n \text{ is even and } n > 1 \end{cases}$$

a Construct a table of the first eight values of $F(n)$.
b Find $F(497)$.
c Find $F(5234)$.

28 In the game Tower of Hanoi, the goal is to move the tower of disks, one disk at a time, from one peg to another peg without ever putting a larger disk on top of a smaller disk.

a Copy and complete the following table.

Number of disks	1	2	3	4
Minimum number of moves needed to finish game				

b To move n disks, you must move $n - 1$ disks to a second peg, move the nth disk to the third peg, then move the $n - 1$ disks on top of the nth disk. Using $H(n)$ to represent the minimum number of moves in a game with n disks, write the preceding argument as a recursive statement involving $H(n)$.
c Test your recursive statement with the data from part **a.**

29 A binary number consists of a string of 0's and 1's. Let $F(n)$ be the number of different n-digit binary numbers in which the first digit is a 1 and no two consecutive digits are 1's. (For example, 1010 qualifies but 1011 does not.)

a Find $F(1)$, $F(2)$, $F(3)$, $F(4)$, $F(5)$, and $F(6)$.
b What do you think might be a recursive definition of F?

MEASURES OF CENTRAL TENDENCY AND PERCENTILES

Objectives

After studying this section, you will be able to
- Determine the mean, the mode, and the median of a set of data
- Interpret percentiles and percentile ranks

Mean, Mode, and Median

A fishing derby was held to see who could catch the greatest number of bass weighing over 2 pounds. Fifteen contestants entered, catching the following numbers of eligible bass.

$$2, 2, 3, 3, 3, 3, 3, 4, 5, 5, 7, 11, 12, 12, 31$$

A newspaper reporter writing a story about the derby asked the contest manager, "What was the average number of bass weighing over 2 pounds caught by the contestants?" The contest manager responded, "Which average do you mean?"

The manager first added the numbers of eligible fish the contestants caught and divided the sum by the number of contestants, 15.

$$\frac{\text{Total number of bass}}{\text{Number of contestants}} = \frac{106}{15} = 7\frac{1}{15}$$

He told the reporter, "The *arithmetic mean* of the numbers of fish caught is $7\frac{1}{15}$." An arithmetic mean is also simply called a *mean*.

"On the other hand," the contest manager said, "three is the most common number of fish caught." The number that occurs the greatest number of times in a set of data is another type of average, called the *mode* of the data.

"Then again," he continued, "the number 4 is at the middle of the set of data. Seven contestants caught more than 4 fish, and 7 caught fewer." The middle number of an ordered set of data is the median.

The mean, the mode, and the median are called *measures of central tendency* of a set of data.

Percentiles and Percentile Ranks

After a medical examination, Vera received this report.

	Triglycerides	Cholesterol
Result	113	248
Percentile rank	79	61

The triglyceride level of 113 with a ***percentile rank*** of 79 means that 79 percent of the people tested had a result less than 113. What does the cholesterol percentile rank of 61 mean?

There are several percentiles commonly used in data reporting. The 25th percentile of a distribution corresponds to Q_1 and is called the ***lower quartile.*** The 75th percentile corresponds to Q_3 and is called the ***upper quartile.*** The 50th percentile is the median (Q_2). A box-and-whisker plot (see Section 4.7) identifies the 25th, 50th, and 75th percentiles of a set of data.

Problem 1   *The following data represent Victor Vector's scores on his first nine quizzes in physics class.*

$$16, 13, 19, 20, 20, 18, 11, 19, 17$$

Arranging the data from smallest to largest gives

$$11, 13, 16, 17, 18, 19, 19, 20, 20$$

a *Determine the mean, the mode, and the median of the quiz scores.*
b *Victor earned a score of 19 on the next quiz. Determine the new mean, mode, and median.*

Solution   **a** The sum of Victor's scores is 153.

$$\text{Mean} = \frac{\text{sum of quiz scores}}{\text{number of quiz scores}} = \frac{153}{9} = 17$$

The scores 19 and 20 appear most often and the same number of times. The data is said to be ***bimodal,*** with the two modes being 19 and 20.

The median (middle) score is 18.

b The data for the 10 quiz scores are

$$11, 13, 16, 17, 18, 19, 19, 19, 20, 20$$

The sum of these scores is 172.

$$\text{Mean} = \frac{\text{sum of quiz scores}}{\text{number of quiz scores}} = \frac{172}{10} = 17.2$$

The mode is 19, since this score occurs the greatest number of times.

Since there is an even number of data, we have two middle scores, 18 and 19. The median is the mean of the two middle scores, $\frac{18 + 19}{2}$, or 18.5.

Problem 2 *In a recent candy drive Dan Teen sold 130 packages of sugarless gum. Dan wanted to know how his sales compared with those of others in his club. The data below represent the numbers of packages of sugarless gum sold by all members in his club. Find the percentile rank of Dan's sales.*

$$22, 35, 67, 71, 88, 92, 100, 112, 130, 145, 155, 171, 188$$

Solution The percentile rank of Dan's total sales of 130 is determined by dividing 8 by 13, because his sales exceeded those of 8 of the 13 club members. Since $\frac{8}{13} \approx 0.615$, Dan's sales exceeded those of 61 percent of the club members. We can therefore say that his percentile rank is 61, although percentile ranks are more meaningful for large sets of data.

Problem Set

1 Ashvin scored 550 on a standardized exam. He was told that his score exceeded the scores of 85,000 of the 113,000 who took the exam. What was his percentile rank?

2 Nachum Oer had the following scores in his first eight games in a recent bowling tournament.

$$194, 223, 246, 235, 267, 211, 229, 271$$

Nachum estimates that he needs a mean of 243 for 12 games in order to win some of the prize money. What must he average in his last four games to win some money?

3 Make a stem-and-leaf plot and a box-and-whisker plot of the following data, which represent the heights, in inches, of students in an eleventh-grade chemistry class.

61, 80, 63, 72, 79, 63, 72, 76, 69, 67, 65, 66,
71, 65, 73, 72, 65, 70, 64, 73, 66, 68, 70, 71, 72

4 In a survey of an advanced algebra class at Apollo High School, the 21 class members reported the numbers of hours per week that they worked at jobs outside of school. The reported hours were as follows:

10, 16, 15, 12, 0, 6, 19, 14, 15, 6,
0, 0, 10, 20, 18, 24, 7, 0, 12, 10, 15

a Determine the mean, the mode, and the median of the data.
b In your opinion, which of the three measures of central tendency best describes the data? Explain your reasoning.
c Bob transferred into the class after the survey was taken. He works 19 hours per week. How much does his presence affect the mean, the median, and the mode?

5 Explain why you can't make a stem-and-leaf plot showing the data represented by a given box-and-whisker plot.

6 So far this basketball season, Devan has made 36% of the field goals he has attempted. If he has attempted 84 field goals, how many shots in a row must he make to raise his percentage to 40%?

7 What means can the scores 126, 160, 90, x, and 120 have if x is a whole number and x is the median of the data?

8 What modes are possible for the data {12, 16, x, 9, x, 15, x} if x is a natural number and the mean is less than 14?

9 Find a table of numerical data in a newspaper or magazine and determine the mean, the mode, and the median of the data.

10 In the frequency graph shown, M_o represents the mode, M_e represents the median, and $\overline{x}$ represents the mean. Copy each of the following frequency graphs and indicate where M_o, M_e, and $\overline{x}$ might be.

M_o M_e $\overline{x}$

a   **b**   **c**

In problems 11 and 12, refer to the chart, which shows the numbers of people scoring various numbers of correct responses on a computer-aptitude exam.

11 Find the mean, the mode, and the median number of correct answers.

12 Choose four scores and find the percentile rank of each.

Number of Correct Responses	Number of People with This Score
15	62
14	320
13	602
12	890
11	1123
10	2365
9	4698
8	7642
7	3537
6	2135
5	1601
4	753
3	351
2	162
1	74
0	19

Problem Set, *continued*

13 Roll 3 dice, noting the total of the numbers on the upturned faces. Do this 25 times and record the 25 totals.

   a Determine the mean, the mode, and the median of the rolls.
   b Draw a box-and-whisker plot to display the data.

14 The values x, 17, y, y, and 23, where x and y are whole numbers, have a mean less than 9. What are the possible values of (x, y)?

CAREER PROFILE

EXPONENTIALS AND STATISTICS IN BANKING
Jessalyn Wilscam evaluates businesses' prospects

"The bank I work for offers training classes in accounting and special classes in statistics and finance," says Jessalyn Wilscam, a vice president with a bank in New York City. Why? "I approve loans to companies, and I need to understand the information they are providing to justify the loan. The customers I work with are largely newspapers, radio, and cable TV. If the company is a newspaper, for example, it may say that its sales will go up 8% in the next year."

Looking at statistical data, Ms. Wilscam must decide whether she agrees with what the company projects. Based on her decision, she works out how much to lend the company.

"I also have to figure out how much money the loan will bring in compared with how much it's costing us, because the money we use to make the loan is itself borrowed."

This involves straightforward calculation using exponentials. Ms. Wilscam uses a computer with a spreadsheet program to do the calculation for her. Her own role is to decide whether the numbers make sense.

What does Ms. Wilscam like most about her job? "I travel, I look at different companies and industries, I meet people. It's an analytical job, which I like."

Ms. Wilscam grew up in Omaha and has a political science degree from Newcome College of Tulane University. Besides the statistics class offered by her bank, she had four years of mathematics in high school. She says she wishes she had taken calculus, since she uses so much mathematics in her job.

This graph shows the money the bank pays out and takes in on $1,000,000 over a twelve-month period. Considering that the bank cannot loan the interest it is paying its depositor or investor, what will happen to the bank's profit margin if the loan is not repaid when it is due?

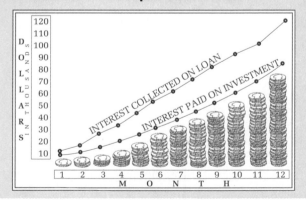

5 CHAPTER SUMMARY

CONCEPTS AND PROCEDURES

After studying this chapter, you should be able to
- Represent relations (5.1)
- Recognize functions (5.1)
- Identify restrictions on the domain of a function (5.2)
- Interpret composite functions (5.2)
- Recognize inverse functions (5.2)
- Find the inverse of a given function (5.3)
- Recognize the relationship between the graphs of a function and its inverse (5.3)
- Perform operations on the outputs of functions (5.4)
- Perform operations on the inputs of functions (5.4)
- Use the factorial function (5.5)
- Use the permutation function (5.5)
- Use the combination function (5.5)
- Interpret recursive definitions of functions (5.6)
- Relate recursive definitions to equivalent closed-form definitions (5.6)
- Determine the mean, the mode, and the median of a set of data (5.7)
- Interpret percentiles and percentile ranks (5.7)

VOCABULARY

arithmetic mean (5.7)
bimodal (5.7)
closed form (5.6)
combination (5.5)
composite (5.2)
composition of functions (5.2)
discrete function (5.5)
domain (5.1)
factorial (5.5)
Fibonacci numbers (5.6)
first differences (5.6)
function (5.1)
inverse functions (5.2)

lower quartile (5.7)
mean (5.7)
measure of central tendency (5.7)
mode (5.7)
percentile rank (5.7)
permutation (5.5)
range (5.1)
recursive definition (5.6)
reflection (5.3)
relation (5.1)
second differences (5.6)
upper quartile (5.7)

REVIEW PROBLEMS

1 Is the relation represented by the following table a function?

Input	−8	−4	0	1	4	5.77
Output	0	0	0	1	0	−1

2 Let $f(x) = 3x - 5$. Write a simplified expression for each of the following.

    a $f(6x)$ **b** $f(x + 3)$ **c** $f(4y + 3)$

3 Identify the domain and the range of each of the following functions.

    a $f(x) = \dfrac{1}{x^2}$ **b** $g(x) = 2x - 2$ **c** $h(x) = |x + 6|$

4 Let $r(x) = 5x + 1$ and $s(x) = x^2 - 5$.

    a Find $r[s(2)]$.   **b** Find $s[r(2)]$.

5 Which of the following functions are discrete?

	Input	Output
a	Annual income	Federal income tax paid
b	Volume of a tree	Number of sheets of paper made from the tree
c	Number of tickets sold	Total revenue from a baseball game
d	Gallons of gasoline	Miles driven
e	Number of minutes spent exercising	Pulse rate

6 If $g(x) = \frac{x}{3} - 2$, what is INV(g)?

7 If C is the combination function and $C(10, 3) = n!$, what is the value of n?

8 Find INV$f \circ f(x)$ for each of the following functions.

    a $f(x) = 2x - 5$ **b** $g(z) = -3z$

    c $p(x) = \sqrt{x}$ **d** $r(y) = -\dfrac{1}{y}$

9 Let $f(0) = 3$ and $f(n) = n[f(n - 1)]$.

    a Find $f(1)$, $f(2)$, $f(3)$, and $f(4)$.

    b Write a closed-form formula for function f.

10 Bill Yard participated in the Nine Ball Pool Tournament. The graph shows the numbers of balls he pocketed in the games he played.

  a How many games did Bill play? How many balls did he pocket all together?
  b Find the mean, the mode, and the median number of balls pocketed by Bill.

In problems 11–15, identify the domain of each function.

11 $g(x) = \dfrac{4x}{x^2 - 4}$

12 $h(x) = \sqrt{6 - 2x}$

13 $F(x) = x!$

14 $t(x) = \dfrac{6}{|x|^5 - 32}$

15 $p(1) = 2,\ p(n + 1) = \dfrac{1}{[p(n)]^2}$

16 Find the following matrix product for $f(x) = x^2$ and $g(x) = 2x + 3$.

$$\begin{bmatrix} f(2) & f(3) \\ f(-1) & f(-6) \end{bmatrix}\begin{bmatrix} g(4) \\ g(-6) \end{bmatrix}$$

17 Which of the following graphs represent y as a function of x? Which represent x as a function of y?

a   **b**   **c**

18 A certain compact-disc player can be programmed to play the songs on a disc in any order.

  a In how many possible orders can the songs on a nine-song disc be played if each is played only once?
  b If it takes 43 minutes to play the whole disc, how long would it take to play the songs on the disc in every possible way?

19 When playing the board game Klu, a player can be any of eight different characters. If three people are to play the game, in how many ways can they choose their characters?

In problems 20–23, graph each function, then sketch the reflection of the graph over the line y = x and indicate whether the reflection represents a function.

20 $f(x) = 4x + 1$

21 $g(x) = (x - 2)^2 + 3$

22 $h(x) = \dfrac{1}{x + 2}$

23 $j(x) = |x| + 2$

Review Problems, *continued*

24 Function f has a domain of $\{0, 1, 2, 3, 4, 5\}$ and a range of $\left\{\frac{1}{3}, \frac{1}{4}, \frac{1}{5}, \frac{1}{6}, \frac{1}{7}, \frac{1}{8}\right\}$. Each element of the range is paired with exactly one element of the domain.

   a What is the domain of INVf?
   b What is the range of INVf?

25 In the figure shown, each smaller square's vertices are the midpoints of the sides of the next larger square. The outer square has sides 4 centimeters long. If a point within the figure is picked at random, what is the probability that the point lies in the shaded region?

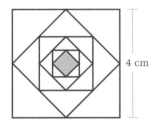

4 cm

In problems 26–29, find the inverse of each function. Specify restrictions on the domain of the function if necessary.

26 $p(x) = 6x - 3$ **27** $r(x) = 2x^2 - 3$

28 $s(x) = \dfrac{1}{\sqrt{x}}$ **29** $t(x) = \frac{1}{2}x + \frac{5}{8}$

30 If $p(x) = \dfrac{x^2 + 3x}{x^2 - 2x - 15}$ and $q(x) = \frac{1}{x}$, what are $q[p(x)]$ and $p[q(x)]$?

31 a Write a function P that represents the perimeter of the rectangle.
    b What are the domain and the range of P?
    c Find INVP.
    d What does the output of INVP represent?

$x + 4$

$2x$

In problems 32 and 33, find a closed-form formula for each function.

32 $f(0) = -1$ **33** $g(1) = 4$
    $f(n - 1) = \frac{1}{2} + f(n)$ $g(n + 1) = 4[g(n - 1)]$

34 Let $g(x) = x^2 - 3$ and $h(x) = 1 - x$. Write a simplified expression for each of the following.

   a $g \circ h(x)$ **b** $h \circ g(x)$ **c** $h(x + 6)$
   d $g(x + 6)$ **e** $g(6x)$ **f** $h(6x)$

35 Write a recursive definition of the function $h(k) = k^2 + 3k + 1$, where k is a positive integer.

36 If $p(x) = 3x^2 - 5$, is $-5[p(x)]$ or $p(-5x)$ greater?

CHAPTER TEST

1 The input values x for the following relation are the set of positive integers.

$$r = \begin{cases} 2 \text{ if x is a multiple of 2} \\ 3 \text{ if x is a multiple of 3} \\ 1 \text{ if x is a multiple of neither 2 nor 3} \end{cases}$$

Is r a function of x?

2 Suppose that $h(y) = \sqrt{y - 5}$ and that $g(x) = x + 2$ for the domain $\{x:1 \le x \le 5\}$.

  a What is the domain of function h?
  b If $R(x) = h[g(x)]$, what is the domain of R?
  c What is the range of R?

3 Refer to the diagram.

  a Write a closed-form formula for F.
  b Write a recursive definition of F.

4 If $f(x) = x^3 + 1$ and $g(x) = |x|$, what are $g \circ f(-3)$ and $f \circ g(-3)$?

5 If two of the following functions are selected at random, what is the probability that they are inverse functions?

$$f(x) = 2x + 10 \qquad g(x) = \sqrt{x} \qquad h(x) = x^2, x \ge 0$$
$$m(x) = \frac{1}{x + 2} \qquad n(x) = \tfrac{1}{2}x - 5 \qquad p(x) = \frac{1}{x} - 2$$

6 A congressional committee is to consist of 3 of the 435 members of the House of Representatives. In how many possible ways can the committee be formed?

7 The data below represent the speeds, in miles per hour, of drivers ticketed on Interstate 314 by Officer "Radar" Gunn.

$$72, 78, 67, 70, 73, 69, 83, 68, 71, 75, 80, 73, 76$$

  a Determine the mean, the mode, and the median of the data.
  b Draw a box-and-whisker plot to represent the data.
  c Use the plot to determine the speeds that have percentile ranks less than 75.

This photo of the distorted reflections of buildings in a set of coordinate axes brings to mind reflections of graphs.

6.1 BEYOND PLOTTING POINTS

Objectives

After studying this section, you will be able to
- Graph parabolas
- Graph absolute-value functions
- Stretch, shrink, and reflect graphs

Part One: Introduction

Graphs of Parabolas

In Section 4.3, we saw that the graph of $f(x) = x^2$ has a vertex at the origin and is ∪-shaped. Some of the ordered pairs on the graph of this function are $(-2, 4)$, $(0, 0)$, $(1, 1)$, and $(3, 9)$. In general, the graph of a function of the form $f(x) = a(x - h)^2 + k$, where a, h, and k are constants, is called a parabola and has a characteristic ∪ shape.

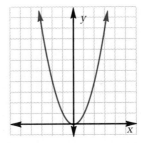

Absolute-Value Graphs

The graph of the absolute-value function $f(x) = |x|$ is similar to the graph of $f(x) = x^2$. The graph has a vertex and a line of symmetry, and $f(x) = f(-x)$. The characteristic shape is a V. Some points on the graph are $(-2, 2)$, $(-1, 1)$, $(0, 0)$, $(1, 1)$, and $(2, 2)$.

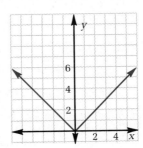

Stretching, Shrinking, and Reflecting

Let's look at the graphs of some functions of the form $y = ax^2$, where $a \neq 1$. How do these graphs differ from the graph of the standard parabola, $f(x) = x^2$?

These graphs suggest that if the output of $f(x) = x^2$ is multiplied by a positive constant a, $a > 1$, the graph will appear to be *stretched* along the y-axis. If $0 < a < 1$, the graph is *shrunk* along the y-axis.

What happens if the coefficient a is negative?

These graphs appear to be similar to the earlier graphs with positive coefficients, except that these are *reflected* over the x-axis.

  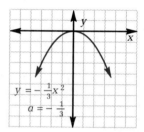

Example

Sketch the graph of $g(x) = -0.5x^2$.

We can accurately draw a graph by using a plotter, or we can sketch the graph without plotting points. Since the coefficient is negative, the graph of g is a transformation of the graph of $f(x) = x^2$. The graph is reflected over the x-axis, opening downward. Because $|a| < 1$, the graph will be shrunk vertically by a factor of 0.5.

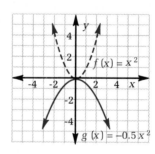

If the output of the standard absolute-value function, $f(x) = |x|$, is multiplied by a constant a, the graph of f will also be transformed.

  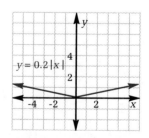

Reflected **Stretched Vertically** **Shrunk Vertically**

Part Two: Sample Problems

Problem 1   *Suppose (5, 1) is a point on the graph of y = h(x). For each of the following, name a point on the graph.*
  a $y = h(2x)$
  b $y = -1.5[h(x)]$

Solution   When the input to *h* is 5, the output is 1.

  a In $y = h(2x)$, the input is 5. Then, $2x = 5$ and $x = \frac{5}{2}$, or 2.5. One point on the graph is (2.5, 1).
  b Since $h(5) = 1$, $-1.5[h(5)] = -1.5(1)$, or -1.5.

  Thus, (5, −1.5) is a point on the graph of $y = -1.5[h(x)]$. In **a,** the input is changed. In **b,** the output is changed.

Problem 2   *Use the graph of f to graph g and h.*
  a $g(x) = 2[f(x)]$
  b $h(x) = f(2x)$

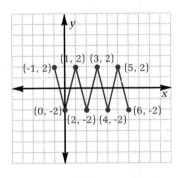

Solution   **a** For each input, the *output* of g is twice the output of *f*, so the graph of g is stretched vertically by a factor of 2.

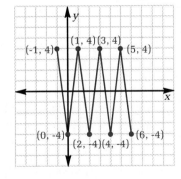

  b For any given output, the *input* of h is one-half the input of *f*, so the graph of h is shrunk horizontally by a factor of $\frac{1}{2}$.

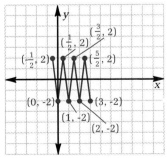

Notice that when the input is multiplied by a constant, the transformation is horizontal. When the output is multiplied by a constant, the transformation is vertical.

Part Three: Exercises and Problems

Warm-up Exercises

In problems 1–4, copy the graph of f, and on the same axes sketch the graph described.

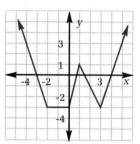

1 The graph of f stretched vertically by a factor of 2

2 The graph of f stretched horizontally by a factor of 3

3 The graph of f shrunk horizontally by a factor of $\frac{1}{3}$

4 The graph of f shrunk vertically by a factor of $\frac{1}{2}$

In problems 5–7, refer to the table of values for $f(x)$, then copy and complete each table.

x	-2.0	-1.5	-1.0	-0.5	0	0.5	1.0	1.5	2.0	2.5	3.0
$f(x)$	7	2	-1	1	2	$-\frac{1}{2}$	-3	-8	-15	-22	-40

5

x	-1	0	1	1.5
$f(2x)$				

6

x	-1	0	1	2
$\frac{1}{2}[f(x)]$				

7

x	-2	-1	0	1	2
$f\left(\frac{1}{2}x\right)$					

8 Copy each diagram and fill in the blanks.

a $f(x) = x^2$

b $f(x) = 3x^2$

c $f(x) = \frac{1}{3}x^2$

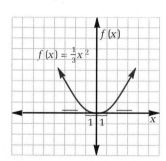

In problems 9 and 10, describe how the graph of *g* or *h* compares with the graph of *f*, where $f(x) = x^2$.

9 $g(x) = f\left(\frac{1}{2}x\right)$

10 $h(x) = \frac{1}{2}[f(x)]$

Problem Set

In problems 11–13, determine the value of *a*, given the graph of $f(x) = a|x|$.

11

12

13

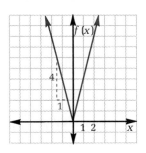

In problems 14 and 15, describe how the graph of each function differs from the graph of $y = x^2$.

14 $f(x) = 2.5x^2$

15 $g(x) = -2.5x^2$

16 Refer to the diagram.
  a Find (x, y).
  b Find AB.

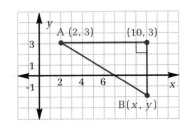

17 Joe saw his image in a mirror. Where do you think the mirror is?

18 Let the domain of $f(x) = |x|$ be {−3, −2, −1, 0, 1, 2, 3}.
  a Find the range of $y = 2[f(x)]$.
  b Graph $y = f(x)$ and $y = -2[f(x)]$ on the same axes.

In problems 19–21, name a point on the graph of each equation if (2, 6) is a point on the graph of $y = f(x)$.

19 $y = 4[f(x)]$

20 $y = -5[f(x)]$

21 $y = \frac{2}{7}[f(x)]$

Problem Set, *continued*

22 For which of the following is *y* a function of *x*?

a

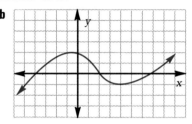

b

c

x	−6	2	8	10
y	−4	−4	0	1

23 Evaluate $\dfrac{x^5 y^{-17}}{x^{-3} y^5} \cdot \dfrac{x^2 y^{18}}{x^9 y^{-3}}$ if $x = 9.6$ and $y = -3.2$.

24 The height of a ball above the ground (in meters) at time *t* seconds is given by $h(t) = -4.9t^2 + 39.2t$.
  a How high is the ball at $t = 0$ seconds?
  b When will the ball again be on the ground?
  c When is the ball 50 meters above the ground?

25 Given $\{(x, f(x)):(x, f(x)) = (-2, 0), (3, 4), (7, 12), (9, -13)\}$, find the set of ordered pairs $(x, 4[f(x)])$.

26 Determine the value of *a* for each function.
  a $f(x) = ax^2$, with a graph passing through (1, 9)
  b $g(x) = a|x|$, with a graph passing through (9, 4)

27 Let $f(x) = 3 + 6x$ and $g(x) = x^2 + 4x$. Evaluate $f(g(1))$ and $g(f(1))$.

28 Refer to the table below. If $g(x) = k[f(x)]$, what is the value of *k*?

x	−3	−2	−1	0	1	2	3
f(x)	1.5	1	0.5	0	0.5	1	1.5
g(x)	18	12	6	0	6	12	18

29 Suppose $f(x) = x^2$ and *b* is a constant greater than 0. List the following range elements from smallest to largest: $f(b)$, $2[f(b)]$, $f(2b)$, $-f(b)$, $-2[f(b)]$, $f(-3b)$.

30 Let $f(x) = k^2 x^2$ and $g(x) = -3kx + 10$.
  a If $k = 1$, where do the graphs of *f* and *g* intersect?
  b Where do the graphs intersect in terms of *k*?

31 Let $f(x) = |x|$.

a Copy and complete the following table, and graph $y = f(x) + 2$.

x	−3	−2	−1	0	1	2	3
f(x) + 2							

b Copy and complete the following table, and graph $y = f(x) - 2$.

x	−3	−2	−1	0	1	2	3
f(x) − 2							

c Describe how the graphs in parts **a** and **b** differ from the graph of f.

32 Let $f(x) = -\frac{1}{3}x^2$ and $g(x) = x - 4$. Find all the values of x for which $f(x) = g(x)$.

In problems 33 and 34, solve for x.

33 $\dfrac{x - 2}{4} = \dfrac{16}{x - 2}$

34 $\dfrac{x + 3}{5} = \dfrac{11}{x - 3}$

35 The total number of children and adults who attended a recent football game was 30,783. Children's tickets cost $4.50 each, and adult tickets cost $6.75 each. The total revenue from the sale of tickets was $180,054. How many of each type of ticket were sold?

36 If $f\left(\begin{bmatrix} a & b \\ c & d \end{bmatrix}\right) = ad - bc$, then what is each of the following?

a $f\left(2\begin{bmatrix} a & b \\ c & d \end{bmatrix}\right)$

b $2\left[f\left(\begin{bmatrix} a & b \\ c & d \end{bmatrix}\right)\right]$

c How do your answers to parts **a** and **b** compare?

37 On January 1, an employee was given two options. Which option should he choose? Explain your answer.

a Double his current income for the coming year.

b Receive 6% increase in salary on the first day of each month, beginning on February 1.

38 a What is the domain of $f(x) = \frac{3x(x - 2)}{(x - 2)}$?

b If the expression $(x - 2)$ is canceled, the result is the function $g(x) = 3x$. What is the domain of g?

39 Find the number of atoms in a copper medallion if its mass is 3.1 grams and each copper atom has a mass of 1.07×10^{-22} grams. Express your answer in scientific notation.

TRANSLATING GRAPHS

Objectives

After studying this section, you will be able to
- Shift graphs vertically
- Shift graphs horizontally

Part One: Introduction

Shifting Graphs Vertically

If we add a value to the output of a function, how is the graph affected? What happens if we subtract a value from the output?

Let $f(x) = |x|$, and define the functions g and h as follows.

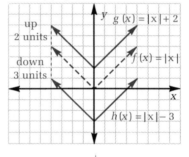

$$g(x) = f(x) + 2 \qquad h(x) = f(x) - 3$$
$$ = |x| + 2 \qquad = |x| - 3$$

In general, when we add a value to the output of a function, the graph is shifted *upward*. When we subtract a value from the output of a function, the graph is shifted *downward*.

Shifting Graphs Horizontally

How does the graph of a function change if the addition or subtraction is performed on the input?

Again, let $f(x) = |x|$, and define the functions p and r as follows.

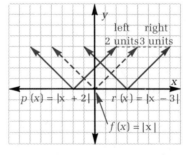

$$p(x) = f(x + 2) \qquad r(x) = f(x - 3)$$
$$ = |x + 2| \qquad = |x - 3|$$

In general, adding to the input of a function shifts the graph *left*, and subtracting from the input of a function shifts the graph *right*.

Now we can combine the vertical and horizontal shifts with the stretches and shrinks, discussed in Section 6.1.

 If $g(x) = a \cdot f(x - h) + k$, where f is a function, then, compared with the graph of f,

1 *The graph of g is stretched vertically by a factor of $|a|$*
2 *The graph of g is shifted right h units and up k units*

Part Two: Sample Problems

Problem 1 *Suppose (3, 3) is a point on the graph of y = f(x). Name a point on the graph of y = f(x − 3) − 7.*

Solution Compared with the graph of $y = f(x)$, the graph of $y = f(x − 3) − 7$ is shifted three units to the right and seven units down. Thus the point (3, 3) becomes (3 + 3, 3 − 7), or (6, −4).

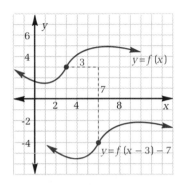

Problem 2 *Sketch the graph of g(x) = x² − 16x + 35.*

Solution If the function were in the form $g(x) = (x − h)^2 + k$, we could describe its graph as the graph of $f(x) = x^2$ translated h units horizontally and k units vertically. To change g into the form $g(x) = (x − h)^2 + k$, we complete the square. (There is a review of this process in Section 4.5.)

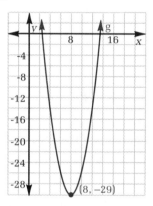

$$g(x) = x^2 − 16x + 35$$

$$= x^2 − 16x + \underline{} − \underline{} + 35$$

$$= x^2 − 16x + \underline{64} − \underline{64} + 35$$

$$= (x − 8)^2 − 29$$

Remember that when we add a number and its opposite to a polynomial, we do not change the value of the polynomial.

Part Three: Exercises and Problems

Warm-up Exercises

In problems 1–4, indicate whether the graph of the equation is a translation up, down, to the left, or to the right of the graph of $y = f(x)$.

1 $y = f(x − 17)$ **2** $y = f(x) − 17$
3 $y = f(x) + 1$ **4** $y = f(x + 3.2)$

In problems 5–8, name a point on the graph of each equation if (20, 5) is a point on the graph of $y = g(x)$.

5 $y = g(x) − 12$ **6** $y = g(x) + 1$
7 $y = g(x + 16)$ **8** $y = g(x − 1)$

In problems 9–12, write the equation of each graph, assuming that each is a translation of the graph of $y = x^2$.

9

10

11

12

Problem Set

In problems 13–16, let $f(x) = x^2$. Determine the vertex of each equation's graph and state whether it is the highest or lowest point on the graph.

13 $2[f(x - 4)] = y$

14 $-5[f(x - 2)] + 3 = y$

15 $-3[f(x + 2)] = y$

16 $4[f(x + 7)] + 3 = y$

In problems 17–22, find the values of x that satisfy each equation, using the graph of $f(x) = y$ shown.

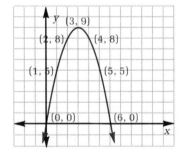

17 $f(x) = 0$

18 $f(x + 4) = 0$

19 $f(x - 2) = 0$

20 $f(x - 9) = 0$

21 $f(x) - 5 = 0$

22 $f(x) - 10 = 0$

23 a Complete the square in $g(x) = x^2 - 8x + 12$ by filling in the blanks.

$$g(x) = (x^2 - 8x + \underline{\hspace{1cm}}) - \underline{\hspace{1cm}} + 12$$

b If $g(x) = (x - h)^2 + k$, what are the values of h and k?

24 Simplify $\sqrt{8} + \sqrt{12} + \sqrt{18} + \sqrt{27} + \sqrt{50}$.

25 a Draw the graph of the reflection of $y = x + 2$ over the line $y = x$.
   b What is the equation of the reflected graph?
   c What is the equation of the reflection of the graph $y = x + b$ over the line $y = x$?

26 Find k.

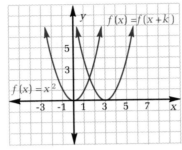

27 Graph each function on the same set of axes.
   a $f(x) = -2$ **b** $g(x) = |x|$ **c** $h(x) = f(x) + g(x)$

In problems 28–31, find the y-intercept of the graph of each equation if
$f(x) = \frac{1}{2}x - 4.$

28 $f(x + 4) = y$ **29** $f(x) - 7 = y$
30 $f(2x) = y$ **31** $f(x - 2) = y$

32 How many arrangements of the given letters are possible?
   a A, B, C   **b** A, B, C, D   **c** A, B, C, D, E

33 Let $f(x) = x^2 + 3$ and $g(x) = -x^2 - 3$.
   a Graph $y = f(x)$ and $y = g(x)$ on the same set of axes.
   b Graph $y = f(x) + g(x)$.

34 Solve $\dfrac{5^{2n + 7}}{5^3} = 5^{14}$ for n.

In problems 35 and 36, refer to the diagram.
35 Find the coordinates of the point symmetric to P with respect to the x-axis.
36 Find the coordinates of the point symmetric to P with respect to the point $(0, 0)$.

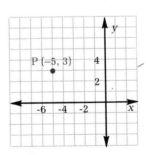

37 Find k so that $x^2 + kx + 25$ will be a perfect square.

38 Complete the square to find the vertex of the parabola described by $f(x) = x^2 + 6x + 12$.

Problem Set, *continued*

In problems 39–42, graph each equation without making a table.

39 $f(x) = \frac{1}{2}|x - 3|$

40 $h(x) = \frac{1}{2}|x + 3|$

41 $g(x) = \frac{1}{2}|x| + 3$

42 $j(x) = \frac{1}{2}|x| - 3$

43 Solve for (x, y).

$$\begin{cases} 5x + 4y = 12 \\ 3x - 5y = 22 \end{cases}$$

44 Let $f(x) = a(x - h)^2 + k$. If the vertex of the graph of f is $(2, -5)$ and the graph passes through $(4, -3)$, what is f?

In problems 45–47, use the graph of $y = f(x)$ to graph each equation.

45 $y = f(x + 3)$
46 $y = f(x) - 2$
47 $y = f(x + 3) - 2$

48 Mr. Ted trots down a different three of seven possible lanes each day. How many days will pass before he must repeat his choice of three lanes?

In problems 49 and 50, rewrite each expression as a power of x.

49 $\dfrac{(x^{a+2})^5}{(x^{2a+1})^4}$

50 $\left(\dfrac{x^{a+1}}{x^{b-1}}\right)^5$

51 Graph $3x - 2y < 19$.

52 Let $f(x) = x + 6$ and $g(x) = 2x - 3$.
   a Find the point of intersection of the graphs of $y = f(x)$ and $y = g(x)$.
   b Find the point of intersection of the graphs of $y = f(x + 4)$ and $y = g(x + 4)$.

53 If $f(x) = a(x - 3)^2 + k$ and the graph of f passes through $(3, 10)$ and $(6, -26)$, what are a and k?

54 Let $f(x) = 2x - 3$ and $g(x) = f(-x)$. Graph f and g on the same set of axes.

55 Let $F(1) = 1$ and $F(n + 1) = 2 \cdot F(n)$, where n is a positive integer.

  a Copy and complete the table.

n	1	2	3	4	5	6	7	8
$F(n)$								

  b Write a closed-form formula for F.

56 In the diagram, ABCD $\sim$ BCFE.

  a Write a proportion relating the sides.

  b Solve your proportion for x.

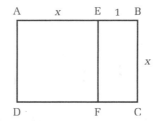

57 The formula $h(x) = -0.0035(x - 160)^2 + 90$ describes the height in feet of a baseball at a horizontal distance of x feet from home plate.

  a How high does the ball go?

  b How far does the ball go?

  c When is the ball 50 feet above the ground?

HISTORICAL SNAPSHOT

FUN WITH GRAPHS
Who was Descartes when he was at home?

Have you ever wondered what fun is to a mathematician? Mathematical fun often means solving problems that have no real applications. Such problems are usually extremely puzzling, and their solutions are often amusing. Two such problems, which you can learn more about on your own, are the seven bridges of Königsburg (see Section 1.3) and Penrose tilings. For now, we will concentrate on playful graphing.

René Descartes (1596–1650) discovered that an equation can be written for every geometric shape and that there is a geometric representation for every

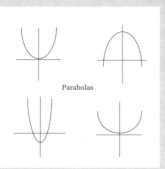

Parabolas

equation. The first set of examples shows the graphs of various quadratics, with which you are now somewhat familiar.

Having made his discovery, Descartes applied himself to writing equations that would yield interesting graphs. Other mathematicians, including Johann Bernoulli (1667–1748), Blaise Pascal (1623–1662), and the eighteenth century Guido Grandi, joined the fun, and the results include the four graphs below.

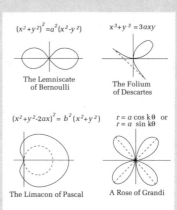

$(x^2+y^2)^2 = a^2(x^2-y^2)$

The Lemniscate of Bernoulli

$x^3+y^3 = 3axy$

The Folium of Descartes

$(x^2+y^2-2ax)^2 = b^2(x^2+y^2)$

The Limacon of Pascal

$r = a\cos k\theta$ or $r = a\sin k\theta$

A Rose of Grandi

REFLECTIONS AND SYMMETRY

Objectives

After studying this section, you will be able to
- Reflect objects graphed on a coordinate system
- Recognize symmetry with respect to a line or a point

Part One: Introduction

Reflections

We are familiar with a *reflection* as a mirror image. In mathematics, an object can be reflected over a line or a point. For the reflections of triangle ABC, only the vertices are labeled, but every point of the triangle is reflected. In the diagram we see that when an object is reflected over the y-axis, each point (a, b) is reflected to $(-a, b)$. When an object is reflected over the x-axis, each point (a, b) is reflected to $(a, -b)$.

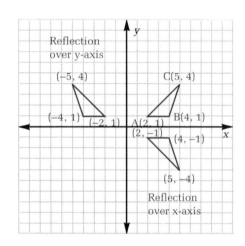

Now look at the following reflections.

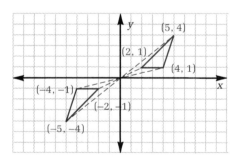

When an object is reflected over the line $y = x$, each point (a, b) is reflected to (b, a). When an object is reflected over the origin, each point (a, b) is reflected to $(-a, -b)$.

Example   *Write an equation for the reflection over the x-axis of the graph of*
$y = (x - 3)^2 + 4$.

The reflection over the x-axis of any point (x, y) is $(x, -y)$. To find the equation of the graph's reflection, we substitute $-y$ for y in the original equation. The value of x is unchanged.

$$-y = (x - 3)^2 + 4$$
$$y = -[(x - 3)^2 + 4]$$
$$y = -(x - 3)^2 - 4$$

To check that $y = -(x - 3)^2 - 4$ is the equation of the reflection, we verify that this graph has the vertex $(3, -4)$ and opens downward.

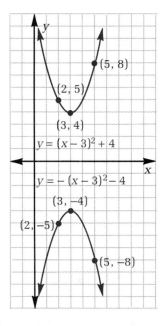

Symmetry

Some graphs appear unchanged when they are reflected over a line or a point.

Example   *Find the reflection over the y-axis of the graph of $f(x) = x^2 + 4$.*

The reflection of a point (x, y) over the y-axis is $(-x, y)$. Let's graph f and reflect several points. In function f, if we replace x with $-x$, the output is unchanged, since $x^2 = (-x)^2$. Therefore, the reflection is the same as the original graph.

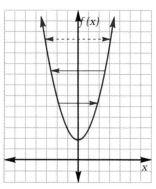

> **When the result of reflecting a graph over a line or point is the same graph, we say that the graph is symmetric with respect to that line or point.**

Part Two: Sample Problems

Problem 1   Which of the following graphs are symmetric with respect to the
x-axis, the y-axis, the line y = x, and the origin?

a

b

c

d

e

f
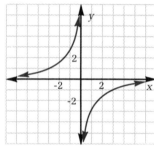

Solution   Graph **c** is symmetric with respect to the x-axis. Graph **b** is symmetric with respect to the y-axis. Graphs **d** and **f** are symmetric with
respect to y = x. Graphs **a, d,** and **f** are symmetric with respect to
the origin.

Although graph **e** is not symmetric with respect to the y-axis,
the x-axis, y = x, or the origin, it is symmetric with respect to the
line x = −4. Recall from Section 4.3 that this line is called the axis
of symmetry of the parabola.

Problem 2   Write the equation of function g, which represents the reflection of the
graph of $f(x) = \frac{1}{4}(x - 5)^2 + 7$ over the origin.

Solution   We can find g graphically or algebraically.

Method 1
Reflect the vertex and several other
points of the graph of f over the origin.
We can see that the reflected parabola
has a vertex at $(-5, -7)$, opens downward, and is stretched vertically by
the same factor as the graph of f.
Therefore, the equation of g is

$$g(x) = -\frac{1}{4}(x + 5)^2 - 7.$$

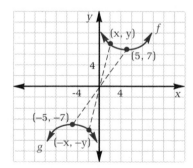

Study the graphs of f and g. A reflection over a point is also called a half-turn. Can you see why?

Method 2

When the graph of $y = \frac{1}{4}(x - 5)^2 + 7$ is reflected over the origin, each point (x, y) is reflected to $(-x, -y)$. To find the equation of the reflected graph, we replace x with $-x$ and y with $-y$, then solve for y.

$$-y = \frac{1}{4}(-x - 5)^2 + 7$$

$$-y = \frac{1}{4}[-1(x + 5)]^2 + 7$$

$$-y = \frac{1}{4}(x + 5)^2 + 7$$

$$y = -\frac{1}{4}(x + 5)^2 - 7$$

Thus, $g(x) = -\frac{1}{4}(x + 5)^2 - 7$.

Problem 3 *Graph $y = 3^x$, its reflection over the y-axis, and its reflection over the line $y = x$.*

Solution

To graph $y = 3^x$, use a graphing device or make a table of values and plot points.

To find the equation of the graph's reflection over the y-axis, replace x with $-x$.

To find the equation of the graph's reflection over the line $y = x$, exchange y and x.

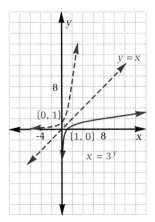

Remember that the reflection of a function's graph over the line $y = x$ is the inverse of the function. The equation of the inverse of $y = 3^x$ is $x = 3^y$, which is graphed at the right above.

Part Three: Exercises and Problems

Warm-up Exercises

In problems 1–4, give the coordinates of each point.

1 Point A reflected over the x-axis

2 Point B reflected over the line $y = x$

3 Point B reflected over the y-axis

4 Point A reflected over the origin

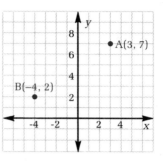

5 Use the graph for problems **1–4.** Is the set of points shown symmetric with respect to the origin? Explain.

In problems 6–9, determine the equation of the axis of symmetry of each graph.

6

7

8

9

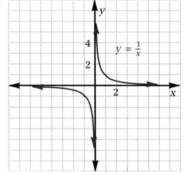

In problems 10–12, write the equation of the reflection of the graph of $y = (x - 6)^2 + 4$ over each line or point.

10 The x-axis   **11** The y-axis   **12** The origin

Problem Set

In problems 13–18, give the coordinates of the reflection of the point (−2, 5) over each line or point.

13 The x-axis

14 The line y = −x

15 The y-axis

16 The line y = 4

17 The line y = x

18 The origin

In problems 19–21, determine the equation of the axis of symmetry of each graph.

19

20

21
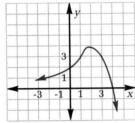

22 Write a linear function in the form $f(x) = ax + b$ to represent the table below.

x	−4	−3	−2	−1	0	1	2	3	4
f(x)	−7	−4	−1	2	5	8	11	14	17

In problems 23–25, graph each set on a number line.

23 {x:−2 < x < 5}

24 {x:x ≥ 2}

25 {x:x ≠ 4}

26 The coordinates of the vertices of a triangle are (−2, 5), (3, 7), and (6, 1). What are the coordinates of the vertices of the triangle's reflection over

a The x-axis?

b The origin?

27 Let $f(5) = 7$.

a If g is the reflection of f over the x-axis, what is g(5)?

b If h is the reflection of f over the y-axis, what is h(−5)?

c If j is the reflection of f over the line y = x, what is j(7)?

d If k is the reflection of f over the origin, what is k(−5)?

28 Dick mixed 6 liters of a solvent with 24 liters of water. What percentage of the solution was solvent?

29 a Graph $y = 2^x$.

b Graph its reflection over the y-axis.

c Graph its reflection over the line y = x.

30 The point $(-4, 3)$ is on the graph of $y = f(x)$. Find the coordinates of a point on the graph of $y = f(x - 2) + 5$.

31 Let $f(x) = x^2$.

a Find the equation of the reflection of the graph of $y = f(x)$ over the y-axis.

b Find the equation of the reflection of the graph of $y = f(x + 2)$ over the y-axis.

32 Paula charges a fee of $55 plus $20 per hour to paint rooms in a house.

a Write a formula to describe the cost if the job takes h hours.

b How many hours must Paula work in order to earn at least $150?

33 Identify at least four characteristics of the figure shown.

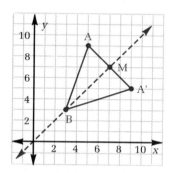

34 Graph the functions f, g, and h on the same axes, where $f(x) = -x + 1$, $g(x) = 3x + 2$, and $h(x) = f(x) + g(x)$.

35 If the point $(-3, 4)$ is reflected in succession about the x-axis, the line $y = x$, and the origin, what will be the coordinates of the final point?

36 If $f(A) = 3A$, where A is a matrix, what is the value of $f(A)$ for the input shown?

$$A = \begin{bmatrix} 1.4 & -4 \\ 6 & \frac{2}{3} \end{bmatrix}$$

37 Half of the parabola $y = f(x)$ is shown, along with the parabola's axis of symmetry. One of the values of x for which $f(x) = 0$ is $4 + \sqrt{3}$. Find the other value of x for which $f(x) = 0$.

In problems 38–41, identify the line(s) of symmetry of the graph of each function.

38 $f(x) = x^2 + 4$

39 $f(x) = \dfrac{1}{x}$

40 $f(x) = |x + 5| - 3$

41 $f(x) = 2x + 3$

42 Let $a = 13$ and $b = 5$.
   a Compute $|a - b|$.
   b Compute $|b - a|$.
   c Is it true that for any x and y, $|x - y| = |y - x|$? Why or why not?

43 a Find the area of $\triangle ABC$.
   b Let A' be the reflection of A over the y-axis. Find the area of $\triangle A'BC$.
   c Let A'' be the reflection of A over the x-axis. Find the area of $\triangle A''BC$.

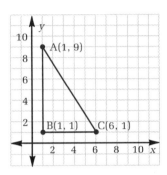

44 Let $N(x) = 4x - 3$. Find $\dfrac{N(a + b) - N(a)}{b}$ for any real a and b such that $b \neq 0$.

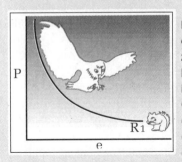

GRAPHING OTHER FUNCTIONS

Objectives

After studying this section, you will be able to
- Graph cubic and quartic polynomial functions
- Graph reciprocal functions
- Graph exponential functions

Part One: Introduction

Cubic and Quartic Polynomial Functions

The graph of the cubic function $f(x) = x^3$ is shown. A *cubic function* is a polynomial function of degree three.

Using what you have seen about stretching, shrinking, reflecting, translating, and symmetry, predict the graphs of
$g(x) = f(x - 4) = (x - 4)^3$,
$h(x) = -5[f(x)] = -5x^3$, and
$j(x) = f(x) + 3 = x^3 + 3$. Check your predictions by graphing these functions.

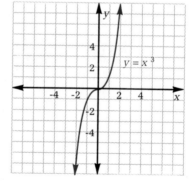

Study this graph of the cubic function $p(x) = x^3 - 6.5x^2 + 0.5x + 35$.

The graph of p has three x-intercepts. As you learned in Chapter 4, these intercepts correspond to the real zeros of p and the real roots of $p(x) = 0$. From a graph, we can estimate the zeros of p to be -2, 3.5, and 5. A cubic function can have at most three real zeros. How many zeros does $f(x) = x^3$ have?

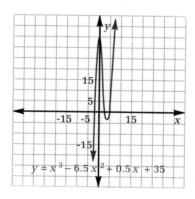

Below are some graphs of polynomial functions of degree four, called *quartic functions*

$y = x^4 - 6x^2$

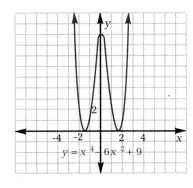

$y = x^4 - 6x^2 + 9$

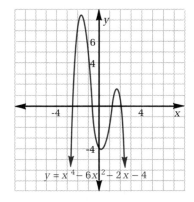

$y = x^4 - 6x^2 - 2x - 4$

The graphs of many quartic functions have a characteristic W shape and at most four x-intercepts.

Reciprocal Functions

Study the graph of $y = \frac{1}{x}$, called a *reciprocal function*, since y is the reciprocal of x. Because this function is undefined for $x = 0$, its domain is all real numbers except 0. Some ordered pairs on the graph are $(1, 1)$, $(-1, -1)$, $\left(2, \frac{1}{2}\right)$, $\left(\frac{1}{2}, 2\right)$, $\left(-2, -\frac{1}{2}\right)$, and $\left(-\frac{1}{2}, -2\right)$. If the values of x and y are interchanged, another point on the graph is always produced, so the graph is symmetric with respect to the line $y = x$.

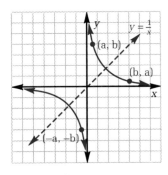

If (x, y) is on the graph, the point $(-x, -y)$ is also on the graph. Therefore, the function is also symmetric with respect to the origin. From the graph we see that the range of the function is all real numbers except 0.

Example   Let $f(x) = \frac{1}{x}$. *Graph the function h, where* $h(x) = f(x - 3)$.

First let's solve for $h(x)$. $h(x) = f(x - 3)$

$$= \frac{1}{x - 3}$$

Since $h(x)$ is undefined when $x = 3$, the domain of h is all real numbers except 3. The graph of h is the graph of f shifted three units to the right. The graph is symmetric with respect to the line $y = x - 3$ and the point $(3, 0)$. From the graph we see that the range of h is all real numbers except 0.

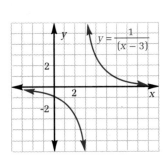

Exponential Functions

Graph the *exponential functions* $f(x) = 2^x$, $g(x) = 10^x$, and $h(x) = 0.5^x$. If you do not have a graphing calculator or a computer with a graphing program, generate tables of values, perhaps using the $\boxed{x^y}$ key on a scientific calculator. Be sure to include negative values, 0, and positive values for x.

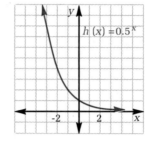

The graphs of f, g, and h all pass through the point (0, 1). The domain of each function is the real numbers. From the graphs, we see that the range of each function is the set of all positive real numbers.

Exponential functions have many applications in the study of natural phenomena. These functions are studied in a later chapter.

Part Two: Sample Problems

Problem 1

Five sets of experimental data are graphed below. Match each graph with the type of function that best describes the data: (i) exponential, (ii) reciprocal, (iii) quadratic, (iv) linear, or (v) cubic.

Solution   **a** iii   **b** v   **c** iv   **d** ii   **e** i

Problem 2   *A piece of corrugated cardboard 10 inches square can be made into an open box with a volume of 48 cubic inches, provided that a square is cut from each corner before the cardboard is folded. What are the possible dimensions of the resulting box?*

Solution   Let's start by sketching the original piece of cardboard and the resulting open box.

The volume of a rectangular box is $V = lwh$. In this problem, $V = 48$, $l = 10 - 2x$, $w = 10 - 2x$, and $h = x$. Substituting these values,

$$48 = (10 - 2x)(10 - 2x)x, \text{ or}$$

$$0 = x(10 - 2x)^2 - 48$$

Let $p(x) = x(10 - 2x)^2 - 48$. The real zeros of this cubic polynomial function are the values of x for which $p(x) = 0$. These are the values of x we are looking for.

We can graph p and approximate the zeros as 3, 0.63, and 6.3. Let's use these values to make a table.

x	h	l	w	V	
3	3	4	4	48	**Exactly!**
0.63	0.63	8.74	8.74	48.12	**Very close!**
6.3	6.3	−2.6			**Impossible!**

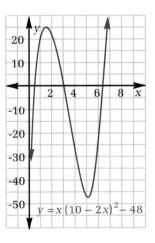

$y = x(10 - 2x)^2 - 48$

There are two sets of possible dimensions, 4 inches by 4 inches by 3 inches and 8.74 inches by 8.74 inches by 0.63 inch.

Part Three: Exercises and Problems

Warm-up Exercises

1 Let $f(x) = x^3$.
  a Graph $g(x) = f(x) + 2$.   **b** Graph $h(x) = f(x - 3)$.

2 From the equations listed, choose one to describe each graph shown.

  i $y = \dfrac{1}{x}$ **ii** $y = \dfrac{1}{x^2}$ **iii** $y = -\dfrac{1}{x}$

a   **b**   **c**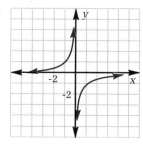

3 The graph of f is shown.
  a Find the real zeros of f.
  b For what values of x does $f(x) = 0$?
  c Find the real zeros of $f(x + 2)$.

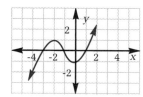

Problem Set

4 Identify each function as (i) linear, (ii) quadratic, (iii) exponential, or (iv) other.

  a $f(x) = 5 + 6x - 2x^2$ **b** $h(x) = 9x - 3$
  c $F(x) = 4^x$ **d** $g(x) = x^3 - 8x$
  e $P(x) = 6 + 4x$ **f** $h(x) = x^4 + 5$
  g $C(x) = 4$ **h** $f(x) = (1 + x^2)^2$

5 How many distinct real zeros does each function have?

  a   **b**   **c**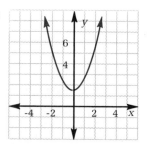

24 Solve each of the following for x if $f(x) = 2^x$.

   a $f(x) = 8$ **b** $f(x) = 16$ **c** $f(x - 1) = 1$

25 Use the graph of $f(x) = \frac{1}{x}$ to sketch the graph of each of the following functions.

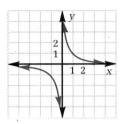

   a $g(x) = f(x + 5)$
   b $h(x) = f(x) + 2$
   c $l(x) = f(x + 3) - 2$

26 Use the graph of $f(x) = \frac{1}{x^2}$ to find the real zeros of each of the following functions.

   a f
   b $g(x) = f(x + 3)$
   c $h(x) = f(x) - 4$
   d $l(x) = -f(x) + 4$

27 Let $f(x) = \frac{1}{x}$ and $g(x) = x$.

   a Find $f \circ g(x)$.   **b** Find $g \circ f(x)$.
   c Explain your answers to parts **a** and **b.**

28 Refer to problem **13.** The intensity of light I is inversely proportional to the square of the distance d from the light source.

   a If the intensity is 12 lumens when the distance is 4 feet, what is the intensity when the distance is 20 feet?
   b Graph the function relating intensity and distance for distances greater than zero.

29 Let $f(x) = x^3$ and $g(x) = x$.
The graphs of these functions intersect at
(0, 0), (1, 1), and (−1, −1) as shown.
Where do the graphs of the following
pairs of functions intersect?

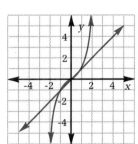

   a $\begin{cases} m(x) = f(x) + 3 \\ k(x) = g(x) + 3 \end{cases}$

   b $\begin{cases} l(x) = f(x - 4) \\ m(x) = g(x - 4) \end{cases}$

   c $\begin{cases} r(x) = f(x + 3) - 2 \\ s(x) = g(x + 3) - 2 \end{cases}$

ASYMPTOTES AND HOLES IN GRAPHS

Objectives

After studying this section, you will be able to
- Recognize asymptotes of graphs
- Recognize holes in graphs

Part One: Introduction

Exploring Graphs

Study the following graphs and the equations they represent, looking for patterns.

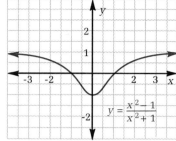

You may have noticed that some of the graphs appear to be symmetrical. What kinds of symmetry do these graphs exhibit? Could you predict whether an equation's graph is symmetrical and, if it is, what type of symmetry it has? Some of the graphs are discontinuous—what characteristics of the equations might account for the gaps?

One of the benefits of graphing calculators and computer graphing programs is that they allow us to quickly generate graphs of complicated functions that would be difficult to graph by hand. If you have access to a function grapher, use it to examine the graphs of a variety of functions. Note how changes in a function affect its graph, and try to draw some conclusions about the relationships between functions and their graphs.

Asymptotes

In some of the preceding diagrams, the graph approaches a horizontal line, called a ***horizontal asymptote,*** or a vertical line, called a ***vertical asymptote.*** A full understanding of asymptotes and their relation to functions requires knowledge that you will gain in future mathematics classes. For now, however, there are some observations we can make and some tentative conclusions we can draw.

The graph of $y = \frac{1}{1 + x^2}$, for example, approaches the line represented by $y = 0$ (the x-axis), since the value of $\frac{1}{1 + x^2}$ becomes closer and closer to 0 as the absolute value of x increases. The line $y = 0$ is therefore a horizontal asymptote of this graph. The easiest way to predict whether a function's graph has a horizontal asymptote is to evaluate the function for several great and small input values and determine whether the outputs approach some specific value.

If a function has a restricted domain, the restriction will be reflected in the function's graph. Frequently, it appears as a vertical asymptote.

For example, the value of $f(x) = \frac{(x - 5)(x + 15)}{x + 5}$ is undefined when $x = -5$, since the denominator of $f(x)$ is equal to 0 for that input. Also, as the x values approach -5, $|x + 5|$ becomes smaller and smaller, so $|f(x)|$ becomes correspondingly greater and greater. The line $x = -5$ is therefore a vertical asymptote of the function's graph.

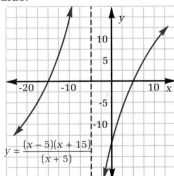

Holes in Graphs

Another way in which a restriction can be reflected in a function's graph is as a *hole*.

Example   *Graph the function* $g(x) = \dfrac{(x + 5)(x + 15)}{x + 5}$.

Since $\frac{x + 5}{x + 5} = 1$ for almost every value of x, the graph is basically the same as the graph of the linear function $p(x) = x + 15$. When x = −5, however, the value of g(x) is undefined, so the graph has a hole at x = −5. We indicate this by an open dot.

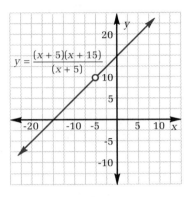

Whenever a function contains a quotient whose numerator and denominator have one or more common factors involving the variable, its graph is likely to have one or more holes. Different graphing calculators and programs react differently to the presence of a hole —many show a continuous graph, ignoring the hole; some start to generate the graph and then stop when they reach the hole; some show a break too small to detect. For this reason, it is useful to be able to identify holes by simply examining the equations of functions.

Part Two: Sample Problem

Problem   *The graph of* $y = \frac{x}{x - 2}$ *has one vertical and one horizontal asymptote. Write the equation of each asymptote.*

Solution   When we use a computer program to generate the graph, it appears that the graph approaches the line y = 1 at the left and right sides of the display. By substituting great and small values for x in the equation, we confirm that y approaches 1 as $|x|$ increases, and thus that y = 1 is the equation of the horizontal asymptote.

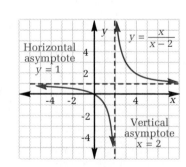

Since the denominator of $\frac{x}{x - 2}$ is 0 when x = 2, and the numerator is not equal to 0, the equation of the vertical asymptote is x = 2.

Part Three: Exercises and Problems

Warm-up Exercises

1 The graph of $y = \frac{1}{(x + 2)(x - 3)}$ has two vertical asymptotes. Write their equations.

2 Let $f(x) = \frac{x(x - 3)(x + 2)}{x(x - 3)(x + 5)}$.

  a What are the equations of the vertical asymptotes of the graph of f?

  b What are the x values of the holes in the graph?

3 Write the equations of the horizontal and vertical asymptotes of the following graphs.

  a   **b**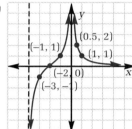

4 The graph of $y = \frac{2x}{x + 1}$ has one horizontal asymptote and one vertical asymptote. Write their equations.

5 What is the value of y if $y = \dfrac{7 - \frac{3}{x}}{1 + \frac{2}{x}}$ and x has the given value?

  a 1000   **b** 10,000

  c 100,000   **d** 1,000,000

Problem Set

6 The graph of $y = \frac{1}{x^2 + 4x - 21}$ has two vertical asymptotes. Write their equations.

7 Write the equations of the horizontal and vertical asymptotes of the following graphs.

  a   **b**

8 Graph $y = \frac{x(x + 1)}{(x + 1)}$.

Problem Set, *continued*

9 The graph of $y = f(x)$ is shown. Sketch the graph of $y = f(x - 2) + 5$.

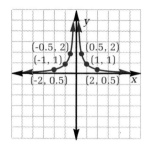

10 Sketch the graph of each function.

a $f(x) = \dfrac{1}{x + 2}$

b $g(x) = \dfrac{x - 2}{x^2 - 4}$

11 Suppose the graph of a function f has vertical asymptotes with equations $x = 2$ and $x = 5$.

a Find the vertical asymptotes of the graph of $f(x + 3)$.

b Find the vertical asymptotes of the graph of $f\left(\tfrac{1}{2}x\right)$.

12 The graph of $y = f(x)$ is shown.

a Sketch the graph of $y = f(x + 1)$.

b Write the equations of the vertical asymptotes of the graph of $y = f(x + 1)$.

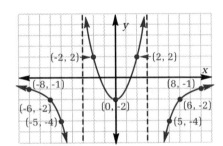

In problems 13–15, solve for x.

13 $2^x = 8$

14 $3^x = \dfrac{1}{81}$

15 $2^x = \sqrt{2}$

16 Sketch a graph of a function with vertical asymptotes at $x = 2$ and $x = 4$ and a horizontal asymptote at $y = 1$.

17 Solve the following system for (x, y).

$$\begin{cases} 3x - 8y = 18 \\ x + 2y = -8 \end{cases}$$

18 In how many ways can nine baseball players be arranged in a batting order?

19 Let $f(x) = \dfrac{4x^2 - 8x}{x^2 + 3x - 10}$.

a Factor completely the numerator and the denominator of $f(x)$.

b What are the equations of the asymptotes of f?

c At what value of x is there a hole in the graph?

20 Write the equation of the axis of symmetry of the graph shown.

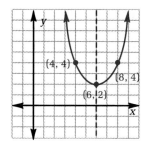

21 Rationalize the numerator of $\dfrac{\sqrt{5} - \sqrt{3}}{2}$.

22 Richard and Mary can paddle a canoe in still water at a rate of 5 miles per hour. A stream has a current of 2.5 miles per hour.

  a How fast can they paddle downstream?
  b How fast can they paddle upstream?
  c If Richard and Mary paddled for 3 hours downstream and then 3 hours upstream, how far were they from where they started?

23 Write an equation of the function with the given graph.

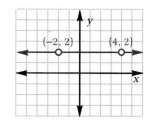

24 Write the equations of the axes of symmetry of the curve shown.

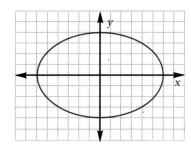

25 Let f be a linear function such that $f(4) = 12$ and $f(5) = 15$.

  a Find $f(6)$.   **b** Find $f(3)$.
  c Write a formula for $f(x)$.

26 Solve the system for (x, y).

$$\begin{cases} y + x^2 = 12 \\ y - x^2 = 4 \end{cases}$$

27 The perimeter of the figure shown becomes 248 if the value of y is increased by 50% and the value of x is increased by 25%. Find x and y.

$P = 200$ $2y + 16$

$4x + 12$

Problem Set, *continued*

28 In three-dimensional graphing, three mutually perpendicular number lines are used as axes. A point is identified by an ordered triplet of the form (x, y, z). Find the coordinates of A, B, C, and D.

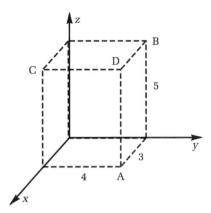

29 Write an equation of the function with the given graph.

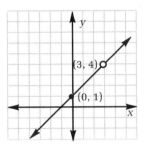

30 The graph of $f(x) = x^3$ is shown. Find the x- and y-intercepts of the graphs of each of the following functions.

a f
b $h(x) = f(x - 3)$
c $g(x) = f(x + 2)$
d $l(x) = f(x) + 8$

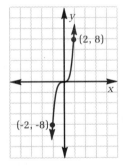

31 Determine the vertical asymptotes of $f(x) = \dfrac{x^3 - x - 5}{x^2 - 5x - 6}$

32 Lines ℓ, m, and n are tangent to the circle. Estimate the slopes of these lines.

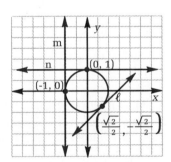

MEASURES OF DISPERSION

Objectives

After studying this section, you will be able to
- Compute the range of a set of data
- Compute the deviation scores and the mean deviation of a set of data

Range

Measures of central tendency provide information only about the "averages" or "centers" of a distribution of data. To find out more, we need to analyze variations of data within the distribution. These variations are analyzed using **measures of dispersion**, which include **range, deviation score,** and **mean deviation.** (You will learn about another important measure of dispersion, called *standard deviation*, in Section 8.5.)

The data below represent the numbers of miles Mary Thon ran during 7 days of preparation for the Mathem City Marathon.

15, 10, 15, 8, 20, 8, 15

The low and high numbers of miles run are 8 and 20. The difference between the highest number and the lowest number of miles run is 20 − 8, or 12, miles. So we say that the **range** of the data is 12.

> **Range = greatest number − smallest number**

Example   *Find the range of each set of data.*

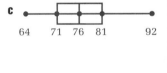

<table>
<tr><td>High number = 87</td><td>High number = 12</td><td>High number = 92</td></tr>
<tr><td>Low number = 45</td><td>Low number = 4</td><td>Low number = 64</td></tr>
<tr><td>Range = 87 − 45</td><td>Range = 12 − 4</td><td>Range = 92 − 64</td></tr>
<tr><td>= 42</td><td>= 8</td><td>= 28</td></tr>
</table>

Deviation Scores and Mean Deviation

At the William Tell Open, the 8 members of the Antelope Valley Archery Club listed their numbers of bull's-eyes from least to greatest.

$$41, 43, 44, 47, 48, 48, 49, 50$$

Hawkeye hit 50 of 50 bull's-eyes, whereas Diana hit 43 of 50 bull's-eyes. Hawkeye and Diana wanted to know how their totals compared with the mean number of bull's-eyes recorded.

The mean number of bull's-eyes recorded was

$$\frac{41 + 43 + 44 + 47 + 48 + 48 + 49 + 50}{8} = 46.25$$

To compare any number in a set of data with the mean, we find its *deviation score*.

> ⟫ *Deviation score = score − mean*

We will determine the deviation score of both archers in order to make comparisons with the mean for all the club members.

$$\text{Hawkeye's deviation score} = 50 - 46.25 = 3.75$$
$$\text{Diana's deviation score} = 43 - 46.25 = -3.25$$

Hawkeye's performance was 3.75 bull's-eyes above the mean. Diana's performance was 3.25 bull's-eyes below the mean.

Aunt Chovie owns 2 pizza parlors in Mathem City. The data below represent the numbers of pizzas sold at the 2 parlors each Saturday night for the past 6 weeks.

Parlor A	16, 12, 22, 21, 43, 54
Parlor B	31, 34, 29, 40, 30, 28

For purposes of scheduling employees, Aunt Chovie needs information about which pizza parlor has been more consistent in its Saturday sales. To do this, she uses the *mean deviation* of the data for each parlor.

> ⟫ *Mean deviation = $\dfrac{\text{sum of absolute values of deviation scores}}{\text{number of scores}}$*

The mean number of pizzas sold at Parlor A was $\frac{168}{6}$, or 28.

Score	Deviation Score (Score − Mean)	Absolute Value of Deviation Score
16	$16 - 28 = -12$	$|-12| = 12$
12	$12 - 28 = -16$	$|-16| = 16$
22	$22 - 28 = -6$	$|-6| = 6$
21	$21 - 28 = -7$	$|-7| = 7$
43	$43 - 28 = 15$	$|15| = 15$
54	$54 - 28 = 26$	$|26| = 26$
Sum = 168	Sum = 0	Sum = 82

The mean deviation $= \dfrac{12 + 16 + 6 + 7 + 15 + 26}{6}$

$= \dfrac{82}{6} = 13\dfrac{2}{3}$

The mean number of pizzas sold at Parlor B was $\dfrac{192}{6}$, or 32.

Score	Deviation Score (Score − Mean)	Absolute Value of Deviation Score
31	$31 - 32 = -1$	$\lvert -1 \rvert = 1$
34	$34 - 32 = 2$	$\lvert 2 \rvert = 2$
29	$29 - 32 = -3$	$\lvert -3 \rvert = 3$
40	$40 - 32 = 8$	$\lvert 8 \rvert = 8$
30	$30 - 32 = -2$	$\lvert -2 \rvert = 2$
28	$28 - 32 = -4$	$\lvert -4 \rvert = 4$
Sum = 192	Sum = 0	Sum = 20

The mean deviation $= \dfrac{1 + 2 + 3 + 8 + 2 + 4}{6}$

$= \dfrac{20}{6} = 3\dfrac{1}{3}$

Since the mean deviation for Parlor B is less than the mean deviation for Parlor A, the Saturday pizza sales of Parlor B tend to be closer to the mean than those of Parlor A. Because Parlor B is more consistent than Parlor A in pizza sales, Aunt Chovie knows that Parlor B will need a more consistent number of employees on Saturday.

Note that for each pizza parlor the sum of the deviation scores was zero. Can you explain why?

Problem Set

1 The graph shows the number of goals scored by Flash Falett during his recent seven-game streak of scoring at least one goal per game.

  a Find the total number of goals Flash scored during the streak.
  b Determine the range of goals scored.
  c Find the mean, the mode, and the median of the data.

2 The mean deviation of the data 10, 12, 17, 25, and x is y.

  a Find x if the mean is 18.
  b Find y if the mean is 18.

Problem Set, *continued*

3 Average monthly temperatures for Twosine and Mathem City are given in the following table. Which city has the more consistent average temperature during these months?

Month	Twosine	Mathem City
May	75	45
June	85	95
July	90	85
August	70	85
September	80	90

4 a Copy and complete the following table.

Scores	Deviation Score	Absolute Value of Deviation Score
23	_____	_____
32	_____	_____
50	_____	_____
54	_____	_____
71	_____	_____

b Find the mean deviation score of the data.

5 In most skewed distributions, the difference between the arithmetic mean and the median is about one-third the difference between the arithmetic mean and the mode. Is this true for the data shown?

6 The mean deviation is found by averaging deviations about the mean. The median deviation is found by averaging deviations about the median. Find the mean and median deviations for the following data.

41, 42, 44, 45, 46, 47, 63, 91, 111

7 Mr. Matt Hematics's test scores are shown.
a Find the range of the scores.
b Find the mean, median, and mode.
c Calculate the mean deviation.

9	3 6 8 9
8	4 5 9
7	0 1 3 4 4 7 8 8
6	3 4 4 6 6 6 8 9
5	3 4 7
4	6
3	4 6

5 | 7   means a score of 57 points

6 CHAPTER SUMMARY

CONCEPTS AND PROCEDURES

After studying this chapter, you should be able to
- Graph parabolas (6.1)
- Graph absolute-value functions (6.1)
- Stretch, shrink, and reflect graphs (6.1)
- Shift graphs vertically (6.2)
- Shift graphs horizontally (6.2)
- Reflect objects graphed on a coordinate system (6.3)
- Recognize symmetry with respect to a line or a point (6.3)
- Graph cubic and quartic polynomial functions (6.4)
- Graph reciprocal functions (6.4)
- Graph exponential functions (6.4)
- Recognize asymptotes of graphs (6.5)
- Recognize holes in graphs (6.5)
- Compute the range of a set of data (6.6)
- Compute the deviation scores and the mean deviation of a set of data (6.6)

VOCABULARY

cubic function (6.4)
deviation score (6.6)
exponential function (6.4)
hole (6.5)
horizontal asymptote (6.5)
mean deviation (6.6)
measures of dispersion (6.6)
quartic function (6.4)
range (6.6)
reciprocal function (6.4)
reflect (6.1, 6.3)
shift (6.2)
shrink (6.1)
stretch (6.1)
symmetry (6.3)
vertical asymptote (6.5)

1 Graph the reflection of $y = f(x)$ over the line $y = x$.

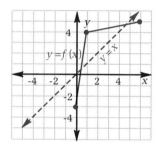

2 a Find the range of the data shown.
  b Find the mean number of free throws made per game.

Number of free throws made per game by Swish Swann

3 Let $f(x) = \frac{x^2 + 3x - 28}{x^2 + 8x - 48}$.
  a Evaluate the numerator if $x = 4$ and $x = -12$.
  b Evaluate the denominator if $x = 4$ and $x = -12$.
  c Describe the behavior of the graph of f at $x = 4$ and $x = -12$.

4 Find the range of the data shown.

43   70   85 90   101

5 An airplane that flies at 425 miles per hour in still air is flying into a head wind of 75 miles per hour. How far will the plane fly in 5.5 hours?

6 The graph of $y = f(x)$ contains the point (3, 2). What point must be on the graph of each of the following functions?

  a $g(x) = \dfrac{1}{f(x)}$ **b** $h(x) = [f(x)]^2$

7 Match each function with its graph.

  a $f(x) = 2^x$
         b $g(x) = \dfrac{1}{x}$
         c $h(x) = \sqrt{x}$

  d $l(x) = x^3 - x$
         e $m(x) = x^4 - 5x^2 + 4$

i

ii

iii

iv

v
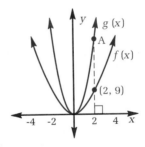

8 a Find the deviation score of each of the following data.

$$16,\ 20,\ 21,\ 28,\ 35$$

  b Find the mean deviation score of the data.

9 If $g(x) = 6[f(x)]$, what are the coordinates of point A?

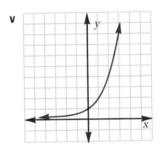

10 Let the domain of $f(x) = 3x - 5$ be $\{-3, -2, -1, 0, 1, 2, 3\}$. Find the range of each function.

  a $y = f(x)$
         b $y = 4[f(x)]$
         c $y = -f(x)$

11 Rex made 48 ounces of a mixture consisting of 60% saline solution and 40% active ingredients.

  a How many ounces of saline were in the mixture? How many ounces of active ingredients?

  b If Rex added 10 ounces of saline solution to the mixture, what percentage of the new mixture was saline?

12 Write an equation of a function whose graph has vertical asymptotes at $x = 3$ and $x = 2$ and a hole at $x = -2$.

13 Use the graph of $f(x) = x^3$ to sketch the graph of each function.

    a $g(x) = f(x + 6)$
    b $h(x) = f(x) - 4$
    c $l(x) = f(x + 3) + 2$

14 The point $(3, 9)$ is on the graph of $f(x) = x^2$. Find the corresponding point on the graph of each of the following functions.

    a $y = f(x + 3)$ **b** $y = f(x - 7)$ **c** $y = f(x) + 4$
    d $y = f(x) - 9$ **e** $y = f(2x)$

15 Supply the missing information for each graph.

a $f(x) = x^2$ **b** $f(x) = 4x^2$ **c** $f(x) = \frac{1}{3}x^2$

16 Find the values of x for which $y = 2x^2 - 3x - 2$ and $y = 0$.

17 Let $f(x) = 2(x - 3)^2 + 6$.

    a Find the vertex of the graph of f.
    b Find the axis of symmetry of the graph of f.
    c If the graph of $y = f(x)$ is reflected over the x-axis, what is the equation of the reflected graph?

18 Let $f(x) = x^2$. Find the vertex of the graph of each of the following equations.

    a $y = f(x + 2)$ **b** $y = f(x - 6)$ **c** $y = f(x) + 5$
    d $y = f(x) - 7$ **e** $y = f(x + 2) - 3$ **f** $y = f(x - 7) + 5$

19 Graph $y = x^2 - 2$ and its reflection over the line $y = x$. What is an equation of the reflection?

20 Let $f(x) = x + 2$ and $g(x) = |x|$. Find all ordered pairs (x, y) such that $y = f(x) = g(x)$.

CHAPTER TEST

In problems 1–3, describe how the graph of each function differs from the graph of $f(x) = x^2$.

1 $f(x) = \dfrac{x^2}{4}$

2 $f(x) = \dfrac{3}{2}x^2$

3 $f(x) = -\dfrac{2}{3}x^2$

4 Let $f(x) = x^2$.

  a Copy and complete the table and graph $y = f(x + 2)$.

x	−4	−3	−2	−1	0
$x + 2$	−2	−1			
$f(x + 2)$	4	1	0	1	4

  b Describe how the graph you drew in part **a** differs from the graph of $y = x^2$.

5 Name a point on the graph of each equation if (3, 17) is a point on the graph of $y = g(x)$.

  a $y = g(x) - 10$ **b** $y = g(x - 10)$
  c $y = g(x + 3) + 5$

6 Use the graph of $f(x) = \left(\dfrac{1}{2}\right)^x$ to find the y-intercept of the graph of each of the following functions.

  a f
  b $g(x) = f(x) - 4$
  c $h(x) = f(x) + 9$
  d $m(x) = f(x - 3)$
  e $n(x) = f(x + 5)$

7 Write the equation of the reflection of the graph of $y = 3(x - 2)^2 + 9$ over each line.

  a The x-axis   **b** The y-axis
  c The line $x = 2$

8 Let $f(x) = \dfrac{x^2 - x - 6}{x^2 - 5x + 6}$.

  a What is the equation of the vertical asymptote of the graph of f?
  b What is the x value of the hole in the graph of f?
  c What are the real zeros of f?

9 The data 5, x, 37, 41, and y are arranged from smallest to largest. If the range is 64 and the mean is 35, what is (x, y)?

SHORT SUBJECT
Conics

Conics with Centers at the Origin

When a plane intersects a double cone, interesting and useful mathematical curves called conic sections are determined. There are four conic sections that we use frequently.

Circle   **Ellipse**   **Parabola**   **Hyperbola**

You are probably familiar with the equations of circles and parabolas.

Example   *Describe the graph of the equation* $x^2 + y^2 = 25$.

The graph is a circle with its center at the origin and a radius of 5.
x-intercepts: -5 and 5
y-intercepts: -5 and 5
Range of x values: $-5 \leq x \leq 5$
Range of y values: $-5 \leq y \leq 5$
Radius, r: 5
Symmetry: The graph is symmetric about the x-axis, the y-axis, and the origin.

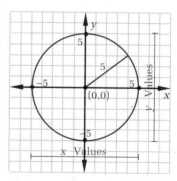

If we divide both sides of the original equation by 25, the equivalent equation is in a form that resembles the intercept form of a line:
$$\frac{x^2}{25} + \frac{y^2}{25} = 1.$$

What happens if we change one of the denominators in this equation?

Example   *Describe the graph of the equation* $\frac{x^2}{9} + \frac{y^2}{25} = 1.$

x-intercepts: ±3
y-intercepts: ±5
Range of x values: $-3 \le x \le 3$
Range of y values: $-5 \le y \le 5$
Symmetry: x-axis, y-axis, origin
The graph of $\frac{x^2}{9} + \frac{y^2}{25} = 1$ is an
ellipse.

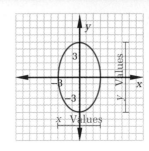

An ellipse is a circle that has been
stretched along a line passing
through its center. An ellipse with a
center at (0, 0), symmetric to the
x- and y-axes, has an equation of
the form $\frac{x^2}{a^2} + \frac{y^2}{b^2} = 1.$

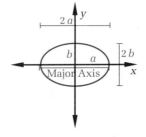

The longest diagonal of the ellipse is
called the ***major axis***; the shortest
diagonal is called the ***minor axis***.
For the ellipse $\frac{x^2}{9} + \frac{y^2}{25} = 1$, the y-axis
is the major axis, and the x-axis is
the minor axis.

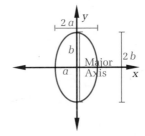

What happens if the x and y terms are subtracted instead of
added?

Example   *Describe the graph of the equation* $\frac{x^2}{9} - \frac{y^2}{25} = 1.$

x-intercepts: ±3
y-intercepts: If x = 0, $\frac{y^2}{25} = -1$, but no real value of y satisfies this
equation, so there are no y-intercepts. In fact, there is no real value
of y for the interval $-3 < x < 3$. Thus, the graph will have values
only for the range of $x \ge |3|$. To see the graph, we can plot some
points.

x	±3	≈±4.2	±4
y	0	±5	≈±4.4

For this equation, x^2 and y^2 have the
same value for any set of four ordered pairs (x, y), (−x, −y), (x, −y),
and (−x, y), and the graph is symmetric about the x-axis, the y-axis,
and the origin.

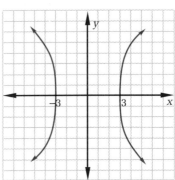

This conic is a **hyperbola,** with an equation of the form $\frac{x^2}{a^2} - \frac{y^2}{b^2} = 1$. As x gets very large, the graph approaches the lines $y = \frac{5}{3}x$ and $y = -\frac{5}{3}x$, which are called **asymptotes.**

If we interchange x and y in the equation, then the hyperbola is rotated 90°, and the resulting equation is $\frac{y^2}{9} - \frac{x^2}{25} = 1$.

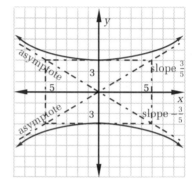

We have already studied the conic with an equation of the form $y = ax^2$: a parabola with a vertex at the origin and a vertical axis of symmetry. The graph of the equation $x = ay^2$ is also a parabola, but one with a horizontal axis of symmetry.

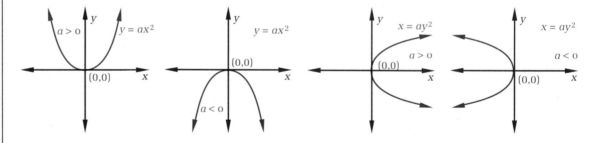

Conics with Centers Not at the Origin

Once we recognize the equation of a conic with a center at the origin, we extend our study to the general equation of a conic.

Remember from our earlier work with parabolas that an equation in the form $y = (x - 4)^2 + 7$, or $y - 7 = (x - 4)^2$, is a parabola that opens upward and has a vertex at (4, 7).

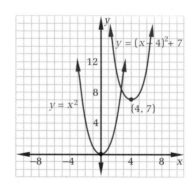

A circle with the equation $(x - h)^2 + (y - k)^2 = r^2$ has a center at (h, k) and radius r.

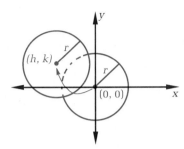

The ellipse $\frac{(x - h)^2}{a^2} + \frac{(y - k)^2}{b^2} = 1$ has a center at (h, k). The vertices are a units right and left of (h, k) and b units up and down from (h, k).

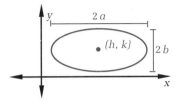

The hyperbola $\frac{(x - h)^2}{a^2} - \frac{(y - k)^2}{b^2} = 1$ has a center at (h, k), has vertices $(h + a, k)$ and $(h - a, k)$, and opens left and right.

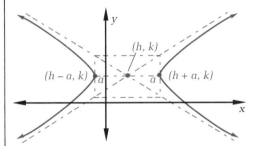

The hyperbola $\frac{(y - k)^2}{b^2} - \frac{(x - h)^2}{a^2} = 1$ has a center at (h, k), has vertices $(h, k + b)$ and $(h, k - b)$, and opens up and down.

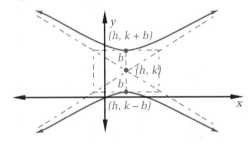

The graph of the hyperbola approaches asymptotes that pass through a center (h, k) and have slopes $\frac{b}{a}$ and $-\frac{b}{a}$.

Sample Problems

Problem 1   *Graph the ellipse $4x^2 + 25y^2 = 400$.*

Solution   Change the equation to the form $\frac{x^2}{a^2} + \frac{y^2}{b^2} = 1$.

$$4x^2 + 25y^2 = 400$$

$$\frac{4x^2}{400} + \frac{25y^2}{400} = 1$$

$\dfrac{x^2}{100} + \dfrac{y^2}{16} = 1$. This is the equation of an ellipse with center $(0, 0)$.

If $y = 0$, $x = 10$ or -10. We move ten units to the left and right of the center. If $x = 0$, $y = 4$ or -4. We move four units up and down from the center. Use these points to sketch the curve. The major axis is horizontal.

Problem 2   *Graph the hyperbola* $25x^2 - 4y^2 = 400$.

Solution   Change the equation to the form $\frac{x^2}{a^2} - \frac{y^2}{b^2} = 1$ by dividing by 400. The resulting equation, $\frac{x^2}{16} - \frac{y^2}{100} = 1$, is

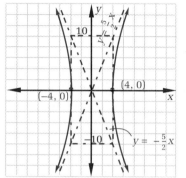

a hyperbola. It opens left and right and has center (0, 0) and vertices (4, 0) and (−4, 0). This hyperbola looks a bit like a parabola but the curves are not the same. The graph of a hyperbola "straightens out" and approaches two asymptotes, determined by the diagonals of the rectangle. The lengths of the sides of the rectangle are $2a$ and $2b$. The slopes of the asymptotes can be seen in the rectangle to be $\pm\frac{10}{4}$, or ± 2.5. The equations of the asymptotes are $y = 2.5x$ and $y = -2.5x$.

Problem Set

In problems 1–6, identify each equation as representing a line, a circle, an ellipse, a parabola, or a hyperbola. Give any information you can about the figure.

1 $9y^2 - 8x^2 = 72$ **2** $9y = (x + 8)^2 + 72$
3 $9y^2 + 8x^2 = 72$ **4** $9y - 8x = 72$
5 $9y^2 + 9x^2 = 72$ **6** $9y - 8x^2 = 72$

7 Find an equation for each conic below.

a   **b**   **c**

In problems 8–13, determine the conic represented by each equation. List any important features, such as center, radius, and vertex. Then graph each conic.

8 $4(x - 6)^2 + (y + 2)^2 = 36$ **9** $\dfrac{(y + 5)^2}{49} - \dfrac{(x + 2)^2}{25} = 1$

10 $x^2 - y^2 - 6y + 7 = 0$ **11** $x^2 + 10x + y^2 - 8y = 0$
12 $x^2 + y^2 = 0$ (Be careful!)   **13** $x - 4 = 2(y + 3)^2$

14 Graph $x^2 + y^2 = 81$ and identify the curve.

15 Which of the following equations have graphs that are conics?
Name the conics.

a $x^2 + y^2 = 41$

b $3x^2 + 75y^2 = 675$

c $4y^2 - 9x^2 = 36$

d $y = \frac{1}{2}(x + 3)^2 + 10$

e $y = 2x^3 + 4x^2 + 7x + 4$

f $x = 3(y - 2)^2 - 5$

In problems 16–19, graph each equation.

16 $(x - 4)^2 + (y + 2)^2 = 36$

17 $\dfrac{(y + 4)^2}{25} + \dfrac{(x - 3)^2}{16} = 1$

18 $\dfrac{(y - 4)^2}{16} - \dfrac{(x + 2)^2}{49} = 1$

19 $\dfrac{(x - 2)^2}{36} + \dfrac{(y + 3)^2}{9} = 1$

20 If one of the following equations is selected at random, what is
the probability that its graph is an ellipse?

a $\dfrac{x^2}{4} = 1 + \dfrac{y^2}{9}$

b $\dfrac{y^2}{16} + \dfrac{x^2}{25} = 1$

c $\dfrac{x^2}{16} - \dfrac{y^2}{9} = 1$

d $\dfrac{x^2}{49} + \dfrac{1}{25} = \dfrac{y^2}{4}$

e $\dfrac{x}{16} + \dfrac{y}{25} = 1$

f $\dfrac{y^2}{5} + \dfrac{x^2}{4} = 1$

21 Write an equation of the hyperbola
shown.

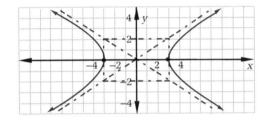

22 Write an equation of the circle with center (6, 1) and containing
the point (2, 1).

23 Graph $\dfrac{(x + 6)^2}{16} - \dfrac{(y - 2)^2}{9} = 1$.

24 Find an equation of the circle centered at $(-3, 7)$ and containing
the point (0, 11).

25 a Find the x-intercepts of $g(x) = -2x^2 + 8$.
b Find the x-intercepts of $y = g(x + 3)$.

26 Graph the following conics on the same set of axes.

a $\dfrac{x^2}{9} - \dfrac{y^2}{9} = 1$

b $\dfrac{x^2}{4} - \dfrac{y^2}{4} = 1$

c $\dfrac{x^2}{1} - \dfrac{y^2}{1} = 1$

d $x^2 - y^2 = 0$

27 Find all x- and y-intercepts of $\dfrac{(x - 3)^2}{4} - \dfrac{y^2}{9} = 1$.

28 a Change $f(x) = x^2 + 3x - 12$ into the form $f(x) = a(x - h)^2 + k$.
b Identify the curve.
c Find the vertex.

Systems

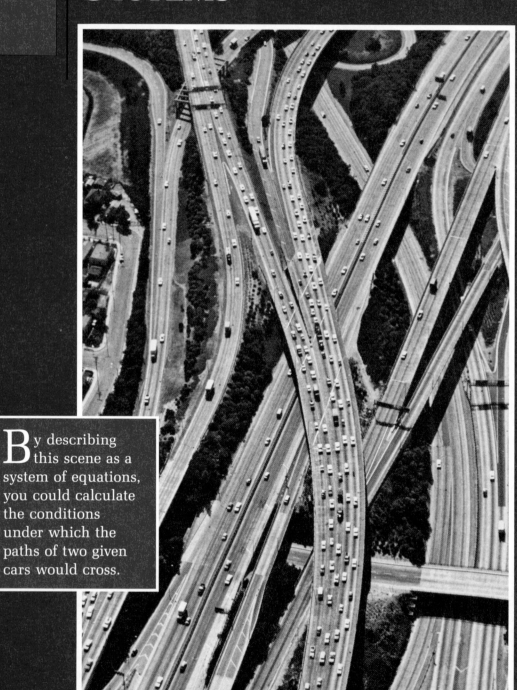

By describing this scene as a system of equations, you could calculate the conditions under which the paths of two given cars would cross.

Solving Problems with Systems of Equations

Objective

After studying this section, you will be able to
- Use systems of equations to solve problems

Part One: Introduction

You have already studied how to solve systems of linear equations by making a graph and by using two algebraic methods. Look carefully at the solution to the following word problem.

Example   *Paul E. Bank has $2.25 in quarters and dimes. He has 15 coins. Find the number of quarters and the number of dimes he has.*

Let d and q be the number of dimes and quarters respectively.

The total value of the coins is $2.25.

Value of dimes + value of quarters = total value
$$10d \qquad + \qquad 25q \qquad = 225 \text{ (cents)}$$

The total number of coins is 15.

$$d + q = 15$$

We have a system of two equations in two unknowns. The system's graph, shown in the diagram, indicates that $(d, q) = (10, 5)$.

We could also solve the system algebraically, using substitution. Since $d = 15 - q$,

$$10(15 - q) + 25q = 225$$
$$150 - 10q + 25q = 225$$
$$15q = 75$$
$$q = 5, \text{ so } d = 15 - 5 = 10$$

There are 10 dimes and 5 quarters.

If we change the total number of coins in the preceding example, the graph of the equation for the total number of coins will change.

If there were 12 coins, $d + q$ would equal 12. (Keep in mind that both d and q must be whole numbers.) The graph shows that $d = 5$ and $q = 7$.

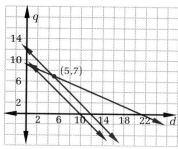

What would happen if there were 10 coins? The intersection of the graph would be $\left(1\frac{2}{3}, 8\frac{1}{3}\right)$. These coordinates are not whole numbers. Even though the system has a solution, the word problem does not. If 10 coins have a value of $2.25, they cannot be all dimes and quarters.

You will find that some systems have no solutions and that others have infinitely many.

Example   *Solve the following system.*

$$\begin{cases} y = 2x - 4 \\ y = 2x + 1 \end{cases}$$

Let's substitute $2x - 4$ for y in the second equation.

$$\begin{array}{r} y = \quad 2x + 1 \\ 2x - 4 = \quad 2x + 1 \\ \underline{-2x \qquad\quad -2x} \\ -4 = 1 \end{array}$$

The statement $-4 = 1$ is false. Therefore, the system has no solution. We get the same result by graphing. The slopes are equal but the y-intercepts are different. The graphs are parallel.

Example   *Solve the following system.*

$$\begin{cases} y = 5x - 3 \\ 2y = 10x - 6 \end{cases}$$

We substitute $5x - 3$ for y in the second equation.

$$2(5x - 3) = 10x - 6$$
$$10x - 6 = 10x - 6$$

This statement is an identity. All points that are solutions of $y = 5x - 3$ are also solutions of $2y = 10x - 6$, since one equation is a multiple of the other. This system has an infinite number of solutions, represented by $\{(x, y):y = 5x - 3\}$.

Part Two: Sample Problems

Problem 1   *Clem Chem needs to make 60 milliliters of a 9% solution of sulfuric acid for an experiment. He has available a 4% and a 12% solution. How many milliliters of each solution should he use?*

Solution   Let x represent the number of milliliters of the 4% solution, and let y represent the number of milliliters of the 12% solution.

Amount of acid $0.04x + 0.12y = 0.09(60) = 5.4$
Amount of solution $x + y = 60$

$$\begin{cases} 4x + 12y = 540 \\ x + y = 60 \end{cases}$$

We can substitute $60 - x$ for y in the first equation.

$$4x + 12(60 - x) = 540$$
$$4x + 720 - 12x = 540$$
$$-8x = -180$$
$$x = 22.5, \text{ so } y = 60 - 22.5 = 37.5$$

Clem needs 22.5 milliliters of the 4% solution and 37.5 milliliters of the 12% solution.

Problem 2   *A 1400-mile flight from Arconia to Citron took 4 hours with a tail wind. On the return flight, with a head wind of the same speed, the flight took 5 hours. What was the wind speed? How long would the flight have taken if there had been no wind?*

Solution   First let's organize the information.

Let p = the speed of the plane in still air,
$\quad w$ = the speed of the wind,
$\quad p + w$ = the speed of the plane with the tail wind,
$\quad p - w$ = the speed of the plane against the head wind.

	Time	Rate	Distance
With the wind	4 hours	$p + w$	1400 miles
Against the wind	5 hours	$p - w$	1400 miles

Remember, time · rate = distance.

$$\begin{cases} 4(p + w) = 1400 \\ 5(p - w) = 1400 \end{cases}$$

We first simplify each equation by dividing out the numerical factors. Then we add the resulting equations.

$$\begin{aligned} p + w &= 350 \\ \underline{p - w} &= \underline{280} \\ 2p\quad &= 630 \\ p\quad &= 315, \text{ so } w = 35 \end{aligned}$$

The wind speed is 35 miles per hour. The plane can travel 315 miles per hour with no wind. The flight would have taken $1400 \div 315$, or ≈ 4.44, hours if there had been no wind.

Part Three: Exercises and Problems

Warm-up Exercises

1 Is $(x, y) = (4, -3)$ a solution of the following system?
$$\begin{cases} 2x + y = 5 \\ 4x + 2y = 10 \end{cases}$$

2 Is $(x, y, z) = (-2, 4, 5)$ a solution of the following system?
$$\begin{cases} x + y + z = 7 \\ 2x - 2y + 3z = 3 \\ x + y - z = -3 \end{cases}$$

3 A plane flies 350 miles per hour with a head wind and 428 miles per hour in the opposite direction when the wind is a tail wind.

   a Find the plane's speed in still air.
   b Find the wind speed.

4 Use the diagrams to solve for (r, c).

In problems 5–7, determine whether each system of equations has no solutions, one solution, or many solutions.

5 $\begin{cases} y = 2x + 5 \\ y = 3x - 7 \end{cases}$ **6** $\begin{cases} y = 3x - 5 \\ y = 3x + 5 \end{cases}$ **7** $\begin{cases} y = 3x - 5 \\ 5 = 3x - y \end{cases}$

8 The sum of the ages of Zelda Zee and her sister Zuider is 45. Zelda's age is three more than twice Zuider's age. How old is each girl?

9 What is the value of x in the following system?
$$\begin{cases} 2x + 3y + 2z = 17 \\ 3x - 3y - 2z = 48 \end{cases}$$

Problem Set

In problems 10–12, determine whether each system of equations has no solutions, one solution, or many solutions.

10 $\begin{cases} y = 2x + 1 \\ y = 2x + 2 \end{cases}$ **11** $\begin{cases} 3x + y = 4 \\ 9x + 3y = 12 \end{cases}$ **12** $\begin{cases} y = 3x - 5 \\ y = 25x - 4 \end{cases}$

13 Use the diagrams to solve for (x, y).

In problems 14–16, solve each system.

14 $\begin{cases} 2x + 3y = 28 \\ 3x - y = 9 \end{cases}$

15 $\begin{cases} x - 3y = 7 \\ -2x + 6y = 13 \end{cases}$

16 $\begin{cases} 2x + 3y = 5 \\ 4x + 6y = 5 \end{cases}$

17 Sam is three times as old as Mary. In six years, Sam will be twice as old as Mary. Find each person's present age.

18 Solve the following system for (x, y, z).

$\begin{cases} x = 2y \\ z = 7y \\ 3x + 5y - z = 13 \end{cases}$

19 Dents Rent-a-Car charges $22.50 per day plus $0.18 per mile. Save-Us Rental charges $28.95 per day plus $0.15 per mile.

  a Write an equation for the total cost C_d (in dollars) of a one-day trip of m miles in a car rented from Dents.

  b Write an equation for the total cost C_s (in dollars) of traveling m miles in one day in a car rented from Save-Us.

  c How many miles would one need to drive in one day in order for the two rental costs to be the same?

20 The perimeter of each rectangle is 22. Find the values of x and y.

21 The graph of y = mx + b has a slope of 3 and contains the point (4, −8). Find the value of b.

22 During the first 10 games of the soccer season, Carlos had a total of 47 shots on goal.

  a How many shots on goal did he average per game?

  b How many shots on goal must he have in the next 4 games to increase his average to 6 shots on goal per game?

23 Port and Starboard are paddling canoes. They travel 20 miles downstream in 4 hours. They return upstream in 6 hours.

  a How fast is the current?

  b How fast can they paddle in still water?

24 Solve the following equation for (x, y), then check your solution by means of matrix multiplication.

$$\begin{bmatrix} 3 & -4 \\ 2 & 5 \end{bmatrix} \begin{bmatrix} x \\ y \end{bmatrix} = \begin{bmatrix} -26 \\ 21 \end{bmatrix}$$

25 Let $f(x) = (x - 3)(x + 4)(x - 9)$.

  a Find the x-intercepts of the graph of y = f(x).

  b Find the x-intercepts of the graph of y = f(2x).

26 If $f(x) = 2x^2$, for what value(s) of x is f(x) + 2 = 9?

Problem Set, *continued*

27 A 140-liter batch of a mixture contains 25 liters of iodine.

  a If 60 liters of iodine is added to the mixture, what percentage of the mixture will be iodine?

  b Find the least number of liters of iodine that must be added to the original mixture to create a mixture that is at least 70% iodine.

28 Find (m, b) if $(2, 5)$ and $(7, 11)$ are points on the graph of $y = mx + b$.

In problems 29 and 30, solve the system.

29 $\begin{cases} y = -3x + 4 \\ 12x + 4y = 2 \end{cases}$

30 $\begin{cases} 3x - 4y = 12 \\ y = \dfrac{3}{4}x - 3 \end{cases}$

31 The perimeters of the square and the triangle are equal. Find (x, y) if three times the perimeter of the square exceeds twice the perimeter of the triangle by 24.

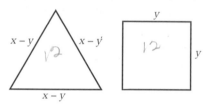

32 Two of the following equations are selected at random to form a system. Find the probability that the system has one solution.

  a $y = 3x + 7$ **b** $y = -5x + 4$ **c** $5x + y = 20$

  d $3x - y = 14$ **e** $y = -15x + 2$

33 If $x = 24$ when $y = 6$ and y varies directly as x, what are the values of x and y when the sum of x and twice y is 36?

34 Carmony Computer Consultants charges a $255 fee plus $85 per hour for its work. Holliday Computer Works charges a flat rate of $115 per hour.

  a Write a cost function for each company, then graph the two functions on the same coordinate system.

  b For jobs of how many hours is it cheaper to hire Carmony?

35 Let $y = -5x^2 - 20x + 6$. Find q if $y = -5(x^2 + qx) + 6$.

36 Let $3x^2 + 5x - 2 = 0$.

  a Solve the equation for x.

  b Find the sum of the equation's roots.

  c Find the product of the equation's roots.

37 Solve the following system for (x, y).

$\begin{cases} 2^{x+y} = 128 \\ 5^{2x-y} = 25 \end{cases}$

38 Refer to the triangle.

a Find the value of z.

b Can you find the values of x and y?

39 Mr. Fairwrench's radiator contains seven quarts of a mixture that is 35% antifreeze and 65% water. He needs a mixture that is 50% antifreeze and 50% water. How many quarts should he drain from his radiator and replace with pure antifreeze?

In problems 40 and 41, solve each system for (*x, y*).

40 $\begin{cases} x^2 = 2y^2 \\ 3x = y^2 \end{cases}$

41 $\begin{cases} y = |x - 2| + 5 \\ y = \dfrac{1}{2}|x| \end{cases}$

HISTORICAL SNAPSHOT

A SURVEYOR'S DREAM
Planning a capital city

In general, large cities have grown spontaneously around an original settlement. As the city grew outward, streets and bridges were built along the paths that best served the needs of the community.

However certain capital cities have been planned from the very beginning. Brasília, the capital of Brazil, is one example. Washington, D.C., is another.

The first capital of the United States was New York City. It was President George Washington who wanted the capital moved to its present location. He hired a French architect named Pierre Charles L'Enfant to create a plan for the new city. Then Washington put together a six-person team to carry out L'Enfant's plan.

Benjamin Banneker, a self-taught mathematician, became the first black presidential appointee when President Washington chose him as the surveyor for this team. Banneker was instrumental in selecting the sites for the White House, the Capitol, and other buildings still standing today. When L'Enfant resigned and left for France with his plans, Banneker reconstructed the plans from memory. It is largely because of Banneker that

we are able to enjoy the beauty of Washington, D.C., today.

Describe situations in which you think linear systems helped Banneker as he faced the tremendous task of helping to design, survey, and lay out the nation's new capital.

LINEAR SYSTEMS WITH THREE VARIABLES

Objectives

After studying this section, you will be able to
- Solve systems of equations in three unknowns
- Graph equations that contain three variables

Part One: Introduction

The strategy for solving systems of three equations in three unknowns involves combining pairs of equations to eliminate one of the variables, leaving a system of two equations in two unknowns.

Example   *Solve the following system.*

$$
\begin{array}{ll}
(1) & \\
(2) & \\
(3) &
\end{array}
\begin{cases}
x + 2y + 4z = 8 \\
x - 2y + 5z = -3 \\
4x + 4y - 3z = 1
\end{cases}
$$

In this problem, it is easiest to eliminate y. Notice that we can obtain an equation that does not contain y by adding equations (1) and (2).

$$
\begin{array}{ll}
(1) & x + 2y + 4z = 8 \\
(2) & \underline{x - 2y + 5z = -3} \\
& 2x + 9z = 5
\end{array}
$$

Next, we multiply (2) by 2 and add the result to (3).

$$
\begin{array}{l}
2x - 4y + 10z = -6 \\
\underline{4x + 4y - 3z = 1} \\
6x + 7z = -5
\end{array}
$$

Now we have two equations in x and z.

$$
\begin{cases}
2x + 9z = 5 \\
6x + 7z = -5
\end{cases}
$$

When we solve this system (by the multiplication-addition method), we find that $z = 1$ and $x = -2$. To find y, we substitute these values in equation (1).

$$x + 2y + 4z = 8$$
$$-2 + 2y + 4(1) = 8$$
$$2y + 2 = 8$$
$$y = 3$$

The solution of the system is therefore $(x, y, z) = (-2, 3, 1)$. To check this answer, substitute -2 for x, 3 for y, and 1 for z in each equation.

We can also use this technique to find the equation of a parabola.

Example   *Write an equation that represents a parabola containing the three points $(-3, -2)$, $(-1, 3)$, and $(5, 6)$.*

Since each point lies on the parabola, each ordered pair must be a solution of an equation of the form $y = ax^2 + bx + c$.

Substitute $(-3, -2)$ $\qquad$ $-2 = a(-3)^2 + b(-3) + c$

Substitute $(-1, 3)$ $\qquad$ $3 = a(-1)^2 + b(-1) + c$

Substitute $(5, 6)$ $\qquad$ $6 = a(5)^2 + b(5) + c$

These equations form a system in a, b, and c.

(1) $\quad \begin{cases} 9a - 3b + c = -2 \\ a - b + c = 3 \\ 25a + 5b + c = 6 \end{cases}$
(2)
(3)

Eliminating c is easiest. We multiply equation (2) by -1 and add the result to (1) and (3).

$$
\begin{array}{ll}
(1) \quad 9a - 3b + c = -2 & -1(2) \quad -a + b - c = -3 \\
-1(2) \quad \underline{-a + b - c = -3} & (3) \quad \underline{25a + 5b + c = 6} \\
\qquad \quad 8a - 2b \quad\;\; = -5 & \qquad\; 24a + 6b \quad\;\; = 3 \\
& \qquad\quad\; 8a + 2b \quad\;\; = 1
\end{array}
$$

Now we add the two new equations.

$$
\begin{array}{r}
8a - 2b = -5 \\
\underline{8a + 2b = 1} \\
16a = -4 \\
a = -\dfrac{1}{4}
\end{array}
$$

We substitute $-\frac{1}{4}$ for a in one of the equations to find b.

$$8a - 2b = -5$$
$$8\left(-\frac{1}{4}\right) - 2b = -5$$
$$-2 - 2b = -5$$
$$-2b = -3$$
$$b = \frac{3}{2}$$

Now we substitute the values of a and b for these variables in (2) to find c.

$$a - b + c = 3$$

$$\left(-\frac{1}{4}\right) - \frac{3}{2} + c = 3$$

$$-\frac{7}{4} + c = 3$$

$$c = \frac{19}{4}$$

An equation that represents the parabola is $y = -\frac{1}{4}x^2 + \frac{3}{2}x + \frac{19}{4}$.

Graphing Equations with Three Variables

If a linear equation contains three variables, its graph is a plane in three-dimensional space. To graph such an equation, we use a three-dimensional coordinate system consisting of three axes, each of which is perpendicular to the other two. Taken two at a time, these axes determine three coordinate planes—an xy plane, a yz plane, and an xz plane.

Example   *Graph x + 2y + 4z = 8.*

Since three points determine a plane, we can locate the graph of this equation by identifying the points at which it intersects the three axes. To find each intercept, we substitute 0 for two of the variables and solve for the third. In this case, the x-intercept is 8, the y-intercept is 4, and the z-intercept is 2.

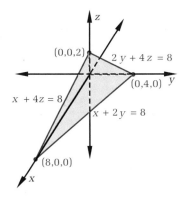

Each of the intersections of this plane with the coordinate planes can be found by substituting 0 for one of the variables and graphing the resulting line. If we let z = 0, we can see that the graph intersects the xy plane along the line x + 2y = 8. In the same way, we can find that it intersects the other coordinate planes along the lines 2y + 4z = 8 and x + 4z = 8. These lines are called *traces*.

The solution of a system of three equations in three variables is the intersection of three planes. This intersection may be a point, a line, or the empty set.

Planes have a point in common—one solution   Planes have a line in common—infinite solutions   Planes have no points in common—no solutions

There is a final possibility. If two equations of the system are multiples of the third, the solution is a plane.

Part Two: Sample Problem

Problem

Tickets for all 1150 seats for the Thespis High School play were sold. Student tickets sold for $1.50 and adult tickets sold for $2.50, with senior citizens getting a $0.50 discount off the adult price. A total of $2450 was taken in. If student and adult tickets had cost $0.30 more, the senior citizens could have got in free, and the total income would have been the same. How many senior-citizen tickets were sold?

Solution

Let x represent the number of student tickets,
  y represent the number of adult tickets,
  z represent the number of senior-citizen tickets.

Total number of tickets	(1)	$x + y + z = 1150$
Actual income	(2)	$1.5x + 2.5y + 2z = 2450$
Income if senior-citizen tickets had been free	(3)	$1.8x + 2.8y + 0z = 2450$

We can easily eliminate z, since it does not appear in the third equation.

Multiply (1) by -2 $-2x - 2y - 2z = -2300$

Add (2) $1.5x + 2.5y + 2z = \ \ \ 2450$

Multiply by 2 to $-0.5x + 0.5y \quad\quad = \ \ \ \ \ 150$

clear the decimals $-x + \ \ y = \ \ \ \ \ 300$

Now we form a system with this equation and (3).

$$\begin{cases} -x + y = 300 \\ 1.8x + 2.8y = 2450 \end{cases}$$

When we solve this system, we find that $x = 350$ and $y = 650$. By substituting these values in (1), we find that $z = 150$, so 150 senior-citizen tickets were sold.

Part Three: Exercises and Problems

Warm-up Exercises

1 Is $(w, x, y, z) = (3, -4, 2, 11)$ a solution of the following system?

$$\begin{cases} w + x + y = 1 \\ x + y + z = 9 \\ wxy = 24 \end{cases}$$

2 Find the value of b in the following system.

$$\begin{cases} a + b + c + d + e = 82 \\ a + c + d + e = 59 \end{cases}$$

3 Find the coordinates of points A, B, and C.

In problems 4 and 5, solve each system for (x, y, z).

4 $\begin{cases} x + y = 8 \\ y + z = 6 \\ x + z = 24 \end{cases}$

5 $\begin{cases} x + y + z = 15 \\ x - y - z = -5 \\ -x - y + z = -1 \end{cases}$

6 A parabola crosses the x-axis at (5, 0) and (−3, 0), and its vertex is at (1, 10). Write an equation that represents the parabola.

7 Solve the following system for (x, y, z).

$\begin{cases} x = 7 - y - z \\ x = 1 - 2y + z \\ x = 1 + 4y - 2z \end{cases}$

Problem Set

In problems 8 and 9, solve for (x, y, z).

8 $\begin{cases} 3x - 4y + 6z = 39 \\ 4x + 2y + z = 2 \\ 2x - 2y + 3z = -4 \end{cases}$

9 $\begin{cases} y = 2x + 1 \\ z = 3x \\ z + 2x - y = 15 \end{cases}$

10 Use the diagram to find (x, y, z).

11 Consider the plane represented by 2x + 3y + z = 12.

    a Find the plane's x-intercept.
    b Find the plane's y-intercept.
    c Find the plane's z-intercept.
    d Use your answers to parts **a, b,** and **c** to graph the plane.

12 The sum of Bill's age and his father's age is 64. In 5 years, Bill's father's age will be 10 less than 3 times Bill's age then. How old is each person now?

13 Write an equation of the parabola that contains the points (3, −1), (0, −7), and (2, 9).

In problems 14 and 15, solve each system.

14 $\begin{cases} x + 2y - 3z = 3 \\ 3x - 4y + 6z = 4 \\ y - 2z = 2 \end{cases}$

15 $\begin{cases} 9x + 3y + z = 5 \\ 4x + 2y + z = 7 \\ x + y + z = 7 \end{cases}$

16 Consider the equations $3x + 4y + 6z = 12$ and $3x + 4y + 6z = 24$.

(4,00) (0,3,0) (0,0,2)

   a Graph the equations on one set of axes.
   b What do you notice about the planes?

(8,00) (0,6,0) (0,0,4)

17 A box of 40 coins contains nickels, dimes, and quarters. The total value of the coins is $4.00. If there were 3 times as many nickels, half as many dimes, and 6 more quarters, the value of the coins would be $5.50. How many quarters are in the box?

18 Show that $\begin{bmatrix} x \\ y \\ z \end{bmatrix} = \begin{bmatrix} 3 \\ -5 \\ 6 \end{bmatrix}$ is a solution of $\begin{bmatrix} 1 & 2 & 3 \\ -2 & 5 & 1 \\ 4 & -1 & 1 \end{bmatrix} \begin{bmatrix} x \\ y \\ z \end{bmatrix} = \begin{bmatrix} 11 \\ -25 \\ 23 \end{bmatrix}$

19 Write the following system as a matrix equation.

$\begin{cases} 3x + 4y + z = 11 \\ 2x - y + 5z = 9 \\ -4x + 7y + 2z = -4 \end{cases}$

20 How many different 5-card poker hands can be dealt from a standard deck of 52 cards?

21 Solve the following system for (x, y).

$\begin{cases} 2^x 2^y = 32 \\ 5^x 5^y = 3125 \end{cases}$

22 Refer to the diagrams.

   a Write a function S for the area of the square.
   b Write a function T for the area of the triangle.
   c For what value of x is $T(x) = S(x)$?

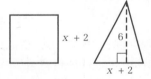

23 Let A, B, and C be three points such that the coordinates of A are (1, 5), the coordinates of B are (6, 3), and C is the intersection of $\overline{AB}$ and the line $y = x$.

   a Find the coordinates of point D, the reflection of B over the line $y = x$.
   b Find the distance from A to B.
   c Find the distance from A to C to D.

Problem Set, *continued*

24 Tickets at a ballpark sell for $4.50, $7.00, and $12.50. One day a total of 24,202 tickets were sold for a total of $151,924. The sum of the numbers of $7.00 tickets and $12.50 tickets sold was 702 less than the number of $4.50 tickets sold. How many of each kind of ticket were sold?

25 Swenson's Bakery sells three kinds of cakes. The amounts of flour, sugar, and eggs used for each cake are shown below, along with the bakery's daily consumption of these ingredients.

	Cake				**Amount Used Daily**
	A	**B**	**C**		
Flour (cups)	5	5	4	**Flour (cups)**	90
Sugar (cups)	3	2	2	**Sugar (cups)**	46
Eggs	1	2	3	**Eggs**	35

How many of each kind of cake are baked each day?

26 Consider the following table of values for a function *f*.

n	3	4	5	6	7	8
f(*n*)	0	2	5	9	14	20

a Does *f* appear to be a quadratic function? Why or why not?
b Write a closed-form formula for *f*.

27 A truck radiator contains 14 quarts of a mixture that is 75% antifreeze and 25% water. How much should be drained and replaced with pure water for the radiator to contain 14 quarts of a mixture that is 60% antifreeze and 40% water?

28 The average of three numbers is 18. If the first number is increased by five, the second number is doubled, and the third number is tripled, the average becomes 34. If the first number is decreased by five, the second number is tripled, and the third number is doubled, the average becomes 48. Find the largest of the three numbers.

29 If the number *y* of angles determined by *n* rays with a common endpoint is given by $y = an^2 + bn + c$, what is (*a*, *b*, *c*)?

| $y = 0$ | $y = 1$ | $y = 3$ | $y = 6$ | $y = 10$ | $y = 15$ |

30 The sum of the digits of a three-digit number is 10. The sum of the tens digit and the units digit equals the hundreds digit. The number represented if the hundreds digit is omitted is one less than three times the hundreds digit. Find the three-digit number.

31 Refer to the diagram.

　a Find the coordinates of the midpoints of $\overline{BC}$, $\overline{AB}$, and $\overline{AC}$.

　b Write an equation that represents the plane that passes through the midpoints found in part **a**.

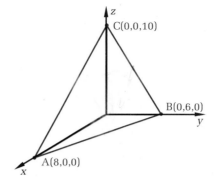

32 Solve the following system for (a, b, c, d, e).

$$\begin{cases} a + b + c + d = 17 \\ a + b + c + e = 19 \\ a + b + d + e = 23 \\ a + c + d + e = 22 \\ b + c + d + e = 15 \end{cases}$$

$e - d = 2$

SYSTEMS OF INEQUALITIES

Objective

After studying this section, you will be able to
- Graph systems of inequalities

Part One: Introduction

In Section 3.3 you learned methods of graphing linear inequalities and their intersections. We will extend these methods to the graphing of systems of inequalities.

Example   *Graph the following system.*

$$\begin{cases} -4 \leq x \leq 12 \\ y \geq \dfrac{3}{4}x - 2 \end{cases}$$

We first graph the vertical lines representing $x = -4$ and $x = 12$. The graph of $y = \frac{3}{4}x - 2$ has a slope of $\frac{3}{4}$ and a y-intercept of -2. Because the point $(0, 0)$ satisfies $y \geq \frac{3}{4}x - 2$, we shade the region above this line and between the two vertical lines.

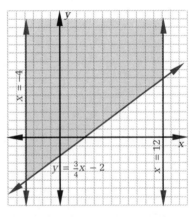

Example   *Graph the following system.*

$$\begin{cases} -3 \leq y \leq 7 \\ y \geq 2x + 3 \\ x \geq -5 \end{cases}$$

The boundaries of the shaded region are the graphs of $y = -3$, $y = 7$, $y = 2x + 3$, and $x = -5$.

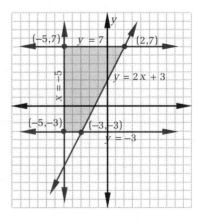

Part Two: Sample Problem

Problem Graph the following system.

$$\begin{cases} y > x + 2 \\ y < 4 - x^2 \end{cases}$$

Solution The boundaries are the line representing $y = x + 2$ and the parabola representing $y = -x^2 + 4$. We graph these with dashes (since they are not parts of the solution set) and test some convenient points to find the solution shown in the graph.

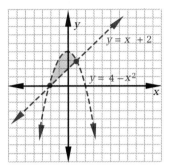

Part Three: Exercises and Problems

Warm-up Exercises

In problems 1 and 2, solve each system by graphing.

1 $\begin{cases} 1 > y > -3 \\ -2 < x < 4 \end{cases}$

2 $\begin{cases} x + y > 8 \\ x + y < 2 \end{cases}$

3 Write an inequality to describe the graph shown.

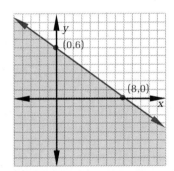

4 Graph the solution set of the following system.

$$\begin{cases} x + 2y \le 10 \\ y \ge 2 \\ x \ge -2 \end{cases}$$

5 Graph the following system and identify the vertices of the region it defines.

$$\begin{cases} -9 \le x \le 4 \\ -2 \le y \le 0 \end{cases}$$

6 Is (0, 0) a solution of all of the following inequalities?

$$2x + 3y \le 5 \qquad x < 2 \qquad y < -3 \qquad y \le \tfrac{1}{2}x + 2$$

7 An investment firm can invest at most \$80,000 in two companies, BIMCO and Amalgamated Snarfs. BIMCO stock sells for \$55 per share, and Amalgamated Snarfs stock sells for \$87 per share. Translate this situation into an inequality. (Let x equal the number of shares of BIMCO purchased, and let y equal the number of shares of Amalgamated Snarfs purchased.)

Problem Set

In problems 8 and 9, graph the solution of each system.

8 $\begin{cases} 3x + 2y \le 6 \\ 3x + 2y \le 12 \end{cases}$

9 $\begin{cases} -2 < x < 6 \\ -4 < y + 2x < 8 \end{cases}$

[handwritten: $y < -2x + 8$, $y > -2x - 4$]

10 What are the coordinates of the vertices of the shaded region in the diagram shown?

11 Graph the solution of the following system.

$\begin{cases} y \ge x \\ 6x + 5y \le 30 \end{cases}$

In problems 12 and 13, solve for (x, y, z).

12 $\begin{cases} x + y = 11 \\ x + z = 17 \\ y + z = 42 \end{cases}$

13 $\begin{cases} x + 2y - z = 9 \\ 3y + z = 26 \\ z = 5 \end{cases}$

14 A toy-manufacturing company has at most 200 pounds of plastic available for producing 2 kinds of toys. Three pounds of plastic are needed to produce a set of toy soldiers, and 7 pounds of plastic are required to produce a set of dolls. Write an inequality to describe this situation. (Let x equal the number of toy soldiers produced and y equal the number of dolls produced.)

[handwritten: $y \le -x + 10$, $y \ge -x + 2$]

15 Graph $2 \le x + y \le 10$.

16 Solve $3y^2 + 2y - 1 = 0$ for y.

17 Graph the following equations on the same set of axes.

    a $y = x^2$ **b** $y = (x - 2)^2$ **c** $y = (x - 2)^2 + 5$

18 Refer to the diagram.

a Find the coordinates of points A, B, C, D, E, F, G, and H.

b Write equations that represent the planes ABCD, EFGH, DCFE, and BCFG.

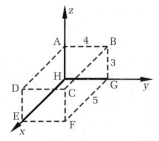

19 Consider the following system.

$$\begin{cases} x \geq 0 \\ y \geq 0 \\ y \leq -\frac{1}{2}x + 5 \\ y \geq x - 3 \end{cases}$$

a Find the coordinates of the vertices of the region defined by the system.

b Evaluate $f(x, y) = 2x + 3y$ at each vertex.

20 Graph the solution set of the following system.

$$\begin{cases} y \leq 2x + 3 \\ 4x - 2y \leq 5 \\ -3 \leq x \leq 5 \end{cases}$$ $y \geq 2x - 2\frac{1}{2}$

21 Write a system of inequalities that represents the shaded region in the diagram shown.

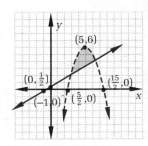

22 Kem E. Cal heated 500 milliliters of an 8% saline solution until all but 400 milliliters of the solution had evaporated. What percentage of the remaining solution was salt?

23 A point is randomly selected from $\{(0, 0), (1, 3), (2, 2), (-2, -2)\}$. What is the probability that the chosen point lies in the region defined by the following system?

$$\begin{cases} y < 2x + 6 \\ y > 2x - 6 \\ y < -2x + 6 \\ y > -2x - 6 \end{cases}$$

24 Snoopy flies his Sopwith Camel from his base to his destination and back, a total of 240 miles. If he had flown 20 miles per hour faster, the trip would have taken an hour less. How fast did Snoopy fly?

25 Refer to the diagram.

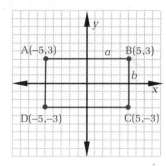

  a Find the ratio of length *b* to length *a*.

  b Write equations that represent the
lines containing the diagonals of the
rectangle.

  c How could you use your answer to
part **b** to answer part **a**?

26 Write a system of inequalities that describes a square region
whose center is at the origin, whose vertices are on the axes, and
whose area is 50 square units.

27 Machine A produces 200 widgets per hour. Machine B produces
375 widgets per hour. Machine A runs at least 2 hours per day,
and machine B runs at least 3 hours per day. The 2 machines
together run no more than 10 hours per day. Write at least 4
inequalities to describe this situation. (Let *x* equal the number of
hours machine A runs and *y* equal the number of hours machine B runs.)

28 If $f(x, y) = 4x + 3y$, what is the minimum value of f for the
domain $\{(-3, 1), (4, 7), (5, -7)\}$?

29 Find the area of the region defined by the following system.
$$\begin{cases} 2 \le y \le 7 \\ 4y < 5x + 3 \\ 5x + 2y < 54 \end{cases}$$

30 Solve the following system for (x, y, z).
$$\begin{cases} 3x + y - 2z = 4 \\ -6x + 4y + 4z = 28 \\ -7x + 2y = 26 \end{cases}$$

31 Plane A leaves New York for London at 8:50 A.M. Plane B leaves
New York for London at 9:40 A.M. When plane B leaves, the
planes are 600 miles apart. One hour later the planes are 550
miles apart. Find the speed of each plane.

32 Find the area of the region defined by the following system.
$$\begin{cases} 0 \le x \le 12 \\ y \ge 0 \\ 2y - x \le 10 \\ 2y + x \le 22 \end{cases}$$

33 Write a system of inequalities that represents the shaded region in the diagram.

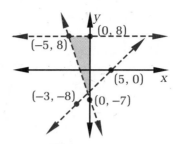

34 Graph the region defined by the following system and find its area.

$$\begin{cases} y \le \dfrac{1}{2}x + 6 \\ y \le -2x + 6 \\ y \ge 2x - 6 \\ y \ge -\dfrac{1}{2}x - 6 \end{cases}$$

35 A matrix can be used to represent a directed graph.

For example, $\begin{bmatrix} 0 & 2 & 1 \\ 0 & 1 & 1 \\ 3 & 0 & 0 \end{bmatrix}$ represents

The number in row a, column b, indicates the number of direct paths from a to b.

a Construct a matrix to represent the digraph shown.

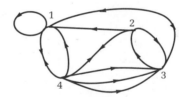

b Draw the digraph represented by the following matrix.

$$\begin{bmatrix} 0 & 1 & 2 & 3 \\ 1 & 0 & 1 & 0 \\ 1 & 1 & 0 & 0 \\ 2 & 1 & 0 & 1 \end{bmatrix}$$

In problems 36 and 37, graph the solution set of each system.

36 $\begin{cases} y \le -x + 3 \\ y \le x + 3 \\ y \ge -x - 3 \\ y \ge x - 3 \\ x \le 2 \\ x \ge -2 \\ y \le 2 \\ y \ge -2 \end{cases}$

37 $\begin{cases} y < x + 2 \\ y < 2 \\ y < -x + 4 \\ y > x - 4 \\ y > -2 \\ y > -x - 2 \end{cases}$

INVERSE VARIATION

Objectives

After studying this section, you will be able to
- Solve inverse-variation problems
- Graph equations of the form $xy = k$

Part One: Introduction

The Graph of $xy = k$

The graph of an equation of the form $xy = k$ or $y = \frac{k}{x}$, where

k is a nonzero constant, can be represented by a hyperbola with its
center at the origin and with the x-axis and y-axis as asymptotes.
If $k > 0$, the hyperbola lies in the first and third quadrants;
if $k < 0$, the hyperbola lies in the second and fourth quadrants.

Example *Graph $xy = -9$.*

The graph is a hyperbola lying in the
second and fourth quadrants. By
plotting a few points and applying a
knowledge of symmetry and asymptotes as discussed in Chapter 6, we
graph the equation as shown.

Inverse-Variation Problems

In Section 3.4, you learned that two quantities x and y are said to
vary directly if they are related by an equation of the form $y = mx$,
where m is the constant of variation. A characteristic of direct
variation with a positive constant of variation is that as the value of
one variable increases, the value of the other variable also increases
proportionally.

Many real-world relationships, however, are different—the faster you travel, the *less* time it takes to reach your destination; the smaller the volume into which a gas is forced, the *greater* the gas's pressure. Such relationships are examples of **inverse variation** and are represented by equations of the form $xy = k$, or $y = \frac{k}{x}$, or $y = k \cdot \frac{1}{x}$, where k is the constant of variation. When two quantities vary inversely, the absolute value of one quantity decreases proportionally as the absolute value of the other increases.

Example

If x varies inversely as y, and if $y = 6$ when $x = 12$, what is the value of x when $y = 9$?

To find the value of k, the constant of variation, we substitute

$$xy = k$$
$$12 \cdot 6 = k$$
$$72 = k$$

Substitute again
$$xy = 72$$
$$x \cdot 9 = 72$$
$$x = 8$$

Part Two: Sample Problems

Problem 1

Bankers use the "rule of 72" to approximate the number of years it will take for an investment to double in value. According to this rule, the number of years is inversely proportional to the percentage value of the annual interest rate, with a constant of variation of approximately 72. If you invest money at 9%, approximately how many years will it take for the money to double?

Solution

$\text{Years} = \frac{72}{\text{interest rate}} = \frac{72}{9} = 8$

The money will double in about eight years.

Problem 2

Graph $xy = 12$ and identify the vertices of the hyperbola.

Solution

In this inverse variation, the constant of variation is 12. Since the constant is positive, the graph will lie in the first and third quadrants.

We plot several points (x, y) such that $xy = 12$ and sketch the graph.

Because the vertices must lie on the diagonal line $y = x$, we can substitute x for y in $xy = 12$, obtaining $x^2 = 12$. Thus, $x = \pm\sqrt{12}$. The vertices are $\left(\sqrt{12}, \sqrt{12}\right)$ and $\left(-\sqrt{12}, -\sqrt{12}\right)$.

Part Three: Exercises and Problems

Warm-up Exercises

1 Graph $xy = -4$.

In problems 2–5, I varies inversely as M. Find the constant of variation.

2 $I = 12$ when $M = 18$.

3 $I = 18$ when $M = 12$.

4 $I = 9$ when $M = 24$.

5 $I = 3$ when $M = 8$.

6 Determine whether the tables represent inverse relationships.

a

x	3	2	1	4	6	8	10	12
y	8	12	24	6	4	3	2.4	2

b

x	1	2	3	4	5	6
y	10	8	6	4	2	0

c

x	$-\frac{5}{4}$	$-\frac{3}{2}$	$-\frac{1}{3}$	5	4	$\frac{8}{5}$	10
y	$\frac{4}{5}$	$\frac{2}{3}$	3	$-\frac{1}{5}$	$-\frac{1}{4}$	$-\frac{5}{8}$	$-\frac{1}{10}$

7 If b varies inversely as P and the constant of variation is 0.4, what is P when $b = 8$?

8 Find the vertices of the graph of $xy = 36$.

Problem Set

In problems 9–12, graph each equation.

9 $xy = 1$

10 $xy = 3$

11 $xy = 9$

12 $yx = -1$

13 Copy and complete the table to show that y varies inversely as x.

x	−2	−1			
y	15		−3	6	60

14 Suppose that Y varies inversely as W and that $Y = 18$ when $W = 16$. Find the value of W when $Y = 24$.

15 The number of teeth in each gear is inversely proportional to its turning speed in revolutions per minute (rpm). Gear 1 has 40 teeth and turns at 440 rpm. Gear 2 has 24 teeth. Find the turning speed of gear 2.

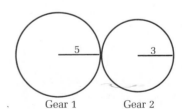

Gear 1   Gear 2

16 Consider the function f such that $f(x) = \frac{16}{x}$.

   a Find the equations of all asymptotes of the graph.

   b Graph f and its asymptotes.

17 Explain why the bases and the heights of all triangles with area 24 are inversely related. Are the bases and heights of triangles of any given area inversely proportional?

18 Suppose $e(x, y) = x^y$. Compute $e(1, 1)$, $e(1, 2)$, $e(1, 4)$, $e(1, -2)$, and $e(1, n)$.

In problems 19 and 20, graph each equation.

19 $\dfrac{x^2}{9} - \dfrac{y^2}{36} = 1$ **20** $\dfrac{y^2}{9} - \dfrac{x^2}{36} = 1$

21 Solve the following system for (x, y).

$$\begin{cases} 9x + 4y = 43 \\ 5x - 8y = 75 \end{cases}$$

22 It costs \$40 for a family to obtain a swimming pass to Lake Minian each summer. Each time the family uses the card, a punch mark is made for each person who goes swimming.

   a Find the cost per punch mark if 20 punches are made and if 80 punches are made.

   b How many punches will need to be made for the cost to be less than \$0.30 per punch?

23 If F varies inversely as r^2, and if F is 25 when r is 3, what is the value of F when r is 6?

24 Graph $xy - 2y = 4$. (Hint: Factor the left side.)

In problems 25 and 26, graph each equation.

25 $\dfrac{x}{4} + \dfrac{y}{9} = 1$ **26** $\dfrac{x^2}{4} + \dfrac{y^2}{9} = 1$

In problems 27–29, factor each expression over the integers.

27 $x^2 - 9x - 10$ **28** $2x^3 - x^2 - 3x$ **29** $x^2 + 9x + 7$

In problems 30 and 31, graph each function.

30 $f(x) = \dfrac{12}{x}$ **31** $f(x) = \dfrac{12x}{x^2}$

32 If y varies inversely as x and x varies inversely as z, does y vary inversely as z? Explain your answer.

33 Let $y = x^2 + 1$.

   a Graph the equation.
   b Interchange x and y and graph the new equation.
   c In the new equation, is y a function of x?

34 Write an equation to represent the inverse variation represented by the graph shown.

                $(-3,-4)$

35 Suppose x varies inversely as y.

   a Graph $xy = k$, where $k = 1$.
   b Graph $xy = k$, where $k = 2$.
   c Find the points of intersection of each of the curves in parts **a** and **b** with the line $y = x$.

36 Graph $(x - 3)(y + 1) = 12$.

37 Solve the following system for (x, y).

$$\begin{cases} y = \dfrac{1}{x} \\ y = \dfrac{1}{2x + 3} \end{cases}$$

38 Brute Force is a member of the Muscle City Health Club. His membership fee is \$160 per year.

   a Find his cost per workout if he works out three days per week.
   b What would his cost per workout be if the membership fee were decreased by 20%?

39 Consider functions f and g such that $f(x) = \frac{4}{x}$ and $g(x) = f(x + 2) + 3$.

   a Graph f.
   b Write the equations of the asymptotes of $y = f(x)$.
   c Graph g.
   d Write the equations of the asymptotes of $y = g(x)$.

40 Bia Thlon rode her bike for 3 hours at a steady rate, then walked for 2 hours at a different steady rate. The next day, she rode her bike for 4 hours and walked for 1 hour at the same rates as on the previous day. She went 42 miles the first day and 51 miles the second. How much faster is Bia's cycling rate than her walking rate?

41 The graph of $y = \frac{40}{x}$ is shown. Point P is on the graph. Find the area of the rectangle.

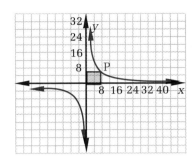

42 Let f be a function whose domain is the positive integers. The following are some of the values of $f(n)$.

$f(1) = 1$
$f(2) = 3 + 5 = 8$
$f(3) = 7 + 9 + 11 = 27$
$f(4) = 13 + 15 + 17 + 19 = 64$

Make a reasonable guess for each value.

a $f(5)$ **b** $f(6)$ **c** $f(10)$
d $f(20)$ **e** $f(100)$

43 The intensity with which an object is illuminated is inversely proportional to d^2, the square of its distance from the source of light. If the intensity I of light on a movie screen is 50 candles when the projector is 15 feet from the screen, what is the intensity of light on the screen when the projector is moved 5 feet farther from it?

In problems 44 and 45, graph each equation.

44 $x^2 + 6x + 4y^2 + 24y = 19$ **45** $x^2 - 4x - y^2 - 8y = 13$

46 Graph the relationship of x to y if the area of the shaded region is 576, $x > 0$, and $y > 0$.

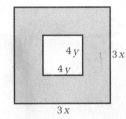

47 Write an equation to represent the ellipse in the diagram.

NONLINEAR SYSTEMS

Objective

After studying this section, you will be able to
- Solve systems containing nonlinear equations

Part One: Introduction

Just as you have used graphing to help solve systems of linear equations, you can use it to help solve systems that contain nonlinear equations.

Example   *Solve the following system.* $\begin{cases} y^2 - x^2 = 16 \\ y^2 + x^2 = 34 \end{cases}$

First, let's sketch the graphs of these equations on the same set of axes. The graph of $y^2 - x^2 = 16$, or $\frac{y^2}{16} - \frac{x^2}{16} = 1$, is a hyperbola that is symmetrical about the y-axis, with vertices (0, 4) and (0, −4). The graph of $x^2 + y^2 = 34$ is a circle with its center at (0, 0) and a radius of $\sqrt{34}$, or ≈5.8. The sketch indicates that the system has four solutions. We can find the solutions algebraically.

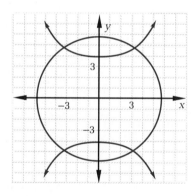

Add the equations to eliminate the x^2 term

$$\begin{aligned} y^2 + x^2 &= 34 \\ y^2 - x^2 &= 16 \\ \hline 2y^2 &= 50 \\ y^2 &= 25 \\ y = 5 \text{ or } y &= -5 \end{aligned}$$

Substitute 5 and −5 for y in either of the original equations and solve for x.

$$\begin{aligned} y^2 + x^2 &= 34 \\ 5^2 + x^2 &= 34 \\ x^2 &= 9 \\ x = 3 \text{ or } x &= -3 \end{aligned}$$ $$\begin{aligned} y^2 + x^2 &= 34 \\ (-5)^2 + x^2 &= 34 \\ x^2 &= 9 \\ x = 3 \text{ or } x &= -3 \end{aligned}$$

The four solutions of the system are (3, 5), (−3, 5), (3, −5), and (−3, −5). These solutions agree with our sketch.

Part Two: Sample Problems

Problem 1   *Solve the following system.* $\begin{cases} 2x - 3y = 6 \\ xy = 12 \end{cases}$

Solution   When we sketch the graphs of the equations, the diagram shows two solutions. Let's use substitution to solve the system algebraically. Solving the first equation for x, we have $x = \frac{3}{2}y + 3$. Now we substitute for x in $xy = 12$ and solve for y.

$$\left(\frac{3}{2}y + 3\right)y = 12$$

$$\frac{3}{2}y^2 + 3y = 12$$
$$y^2 + 2y = 8$$
$$y^2 + 2y - 8 = 0$$
$$(y - 2)(y + 4) = 0$$
$$y = 2 \text{ or } y = -4$$

$$\begin{array}{ll} \text{If } y = 2 & \text{If } y = -4 \\ 2x = 12 & -4x = 12 \\ x = 6 & x = -3 \end{array}$$

The two solutions of the system are $(6, 2)$ and $(-3, -4)$.

Problem 2   *Solve the following system.* $\begin{cases} y = 1 - x^2 \\ 4x^2 + y^2 = 16 \end{cases}$

Solution   The graph of $y = -x^2 + 1$ is a parabola opening downward with a vertex at $(0, 1)$. The graph of $4x^2 + y^2 = 16$, or $\frac{x^2}{4} + \frac{y^2}{16} = 1$, is an ellipse centered at $(0, 0)$. The diagram shows two solutions.

Let's solve the system by substitution. Either we can substitute $1 - x^2$ for y in $4x^2 + y^2 = 16$ to get a fourth-degree equation (try it and see), or we can substitute $1 - y$ for x^2 in $4x^2 + y^2 = 16$ to get the quadratic equation $4(1 - y) + y^2 = 16$. The latter method is easier.

$$4(1 - y) + y^2 = 16$$
$$4 - 4y + y^2 = 16$$
$$y^2 - 4y - 12 = 0$$
$$(y - 6)(y + 2) = 0$$
$$y = 6 \text{ or } y = -2$$

Our graph shows that y must be negative, so 6 is not a possible value of y. (Try substituting 6 for y in the first equation to see why.) We substitute -2 for y in the first equation and solve for x.

$$1 - x^2 = y$$
$$1 - x^2 = -2$$
$$x^2 = 3$$
$$x = \sqrt{3} \text{ or } x = -\sqrt{3}$$

The two points of intersection are $\left(\sqrt{3}, -2\right)$ and $\left(-\sqrt{3}, -2\right)$.

Part Three: Exercises and Problems

Warm-up Exercises

1 Estimate the solutions of the system represented in each diagram.

a

b

c

2 Consider the following system.

$$\begin{cases} x^2 - y^2 = 36 \\ x^2 + y^2 = 4 \end{cases}$$

  a Solve the system for (x^2, y^2).
  b Solve the system for (x, y).

3 Is $(x, y) = (-3, 4)$ a solution of the following system?

$$\begin{cases} x^2 + y^2 = 25 \\ y = -2x - 2 \end{cases}$$

In problems 4 and 5, solve for (x, y).

4 $\begin{cases} y = 2 \\ x^2 + y^2 = 25 \end{cases}$

5 $\begin{cases} y^2 - x^2 = 5 \\ x^2 + y^2 = 13 \end{cases}$

6 Find the points of intersection of the graphs of $\frac{x^2}{9} + \frac{y^2}{16} = 1$ and $\frac{x^2}{9} - \frac{y^2}{16} = 1$.

7 Solve the following system for (x, y).

$$\begin{cases} 9x^2 + 16y^2 = 1 \\ 9x^2 - 16y^2 = 1 \end{cases}$$

Problem Set

In problems 8–11, solve each system for (x, y).

8 $\begin{cases} 2x^2 + y^2 = 36 \\ y = 2x \end{cases}$

9 $\begin{cases} x^2 + y^2 = 36 \\ 2x^2 - y^2 = 12 \end{cases}$

10 $\begin{cases} x^2 + 8y = 33 \\ y = x - 9 \end{cases}$

11 $\begin{cases} y = x^2 \\ x^2 + y^2 = 6 \end{cases}$

12 Find the points of intersection of the graphs of $y = x^2$ and $x^2 - y^2 = -2$.

13 The wavelength w, in meters, of a radio wave varies inversely as its frequency f, in kilocycles per second, according to the equation $wf = 300{,}000$.

    a Find the wavelength of the transmissions of radio station WINK, which broadcasts at a frequency of 800 kilocycles per second.

    b Find the wavelength of the transmissions of radio station WONK, which broadcasts at a frequency of 1120 kilocycles per second.

    c Find the frequency, in kilocycles per second, at which radio station WAIT broadcasts, given that the wavelength of the transmissions of the station is 400 meters.

14 Graph, on the same coordinate system, the two lines described by the matrix equation.

$$\begin{bmatrix} 2 & 3 \\ -4 & -6 \end{bmatrix} \begin{bmatrix} x \\ y \end{bmatrix} = \begin{bmatrix} 12 \\ -12 \end{bmatrix}$$

In problems 15–17, factor each expression.

15 $4 - x^2$ **16** $4 - (5x)^2$ **17** $4 - (5x - 3)^2$

18 Suppose that x and y vary inversely. For positive values of x, as x increases, y also increases. For negative values of x, as x increases, y also increases. Give an example of such a relationship and sketch its graph.

In problems 19–22, solve each system for (x, y).

19 $\begin{cases} y = x + 10 \\ x^2 + y^2 = 4 \end{cases}$ **20** $\begin{cases} x^2 - y^2 = 4 \\ y^2 = 3x \end{cases}$

21 $\begin{cases} x^2 + y^2 = 1 \\ x^2 + y^2 = 3 \end{cases}$ **22** $\begin{cases} y^2 - 9x^2 = 16 \\ y = -5x \end{cases}$

23 Seven points lie on a circle. How many chords are determined by the points?

24 Consider the following multiplication table.

    a Find the sum of the elements in each region.

    b Find the sum of the elements in the nth such region.

	1	2	3	4	5
1	1	2	3	4	5
2	2	4	6	8	10
3	3	6	9	12	15
4	4	8	12	16	20
5	5	10	15	20	25

Problem Set, *continued*

25 The product of the x- and the y-coordinate of each point on a certain graph is 24.

   a Write an equation that corresponds to the graph.
   b Draw the graph.

26 Find each product.

   a $(a - b)(a^2 + ab + b^2)$
   b $(a - b)(a^2 + 2ab + b^2)$

27 If f is a discrete function such that $f(1) = 0$ and $f(n + 1) = 100 \cdot f(n)$, what is $f(78)$?

28 Two pounds of candy valued at $3.60 per pound are mixed with eight pounds of candy valued at $4.40 per pound.

   a Find the value of the mixture.
   b Find the value per pound of the mixture.

29 If $f(x) = 8x + 13$ and $g(x) = 2x - 7$, for what value of x is $f(x) = g(x)$?

In problems 30–32, factor each expression over the integers.

30 $10x^2 - 7x + 1$ **31** $x^3 - 25x$ **32** $81 - 4x^2y^4$

33 A linear function f is of the form $f(x) = mx + b$, with $f(3) = 8$ and $f(-6) = 3$.

   a Find m and b.
   b Draw the graph of f.
   c Draw the graph of function n such that $n(x) = f(x - 2)$.

34 Suppose that x and y vary inversely and that $y = 3.7$ when $x = 5$. What is the value of x when $y = 7.4$?

35 Maggie Zeen sold 150 magazine subscriptions, some at $12 and the rest at $19, during the month of June.

   a How many subscriptions of each type did she sell if the total amount of her sales was $2059?
   b Find Maggie's commission rate if the amount of her commission was $617.70.

36 Use the process of completing the square to find the vertex of the parabola described by each function.

   a $f(x) = x^2 - 12x - 16$ **b** $f(x) = -x^2 - 12x - 16$
   c $f(x) = -2x^2 - 12x - 16$ **d** $f(x) = 2x^2 - 12x - 16$

37 The sum of two numbers x and y is 23, and the sum of the squares of the numbers is 289. Find (x, y).

38 Use the data displayed at the right.

    a Find the mode of the data shown.
    b Find the mean.
    c Find the median.

39 Consider the following table.

x	16			
y	8	4	2	1

    a Copy and complete the table to show that x varies directly as y.

    b Copy and complete the table to show that x varies inversely as y.

40 Find the points of intersection of the graphs of $\frac{x^2}{9} + \frac{y^2}{16} = 1$ and $\frac{x^2}{16} + \frac{y^2}{9} = 1$.

41 Determine the value of a, given each graph of $f(x) = ax^2$.

  a

  b

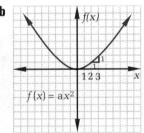

42 Solve the following system for (x, y).

$$\begin{cases} \dfrac{(x - 2)^2}{4} + \dfrac{(y - 3)^2}{9} = 1 \\ \dfrac{(x + 2)^2}{4} + \dfrac{(y + 3)^2}{9} = 1 \end{cases}$$

43 Solve the following system for (x, y).

$$\begin{cases} x^2 + y^2 = 5 \\ x^2 + y^2 - x - y = 4 \end{cases}$$

44 Graph the following system.

$$\begin{cases} \dfrac{(x - 4)^2}{36} + \dfrac{(y - 3)^2}{16} \geq 1 \\ 2y + x \geq 1 \end{cases}$$

OTHER SYSTEMS OF EQUATIONS

Objective

After studying this section, you will be able to
▪ Solve systems of equations involving rational expressions

Part One: Introduction

Systems in which one or more variables are in the denominator of a fraction can be solved by using methods similar to those you have used to solve other nonlinear systems.

Example   *Solve the following system.*

$$\begin{cases} \dfrac{20}{x} - \dfrac{1}{y} = 3 \\ \dfrac{8}{x} + \dfrac{5}{y} = 12 \end{cases}$$

If we let $P = \frac{1}{x}$ and $Q = \frac{1}{y}$, we can rewrite the system as follows.

$$\begin{cases} 20P - Q = 3 \\ 8P + 5Q = 12 \end{cases}$$

To solve this system for P and Q, we multiply the first equation by 5 and add it to the second.

$$\begin{array}{r} 100P - 5Q = 15 \\ 8P + 5Q = 12 \\ \hline 108P \qquad = 27 \end{array}$$

$$P = \frac{27}{108} = \frac{1}{4}$$

We now substitute $\frac{1}{4}$ for P in the first equation and solve for Q.

$$20P - Q = 3$$
$$20\left(\tfrac{1}{4}\right) - Q = 3$$
$$5 - 3 = Q$$
$$2 = Q$$

Since $P = \frac{1}{x}$ and $Q = \frac{1}{y}$, $x = 4$ and $y = \frac{1}{2}$.

Part Two: Sample Problems

Problem 1   John, George, and Paul always enter the annual pie-eating contest in their hometown, Ringo. One year, John and Paul together ate 18 pies in 16 minutes. The next year, George and Paul together ate 20 pies in 16 minutes. Last year, the 3 together ate 30 pies in 16 minutes. How long does it take each to eat 1 pie?

Solution   If John eats a pie in J minutes, then his rate is $\frac{1}{J}$ pie per minute. In the same way, George's rate is $\frac{1}{G}$, and Paul's rate is $\frac{1}{P}$. The individual rates for each year add up to the combined rate for that year.

$$\begin{cases} \dfrac{1}{J} + \dfrac{1}{P} = \dfrac{18}{16} \\ \dfrac{1}{G} + \dfrac{1}{P} = \dfrac{20}{16} \\ \dfrac{1}{J} + \dfrac{1}{G} + \dfrac{1}{P} = \dfrac{30}{16} \end{cases}$$

We can clear some fractions by multiplying each equation by 16.

$$\begin{cases} \dfrac{16}{J} + \dfrac{16}{P} = 18 \\ \dfrac{16}{G} + \dfrac{16}{P} = 20 \\ \dfrac{16}{J} + \dfrac{16}{G} + \dfrac{16}{P} = 30 \end{cases}$$

If we now let $A = \frac{16}{J}$, $B = \frac{16}{G}$, and $C = \frac{16}{P}$, we can write the following system.

$$\begin{cases} A + C = 18 \\ B + C = 20 \\ A + B + C = 30 \end{cases}$$

By subtracting the second equation from the third equation, we find that $A = 10$. By subtracting the first equation from the third equation, we find that $B = 12$. If we substitute these values for A and B in the third equation, we find that $C = 8$. Now that we know the values of A, B, and C, we can find the values of J, G, and P.

We know that $\frac{16}{J} = A$ and $A = 10$, so $J = \frac{16}{10}$. It takes John $1\frac{3}{5}$ minutes to eat a pie.

We know that $\frac{16}{G} = B$ and $B = 12$, so $G = \frac{16}{12}$. It takes George $1\frac{1}{3}$ minutes to eat a pie.

We know that $\frac{16}{P} = C$ and $C = 8$, so $P = \frac{16}{8}$. It takes Paul 2 minutes to eat a pie.

Problem 2   *Solve the following system.*

$$\begin{cases} x = y^2 \\ \dfrac{14}{x} = \dfrac{5}{y} + 1 \end{cases}$$

Solution   We can simplify this system by multiplying the corresponding sides of the equations.

$$x\left(\frac{14}{x}\right) = y^2\left(\frac{5}{y} + 1\right)$$
$$14 = 5y + y^2$$
$$0 = y^2 + 5y - 14$$
$$0 = (y + 7)(y - 2)$$
$$y = -7 \text{ or } y = 2$$

If $y = -7$, then $x = 49$. If $y = 2$, then $x = 4$. The solutions are $(49, -7)$ and $(4, 2)$. Check these solutions in each equation of the system.

Part Three: Exercises and Problems

Warm-up Exercises

In problems 1 and 2, solve for (x, y).

1 $\begin{cases} \dfrac{1}{x} + \dfrac{1}{y} = 6 \\ \dfrac{1}{x} - \dfrac{1}{y} = 12 \end{cases}$

2 $\begin{cases} \dfrac{1}{x} - \dfrac{2}{y} = 1 \\ \dfrac{5}{x} + \dfrac{6}{y} = -1 \end{cases}$

3 The sum of the reciprocals of two numbers is $\frac{1}{2}$. The difference of their reciprocals is $\frac{1}{3}$. Find the two numbers.

4 Solve the following system for (x, y).

$$\begin{cases} \dfrac{1}{x} + \dfrac{1}{3} = \dfrac{2}{y} \\ x = y \end{cases}$$

Problem Set

5 Solve the following system for (x, y).

$$\begin{cases} \dfrac{3}{x} - \dfrac{2}{y} = 5 \\ \dfrac{4}{x} + \dfrac{5}{y} = 22 \end{cases}$$

6 Solve the following system. (Hint: Factor and divide.)

$$\begin{cases} x^2 - y^2 = 20 \\ x + y = 4 \end{cases}$$

7 Solve the following system for (x, y). (Hint: Start by dividing the sides of one equation by the corresponding sides of the other.)

$$\begin{cases} (x + y)(x - y) = y^3 \\ x + y = y^2 \end{cases}$$

8 Teri Yaki can make a dozen egg rolls in three hours. Her sister Suki can make a dozen rolls in five hours. How long would it take them to make a dozen rolls if they worked together?

9 Suppose that f and g are functions such that $f(x) + g(x) = 3x^2 + 2x + 7$ and $f(x) - g(x) = 2x^2 - 3x + 1$. Write formulas to represent f and g.

10 In the figure, A is at $(2, y)$ and B is at $(3, 4)$. Find the value of y for which $d_1 = d_2$.

11 If it takes five workers six hours to paint an office, how long will it take eight workers to paint the office, assuming all the workers work at the same rate?

12 Solve $q^2 + 7731q = 0$ for q.

13 The area of a rectangle is 32 square units. Its sides have integral lengths. Find the probability that its perimeter is greater than 30 units.

14 Solve $w(w - 1)(w + 2)(w - 3) = 0$ for w.

15 A military squad leader wants to select three of ten soldiers for a special mission. In how many ways can the three be chosen?

16 If pump A can fill a pool in six hours and pump B can fill the pool in four hours, how long will filling the pool take if the two pumps work together?

17 Consider the discrete function F for which $F(1) = 1$ and $F(n) = \frac{1}{10}[F(n - 1)]$. Find the values of the following.

a $F(1), F(2), F(3), F(4),$ and $F(5)$

b $\displaystyle\sum_{n=1}^{5} F(n)$

Problem Set, *continued*

18 Solve the following system for (x, y).

$$\begin{cases} 2x + \dfrac{3}{y} = 4 \\ 5x - \dfrac{2}{y} = 29 \end{cases}$$

In problems 19 and 20, solve for (x, y).

19 $\begin{cases} 3(x + 4) + 8(y - 2) = -48 \\ 2(x + 4) - 4(y - 2) = -4 \end{cases}$

20 $\begin{cases} \dfrac{2}{x + 1} + \dfrac{5}{y - 1} = 12 \\ \dfrac{5}{x + 1} + \dfrac{2}{y - 1} = 9 \end{cases}$

21 Pump A can fill a swimming pool in 6 hours, and pump B can fill the pool in 4 hours. The two pumps began working together to fill an empty pool, but after 40 minutes pump B broke down, and pump A had to complete the job alone. The pool was scheduled to open 4 hours after the pumping started. Was it full by then, or did the opening have to be delayed?

22 The voltage across each coil of a transformer varies directly as the number of turns in the coil.

   a Write a proportion to describe the relationship involving V_1, V_2, T_1, and T_2.
   b V_1, the voltage across the primary coil, is 120 volts. If the primary coil consists of 200 turns and the secondary coil consists of 40 turns, what is V_2?

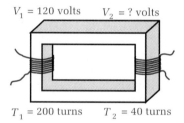

$V_1 = 120$ volts $V_2 = ?$ volts

$T_1 = 200$ turns $T_2 = 40$ turns

23 Solve the following system for (x, y).

$$\begin{cases} x^2 = 8y \\ \dfrac{16}{x} = \dfrac{8}{y} \end{cases}$$

24 Suppose that f and g are functions such that $3[f(x)] + 4[g(x)] = 2x^2 + 3x - 5$ and $2[f(x)] + 3[g(x)] = x^2 - 2x + 7$. Write formulas to represent f and g.

25 Solve the following system for (A, B, C, D).

$$\begin{cases} A + B + C + D = 15 \\ A + B + C = 9 \\ A + B + D = 3 \\ A + C + D = 14 \end{cases}$$

26 Tom, Dick, and Harry paint houses. If all three work together, they finish in five days. If Tom and Dick work together, they finish in seven days. If Tom and Harry work together, they finish in ten days. How long would it take each one alone to paint a house?

27 Suppose that $f(x) = 3x + 12$ and $g(x) = 4x - 15$. Find all values of x for which $f(x) \cdot g(x) = f(x) + g(x)$.

28 A go-cart race goes up Grand Mesa for four kilometers, across the level top for eight kilometers, and down the other side for three kilometers. Poncho Carter completed the entire race in two hours. His time going up Grand Mesa was the same as his time for the rest of the race. The sum of the time it took him to go up the mesa and the time he spent on the mesa's top was ten times the time it took him to go down the other side. How fast did Poncho go up the mesa? How fast did he go on the level top? How fast did he go down the mesa?

29 Let $f(x) = \frac{1}{x - 3}$.
a Find INVf.
b Show that $f \circ \text{INV}f(x) = x$ and that $\text{INV}f \circ f(x) = x$.
c Show graphically that the function you found in part **a** is the inverse of f.

30 For each of the following graphs, tell whether y varies inversely as x. If it does, write an equation for the inverse variation represented by the graph.

a

b

c

d

Problem Set, *continued*

In problems 31–33, solve each system.

31 $\begin{cases} \dfrac{3}{|x|} + \dfrac{5}{|y|} = 18 \\ \dfrac{2}{|x|} - \dfrac{3}{|y|} = 50 \end{cases}$

32 $\begin{cases} x = y^2 \\ x^2 + 2x = y^3 \end{cases}$

33 $\begin{cases} \dfrac{4}{x} + \dfrac{2}{y} + \dfrac{10}{z} = 2 \\ \dfrac{6}{x} + \dfrac{1}{y} + \dfrac{5}{z} = 2 \\ \dfrac{-4}{x} + \dfrac{10}{y} - \dfrac{5}{z} = -7 \end{cases}$

34 Consider the following system.

$$\begin{cases} \sqrt{x} + 2\sqrt{y} = 7 \\ 2\sqrt{x} + \sqrt{y} = 8 \end{cases}$$

  a Solve the system for $\left(\sqrt{x}, \sqrt{y}\right)$.
  b Solve the system for (x, y).

35 Suppose that the function $f(x, y) = 5x + 3y$ has as its domain the set of values (x, y) represented by the lattice points in the shaded region shown.

  a What is the greatest possible output of function f?
  b What is the least possible output of function f?

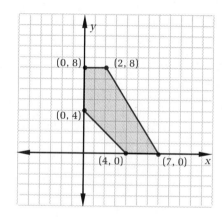

36 Solve the following system for (x, y).

$$\begin{cases} \dfrac{10}{x} + \dfrac{5}{y} = 20 \\ \dfrac{1}{4x} - \dfrac{2}{5y} = -3 \end{cases}$$

37 The following data represent the mean daily high temperatures (in degrees Fahrenheit) in Edinburgh, Scotland, for 12 months.

  43, 43, 47, 50, 55, 62, 65, 64, 60, 53, 47, 44

  a Find the mean, the mode, and the median of the data.
  b Find the range of the data.
  c Find the mean deviation of the data.

Chapter Summary

Concepts and Procedures

After studying this chapter, you should be able to
- Use systems of equations to solve problems (7.1)
- Solve systems of equations in three unknowns (7.2)
- Graph equations that contain three variables (7.2)
- Graph systems of inequalities (7.3)
- Solve inverse-variation problems (7.4)
- Graph equations of the form $xy = k$ (7.4)
- Solve systems containing nonlinear equations (7.5)
- Solve systems of equations involving rational expressions (7.6)

Vocabulary

inverse variation (7.4)
trace (7.2)

REVIEW PROBLEMS

1 Consider the parabolic function $f(x) = 2(x - h)^2 + k$, with $f(1) = 76$, $f(9) = 12$, and $h > 0$.
  a Find the values of h and k.
  b Draw the graph of $f(x)$.

2 Solve the following matrix equation for (x, y) and check your answer by matrix multiplication.
$$\begin{bmatrix} 3 & -4 \\ 2 & 5 \end{bmatrix} \begin{bmatrix} x \\ y \end{bmatrix} = \begin{bmatrix} 16 \\ 3 \end{bmatrix}$$

3 The speeds (in revolutions per minute) of two pulleys are inversely proportional to the pulleys' diameters. One pulley's diameter (D_1) is 12, and that pulley's speed (S_1) is 160 rpm. If the other pulley's diameter (D_2) is 4, what is S_2?

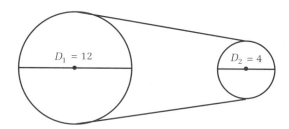

4 An airplane flies 480 miles in 3.2 hours with a tail wind. The return trip, against the same wind, takes $5\frac{1}{3}$ hours.
  a What is the speed of the plane in still air?
  b What is the wind speed?

5 The sum of the squares of two numbers is 88. The difference of the squares of the two numbers is 10. What might the two numbers be?

6 Solve the following system for (x, y).
$$\begin{cases} y = x^2 + 2x \\ y = 5x + 10 \end{cases}$$

7 Factor each expression completely.
  a $x^2 - y^2$ **b** $x^4 - y^4$

8 When Jim works in the ticket booth, he can collect $50 in 30 minutes. When Jim and Tony work together, they can collect $50 in 10 minutes. How long would it take Tony alone to collect $50?

9 Solve the following system for (x, y, z).

$$\begin{cases} x - 4y + 5z = 1 \\ -2x + 6y - 3z = 19 \\ 7x + 10y + z = 4 \end{cases}$$

10 In a swimming-and-running biathlon, participants swim for 2 kilometers and then run for 10 kilometers. Suzy Swift completed the biathlon in 2.9 hours. If she had swum at her running rate and run at her swimming rate, she would have finished in 8.7 hours. How fast can Suzy run and swim?

11 Find the equation of the axis of symmetry of the graph of each equation.

a $y = 2(x - 4)^2 + 5$ **b** $y = \frac{1}{2}(x + 7)^2 - 3$

c $y = x^2 - 6x + 5$

12 The data 2x, 2x + 7, 2x + 13, 2x + 15, and 3x − 10 have a range of 24. Find the mean of the data.

13 Consider the following system.

$$\begin{cases} x \cdot y = 36 \\ y = x \end{cases}$$

a Solve the system for (x, y).

b What do you notice about your answer to part **a?**

14 Write a system of inequalities to describe the shaded region in the diagram.

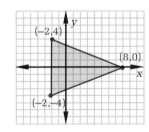

15 Pop and Zeb have gone fishing in their small motorboat. They traveled 19.5 miles downstream to a fishing hole in 3 hours. After 3 hours on the way back upstream, they have traveled only 8.7 miles.

a How much longer will it take them to return to their starting point?

b How fast is the current? What is the speed of the boat in still water?

16 Solve the matrix equation AX = B for X.

$$A = \begin{bmatrix} 6 & 9 & -1 \\ 3 & 4 & 2 \\ 0 & 5 & 8 \end{bmatrix} \quad X = \begin{bmatrix} p \\ q \\ r \end{bmatrix} \quad B = \begin{bmatrix} 16 \\ 19 \\ 55 \end{bmatrix}$$

Review Problems, *continued*

17 The product of two numbers is 12. If one number is increased by 20%, the second number must be decreased by $n\%$ for the product to remain 12. What is the value of n?

18 Factor each expression.

a $x^2 - 5x - 14$ **b** $(3x)^2 - 5(3x) - 14$

c $(x + 4)^2 - 5(x + 4) - 14$

19 Graph $\dfrac{(x-2)^2}{4} + \dfrac{(y+1)^2}{9} = 1$ and $\dfrac{(x+2)^2}{4} + \dfrac{(y-1)^2}{9} = 1$ on the same coordinate system.

20 The measure of an exterior angle of a regular polygon varies inversely as the number of the polygon's sides. We know that each exterior angle of an equilateral triangle is 120°.

a Find the constant of variation for this inverse relationship.

b Write a formula that can be used to find the measure E of an exterior angle of a polygon with n sides.

c What is the measure of each exterior angle of a dodecagon (12-sided polygon)?

21 Solve the following matrix equation for (x, y).

$$\begin{bmatrix} 2 & 9 \\ -3 & 1 \end{bmatrix} \begin{bmatrix} x \\ y \end{bmatrix} = \begin{bmatrix} -52 \\ 20 \end{bmatrix}$$

22 The diagram shows the graph of $y = f(x)$. Sketch the reflection of this graph over the line $y = x$.

23 Buns Might Candy Company sells a four-pound mixture of peanuts and cashews that is 25% cashews for $14.20. It also sells a four-pound mixture of peanuts and cashews that is 40% cashews and costs $17.50. What would you expect to pay for one pound of cashews at Buns Might?

24 The numerator of a fraction is five more than the denominator. The sum of the numerator and denominator is 73. Find the fraction.

25 The points $(-4, 6)$, $(-1, -3)$, and $(1, 21)$ are on a parabola. Find an equation of the parabola.

7

CHAPTER TEST

1 Cool Cash has 125 coins, all dimes and quarters, in a milk bottle. If he added 10 quarters and 12 dimes, the total value of the coins would be $24.45. How many dimes are in the bottle?

2 Solve the following system for (x, y, z).
$$\begin{cases} 2x - y + 3z = 13 \\ 4x + 3y - 2z = 5 \\ x - y - 4z = -4 \end{cases}$$

3 Graph the equation $3x + 2y + 4z = 12$.

In problems 4 and 5, graph the solution set of each system.

4 $\begin{cases} 2x + 3y \leq 6 \\ 2x - y \geq 4 \end{cases}$

5 $\begin{cases} y \leq x + 3 \\ y > (x - 1)^2 - 5 \end{cases}$

In problems 6–8, graph each equation.

6 $xy = -12$ **7** $xy = 9$ **8** $|xy| = 4$

9 A *power function* is a function of the form $f(x) = ax^n$, where $a \neq 0$. Newton's law of gravitation says that two objects of unit mass attract each other with a gravitational force F, which varies inversely as the square of the distance d between the objects. The constant of variation is called Newton's gravitational constant, g. Express F as a power function of d.

In problems 10 and 11, solve each system of equations for (x, y).

10 $\begin{cases} x^2 + y^2 = 32 \\ x^2 + y^2 = 4x + 4y \end{cases}$

11 $\begin{cases} xy = 2 \\ x^2 + y^2 = 5 \end{cases}$

In problems 12 and 13, solve each system for (x, y).

12 $\begin{cases} \dfrac{3}{x} - \dfrac{1}{y} = 2 \\ \dfrac{1}{x} - \dfrac{2}{y} = -10 \end{cases}$

13 $\begin{cases} \dfrac{2}{x - 5} + \dfrac{7}{y + 3} = 9 \\ \dfrac{3}{x - 5} - \dfrac{4}{2y + 6} = 1 \end{cases}$

14 Find the vertices of the region defined by the inequalities $x \geq 0$, $y \geq 2x - 2.5$, and $y \leq \frac{1}{2}x + 2$.

SHORT SUBJECT

Factoring to Solve Equations and Inequalities

Solving Equations by Factoring

In Section 4.4, you found that you could solve a number of quadratic equations by factoring and applying the Zero Product Property. Some cubic and quartic equations can be solved in a similar fashion.

Example   *Solve $5x^3 - 10x^2 + 9x - 18 = 0$ for x.*

To factor the polynomial on the left side, we group the terms in twos, remove a common factor from each group, and use the Distributive Property of Multiplication over Addition or Subtraction in reverse.

$$5x^3 - 10x^2 + 9x - 18 = 0$$

Group terms $\qquad (5x^3 - 10x^2) + (9x - 18) = 0$

Remove common factors $\qquad 5x^2(x - 2) + 9(x - 2) = 0$

Distributive Property
of Mult. over Add. $\qquad\qquad (5x^2 + 9)(x - 2) = 0$

Zero Product Property $\qquad\qquad 5x^2 + 9 = 0 \text{ or } x - 2 = 0$

$$x^2 = -\frac{9}{5} \qquad x = 2$$

Since there is no real value of x for which x^2 is negative, the only real solution of the equation is x = 2.

Example   *Solve $y^4 - 5y^2 + 4 = 0$ for y.*

We can factor the degree-four polynomial in this equation by thinking of it as a quadratic with a variable of y^2.

$$y^4 - 5y^2 + 4 = 0$$
$$(y^2)^2 - 5(y^2) + 4 = 0$$
$$(y^2 - 4)(y^2 - 1) = 0$$

Difference of squares
$$(y - 2)(y + 2)(y - 1)(y + 1) = 0$$

$$y - 2 = 0 \text{ or } y + 2 = 0 \text{ or } y - 1 = 0 \text{ or } y + 1 = 0$$

$$y = 2 \qquad y = -2 \qquad y = 1 \qquad y = -1$$

The solution set is $\{-2, -1, 1, 2\}$.

Example   Solve $y^4 + 3y^2 + 4 = 0$ for y.

This equation appears similar to the equation in the preceding example, but a little experimentation will show that the polynomial cannot be factored in the same way. To factor this polynomial, we will complete the square by adding and subtracting y^2.

$$y^4 + 3y^2 + 4 = 0$$

Add and subtract y^2
$$y^4 + 3y^2 + y^2 + 4 - y^2 = 0$$
$$(y^4 + 4y^2 + 4) - y^2 = 0$$
$$(y^2 + 2)^2 - y^2 = 0$$

Difference of squares
$$[(y^2 + 2) - y][(y^2 + 2) + y] = 0$$
$$(y^2 - y + 2)(y^2 + y + 2) = 0$$

Since neither $y^2 - y + 2 = 0$ nor $y^2 + y + 2 = 0$ has real solutions (the discriminants of both equations are negative), the original equation has no real solutions.

In Chapter 4, you were introduced to two useful factoring patterns—the perfect-square-trinomial pattern and the difference-of-squares pattern. The factoring patterns for sums and differences of perfect cubes are also useful in the solution of certain equations.

Factors of a Sum or a Difference of Two Cubes

$$x^3 + a^3 = (x + a)(x^2 - ax + a^2)$$
$$x^3 - a^3 = (x - a)(x^2 + ax + a^2)$$

Example   Solve $z^3 = -64$ for z.

$$z^3 = -64$$
$$z^3 + 64 = 0$$
$$z^3 + 4^3 = 0$$

Sum of cubes
$$(z + 4)(z^2 - 4z + 16) = 0$$

$$z + 4 = 0 \text{ or } z^2 - 4z + 16 = 0$$

$$z = -4$$

The equation $z^2 - 4z + 16 = 0$ has no real solutions, so the only solution is $z = -4$.

Solving Inequalities by Factoring

As the accompanying graph shows, the value of a polynomial $P(x)$ changes sign only at certain values of x—the values for which $P(x) = 0$. For inputs in each of the intervals bounded by these values, the value of $P(x)$ is always positive or always negative. This characteristic suggests that higher-degree polynomial inequalities can be solved by a boundary-value method similar to the methods used to solve linear inequalities.

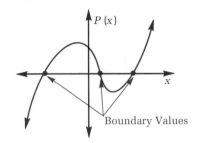

Boundary Values

Example   *Find the solution set of $x^2 + 3x > 10$.*

We first rewrite the inequality in the form $P(x) > 0$ and factor $P(x)$.

$$x^2 + 3x > 10$$
$$x^2 + 3x - 10 > 0$$
$$(x + 5)(x - 2) > 0$$

The boundary values are the values of x for which $x + 5 = 0$ or $x - 2 = 0$—that is, -5 and 2. We can plot these values on a number line, using open dots because neither value satisfies the inequality.

We choose a value from each of the three regions determined by the boundary points and test it to see whether it satisfies the original inequality. We will use -7, 0, and 5.

$x^2 + 3x$	$> 10?$
$(-7)^2 + 3(-7) = 49 - 21 = 28$	Yes
$0^2 + 3(0) = 0$	No
$5^2 + 3(5) = 25 + 15 = 40$	Yes

We shade the regions containing -7 and 5. The solution set of the inequality is $\{x : x < -5 \text{ or } x > 2\}$, as shown in the resulting graph.

The method used in the preceding example can be summarized as follows.

Boundary Algorithm for Solving Polynomial Inequalities

1. Rewrite the inequality so that one side is zero, then factor the polynomial on the other side.

2. Identify each value of the variable for which a factor equals zero. Plot these boundary values on a number line, using solid dots if the values satisfy the inequality or open dots if they do not.

3. Test a value from each region determined by the boundary points to see whether it satisfies the original inequality.

4. Shade each region in which a test value satisfies the inequality.

Sample Problems

Problem 1   Solve $3x^3 + 5x^2 - 27x - 45 = 0$ for x.

Solution

$$3x^3 + 5x^2 - 27x - 45 = 0$$

Factor by grouping

$$x^2(3x + 5) - 9(3x + 5) = 0$$
$$(x^2 - 9)(3x + 5) = 0$$

Difference of squares

$$(x - 3)(x + 3)(3x + 5) = 0$$

$$x - 3 = 0 \text{ or } x + 3 = 0 \text{ or } 3x + 5 = 0$$
$$x = 3 \qquad x = -3 \qquad x = -\frac{5}{3}$$

Problem 2   Solve $81b^3 = 24$ for b.

Solution

$$81b^3 = 24$$
$$81b^3 - 24 = 0$$

Remove common factor

$$3(27b^3 - 8) = 0$$
$$3[(3b)^3 - 2^3] = 0$$

Difference of cubes

$$3(3b - 2)(9b^2 + 6b + 4) = 0$$

Since $9b^2 + 6b + 4$ has no real zeros, the only solution is given by $3b - 2 = 0$. The solution is $b = \frac{2}{3}$.

Problem 3   Solve $x^4 - 12x^2 + 16 \leq 0$ for x.

Solution

$$x^4 - 12x^2 + 16 \leq 0$$

Add and subtract $4x^2$

$$x^4 - 12x^2 + 4x^2 + 16 - 4x^2 \leq 0$$
$$(x^4 - 8x^2 + 16) - 4x^2 \leq 0$$
$$(x^2 - 4)^2 - 4x^2 \leq 0$$

Difference of squares

$$[(x^2 - 4) - 2x][(x^2 - 4) + 2x] \leq 0$$
$$(x^2 - 2x - 4)(x^2 + 2x - 4) \leq 0$$

By applying the quadratic formula to each trinomial factor, we identify the boundary values as $-1 \pm \sqrt{5}$ and $1 \pm \sqrt{5}$, or ≈ -3.24, ≈ -1.24, ≈ 1.24, and ≈ 3.24. Each of these values satisfies the original inequality, but when we test the values -4, -2, 0, 2, and 4 (from the regions determined by the boundary values), we find that only -2 and 2 satisfy the inequality. The solution set can therefore be represented as follows.

$$-1 - \sqrt{5} \qquad 1 - \sqrt{5} \qquad -1 + \sqrt{5} \qquad 1 + \sqrt{5}$$

Problem Set

In problems 1–6, find the real zeros of each function.

1 $P(x) = (x + 6)(x - 2)(x + 2)$

2 $Q(x) = (x - 1)(x^2 - 5)(x + 3)$

3 $R(x) = (x + 4)(x + 2)(x^2 - 7)$

4 $S(x) = (x - 3)(x - 5)(x^2 + 4)$

5 $T(x) = (x - 7)(x^2 - 12x + 33)$

6 $U(x) = (x - 2)^2(x^2 - 17)$

Problem Set, *continued*

7 Graph the solution set of each equation or inequality on a number line.

   a $x^2 - 3x - 4 = 0$ **b** $x^2 - 3x - 4 < 0$ **c** $x^2 - 3x - 4 > 0$

8 Factor $y^4 - 7y^3 + 10y^2$ completely.

9 Solve $(x^2 - 4)(x^2 + 6x + 8) = 0$ for x.

In problems 10–17, factor each expression over the integers.

10 $3x^3 + 6x^2 - x - 2$ **11** $x^3 + 1$

12 $x^4 - 81$ **13** $8x^3 - 125$

14 $x^4 - 4x^2 - 5$ **15** $x^3 - 12x^2 + 36x$

16 $(x - 3)^2 - 64$ **17** $x^4 + x^2 + 25$

18 The diagram shows the graph of the function $P(x) = x^3 - x^2 - 5x + 5$.

   a Factor $P(x)$ over the integers.
   b Find the solution set of $P(x) < 0$.
   c What is the relationship between your answer to part **b** and the graph of P?

In problems 19 and 20, graph the solution set of each inequality on a number line.

19 $(x - 5)(x - 10)(x + 4) > 0$ **20** $x^3 - 4x^2 + 3x^2 - 12x \leq 0$

21 a Write an expression for the sum of the volumes of the two cubes shown.
      b Factor the expression you wrote in part **a.**

In problems 22 and 23, factor the polynomial represented by each expression.

22 $\displaystyle\sum_{n=0}^{3} 2^n x^n$ **23** $\displaystyle\sum_{n=1}^{4} (-1)^n x^{n-1}$

24 What is the solution set of $a^4 + 32 \geq 12a^2$?

In problems 25–30, solve each equation for z.

25 $z^4 + 10z^2 + 25 = 0$

26 $4z^3 + 6z^2 - 12z - 18 = 0$

27 $z^4 - 13z^2 + 36 = 0$

28 $6z^4 = 150$

29 $z^4 - 45z^2 = -4$

30 $15z^3 - 1 = 5z^2 - 3z$

31 Factor $b^4 + 3b^3 - 27b - 81$ over the integers.

32 a Write an expression for the area of the shaded region of the circle.
 b Write an expression for the area of the rectangle.
 c Show that the ratio of the area of the shaded region to the area of the rectangle is $\pi{:}1$.

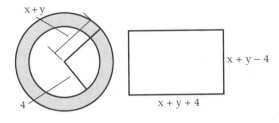

33 Let $f(x) = x^2 + ax + p$, where p is prime and a is an integer.

 a For what values of a is $f(x)$ factorable?
 b If $f(x)$ is factorable, can a be prime? Explain your answer.

34 George made graphs of the following equations. Unfortunately, he forgot to write the equations alongside their corresponding graphs. Which equation corresponds to each graph?

$y = 3x^4 - 2x^2 - 1$

$y = x^3 - 2x^2 - 8x$

$y = x^3 - 1$

$y = x^3 - 3x^2 - x + 3$

a **b** **c** **d**

In problems 35–38, solve each inequality for x. Express each solution in set notation and as a number-line graph.

35 $125x^3 - 1000 > 0$

36 $x^4 + 9x^2 + 18 \geq 0$

37 $2x^3 + 5x^2 - 8x \leq 20$

38 $x^3 - \dfrac{1}{8} + x^2 - \dfrac{1}{4} < 0$

39 Solve each of the following for y and graph each solution on a number line.

 a $|y|^2 - |y| = 0$
 b $|y|^2 - 5|y| + 4 = 0$
 c $|y|^2 - 5|y| + 4 \geq 0$

This print by Paul Klee presents a combination of realistic and imaginary forms that is symbolic of the extended number system, which includes imaginary numbers.

RATIONAL EXPONENTS

Objectives

After studying this section, you will be able to
- Apply the properties of exponents to expressions with fractional exponents
- Understand the restrictions that apply to exponential expressions with negative bases

Part One: Introduction

An Investigation of Fractional Exponents

If we look at the first-quadrant sections of the graphs of the power functions $y = x^2$, $y = x^3$, $y = x^4, \ldots$, we see that as the exponent gets larger, the graph becomes steeper and lies closer to the y-axis. The spaces between these graphs, moreover, suggest that graphs of fractional-power functions, such as $y = x^{2.5}$ and $y = x^{3.5}$, can be inserted between the graphs of the integral-power functions.

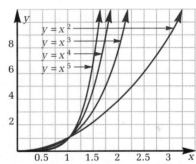

To learn more about fractional exponents, let's assume that the rules of exponents still apply and look at a particular case. For now, we will focus on nonnegative values of x.

Example   *Evaluate $9^{\frac{1}{2}}$.*

According to the Power Rule, $\left(9^{\frac{1}{2}}\right)^2 = 9^{\frac{1}{2} \cdot 2} = 9^1 = 9$. Since we know that $(\sqrt{9})^2$ is also equal to 9, we can conclude that $9^{\frac{1}{2}} = \sqrt{9}$. Therefore, the value of $9^{\frac{1}{2}}$ is 3.

This example indicates that $\left(x^{\frac{1}{2}}\right)^2 = x$. Similarly, the Power Rule tells us that $\left(x^{\frac{1}{3}}\right)^3 = x$, so $x^{\frac{1}{3}} = \sqrt[3]{x}$, the cube root of x, and $\left(x^{\frac{1}{4}}\right)^4 = x$, so $x^{\frac{1}{4}} = \sqrt[4]{x}$, and so on. In general, $x^{\frac{1}{n}} = \sqrt[n]{x}$.

We can apply this reasoning to other fractional exponents. The Product Rule implies that $\left(x^{\frac{1}{n}}\right)^m = x^{\frac{1}{n} \cdot m} = x^{\frac{m}{n}}$. This observation leads us to a general definition of rational exponentiation.

⟩⟩ *If $x \geq 0$ and m and n are positive integers, then*
$$x^{\frac{m}{n}} = \left(\sqrt[n]{x}\right)^m.$$

The number n in an expression of the form $\sqrt[n]{x}$ is called the **root index**, and x is called the **radicand**.

Example   *Evaluate $16^{\frac{5}{4}}$.*

$$16^{\frac{5}{4}}$$
$$= \left(\sqrt[4]{16}\right)^5$$
$$= 2^5$$
$$= 32$$

Exponential Expressions with Negative Bases

So far, we have looked at expressions with nonnegative bases. What happens when a negative base is raised to a fractional power?

According to the definition of rational exponentiation, $(-4)^{\frac{1}{2}} = \sqrt{-4}$, but there is no real number equal to $\sqrt{-4}$. Indeed, for any negative value of x, $x^{\frac{1}{2}}$ is not defined over the real numbers. However, $(-8)^{\frac{1}{3}} = -2$, since $(-2)^3 = -8$. In fact, whenever a negative base is raised to the third power, the result is a negative number. It follows that negative numbers will always have real cube roots.

By extension, a negative number has a real root when the root index is odd but does not have a real root when the index is even. In general, if the value of y in an expression of the form $x^{\frac{z}{y}}$ is odd, we include negative values of x, but if the value of y is even or is unspecified, we must restrict the value of x to $\{x : x \geq 0\}$.

Trying to evaluate an expression such as $(-3)^{\frac{2}{5}}$ by entering
3 $\boxed{\pm}$ $\boxed{x^y}$ .4 $\boxed{=}$ on a calculator will often produce an error message. A better way to proceed is to determine whether the result should be positive or negative, and then use a calculator to evaluate the corresponding expression with a positive base.

Example   *Evaluate each of the following expressions.*

a $(-3)^{\frac{2}{5}}$

$(-3)^{\frac{2}{5}} = \left(\sqrt[5]{-3}\right)^2$

An even power of a negative real number is a positive number.

When we enter 3 $\boxed{x^y}$ .4 $\boxed{=}$, the output is ≈ 1.55, so $(-3)^{\frac{2}{5}} \approx 1.55$.

b $(-3)^{\frac{3}{5}}$

$(-3)^{\frac{3}{5}} = \left(\sqrt[5]{-3}\right)^3$

An odd power of a negative real number is a negative number.

When we enter 3 $\boxed{x^y}$ .6 $\boxed{=}$, the output is ≈ 1.93, so $(-3)^{\frac{3}{5}} \approx -1.93$.

c $(-3)^{\frac{3}{4}}$

$(-3)^{\frac{3}{4}} = \left(\sqrt[4]{-3}\right)^3$

An even root of a negative real number is not a real number. This expression has no real equivalent.

Part Two: Sample Problems

Problem 1 Evaluate $\left(\frac{5}{3}\right)^{-3} \cdot \left(\frac{3}{5}\right)^{\frac{3}{2}}$.

Solution We can evaluate this expression in two ways.

Method 1

$$\left(\frac{5}{3}\right)^{-3} \cdot \left(\frac{3}{5}\right)^{\frac{3}{2}}$$
$$\approx 0.216(0.464758)$$
$$\approx 0.1003877$$

Method 2

$$\left(\frac{5}{3}\right)^{-3} \cdot \left(\frac{3}{5}\right)^{\frac{3}{2}}$$
$$= \left(\frac{3}{5}\right)^{3} \cdot \left(\frac{3}{5}\right)^{\frac{3}{2}}$$
$$= \left(\frac{3}{5}\right)^{\frac{9}{2}}$$
$$= 0.6^{4.5}$$
$$\approx 0.1003877$$

Simplifying the expression first (Method 2) often produces an expression that is easier to evaluate with a calculator.

Problem 2 *The temperature of an egg that has just been hard-boiled is 98°C. If this egg is put into water with a constant temperature of 18°C, we can use the formula $T(x) = 18 + 80(2.73)^{-0.28x}$ to find the temperature of the egg after x minutes in the water. What is the temperature of the egg*

a *After 5 minutes?* **b** *After 10 minutes?* **c** *After 15 minutes?*

Solution We can use a calculator to find $T(5)$, $T(10)$, and $T(15)$.

a Enter 18 $\boxed{+}$ 80 $\boxed{\times}$ 2.73 $\boxed{x^y}$ $\boxed{(}$ .28 $\boxed{\pm}$ $\boxed{\times}$ 5 $\boxed{)}$ $\boxed{=}$.
The output is $\approx$37.609, so the temperature after 5 minutes is about 38°C.

b Enter 18 $\boxed{+}$ 80 $\boxed{\times}$ 2.73 $\boxed{x^y}$ $\boxed{(}$ .28 $\boxed{\pm}$ $\boxed{\times}$ 10 $\boxed{)}$ $\boxed{=}$.
The output is $\approx$22.807, so the temperature after 10 minutes is about 23°C.

c Enter 18 $\boxed{+}$ 80 $\boxed{\times}$ 2.73 $\boxed{x^y}$ $\boxed{(}$ .28 $\boxed{\pm}$ $\boxed{\times}$ 15 $\boxed{)}$ $\boxed{=}$.
The output is $\approx$19.178, so the temperature after 15 minutes is about 19°C.

Notice that in the first 5 minutes the temperature decreases by 60°C, in the next 5 minutes it decreases by 15°C, and in the last 5 minutes it decreases by 4°C. This is an example of *exponential change*.

Part Three: Exercises and Problems

Warm-up Exercises

1 Evaluate each expression.

a $6^{\frac{1}{2}} \cdot 6^{\frac{1}{2}}$

b $4^{\frac{1}{3}} \cdot 4^{\frac{1}{3}} \cdot 4^{\frac{1}{3}}$

c $(2^8)^{\frac{1}{2}}$

d $\left(2^{\frac{1}{2}}\right)^6$

e $36^{-\frac{1}{2}}$

f $\left(\sqrt[3]{-8}\right)^2$

2 Rewrite each expression as a fractional power of x.

   a $\sqrt{x} \cdot x$ **b** $\sqrt[3]{x^2} \cdot \sqrt[4]{x}$

3 Evaluate each expression without using a calculator.

   a $\sqrt{(-3)^2}$ **b** $\sqrt[3]{8^2}$ **c** $\sqrt[3]{-1000}$

4 Use a calculator to evaluate each expression. Round your answers to the nearest hundredth.

   a -1.35^6 **b** $5200\,(1.03)^{2.5}$ **c** $2^{-5.3}$

5 Which of the lettered curves could be the graph of $y = x^{\frac{5}{4}}$?

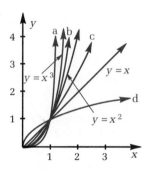

Problem Set

6 Explain how you would determine the value of $27^{\frac{5}{3}}$.

In problems 7 and 8, simplify each expression.

7 $\sqrt[3]{x^6}$ **8** $7^{1.6} \cdot 7^{0.4}$

9 Match each number with the set or sets of which it is a member.

   a -6 **i** Natural numbers
   b $\dfrac{22}{7}$ **ii** Rational numbers
                                      iii Integers
   c $\sqrt{2}$ **iv** Real numbers
   d π **v** Irrational numbers
   e $0.\overline{45}$ **vi** Whole numbers

10 Evaluate each expression.

   a $\sqrt[4]{81}$ **b** $81^{\frac{3}{4}}$ **c** $81^{-\frac{3}{4}}$

11 Find the length of $\overline{AB}$.

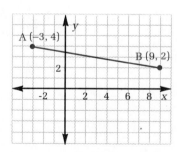

12 If one of the expressions below is chosen at random, what is the probability that it is negative? That it is undefined?

$$(-5)^{\frac{2}{3}} \qquad (-3)^{\frac{3}{4}} \qquad \sqrt[6]{(-7)^2} \qquad \left(\sqrt[6]{-7}\right)^8 \qquad (-22.2)^{\frac{5}{2}}$$

13 Consider the cube in the figure.

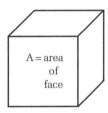

A = area of face

  a Write an expression for the volume of the cube in terms of A.

  b Calculate the cube's volume to the nearest tenth if the area of each face is 15 square centimeters.

In problems 14–17, solve each equation for *n*.

14 $\left(3^{\frac{5}{7}}\right)^n = 3$

15 $\left(\dfrac{2}{3}\right)^n = \left(\dfrac{3}{2}\right)^2$

16 $(-27)^n = 9$

17 $4\left(16^{\frac{1}{3}}\right) = 2^n$

In problems 18 and 19, evaluate each expression.

18 $16^{0.25}$

19 $25^{1.5}$

20 Suppose that $\ell(a, b)$ means "the power of a that produces an expression equal to b." For example, $\ell(3, 9) = 2$, since $3^2 = 9$; and $\ell(2, 16) = 4$, since $2^4 = 16$. Evaluate each of the following.

  a $\ell(2, 8)$ **b** $\ell(2, 64)$ **c** $\ell(4, 64)$ **d** $\ell(4, 2)$ **e** $\ell(5, 1)$

In problems 21 and 22, evaluate each expression.

21 $\left(7^{\frac{1}{2}} + 5^{\frac{1}{2}}\right)\left(7^{\frac{1}{2}} - 5^{\frac{1}{2}}\right)$

22 $4^{-\frac{2}{3}}\left(4^{\frac{2}{3}} + 4^{\frac{5}{3}}\right)$

23 Factor each expression over the integers.

  a $x^2 - 13x - 30$ **b** $y^2 - 289$

  c $3a^2 + 33a + 84$ **d** $5n^2 - 16n - 16$

24 Rewrite each expression as a rational power of x.

  a $\sqrt[3]{x^5}$ **b** $\sqrt[5]{x^{20}}$

In problems 25–28, simplify each expression.

25 $\left(8x^6y^9\right)^{\frac{2}{3}}$

26 $\left[\left(x^{\frac{2}{3}}\right)^6\left(y^{\frac{1}{3}}\right)^{12}\right]^{\frac{1}{2}}$

27 $\dfrac{3x^{-1}y}{2xy^{-1}}$

28 $\dfrac{5x^2y^7}{10x^{-2}y^{10}}$

29 Which of the following expressions are equivalent to $x^{\frac{4}{7}}$?

  a $\left(x^4\right)^{\frac{1}{7}}$ **b** $\left(x^{\frac{1}{7}}\right)^4$ **c** $\left(\sqrt[7]{x}\right)^4$

  d $\left(\sqrt[4]{x}\right)^7$ **e** $\sqrt[4]{x^7}$ **f** $\sqrt[7]{x^4}$

Problem Set, *continued*

30 Indicate whether each statement is True or False.

  a Every rational number is a real number.
  b Every irrational number is a real number.
  c The number 0 is both rational and irrational.
  d The sum of two rational numbers is always a rational number.
  e The sum of two irrational numbers is always an irrational number.

31 A pot of 90°C coffee is placed in a room with an air temperature of 30°C. The formula $T(x) = 30 + 60(2.72)^{-0.07x}$ can be used to find the temperature of the coffee x minutes after it is placed in the room.

  a Find the temperature of the coffee after 5 minutes.
  b Find the temperature of the coffee after 20 minutes.
  c To the nearest minute, how long will it take the coffee to cool to 33°C?

In problems 32 and 33, copy each equation, supplying the missing terms.

32 $x^{-12} + x^{-5} = x^{-12}(? + ?)$ **33** $x^{\frac{1}{2}} + x^{\frac{5}{2}} = x^{\frac{1}{2}}(? + ?)$

34 When the number 0.01001000100001 . . . is added to an irrational number x, the sum is rational. Find at least two possible values of x.

In problems 35 and 36, expand and simplify.

35 $\left(x^{\frac{1}{3}} + y^{\frac{1}{3}}\right)\left(x^{\frac{2}{3}} - x^{\frac{1}{3}}y^{\frac{1}{3}} + y^{\frac{2}{3}}\right)$

36 $\left(x^{\frac{1}{4}} + y^{\frac{1}{4}}\right)\left(x^{\frac{3}{4}} - x^{\frac{2}{4}}y^{\frac{1}{4}} + x^{\frac{1}{4}}y^{\frac{2}{4}} - y^{\frac{3}{4}}\right)$

37 Consider $50^{\frac{n}{n+1}}$, where n is a positive integer.

  a Compute decimal approximations of $50^{\frac{1}{2}}$, $50^{\frac{2}{3}}$, $50^{\frac{3}{4}}$, $50^{\frac{4}{5}}$, $50^{\frac{100}{101}}$, and $50^{\frac{10,000}{10,001}}$.

  b What seems to happen to the value of $50^{\frac{n}{n+1}}$ as the value of n increases?

38 Table salt (NaCl) is a compound consisting of sodium ions (Na^+) and chloride ions (Cl^-) bound in a cubic arrangement.

  a Find the volume of the cube pictured.
  b How many such cubes would be needed to make a grain of table salt (0.1 cubic millimeter)?
  c About how many sodium atoms does a grain of salt contain? (Hint: The answer is not four times your answer in part **b**.)

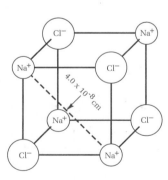

SOLVING RADICAL EQUATIONS

Objectives

After studying this section, you will be able to
- Solve equations that contain square roots
- Solve equations that contain rational exponents

Part One: Introduction

Equations That Contain a Square Root

The strategy we use to solve equations that contain radical expressions is similar to the strategy you use to solve linear equations.

Strategy for Solving Radical Equations
1. Isolate the radical expression on one side of the equation.
2. Square both sides to eliminate the radical.
3. Solve the resulting equation for the variable.
4. Check the solutions.

As you will see, checking is an essential step in solving equations that contain radicals or fractional exponents.

Example   *Solve $9 + 2\sqrt{4 + 3q} = 29$ for q.*

$$9 + 2\sqrt{4 + 3q} = 29$$

Add -9 to each side $2\sqrt{4 + 3q} = 20$

Divide by 2 to isolate the radical $\sqrt{4 + 3q} = 10$

Square both sides $4 + 3q = 100$

Solve for q $3q = 96$

$$q = 32$$

Check

Left Side

$$9 + 2\sqrt{4 + 3q}$$
$$= 9 + 2\sqrt{4 + 3(32)}$$
$$= 9 + 2\sqrt{100}$$
$$= 9 + 20$$
$$= 29$$

Right Side
$$= 29$$

If $q = 32$, the sides are equal, so the answer checks.

Example   *Solve* $m + \sqrt{m} = 90$ *for m.*

Method 1 $\qquad\qquad\qquad\qquad m + \sqrt{m} = 90$

Isolate the radical $\qquad\qquad\qquad\qquad \sqrt{m} = 90 - m$

Square both sides $\qquad\qquad\qquad\qquad m = (90 - m)^2$

$\qquad\qquad\qquad\qquad\qquad\qquad\qquad\quad m = 8100 - 180m + m^2$

$\qquad\qquad\qquad\qquad\qquad\qquad\qquad\quad 0 = 8100 - 181m + m^2$

Factor $\qquad\qquad\qquad\qquad\qquad\qquad\quad 0 = (81 - m)(100 - m)$

Zero Product Property $\qquad\quad m = 81 \text{ or } m = 100$

Check

$m = 81$ $\qquad\qquad\qquad\qquad\qquad\qquad\quad m = 100$

Left Side	**Right Side**	**Left Side**	**Right Side**
$m + \sqrt{m}$	$= 90$	$m + \sqrt{m}$	$= 90$
$= 81 + \sqrt{81}$		$= 100 + \sqrt{100}$	
$= 81 + 9$		$= 100 + 10$	
$= 90$		$= 110$	

If $m = 81$, the sides are equal. If $m = 100$, the sides are not equal. Therefore, $m = 81$ is the only correct answer. One reason why it is essential to check answers is that squaring both sides of an equation may introduce an ***extraneous root***—an apparent solution that does not in fact satisfy the original equation.

Method 2 $\qquad\qquad\qquad\qquad m + \sqrt{m} = 90$

Let $p = \sqrt{m}$ $\qquad\qquad\qquad\qquad\quad p^2 + p = 90$

$\qquad\qquad\qquad\qquad\qquad\qquad\quad p^2 + p - 90 = 0$

Factor $\qquad\qquad\qquad\qquad\qquad (p - 9)(p + 10) = 0$

Zero Product Property $\qquad\qquad p = 9 \text{ or } p = -10$

Substitute $\sqrt{m}$ for p $\qquad\quad \sqrt{m} = 9 \text{ or } \sqrt{m} = -10$

Since $\sqrt{m}$ cannot be negative, $\sqrt{m} = 9$—that is, $m = 81$—is the only solution. Check as before to ensure that 81 is the correct answer.

Note If the rewritten equation cannot be solved by factoring, use the quadratic formula.

Equations That Contain Rational Exponents

We solve equations that contain rational exponents in much the same way as those containing radicals, isolating the exponential term on one side of the equation and raising both sides to the power of the reciprocal of the exponent.

Example   *Solve* $(2c + 1)^{\frac{3}{4}} = 8$ *for c.*

$$(2c + 1)^{\frac{3}{4}} = 8$$

Raise both sides to the $\frac{4}{3}$ power $\qquad\left[(2c + 1)^{\frac{3}{4}}\right]^{\frac{4}{3}} = 8^{\frac{4}{3}}$

Use the Product Rule $\qquad\qquad (2c + 1)^{\frac{3}{4} \cdot \frac{4}{3}} = 8^{\frac{4}{3}}$

$$2c + 1 = 16$$

$$c = 7.5$$

Check

Left Side

$$(2c + 1)^{\frac{3}{4}}$$
$$= [2(7.5) + 1]^{\frac{3}{4}}$$
$$= 16^{\frac{3}{4}}$$
$$= 2^3$$
$$= 8$$

Right Side

$$= 8$$

If $c = 7.5$, the sides are equal, so the answer checks.

Example

Solve $5 + (j^2 - 1)^{\frac{-2}{3}} = 21$ for j.

$$5 + (j^2 - 1)^{-\frac{2}{3}} = 21$$

Isolate the exponential term

$$(j^2 - 1)^{-\frac{2}{3}} = 16$$

Raise both sides to
the inverse power

$$(j^2 - 1)^{\left(-\frac{2}{3}\right)\left(-\frac{3}{2}\right)} = 16^{-\frac{3}{2}}$$

Use absolute-value symbols,
since the inverse power has
an even denominator

$$|j^2 - 1| = \frac{1}{64}$$

$$j^2 - 1 = \frac{1}{64} \text{ or } j^2 - 1 = -\frac{1}{64}$$

$$j^2 = \frac{65}{64} \text{ or } j^2 = \frac{63}{64}$$

$$j = \frac{\sqrt{65}}{8} \text{ or } j = -\frac{\sqrt{65}}{8} \text{ or } j = \frac{\sqrt{63}}{8} \text{ or } j = -\frac{\sqrt{63}}{8}$$

$$j \approx 1.0078 \text{ or } j \approx -1.0078 \text{ or } j \approx 0.9922 \text{ or } j \approx -0.9922$$

Let's check an approximate answer, 1.0078, and the corresponding
exact value, $\frac{\sqrt{65}}{8}$.

Check

Left Side

$$5 + \left[\left(\frac{\sqrt{65}}{8}\right)^2 - 1\right]^{-\frac{2}{3}}$$
$$= 5 + \left(\frac{65}{64} - 1\right)^{-\frac{2}{3}}$$
$$= 5 + \left(\frac{1}{64}\right)^{-\frac{2}{3}}$$
$$= 5 + 16$$
$$= 21$$

Right Side

$$= 21$$

Left Side

$$5 + (1.0078^2 - 1)^{-\frac{2}{3}}$$
$$= 5 + (1.01566084 - 1)^{-\frac{2}{3}}$$
$$= 5 + 0.01566084^{-\frac{2}{3}}$$
$$= 5 + 15.9755799$$
$$= 20.9755799$$

Right Side

$$= 21$$

When we check the approximation 1.0078, the result is close to, but
not equal to, 21. In many cases, it is difficult to determine whether
such a discrepancy is due to rounding or indicates an incorrect
solution. It is therefore better to check exact solutions whenever
possible. Checking will verify that the other three results are also
solutions. The solution set is $\left\{\frac{\sqrt{65}}{8}, -\frac{\sqrt{65}}{8}, \frac{\sqrt{63}}{8}, -\frac{\sqrt{63}}{8}\right\}$.

Part Two: Sample Problems

Problem 1 Solve $3\sqrt{v^3 - v + 1} + v = 4\sqrt{v^3 - v + 1}$ for v.

Solution

$$3\sqrt{v^3 - v + 1} + v = 4\sqrt{v^3 - v + 1}$$

Isolate the radical
$$v = \sqrt{v^3 - v + 1}$$

Square both sides
$$v^2 = v^3 - v + 1$$
$$0 = v^3 - v^2 - v + 1$$

Factor by grouping
$$0 = v^2(v - 1) - 1(v - 1)$$
$$0 = (v^2 - 1)(v - 1)$$
$$0 = (v + 1)(v - 1)^2$$
$$v = -1 \text{ or } v = 1$$

Check
If $v = -1$, the left side is equal to 2 and the right side is equal to 4, so $v = -1$ is not a solution. If $v = 1$, both sides are equal to 4, so $v = 1$ is the only solution.

Problem 2 Solve $\sqrt{z + 9} + \sqrt{z} = 9$ for z.

Solution

$$\sqrt{z + 9} + \sqrt{z} = 9$$

Isolate one radical term
$$\sqrt{z + 9} = 9 - \sqrt{z}$$

Square both sides
$$z + 9 = 81 - 18\sqrt{z} + z$$

Isolate the remaining radical term
$$18\sqrt{z} = 72$$
$$\sqrt{z} = 4$$

Square both sides
$$z = 16$$

Check

Left Side
$$\sqrt{z + 9} + \sqrt{z}$$
$$= \sqrt{16 + 9} + \sqrt{16}$$
$$= 5 + 4$$
$$= 9$$

Right Side
$$= 9$$

If $z = 16$, the sides are equal, so the answer checks.

Part Three: Exercises and Problems

Warm-up Exercises

1 Solve for y.

  a $\sqrt{y} = 9$ **b** $\sqrt{y + 1} = 3$ **c** $2\sqrt{y + 3} = 5$

2 Solve for k.

  a $\sqrt{k + 1} = 10$ **b** $\sqrt{k} = -15$

3 Solve for p.

a $\sqrt{p} = -5$ **b** $\sqrt[3]{p} = 5$ **c** $\sqrt[3]{p} = -5$

4 Solve for x.

a $x^{\frac{1}{3}} = 2$ **b** $x^{\frac{1}{3}} = \sqrt[3]{5}$

c $2\sqrt{x} + 3 = 5$ **d** $\sqrt[3]{x + 2} - 3 = 4$

5 If the area of the larger rectangle is 91 square feet, what is the area of the smaller rectangle?

Problem Set

6 Find a if $\left(x^{\frac{3}{7}}\right)^a = x$.

7 Find b if $\left(y^{-\frac{3}{4}}\right)^b = y$.

8 Refer to the diagram. Find the value of x for which $AB = \sqrt{58}$.

9 Suppose that $\ell(p, q)$ means "the power of p that produces an expression equal to q." For example, $\ell(16, 2) = \frac{1}{4}$, since $16^{\frac{1}{4}} = 2$. Evaluate each of the following.

a $\ell\left(2, \dfrac{1}{16}\right)$ **b** $\ell(x, x)$ **c** $\ell(10, 1000)$

d $\ell(4, 8)$ **e** $\ell(2, 8)$ **f** $\ell(x, x^5)$

In problems 10 and 11, solve for x.

10 $(2x + 1)^{\frac{2}{3}} = 4$ **11** $\sqrt[3]{1 - 2x} = -3$

12 Refer to the circle.

a Find the radius r if the area of the circle is 36π.

b Find the radius r if the area of the circle is 36.

Problem Set, *continued*

13 If the volume of the sphere shown is 1773, what is the value of m?

$$V = \frac{4}{3}\pi r^3$$

In problems 14–19, solve for x.

14 $x^{\frac{1}{5}} = 2$

15 $x^{\frac{1}{2}} = 16$

16 $x^{\frac{1}{7}} = 1.64$

17 $x^{0.15} = 2$

18 $x^{\frac{5}{6}} = 32$

19 $x^{-\frac{3}{4}} = 8$

In problems 20–23, write each expression in standard radical form.

20 $\sqrt{54}$

21 $\dfrac{\sqrt{3}}{\sqrt{5}}$

22 $\sqrt{288}$

23 $\dfrac{10}{\sqrt{2}}$

In problems 24–27, solve for y.

24 $2^y = 32$

25 $8^y = 2$

26 $27^y = 9$

27 $x^y = \sqrt[5]{x^3}$

28 Find the value of n for which the distance from the point A(n, 5) to the point B(1, −3) is 17.

In problems 29–31, determine side length x for each triangle.

29

30

31
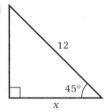

32 Solve $\sqrt{x^2 + 1} = x - 3$ for x.

33 Determine the height of an equilateral triangle that has a perimeter of 18 centimeters.

34 Determine the perimeter of the square shown.

35 Solve $\left(\sqrt{n + 1} - 5\right)\left(\sqrt{n + 1} - 7\right) = 0$ for n.

36 If the volume of the box shown is 66 cubic centimeters, what is the area of the right face to the nearest square centimeter?

37 Estimate the value of $\dfrac{50}{\sqrt{48}}$ without using a calculator.

38 Write each expression in standard radical form.

  a $\sqrt{16x^{16}}$ **b** $\sqrt{25x^{25}}$ **c** $\sqrt{32x^{12}}$ **d** $\sqrt{24x^{10}y^7}$

39 Determine, to the nearest hundredth, the length of the hypotenuse of the triangle.

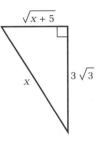

40 Find the geometric mean between $5\sqrt{2} + 1$ and $5\sqrt{2} - 1$. (Recall that the geometric mean between two positive numbers a and b is equal to $\pm\sqrt{ab}$.)

41 Explain why $\left(\sqrt[4]{x}\right)^2 = \sqrt{x}$.

42 Use the distance formula to prove that the points $(-2, 3)$, $(0, 6)$, and $(3, 4)$ are vertices of a right triangle.

43 On your calculator is a key labeled $\boxed{\text{log}}$. To apply the log function to a numerical input, enter the number and then press the $\boxed{\text{log}}$ key.

  a Evaluate log 100.   **b** Evaluate log 10^2.
  c Evaluate log 10^5.   **d** Evaluate log $\sqrt{10}$.
  e What do you suppose *log* means?

44 If the area of the rectangle shown is 15 square microns, what are the dimensions of the rectangle?

In problems 45–48, solve for x.

45 $x + \sqrt{x} = 30$ **46** $x - 8\sqrt{x} + 15 = 0$

47 $x + 4\sqrt{x} + 3 = 0$ **48** $x = 5\sqrt{x} + 24$

49 Evaluate $\left(12^{\frac{1}{4}} + 6^{\frac{1}{4}}\right)\left(12^{\frac{1}{4}} - 6^{\frac{1}{4}}\right)\left(12^{\frac{1}{2}} + 6^{\frac{1}{2}}\right)$.

50 Consider the equation $S = 1 + 3 + 3^2 + 3^3 + \ldots + 3^{10}$.

  a What equation do you obtain if you multiply each side of this equation by 3?
  b What is the result of subtracting the given equation from the equation you obtained in part **a**?
  c Use your answer to part **b** to solve for S.

Problem Set, *continued*

51 Solve for x.

    a $x^{\frac{2}{3}} + x^{\frac{1}{3}} - 12 = 0$
                         b $-\sqrt{x^2 + 9x + 3} = x + 5$

52 Factor $x^{2n+1} + 5x^{n+1} + 4x$.

In problems 53 and 54, solve for x.

53 $(x - 4)^{-2}(x + 2)^3(x - 3)^2 = 0$
                      54 $15x^{-2} - 16x^{-1} = 15$

55 Suppose that $2^a = 5$ and $2^b = 6$. Determine, in terms of a and b, the value of x for which $2^x = 15$.

56 Suppose that $R = \sqrt{\frac{(s - a)(s - b)(s - c)}{s}}$ and
$A = \sqrt{s(s - a)(s - b)(s - c)}$.

    a What is the value of A if $R = 3$ and $s = 18$?
    b What is the value of R if $A = 24$ and $s^2 = 144$?

HISTORICAL SNAPSHOT

WHEN IS A NUMBER NOT REAL?
The complex number system

representation of a complex number and that of a

Why do we bother with complex numbers, since they are based on an imaginary quantity, the square root of −1? If mathematics arose out of real needs—to count herds, measure fields, and keep accounts—then what factors created a need for complex numbers?

While the earliest need for these numbers is unclear, we do know that around A.D. 100, Hero of Alexandria identified numbers that were the even roots of negative numbers. Girolamo Cardano (1501–1576) included calculations using imaginary numbers in his *Ars Magna* (Great Art). Leonhard Euler (1707–1783) gave us the notation *i* for the square root of −1 used in representing complex numbers.

In 1806, the Swiss mathematician Jean Robert Argand developed a means of graphically representing complex numbers. In the Argand diagram, one axis represents the imaginary component of a number, and the other axis, the real component. The similarity between the vector led to the discovery that complex numbers could be used to solve problems related to alternating electrical current. The discovery and use of alternating current has made possible most of our present-day uses of electricity, in powering everything from household appliances to sound systems, from lighting to food processors and computers.

INTRODUCTION TO COMPLEX NUMBERS

Objectives

After studying this section, you will be able to
- Identify pure imaginary numbers
- Perform operations on pure imaginary numbers
- Identify complex numbers
- Determine the conjugate of a complex number

Part One: Introduction

Pure Imaginary Numbers

Quadratic equations such as $x^2 - 6x - 16 = 0$ have two distinct real roots—in this case, $x = 8$ and $x = -2$. Other quadratics, such as $x^2 - 4x + 4 = 0$, have two equal real roots—in this case, $x = 2$. Some quadratic equations, however, have no real roots.

Example   *Solve the following equations for x.*

a $x^2 - 6x + 16 = 0$ **b** $x^2 + 4x + 5 = 0$

Let's use two different techniques to solve these equations.

The Quadratic Formula

$$x^2 - 6x + 16 = 0$$
$$x = \frac{6 \pm \sqrt{36 - 64}}{2}$$
$$x = \frac{6 \pm \sqrt{-28}}{2}$$

Complete the Square

$$x^2 + 4x + 5 = 0$$
$$x^2 + 4x + 4 = -5 + 4$$
$$(x + 2)^2 = -1$$
$$x + 2 = \pm \sqrt{-1}$$
$$x = -2 \pm \sqrt{-1}$$

No real number has a negative square, so the square roots of numbers such as -28 and -1 are not real numbers. These equations have no real roots.

In order to work with the solutions of equations such as those in the preceding example, mathematicians use the symbol i to represent the nonreal quantity $\sqrt{-1}$. Since $i = \sqrt{-1}$, we can say that $i^2 = -1$ and define the nonreal number i such that $i = \sqrt{-1}$ and $i^2 = -1$. If a is a positive real number, then $\sqrt{-a} = i\sqrt{a}$.

Using these definitions, we can evaluate expressions that contain square roots of negative numbers. For example,

$$\sqrt{-4} = i\sqrt{4} = 2i \qquad\qquad \sqrt{-100} = i\sqrt{100} = 10i$$
$$(2i)^2 = -4 \qquad\qquad\qquad (10i)^2 = -100$$

The Arithmetic of Pure Imaginary Numbers

Numbers of the form ki, where k is real and nonzero—such as $6i$, $\sqrt{5}i$, and $-12.5i$—form a set of nonreal numbers known as the **pure imaginary numbers**. Do the properties of real numbers also apply to pure imaginary numbers? Let's look at the property stating that $\sqrt{x}\sqrt{y} = \sqrt{xy}$, where $x \geq 0$ and $y \geq 0$, and see whether it applies to roots of negative as well as positive real numbers.

If this property holds for negative radicands, then

$$\sqrt{-9}\sqrt{-4} = \sqrt{-9(-4)} = \sqrt{36} = 6$$

but by definition,

$$\sqrt{-9}\sqrt{-4} = 3i \cdot 2i = 6i^2 = -6$$

This is one property of radicals that does not extend to radical expressions that represent pure imaginary numbers. In fact, neither do the other properties of radicals. It is therefore important to rewrite such expressions in the form ki before performing operations.

Example   *Simplify each expression.*

a $\sqrt{-2}\sqrt{-8}$

$\sqrt{-2}\sqrt{-8}$

$= \sqrt{2}\sqrt{-1}\sqrt{8}\sqrt{-1}$

$= \sqrt{2}i \cdot \sqrt{8}i$

$= \sqrt{16}i^2$

$= 4(-1)$

$= -4$

b $\sqrt{\dfrac{-4}{9}}$

$\sqrt{\dfrac{-4}{9}}$

$= \sqrt{\dfrac{4}{9}}\sqrt{-1}$

$= \dfrac{2}{3}i$

c $\sqrt{\dfrac{24}{-25}}$

$\sqrt{\dfrac{24}{-25}}$

$= \sqrt{\dfrac{24}{25}}\sqrt{-1}$

$= \dfrac{2\sqrt{6}}{5}i$

Example   *Simplify each expression.*

a $2i + 5i - 9i$

$\quad 2i + 5i - 9i$

$= -2i$

b $(5i)(-5i)$

$\quad (5i)(-5i)$

$= -25i^2$

$= -25(-1)$

$= 25$

c $\sqrt{-16} - \sqrt{-9}$

$\quad \sqrt{-16} - \sqrt{-9}$

$= i\sqrt{16} - i\sqrt{9}$

$= 4i - 3i$

$= i$

Complex Numbers

Let's look again at the two quadratic equations with nonreal roots we saw at the beginning of this section. We can now simplify the roots of these equations.

$$x^2 - 6x + 16 = 0 \qquad\qquad x^2 + 4x + 5 = 0$$

$$x = \frac{6 \pm \sqrt{-28}}{2} \qquad\qquad x = -2 \pm \sqrt{-1}$$

$$= \frac{6 \pm \sqrt{28}i}{2} \qquad\qquad = -2 \pm i$$

$$= \frac{6 \pm 2\sqrt{7}i}{2}$$

$$= 3 \pm \sqrt{7}i$$

These roots are examples of **complex numbers.** A number that can be expressed in the form $a + bi$, where $i = \sqrt{-1}$ and a and b are real numbers, is called a **complex number.**

The term a in a complex number $a + bi$ is known as the number's **real part,** and the term bi is known as the number's **imaginary part.** Both the real numbers and the pure imaginary numbers are subsets of the complex-number system. For example, we can think of 7 as $7 + 0i$, and we can think of $3i$ as $0 + 3i$.

Complex Conjugates

For every complex number there exists another complex number called its **conjugate.** The **conjugate** of a complex number $a + bi$ is $a - bi$.

Complex Number	Real Part	Imaginary Part	Conjugate
$-6 + 2i$	-6	$2i$	$-6 - 2i$
$-4i$	0	$-4i$	$4i$
10	10	$0i$	10
$5 - 2i$	5	$-2i$	$5 + 2i$
$3i - 7$	-7	$3i$	$-7 - 3i$

Conjugates play an important role in the arithmetic of complex numbers, as you will see in the next section.

Part Two: Sample Problems

Problem 1   Simplify $\frac{2}{3i}$.

Solution   Although this expression is in a simple form, pure imaginary numbers are usually written in the form ki, where k is a nonzero real number. We can rewrite $\frac{2}{3i}$ in this form by multiplying both the numerator and the denominator by i.

$$\frac{2}{3i} = \frac{2}{3i} \cdot \frac{i}{i}$$

$$= \frac{2i}{3i^2}$$

$$= \frac{2i}{3(-1)}$$

$$= -\frac{2}{3}i$$

Problem 2 Factor $x^2 + 36$ *over the complex numbers.*

Solution Since we can now interpret square roots of negative numbers, we can rewrite this sum of two squares as a difference of two squares and factor it accordingly.

$$x^2 + 36$$
$$= x^2 - (-36)$$
$$= x^2 - (6i)^2$$
$$= (x + 6i)(x - 6i)$$

Problem 3 *Solve $x^2 + 25 = 0$ for x.*

Solution

$$x^2 + 25 = 0$$
$$x^2 = -25$$

Take the square root of each side
$$x = \pm\sqrt{-25}$$
$$x = \pm 5i$$

The solutions are $x = 5i$ and $x = -5i$. We also could have solved this equation by factoring $x^2 + 25$ into the expression $(x + 5i)(x - 5i)$ and using the Zero Product Property to determine that $x = \pm 5i$.

Part Three: Exercises and Problems

Warm-up Exercises

1 Copy and complete the following table.

Complex Number	Real Part	Imaginary Part	Conjugate
2 + 5i			
3 − 4i			
−2 + 7i			
5 − 4i			
9i + 3			
−6 − 5i			
−4i			
16			

2 Simplify each expression.

a $\sqrt{-64}$

b $-\sqrt{-25}$

c $-\sqrt{-4} + \sqrt{-9}$

d $\sqrt{\dfrac{-9}{25}}$

e $\sqrt{-12}$

f $\sqrt{-3}\sqrt{-3}$

g $\sqrt{\dfrac{-1}{4}}$

h $3i \cdot 5i$

i $(7i)^2$

3 Does calling the number *i* imaginary mean that such a number does not exist?

4 Simplify each expression.

a $\dfrac{1}{i}$ **b** $\dfrac{-1}{i}$ **c** $\dfrac{2}{i}$ **d** $\dfrac{-2}{i}$

5 Multiply $\begin{bmatrix} i & 0 \\ 0 & i \end{bmatrix}\begin{bmatrix} i & 0 \\ 0 & i \end{bmatrix}$.

Problem Set

6 Simplify each expression.

a $-\sqrt{25}$ **b** $\sqrt{-20}$ **c** $-\sqrt{-40}$ **d** $2\sqrt{-36}$

7 Rewrite each expression in the form ki.

a $\dfrac{4}{2i}$ **b** $\dfrac{-9}{3i}$ **c** $\dfrac{-5}{-4i}$

8 Find the distance between O and A.

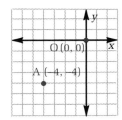

9 Explain why $i^4 = 1$.

10 Simplify each expression.

a $\sqrt{\dfrac{-25}{16}}$ **b** $-\sqrt{\dfrac{-25}{16}}$ **c** $\left(\sqrt{-4}\right)^2$

11 Find the conjugate of each number.

a $i(2i - 7)$ **b** $4i + 3$ **c** $7 - i^2$

12 If a number is selected at random from the set
$\{-6i^2, 8i, -4, -\sqrt{-4}, 8\sqrt{-1}i, -\sqrt{9}\}$, what is the probability that
the number is a pure imaginary number?

13 Find each product.

a $(x + 3i)(x - 3i)$ **b** $(x + i)(x - i)$ **c** $(x + i)(x + i)$

14 Use the graph of $y = f(x) = x^2 - 4$ to
help you sketch the graph of each of the
following equations.

a $y = g(x) = f(2x)$
b $y = h(x) = f(x - 3)$
c $y = s(x) = f(x) + 5$
d $y = t(x) = \frac{1}{2}[f(x)] + 1$

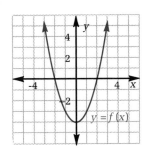

Problem Set, *continued*

15 Factor each expression over the complex numbers.

    a $y^2 + 4$ **b** $9 + 4x^2$

16 Solve for x.

    a $x^2 = 25$ **b** $x^2 = -36$

    c $x^2 - 49 = 0$ **d** $x^2 + 49 = 0$

17 Simplify each expression.

    a $4\sqrt{-3}\sqrt{-12}$ **b** $-2i + 6i - 7i$ **c** $-\left(\sqrt{-3}\right)^2$

    d $\left(\sqrt{-8}\right)^2$ **e** $2i\left(4i + 3\sqrt{2}i\right)$ **f** $\sqrt{2}\left(\sqrt{-8} - \sqrt{-27}\right)$

18 Tom said that $\sqrt{-\frac{1}{9}} = \frac{\sqrt{1}}{\sqrt{-9}} = \frac{1}{3i} = \frac{1}{3i} \cdot \frac{i}{i} = \frac{i}{-3}$.

    Marianne said that $\sqrt{-\frac{1}{9}} = \frac{\sqrt{-1}}{\sqrt{9}} = \frac{i}{3}$. Ezra said that both Tom and Marianne had done the work wrong. Who was right, and why?

19 Multiply $\begin{bmatrix} 2i & 3i \\ -i & 4i \end{bmatrix}\begin{bmatrix} i & 0 \\ 0 & i \end{bmatrix}$.

20 If one of the following equations is selected at random, what is the probability that its graph is a hyperbola?

    a $9x^2 - 4y^2 = 36$ **b** $\left(\frac{x}{3}\right)^2 = \left(\frac{y}{2}\right)^2 + 1$ **c** $y^2 - \frac{x^2}{9} = 1$

    d $x^2 - y^2 = 16$ **e** $(x - y)(x + y) = 25$ **f** $\frac{x^2}{4} + \frac{y^2}{9} = 1$

21 Match each number with an equivalent expression.

    a 4   **i** $(-2i)^2$

    b $4i$ **ii** $-(2i)^2$

    c -4 **iii** $\frac{12}{3i}$

    d $-4i$ **iv** $\sqrt{-16}$

22 Factor each expression over the complex numbers.

    a $x^2 - 25$ **b** $x^2 + 25$ **c** $4x^2 - 49$

    d $4x^2 + 49$ **e** $4x^2 - 16$ **f** $4x^2 + 16$

23 What, in terms of a, is the volume of the cone produced by rotating the shaded triangle about the x-axis?

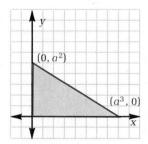

24 Explain why $i^{-1} = -i$.

25 Simplify each expression.
    a $\sqrt{-0.04} + \sqrt{-0.09}$ **b** $\sqrt{-6.25}$
    c $6i(-6i)$ **d** $2i\left(3i - \sqrt{2}i\right)$

In problems 26–30, solve for x.

26 $x^2 + 7 = 0$ **27** $x^2 + 12 = 0$ **28** $4x^2 + 4x = 0$
29 $x^2 + 8x + 17 = 0$ **30** $x^2 - 10x + 29 = 0$

31 Find a complex number $x + yi$ such that the value of x is twice the value of y and $2x - 3y = 5$.

32 Let $f(x) = \dfrac{x(x - 5)(x + 6)}{x(x - 4)(x - 5)(x + 1)}$.
    a What are the equations of the vertical asymptotes of the graph of f?
    b What are the x-coordinates of the holes in the graph?

In problems 33–37, solve for x.

33 $-2x = 16i$ **34** $-2ix = 16i$ **35** $ix = 12$
36 $3i + 12x = 4x - 15i$ **37** $12 - 3ix = 2ix - 8$

38 Solve each system for (x, y).
    a $\begin{cases} x + 2y = 3i \\ x - 2y = i \end{cases}$ **b** $\begin{cases} 2x + yi = 4 \\ 3x - yi = 1 \end{cases}$

39 **a** Write an equation with roots $10i$ and $-10i$.
    b Write an equation with roots 0, $5i$, and $-5i$.

40 Find the sum and the product of the roots of $x^2 - 8x + 9 = 0$.

41 The area of an ellipse is equal to πab, where a is half the length of the major axis and b is half the length of the minor axis. Find the areas of the base and the elliptical cross section of the cylinder shown.

42 Solve $x^3 + 100x = 0$ for x.

43 If 3 is a root of $x^3 - 3x^2 + 4x - 12 = 0$, what are the other two roots?

In problems 44 and 45, solve for x.

44 $x^4 + 13x^2 + 36 = 0$ **45** $(3^x)^2 - 12(3^x) + 27 = 0$

ALGEBRA OF COMPLEX NUMBERS

$$(3 + 2i)(2 - i) = 8 + i$$

Objectives

After studying this section, you will be able to

- Identify equal complex numbers
- Perform operations on complex numbers

Part One: Introduction

Equal Complex Numbers

What does it mean to say that two complex numbers are equal? The complex numbers $a + bi$ and $c + di$ (where a, b, c, and d are real) are equal if and only if their real parts are equal ($a = c$) and their imaginary parts are equal ($bi = di$).

One reason for expressing complex numbers in the form $a + bi$, known as **standard complex form**, is to make comparison easier. Thus, $2 + 7i = \frac{6}{3} + \sqrt{49}i$, since $2 = \frac{6}{3}$ and $7i = \sqrt{49}i$. However, $2 + 7i \neq 7 + 2i$ because $2 \neq 7$ and $7i \neq 2i$.

Example Find a pair of real numbers (x, y) for which $6y + 2xi = -30 + 18i$.

Each side of the equation represents a complex number. We can use the definition of equal complex numbers to solve for (x, y).

Equal Real Parts	**Equal Imaginary Parts**
$6y = -30$	$2x = 18$
$y = -5$	$x = 9$

Thus, $(x, y) = (9, -5)$.

The Arithmetic of Complex Numbers

Arithmetic operations can be performed on complex numbers in much the same way that they are performed on real monomials and binomials.

> **To find the sum of two complex numbers, add their real parts and add their imaginary parts.**

For example, $(3 + 7i) + (-8 + 4i) = -5 + 11i$

> **To find the difference of two complex numbers, subtract their real parts and subtract their imaginary parts.**

For example, $(2 - 6i) - (4 - 9i) = 2 - 6i - 4 + 9i$
$$= -2 + 3i$$

> **To find the product of two complex numbers, multiply them as you would monomials or binomials.**

For example, $(2 + 3i)(4 - 5i) = 8 - 10i + 12i - 15i^2$
$$= 8 - 10i + 12i - 15(-1)$$
$$= 8 - 10i + 12i + 15$$
$$= 23 + 2i$$

> **To find the quotient of two complex numbers, multiply the numerator and the denominator by the conjugate of the denominator.**

For example, $\dfrac{2 - 3i}{3 - 4i} = \dfrac{2 - 3i}{3 - 4i} \cdot \dfrac{3 + 4i}{3 + 4i}$
$$= \dfrac{6 + 8i - 9i - 12i^2}{9 + 12i - 12i - 16i^2}$$
$$= \dfrac{18 - i}{25}$$
$$= \dfrac{18}{25} - \dfrac{1}{25}i$$

This method of finding a quotient is based on the fact that the product of a complex number and its conjugate is always a real number. Can you prove that this is so?

Example *Simplify each expression.*

a $2(3 - 7i) - 6(-2 + 5i)$
$2(3 - 7i) - 6(-2 + 5i) = 6 - 14i + 12 - 30i$
$$= 18 - 44i$$

b $(-5 + 4i)(-5 - 4i)$
$(-5 + 4i)(-5 - 4i) = 25 + 20i - 20i - 16i^2$
$$= 25 + 20i - 20i - 16(-1)$$
$$= 41$$

Notice once again that the product of a complex number and its conjugate is a real number.

c i^{59}

To simplify i^{59}, let's try some simpler cases and look for a pattern.

$i^0 = 1$
$i^1 = i$
$i^2 = -1$
$i^3 = i^2 i = -i$
$i^4 = i^2 i^2 = -1(-1) = 1$
$i^5 = i^4 i = 1i = i$
$i^6 = i^4 i^2 = 1(-1) = -1$
$i^7 = i^4 i^3 = 1(-i) = -i$

The powers of i generate a pattern of four repeating numbers $(1, i, -1, -i, 1, i, -1, -i, 1, i, \ldots)$ with i raised to the fourth power being equal to 1. To simplify i^{59}, we can divide 59 by 4 and use the result and the remainder to rewrite i^{59} in an easily evaluated form.

$$i^{59} = (i^4)^{14} \cdot i^3 = 1^{14}(-i) = -i$$

Part Two: Sample Problems

Problem 1   *Find the complex zeros of the function $f(x) = x^3 + 8$.*

Solution   Remember, to find the zeros of a function, we set the function equal to zero and solve the resulting equation.

$$x^3 + 8 = 0$$
$$(x + 2)(x^2 - 2x + 4) = 0$$
$$x + 2 = 0 \text{ or } x^2 - 2x + 4 = 0$$
$$x = -2 \text{ or } x = \frac{2 \pm \sqrt{4 - 16}}{2}$$
$$= \frac{2 \pm \sqrt{-12}}{2}$$
$$= \frac{2 \pm \sqrt{12}\sqrt{-1}}{2}$$
$$= \frac{2 \pm 2\sqrt{3}i}{2}$$
$$= 1 \pm \sqrt{3}i$$

The zeros are -2, $1 + \sqrt{3}i$, and $1 - \sqrt{3}i$.

Problem 2   *Find a complex number x such that $3x = 4ix - 10$.*

Solution   We rearrange the x terms so that they are on one side of the equation, then solve for x.

$$3x = 4ix - 10$$
$$3x - 4ix = -10$$
$$(3 - 4i)x = -10$$
$$x = \frac{-10}{3 - 4i}$$
$$= \frac{-10}{3 - 4i} \cdot \frac{3 + 4i}{3 + 4i}$$
$$= \frac{-10(3 + 4i)}{9 - 16i^2}$$
$$= \frac{-30 - 40i}{25}$$
$$= -\frac{6}{5} - \frac{8}{5}i$$

Problem 3   Solve $x^2 - 3ix - 2 = 0$ for x.

Solution   We can use the quadratic formula, with $a = 1$, $b = -3i$, and $c = -2$.

$$x = \frac{3i \pm \sqrt{(-3i)^2 - 4(1)(-2)}}{2(1)}$$

$$= \frac{3i \pm \sqrt{9i^2 + 8}}{2}$$

$$= \frac{3i \pm \sqrt{-9 + 8}}{2}$$

$$= \frac{3i \pm \sqrt{-1}}{2}$$

$$= \frac{3i \pm i}{2}$$

Thus, $x = 2i$ or $x = i$. We could also have solved this problem by using the Zero Product Property, rewriting $x^2 - 3ix - 2$ as $x^2 - 3ix + 2i^2$, which can be factored into $(x - 2i)(x - i)$.

Problem 4   Write an equation whose roots are $2 + i$ and $2 - i$.

Solution   For an equation of the form $ax^2 + bx + c = 0$ to have roots of $2 + i$ and $2 - i$, the polynomial on the left side must have factors of $x - (2 + i)$ and $x - (2 - i)$. We can therefore set the product of these two factors equal to zero and then multiply and simplify to find such an equation.

$$[x - (2 + i)][x - (2 - i)] = 0$$
$$[(x - 2) - i][(x - 2) + i] = 0$$
$$(x - 2)^2 - i^2 = 0$$
$$x^2 - 4x + 4 - i^2 = 0$$
$$x^2 - 4x + 4 - (-1) = 0$$
$$x^2 - 4x + 5 = 0$$

Part Three: Exercises and Problems

Warm-up Exercises

1 Copy and complete the following table.

Complex Number	$a + bi$ Form	Real Part	Imaginary Part	Conjugate
$-5i - 7$				
$19i$				
$2(5 + 3i)$				
27				
$\sqrt{3} + \sqrt{-3}$				

2 Factor each expression over the complex numbers.

    a $x^2 + 121$ **b** $x^2 - 121$

    c $9x^2 + 4$ **d** $9x^2 + 36$

3 Solve each equation for x.

    a $ix = 3i$ **b** $ix = 3$

4 Solve each equation for (x, y).

    a $x + iy = 5 + 7i$ **b** $x + iy = (6 + 7i)(9 - 4i)$

    c $x + yi = -2(3 - 4i)$ **d** $x + yi = (2 \div i)(2 + i)$

5 Write a quadratic equation with the given roots.

    a 7 and −5   **b** $5i$ and $-5i$

Problem Set

6 Rewrite each expression as a number in standard complex form.

    a $\dfrac{5}{2i}$ **b** $\dfrac{2}{3 - i}$ **c** $i^{10} + i^6 + i^5 - i^3$

    d $(4 - 5i)(2 - i)$ **e** $3i(2 - 4i)$

7 Evaluate each expression.

    a i^4 **b** i^{24} **c** i^{37} **d** i^{803}

8 Perform the indicated operations.

    a $(8 + 7i) + (4 - 2i)$ **b** $(3 - 6i) - (8 - 2i)$

    c $(3 + 4i)(3 - 4i)$ **d** $\dfrac{2 + 3i}{3 + 2i}$

9 Simplify each expression.

    a $2i^3 - 3i^9 + 4i^{15}$ **b** $(2i)^3 - (5i)$ **c** $\dfrac{i^5 - i}{-i^3}$

10 The graph shows the results of an experiment in which five coins were tossed a number of times.

    a How many heads were recorded all together?

    b In what percentage of the trials were more than two heads recorded?

    c In what percentage of the trials was at least one tail recorded?

11 Simplify each expression.

    a $\sqrt{\dfrac{-16}{9}}$ **b** $\sqrt{\dfrac{16}{-9}}$ **c** $\sqrt{-\dfrac{16}{9}}$

12 Solve each equation for x by factoring.

a $4x^2 + 9 = 0$ **b** $x^2 + 49 = 0$

13 Solve the system for (x, y).

$$\begin{cases} x + 3y = 6i \\ x - 3y = 4 \end{cases}$$

In problems 14–16, simplify each expression.

14 $(3i)^2 - (4i)^2 - 6i^2$ **15** $3^2 i^2 + (2i)^2$ **16** $\sqrt{-8}\sqrt{-3}$

17 a What is the discriminant of $x^2 - 4x + 8 = 0$?
b What are the roots of $x^2 - 4x + 8 = 0$?

18 Solve each equation for x.

a $x^2 + 49 = 0$ **b** $x^2 - 2x + 2 = 0$ **c** $x^2 - 6x + 9 = -25$

19 Perform the indicated operations. Write your answers in standard complex form.

a $(3 - 4i)(2 + i)$ **b** $(6 - 4i) - (-3 - 9i)$
c $(2 + 6i) \div (3 - i)$

20 Refer to the graph. Write an equation corresponding to the reflection of this curve over

a The x-axis
b The y-axis
c The origin
d The line $x = y$

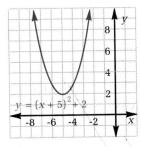

$y = (x + 5)^2 + 2$

In problems 21–26, simplify each expression.

21 $i^{17} + i^{15} + i^{13} + i^{11}$ **22** $2i^7 - 3i^{13}$
23 $(2 + i) - 3(5 - 7i)$ **24** $(1 + i)^2 - (1 - i)^2$
25 $4i - 8i^3 + 16i^5 - 10i^7$ **26** $(2i)^2 - 4i^2 - (-3i)^2$

27 Find the real numbers x and y that satisfy each equation.

a $(x - 7) + 4yi = 9 + (y - 21)i$
b $(x + 2y) + (x - y)i = 11 + i$
c $(x - 3y)i = 4x - 12y$

28 Let z and z̄ be conjugates.

a Find $z + \bar{z}$ if $z = 2 - 3i$.
c Find $\bar{z} - z$ if $z = 6 - 3i$.
e Find $z \cdot \bar{z}$ if $z = \sqrt{2} - \sqrt{3}i$.

b Find $z - \bar{z}$ if $z = -3 - 4i$.
d Find $z \cdot \bar{z}$ if $z = 3 - 4i$.

Problem Set, *continued*

29 Simplify each expression.

  a $4i^{-3} + i^{-1}$

  b $5i^{-5} - 7i^{-1}$

In problems 30–33, find all the complex solutions of each equation.

30 $x^2 - 6x + 25 = 0$

31 $2x^2 + 3x + 4 = 0$

32 $5x^2 + 45 = 0$

33 $2x^2 = 6x - 5$

34 Solve $\frac{5x + 3}{2 - 5i} = \frac{2 + 5i}{2}$ for x.

35 Find the complex zeros of $f(x) = x^2 + 20$.

36 Evaluate each expression.

  a $\displaystyle\sum_{k=1}^{8} i^k$

  b $\displaystyle\sum_{k=1}^{10} i^k$

  c $\displaystyle\sum_{k=1}^{100} i^k$

  d $\displaystyle\sum_{k=1}^{102} i^k$

37 Find the sum and the product of the roots of the equation $x^2 + 10x + 26 = 0$.

38 For what values of (x, y) is $x + yi = 3(2 - 4i) - 6(x - yi)$?

39 Write an equation that describes the conic section shown.

a   **b**   **c**   **d**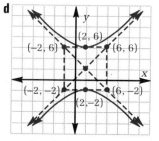

40 Find the real values of x and y that solve each equation.

  a $12x + 5y + xi - yi = -9 + 12i$

  b $4x - 3y + 2 = (x - 2y + 13)i$

41 Solve the system for (x, y).

$$\begin{cases} ix + 2y = 6i \\ ix - 2y = 4 \end{cases}$$

42 The Riddler said, "I'm thinking of two complex numbers that have a sum of $1 + 3i$ and a difference of $7 - 5i$." What is the product of the Riddler's two numbers?

43 If $g(1) = i$ and $g(n + 1) = i^{n+1} + g(n)$ for all positive integers n, what are the values of g(2), g(3), g(4), g(5), g(6), g(7), g(8), and g(57)?

44 Solve each equation for x.

a $x - 8 = 0$ **b** $x^2 - 8 = 0$ **c** $x^3 - 8 = 0$

d $x^2 - 10ix + 9i^2 = 0$ **e** $x^2 - 6ix - 5 = 0$

45 Find the complex zeros of $f(x) = x^4 + 8x^2 + 16$.

46 Find each product.

a $[6 + (3 + i)][6 + (3 - i)]$

b $[5 + (4 - 2i)][5 + (4 + 2i)]$

47 Find all values of a and b for which $(a + bi)(3 - 2i)$ is a real number.

USING A CURVE TO TRACE DISEASE

Dr. Richard Dicker applies statistics to epidemics

"I'm the director of the Epidemic Intelligence Service, a two-year program of service and training for people who want to explore a career in epidemiology," says Richard Dicker, an epidemiologist with the Center for Disease Control.

Epidemiologists try to find the origins of epidemics (such as of flu and measles), to identify who is at risk, and to take action to protect susceptible people from the disease. One model of an epidemic's progression is the *point source* model, based on the hypothesis that the epidemic originated at a specific time and location.

For example, explains Dr. Dicker, "there was a measles outbreak in Chicago that was traced to an emergency room. A child with measles had been brought to a hospital emergency room, and other children who were there at the same time caught the measles."

A normal curve can be used in identifying the time and location of the origin of the epidemic. Dr. Dicker explains, "The epidemic curve from a point source is a skewed normal curve where, if you plot time on the x-axis and onset (number of cases) on the y-axis, there is a sharp rise in the number of cases followed by a trailing off. If you

know the incubation period of the disease, you can figure out the time at which a great number of people became exposed to the disease. By finding out where they were at that time, it is possible to identify the epidemic's origin."

Dr. Dicker is a physician with training in preventive medicine. He has a bachelor's degree in chemistry from Tufts University in Medford, Massachusetts, a medical degree from the University of Massachusetts at Amherst, and a master's degree in epidemiology from Harvard.

Registered Deaths per Day during the Plague, 1400

Daily Count Recorded by the Grascia Scribe

From Ann G. Carmichael, *Plague and the Poor in Renaissance Florence.* Copyright © 1986 by Cambridge University Press.

THE NORMAL CURVE

Objective

After studying this section, you will be able to
- Recognize some characteristics of a normal distribution of data

The diagram at the right represents a group of test scores. The smooth curve drawn over the data has a shape that statisticians call a *bell-shaped curve*. This curve serves as a basis for much of the formal work in statistics.

In many large collections of data, the frequency of individual data values decreases symmetrically about a single value that corresponds to the mean, the mode, and the median of the data. This is known as a ***normal distribution*** of data, and the graph is a symmetrical bell-shaped curve called a ***normal curve***.

By using the mean and a nonnegative measure of dispersion known as the ***standard deviation*** (SD), we can identify some of the characteristics of data in a normal distribution. (In the next chapter, you will learn how to calculate the standard deviation of a set of data.)

Notice that the area under the curve has been divided by vertical segments at points that correspond to the mean and to values that are one, two, and three standard deviations on either side of the mean.

Mathematicians have calculated the relative areas of these eight regions, and this information is used to analyze the distribution of values in a set of data. The following diagram shows what percentage of the entire area under the curve lies within each of the regions. For example, the area of region III is approximately 13.6% of the total area under the curve, so about 13.6% of the data fall between 1 and 2 standard deviations below the mean. The combined areas of regions IV and V make up about 68.2% of the total area, so about 68.2% of the data lie within 1 standard deviation of the mean.

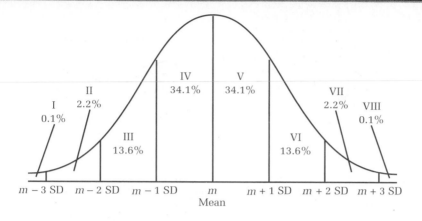

Sample Problem

Problem   *A set of normally distributed data has a mean of 26 and a standard deviation of 4.*

    a *What values are 1, 2, and 3 standard deviations from the mean?*
    b *What percentage of the total area under the curve lies between 18 and 30?*
    c *What percentage of the values are between 18 and 30?*
    d *What percentile rank does a value of 30 have?*

Solution   **a** We sketch a representative normal curve and label the horizontal axis. The values 22 and 30 are 1 SD from the mean of 26. The values 18 and 34 are 2 SD from the mean, and the values 14 and 38 are 3 SD from the mean.

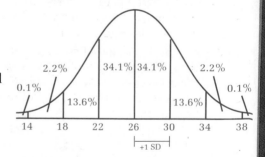

    b The region between 18 and 22 occupies 13.6% of the total area under the curve, and the regions between 22 and 26 and between 26 and 30 occupy 34.1% of the total area each. The region between 18 and 30 constitutes approximately 13.6 + 34.1 + 34.1, or 81.8, percent of the total area.
    c The percentage of values between 18 and 30 is the same as the corresponding percentage of area under the curve. Thus, about 81.8% of the data are between 18 and 30.
    d The percentile rank of a value of 30 is the percentage of the values that are less than or equal to 30. Since 30 is 1 SD to the right of the mean, approximately 50 + 34.1, or 84.1, percent of the area under the curve is to the left of 30. Thus a value of 30 has a percentile rank of about 84.

Problem Set

1 In the normal distribution shown, region 1 has an area of 50 square units; region 2, an area of 200 square units; region 3, an area of 250 square units; region 4, an area of 350 square units; and region 5, an area of 150 square units.

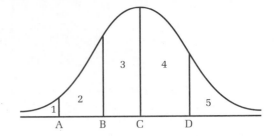

a Find the total area under the curve.
b What percentage of the total area is to the left of B?
c What is the percentile rank of the value at B?
d What percentage of the total area is to the left of D?
e What is the percentile rank of the value at D?

2 The area under the normal curve shown is 400. Find the areas of regions I, II, III, and IV.

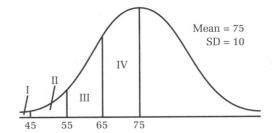

3 The data represented by the normal curve have a mean of 50 and a standard deviation of 10.

a What percentage of the total area under the curve lies in the shaded region?
b What is the percentile rank of a value of 60?

4 Copy and complete the following table for a normal distribution of data having a mean of 500 and a standard deviation of 100.

Data value	200	300	400	500	600	700	800
Percentile rank							

5 What percentage of the area under the normal curve lies in the shaded region?

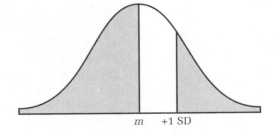

6 A normal distribution has a mean of 60 and a standard deviation of 8.

  a What percentage of the area under the distribution's graph is between the values of 44 and 68?

  b What percentage of the data have a value greater than 52?

7 A set of normally distributed data has a mean of 220 and a standard deviation of 60. Find the percentile rank of each of the following values.

  a 100   **b** 160   **c** 280   **d** 340   **e** 400

In problems 8–11, find the percentage of the total area under the curve contained by the shaded region.

8

9

10

11

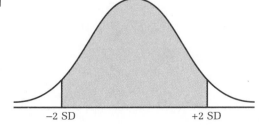

CHAPTER SUMMARY

CONCEPTS AND PROCEDURES

After studying this chapter, you should be able to

- Apply the properties of exponents to expressions with fractional exponents (8.1)
- Understand the restrictions that apply to exponential expressions with negative bases (8.1)
- Solve equations that contain square roots (8.2)
- Solve equations that contain rational exponents (8.2)
- Identify pure imaginary numbers (8.3)
- Perform operations on pure imaginary numbers (8.3)
- Identify complex numbers (8.3)
- Determine the conjugate of a complex number (8.3)
- Identify equal complex numbers (8.4)
- Perform operations on complex numbers (8.4)
- Recognize some characteristics of a normal distribution of data (8.5)

VOCABULARY

complex number (8.3)
conjugate (8.3)
extraneous root (8.2)
imaginary part (8.3)
normal curve (8.5)
normal distribution (8.5)
pure imaginary number (8.3)
radicand (8.1)
real part (8.3)
root index (8.1)
standard complex form (8.4)
standard deviation (8.5)

REVIEW PROBLEMS

In problems 1–6, evaluate each expression.

1 $5^{\frac{1}{3}} \cdot 5^{\frac{2}{3}}$

2 $(2^6)^{\frac{1}{3}}$

3 $\left(2^{\frac{1}{4}}\right)^8$

4 $49^{-\frac{1}{2}}$

5 $81^{-\frac{3}{4}}$

6 $4^{-\frac{5}{2}}$

7 A circle with a radius of $3^{\frac{1}{4}}$ is inscribed in a square as shown. What is the area of the shaded portion of the figure?

8 Solve $\sqrt[3]{5x + 7} = -2$ for x.

9 Rewrite each expression as a number in standard complex form.

a $\dfrac{4}{-3i}$

b $2i(3 + i)$

c $\dfrac{5}{6 + i}$

d $(12i^2)^2$

In problems 10–12, evaluate each expression.

10 $2 \cdot 3^{\frac{1}{3}} \cdot 5 \cdot 3^{-\frac{4}{3}}$

11 $\left(2^{\frac{2}{5}} \cdot 2^{\frac{1}{5}}\right)^{10}$

12 $\left(4^{\frac{3}{2}} \cdot 4^{\frac{5}{2}}\right)^{\frac{1}{2}}$

13 A normally distributed set of data has a mean of 480 and a standard deviation of 50. Which of the data values are

a 1.5 SD from the mean?

b 2.4 SD from the mean?

In problems 14–19, simplify each expression.

14 $\sqrt{-2}\sqrt{-32}$

15 $\dfrac{10}{7i}$

16 $-7i + 6i - 3i$

17 $4\left(\sqrt{-49} - \sqrt{-16}\right)$

18 $-\left(\sqrt{-5}\right)^2$

19 $3i\left(i + 2\sqrt{7}i\right)$

20 Find the conjugate of each complex number.

a $2 - 9i$

b $\dfrac{1}{2} + \sqrt{3}i$

c $15i$

d $-3i - 5$

e $\sqrt{23}$

f $\dfrac{5}{7} - \dfrac{5}{7}i$

21 Simplify each expression.

a $x^{\frac{1}{3}} \cdot x^{\frac{4}{5}}$

b $y^{3.7}\left(y^{-5.2}\right)$

c $\left(a^{9.5}\right)^2$

Review Problems, *continued*

22 What percentage of the total area under the normal curve lies in the shaded portion of the diagram?

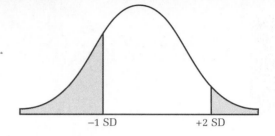

−1 SD   +2 SD

In problems 23–26, perform the indicated operations. Write your answers in standard complex form.

23 $(6 + 3i) − (−1 + 5i)$

24 $(3 − 3i)(5 − i)$

25 $\dfrac{2 + 5i}{5 + 2i}$

26 $(2 − 3i)^2 + (4 + 12i)$

In problems 27–30, solve each equation for (x, y).

27 $2x + 7iy = 14 − 28i$

28 $(2y + 3) − 5i = 3 − 10xi$

29 $\dfrac{x}{5} − 3i = (y + 5)i − 14$

30 $(x + y) + (2x − 3y)i = 15 + 15i$

31 What are the complex zeros of the function $g(x) = x^4 − 16$?

32 Simplify $\begin{bmatrix} 3i & 8i \\ -8i & i \end{bmatrix} + \begin{bmatrix} 7i & i \\ -3i & -4i \end{bmatrix}\begin{bmatrix} 0 & 2i \\ i & 0 \end{bmatrix}$.

In problems 33–38, solve each equation for a.

33 $\sqrt{3a − 7} + 6 = 10$

34 $5(a + 1)^{\frac{4}{3}} = 80$

35 $15 = 12 + (a^2 − 7)^{\frac{1}{5}}$

36 $\sqrt{a − 3} = \sqrt{a + 3} − 3$

37 $(a^2 − 100)^{\frac{2}{3}} = 16$

38 $3a + 2\sqrt{a} = 10$

39 Write an equation that has the given roots.

    a $11i$ and $−11i$

    b $3, 2 + 2i,$ and $2 − 2i$

In problems 40–43, find the complex solutions of each equation.

40 $5x^2 + 3x + 1 = 0$

41 $x^2 − 6x + 18 = 0$

42 $4x^3 = 25x$

43 $x^4 + 14x^2 = −49$

44 If a right triangle has the side measures shown, what are the possible values of x?

$2\sqrt{2}$

$\sqrt{x}$

$\sqrt[4]{2x − 1}$

CHAPTER TEST

1 When is $\left(\sqrt[n]{x}\right)^n = \sqrt[n]{x^n}$?

In problems 2 and 3, simplify each expression.

2 $\dfrac{10x^{\frac{8}{5}} + 30x^{\frac{4}{5}}}{5x^{\frac{6}{5}} + 15x^{\frac{2}{5}}}$

3 $\dfrac{10x^{\frac{9}{4}} + 25x^{\frac{5}{4}}}{-5x^{\frac{1}{4}}}$

In problems 4 and 5, find the real roots of each equation.

4 $\sqrt{x^2 + 9} - 1 = x$

5 $9x^{\frac{2}{3}} + 3x^{\frac{1}{3}} = 6$

In problems 6–8, match each number with all the phrases that correctly describe it.

6 $3 - 2i$

7 $2i - 3$

8 $\dfrac{\sqrt{3}}{5}i$

a Pure imaginary number
b Complex number
c Conjugate of $2i + 3$
d Additive inverse of $3 - 2i$

In problems 9–11, simplify each expression.

9 $3i - 2i + \dfrac{7i}{-7}$

10 $(5i)(-3i)$

11 $i + i^2 + i^3$

In problems 12–14, simplify each expression. Write your answer in the form _a + bi_.

12 $(6 - i)(3 - 2i)$

13 $(8 - 7i) - (3 + 6i)$

14 $\dfrac{8 + 3i}{1 - 2i}$

15 Find the values of x_1, x_2, x_3, and x_4.

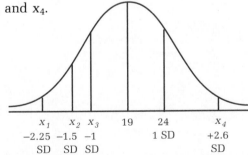

	x_1	x_2	x_3		19	24		x_4
	−2.25	−1.5	−1			1 SD		+2.6
	SD	SD	SD					SD

16 Is there a complex number that is equal to the square of its conjugate? If so, how many such complex numbers are there, and what numbers are they?

POLYNOMIALS AND POLYNOMIAL FUNCTIONS

The curves in this photograph of a roller coaster resemble the graphs of polynomials.

THE REMAINDER AND FACTOR THEOREMS

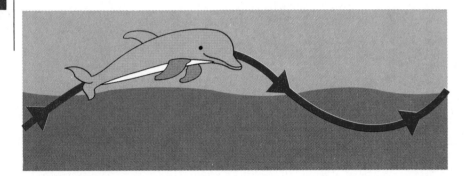

Objectives

After studying this section, you will be able to
- Write a polynomial in nested form
- Divide a polynomial by a binomial
- Apply the remainder and factor theorems

Part One: Introduction

The Nested Form of a Polynomial

We usually write a polynomial such as $6x - 5x^2 - 4 + 2x^3$ in *descending order of powers*—$2x^3 - 5x^2 + 6x - 4$. A polynomial can be written in another useful form, called **nested form.** The following example shows how x was repeatedly factored out of all the x terms.

Example   *Rewrite $7x^4 - 3x^3 + 2x^2 + 9x - 5$ in nested form.*

$$7x^4 - 3x^3 + 2x^2 + 9x - 5$$
$$= (7x^3 - 3x^2 + 2x + 9)x - 5$$
$$= ((7x^2 - 3x + 2)x + 9)x - 5$$
$$= (((7x - 3)x + 2)x + 9)x - 5$$
$$= ((((7)x - 3)x + 2)x + 9)x - 5$$

The following procedure can be used to write a polynomial in nested form.

Converting a Polynomial to Nested Form

1. Write the polynomial in descending order of powers.

2. Factor x out of all terms in which it appears.

3. Repeat step 2 for the expression in parentheses. Continue the process until no power of x greater than the first appears.

Nested form allows us to write an efficient computer program to evaluate polynomials for values of x. One such program is given at the beginning of this section's problem set.

Example   *If $P(x) = (((5)x - 3)x - 4)x + 9$, what is $P(2)$?*

Method 1
$$P(x) = (((5)x - 3)x - 4)x + 9$$
$$P(2) = (((5)2 - 3)2 - 4)2 + 9$$
$$= ((7)2 - 4)2 + 9$$
$$= (10)2 + 9$$
$$= 29$$

Method 2
We can also use a calculator to evaluate this function. First we store the value 2 in the calculator's memory by entering 2 $\boxed{\text{Min}}$. With the value of x stored in the memory, we can press $\boxed{\text{MR}}$ any time we need this value. To evaluate $P(x)$ for $x = 2$, we enter

5 $\boxed{\times}$ $\boxed{\text{MR}}$ $\boxed{-}$ 3 $\boxed{=}$ $\boxed{\times}$ $\boxed{\text{MR}}$ $\boxed{-}$ 4 $\boxed{=}$ $\boxed{\times}$ $\boxed{\text{MR}}$ $\boxed{+}$ 9 $\boxed{=}$

Once again, the output is 29. The $\boxed{\text{Min}}$ and $\boxed{\text{MR}}$ keys may have different names on your calculator, such as $\boxed{\text{M+}}$ and $\boxed{\text{RM}}$ or $\boxed{\text{STO}}$ and $\boxed{\text{RCL}}$

Long Division of a Polynomial by a Binomial

Long division of polynomials is like long division of real numbers. Study and compare the following two procedures.

Division of 298 by 14	**Division of $2x^2 + 9x + 8$ by $x + 4$**

$$\begin{array}{r} 2\ 1 \\ 14\overline{\smash{\big)}2\ 9\ 8} \\ \underline{2\ 8} \\ 1\ 8 \\ \underline{1\ 4} \\ 4 \end{array} \qquad \begin{array}{r} 2x + 1 \\ x + 4\overline{\smash{\big)}2x^2 + 9x + 8} \\ \underline{2x^2 + 8x} \\ x + 8 \\ \underline{x + 4} \\ 4 \end{array}$$

Recall that dividend = divisor · quotient + remainder. For these two examples,

$$298 = 14 \cdot 21 + 4 \qquad\qquad 2x^2 + 9x + 8 = (x + 4)(2x + 1) + 4$$

Example   *Divide $2x^3 - 19x^2 + 29x - 40$ by $x - 8$.*

$$\begin{array}{r} 2x^2 - 3x + 5 \\ x - 8\overline{\smash{\big)}2x^3 - 19x^2 + 29x - 40} \\ \underline{2x^3 - 16x^2} \\ -3x^2 + 29x \\ \underline{-3x^2 + 24x} \\ 5x - 40 \\ \underline{5x - 40} \\ 0 \end{array}$$

Thus, $2x^3 - 19x^2 + 29x - 40$ can be written as $(x - 8)(2x^2 - 3x + 5) + 0$. Since the remainder is zero, $x - 8$ is a factor of $2x^3 - 19x^2 + 29x - 40$.

Example Divide $x^3 - 12$ by $x - 2$.

Because the dividend has no terms of degree one or two, we save places for them by rewriting the polynomial as $x^3 + 0x^2 + 0x - 12$.

$$
\begin{array}{r}
x^2 + 2x + 4 \\
x - 2 \overline{)\, x^3 + 0x^2 + 0x - 12} \\
\underline{x^3 - 2x^2} \\
2x^2 + 0x \\
\underline{2x^2 - 4x} \\
4x - 12 \\
\underline{4x - 8} \\
-4
\end{array}
$$

Thus, $x^3 - 12 = (x - 2)(x^2 + 2x + 4) - 4$.

The Remainder Theorem and the Factor Theorem

There is an interesting relationship between long division and evaluating a polynomial in nested form. See if you can recognize it in the following example.

Example Let $P(x) = 5x^3 - x^2 + 3x - 4$.

a Find $P(2)$ by using the nested form of the polynomial.
$P(x) = (((5)x - 1)x + 3)x - 4$
$P(2) = (((5)2 - 1)2 + 3)2 - 4$
$ = ((9)2 + 3)2 - 4$
$ = (21)2 - 4$
$ = 38$

b Divide $P(x)$ by $x - 2$.

$$
\begin{array}{r}
5x^2 + 9x + 21 \\
x - 2 \overline{)\, 5x^3 - x^2 + 3x - 4} \\
\underline{5x^3 - 10x^2} \\
9x^2 + 3x \\
\underline{9x^2 - 18x} \\
21x - 4 \\
\underline{21x - 42} \\
38
\end{array}
$$

The numbers in red in part **a** match the numerical values in $5x^2 + 9x + 21$—the quotient when $P(x)$ is divided by $x - 2$. Moreover, the remainder when $P(x)$ is divided by $x - 2$ is equal to the numerical value of $P(2)$. This suggests the following theorem, called the *Remainder Theorem.*

> When a polynomial $P(x)$ is divided by $x - a$, the remainder is equal to $P(a)$.

One conclusion we draw from the Remainder Theorem is that if $P(a) = 0$, $x - a$ is a factor of $P(x)$. This conclusion is known as the *Factor Theorem*.

> ➤ **If $P(x)$ is a polynomial and $P(a) = 0$, then $x - a$ is a factor of $P(x)$.**

Example   *Is $x - 3$ a factor of $2x^2 + x - 21$?*

$$P(x) = ((2)x - 1)x - 21$$
$$P(3) = ((2)3 + 1)3 - 21$$
$$= (7)3 - 21$$
$$= 0$$

Since $P(3) = 0$, $x - 3$ is a factor of $2x^2 + x - 21$. By referring to the red numbers in the evaluation of $P(3)$, we see that the other factor is $2x + 7$.

Part Two: Sample Problems

Problem 1   *Rewrite $x^2 - 4$ in nested form.*

Solution   This polynomial has no first-degree term, so we rewrite it as $x^2 + 0x - 4$.

$$x^2 + 0x - 4$$
$$= (x + 0)x - 4$$
$$= ((1)x + 0)x - 4$$

Problem 2   *Let $P(x) = 2x^3 + 5x^2 - 2x - 7$. Find the quotient and the remainder when $P(x)$ is divided by $x + 3$.*

Solution   We rewrite $P(x)$ in nested form, as $P(x) = (((2)x + 5)x - 2)x - 7$, and evaluate $P(-3)$.

$$P(x) = (((2)x + 5)x - 2)x - 7$$
$$P(-3) = (((2)(-3) + 5)(-3) - 2)(-3) - 7$$
$$= ((-1)(-3) - 2)(-3) - 7$$
$$= (1)(-3) - 7$$
$$= -10$$

The quotient is $2x^2 - x + 1$, and the remainder is -10. Since the remainder is not zero, we know that $x + 3$ is not a factor of $P(x)$.

If we use a calculator to evaluate $P(-3)$, we need to record the output each time we press the $\boxed{=}$ key. First we store -3 in the memory by entering 3 $\boxed{\pm}$ $\boxed{\text{Min}}$. Then we enter

2 $\boxed{\times}$ $\boxed{\text{MR}}$ $\boxed{+}$ 5 $\boxed{=}$ $\boxed{\times}$ $\boxed{\text{MR}}$ $\boxed{-}$ 2 $\boxed{=}$ $\boxed{\times}$ $\boxed{\text{MR}}$ $\boxed{-}$ 7 $\boxed{=}$

  2 -1 1 -10

Again, the quotient is $2x^2 - x + 1$, and the remainder is -10.

Part Three: Exercises and Problems

Warm-up Exercises

In problems 1 and 2, write each polynomial in nested form.

1 $x^2 - 3x + 5$

2 $3x^4 - 2x^2 + 5x - 9$

3 Write the polynomial $(((4)x - 3)x + 2)x - 7$ in descending order of powers.

4 Consider the polynomial $2x^3 - 13x^2 - 7x + 4$.

    a Use long division to find the quotient and the remainder when $2x^3 - 13x^2 - 7x + 4$ is divided by $x - 5$.

    b Evaluate $P(x) = 2x^3 - 13x^2 - 7x + 4$ when $x = 5$ using the nested form of $P(x)$. How does your answer compare with your answer to part **a**?

5 Use long division to divide $x^5 - y^5$ by $x - y$.

Problem Set

The following BASIC program evaluates a polynomial $P(x)$ for a given value of x. If you have access to a computer, you may use it to solve some of the problems in this chapter.

```
10  REM This program evaluates polynomials for various values
20  REM of x. It also gives quotient coefficients and remainder
30  REM during the evaluation.
40  GOSUB 190
50  REM ---X Value Data Entry---
60  INPUT "Enter a value of x. ==>";X
70  REM ---Nested-Form Polynomial Evaluation---
80  LET Y = A(N)
90  PRINT: PRINT Y,
100 FOR I = N - 1 TO 0 STEP -1
110 LET Y = Y * X + A(I)
120 PRINT Y,
130 NEXT I
140 PRINT
150 PRINT "When x is ";X;", the polynomial's value is ";Y;"."
160 INPUT "Do you want to try another x value? ==>";A$
170 IF A$ = "Y" OR A$ = "y" THEN 50
180 END
190 REM ---Polynomial Input Section---
200 INPUT "Enter the degree of the polynomial. ==>";N: DIM A(N)
210 FOR I = N TO 0 STEP -1
220 PRINT "Enter the coefficient of the term"
230 PRINT "of degree ";I;". ==>";: INPUT A(I)
240 NEXT I
250 RETURN
```

Problem Set, *continued*

6 If $x + 7$ is a factor of the polynomial $Q(x)$, what is the value of $Q(-7)$?

In problems 7 and 8, rewrite each polynomial in nested form.

7 $5x^3 + 2x^2 + 6x + 1$ **8** $7x^3 - 3x^2 - 6x + 5$

In problems 9–12, rewrite each expression as a polynomial in descending order of powers.

9 $(((3)x + 6)x - 7)x + 9$ **10** $((((3)x + 5)x + 0)x + 7)x - 9$

11 $(((2)x + 0)x - 5)x - 7$ **12** $((((4)y - 9)y + 2)y + 5)y - 2$

In problems 13 and 14, evaluate each expression for $x = 2$.

13 $((7)x + 5)x + 1$ **14** $(((2)x + 5)x + 3)x + 9$

15 Consider the polynomial $((((3)x_1 + 2)x_1 - 4)x_1 + 5)x_1 - 6$.
    a What is the degree of the polynomial?
    b What is the coefficient of its linear term?
    c What is its constant term?
    d What is its quadratic term?
    e What is its cubic term?
    f What is its leading coefficient?

In problems 16 and 17, factor each expression.

16 $x^4 - 8x^2 - 9$ **17** $x^4 - 6x^2 + 9$

18 The area of the shaded region of the diagram is 12. Draw a graph that shows the relationship between x and y.

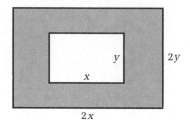

19 Divide $2x^3 - 5x^2 + 2x + 20$ by $2x + 3$.

In problems 20–23, factor each expression.

20 $x^3 - 64$ **21** $2x^3 - 128$ **22** $4x^3 - 64$ **23** $8x^3 - 27$

24 What is the remainder when $4x^3 - 3x^2 - x - 7$ is divided by each binomial?
    a $x - 1$ **b** $x + 1$ **c** $x - 3$

25 Consider the rectangles shown in the diagram.

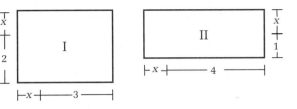

a Write an expression for the area of each rectangle.
Which has the greater area?
How much greater?

b Divide your expression for the area of the larger rectangle by x + 1.

c How does the remainder in your answer to part **b** relate to your answer to part **a?**

26 If the polynomial P(x) is divided by x − 4, the degree of the quotient is 5 and the remainder is 2.

a What is the degree of P(x)?   **b** What is P(4)?

27 Find the cubic term and the constant term of each product.

a (3x − 2)(x + 2)(6x − 5)   **b** (3x + 5)(2x + 1)(3x + 4)
c (x − 2)(x − 10)(x + 1)

In problems 28–30, factor each expression completely.

28 10x² + x − 2   **29** 27x² − 36x − 15   **30** (2x − 1)² − 9y²

31 Divide x³ − 2x² − 3x − 5 by x² − 2.

32 What are the roots of (x − 4)(2x + 3)(3x − 5) = 0?

33 Use the following table of values to approximate the zeros of f.

x	−4	−3	−2	−1	0	1	2	3	4
f(x)	1.5	1	−1	−3	−2	4	8	1	−5

34 Let P(x) = 2x⁴ − 9x² + 5x + 4 and Q(x) = x + 2. Find the quotient and the remainder when P(x) is divided by Q(x).

35 Write an expression for the total area of the two rectangles shown.

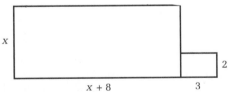

36 There are 28 students in a geometry class. Each day, a different group of 4 students goes to the board to demonstrate problems. How many classes must there be before one of these groups is forced to repeat?

In problems 37–39, factor each expression over the integers.

37 x⁴ − 25   **38** x⁴ − 10x² + 9   **39** x⁴ − 16

Problem Set, *continued*

40 a Write a nested polynomial expression for the sum of the volumes of the two solids shown.

  b Rewrite your answer to part **a** as a polynomial in descending order of powers.

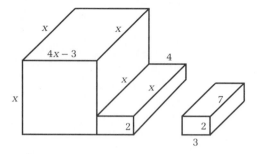

41 Let $P(x) = x^{15} + 1$.

  a Find $P(-1)$.

  b Is $P(x)$ factorable over the integers? Explain your answer.

42 Let $P(x) = (3x - 2)(4x + 5)(x - 6)$.

  a Find the constant term of $P(x)$.

  b Find the leading coefficient of $P(x)$.

43 Divide $2x^3 - 8x^2 + 6x + 5$ by $x + 3$.

44 Solve $\frac{3}{40}x^2 + \frac{1}{4}x - \frac{1}{5} = 0$ for x. (Hint: Multiply both sides by 40.)

45 The zeros of a cubic function Q are 3, -2, and 2. What is a possible factored form of the polynomial $Q(x)$?

46 Find the quotient and the remainder for $(x^3 - 8) \div (x - 2)$.

47 Suppose that $P(x) = ax^2 + bx + c$ and that $P(0) = 4$, $P(1) = 8$, and $P(-1) = 12$. Find (a, b, c).

48 Find the quotient and the remainder when the polynomial $ax^3 + bx^2 + bx + a$ is divided by $x - 1$.

49 Let $P(x) = ax^5 + bx^3 + cx$, where a, b, and c are negative. Explain why P cannot have any negative zeros.

50 The diagram shows the graphs of $y = P(x)$ and $y = g(x)$, where P is a cubic function and g is a quadratic function.

  a Write a formula for function P.

  b Write a formula for function g.

  c Write a function H such that $H(x) = P(x) - g(x)$.

  d Show that -2 is a zero of H.

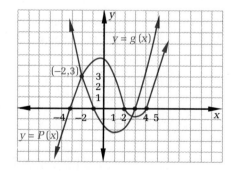

51 When polynomial $P(x)$ is divided by $x - 1$, the remainder is 3. When $P(x)$ is divided by $x - 2$, the remainder is 5. Find the remainder when $P(x)$ is divided by $x^2 - 3x + 2$.

THE RATIONAL-ZEROS THEOREM

Objectives

After studying this section, you will be able to
- Perform synthetic division
- Find zeros of functions by factoring and using the quadratic formula
- Apply the Rational-Zeros Theorem

Part One: Introduction

Synthetic Division

Before computers and calculators were developed, mathematicians frequently evaluated polynomials by using *synthetic division*. Synthetic division is closely related to nested-form evaluation. Synthetic division also provides the quotient and the remainder when a polynomial is divided by a binomial.

Example   Let $P(x) = 3x^3 - 4x^2 + 5x - 7$. *Use nested-form evaluation and synthetic division to divide $P(x)$ by $x - 2$.*

Nested Form

$P(x) = (((3)x - 4)x + 5)x - 7$
$P(2) = (((3)2 - 4)2 + 5)2 - 7$
$\quad\ = ((2)2 + 5)2 - 7$
$\quad\ = (9)2 - 7$
$\quad\ = 11$

Synthetic Division

$P(x) = 3x^3 - 4x^2 + 5x - 7$

$$\begin{array}{r|rrrr} 2 & 3 & -4 & 5 & -7 \\ & & 6 & 4 & 18 \\ \hline & 3 & 2 & 9 & 11 \end{array}$$

The results of both methods are the same. When $P(x)$ is divided by $x - 2$, the quotient is $3x^2 + 2x + 9$ and the remainder is 11.

The following steps make up the synthetic-division algorithm for dividing a polynomial $P(x)$ by a binomial of the form $x - a$.

Synthetic-Division Algorithm

1. Write the value of *a*, then write the coefficients and constant of $P(x)$ in a row to the right of that value.

2. Bring down the first coefficient below the addition line.

3. Multiply this number by *a*, and write the product under the next coefficient.

4. Add, writing the sum below the addition line.

5. Repeat steps 3 and 4 until all the coefficients and the constant have been dealt with. The numbers below the addition line are the quotient coefficients and the remainder.

Using Factoring and the Quadratic Formula to Find Zeros

In previous chapters, we solved linear and quadratic functions by setting the function equal to 0 and solving the resulting equation. Remember that the zeros of a function are the input values for which the output of the function is zero.

When the degree of a function is greater than two, finding the function's zeros is usually more difficult. In Section 6.4, we approximated the zeros of such functions by graphing them and estimating the values of the graphs' x-intercepts. In this section and the next, we introduce algebraic methods that are more accurate than graphing.

Example   *One of the zeros of $P(x) = x^3 - 2x^2 - 4x + 5$ is 1. Find two other zeros of P.*

Since $P(1) = 0$, we know that $x - 1$ is a factor of $P(x)$. To find the other factor, we use synthetic division.

$$
\begin{array}{r|rrrr}
1 & 1 & -2 & -4 & 5 \\
  &   & 1 & -1 & -5 \\
\hline
  & 1 & -1 & -5 & 0
\end{array}
$$
← The zero remainder shows that 1 really is a zero of P.

Thus, $P(x) = (x - 1)(x^2 - x - 5)$. To find other zeros of P, we use the quadratic formula to solve $x^2 - x - 5 = 0$. We find $x = \frac{1 + \sqrt{21}}{2}$ and $x = \frac{1 - \sqrt{21}}{2}$.

If you can rewrite a polynomial function as a product of linear and quadratic factors, you can find its zeros. Set each of the factors equal to 0 and solve the resulting equations.

The Rational-Zeros Theorem

In the preceding example, we could find two irrational zeros of function P because we already knew a rational zero of the function. The **Rational-Zeros Theorem** will help us find all the rational zeros of any polynomial function with integral coefficients.

 If F is a polynomial function with integral coefficients and if $\frac{p}{q}$ (a rational number in lowest terms) is a zero of F, then p is a factor of the constant term of F(x) and q is a factor of the leading coefficient of F(x).

Proof of the Rational-Zeros Theorem:
Let $F(x) = a_n x^n + a_{n-1} x^{n-1} + \ldots + a_1 x + a_0$, where each value of a_i is an integer. If $\frac{p}{q}$ is a zero of F,

$$a_n \left(\frac{p}{q}\right)^n + a_{n-1} \left(\frac{p}{q}\right)^{n-1} + \ldots + a_1 \left(\frac{p}{q}\right) + a_0 = 0$$

We multiply both sides of this equation by q^n.

$$a_n p^n + a_{n-1} p^{n-1} q + \ldots + a_1 p q^{n-1} + a_0 q^n = 0$$
$$a_{n-1} p^{n-1} q + \ldots + a_1 p q^{n-1} + a_0 q^n = -a_n p^n$$
$$q(a_{n-1} p^{n-1} + \ldots + a_1 p q^{n-2} + a_0 q^{n-1}) = -a_n p^n$$

Because q is a factor of the left side, it must also be a factor of the right side. Since $\frac{p}{q}$ is in lowest terms, q is not a factor of p^n, so q must be a factor of a_n, the leading coefficient of $F(x)$. Now let's reconsider the equation in which both sides were multiplied by q^n.

$$a_n p^n + a_{n-1} p^{n-1} q + \ldots + a_1 p q^{n-1} + a_0 q^n = 0$$
$$a_n p^n + a_{n-1} p^{n-1} q + \ldots + a_1 p q^{n-1} = -a_0 q^n$$
$$p(a_n p^{n-1} + a_{n-1} p^{n-2} q + \ldots + a_1 q^{n-1}) = -a_0 q^n$$

Applying the same argument for p that we used for q, we can show that p is a factor of a_0, the constant term of $F(x)$.

All this may seem a little abstract to you. The important thing, however, is to be able to apply the Rational-Zeros Theorem to identify the possible zeros of a function.

Example

Let $F(x) = 3x^4 - x^3 - 15x^2 - x + 2$. Find all the rational zeros of F and, if possible, all the other zeros of F.

According to the Rational-Zeros Theorem, if there is a rational zero $\frac{p}{q}$ of F, then p must be a divisor of 2 and q must be a divisor of 3. The only possible values of p are ± 1 and ± 2, and the only possible values of q are ± 1 and ± 3. The possibilities for $\frac{p}{q}$ are therefore ± 1, ± 2, $\pm \frac{1}{3}$, and $\pm \frac{2}{3}$.

Let's evaluate $F(1)$ and $F(-1)$.

$$F(1) = 3(1^4) - 1^3 - 15(1^2) - 1 + 2 = -12$$
$$F(-1) = 3(-1)^4 - (-1)^3 - 15(-1)^2 - (-1) + 2 = -8$$

Neither 1 nor -1 is a zero. Let's evaluate $F(-2)$ next, using synthetic division.

```
-2 | 3   -1   -15   -1    2
   |     -6    14    2   -2
   ----------------------------
     3   -7   -1     1    0   ← A zero!
```

So $F(x)$ can be factored as $(x + 2)(3x^3 - 7x^2 - x + 1)$. Applying the Rational-Zeros Theorem again, we find that the only possible rational zeros of $3x^3 - 7x^2 - x + 1$ are $\pm \frac{1}{3}$ and ± 1. We eliminate 1 and -1, since these are not zeros of F.

Let's try $\frac{1}{3}$.

```
 1  | 3   -7   -1    1
 3  |       1   -2   -1
    ----------------------
      3   -6   -3    0   ← Another zero!
```

Now we know that $F(x) = (x + 2)\left(x - \frac{1}{3}\right)(3x^2 - 6x - 3)$, or $F(x) = 3(x + 2)\left(x - \frac{1}{3}\right)(x^2 - 2x - 1)$. We can use the quadratic formula to solve $x^2 - 2x - 1 = 0$ and find $x = 1 \pm \sqrt{2}$. The four zeros of F are -2, $1 - \sqrt{2}$, $\frac{1}{3}$, and $1 + \sqrt{2}$.

Part Two: Sample Problems

Problem 1   Use synthetic division to find the quotient and the remainder when $2x^3 - 3x^2 + 100$ is divided by $x + 4$.

Solution

$$
\begin{array}{r|rrrr}
-4 & 2 & -3 & 0 & 100 \\
   &   & -8 & 44 & -176 \\
\hline
   & 2 & -11 & 44 & -76
\end{array}
$$

The quotient is $2x^2 - 11x + 44$. The remainder is -76.

Problem 2   Let $P(x) = \frac{1}{15}x^4 - \frac{1}{5}x^3 - x^2 - x + \frac{10}{3}$. Write a polynomial function Q that has integral coefficients and the same zeros as P.

Solution   The zeros of P are the solutions of the equation $P(x) = 0$. When we multiply both sides of this equation by a number, the right side remains zero, so we can multiply $P(x)$ by any number without changing the zeros. The least common denominator of the terms of $P(x)$ is 15, so if we let $Q(x) = 15[P(x)]$, function Q will have integral coefficients and the same zeros as P. Thus, $Q(x) = x^4 - 3x^3 - 15x^2 - 15x + 50$.

Problem 3   Write a cubic polynomial function whose zeros are -2, 3, and $\frac{2}{3}$.

Solution   According to the Factor Theorem, a polynomial function with the factors $x + 2$, $x - 3$, and $x - \frac{2}{3}$ will have the required zeros.

$$P(x) = (x + 2)(x - 3)\left(x - \frac{2}{3}\right)$$

$$= x^3 - \frac{5}{3}x^2 - \frac{16}{3}x + 4$$

Another answer is $P(x) = 3x^3 - 5x^2 - 16x + 12$. There are an infinite number of polynomial functions with these three zeros.

Part Three: Exercises and Problems

Warm-up Exercises

1 Consider the following example of synthetic division.

$$
\begin{array}{r|rrrr}
-4 & 2 & 3 & -18 & 5 \\
   &   & -8 & 20 & -8 \\
\hline
   & 2 & -5 & 2 & -3
\end{array}
$$

a What polynomial is the dividend?
b What is the binomial divisor?
c What is the remainder?
d What is the quotient?

2 What are the quotient and the remainder when $3x^2 - 6x + 7$ is divided by $x - 4$?

3 Use synthetic division to divide $2x^2 - 3x + 5$ by $x - 1$.

4 Find all the rational zeros of the function
$f(x) = 3x^4 - 7x^3 - x^2 + 7x - 2$.

5 The zeros of a function P are 4, -3, $\frac{2}{3}$, and 7. Write an expression with integral coefficients that might represent $P(x)$.

Problem Set

6 Use synthetic division to divide $3x^3 + x^2 - 2x + 6$ by $x + 1$.

7 List the possible rational zeros of $P(x) = 2x^3 + ax + 5$, where a is an integer.

8 Find the product $(x - 1)(x - 2)(x - 3)$, then use the product to write a polynomial function having the zeros 1, 2, and 3.

9 Solve $4x^3 + 12x^2 - 9x - 27 = 0$ for x.

10 Write an expression to represent the base of the rectangle shown.

Area $= x^3 - 5x^2 + 8x - 4$ $x - 2$

base

11 Use the graph to approximate the zeros of f.

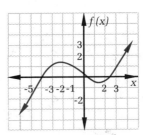

12 The difference between the numerical value of the volume of the cylinder and the numerical value of the area of one of its bases is $\frac{4}{27}\pi$. Find the radius of the cylinder's base.

13 Write an equation whose roots are -2, 4, and 9.

14 Use synthetic division to find the remainder for $(3x^2 - 5x + 7) \div (x - 2)$.

15 List the possible rational zeros of the function $P(x) = 4x^3 + ax^2 + bx + 6$, where a and b are integers.

16 Explain why the following statement is false: According to the Rational-Zeros Theorem, in any rational root $\frac{p}{q}$ of the function $P(x) = 9x^3 - \frac{2}{3}x^2 + 4x - 5$ the numerator p will be a factor of 9 and the denominator q will be a factor of -5.

17 When polynomial s is divided by $x + 4$, the quotient is $4x^2 - 7x + 5$ and the remainder is -4. What is the polynomial?

18 The graph of $y = P(x)$ is shown. Between what pairs of consecutive integers can the zeros of P be found?

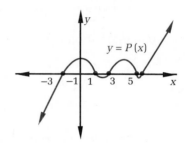

19 If $P(x) = x^3 - 4x^2 + cx + 6$, for what value of c is $P(3) = 0$?

In problems 20–22, solve for x in terms of the other variables.

20 $ax = c - b$ **21** $(a + b)x = 7$ **22** $ax - bx = 9$

23 Show that $x - 2$ is a factor of $x^3 - 5x^2 + 7x - 2$.

In problems 24 and 25, factor each expression completely.

24 $12x^3 - 21x^2 - 6x$ **25** $18x^4 - 50x^2$

26 Write a function whose zeros are 2, 3, −2, and −3.

27 Let $P(x) = x^3 - 4x^2 - 6x + 9$. Given that $x - 1$ is a factor of $P(x)$, find all the zeros of P.

28 Solve $6y^4 + 7y^3 - 37y^2 - 8y + 12 = 0$ for y.

29 A certain polynomial is evenly divisible by $x - 3$, with the quotient being $2x^2 - 5x + 7$. What is the polynomial?

30 Write a cubic polynomial function that has integral coefficients and the given zeros.

    a 2, −5, and −1   **b** $\frac{2}{3}, \frac{1}{3}$, and 1

31 The numbers in one of the rows of Pascal's triangle are 1, 7, 21, 35, 35, 21, 7, 1. Determine the numbers in the next row.

32 What are the zeros of $P(x) = x^4 - 12x^2 + 35$?

33 A quadratic equation has two roots, one of which is twice the other. If the sum of the roots is 30, what is the equation?

34 Let $P(x) = (x - 4)(x^2 - 7)$.
   a What are the zeros of P?
   b If $Q(x) = P(x - 6)$, what are the zeros of Q?
   c If $R(x) = P(2x)$, what are the zeros of R?

In problems 35 and 36, solve for x.

35 $x^2 + ax + bx + ab = 0$ **36** $x^3 - 6x^2 + 12x - 9 = 0$

37 What is the domain of the function $f(x) = \dfrac{2x + 3}{x^3 - 3x^2 - 4x + 12}$?

38 Let $Q(x) = 6x^3 - 5x^2 + kx - 2$.
   a List all the possible rational zeros of Q.
   b If 2 is a zero of Q, what is the value of k?

STATISTICAL ANALYSIS OF SUCCESS
Leonard Ramist assesses students' prospects

Your score on a college entrance examination is a function of the mean and the standard deviation for the scores of all the students taking the test. The purpose of such examinations is to help predict how you will do in college.

One career in statistics involves determining how the test results themselves will be evaluated and how the scores will be used. This is Leonard Ramist's career. He is a Program Director in the Admission Testing Program of the Educational Testing Service in Princeton, New Jersey.

"One of the major mathematical aspects of my job is to find an equation based on SAT scores and grades in high school that will best predict a student's success as a freshman at a particular college," says Ramist. "We provide that information to colleges, as well as a statistical program that helps them determine how well grades and SAT's work in predicting success at that college."

The statistical tools Ramist uses most often are correlation and regression analysis.

Regression analysis involves finding a function that best fits a set of data.

Mr. Ramist has a bachelor's degree in economics and accounting and a master's degree in operations research, both from the University of Pennsylvania. "Operations research," he says, "is a combination of mathematics and statistics and involves modeling real-life situations."

REAL ZEROS OF POLYNOMIAL FUNCTIONS

Objectives

After studying this section, you will be able to
- Identify upper and lower bounds of the zeros of a polynomial function
- Determine the approximate values of real zeros

Part One: Introduction

Upper and Lower Bounds of Zeros

In the preceding section, you learned how to find rational zeros of a polynomial function. What happens if real zeros are not rational numbers?

A useful way to begin to approximate any real zero of a function is to identify an ***upper bound***—a value of x above which there are definitely no zeros—and a ***lower bound***—a value of x below which there are definitely no zeros. We can then search for zeros between these two bounds.

Consider the function $P(x) = 2x^3 - 11x^2 - 10x + 55$. Let's try to find a positive value of x that is an upper bound. Choosing $x = 7$, we evaluate $P(7)$ using synthetic division.

$$
\begin{array}{r|rrrr}
7 & 2 & -11 & -10 & 55 \\
 &   & 14 & 21 & 77 \\
\hline
 & 2 & 3 & 11 & 132
\end{array}
$$

When $P(x)$ is divided by $x - 7$, the quotient is $2x^2 + 3x + 11$ and the remainder is 132. In other words,

$$P(x) = (x - 7)(2x^2 + 3x + 11) + 132.$$

Since all the terms of $2x^2 + 3x + 11$ are positive, its value will be positive for any positive value of x. In addition, $x - 7$ will have a positive value for any x greater than 7. We have identified an upper bound of the function's zeros.

 When a polynomial P(x) is divided by x − a, where a > 0, if all the terms of the quotient are nonnegative and the remainder is nonnegative, then a is an upper bound of the zeros of P.

Now let's find a lower bound of the zeros of P by looking at negative values of x. We will try $x = -3$.

$$
\begin{array}{r|rrrr}
-3 & 2 & -11 & -10 & 55 \\
   &   & -6 & 51 & -123 \\
\hline
   & 2 & -17 & 41 & -68
\end{array}
$$

Thus, $P(x) = (x + 3)(2x^2 - 17x + 41) - 68$. In this case, the value of $2x^2 - 17x + 41$ will be positive for any negative value of x, but $x + 3$ will be negative for any value of x less than -3. Therefore, $P(x)$ will be negative for any x less than -3. We have identified a lower bound of the function's zeros.

> ⏩ **When a polynomial $P(x)$ is divided by $x - a$, where $a < 0$, if the terms of the quotient and the remainder alternate in sign, then a is a lower bound of the zeros of P.**

To simplify our calculations, in the examples in this section we will work with a function that has a positive leading coefficient. If a polynomial function P has a negative leading coefficient, we can always write a function Q, $Q(x) = -[P(x)]$. This function Q will have a positive leading coefficient and, as the graph shows, the same zeros as P.

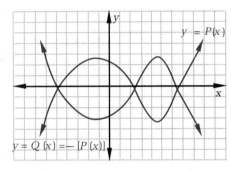

Example

Let $P(x) = 2x^4 + 5x^3 - 13x^2 - 25x + 15$. *Find an upper bound and a lower bound of the zeros of P.*

When we evaluate $P(1)$ or $P(2)$, some of the terms in the quotient are negative or the remainder is negative. Let's try evaluating the function for $x = 3$.

$$
\begin{array}{r|rrrrr}
3 & 2 & 5 & -13 & -25 & 15 \\
  &   & 6 & 33 & 60 & 105 \\
\hline
  & 2 & 11 & 20 & 35 & 120
\end{array}
$$

Since all the terms of the quotient and the remainder are positive, 3 is an upper bound of the zeros.

When we test negative values of x to find a lower bound, we find that for $x = -1$ through $x = -4$ the quotient terms and remainder do not alternate in sign. Let's try $x = -5$.

$$
\begin{array}{r|rrrrr}
-5 & 2 & 5   & -13 & -25 & 15 \\
   &   & -10 & 25 & -60 & 425 \\
\hline
   & 2 & -5 & 12 & -85 & 440
\end{array}
$$

Since the terms of the quotient and the remainder alternate in sign, -5 is a lower bound of the zeros.

Approximating the Real Zeros of a Function

Once we find upper and lower bounds of the zeros of P, we can make a table of values and graph P over the domain defined by these bounds. (A BASIC program that generates sets of ordered pairs for polynomial functions is included in the problem set.)

Example   *Roughly estimate the values of the zeros of the function*
$P(x) = 2x^4 + 5x^3 - 13x^2 - 25x + 15.$

From the previous example, we know that a lower bound of the zeros of this function is -5 and an upper bound is 3. We make a table for inputs between these bounds and sketch the graph.

x	P(x)
-5.0000000	440.00000
-4.6000000	263.73120
-4.2000000	142.57920
-3.8000000	64.947200
-3.4000000	20.467200
-3.0000000	0.00000000
-2.6000000	-4.3648000
-2.2000000	0.69120000
-1.8000000	9.7152000
-1.4000000	18.483200
-1.0000000	24.000000
-0.60000000	24.499200
-0.20000000	19.443200
0.20000000	9.5232000
0.60000000	-3.3408000
1.0000000	-16.000000
1.4000000	-24.076800
1.8000000	-21.964800
2.2000000	-2.8288000
2.6000000	41.395200
3.0000000	120.00000

The table and the graph show that -3 is one of the zeros of P. There is another zero between -2.6 and -2.2, a third between 0.2 and 0.6, and a fourth between 2.2 and 2.6.

Now we can increase the accuracy of the approximations by using a process known as ***bisection***. As you have seen, if the values of $P(x)$ have different signs for two inputs x_1 and x_2, a zero of P must lie somewhere between x_1 and x_2. Bisection is a technique that uses this fact repeatedly to approach closer approximations of a zero.

The Bisection Method of Locating a Zero

1. Evaluate the function for two *x* values, one slightly to the left of the zero on the x-axis and one slightly to the right of the zero.

2. Find the average of the two *x* values and evaluate the function for this third value.

3. Of the three *x* values, choose the two on either side of the zero.

4. Repeat steps 1-3 until the desired accuracy is reached.

A BASIC program that approximates zeros by bisection appears in the problem set.

Example   Let $P(x) = 2x^4 + 5x^3 - 13x^2 - 25x + 15$. *Use the bisection method to find, to the nearest thousandth, the value of the zero of P that lies between 2.2 and 2.6.*

We first define the following variables.

x_L = the x value to the left of the zero
x_R = the x value to the right of the zero
x_M = the average of x_L and x_R
P_L = the value of $P(x)$ at x_L
P_R = the value of $P(x)$ at x_R
P_M = the value of $P(x)$ at x_M

The following table summarizes our calculations.

x_L	x_M	x_R	P_L	P_M	P_R	Bounds of Zero
2.2	2.4	2.6	−2.828	15.595	41.395	x_L, x_M
2.2	2.3	2.4	−2.828	5.533	15.595	x_L, x_M
2.2	2.25	2.3	−2.828	1.148	5.533	x_L, x_M
2.2	2.225	2.25	−2.828	−0.890	1.148	x_M, x_R
2.225	2.2375	2.25	−0.890	0.117	1.148	x_L, x_M
2.225	2.3125	2.2375	−0.890	−0.390	0.117	x_M, x_R
2.23125	2.23438	2.2375	−0.390	−0.137	0.117	x_M, x_R
2.23438	2.23594	2.2375	−0.137	−0.011	0.117	x_M, x_R
2.23594	2.23672	2.2375	−0.011	0.053	0.117	x_L, x_M
2.23594	2.23633	2.23672	−0.011	0.021	0.053	x_L, x_M
2.23594	2.23614	2.23633	−0.011	0.005	0.021	x_L, x_M

The value of the zero to three decimal places is 2.236.

Part Two: Sample Problem

Problem   *If the box shown has a volume of 50 cubic units, what is the value of x to three decimal places?*

Solution   We write the equation $(x + 3)(x - 2)(x - 4) = 50$ and simplify to obtain $x^3 - 3x^2 - 10x - 26 = 0$. The real roots of this equation are the same as the real zeros of $P(x) = x^3 - 3x^2 - 10x - 26$. We use the procedures shown in the examples.

     When we evaluate $P(x)$ for various values of x we find that −3 is a lower bound and 6 is an upper bound. Making a table of values for inputs between these bounds shows us that P has only one real zero and that this zero is between 5.4 and 5.6. We then use the bisection method to approximate this zero to three decimal places and find that $x \approx 5.589$.

Part Three: Exercises and Problems

Warm-up Exercises

1 Let $P(x) = 3x^4 + 5x^3 - x^2 - 4x - 10$. Explain why -2 is a lower bound of the zeros of P.

2 Find an upper bound and a lower bound of the zeros of $P(x) = x^3 - 6x^2 - 10x + 60$.

3 Let $P(x) = 2x^4 + 5x^3 - 13x^2 - 25x + 15$. (This is the function used in the examples in this section.) Use the bisection method to calculate the zero located between -2.6 and -2.2 to two decimal places.

Problem Set

If you have access to a computer, you may use the following two programs to solve some of the problems in this set.

```
10  REM This program prints lists of ordered pairs for
20  REM polynomial functions
30  GOSUB 170
40  GOSUB 240
50  REM --- Ordered Pair Loop ---
60  FOR X = LB TO UB STEP INC
70  GOSUB 110
80  PRINT "(";X;", ";Y;")"
90  NEXT X
100 END
110 REM --- Nested-Form Polynomial Evaluation ---
120 LET Y = A(N)
130 FOR I = N - 1 TO 0 STEP -1
140 LET Y = Y * X + A(I)
150 NEXT I
160 RETURN
170 REM --- Polynomial Input Section ---
180 INPUT "Enter the degree of the polynomial. ==>";N: DIM A(N)
190 FOR I = N TO 0 STEP -1
200 PRINT "Enter the coefficient of"
210 PRINT "the term of degree ";I;". ==>";: INPUT A(I)
220 NEXT I
230 RETURN
240 REM --- Loop Data Input Section ---
250 INPUT "Enter the lower-bound value of x. ==>";LB
260 INPUT "Enter the upper-bound value of x. ==>";UB
270 INPUT "Enter the increment. ==>";INC
280 RETURN

10  REM This program finds values of zeros by bisection
20  GOSUB 140
```

```
 30 GOSUB 210
 40 REM --- Bisection Calculations ---
 50 PRINT "X-MID", "Y-MID"
 60 LET X = XL: GOSUB 270: LET YL = Y
 70 LET X = XR: GOSUB 270: LET YR = Y
 80 IF (XR - XL) < A THEN PRINT "The zero is ";XL".": END
 90 LET X = (XR + XL)/2: GOSUB 270
100 PRINT X, Y
110 IF Y * YL < 0 THEN XR = X
120 IF Y * YL >= 0 THEN XL = X
130 GOTO 60
140 REM --- Polynomial Input Section ---
150 INPUT "Enter the degree of the polynomial. ==>";N: DIM A(N)
160 FOR I = N TO 0 STEP -1
170 PRINT "Enter the coefficient of"
180 PRINT "the term of degree ";I;". ==>";: INPUT A(I)
190 NEXT I
200 RETURN
210 REM --- Initial Approximations Data Entry ---
220 INPUT "Enter an x value to the left of the zero. ==>";XL
230 INPUT "Enter an x value to the right of the zero. ==>";XR
240 INPUT "To how many places do you want the zero (1-5)? ==>";A
250 LET A = 1/10 ^ (A + 1)
260 RETURN
270 REM --- Nested-Form Polynomial Evaluation ---
280 LET Y = A(N)
290 FOR I = N - 1 TO 0 STEP -1
300 LET Y = Y * X + A(I)
310 NEXT I
320 RETURN
```

4 Let $P(x) = 2x^4 + 5x^3 - 16x^2 - 3x - 1$. Are there any real roots of P greater than

   a 1?   **b** 2?   **c** 3?   **d** 4?

5 Find an upper bound and a lower bound of the zeros of
$f(x) = 2x^3 - 9x^2 - 16x + 72$.

6 Determine the zeros of $f(x) = x^2 - 2$ to the nearest thousandth.

7 The function $f(x) = x^3 - x - 2$ has a zero between 1 and 2. Approximate the value of this zero to three decimal places.

8 Given that 5 is an upper bound of the zeros of a polynomial function P, identify 12 other upper bounds for P.

In problems 9–11, factor each expression over the integers.

  9 $12y^2 - 3y^4$ **10** $a^4 - 1$ **11** $8 - b^3$

Problem Set, *continued*

12 Find the quotient and the remainder when $x^3 - 7x^2 + 9x + 8$ is divided by $x - 5$.

In problems 13 and 14, approximate the real zeros of each function to the nearest thousandth.

13 $f(x) = 3x^4 - x^3 + 5x - 1$

14 $g(x) = x^4 - 2x^3 - 7x^2 + 6x + 12$

15 Solve $x^3 + 5x^2 - 13x - 65 = 0$ for x.

16 The volume of the box shown is 140 cubic units. Find integral upper and lower bounds of the possible values of x.

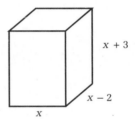

17 Solve the following system for (x, y).
$$\begin{cases} x^2 - y^2 = 4 \\ 3x^2 + y^2 = 12 \end{cases}$$

18 Suppose that y varies inversely as the reciprocal of x and that $y = 36$ when $x = 12$. What is the value of y when $x = 6$?

19 Find the greatest nonpositive integral lower bound of the zeros of each function.
 a $f(x) = x^4 - 2x^3 + x^2 - 3x + 4$
 b $g(x) = x^4 - 2x^3 + x^2 - 3x - 5$
 c $h(x) = x^4 - 2x^3 + x^2 - 3x - 35$
 d $k(x) = x^4 - 2x^3 + x^2 - 3x - 120$

20 Expand each exponential expression.
 a $(x + y)^0$ **b** $(x + y)^1$ **c** $(x + y)^2$ **d** $(x + y)^3$

21 Let $f(z) = \frac{z^2 + z}{z}$ and $g(z) = z + 1$. Find each of the following.
 a $f(3)$ **b** $f(2)$ **c** $f(-1)$
 d $g(3)$ **e** $g(2)$ **f** $g(-1)$

22 Let $P(x) = 5x^2 - 7x + 11$.
 a Rewrite $P(x)$ in nested form.   **b** Find $P(2x)$.

23 If the volume of the cylinder shown is 100 cubic units, what is the value of x to two decimal places?

In problems 24 and 25, solve each inequality for x.

24 $x(x^2 - 6x + 8) < 0$ **25** $x^2 \geq 6x$

26 Sketch the graphs of the following equations on the same coordinate system.

    a $\dfrac{x^2}{4} + \dfrac{y^2}{9} = 1$ **b** $\dfrac{x^2}{4} - \dfrac{y^2}{9} = 1$ **c** $\dfrac{y^2}{9} - \dfrac{x^2}{4} = 1$

27 Let P be a polynomial function such that $P(2) = -8$ and $P(3) = 12$.

    a Explain why P must have at least one zero between 2 and 3.
    b Draw a diagram to show that P could have more than one zero between 2 and 3.
    c Can P have exactly two zeros between 2 and 3?

28 Let $P(x) = 5x^3 - 31x^2 + 49x - 11$.

    a Between what pairs of consecutive integers can the real zeros of P be found?
    b Use the Rational-Zeros Theorem and the quadratic formula to find the exact values of the zeros of P.

29 If $P(x) = 2x^4 - 4x^3 - 5x^2 + ax - 6$ and if 3 is an upper bound of the zeros of P, what are the possible values of a?

30 Clem divided $x^4 - 3x^3 + 4x^2 - 7x + 12$ by $x - 5$ and obtained a quotient of $x^3 + 2x + 14x + 63$ with no remainder. Did Clem divide correctly? How do you know?

31 Let $P(x) = x^4 + 2x^3 - 12x^2 - 16x + 32$.

    a Find $P(2)$.   **b** Find $P(3)$.
    c Why must there be a zero of P between $x = 2$ and $x = 3$?

32 Let $P(x) = ((((2)x + 4)x - 13)x - 5)x - 2$ and $Q(x) = 2x^4 + 4x^3 - 13x^2 - 5x - 3$.

    a Find $P(2)$.   **b** Find $Q(2)$.
    c Is $x - 2$ a factor of $P(x)$?   **d** Is $x - 2$ a factor of $Q(x)$?

33 Suppose that $f(x) = ax^3 + bx^2 + cx + d$ and that $f(0) = 0$.

    a Find the value of d.
    b If $f(1) = f(-1) = 0$ and $a = 1$, what is (b, c)?
    c If $f(1) = f(-1) = 0$, what is b?
    d If $f(w) = f(-w) = 0$, where $w \neq 0$, what is b?

34 Let $P(x) = 2x^4 - 3x^2 + 2x - 8$.

    a Demonstrate that there is a zero of P between 1 and 2.
    b Find this zero to two decimal places.

FOUR USEFUL THEOREMS

Objectives

After studying this section, you will be able to
- Determine the number of complex zeros of a polynomial function
- Determine the sum and the product of the roots of a quadratic equation
- Apply the Conjugate-Zeros Theorem

Part One: Introduction

The Fundamental Theorem of Algebra

By factoring over the integers, we find that the function $f(x) = x^2 - 3x - 4$ has two distinct real zeros, 4 and -1. By factoring over the complex numbers, we find that the function $g(x) = x^2 + 4$ has two distinct complex zeros, $-2i$ and $2i$.

Example   *How many zeros does $h(x) = x^2 - 6x + 9$ have?*

We set $h(x)$ equal to zero and solve for x.

$$x^2 - 6x + 9 = 0$$
$$(x - 3)(x - 3) = 0$$
$$x = 3 \text{ or } x = 3$$

The function has two identical zeros, 3 and 3. We say that 3 is a zero of *multiplicity* two.

One of the greatest mathematicians of all time, Carl Friedrich Gauss (1777–1855), proved the following theorem, known as the *Fundamental Theorem of Algebra.*

> ➤ *Every polynomial function of positive degree with complex coefficients has at least one complex zero.*

Based on this theorem is the following, more useful theorem.

> ➤ *Every polynomial function of positive degree n with complex coefficients has exactly n complex zeros (counting multiplicities).*

Since $f(x) = x^4 - 16$ is a fourth-degree function, we know that it has exactly four complex zeros. We also know that $g(x) = ix^3 + 7x - 2 + 3i$, a cubic function, has exactly three complex zeros. Although this theorem tells us the *number* of zeros a function has, it may be difficult or impossible to determine the exact *values* of all the zeros. Generalized techniques have been developed for finding the complex zeros of linear, quadratic, cubic, and quartic functions, but the Norwegian mathematician Niels Henrik Abel proved that there is no generalized technique for finding the complex zeros of a function of degree greater than four. We can, however, approximate the zeros of such functions.

The Sum and the Product of the Roots of a Quadratic Equation

The following theorem states an important characteristic of the roots of a quadratic equation.

> ➤ *The sum of the roots of a quadratic equation*
> $ax^2 + bx + c = 0$ *is equal to* $-\frac{b}{a}$, *and the product of the equation's roots is equal to* $\frac{c}{a}$.

Example   Find the sum and the product of the roots of $x^2 - 4x + 5 = 0$.

In this equation, $a = 1$, $b = -4$, and $c = 5$, so the sum of the roots $\left(-\frac{b}{a}\right)$ is $-\frac{-4}{1}$, or 4, and the product of the roots $\left(\frac{c}{a}\right)$ is $\frac{5}{1}$, or 5.

We can check these answers by using the quadratic formula to find that the equation's roots are $2 + i$ and $2 - i$. Since $(2 + i) + (2 - i) = 4$ and $(2 + i)(2 - i) = 4 - i^2 = 5$, our results are correct.

We can demonstrate the preceding theorem by dividing both sides of $ax^2 + bx + c = 0$ by a, producing $x^2 + \frac{b}{a}x + \frac{c}{a} = 0$, or

$$x^2 - \left(-\frac{b}{a}\right)x + \frac{c}{a} = 0 \qquad\qquad (1)$$

Now we write a quadratic equation with the two roots r_1 and r_2.

$$(x - r_1)(x - r_2) = 0$$
$$x^2 - (r_1 + r_2)x + r_1r_2 = 0 \qquad\qquad (2)$$

Comparing equations (1) and (2), $r_1 + r_2 = -\frac{b}{a}$ and $r_1r_2 = \frac{c}{a}$.

The Conjugate-Zeros Theorem

Let's look at some functions and their zeros.

Function	Zeros
$p(x) = x^2 - 4x + 20$	$2 + 4i$, $2 - 4i$
$q(x) = x^3 - 2x^2 + 9x - 18$	2, $3i$, $-3i$
$r(x) = x^4 + 5x^2 + 4$	i, $-i$, $2i$, $-2i$
$s(x) = x^4 + x^3 - 11x^2 - 31x - 20$	4, -1, $-2 + i$, $-2 - i$

Notice that whenever a nonreal complex number is a zero, its conjugate is also a zero. This is not always the case—the zeros of $f(x) = x^2 - 3ix - 2$, for example, are $2i$ and i, which are not conjugates. But it is always the case for polynomial functions with real coefficients.

> ➤ *If $P(x)$ is a polynomial with real coefficients and if $a + bi$ (where a and b are real and $b \neq 0$) is a zero of P, then $a - bi$ is also a zero of P.*

Example   *If 3 and $-2 + 5i$ are zeros of a cubic function with real coefficients, what is the third zero?*

Since the coefficients in the cubic function are real, the conjugate of $-2 + 5i$ must also be a zero of the function. The third zero is $-2 - 5i$.

Part Two: Sample Problems

Problem 1   *Write a quadratic equation whose roots are $3 + 2i$ and $3 - 2i$.*

Solution   We could use the Zero Product Property in reverse, but it is simpler to use the sum-and-product theorem. The given roots have a sum of 6 and a product of 13, so the equation $x^2 - 6x + 13 = 0$ will have these two roots.

Problem 2   *One of the zeros of $P(x) = x^4 - 3x^3 + 5x^2 - 27x - 36$ is $-3i$. What are the other zeros of P?*

Solution   Since the polynomial $P(x)$ has real coefficients, $3i$ (the conjugate of $-3i$) must also be a zero of P. Since the numbers $-3i$ and $3i$ are the zeros of the quadratic function $f(x) = x^2 + 9$, we divide $P(x)$ by $x^2 + 9$, finding the quotient $x^2 - 3x - 4$. The value of this polynomial is 0 when $x = 4$ or $x = -1$, so the four zeros of $P(x)$ are $-3i$, $3i$, 4, and -1.

Part Three: Exercises and Problems

Warm-up Exercises

1 How many complex zeros does the function $f(x) = 6x^2 - 3x + 5$ have?

2 Find the sum and the product of the roots of the equation $x^2 + 15x + 50 = 0$.

3 Find all the zeros of $q(x) = 25x^2 - 20x + 4$.

4 If $a + bi$ is a root of $c_4x^4 + c_3ix^3 + c_2x^2 + c_1ix + c_0 = 0$, is $a - bi$ necessarily a root of the equation?

Problem Set

In problems 5 and 6, determine how many complex zeros each function has.

5 $f(x) = x^7 - 6x^5 + 3$ **6** $g(x) = x^2(x^2 + 4x + 1)(x - 3)^4$

In problems 7 and 8, find the sum and the product of the roots of each equation.

7 $2x^2 - 3x - 6 = 0$ **8** $5x^2 + 6x - 7 = 0$

In problems 9–12, write a quadratic equation with the given roots.

9 5 and −5

10 $2 + \sqrt{5}$ and $2 - \sqrt{5}$

11 $5i$ and $-5i$

12 $2 + i$ and $2 - i$

13 Suppose that the equation $x^2 + 12x + c = 0$ has a root of multiplicity two.

   a Find this root.   **b** What is the value of c?

14 Write each expression as a number in standard complex form.

   a $i^7 \cdot i^5$ **b** $i^{11} \cdot i^9$ **c** $i^8 \cdot i^{12}$

15 Solve $z = 3iz + 50$ for z.

16 Write a quadratic equation that has complex coefficients and the roots $4 + i$ and $-i$.

17 Consider the following two matrices.

$$A = \begin{bmatrix} 3 + 2i & 4 - i \\ 6 + 5i & 6 - 6i \end{bmatrix} \qquad B = \begin{bmatrix} 6i & -4 \\ 9 - 3i & -5 - i \end{bmatrix}$$

   a Find $A + B$.   **b** Find $A - B$.

18 There are 20 elements in set A and 16 elements in set B. If there are 30 elements in $A \cup B$, how many elements are in $A \cap B$?

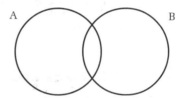

19 Write a quartic (degree-four) equation with integral coefficients such that two of the equation's roots are $3 - i$ and $2i$.

In problems 20 and 21, determine the degree of the polynomial in each equation and the number of complex roots the equation has. Then list each root with its multiplicity.

20 $x^2 (x + 5)(x - 3) = 0$

21 $(x - 2)(x^2 + 4)(x^2 - 4) = 0$

22 Solve the matrix equation for (x, y).

$$\begin{bmatrix} i & 1 \\ 1 & -i \end{bmatrix} \begin{bmatrix} x \\ y \end{bmatrix} = \begin{bmatrix} 1 \\ -i \end{bmatrix}$$

23 Claire has a penny, a nickel, a dime, a quarter, a half dollar, and a silver dollar. If she chooses three of the coins at random, how many different amounts of money might she choose?

24 Identify the real part and the imaginary part of each complex number.

   a $2(8 - 3i)$ **b** $\dfrac{16 - 5i}{2}$ **c** $\dfrac{5 + 3i}{i}$

Problem Set, *continued*

25 If one of the following pairs of numbers is selected at random, what is the probability that the numbers are the zeros of a quadratic function with at least one nonreal coefficient?

a -3 and -6 **b** $2 + i$ and $2 - i$

c $1 + \sqrt{3}$ and $1 - \sqrt{5}$ **d** $2i$ and $-2i$

e $2 + 3i$ and $3 - 2i$

26 Multiply $\begin{bmatrix} i & 0 \\ 0 & i \end{bmatrix}\begin{bmatrix} -i & 0 \\ 0 & -i \end{bmatrix}$.

27 The six points are equally spaced on the circle shown.

a How many triangles can be formed by choosing three of these points as vertices?

b If one of these triangles is chosen at random, what is the probability that it is equilateral?

c If one of the triangles is chosen at random, what is the probability that it is isosceles?

28 If a number is selected at random from $\{-4, (2 + 2i)^2, (3 - i)^2, (2i)^6, 0, (-\sqrt{3} - \sqrt{3}i)^2\}$, what is the probability that the number is real?

29 Consider the equation $(x^2 + 9)^2(x^2 - 9)(x^2 + 6x + 9) = 0$.

a How many roots does the equation have?

b Find each root and its multiplicity.

30 Multiply $\begin{bmatrix} 3 & 2i \\ 4 & 5i \\ -2 & i \\ 8 & -3i \end{bmatrix}\begin{bmatrix} 2 \\ 3i \end{bmatrix}$.

31 Solve each equation for z.

a $iz + iz = 6$ **b** $2iz - 6i = iz + 10i$

32 Solve $ix^2 + 5x + 24i = 0$ for x.

33 Find the sum and the product of the zeros of the function $P(x) = \sqrt{2}x^2 - \sqrt{6}x + \sqrt{10}$.

34 Solve each equation for w.

a $\sqrt{w^2 + 5} = 2$ **b** $\sqrt{w^2 + 5}\sqrt{w^2 + 8} = 2$

35 Find the complex number $x + yi$ such that $(x + yi)^2 = i$.

36 The graph of the function $P(x) = x^3 - 3x^2 + x - 3$ intersects the x-axis at only one point.
  a How many real zeros does P have?
  b How many complex zeros does P have?
  c What are the zeros of P?

37 Write a degree-four equation that has real coefficients and the roots $-3i$ and $6i$.

38 Find the sum and the product of the roots of the equation $ix^2 - 6ix + 8 = 0$.

HISTORICAL SNAPSHOT

HOW MUCH PROOF IS ENOUGH?
A life of work dismissed

Niels Henrik Abel (1802–1829) spent much of his short life in obscurity and poverty. But although his accomplishments went largely unnoticed during his lifetime, he made many important contributions to mathematics. One of Abel's most significant contributions was his demonstration that Leonhard Euler's proof of the binomial theorem applied to rational powers only. Euler (1707–1783) was one of the greatest mathematicians of all time and made many lasting contributions to mathematics. Abel proved the binomial theorem for all cases, including for irrational powers (such as π and the square root of 2).

Abel went on to prove that no solution is possible for the quintic equation. He published a series of papers on equation theory, function theory, and power series. In Paris, he presented a theorem on integrals of algebraic functions, but the paper he presented was mislaid, and not until after his death was what is now called Abel's Theorem acknowledged.

While ill with tuberculosis, Abel wrote papers on elliptic functions, a generalization of trigonometric functions.

THE BINOMIAL THEOREM

Objective

After studying this section, you will be able to
- Use the binomial theorem to expand powers of binomials

Part One: Introduction

Remember that $(x + y)^n = (x + y)(x + y) \cdot \ldots \cdot (x + y)$, with the $x + y$ a factor n times in the product. For example,

$$(x + y)^4$$
$$= (x + y)(x + y)(x + y)(x + y)$$
$$= (x + y)(x + y)(x^2 + 2xy + y^2)$$
$$= (x + y)(x^3 + 3x^2y + 3xy^2 + y^3)$$
$$= x^4 + 4x^3y + 6x^2y^2 + 4xy^3 + y^4$$

Let's look for a pattern in the expansions of powers of a binomial.

$$(x + y)^0 = 1$$
$$(x + y)^1 = 1x + 1y$$
$$(x + y)^2 = 1x^2 + 2xy + 1y^2$$
$$(x + y)^3 = 1x^3 + 3x^2y + 3xy^2 + 1y^3$$
$$(x + y)^4 = 1x^4 + 4x^3y + 6x^2y^2 + 4xy^3 + 1y^4$$
$$(x + y)^5 = 1x^5 + 5x^4y + 10x^3y^2 + 10x^2y^3 + 5xy^4 + 1y^5$$
$$(x + y)^6 = 1x^6 + 6x^5y + 15x^4y^2 + 20x^3y^3 + 15x^2y^4 + 6xy^5 + 1y^6$$

Some of the following patterns can be observed.

1. There are $n + 1$ terms in the expansion of $(x + y)^n$. For example, the expansion of $(x + y)^4$ consists of five terms.
2. The degree of each term in the expansion of $(x + y)^n$ is n. For example, in the expansion of $(x + y)^4$, the sum of the exponents in each term is 4.
3. In each successive term in the expansion of $(x + y)^n$, the exponent of x decreases by 1 and the exponent of y increases by 1. The first term is always x^n and the last is always y^n.

The pattern of coefficients is known as *Pascal's triangle.*

Row 0							1						
Row 1						1		1					
Row 2					1		2		1				
Row 3				1		3		3		1			
Row 4			1		4		6		4		1		
Row 5		1		5		10		10		5		1	
Row 6	1		6		15		20		15		6		1

Each row of Pascal's triangle begins and ends with the number 1. Each interior element of the row is the sum of the two adjacent elements in the preceding row.

Example   **a** *Write row 7 of Pascal's triangle.*

The first and last elements of the row are 1's, and each of the other elements is the sum of two elements of row 6. Therefore, row 7 is 1, 7, 21, 35, 35, 21, 7, 1.

b *Expand* $(x + y)^7$.

$$(x + y)^7$$
$$= x^7 + 7x^6y + 21x^5y^2 + 35x^4y^3 + 35x^3y^4 + 21x^2y^5 + 7xy^6 + y^7$$

Of course, we can find the terms of an expansion by actually multiplying all the factors.

$$\overset{\textbf{1}\qquad\textbf{2}\qquad\textbf{3}\qquad\textbf{4}}{(x + y)^4 = (x + y)(x + y)(x + y)(x + y)}$$

The terms in the product of the four factors of $(x + y)^4$ consist of all the ways that a group of four x's and y's can be formed, taking one variable from each factor. The x^3y terms, for example, are found as shown.

Factor Number

1	2	3	4		
x	x	x	y	=	x^3y
x	x	y	x	=	x^3y
x	y	x	x	=	x^3y
y	x	x	x	=	x^3y
		Total			$4x^3y$

This process is the same as selecting one y from the four factors in every possible way. In Chapter 5, you saw that the number of groups of r items that can be selected from a set of n items is given by the combination function C.

$$C(n, r) = \frac{n!}{(n - r)!r!}, \text{ so } C(4, 1) = \frac{4!}{(4 - 1)!1!} = 4.$$

Thus, the coefficient of x^3y in the expansion is 4.

Let's try using the combination function for the other terms. (Remember that $0! = 1$.)

$$C(4, 0) = \frac{4!}{(4 - 0)!0!} = 1 \quad \text{(the coefficient of } x^4)$$

$$C(4, 2) = \frac{4!}{(4 - 2)!2!} = 6 \quad \text{(the coefficient of } x^2y^2)$$

$$C(4, 3) = \frac{4!}{(4 - 3)!3!} = 4 \quad \text{(the coefficient of } xy^3)$$

$$C(4, 4) = \frac{4!}{(4 - 4)!4!} = 1 \quad \text{(the coefficient of } y^3)$$

A general rule is: The coefficient of the $(r + 1)$th term of the expansion of $(x + y)^n$ is equal to $C(n, r)$.

Example   *Find the fourth term of the expansion of $(x + y)^{12}$.*

We are looking for the fourth term, $r + 1 = 4$, so $r = 3$. The coefficient of this term is equal to $C(12, 3)$.

$$C(12, 3) = \frac{12!}{(12 - 3)!3!} = 220 \qquad \frac{5!}{4!}$$

In the fourth term, the exponent of y is 3—the value of r—and the exponent of x is 9. (To check this, study the expansions of consecutive binomial powers listed at the beginning of this section and review patterns 2 and 3.) The fourth term of the expansion of $(x + y)^{12}$ is $220x^9y^3$.

All of our observations about expansions of powers of binomials can be summarized in the **binomial theorem**.

> **For any positive integer n, the expansion of $(x + y)^n$ is $[C(n, 0)]x^n + [C(n, 1)]x^{n-1}y + [C(n, 2)]x^{n-2}y^2 + \ldots + [C(n, n)]y^n$.**

Part Two: Sample Problems

Problem 1   *Expand $(3x - 2y)^4$.*

Solution   If we think of $(3x)$ as the x term in the binomial and $(-2y)$ as the y term, we can use the binomial theorem.

$(3x - 2y)^4$
$= [(3x) + (-2y)]^4$
$= [C(4, 0)](3x)^4 + [C(4, 1)](3x)^3(-2y) + [C(4, 2)](3x)^2(-2y)^2$
$\quad + [C(4, 3)](3x)(-2y)^3 + [C(4, 4)](-2y)^4$
$= 1(81x^4) + 4(27x^3)(-2y) + 6(9x^2)(4y^2) + 4(3x)(-8y^3) + 1(16y^4)$
$= 81x^4 - 216x^3y + 216x^2y^2 - 96xy^3 + 16y^4$

Problem 2   *Show that for any nonnegative integral value of n, $C(n, 0) + C(n, 1) + C(n, 2) + \ldots + C(n, n) = 2^n$.*

Solution   According to the binomial theorem,

$(x + y)^n = [C(n, 0)]x^n + [C(n, 1)]x^{n-1}y$
$\qquad\qquad + [C(n, 2)]x^{n-2}y^2 + \ldots + [C(n, n)]y^n$

If we let $x = 1$ and $y = 1$, we have

$(1 + 1)^n = [C(n, 0)](1^n) + [C(n, 1)](1^{n-1})(1)$
$\qquad\qquad + [C(n, 2)](1^{n-2})(1^2) + \ldots + [C(n, n)](1^n)$
$\qquad 2^n = C(n, 0) + C(n, 1) + C(n, 2) + \ldots + C(n, n)$

Part Three: Exercises and Problems

Warm-up Exercises

1 Write rows 8–10 of Pascal's triangle.

2 Expand $(2x + 5y)^5$.

3 What is the tenth term of the expansion of $(x - 2y)^{13}$?

4 Show that $C(n, r + 1) = C(n, r) \cdot \frac{n - r}{r + 1}$. How can this relationship be used in writing the expansion of $(x + y)^n$?

Problem Set

In problems 5 and 6, expand each expression.

5 $(p + q)^3$

6 $(2x + y)^3$

7 Consider the expression $(x + y)^{12}$. Write the first four terms and the last four terms of the expansion of the expression.

8 Find the sixth term of the expansion of $(y - 3)^{11}$.

9 What term of the expansion of $(x^2 + 2)^5$ contains x^6?

10 Match each factored expression with the correct expansion.

　a $(a + b)^3$ 　　　　　　　　　　　　**i** 　$a^3 + b^3$
　b $(a - b)^3$ 　　　　　　　　　　　　**ii** 　$a^3 - 3a^2b + 3ab^2 - b^3$
　c $(a + b)(a^2 - ab + b^2)$ 　　　　**iii** 　$a^3 + 3a^2b + 3ab^2 + b^3$
　d $(a - b)(a^2 + ab + b^2)$ 　　　　**iv** 　$a^3 - b^3$

11 Indicate whether each statement is True or False.

　a $(a + b)^4 = a^4 + b^4$
　b $a^3 + b^3 = (a + b)(a^2 + b^2)$
　c $(a + b)^3 = a^3 + 3a^2b + 3ab^2 + b^3$
　d $a^3 + b^3 = (a + b)(a^2 + 2ab + b^2)$

12 Find, to the nearest thousandth, the value of x for which the volume of the box shown is 50.

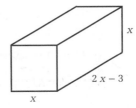

13 If $f(x) = (x + 5)^3$ and $g(x) = x^3 + 5^3$, for what values of x is $f(x) = g(x)$?

Problem Set, *continued*

In problems 14 and 15, factor each expression over the integers.

14 $x^3 + 3x^2y + 3xy^2 + y^3$

15 $x^4 + 4x^3y + 6x^2y^2 + 4xy^3 + y^4$

16 Consider the first six rows of Pascal's triangle.
  a Find the sum of the numbers in each row.
  b Predict the sum of the numbers in the twelfth row.

17 Let C be the combination function and n be a nonnegative integer. Explain why each of the following statements is true.
  a $C(n, 0) = 1$
  b $C(n, n) = 1$

18 Consider the expansion of $(a + b)^{22}$.
  a What is the eighteenth term?
  b What is the sixth term?

19 Write the first three terms of $(3x - 5y)^{10}$.

In problems 20–23, expand each expression.

20 $(x + 2y)^5$

21 $(x - 2y)^5$

22 $(2x + y)^5$

23 $(2x - y)^5$

24 Factor $x^2 + 24x + 144$ completely.

25 Divide each of the following expressions by $x + 2$.
  a $x^2 + 4$
  b $x^4 + 16$

26 The polynomial function $P(x) = x^3 - x^2 - 14x + 18$ has three real zeros. Find these zeros to two decimal places.

27 Find the sum of all the terms in the expansion of $\left(\frac{1}{3} + \frac{2}{3}\right)^5$.

28 Write the first four terms of $(2w + 3)^9$.

29 Adam Ant starts at level 1 and travels downward through the maze by moving to the left (L) or to the right (R). To reach level 2, for example, he can move R or move L. To reach level 3, he can move RR, RL, LR, or LL.

Level 1
Level 2
Level 3
Level 4
Level 5

  a List all the ways in which he can reach level 4.
  b List all the ways in which he can reach level 5.
  c What is the relationship between the number of ways in which Adam can reach the various levels and the numbers in Pascal's triangle?

30 Solve $(x + 2)^3 = (x + 2)^4$ for x.

31 **a** Write a formula for the volume V of
the cube shown.
b If the volume is 100, what is the value
of x (to the nearest hundredth)?

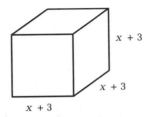

x + 3

x + 3

x + 3

32 In how many different orders can seven golfers tee off at the first
hole on a course?

33 Expand $\left(2x + \frac{1}{2}y\right)^5$.

In problems 34–39, factor each expression over the integers.

34 $x^3 + 5x^2 + 4x + 20$ **35** $x^3 + 2x^2y - 16x - 32y$

36 $x^3 - x^2 - 25x + 25$ **37** $x^2 - 4y^2 + 3x - 6y$

38 $x^2 - y^2 - x - y$ **39** $x^3 + 2x^2 - 6x - 12$

40 Consider the following system.

$$\begin{cases} x + y = 5 \\ xy = 2 \end{cases}$$

a Find the value of $x^2 + y^2$.
b Find the value of $x^3 + y^3$.

41 Multiply $(x - a)(x - b)(x - c)(x - d) \ldots (x - z)$.

**In problems 42 and 43, find the sum of the coefficients in the expansion
of each binomial power.**

42 $(2x + y)^5$ **43** $(3x + 2y)^{20}$

44 Show that for any positive integral value of n,
$C(n, 0) - C(n, 1) + C(n, 2) + \ldots + (-1)^n[C(n, n)] = 0$.

45 Show that $C(n, r) = C(n, n - r)$.

46 Consider the number pattern shown.
a Describe the procedure by which the
successive rows of the pattern are generated, and find the next three rows.
b What is the largest number that will
occur in the pattern?

```
1
1  1
2  1
1  2  1  1
1  1  1  2  2  1
3  1  2  2  1  1
1  3  1  1  2  2  2  1
```

47 If the product of $(x - 4)(x + 2)^5$ is written in descending order of
powers, what is its second term?

STANDARD DEVIATION AND CHEBYSHEV'S THEOREM

Objectives

After studying this section, you will be able to
- Calculate the standard deviation of a set of data
- Apply Chebyshev's theorem

Calculating Standard Deviation

In Section 8.5, you were introduced to an extremely useful measure of dispersion—standard deviation. In this section, you will find out how to calculate the standard deviation of a set of data and will explore the relationship between the standard deviation and the data.

Suppose that Wanda the waitress collected the following amounts in tips (to the nearest dollar) during ten days of work at the Longbranch Steak House.

$$19, 23, 29, 27, 35, 16, 22, 28, 29, 42$$

The mean of these data is $\frac{270}{10}$, or 27. The following table will help us calculate the standard deviation of the data.

Value	Value − Mean	(Value − Mean)^2
19	$19 - 27 = -8$	$(-8)^2 = 64$
23	$23 - 27 = -4$	$(-4)^2 = 16$
29	$29 - 27 = 2$	$2^2 = 4$
27	$27 - 27 = 0$	$0^2 = 0$
35	$35 - 27 = 8$	$8^2 = 64$
16	$16 - 27 = -11$	$(-11)^2 = 121$
22	$22 - 27 = -5$	$(-5)^2 = 25$
28	$28 - 27 = 1$	$1^2 = 1$
29	$29 - 27 = 2$	$2^2 = 4$
42	$42 - 27 = 15$	$15^2 = 225$
		Total 524

The average of the (value − mean)^2 quantities is called the *variance* of the data. The variance of these data is $\frac{524}{10}$, or 52.4. We can now use the following rule to calculate the standard deviation of the data.

>> ***Standard deviation = $\sqrt{variance}$.***

In this case,

$$SD = \sqrt{52.4} \approx 7.239$$

Many calculators have built-in functions for mean and standard deviation. (Some use $\bar{x}$ to symbolize mean and σ_n to stand for standard deviation.) Almost all mathematicians use calculators or computers for statistical work. They are great time savers!

What does the standard deviation mean in terms of Wanda's data? Let's draw and label a number line.

Point	Coordinate
A	Mean − 3 SD ≈ 27 − 3(7.239) = 5.283
B	Mean − 2 SD ≈ 27 − 2(7.239) = 12.522
C	Mean − 1 SD ≈ 27 − 1(7.239) = 19.761
M	Mean = 27
D	Mean + 1 SD ≈ 27 + 1(7.239) = 34.239
E	Mean + 2 SD ≈ 27 + 2(7.239) = 41.478
F	Mean + 3 SD ≈ 27 + 3(7.239) = 48.717

If we associate the number line with a bell-shaped curve representing a normal distribution, we can use the area under the curve to make predictions about Wanda's income from tips.

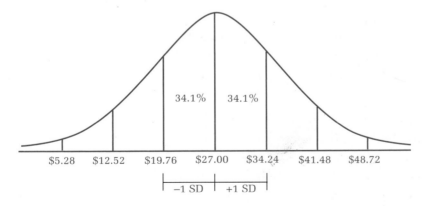

Wanda can expect to earn between $19.75 and $34.25 per day in tips approximately 68% of the time.

Problem *Suppose that scores on the mathematics section of the Test of Basic Understanding (TBU) are normally distributed, with a mean of 500 and a standard deviation of 100.*

a *Draw a bell-shaped curve that represents the data, indicating scores that are 1 SD, 2 SD, and 3 SD from the mean.*
b *Find the percentile rank of a score that is 1 SD below the mean.*
c *Find the percentile ranks of scores of 450 and 650.*
d *If a score of 660 is k SD from the mean, what is the value of k?*
e *Which scores have percentile ranks of less than 78?*

Solution **a**

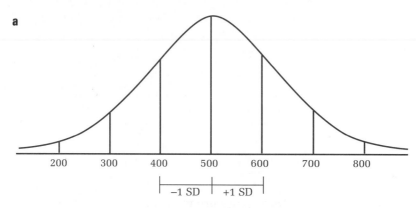

b The Normal Distribution Table on page 732 shows the area under the curve to the left of a data point and the associated percentile rank for values at various distances from the mean. According to the table, a value −1 SD from the mean (in this case, a score of 400) has a percentile rank of 15.

c A score of 450 is −0.5 SD from the mean, so according to the table, its percentile rank is 30. A score of 650 is +1.5 SD from the mean and has a percentile rank of 93.

d Since a score of 660 is 160 points, or 1.6 SD, above the mean, $k = 1.6$.

e According to the Normal Distribution Table, a score that is +0.8 SD from the mean has a percentile rank of 78. Thus, any score less than 0.8 SD above the mean will have a percentile rank less than 78. Since in this case m + 0.8 SD is 500 + 0.8(100), or 580, scores less than 580 have percentile ranks less than 78.

Chebyshev's Theorem

If the value of the standard deviation of a distribution is small, we can conclude that many of the data values are clustered close to the mean. A large standard deviation, on the other hand, indicates the data values are more widely dispersed from the mean. In any case, as you saw in Section 8.5, almost all the values in a normal distribution lie within 3 SD of the mean.

To get a sense of the dispersion of values in *any* distribution of data, normal or not, mathematicians use the following rule, known as *Chebyshev's theorem.*

⟫ **In any distribution, the percentage of the data values that lie within k standard deviations of the mean (where k > 1) is at least**

$$\frac{k^2 - 1}{k^2} \cdot 100$$

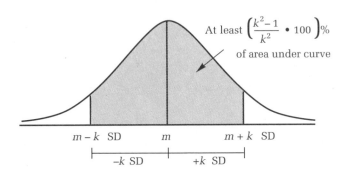

At least $\left(\frac{k^2-1}{k^2} \cdot 100\right)\%$ of area under curve

$m - k$ SD $\qquad m \qquad m + k$ SD

$-k$ SD $\qquad +k$ SD

Problem

A nonnormal distribution of data has a mean of 60 and a standard deviation of 15.

a What data values are within 2 SD of the mean?
b What percentage of the values must be between 37.5 and 82.5?
c If at least 40% of the data lie within k SD of the mean, what are the possible values of k?

Solution

a The standard deviation is 15, so 2 SD = 30. Thus, all values from 30 to 90 are within 2 SD of the mean.

b Since 37.5 is $\frac{37.5 - 60}{15}$, or -1.5, SD from the mean and 82.5 is $\frac{82.5 - 60}{15}$, or $+1.5$, SD from the mean, according to Chebyshev's theorem at least

$$\frac{1.5^2 - 1}{1.5^2} \cdot 100, \text{ or } \approx 55.56,$$

percent of the distribution lies between these values.

c The following diagram will help us visualize the problem.

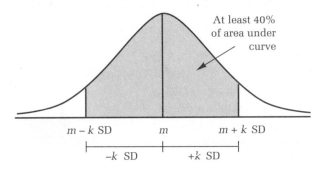

At least 40% of area under curve

$m - k$ SD $\qquad m \qquad m + k$ SD

$-k$ SD $\qquad +k$ SD

We use Chebyshev's theorem.

$$\frac{k^2 - 1}{k^2} \cdot 100 \geq 40$$

Solve for k
$$100k^2 - 100 \geq 40k^2$$
$$60k^2 \geq 100$$
$$k^2 \geq \frac{5}{3}$$
$$k \leq -\frac{\sqrt{15}}{3} \text{ or } k \geq \frac{\sqrt{15}}{3}$$

Since Chebyshev's theorem specifies that $k > 1$, we are interested only in the positive solutions of the inequality. At least 40% of the data will be within k SD of the mean if $k \geq \frac{\sqrt{15}}{3}$, or ≈ 1.291.

Problem Set

1 For what value of x is the mean of the following data 30?

10, 25, x, 17, 90, 21, 35, 6, 42, 13

2 Refer to the distribution curve.

a How many SD from the mean is a data value of 95?

b How many SD from the mean is a data value of 30?

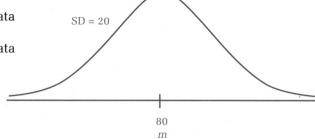

SD = 20

80
m

3 The diagram represents a normal distribution.

a Use the Normal Distribution Table to find the percentage of the area under the curve that is to the left of point A.

b What percentage of the area under the curve is to the *right* of point B?

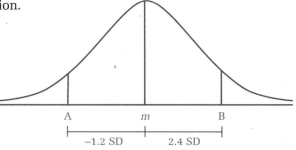

A   *m*   B

−1.2 SD   2.4 SD

4 Consider the data values 6, 8, 12, 14, 18, and 20.

a What is the variance of the data?

b What is the standard deviation of the data?

5 Find the mean and the standard deviation of the following data.

17, 23, 39, 47, 51, 59, 67

6 Determine the data values that correspond to points m, A, B, and C in the diagram.

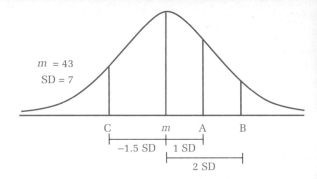

$m = 43$

$SD = 7$

C m A   B

−1.5 SD   1 SD

2 SD

7 If the scores on an examination are normally distributed and Amy's score is located at $m + 1.7$ SD, what is the percentile rank of her score?

8 In a nonnormal distribution of data, the mean of the data is 140 and the standard deviation is 30. What percentage of the data must lie between the values in each of the following pairs?

a 50 and 230

b 150 and 170

9 What percentage of the area under the normal curve shown is in the shaded region?

$SD = 10$

64.2   78.6

m

10 If the shaded region contains at least 60% of the area under the curve shown, what is the value of k?

$-k$ SD   0 $+k$ SD

11 The diagram represents a set of normally distributed test scores. What percentage of the people taking the test scored between 400 and 650?

$SD = 100$

400   500   650

12 A study showed that automobiles arrive at a certain intersection at an average rate of 10 per minute. If the data collected in the study form a normal distribution with a standard deviation of 2.64, what is the probability that 15 or more cars will arrive at the intersection in any given minute?

CHAPTER SUMMARY

CONCEPTS AND PROCEDURES

After studying this chapter, you should be able to
- Write a polynomial in nested form (9.1)
- Divide a polynomial by a binomial (9.1)
- Apply the remainder and factor theorems (9.1)
- Perform synthetic division (9.2)
- Find zeros of functions by factoring and using the quadratic formula (9.2)
- Apply the Rational-Zeros Theorem (9.2)
- Identify upper and lower bounds of the zeros of a polynomial function (9.3)
- Determine the approximate values of real zeros (9.3)
- Determine how many complex zeros a polynomial function has (9.4)
- Determine the sum and the product of the roots of a quadratic equation (9.4)
- Apply the Conjugate-Zeros Theorem (9.4)
- Use the binomial theorem to expand powers of binomials (9.5)
- Calculate the standard deviation of a set of data (9.6)
- Apply Chebyshev's theorem (9.6)

VOCABULARY

binomial theorem (9.5)
bisection (9.3)
Chebyshev's theorem (9.6)
Factor Theorem (9.1)
Fundamental Theorem of Algebra (9.4)
lower bound (9.3)
multiplicity (9.4)

nested form (9.1)
Pascal's triangle (9.5)
Rational-Zeros Theorem (9.2)
Remainder Theorem (9.1)
synthetic division (9.2)
upper bound (9.3)
variance (9.6)

REVIEW PROBLEMS

1 Use the graph of $y = f(x)$ to estimate the zeros of f.

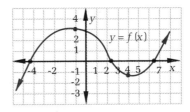

In problems 2 and 3, rewrite each polynomial in nested form.

2 $2x^5 - x^3 + 4x + 15$

3 $x - 3x^3 - 4x^2 + 7$

4 What is the remainder when $x^4 - 2x^3 + 4x^2 - 8x + 16$ is divided by $x - 2$?

In problems 5 and 6, use synthetic division to find each quotient and remainder.

5 $(4x^4 - 6x^3 + x^2 - 8x - 15) \div (x - 3)$

6 $(x^5 + 2x^3 - 5x^2 + 3x + 4) \div (x + 2)$

7 If the total area under the normal curve shown is 86 square units, what is the area of the shaded region?

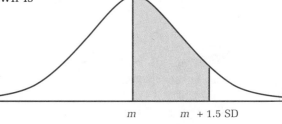

8 Is $x + 2$ a factor of $2x^4 + x^3 - 16x^2 - 27x - 14$?

In problems 9–14, write a polynomial function with integral coefficients and the given zeros.

9 -3, 1, and 4

10 -2, -1, 1, and 2

11 $3 - \sqrt{7}$ and $3 + \sqrt{7}$

12 $5 - 3i$ and $5 + 3i$

13 -6, $-\dfrac{1}{4}$, and $\dfrac{2}{3}$

14 $\dfrac{1}{2}$, 3, $-i$, and i

15 Let $f(x) = x^3 - 6x^2 - 13x + 42$. Use synthetic division to find an integral lower bound and an integral upper bound of the zeros of f.

16 List all the rational numbers that might be zeros of the function $g(x) = 2x^4 + 5x^3 - 25x^2 + x + 5$. Then find all the zeros of g.

Review Problems, *continued*

17 How many complex roots does the equation
$2x^4 - ix^2 - 1 + 3i = 0$ have?

In problems 18 and 19, expand each expression.

18 $(x + y)^4$ **19** $(x - y)^4$

20 One of the zeros of $P(x) = 2x^3 - 8x^2 - 7x + 25$ is between 4 and 4.4. Use the bisection method to approximate the value of this zero to two decimal places.

21 Let $P(x) = ax^4 + bx^3 + cx^2 + dx + e$, where a, b, c, d, and e are positive. Explain why P cannot have any positive zeros.

22 The scores on a standardized test are normally distributed, with a mean of 500 and a standard deviation of 100. What is the percentile rank of a score of 670?

23 Consider the equation $x^3 - 3x^2 + 3x - 1 = 0$.
  a What is the degree of the polynomial in the equation?
  b List the roots of the equation with their multiplicities.

24 Find the greatest nonpositive integral lower bound of the zeros of $f(x) = x^4 - 2x^3 + x^2 - 3x - 160$.

25 Calculate the mean, the variance, and the standard deviation of the following set of data.

$$17, \ 25, \ 9, \ 31, \ 25, \ 22, \ 15, \ 16$$

26 Consider the polynomial $x^5 + 32$.
  a Divide $x^5 + 32$ by $x + 2$.
  b Is -2 a root of the equation $x^5 + 32 = 0$?

27 Write the first four terms of the expansion of $(3x + 5y)^9$.

28 Find all the complex roots of $x^4 - 1 = 0$.

29 The diagram shown represents a nonnormal distribution. What minimum percentage of the total area under the curve is in the shaded·region?

30 Find the least nonnegative integral upper bound of the zeros of $f(x) = x^4 + 2x^3 + x^2 + 3x - 160$.

CHAPTER TEST

1 Rewrite $-10x^3 + 7x^2 + \frac{3}{2}x - 8$ in nested form.

2 Find the quotient and remainder when $x^3 - 3x^2 - 5x + 15$ is divided by $x - 3$.

3 Show that $x - 1$ is a factor of $x^n - 1$ for every positive integer n.

4 Use synthetic division to show that $x - 2$ is *not* a factor of $x^4 + 6x^2 - 7x - 6$.

5 Find all of the rational roots of $3x^3 + x^2 + x - 2 = 0$.

6 Find all of the real roots of $2x^3 + 5x^2 - 7x + 2 = 0$.

7 Find the least nonnegative integral upper bound of the zeros of the function $q(x) = x^4 + 2x^3 + x^2 + 3x + 1$.

8 Use a calculator to help you find the real zero of $f(x) = 4x^3 - 3x^2 + 2$ to the nearest tenth.

9 Counting multiplicities, how many complex zeros are there for the polynomial function $P(x) = 3x^5 - x^3 + 2x^2 + 6$?

10 Find the sum and product of the roots of $-2x^2 + 3x + 1 = 0$.

11 A polynomial function $P(x)$ of degree three has 7 and $3i$ as two of its zeros. What is the other zero, and what polynomial represents the function?

12 What is the fourth term in the expansion of $(2x + 3)^5$?

13 In a normal distribution of data, the mean of the data is 140 and the standard deviation is 30. What percentage of the data must lie between the values 35 and 245?

In problems 14–17, write a quadratic equation with the given roots.

14 12 and -3

15 $3 + 2i$ and $3 - 2i$

16 $3 + \sqrt{2}$ and $3 - \sqrt{2}$

17 $\sqrt{2} + \sqrt{5}i$ and $\sqrt{2} - \sqrt{5}i$

18 Let $P(x) = 2x^5 - 7x^4 + 9x^3 + x^2 + 2x - 4$.

   a Find the quotient and the remainder when $P(x)$ is divided by $x - 1$.

   b Find $P(1)$.

RATIONAL EXPRESSIONS, EQUATIONS, AND FRACTIONS

Like the forms used in this construction, the elements of rational expressions are simple, but the expressions can be complex and varied.

MULTIPLYING AND DIVIDING RATIONAL EXPRESSIONS

Objectives

After studying this section, you will be able to
- Recognize rational expressions
- Simplify rational expressions
- Multiply and divide rational expressions

Part One: Introduction

Recognizing Rational Expressions

A *rational expression* is any expression that can be written as a ratio of polynomials. Here are some examples of rational expressions.

$$\frac{x + 2}{x - 3} \qquad 1 + \frac{t}{h} \qquad \frac{x^2 - 10x - 75}{x + 5} \qquad \frac{y_2 - y_1}{x_2 - x_1} \qquad x^2 + 3$$

When working with rational expressions, we need to check for restrictions. *Restricted values* are values that make the denominator of a rational expression equal to zero. For example, if $f(x) = \frac{x + 2}{x - 3}$, the domain of f must exclude $x = 3$, because $f(3)$ is undefined. Any other real number can be used. The restrictions on the variables of the first four examples above are $x \neq 3$, $h \neq 0$, $x \neq -5$, and $x_1 \neq x_2$.

Simplifying Rational Expressions

When the numerator and denominator of a rational expression have no factor in common, the expression is *simplified.* To simplify a rational expression, we factor the numerator and the denominator and look for any common factors.

Example Give all restrictions and simplify $\frac{4x^2 + 6x}{2x^2 + x - 3}$.

Factor both the numerator and the denominator to find common factors.

$$\frac{4x^2 + 6x}{2x^2 + x - 3} = \frac{2x(2x + 3)}{(x - 1)(2x + 3)}; \ x \neq 1, x \neq -1.5$$

$$= \frac{2x}{x - 1} \cdot 1, \text{ since } \frac{2x + 3}{2x + 3} = 1$$

$$= \frac{2x}{x - 1}; \ x \neq 1, x \neq -1.5$$

It is very important to remember that although the simplified
expression has only one value that makes it undefined,
all restrictions found in the problem are included in the answer.
Only under these conditions are the original expression and the
simplified expression equal.

Multiplying and Dividing Rational Expressions

Multiplying and dividing rational expressions is similar to multiplying and dividing numerical fractions. However, we must always note
restrictions when using variables.

Example   *Multiply the following rationals.*

a $\dfrac{256}{81} \cdot \dfrac{27}{16}$

b $\dfrac{x^2 - 4}{x^2y} \cdot \dfrac{xy^2}{x + 2}$

$$\dfrac{256}{81} \cdot \dfrac{27}{16}$$

Factor
$$= \dfrac{16 \cdot 16}{3 \cdot 27} \cdot \dfrac{27}{16}$$

Find forms
of 1
$$= \dfrac{16}{16} \cdot \dfrac{27}{27} \cdot \dfrac{16}{3}$$

$$= (1)(1)\dfrac{16}{3}$$

$$= \dfrac{16}{3}$$

The restrictions on the
rational expression are
$x \neq 0$, $y \neq 0$, and $x \neq -2$.

$$\dfrac{x^2 - 4}{x^2y} \cdot \dfrac{xy^2}{x + 2}$$

$$= \dfrac{(x + 2)(x - 2)}{x^2y} \cdot \dfrac{xy^2}{x + 2}$$

$$= \dfrac{x + 2}{x + 2} \cdot \dfrac{xy}{xy} \cdot \dfrac{y(x - 2)}{x}$$

$$= (1)(1)\dfrac{y(x - 2)}{x}$$

$$= \dfrac{y(x - 2)}{x}; \ x \neq 0, \ x \neq -2, \ y \neq 0$$

To divide rational expressions, we multiply the dividend by the
reciprocal of the divisor.

Example   *Divide the following.*

a $\dfrac{46}{9}$ by $\dfrac{23}{3}$

b $\dfrac{2x + 12}{x^2}$ by $\dfrac{x + 6}{x}$

$$\dfrac{46}{9} \div \dfrac{23}{3}$$

Multiply by
the reciprocal
of the divisor
$$= \dfrac{46}{9} \cdot \dfrac{3}{23}$$

$$= \dfrac{2 \cdot 23 \cdot 3}{3^2 \cdot 23}$$

$$= \dfrac{2}{3}$$

$$\dfrac{2x + 12}{x^2} \div \dfrac{x + 6}{x}; \ x \neq 0$$

$$= \dfrac{2x + 12}{x^2} \cdot \dfrac{x}{x + 6}; \ x \neq 0, \ x \neq -6$$

$$= \dfrac{2(x + 6)x}{x^2(x + 6)}$$

$$= \dfrac{2}{x}; \ x \neq 0, \ x \neq -6$$

In this case we have two restrictions, $x \neq 0$ and $x \neq -6$. The second restriction, $x \neq -6$, is necessary when we multiply by $\frac{x}{x+6}$, the reciprocal of the divisor.

Part Two: Sample Problems

Problem 1   *Divide $\frac{x^2-49}{x^2}$ into $3x + 21$.*

Solution   Since we are to divide $\frac{x^2-49}{x^2}$ into $3x + 21$, $\frac{x^2-49}{x^2}$ is the divisor, and the problem is rewritten as $(3x + 21) \div \left(\frac{x^2-49}{x^2}\right)$.

Write $3x + 21$ as
a fraction
$$\frac{3x+21}{1} \div \frac{x^2-49}{x^2}; \ x \neq 0$$

Multiply by
the reciprocal
of the divisor
$$= \frac{3x+21}{1} \cdot \frac{x^2}{x^2-49}$$

Factor
$$= \frac{3(x+7)}{1} \cdot \frac{x^2}{(x+7)(x-7)}; \ x \neq 7, \ x \neq -7$$

Multiply
$$= \frac{3(x+7)x^2}{1(x-7)(x+7)}$$

Simplify
$$= \frac{3x^2}{x-7}; \ x \neq 0, \ x \neq 7, \ x \neq -7$$

There are three restrictions because the solution uses the divisor and its reciprocal. Neither the numerator nor the denominator of the divisor can be zero.

Problem 2   *Multiply and give all restrictions.*

$$\frac{x^2-2x-15}{x^2y-25y} \cdot \frac{x^2+5x}{x^3+27}$$

Solution   Remember: Before simplifying, check for restrictions by finding the zeros of each polynomial in a denominator.

$$\frac{x^2-2x-15}{x^2y-25y} \cdot \frac{x^2+5x}{x^3+27}$$

$$= \frac{(x-5)(x+3)}{y(x+5)(x-5)} \cdot \frac{x(x+5)}{(x+3)(x^2-3x+9)}; \ y \neq 0, \ x \neq -5, \ x \neq 5, \ x \neq -3$$

We use the quadratic formula to determine further restrictions on x.

Let $x^2 - 3x + 9 = 0$.

$$x = \frac{3+\sqrt{-27}}{2} \text{ and } x = \frac{3-\sqrt{-27}}{2}$$

$$x = \frac{3+i \cdot 3\sqrt{3}}{2} \text{ and } x = \frac{3-i \cdot 3\sqrt{3}}{2}$$

Now we can simplify.

$$\frac{(x-5)(x+3)}{y(x+5)(x-5)} \cdot \frac{x(x+5)}{(x+3)(x^2-3x+9)}$$

$$= \frac{x}{y(x^2-3x+9)}; \; y \neq 0, \; x \neq -5, \; x \neq 5, \; x \neq -3,$$

$$x \neq \frac{3+3\sqrt{3}i}{2}, \; x \neq \frac{3-3\sqrt{3}i}{2}$$

Part Three: Exercises and Problems

Warm-up Exercises

In problems 1–8, tell whether each expression is rational.

1 $n + 5$

2 $\dfrac{\sqrt{x}}{x+3}$

3 $\dfrac{\frac{1}{a}}{b}$

4 $\dfrac{\sqrt{(x-y)^2}}{x}$

5 $\dfrac{n+4}{n+2}$

6 $\dfrac{x^2-9}{x+3}$

7 $\dfrac{5x^2-10x}{x^2+x-6}$

8 $\dfrac{a^2+b^2}{a+b}$

9 Divide 1 by $\frac{a}{b}$ and give restrictions.

10 Multiply $\frac{x-5}{x+2}$ by $x^2 - 5x - 14$ and give restrictions.

Problem Set

11 If one of the following functions is selected at random, what is the probability that it is a rational expression?

a $f(x) = \dfrac{x+5}{2\sqrt{x}}$

b $g(x) = \dfrac{x^2+2x-\sqrt{3}}{x}$

c $h(x) = 15 + \dfrac{3}{x}$

d $j(x) = \left[\dfrac{2}{3}\left(x+\dfrac{3}{5}\right)x + \dfrac{5}{8}\right]x$

e $k(x) = \dfrac{x^2-1}{1-x^2}$

In problems 12–15, simplify and state restrictions.

12 $\dfrac{3-5}{5-3}$

13 $\dfrac{x-y}{y-x}$

14 $\dfrac{x-5}{5-x}$

15 $\dfrac{(x+5)^4}{(x+5)^2}$

16 Find the domain of f.

$$f(x) = \frac{3x+4}{3x^3+18x^2+24x}$$

In problems 17–20, simplify and state restrictions.

17 $\dfrac{xy^2z}{xy}$ 　　　　　 **18** $\dfrac{x}{y} \cdot \dfrac{x^2}{y}$ 　　　　　 **19** $\dfrac{3xy}{6y^2}$ 　　　　　 **20** $\dfrac{x}{y} \div \dfrac{x^2}{y}$

21 Study the example, then copy and complete the chart.

Expressions	Greatest Common Factor	Least Common Multiple
4, 6, 8	2	24
9, 12, 6		
$4x^2$, $6xy$, $2x^2y$		
$x(x-2)$, $4(x-2)$		

In problems 22–25, simplify and state restrictions.

22 $\dfrac{(x+2)(x+3)}{(x+1)(x+2)}$ 　　　　　　　 **23** $\dfrac{x^3 - 3x^2}{x}$

24 $\dfrac{x^2 - 9}{x^2 + 2x - 3}$ 　　　　　　　 **25** $\dfrac{2x^3 + 12x^2 + 16x}{x^3 + 4x}$

26 Multiply $\dfrac{x+5}{x-2} \cdot \dfrac{x+3}{x+5} \cdot \dfrac{x-2}{x+3}$ and write your answer in simplest form.

27 Divide $\dfrac{x^2 + 9x + 20}{x^2 - 9x + 20}$ into $\dfrac{x^2 + 10x + 25}{x^2 - 16}$ and write your answer in simplest form.

28 The length of a rectangle is $x + 2$, and its area is $x^2 + 7x + 10$. Find its width.

29 Let $f(x) = \dfrac{x^2 - 25}{x + 2}$ and $g(x) = \dfrac{x^2 + 4}{x + 5}$. Simplify $f(x) \cdot g(x)$.

30 Let $f(x) = \dfrac{6x^2(x+2)(x-3)}{(x^2-1)(x+2)(x+3)}$. Evaluate each of the following.
　a $f(0)$ 　　　　　　 **b** $f(3)$ 　　　　　　 **c** $f(-2)$
　d $f(-3)$ 　　　　　　 **e** $f(2)$

31 Given $f(x) = \dfrac{x+1}{x+2}$ and $g(x) = \dfrac{x+2}{x+1}$, find the domains of functions h and j.
　a $h(x) = f(x) \cdot g(x)$ 　　　　　　 **b** $j(x) = \dfrac{g(x)}{f(x)}$

32 Find all values of y that make each statement true.
　a $\dfrac{1}{y} = \dfrac{1}{5}$ 　　　　　 **b** $\dfrac{2}{y} = \dfrac{8}{12}$ 　　　　　 **c** $\dfrac{y}{2} = \dfrac{2}{y}$

33 Determine whether each statement is True or False when $a \neq 0$ and $b \neq 0$.
　a $a\left(\dfrac{1}{a}\right) = 1$ 　　　　 **b** $a\left(\dfrac{1}{a} + \dfrac{1}{b}\right) = 1 + \dfrac{1}{b}$ 　　　　 **c** $ab\left(\dfrac{1}{a} + \dfrac{1}{b}\right) = b + a$

34 The numerator of a fraction is three more than the denominator. If both the numerator and the denominator are increased by three and the resulting fraction is multiplied by the original fraction, the product is equal to $\frac{7}{5}$. Find the original fraction.

35 Solve $\frac{x^2 + 11x + 28}{x - 5} \cdot \frac{x^2 - 8x + 15}{x + 7} = 2x$ for x.

36 Find all vertical asymptotes of the graph of $f(x) = \frac{x + 1}{x^2 - 6x + 8}$.

37 The numerator of a fraction is five more than the denominator. Both the numerator and the denominator are increased by five, and the resulting fraction is multiplied by the original one. What is the relationship between the numerator and the denominator of the product?

38 Expand $(2x + 3y)^3$.

39 Solve $\frac{2x^3 - x^2 - 6x}{x^2 - 2x} = x - 1$ for x.

40 In the trapezoid shown, $b_1 = 2x^2 + 2$, $b_2 = 4x + 6$, and the area is $x^3 - 8$. Find the height h.

41 By what rational expression should we multiply $\frac{x^2 - 3x - 10}{x^2 - 16}$ to get an answer of $\frac{x + 2}{x - 4}$?

42 Simplify $\frac{x^2 - 4}{x^2 + 2x + 3}$ and state restrictions.

43 Working alone, Private I can dig a hole in 20 minutes. Working alone, Corporal Punishment can dig a hole in 15 minutes. How long will it take them if Sergeant Pepper has them work together to dig the hole?

44 Explain why $f(x)$ and $g(x)$ are not the same if $f(x) = \frac{x(x + 2)}{(x - 1)(x + 2)}$ and $g(x) = \frac{x}{x - 1}$.

45 Write $\left(x + \frac{1}{x}\right)^6$ in expanded form.

46 Simplify $\frac{x^2 + 3xy + 2x + 6y}{x + 3y}$.

In problems 47 and 48, use the computer programs in Section 9.3 to estimate the roots of each equation to the nearest hundredth.

47 $x^5 - 2x^4 + 2x^3 + 30x^2 - 60x - 60 = 0$

48 $2x^4 + 4x^3 + 3x^2 - 6x - 9 = 0$

49 If $x + \frac{1}{x} = 5$, what is the value of $x^2 + \frac{1}{x^2}$? (Hint: Square both sides of the original equation.)

TEACHING MATHEMATICS

Joan Hairston communicates the beauty and joy of mathematics

"I emphasize that mathematics is a language," says Joan Hairston, a mathematics teacher at Dorsey Senior High School in Los Angeles, California. "I not only give my students problems to solve but also ask the students to write about how they have solved a given problem. They must describe both the problem and the solution. This enables me to see the depth of their understanding and their thinking process."

One of Ms. Hairston's primary goals is to nurture her students' analytical abilities and to help them see that patience and persistence

can lead them to a solution to almost any problem.

As a teacher coordinator of the Urban Math Collaborative, a national organization, Ms. Hairston is working for positive change in the mathematics curriculum. She is trying to promote more critical thinking and greater use of language activities—discussions and writing—in the study of mathematics. She also gives her students assignments to research the contributions made in science and mathematics by members of underrepresented minorities.

As a teacher, she keeps herself alert to mathematical relationships that exist in the world and shares them with her students. She teaches all levels of high school mathematics, from general mathematics through algebra, geometry, and advanced algebra. "I try to make my geometry class a lab, with opportunities for exploration that allow students to see the beauty of the structure of geometry," she says. "I also like giving the students graphs and asking why they think certain things occur." In short, she wants her students to want to learn and to share her excitement about mathematics.

Ms. Hairston has a bachelor's degree from Smith College in Northampton, Massachusetts, with a double major in mathematics and psychology. She received her teaching credentials through the California state university system.

10.2 RATIONAL EQUATIONS AND INEQUALITIES

Objectives

After studying this section, you will be able to
- Find zeros of rational functions
- Solve rational equations and inequalities

Part One: Introduction

Zeros of Rational Functions

Finding the real zeros of rational functions is similar to finding the real zeros of polynomial functions.

Example   Find the real zeros of $f(x) = \frac{x^2 - 5x - 36}{x - 3}$.

There is a restriction on the domain of f—$x \neq 3$.

Recall that $f(x) = 0$ only when the *numerator* of the rational expression is zero. If we find the zeros of the polynomial in the numerator and if function f is defined at these values, then these values are the zeros of f.

$$x^2 - 5x - 36 = 0$$
$$(x - 9)(x + 4) = 0$$
$$x = 9 \text{ or } x = -4$$

The rational function f is defined at these two values of x, so the zeros of f are 9 and -4.

What happens if an expression cannot be factored?

Example   Find all complex zeros of $f(x) = \frac{x^3 - 5x^2 + 9x - 6}{x - 3}$.

The domain of f has one restriction—$x \neq 3$. We need to find the values of x that make the numerator 0. If f is defined at these values, the values are zeros of f.

According to the Rational-Zeros Theorem, ± 1, ± 2, ± 3, or ± 6 could be zeros. Using synthetic division, we check 2.

$$
\begin{array}{r|rrrr}
2 & 1 & -5 & 9 & -6 \\
  &   & 2 & -6 & 6 \\
\hline
  & 1 & -3 & 3 & 0 \\
\end{array}
$$

The remainder is 0, so 2 is a zero. The quotient, $x^2 - 3x + 3$, cannot be factored. We use the quadratic formula to find its roots:

$$x = \frac{3 + \sqrt{3}i}{2} \text{ and } x = \frac{3 - \sqrt{3}i}{2}$$

The zeros of f are 2, $\frac{3}{2} + \frac{\sqrt{3}}{2}i$, and $\frac{3}{2} - \frac{\sqrt{3}}{2}i$.

Solving Rational Equations and Inequalities

In our work with rational functions, we often need to solve *rational equations.* Rational equations are equations that contain at least one rational expression.

Example   *If $f(x) = \frac{1}{x}$ and $g(x) = \frac{2}{x^2}$, for what values of x does the sum of $f(x)$ and $g(x)$ equal 3?*

We are asked to find the values of x for which $f(x) + g(x) = 3$.

Substituting	$\dfrac{1}{x} + \dfrac{2}{x^2} = 3$
Multiply both sides by x^2	$\dfrac{x^2}{x} + \dfrac{2x^2}{x^2} = 3x^2$
Simplify terms	$x + 2 = 3x^2$
	$0 = 3x^2 - x - 2$
	$0 = (3x + 2)(x - 1)$
	$x = -\dfrac{2}{3} \text{ or } x = 1$

The functions $f(x)$ and $g(x)$ are both defined at these values of x. The sum of $f(x)$ and $g(x)$ is 3 at $x = -\frac{2}{3}$ and $x = 1$.

Example   *Given $f(x) = \frac{x^2 - 5x + 6}{x^2 - 4}$, find all values of x such that $f(x) \leq 0$.*

We are asked to solve the inequality $\frac{x^2 - 5x + 6}{x^2 - 4} \leq 0$. To do this, we factor the rational expression and graph the solutions of the resulting *rational inequality.*

$$\frac{x^2 - 5x + 6}{x^2 - 4} \leq 0$$

Factor $$\frac{(x - 2)(x - 3)}{(x - 2)(x + 2)} \leq 0$$

Each factor gives a boundary value. The boundary values are $x = 2$, $x = 3$, and $x = -2$. At $x = -2$ and $x = 2$, the left side of the inequality is undefined. Only $x = 3$ makes the inequality a true statement. So only this point is marked with a solid dot on the number line below.

We choose a test point from each region determined by the boundary values. Let's test -3, 0, 2.5, and 5.

Test Point	Left Side	Is $f(x) \leq 0$?
$x = -3$	6	No, $\quad 6 > 0$
$x = 0$	-1.5	Yes, $-1.5 \leq 0$
$x = 2.5$	$-\dfrac{1}{9}$	Yes, $\quad -\dfrac{1}{9} \leq 0$
$x = 5$	$\dfrac{2}{7}$	No, $\quad \dfrac{2}{7} > 0$

The solutions of the inequality are shown on the following graph.

Let's look at the graph of f on the coordinate plane. Notice that $f(x) \leq 0$ for the same values of x that were graphed on the number line.

Part Two: Sample Problems

Problem 1 If $f(x) = \dfrac{3x - 1}{x} + \dfrac{3}{x - 3}$ and $g(x) = \dfrac{9}{x^2 - 3x}$, what are the values of x for which $f(x) = g(x)$?

Solution The restrictions are $x \neq 0$ and $x \neq 3$.
We are asked to find the values of x that make $f(x) = g(x)$.

$$\frac{3x - 1}{x} + \frac{3}{x - 3} = \frac{9}{x^2 - 3x}$$

Factor the denominator
$$\frac{3x - 1}{x} + \frac{3}{x - 3} - \frac{9}{x(x - 3)} = 0$$

Multiply both sides by the least common multiple (LCM) of the denominators, $x(x - 3)$.

$$\left(\frac{3x - 1}{x} + \frac{3}{x - 3} - \frac{9}{x(x - 3)}\right) \cdot x(x - 3) = 0 \cdot x(x - 3)$$

$$(3x - 1)(x - 3) + 3x - 9 = 0$$

$$3x^2 - 10x + 3 + 3x - 9 = 0$$

$$3x^2 - 7x - 6 = 0$$

$$(3x + 2)(x - 3) = 0$$

$$x = -\frac{2}{3} \text{ or } x = 3$$

Since $f(x)$ and $g(x)$ are undefined at $x = 3$, there is only one solution, $x = -\frac{2}{3}$.

Problem 2

Bill and Tom washed cars to raise money for a school fund drive. It took Tom three minutes longer to wash a car than it took Bill. Together they washed nine cars per hour. How long did it take Bill to wash a car by himself?

Solution

If m = the number of minutes it takes Bill to wash a car, then $m + 3$ = the number of minutes it takes Tom to wash a car. The number of cars Bill and Tom washed in 60 minutes is $\frac{60}{m}$ and $\frac{60}{m + 3}$ respectively.

$$\frac{60}{m} + \frac{60}{m + 3} = 9$$

Multiply both sides by $m(m + 3)$

$$60(m + 3) + 60m = 9m(m + 3)$$
$$60m + 180 + 60m = 9m^2 + 27m$$
$$0 = 9m^2 - 93m - 180$$
$$0 = 3m^2 - 31m - 60$$

By the quadratic formula, $m = \frac{-5}{3}$ or $m = 12$. Since m must be positive, it took Bill 12 minutes to wash a car.

Problem 3

A baseball team has a record of 47 wins and 39 losses. How many games must the team win in a row in order for its winning percentage to be above .650?

Sports Page

Central Division	W	L
Centerville Cardinals	47	39
Beantown Bombers	45	41

Solution

Let w = the number of games the team must win in a row.
Then $\frac{47 + w}{47 + 39 + w}$ is the ratio of $\frac{\text{total wins}}{\text{total games}}$.
Find the value of w when this ratio is greater than 0.650.

$$\frac{47 + w}{86 + w} > 0.650$$

Multiply both sides by $(86 + w)$

$$\frac{(47 + w)(86 + w)}{(86 + w)} > 0.650(86 + w)$$
$$47 + w > 55.9 + 0.65w$$
$$0.35w > 8.9$$
$$w > \frac{8.9}{0.35} \approx 25.43$$

The team must win at least 26 games in a row for its winning percentage to be above .650.

Part Three: Exercises and Problems

Warm-up Exercises

In problems 1–4, find the LCM of each pair of numbers.

1 6, 7   **2** x, y   **3** x, xy   **4** $x + 1, x^2 - 1$

In problems 5 and 6, solve each equation.

5 $\dfrac{4}{x} + \dfrac{3}{x^2} = 1$

6 $\dfrac{27}{(x + 1)^2} - \dfrac{3}{x + 1} = 4$

7 Find the zeros of $f(x) = \dfrac{(x + 2)(2x - 3)(3x + 1)}{(x - 2)(3x - 1)}$.

8 Bill can word-process text in three-fourths the time it takes Marsha. Bill worked on a project for two hours, and then Marsha joined him. Working together, they finished in one hour.

   a How long did Bill work?
   b How long did Marsha work?
   c How long would it take Marsha to do the project alone?
   d How long would it take Bill to do the project alone?
   e How long would it take if they worked together the entire time?

9 Solve $\dfrac{x}{x + 1} > 5$ for x.

10 Solve $\dfrac{x - 3}{x - 5} \geq 0$ for x and graph the solution on a number line.

Problem Set

11 Solve $\dfrac{x^2 + x - 12}{x + 5} = 0$ for x.

In problems 12–15, solve for x.

12 $(x + 3)(x - 5) = 0$ **13** $(x + 3) \div (x - 5) = 0$
14 $(x + 3) + (x - 5) = 0$ **15** $(x + 3) \cdot (x - 5) = 9$

In problems 16–19, solve for x.

16 $\dfrac{1}{x} + \dfrac{2}{x} = 1$

17 $\dfrac{2}{x} = \dfrac{3}{x + 4}$

18 $\dfrac{2}{3x + 5} + \dfrac{6}{3x + 5} = 1$

19 $\dfrac{1}{2} + \dfrac{3}{x + 2} = 2$

20 Solve $\dfrac{a}{x} = \dfrac{3}{4}$ for a in terms of x.

21 Find the zeros of the function $g(x) = \dfrac{(x + 2)(x + 3)^2}{(x + 3)(x + 4)}$.

In problems 22–24, simplify and state restrictions.

22 $\dfrac{x^2 + x}{x}$ **23** $\dfrac{x^3 - 5x^2 - 4x + 20}{(9 - x^2)(4 - x^2)}$ **24** $\dfrac{x^2 - 5x - 6}{x + 1}$

25 a If Bob can do a job in 10 minutes, what portion of the job can he do in 1 minute?

b If Bill can do a job in 20 minutes, what portion of the job can he do in 1 minute?

c If Jill can do a job in x minutes, what portion of the job can she do in 1 minute?

In problems 26–29, solve for x.

26 $\dfrac{x}{6} - \dfrac{3x}{4} = \dfrac{5}{2}$

27 $\dfrac{5}{x} + \dfrac{7}{x^2} = 2$

28 $\dfrac{6}{x+2} + \dfrac{8}{x+2} = 1$

29 $\dfrac{6}{x-5} = \dfrac{8}{x-5} - \dfrac{1}{2}$

30 Find the zeros of the function $h(x) = \dfrac{x^2 + 9x - 36}{x^2 - 36}$.

In problems 31 and 32, divide.

31 $\dfrac{x^2 - 5x}{x} \div (3x - 15)$

32 $\dfrac{x^2 + x + 1}{x^2 - 1} \div \dfrac{x^3 - 1}{(x - 1)^2}$

In problems 33–35, solve for x.

33 $\dfrac{5}{x} + \dfrac{7}{x} < 1$

34 $\dfrac{2x^2 - x + 5}{3x^2 + x + 7} < \dfrac{2}{3}$

35 $\dfrac{5}{x} \le \dfrac{7}{x} + \dfrac{2}{3}$

36 Alex can finish a job in six hours, and Biff can do the same job in eight hours. What fraction of the job is completed by both working together for

a One hour?   **b** Two hours?   **c** Three hours?

In problems 37 and 38, simplify.

37 $\dfrac{42x^6}{21x^4 + 63x^2}$

38 $\dfrac{16x^4 + 32x^3}{10x^2 + 20x}$

In problems 39–41, solve and graph the solution on a number line.

39 $\dfrac{(x - 3)(x + 4)}{(x + 1)} \ge 0$

40 $\dfrac{5 - x}{x^2} \le 0$

41 $\dfrac{x}{x + 5} < 0$

42 Solve $\dfrac{9}{x - 3} - \dfrac{6}{x} = \dfrac{57}{x(x - 3)}$ for x.

43 Machine 1 can do a job in three hours, machine 2 can do the same job in four hours, and machine 3 can do the job in five hours. How many hours will the job take if all three machines work together?

44 Solve $A = p + prt$ for p.

45 Find the value(s) of c so that $x^3 + 2x^2 + cx + 4$ is divisible by $x - 1$.

Problem Set, *continued*

46 Find all complex zeros of $f(x) = x^4 + x^3 + x^2 + 3x - 6$.

47 A number less the product of its reciprocal and 12 is 4. Find the number.

In problems 48 and 49, solve for x.

48 $\dfrac{5}{x-7} + \dfrac{3}{x+4} = \dfrac{8x-1}{(x-7)(x+4)}$

49 $\dfrac{3}{2x+1} + \dfrac{5}{x-3} = \dfrac{13x-5}{(2x+1)(x-3)}$

50 Find all complex zeros of $p(x) = x^4 + 5x^3 + 9x^2 - x - 14$.

51 The Cubics won x games during the month of April and lost three fewer than they won. The ratio of wins to losses was 5:4.

   a How many wins did they have in April?
   b How many games did they play in April?

52 Refer to the diagram.

   a Find the coordinates of A.
   b Find the coordinates of B.
   c Find the slope m of $\overline{AB}$.

In problems 53–55, solve for x. (Hint: Factor each side.)

53 $ax + 2x = a^2 - 4a - 12$ **54** $ax + a^2 = 16 - 4x$

55 $ax - 3x = a^3 - 27$

56 For what values of a is $x = 2$ a solution of the inequality $\dfrac{3a+x}{x-3a} < 1$?

57 One personal computer has a printer that can print a page in 30 seconds. A second computer has a printer that can print a page in 20 seconds.

   a How long will it take to print a 500-page document if both printers work together?
   b If the first printer starts on page 1, on what page should the second printer start in order for them to finish at approximately the same time?

58 The sum of the reciprocals of two consecutive integers is $-\frac{9}{20}$. Find the integers.

59 Let $f(x) = x^2 + x$ and $g(x) = x^2 - x$. Simplify each expression.

   a $\dfrac{f(x)}{g(x)}$
      b $\dfrac{f(x-2)}{g(x-2)}$
      c $\dfrac{f(3x)}{g(3x)}$

60 Let $(x + 3) \cdot f(x) = x^2 - 9$.

   a Solve for $f(x)$.
            b Graph $y = f(x)$.

61 Find the values of k so that $f(x) = \dfrac{x^2 + kx - 32}{x - 2}$ is a polynomial function.

HISTORICAL SNAPSHOT

ANCIENT PROBLEMS
They don't get easier

The Rhind Papyrus is an Egyptian text on mathematics that was recorded by a scribe named Ahmes around 1650 B.C. It was named after Henry Rhind, a Scottish antiquary who sold the document to the British Museum, where it is now displayed. The text, written on papyrus, is believed to be a revised copy of an earlier treatise.

The first part of the work involves unit fractions—fractions with a numerator of 1. In this treatise, any fraction other than a unit fraction or $\frac{2}{3}$ is expressed as the sum of unit fractions with unlike denominators. For example, the fraction $\frac{2}{29}$ would be written as $\frac{1}{24} + \frac{1}{58} + \frac{1}{174} + \frac{1}{232}$. The fraction $\frac{2}{3}$ was expressed directly as "$\frac{2}{3}$".

The second part of the work consists of eighty-five problems. Many of the problems had practical applications, but others apparently were written to be solved for fun.

Egyptian fractions were always one part of something. The sign for 'one part of' was �open-oval⌣. Fractions shown below are $\frac{1}{10}$, $\frac{1}{9}$, $\frac{1}{8}$ and $\frac{1}{7}$.

Here are three examples of problems from the papyrus. The examples show how algebra problems were written before Diophantus developed his system of algebraic notation. (See the Historical Snapshot on page 134.) For each problem, write an equation that you think represents what is described in the problem. Then solve the equation.

1 "A quantity and its seventh added together give 19. What is the quantity?"

2 "A quantity and its two thirds are added together, one third of this is added, then one third of this sum is taken, and the result is 10. What is the quantity?"

3 "I have gone three times into the hekat measure, my one third has been added to me, [and I return], having filled the hekat measure. What is it, that this says?"

ADDING AND SUBTRACTING RATIONAL EXPRESSIONS WITH LIKE DENOMINATORS

$$(3x + 21) \div \left(\frac{x^2 - 4}{x^2} \right)$$

Objectives

After studying this section, you will be able to
- Add rational expressions with like denominators
- Subtract rational expressions with like denominators

Part One: Introduction

Addition of Rational Expressions

To add two or more rational expressions with like denominators, we add the numerators, just as we do with numeric fractions. We still must note restrictions, however.

Example *Add the following.*

a $\dfrac{2}{9} + \dfrac{5}{9}$

$\dfrac{2}{9} + \dfrac{5}{9}$

$= \dfrac{2 + 5}{9}$

$= \dfrac{7}{9}$

b $\dfrac{2x}{x + 3} + \dfrac{3}{x + 3}$

$\dfrac{2x}{x + 3} + \dfrac{3}{x + 3}$

$= \dfrac{2x + 3}{x + 3}; x \neq -3$

The denominators remain unchanged.

When we multiplied rational expressions, we factored first, which guaranteed that the answers were in simplified form. When we add rational expressions, the sum may need to be simplified further. Consider the following example.

Example   *Add the following.*

a $\dfrac{2}{9} + \dfrac{4}{9}$

$$\dfrac{2}{9} + \dfrac{4}{9}$$

$$= \dfrac{2 + 4}{9}$$

$$= \dfrac{6}{9}$$

$$= \dfrac{2}{3}$$

b $\dfrac{2x}{x + 3} + \dfrac{6}{x + 3}$

$$\dfrac{2x}{x + 3} + \dfrac{6}{x + 3}$$

$$= \dfrac{2x + 6}{x + 3}$$

$$= \dfrac{2(x + 3)}{x + 3}$$

$$= 2; \ x \neq -3$$

Again, we note restrictions.

Subtraction of Rational Expressions

To subtract rational expressions with like denominators, subtract their numerators. The answer will often need to be simplified further.

Example   *Subtract* $\dfrac{x + 2}{x + 1}$ *from* $\dfrac{x^2}{x + 1}$.

Rewrite the problem $\dfrac{x^2}{x + 1} - \dfrac{x + 2}{x + 1}$

Subtract numerators $= \dfrac{x^2 - (x + 2)}{x + 1}$

Distribute $= \dfrac{x^2 - x - 2}{x + 1}$

Factor $= \dfrac{(x + 1)(x - 2)}{x + 1}$

Simplify $= x - 2; \ x \neq -1$

Example   *Subtract* $\dfrac{x^3 - x + 5}{x + 5}$ *from* $\dfrac{x^3 + x^2 - 15}{x + 5}$.

Note that $x \neq -5$ is a restriction.

$$\dfrac{x^3 + x^2 - 15}{x + 5} - \dfrac{x^3 - x + 5}{x + 5}$$

$$= \dfrac{(x^3 + x^2 - 15) - (x^3 - x + 5)}{x + 5}$$

Remember to subtract every term of the polynomial being subtracted.

$$= \dfrac{x^3 + x^2 - 15 - x^3 + x - 5}{x + 5}$$

$$= \dfrac{x^2 + x - 20}{x + 5}$$

$$= \dfrac{(x + 5)(x - 4)}{x + 5}$$

$$= x - 4; \ x \neq -5$$

Part Two: Sample Problems

Problem 1   Let $f(x) = \dfrac{(x + 4)^2}{x - 3}$ and $g(x) = \dfrac{2x^2 - 12x - 31}{x - 3}$.

   a Express the function h, the sum of f and g, in simplified form.
   b Graph the function h.

Solution   **a** $h(x) = f(x) + g(x)$

$$= \frac{(x + 4)^2}{x - 3} + \frac{2x^2 - 12x - 31}{x - 3}$$

$$= \frac{x^2 + 8x + 16 + 2x^2 - 12x - 31}{x - 3}$$

$$= \frac{3x^2 - 4x - 15}{x - 3}$$

$$= \frac{(3x + 5)(x - 3)}{x - 3}$$

$$= 3x + 5; \ x \neq 3$$

   b

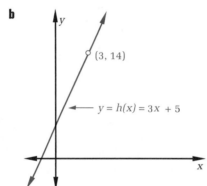

(3, 14)

$y = h(x) = 3x + 5$

Problem 2   Given the functions $f(x) = \dfrac{x^2 - 4x + 3}{(x - 3)(x^2 - x - 1)}$ and $g(x) = \dfrac{-3x + 9}{(x - 3)(x^2 - x - 1)}$, find the zeros of h, where $h(x) = f(x) - g(x)$.

Solution $f(x) - g(x) = h(x)$ and $h(x) = 0$, so

$$\frac{x^2 - 4x + 3}{(x - 3)(x^2 - x - 1)} - \frac{-3x + 9}{(x - 3)(x^2 - x - 1)} = 0$$

$$\frac{x^2 - 4x + 3 - (-3x + 9)}{(x - 3)(x^2 - x - 1)} = 0$$

$$\frac{x^2 - 4x + 3 + 3x - 9}{(x - 3)(x^2 - x - 1)} = 0$$

$$\frac{x^2 - x - 6}{(x - 3)(x^2 - x - 1)} = 0$$

$$\frac{(x - 3)(x + 2)}{(x - 3)(x^2 - x - 1)} = 0$$

The numerator is zero when $x = 3$ or $x = -2$. Our work seems to be finished. But be careful! What are the restrictions on h's domain? We can use the quadratic formula to find the restrictions.

$$x \neq 3,\ x \neq \frac{1 + \sqrt{5}}{2},\ x \neq \frac{1 - \sqrt{5}}{2}$$

Since $h(3)$ is undefined, $x = 3$ must be rejected. So $x = -2$ is the only zero of h.

Part Three: Exercises and Problems

Warm-up Exercises

1 Match each expression on the left with an equivalent expression on the right.

a $\dfrac{x + 4}{2}$

b $\dfrac{9}{2} + \dfrac{\sqrt{3}}{2}$

c $\dfrac{7}{x}$

d $\dfrac{5}{3}$

i $\dfrac{3}{x} + \dfrac{4}{x}$

ii $\dfrac{x}{2} + \dfrac{4}{2}$

iii $\dfrac{x + 5}{3} - \dfrac{x}{3}$

iv $\dfrac{9 + \sqrt{3}}{2}$

In problems 2–6, simplify.

2 $\dfrac{9}{5} - \dfrac{3}{5}$

3 $\dfrac{7}{3} + \dfrac{8}{3}$

4 $\dfrac{x}{y} - \dfrac{1}{y}$

5 $\dfrac{7x}{3} + \dfrac{8x}{3}$

6 $\dfrac{7}{x} + \dfrac{8}{x}$

In problems 7–9, solve each equation and simplify each expression.

7 $\dfrac{2x}{3} + \dfrac{x}{3}$

8 $\dfrac{5}{x} - \dfrac{x - 7}{x} = \dfrac{2x - 12}{x}$

9 $\dfrac{21}{x - 5} - \dfrac{5x - 4}{x - 5}$

Problem Set

10 If two of the following expressions are chosen at random, what is the probability that they are equal?

$$\dfrac{7}{3} + \dfrac{4}{3} \qquad \dfrac{11}{6} \qquad \dfrac{11}{3} \qquad \dfrac{10}{3} + \dfrac{1}{3} \qquad 3 + \dfrac{2}{3}$$

In problems 11–16, solve each equation and simplify each expression.

11 $\dfrac{4}{3x} = \dfrac{x}{3x}$

12 $\dfrac{5x}{2y} + \dfrac{3x}{2y} - \dfrac{14x}{2y}$

13 $\dfrac{4}{3x} + \dfrac{x}{3x}$

14 $\dfrac{15x}{3x + 5} + \dfrac{25}{3x + 5}$

15 $\dfrac{6}{5y} = \dfrac{3y}{5y}$

16 $\dfrac{4x + 2}{6x - 3} - \dfrac{6 - 4x}{6x - 3}$

Problem Set, *continued*

In problems 17 and 18, solve for x.

17 $\dfrac{7}{a} + x = \dfrac{4}{a}$

18 $x + \dfrac{a}{2b} = \dfrac{3a}{2b}$

19 a Find the ratio of the perimeter of rectangle A to that of rectangle B.
   b For what value of x will the ratio be 2:1?

In problems 20–22, simplify and give the restrictions.

20 $\dfrac{-5 + 14}{5 - 14}$

21 $\dfrac{-2x + 3}{2x - 3}$

22 $\dfrac{x + 3}{2x - 8} - \dfrac{3x - 5}{2x - 8}$

23 Find the value of three fourths divided by one half.

24 Simplify and give any restrictions.

   a $x^2 \cdot x^3$

   b $\dfrac{x^2}{\left(\dfrac{1}{x^3}\right)}$

   c $x^2 \div \dfrac{1}{x^3}$

25 Simplify and give the restrictions.

   a $\dfrac{x^2}{x + 3} + \dfrac{2x - 3}{x + 3}$

   b $\dfrac{x^2}{x + 3} - \dfrac{2x - 3}{x + 3}$

26 Find the least common multiple of each group.

   a 4, 7, 14
   b $x, x - 1, x + 1$
   c $x - 1, x + 1, x^2 - 1$

27 Let $f(x) = \dfrac{x}{x^2 + 1}$ and $g(x) = \dfrac{-1}{x^2 + 1}$.

   a Find $f(x) + g(x)$.
   b Find x such that $f(x) - g(x) = 0$.

In problems 28–30, solve each equation or inequality and simplify each expression.

28 $\dfrac{x^2}{x - 7} - \dfrac{49}{x - 7}$

29 $\dfrac{x^2}{x - 7} = \dfrac{49}{x - 7}$

30 $\dfrac{x^2}{x - 7} \leq \dfrac{49}{x - 7}$

In problems 31–34, solve each equation and simplify each expression.

31 $\dfrac{4y}{3x} - \dfrac{2y}{3x} + \dfrac{10y}{3x}$

32 $\dfrac{6}{x - y} + \dfrac{5}{x - y} + \dfrac{3}{y - x}$

33 $\dfrac{4}{x - 4} = \dfrac{6}{x - 4} + 1$

34 $\dfrac{x^2}{x^2 - 8x} - \dfrac{4x}{x^2 - 8x}$

35 Simplify $\dfrac{1}{x^2} + \dfrac{9}{x}$.

36 Solve $\frac{1}{x^2} + \frac{9}{x} + 8 = 0$.

In problems 37 and 38, find the zeros of each function.

37 $f(x) = \dfrac{x^2 - 49}{x} \cdot \dfrac{x^2 + x}{x + 7}$

38 $g(x) = \dfrac{x^2 - 4x - 21}{x^2 - 9}$

39 The distance between a point (x_1, y_1) and a line in the form $ax + by + c = 0$ is given by the rational expression

$$\frac{|ax_1 + by_1 + c|}{\sqrt{a^2 + b^2}}$$

Find the distance between the line $3x - 4y + 6 = 0$ and the point $(-6, 2)$.

In problems 40 and 41, simplify.

40 $\dfrac{2x}{x^2 - 3x - 18} - \dfrac{12}{x^2 - 3x - 18}$

41 $\dfrac{x^2}{x^3 - 27} + \dfrac{9}{27 - x^3}$

42 Solve $\frac{9}{2x} + \frac{4}{x} = 34$ for x.

43 Use the function $h(x) = f(x) - g(x)$, where $f(x) = \frac{x^3 - 2x^2}{x + 3}$ and $g(x) = \frac{9x - 18}{x + 3}$.
 a Find the zeros of h.   **b** Graph $y = h(x)$.

In problems 44–46, add or subtract and simplify.

44 $\dfrac{3x - 1}{8x^3 + 1} - \dfrac{x - 2}{8x^3 + 1}$

45 $\dfrac{x^3 - x^2}{x + 2} - \dfrac{4x - 4}{x + 2}$

46 $\dfrac{9}{x + 3} - \dfrac{x^2}{x + 3}$

47 Simplify $p(x) - q(x)$, where $p(x) = \frac{3}{x + 7}$ and $q(x) = \frac{3 - x}{x + 7}$.

48 Hose A fills a pool in 1 hour 25 minutes. A second hose, B, fills the pool in 2 hours. How long will it take to fill the pool if both hoses are used?

49 Solve the inequality $\frac{x^2 + 2x + 1}{x^2 - 1} > 0$.

50 Simplify $\frac{x^3 - 5x^2}{x^3 - 5x^2 - 14x} + \frac{4x^2}{x^3 - 5x^2 - 14x} + \frac{x^2 + 8}{x^3 - 5x^2 - 14x}$.

51 Solve $\frac{x + 4}{x + 1} + \frac{2x}{x - 1} = 6$ for x.

52 Let $f(x) = \frac{x^2 + 9}{x^3 + 6x^2 + 18x + 27}$ and $g(x) = \frac{6x}{x^3 + 6x^2 + 18x + 27}$.
 a Find $f(x) + g(x)$.
 b Find x such that $f(x) - g(x) = 0$.

In problems 53 and 54, simplify.

53 $\dfrac{(x + 1)^2 - 2(x + 1)}{(x + 1)^2 + (x + 1)}$

54 $\dfrac{(x + 2)(x^2 - 3x - 7) + 3(x + 2)}{(x - 4)(x^2 + 3x + 7) - 5(x - 4)}$

ADDING AND SUBTRACTING RATIONAL EXPRESSIONS WITH UNLIKE DENOMINATORS

Objectives

After studying this section, you will be able to
- Add rational expressions with unlike denominators
- Subtract rational expressions with unlike denominators

Part One: Introduction

Adding and Subtracting Rational Expressions with Unlike Denominators

To add or subtract rational expressions with different denominators, we first write them as equivalent fractions that have the same, or common, denominators. Then we can add or subtract numerators as we did in the last section.

To find a common denominator, we factor the denominators and look for a common multiple. In some cases, our work may go more quickly if we use the least common denominator, the smallest multiple of the denominators. But often we just find a common denominator. Then we multiply each term by a form of 1. Let's look at an example.

Example   *Add the numeric fractions $\frac{5}{7}$ and $\frac{1}{21}$.*

$$\frac{5}{7} + \frac{1}{21}$$

Factor denominators

$$= \frac{5}{7} + \frac{1}{3 \cdot 7}$$

A common denominator is 21.
Multiply the first term by $\frac{3}{3}$.

$$= \frac{5}{7} \cdot \frac{3}{3} + \frac{1}{21}$$

$$= \frac{15}{21} + \frac{1}{21}$$

$$= \frac{16}{21}$$

Example   *Add the rational expressions $\frac{3}{2x}$ and $\frac{1}{xy}$.*

$$\frac{3}{2x} + \frac{1}{xy}$$

A common denominator is 2xy $= \dfrac{3}{2x} \cdot \dfrac{y}{y} + \dfrac{1}{xy} \cdot \dfrac{2}{2}$

$$= \dfrac{3y + 2}{2xy}; \ x \neq 0, \ y \neq 0$$

Example   *Add $\dfrac{5}{x+2} + \dfrac{3}{x-2}$.*

A common denominator is $(x + 2)(x - 2)$.

$$\dfrac{5}{x + 2} + \dfrac{3}{x - 2} = \dfrac{5}{x + 2} \cdot \dfrac{x - 2}{x - 2} + \dfrac{3}{x - 2} \cdot \dfrac{x + 2}{x + 2}$$

$$= \dfrac{5(x - 2)}{(x + 2)(x - 2)} + \dfrac{3(x + 2)}{(x + 2)(x - 2)}$$

$$= \dfrac{5x - 10}{(x + 2)(x - 2)} + \dfrac{3x + 6}{(x + 2)(x - 2)}$$

Add numerators $= \dfrac{8x - 4}{(x + 2)(x - 2)}$

$$= \dfrac{4(2x - 1)}{(x + 2)(x - 2)}; \ x \neq 2, \ x \neq -2$$

Part Two: Sample Problems

Problem 1   *Simplify $\dfrac{16}{x^2 - 2x} - \dfrac{1}{2 - x}$.*

Solution

$$\dfrac{16}{x^2 - 2x} - \dfrac{1}{2 - x}$$

Factor denominators $= \dfrac{16}{x(x - 2)} - \dfrac{1}{2 - x}$

Notice opposite factors $(x - 2)$ and $(2 - x)$ $= \dfrac{16}{x(x - 2)} - \dfrac{1}{-(x - 2)}$

Multiply by a form of 1 $= \dfrac{16}{x(x - 2)} + \dfrac{1}{x - 2} \cdot \dfrac{x}{x}$

$$= \dfrac{16}{x(x - 2)} + \dfrac{x}{x(x - 2)}$$

$$= \dfrac{16 + x}{x(x - 2)}; \ x \neq 0, \ x \neq 2$$

Problem 2   *Simplify $\dfrac{4}{x^2} - \dfrac{16}{x^2 - 2x} - \dfrac{1}{x - 2}$.*

Solution

$$\dfrac{4}{x^2} - \dfrac{16}{x^2 - 2x} - \dfrac{1}{x - 2}$$

Factor denominators $= \dfrac{4}{x(x)} - \dfrac{16}{x(x - 2)} - \dfrac{1}{x - 2}$

In this case, it is most convenient to use the least common denominator (LCD), the smallest multiple of the denominators $x(x)$, $x(x - 2)$, and $x - 2$. The smallest multiple of the denominators is $x(x)(x - 2)$.

$$= \frac{4}{x^2} \cdot \frac{(x - 2)}{(x - 2)} - \frac{16}{x(x - 2)} \cdot \frac{x}{x} - \frac{1}{x - 2} \cdot \frac{x^2}{x^2}$$

$$= \frac{4(x - 2)}{x^2(x - 2)} - \frac{16x}{x^2(x - 2)} - \frac{x^2}{x^2(x - 2)}$$

$$= \frac{4x - 8 - 16x - x^2}{x^2(x - 2)}$$

$$= \frac{-8 - 12x - x^2}{x^2(x - 2)}; \ x \neq 0, \ x \neq 2$$

Part Three: Exercises and Problems

Warm-up Exercises

In problems 1 and 2, find the least common multiple.

1 12, 16, 24

2 $x^2 - x$, $x^2 + x$

In problems 3 and 4, find the greatest common factor.

3 12, 16, 24

4 $x^2 - x$, $x^2 + x$

In problems 5–8, find a common denominator.

5 $\dfrac{x^2}{x(x - 3)} + \dfrac{9}{x - 3}$

6 $\dfrac{x - 3}{27} - \dfrac{x}{3}$

7 $\dfrac{3x - 4}{x^2 - 5x + 6} - \dfrac{2x}{x^2 - 2x}$

8 $\dfrac{x}{4x + 8} + \dfrac{16}{8x^2 - 32}$

In problems 9 and 10, add or subtract.

9 $\dfrac{x^2 + 3x - 6}{x^2 - 2x - 3} - \dfrac{3}{x - 3}$

10 $\dfrac{x^2 + 25}{x^2 - 25} + \dfrac{-25}{x^2 + 5x}$

Problem Set

In problems 11–13, add or subtract.

11 $\dfrac{3}{x} + \dfrac{4}{y}$

12 $\dfrac{x}{4} + \dfrac{2}{x}$

13 $\dfrac{3x}{2y} - \dfrac{4y}{x}$

14 Explain why it is necessary to have a common denominator for fractions before they can be added or subtracted.

In problems 15–17, simplify.

15 $\dfrac{x \cdot x - 3 \cdot 3}{x - 3}$

16 $\dfrac{x \cdot x \cdot x - 3 \cdot 3 \cdot 3}{x - 3}$

17 $\dfrac{x \cdot x \cdot x - 3 \cdot 3 \cdot 3}{x \cdot x - 3 \cdot 3}$

18 Find the total surface area of the rectangular box.

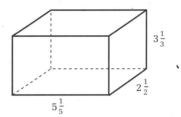

$3\frac{1}{3}$

$2\frac{1}{2}$

$5\frac{1}{5}$

In problems 19–22, find a common denominator.

19 $\dfrac{2}{x(x + 1)} - \dfrac{3x}{x + 1}$

20 $\dfrac{1}{x^2 + 2x} + \dfrac{3}{x^2 - 4}$

21 $\dfrac{2}{xy^3} + \dfrac{5}{x^2y}$

22 $\dfrac{6}{x^3 - x^2} + \dfrac{1}{x^2 + x}$

23 If there are two poles of heights a and b, with a wire stretched from the top of each to the bottom of the other, the wires meet at height h, such that $\frac{1}{a} + \frac{1}{b} = \frac{1}{h}$. If the poles have heights of 20 feet and 30 feet, at what height do the wires meet?

a

b

h

In problems 24 and 25, add or subtract.

24 $\dfrac{4}{x - 3} + \dfrac{5}{3 - x}$

25 $\dfrac{2}{x^2 - 3x} - \dfrac{5}{3 - x}$

26 Multiply the matrix by the scalar.

$$\dfrac{x}{x - 1} \cdot \begin{bmatrix} x^2 - 1 & x^2 - 2x + 1 \\ \dfrac{x - 1}{x} & \dfrac{x + 1}{x} \end{bmatrix}$$

27 Solve $\frac{1}{x} = \frac{1}{x + 1}$ for x.

28 Find the product $(x + y)^3$.

In problems 29–31, simplify.

29 $\dfrac{4}{x + 3} + \dfrac{2}{3x - 2}$

30 $\dfrac{1}{y} - \dfrac{1}{x} + \dfrac{2}{xy}$

31 $\dfrac{4}{x + 3} - \dfrac{2}{3x - 2}$

Problem Set, *continued*

32 Fill in the missing factor. _____ $\dfrac{(x-3)(x+2)}{x^2(x-1)} = \dfrac{x-1}{x+2}$

33 Find the reciprocal of the sum of the reciprocals of 2 and 3.

34 The ratio of the area of square A to the area of square B is 3:2. Find x.

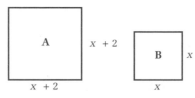

35 Find the reciprocal of the sum of the reciprocals of x and y.

In problems 36 and 37, solve for x.

36 $\dfrac{5}{x+2} = \dfrac{7}{x-4}$

37 $\dfrac{1}{2x} + \dfrac{5}{6x} = \dfrac{3}{4x^3}$

38 Solve $x\left(\dfrac{1}{x_1} + \dfrac{1}{x_2}\right) = 1$ for x.

39 Solve $\dfrac{1}{x} + \dfrac{1}{x+1} \geq 0$ for x and graph the solution on a number line.

In problems 40 and 41, solve for x.

40 $\dfrac{3}{x} + \dfrac{5}{2x} = \dfrac{7}{4}$

41 $2ax + 3x = 4a^2 - 9$

42 $\triangle ABC \sim \triangle DEF$.

    a Set up a correct proportion.
    b Solve your proportion for x.

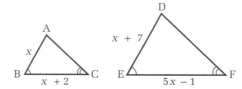

In problems 43–46, simplify.

43 $\dfrac{9}{x^2-2x} - \dfrac{3}{2-x}$

44 $\dfrac{3}{x} + \dfrac{5}{x-1}$

45 $\dfrac{2}{x} + \dfrac{5}{x} + \dfrac{7}{x+1}$

46 $\dfrac{x^2-xy-6y^2}{x^2-9y^2} \cdot \dfrac{4x+12y}{x^2+4xy+4y^2}$

47 Solve $\dfrac{x}{x-1} - \dfrac{2}{x+1} + x = 4$ for x.

48 Find a linear function in the form $f(x) = ax + b$ such that $f(2) = 9$ and $f(4) = 17$.

49 Solve the inequality $\dfrac{x^2-25}{x^2-9} \leq 0$.

In problems 50 and 51, let $f(x) = x^2$ and $g(x) = 3x + 10$. Find the following.

50 $\dfrac{f(x) - g(x)}{x+2}$

51 $\dfrac{f(x+3) - g(x+3)}{(x+3)+2}$

52 Refer to the diagram.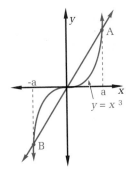

   a Find the coordinates of A and B.

   b Find the slope of $\overleftrightarrow{AB}$.

   c For what values of a is the slope greater than 2?

In problems 53–55, simplify.

53 $\dfrac{x-1}{x+1} + \dfrac{x+1}{x-1}$ **54** $\dfrac{x-1}{x+1} - \dfrac{x+1}{x-1}$ **55** $\dfrac{\dfrac{x-1}{x+1} + \dfrac{x+1}{x-1}}{\dfrac{x-1}{x+1} - \dfrac{x+1}{x-1}}$

56 Graph $f(x) = \dfrac{x-1}{x(x+1)}$.

In problems 57 and 58, let $f(x) = \dfrac{1}{x}$. Find each value.

57 $f(x+3) - f(x)$ **58** $f(x+h) - f(x)$

59 Solve $\dfrac{1}{x} + \dfrac{1}{x+1} = \dfrac{2x+1}{x(x+1)}$ for x.

60 It takes machine A twice as long to produce 10,000 bolts as it takes machine B. Together they do the job in 8 hours. How long will it take each machine to produce 5000 bolts if each works separately?

61 The expression $\dfrac{x}{x+5} + \dfrac{2}{x+2} - \dfrac{15}{(x+5)(x+2)}$ can be simplified to $\dfrac{B(x)}{x+2}$; $x \neq -2$, $x \neq -5$.

   a Find the binomial $B(x)$.

   b The result $\dfrac{B(x)}{x+2}$ has the obvious restriction $x \neq -2$, but why must we also restrict the answer to $x \neq -5$?

62 Refer to the diagram.

   a Use congruent triangles to find a and b if $\dfrac{h}{h_1} = \dfrac{a}{x+y}$ and $\dfrac{h}{h_2} = \dfrac{b}{x+y}$.

   b Add the equations in part **a** and solve for h.

 63 Find all ordered pairs of positive integers (a, b), with $a \geq 3$ and $b \geq 3$, so that $\dfrac{1}{a} + \dfrac{1}{b} > \dfrac{1}{2}$.

10.5 | COMPLEX FRACTIONS

Objective

After studying this section, you will be able to
- Simplify complex fractions

Part One: Introduction

Simplify Complex Fractions

In later work with mathematics, you will often see **complex fractions.**
Complex fractions are rational expressions that have fractions in
the numerator, the denominator, or both. Here are three examples.

$$\frac{1 + \frac{5}{n}}{n - \frac{1}{3}} \qquad \frac{\frac{a}{b} - \frac{b}{a}}{\frac{a}{b^2} - \frac{b}{a^2}} \qquad \frac{1}{1 - \frac{1}{x}}$$

In this section, you will learn two methods for simplifying complex
fractions into simpler rational expressions.

Example   *Simplify* $\dfrac{1 + \frac{5}{n}}{n - \frac{1}{3}}$.

Method 1

The numerator is a sum of rational expressions, and the denominator is a difference of rational expressions. We can add and subtract
respectively. The result will be a division problem.

$$\frac{1 + \dfrac{5}{n}}{n - \dfrac{1}{3}} = \frac{1 \cdot \dfrac{n}{n} + \dfrac{5}{n}}{n \cdot \dfrac{3}{3} - \dfrac{1}{3}}$$

Simplify numerator
Simplify denominator
$$= \frac{\dfrac{n + 5}{n}}{\dfrac{3n - 1}{3}}$$

$$= \frac{n + 5}{n} \div \frac{3n - 1}{3}$$

Multiply by
reciprocal of divisor
$$= \frac{n + 5}{n} \cdot \frac{3}{3n - 1}$$

$$= \frac{3(n + 5)}{n(3n - 1)} \text{ or } \frac{3n + 15}{3n^2 - n}; n \neq 0, n \neq \frac{1}{3}$$

454   Chapter 10   Rational Expressions, Equations, and Functions

Method 2

In this method we find a common denominator of the fractions in the numerator and denominator of the complex fraction and multiply the complex fraction by an appropriate form of 1.

We multiply by this form of 1 because $3n$ is a common multiple of n and 3

$$\dfrac{1 + \dfrac{5}{n}}{n - \dfrac{1}{3}} = \dfrac{1 + \dfrac{5}{n}}{n - \dfrac{1}{3}} \cdot \dfrac{3n}{3n}$$

Distribute

$$= \dfrac{3n + \dfrac{15n}{n}}{3n^2 - \dfrac{3n}{3}}$$

Simplify

$$= \dfrac{3n + 15}{3n^2 - n} \text{ or } \dfrac{3(n + 5)}{n(3n - 1)};$$

$$n \neq 0, n \neq \dfrac{1}{3}$$

In summary, in Method 1 we simplify the numerator and denominator and then divide. In Method 2 we multiply by a form of 1 and simplify. The form of 1 is determined by finding a common multiple of all denominators within the complex fraction.

Part Two: Sample Problems

Problem 1   Simplify $\dfrac{\dfrac{1}{b} - \dfrac{1}{a}}{\dfrac{1}{b^2} - \dfrac{1}{a^2}}$.

Solution   We will use Method 2.

$$\dfrac{\dfrac{1}{b} - \dfrac{1}{a}}{\dfrac{1}{b^2} - \dfrac{1}{a^2}} \cdot \dfrac{a^2b^2}{a^2b^2}$$

$$= \dfrac{\dfrac{a^2b^2}{b} - \dfrac{a^2b^2}{a}}{\dfrac{a^2b^2}{b^2} - \dfrac{a^2b^2}{a^2}}$$

$$= \dfrac{a^2b - b^2a}{a^2 - b^2}$$

$$= \dfrac{ab(a - b)}{(a + b)(a - b)}$$

$$= \dfrac{ab}{a + b}; a \neq 0, b \neq 0, a \neq -b, a \neq b$$

Problem 2   Solve $\dfrac{1}{1 - \frac{1}{x}} = x$ *for x.*

Solution
$$\frac{1}{1 - \dfrac{1}{x}} = x;\ x \neq 0;\ x \neq 1$$

$$\frac{1}{1 - \dfrac{1}{x}} \cdot \frac{x}{x} = x$$

$$\frac{x}{x - 1} = x;\ x \neq 1$$

$$\frac{x}{x - 1} \cdot (x - 1) = x \cdot (x - 1)$$

$$x = x^2 - x$$
$$0 = x^2 - 2x$$
$$0 = x(x - 2)$$

This implies that $x = 0$ or $x = 2$. Since $x \neq 0$ is a restriction, $x = 0$ is not a solution. The only solution is $x = 2$.

Problem 3   Given $f(x) = \frac{1}{x};\ x > 0$.

Write a general formula for the slope of $\overline{AB}$.

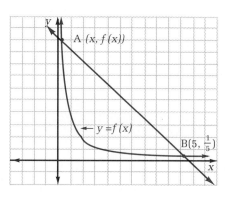

Solution
$$\text{Slope of } \overline{AB} = \frac{\dfrac{1}{x} - \dfrac{1}{5}}{x - 5};\ x \neq 5$$

Multiply by $\dfrac{5x}{5x}$
$$= \frac{\dfrac{1}{x} - \dfrac{1}{5}}{x - 5} \cdot \frac{5x}{5x}$$

$$= \frac{\dfrac{5x}{x} - \dfrac{5x}{5}}{(x - 5)5x}$$

$$= \frac{5 - x}{(x - 5)5x}$$

$$= \frac{-(x - 5)}{(x - 5)5x}$$

$$= \frac{-1}{5x};\ x \neq 5,\ x > 0$$

Part Three: Exercises and Problems

Warm-up Exercises

In problems 1–7, simplify.

1 $\dfrac{\dfrac{1}{2}}{\dfrac{2}{3}}$

2 $\dfrac{\dfrac{1}{a}}{\dfrac{b}{b}}$

3 $\dfrac{\dfrac{2}{3}}{\dfrac{5}{2}}$

4 $\dfrac{\dfrac{6}{5}}{\dfrac{2}{5}}$

5 $\dfrac{1 + \dfrac{2}{5}}{1 - \dfrac{3}{10}}$

6 $\dfrac{\dfrac{1}{2} - \dfrac{1}{5}}{\dfrac{1}{10}}$

7 $\dfrac{2 - \dfrac{3}{5}}{1 - \dfrac{1}{15}}$

In problems 8–10, write a common denominator in order to use Method 2.

8 $\dfrac{\dfrac{1}{x} + \dfrac{1}{5}}{1 + \dfrac{5}{x}}$

9 $\dfrac{1 - \dfrac{6}{x - 2}}{1 + \dfrac{5}{x + 2}}$

10 $\dfrac{\dfrac{x}{x - 3} + \dfrac{2}{x}}{1 - \dfrac{4}{x - 3}}$

Problem Set

In problems 11–14, simplify.

11 $\dfrac{1 + \dfrac{1}{x}}{1 - \dfrac{1}{x}}$

12 $\dfrac{1 + \dfrac{1}{x^2}}{1 - \dfrac{1}{x^2}}$

13 $\dfrac{1 + \dfrac{x}{x + 1}}{1 - \dfrac{x}{x + 1}}$

14 $\dfrac{1 + \dfrac{2}{3}}{1 - \dfrac{2}{3}}$

15 State all restrictions for the expression $\dfrac{\dfrac{3}{x} + \dfrac{1}{x + 2}}{\dfrac{1}{2x} - \dfrac{1}{x + 1}}$.

16 a Find the ratio of the area of the triangle to its hypotenuse.
b What are the restrictions on x?

3 x

4 x

In problems 17 and 18, simplify, using either Method 1 or 2.

17 $\dfrac{x - 3}{\dfrac{1}{x} - \dfrac{1}{3}}$

18 $\dfrac{3 + \dfrac{1}{x - 2}}{3 - \dfrac{1}{x - 2}}$

Problem Set, *continued*

In problems 19 and 20, simplify or solve.

19 $\dfrac{2x - 3}{4x} - \dfrac{2x - 1}{2x}$

20 $\dfrac{2x - 3}{4x} - \dfrac{2x - 1}{2x} = 0$

21 The harmonic mean of two numbers a and b is defined as $\dfrac{2}{\frac{1}{a} + \frac{1}{b}}$.

The harmonic mean of three numbers a, b, and c is $\dfrac{3}{\frac{1}{a} + \frac{1}{b} + \frac{1}{c}}$.

a Find the harmonic mean of 3 and 4.
b Find the harmonic mean of 2, 3, and 4.
c Find the harmonic mean of 2, 3, 4, and 5.

In problems 22 and 23, simplify.

22 $\dfrac{4}{x - 2} + \dfrac{6}{2 - x}$

23 $\dfrac{5}{2(x + 1)} + \dfrac{3}{x + 1}$

24 Given $f(x) = \frac{x + 3}{2x + 5}$. Find the slope of the line joining $(2, f(2))$ to $(4, f(4))$.

In problems 25–27, simplify.

25 $\dfrac{\frac{1}{x} + \frac{1}{y}}{\frac{1}{x} - \frac{1}{y}}$

26 $\dfrac{\frac{1}{x^3} + 8}{\frac{1}{x} + 2}$

27 $\dfrac{\frac{5}{x} - \frac{1}{2}}{\frac{25}{x^2} - \frac{1}{4}}$

28 The focal length f of a thin lens is given by

$$\frac{1}{f} = \frac{1}{d_o} + \frac{1}{d_i}$$

where d_o is the distance between the object and the lens and d_i is the distance between the image and the lens.

a Solve for f.
b Solve for d_i.

In problems 29 and 30, solve for x and graph the solution on a number line.

29 $\dfrac{x^2 - 9}{x^2 - 6x} \geq 0$

30 $\dfrac{x^2 - 9}{x^2 + 3x} \geq 0$

31 Let $f(x) = \frac{1}{x - 3}$. Find the general formula for the slope of the line joining $A(x, f(x))$ to $B(x + 5, f(x + 5))$ when $x > 3$.

32 Simplify $\dfrac{x - \frac{3}{x + 2}}{x - \frac{4}{x + 3}}$.

33 Solve $\dfrac{1}{1 + \frac{2}{x}} = x$.

34 Given $f(x) = 3 + \frac{2}{x}$, write a simplified expression for $f(f(x))$.

35 The sum of the slopes of lines l_1 and l_2 is $\frac{3}{4}$. Find the slope of the steeper line.

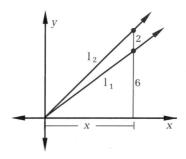

36 Let $g(x) = \frac{2 - 3x}{9x - 6}$. Write a simplified expression for $g\left(\frac{1}{x + 3}\right)$.

In problems 37–39, simplify.

37 $\dfrac{2}{x} + \dfrac{2 + \dfrac{4}{x}}{3 + \dfrac{6}{x}}$

38 $\dfrac{\dfrac{6}{x^2} + \dfrac{1}{x} - 1}{x - \dfrac{9}{x}}$

39 $\left(1 - \dfrac{1}{x}\right)\left(\dfrac{4x^2}{x^2 - 1}\right)$

In problems 40 and 41, find the values of x that make each statement true.

40 $x + 4 + \dfrac{6}{x - 1} = 0$

41 $\dfrac{\dfrac{1}{x} + \dfrac{1}{2}}{\dfrac{1}{x^2} - \dfrac{1}{4}} = 1$

42 After a rainstorm, pipeline A fills a reservoir in two hours. Pipeline B can fill the same reservoir in five hours, and pipeline C drains the reservoir in three hours.

 a If the reservoir is empty and all three pipelines are operating, how full will the reservoir be after one hour? After two hours?

 b Under the same conditions, after how long will the reservoir be filled?

43 Given $c^2 - s^2 = 2$, simplify $\dfrac{\dfrac{2s}{c}}{1 - \dfrac{s^2}{c^2}}$.

44 Given $f(x) = \dfrac{x}{x + 1}$, simplify.

 a $f(f(x))$

 b $\begin{bmatrix} 1 & 0 \\ 1 & 1 \end{bmatrix}\begin{bmatrix} 1 & 0 \\ 1 & 1 \end{bmatrix}$

 c $f(f(f(x)))$

 d $\begin{bmatrix} 1 & 0 \\ 1 & 1 \end{bmatrix}\begin{bmatrix} 1 & 0 \\ 1 & 1 \end{bmatrix}\begin{bmatrix} 1 & 0 \\ 1 & 1 \end{bmatrix}$

 e $f(f(f(f(x))))$

 f $\begin{bmatrix} 1 & 0 \\ 1 & 1 \end{bmatrix}\begin{bmatrix} 1 & 0 \\ 1 & 1 \end{bmatrix}\begin{bmatrix} 1 & 0 \\ 1 & 1 \end{bmatrix}\begin{bmatrix} 1 & 0 \\ 1 & 1 \end{bmatrix}$

Problem Set, *continued*

45 Find the slope of $\overline{AB}$.

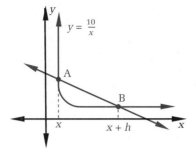

46 Find real numbers A, B, and C if

a $x^2 - 2x + 5 = Ax^2 + Bx + C$

b $6x + 9 = (A + B)x + (2A - B)$

c $\dfrac{A}{x - 4} + \dfrac{B}{x + 3} = \dfrac{3x + 2}{(x - 4)(x + 3)}$

47 Simplify $\dfrac{\frac{4}{x + h} - \frac{4}{x}}{h}$.

48 In the expansion of $\left(x + \frac{1}{x}\right)^6$, what is the coefficient of the term that does not contain x?

49 Let $f(x) = \dfrac{x}{x + 3}$. Find the value of a so that the slope of the line through $(a, f(a))$ and $(-2, f(-2))$ is 1.

In problems 50 and 51, graph each equation.

50 $x^2 - y^2 - 4(x - y) = 0$

51 $\dfrac{x^2 - y^2}{x - y} = 4$

52 Consider $f(x) = \dfrac{\frac{5}{x} + 3}{6 + \frac{2}{x}}$.

a As positive values of x get extremely large, what happens to the value of $f(x)$?

b As positive values of x get closer to zero, what happens to the value of $f(x)$? (Hint: Simplify the expression first.)

53 The expression $n = 2 + \cfrac{3}{2 + \cfrac{3}{2 + \cfrac{3}{2 + \ \cdots}}}$ is called an infinite continued fraction. The value of n can be determined by observing that $n = 2 + \frac{3}{n}$.

a Solve for n and check your result. Why does only one answer work?

b Find the value of $n = 1 + \cfrac{6}{1 + \cfrac{6}{1 + \cfrac{6}{1 + \cfrac{6}{1 + \ \cdots}}}}$.

CHAPTER SUMMARY

CONCEPTS AND PROCEDURES

After studying this chapter, you should be able to
- Recognize rational expressions (10.1)
- Simplify rational expressions (10.1)
- Multiply and divide rational expressions (10.1)
- Find zeros of rational functions (10.2)
- Solve rational equations and inequalities (10.2)
- Add and subtract rational expressions with like denominators (10.3)
- Add and subtract rational expressions with unlike denominators (10.4)
- Simplify complex fractions (10.5)

VOCABULARY

complex fraction (10.5)
rational equation (10.2)
rational expression (10.1)
rational inequality (10.2)
restricted value (10.1)
simplify (10.1)

1 Which of the following are rational expressions?

a $\sqrt{x} + \dfrac{1}{x + 2}$

b $\dfrac{x_1 + x_2 + x_3 + x_4}{4}$

c $\dfrac{x + 2}{1 + x^2}$

d $\dfrac{\sqrt{2} + x}{\sqrt{3} + x}$

e $\dfrac{5x^2 - 7x}{x + 4}$

f $x^3 - x + 1$

In problems 2–5, add or subtract.

2 $\dfrac{5x(x + 1)}{3x - 5} + \dfrac{(x - 5)(x + 5)}{3x - 5}$

3 $\dfrac{25x^2 + 6x}{5x + 7} - \dfrac{6x + 49}{5x + 7}$

4 $\dfrac{x^2}{x^2 - 6x + 5} - \dfrac{4x + 5}{x^2 - 6x + 5}$

5 $\dfrac{2x + 1}{(x + 3)(x - 3)} - \dfrac{x - 2}{(x + 3)(x - 3)}$

In problems 6–9, simplify.

6 $\dfrac{\dfrac{1}{3} + \dfrac{1}{4}}{\dfrac{1}{6} - \dfrac{1}{2}}$

7 $\dfrac{2 + \dfrac{3}{5}}{4 - \dfrac{1}{5}}$

8 $\dfrac{\dfrac{4}{5} - \dfrac{2}{3}}{\dfrac{1}{7} + \dfrac{1}{2}}$

9 $\dfrac{2 \cdot 5 + 3}{4 \cdot 5 - 1}$

10 Refer to the diagram.

a Find the ratio of the area of rectangle A to the area of rectangle B.

b For what values of x will the ratio be equal to 2?

11 Study the example, then copy and complete the chart.

Expressions	Greatest Common Factor	Least Common Multiple
$2(x - 1)$, $(x + 1)(x - 1)$	$x - 1$	$2(x + 1)(x - 1)$
$3(x + 4)$, $6(x + 4)(x - 2)$		
$3x - 21$, $x^2 - 49$		
$x^2 + 3x$, $x^2 + 6x + 9$		

In problems 12–15, solve for y.

12 $\dfrac{5}{y} - \dfrac{9}{y} = 2$

13 $\dfrac{y(y - 2)}{y - 4} = 0$

14 $\dfrac{2}{y} + \dfrac{3}{y + 1} = \dfrac{-8}{y(y + 1)}$

15 $\dfrac{y(y - 2)}{y - 2} = 0$

In problems 16 and 17, solve for x.

16 $\dfrac{12}{x+2} = \dfrac{3}{x-2} + \dfrac{6}{x^2-4}$

17 $\dfrac{8}{x-8} + \dfrac{2}{5} = \dfrac{x}{x-8}$

18 Simplify and state restrictions.

$$\dfrac{x^2-4}{x+3} \cdot \dfrac{x^2+5x+6}{x+1} \cdot \dfrac{x^2+3x+2}{x-1} \cdot \dfrac{x^2+x-2}{x-2}$$

19 Find the zeros of $f(x) = \dfrac{x^2+x-20}{x-3}$.

In problems 20–22, simplify.

20 $3 + \dfrac{4}{7}$

21 $x + \dfrac{3}{x}$

22 $x - 5 + \dfrac{2}{x+5}$

23 Find the zeros of the function $f(x) = \dfrac{3x^2-2x-8}{x-2}$.

In problems 24–26, simplify.

24 $\dfrac{2x-3}{3-2x}$

25 $\dfrac{(2-3x)^2}{(3x-2)^2}$

26 $\dfrac{(2-3x)^3}{(3x-2)^2}$

In problems 27 and 28, perform the indicated operations and state restrictions.

27 $\dfrac{x(x+1)}{x+2} \div \dfrac{x(x-1)}{x+2}$

28 $\dfrac{3x^2+15x}{x^2+2x-15} \cdot \dfrac{x^2-9}{x+3}$

29 Graph $\dfrac{2}{x} + \dfrac{3}{y} = \dfrac{12}{xy}$.

30 The volume of the box shown is $x^3 + 2x^2 - 8x$, its length is $x + 4$, and its width is x. Find its height.

In problems 31–33, simplify.

31 $\dfrac{1}{x+y} + \dfrac{1}{x-y}$

32 $\dfrac{x}{x+y} + \dfrac{y}{x-y}$

33 $\dfrac{x}{x+y} - \dfrac{y}{x-y}$

34 Find all vertical asymptotes of the graph of $f(x) = \dfrac{x^2+2x}{x^2-3x-10}$.

35 Solve for (x, y, z).

$$\begin{cases} 3x + y - 2z = 8 \\ 2x - y + 3z = 25 \\ x - 3y - 4z = 6 \end{cases}$$

36 Find all complex zeros of $f(x) = \dfrac{x^3 - 7x^2 + 16x - 16}{x - 5}$.

37 Simplify $\dfrac{x + 1 - \dfrac{9}{x + 1}}{x + 2 - \dfrac{6}{x + 1}}$.

38 Simplify $\dfrac{3 + x}{2 - 3x} \cdot \dfrac{3x^2 - 2x}{x^2 + 6x + 9}$ and note restrictions.

39 The denominator of a fraction is two more than its numerator. If the fraction is added to its reciprocal, the sum will be twice the original numerator. Find the original numerator.

40 Let $f(x) = \dfrac{x^2 - 7x + 12}{x^2 - 9}$. Find all values of x such that $f(x) \leq 0$.

In problems 41–44, solve for x.

41 $\dfrac{15}{x^2} - \dfrac{2}{x} - 1 = 0$

42 $\dfrac{5}{x - 3} - \dfrac{4}{x + 4} = 0$

43 $\dfrac{4}{(x - 3)^2} - \dfrac{5}{x - 3} = -1$

44 $6ax = 5ax + 16a^2$

45 Let $x + y = 1$. Write $\dfrac{\frac{1}{x} + 1}{\frac{1}{x} - x}$ in terms of y.

In problems 46 and 47, let $f(x) = \dfrac{2x + 3}{3x - 1}$ and $g(x) = \dfrac{2x - 1}{3x + 4}$.

46 Simplify $f(g(x))$.

47 Simplify $g(f(x))$.

48 Let $s^2 + c^2 = 1$. Simplify $\dfrac{1}{s^2} + \dfrac{1}{c^2}$.

49 Let $f(x) = \dfrac{x^2 + cx + b}{x + 4}$. Find b and c if $f(-3) = 31$ and $f(-5) = -59$.

50 Divide $f(x + 3)$ by $f(x - 3)$ if $f(x) = x^2 - 9$.

51 N. Vestor purchased $20,000 worth of bonds, some at 10% and the rest at 9%. His investment yields $1930 a year.

  a Determine how much he invested at each rate.
  b Explain why he might not have wanted to invest all $20,000 at the higher rate of return.

52 Of the 57 test questions Irma Wisdom has answered, she has 48 right.

  a If she makes no more mistakes, how many more questions must she answer so that she will have answered 90% or more correctly?
  b If the exam has 75 questions, can she get a score higher than 90%?

In problems 1–4, simplify and state restrictions.

1 $\dfrac{(x + 3)(x + 4)}{(x + 2)(x + 3)}$

2 $\dfrac{x^3 + 2x^2}{x}$

3 $\dfrac{x^2 - 4}{x^2 + 3x + 2}$

4 $\dfrac{3x^3 + 15x^2 + 18x}{x^3 - 9x}$

5 Multiply $\dfrac{x + 7}{3 - x} \cdot \dfrac{x + 4}{x + 7} \cdot \dfrac{x - 3}{x - 4}$ and write your answer in simplest form.

In problems 6 and 7, solve for x.

6 $\dfrac{6}{x - 2} = \dfrac{5}{x - 3}$

7 $\dfrac{3}{x^2 - 4} = \dfrac{-2}{5x + 10}$

8 A baseball team has a record of 35 wins and 20 losses. How many games must the team win in a row in order for its winning percentage to be above .750?

9 Let $f(x) = \dfrac{x^2 + 16}{x^2 + 9x + 20}$ and $g(x) = \dfrac{8x}{x^2 + 9x + 20}$.

   a Find $f(x) + g(x)$.

   b Find x such that $f(x) - g(x) = 0$.

In problems 10–12, perform the indicated operations.

10 $\dfrac{2x}{x - 7} + 3$

11 $x + \dfrac{3}{x}$

12 $x - 5 + \dfrac{2}{x + 5}$

In problems 13 and 14, add or subtract.

13 $\dfrac{x}{x - y} - \dfrac{2x}{x + y} - \dfrac{2xy}{x^2 - y^2}$

14 $\dfrac{2}{x^2 - y^2} + \dfrac{2}{(x + y)^2}$

In problems 15 and 16, simplify.

15 $\dfrac{1 + \dfrac{x}{y}}{1 - \dfrac{x}{y}}$

16 $\dfrac{\dfrac{1}{x - y} - 1}{2 - \dfrac{x}{x - y}}$

17 Simplify $\dfrac{\dfrac{x + 3}{x - 3} + \dfrac{x - 3}{x + 3}}{\dfrac{x + 3}{x - 3} - \dfrac{x - 3}{x + 3}}$.

18 Let $f(x) = \dfrac{2}{x}$. Simplify $\dfrac{f(x + h) - f(x)}{h}$.

Linear Programming

In Section 7.3, you saw how the solutions of systems of inequalities can be graphically represented on the coordinate plane. Now consider the following system of inequalities and the graph of its solution set (the shaded region in the diagram).

$$\begin{cases} x \geq 3 \\ y \geq 2 \\ x \leq 3y \\ x + y \leq 12 \end{cases}$$

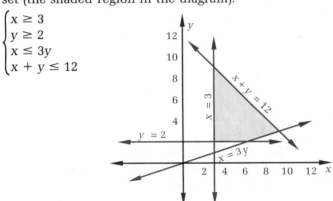

Suppose we define the function $p(x, y) = 6x + 3y$ in such a way that the function's domain is restricted to values of x and y that are in the solution set of this system. Is there a particular input (x, y) that yields the maximum possible output of function p? Is there another input for which the value of p is at a minimum? Let's test the coordinates of some of the points in the region that represents the domain.

Point	(x, y)	$6x + 3y$
A	(3, 9)	$6(3) + 3(9) = 45$
B	(4, 6)	$6(4) + 3(6) = 42$
C	(7, 5)	$6(7) + 3(5) = 57$
D	(5, 3)	$6(5) + 3(3) = 39$
E	(9, 3)	$6(9) + 3(3) = 63$
F	(3, 2)	$6(3) + 3(2) = 24$
G	(6, 2)	$6(6) + 3(2) = 42$

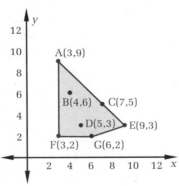

This listing, of course, is not exhaustive—there are infinitely many points in the solution set of the system, and we cannot test them all. We do notice, however, that both the greatest output we found (63) and the least output we found (24) were produced by inputs—(9, 3) and (3, 2)—that correspond to vertices of the shaded region. In fact, it has been proved that in cases such as this, the maximum and minimum values of a function will always correspond to vertices of the region representing the function's domain.

> *If a linear function has a domain of ordered pairs (x, y) that corresponds to a polygonal region of the coordinate plane, the maximum and minimum values of the function will occur at vertices of the region.*

The preceding theorem is the basis of a technique, called *linear programming,* that is frequently used by businesses to determine the best way of allocating their resources to minimize costs or to maximize profits.

Example   *Charlotte Russe earns money by crafting and selling wooden toys. She makes two kinds of toys—trains, on which she makes a profit of $6 each, and trucks, on which she makes a profit of $3 each. To satisfy the demand, she must produce at least 3 trains and 2 trucks each day, and at least one fourth of the toys she produces must be trucks. If she can produce no more than 12 toys in a day and if she can sell all that she produces, how many of each kind of toy should Charlotte make each day to maximize her profits?*

This problem can be modeled by the graph that we have already considered. We let x = the number of trains Charlotte makes and y = the number of trucks she makes. She must make at least 3 trains and 2 trucks, so $x \geq 3$ and $y \geq 2$. At least one fourth of the toys must be trucks, so $x \leq 3y$; and because her maximum daily output is 12 toys, $x + y \leq 12$. Thus, the restrictions on Charlotte's production, known as *constraints,* correspond to the system of inequalities presented at the beginning of this section.

Charlotte's profits can be represented by the function $p(x, y) = 6x + 3y$. As we have seen, under the given constraints the maximum value of this function is yielded by the input (9, 3), so Charlotte should produce 9 trains and 3 trucks each day to maximize her profits.

Linear-programming problems that involve only a few constraints in two variables can be solved by simply graphing the corresponding system of inequalities and testing the coordinates of the vertices in the function to be maximized or minimized. Most real-world applications of linear programming, however, involve so many variables that they must be dealt with by computer programs utilizing matrix operations.

Sample Problems

Problem 1   *The Kepler Model Company is planning to market a variety of electric racing-car sets. Each set will contain at least 8 sections of curved track and 4 sections of straight track. No set will contain more than 36 sections in all or more than 20 sections of either type. If the company makes a profit of $0.40 on each straight section and $0.65 on each curved section, what combination of track sections will be most profitable for the company?*

Solution   We let x = the number of curved sections in a set and y = the number of straight sections. Since there will be at least 8 and no more than 20 curved sections, $8 \leq x \leq 20$. Since there will be at least 4 and no more than 20 straight sections, $4 \leq y \leq 20$. The greatest number of sections will be 36, so $x + y \leq 36$. The following system and graph, therefore, represent the constraints.

$$\begin{cases} 8 \leq x \leq 20 \\ 4 \leq y \leq 20 \\ x + y \leq 36 \end{cases}$$

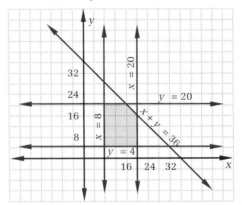

The profit function is $p(x, y) = 0.65x + 0.4y$, which we evaluate for the coordinates of the five vertices of the region—(8, 4), (8, 20), (16, 20), (20, 16), and (20, 4).

Vertex	0.65x + 0.40y
(8, 4)	0.65(8) + 0.4(4) = 6.8
(8, 20)	0.65(8) + 0.4(20) = 13.2
(16, 20)	0.65(16) + 0.4(20) = 18.4
(20, 16)	0.65(20) + 0.4(16) = 19.4
(20, 4)	0.65(20) + 0.4(4) = 14.6

The profit will be greatest ($19.40) for a combination of 20 curved sections and 16 straight sections.

Problem 2   *A certain publisher ships 300–450 books each week to a national chain of bookstores. Some of the books are shipped from the publisher's eastern warehouse, and some are shipped from the publisher's western warehouse, but at least one third of them must be shipped from each warehouse. The shipping cost per book is $0.37 from the eastern warehouse and $0.55 from the western warehouse. Find the minimum weekly shipping cost for these orders.*

Solution   If we let x = the number of books shipped from the eastern warehouse and y = the number of books shipped from the western warehouse, we can represent the constraints as follows.

$$\begin{cases} x + y \geq 300 \\ x + y \leq 450 \\ x \leq 2y \\ y \leq 2x \end{cases}$$

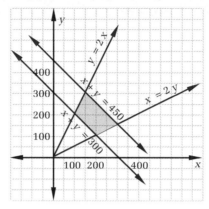

The vertices of the shaded region are at (100, 200), (150, 300), (300, 150), and (200, 100). We test these coordinates in the cost function, c(x, y) = 0.37x + 0.55y.

Vertex	0.37x + 0.55y
(100, 200)	0.37(100) + 0.55(200) = 147
(150, 300)	0.37(150) + 0.55(300) = 220.5
(300, 150)	0.37(300) + 0.55(150) = 193.5
(200, 100)	0.37(200) + 0.55(100) = 129

The minimum cost is $129, incurred when 200 books are shipped from the eastern warehouse and 100 are shipped from the western warehouse.

Problem Set

1 Graph the following system of inequalities, indicating the coordinates of the vertices of the region that represents the solution set.

$$\begin{cases} 0 \leq y \leq 8 \\ x \geq 1 \\ 2x + y \leq 16 \end{cases}$$

2 Refer to the graph shown.
   a What are the coordinates of points A, B, C, D, and E?
   b Use your answers to part **a** to find the maximum value of f(x, y) = 3x + 2y for the domain represented by the shaded region.

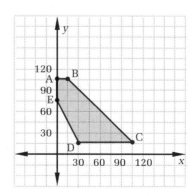

Problem Set, *continued*

3 If line ℓ has a slope of $-\frac{3}{2}$ and a y-intercept of 2 and line $\mathcal{M}$ has a slope of -2 and a y-intercept of 6, what are the coordinates of the point where ℓ and $\mathcal{M}$ intersect?

4 A milling machine can be used to produce either widgets or gimcracks. It takes 5 minutes to produce a widget and 6 minutes to produce a gimcrack, and the machine is in operation no more than 55 hours a week. Write a linear inequality to describe this situation, identifying the meaning of each variable used.

5 Let $c(x, y) = 15x - 5y$, with the following restrictions.

$$x \geq 1 \qquad y \geq 0 \qquad x \leq 4 \qquad y \leq 2x + 5$$

a Find the maximum output of function c.
b Find the minimum output of function c.

6 Maximize and minimize the function $g(x, y) = 3x - 4y$ for the values of (x, y) in the shaded region.

7 A jewelry craftsman produces bracelets and necklaces that contain both gold and platinum. The following table shows the amounts of precious metals used in the production of these items.

	Metal Content (Grams)		Grams Available
	Bracelet	Necklace	per Week
Gold	12	6	120
Platinum	9	18	144

a Write a system of inequalities that represents the given constraints, using x to represent the number of bracelets produced and y to represent the number of necklaces produced.
b Suppose that the craftsman makes a profit of $130 on each bracelet and $90 on each necklace. Write an expression that represents his total profit on the two items.
c Use your answers to parts **a** and **b** to calculate the craftsman's maximum weekly profit.
d How many of each item should he produce per week to obtain the maximum profit?

8 Graph the region represented by the following system of inequalities. What are the coordinates of the region's vertices?

$$\begin{cases} 0 \leq x \leq 6 \\ 0 \leq y \leq 11 \\ y \leq 2x + 3 \\ 3y \geq 2x \end{cases}$$

9 An electronics company manufactures personal tape players, on which it makes a profit of $28 each, and personal CD players, on which it makes a profit of $33 each. The company intends to produce at least 60 tape players and 100 CD players per day, but its factory is not equipped to assemble more than a total of 200 of these items each day. What should the company's daily production of these items be if profits are to be as great as possible?

10 If $z = 0.60x + 0.95y$ for the set of values of (x, y) represented by the shaded polygonal region, what are the maximum and minimum values of z?

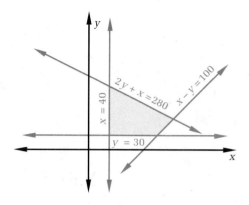

11 Waste Schleppers, Inc., transports sealed containers of aluminum and glass refuse to a recycling plant. Each full container of aluminum weighs 800 pounds and occupies 60 cubic feet of space, and each full container of glass weighs 900 pounds and takes up 75 cubic feet. The firm charges $100 per container for hauling aluminum and $80 per container for hauling glass. If the Waste Schleppers truck has a load limit of 22,000 pounds and only 1740 cubic feet of cargo space, what is the firm's maximum revenue for a single haul?

12 Penny Black, a stamp collector, purchases mixed lots of stamps from two suppliers, Commemorative Corner and House of Postage. She has found that each 100-stamp lot is likely to be made up of the following types of stamps.

	United States Stamps	Foreign Stamps
Commemorative Corner	75%	25%
House of Postage	40%	60%

If Commemorative Corner charges $5.50 per lot and House of Postage charges $4.75 per lot, and if Penny wants to add at least 400 United States stamps and 300 foreign stamps to her collection, what is the minimum amount she should expect to pay?

EXPONENTIAL AND LOGARITHMIC FUNCTIONS

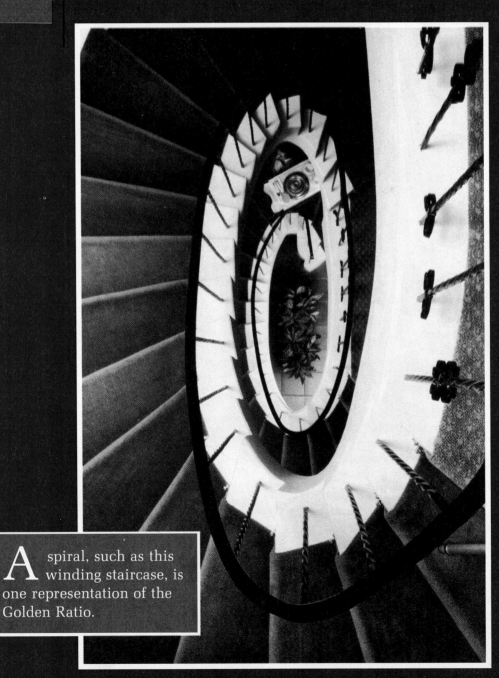

A spiral, such as this winding staircase, is one representation of the Golden Ratio.

11.1 | DEFINITIONS AND GRAPHS OF THE EXPONENTIAL AND LOGARITHMIC FUNCTIONS

Objectives

After studying this section, you will be able to
- Graph exponential functions
- Graph logarithmic functions
- Use the definition of the logarithmic function

Part One: Introduction

The Graph of the Exponential Function

Recall the definition of an exponential function.

 An exponential function is a function that can be written in the form $f(x) = a^x$, where a is a positive constant and $a \neq 1$. The positive constant a is called the base.

Let's graph several exponential functions on the same coordinate system and look for patterns.

Shown are the graphs of $f(x) = 2^x$, $g(x) = 3^x$, and $h(x) = 4^x$.

Notice the following similarities among these exponential functions.

All have domain $\{x : x \in \mathscr{R}\}$.
All have range $\{y : y > 0\}$.
All have y-intercepts of 1.
They all have $y = 0$ as a horizontal asymptote.
None of the graphs has an x-intercept.

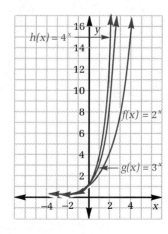

So far the base a has always been chosen greater than 1. What happens if we use a base a such that $0 < a < 1$? Again look for patterns as we graph $f(x) = \left(\frac{1}{2}\right)^x$, $g(x) = \left(\frac{1}{3}\right)^x$, and $h(x) = \left(\frac{1}{4}\right)^x$ on the same coordinate system. Notice that all five patterns seen when $a > 1$ are also true when $0 < a < 1$.

When $a > 1$, the function $f(x) = a^x$ increases as x increases. The larger the value of a the more rapidly the function increases.

When $0 < a < 1$, the function $f(x) = a^x$ decreases when x increases. The smaller the value of a the more rapidly the function decreases.

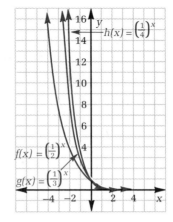

Notice that $f(x) = 2^x$ and $g(x) = \left(\frac{1}{2}\right)^x$ are reflections over the y-axis.

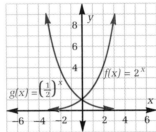

The Graph of the Logarithmic Function

The inverse of the exponential function is called the *logarithmic function.* To graph the inverse of a function of x we reflect the graph of the function about the line $y = x$. Thus, to graph the logarithmic function we reflect the exponential function about the line $y = x$.

Algebraically, we reverse the coordinates of the ordered pairs (x, y) of the original function to obtain the inverse function. So if $y = a^x$ is our original function, the equation with x and y reversed is $x = a^y$. Let's graph the exponential function $y = 2^x$ and its inverse, the logarithmic function $x = 2^y$.

Notice the following about the logarithmic function.

The domain is $\{x : x > 0\}$.

The range is $\{y : y \in \mathcal{R}\}$.

The x-intercept is 1.

There is no y-intercept.

$x = 0$ is a vertical asymptote.

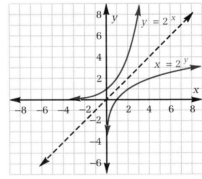

The Definition of the Logarithmic Function

Normally, when we write the equation of the inverse of $y = a^x$ we would reverse the roles of x and y to get $x = a^y$ and then solve for y. Unfortunately, we do not yet know how to solve this equation for y. Instead we state the following very important definition.

The equation $y = \log_a (x)$ is equivalent to the exponential equation $x = a^y$. $y = \log_a (x)$ is read "y equals the logarithm to the base a of the number x." The base a is always positive, and $a \neq 1$.

Note Sometimes we write $\log_a (x)$ as $\log_a x$, without parentheses. We will use parentheses when they clarify the expression.

An important observation: Notice that since $y = \log_a x$ means $x = a^y$, a logarithm is an exponent. It is the exponent that the base a requires in order to equal the number x.

Example *Evaluate y in each equation.*

a $y = \log_2 8$

$y = \log_2 8$ is equivalent to $8 = 2^y$, so $y = 3$.

b $y = \log_4 \left(\frac{1}{16}\right)$

$y = \log_4 \left(\frac{1}{16}\right)$ means $\frac{1}{16} = 4^y$, so $y = -2$.

c $y = \log_{10} -10$

$y = \log_{10} -10$ is equivalent to $-10 = 10^y$. No matter what value is chosen for y, 10^y is greater than zero. *There is no real-number logarithm for a nonpositive number.*

Part Two: Sample Problems

Problem 1 *Solve for the indicated variable.*

a $\log_b 16 = 2$ **b** $\log_{\frac{1}{2}} c = -3$ **c** $\log_x 9 = \frac{2}{3}$

Solution **a** $\log_b 16 = 2$ means $b^2 = 16$. Therefore, $b = 4$ or $b = -4$. Since the base must be positive, the only correct answer is $b = 4$.

b $\log_{\frac{1}{2}} c = -3$ means $c = \left(\frac{1}{2}\right)^{-3}$, or $c = \frac{1^{-3}}{2^{-3}} = 2^3 = 8$. Therefore, $c = 8$.

c $\log_x 9 = \frac{2}{3}$ is equivalent to $x^{\frac{2}{3}} = 9$. Raise each side to the $\frac{3}{2}$ power.

$\left(x^{\frac{2}{3}}\right)^{\frac{3}{2}} = 9^{\frac{3}{2}}$

$x = 27$

Problem 2 *Evaluate the following for $a > 0$ and $a \neq 1$.*

a $\log_a a$ **b** $\log_a 1$

Solution **a** Let $y = \log_a a$. This is equivalent to $a = a^y$, so $y = 1$. Therefore, $\log_a a = 1$ for $a > 0$, $a \neq 1$.

b Let $y = \log_a 1$. This is equivalent to $1 = a^y$. Since $a^0 = 1$, we have $y = 0$. Therefore, $\log_a 1 = 0$ for $a > 0$, $a \neq 1$.

Problem 3   Write each of the following exponential equations in logarithmic form.

   a $3^y = 12$ **b** $a^5 = 100$ **c** $4^{\log_4 16} = x$

Solution   **a** $3^y = 12$ is equivalent to $\log_3 12 = y$.
   b $a^5 = 100$ is equivalent to $\log_a 100 = 5$.
   c $4^{\log_4 16} = x$ is equivalent to $\log_4 x = \log_4 16$. In this case, we see that x must equal 16.

Problem 4   Evaluate each of the following, where $a > 0$ and $a \neq 1$.

   a $a^{\log_a x}$ **b** $\log_a (a^x)$

Solution   **a** We convert to logarithmic form. We let $y = a^{\log_a x}$, which is equivalent to $\log_a x = \log_a y$. Therefore, y must equal x. We have shown that $a^{\log_a x} = x$ for all $a > 0$, $a \neq 1$.
   b We convert to exponential form. We let $y = \log_a (a^x)$, which means the same as $a^y = a^x$. Therefore, y must equal x. We have shown that $\log_a (a^x) = x$ for all $a > 0$, $a \neq 1$.

Part Three: Exercises and Problems

Warm-up Exercises

1 Complete the following statement with one word. A logarithm is an _____ .

2 Rewrite $x^y = z$ in logarithmic form.

3 Rewrite $\log_m n = w$ in exponential form.

4 Solve for w.
   a $\log_6 w = 3$ **b** $\log_5 w = 3$ **c** $\log_2 w = -3$

5 If a function is randomly selected from the list below, what is the probability that it is an exponential function?
   $g(x) = 3x$ $h(x) = x^4$ $k(x) = 4^x$ $j(x) = 3^2$ $m(x) = 10^x$

6 Copy and complete the following tables.

a x	0	1	2	3	4	−1	−2	−3	−4
10^x									

b x									
$\log_{10} x$	0	1	2	3	4	−1	−2	−3	−4

Problem Set

7 Solve for x.

   a $\log_2 x = \log_2 16$ **b** $\log_2 x = \log_4 16$

8 Solve for M.

   a $M = \log_7 7$ **b** $M = \log_7 1$

9 Evaluate.

   a $2^{\log_2 8}$ **b** $10^{\log_{10} 1000}$ **c** $3^{\log_3 81}$

10 Evaluate.

   a $\log_2 2^8$ **b** $\log_5 5^3$ **c** $\log_{10} 10^{-4}$

11 Solve for y.

   a $y = \log_5 125$ **b** $5 = \log_{125} y$ **c** $3 = \log_y 125$

12 Solve for x.

   a $\log_x 125 = 3$ **b** $\log_x 0.25 = -2$
   c $\log_4 x = 12$ **d** $x = \log_8 -8$

13 Complete each table.

   a

x	0	1	2	3	−1	−2	−3		
2^x								32	$\frac{1}{16}$

   b

x	1	2	4	8	$\frac{1}{2}$	$\frac{1}{4}$	$\frac{1}{8}$		
$\log_2 x$								−3	5	−4

14 Write 3^{12} as a power of each of the following.

   a 9   **b** 27   **c** 81

15 Solve each equation for y.

   a $y = \log_8 2$ **b** $y = \log_2 \frac{1}{8}$ **c** $y = \log_8 \frac{1}{2}$

16 Simplify $8^{n-2} \cdot 2^{n+5} \cdot 4^{3n}$.

17 **a** Graph $f(x) = 10^x$ and $g(x) = \log_{10} x$ on the same coordinate plane.
     b The graphs are symmetrical with respect to what line?

In problems 18–21, evaluate each expression.

18 $\log_6 216$ **19** $\log_{0.01} 100$ **20** $\log_7 (7^{-9})$ **21** $\log_2 -4$

In problems 22–25, write the equivalent logarithmic form.

22 $4^3 = 64$ **23** $3^{-4} = \dfrac{1}{81}$ **24** $x = 2^{4.5}$ **25** $2^n = 363$

26 Solve $\log_4 (4^{10}) = x$ for x.

27 Rationalize the denominator. $\dfrac{5 + \sqrt{3}}{5 - \sqrt{3}}$

28 Explain what is wrong with the following solution.

Given: $\log_x 16 = 2$ Solution: $x^2 = 16$, so $x = 4$ or $x = -4$

29 Evaluate each expression.

    a $\log_{10} 10 + \log_{10} 100 + \log_{10} 1000$ **b** $\log_{10} 1{,}000{,}000$

    c $\log_3 81 - \log_3 9$ **d** $\log_3 \left(\dfrac{81}{9}\right)$

30 Match each graph with its corresponding function.

    a $f(x) = 2^x$ **b** $g(x) = \log_2 x$

    c $h(x) = 2^{-x}$ **d** $k(x) = -\log_2 x$

i   **ii**   **iii**   **iv**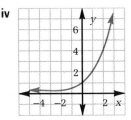

31 Evaluate.

    a $\log_2 \sqrt{64}$ **b** $\dfrac{1}{2}(\log_2 64)$ **c** $\sqrt{\log_2 64}$

32 Rewrite $5^7 = 78{,}125$ in logarithmic form.

33 The volume of the larger cube exceeds the volume of the smaller cube by 10. Find x.

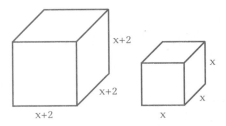

34 Sketch the graph of each logarithmic function.

    a $y = \log_2 (x + 5)$ **b** $y = (\log_2 x) + 5$

35 Sketch the following functions on the same coordinate system.

    a $f(x) = \log_2 x + \log_2 8$ **b** $h(x) = \log_2 (8x)$

    c $g(x) = \log_2 (x + 8)$

36 Suppose $\log_a 2 \approx 0.333$ and $\log_a 3 \approx 0.528$. Approximate $\log_a 6$.

37 Specify the domain and range of each function.

    a $f(x) = \log_3 x$ **b** $g(x) = 3^x$ **c** $h(x) = \log_5 |x|$

38 Graph $f(x) = \log_2 x$ and the inverse of $f(x)$.

39 Which of the following is the graph of the inverse of $f(x) = 2^x$?

a

b

c

d

40 Simplify $\left(\dfrac{3^2 - 3^0}{9^{\frac{3}{2}}}\right)^{\frac{-1}{3}}$.

41 Graph $y = \log_{\frac{1}{4}} x$.

42 **a** Graph $f(x) = 5^{-x}$ and $g(x) = \log_{\frac{1}{5}} x$ on the same plane.
    b Explain why the two graphs are symmetrical with respect to the line $y = x$.

43 Find the x- and y-intercepts and the asymptotes of the graphs of the following functions.

    a $y = 7^x$ **b** $y = \log_7 x$

44 The graph of $y = f(x)$ is shown. Sketch a graph of each of the following equations.

    a $y = -f(x)$
    b $y = f(-x)$
    c $y = |f(x)|$

45 Solve $\log_x 16 = \frac{3}{4}$ for x.

Two Important Exponential and Logarithmic Functions

Objectives

After studying this section, you will be able to

- Solve problems involving exponential and logarithmic functions with base 10
- Solve problems involving exponential and logarithmic functions with base *e*

Part One: Introduction

Exponential and Logarithmic Functions with Base 10

In this section, we study the most often used logarithmic functions, those with bases of 10 and *e*.

> ➤ **The logarithmic function $f(x) = log_{10} x$ is called the common logarithmic function.**

In fact, this logarithmic function is so common that the base 10 is often omitted. The function is written as $f(x) = \log x$.

Example   *Evaluate each of the following expressions.*

a $\log 100$

$y = \log 100$ is equivalent to $10^y = 100 = 10^2$, so $y = 2$. Therefore, $\log 100 = 2$.

b $\log 0.001$

$y = \log 0.001$ is equivalent to $10^y = 0.001 = 10^{-3}$, so $y = -3$. Therefore, $\log 0.001 = -3$.

c $\log 27$

$y = \log 27$ means $10^y = 27$. The solution for y is somewhere between 1 and 2, since $10^1 = 10$ and $10^2 = 100$. Fortunately, we can obtain a very close approximation to $\log 27$ using a scientific calculator's $\boxed{\text{LOG}}$ key, which evaluates base 10 logarithms. To find $\log 27$ we enter 27 $\boxed{\text{LOG}}$. The display shows $\boxed{1.431363764}$. The exact value of $\log 27$ is an irrational number, so we say, $\log 27 \approx 1.431363764$.

Example   *Find log 324.78.*

$y = \log 324.78$ is equivalent to $10^y = 324.78$. The answer must be between 2 and 3. Why? Using a calculator to find a closer approximation, we enter 324.78 $\boxed{\text{LOG}}$. The calculator displays $\boxed{2.511589277}$. So $\log 324.78 \approx 2.511589277$. This answer means that $324.78 \approx 10^{2.511589277}$. Let's check using either the calculator's $\boxed{x^y}$ key or its $\boxed{10^x}$ key. We enter 2.511589277 $\boxed{10^x}$ and get $\boxed{324.7799996}$. This is very close to 324.78.

Example   *If log x = 2.4516, what is x?*

$\log x = 2.4516$ is equivalent to $10^{2.4516} = x$. We know that x must be between 100 and 1000. Why? To find a closer approximation, we use our calculator and enter 2.4516 $\boxed{10^x}$. The display shows $\boxed{282.8785388}$. Therefore, if $\log x = 2.4516$, then $x \approx 282.88$.

Note   In the last example, we knew the logarithm of a number and were asked to find the number. This is sometimes called finding an *antilogarithm.*

Exponential and Logarithmic Functions with Base *e*

Logarithms and powers using a base of 10 are important because of our base-10 numeration system. Logarithms and powers in formulas that model real-world situations often involve another important base. This base, denoted by the letter *e*, is an irrational number whose value is approximately 2.718281828. Logarithms that use base *e* are called *natural logarithms.* Natural logarithms are used extensively in economics, engineering, physics, astronomy, anthropology, and biology.

 The logarithmic function $f(x) = \log_e (x)$, usually written $f(x) = \ln x$, is called the natural logarithmic function. The irrational number e has an approximate value of 2.718281828.

Remember, logarithms can have any positive number that is not 1 as a base. The definition of a logarithm works just the same for the irrational number *e* as it does for 10 or any other base. When the letter *e* is used in the rest of this chapter, it will always represent the number *e*.

Example   *Evaluate the following expressions.*

a $\ln e^4$
   Remember, $\ln x$ really means $\log_e x$. Let $y = \ln e^4$, which means $e^y = e^4$, so $y = 4$. Therefore, $\ln e^4 = 4$.

b $e^{\ln 2}$
   Let $y = e^{\ln 2}$. Now we convert this to logarithmic form using the definition of a logarithm in reverse.
   $\ln y = \ln 2$, so $y = 2$.

c $\ln 1$
   $y = \ln 1$ is equivalent to $e^y = 1$. Since any number to the zero power is 1, we have $y = 0$. Therefore, $\ln 1 = 0$.

Scientific calculators have the keys ⌊In⌋ and ⌊eˣ⌋, often as inverses on the same key, to calculate base e logarithms and antiloga-
rithms respectively. Enter 1 ⌊eˣ⌋ to see the value of e in the display
of your calculator.

Example   *Solve for x.*

a x = ln 100
   Remember, ln x means $\log_e x$. x = ln 100 is equivalent to
   $e^x = 100$. Since e is less than 3 and $3^4 = 81$, we expect the value
   of x to be somewhat more than 4. We can use a calculator for a
   closer approximation by entering 100 ⌊In⌋. The display is
   ⌊4.605170186⌋. Therefore, x ≈ 4.6052.

b ln x = 4
   Since ln x = 4 is equivalent to $e^4 = x$, to find x we use
   the ⌊eˣ⌋ key and enter 4 ⌊eˣ⌋. The display shows ⌊54.59815003⌋
   so x ≈ 54.6.

Part Two: Sample Problems

Problem 1   *Solve each of the following for x.*

a 400 = 50 *log* (10x)   **b** 900 = 15e^{12x}

Solution

a 400 = 50 log (10x)
       8 = log (10x)
   Convert to exponential form
       $10^8 = 10x$
       $10^7 = x$

b 900 = 15e^{12x}
       60 = e^{12x}
   Convert to logarithmic form
       ln 60 = 12x

       $\dfrac{\ln 60}{12} = x$

       0.3412 ≈ x

Problem 2   *The loudness L, measured in decibels (so called after Alexander
   Graham Bell), of a sound of intensity I is given by the logarithmic
   function $L(I) = 10 \log \left(\frac{I}{I_0}\right)$, where I_0, the threshold of hearing, is the
   faintest audible sound.*

a *If the faintest audible sound is made, how many decibels is that
   sound?*
b *Noise on a city street measures approximately 75 decibels. How
   many times as intense is this sound than the faintest audible sound?*
c *The noise produced in a thunderstorm is approximately 10^{11} times
   as intense as the faintest audible sound. What is the loudness of the
   sound in decibels?*

Solution

a Since the faintest sound has intensity $I = I_0$, we have
$L(I_0) = 10 \log \left(\frac{I_0}{I_0}\right) = 10 \log 1 = 10 \cdot 0 = 0$. The faintest possible sound has a loudness of 0 decibels.

b $75 = 10 \log \left(\frac{I}{I_0}\right)$, or $7.5 = \log \left(\frac{I}{I_0}\right)$. This is equivalent to $10^{7.5} = \frac{I}{I_0}$, or $10^{7.5}I_0 = I$.
Therefore, the intensity is $10^{7.5}$, or $\approx 31{,}622{,}777$, times as great as that of the faintest audible sound.

c The intensity is $I = 10^{11}I_0$ for a thunderstorm.
Therefore, $L = 10 \log \left(\frac{10^{11}I_0}{I_0}\right)$, or $L = 10 \log (10^{11})$
$$= 10 \cdot 11$$
$$= 110 \text{ decibels}$$

Problem 3

The Euler Bank compounds interest continuously.

a *If $5000 is invested in the Euler Bank at 7.85%, how much money will be in the account after 12 years?*
b *Susan invests $10,000 at the Euler Bank at 8.65%. In how many years will she have $250,000 in the bank?*

Solution

The formula for computing the amount in an account when interest is compounded continuously is

$A = Pe^{rt}$, where $P =$ the amount of the original deposit,
$\qquad\qquad r =$ the yearly interest rate, and
$\qquad\qquad t =$ the number of years the money has been in the account.

This is an example of the base e occurring in a business formula.

a $A = Pe^{rt}$
$\quad = 5000e^{0.0785(12)}$
$\quad = 5000e^{0.942}$
$\quad \approx 5000(2.5651)$
$\quad \approx \$12{,}825.53$

b $\qquad A = Pe^{rt}$
$250{,}000 = 10{,}000e^{0.0865t}$
$\qquad 25 = e^{0.0865t}$
$\qquad \ln 25 = 0.0865t$
$\qquad 3.2189 \approx 0.0865t$
$\qquad 37.2 \approx t$

Susan will have $250,000 in the bank after approximately 37.2 years.

Part Three: Exercises and Problems

Warm-up Exercises

1 Arrange in order from smallest to largest.
   a $\log 100$ **b** $10 \cdot \log 10$ **c** $(\log 10) \cdot (\log 10)$ **d** $\log (10^5)$

2 Evaluate.
   a $\ln \left(\dfrac{e^5}{e^2}\right)$ **b** $\ln e^5 - \ln e^2$ **c** $\ln e^3$

3 Evaluate the following expressions.

    a $\log 1$ **b** $\ln 1$ **c** $\log_2 1$ **d** $\log_8 1$

In problems 4–7, evaluate each expression without using a calculator.

    4 $\log 10{,}000$ **5** $\log 0.0001$ **6** $\ln\left(e^{\frac{1}{2}}\right)$ **7** $e^{\ln 5}$

In problems 8–11, use a calculator to evaluate each expression.

    8 $\log 0.000157$ **9** $\log 353$ **10** $\ln 0.0015$ **11** $\ln 53.4$

12 The noise produced by normal conversation is about 10^6 times as loud as the faintest audible sound. What is the loudness of this sound in decibels? (Hint: Use the formula in Sample Problem 2.)

Problem Set

13 Approximate each of the following to four decimal places.

    a $\log 27$ **b** $\log 3$ **c** $\log \dfrac{1}{3}$ **d** $\log \dfrac{1}{27}$

    e $\log 9$ **f** $\log 1$ **g** $\log \dfrac{1}{9}$

14 Solve for x.

    a $x = \ln 50$ **b** $x = \log 50$ **c** $\ln x = 6$ **d** $\log x = 6$

15 Solve for y.

    a $y = \ln -6$ **b** $-6 = \ln y$

16 Rectangle ABCD ~ rectangle PQRS
$AB = 40$, $AD = 35$, $PQ = 8$

    a Find the ratio AD:PS.
    b Find the ratio of the area of ABCD to the area of PQRS.
    c Find the ratio of the log of the area of ABCD to the log of the area of PQRS.

17 For what values of x does $\log x = \ln x$?

18 Solve $b = \log_4 \sqrt{2}$ for b.

19 If $\log x \approx 72.514$, how many digits does x have to the left of the decimal place?

20 Evaluate each expression to five decimal places.

    a $4(\log 3)$ **b** $2(\log 9)$ **c** $\log 81$ **d** $8\left(\log \sqrt{3}\right)$

21 Find the base e antilogarithm of 2.17 to the nearest thousandth.

22 The Last Chance National Bank compounds interest continuously. If Big Bucks deposits $15,000 at 6.57%, how long must he leave the money in the bank to become a millionaire?

23 If one of the following expressions is selected at random, what is the probability that it is negative?

$$\log 7 \qquad \log 0.7 \qquad \log \frac{1}{7} \qquad \log -7 \qquad \log 7.7$$

24 The threshold of pain from sound is 10^{12} times as intense as the faintest audible sound. What is the measure of this sound in decibels? (Hint: Use the formula in Sample Problem 2.)

25 Evaluate.
   a $\log_2 4$ **b** $\log_2 8$ **c** $\log_2 16$ **d** $\log_2 32$

26 Evaluate to four decimal places.
   a $\log 6 + \log 4$ **b** $\log 8 + \log 3$
   c $\log 12 + \log 2$ **d** $\log 24 + \log 1$

27 Evaluate.
   a $\log_3 81$ **b** $\log_{\frac{1}{3}} 81$ **c** $\log_{81} 3$

28 Calculate the following.
   a $\ln e^6$ **b** $e^{\ln e}$ **c** $4 \cdot \ln 1$

29 Evaluate to four decimal places.
   a $\log 10$ **b** $\log 20$ **c** $\log 40$ **d** $\log 80$

30 Evaluate to three decimal places.
   a $\ln 52,791$ **b** $\log -2151$ **c** $\log 11,235,813$ **d** $\ln 0.00000005$

31 The amount of money A in a savings account at time t is given by the formula $A = P\left(1 + \frac{r}{n}\right)^{nt}$, where P = the amount of money deposited, r = the yearly interest rate, n = the number of compounding periods per year, and t = the number of years the money has been in the bank. If $7000 was placed in a bank at 7.45% interest compounded quarterly for 12 years, how much will be in the bank at the end of that time?

32 Find the amount of money in an account in which $7000 has been earning 7.45% interest, compounded continuously, for 12 years. How does this answer compare with your answer to problem **31**?

33 Solve for x.
   a $65 = 10e^x$ **b** $750 = 15 \cdot 10^x$ **c** $\log 1000 = x$
   d $\log x = 9.54$ **e** $3.4 = \ln 2 + \ln x$ **f** $x = \ln e^3$

Problem Set, *continued*

34 a Find x if ln (3x + 4) = 2.
  b Find x if log (3x − 700) = 3.

35 Suppose $10,000 has been earning interest at 6% for eight years. Use the compound interest formula (see problem **31**) and the continuous compound interest formula $A = Pe^{rt}$ to calculate the amount in the bank

  a If interest is compounded quarterly
  b If interest is compounded monthly
  c If interest is compounded daily
  d If interest is compounded continuously

36 Solve $(\log_{10} x)^2 = 5 \log_{10} x + 6$ for x.

37 The noise in an office is 3162 times as intense as the faintest audible sound. The noise on a city street is 10 million times as intense as the faintest audible sound.

  a Find the number of decibels for each sound.
  b How many times as intense is the noise on a city street than the noise in an office?

38 Find the base 5 logarithm of 0.008.

39 Find y by finding the antilogarithm of the following.
  a log y = 3.2465   **b** log y = −3.9764
  c log y = 1.5796   **d** log y = −2.75

40 Solve $(\log_9 x)^2 = 81$ for x.

41 Find ln x if $\log_{10}$ x = 3.

42 Solve $\sqrt{w} + \sqrt{w + 3} = 3$ for w.

In problems 43–46, use a calculator to solve for x.
43 $40 = 10e^x$ **44** 0.815 = log x
45 $9000 = 5 \cdot 10^x$ **46** 3.4 = ln (2x)

47 Using the data in Sample Problem 3, part **a,** calculate the amount that would be in the account if interest were compounded monthly using the formula $A = P\left(1 + \frac{r}{n}\right)^{nt}$, where
  P = amount originally deposited,
  r = the yearly interest rate,
  n = the number of compoundings per year, and
  t = the number of years.

11.3 PROPERTIES OF LOGARITHMS

Objective

After studying this section, you will be able to
- Use seven properties of logarithms

Part One: Introduction

In this section we develop some properties of logarithms. We assume the base $a > 0$ and $a \neq 1$. We also assume we are finding logarithms of only positive numbers.

Since $a^0 = 1$ and $a^1 = a$, we have the following.

Property 1: $\log_a 1 = 0$ **Property 2:** $\log_a a = 1$

Recall that logarithmic and exponential functions are inverses and that if f and g are inverse functions, then $g[f(x)] = x$ and $f[g(x)] = x$. So if $f(x) = a^x$ and $g(x) = \log_a x$, then $\log_a (a^x) = a^{\log_a x} = x$. This gives us the following two properties.

Property 3: $\log_a (a^x) = x$ **Property 4:** $a^{\log_a x} = x$

We now develop three additional theorems that give us very important properties of logarithms.

Example   *Let $M = 10^4$ and $N = 10^3$. Evaluate $\log (M \cdot N)$ and $\log M + \log N$.*

$$\log (M \cdot N) \qquad\qquad \log M + \log N$$
$$= \log (10^4 \cdot 10^3) \qquad = \log 10^4 + \log 10^3$$
$$= \log (10^7) \qquad\qquad = 4 + 3$$
$$= 7 \qquad\qquad\qquad\quad = 7$$

This example suggests that the logarithm of the product of two numbers is equal to the sum of the logarithms of the two numbers.

Property 5: $\log_a (M \cdot N) = \log_a M + \log_a N$

Proof of Property 5: Let $x = \log_a M$ and let $y = \log_a N$.
          Then $a^x = M$ and $a^y = N$.
          Therefore, $M \cdot N = a^x \cdot a^y$
$$M \cdot N = a^{x+y}$$

Using the definition of a logarithm, we have
$$\log_a (M \cdot N) = x + y$$
$$= \log_a M + \log_a N$$

Example   Find log (4.75×10^5).

$$\log (4.75 \times 10^5) = \log 4.75 + \log (10^5)$$
$$\approx 0.6767 + 5$$
$$\approx 5.6767$$

Thus, log $(4.75 \times 10^5) \approx 5.6767$.

Now consider the following example, which will lead to our next property of logarithms.

Example   Let $M = 10^9$ and $N = 10^3$. Evaluate $\log \left(\frac{M}{N}\right)$ and $\log M - \log N$.

$$\log \left(\frac{M}{N}\right) \qquad\qquad\qquad \log M - \log N$$

$$= \log \left(\frac{10^9}{10^3}\right) \qquad\qquad\qquad = \log 10^9 - \log 10^3$$

$$= \log (10^6) \qquad\qquad\qquad\qquad = 9 - 3$$
$$= 6 \qquad\qquad\qquad\qquad\qquad = 6$$

This illustrates that the logarithm of the quotient of two numbers is equivalent to the difference of the logarithms of the two numbers.

Property 6: $\log_a \left(\frac{M}{N}\right) = \log_a M - \log_a N$

Proof of Property 6: Let $x = \log_a M$ and let $y = \log_a N$.
Then $a^x = M$ and $a^y = N$.
Therefore, $\frac{M}{N} = \frac{a^x}{a^y}$, or $\frac{M}{N} = a^{x-y}$.
Using the definition of a logarithm, we write

$$\log_a \left(\frac{M}{N}\right) = x - y, \text{ or } \log_a \left(\frac{M}{N}\right) = \log_a M - \log_a N$$

Example   Evaluate.

a $\ln \left(\frac{2}{e^5}\right)$

$\ln \left(\frac{2}{e^5}\right)$
$= \ln 2 - \ln (e^5)$
$\approx 0.6931 - 5$
≈ -4.3069

b $\log 500 - \log 5$
$\log 500 - \log 5$

$= \log \left(\frac{500}{5}\right)$
$= \log 100$
$= 2$

The final theorem presented in this section can be seen in the following example.

Example   Let $M = 10^6$ and $p = 2$. Evaluate $\log (M^p)$ and $p \cdot \log M$.

$\log (M^p)$ $\qquad\qquad\qquad\qquad$ $p \cdot \log M$
$= \log (10^6)^2$ $\qquad\qquad\qquad$ $= 2 \cdot \log (10^6)$
$= \log (10^{12})$ $\qquad\qquad\qquad$ $= 2 \cdot 6$
$= 12$ $\qquad\qquad\qquad\qquad$ $= 12$

This suggests that the logarithm of a number raised to a power is equal to the power times the logarithm of the number.

Property 7: $\log_a (M^p) = p \cdot \log_a M$

Proof of Property 7: Let $x = \log_a M$. Then $M = a^x$.
Therefore, $M^p = (a^x)^p$, or $M^p = a^{px}$.
Using the definition of a logarithm, we write
$\log_a (M^p) = px$, or $\log_a (M^p) = p \cdot \log_a M$

Example   *Evaluate* $\log 4^5$.

$\log 4^5 = 5 \cdot \log 4$
$\approx 5 \cdot (0.60206)$
≈ 3.0103

Notice that since logarithms are exponents, each property of logarithms has a corresponding property of exponents. For example, if $x = \log_a M$ and $y = \log_a N$, the following are true.

Logarithmic Property	**Exponent Property**
$\log_a (M \cdot N) = \log_a M + \log_a N$	$a^x \cdot a^y = a^{x+y}$
$\log_a \left(\dfrac{M}{N}\right) = \log_a M - \log_a N$	$\dfrac{a^x}{a^y} = a^{x-y}$
$\log_a (M^p) = p \cdot \log_a M$	$(a^x)^y = a^{xy}$

Part Two: Sample Problems

Problem 1   Let $\log 2 \approx 0.3010$ and $\log 3 \approx 0.4771$. Evaluate the following by using the properties instead of a calculator.

a $\log 2^3$ **b** $\log 12$ **c** $\log \sqrt[3]{4}$ **d** $\log 50$

Solution

a $\log 2^3$
$= 3 \log 2$
$\approx 3(0.3010)$
≈ 0.9030

b $\log 12$
$= \log (2^2 \cdot 3)$
$= 2 \log 2 + \log 3$
$\approx 2(0.3010) + 0.4771$
≈ 1.0791

c $\log \sqrt[3]{4}$
$= \log (4)^{\frac{1}{3}}$
$= \log (2^2)^{\frac{1}{3}}$
$= \log (2^{\frac{2}{3}})$
$= \dfrac{2}{3} \log 2$
$\approx \dfrac{2}{3}(0.3010)$
≈ 0.2007

d $\log 50$
$= \log \dfrac{100}{2}$
$= \log 100 - \log 2$
$\approx 2 - 0.3010$
≈ 1.6990

Problem 2   Write $2 \ln x + \ln (x + 2) - 3 \ln \pi$ as a single logarithm.

Solution

$$2 \ln x + \ln (x + 2) - 3 \ln \pi$$
$$= \ln (x^2) + \ln (x + 2) - \ln (\pi^3)$$
$$= \ln [x^2(x + 2)] - \ln (\pi^3)$$
$$= \ln \left[\frac{x^2(x + 2)}{\pi^3} \right]$$

Problem 3   The formula for the depreciated value V of a car is $V = C(0.87)^t$, where C is the original price and t is the age of the car.

a What is the value of a five-year-old car that originally cost $11,451?

b A car has a current blue-book value of $4700, and the original price of the car was $13,450. How old is the car?

Solution

a $V = C(0.87)^t$; therefore
$$V = 11{,}451(0.87)^5$$
$$\approx 11{,}451(0.4984)$$
$$\approx \$5707$$
The approximate value of the car is $5707.

b $V = C(0.87)^t$, therefore
$$4700 = 13{,}450(0.87)^t$$
$$0.3494 \approx (0.87)^t$$
$$\log 0.3494 \approx \log (0.87)^t$$
$$\log 0.3494 \approx t \cdot \log 0.87$$
$$-0.4566 \approx t(-0.0605)$$
$$7.55 \approx t$$

The car is about $7\frac{1}{2}$ years old.

Note   In part **b** above, we used the fact that if two quantities are equal, then the logarithms of these two quantities must also be equal.

Part Three: Exercises and Problems

Warm-up Exercises

In problems 1–6, use the values $\log 2 \approx 0.3010$ and $\log 3 \approx 0.4771$ to evaluate each expression without using a calculator.

1 $\log 6$

2 $\log 18$

3 $\log \dfrac{100}{6}$

4 $\log 4^3$

5 $\log \sqrt[4]{2}$

6 $\dfrac{\log 3}{\log 10}$

7 Match each lettered expression with an equivalent expression.

a $\log_3 (5 \cdot 7)$

b $\log_3 5^7$

c $\log_3 \left(\dfrac{5}{7} \right)$

d $\log_3 3^{57}$

e $\log_{357} 357$

i $7 \cdot \log_3 5$

ii 57

iii $\log_3 5 + \log_3 7$

iv 1

v $\log_3 5 - \log_3 7$

Problem Set

8 Find the exact value of each expression.

  a $\log_2 96 - \log_2 3$ **b** $\log_6 2 + \log_6 18$ **c** $\log_6 6^5$

9 The coordinates of A are (log 4, log 5). AB = log 20 and BC = log 250. Find the coordinates of C.

10 Write as a single logarithm.

  a $\log_2 7 + \log_2 6 - \log_2 4$ **b** $3 \log_4 5 - \dfrac{1}{2} \log_4 12$

  c $2 \log_4 (9) - 1$ **d** $4 \log_2 3 + \log_2 9 - \log_2 12$

11 Arrange the following expressions in order from smallest to largest.

  a $\log (4 \cdot 3)$ **b** $\log 4 \cdot \log 3$ **c** $\log 4 + \log 3$ **d** $\log 4 - \log 3$

12 Evaluate $(\log 2 + \log 5)^6$.

In problems 13 and 14, write each expression as a sum and difference of logarithms.

13 $\log_2 \dfrac{x^3 \sqrt{x - 3}}{y}$ **14** $\ln \dfrac{x}{x^5(x - 7)}$

15 Write $\frac{1}{2}(3 \ln x - \ln z)$ as a single logarithm.

16 If $A = P\left(1 + \dfrac{r}{n}\right)^{nt}$ and $A = \$1,000,000$, $P = \$35,000$, $n = 4$, and $r = 8.5\%$, what is t?

In problems 17–22, evaluate each expression.

17 $\log_2 (2^5)$ **18** $(\log_2 2)^5$ **19** $\log_3 \left(\dfrac{243}{27}\right)$

20 $\dfrac{\log_3 243}{\log_3 27}$ **21** $\log_2 (8^5)$ **22** $(\log_2 8)^5$

23 Find the average of $\log_4 8$, $\log_4 2$, and $\log_4 4$.

24 If two of the following expressions are selected at random, what is the probability that they will be equal?

  $\log 4 + \log 16$ $6 \log 2$ $\log 128 - \log 2$

  $3 \log 4$ $2 \log 8$ $\log 64$

Problem Set, *continued*

25 Multiply.
$$\begin{bmatrix} \log 2 & \log 3 \\ \log 5 & \log 2 \end{bmatrix} \cdot \begin{bmatrix} 2 \\ 3 \end{bmatrix}$$

26 Simplify the following expressions.

a $\dfrac{(-2)^4}{-2^3}$ **b** $\dfrac{-x^{60}}{x^2 \cdot x^{15}}$ **c** $\dfrac{(x^2)^3 \, (x^2 \cdot x^4)}{x^{20}}$

27 Evaluate.

a $\log_2 64$ **b** $\log_2 8$ **c** $\log_8 64$

d Is $(\log_2 8)(\log_8 64) = \log_2 64$ a true statement?

28 Find the area of the shaded region.

29 Let $f(x) = \log x$ and $g(x) = 10^x$.

a Find $f[g(x)]$.
b Find $g[f(x)]$.
c Is $f[g(x)] = g[f(x)]$? (Hint: Think about domains.)

30 The population P of a town is growing exponentially according to the equation $P = P_0 e^{\frac{t}{30}}$.

a If at $t = 0$ there are 10,000 people in the town, what is P_0?
b How many people are in the town when $t = 15$?
c When will there be 35,000 people in the town?

31 $y = \log_a b$ is equivalent to $a^y = b$. Use the equation $a^y = b$ and natural logarithms to express y in terms of the quotient of two natural logarithms.

32 Let $\log 2 = c$ and $\log 3 = d$. Find the following values in terms of c and d.

a $\log 12$ **b** $\log \dfrac{1}{8}$ **c** $\log 81$ **d** $\log \dfrac{4}{27}$

33 Write the following expression as a single logarithm.
$$\ln \sqrt{x^2 - 1} - \ln \sqrt{x + 1}$$

34 Suppose $\log_2 3 = a$ and $\log_2 5 = b$. Find each of the following values in terms of a and b.

a $\log_2 15$ **b** $\log_2 6$ **c** $\log_2 2.5$

35 Evaluate each expression to three decimal places.

   a $\log (2 \times 10^5)$ **b** $\log (2 \times 10^{38})$

   c $\log (2 \times 10^7)$ **d** $\log (2 \times 10^{472})$

36 The graph of the function $f(x) = \log_6 x$ is shown.

Find the area of the trapezoid ABCD.

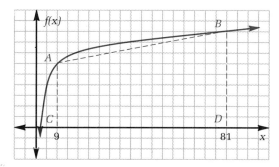

37 Write the following expression as a single logarithm.

$$\ln \left(\frac{x}{x^2 - 1}\right) + \ln \left(\frac{x^2 + 2x + 1}{3x}\right)$$

38 Solve $12 = 5^{(x + 3)}$ for x.

39 Boris and Emil each inherited $8000 from Uncle Horace. Boris deposited his inheritance in a bank that paid 6.85% interest, compounded continuously, whereas Emil deposited his in a bank that paid 7.6% interest, compounded continuously. How long will it be until Emil has twice as much money as Boris? How long would it be if Uncle Horace had given them $4000 instead?

40 Sketch each function on the same coordinate system.

   a $f(x) = \log_2 x + \log_2 8$ **b** $f(x) = \log_2 (x + 8)$ **c** $f(x) = \log_2 8x$

41 Evaluate $\log \frac{1}{2} + \log \frac{2}{3} + \log \frac{3}{4} + \log \frac{4}{5} + \ldots + \log \frac{9}{10}$.

42 Simplify.

   $(\log 4)^3 + 3(\log 4)^2(\log 25) + 3(\log 4)(\log 25)^2 + (\log 25)^3$

43 Determine whether each statement is True or False.

   a $\log_5 x + \log_8 x = \log_{13} x$ **b** $\log_5 x + \log_8 x = \log_{40} x$

   c $\log_5 x + \log_8 x = \dfrac{\ln 5 + \ln 8}{(\ln 5)(\ln 8)} \cdot \ln x$

44 One measure of the quality of an egg is the Haugh unit. An egg's Haugh rating is given by

$$100 \log \left[H - \frac{1}{100}\sqrt{32.2} \ (30w^{0.37} - 100) + 1.9 \right]$$

where w is the weight of the egg in grams and H is the height of the albumen in millimeters when the egg is broken on a flat surface. Find the Haugh rating of an egg that weighs 48.7 grams if $H = 5$ millimeters.

SOLVING EXPONENTIAL AND LOGARITHMIC EQUATIONS

Objectives

After studying this section, you will be able to
- Use the base-change formula
- Solve exponential equations
- Solve logarithmic equations

Part One: Introduction

The Base-Change Formula

As seen earlier, a calculator can be used to compute logarithms and powers when the base is either 10 or e. We can also calculate powers of any positive base by using the $\boxed{x^y}$ key.

Example Use a calculator to find $2^{4.53}$.

Enter 2 $\boxed{x^y}$ 4.53 $\boxed{=}$. The display is $\boxed{23.10286713}$
Therefore, $2^{4.53} \approx 23.10$.

How can we use the calculator to find logarithms with bases other than 10 or e? Consider the following example.

Example Evaluate.

a $\log_2 23.10$
From the example above, we know that $\log_2 23.10 \approx 4.53$.

b $\dfrac{\log 23.10}{\log 2}$

$\dfrac{\log 23.10}{\log 2}$

$\approx \dfrac{1.36361198}{0.301029995}$

≈ 4.529820957

c $\dfrac{\ln 23.10}{\ln 2}$

$\dfrac{\ln 23.10}{\ln 2}$

$\approx \dfrac{3.139832617}{0.69314718}$

≈ 4.529820949

All three of these answers are the same. This is not just a coincidence. This example illustrates another property, known as the base-change formula.

Property 8:
The Base-Change Formula

$$\log_a M = \frac{\log_b M}{\log_b a}, \text{ where } b \text{ can be any legitimate base.}$$

Proof of Property 8: Let $x = \log_a M$. This is equivalent to

$$a^x = M$$

Take $\log_b$ of both sides $\qquad \log_b a^x = \log_b M$

Use Property 7 $\qquad\qquad x \cdot \log_b a = \log_b M$

$$x = \frac{\log_b M}{\log_b a}$$

Now substitute for x $\qquad\quad \log_a M = \frac{\log_b M}{\log_b a}$

Example   *Evaluate.*

a $\log_5 36$

$$\log_5 36 = \frac{\log 36}{\log 5}$$

$$\approx 2.2266$$

Use $\boxed{x^y}$ to check:

$$5^{2.2266} \approx 36.002$$

b $\log_{\frac{1}{2}} 0.007$

$$\log_{\frac{1}{2}} 0.007 = \frac{\ln 0.007}{\ln 0.5}$$

$$\approx 7.1584$$

$$0.5^{7.1584} \approx 0.007$$

Note   We used base 10 and base e because we could then use a calculator to calculate the logarithms. It doesn't matter which of these two bases you use. Try each problem using alternate bases.

Solving Exponential Equations

An ***exponential equation*** is any equation with a variable in an exponent. To solve an exponential equation we usually take the logarithm, to an appropriate base, of both sides of the equation.

Example   *Solve $5^x = 12$ for x.*

$$5^x = 12$$

Take the base-5 log
of both sides $\qquad\quad \log_5 (5^x) = \log_5 12$

$$x \log_5 5 = \log_5 12$$

Base-change formula $\qquad x = \frac{\log 12}{\log 5}$

$$\approx 1.54396$$

Check
$5^x \approx 5^{1.54396} \approx 12.00001331 \approx 12$. For a closer approximation, use the value of x that is stored in the calculator after dividing log 12 by log 5.

Example   *Solve $4e^{3x} = 100$ for x.*

$$4e^{3x} = 100$$
$$e^{3x} = 25$$

Take ln of both sides $$\ln(e^{3x}) = \ln 25$$
$$3x = \ln 25$$
$$3x \approx 3.2189$$
$$x \approx 1.0730$$

Note   Here it makes sense to use base e logarithms, since the exponential equation involves the number e.

Check
$$4e^{3x} \approx 4e^{3 \cdot 1.0730} \approx 4e^{3.219} \approx 100.0124183 \approx 100$$

Solving Logarithmic Equations

We solve a logarithmic equation by using the properties of logarithms to obtain a form where we can eliminate the logarithms. Check your answers. Remember that we can find logarithms only of positive numbers and that the base must be positive and not 1.

Example   *Solve $\log_4 x + \log_4 (x + 6) = 2$ for x.*

$$\log_4 x + \log_4 (x + 6) = 2$$
$$\log_4 [x(x + 6)] = 2$$

Change to exponential form $$x(x + 6) = 4^2$$
$$x^2 + 6x = 16$$
$$x^2 + 6x - 16 = 0$$
$$(x + 8)(x - 2) = 0$$
$$x + 8 = 0 \text{ or } x - 2 = 0$$
$$x = -8 \text{ or } x = 2$$

$x = -8$ is not a solution of the original logarithmic equation, since we cannot find logarithms of negative numbers. The only solution is $x = 2$. You should check it yourself.

Example   *Solve $\ln P - \ln P_0 = kt$ for P.*

$$\ln P - \ln P_0 = kt$$

$$\ln \frac{P}{P_0} = kt$$

Write in equivalent exponential form $$\frac{P}{P_0} = e^{kt}$$

$$P = P_0 e^{kt}$$

Note   This is an important formula in science. It describes such things as population growth and radioactive decay.

Part Two: Sample Problems

Problem 1   Solve $4^{x^2} \cdot 4^{-2x} = 7$ for x.

Solution   We first use the properties of exponents.

$$4^{x^2} \cdot 4^{-2x} = 7$$

$$4^{x^2 - 2x} = 7$$

Take $\log_4$ of both sides $\log_4 (4^{x^2 - 2x}) = \log_4 7$

Base-change formula $x^2 - 2x = \dfrac{\log 7}{\log 4}$

$$x^2 - 2x \approx 1.404$$

$$x^2 - 2x - 1.404 \approx 0$$

Quadratic formula $x \approx \dfrac{2 \pm \sqrt{4 + 5.615}}{2}$

$$x \approx 2.550 \text{ or } x \approx -0.550$$

Checking each solution gives approximately $4^{1.4025} \approx 6.989$.

Problem 2   Solve $(\log x)^2 + \log (x^3) - 12 = 0$ for x.

Solution $(\log x)^2 + \log (x^3) - 12 = 0$
$(\log x)^2 + 3 \log x - 12 = 0$

This is a quadratic equation in log x. Using the quadratic formula, we solve for log x and obtain $\log x \approx 2.28$ or $\log x \approx -5.28$.

$x \approx 10^{2.28}$ or $x \approx 10^{-5.28}$
$x \approx 190.55$ or $x \approx 5.25 \times 10^{-6}$

Problem 3   Solve $\log_5 x = \log_5 (x + 5) - \log_5 2$ for x.

Solution   We first use properties of logarithms.

$$\log_5 x = \log_5 (x + 5) - \log_5 2$$

$$\log_5 x = \log_5 \left(\frac{x + 5}{2} \right)$$

Since the logarithms are equal, the quantities must be equal.

$$x = \frac{x + 5}{2}$$

$$2x = x + 5$$

$$x = 5$$

You should check to see whether the answer is correct.

Part Three: Exercises and Problems

Warm-up Exercises

In problems 1–5, solve for x. Do not use a calculator.

1 $3^{2x-1} = 9$ **2** $4^x \cdot 2^{-3} = 32$ **3** $\log_3 (x + 2) = 2$

4 $(\ln x)^2 - \ln x = 0$ **5** $4^{x^3} = 2^{16}$

6 Show that the two lines are parallel.

7 The number of bacteria b on a petri dish is given by $b = 500e^{0.04t}$, where t is time measured in minutes.

   a How many bacteria are there at $t = 0$?

   b How many bacteria will there be when $t = 30$ minutes?

8 A square with side 2^x has area 512. What is the area of a square with side x?

Problem Set

9 Use a calculator to find the values of the following expressions.

   a $\log_2 28$ **b** $\log_{\frac{1}{2}} 36$ **c** $\log_5 130$

10 Solve for b.

   a $3^b = 19$ **b** $7^b = \dfrac{3}{5}$ **c** $\log b = \dfrac{2}{5}$

In problems 11 and 12, solve for x. Do not use a calculator.

11 $\ln (x + 5) - \ln x = \ln \left(\dfrac{4}{3}\right)$ **12** $\log_3 x + \log_3 (x - 2) = 1$

13 Evaluate $\log_2 3 \cdot \log_3 64$.

14 Prove that $\log_{a^n} x = \dfrac{\log_a x}{n}$.

15 Find the area of the rectangle.

16 Solve for x.

   a $2^x = \log 12$ **b** $\log_7 x = \log 125$

17 Solve $\log_5 x + \log_5 (x + 20) = 3$ for x.

18 Evaluate each of the following expressions.

   a $\log_2 4^5$ **b** $\log_3 (81 \cdot 27)$ **c** $\log_5 \left(\dfrac{625}{25} \right)$

19 **a** Solve $\log_7 x = \log_7 (x + 9) - \log_7 3$ for x.
    b Solve $\log_7 x = \log_7 (x + a) - \log_7 3$ for x in terms of a.

20 Simplify $(\log 5 + \log 2)(\log 20 - \log 2)$.

21 Write in simple form.

   a $\log_2 3 \cdot \log_3 4$
   b $\log_2 3 \cdot \log_3 4 \cdot \log_4 5 \cdot \log_5 6 \cdot \log_6 7 \cdot \log_7 8$

 22 Place in order from smallest to largest.

   $\log_6 21$ $\log_{10} 55$ $\log_4 10$ $\log_5 15$

23 Find the point at which the graphs intersect.

 24 The base sticker price of an automobile rises at about 6% per year. The formula $B = B_0(1.06)^t$ relates the base sticker price B to time t in years.

   a At $t = 0$ (1950) the base sticker price was \$1500. Find B_0.
   b What would the base sticker price of the same 1950 car have been in 1970?

25 **a** Solve $\log (\log x) = 3$ for x.
    b How many digits does x have?

26 Solve $\log_{x^2 + 6} 2 + \log_{x^2 + 6} 5 = 1$ for x.

27 Solve $5^{x^2} \cdot 5^{-9x} = 5^{-18}$ for x.

28 Write as a sum or difference of logarithms.

   a $\ln \dfrac{x^2 y}{x + 5}$ **b** $\ln \sqrt{\dfrac{x^2}{y}}$

29 Solve $x = \log_4 9 \cdot \log_9 12 \cdot \log_{12} 16$ for x.

 30 Solve each of the following equations for x.

   a $6^x = 12$ **b** $5e^{3x} = 10$ **c** $16 \cdot 10^{x^2} = 144$

Problem Set, *continued*

31 The formula $P = P_0 e^{kt}$ can be used to predict the number of grams P of a radioactive element remaining after t hours. P_0 is a constant and is the number of grams of the element at $t = 0$. k is a constant specific to a given radioactive element. Consider the following data.

t	0	1	2	3	4	. . .
P	5	≈ 3.533	2.5	≈ 1.7678	1.25	. . .

  a What is P_0?
  b Find k.
  c How much of the element remains after nine hours?

32 Solve $\log_9 x + \log_9 (x + 6) = \frac{3}{2}$ for x.

33 The function f is defined so that $f(0) = 1$ and $f(n + 1) = f(n) \cdot 3$ for every integer n.

  a Find $f(2)$.   **b** If $f(n) = 19{,}683$, what is n?
  c Find $f(3)$.   **d** Find $f(-3)$.
  e Find $f(4)$.   **f** If $f(n) = 30{,}000$, what is n?

34 Solve $\log_2 [\log_3 (\log_4 x)] = 0$ for x.

35 Solve for x.

  a $(\log_4 x)^2 = 16$ **b** $(\log_4 x)^2 - 15 \log_4 x = 16$

36 The area of the trapezoid is 12 square units. Find b.

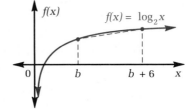

37 Solve $\sqrt{\log x} = \log \sqrt{x}$ for x.

38 The graphs of $y = e^x$ and $y = e^{-x}$ are pictured. Note that they intersect at $(0, 1)$.

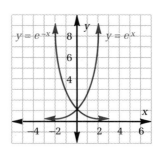

  a If the curve $y = e^x$ is shifted three units to the left and the curve $y = e^{-x}$ is shifted three units to the right, where do the curves intersect?
  b If the curve $y = e^x$ is shifted three units to the left and the curve $y = e^{-x}$ is shifted five units to the right, where do the curves intersect?

11.5 APPLICATIONS OF EXPONENTIAL AND LOGARITHMIC FUNCTIONS

Objectives

After studying this section, you will be able to
- Use exponential and logarithmic functions as mathematical models
- Analyze exponentially related data

Part One: Introduction

Applications as Mathematical Models

In many real-world situations the mathematical model that best describes the relationship between two quantities is an exponential or logarithmic function.

Example   *An earthquake's magnitude, as measured by the Richter energy number R, is the base-10 logarithm of the intensity I of the quake's vibrations. The equation relating the Richter number R and the intensity of the quake I is $R = \log\left(\frac{I}{I_0}\right)$, where I_0 is the minimum detectable intensity of an earthquake.*

a *Write the Richter earthquake equation in exponential form.*

$R = \log\left(\dfrac{I}{I_0}\right)$ is equivalent to $10^R = \left(\dfrac{I}{I_0}\right)$, so $I = 10^R I_0$.

b *The atomic bomb tested on Bikini Atoll had a Richter number of 5.0, and the San Francisco earthquake of 1906 had a Richter number of 8.25. How many times more intense were the vibrations of the San Francisco quake than those at Bikini?*

I(Bikini) = $10^5 I_0$ and I(San Fran.) = $10^{8.25} I_0$

$$\frac{\text{I(San Fran.)}}{\text{I(Bikini)}} = \frac{10^{8.25} I_0}{10^5 I_0} = 10^{3.25} \approx 1778$$

Therefore, I(San Fran.) $\approx 1778 \cdot$ I(Bikini). The San Francisco earthquake was about 1778 times as intense as the atomic bomb vibrations at Bikini Atoll.

Example *Population growth is very often exponentially related to time. That is, the population P is given by the equation $P = P_0 e^{kt}$, where P_0 and k are constants. The prairie dog population of Dry Gulch was 24 in 1975 and 90 in 1980.*

a *From the given data, determine P_0 and k.*

Let $t = 0$ in 1975. Then $24 = P_0 e^{k(0)}$
$$24 = P_0$$

In 1980, 5 years later, there were 90 prairie dogs, so

$$90 = 24e^{k(5)}$$
$$3.75 = e^{5k}$$
$$\ln 3.75 = \ln \left(e^{5k}\right)$$
$$1.322 \approx 5k$$
$$0.2644 \approx k$$

The prairie dog population equation is $P \approx 24e^{0.2644t}$.

b *Assuming continued exponential growth of the prairie dog population, what is the expected population of prairie dogs in Dry Gulch in the year 2000?*

Since $t = 0$ in 1975, in the year 2000, $t = 25$.

$$P \approx 24e^{0.2644(25)}$$
$$P \approx 24 \cdot 742.48$$
$$P \approx 17{,}820$$

There will be about 17,820 prairie dogs in the year 2000.

Analyzing Exponentially Related Data

We have seen several formulas of the form $y = ka^{mx}$. When such a formula occurs, we say that x and y are exponentially related. If we let $a = 10$, so that we have $y = k10^{mx}$, and take the log of both sides, an interesting thing happens.

$$y = k10^{mx}$$
$$\log y = \log (k10^{mx})$$
$$\log y = \log k + \log (10^{mx})$$
$$\log y = \log k + mx$$

If we let $Y = \log y$ and $b = \log k$, we obtain

$$Y = mx + b, \text{ a linear equation!}$$

This means that the ordered pairs (x, y) are exponentially related by $y = k10^{mx}$ if and only if the ordered pairs $(x, \log y)$ are linearly related by $\log y = mx + b$. Graphically, this says that the pairs (x, y) form an exponential curve if and only if the pairs $(x, \log y)$ form a straight line.

Example

Are the data in the table exponentially related?

x	10	20	30	40	50	60
y	910	390	170	72	31	14

We will make a table of x and log y and then graph the ordered pairs.

x	log y
10	≈2.96
20	≈2.59
30	≈2.23
40	≈1.86
50	≈1.49
60	≈1.15

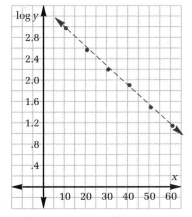

Since the graph of the ordered pairs (x, log y) is approximately a straight line, the original data are exponentially related.

Part Two: Sample Problems

Problem 1

At 8:00 A.M. on a spring day, with the temperature constant at 20°C, Sherlock Holmes found a corpse lying in an alley. To determine the time of death, Holmes had Watson measure the body temperature immediately and again one hour later. The body temperature at 8:00 A.M. was 32°C, and the temperature at 9:00 A.M. was 31°C. Determine the approximate time of death.

Solution

An equation known as Newton's law of cooling enables us to determine the time of death.

The equation is $\ln \dfrac{T - A}{T_0 - A} = -kt$, where $\qquad T = (T_0 - A)(-kt) + A$

T = the temperature of the body at any time after death
T_0 = the temperature of the body at time of death. In our problem this is normal body temperature, 37°C.
A = the temperature of the surrounding medium, known as ambient temperature. In our problem it is 20°C.
k = a constant that corresponds to the human body's cooling rate
t = the length of time that the body has been cooling

At the time of death, $t = 0$, $T_0 = 37°C$, and $A = 20°C$.
At 8:00 A.M. let time $= t$.

$$T = 32°C, \text{ so } \quad \ln \frac{32 - 20}{37 - 20} = -kt$$

$$-0.3483 \approx -kt \qquad (1)$$

At 9:00 A.M. time $= t + 1$.

$$T = 31°C, \text{ so } \quad \ln \frac{31 - 20}{17} = -k(t + 1)$$

$$-0.4353 \approx -k(t + 1) \qquad (2)$$

Dividing equation (2) by equation (1) yields

$$\frac{-0.4353}{-0.3483} \approx \frac{-k(t + 1)}{-kt}, \qquad \text{or } 1.25 \approx \frac{t + 1}{t}$$

$$1.25t \approx t + 1$$
$$0.25t \approx 1$$
$$t \approx 4$$

At 8:00 A.M. the person had been dead for about four hours. The time of death was approximately 4:00 A.M.

Problem 2   *The following table shows the height h, in inches, of a plant as a function of w weeks.*

w	1	2	3	4	5	6	7	8	9	10
h	0.5	0.7	1.1	1.5	2.4	3.5	5.0	7.4	10.0	17.0

   a *Find an exponential function to fit the data.*
   b *Predict the height of the plant by week 12.*

Solution   **a** Let's assume an equation of the form $h = k10^{mw}$ and take the log of both sides to obtain $\log h = \log k + mw$. Using the first and last columns of data, we have the following linear system.

Using $(w, h) = (10, 17)$ $\qquad\qquad$ $1.2304 \approx \log k + 10m$
Using $(w, h) = (1, 0.5)$ $\qquad\qquad$ $\underline{-0.3010 \approx \log k + 1m}$
Subtract $\qquad\qquad\qquad\qquad\qquad\quad$ $1.5314 \approx 9m$

$\qquad\qquad\qquad\qquad\qquad\qquad\qquad\quad 0.1702 \approx m$

Substituting the value of m into the second equation yields

$$-0.3010 \approx \log k + 0.1702$$
$$-0.4712 \approx \log k$$
$$10^{-0.4712} \approx k$$
$$0.3379 \approx k$$

The exponential function for the data is $h \approx 0.3379 \cdot 10^{0.1702w}$. Let's see whether this equation does approximately fit the data by checking $(w, h) = (6, 3.5)$.

$$h \approx 0.3379 \cdot 10^{0.1702(6)}$$
$$\approx 0.3379(10.5)$$
$$\approx 3.55 \approx 3.5$$

   b We use the equation $h \approx 0.3379 \cdot 10^{0.1702w}$, where $w = 12$.

$$h \approx 0.3379 \cdot 10^{0.1702(12)}$$
$$h \approx 0.3379(110.255)$$
$$h \approx 37.3 \text{ inches}$$

Part Three: Exercises and Problems

Warm-up Exercises

1 The earthquake at Hebgen Lake, Montana, in 1959 was 12,589,254 times as intense as the minimum detectable earthquake. What was its Richter energy number?

2 The atmospheric pressure P decreases exponentially with the height above sea level. The equation relating the pressure P and the height h is $P = 14.7e^{-kh}$, where k is a positive constant.

a Find k if the pressure is 11.9 pounds per square inch at an altitude of 5000 feet.

b Find the atmospheric pressure outside an airplane that is flying at an altitude of 22,000 feet.

3 The mass of a radioactive substance decreases exponentially with time according to the equation $M = M_0 e^{-kt}$, where M_0 is the amount of the radioactive substance at $t = 0$ and k is a positive constant that depends on the type of radioactive substance.

a Find k for carbon-14 if the half-life of carbon-14 is 5600 years. (Note that half-life is the time it takes for half of the mass M_0 to decay. So $M = 0.5M_0$ when $t = 5600$ years for this problem.)

b A bone is found with 30% of its carbon-14 remaining. How old is the bone?

4 The following table gives the temperature of a jar of water in a room after t minutes.

t	0	10	20	30	40	50	60	70	80
Temp.	125	115	106	100	95	91	87	85	83

a Are the data exponentially related?

b Predict the temperature after two hours.

Problem Set

5 The largest Richter number for an earthquake was 8.9. How many times more intense was this earthquake than the San Francisco earthquake of 1906? (See the example on page 501.)

6 Using $P = 14.7e^{-kh}$, find the atmospheric pressure at the top of Mt. Everest, which is 29,028 feet high. (See problem **2**, above.)

7 The number of bacteria B in a culture increases according to the equation $B = B_0 e^{kt}$. There were 400 bacteria at time $t = 0$ and 700 bacteria at time $t = 3$ hours. How many bacteria will there be after 12 hours?

Problem Set, *continued*

8 The data shown represent the sales S for each week *w* for a recently released Rolling Rocks album.

a Determine an exponential function that fits the data.
b What would you predict the sales of the Rolling Rocks album will be for the eighth week?

9 Rationalize the denominator.

$$\frac{3}{\sqrt{2} - 1}$$

10 A tray of water is placed in a freezer in order to make ice cubes. The water is initially at 60°F. The freezer is at 0°F. If the ice cubes are formed in two hours, what is the constant *k* in Newton's cooling formula? (Hint: Ice freezes at 32°F.)

11 The following data show the increasing cost of certain goods from 1980 to 1985.

Year	1980	1981	1982	1983	1984	1985
Cost	$100	$105.30	$110.88	$116.76	$122.95	$129.46

a Is the cost exponentially related to time?
b If the cost continues to rise according to the same pattern, how much will the goods cost in 1999?

12 Solve for *x*.

a $6^{x^2 - 2} = 1$

b $6^{x^2 - 2} = \dfrac{1}{36}$

c $6^{x^2 - 2} = 36$

d $6^{x^2 - 2} = \dfrac{1}{216}$

13 Humberto deposited $785 in an account that pays $8\frac{3}{4}$% interest, compounded continuously. How long will it take until Humberto has $1000?

14 Multiply $(x + 3 + \sqrt{5})(x + 3 - \sqrt{5})$ and combine terms.

15 Multiply $(x + y + 3)(x + y - 3)$.

16 Four girls are trying out for the female lead in the school play, and three boys are trying out for the male lead. How many different female-male lead combinations are there?

17 The graph shows the average number of items in a supermarket for each year since 1978. Assume the data are exponentially related according to $I = I_0 e^{kt}$, where I = the number of items in the store, I_0 = the number of items in 1978, and t = the number of years since 1978.

a Use the data from 1978 and 1987 to find I_0 and k.

b At this rate of growth, approximately how many items will be in the supermarket in 2025?

18 A hard-boiled egg has a temperature of 98°C. If it is put into a sink that maintains a temperature of 18°C, its temperature x minutes later is given by

$$T(x) = 18 + 80e^{-0.28x}$$

Hilda needs her egg to be at exactly 30°C for decorating. How long should she leave it in the water?

19 A satellite has a radioisotope power supply. The power output in watts is given by the equation $P = 50e^{\frac{-t}{250}}$, where t is the time in days since the power supply was placed in service.

a How much power will be available at the end of one year?

b What is the half-life of the power supply?

c The equipment aboard the satellite requires 10 watts of power to operate properly. What is the operational life of the satellite?

20 Consider the graph of $y = \frac{1}{x}$.

$A(1, 1)$, $B\left(10, \frac{1}{10}\right)$, $C\left(100, \frac{1}{100}\right)$, and $D\left(1000, \frac{1}{1000}\right)$ are all points on the graph corresponding to the points $E(1, 0)$, $F(10, 0)$, $G(100, 0)$, and $H(1000, 0)$ on the x-axis. Find the area of each trapezoid.

a ABFE

b BCGF

c CDHG

21 A 35-millimeter camera has f-stops numbered as follows: 1.4, 2, 2.8, 4, 5.6, 8, 11, 16, 22. These numbers relate to the amount of light that strikes the film; the smaller the number, the larger the lens aperture.

a Make a table of the base-10 logarithms of these numbers.

b Are these numbers exponentially related to the stops they designate?

Problem Set, *continued*

22 Multiply $(1 + \log 2)(1 - \log 2)$.

23 Solve $x^2 + (\log 20)x + \log 2 = 0$ for x.

24 The number of people in the Denver suburban area has grown exponentially since 1950 according to the equation $P = P_0e^{kt}$. In 1950 there were 350,000 people. In 1960 there were 600,000 people. How many people lived in the Denver suburban area in 1989?

25 The graphs show $y = 3^x$ and $y = 2^{-x}$. They intersect at $(0, 1)$. If the graph of $y = 3^x$ is shifted four units to the right and the graph of $y = 2^{-x}$ is shifted five units to the left, where will the curves meet?

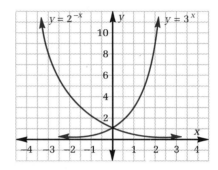

MATHEMATICAL EXCURSION

SOMETHING EARTHSHAKING
The magnitude of an earthquake

On Tuesday, October 17, 1989, at about 5:00 P.M. Pacific time, people all over the United States saw their television screens go blank as an earthquake interrupted the third game of the World Series. Measuring 7.1 on the Richter scale, the earthquake was one of the largest in United States history.

The Richter scale, the system we use for reporting earthquake magnitudes, was developed by Charles Francis Richter (1900–1985). His scale describes an earthquake's magnitude according to changes in ground motion.

Although no magnitude greater than 8.7 has been recorded, the Richter scale is an open-ended logarithmic scale. (See the Career Profile on page 518.) The Richter magnitude of an earthquake is the log to the base 10 that corresponds to the amount of ground motion measured in the earthquake. This means that each unit of increase on the Richter scale represents a tenfold increase in ground motion.

Compare the amounts of ground motion in Richter magnitudes 7.7 and 4.7.

BINOMIALS AND BINOMIAL DISTRIBUTIONS

Objectives

After studying this section, you will be able to
- Recognize a binomial probability experiment
- Find the mean, variance, and standard deviation of a binomial distribution

Binomials and Their Distributions

In earlier sections we have worked with binomials of the form $(a + b)^n$. We now turn our attention to binomials of the form $(pa + qb)^n$.

We begin our discussion by considering the expansion of $\left(\frac{2}{5}h + \frac{3}{5}t\right)^3$.

We write

$$\left(\frac{2}{5}h + \frac{3}{5}t\right)^3 = \left(\frac{2h + 3t}{5}\right)^3 = \frac{8h^3t^0 + 36h^2t^1 + 54h^1t^2 + 27h^0t^3}{125}$$

$$= \frac{8}{125}h^3t^0 + \frac{36}{125}h^2t^1 + \frac{54}{125}h^1t^2 + \frac{27}{125}h^0t^3$$

The expansion above models the tossing of a weighted coin three times. In the binomial $\left(\frac{2}{5}h + \frac{3}{5}t\right)$, the coefficient of h, $\frac{2}{5}$, is the probability of the weighted coin's landing heads. The coefficient of t, $\frac{3}{5}$, is the probability of the weighted coin's landing tails. The exponent 3 on the binomial models the tossing of the coin three times.

Let us now look at one of the terms of the expansion, say $\frac{54}{125}h^1t^2$. The expression h^1t^2 models the outcome where the coin lands heads once and tails twice. The coefficient, $\frac{54}{125}$, is the probability of this outcome. In a like manner, the term $\frac{27}{125}h^0t^3$ tells us that the probability is $\frac{27}{125}$ that the coin will land heads zero times and tails three times when tossed three times. What is the sum of the probabilities of the four outcomes? Why?

The graphs on the next page represent the four outcomes of tossing the weighted coin three times and the corresponding probabilities.

The above is an example of a **binomial probability experiment**.

In order for an experiment to be a binomial probability experiment, the following conditions must be satisfied:

1 There must be a fixed number n of repeated trials whose outcomes are independent. (In our experiment, there were three tossings of a coin. The outcome of each coin toss was independent of the other outcomes.)

2 Each of the repeated trials must result in one of two possible outcomes. Each outcome must have the same probability as the other trials. (In our experiment, each trial had the probability of tossing a head as $\frac{2}{5}$ and the probability of tossing a tail as $\frac{3}{5}$.)

Observe that $(pa + qb)^n$ has probability p for outcome a and probability q for outcome b and that $p + q$ must equal 1.

Example *In any shipment of automobile tires from the Badmonth Tire Company, it is known that the probability of a tire's being defective is .3.*

    a *Find the probability that at least two of four purchased tires are defective.*

    Let $(.3d + .7n)^4$ be the binomial representation that models the purchase of four tires. The variable d models defective tires, while the variable n models nondefective tires.
The expansion of $(.3d + .7n)^4$ yields

$$.0081d^4n^0 + .0756d^3n^1 + .2646d^2n^2 + .4116d^1n^3 + .2401d^0n^4$$

The probability that at least two of the tires are defective is $.0081 + .0756 + .2646 = .3483$, or at least two of four tires are defective in 34.83% of cases.

    b *Draw the binomial distribution graph.*
The graph for the distribution is shown below.

Mean and Standard Deviation of a Binomial Distribution

We have worked with the mean and standard deviation of a normal distribution. The tire example will aid us in working with the mean and standard deviation of a binomial distribution.

Example   *The Keepon Trucking Company bought 300 tires from the Badmonth Tire Company. According to the preceding example, how many defective tires might they expect to receive?*

Finding the **expected value** or **expected number** of defective tires is the same as answering the question "What is the mean of the binomial distribution where the probability of getting a single defective tire is .3 and the experiment is repeated 300 times?"

The expected number of defective tires is found by multiplying .3 (the probability of getting a defective tire) by 300 (the number of tires to be purchased). The expected number (mean) of defective tires is .3(300) = 90.

Summarizing: The **mean of a binomial distribution** is found by multiplying the number of trials n by the probability p of success on each trial.

> **Mean of a binomial distribution = np**

The **variance of a binomial distribution** represented by $(pa + qb)^n$ is defined to be npq.

> **Variance = npq**

The **standard deviation of a binomial distribution** is defined to be $\sqrt{\text{variance}}$, or $\sqrt{npq}$.

> **Standard deviation = $\sqrt{\text{variance}}$ = $\sqrt{npq}$**

The standard deviation for the distribution of defective tires when 300 are purchased is $\sqrt{300(.3)(.7)} = \sqrt{63} \approx 7.94$.

Example   *Find the probability that exactly 100 tires out of a purchase of 300 tires will be defective.*

We will use the Normal Distribution Table to aid us in solving this problem. We can associate the following bell-shaped curve with the problem.

Observe that all the values that are greater than or equal to 99.5 and less than 100.5 would round to the value 100. We need to determine what percentage of the area under the curve is between the data values 99.5 and 100.5.

We first need to find how many standard deviations 99.5 and 100.5 are from the mean, 90, when the standard deviation is 7.94.

$$\frac{99.5 - 90}{7.94} \approx 1.2 \text{ SD} \qquad \frac{100.5 - 90}{7.94} \approx 1.3 \text{ SD}$$

The Normal Distribution Table indicates that 0.8849 and 0.9032 of the area under the curve is to the left of $m + 1.2$ SD and $m + 1.3$ SD respectively.

Thus, the area between the values 99.5 and 100.5 is approximately $0.9032 - 0.8849$, or 0.0183, of the total area under the curve. We conclude that there is a probability of $\approx .02$ that exactly 100 of the tires will be defective.

Perhaps you wondered how it can be possible to approximate a binomial distribution by using a normal distribution. It has been shown mathematically that such approximations are quite accurate as long as $p \le .5$ and $np > 5$, or $p > .5$ and $nq > 5$. In our example, $n = 300$, $p = .7$, and $q = .3$. Since

$$nq = 300(.3) > 5$$

our approximations are acceptable.

Problem Set

1 a Write out the five terms of $(0.7W + 0.3L)^4$.
   b If .7 is the probability of winning a game and .3 is the probability of losing a game, what is the probability of winning two games and losing two games in a four-game series?

2 A random-number generator has an equal probability of generating a 1, 2, 3, or 4. Find the probability that five 4's are generated out of ten numbers.

3 On a 100-item true-false test, Randy Number knows 64 of the answers and guesses on the rest. What is her expected score?

4 Find the coefficient of the term containing a^4b^2 in the expansion of $\left(\frac{1}{4}a + \frac{3}{4}b\right)^6$.

5 Two marbles are to be drawn at random from a bag containing eight red marbles and five green marbles. Use the tree diagram shown to determine the probability that one of the marbles will be red and one will be green.

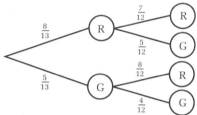

6 A certain coin is weighted so that when it is tossed, it will turn up heads more frequently than tails. If the coin turns up heads, on the average, two thirds of the time and if it is tossed five times, what is the probability that it will turn up heads

    a Exactly four times?   **b** At least four times?

7 Ten percent of a batch of manufactured items are defective. If five items are selected at random from this batch, what is the probability that

    a None is defective?
    b Exactly one is defective?
    c At least three are defective?
    d Less than three are defective?

8 Roo Lett has an $\frac{18}{38}$ probability of winning any one game. If she plays seven games, what is the probability that Roo

    a Loses all seven?   **b** Loses six of seven?

9 A weighted coin comes up heads $\frac{3}{5}$ of the time. The coin is flipped 270 times.

    a Find the expected number of heads (the mean).
    b Find the standard deviation of the number of heads.

10 On a true-false test, Gil guessed on every problem. The test had 80 questions.

    a Find the probability that he gets each question right.
    b Find the expected number of correct answers.
    c Use a normal distribution to find the standard deviation of his number of correct responses.
    d What percentage of the time will he get at least 35 correct?

CHAPTER SUMMARY

CONCEPTS AND PROCEDURES

After studying this chapter, you should be able to
- Graph exponential functions (11.1)
- Graph logarithmic functions (11.1)
- Use the definition of the logarithmic function (11.1)
- Solve problems involving exponential and logarithmic functions with base 10 (11.2)
- Solve problems involving exponential and logarithmic functions with base e (11.2)
- Use seven properties of logarithms (11.3)
- Use the base-change formula (11.4)
- Solve exponential equations (11.4)
- Solve logarithmic equations (11.4)
- Use exponential and logarithmic functions as mathematical models (11.5)
- Analyze exponentially related data (11.5)
- Recognize a binomial probability experiment (11.6)
- Find the mean, variance, and standard deviation of a binomial distribution (11.6)

VOCABULARY

antilogarithm (11.2)
base (11.1)
base-change formula (11.4)
binomial probability experiment (11.6)
common logarithmic function (11.2)
expected number (11.6)
expected value (11.6)
exponential equation (11.4)

exponential function (11.1)
logarithmic function (11.1)
mean of a binomial distribution (11.6)
natural logarithm (11.2)
natural logarithmic function (11.2)
standard deviation of a binomial distribution (11.6)
variance of a binomial distribution (11.6)

PROPERTIES

$\log_a 1 = 0$
$\log_a a = 1$
$\log_a (a^x) = x$
$a^{\log_a x} = x$
$\log_a (M \cdot N) = \log_a M + \log_a N$

$\log_a \left(\dfrac{M}{N}\right) = \log_a M - \log_a N$

$\log_a (M^p) = p \cdot \log_a M$

$\log_a M = \dfrac{\log_b M}{\log_b a}$

REVIEW PROBLEMS

In problems 1–3, write the equivalent exponential form.

1 $\log_3 81 = 4$

2 $\log_5 (5^{10}) = x$

3 $\log_a (a^t) = t$

In problems 4–6, solve for x.

4 $\log_x 32 = 5$

5 $\log_5 0.008 = x$

6 $9^{\log_9 x} = 35$

7 Rectangle ABCD ~ rectangle PQRS.
AB = 90, BC = 48, and PQ = 15

  a Find QR.
  b Find the ratio of the perimeter of ABCD to the perimeter of PQRS.
  c Find the ratio of the area of ABCD to the area of PQRS.
  d Find the ratio of the log of your answer to part **c** to the log of your answer to part **b**.

8 Approximate to three decimal places.

  a $\dfrac{\log 30}{\log 20}$

  b $\dfrac{\ln 30}{\ln 20}$

9 Find $\frac{x}{y}$ if $\log_{10} x = 2.5$ and $\ln y = 4$.

10 Determine whether each statement is True or False.

  a $\ln A + \ln B = \ln (A + B)$
  b $\ln A + \ln B = \ln (A \cdot B)$
  c $(\ln A)(\ln B) = \ln (A \cdot B)$
  d $(\ln A)(\ln B) = \ln B^{\ln A}$
  e $(\ln A)(\ln B) = (\ln B)^{\ln A}$

11 Solve for x.

  a $x^2 + 5x - 6 = 0$
  b $(9^x)^2 + 5(9^x) - 6 = 0$
  c $(\ln x)^2 + 5 \ln x - 6 = 0$

12 Radium has a half-life of 1660 years. If the initial amount of radium is 200 grams, how much will remain in 500 years?

Review Problems, *continued*

13 Find the perimeter of the rectangle.

$\log_{25} 5$

$\log_4 8$

14 Find the coefficient of the $d^2 n^6$ term of $\left(\frac{2}{3}d + \frac{1}{3}n\right)^8$.

15 Approximate each of the following expressions to six decimal places.

   a log 500   **b** log 5   **c** log 0.05
   d log 50   **e** log 0.5

16 Evaluate to three decimal places.

   a log 60 − log 10   **b** log 12 − log 2   **c** log 6 − log 1
   d log 36 − log 6   **e** log 42 − log 7

17 The cost of 4 years of education at a private college is now approximately $64,000. How much would Chip's parents have had to invest at 6.5% 18 years ago to have that amount today, assuming the interest was compounded continuously?

18 Sales of a new breakfast cereal, Toasty Twigs, increased according to the formula $S = S_0 \log 5M$, where S_0 is the number of boxes sold when the cereal was first placed on the market, M is the number of months since the cereal was introduced, and S is the number of boxes sold during the Mth month. How many months did it take for sales of Toasty Twigs to double?

19 A certain weighted coin has a $\frac{3}{5}$ probability of turning up heads each time it is tossed. The coin is tossed five times.

   a Copy and complete the following table.

Number of heads	0	1	2	3	4	5
Probability						

   b Construct a bar graph showing the probabilities for this experiment.

20 If log $n \approx 115.11$, how many digits are to the left of the decimal point in the number n?

21 A cup of coffee is poured when its temperature is 125°F. The room temperature is 68°F. After 5 minutes, the coffee has cooled to 105°F. What is the temperature of the coffee after 12 minutes?

22 Copy and complete the tables.

a
x	1	2	4	8	64	$\frac{1}{2}$	$\frac{1}{4}$		
$\log_2 x$								4	−3

b
x	0	1	2	3	−2	−1	−3		
2^x								16	$\frac{1}{64}$

23 Solve $\log_2 x = \log_2 (x + 8) - \log_2 5$ for x.

24 Most airplanes fly at altitudes from 30,000 to 35,000 feet above the ground. Using the equation for atmospheric pressure, $P = 14.7e^{-kh}$, and the fact that at 5000 feet the atmospheric pressure is 11.9 pounds per square inch, find the range of pressures outside a plane flying at the given altitudes.

25 If each question on a multiple-choice test has five choices, there is a 20% probability of answering a question correctly by guessing. Suppose that Lois Kohr guesses on all 60 questions of such a test.
  a What is her expected score?
  b What is the probability that she will answer at least 20 of the questions correctly?

26 a Graph $y = 2^x$.   **b** Graph $y = x^2$.

27 Solve $2^w = 7^{w+3}$ for w.

28 Approximate $\log 1 + \log 2 + \log 3 + \log 4 + \ldots + \log 39$ to the nearest tenth. (Hint: Using the factorial key on a calculator will save you a lot of time on this one.)

29 Solve $(\log_4 x)^2 = 4$ for x.

30 The formula for compound interest is $A = P\left(1 + \frac{r}{n}\right)^{nt}$. If you deposit $25,000 at 7%, compounded quarterly, how long will it take to become a millionaire?

31 A fair coin is tossed eight times. Find the probability that four of the coin tosses land heads and four of the tosses land tails.

32 A certain virus has infected 10,000 people in a geographical area. The treatment for the virus can reduce the number of infected people by 10% each week, so the decrease is exponential. The following data have been collected for the first three weeks. How many weeks will pass until only 10% of the original 10,000 have the virus?

t	0	1	2	3
N	10,000	9000	8100	7300

33 The area of the rectangle is 500 square units. Find a.

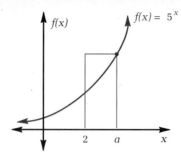

34 Write as a single logarithm.

a $3 \ln x + \ln \pi - 2 \ln (x - 2)$

b $\frac{1}{2} \ln x + \frac{1}{2} \ln y - \ln (x - 5)$

35 Solve for x.

a $2^{x+2} = 4^x$

b $2^{x+2} = 3^x$

c $2^{x+2} = 2^x$

36 The decline in the buffalo population was exponential in the 1800's. In 1800 it was estimated that there were 6,000,000 buffalo roaming the plains. By 1830 this number had declined to 500,000. Assuming the same rate of decline, how many buffalo were there in 1930? (Use $B = B_0 e^{-kt}$.)

LOGARITHMIC INTUITION
Richard Harris reports science on the radio

"One thing people often ask me is how much more powerful the San Francisco earthquake of October 1989 was than another particular quake," says Richard Harris. Mr. Harris, as National Public Radio's science correspondent, spent ten days in San Francisco reporting on that earthquake.

Mr. Harris explains that the earthquake that occurred in southern California in February 1990, for example, measured 5.5. To compare that one with the 1989 San Francisco quake, which measured 7.1, you would divide $10^{7.1}$ by $10^{5.5}$. The quotient, $10^{1.6}$, is about 40. This means there was about forty times as much ground motion in the San Francisco quake as in the more recent California quake. (See the Mathematical Excursion on p. 508.)

"What I like best about my job is that I do different things every day," Mr. Harris says. Within one year he traveled to San Francisco,

then to Brazil to do a series of stories on the Amazon rain forest, then to Florida for a space shuttle launch.

Mr. Harris graduated from the University of California at Santa Cruz. "I was a biology major, but I studied a little bit of everything. I took mathematics through calculus in order to understand my other science courses," he says. "To report a story involving science, I have to understand math."

CHAPTER TEST

1 Solve for P.

    a $P = \log_{10} 10,000,000$ **b** $P = \log_8 64$

    c $P = \log_2 256$ **c** $P = \log_{\frac{1}{2}} 8$

2 Approximate to three decimal places.

    a $\log 20 + \log 30$ **b** $\log (20 + 30)$

    c $\log 20 + 30$ **d** $20 + \log 30$

3 Evaluate each of the following expressions.

    a $\log_2 48 - \log_2 3$ **b** $\log_3 72 - 3 \log_3 2$ **c** $1 - \log_2 32$

4 Write each expression as a sum and difference of logarithms.

    a $\ln \dfrac{e^2 x}{(x - 2)}$ **b** $\log \sqrt[3]{\dfrac{x^5}{y^2}}$

5 If \$10,000 is invested at 7.85%, compounded continuously, how much money will be in the account after six years?

6 Solve $6^{x^2 + 3x} = 25$ for x.

7 Solve $x = \log_3 6 \cdot \log_6 8 \cdot \log_8 27$ for x.

8 Noise from a Chicago elevated train measures 95 decibels. Noise in an automobile at highway speed measures 50 decibels. How many times more intense is the sound from the elevated train than the sound in the automobile?

9 The atomic bomb dropped on Hiroshima had a Richter number of 5.7. The Alaska earthquake of 1964 was 631 times as intense as the Hiroshima bomb. What was the Richter number for the Alaska earthquake?

10 A weighted coin comes up heads $\frac{4}{5}$ of the time. The coin is flipped 180 times.

    a Find the expected number of heads (the mean).

    b Find the standard deviation of the distribution.

11 Write as a single logarithm.

    $\dfrac{1}{2} \ln y - 3 \ln x^2$

COUNTING AND PROBABILITY

W hile enjoying David Hockney's beautiful *Japanese Rain on Canvas* for its own sake, we are nonetheless tempted to speculate on probabilities related to the raindrops and the spots.

SYSTEMATIC COUNTING

Objectives

After studying this section, you will be able to
- Apply the Fundamental Counting Principle
- Relate the numbers of elements in two sets to the numbers of elements in their union and intersection
- Use the combination and permutation functions to solve counting problems

Part One: Introduction

The Fundamental Counting Principle

In Chapter 1, you explored various ways of solving the handshake problem. That problem and others like it are called counting problems or problems in *combinatorics.* Here is another:

Suppose Moe picks a number from 1 to 4, Larry picks a number from 5 to 7, and Curly picks the number 8 or 9. How many sets of three numbers are possible?

For each of Moe's four possible choices, Larry has three possible choices, and Curly has two. The total number of possible triples is therefore $4 \cdot 3 \cdot 2$, or 24. This solution illustrates the *Fundamental Counting Principle.*

> ▶ *If one event can happen in m ways and another event can happen in n ways, then the number of ways in which both can happen is equal to m · n.*

One way of visualizing this principle is to use a tree diagram to represent the possibilities. The following diagram shows each of Moe's four choices, Larry's three choices, and Curly's two choices in the problem described above. By counting the possible paths in the diagram, we can verify that the total number of possibilities is 24.

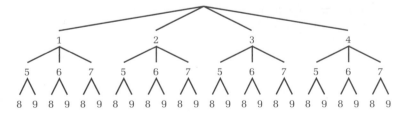

Unions and Intersections

Consider the sets A = {1, 2, 3, 4} and B = {3, 4, 5, 6, 7}. The union of the sets, A ∪ B, is {1, 2, 3, 4, 5, 6, 7} and the intersection of the sets, A ∩ B, is {3, 4}. (Recall that A ∪ B consists of the elements that are in either A *or* B and that A ∩ B consists of the elements that are in both A *and* B.)

A useful way of representing this situation is a **Venn diagram.** The region that is included in both circles represents the intersection of the sets. The entire region enclosed by the circles represents the union of the sets.

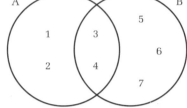

We use the notation #(S) to refer to the number of elements in a set S. In this case, #(A) = 4, #(B) = 5, #(A ∪ B) = 7, and #(A ∩ B) = 2. Notice, moreover, that 4 + 5 = 7 + 2. This relationship suggests an important theorem that can be used to solve a variety of counting problems.

> *For any two sets* A *and* B,
> #(A) + #(B) = #(A ∪ B) + #(A ∩ B).

Example

How many cards in a standard deck are either aces or hearts?

If we let A = {aces} and B = {hearts}, we know that #(A) = 4 and #(B) = 13. Since A ∩ B = {aces and hearts} and the only element in this set is the ace of hearts, #(A ∩ B) = 1.

We want the number of elements in A ∪ B. According to the theorem presented in this section,

$$\#(A) + \#(B) = \#(A \cup B) + \#(A \cap B)$$
$$4 + 13 = \#(A \cup B) + 1$$
$$16 = \#(A \cup B)$$

Alternative solution: Let's see which cards satisfy the conditions of the problem. Certainly all 13 hearts do. There are 4 aces, but since 1 is the ace of hearts, we only count 3. Therefore, 16 cards are either aces or hearts.

Permutations and Combinations

In Chapter 5, you were introduced to two functions that simplify counting. The combination function, $C(n, r) = \frac{n!}{(n - r)!r!}$, is used to determine the number of *groups* of r elements that can be selected from a set of n elements. We can apply this function whenever we are dealing with a situation in which the order of selection does not matter.

The permutation function, $P(n, r) = \frac{n!}{(n - r)!}$, is used to determine the number of *arrangements* of r elements that can be selected from a set of n elements. We use this function when the order of selection does matter.

Example

How many different three-digit numbers can be formed from the digits 1, 2, 3, 4, 5, 6, and 7 if no digit is used twice?

Because order does matter (324 is different from 234, for example), we use permutations. We are looking for the number of arrangements of three items chosen from a set of seven.

$$P(7, 3) = \frac{7!}{(7 - 3)!} = \frac{7!}{4!} = 7 \cdot 6 \cdot 5 = 210$$

There are 210 such three-digit numbers.

Part Two: Sample Problems

Problem 1

How many different 13-card bridge hands can be dealt from a standard deck of 52 cards?

Solution

We are not concerned with the order in which the cards are dealt, so we use the combination function.

$$C(52, 13) = \frac{52!}{(52 - 13)!13!} = \frac{52!}{39! \cdot 13!} \approx 6.35 \times 10^{11}$$

There are over 600 billion possible bridge hands.

Problem 2

A box contains 20 muffins, 5 of which are blueberry and the rest of which are raisin.

a How many groups of 2 blueberry muffins and 3 raisin muffins can be chosen from the box?

b In how many ways can a person choose 2 blueberry muffins and 3 raisin muffins if the first choice must be a raisin muffin and the two kinds must be chosen alternately?

Solution

a We are looking for the number of ways in which 2 muffins can be chosen from 5 and 3 muffins can be chosen from 15. The order of choosing the muffins does not matter, so we use combinations and apply the Fundamental Counting Principle.

$C(5, 2) \cdot C(15, 3) = 10 \cdot 455 = 4550$

b In this case, the order of choice does matter, so we cannot use combinations. The only order that satisfies the given conditions is (1) raisin, (2) blueberry, (3) raisin, (4) blueberry, (5) raisin.

There are 15 raisin muffins from which the first muffin can be chosen. There are 5 blueberry muffins from which the second can be chosen. There are 14 raisin muffins left for the third selection. There are 4 blueberry muffins left for the fourth selection. There are 13 raisin muffins left for the fifth choice. The number of ways in which the muffins can be chosen is therefore $15 \cdot 5 \cdot 14 \cdot 4 \cdot 13$, or 54,600.

Problem 3 *Bali High School has a student population of 2400. Of these students, 2135 are taking math, 1857 are taking science, and 1664 are taking both math and science. How many students are taking neither math nor science?*

Solution We can draw a chart to clarify the way in which the students are grouped. The first row represents the students taking math, and the second row represents those not taking math. The first column represents those taking science; the second column, those not taking science. We know that 1664 students take both courses.

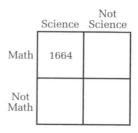

Now we can begin to fill in the other boxes. The total taking math is 2135, and 2135 − 1664 = 471; so 471 students are taking math but not science. There are 1857 students taking science, so 1857 − 1664, or 193, students take science but not math.

Since the total number of students is 2400 and the three categories filled in so far total 2328, there must be 72 students who are taking neither math nor science.

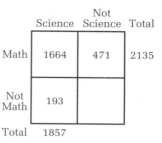

Part Three: Exercises and Problems

Warm-up Exercises

In problems 1–3, identify each situation as involving combinations, permutations, or neither.

1 Picking a committee of seven members of the U.S. Senate
2 Lining up in a cafeteria line
3 Lining up members of a baseball team according to height

In problems 4 and 5, evaluate each expression.
4 $P(10, 2)$ **5** $C(15, 4)$

6 Let A = {students in your math class who also take history} and B = {students in your math class who also take a foreign language}. Find #(A), #(B), #(A ∩ B), and #(A ∪ B). Do your results agree with the theorem presented in this section?

7 A basketball team has three centers, four forwards, and five guards on its roster. How many different squads of one center, two forwards, and two guards can the coach put on the court?

8 Goo Lash Caterers provided a seven-course dinner for a party. Unfortunately, they forgot to label the containers of food, so the courses had to be served in a random order. In how many different orders could the courses have been served?

Problem Set

9 Let C be the combination function and P be the permutation function.

   a Evaluate $C(12, 7)$.   **b** Evaluate $P(12, 7)$.

10 If $\#(A) = 16$, $\#(B) = 31$, and $\#(A \cup B) = 39$, what is $\#(A \cap B)$?

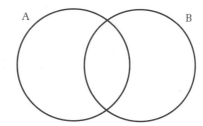

11 Pete's Pizza Parlor offers ten pizza toppings. Pete's Special includes a choice of any three toppings. How many three-topping combinations can be ordered?

12 In how many orders can the numbers 1, 2, 3, 5, 8, 13, and 21 be listed?

13 If $m_1 \in \{3, 5, 7, 9\}$ and $m_2 \in \left\{-3, -5, -\frac{1}{7}, -9\right\}$, for how many pairs (m_1, m_2) will the graphs of $y = m_1 x$ and $y = m_2 x$ be perpendicular?

14 Evaluate each expression.

   a $C(10, 3)$ **b** $C(10, 7)$ **c** $C(15, 2)$
   d $C(15, 13)$ **e** $C(18, 4)$ **f** $C(18, 14)$

15 Superstitious Sandy, the coach of a baseball team, starts the same nine players in every game but arranges them in a different batting order each time. How many games must the team play in order for Sandy to use all possible batting orders?

16 There are 85 athletes at Wassamatta U. Sixteen are on the basketball team, 75 are on the football team, and 12 are on both these teams. How many are on neither the basketball team nor the football team?

17 Use the Venn diagram to find each number.

   a #(A)

   b #(A ∩ B)

   c #(A ∩ B ∩ C)

   d #(B ∩ C)

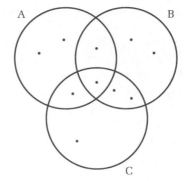

18 Radio station WOLD plays ten requests between 10:00 and 11:00. In how many different orders can each group of ten songs be played?

19 A sergeant needs to select 6 "volunteers" from his unit of 52 soldiers for KP duty. To find the number of ways in which the KP detail can be selected, should Sarge use combinations, permutations, neither, or both?

20 Eight horses are competing in a race. The first prize is $500, the second is $400, and the third is $200. To determine the number of ways in which the prizes could be awarded, would you use combinations, permutations, neither, or both?

21 Let A = {x:x ≤ 5} and B = {x:x > 0}. Graph the following sets on a number line.

   a A ∩ B   **b** A ∪ B

22 If a point within the larger square is chosen at random, what is the probability that the point is in the smaller, shaded square?

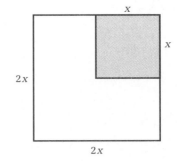

23 The Thirty-seven Flavors ice cream shop offers 37 different kinds of ice cream. How many different 2-scoop cones can be ordered if customers are given a choice of plain or sugar cones? (Assume that customers asking for 2 different flavors can specify the order in which the flavors are put on the cone.)

24 A key has five zones of indentation, each of which can be indented to any of four depths. How many different keys can be made?

25 a How many seven-digit numbers can be formed from the digits 0–9 if each digit can be used more than once?
b Are all of these possible telephone numbers in the United States?

26 If $m \in \{2, 4, 6, 7, 9\}$ and $n \in \{1, 3, 4, 6\}$, for how many pairs (m, n) will i^{mn} be a real number?

27 If $\#(\mathrm{I}) = 16$, $\#(\mathrm{II}) = 10$, and $\#(\mathrm{III}) = 20$, what is $\#(\mathrm{A} \cup \mathrm{B})$?

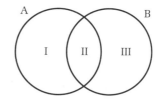

28 In poker, a flush is a hand containing five cards of the same suit. How many different flushes can be dealt from a 52-card deck?

29 Consider the sets $\mathrm{A} = \{1, 3, 5, 7, 9\}$ and $\mathrm{B} = \{2, 4, 6, 8, 10, 12, 14\}$.
a Find $\#(\mathrm{A})$.   **b** Find $\#(\mathrm{B})$.   **c** Find $\#(\mathrm{A} \cap \mathrm{B})$.
d Find $\#(\mathrm{A} \cup \mathrm{B})$.   **e** Is $\#(\mathrm{A}) + \#(\mathrm{B}) = \#(\mathrm{A} \cup \mathrm{B})$? Why?

30 If $a \in \{-2, 0, 2, 4\}$ and $b \in \{1, 3, 5\}$, for how many ordered pairs (a, b) is $a^b > 0$?

31 Ten boys and eight girls are in a class. In how many ways can four of the boys and three of the girls line up in alternate order?

32 Explain why $\#(\mathrm{A}) + \#(\mathrm{B}) = \#(\mathrm{A} \cup \mathrm{B}) + \#(\mathrm{A} \cap \mathrm{B})$ is a true statement.

33 How many triangles are in the figure shown?

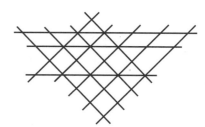

34 Explain why a set consisting of n elements has 2^n subsets.

12.2 SAMPLE SPACES, EVENTS, AND PROBABILITY

Objectives

After studying this section, you will be able to
- Determine the sample space for an experiment
- Identify events and calculate their probabilities

Part One: Introduction

Sample Spaces

When you have solved probability problems in the past, you have started by determining the number of possible outcomes. The set of all possible outcomes of an experiment is called the ***sample space*** for that experiment. Although the outcomes in a sample space need not be equally likely, *in this book we will work only with sample spaces made up of equally likely outcomes.* Such a space is said to have ***equal elemental probabilities.***

Example When *two dice are rolled, the possible sums of the numbers on the upturned faces of the dice are {2, 3, 4, 5, 6, 7, 8, 9, 10, 11, 12}. Is this an appropriate sample space for the experiment of rolling two dice?*

No—the elements are not equally likely. (Rolling a 6, for example, is more likely than rolling a 2.) The appropriate sample space is the following set of 36 equally likely outcomes.

{(1, 1), (1, 2), (1, 3), (1, 4), (1, 5), (1, 6),
 (2, 1), (2, 2), (2, 3), (2, 4), (2, 5), (2, 6),
 (3, 1), (3, 2), (3, 3), (3, 4), (3, 5), (3, 6),
 (4, 1), (4, 2), (4, 3), (4, 4), (4, 5), (4, 6),
 (5, 1), (5, 2), (5, 3), (5, 4), (5, 5), (5, 6),
 (6, 1), (6, 2), (6, 3), (6, 4), (6, 5), (6, 6)}

Sometimes it is inconvenient to list all the elements of a sample space, so other methods of representation are used. We could, for example, show the 36 elements of the sample space for the rolling of two dice in any of the following forms.

A Lattice
(Each dot represents an element.)

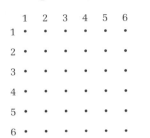

A Chart
(Each box represents an element.)

A Tree Diagram
(Each path represents an element.)

Probabilities of Events

Suppose that we are going to roll two dice and want to know the probability of rolling a 6. We have already determined the sample space for the rolling of two dice, but we now need to identify the *event*—the element or elements of the sample space that satisfy the given conditions.

In this case, the event consists of every ordered pair whose sum is 6. We can represent this event in any of the ways we used to represent the sample space. A lattice representation is shown at the right. The equivalent set notation is

$\{(1, 5), (2, 4), (3, 3), (4, 2), (5, 1)\}$

If an event A is a subset of a sample space S, then we can find the probability of event A, symbolized P(A), by means of the following formula.

$$P(A) = \frac{\#(A)}{\#(S)}$$

Example   *What is the probability that when two dice are rolled, the sum of the numbers on the upturned faces will be 6?*

As we have seen, the event (a roll of 6) contains 5 elements and the sample space contains 36 elements. Therefore, the probability is $\frac{5}{36}$.

Example   *A die is rolled and a coin is flipped. Find the probability that the number on the die is even and the coin shows heads.*

We can represent the sample space by means of a lattice and circle the elements that satisfy the given conditions (the event). The probability is $\frac{3}{12}$, or $\frac{1}{4}$.

```
      H  T
  1   ·  ·
  2   ⊙  ·
  3   ·  ·
  4   ⊙  ·
  5   ·  ·
  6   ⊙  ·
```

Part Two: Sample Problems

Problem 1   *A bag contains six red marbles and five blue marbles. Three marbles are drawn at random from the bag. Find the probability that all three are red.*

Solution   The sample space—the set of all groups of 3 marbles that can be drawn from 11—consists of $C(11, 3)$, or 165, elements. The event is made up of the groups of 3 marbles that can be drawn from the 6 red ones. There are $C(6, 3)$, or 20, such groups, so the probability is $\frac{20}{165}$, or $\frac{4}{33}$.

Problem 2   *Five cards are drawn at random from a standard deck. Find the probability that two are hearts and three are spades.*

Solution   The number of groups of five cards that can be chosen from a deck is $C(52, 5)$, or 2,598,960. The number of possible groups of two hearts is $C(13, 2)$, or 78, and the number of possible groups of three spades is $C(13, 3)$, or 286. To find the number of elements in the event, we apply the Fundamental Counting Principle, multiplying these two results. The event therefore consists of $78 \cdot 286$, or 22,308, elements. Thus, the probability is $\frac{22,308}{2,598,960}$, or $\approx$.0086.

Note It is frequently most convenient to express probabilities in decimal form. This probability is a little less than .01, so there is less than one chance in a hundred of drawing two hearts and three spades.

Problem 3   *Five different cards are drawn at random, one at a time, from a standard deck. Find the probability that the selection consists of two hearts and three spades chosen alternately.*

Solution   Since we are looking for the probability of choosing cards in a certain order, the sample space consists of all the possible *arrangements* of 5 cards chosen from a deck of 52. Thus, there are $P(52, 5)$, or 311,875,200, elements in the sample space.

The event is the set of outcomes in which a spade, a heart, a spade, a heart, and a spade are chosen in sequence. There are 13 choices for the first card, 13 for the second, 12 for the third, then 12, then 11, so the event contains $13 \cdot 13 \cdot 12 \cdot 12 \cdot 11$, or 267,696, elements. The probability is $\frac{267,696}{311,875,200}$, or $\approx .00086$.

Problem 4   *Two real numbers between −1 and 1 are randomly chosen. Find the probability that the sum of their squares is less than 1.*

Solution   We can represent the sample space and the event on a coordinate system. Each point in the square represents an ordered pair (x, y) of numbers between −1 and 1.

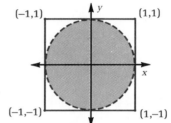

    The points for which $x^2 + y^2 < 1$ are those in the interior of the dashed circle.

    In this case we can't count the elements of the sample space and the event (each has infinitely many elements). The probability, however, does correspond to the ratio of the regions' areas. Since the area of the region corresponding to the event (the circle) is π and the area of the region corresponding to the sample space (the square) is $2 \cdot 2$, or 4, the probability is $\frac{\pi}{4}$, or $\approx .785$.

Part Three: Exercises and Problems

Warm-up Exercises

In problems 1–3, explain why each statement is true.

1 For any event A, $0 \le P(A) \le 1$.

2 $P(\phi) = 0$, where ϕ represents the empty set.

3 For any events A and B, $P(A) + P(B) = P(A \cup B) + P(A \cap B)$.

4 In poker, a flush is a hand consisting of five cards of the same suit. If you are dealt five cards, what is the probability that you have a diamond flush?

5 A dart thrown at the dart board shown lands in a random spot on the board. What is the probability that it lands in the bull's-eye?

6 Represent, in as many ways as you can, the sample space for rolling one die and tossing two coins.

7 In the game Castles and Creatures, one 12-sided die (with sides numbered 1–12) and one 4-sided die (with sides numbered 1–4) are used.

    a Represent the sample space for rolling both dice.
    b When a player rolls the dice, his or her character receives the powers of a wizard if the sum of the numbers on the dice is greater than 10. Find the probability of such a roll.

Problem Set

8 Two dice are rolled.

    a How many possible outcomes are there?
    b How many distinct sums of the numbers on the upturned faces are possible?

9 Three of the elements of {1, 2, 3, 5, 7, 9, 11} are chosen at random.

    a What is the probability that their sum is even?
    b What is the probability that their product is even?

10 In a standard deck, how many cards are aces or kings or hearts?

11 Let C be the combination function.

    a Find $C(8, 1)$.   **b** Find $C(15, 1)$.
    c Find $C(32, 1)$.   **d** Find $C(13, 1)$.
    e What conclusion can you draw from your answers to parts **a–d?**

12 David has twelve 25-cent stamps and eight 13-cent stamps in his drawer. He reaches in without looking and selects five stamps. What is the probability that he takes three 25-cent stamps and two 13-cent stamps?

13 A square is inscribed in a circle as shown.

    a What is the probability that a randomly chosen point in the interior of the circle also lies inside the square?
    b What is the probability that a randomly chosen point inside the square is also inside the circle?

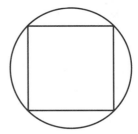

14 You have 10 tickets for a raffle. If 120 raffle tickets have been sold and 2 tickets are drawn at random to determine the winners of 2 prizes, what is

    a The probability that you will win no prize?
    b The probability that you will win one prize?
    c The probability that you will win both prizes?
    d What is the sum of your answers to parts **a–c?** What is the meaning of this sum?

15 Let A = {1, 2, 3, 5, 7} and B = {perfect squares less than 30}.

   a Find A ∪ B.   **b** Find A ∩ B.

16 A bag contains eight American League baseballs and five National League baseballs. Umpire Streichsbach reaches in and selects three balls without looking.

   a What is the probability that all three are American League baseballs?

   b What is the probability that all three are National League baseballs?

17 Suppose that segments are drawn to points S and R from a point somewhere on $\overline{PQ}$, forming a triangle with base $\overline{RS}$. If a point inside square PQRS is selected at random, what is the probability that it is also inside the triangle?

18 On the TV game show *Jewel of Fortune*, the winner gets to select, without looking, 3 gems from a bag containing 5 diamonds, 10 emeralds, and 20 zircons.

   a What is the probability that a winner will select 3 zircons?

   b What is the probability that a winner will select a gem of each type?

19 James is gluing legs onto a table. Five red and eight blue legs are available. James randomly picks four of these legs. Find the probability that James's table will have four red legs.

20 Let M = {prime integers less than 50} and N = {odd positive integers less than 50}.

   a Find #(N).   **b** Find #(M).

   c Find #(M ∩ N).   **d** Find #(M ∪ N).

   e Is #(N) + #(M) = #(M ∪ N) + #(M ∩ N)?

21 A bag contains ten red marbles, four green marbles, and eight blue marbles. If four marbles are chosen at random from the bag, what is the probability that two are red and two are blue?

22 Two congruent squares overlap as shown. What is the probability that a randomly chosen point in the interior of the figure is in the shaded region?

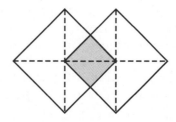

Problem Set, *continued*

23 Six cards are drawn at random from a standard deck. Find the probability that four are hearts and two are clubs.

24 What is the greatest number of ancestors a person can have in the five generations preceding his or her own?

25 An aviary contained 12 birdies and 15 eagles. Bogey left the window open, and before Paar shut it, 7 of the aviary's inhabitants had flown out. Find the probability that 4 birdies and 3 eagles had escaped in alternate order.

26 Two different numbers are randomly chosen from $\{1, \sqrt{2}, \sqrt{3}, 2, \sqrt{5}, \sqrt{6}\}$.

  a Represent the sample space for this experiment.
  b Find the probability that at least one of the numbers selected is rational.

27 Solve $\displaystyle\sum_{k=1}^{3} (kx + 5) = 20$ for x.

28 A natural number x is randomly selected from set A, and a natural number y is randomly selected from set B. Find the probability that $|x - y| \geq 3$.

29 Consider the sequence 3, 7, 11, 15, 19, 23, ... If the pattern continues and three of the next five numbers in the sequence are chosen at random, what is the probability that none of the three is a multiple of 3?

30 How many lattice points (x, y) satisfy the inequality $x^2 + y^2 \leq 25$?

31 Bade Woggs has 25 red socks and 30 white socks in a drawer. Since it is dark, he can't tell them apart.

  a How many socks must he take from the drawer to be sure that he has a matching pair of socks?
  b How many socks must he take to be sure that he has a pair of red socks?

32 If four points are selected at random from the square lattice shown, what is the probability that the four points are vertices of a square?

33 If a Christmas pie is 9 inches in diameter and contains 30 spherical plums, each of which is $\frac{3}{4}$ inch in diameter, what is the probability that Jack Horner will prick a plum if he sticks a pin into the pie at random?

PROBABILITIES OF UNIONS

Objectives

After studying this section, you will be able to
- Understand disjunctions and unions of sets
- Calculate probabilities of mutually exclusive events

Part One: Introduction

Disjunctions

Suppose that one card is drawn at random from a standard deck. What is the probability that it is either an ace or a heart?

A statement in which two possible outcomes are connected by the word *or* is called a ***disjunction.*** When we are asked to find the probability of a disjunction, the event is the union of the two sets of outcomes, since the union consists of all the elements that are in one set *or* in the other set.

If we let A = {aces} and B = {hearts}, we know that

$$P(A \cup B) = \frac{\#(A \cup B)}{\#(\text{sample space})} = \frac{\#(A \cup B)}{52}$$

In Section 12.1, we found that #(A ∪ B) + #(A ∩ B) = #(A) + #(B). In this case, #(A) = 4, #(B) = 13, and #(A ∩ B) = 1, so #(A ∪ B) = 16. The probability of drawing either an ace or a heart is $\frac{16}{52}$, or $\frac{4}{13}$.

When we apply the theorem presented in Section 12.1 to probabilities, we obtain the following theorem.

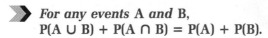

> ***For any events A and B,***
> **P(A ∪ B) + P(A ∩ B) = P(A) + P(B).**

Example   *If a single die is rolled, what is the probability that the roll is a multiple either of 2 or of 3?*

If we let A = {multiples of 2} and B = {multiples of 3}, we need to find the probability of A ∪ B. The sample space is {1, 2, 3, 4, 5, 6}. Since A = {2, 4, 6} and B = {3, 6} and the intersection of A and B is {6}, $P(A) = \frac{3}{6}$, $P(B) = \frac{2}{6}$, and $P(A \cap B) = \frac{1}{6}$.

$$P(A \cup B) + P(A \cap B) = P(A) + P(B)$$

$$P(A \cup B) + \frac{1}{6} = \frac{3}{6} + \frac{2}{6}$$

$$P(A \cup B) = \frac{2}{3}$$

Alternative Solution: Which of the elements of the sample space satisfy the given conditions?

1 is not a multiple of 2 or 3.
2 is a multiple of 2.
3 is a multiple of 3.
4 is a multiple of 2.
5 is not a multiple of 2 or 3.
6 is a multiple of both 2 and 3.

Four of the six rolls are multiples either of 2 or of 3, so the probability is $\frac{4}{6}$, or $\frac{2}{3}$.

Mutually Exclusive Events

When two events A and B cannot occur together, they are said to be *mutually exclusive.* In such a case, $P(A \cap B) = 0$, since the intersection of A and B is the empty set. For mutually exclusive events, therefore, the preceding theorem has the following form.

> **If A *and* B *are mutually exclusive events, then***
> **$P(A \cup B) = P(A) + P(B)$.**

Example   *If a card is randomly chosen from a standard deck, what is the probability that it is either an ace or a king?*

Let A = {aces} and B = {kings}. These events are mutually exclusive (the card cannot be both an ace and a king), so

$$P(A \cup B) = P(A) + P(B) = \frac{1}{13} + \frac{1}{13} = \frac{2}{13}$$

Part Two: Sample Problems

Problem 1   *A bag contains three chicken-salad sandwiches, four Limburger cheese sandwiches, and five ham sandwiches. If you reach into the bag and pick one sandwich at random, what is the probability that it is a chicken-salad sandwich or a ham sandwich?*

Solution $P(\text{chicken salad}) = \frac{3}{12}$, and $P(\text{ham}) = \frac{5}{12}$. Since choosing a chicken-salad sandwich and choosing a ham sandwich are mutually exclusive events (you can take only one sandwich), we add the two probabilities.

$$P(\text{chicken salad or ham}) = \frac{3}{12} + \frac{5}{12} = \frac{8}{12} = \frac{2}{3}$$

Problem 2　Robin Finch has an aviary containing two kinds of birds, jays and bulbuls. Each bird is either gray or blue. She has 23 gray birds and 15 blue birds. Of the blue birds, 10 are bulbuls, and there are 18 bulbuls all together. One day, Robin's friend Martin came by and randomly selected a bird. What is the probability that he selected a gray bird or a jaybird?

Solution　If we let A = {gray birds} and B = {jays}, what we are trying to find is P(A ∪ B). Let's use a diagram to organize the information in the problem.

	Gray	Blue	Total
Jays			
Bulbuls		10	18
Total	23	15	

　　We start by entering the given values. Note that there are 23 + 15, or 38, birds in all.

　　Since there are 18 bulbuls and 10 of them are blue, 8 of them must be gray. Since 8 of the 23 gray birds are bulbuls, the other 15 must be jays. The remaining 5 jays are blue.

　　The first column in the diagram represents set A, and the first row represents set B. Therefore, #(A ∪ B) = 8 + 15 + 5, or 28, and P(A ∪ B) = $\frac{28}{38}$, or ≈.74.

	Gray	Blue	Total
Jays	15	5	
Bulbuls	8	10	18
Total	23	15	

Part Three: Exercises and Problems

Warm-up Exercises

1 Suppose that two cards are picked from a deck. Are the following events mutually exclusive?

　a {black cards} and {kings}　　　　**b** {spades} and {diamonds}

2 Suppose that two dice are rolled. Are the following events mutually exclusive?

　a {even numbers} and {odd numbers}
　b {multiples of 3} and {multiples of 2}
　c {1} and {prime numbers} and {composite numbers}

3 At the annual dance of the Superheroes Club one year, each member showed up dressed either as Batman or as Superman. Of the 100 members attending, 76 were dressed as Batman, and 44 of these wore masks. All together, 51 members wore masks. What is the probability that a randomly selected member at the dance was dressed as Superman and wore no mask?

4 The figure at the right is known as Lewis Carroll's squares. If a point inside the figure is picked at random, what is the probability that it is in the shaded area?

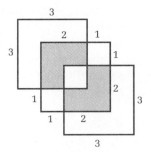

Problem Set

5 In rectangle ABCD, AB = 2(AD) and M and N are the midpoints of $\overline{AB}$ and $\overline{DC}$. If a point inside ABCD is selected at random, what is the probability it is inside △DMC or inside △ANB?

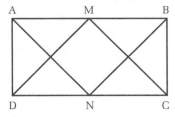

6 Suppose that the ace of spades is removed from a standard deck and a card is then selected at random. Find the probability that the card is either an ace or a spade.

7 If two of the numbers $3 + 2\sqrt{5}$, $4 - 2\sqrt{5}$, $5 + \sqrt{5}$, $4 + 2\sqrt{5}$, $3\sqrt{5}$, $3 - 2\sqrt{5}$, and $-3\sqrt{5}$ are chosen at random, what is the probability that they are

   a Conjugates?   **b** Opposites?
   c Opposites or conjugates?   **d** Opposites and conjugates?

8 PQRS is a 2 × 2 square. PQM and SNR are equilateral triangles. If a point inside PQRS is selected at random, what is the probability that it is inside either △PQM or △SNR?

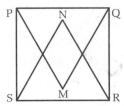

9 If four dice are rolled, what is the probability that the sum of the numbers on the dice is either odd or even?

10 A group of six adults and seven children was waiting in line for popcorn. If they had lined up randomly, what is the probability that the sequence was child, adult, child, adult, child, etc.?

11 **a** What is the sample space for the rolling of two dice?
     b If the dice are loaded so that each always shows an even number, what is the sample space?
     c If the two dice described in part **b** are rolled, what is the probability that at least one of them shows a 2?

12 If two dice—one red, the other green—are rolled, what is the probability of each event?

   a {red 2 or green 5}
   b {red 2 and sum of 6}
   c {red 2 and green greater than 2}
   d {red 2 and sum of 2}

13 If $P(A) = \frac{8}{15}$ and $P(B) = \frac{2}{15}$, is $P(A \cup B) = \frac{10}{15} = \frac{2}{3}$?

14 Lectoral College has 2800 students, of whom 1910 take English, 1400 take math, and 820 take both math and English. If one of the students is chosen at random, what is the probability that he or she takes neither math nor English?

15 Seven rays have their endpoints at the origin of a coordinate system and lie in Quadrant I. How many acute angles are formed by the rays?

16 A die is rolled. Let A = {multiples of 4} and B = {multiples of 2}. Find each of the following probabilities.

   a $P(A)$ **b** $P(B)$ **c** $P(A \cup B)$ **d** $P(A \cap B)$

17 As a practical joke, Calvin took the labels off all 27 cans of food his family had in the cupboard. There were 13 cans of vegetables, 8 cans of soup, and 6 cans of baking soda. His father selected 3 cans from the shelf to use in preparing a dinner. What is the probability he got one can of soup and two of vegetables or two cans of soup and one of vegetables?

18 Suppose that $f(1) = 2$ and $f(n + 1) = 3[f(n)]$. Evaluate the following.

   a $f(1)$ **b** $f(2)$ **c** $f(3)$ **d** $f(4)$

19 Evaluate each of the following expressions.

   a $\sum_{k=1}^{10} \left(\sqrt{-1}\right)^k$ **b** $\sum_{k=1}^{11} \left(\sqrt{-1}\right)^k$

20 Let A = {positive integers less than or equal to 20}. If three positive integers are randomly selected from A, what is the probability that all will be odd?

21 Suppose that the odds of winning a game are 5 to 3. (This means that over a long series of trials, you will win 5 times for every 3 times you lose.)

   a If you play the game once, what is the probability that you will win?
   b What is the probability that you will lose?

Problem Set, *continued*

22 How many triangles are in the diagram shown?

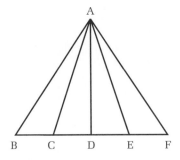

23 If the probability of a certain NFL team's winning the Super Bowl is $\frac{4}{11}$, what are the odds that the team will win the Super Bowl?

24 The penny gum-ball machine at the Big Store contains 55 gum balls and 10 prizes. Groucho puts 3 cents into the machine and gets 3 items. Find the probability that they are either all prizes or all gum balls.

25 If three of the ten points shown are selected at random, what is the probability that the points are collinear?

26 Namor's Submarine Sandwich Shop offers a "special surprise" meal for $0.50. You pick one sandwich at random from a box containing 8 liverwurst sandwiches, 2 ham sandwiches, and 4 roast beef sandwiches.

  a What is the probability that you will get a ham sandwich or a roast beef sandwich for your $0.50?

  b How much would you have to spend to guarantee getting at least one ham or roast beef sandwich?

27 At Thirty-seven Flavors, 37 kinds of ice cream, 6 kinds of syrup, and 4 kinds of nuts are available. If a person can order a sundae with or without whipped cream, how many different sundaes containing 3 scoops of ice cream and 1 kind of syrup can be ordered? (Assume that the order of stacking the scoops does not matter.)

28 A card is chosen from a standard deck. Let A = {jacks} and B = {queens}.

  a Find P(A).   **b** Find P(B).   **c** Find P(A ∪ B).   **d** Find P(A ∩ B).

29 Draw a Venn diagram to represent

  a Two events, A and B, that are mutually exclusive

  b Two events, A and B, that are not mutually exclusive

30 If three of the points shown are selected at random, what is the probability that they are collinear?

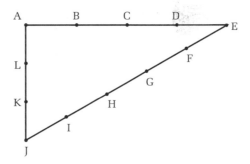

31 Find the next two numbers in each sequence.
  a 3, 9, 15, 21, 27, ___?___ , ___?___
  b 4, 9, 19, 39, 79, ___?___ , ___?___
  c 1, 1, 2, 3, 5, 8, 13, 21, 34, ___?___ , ___?___

32 If two of the six binomials $a + b$, $x + 2y$, $3x - y$, $x + y$, $a - b$, and $2y - x$ are chosen at random, what is the probability that their product is a difference of two squares?

33 A rectangle is inscribed in a square in such a way that four isosceles triangles are formed. What is the probability that

  a The area of the rectangle is greater than half the area of the square?
  b The area of the rectangle is less than half the area of the square?
  c The area of the rectangle is equal to half the area of the square?

34 Consider the words *rhyme, slime, time, crime, lime, name, fame, game, same, tame,* and *blame.*
  a If 2 of the 11 words are chosen at random, what is the probability that they rhyme?
  b If 2 of the 11 words are chosen at random, what is the probability that they have the same number of letters?

35 A number a is selected at random from {3, 7, 10, 12, 15}. Then a different number, b, is selected from the set, again at random. What is the probability that $\log_a b > 1$?

36 Let A = {multiples of 3 between 0 and 100}, B = {multiples of 5 between 0 and 100}, and C = {multiples of 3 or 5 between 0 and 100}. Find each number.
  a #(A)   **b** #(B)   **c** #(C)

37 Consider eight coplanar points, no three of which are collinear and no four of which lie on the same circle. How many circles pass through three of the eight points?

PROBABILITIES OF INTERSECTIONS

Objectives

After studying this section, you will be able to
- Determine probabilities of intersections of independent events
- Solve problems involving conditional probabilities

Part One: Introduction

Intersections of Independent Events

Suppose that a die is rolled and a coin is tossed. What is the probability that the die shows 4 and the coin shows heads?

A statement in which two possible outcomes are connected by the word *and* is called a ***conjunction.*** The event corresponding to a conjunction is the intersection of the two sets of outcomes, since the intersection consists of all the elements that are in one set *and* in the other set.

If we let A = {4} and B = {heads}, then P(4 and heads) is P(A ∩ B). It is important to recognize that in this case A and B are ***independent events***—the rolling of the die has no effect on the tossing of the coin, and the tossing of the coin has no effect on the rolling of the die. When events are independent, we can find the probability of their intersection by simply multiplying the probabilities of the individual events.

> *If two events* A *and* B *are independent, then*
> P(A ∩ B) = P(A) · P(B).

Thus, since $P(4) = \frac{1}{6}$ and $P(\text{heads}) = \frac{1}{2}$, the probability that the die shows 4 and the coin shows heads is $\frac{1}{6} \cdot \frac{1}{2}$, or $\frac{1}{12}$. Remember, *this "multiplication rule" applies only to independent events.*

Example *Two cards are drawn at random from different standard decks. Find the probability that the first is an ace and the second is a king.*

We let A represent the event in which the first card is an ace and B represent the event in which the second is a king. The events are independent, since the choice of a card from one deck will have no effect on the choice of a card from the other deck. Thus,

$$P(A \cap B) = P(A) \cdot P(B) = \frac{4}{52} \cdot \frac{4}{52} = \frac{1}{13} \cdot \frac{1}{13} = \frac{1}{169}$$

Dependent Events and Conditional Probabilities

Now suppose we draw a card from a standard deck and then, without replacing that card, we draw a second card from the deck. What is the probability that the first is an ace and the second is a king?

This situation is different from that in the preceding example. The choosing of the first card affects the probability for the choosing of the second—there are only 51 cards, rather than 52, from which the second can be chosen. If we let A represent the event in which the first card is an ace and B represent the event in which the second is a king, we say that A and B are *dependent events.* We want to find the probability that the first card is one of the four aces in the entire deck of 52 cards and that the second card is one of the four kings in the remaining 51 cards. Thus,

$$P(A \cap B) = \frac{4}{52} \cdot \frac{4}{51} = \frac{4}{663}$$

The factor $\frac{4}{51}$ represents the *conditional probability* that B will occur, *given that A has occurred,* denoted $P(B|A)$. To find the probability of the intersection of two dependent events, therefore, we use the following rule.

> **If event A *is a condition for event* B,**
> $P(A \cap B) = P(A) \cdot P(B|A)$.

Note that when A and B are independent events, $P(B|A)$ is simply $P(B)$, so this rule becomes equivalent to the previously discussed multiplication rule. Notice also that when A and B are mutually exclusive events (a special case of dependent events), $P(B|A) = 0$, so $P(A \cap B) = 0$.

If we rewrite the formula $P(A \cap B) = P(A) \cdot P(B|A)$ in the form $P(B|A) = \frac{P(A \cap B)}{P(A)}$, we can use it to find conditional probabilities.

Example

Imagine two men, each of whom tells the truth only two thirds of the time. If both men say that it is raining, what is the probability that it really is raining?

It might appear that the probability is merely the product of the probability that one man is telling the truth and the probability that the other is telling the truth, $\frac{2}{3} \cdot \frac{2}{3}$, or $\frac{4}{9}$.

The problem, however, indicates that the men *agree* that it is raining, so what we really need to find is the probability that one is telling the truth (that is, the probability that it is raining), *given that* they agree.

If we let A represent the event in which the men agree and B represent the event in which one of them tells the truth, therefore, we are looking for P(B|A). Now, P(A) is the probability that both men are telling the truth or both are lying, so $P(A) = \frac{2}{3} \cdot \frac{2}{3} + \frac{1}{3} \cdot \frac{1}{3} = \frac{5}{9}$. $P(A \cap B)$ is $\frac{4}{9}$, the probability that both men are telling the truth. Thus,

$$P(B|A) = \frac{P(A \cap B)}{P(A)} = \frac{\dfrac{4}{9}}{\dfrac{5}{9}} = \frac{4}{5}$$

Alternative solution: We can use a chart to model the problem. On the average, each man tells the truth two times out of three. Since we know that the men agree, we do not need to consider the four cases that are crossed out. Of the remaining five cases, four involve the men telling the truth. The probability is therefore $\frac{4}{5}$.

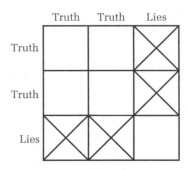

Part Two: Sample Problem

Problem

Tom, Dick, and Harry independently answer a question on a test. The probability that Tom answers correctly is .8, the probability that Dick answers correctly is .6, and the probability that Harry answers correctly is .3. What is the probability that

a All three answer the question correctly?
b At least two of them answer the question correctly?
c At least one answers the question correctly?

Solution

We will let T = {cases in which Tom answers correctly}, D = {cases in which Dick answers correctly}, and H = {cases in which Harry answers correctly}. These three events are independent, and we know that P(T) = .8, P(D) = .6, and P(H) = .3. Also, the probability that Tom answers incorrectly [denoted P(T′)] is 1 − .8, or .2. Similarly, P(D′) = .4 and P(H′) = .7.

a Here we want the probability of the conjunction of T and D and H—that is, P(T ∩ D ∩ H).

$$P(T \cap D \cap H)$$
$$= P(T) \cdot P(D) \cdot P(H)$$
$$= .8(.6)(.3)$$
$$= .144$$

b This part is tricky. There are several ways in which at least two can answer the question correctly—the correct answerers could be Tom and Dick, Tom and Harry, Dick and Harry, or all three. We can represent these possibilities as the following four mutually exclusive events.

1 Tom and Dick answer correctly, but not Harry—$T \cap D \cap H'$.
2 Tom and Harry answer correctly, but not Dick—$T \cap H \cap D'$.
3 Dick and Harry answer correctly, but not Tom—$D \cap H \cap T'$.
4 All three answer correctly—$T \cap D \cap H$.

Therefore,

P(at least two answer correctly)

$= P[(T \cap D \cap H') \cup (T \cap H \cap D') \cup (D \cap H \cap T') \cup (T \cap D \cap H)]$
$= P(T \cap D \cap H') + P(T \cap H \cap D') + P(D \cap H \cap T') + P(T \cap D \cap H)$
$= P(T) \cdot P(D) \cdot P(H') + P(T) \cdot P(H) \cdot P(D')$
$\quad + P(D) \cdot P(H) \cdot P(T') + P(T) \cdot P(D) \cdot P(H)$
$= .8(.6)(.7) + .8(.3)(.4) + .6(.3)(.2) + .8(.6)(.3)$
$= .336 + .096 + .036 + .144$
$= .612$

c P(at least one is correct) $= 1 - $ P(all are wrong)
$= 1 - P(T' \cap D' \cap H')$
$= 1 - .2(.4)(.7)$
$= 1 - .056$
$= .944$

Part Three: Exercises and Problems

Warm-up Exercises

In problems 1–4, indicate whether events A and B are independent.

1 One die is rolled; $A = \{5\}$ and $B = \{4\}$.
2 Two dice are rolled; for the first die, $A = \{5\}$, and for the second die, $B = \{4\}$.
3 Two cards are drawn from a standard deck; for the first card, $A = \{kings\}$, and for the second card, $B = \{kings\}$.
4 One card is drawn from a standard deck; $A = \{kings\}$ and $B = \{spades\}$.

5 If the probability that it will rain today is .6 and the probability that it will rain tomorrow if it rains today is .35, what is the probability that it will rain both today and tomorrow?

6 Two cards are chosen at random from a standard deck. Find the probability that the first card is a king and the second is a spade.

7 On a multiple-choice test, each item includes four choices, of which one is correct. If the test consists of six items, what is the probability that you can answer all of them correctly by guessing?

Problem Set

8 A die is rolled and a coin is tossed. Indicate whether each outcome is best described as consisting of independent events, dependent events, or mutually exclusive events.
  a The die shows 5 and the coin shows heads.
  b The die shows 5 and the die shows an even number.
  c The coin shows heads, given that the coin shows heads and the die shows 3.
  d The die shows 2 and the die shows 3.

9 Three cards are chosen from a standard deck. Find the probability that the first is a king, the second is a queen, and the third is a jack.

10 All eight children in the P. R. Olific family are female. If Mr. and Mrs. Olific have a ninth child, what is the probability that it will be female?

11 Each of three musicians plays a note independently. The probability that the first plays a C is $\frac{2}{3}$; the probability that the second plays a C is $\frac{1}{4}$; the probability that the third plays a C is $\frac{3}{8}$. What is the probability that
  a All three play a C?
  b None of the three plays a C?
  c At least one of the three plays a C?
  d At least two of the three play a C?

12 A gum-ball machine contains 45 gum balls and 5 prizes. If you put in 6 cents and receive 6 items, what is the probability that you will get
  a All gum balls?   **b** 4 gum balls and 2 prizes?

13 Two points inside the figure shown are chosen at random. Find the probability that the first is in square A and the second is in rectangle B.

14 A die is rolled. Consider the events A = {odd numbers}, B = {even numbers}, and C = {2}.

    a Find P(A ∩ B).   **b** Find P(A ∩ C).   **c** Find P(B ∩ C).

15 If $P(A) = \frac{1}{2}$ and $P(A|B) = \frac{2}{3}$, what is $P(A \cap B)$?

16 Suppose that a card is drawn from a standard deck. Indicate whether each of the following outcomes consists of independent events or dependent events. Explain your answers.

    a The card is a heart and the card is a 4.
    b The card is a heart and the card is a spade.
    c The card is a queen and the card is a king.

17 Suppose that two cards are drawn from a standard deck. Indicate whether each of the following outcomes consists of independent events or dependent events. Explain your answers.

    a The first card is a jack and the second card is an ace.
    b The first card is a club and the second card is black.

18 The Buffalo Chips Snack Food Co. produces bags containing a mixture of 35 potato chips, 24 taco chips, and 11 banana chips. Dale reaches into the bag and grabs 15 chips. Find the probability that he gets 5 of each kind.

19 Evaluate each expression.

    a $\displaystyle\sum_{k=1}^{n} \left(\sqrt{-1}\right)^k$, where n is odd

    b $\displaystyle\sum_{k=1}^{n} \left(\sqrt{-1}\right)^k$, where n is even

20 **a** Evaluate $\frac{1}{1 \cdot 2}$.

    b Evaluate $\frac{1}{1 \cdot 2} + \frac{1}{2 \cdot 3}$.

    c Evaluate $\frac{1}{1 \cdot 2} + \frac{1}{2 \cdot 3} + \frac{1}{3 \cdot 4}$.

    d Evaluate $\frac{1}{1 \cdot 2} + \frac{1}{2 \cdot 3} + \frac{1}{3 \cdot 4} + \frac{1}{4 \cdot 5}$.

    e Evaluate $\frac{1}{1 \cdot 2} + \frac{1}{2 \cdot 3} + \frac{1}{3 \cdot 4} + \frac{1}{4 \cdot 5} + \frac{1}{5 \cdot 6}$.

    f Use the pattern you developed in parts **a–e** to predict the value of $\frac{1}{1 \cdot 2} + \frac{1}{2 \cdot 3} + \frac{1}{3 \cdot 4} + \ldots + \frac{1}{98 \cdot 99} + \frac{1}{99 \cdot 100}$.

21 A bag contains 15 marbles, of which 6 are red and 9 are green. Suppose that 5 marbles are drawn at random from the bag.

    a What is the probability that all 5 are the same color?
    b What is the probability that all 5 are green?
    c If all 5 are the same color, what is the probability that they are green?

Problem Set, *continued*

22 If $P(A) = \frac{2}{3}$ and $P(B) = \frac{1}{2}$, is $P(A \cap B) = \frac{2}{3} \cdot \frac{1}{2} = \frac{1}{3}$?

23 When the Wassamatta U. Mooses score a touchdown, they kick for an extra point 80% of the time. On the average, 75% of their kick attempts are successful. About what percentage of the Mooses' touchdowns are followed by a successfully kicked extra point?

24 For each of the following equilateral triangles, find the values of x and y and the measure of $\angle \theta$.

a

b
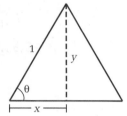

25 The probability that Mary Curd will score on a free-throw attempt is .85. If she is fouled and is awarded two free throws, what is the probability that she makes at least one free throw?

26 If $P(A) = .8$, $P(A|B) = .64$, and $P(B|A) = .4$, what is $P(B)$?

27 A piggy bank contains six pennies, five nickels, four dimes, three quarters, and two worthless slugs. If the bank is shaken until three of the items drop out, what is the probability that their total value is $0.25?

28 On the dart board shown, the smallest of the concentric circles has a radius of 2 inches. Each of the other circles has a radius 2 inches greater than that of the next smaller circle. What is the probability that two darts hitting the board at random will score exactly 25 points?

29 A bag contains red, green, and blue marbles. Is it possible that the probability of choosing a red marble is $\frac{1}{3}$, the probability of choosing a green marble is $\frac{1}{2}$, and the probability of choosing a blue marble is $\frac{1}{4}$? Why or why not?

30 Ten decks of cards (520 cards in all) are shuffled together, and 5 cards are dealt. Find the probability that at least 2 of the cards are of the same suit.

31 A dart board for the game of skill darts is shown. If a player's first dart lands inside the larger square, the player throws another. If the second dart lands inside the circle, the player throws a third time. If the third dart lands inside the smaller square, the player wins. If all of a player's throws land somewhere inside the larger square, what is the probability that the player wins?

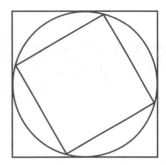

HISTORICAL SNAPSHOT

A LUCKY COLLABORATION
Fermat and Pascal: A co-theory of probabilities

What are the odds that two people, neither of whose interests were exclusively mathematical, would develop through correspondence the fundamentals of future probability theory? It happened in France in the 1600's.

Pierre de Fermat (1602?–1665) was a magistrate by profession and a mathematician at his leisure. Blaise Pascal (1623–1662) is well known not only as a mathematician but also as a religious philosopher and especially as a scientist. The two wrote letters back and forth in which they developed the fundamental principles of probabilities. Their correspondence provided each with a sounding board. Their exchange of ideas helped them revise hypotheses, spot logical errors, and correct them. Although their solutions to the same problems varied in details, both are credited as the originators of a single theory.

Fermat and Pascal began their work together at the request of a gambler. Interest in probability later grew as the insurance industry developed. Probability theory now has many applications, particularly in business and science. In short, a theory with seedy beginnings has become a respected area of mathematics.

Pascal himself did not develop the triangle shown below, but because of the applications he developed for it, the triangle now bears his name.

Use Pascal's triangle to find the possible outcomes of tossing a coin. Continue the triangle to show ten tosses. Do you see a pattern?

12.5 | INTERPRETING PROBABILITIES

Objectives

After studying this chapter, you will be able to

- Understand the significance of probabilities
- Understand how Monte Carlo methods are used to estimate probabilities
- Judge sampling techniques

Part One: Introduction

What Does a Probability Mean?

Imagine that there is an outbreak of influenza among the students in your school and your doctor has told you that if you continue to attend classes, there is a probability of $\frac{1}{10}$ that you will catch the flu.

What does this probability mean? Does it mean that out of any group of ten students, one will certainly get sick? Does it mean that if you go to school nine days without catching the flu, you are sure to catch it on the next day? Does it mean that if two of the twenty students in your homeroom are sick, you have nothing to worry about?

Actually, it means none of these things. What your doctor is telling you is that she estimates, on the basis of her previous experience with the disease, that about one tenth of the students attending your school will catch the flu. She has no way of knowing whether you will be one of them.

It is important to realize that a probability indicates what fraction of a great number of cases are likely to involve a certain outcome; it does not predict what the outcome will be in any individual case or group of cases.

Example   *A coin is tossed 13 times and turns up heads each time. What is the probability that the next toss will result in heads?*

The probability is $\frac{1}{2}$. The outcomes of the first 13 tosses do not change the probability of heads on the fourteenth toss, since each toss is independent of the preceding tosses.

Example   *A coin is tossed 14 times. What is the most likely distribution of heads and tails?*

The most likely distribution is 7 heads and 7 tails. Although this outcome has a probability of only $\approx .209$, it is still more likely than any of the other possible outcomes. Since for any given toss $P(\text{heads}) = \frac{1}{2}$ and $P(\text{tails}) = \frac{1}{2}$, the most likely outcome will be half heads and half tails whenever a coin is tossed an even number of times.

Monte Carlo Methods

In the early days of gambling casinos, sophisticated techniques for calculating probabilities had not yet been developed. How did the casino owners determine the odds of winning a game?

What they did was to play the game thousands of times and record the results. Then they used the data they had collected to estimate the probability. Such methods of estimating probabilities are called Monte Carlo techniques.

Example   *Suppose that we didn't know the probabilities of the possible outcomes of rolling two dice. How could we approximate them?*

We could have a computer simulate the rolling of two dice several thousand times. Suppose the computer produced the following data.

Roll	2	3	4	5	6	7	8	9	10	11	12
Frequency	453	912	1332	1815	2262	2710	2259	1822	1330	899	444

We might notice that rolls of 2 and 12 occurred about the same number of times, as did rolls of 3 and 11, 4 and 10, 5 and 9, and 6 and 8. Moreover, the number of 2's divided by the total number of trials is approximately $\frac{1}{36}$, the number of 3's divided by the total number of trials is about $\frac{2}{36}$, and so on. By repeated experimentation, we could closely approximate the probability of each outcome.

Many real-life probability problems are so complex that they cannot be solved by means of formulas and theorems. In such cases, mathematicians use Monte Carlo techniques to obtain accurate estimates of the probabilities. Of course, the mathematicians usually use computers to model the experiments instead of carrying out actual trials.

Sampling

You have probably seen polls that predict the results of political elections. How are these predictions made? The pollsters clearly cannot ask every voter in the country whom he or she will vote for. Instead, they select a group of people they hope will be representative of the entire population. Such a group is called a **sample.**

Example   *Wanting to know how people in the United States feel about mass transit, we decide to stop people at a commuter train station and ask their opinion. Will our sample be a good one?*

Probably not. We would be questioning only people who actually use a mass-transit facility. The sample would not include people who prefer to ride a bike, drive a car, or walk.

Example   *In 1936, the Literary Digest sent out questionnaires asking people whether they were going to vote for Franklin D. Roosevelt or Alf Landon. The magazine reported that Landon would win by a three-to-two margin. Instead, Roosevelt won by a landslide. What might have been wrong with the magazine's polling technique?*

In fact, only 23% of those to whom the questionnaires were sent mailed them back to the magazine, and most of these were wealthy people more likely to vote for the Republican Landon. To be sure of accurate results, the magazine should have tried to poll a sample that was more representative of the whole electorate.

Example   *The results of political elections are frequently projected by means of exit polls—that is, by asking voters leaving polling places in selected precincts whom they voted for. Usually, such projections are fairly accurate. Why?*

There are two main reasons. First, the samples consist only of people who actually voted. Second, the pollsters select precincts in which, according to the results of previous elections, the voters are reflective of the electorate as a whole.

Part Two: Sample Problem

Problem   *A cereal manufacturer puts a prize in each box of cereal. There are ten different prizes, and the prizes are randomly distributed. How might we determine the average number of boxes of cereal a person would have to buy to get all ten prizes?*

Solution   One way would be to write the numbers 1–10 on slips of paper to represent the ten prizes. We could pick slips at random, recording the number on each and then replacing it with the others before drawing again, until we had recorded each number at least once. By repeating this experiment many times and calculating the mean number of draws necessary to obtain all ten numbers, we would obtain an approximate value for the number of cereal boxes one would need to buy.

Part Three: Exercises and Problems

Warm-up Exercises

1 Suppose that you wished to conduct a poll to determine the average number of hours students study each night. How would you conduct the poll to be sure that your sample was not biased?

2 A die is to be rolled repeatedly and a running total of the outcomes kept until the total exceeds 30. Design a Monte Carlo experiment to determine the probability that the total will be 32.

3 If the makers of Sneezarrest capsules claimed that in a poll of doctors, 90% of the physicians surveyed preferred their product, why might you be skeptical of their claim?

Problem Set

4 A high-school counselor sent a letter to each member of the preceding year's graduating class, asking how well he or she was doing in college. Of the 52% of the graduates that responded, 93% said that they were "having a great year" or "doing well." What conclusions can be drawn from this survey?

5 Sandy enters 6 $\boxed{\times}$ into her calculator. She then enters a random digit and hits $\boxed{=}$. What is the probability that the units digit of the displayed value is

a 6? **b** 8? **c** 3?

6 Flip four coins, recording the outcome, then repeat the experiment.
   a Were the results of your two trials the same?
   b What is the most probable outcome of the flipping of four coins?
   c Would you expect the most probable outcome to occur each time you flipped four coins? Why or why not?

7 A school's librarian was concerned because not many students were using the library. To find out why, she carefully composed a questionnaire about library use and during one week asked every student entering the library to fill out the questionnaire. Discuss the validity of her approach.

8 Evaluate $\sum_{k=1}^{7} (3k - 2)$.

9 If you were in charge of marketing a new hair-coloring product and needed to know how many people currently use such a product, how would you go about obtaining this information?

10 A box contains four bananas, three apples, five pears, and a pomegranate. If one fruit is chosen at random from the box, what is the probability that it is an apple?

11 If you were a pollster who wanted to determine people's feelings about the writings of Charles Dickens, how would you go about conducting a survey?

12 Let $a(n) = n^2 - 1$.

    a Find $a(1)$.   **b** Find $a(2)$.   **c** Find $a(4)$.

    d Find $a(5)$.   **e** Find $a(k)$.   **f** Find $a(k + 1)$.

13 Every box of Defeaties, the Breakfast of Also-rans, contains a prize. There are three types of prizes, and these are randomly distributed. If Mr. I.M.A. Loser buys three boxes of Defeaties, what is the probability that he gets one prize of each type?

14 A bag contains 5 red marbles and 15 green marbles. Four of the marbles are chosen at random, and the number that are green is recorded. This process is repeated several thousand times. How many green marbles would you expect to be chosen, on the average, in each trial?

15 A bag contains five red marbles and eight green marbles. If four of the marbles are chosen at random, what is the probability that

    a All are red?   **b** All are green?

    c Two are red and two are green?

16 Each of the squares shown has sides 4 units long. If a point inside the figure is chosen at random, what is the probability that it lies in a shaded region?

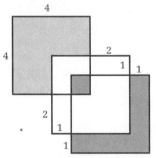

17 The scores for a certain college aptitude test are assigned a margin of error of ±50. Judy took the test and received a score of 1670. She decided to study for the test and retake it. On her second try, she scored 1710. Explain whether the time and money invested in the retake were worthwhile.

18 What does a weather forecaster mean by saying that there is a 30% chance of rain?

19 Every package of cigarettes sold in the United States must bear a warning, such as "Cigarette Smoking May Be Hazardous to Your Health." The law requiring such warnings is a result of a report in which the Surgeon General concluded that there is a 99.9% certainty that a link exists between smoking and the incidence of cancer. Which of the following best describes the meaning of the Surgeon General's conclusion?

a Out of each 1000 smokers, 999 have contracted cancer.
b Out of 1000 randomly selected smokers, 999 will get cancer.
c On the average, 999 out of every thousand smokers will get cancer.
d The probability is .999 that people who smoke are more likely to get cancer than people who do not.
e The probability is .999 that smoking causes cancer.

20 In the addition table shown, a, b, c, d, e, and f represent real numbers. Each of the other numbers is the sum of the numbers heading its row and column (for example, $7 = a + e$). Find $x + y$.

+	a	b	c
d	1	−5	y
e	7	x	10
f	0	−6	3

21 In Monte Cristo County, 15% of the voters are Republicans; the rest are Democrats. Of the Republicans, 80% earn over $100,000 a year. Only 5% of the Democrats earn over $100,000 a year. If one person who earns over $100,000 a year is chosen at random from the county's voters, what is the probability that the person is a Republican?

22 A $3 \times 3 \times 3$ cube is painted on all six faces, then cut into 27 identical $1 \times 1 \times 1$ cubes. If three of the small cubes are selected at random, what is the probability that one of them has three painted faces and the other two have exactly two painted faces?

23 Investigate the sampling method used to determine at least one of the following. Discuss the significance of the results obtained.

a The Nielsen ratings of television programs
b *Rolling Stone*'s list of the top 100 songs
c The results of a Gallup poll
d The winners of the Academy Award
e The members of the Baseball Hall of Fame
f The *New York Times*'s list of best-selling books

CHAPTER SUMMARY

CONCEPTS AND PROCEDURES

After studying this chapter, you should be able to
- Apply the Fundamental Counting Principle (12.1)
- Relate the numbers of elements in two sets to the numbers of elements in their union and intersection (12.1)
- Use the combination and permutation functions to solve counting problems (12.1)
- Determine the sample space for an experiment (12.2)
- Identify events and calculate their probabilities (12.2)
- Understand the relationship between disjunctions and unions of sets (12.3)
- Calculate probabilities of mutually exclusive events (12.3)
- Determine probabilities of intersections of independent events (12.4)
- Solve problems involving conditional probabilities (12.4)
- Understand the significance of probabilities (12.5)
- Understand how Monte Carlo methods are used to estimate probabilities (12.5)
- Judge sampling techniques (12.5)

VOCABULARY

combinatorics (12.1)
conditional probability (12.4)
conjunction (12.4)
dependent events (12.4)
disjunction (12.3)
equal elemental probabilities (12.2)
event (12.2)
Fundamental Counting Principle (12.1)
independent events (12.4)
mutually exclusive (12.3)
sample (12.5)
sample space (12.2)
Venn diagram (12.1)

REVIEW PROBLEMS

1 Evaluate each expression.

   a 5!   **b** 4!   **c** 3!   **d** 2!   **e** 1!   **f** 0!

2 Copy the chart shown, which represents the 36 possible outcomes when two dice are rolled.

   a Put an *X* in each box that represents a roll with a sum of 5.

   b Put an *O* in each box that represents a roll in which at least one die shows an even number.

   c How many boxes contain both an *X* and an *O*?

3 A single die is rolled.

   a What is the sample space?

   b Find the probability that the roll is a multiple of 2.

   c Find the probability that the roll is a multiple of 3.

   d Find the probability that the roll is a multiple of either 2 or 3.

   e Find the probability that the roll is a multiple of 6 (that is, of both 2 and 3).

   f What is the sum of your answers to parts **b** and **c**?

   g What is the sum of your answers to parts **d** and **e**?

4 Copy the Venn diagram shown, shading the region that represents the specified set.

   a $(A \cap B) \cup (B \cap C)$

   b $(A \cup B) \cap (B \cup C)$

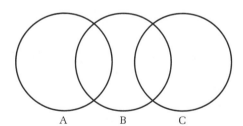

5 How many different radio-station call signs are possible in which the first letter is a *K* or a *W* and exactly four different letters are used?

6 A red die and a green die are rolled. What is the probability that

  a The red one shows 5 and the green one shows 2?
  b The red one shows an even number and the green one shows 3 or 4?
  c The red one shows a number less than 3 and the green one shows an odd number?
  d The red one shows 5 and the total roll is 4?
  e The red one shows 3 and the total roll is 10?
  f The red one shows 4 and the total roll is 6?

7 If you randomly choose a number from {2, 3, 4, 5, 6, 7, 8, 9, 10, 11, 12, 13, 14, 15, 16}, two of the possible events are A = {multiples of 5} and B = {multiples of 2}.

  a Find P(A).　　　　　**b** Find P(B).　　　　　**c** Find P(A ∪ B).
  d Find P(A ∩ B).　　　**e** Is P(A) + P(B) = P(A ∪ B) + P(A ∩ B)?

8 The drawing for the Lot o' Money Lottery consists of five numbers chosen from {1, 2, 3, . . . , 50}. How many different five-number choices are possible?

9 Point P is somewhere in the interior of rectangle ABCD. If another point in the interior of ABCD is selected at random, what is the probability that it is inside either △APD or △BCP?

10 If two of the numbers in {1, 3, 5, 7, 9, 11, 13, 15} are chosen at random, what is the probability that their sum is even?

11 If a card is chosen at random from a standard deck, what is the probability that it is either a heart or the jack of diamonds?

12 If P(A) = .5 and P(A ∩ B) = .4, what is P(B|A)?

13 The service manager of an automobile dealership reported to the dealership's owner that 95% of those who bought new cars at the dealership during 1989 were "extremely satisfied" with the service department. Why might the owner have cause for concern?

14 A die is rolled and a coin is tossed. Find the probability that the die shows an odd number and the coin shows heads.

15 Consider the sets A = {3, 5, 7, 9, 11} and B = {3, 6, 9, 12}.

  a Find A ∪ B.　　　　　**b** Find A ∩ B.　　　　　**c** Find #(A ∪ B).
  d Find #(A ∩ B).　　　**e** Find #(A) + #(B).

16 A lottery pays $500 to the holders of the first number drawn, $300 to the holders of the second number, $200 to the holders of the third number, and $100 to the holders of the fourth number. If the numbers are chosen from the set {1, 2, 3, . . . , 50}, how many possible outcomes are there?

17 How many lines can be drawn through the point (1, 5) in such a way that one intercept is three greater than the other?

18 If n is a randomly chosen natural number and $i = \sqrt{-1}$, what is the probability that the following sum is a real number?

$$\sum_{k=1}^{n} i^k$$

19 Suppose that Joe and Mary play a game in which Joe can win $1, $2, $3, or $4 and Mary can win $1, $2, or $3.

a List all of the possible outcomes.
b List all the sums of money that can be won.

20 In the diagram, D, E, and F are the midpoints of $\overline{AC}$, $\overline{CB}$, and $\overline{BA}$.

a If a point in the interior of right triangle ABC is selected at random, what is the probability that it is in the interior of $\triangle DEF$?
b If a point in the interior of $\triangle DEF$ is selected at random, what is the probability that it is in the interior of $\triangle ABC$?

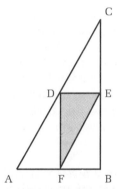

21 On the average, 1.5% of the widgets manufactured at a certain plant are defective. If an inspector selects two of the widgets at random for examination, what is the probability that neither is defective?

22 A baseball team has five starting pitchers and four relief pitchers. In how many ways can one starter and two relievers be selected to pitch in a game?

23 A bag contains eight red marbles and three blue marbles. If two marbles are drawn at random from the bag, what is the probability that both are blue?

24 Find the probability that exactly six cards in a ten-card gin-rummy hand will be hearts.

25 How many subsets does {1, 2, 3, 4, 5, 6, 7} have?

26 If a point in the interior of rectangle ABCD is selected at random, what is the probability that it is in Quadrant I or Quadrant III?

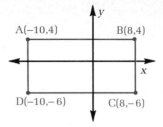

STATISTICS AND THE PUBLIC MIND
Dave Petts crunches numbers to find out how we feel

Television and electronic communications have generated an overabundance of numbers and statistics calling attention to what Americans think about many different subjects. Political polling is the science of representing as accurately as possible the central tendencies in the public's opinions about politics. Hence, solid statistical methods are essential to Dave Petts, a political pollster with a Washington, D.C., polling firm.

"A lot of statistics is involved because statistics and probability theory undergird political polling," says Mr. Petts. His work primarily involves recording and analyzing voters' attitudes toward the candidates represented by his firm. He employs factor analysis and regression analysis "to try to understand what's driving the voter."

The greatest challenge Mr. Petts faces is "to make decisions very quickly, based on less than perfect information. Are the voters hearing the candidate's message? What is causing misperceptions? Or, if she's doing well in polls, what do we need to do to keep it that way?"

Do you think labor unions today have too much power?

Too much power	40%
Not enough power	22%
Right amount	33%

Do you think American workers still need labor unions?

Still need them	73%
No longer necessary	22%

Should private-sector workers have the right to strike without losing their jobs or is this the chance they take?

Have the right to strike	47%
It's the chance they take	50%

After the strike, should Greyhound be required to rehire the striking workers?

Yes	57%
No	31%

From a telephone poll of 500 adult Americans taken for TIME/CNN on March 14 by Yankelovich Clancy Shulman. Sampling error plus or minus 4.5%.

TIME Chart by Steve Hart

12

CHAPTER TEST

1 At Slick Sal's car dealership, customers are given a choice of four different colors, three different models, six different body styles, and two different radios. How many different kinds of cars can be ordered?

2 There are 385 students in the junior class at Hyde Park High, of which 80% take both math and English. Fifteen juniors take math but not English, and 55 take English but not math.
a How many juniors take neither math nor English?
b How many juniors take math?
c How many juniors take English?

3 S. Peller is playing Skrabull and has the letters *F*, *E*, *I*, *R*, *S*, and *T* in her rack. In how many ways can she select three letters to play?

4 A die is rolled and a coin is tossed. Find the probability that the number on the die is odd and the coin shows heads.

5 Scarlett threw 5 balloons into the air. Rhett threw 9 balloons into the air. Two of the balloons flew off, but the other 12 fell to the ground. Find the probability that both of the balloons that were gone with the wind were thrown either by Rhett or by Scarlett.

6 After scoring a touchdown, the Decatur Sallies attempt to kick for an extra point 85% of the time. The other 15% of the time, they attempt a running or passing play for two extra points. They are successful in 90% of their tries for one extra point and 40% of their tries for two extra points. If the Sallies score a touchdown, what is the probability that they add at least one extra point?

7 Suppose two dice are rolled at the same time two coins are tossed. What is the probability that both coins show heads and the dice show a total of 10?

8 A newspaper columnist wanted to find out how most people felt about gun control. So she invited her readers to write a letter, telling her whether they were for it or against it and explaining why. Why should we be skeptical of the results of her poll?

9 How many positive integers are divisors of 7007?
(Hint: $7007 = 7^2 \cdot 11 \cdot 13$)

SEQUENCES AND SERIES

The sizes of the pipes in an organ form a geometric series such that the larger the pipe, the lower the tone it produces.

13.1 SEQUENCES

Objectives

After studying this section, you will be able to
- Apply the definition of a sequence
- Describe a sequence
- Form sequences of partial sums

Part One: Introduction

The Definition of a Sequence

Consider the following infinite list of numbers.

$$2, 5, 8, 11, 14, \ldots, 3n - 1, \ldots$$

The ellipsis (. . .) indicates that the list continues using the $3n - 1$ pattern. This list actually consists of the values of the function a,

$$a(n) = 3n - 1, \text{ where } n \text{ is chosen from the set of}$$
$$\text{natural numbers, } \{1, 2, 3, \ldots\}$$

In this chapter, the letter n will always represent a positive integer.

We often use a_n instead of $a(n)$ when discussing a function whose domain is the natural numbers.

For the function

$$a(n) = 3n - 1$$
$$a_1 = a(1) = 3(1) - 1 = 2$$
$$a_2 = a(2) = 3(2) - 1 = 5$$
$$a_3 = a(3) = 3(3) - 1 = 8$$
$$\vdots$$
$$a_n = a(n) = 3(n) - 1 = 3n - 1$$

The function a is an example of a **sequence**. A **sequence** is a function whose domain is the set of natural numbers. The values of this function are called **terms**. Sometimes a sequence is called a **progression**.

The notation $\{a_n\}$ is used to denote the sequence $a_1, a_2, a_3, \ldots, a_n, \ldots$, where the nth term of the sequence is a_n.

Example Write the first three terms and the nth term of the sequence $\{a_n\}$, where $a_n = n^2 - 1$.

$$a_1, a_2, a_3, \ldots, a_n, \ldots = 0, 3, 8, \ldots, n^2 - 1, \ldots$$

All sequences have an infinite number of terms. In some cases, however, we want to consider only a finite number of terms. We call such a function—whose domain is a finite subset of the natural numbers—an *array*.

Example Write the array consisting of the first six terms of the sequence $\{a_n\} = \{5n - 3\}$.

n	1	2	3	4	5	6
a_n	2	7	12	17	22	27

Arrays are commonly used in computer programming.

Ways to Describe a Sequence

What is the next term in the sequence 2, 3, 5, . . . ?

  "Seven," said Aiko. "It is the sequence of prime numbers."

  "Eight," said Bob. "Each term is the sum of the preceding two terms—$a_1 = 2$, $a_2 = 3$, $a_n = a_{n-1} + a_{n-2}$."

  "Nine," said Cathy. "The sequence is $\{a_n\} = \{2^{n-1} + 1\}$."

All three answers are reasonable, which means that the sequence 2, 3, 5, . . . was not well-defined.

  A sequence must be described so that it is possible to determine any term accurately. Aiko described a sequence in *words*. Bob described a different sequence *recursively*. Cathy gave a *closed-form* formula for the nth term. All three ways of describing a sequence are acceptable. Listing a few terms is *not* a good way to describe a sequence, because different interpretations are always possible.

Example Find the fourth term of each of the following sequences.

a 5, 25, 125, . . . , 5^n, . . .

The formula that describes the function for this sequence is $a_n = 5^n$. Since the fourth term occurs when $n = 4$, $a_4 = 5^4 = 625$.

b $\{a_n\} = \{n^2 - 2n\}$

The formula that describes the function for the sequence is $a_n = n^2 - 2n$. The fourth term occurs when $n = 4$, so $a_4 = 4^2 - 2 \cdot 4 = 8$.

c {nth prime number}

There is no known formula for obtaining the prime numbers, so this sequence is described verbally. The first eight prime numbers are 2, 3, 5, 7, 11, 13, 17, and 19. The fourth prime is 7.

Sequences of Partial Sums

Associated with every sequence $\{a_n\}$ is another sequence, $\{S_n\}$, called the *sequence of partial sums* of the original sequence. For example, looking at the figure on the next page, find the pattern that describes the sequence $\{a_n\}$ and the sequence of partial sums, $\{S_n\}$.

If $\{a_n\} = \{2n - 1\} = 1, 3, 5, \ldots, 2n - 1, \ldots$, then

$$S_1 = a_1 = 1$$
$$S_2 = a_1 + a_2 = 1 + 3 = 4$$
$$S_3 = a_1 + a_2 + a_3 = 1 + 3 + 5 = 9$$
$$S_4 = a_1 + a_2 + a_3 + a_4 = 1 + 3 + 5 + 7 = 16$$

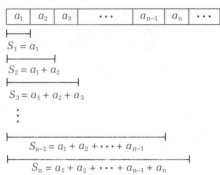

.
.
.

$$S_{n-1} = a_1 + a_2 + a_3 + \ldots + a_{n-1}$$
$$= 1 + 3 + 5 + \ldots + [2(n - 1) - 1]$$
$$= (n - 1)^2$$
$$S_n = a_1 + a_2 + a_3 + \ldots + a_{n-1} + a_n$$
$$= 1 + 3 + 5 + \ldots + (2n - 1)$$
$$= n^2$$

In the sequence of partial sums, $\{S_n\}$, the nth term is the sum of the first n terms of the original sequence, $\{a_n\}$.

If $\{a_n\}$ is any sequence, then the sequence $\{S_n\}$, defined by $S_n = a_1 + a_2 + a_3 + \ldots + a_n$, is called the sequence of partial sums of the sequence $\{a_n\}$. This is a closed-form definition.

If we look at the pattern for the terms S_{n-1} and S_n, we see

$$S_{n-1} = a_1 + a_2 + a_3 + \ldots + a_{n-1}$$
$$S_n \quad = a_1 + a_2 + a_3 + \ldots + a_{n-1} + a_n$$

Since $S_n = S_{n-1} + a_n$, we can define $\{S_n\}$ recursively. If $\{a_n\}$ is any sequence, then the sequence $\{S_n\}$, defined by $S_1 = a_1$ and $S_n = S_{n-1} + a_n$, is called the sequence of partial sums of the sequence $\{a_n\}$. This is a recursive definition.

Example

If $\{S_n\} = \{n^2\}$ is the sequence of partial sums of a sequence $\{a_n\}$, what is the formula describing a_n?

We know that $S_n = n^2$, $S_{n-1} = (n - 1)^2$, and $S_n = S_{n-1} + a_n$

If	$S_n = S_{n-1} + a_n,$
then	$n^2 = (n - 1)^2 + a_n$
That is,	$a_n = n^2 - (n - 1)^2$
	$a_n = n^2 - (n^2 - 2n + 1)$
	$a_n = n^2 - n^2 + 2n - 1$
	$a_n = 2n - 1$

Part Two: Sample Problem

Problem   A cell divides into two cells, each of which divides, to produce a total of four cells. This process continues as shown in the diagram. Each level of the diagram is called a generation. How many cells are there in the 100th generation?

First Generation

Second Generation

Third Generation

Solution   Let $\{G_n\}$ be the sequence of the number of cells in each generation n.

$G_1 = 1 = 2^0$, $G_2 = 2 = 2^1$, $G_3 = 4 = 2^2$, $G_4 = 8 = 2^3$, ...

The number of cells in each generation is a power of 2. The nth generation has 2^{n-1} cells. Since $G_n = 2^{n-1}$,

$G_{100} = 2^{100-1} = 2^{99} \approx 6.34 \times 10^{29}$ cells

How could you describe this sequence recursively?

Part Three: Exercises and Problems

Warm-up Exercises

In problems 1–3, list the first six terms of each sequence.

1 $\{2n - 7\}$ **2** $\{n^2 - 1\}$ **3** {the nth prime number}

4 If $\{a_n\} = \{2^n\}$ and $\{S_n\}$ is the sequence of partial sums for $\{a_n\}$, what are the first five terms of $\{S_n\}$?

5 $\{a_n\}$ is a sequence and $\{S_n\}$ is its sequence of partial sums. If $S_{10} = 35$ and $S_{11} = 31$, what is a_{11}?

In problems 6–9, give the fourth through the eighth terms of the sequence.

6 $32, 8, 2, \ldots, 2^{7-2n}, \ldots$ **7** $a_1 = 3$, $a_n = 2a_{n-1}$

8 $a(1) = 1$, $a(n) = n + a(n - 1)$ **9** $\{a_n\} = \{n^2 - 2n\}$

Problem Set

10 The diagram illustrates the first four triangular numbers. Write the next four triangular numbers.

1   3   6   10

11 Find a formula that describes the terms a_n of the array.

n	1	2	3	4
a_n	4	8	12	16

In problems 12 and 13, list the fourth through eighth terms of the sequences.

12 $\{n^2\}$

13 $a_1 = 5$, $a_n = 2a_{n-1}$

14 Use a calculator to find a_1, a_{10}, and a_{100} to the nearest ten-thousandth if $a_n = \frac{3n + 1}{2n + 1}$.

In problems 15–17, compute the sum.

15 $\displaystyle\sum_{n=1}^{5} n^2$

16 $\displaystyle\sum_{n=1}^{5} n$

17 $\displaystyle\sum_{n=1}^{5} (n^2 + n + 3)$

18 The approximate monthly cost in dollars of producing the nth bicycle is given by the formula $c = 25 - 0.01n^2$.

   a Find the cost of producing the first bike, the second bike, and the third bike.

   b Find the total cost of producing the first three bikes.

In problems 19 and 20, write the first five terms of each sequence.

19 $\left\{\dfrac{n}{n + 1}\right\}$

20 $\left\{\dfrac{n^2}{n + 1}\right\}$

21 Life is found on the planet Trips. On Trips, each generation of cells divides into three cells instead of two.

   a How many cells will be in the fifth generation?

   b In what generation will the number of cells first exceed 3000?

22 Let $a_n = n$ and $b_n = \dfrac{n(n + 1)}{2}$.

   a Find the first four terms of $\{a_n \cdot b_n\}$.

   b Find the first four terms of the sequence $\{S_n\}$ of partial sums for $\{a_n \cdot b_n\}$.

23 In the sample problem, after how many cell divisions will the total population first exceed 1 million?

24 Refer to the diagram.

   a Write the area of the rectangle as a function $A(t)$, where t is a natural number less than 10.

   b Write the sequence of area values $A(t)$.

10−t

10+t

Problem Set, *continued*

25 In the figure at the right, a_n is the distance from $(0, 1)$ to $(n, 0)$.

   a Calculate the first four terms of the sequence $\{a_n\}$.

   b Predict the next three terms without actually calculating them.

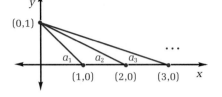

26 Solve $\displaystyle\sum_{n=1}^{5} (2nj + 3) = 105$ for j.

27 If $\{S_n\} = \{3n - 2\}$ is the sequence of partial sums for $\{a_n\}$, what is a formula that describes $\{a_n\}$?

28 Find a_1, a_2, a_3, and a_4 so the levers are in balance.

29 To find the next term of the sequence pictured, find the area of a square whose sides are half as long as the sides of the previous square.

   a Describe this sequence by the recursive method.

   b Describe this sequence by the closed-form method.

   c What is the 25th term?

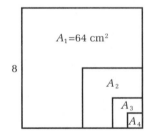

30 The sequence $\{a_n\} = \{1000(1 + 0.06)^n\}$ represents the amounts of money in a bank after n years if $1000 is deposited at 6% interest. Find a_1, a_2, a_3, a_4, and a_5.

31 An equilateral triangle has sides with length 1024. The midpoints of the sides are connected to form another equilateral triangle. This second triangle's midpoints are connected to form a third equilateral triangle, and so on. Write the array consisting of the areas of the first eight triangles.

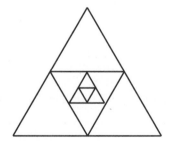

32 11, 101, 1001, 10,001, . . . has the pattern that each successive term places one more zero between the 1's.

  a Write a recursive formula for the sequence.

  b Write a closed-form formula for the nth sequence.

33 Write the first five terms of $\{a_n\}$, where $a_1 = 1$, $a_2 = 3$, and $a_n = \frac{a_{n-1}}{a_{n-2}}$.

In problems 34 and 35, find a formula to describe the terms of each array.

34

n	1	2	3	4	5
a_n	2	5	10	17	26

35

n	1	2	3	4	5	6
a_n	5	−10	15	−20	25	−30

36 Describe as many sequences as you can whose first three terms are 4, 6, and 8.

37 Consider the sequence $\{a_n\} = \left\{ 3\left(\frac{1}{10}\right)^n \right\}$.

  a Write the first six terms of this sequence.

  b Write the first six terms of $\{S_n\}$, the sequence of partial sums of $\{a_n\}$.

  c What value do the values of S_n approach as n gets larger?

38 For the sequence pattern 1, 8, 15, . . . , find as many functions as you can that match the first three terms listed. What is the fourth term for each of your functions? Give a valid description of your sequence.

39 In the game Tower of Hanoi, the object is to move the rings from Peg 1 to Peg 3. The rules allow you to move one ring at a time. You may use Peg 2, and you must never place a wider ring on top of a smaller ring. If a_n is the number of moves required to move a stack of n rings from Peg 1 to Peg 3, what are a_1, a_2, a_3, a_4, and a_5? Guess a formula for a_n.

SERIES

Objectives

After studying this section, you will be able to
- Compute finite series
- Use sigma notation to express a series
- Find the values of infinite series

Part One: Introduction

Finite Series

In common usage, the words *sequence* and *series* are almost interchangeable. In mathematics, however; the words mean different things. Consider these examples.

$$\begin{aligned}
\textbf{Sequence:} \quad & 2, 4, 6, \ldots, 2n, \ldots \\
\textbf{Related finite series:} \quad & 2 + 4 + 6 + 8 \\
\textbf{Related infinite series:} \quad & 2 + 4 + 6 + \ldots + 2n + \ldots
\end{aligned}$$

You may recognize that the finite series above is a partial sum of the sequence $\{a_n\} = \{2n\}$. Every *finite series* represents a partial sum S_n of a sequence $\{a_n\}$. We often use the term *series* when we really mean *finite series*.

Example   *If $\{a_n\} = \left\{\frac{n}{2}\right\}$, what is the sum of the finite series S_5 formed by adding the first five terms of the sequence $\{a_n\}$?*

$$S_5 = a_1 + a_2 + a_3 + a_4 + a_5$$

$$= \frac{1}{2} + 1 + \frac{3}{2} + 2 + \frac{5}{2} = 7.5$$

Sigma Notation and Series

The sigma notation introduced in Chapter 1 is particularly useful for describing series. The nth partial sum, S_n, of a sequence $\{a_n\}$ can be written as

$$S_n = \sum_{k=1}^{n} a_k = a_1 + a_2 + a_3 + \ldots + a_n$$

The Σ means to sum the terms, the $k = 1$ means that the first term to add is a_1, and the n means to continue summing terms up to and including a_n.

Example   Evaluate the finite series $\displaystyle\sum_{k=1}^{6}(2k + 1)$.

$$\sum_{k=1}^{6}(2k + 1) = 3 + 5 + 7 + 9 + 11 + 13$$
$$= 48$$

Infinite Series

What would happen if we were to add all the terms of an infinite sequence? While it may be physically impossible to add an infinite number of terms, we can often determine what the sum would be.

For a sequence $\{a_n\}$, the series $\displaystyle\sum_{n=1}^{\infty}a_n$ is called an ***infinite series.***

The symbol ∞, representing infinity, is used to indicate that all terms of the sequence are to be added together.

Example   Evaluate $\displaystyle\sum_{n=1}^{\infty}3 \cdot \left(\tfrac{1}{2}\right)^{n-1}$.

This is an infinite series equivalent to

$$3 + \frac{3}{2} + \frac{3}{4} + \frac{3}{8} + \ldots + \frac{3}{2^{n-1}} + \ldots$$

Let's calculate a few partial sums, S_n, and make a graph of the ordered pairs (n, S_n) for $n = 1, 2, \ldots, 9$.

n	S_n
1	3
2	4.5
3	5.25
4	≈ 5.63
5	≈ 5.81
6	≈ 5.91
7	≈ 5.95
8	≈ 5.98
9	≈ 5.99

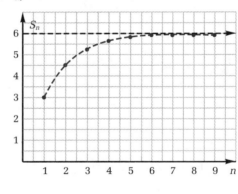

The ordered pairs described in the table above seem to approach a horizontal asymptote. The sum of the terms of $\{a_n\}$ gets closer and closer to 6.

If the graph of the sequence of partial sums, $\{S_n\}$, of a sequence $\{a_n\}$ approaches a horizontal asymptote $y = S$, we write $S = \displaystyle\sum_{n=1}^{\infty}a_n$ and call S the ***sum of the infinite series.*** In the preceding example, we would say that $6 = \displaystyle\sum_{n=1}^{\infty}3 \cdot \left(\tfrac{1}{2}\right)^{n-1}$. If the graph of a sequence of partial sums does not approach a horizontal asymptote, then we say that the infinite series does not have a sum.

Part Two: Sample Problems

Problem 1   If $\displaystyle\sum_{k=1}^{n} a_k = n(n + 1)$, what is the nth term of the original sequence $\{a_n\}$?

Solution   **Method 1**
Let's look for patterns.

Number of Terms (n)	Series $\displaystyle\sum_{k=1}^{n} a_k$	Sum of Series $n(n + 1)$	a_n
1	a_1	$1(1 + 1) = 2$	$a_1 = 2$
2	$a_1 + a_2$	$2(2 + 1) = 6$	$a_2 = 4$
3	$a_1 + a_2 + a_3$	$3(3 + 1) = 12$	$a_3 = 6$
4	$a_1 + a_2 + a_3 + a_4$	$4(4 + 1) = 20$	$a_4 = 8$

The pattern in the last column suggests that $a_n = 2n$.

Method 2
Let $S_n = \displaystyle\sum_{k=1}^{n} a_k$, so $S_n = n(n + 1)$ and $S_{n-1} = (n - 1)n$.

We know that $S_n = S_{n-1} + a_n$

Substituting $n(n + 1) = (n - 1)n + a_n$

or $n(n + 1) - (n - 1)n = a_n$

$$n^2 + n - n^2 + n = a_n$$
$$2n = a_n$$

Problem 2   Estimate the sum $\displaystyle\sum_{n=1}^{\infty}\left(\frac{1}{n} - \frac{1}{n + 1}\right)$.

Solution $S_1 = \left(1 - \dfrac{1}{2}\right) = \dfrac{1}{2}$

$S_2 = \left(1 - \dfrac{1}{2}\right) + \left(\dfrac{1}{2} - \dfrac{1}{3}\right) = 1 - \dfrac{1}{3} = \dfrac{2}{3}$

$S_3 = \left(1 - \dfrac{1}{2}\right) + \left(\dfrac{1}{2} - \dfrac{1}{3}\right) + \left(\dfrac{1}{3} - \dfrac{1}{4}\right) = 1 - \dfrac{1}{4} = \dfrac{3}{4}$

$S_4 = 1 - \dfrac{1}{5} = \dfrac{4}{5}$

$S_5 = 1 - \dfrac{1}{6} = \dfrac{5}{6}$

.
.
.

$S_n = 1 - \dfrac{1}{(n + 1)} = \dfrac{n}{n + 1}$

Now graph the ordered pairs (n, S_n). The points approach a horizontal asymptote of $S_n = 1$. The sum of the infinite series appears to be 1.

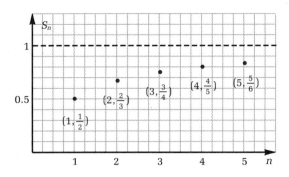

Part Three: Exercises and Problems

Warm-up Exercises

1 Let $\{a_n\} = \{n!\}$. Use sigma notation to express the fourth term of the sequence of partial sums for $\{a_n\}$. Evaluate your expression.

2 Given the sequence $\{a_n\}$, where a_n is the perimeter of a rectangle with sides n and $2n$.

a Find $a_1, a_2, a_3, a_4,$ and a_5.

b If $S_5 = \displaystyle\sum_{n=1}^{5} a_n$, what is S_5?

3 Let $\{a_n\} = \{3n - 1\}$. Write the first five terms of the sequence of partial sums of $\{a_n\}$.

In problems 4 and 5, evaluate each finite series.

4 $\displaystyle\sum_{n=1}^{4} 6n$

5 $\displaystyle\sum_{n=1}^{10} (2n - 1)$

6 If $\{S_n\}$ is the sequence of partial sums of $\{a_n\}$ and $S_n = n^2 + 2n$, what is $\{a_n\}$? Write its first five terms.

7 If $\displaystyle\sum_{k=1}^{n} a_k = n^2$, what is the nth term of the sequence $\{a_n\}$?

Problem Set

In problems 8–11, evaluate each finite series.

8 $\displaystyle\sum_{n=1}^{7} (2n + 3)$

9 $\displaystyle\sum_{n=1}^{8} 3n$

10 $\displaystyle\sum_{n=1}^{10} (-1)^n$

11 $\displaystyle\sum_{n=1}^{5} \log n$

Problem Set, *continued*

In problems 12 and 13, write the first five terms of the sequence.

12 $\{a_n\} = \{3n\}$

13 $\{a_n\} = \{(-1)^{n+1}\}$

14 Evaluate the following series.

a $\displaystyle\sum_{n=1}^{10} n^2$

b $\displaystyle\sum_{n=2}^{11} n^2$

c $\displaystyle\sum_{n=1}^{11} (n^2 + 2n + 1)$

d What method did you use to evaluate part **c**?
What is another method?

15 Evaluate $\displaystyle\sum_{j=1}^{4} a_j$ if $a_j = 3j + 1$.

16 Draw the fourth and fifth terms of the
sequence of points. Write a formula in
closed form for the sequence.

In problems 17–20, evaluate each finite series.

17 $\displaystyle\sum_{n=1}^{5} [(n + 2)(n + 1)]$

18 $\displaystyle\sum_{n=2}^{4} (4.1n + 2.5)$

19 $\displaystyle\sum_{n=1}^{5} 6\left(\frac{1}{10}\right)^{n-1}$

20 $\displaystyle\sum_{n=3}^{5} n^n$

21 Find x if $\displaystyle\sum_{j=1}^{3} (5 - 2jx) = 51$.

22 Let a_n = area of an equilateral triangle with side n.

a Write the first four terms of the sequence $\{a_n\}$.
b Find the value of the finite series formed by adding the first
four terms of the sequence.

23 Evaluate $\displaystyle\sum_{n=1}^{20} 7\left(\frac{1}{10}\right)^n$.

24 Let $\{c_n\} = \{a_n + b_n\}$, where $\{a_n\} = \{n - 2\}$ and $\{b_n\} = \{n!\}$. Write
the first five terms of $\{c_n\}$.

**In problems 25 and 26, find the sum of each infinite series, if that sum
exists.**

25 $\displaystyle\sum_{n=1}^{\infty} 18\left(\frac{1}{10}\right)^n$

26 $\displaystyle\sum_{n=1}^{\infty} n$

27 The eighth term of the sequence $\{a_n\}$ is 7, and $a_n = a_{n-1} + 2$ for $n \geq 2$. Determine a_7, a_6, and a_1.

28 The sequence $\{a_n\}$ is pictured in triangle ABC.

  a Find the first four terms.
  b What is the geometric interpretation

  of $\displaystyle\sum_{n=1}^{\infty} a_n$?

29 Let a_1 = area of equilateral triangle with side 8,
    a_2 = area of equilateral triangle with side 4, and so on.
  a Find $a_1, a_2, \ldots, a_5$.   **b** Find S_5.

In problems 30 and 31, evaluate each series.

30 $\displaystyle\sum_{n=1}^{5} [(n-3)(n-1)]$

31 $\displaystyle\sum_{n=4}^{10} \log n$

In problems 32–35, let $\{S_n\}$ be the sequence of partial sums of $\{a_n\}$. Graph the points (n, S_n) for $n = 1, 2, 3, \ldots, 7$. Does the associated infinite series appear to have a sum? If so, what is the sum?

32 $\{a_n\} = \left\{\left(\dfrac{1}{2}\right)^{n-1}\right\}$

33 $\{a_n\} = \{1^n\}$

34 $\{a_n\} = \{3(0.1)^{n-1}\}$

35 $\{a_n\} = \{n\text{th digit in } \pi\}$

In problems 36 and 37, evaluate.

36 $\displaystyle\sum_{n=1}^{\infty} \left(-\dfrac{1}{2}\right)^{n-1}$

37 $\displaystyle\sum_{n=1}^{\infty} 0^n$

38 The array 5, 10, 15, 20, 25 has an obvious pattern—the multiples of 5. Find both a closed form and a recursive form for the general formula of the sequence.

39 If $\displaystyle\sum_{k=1}^{n} a_k = n(2n+1)$, what is a_n?

40 Let $a_6 + a_5 = 29$, $a_6 - a_5 = 7$, and $a_n = a_{n-1} + a_{n-2}$ for $n \geq 3$.
    Find $\displaystyle\sum_{k=1}^{6} a_k$.

In problems 41–43, find the sum of each series, if possible.

41 $\displaystyle\sum_{n=1}^{\infty} \left(\dfrac{1}{5}\right)^{n-1}$

42 $\displaystyle\sum_{n=1}^{\infty} 2^{n-1}$

43 $\displaystyle\sum_{n=1}^{15} i^n$, where $i = \sqrt{-1}$

44 Estimate $\displaystyle\sum_{n=1}^{\infty} 4\left(\dfrac{1}{2n+1} - \dfrac{1}{2n+3}\right)$. $\dfrac{8}{15}$

ARITHMETIC SEQUENCES AND SERIES

Objectives

After studying this section, you will be able to
- Compute any term in an arithmetic sequence
- Compute arithmetic means
- Evaluate arithmetic series

Part One: Introduction

Arithmetic Sequences

Consider the sequence 2, 5, 8, 11, 14, . . . , $3n - 1$, . . . The difference between any two successive terms is 3. Therefore, we obtain any term of the sequence by adding 3 to the previous term. This is an example of an **arithmetic sequence.** An **arithmetic sequence** is any sequence $\{a_n\}$ in which the difference between each two successive terms is the same. The difference, d, is called the **common difference.**

The definition can be translated into a recursive formula for the nth term.

Definition: $\qquad\qquad a_n - a_{n-1} = d$
Recursive formula: $\qquad\quad a_n = a_{n-1} + d$

To go from the first term to the nth term, we add d, the difference, $(n - 1)$ times to the first term. This process can be translated into a closed-form formula.

Closed-form formula: $\quad a_n = a_1 + (n - 1)d$

We use the closed form to derive an equation relating any two elements in the series, a_n and a_{n-k}.

$$
\begin{array}{ll}
\text{Formula for } a_n & \boldsymbol{a_n = a_1 + (n - 1)d} \\
\text{Formula for } a_{n-k} & \underline{\boldsymbol{a_{n-k} = a_1 + (n - k - 1)d}} \\
\text{Subtract} & \boldsymbol{a_n - a_{n-k} = kd} \\
& \boldsymbol{a_n = a_{n-k} + kd}
\end{array}
$$

Example   *Find the value of the 48th term of an arithmetic sequence with first term -20 and common difference 3.*

In this case, $a_1 = -20$, $d = 3$, and $n = 48$. The 48th term is a_{48}.

Closed form
$$\boldsymbol{a_n = a_1 + (n - 1)d}$$
$$\boldsymbol{a_{48} = -20 + (48 - 1)3}$$
$$\boldsymbol{= -20 + 141}$$
$$\boldsymbol{a_{48} = 121}$$

Example   The 18th term of an arithmetic sequence is 54 and the 24th term is 36. Find the first term and the common difference.

Use the formula $a_n = a_{n-k} + kd$.
$$a_{24} = a_{18} + 6d$$
$$36 = 54 + 6d$$
$$-18 = 6d$$
$$-3 = d$$

Now use the closed form.
$$a_n = a_1 + (n-1)d$$
$$a_{18} = a_1 + 17d$$
$$54 = a_1 + 17(-3)$$
$$54 = a_1 - 51$$
$$105 = a_1$$

The first term is 105 and the common difference is -3.

Arithmetic Means

You may be familiar with the arithmetic mean as an average of two numbers. The term has a broader definition based on arithmetic sequences. In an arithmetic sequence, **arithmetic means** are the terms between any two designated terms.

Example   A portion of an arithmetic sequence is given. Fill in the blanks.

$$12, \underline{\hspace{1cm}}, \underline{\hspace{1cm}}, \underline{\hspace{1cm}}, 26$$

In this problem, we need to find three arithmetic means between 12 and 26. Let $a_1 = 12$; then $a_5 = 26$.

$$a_5 = a_1 + 4d$$
$$26 = 12 + 4d$$
$$14 = 4d$$
$$3.5 = d$$

The sequence is 12, 15.5, 19, 22.5, 26.

Arithmetic Series

We can derive a formula for the partial sum of an **arithmetic series.** Let's consider the following example.

Example   Find the partial sum S_{10} of the first ten terms of the arithmetic sequence $\{a_n\} = \{2 + (n-2)3\}$.

We could solve this by adding up all the terms.

$$S_{10} = -1 + 2 + 5 + 8 + 11 + 14 + 17 + 20 + 23 + 26$$

Let's try a more creative way. We write down the terms twice—once from first to last and once from last to first—and then add vertically.

$$
\begin{array}{rl}
S_{10} = & -1 + 2 + 5 + 8 + 11 + 14 + 17 + 20 + 23 + 26 \\
S_{10} = & 26 + 23 + 20 + 17 + 14 + 11 + 8 + 5 + 2 + (-1) \\
\hline
2 \cdot S_{10} = & 25 + 25 + 25 + 25 + 25 + 25 + 25 + 25 + 25 + 25 \\
= & 10 \cdot 25
\end{array}
$$

$$S_{10} = \frac{10 \cdot 25}{2}$$

$$= 125$$

In the example, 25 was the sum of the first and tenth terms of the sequence. We can make the following generalization.

> ▶ **The sum of the first n terms, S_n, of the arithmetic sequence a_n with common difference d is**
> $$S_n = n\left(\frac{a_1 + a_n}{2}\right)$$

Proof: We proceed as in the example.

$$
\begin{aligned}
S_n &= \quad a_1 + \; (a_1 + d) + (a_1 + 2d) + (a_1 + 3d) + \ldots + a_n \\
S_n &= \quad a_n + (a_n - d) + (a_n - 2d) + (a_n - 3d) + \ldots + a_1 \\
\hline
2S_n &= (a_1 + a_n) + (a_1 + a_n) + (a_1 + a_n) + (a_1 + a_n) + \ldots + (a_1 + a_n) \\
2S_n &= n \cdot (a_1 + a_n) \\
S_n &= n\left(\frac{a_1 + a_n}{2}\right)
\end{aligned}
$$

Since $a_n = a_1 + (n - 1)d$, we can substitute for a_n.

> ▶ $S_n = n\left(\dfrac{2a_1 + (n - 1)d}{2}\right)$

Example   An arithmetic sequence has $a_1 = -10$ and a common difference of 0.25. Find the sum of the first 75 terms of this sequence.

$$S_n = n\left(\frac{2a_1 + (n - 1)d}{2}\right)$$

$$S_{75} = 75\left(\frac{2(-10) + 74(0.25)}{2}\right)$$

$$= -56.25$$

Part Two: Sample Problem

Problem   The sum of three consecutive terms of an arithmetic sequence is 27, and their product is 405. Find the three terms.

Solution   Let a be the second of the three terms, and let d be the common difference. Then $a - d$ is the first term and $a + d$ is the third term.

The sum is 27
$$(a - d) + a + (a + d) = 27$$
$$3a = 27$$
$$a = 9$$

The product is 405
$$(9 - d)(9)(9 + d) = 405$$
$$9(81 - d^2) = 405$$
$$81 - d^2 = 45$$
$$36 = d^2$$
$$d = 6 \text{ or } d = -6$$

When $d = 6$, the terms are 3, 9, 15.
When $d = -6$, the terms are 15, 9, 3.

Part Three: Exercises and Problems

Warm-up Exercises

In problems 1 and 2, a_n represents the nth term of an arithmetic sequence and d represents the common difference. Write the first five terms of each sequence.

1 $a_1 = 10$, $d = 3$

2 $a_4 = 6$, $d = -3$

3 An arithmetic series S is written twice below, once first to last and once last to first. Add vertically and solve for S.

$$S = \ \ 2 + \ \ 4 + \ \ 6 + \ldots + 22 + 24$$
$$\underline{S = 24 + 22 + 20 + \ldots + \ \ 4 + \ \ 2}$$

4 Insert two arithmetic means between 12 and 22.

5 Which of the following are arithmetic sequences?

a $7, -4, -15, -26, \ldots$

b $2 + \sqrt{3}, 4 + \sqrt{3}, 8 + \sqrt{3}, \ldots$

6 Find the common difference of each arithmetic sequence.

a $7, 10, 13, 16, \ldots$

b $3\sqrt{5}, -\sqrt{5}, -5\sqrt{5}, -9\sqrt{5}, \ldots$

In problems 7 and 8, find the seventh term of the arithmetic sequence.

7 $2 + \pi, 3 + 3\pi, 4 + 5\pi, \ldots$

8 $-10, -8, -6, \ldots$

Problem Set

In problems 9–11, write the first four terms of each sequence.

9 $\{5n\}$

10 $\{3n + 2\}$

11 $\{-2n - 4\}$

In problems 12 and 13, a_n represents the nth term in an arithmetic sequence and d represents the common difference. Write the first five terms of each arithmetic sequence.

12 $a_1 = -4$, $d = \dfrac{1}{2}$

13 $a_{19} = 21$, $d = \dfrac{1}{4}$

In problems 14–16, list the next three terms of each arithmetic sequence.

14 $3, 9, 15, \ldots$

15 $-5, -1, 3, \ldots$

16 $\dfrac{1}{2}, \dfrac{1}{3}, \dfrac{1}{6}, \ldots$

17 Consider the arithmetic series $5 + 7 + 9 + \ldots + 99 + 101$.

a What is the first term?
b What is the common difference?
c How many terms are there?
d Compute the sum.

Problem Set, *continued*

18 Find the first five partial sums—S_1, S_2, S_3, S_4, and S_5—of $\{a_n\} = \{3n + 1\}$.

In problems 19–21, find the fiftieth term of each arithmetic sequence.

19 3, 9, 15, . . .   **20** −5, −1, 3, . . .   **21** $\dfrac{1}{2}, \dfrac{1}{3}, \dfrac{1}{6}, \ldots$

22 The first term of an arithmetic series is 2 and the common difference is 3. The sum is 187. How many terms are in the series?

23 Let A_n be the surface area of the box shown.

    a Find A_1, A_2, A_3, A_4, and A_5.
    b Write an expression for A_n.

24 What values are printed by the following BASIC program?

```
10 LET Sum = 0
20 FOR K = 1 TO 4
30 LET Sum = Sum + 3 * K
40 PRINT Sum
50 NEXT K
60 END
```

25 The seventh term of an arithmetic sequence is 80, and the eleventh term is 90. Find the ninth term.

26 The average of three successive terms of an arithmetic sequence is 47.2. What is the second of the three terms?

27 Find the three arithmetic means between 16 and 32.

In problems 28–30, find each sum.

28 $\displaystyle\sum_{k=1}^{15} 3k$ **29** $\displaystyle\sum_{k=1}^{100} (2k - 1)$ **30** $\displaystyle\sum_{k=8}^{40} (3k + 1)$

In problems 31 and 32, find the 25th term and the sum of the first 25 terms of the arithmetic sequence, where a_n is the nth term and d is the common difference.

31 $a_1 = 4, d = 2$ **32** $a_{10} = 32, a_{15} = 44.5$

33 Find five arithmetic means between 15 and 39.

In problems 34–36, rewrite each sum, using sigma notation.

34 $1 + 2 + 3 + 4 + \ldots + 162$

35 $1^2 + 2^2 + \ldots + 15^2$

36 $3^4 + 5^4 + 7^4 + \ldots + 43^4$

37 "Diamond" Jim McGillicuddy has $150 in his piggy bank. He puts $15 in the bank, and each successive week he puts $15 more than the week before into the piggy bank. How much is in the bank at the end of two years?

In problems 38 and 39, identify the first term, the common difference, and the sum of each arithmetic series.

38 $\displaystyle\sum_{k=1}^{10} 8 + 5(k - 1)$

39 $\displaystyle\sum_{k=1}^{8} \left(-5k\sqrt{2} + 12\sqrt{2}\right)$

40 Let A_n be the area of the shaded region. Find the first six terms of $\{A_n\}$.

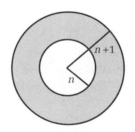

41 The first term of an arithmetic sequence is 325, and the 82nd term is 352. Find the common difference and the sum of the 12th through the 82nd terms.

42 Let A_n be the sum of the shaded areas.

   a Find A_1, A_2, A_3, and A_4.

   b Write an expression for A_n.

43 The sum of two consecutive terms of an arithmetic sequence is 2. Their product is -24. The first of the two terms is smaller than the second. Find the two terms.

44 The first six terms of an arithmetic sequence are 2, 5, 8, 11, 14, and 17. Three of the six numbers are selected at random and placed in the order of selection. Find the probability that these three numbers form an arithmetic progression.

Problem Set, *continued*

45 The lengths of a sequence of rectangles have common difference 3, and the widths have common difference 1. The first rectangle is a 4-by-1 rectangle.

   a What are the dimensions of the tenth rectangle in the sequence?

   b What is the sum of the perimeters of the first ten rectangles?

   c What is the sum of the areas of the first ten rectangles?

```
      4              7                10
   ┌──────┐     ┌──────────┐    ┌────────────────┐
   └──────┘1    └──────────┘2   └────────────────┘3   ···
```

STATISTICS IN PREDICTING LONGEVITY

C. David Williams calculates retirement needs

For most people who work, either they contribute to a pension plan that will provide money for them when they retire, or their employers contribute money on their behalf. An actuary, like C. David Williams of Detroit, applies mathematics in predicting how much money a pension plan will need to pay out over a period of time many years in the future. Into these calculations go statistical data that help determine how long people will live, what will happen to interest rates, and other factors.

An actuary advises companies in formulating retirement plans. The effects of those plans often will not be felt for as long as another forty years. Calculus, a form of mathematics that describes a curve at any given point on the curve, helps the actuary predict how much money will be available in a given year on a given investment and to how many people that money must be distributed.

"We evaluate risk with respect to mortality, economics, and demographics," says Mr. Williams. "We employ elaborate models to make sure a plan can pay according to its terms."

Furthermore, the benefits from most plans are determined by law. This places a burden on actuaries to determine the employer and employee contributions necessary to support the benefits.

Mr. Williams holds a master's degree in mathematics from Northeastern University in Boston. As an example of the importance of mathematics to the work of an actuary: to become certified, Mr. Williams had to pass five mathematics examinations.

GEOMETRIC SEQUENCES AND SERIES

Objectives

After studying this section, you will be able to
- Compute any term in a geometric sequence
- Compute geometric means
- Evaluate finite and infinite geometric series

Part One: Introduction

Geometric Sequences

In the preceding section, we looked at arithmetic sequences, formed by repeated addition. Now let's consider a sequence formed by repeated multiplication.

$$3, 6, 12, 24, 48, \ldots, 3 \cdot 2^{n-1}, \ldots$$

Each term is twice the preceding one, and the *ratio* of any two successive terms is always 2. This is an example of a **geometric sequence.** A **geometric sequence** is any sequence $\{a_n\}$ with the property $\frac{a_n}{a_{n-1}} = r$, where r is a constant and n is an integer larger than 1. The number r is called the **common ratio.**

Let's write some terms of the geometric sequence with first term $a_1 = 4$ and common ratio $r = 3$ and look for patterns.

$$a_1 = 4 = 4 \cdot 3^0$$
$$a_2 = a_1 \cdot r = 4 \cdot 3 = 4 \cdot 3^1$$
$$a_3 = a_2 \cdot r = (4 \cdot 3^1) \cdot 3 = 4 \cdot 3^2$$
$$a_4 = a_3 \cdot r = (4 \cdot 3^2) \cdot 3 = 4 \cdot 3^3$$
$$a_5 = a_4 \cdot r = (4 \cdot 3^3) \cdot 3 = 4 \cdot 3^4$$

The power of the common ratio is always one less than the number of the term.

In general, the nth term of a geometric sequence $\{a_n\}$ with common ratio r is given by

$$a_n = a_1 \cdot r^{n-1} \text{ (closed form) or}$$
$$a_n = a_{n-1} \cdot r^1 \text{ (recursive form)}$$

Using the recursive form, we can develop an alternative recursive form.

$$a_n = a_{n-1} \cdot r^1$$
$$a_n = (a_{n-2} \cdot r^1)r^1 = a_{n-2} \cdot r^2$$
$$a_n = (a_{n-3} \cdot r^1)r^2 = a_{n-3} \cdot r^3$$

$$\vdots$$

$$a_n = a_{n-k} \cdot r^k$$

Example
The fifth term of a geometric sequence is 48 and the ninth term is 768. Find the first term and the common ratio.

Use the recursive form of nth term
$$a_n = a_{n-k} \cdot r^k$$
$$a_9 = a_5 \cdot r^4$$
$$768 = 48 \cdot r^4$$
$$16 = r^4$$
$$\pm 2 = r$$

Now use the closed form
$$a_n = a_1 \cdot r^{n-1}$$
$$a_5 = a_1 \cdot r^4$$
$$48 = a_1 \cdot (\pm 2)^4$$
$$48 = a_1 \cdot 16$$
$$3 = a_1$$

Geometric Means

Geometric means have the same relationship to geometric sequences that arithmetic means have to arithmetic sequences.

Example
Insert one positive geometric mean between 3 and 12.

Think of a geometric sequence 3, ___, 12, or 3, 3r, 3r².

Solve for r
$$3r^2 = 12$$
$$r^2 = 4$$
$$r = \pm 2$$

The positive geometric mean is $3 \cdot 2 = 6$.

A single positive geometric mean between two terms is the square root of the product of the two numbers. In the preceding example, the mean is $\sqrt{3 \cdot 12} = \sqrt{36} = 6$.

As you know from geometry, the altitude to the hypotenuse of a right triangle is the geometric mean between the two segments of the hypotenuse. Also, the length of either leg of the right triangle is the geometric mean between the entire hypotenuse and the portion of the hypotenuse adjacent to that leg.

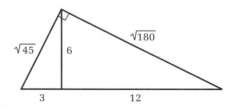

Example   *Insert three real geometric means between 96 and 6.*

The geometric sequence is 96, —, —, —, 6, with $a_1 = 96$ and $a_5 = 6$.

$$a_5 = a_1 \cdot r^4$$
$$6 = 96 \cdot r^4$$

$$\frac{1}{16} = r^4$$

$$\pm\frac{1}{2} = r$$

If $r = \frac{1}{2}$, the geometric sequence is 96, 48, 24, 12, 6.

If $r = -\frac{1}{2}$, the geometric sequence is 96, -48, 24, -12, 6.

Geometric Series

When we find the sum of the first n terms of a geometric sequence $\{a_n\}$ we are finding S_n, the value of a finite **geometric series** of n terms.

> **The sum of the first n terms, S_n, of the geometric sequence $\{a_n\}$ with common ratio r is**
> $$S_n = \frac{a_1(r^n - 1)}{r - 1}$$

Proof: $S_n = a_1 + a_1 \cdot r + a_1 \cdot r^2 + a_1 \cdot r^3 + \ldots + a_1 \cdot r^{n-1}$
$rS_n = a_1 r + a_1 \cdot r^2 + a_1 \cdot r^3 + \ldots + a_1 \cdot r^{n-1} + a_1 \cdot r^n$

Subtracting the first equation from the second, we get

$$rS_n - S_n = a_1 \cdot r^n - a_1$$
$$(r - 1)S_n = a_1(r^n - 1)$$

$$S_n = \frac{a_1(r^n - 1)}{r - 1}$$

Example   *Evaluate $\displaystyle\sum_{n=1}^{7} 96\left(\frac{1}{4}\right)^{n-1}$.*

$$\sum_{n=1}^{7} 96\left(\frac{1}{4}\right)^{n-1} = 96 + 24 + 6 + \ldots + \frac{3}{128}$$

This is a geometric series with $a_1 = 96$ and $r = \frac{1}{4} = 0.25$.

$$S_n = \frac{a_1(r^n - 1)}{r - 1}$$

$$S_7 = \frac{96(0.25^7 - 1)}{0.25 - 1}$$

$$\approx \frac{96(0.000061035 - 1)}{-0.75}$$

≈ 127.992 The sum of the seven terms is about 127.992.

Infinite Geometric Series

The expression $\displaystyle\sum_{n=1}^{\infty} (a_1 \cdot r^{n-1})$ represents an infinite geometric series.

Remember that the sum of an infinite series is defined only if the graph of the sequence of partial sums, $\{S_n\}$, approaches a horizontal asymptote.

Example Evaluate $\displaystyle\sum_{n=1}^{\infty} 96\left(\tfrac{1}{4}\right)^{n-1}$.

The related sequence $\{a_n\}$ is 96, 24, 6, $\tfrac{3}{2}$, $\tfrac{3}{8}$, $\tfrac{3}{32}$, $\tfrac{3}{128}$, ... We generate a table of values of n and S_n, the sum of the terms of $\{a_n\}$, and graph the ordered pairs (n, S_n) for $n = 1, 2, \ldots, 7$.

n	S_n
1	96
2	120
3	126
4	127.5
5	127.875
6	127.96875
7	127.9921875

The points appear to approach an asymptote at 128. Therefore, the sum of the infinite series is 128.

Look at the formula for the sum, S_n, of n terms of a geometric sequence.

$$S_n = \frac{a_1(r^n - 1)}{r - 1}$$

What happens when n is large and $|r| < 1$? Let's examine what happens when $a_1 = 200$ and $r = 0.9$.

n	1	10	100	1000
r^n	0.9	≈ 0.35	$\approx 2.66 \times 10^{-5}$	$\approx 1.75 \times 10^{-46}$
S_n	200	≈ 1302.64	≈ 1999.94	≈ 2000

We notice from the table that if $|r| < 1$ and n is very large, the value of r^n is very small, so S_n approaches $\frac{a_1(0 - 1)}{r - 1}$, or $\frac{a_1}{1 - r}$. When $|r| < 1$, therefore, the sum, S, of the infinite geometric series $\displaystyle\sum_{n=1}^{\infty} a_1 \cdot r^{n-1}$ is given by $S = \frac{a_1}{1 - r}$.

Part Two: Sample Problems

Problem 1   A rubber ball is shot vertically to a height of 20 feet and allowed to · drop. Each bounce is 80% as high as the previous bounce. What is the total distance the ball travels?

Solution   The ball travels up and down on each bounce. On each successive bounce it travels 80% (0.8) as high as on the previous bounce.

Bounce	Distance Up (in feet)	Up-Down Total (in feet)
1	20	40
2	20(0.8) = 16	32
3	16(0.8) = 12.8	25.6
4	12.8(0.8) = 10.24	20.48

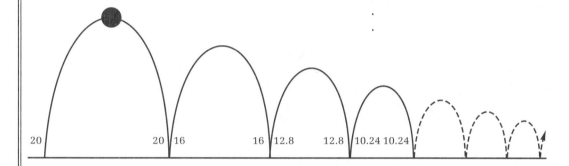

The up-down total is a geometric series with first term $a_1 = 40$ and common ratio $r = 0.8$. The total distance traveled is the sum of all these numbers.

$$S = \frac{a_1}{1 - r} = \frac{40}{1 - 0.08} = 200$$

The ball travels 200 feet.

Problem 2   Evaluate $\displaystyle\sum_{k=1}^{\infty} \frac{2}{3}\left(\frac{4}{3}\right)^k$.

Solution   This is an infinite geometric series with a common ratio of $\frac{4}{3}$. Since $\frac{4}{3} > 1$, the sum does not exist.

Part Three: Exercises and Problems

Warm-up Exercises

In problems 1–3, find the seventh term and the sum of the first seven terms of the following geometric sequences, where a_n is the nth term and r is the common ratio.

1 $a_1 = \sqrt{2}, r = \sqrt{2}$ **2** $a_3 = 24, a_7 = 1.5$ **3** $a_1 = 3i, r = i$

4 Find the sum of each of the following infinite series.

a $\displaystyle\sum_{n=1}^{\infty} 4\left(\frac{1}{2}\right)^n$ **b** $\displaystyle\sum_{n=1}^{\infty} 4(2^n)$

5 Find the sum of the infinite geometric series whose third term is 125 and whose sixth term is 1.

6 Find the geometric mean between 12 and 8.

7 A ball is dropped from a building 65 feet tall. If on each bounce the ball rebounds to 75% of the height of the previous bounce, how far does it travel?

Problem Set

In problems 8–10, write the first six terms of each geometric sequence, given the first term and common ratio.

8 $a_1 = 6, r = 2$ **9** $a_1 = 5, r = 0.3$

10 $a_1 = 16, r = \dfrac{1}{2}$

In problems 11 and 12, find the next three terms of each geometric sequence.

11 4, 2, 1, . . .   **12** 8, −12, 18, . . .

In problems 13–15, state whether each sum is an arithmetic or a geometric series, then give the first term and the common difference or common ratio.

13 $\displaystyle\sum_{k=1}^{10} (5k + 3)$ **14** $\displaystyle\sum_{k=3}^{23} 6\left(\frac{1}{2}\right)^k$ **15** $\displaystyle\sum_{k=1}^{8} \left(\frac{1}{k}\right)$

16 A 12-inch-by-12-inch sheet of paper, 0.004 inch thick, is folded as shown.

    a How thick is the folded paper after the eighth fold?
    b What is the top area after the eighth fold?

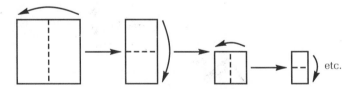

etc.

17 Let d_n = the length of a diagonal of a square with side n.

    a Find d_1, d_2, d_3, d_4, and d_5.   **b** Find $\left\{\dfrac{d_{n+1}}{d_n}\right\}$ for $n = 1, 2, 3, 4$.

In problems 18–20, find the sum of each series.

18 $\displaystyle\sum_{k=1}^{4} 3\left(\frac{1}{10}\right)^k$ **19** $\displaystyle\sum_{k=1}^{\infty} 3\left(\frac{1}{10}\right)^k$ **20** $\displaystyle\sum_{n=1}^{\infty} 8\left(\frac{1}{2}\right)^{n-1}$

In problems 21 and 22, find three geometric means between the given numbers.

21 16 and 0.0625

22 8 and 16.5888

23 7, 7, 7, . . . is an arithmetic sequence. Could it also be a geometric sequence?

24 The lengths of the sides of a right triangle form an arithmetic sequence with common difference 3. Find the lengths of the sides.

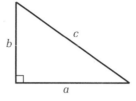

25 Solve $\displaystyle\sum_{n=1}^{3} (nx + 30) = x + 15$ for x.

26 Find the average value of the first four terms of the sequence $\{a_n\} = \{\log (n + 1)\}$.

27 Given: AC = 4,
      DC = 9
Find AB.

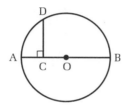

28 Ann T. Gravity has developed Wacko Putty, which, if dropped, rebounds to 108% of its previous height. A ball of Wacko Putty is dropped from a height of 6 feet.

a How high does it bounce on the tenth bounce?
b How far has it traveled up and down from when it was dropped to the top of the tenth bounce?

In problems 29 and 30, find each sum.

29 $5 - \dfrac{5}{2} + \dfrac{5}{4} - \dfrac{5}{8} + \dfrac{5}{16} - \cdots$

30 $\displaystyle\sum_{r=1}^{\infty} \left(\dfrac{7}{4^r}\right)$

31 Given: BC = 8,
      CD = 10;
$\overline{AB}$ is tangent to circle O.
Find x.

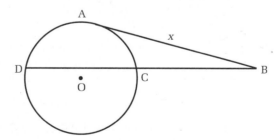

32 The positive geometric mean of two numbers is 12, and the arithmetic mean is 12.5. Find the two numbers.

33 Insert three geometric means between 2i and 162i, if $i^2 = -1$.

Problem Set, *continued*

34 Explain why if one term in a geometric sequence is zero, then all terms but the first term must also be zero. (Hint: Try to find two geometric means between 4 and 0.)

35 The 452nd term of an arithmetic sequence is −893 and the 84th is 27. Find the sum of the first five terms of the sequence.

36 Right triangle PLM is inscribed in circle O.

a Under what circumstances, if any, would the altitude x and the radius r be equal?

b Write an expression for r in terms of a and b.

c Write an expression for x in terms of a and b.

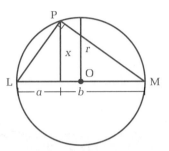

CONVERGING ON π
Mathematicians rise to a challenge

Writing a series that approaches the value of π seemed to be the challenge of the day for seventeenth-century mathematicians. Two mathematicians who addressed themselves to that problem were the Scotsman James Gregory (1638–1675) and the German Gottfried Wilhelm Leibniz (1646–1716). Working independently, each came up with the series

$$\pi = 4\left(1 - \frac{1}{3} + \frac{1}{5} - \frac{1}{7} + \frac{1}{9} - \frac{1}{11}\cdots\right)$$

This series converges slowly. The value for the terms given above is about 2.98.

Two other series that converge on π are

$$\pi = 2\left(\frac{2}{1}\cdot\frac{2}{3}\cdot\frac{4}{3}\cdot\frac{4}{5}\cdot\frac{6}{5}\cdot\frac{6}{7}\cdot\frac{8}{7}\cdot\frac{8}{9}\cdots\right)$$

$$\pi = 4\cdot\cfrac{1}{1 + \cfrac{1^2}{2 + \cfrac{3^2}{2 + \cfrac{5^2}{2 + 9^2}}}}$$

Following the discovery of these series, mathematicians applied themselves to proving that the value of pi could be expressed as a finite series. If it could, of course, π would be rational, which it is not. In 1761, a German physicist named Johann Heinrich Lambert

"SORRY I'M LATE — I WAS WORKING OUT PI TO 5,000 PLACES."

(1728–1777) proved that π is irrational and can only be expressed as an infinite series.

Do a number of calculations in each of the series above to convince yourself that the series do indeed converge on π. Which series converges on π most quickly? Describe how each series converges on π.

CHAPTER SUMMARY

CONCEPTS AND PROCEDURES

After studying this chapter, you should be able to
- Apply the definition of a sequence (13.1)
- Describe a sequence (13.1)
- Form sequences of partial sums (13.1)
- Compute finite series (13.2)
- Use sigma notation to express a series (13.2)
- Find the values of infinite series (13.2)
- Compute any term in an arithmetic sequence (13.3)
- Compute arithmetic means (13.3)
- Evaluate arithmetic series (13.3)
- Compute any term in a geometric sequence (13.4)
- Compute geometric means (13.4)
- Evaluate finite and infinite geometric series (13.4)

VOCABULARY

arithmetic means (13.3)
arithmetic sequence (13.3)
arithmetic series (13.3)
array (13.1)
common difference (13.3)
common ratio (13.4)
finite series (13.2)
geometric means (13.4)
geometric sequence (13.4)
geometric series (13.4)
infinite series (13.2)
progression (13.1)
sequence (13.1)
sequence of partial sums (13.1)
sum of an infinite series (13.2)
term (13.1)

REVIEW PROBLEMS

In problems 1–4, list the first five terms of each sequence.

1 $3, 6, \ldots, n^2 + 2, \ldots$

2 $\{a_n\} = \{5n - 1\}$

3 $\{a_n\} = \{\text{nth prime number}\}$

4 $a_1 = 2, a_{n+1} = 9 - 2a_n$

In problems 5–8, list the first five partial sums of each sequence.

5 $\{a_n\} = \{n^2 + 2\}$

6 $\{a_n\} = \{5n - 1\}$

7 $\{a_n\} = \{\text{nth prime number}\}$

8 $a_1 = 2, a_{n+1} = 9 - 2a_n$

9 Let $S_7 = 15$ and $S_8 = 9$, where $\{S_n\}$ is the sequence of partial sums of $\{a_n\}$.

    a Find a_8.

    b If $\{a_n\}$ is an arithmetic sequence, what is a_1?

In problems 10–13, find the sum.

10 $\displaystyle\sum_{n=1}^{10} \left(\frac{1}{n}\right)$

11 $\displaystyle\sum_{n=1}^{10} \left(\frac{1}{n^2}\right)$

12 $\displaystyle\sum_{k=5}^{8} (k^3 + 3k^2)$

13 $\displaystyle\sum_{k=1}^{10} 6k$

14 Suppose that at the beginning of the year, your savings account contains $4250. If you withdraw $350 per month from the account, how much will it contain at the end of the year?

15 A ball is dropped from a height of 6 feet. Each time it bounces, it rises to 90% of the height from which it fell.

    a How high does it rise on the fourth bounce?

    b How far has it traveled up and down by the top of the fourth bounce?

16 Given $a_1 = 8, a_n = a_{n-1} + 3$, where $n \geq 2$.

    a Write the first four terms of the sequence.

    b Find a_9.   **c** Find S_9.

17 Write $\displaystyle\sum_{k=1}^{6} (-1)^{k+1}k$ in expanded form.

18 Insert five arithmetic means between 17 and 47.

19 The common ratio of a geometric sequence is -4 and the third term is 400. Find the first five terms of the sequence.

20 Insert four geometric means between -2 and 64.

21 How many factors of 4 does the fifteenth term of the geometric series 3, 12, 48, . . . have?

22 Find the sum of the following geometric series.
$$3 + \frac{3}{4} + \frac{3}{16} + \frac{3}{64} + \ldots$$

23 Write a formula that describes the terms of this array.

n	1	2	3	4	5
a_n	3	7	11	15	19

24 Find x if $10 = 1 + x + x^2 + x^3 + \ldots$

25 Construct a table of values for $\sum\limits_{n=1}^{\infty} \left(\frac{1}{2^n}\right)$, listing values of S_n for $\{n : n \le 7\}$. Then graph the ordered pairs (n, S_n). What is the sum of the infinite series?

26 Let $S_n = \sum\limits_{k=1}^{n} a_k = \frac{2n}{n+2}$.
  a Find a_4.
  b Find a formula for a_k in terms of k.
  c Plot (n, S_n) for $n = 2, 4, 6, \ldots, 12$. If $S = \sum\limits_{k=1}^{\infty} a_k$ seems to exist, describe what you think it is. If it does not, explain why you think it does not.

27 Starting with an equilateral triangle with sides of length 1, new triangles are formed by joining the midpoints of the sides of each preceding triangle.

  a What is the length of a side of the sixth triangle?
  b What is the sum of the perimeters of the first six triangles?
  c What is the sum of the areas of all triangles if the process is repeated forever?

28 Find the sum of the infinite geometric series $1 + \frac{3}{2} + \frac{9}{4} + \ldots$ if possible.

29 Find the sums of all multiples of 3 between 27 and 276, inclusive.

In problems 30–32, simplify each sum if possible.

30 $\sum\limits_{k=1}^{n} k$

31 $\sum\limits_{k=1}^{n} \left(\frac{1}{k} - \frac{1}{k+1}\right)$

32 $\sum\limits_{k=1}^{n} \log \frac{k}{k+1}$

33 Find p if $\sum\limits_{j=1}^{5} pj = 14$.

Review Problems, *continued*

In problems 34 and 35, tell whether each statement is True or False.

34 $\displaystyle\sum_{k=2}^{10} a_k = \sum_{k=4}^{12} a_{k-2}$

35 $\displaystyle\sum_{t=1}^{4} [(t^2 - 2)(t - 1)] = \sum_{r=-1}^{4} (r^2 - 1)(r)$

36 Write $x^2 + x^3 + x^4 + \ldots$ in sigma notation.

In problems 37–40, find the first term and common ratio of a geometric sequence matching the given information.

37 $a_6 = 42$, $a_7 = 24$

38 $a_4 = 1$, $a_8 = \dfrac{1}{81}$

39 $\dfrac{a_7}{a_9} = 9$, $r < 0$, $a_8 = 243$

40 $a_1 + a_2 + a_3 = 18 + 12i$, $a_1 + a_2 + a_3 + a_4 = 18 + 9i$, $a_2 = 12i$

41 Find the general term of a sequence whose first four terms are
$x, \dfrac{x^2}{2}, \dfrac{x^3}{3}, \dfrac{x^4}{4}, \ldots$

For problems 42 and 43, find the sum of each geometric series if possible.

42 $\displaystyle\sum_{k=1}^{\infty} \left(\dfrac{2}{3}\right)^k$

43 $\displaystyle\sum_{n=1}^{8} 12\left(-\dfrac{1}{2}\right)^{n-1}$

44 A fungus culture growing under controlled conditions triples in size each day. How many units will the culture contain after six days if it originally contained five units?

45 A town with a population of 2500 people has a predicted yearly growth of 5% over the preceding year for the next ten years. How many people are expected to live in that town at the end of ten years?

46 Phil T. Rich deposits $2 million in a money market account at 10.9% interest, compounded annually. For ten years he allows the interest to accumulate.

a How much money does he have at the end of ten years?
b Do the amounts of money in the bank each year form an arithmetic sequence, an arithmetic series, a geometric sequence, or a geometric series?

47 The snowflake curve is a type of fractal. To make a snowflake curve, begin with an equilateral triangle. Divide each side into three equal segments and replace the middle segment of each side with an equilateral triangle. Find the area enclosed by the snowflake curve if the process is allowed to continue indefinitely.

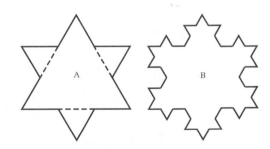

48 Find the perimeter of the snowflake curve described in problem **47**.

13

CHAPTER TEST

In problems 1 and 2, list the first five terms of the sequence.

1 $\{a_n\} = \{n^3 - n\}$

2 $a_1 = 6$, $a_n = 2a_{n-1} + 3$

3 Find a formula to describe the terms a_n of the array below.

n	1	2	3	4
a_n	2	5	8	11

4 $\{S_n\}$ is the sequence of partial sums of $\{a_n\}$. If $S_7 = 63$ and $S_8 = 70$, what is a_8?

In problems 5 and 6, evaluate the finite series.

5 $\displaystyle\sum_{n=1}^{5} (2^n - n)$

6 $\displaystyle\sum_{n=5}^{7} (-1)^n(n - 1)$

7 Determine whether each sequence is arithmetic, geometric, or neither.

    a 1, 3, 9, 27, 81, . . .

    b $\{a_n\} = \{5n + 3\}$

    c $\{a_n\} = \{\sqrt{n}\}$

    d $a_1 = 5$, $a_n = 7a_{n-1}$

8 Give the closed-form formula and the eighth term for each sequence.

    a The arithmetic sequence 5, 9, 13, . . .

    b The geometric sequence 2, 6, 18, . . .

9 Insert five arithmetic means between 14 and 50.

10 Insert two positive geometric means between 40 and 320.

11 Given: $m\angle ADC = 90°$,
              $AB = 10$,
              $BC = 3$
     Find DB.

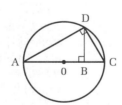

In problems 12 and 13, evaluate the series.

12 $\displaystyle\sum_{n=1}^{8} (3 \cdot 2^{n-1})$

13 $\displaystyle\sum_{k=1}^{40} (5k - 8)$

In problems 14 and 15, find the sum of each series, if it exists.

14 $\displaystyle\sum_{n=1}^{\infty} 3\left(\frac{4}{3}\right)^{n-1}$

15 $\displaystyle\sum_{n=1}^{\infty} 25\left(\frac{4}{5}\right)^{n-1}$

Mathematical Induction

Recall the handshake problem that was discussed in Chapter 1. In Section 1.4, we determined that the number of handshakes exchanged by any number n of people when each person shakes hands with each of the others is equal to

$$\sum_{k=2}^{n}(k-1)$$

that is, to the sum $1 + 2 + 3 + \ldots + (n - 1)$, which is in turn equal to $0 + 1 + 2 + \ldots + (n - 1)$. In Section 1.3, on the other hand, we solved the handshake problem geometrically, finding that the number of handshakes exchanged by n people is equal to $\frac{n^2 - n}{2}$. Therefore, the following statement should be true.

$$0 + 1 + 2 + \ldots + (n - 1) = \frac{n^2 - n}{2}$$

Suppose, however, that you were asked to *prove* that this statement is true for every natural number n. It is easy to show that it is true when $n = 1$, when $n = 2$, when $n = 3$, and so forth, but the set of natural numbers is infinite, so it is impossible to prove the statement by testing it for each possible value of n. What is needed is a general demonstration—one that will apply to the set of natural numbers as a whole.

To see how such a demonstration might be developed, we need to look at the set of natural, or counting, numbers in a new way. As you know, these numbers can be represented by $\{1, 2, 3, \ldots \}$. This set can, however, also be defined recursively:

 If $\mathcal{N}$ is a set such that

    1   **The number 1 is an element of $\mathcal{N}$**
    2   **The number $n + 1$ is an element of $\mathcal{N}$
    whenever n is an element of $\mathcal{N}$**

    then $\mathcal{N}$ is the set of natural numbers.

In the definition, statement 1 establishes that 1 is in $\mathcal{N}$. Statement 2 establishes that since 1 is in $\mathcal{N}$, 2 is also in $\mathcal{N}$. Similarly, since 2 is in $\mathcal{N}$, statement 2 establishes that 3 is also in $\mathcal{N}$. We can continue in this manner, using statement 2 recursively to verify that any natural number is in set $\mathcal{N}$.

By applying this recursive definition, we can determine whether a given statement is true of every member of the natural numbers.

Example   *Prove that* $0 + 1 + 2 + \ldots + (n - 1) = \frac{n^2 - n}{2}$ *for any natural number n.*

Our recursive definition of *natural number* suggests the given statement will be true for every member of the set of natural numbers if

1   It is true when $n = 1$
2   It is true for $n + 1$ whenever it is true for n

To prove that the statement is true when $n = 1$, we simply substitute 1 for n in the statement.

$$0 + 1 + 2 + \ldots + (n - 1) = \frac{n^2 - n}{2}$$

$$1 - 1 = \frac{1^2 - 1}{2}$$

$$0 = 0$$

Since $0 = 0$ is a true statement, the given statement is true for $n = 1$.

Now, to show that the given statement is true for $n + 1$ whenever it is true for n, we *assume* that it is true for some value of n, then see whether it is also true for $n + 1$. In this case, we assume that $0 + 1 + 2 + \ldots + (n - 1) = \frac{n^2 - n}{2}$ and try to show that $0 + 1 + 2 + \ldots + [(n + 1) - 1] = \frac{(n + 1)^2 - (n + 1)}{2}$.

Given

$$0 + 1 + 2 + \ldots + (n - 1) = \frac{n^2 - n}{2}$$

Add n to
each side

$$\underline{\qquad\qquad + n \qquad + n \qquad}$$

$$0 + 1 + 2 + \ldots + n = \frac{n^2 - n}{2} + n$$

$$0 + 1 + 2 + \ldots + [(n + 1) - 1] = \frac{n^2 - n}{2} + \frac{2n}{2}$$

$$= \frac{n^2 + 2n + 1 - n - 1}{2}$$

$$= \frac{(n + 1)^2 - (n + 1)}{2}$$

Since the given statement is true when $n = 1$ and is true for $n + 1$ whenever it is true for n, it must be true for the entire set of natural numbers.

The method of proof used in the preceding example is known as ***mathematical induction.*** It is a powerful technique of demonstration, much used in advanced mathematics. The principle on which proofs by mathematical induction are based can be stated formally as follows.

Principle of Mathematical Induction

If S is a statement that applies to the set $\mathcal{N}$ of natural numbers and

    1. S is true when $n = 1$

    2. When S is true for some natural number n, it is
       also true for $n + 1$

then S is true for every natural number n.

It is important to remember that *both* part 1 and part 2 of the principle must be verified for a proof by mathematical induction to be valid. In Sample Problems 3 and 4 you will see cases in which a statement satisfies only one of the parts and is therefore false.

Sample Problems

Problem 1   *Prove, by mathematical induction, that for every natural number n,*

$$\sum_{k=1}^{n} 2k = n(n + 1).$$

Solution   When $n = 1$, the equation becomes $2(1) = 1(1 + 1)$, or $2 = 2$, which is a true statement, so the given statement is true for $n = 1$.

        To verify part 2 of the principle of mathematical induction, we assume that the given statement is true for some n and show that

$$\sum_{k=1}^{n+1} 2k = (n + 1)[(n + 1) + 1].$$

Given

$$\sum_{k=1}^{n} 2k = n(n + 1)$$

Add $2(n + 1)$
to each side

$$\sum_{k=1}^{n} 2k + 2(n + 1) = n(n + 1) + 2(n + 1)$$

$$\sum_{k=1}^{n+1} 2k = (n + 1)(n + 2)$$

$$= (n + 1)[(n + 1) + 1]$$

    By the principle of mathematical induction, the given statement is true for any natural number n.

Problem 2   *Prove that if n is a natural number, then $n^5 - n$ is divisible by 10.*

Solution   The first step is to show that $n^5 - n$ is divisible by 10 when $n = 1$. Since $1^5 - 1 = 0$ and 0 is divisible by 10, the statement is true for $n = 1$.

Next, we assume that $n^5 - n$ is divisible by 10 for some value of n and show that $(n + 1)^5 - (n + 1)$ is also divisible by 10.

Expand, using the
binomial theorem

Regroup

$$(n + 1)^5 - (n + 1)$$
$$= (n^5 + 5n^4 + 10n^3 + 10n^2 + 5n + 1) - n - 1$$
$$= (n^5 - n) + (5n^4 + 5n) + (10n^3 + 10n^2)$$
$$= (n^5 - n) + 5n(n^3 + 1) + 10n^2(n + 1)$$
$$= (n^5 - n) + 5n(n + 1)(n^2 - n + 1) + 10n^2(n + 1)$$

Examining the final expression, we notice that (1) according to the given statement, $n^5 - n$ is divisible by 10, (2) since either n or $n + 1$ must be an even number, $5n(n + 1)(n^2 - n + 1)$ contains factors of 5 and 2 and therefore is divisible by 10, and (3) $10n^2(n + 1)$ is divisible by 10. According to the distributive property, since each term of the sum contains a factor of 10, the sum itself must contain a factor of 10, so $(n + 1)^5 - (n + 1)$ is divisible by 10.

By the principle of mathematical induction, then, $n^5 - n$ is divisible by 10 whenever n is a natural number.

Problem 3 *Show that the statement $n + 2 = 3n$ satisfies part 1 of the principle of mathematical induction but is not true for every natural number n.*

Solution When $n = 1$, $n + 2 = 1 + 2 = 3$ and $3n = 3(1) = 3$, so the statement is true for $n = 1$.

Given that the statement is true for some value of n, we now can try to show that $(n + 1) + 2 = 3(n + 1)$.

$$(n + 1) + 2 = 3(n + 1)$$
$$n + 3 = 3n + 3$$
$$n = 3n$$

Since this statement is false for every real value of n except 0, the given statement does not satisfy part 2 of the principle. The given statement is not true for every natural number, even though it is true when $n = 1$.

Problem 4 *Show that the statement $n = n + 1$ satisfies part 2 of the principle of mathematical induction but is not true for every natural number n.*

Solution Clearly, $1 \neq 1 + 1$, so the statement fails to satisfy part 1 of the principle.

If there were some value of n for which the statement were true, however, $n + 1 = (n + 1) + 1$ would also be a true statement.

Given $n = n + 1$

Add 1 to each side $n + 1 = n + 2$
$$= (n + 1) + 1$$

Therefore, the given statement is false, even though it satisfies part 2 of the principle.

Problem Set

In problems 1–4, show that each statement is true when $n = 1$.

1 $(1 + h)^n \geq 1 + hn$

2 $\displaystyle\sum_{k=1}^{n}(2k - 1) = n^2$

3 $n < 2^n$

4 $n^2 - n + 6$ is divisible by 2.

5 Rewrite the statements in problems 1–4, replacing n with $n + 1$.

6 Prove that $1 + 5 + 9 + \ldots + (4n - 3) = n(2n - 1)$ for every natural number n.

7 Prove that $n^3 - n$ is divisible by 3 for $\{n : n \in \mathcal{N}\}$.

8 Prove that the sum of the first n natural numbers is equal to $\dfrac{n(n + 1)}{2}$.

9 Use mathematical induction to show that $x^n \cdot y^n = (xy)^n$, where x and y are real numbers and n is a natural number. (Hint: $a^{n+1} = a \cdot a^n$)

10 Is $n + 5 > (n - 2)^2$ for every natural number n? Explain your answer.

11 Prove, by means of mathematical induction, that the sum of the first n terms of a geometric sequence $\{a_n\}$ can be found with the formula

$$S_n = \frac{a_1(r^n - 1)}{r - 1}$$

where r is the common ratio.

12 Prove that the number of diagonals that can be drawn in an n-sided polygon, where $n \geq 3$, is equal to $\dfrac{n(n - 3)}{2}$. (Hint: As your first step, prove the statement true for $n = 3$.)

13 Prove that $a^n - b^n$ always contains a factor of $a - b$ if a and b are real numbers and n is a natural number.

14 Show that each of the following properties of exponents applies to all positive integral exponents m and n.

a $a^m \cdot a^n = a^{m+n}$

b $(a^m)^n = a^{mn}$

c $\dfrac{a^m}{a^n} = a^{m-n}$

In problems 15–18, use mathematical induction to determine whether each statement is True or False for $\{n{:}n \in \mathcal{N}\}$.

15 $2^n \geq n + 1$

16 $n! + (n + 1)! + (n + 2)!$ is divisible by $(n + 1)^2$.

17 $1^3 + 2^3 + 3^3 + \ldots + n^3 = n^2(n + 1)^2 - 4$

18 $1(1!) + 2(2!) + 3(3!) + \ldots + n(n!) = (n + 1)! - 1$

19 Prove that $n^2 \geq \dfrac{n(n + 1)}{2}$ for every natural number n.

20 Prove that the number represented by $n^2 + n$ contains a factor of 2 for every positive integral value of n.

21 Prove that for every element of $\{n{:}n \in \mathcal{N}$ and $n \geq 2\}$,
$$\log (a_1 \cdot a_2 \cdot \ldots \cdot a_n) = \log a_1 + \log a_2 + \ldots + \log a_n$$
where each value of a_k is a positive real number.

22 Let z represent a complex number and $\bar{z}$ represent its conjugate. Prove that $\overline{z^n} = \bar{z}^n$ for every natural number n. (Hint: For any two complex numbers v and w, $\bar{v} \cdot \bar{w} = \overline{vw}$.)

23 Prove that for all positive integral values of n, $5^n - 1$ is divisible by 4.

24 Prove that if n is a natural number greater than 2, the sum of the measures of the interior angles of an n-sided polygon is equal to $180(n - 2)$.

25 Prove that for every natural number n,
$$\sum_{k=1}^{n} \left(\frac{1}{(2k - 1)(2k + 1)} \right) = \frac{n}{2n + 1}.$$

26 Refer to the description of the game Tower of Hanoi in Section 5.6, problem 28. Use mathematical induction to prove that the minimum number of moves needed to transfer an n-disk tower is equal to $2^n - 1$.

27 Use mathematical induction to prove the binomial theorem. That is, show that for all real values of x and y and all positive integral values of n,
$$(x + y)^n = [C(n, 0)]x^n + [C(n, 1)]x^{n-1}y$$
$$+ [C(n, 2)]x^{n-2}y^2 + \ldots + [C(n, n)]y^n$$

CHAPTER

14

INTRODUCTION TO TRIGONOMETRY

The triangles associated with circles in Naum Gabo's mystical *Construction in Space with Balance on Two Points* represent the basic principles of trigonometry.

14.1 THE UNIT CIRCLE

Objectives

After studying this section, you will be able to
- Measure angles as rotations
- Determine points of intersections of rays and the unit circle

Part One: Introduction

Recall that the distance around a circle is called the *circumference* and that a portion of the circle is an *arc*. An angle with its vertex at the center of the circle is called a **central angle.**

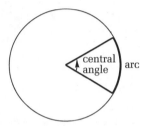

Example   *The circle shown has a radius of 12 and central ∠AOB = 45°. Find the length of arc AB.*

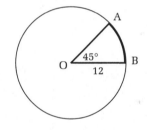

Circumference = $2\pi \cdot$ radius, so the circumference of the circle is 24π. Since the central angle is 45°, arc AB is a fractional part of the circle. It is $\frac{45}{360}$, or $\frac{1}{8}$, of the circle. The length of arc AB is $\frac{1}{8} \cdot 24\pi$, or 3π.

In geometry, an angle was defined to be two rays with a common endpoint. In trigonometry, *an angle is a rotation* from one ray to another. The rotation starts at the **initial ray** and stops at the **terminal ray.**

In this book, the initial ray of an angle will be the positive x-axis unless stated otherwise. Such an angle is said to be in **standard position.** For an angle in standard position, we only need to show the terminal ray and the rotation.

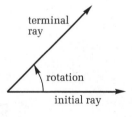

The angle shown as θ is 210° and is in standard position. (Greek letters are commonly used for angles. The letter θ is called theta.)

Using rotations, we can have angles greater than 180°. We can also have negative angles. We define counter-clockwise rotations as positive and clockwise rotations as negative.

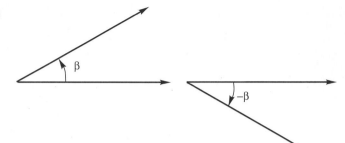

By choosing negative angles, and by adding multiples of 360° to an angle, it is possible to find more than one angle with the same terminal ray.

Example   *The diagram shows a 30° angle. Name two other angles with the same terminal ray.*

We can arrive at the same terminal ray by rotating in the opposite direction. The angle measuring −330° has the same terminal ray.

Another way is to go around more than once. One revolution is 360°, so the angle measuring (30 + 360)°, or 390°, also has the same terminal ray.

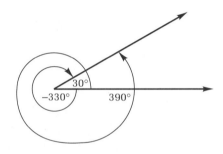

Thus the angles measuring 30°, −330°, and 390° all have the same terminal ray. Angles in standard position that have the same terminal ray are called ***coterminal angles.***

Points on the Unit Circle

The study of trigonometry is based on the circle with equation $x^2 + y^2 = 1$, called the ***unit circle.*** The unit circle has its center at the origin and a radius of 1 unit.

Example   *Find the point of intersection of the unit circle and the ray* $\left\{(x, y): y = \frac{4}{3}x,\ x \geq 0\right\}.$

To find the point of intersection of the circle and ray, we solve the system of equations
$$\begin{cases} x^2 + y^2 = 1 \\ y = \dfrac{4}{3}x \end{cases}$$

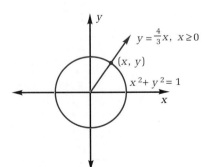

By substitution, we get
$$x^2 + \left(\frac{4}{3}x\right)^2 = 1$$

$$x^2 + \frac{16}{9}x^2 = 1$$

$$\frac{25}{9}x^2 = 1$$

$$x^2 = \frac{9}{25}$$

$$|x| = \frac{3}{5}$$

Since the point is in the first quadrant, $x = \frac{3}{5}$. Then $y = \frac{4}{3} \cdot \frac{3}{5} = \frac{4}{5}$. The point is $\left(\frac{3}{5}, \frac{4}{5}\right)$.

Example   *Find the coordinates of the point of intersection of the unit circle and the terminal ray of a 120° angle.*

Drop a perpendicular to the x-axis to form a 30°-60°-90° triangle. The hypotenuse is 1, the shorter leg is $\frac{1}{2}$, and the longer leg is $\frac{1\sqrt{3}}{2}$. Since the ray is in the second quadrant, the x-coordinate will be negative and the y-coordinate will be positive. The coordinates of the point of intersection are $\left(-\frac{1}{2}, \frac{\sqrt{3}}{2}\right)$.

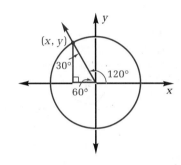

Part Two: Sample Problems

Problem 1   *Find the point of intersection of the unit circle and the angle whose terminal ray contains the point P(5, −12).*

Solution   **Method 1**

By the Pythagorean Theorem, OP = 13. Drop perpendiculars to the x-axis as shown. The result is two similar right triangles and $\frac{5}{x} = \frac{12}{y} = \frac{13}{1}$. Solving, we find $x = \frac{5}{13}$ and $y = \frac{12}{13}$, but these are only distances. Since the point is in the fourth quadrant, the y-coordinate must be *negative*. Thus the point of intersection is $\left(\frac{5}{13}, \frac{-12}{13}\right)$.

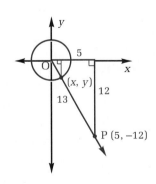

Method 2

The equation of the ray is $y = \frac{-12}{5}x$. The equation of the circle is $x^2 + y^2 = 1$. We could solve the system of equations as in the example at the bottom of the preceding page.

Problem 2   The circle shown has radius 9, and arc AB has length 2π. Find the measure of central angle AOB.

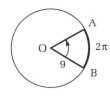

Solution   The circumference of the circle is 18π. Arc AB is $\frac{2\pi}{18\pi}$, or $\frac{1}{9}$, of the circle. This means that $\angle AOB = \frac{1}{9}(360°) = 40°$.

Part Three: Exercises and Problems

Warm-up Exercises

1 Find the value of r.

2 Find the coordinates of the point of intersection of the unit circle and the terminal ray of a 210° angle.

3 Find the value of x.

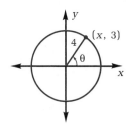

4 Find (x, y) in the third quadrant.

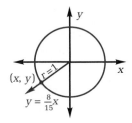

In problems 5–10, find the point of intersection of the unit circle and the terminal ray of each angle.

5 30°   **6** 45°   **7** 60°
8 −30°   **9** −45°   **10** −60°

Problem Set

In problems 11–16, find the point of intersection of the unit circle and the terminal ray of each angle.

11 90°   **12** 180°   **13** 270°
14 360°   **15** 0°   **16** −90°

17 Refer to the diagram.

  a Find the length of arc AB.
  b Find the length of arc ACB.

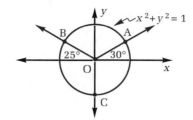

18 The point $(-3, 4)$ is on the terminal ray of an angle in standard position. At what point does the terminal ray of the angle intersect the unit circle?

19 Refer to the diagram.

  a Find the number of degrees in angle θ.
  b Find the length of arc AB if the circle is a unit circle.

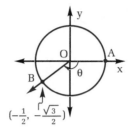

20 Find the value of β and γ if $\alpha = 75°$.

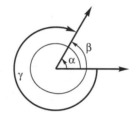

21 Find the point Q on the unit circle that lies on the terminal ray OP of angle ROP.

22 Name the coordinates of points A, B, and C.

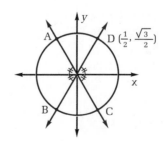

23 Find the point of intersection of the unit circle and the ray $y = \frac{5}{12}x$, $x \geq 0$.

24 a If OA = 4, what is $\dfrac{\text{length of } \overset{\frown}{AB}}{\text{OA}}$?

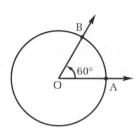

   b If OA = 20, what is $\dfrac{\text{length of } \overset{\frown}{AB}}{\text{OA}}$?

   c If OA = 1, what is $\dfrac{\text{length of } \overset{\frown}{AB}}{\text{OA}}$?

25 Find all other angles θ in standard position, where $-360° \le \theta \le 360°$, such that the point of intersection of the terminal ray of the angle and the unit circle has the same x-coordinate as that of the 50° angle shown.

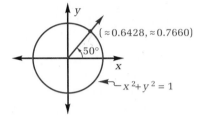

26 a Name the coordinates of point B.
   b Name the coordinates of point C.

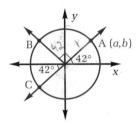

27 Solve the system.

$$\begin{cases} x^2 + y^2 = 1 \\ y = \dfrac{1}{2}x \end{cases}$$

28 A bicycle wheel has a diameter of 27 inches. There are 14 teeth on the gear of the rear wheel. There are 48 teeth on the pedal gear. How many revolutions (to the nearest whole revolution) does the pedal gear make when the bike travels one mile?

29 In the circles shown, find each of the following.

   a The length of $\overset{\frown}{AB}$.
   b The length of $\overset{\frown}{CD}$.
   c The ratio of the length of $\overset{\frown}{CD}$ to the length of $\overset{\frown}{AB}$.
   d The ratio O'D:OB.

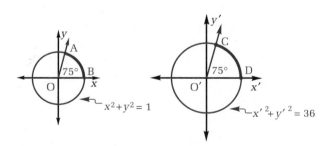

30 In a circle, a central angle of 60° cuts off an arc of length 10π. Find the radius of the circle.

31 Find the point(s) on the unit circle $x^2 + y^2 = 1$ where the line $y = \frac{2}{5}x$ intersects the circle.

32 Arc AB is 14 inches long. O is the center of the circle. What is the length of $\overline{AB}$?

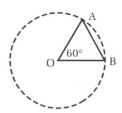

SYSTEMS AND PROFITABILITY
The break-even point

The goal of a business is to make a profit. Even a not-for-profit venture such as a day-care center or a theater company needs to have income that at least equals expenses. Income that exceeds expenses enables a not-for-profit organization to expand its services to the community.

The Parabolic Theater Company is a not-for-profit organization that tries to provide quality productions at the lowest possible ticket prices. It wants to raise money for its productions by selling original T-shirts. The company decides to hire a designer to design and make a silk screen for the shirts. What it pays for the design and for the silk screen will be fixed costs— one-time costs that will never vary, no matter how many T-shirts are sold. The company will also rent a studio where company members will print the T-shirts each Saturday. The rent will be another fixed cost. The

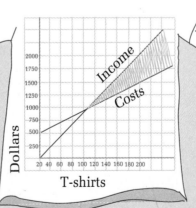

company decides to spend $500 on fixed costs.

There will also be costs that will vary as a function of how many T-shirts are sold. These variable costs are the costs of the shirts and the ink. The company can buy plain T-shirts for $4.00 each and has found that the cost of ink per T-shirt will be $.50. Therefore, the variable, or unit, cost of each T-shirt will be $4.50. The company decides to sell its T-shirts for $10.00 each.

The income and expenses for this venture can be represented as a system of linear equations where number of T-shirts is graphed against dollars, as shown at the left.

How many T-shirts must the company sell simply to break even—that is, to recover its investment in the design and the silk screen? How many must it sell to make $1000 for its theater productions?

THE CIRCULAR FUNCTIONS

Objectives

After studying this section, you will be able to
- Calculate the sine, cosine, tangent, cotangent, secant, and cosecant of an angle
- Use the Pythagorean identities

Part One: Introduction

Sine and Cosine

In the previous section, you saw how the terminal ray of an angle intersects the unit circle at exactly one point. It is extremely useful to be able to compute the x- and y-coordinates of the point of intersection for any angle θ. We define the function ***cosine*** of θ—abbreviated $\cos(\theta)$—to be the x-coordinate, and ***sine*** of θ—abbreviated $\sin(\theta)$—to be the y-coordinate. Sine and cosine are two of six trigonometric functions.

 If the terminal ray of angle θ in standard position contains (x, y) on the unit circle, then $\cos(\theta) = x$ and $\sin(\theta) = y$, or $(\cos(\theta), \sin(\theta)) = (x, y)$.

Example *Use the circle shown to evaluate $\cos(\theta)$ and $\sin(\theta)$.*

The coordinates of the points of intersection of the terminal ray of θ and the unit circle are $(-0.8, 0.6)$. This tells us that $\cos(\theta) = -0.8$ and $\sin(\theta) = 0.6$.

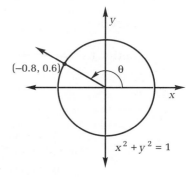

The sine and cosine functions take an angle as input and then output a coordinate from the unit circle. Thus, the range of these two functions is $-1 \leq \cos(\theta) \leq 1$ and $-1 \leq \sin(\theta) \leq 1$.

It is helpful to use a calculator to evaluate trigonometric functions.

Example *Approximate $\sin(39°)$ and $\cos(39°)$.*

Be sure that your calculator is in ***degree mode*** and enter 39 $\boxed{\sin}$

Your calculator should read $\boxed{0.62932039}$, so $\sin(39°) \approx 0.629$.

(We round off to the accuracy that is appropriate for each problem.)

Then we enter 39 $\boxed{\cos}$ and read that $\cos(39°) \approx 0.777$.

If a calculator is not available, you can look up sines and cosines in the table on pages 738–743.

In the preceding example, we were given the angle and asked to find the sine and cosine. Now, we try the reverse—given the sine or cosine, what is the angle?

Example   *If $\sin(\theta) = 0.8296$, with $0° < \theta < 90°$, what is θ?*

To solve this, we use a key labeled either $\boxed{\text{INV}}$ or $\boxed{\text{ARC}}$ or $\boxed{\text{2nd}}$ or $\boxed{\sin^{-1}}$ on most calculators. (We will use the $\boxed{\text{INV}}$ notation.) When we enter .8296 $\boxed{\text{INV}}$ $\boxed{\sin}$, the display is $\boxed{56.0576702}$. Thus, angle $\theta \approx 56°$. (Again, the degree of accuracy of rounding off depends on the application of the answer.)

To use the table on pages 738–743, we look for 0.8292 in the sine column. The closest value is 0.8290, which corresponds to sin (56°), so $\theta \approx 56°$.

Tangent, Cotangent, Secant, and Cosecant

Four other functions are defined in terms of cosine and sine.

Name of Function	Abbreviation and Definition
Tangent	$\tan(\theta) = \dfrac{\sin(\theta)}{\cos(\theta)} = \dfrac{y}{x}$
Cotangent	$\cot(\theta) = \dfrac{\cos(\theta)}{\sin(\theta)} = \dfrac{x}{y}$
Secant	$\sec(\theta) = \dfrac{1}{\cos(\theta)} = \dfrac{1}{x}$
Cosecant	$\csc(\theta) = \dfrac{1}{\sin(\theta)} = \dfrac{1}{y}$

The definitions of the six trigonometric functions are so important that you should memorize them.

Example   *The terminal ray of ϕ contains $(4, -3)$. Evaluate the six trigonometric functions of ϕ.*

By similar triangles, the point of intersection of the terminal ray and the unit circle is $\left(\frac{4}{5}, -\frac{3}{5}\right)$.

From the definitions, $\cos(\phi) = \frac{4}{5}$, $\sin(\phi) = -\frac{3}{5}$, $\tan(\phi) = -\frac{3}{4}$, $\cot(\phi) = -\frac{4}{3}$, $\sec(\phi) = \frac{5}{4}$, and $\csc(\phi) = -\frac{5}{3}$.

$(4, -3)$

Example   *Find $\csc(128°)$.*

Most calculators have no $\boxed{\text{csc}}$ button, but by definition, $\csc(128°)$ is the reciprocal of $\sin(128°)$. Be sure your calculator is in degree mode. Enter 128 $\boxed{\sin}$ $\boxed{1/x}$ to find that $\csc(128°) \approx 1.269$.

Example   If $0° < \theta < 90°$ and $\cot(\theta) = 1.92$, what is θ?

This is a two-stage problem. There is no ⬚cot button, so we use the reciprocal of tangent. The reciprocal of 1.92 is the value of $\tan(\theta)$. Then to find the angle, we use the inverse key and the tangent key.

Entering 1.92 ⬚1/x ⬚INV ⬚tan , we find that $\theta \approx 27.5°$.

Since sin, cos, tan, cot, sec, and csc are functions, we have used parentheses around the arguments of the functions. Often, we leave out the parentheses. For example, we write sin 35° instead of sin(35°).

Pythagorean Identities

The coordinates of the points (x, y) on the unit circle satisfy the equation $x^2 + y^2 = 1$ and $(\cos \theta, \sin \theta)$ is a point on the unit circle. These two relationships lead us to the following theorem.

⟫ **For any angle θ, $(\cos \theta)^2 + (\sin \theta)^2 = 1$.**

To simplify the writing of exponents with trigonometric functions, we usually write $\cos^2 \theta + \sin^2 \theta = 1$. From this first identity it is possible to prove the following identities. (Problem **24** in the Problem Set asks you to develop these proofs.)

⟫ **For any angle θ, $1 + \tan^2 \theta = \sec^2 \theta$.**
⟫ **For any angle θ, $1 + \cot^2 \theta = \csc^2 \theta$.**

These three theorems are called the *Pythagorean identities*.

Part Two: Sample Problems

Problem 1   If $\cos \alpha = \frac{2}{3}$, what is the exact value of sin α?

Solution   There are two points on the unit circle with x-coordinate $\frac{2}{3}$. Using the equation of the unit circle, and substituting,

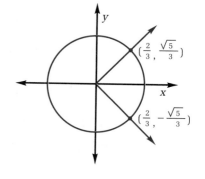

$$\left(\frac{2}{3}\right)^2 + y^2 = 1$$

$$y = \pm \frac{\sqrt{5}}{3}$$

$$\sin \alpha = \frac{\sqrt{5}}{3} \text{ or } \sin \alpha = -\frac{\sqrt{5}}{3}$$

Problem 2   Find the exact value of csc 135°.

Solution   The triangle formed in the second quadrant is a 45°-45°-90° triangle. The point on the unit circle is $\left(\frac{-1}{\sqrt{2}}, \frac{1}{\sqrt{2}}\right) = (\cos 135°, \sin 135°)$. Thus, $\csc 135° = \frac{1}{\sin 135°} = \sqrt{2}$. Since we are asked to find the exact value of csc 135°, the answer is $\sqrt{2}$. A decimal value would be an approximation.

Problem 3 The terminal ray of β is $\{(x, y): y = 3x \text{ and } x \leq 0\}$. Evaluate $\tan \beta$.

Solution Let's find the point of intersection of the line and the unit circle by solving a system.

$$\begin{cases} y = 3x \\ x^2 + y^2 = 1 \end{cases}$$

Substitute for y $\quad x^2 + 9x^2 = 1$

$$x = \pm \frac{1}{\sqrt{10}}$$

Since $x \leq 0$, $x = -\dfrac{1}{\sqrt{10}}$.

The point of intersection is $\left(\dfrac{-1}{\sqrt{10}}, \dfrac{-3}{\sqrt{10}} \right)$ and $\tan \beta = \dfrac{\sin \beta}{\cos \beta} = \dfrac{y}{x} = 3$.

The tangent value is the same as the slope of the line. This is not a surprise, since the definition of tangent is $\frac{y}{x}$.

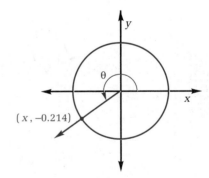

$y = 3x, \ x \leq 0$

$x^2 + y^2 = 1$

Problem 4 The pitch of the roof of a house is $\frac{4}{12}$. What angle does the roof make with the horizontal?

Solution The slope of the roof, $\frac{4}{12}$, is the tangent of angle θ, so angle $\theta \approx 18°$.

Problem 5 Estimate θ to the nearest degree if $\sin \theta = -0.214$, the terminal ray of θ is in Quadrant III, and $\theta > 0°$.

Solution When we enter 0.214 $\boxed{\pm}$ $\boxed{\text{INV}}$ $\boxed{\text{sin}}$ into a calculator, we read an angle of about $-12°$. But the figure shows that the angle we want is in Quadrant III, so it must be greater than $180°$. We know that two angles can have the same y-coordinates. The angle we want must be the same distance below the x-axis as $-12°$. So angle θ is about $180 + 12$, or 192, degrees.

$(x, -0.214)$

Problem 6 Write $\cos \theta$ in terms of $\tan \theta$.

Solution We are asked to write $\cos \theta$ as an expression that includes only "$\tan \theta$" and constants.

Remember that $\cos \theta = \frac{1}{\sec \theta}$, so $\cos^2 \theta = \frac{1}{\sec^2 \theta}$.

We use the identity $1 + \tan^2 \theta = \sec^2 \theta$ to write

$$\cos^2 \theta = \frac{1}{1 + \tan^2 \theta}$$

$$\cos \theta = \pm \sqrt{\frac{1}{1 + \tan^2 \theta}}$$

$$= \pm \frac{1}{\sqrt{1 + \tan^2 \theta}}$$

Part Three: Exercises and Problems

Warm-up Exercises

1 Find all six trig function values of θ.
(The coordinates shown are approximate.)

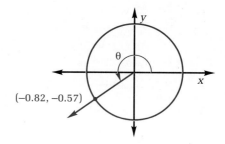

(−0.82, −0.57)

2 Find the point on the unit circle that is on the terminal ray of each angle.
  a 60°   **b** 135°   **c** −30°   **d** 100° (to nearest hundredth)

3 Refer to the figure.
  a Find the coordinates of point A to the nearest hundredth.
  b Find the slope of the ray pictured.

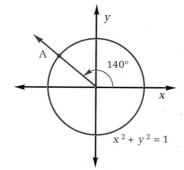

In problems 4–6, use the Pythagorean identities to find the value of each trig function.

4 $\sin \alpha$, if $\cos \alpha = \dfrac{1}{4}$ **5** $\sec \theta$, if $\tan \theta = \sqrt{3}$ **6** $\cot \beta$, if $\csc \beta = \dfrac{5}{3}$

7 Match each angle with the point through which its terminal ray passes.
  a −62°   **i** $(\approx-0.47, \approx0.88)$
  b 118°   **ii** $(\approx0.47, \approx0.88)$
  c 62°   **iii** $(\approx0.47, \approx-0.88)$
  d 242°   **iv** $(\approx-0.47, \approx-0.88)$

8 What is the value of $\sin \theta$ if $\cos \theta = \frac{3}{4}$?

Problem Set

9 Find each first-quadrant angle described.
  a $\sin \alpha = 0.3874$ **b** $\cos \beta = \dfrac{8}{17}$ **c** $\sin \theta = \dfrac{1}{7}$

  d $\tan \lambda = \dfrac{4}{3}$ **e** $\cos \delta = \dfrac{1}{10}$ **f** $\sin \omega = 1.342$

10 a Find $\cos \theta$ if $\tan \theta = 2\frac{1}{8}$.   **b** Find $\cos \theta$ if $\tan \theta = \frac{\sqrt{3}}{3}$.

    c Find $\tan \theta$ if $\sin \theta = \frac{1}{3}$.

11 Given that $\theta = 72°$, calculate each value to the nearest thousandth.

   a $\sin \theta$ **b** $\cos (90° - \theta)$

   c $\tan \theta$ **d** $\cot (90° - \theta)$

12 The terminal ray of θ contains $(7, -24)$. Evaluate the six trig functions of θ.

13 The area of triangle OAC is 5. Find each of the following.

   a The coordinates of point C

   b OC

   c The coordinates of point B

   d $m\angle AOC$

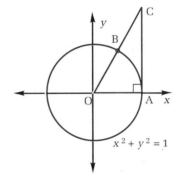

14 Find all six trig function values for θ.

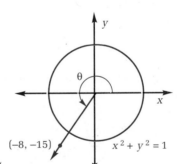

15 Refer to the figure.

   a Find the value of y.

   b Find $\cos \theta$.

   c Find $\sin \theta$.

   d Find the measure of θ.

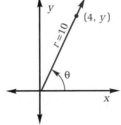

16 Find the first ten terms of the sequence $\{\cos (10k)°\}$ to the nearest hundredth.

Problem Set, *continued*

17 Find each value to the nearest thousandth.

a The coordinates of point A
b The area of triangle AOB

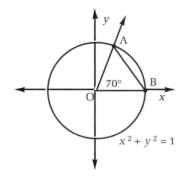

18 Find the value of θ if $\sin \theta \approx 0.4695$.

19 Find each value if $\sin \theta = -0.469$.

a θ
b The coordinates of point A

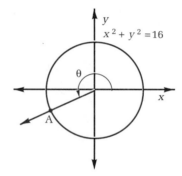

20 Find each of the following for $0° \le \theta \le 360°$.

a The value of θ for which $\sin \theta$ is largest
b The value of θ for which $\sin \theta$ is smallest
c The values of θ for which $\sin \theta = 0$

21 For each point on the unit circle, find the measure of the angle whose terminal ray passes through the point.

a $(0, -1)$

b $\left(-\dfrac{\sqrt{2}}{2}, -\dfrac{\sqrt{2}}{2}\right)$

c $\left(\dfrac{4}{5}, -\dfrac{3}{5}\right)$

d $(\approx 0.819, \approx 0.573)$

22 Evaluate all six trigonometric functions for the angle whose terminal ray passes through $(-0.5, \approx 0.866)$ on the unit circle.

23 If $\cos \theta = 0.695$, what is the value of each of the following?

a $\sin \theta$ **b** $\tan \theta$ **c** $\sec \theta$

24 Use the statement $\cos^2 \theta + \sin^2 \theta = 1$ to prove each of the following.

a $1 + \tan^2 \theta = \sec^2 \theta$ **b** $1 + \cot^2 \theta = \csc^2 \theta$

25 Explain why it is not possible for $\sin \theta$ to be 0.625 and $\cos \theta$ to be 0.54 if $0° \le \theta \le 360°$.

26 Find the point(s) on the unit circle through which the terminal ray of each angle θ might pass.

a $\tan \theta = 1$ **b** $\sin \theta = -\dfrac{\sqrt{2}}{2}$

c $\cos \theta = -1$ **d** $\sec \theta = -2$

27 Let $\sec \theta = 4.25$. Find all possible values of θ such that $0° \le \theta \le 360°$.

28 Name the quadrant that contains the terminal ray of angle θ, given the specified conditions.

a $\cos \theta < 0$ and $\sin \theta > 0$ **b** $\tan \theta > 0$ and $\sin \theta < 0$

29 Write an equation of the line that passes through $(0, 0)$ and forms the given angle.

a 30° with the positive x-axis   **b** 150° with the positive x-axis

30 Refer to the figure and find each value.

a $\cos \theta$ **b** $\sin \theta$
c $\tan \theta$ **d** $\cos (\theta + \alpha)$
e $\sin (\theta + \alpha)$ **f** $\tan (\theta + \alpha)$

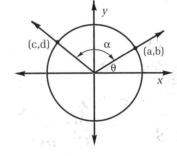

31 Simplify each expression in terms of a single trig function.

a $(1 - \sin \theta)(1 + \sin \theta)$ **b** $\sin^2 \theta + \dfrac{\sin^2 \theta}{\cos^2 \theta} + \cos^2 \theta$ **c** $(\sec \theta)\left(\cos \theta - \dfrac{1}{\cos \theta}\right)$

32 Solve for θ.

a $\tan \theta = -1, 90° < \theta < 270°$ **b** $\cos \theta = \dfrac{1}{2}, -90° < \theta < 90°$

c $\cos \theta = \dfrac{1}{2}, 0° < \theta < 360°$ **d** $\sec \theta = \dfrac{-2}{\sqrt{2}}, 0° < \theta < 360°$

33 Given that $0° \le \theta \le 360°$, find θ for each of the following.

a $\sin \theta = 1$ **b** $\sin \theta = -1$
c $\sin^2 \theta = 1$ **d** $\cos^2 \theta = 1$

34 Write an expression for $\tan \theta$ in terms of $\cos \theta$.

COORDINATE DEFINITIONS

Objectives

After studying this section, you will be able to
- Define the trigonometric functions in terms of coordinates
- Use special angles to compute trigonometric functions

Part One: Introduction

Defining Trig Functions in Terms of Coordinates

In the last section, we used points on the unit circle to define the trig functions. However, we can evaluate the trigonometric functions given *any* point on the terminal ray. The point need not be on the unit circle.

Example   *The terminal ray of θ contains the point (12, 5). Evaluate the trig functions of θ.*

The point (12, 5) is 13 units from the origin. A point on this ray that is only 1 unit from the origin (on the unit circle) is $\frac{1}{13}$ of the distance to the point (12, 5), and so its coordinates will be $\left(\frac{12}{13}, \frac{5}{13}\right)$. Thus,
$\cos \theta = \frac{12}{13}$, $\sin \theta = \frac{5}{13}$, $\tan \theta = \frac{5}{12}$, $\cot \theta = \frac{12}{5}$, $\sec \theta = \frac{13}{12}$, and $\csc \theta = \frac{13}{5}$.

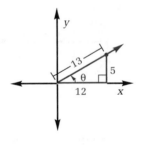

In general, if the terminal ray of an angle θ contains the point (x, y), and if the distance from the origin to (x, y) is r, then

$$\cos \theta = \frac{x}{r} \qquad \sec \theta = \frac{r}{x}$$

$$\sin \theta = \frac{y}{r} \qquad \csc \theta = \frac{r}{y}$$

$$\tan \theta = \frac{y}{x} \qquad \cot \theta = \frac{x}{y}$$

By the Pythagorean Theorem, $r = \sqrt{x^2 + y^2}$.

Quadrants

The trigonometric functions are based on the position of the terminal ray. The functions will be positive or negative depending on which quadrant the terminal ray lies in.

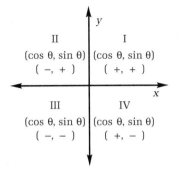

Example *If an angle α terminates in Quadrant III, will its tangent be positive or negative?*

$\tan \alpha = \frac{y}{x}$. In Quadrant III, x and y are both negative. The quotient of two negatives is positive, so $\tan \alpha$ is positive.

Special Angles and Reference Angles

For angles that are multiples of 30° or 45°, we can figure out the exact coordinates of the points on the unit circle by using the special 30°-60°-90° or 45°-45°-90° triangles as shown in the figures. Since these values are used quite often, it is helpful to memorize the values in the first quadrant. To find the values in the other quadrants, we use the symmetry of the circle as shown.

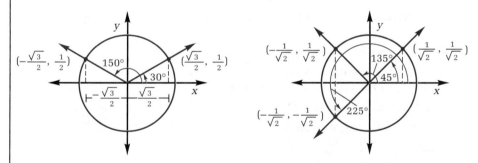

The first-quadrant angles are called the ***reference angles*** for the other angles. The ***reference angle*** for an angle θ is the first-quadrant angle (between 0° and 90°) that forms the same acute angle with the x-axis as θ.

Example *Find the value of each function.*

a *cos 150°*

$\cos 150° = -\cos 30°$

$\quad = -\dfrac{\sqrt{3}}{2}$

b *sin 135°*

$\sin 135° = \sin 45°$

$\quad = \dfrac{1}{\sqrt{2}}$

c sin 225°

$$\sin 225° = -\sin 45°$$

$$= -\frac{1}{\sqrt{2}}$$

For an angle that is not a multiple of 30° or 45°, we proceed as before.

Consider angles of 25°, 155°, 205°, and 335°. Each terminal ray forms an acute angle of 25° with the x-axis. By symmetry, the coordinates on the unit circle for the 25° angle are (a, b), the coordinates for 155° are (−a, b), for 205° they are (−a, −b), and for 335° they are (a, −b). The reference angle is 25°.

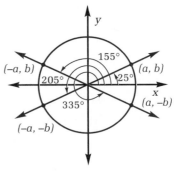

If we know the cosine and sine of the reference angle, we can adjust the sign of one or both coordinates for the cosine or sine of the symmetric angles in the other quadrants.

Example   *Find the reference angle for 250°.*

The figure shows that the terminal ray for 250° makes a 70° angle with the negative x-axis. So the reference angle for 250° is 70°.

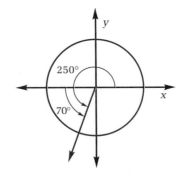

Part Two: Sample Problems

Problem 1   *Find the exact values of sin θ and cos θ if tan θ = $\frac{3}{5}$.*

Solution   There are two quadrants in which tangent is positive: Quadrants I and III. Let's first consider Quadrant I.

Remember, tan θ = $\frac{y}{x}$. The terminal ray of angle θ passes through point (5, 3). The distance from the origin to (5, 3) is $\sqrt{34}$.

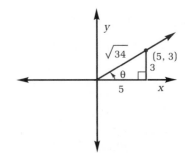

$$\cos θ = \frac{x}{r} = \frac{5}{\sqrt{34}}$$

$$\sin θ = \frac{y}{r} = \frac{3}{\sqrt{34}}$$

If θ is in Quadrant III, the only change is in the signs of the coordinates—
$\sin \theta = -\frac{3}{\sqrt{34}}$ and $\cos \theta = -\frac{5}{\sqrt{34}}$.

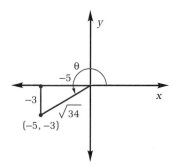

Problem 2   *Evaluate tan 90°.*

Solution   The terminal ray of a 90° angle contains (0, 1). By definition,
$\tan 90° = \frac{y}{x} = \frac{1}{0}$, which is undefined.
So tan 90° is undefined.

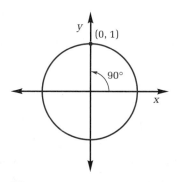

Problem 3   *Point P is ten units from the origin on the terminal ray of a 72° angle. To the nearest hundredth, find the coordinates of P.*

Solution   Let (x, y) be the coordinates of P. We use the definitions of sine and cosine to solve for x and y.

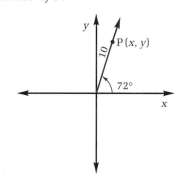

$$\cos 72° = \frac{x}{10} \qquad \sin 72° = \frac{y}{10}$$

$$0.309017 \approx \frac{x}{10} \qquad 0.9510565 \approx \frac{y}{10}$$

$$3.09 \approx x \qquad\qquad 9.51 \approx y$$

Point P is at approximately (3.09, 9.51).

Part Three: Exercises and Problems

Warm-up Exercises

1 State the reference angle for each angle.

  a 245°   **b** 320°   **c** −160°
  d 142°   **e** 57°   **f** 272°

2 Find the exact value of each of the following.

  a cos 210°   **b** sin 240°   **c** tan 150°
  d sec 300°   **e** cot 180°   **f** sin −30°

In problems 3–5, let (x, y) be a point on the terminal ray of θ, and let (x, y) be r units from the origin.

3 Find sin θ if $x = 5$ and $r = 13$.
4 Find cos θ if $x = 8$ and $y = 15$.
5 Find tan θ if $x = 8$ and $r = 10$.

In problems 6 and 7, refer to the figure.

6 Find the value of sin θ, cos θ, and tan θ.
7 Find the value of θ.

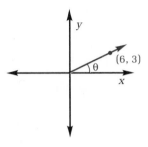

8 In what quadrant is the terminal ray of angle θ if θ is in standard position?

a sin θ > 0, cos θ > 0
b sin θ > 0, tan θ < 0
c sec θ < 0, csc θ < 0
d tan θ < 0, sec θ > 0

9 Let (−7, 24) be a point on the terminal ray of an angle θ in standard position. Find the six trig functions of θ.

10 Refer to the figure.

a Find cos θ, sin θ, and tan θ.
b Find the value of θ.

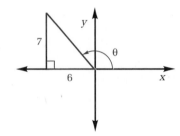

Problem Set

11 Let 0° < θ < 90°.

a If sec θ = 5, what is csc θ?
b If tan θ = $\frac{1}{3}$ and sin θ = $\frac{1}{\sqrt{10}}$, what is cos θ?

12 If θ = 208°, what are the coordinates of point A on the unit circle?

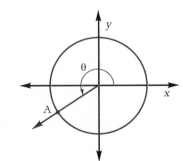

13 Which of the six trigonometric functions have undefined values? For what angles are each of these undefined?

14 If tan θ = 4, what are the coordinates of point A?

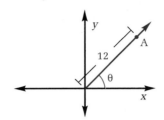

15 Solve for y, where 0° ≤ y ≤ 360°.

  a tan² y = 1   **b** sec² y = 1   **c** sin y = cos y

16 Angle θ = 35°.

  a Find the coordinates of point A.
  b Find the area of △ABC.

17 If cot $\alpha = \frac{2}{3}$ and α is in the third quadrant, what is sin α?

18 In the diagram, $\alpha = \angle POR$, $\beta = \angle QOR$, and the y-axis bisects $\overline{QP}$.

  a What is the relationship between sin α and sin β?
  b What is the relationship between cos α and cos β?
  c What is the relationship between α and β?
  d What is the measure of θ?

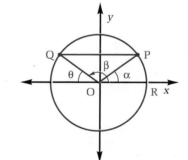

19 Find an expression in terms of a and b for each of the following.

  a tan θ
  b sin (180° − θ)
  c cos (360° − θ)
  d tan (θ + 180°)
  e cos (180° + θ)
  f sin (360° − θ)

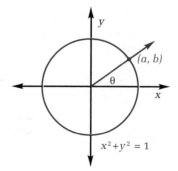

20 Find all values of α for which −360° < α < 360° and

  a cos $\alpha = \dfrac{-\sqrt{2}}{2}$ **b** tan α = −1

Problem Set, *continued*

21 Find the exact coordinates of point Q.

22 If $0° \leq \theta \leq 360°$, what values of θ satisfy each equation?

a $\cos \theta = \dfrac{1}{2}$

b $\cos^2 \theta = \dfrac{1}{2}$

c $\cos^2 \theta - 1 = 0$

d $\cos^2 \theta - \cos \theta = 0$

23 Sketch a large copy of the unit circle shown and label the coordinates of each indicated point on the circle. Explain why you need only determine the coordinates of the points in the first quadrant in order to identify the coordinates of the others.

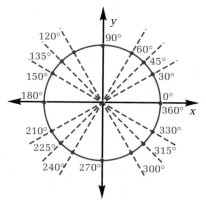

24 Solve each equation for the indicated variable.

a $2S^2 + S - 1 = 0$ for S

b $2(\sin x)^2 + \sin x - 1 = 0$ for sin x (not for x)

c $2 \sin^2 x + \sin x - 1 = 0$ for x, where $0° \leq x \leq 360°$

25 Find the exact values of sec α for which $\tan \alpha = \frac{12}{13}$.

26 Circle O has a radius of 6, and sin $\angle ACB = 0.87$. Find the ratio of the area of $\triangle ADC$ to the area of $\triangle ADB$.

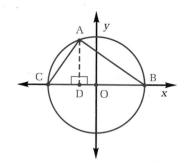

27 Find, to the nearest tenth, all angles that satisfy the given conditions.

a $-360° < \alpha < 360°$ and cos $\alpha = 0.88$

b $-360° < \theta < 360°$ and csc $\theta = 10$

28 Chuck owns a lot that borders Dempster Street and Benson Avenue.

   a What is the frontage of his lot on Benson Avenue?
   b What is the frontage of his lot on Dempster Street?

29 MNPQ is a square. If AO = 4 and θ = 145°, what is the ratio MA:AQ?

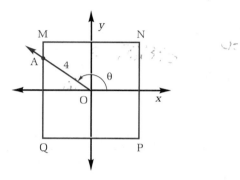

30 The area of a triangle can be computed if the measures of two sides (*a* and *b*) and the included angle (θ) are known.

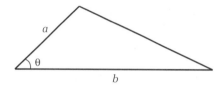

   a Find the area, to the nearest hundredth, of a triangle with sides 8 and 18 and included angle 70°.
   b At what angle, to the nearest degree, should the same two sides intersect so that the area would be 50?

31 Find the exact value of the area of △OAB.

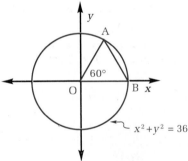

32 After a storm, Pete noticed that a tree had been blown 20° from the vertical and that when he stood directly under the top of the tree, he was 3 meters from its base. How tall had the tree been? How far above the ground was the top of the tree after the storm?

33 Express each of the six trig functions of x, where 0° < x < 90°, in terms of sin x. For example, $\cot x = \frac{\cos x}{\sin x} = \frac{\sqrt{1 - \sin^2 x}}{\sin x}$.

14.4 INVERSE TRIGONOMETRIC FUNCTIONS

Objective

After studying this section, you will be able to
- Compute the inverse trigonometric functions

Part One: Introduction

In earlier sections, you have seen that many angles can have the same terminal ray. Therefore, many angles can have the same sine and cosine.

Example Let θ be a first-quadrant angle with $\sin \theta = \frac{1}{2}$. Determine the measure of θ.

The obvious answer is $\theta = 30°$, but this is *not* the only answer. For example, 390°, −330°, 750°, and infinitely many others all have the same terminal ray. Because they differ by multiples of 360°, we can write
$$\theta = 30° + n \cdot 360°$$
where n is any integer.

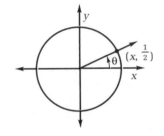

In the previous example we restricted θ to the first quadrant. What if we remove the restriction?

Example Find all angles α such that $\sin \alpha = \frac{1}{2}$.

Two points on the unit circle have y-coordinate $\frac{1}{2}$. The angles corresponding to those points include 30°, 150°, and any angle of the form $30° + n \cdot 360°$ or $150° + n \cdot 360°$, where n is any integer.

An equation like $\sin \theta = 0.6$ has infinitely many solutions for θ. In most cases, however, one solution is enough. If you use the [INV] [sin] keys, the calculator will always display one angle between −90° and 90°. We will define Arcsin, Arccos, and Arctan as the respective *inverse functions* of sine, cosine, and tangent. Recall that a function yields one output for each input. Therefore, the output of each function is one angle within the following ranges.

$$-90° \le \text{Arcsin}(x) \le 90°$$
$$0° \le \text{Arccos}(x) \le 180°$$
$$-90° < \text{Arctan}(x) < 90°$$

Try some values on your calculator and see what happens.

Example   Find the exact value of $\text{Arcsin}\left(\frac{1}{2}\right) + \text{Arccos}\left(\frac{1}{2}\right)$.

$\text{Arcsin}\left(\frac{1}{2}\right) + \text{Arccos}\left(\frac{1}{2}\right) = 30° + 60° = 90°$

Part Two: Sample Problems

Problem 1   Angle θ contains $\left(-3, -3\sqrt{3}\right)$. Find all possible values of θ.

Solution $\tan \theta = \frac{-3\sqrt{3}}{-3} = \sqrt{3}$, so θ has reference angle 60°. But $\left(-3, -3\sqrt{3}\right)$ is in Quadrant III. The angle in Quadrant III is 240°. So $\theta = 240° + n \cdot 360°$.

Problem 2   Romeo and Juliet met but had an argument. Romeo drove due east at 40 mph, and Juliet drove approximately northeasterly at 52 mph. After exactly 45 minutes, each stopped and looked for the other. Amazingly, Juliet was exactly due north of Romeo. To the nearest degree, at what angle from due east did Juliet travel?

Solution   In 45 minutes, Romeo traveled 30 miles, while Juliet traveled 39 miles. Let the positive x-axis represent Romeo's direction, and let P represent Juliet's stopping point. The x-coordinate of P is 30, and the distance from the origin is 39. So $\cos \theta = \frac{x}{r} = \frac{30}{39}$ and $\text{Arccos}\left(\frac{30}{39}\right) \approx 40°$. Juliet traveled about 40° north of due east.

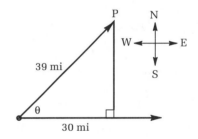

Problem 3   Find each of the following.

a $\text{Arccos}\dfrac{\sqrt{3}}{2}$ **b** $\text{arccos}\dfrac{\sqrt{3}}{2}$

Solution   **a** Recall that $\text{Arccos}\frac{\sqrt{3}}{2}$ refers to a function. We are looking for one angle in the first quadrant whose cosine is $\frac{\sqrt{3}}{2}$. $\text{Arccos}\frac{\sqrt{3}}{2} = 30°$.

b This is *not* the same as part **a.** The lowercase a in *arccos* indicates that we seek a *relation*, not a function. In this case, we are looking for all the first-quadrant and all the fourth-quadrant angles whose cosine is $\frac{\sqrt{3}}{2}$. Thus, $\text{arccos}\frac{\sqrt{3}}{2} = 30° + n \cdot 360°$ or $330° + n \cdot 360°$, where n is any integer.

Part Three: Exercises and Problems

Warm-up Exercises

1 Which of the following denote the set of all angles for which tan θ = −1?
  a $\{\theta : \theta = 135° + (360k)°$ or $\theta = 315° + (360k)°$, k is an integer$\}$
  b $\{\theta : \theta = 135° + (180k)°$, k is an integer$\}$
  c $\{\theta : \theta = 45° + (90k)°$, k is an integer$\}$

2 Write single expressions, in terms of integers k, to represent every angle coterminal with those in the diagrams.

a   **b**   **c**

3 a Find Arccos (cos 60°).
  b Find Arccos (cos 120°).
  c Find Arccos (cos 225°).
  d Does Arccos (cos x) always equal x? Why or why not?

4 Find each of the following.
  a Arccos $\dfrac{\sqrt{2}}{2}$ **b** arccos $\dfrac{\sqrt{2}}{2}$

  c Arcsin $\dfrac{\sqrt{3}}{2}$ **d** arcsin $\dfrac{\sqrt{3}}{2}$

Problem Set

5 Evaluate each of the following.
  a sin (Arccos 0.67)   **b** csc [Arcsin (−0.62)]

6 a List five positive angles coterminal with 80°.
  b List four negative angles coterminal with 80°.

7 Find each of the following.
  a Arctan −1   **b** arctan −1

8 a Find tan θ.
  b Find θ to the nearest hundredth of a degree.

9 Find all positive measures of θ less than $1000°$ for which $\cos \theta = \frac{1}{2}$.

10 Find all angles θ, where $0° \leq \theta \leq 360°$, that make each equation true.

a $\sin \theta = 0.75$ **b** $\sec \theta = 2.45$

c $\cos \theta = -0.43$ **d** $\csc \theta = \frac{2\sqrt{3}}{3}$

11 Arc-function outputs are usually restricted to angles terminating in certain quadrants in order to have a connected region over which all values of the function—both positive and negative—may be obtained. Copy each diagram and write the name of an Arc function near the diagram to which it applies.

  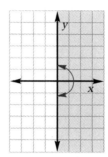

12 Angle θ contains $(6, 8)$. Find all possible values of θ.

13 Find all θ, where $0° < \theta < 360°$, for which $|\sin \theta| = \frac{\sqrt{3}}{2}$.

14 Evaluate.

a 0.63 | INV | | COS | **b** 0.63 | INV | | COS | | SIN |

c Write trigonometric expressions to describe parts **a** and **b**.

15 $\sin A = \frac{9}{13}$ and $\sin B = \frac{3}{13}$.

a Find $\frac{\sin A}{\sin B}$.

b Find $\frac{A}{B}$, where A and B are both acute.

16 Find the exact value of $\text{Arccos}\left(-\frac{1}{2}\right) + \text{Arcsin}\left(\frac{\sqrt{3}}{2}\right)$.

17 Find θ.

18 Evaluate.

a Arccos (cos 140°)   **b** Arctan (tan 210°)

c Arcsin (cos 60°)   **d** Arccos (sin 120°)

e Arcsin (cos 120°)

Problem Set, *continued*

19 Evaluate.

a $\cos\left(\text{Arccos }\dfrac{1}{2}\right)$

b Arccos (cos 300°)

20 **a** Find the length of arc AB if $\theta = 120°$.
 b Find the length of arc AB if $\theta = 480°$.
 c By what amount does your answer to part **b** exceed your answer to part **a?**

21 tan A = 6 and tan B = 3, where A and B are acute.

a Find $\dfrac{\tan A}{\tan B}$.

b Find $\dfrac{A}{B}$.

22 Bonnie and Clyde left town. Bonnie drove due west at 55 miles per hour and Clyde drove northwesterly at 64 miles per hour. After 3 hours Clyde was directly north of Bonnie. To the nearest second, what angle did Clyde's path form with Bonnie's?

23 Find each of the following.
 a sin (Arccos 0.65)
 c sec (2 Arcsin 0.39)
 b cos [Arctan (−4.62)]
 d tan [Arccos (−0.43)]

24 Find the exact value of each of the following.

a $\sin\left(\text{Arccos }\dfrac{1}{2}\right)$

b $\cos\left(2\text{ Arcsin }\dfrac{\sqrt{2}}{2}\right)$

c tan [Arctan (−1)]

d $\sec\left[\text{Arcsin}\left(-\dfrac{1}{2}\right)\right]$

e $\sin\left[\text{Arccos}\left(-\dfrac{\sqrt{3}}{2}\right)\right]$

25 Find an expression, using the variable *n* to stand for any integer, that gives all angles θ for which

a $\cos\theta = \dfrac{2}{3}$

b $\tan\theta = -1$

26 Evaluate Arccos 0.0123 to the nearest minute.

27 Find the measure of angle θ if $90° \le \theta \le 180°$.

28 Find all values of θ between 0° and 720° for which
$\sin (\theta - 20°) = \frac{1}{2}$.

29 a Find the value of the expression tan (arctan 2 + arctan 3).
  b Find the value of $\frac{2 + 3}{1 - 2 \cdot 3}$.
  c What do you notice about these two values?

30 a Solve $10(\sin x)^2 + (\sin x) - 3 = 0$ for sin x.
  b Solve the equation in part **a** for x, where $0° \le x \le 360°$.

31 The terminal ray of angle θ contains $\left(1, \sqrt{3}\right)$. Find all possible values of θ.

32 Evaluate cos (arctan 2 + arctan 3).

33 Find θ.

34 Find all values of θ for which tan $(\theta + 10°) = 1$.

35 Without using a calculator, evaluate Arccos 0.643 + Arcsin 0.643 to the nearest minute.

36 Using a calculator, try different values of x in the function
$f(x) = $ arccos (sec x). For what values is the function defined? Why is this so?

37 The length of arc BAC is 16.1 units. Find the measure of angle θ.

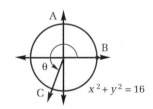

38 Find an angle θ, where $0° \le \theta \le 360°$, such that cos θ is twice as large as sin θ.

39 a Find θ in $\triangle ABC$.
  b Find DB.

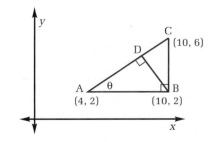

RIGHT TRIANGLES

Objectives

After studying this section, you will be able to
- Define the trigonometric functions in terms of right triangles
- Use the cofunction identities

Part One: Introduction

Trigonometric Functions and Right Triangles

The three sides of a right triangle can be classified in terms of either acute angle. Refer to △ABC in the diagram.

$\overline{AB}$ is the hypotenuse.
$\overline{BC}$ is the leg opposite ∠A.
$\overline{AC}$ is the leg adjacent to ∠A.

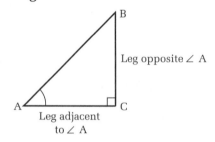

Leg opposite ∠ A

Leg adjacent to ∠ A

Example   *Refer to the triangle in the diagram and identify each of the following.*

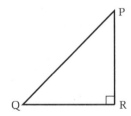

a *The hypotenuse*
$\overline{PQ}$ is the hypotenuse.

b *The leg adjacent to ∠P*
$\overline{PR}$ is the leg adjacent to ∠P.

c *The leg opposite ∠Q*
$\overline{PR}$ is the leg opposite ∠Q.

d *The leg opposite ∠P*
$\overline{QR}$ is the leg opposite ∠P.

By our previous definitions, in right triangle ABC on the coordinate plane, $\sin \angle A = \frac{BC}{AC}$, $\cos \angle A = \frac{AB}{AC}$, and so on.

Now, let's remove the axes. Since the angles and sides are unchanged, the values of the sine and cosine shouldn't change. Furthermore, the position of the triangle shouldn't matter.

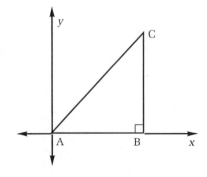

We define the following trigonometric relationships for an acute angle θ in a right triangle.

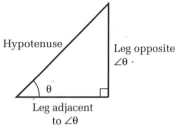

$$\sin \theta = \frac{\text{leg opposite } \theta}{\text{hypotenuse}} \qquad \cos \theta = \frac{\text{leg adjacent to } \theta}{\text{hypotenuse}} \qquad \tan \theta = \frac{\text{leg opposite } \theta}{\text{leg adjacent to } \theta}$$

From these we can write the definitions for cot θ, sec θ, and csc θ.

Example   *Refer to the right triangle and evaluate each of the following.*

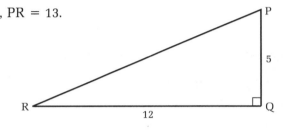

a *cos* $\angle$P
By the Pythagorean Theorem, PR = 13.
$$\cos \angle P = \frac{\text{adjacent leg}}{\text{hypotenuse}} = \frac{5}{13}$$

b *tan* $\angle$R
$$\tan \angle R = \frac{\text{opposite leg}}{\text{adjacent leg}} = \frac{5}{12}$$

c *sin* $\angle$R
$$\sin \angle R = \frac{\text{opposite leg}}{\text{hypotenuse}} = \frac{5}{13}$$

Cofunction Identities

In the preceding example cos $\angle$P and sin $\angle$R had the same value and $\angle$P and $\angle$R were complementary. Previously, we saw that $\cos 30° = \sin 60° = \frac{\sqrt{3}}{2}$ and $\cos 60° = \sin 30° = \frac{1}{2}$. In general, we have the following theorem.

> **If two angles α and β are complementary, then $\sin \alpha = \cos \beta$.**

We can see this by looking at a right triangle. The two acute angles are complementary, and the leg *opposite* one acute angle is *adjacent* to the other acute angle.

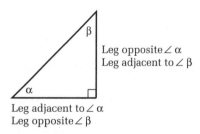

The following theorem expresses a similar relationship.

> **If two angles α and β are complementary, then $\tan \alpha = \cot \beta$ and $\sec \alpha = \csc \beta$.**

The pairs of functions that have the same values for complementary angles are sine and **co**sine, tangent and **co**tangent, and secant and **co**secant. These pairs are called **cofunctions.**
    Here is another way of expressing these cofunction theorems.

$\cos \theta = \sin (90° - \theta)$ $\cot \theta = \tan (90° - \theta)$ $\csc \theta = \sec (90° - \theta)$

Part Two: Sample Problems

Problem 1   A plane at a height of 5000 feet begins descending in a straight line toward a runway. The horizontal distance between the plane and the runway is 45,000 feet. What angle of depression must the plane use?

Solution   Since $\tan \theta = \frac{\text{opposite}}{\text{adjacent}} = \frac{5000}{45,000} \approx 0.1111$, Arctan $0.1111 \approx 6°$. The angle of depression and θ are congruent alternate interior angles. Therefore, the plane should use about a 6° angle of depression.

Problem 2   Two forest-ranger stations are 20 miles apart on a straight east-west ranger road. A forest fire is spotted. Each station spots the fire and gives its angle from the other station. From station 1, the angle is 38° north of east. From station 2, the angle is 133° measured clockwise from west. How far is the fire from the ranger road?

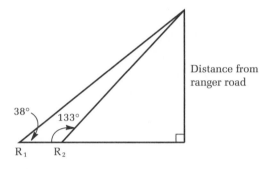

Distance from ranger road

Solution   There are two right triangles in the diagram, so we can get two equations. We have $\tan 38° = \frac{d}{x + 20}$ and $\tan 47° = \frac{d}{x}$. From the first equation, $x(\tan 38°) + 20(\tan 38°) = d$. From the second equation, $x = \frac{d}{\tan 47°} = d(\cot 47°)$. Substitute the second equation into the first, and solve.

$$d(\cot 47°)(\tan 38°) + 20(\tan 38°) = d$$
$$0.72856d + 15.6257 \approx d$$
$$d \approx 57.566 \text{ miles}$$

Part Three: Exercises and Problems

Warm-up Exercises

1 If $\cos \angle D = \frac{4}{5}$, what is EF?

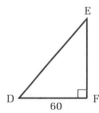

2 Simplify each expression to a single trigonometric function in a single variable.

    a $\tan (90° - \theta)$ **b** $\cos (90° - \theta)$
    c $\sec (90° - \theta)$ **d** $\cot (90° - \theta)$

3 Solve for the indicated side or angle.

a

20
68°
x

b

12
x
48°

c

θ
16
10

4 Find θ.

500
375
θ

Problem Set

5 Given that $\sin \theta = \frac{3}{5}$ and that $90° < \theta < 180°$, without using a calculator, find

    a $\cos \theta$ **b** $\tan \theta$ **c** $\cos (90° - \theta)$

    d $\cot (90° - \theta)$ **e** $\sin (90° - \theta)$

6 Find m∠ABC.

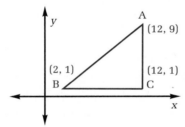

y
A
(12, 9)
(2, 1)
(12, 1)
B
C
x

7 In △FGH, ∠G is a right angle and $\tan \angle F = \frac{3}{4}$.

    a Find $\sin \angle F$.   **b** Find $\cos \angle H$.

8 Given $\tan \theta = 2$, find all values of θ to the nearest tenth of a degree.

9 What is the height of the flagpole?

12°
400'

10 Find θ.

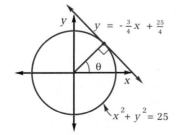

y
$y = -\frac{3}{4}x + \frac{25}{4}$
θ
x
$x^2 + y^2 = 25$

Problem Set, *continued*

11 Refer to the diagram.

    a If ∠BAO = 55°, what is sin ∠ABO?

    b If cos ∠BAO = $\frac{5}{8}$, what is sin ∠ABO?

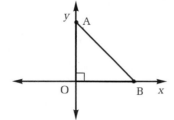

12 a Find BC.

    b Calculate the area of △ACB.

13 △ABC ~ △PQR.

    a If sin ∠A = 0.8, what is sin ∠P?

    b If BC = 8, QR = 12, and PR = 9, why is tan ∠A = tan ∠P?

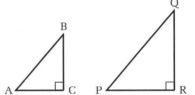

14 How much longer is $\overline{CD}$ than $\overline{BE}$?

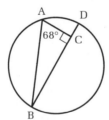

15 Find AC if AB = 52.1.

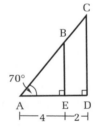

16 What is the shortest side of this figure?

17 Find θ to the nearest tenth of a degree.

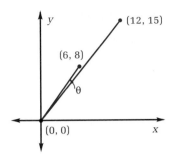

18 Jamie is 6 feet tall and is standing 500 feet from the base of a building. He looks up and sees Jason and Jessie looking out the windows of their apartments. Jason is 100 feet above the ground, and Jessie is 20 feet directly above him. Find θ.

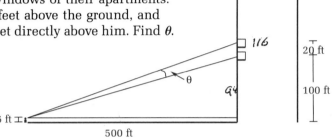

19 Find the length of arc AB.

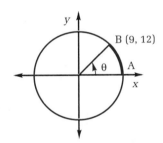

20 Segments AD and DC are tangent to circle O. $\overset{\frown}{ABC} = 200°$. The radius of circle O is 10 units. Find the area of AOCD.

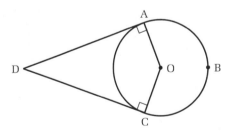

21 Consider regular pentagon PENTA. If the perimeter is 20, what is the length of apothem $\overline{GO}$?

22 If AF = 2, AE = 3, ∠B = 20°, and ∠C = 10°, what is the area of ABDC?

23 Find the ratio h_1:h_2 of the heights of the two buildings, given the angles of elevation shown. If the height h_2 is 250 feet, what is the height h_1?

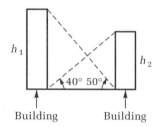

24 a Find $\sin \theta_1$ and $\sin \theta_2$.
   b Find $\frac{\sin \theta_1}{\sin \theta_2}$.
   c Find θ_1 and θ_2.
   d Find $\frac{\theta_1}{\theta_2}$.

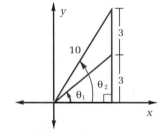

25 Starting at point A on Skull's treasure map, face due east. Rotate 45° counterclockwise. Now take 20 paces to arrive at point B. Rotate another 45° counterclockwise and take 50 paces to point C. The buried treasure is located at the midpoint of $\overline{AC}$. If you start at point A, how many degrees should you rotate counterclockwise, and then how many paces should you take, to arrive directly at the point where the treasure is buried?

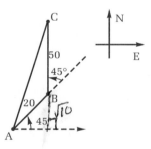

26 The equation of a line is $y = \frac{3}{7}x + 2$. What is the angle between the line and the x-axis?

27 ABCD is a parallelogram. What is the area of ABCD?

28 Find the measure of ∠θ.

29 Find m∠θ.

30 a Find ∠DBC.
   b Find the area of △BCD.

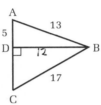

31 $\overline{PQ}$ is a tangent to circles M and N, whose radii are 6 and 3 respectively. Find m∠POM.

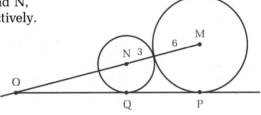

32 Find sin θ if O is the center of the circumscribed circle of regular pentagon ABCDE.

33 The graph of $\frac{x^2}{25} + \frac{y^2}{9} = 1$ is shown.
   a Find ∠ABC.
   b Find ∠ABF if F is a focus of the ellipse.

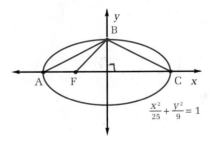

$$\frac{x^2}{25} + \frac{y^2}{9} = 1$$

34 A rhombus has diagonals of lengths 16 and 22. Find the angle measures of the rhombus.

14.6 RADIAN MEASURE

Objective

After studying this section, you will be able to
- Express angles in radians

Part One: Introduction

Arc Lengths and Radians

Until now, we have used degrees to measure angles. In this section, we will learn another way to measure angles.

In the diagram, we denote the radius of the circle by r, the central angle by θ, and the arc length by s.

Example   *If $r = 1$ and $s = 1$, what is θ?*

The circumference C is 2π. Therefore, the arc is $\frac{1}{2\pi}$ of the circle. So the angle is $\frac{1}{2\pi} \cdot 360° = \left(\frac{180}{\pi}\right)° \approx 57.2958°$.

In this example, using degrees as units was extremely inconvenient. With the radius of 1 and an arc length of 1, it seems that the central angle should also be a simple number.

We will define a new angle-measuring unit. With this new unit, the measure of the central angle in the above example is 1 unit. We call this unit a *radian.*

> **One radian is the measure of the central angle of a 1-unit arc of a unit circle.**

What if we don't have a *unit* circle? Suppose the radius were 2. Then the arc length of the same central angle would double. In general, for radius r the arc length is multiplied by r.

> **In a circle with radius r, the relation between an arc s and its central angle θ is $s = r\theta$, where θ is in radians.**

Compare this formula with the formula in degrees, $s = \frac{\theta°}{360°}(2\pi r)$.

You will find that using radians will make your work much easier. Also, radians are used in almost all mathematical applications and most computers.

Here are some basic facts about radian measure.

- A full circle is 2π radians (360°). Half a circle is π radians (180°).
- A right angle is $\frac{\pi}{2}$ radians (90°).
- We can write 2^R to denote two radians, but usually we just write 2, with no symbol. For example, we write sin 2, instead of sin 2^R. Be careful. If you write an angle measure with no degree symbol, it will be interpreted as radians.
- Your calculator has a radian mode. Be sure that you know how to put your calculator in this mode.

Example   *Evaluate.*

a *sin 1*

With your calculator in radian mode, enter 1 $\boxed{\text{sin}}$ The display on the calculator should read about 0.84147.

b *sin 1°*

With your calculator in degree mode, enter 1 $\boxed{\text{sin}}$ The display on the calculator should read about 0.01745.

Example   *What radian measure corresponds to 30°?*

Method 1 Since 30° is $\frac{1}{12}$ of a circle, the radian measure is $\frac{1}{12} \cdot 2\pi$, or $\frac{\pi}{6}$.

Method 2 The portion of the circle is the same in degrees as in radians, so $\frac{30°}{360°} = \frac{\theta}{2\pi}$. If we solve the equation, we get $\theta = \frac{\pi}{6}$.

In general, to convert between radians and degrees, we use the proportion $\frac{\theta°}{360°} = \frac{\theta^R}{2\pi^R}$.

Special Angles

The divisions between the quadrants in degrees are 0°, 90°, 180°, 270°, and 360°. In radians, these angles are 0, $\frac{\pi}{2}$, π, $\frac{3\pi}{2}$, and 2π.

The special angles we studied before were the multiples of 30° and 45°. We now wish to express these in radians, as shown in the figure. You will need to learn the values in the first quadrant and to understand how the reference angles relate to the angles in the other quadrants.

Part Two: Sample Problems

Problem 1   *Evaluate cos* (3.14^R).

Solution   Put your calculator in radian mode. Now enter 3.14 $\boxed{\cos}$. The result should be approximately -0.99999872. It makes sense that cos 3.14 is close to -1, since the angle is very close to π. Therefore, the x-coordinate of the point on the unit circle is very close to -1.

Problem 2   *What is the range of values for Arcsin x in radians?*

Solution   In degrees, we had $-90° \le$ Arcsin x $\le 90°$. Changing to radians, we have $\frac{-\pi}{2} \le$ Arcsin x $\le \frac{\pi}{2}$.

Problem 3   *Using radians, find the exact value of Arccos* $\left(\frac{-1}{2}\right)$.

Solution   In radians, Arccos will be between 0 and π. So Arccos $\left(\frac{-1}{2}\right) = \frac{2\pi}{3}$.

Part Three: Exercises and Problems

Warm-up Exercises

1 Convert the following angles measured in degrees to radian measure. Leave your answer in terms of π.

   a 60°   **b** 210°   **c** $-75°$ **d** 450°   **e** $-30°$

2 Convert the following angles given in radians to degree measure.

   a $\frac{\pi}{4}$ **b** $\frac{-7\pi}{6}$ **c** $\frac{24\pi}{9}$ **d** $\frac{-\pi}{3}$ **e** $\frac{-2\pi}{3}$

3 Find the length of arc AB if $\theta = 110°$.

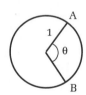

Problem Set

4 A bicycle wheel is 27 inches in diameter. How far does the wheel travel in 15 revolutions?

5 Give the coordinates of points A and B.

6 Convert each angle in degrees to its decimal approximation in radians. Give your answer to the nearest hundredth.

   a 50°   **b** $-400°$ **c** 25°   **d** 206°   **e** $-75°$

7 Find sin ∠B.

8 Express each angle in radians.

  a Full rotation   **b** $\frac{1}{2}$ rotation

  c $\frac{1}{3}$ rotation   **d** $\frac{2}{5}$ rotation

In problems 9–23, find the value of each.

9 $\sin \dfrac{3\pi}{2}$ **10** $\cos \pi$ **11** $\tan \dfrac{\pi}{4}$ **12** $\cos\left(-\dfrac{\pi}{2}\right)$ **13** $\cot \dfrac{\pi}{6}$

14 $\sin\left(-\dfrac{5\pi}{6}\right)$ **15** $\cos \dfrac{3\pi}{4}$ **16** $\sin \dfrac{4\pi}{3}$ **17** $\tan\left(\dfrac{-\pi}{6}\right)$ **18** $\sec \dfrac{\pi}{4}$

19 $\csc \dfrac{2\pi}{3}$ **20** $\tan\left(-\dfrac{7\pi}{6}\right)$ **21** $\sec \dfrac{5\pi}{3}$ **22** $\cos\left(\dfrac{-5\pi}{2}\right)$ **23** $\sin \dfrac{11\pi}{3}$

24 2^R is approximately how many degrees?

25 Find the length of arc s.

26 a Find tan ∠CBD and tan ∠ABD.

  b Find $\dfrac{\tan \angle CBD}{\tan \angle ABD}$.

  c Find ∠CBD and ∠ABD.

  d Find $\dfrac{\angle CBD}{\angle ABD}$.

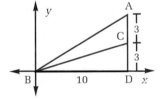

27 Find the length of arc AB.

28 Find the exact value of each of the following.

  a $\sin \dfrac{\pi}{6}$ **b** $\tan \dfrac{\pi}{3}$ **c** $\cos \pi$ **d** $\sec\left(\dfrac{-\pi}{6}\right)$ **e** $\cot \dfrac{\pi}{4}$

29 Evaluate.

  a $\sin 0.7^R$ **b** $\cos 1.2^R$ **c** $\tan 4.2^R$

30 Find x in radians.

  a Arcsin $0.1357 = x$ **b** Arctan $-0.487 = x$

Problem Set, *continued*

31 If $\sin \theta^R = 0.8479$, what is the measure at θ in degrees, where $0° < \theta < 90°$?

32 Solve for x in each triangle. Angles are in radian measure.

a   **b**   **c**

d   **e**

33 Solve x Arcsin $0.5 = (x - 1)$ Arccos 0.5 for x.

34 AB = AC. Find θ^R and θ in degrees.

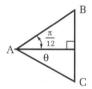

In problems 35–38, consider an angle θ whose terminal ray passes through $\left(\frac{7}{25}, \frac{24}{25}\right)$.

35 Explain why the point $\left(\frac{7}{25}, \frac{24}{25}\right)$ must lie on the unit circle.

36 Explain why $\cos \theta = \frac{7}{25}$ if $\sin \theta = \frac{24}{25}$ and $0° \leq \theta \leq 90°$.

37 Find the value of $\tan \theta$.

38 Find the value of $\sec \theta$.

39 Which triangle has the greater area?

40 Find the perimeter of the shaded region.

41 Solve for $0 \le x \le 2\pi$.

    a $\sin^2 x = \dfrac{3}{4}$
                  b $2 \cos^2 x + \cos x = 0$
               c $\sqrt{3} \sin x = \cos x$

42 A line has a slope of $-\frac{2}{3}$ and passes through the origin. What angle does it form with the positive x-axis, measured counterclockwise?

43 The graph shown represents the equation $y = \sin x$. Find the values of y indicated by the letters A, B, C, D, E, and F.

44 Find $\angle ABC$.

45 **a** Find $\cos \theta$.
    b Find $(\cos \theta)^2 + (\sin \theta)^2$.

46 Arc AQ is an arc of circle O. Arc ABQ is an arc of circle P.
Length of arc AQ = 16″
OA = 24″
$\angle APQ = 2.5 \angle AOQ$
Find the area of the shaded region.

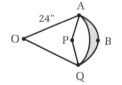

47 If $\angle A = 1.2^R$, AB = AC, and A is the center of arc BC, what is the length of $\overline{BC}$?

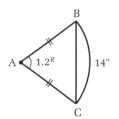

TRIGONOMETRIC RELATIONSHIPS

Objectives

After studying this section, you will be able to
- Recognize odd and even functions
- Identify relationships between trigonometric functions of special angles

Part One: Introduction

Odd and Even Functions

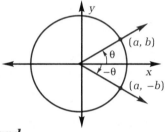

In the figure, we have marked the angles θ and $-\theta$. The points of intersection of these angles and the unit circle have the same x-coordinates and opposite y-coordinates. This relationship suggests the following theorems.

> *For all angles θ, cos $(-\theta)$ = cos θ, and sin $(-\theta)$ = $-$sin θ.*

> *For all angles θ (where cos $\theta \neq 0$), tan $(-\theta)$ = $-$tan θ and sec $(-\theta)$ = sec θ.*

> *For all angles θ (where sin $\theta \neq 0$), cot $(-\theta)$ = $-$cot θ and csc $(-\theta)$ = $-$csc θ.*

Mathematicians sometimes distinguish between **odd functions** and **even functions**. A function f is said to be odd if $f(-x) = -f(x)$ for all values of x. The graph of an odd function is symmetric about the origin. In an even function, $f(-x) = f(x)$ for all values of x. The graph of an even function is symmetric about the y-axis.

The preceding theorems indicate that of the trigonometric functions, sine, tangent, cotangent, and cosecant are odd, whereas cosine and secant are even. You will find a knowledge of these properties useful when you are introduced to the graphs of the trigonometric functions in Chapter 16.

Example   *Simplify the expression cos $(-\theta)$ tan $(-\theta)$.*

$$\cos (-\theta) \tan (-\theta)$$

$$= \cos (-\theta) \cdot \frac{\sin (-\theta)}{\cos (-\theta)}$$

$$= \sin (-\theta)$$
$$= -\sin \theta$$

Supplementary and Complementary Angles

Let's restate the cofunction identities in terms of radians.

$$\sin \theta = \cos \left(\frac{\pi}{2} - \theta\right) \qquad \tan \theta = \cot \left(\frac{\pi}{2} - \theta\right) \qquad \sec \theta = \csc \left(\frac{\pi}{2} - \theta\right)$$

The cofunctions of complementary angles are equal.

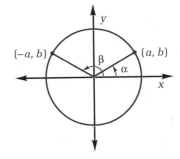

Now let's look at supplementary angles. Remember, two angles are supplementary if the sum of their measures is π. In the figure shown, angles α and β are supplementary. For these angles, the x-coordinates on the unit circle are opposites, and the y-coordinates are equal.

> **For all θ, $\sin (\pi - \theta) = \sin \theta$ and $\cos (\pi - \theta) = -\cos \theta$.**

Can you state the appropriate theorems for the other four trigonometric functions?

Other Relationships

Is there a relationship between $\cos \theta$ and $\cos (\theta + \pi)$?

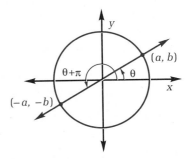

In the figure, we see that the angles differ by π, or half a circle. Thus, the x-coordinates are opposite and $\cos (\theta + \pi) = -\cos \theta$.

Many such relationships exist. The idea is not to memorize all of them but to understand them and be able to look at the unit circle and work them out for yourself when you need them.

Part Two: Sample Problems

Problem 1   Evaluate $\tan \left(\frac{13\pi}{7}\right) - \tan \left(\frac{13\pi}{7} + 2\pi\right)$.

Solution   The two angles differ by 2π. Thus, they are coterminal and have the same tangent. This difference is 0.

Problem 2   Use congruent triangles to justify that $\sin \theta = \cos \left(\frac{\pi}{2} - \theta\right)$.

Solution   If we draw a diagram as shown, we see that both triangles are right triangles having an acute angle θ and congruent hypotenuses of length 1. Thus, the two triangles are congruent. The y-coordinate of point A is therefore equal to the x-coordinate of point B, so $\sin \theta = \cos \left(\frac{\pi}{2} - \theta\right)$.

Part Three: Exercises and Problems

Warm-up Exercises

1 Use a calculator to decide whether each of the following is True or False for $\theta = 125°$.

a $\cos(-\theta) = \cos\theta$ **b** $\sin(-\theta) = -\sin\theta$ **c** $\tan(-\theta) = -\tan\theta$

d $\sec(-\theta) = \sec\theta$ **e** $\cot(-\theta) = -\cot\theta$

2 Use the unit circle shown to evaluate each of the following in terms of a and b.

a $\cos\theta$ **b** $\cos(\pi - \theta)$

c $\sin\theta$ **d** $\sin(\pi - \theta)$

e $\sin(\theta + \pi)$ **f** $\cos(\theta + \pi)$

g $\cos(-\theta)$ **h** $\sin(-\theta)$

3 Evaluate each of the following. What do you observe?

a $\cos\left(\dfrac{\pi}{6}\right)$ **b** $\cos\left(\dfrac{-\pi}{6}\right)$ **c** $\cos\left(\dfrac{\pi}{4}\right)$

d $\cos\left(\dfrac{-\pi}{4}\right)$ **e** $\cos\left(\dfrac{-2\pi}{3}\right)$ **f** $\cos\left(\dfrac{2\pi}{3}\right)$

4 Evaluate each of the following. What do you observe?

a $\sin\left(\dfrac{\pi}{6}\right)$ **b** $\sin\left(\dfrac{-\pi}{6}\right)$ **c** $\sin\left(\dfrac{\pi}{4}\right)$

d $\sin\left(\dfrac{-\pi}{4}\right)$ **e** $\sin\left(\dfrac{-2\pi}{3}\right)$ **f** $\sin\left(\dfrac{2\pi}{3}\right)$

5 Refer to the figure.

a Find $\sin(-\theta)$.

b Find $\cos(-\theta)$.

c Find $\tan(-\theta)$.

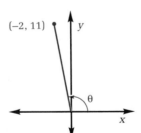

6 Indicate whether each statement is True or False.

a $\sin(-65°) = -\sin 65°$ **b** $\tan 140° = -\tan(-140°)$

c $\cos 47° = -\cos(-47°)$ **d** $\sin 62° + \sin(-57°) = -\sin(-62°) - \sin 57°$

7 Copy the figure and sketch $\pi - \theta$, $\pi + \theta$, and $-\theta$.

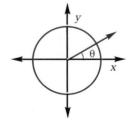

Problem Set

8 Rewrite each expression in terms of $\sin \theta$ or $\cos \theta$.

a $\sin (90° - \theta)$ **b** $\cos (270° - \theta)$

c $\sin \left(\dfrac{\pi}{2} - \theta\right)$ **d** $\cos \left(\dfrac{\pi}{2} + \theta\right)$

e $\sin (\pi + \theta)$

9 Evaluate each of the following for $\sin \alpha = 0.2$.

a $\sin (\pi - \alpha)$ **b** $\sin (\pi + \alpha)$ **c** $\sin (2\pi + \alpha)$

d $\sin (4\pi + \alpha)$ **e** $\sin (6\pi + \alpha)$

10 For each graph, indicate whether the function represented is even or odd.

a   **b**   **c**

d   **e**   **f**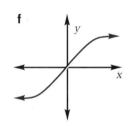

11 Write each of the following as a function of a positive acute angle.

a $\dfrac{\sin (-35°)}{\cos 35°}$ **b** $\tan (-80°)$

12 Refer to the figure to find each of the following.

a $\cos \alpha$
b $\sin \beta$
c $\alpha + \beta$

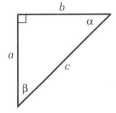

13 Copy and complete the table.

θ	2π	$\dfrac{13\pi}{6}$	$\dfrac{9\pi}{4}$	$\dfrac{7\pi}{3}$	$\dfrac{5\pi}{2}$
$\sin \theta$					
$\cos \theta$					
$\tan \theta$					
$\cot \theta$					

Problem Set, *continued*

14 Refer to the figure.

    a Express α in terms of θ.
    b Find the value of sin θ.
    c Find $\angle$AOB.
    d Find the value of cos α.

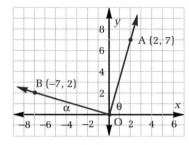

15 Find the exact value of each of the following.

    a CE
    b cos $\angle$BAC
    c tan $\angle$ACB
    d sin $\angle$AEC

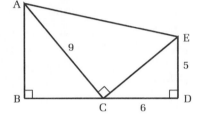

16 Rewrite each expression in terms of sin θ.

    a $3 \sin \theta + 5 \cos \left(\dfrac{\pi}{2} - \theta\right)$
          b $4 \sin (\pi - \theta) - 2 \sin (\pi + \theta)$

17 Show that each statement is true.

    a $\sin (90° - \theta) = \sin 90° \cos \theta - \cos 90° \sin \theta$
    b $\cos (90° - \theta) = \cos 90° \cos \theta + \sin 90° \sin \theta$

18 Use the diagram to find each of the following.

    a $\tan (180° - \theta)$
    b $\tan (180° + \theta)$
    c $\tan \theta$
    d $\tan (-\theta)$

 19 Which is longer—$\overline{BC}$ or $\overline{CD}$?

 20 Evaluate each of the following.

    a $2 \sin 170° + \sin 10° + 3 \cos 80°$
    b $\cos 200° + \cos 20° + 2 \sin 50° + 3 \cos 40°$

21 Prove that $\sin\left(\theta + \frac{\pi}{3}\right)$ and $\cos\left(\frac{\pi}{6} - \theta\right)$ are equal.

22 The terminal ray of θ contains the point $(-3, 4)$.

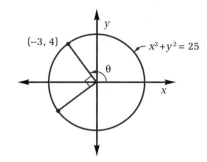

   a What point on the same circle is on the terminal ray of $90° + \theta$?

   b Find $\cos(90° + \theta)$, $\sin(90° + \theta)$, and $\tan(90° + \theta)$.

23 Refer to the figure.

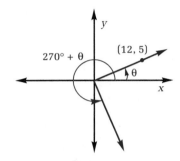

   a Identify a point on the terminal side of $270° + \theta$.

   b Find the exact values of $\cos(270° + \theta)$ and $\sin\theta$.

24 State whether each of the following functions is even or odd.

   a $f(x) = |x^2 - 4|$ **b** $f(x) = x^3 - 2x$

   c $f(x) = x^2 + \cos x$ **d** $f(x) = \cos^2 x$

   e $f(x) = \sin x^2$ **f** $f(x) = x + \sin x$

25 Express each of the following as an equivalent function of an angle between 0 radians and $\frac{\pi}{2}$ radians.

   a $\sin\left(\dfrac{1991\pi}{4}\right)$ **b** $\cos\left(\dfrac{-542\pi}{12}\right)$ **c** $\tan\left(\dfrac{-32\pi}{9}\right)$

26 Simplify $\displaystyle\sum_{n=1}^{9} \sin[(-1)^n x]$.

27 Find the following for $\theta = \frac{\pi}{6}$.

   a $\sin\theta$ **b** $\cos\theta$ **c** $\sin\left(\dfrac{\pi}{2} - \theta\right)$

   d $\cos\left(\dfrac{\pi}{2} - \theta\right)$ **e** $\sin(\pi + \theta)$ **f** $\cos(\pi + \theta)$

28 A tunnel is being dug through a mountain, a distance of two miles. The work team starting at A digs directly toward B at a rate of 4 feet per hour and an angle of depression of θ. The team at B, progressing 5 feet per hour, miscalculates and digs at an angle (α) that is $\left(\frac{1}{60}\right)°$ smaller than θ. What is the vertical error at the point where the tunnels meet?

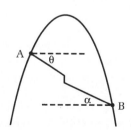

Problem Set, *continued*

29 An approximation for sin x, where x is in radians, is
$\sin x \approx f(x) = \frac{x}{1!} - \frac{x^3}{3!} + \frac{x^5}{5!} - \frac{x^7}{7!} + \frac{x^9}{9!}$. Prove that f is an odd function.

30 An approximation for cos x, where x is in radians, is
$\cos x \approx f(x) = 1 - \frac{x^2}{2!} + \frac{x^4}{4!} - \frac{x^6}{6!} + \frac{x^8}{8!} - \frac{x^{10}}{10!}$. Prove that f is an even function.

CAREER PROFILE

GRAPHING THE WAVES OF THE HEART
Beba Ugarriza provides an image of electrical impulses

Beba Ugarriza is manager of the noninvasive cardiovascular laboratory at a Miami-area hospital. Her position involves overseeing the work of *electrocardiogram* (EKG) specialists. One of an EKG specialist's responsibilities is to operate an *electrocardiograph,* a machine that records the electrical impulses associated with the contraction and relaxation of the heart. The electrocardiogram is a graph of the amount of voltage generated by the heart against the time required for that voltage to travel through the heart. The units represented on the graph are thousandths of volts against tenths of seconds. Like the graphs of trigonometric functions, a normal EKG is periodic.

"The EKG specialist's primary responsibility, which is crucial," says Ms. Ugarriza, "is to ensure that the recordings are diagnostically pure and consistently accurate. Each EKG machine must be calibrated so that a one-millivolt standardization signal produces a deflection of exactly ten millimeters."

Some of the problems that an EKG can help identify include blocked vessels, high blood pressure, thyroid disease, and even certain kinds of malnutrition. An EKG can both identify and locate enlargement or irregularity.

To ensure accuracy, the specialist must be able to recognize variations from normal that might be caused by improper calibration of the electrocardiograph or improper administration of the EKG. Hence, the specialist must be familiar with the several distinct waves produced by

each heartbeat. In a healthy heart, these are the P, Q, R, S, and T waves. The P wave represents the contraction of the atrium, which pushes blood into the ventricle. Waves Q, R, and S represent contraction of the ventricle, which pushes blood out into the body. The T wave represents the *repolarization* of the heart as the cells recharge themselves in preparation for another impulse. Sometimes, a U wave follows the T wave. A U wave can indicate low levels of potassium.

Ms. Ugarriza studied pharmaceutical science at the University of Havana. Her education and training have been rich in mathematics.

CHAPTER SUMMARY

CONCEPTS AND PROCEDURES

After studying this chapter, you should be able to
- Measure angles as rotations (14.1)
- Determine intersections of rays with the unit circle (14.1)
- Calculate the sine, cosine, tangent, cotangent, secant, and cosecant of an angle (14.2)
- Use the Pythagorean identities (14.2)
- Define the trigonometric functions by coordinates (14.3)
- Use special angles and reference angles to compute trigonometric functions (14.3)
- Compute the inverse trigonometric functions (14.4)
- Define the trigonometric functions in terms of right triangles (14.5)
- Use the cofunction identities (14.5)
- Describe angles in radians (14.6)
- Recognize odd and even functions (14.7)
- Identify relationships between trigonometric functions of special angles (14.7)

VOCABULARY

central angle (14.1)
cofunction (14.5)
cosecant (14.2)
cosine (14.2)
cotangent (14.2)
coterminal angles (14.1)
degree mode (14.2)
even function (14.7)
initial ray (14.1)
inverse trigonometric function (14.4)

odd function (14.7)
Pythagorean identities (14.2)
radian (14.6)
reference angle (14.3)
secant (14.2)
sine (14.2)
standard position (14.1)
tangent (14.2)
terminal ray (14.1)
unit circle (14.1)

THEOREMS

$\cos^2 \theta + \sin^2 \theta = 1$
$\sec^2 \theta = 1 + \tan^2 \theta$
$\csc^2 \theta = 1 + \cot^2 \theta$
$\cos \theta = \sin (90° - \theta)$
$\cot \theta = \tan (90° - \theta)$
$\csc \theta = \sec (90° - \theta)$
$s = r\theta$

$\cos (-\theta) = \cos \theta$
$\sin (-\theta) = -\sin \theta$
$\tan (-\theta) = -\tan \theta$
$\sec (-\theta) = \sec \theta$
$\cot (-\theta) = -\cot \theta$
$\csc (-\theta) = -\csc \theta$
$\sin (\pi - \theta) = \sin \theta$
$\cos (\pi - \theta) = -\cos \theta$

REVIEW PROBLEMS

1 The terminal ray of an angle passes through the point $(-5, 12)$. Find the values of the six trigonometric functions for this angle.

2 Find all angles between $-360°$ and $360°$ that have a reference angle of $48°$.

3 Evaluate each of the following.

  a $\sin\left(\arcsin\dfrac{1}{2}\right)$

  b $\sin\left(\text{Arcsin}\,\dfrac{1}{2}\right)$

  c $\cos\left(\text{Arcsin}\,\dfrac{1}{2}\right)$

  d $\cos\left(\arcsin\dfrac{1}{2}\right)$

4 The angle of elevation from a boat to the top of a cliff is $23°$. A sign is directly on top of the cliff. The angle of elevation from the boat to the top of the sign is $24°$. If the sign is 40 feet high, how far is the boat from the cliff?

5 The graph represents the function $y = \cos x$, where each x is an angle measure in degrees. What values of x are represented by points A, B, C, D, E, F, G, and H?

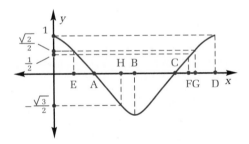

6 Evaluate each of the following.

  a $\cos\left(\dfrac{35\pi}{7}\right) - \sin 12\pi$

  b $\tan\left(2\pi + \dfrac{5\pi}{4}\right)$

  c $\sec\left(\dfrac{15\pi}{2}\right)$

  d $\tan\left(\dfrac{13\pi}{2}\right)$

7 Find the area of the rectangle shown.

8 A point on the terminal side of angle θ is $(-18, 15)$. If $0° \le \theta < 360°$, what is the measure of θ?

9 Find the value of each function.

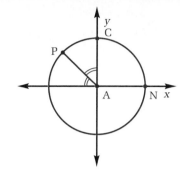

   a sin ∠CAN
   b cos ∠CAN
   c sin ∠PAN
   d cos ∠PAN
   e tan ∠PAN
   f sin ∠CAP

10 If $\ell_1 \parallel \ell_2$, what is $\sin \theta$?

11 The function $y = f(x)$, graphed at right, is odd.

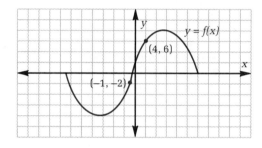

   a Find $f(-4)$.
   b Find $f(1)$.

12 In circle O with radius 18, arc AB has a length of 3π. Find the measure of central angle AOB.

13 Suppose that $\sin \theta = -0.3542$.

   a Let $270° < \theta < 360°$. Find $\cos \theta$ without actually finding the value of θ.
   b If $180° < \theta < 270°$, what is $\cos \theta$?

14 Sig elevates his telescope 55° to spot the top of a building from a point on the ground 200 feet away.

   a What trigonometric function of the 55° angle is equal to $\frac{h}{200}$?
   b Use this function to find the height of the building.

15 Convert each of the following radian measures to degrees. Round your answers to the nearest hundredth.

   a 4.56   **b** −3.79   **c** 15.28   **d** −5.25   **e** −1

Review Problems, *continued*

16 If the pendulum shown swings through a 10° arc, θ = 5°. If the pendulum is on a 33-inch long string, what is the vertical difference between its position at the bottom of a swing and at the end of a swing?

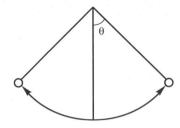

17 Find the points on the unit circle, $x^2 + y^2 = 1$, that are also on the graph of $y = -\frac{3}{4}x$.

18 If sin x = $\frac{1}{3}$ and tan x is negative, what is cos x?

19 If cos x = $\frac{4}{5}$ and csc x < 0, what is tan x?

20 Simplify each of the following in terms of the given function of θ.

   a 3 tan θ − 5 tan (−θ)   **b** −6 sin (−θ) + 3 sin θ

   c 4 cos (−θ) − 2 cos θ

21 For each triangle, find the radian measure of ∠P in terms of π.

   a   **b**   **c**

22 Write an expression representing the values of θ for which tan 2θ = 1.

23 Find the exact value of each of the following.

   a sin 45°   **b** tan 135°   **c** cos 225°

   d sin 315°   **e** cos −135°   **f** tan 225°

24 Find the missing side lengths in each triangle.

   a   **b**   **c**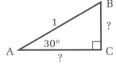

25 If cos θ = 0.76 and 0° ≤ θ < 90°, what is the degree measure of θ?

CHAPTER TEST

1 Find the value of r.

2 Find the values of the six trigonometric functions for $\theta = 200°$.

3 Which function has a greater value?
  a $\sin \theta$ or $\csc \theta$ (where $0° < \theta < 90°$)
  b $\sin \theta$ or $\cos \theta$ (where $90° < \theta < 180°$)
  c $\tan \theta$ or $\tan (180° + \theta)$

4 Refer to the figure to find the following.
  a $\sin \angle A$ and $\sin \angle B$

  b $\dfrac{\sin \angle A}{\sin \angle B}$

  c $\dfrac{m\angle A}{m\angle B}$

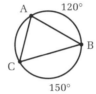

5 Find the measure of θ.

6 Explain why $\cos \theta = \sin \alpha$.

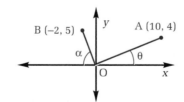

7 Find the coordinates of point P to the nearest hundredth.

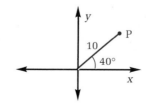

TRIGONOMETRIC IDENTITIES AND EQUATIONS

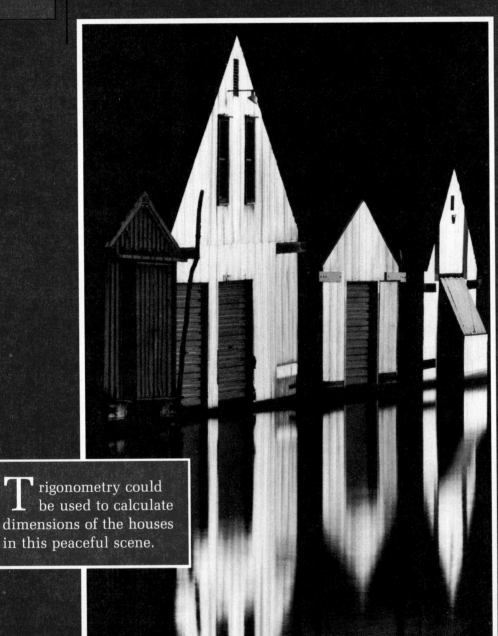

Trigonometry could be used to calculate dimensions of the houses in this peaceful scene.

BASIC TRIGONOMETRIC IDENTITIES

Objective

After studying this section, you will be able to
- Prove trigonometric identities

Part One: Introduction

By using the identities presented in Chapter 14 together with some algebra, it is possible to prove many additional identities involving the trigonometric functions. Working these proofs will show you how to transform complicated trigonometric expressions into simpler forms.

To prove that an equation is an identity, we must show that the equation holds for *every* angle θ for which both sides of the equation are defined. That is, the object is to show that the expression on the left side of the equation really does equal the expression on the right side of the equation for all possible values of θ. You may do this by performing any valid operations on these separate expressions. You may *not* use the algebraic properties of equations, however. Consider the following examples.

Example Prove that $\frac{1}{\sec^2 \theta} + \frac{1}{\csc^2 \theta} = 1$.

Often it is a good idea to change the problem into terms involving only $\sin \theta$ and $\cos \theta$.

	Left Side	**Right Side**
	$\dfrac{1}{\sec^2 \theta} + \dfrac{1}{\csc^2 \theta}$	$= 1$
Use the definitions of $\sec \theta$ and $\csc \theta$	$= \cos^2 \theta + \sin^2 \theta$	
Use a Pythagorean identity	$= 1$	

We have shown the left side to be the same as the right side, so the equation is an identity.

Example   *Prove that $(\sin \theta)(\csc \theta - \sin \theta) = \cos^2 \theta$. Note any restrictions.*

	Left Side	**Right Side**
	$(\sin \theta)(\csc \theta - \sin \theta)$	$= \cos^2 \theta$
Distribute	$= \sin \theta \cdot \csc \theta - \sin^2 \theta$	
Use the definition of $\csc \theta$	$= \sin \theta \cdot \dfrac{1}{\sin \theta} - \sin^2 \theta$	
	$= 1 - \sin^2 \theta$	
Use a Pythagorean identity	$= \cos^2 \theta$	

Since the left side is identical to the right side, the equation is an identity. Note that because $\csc \theta = \frac{1}{\sin \theta}$, the left side of the original equation is not defined when $\sin \theta = 0$. So $\sin \theta \neq 0$ is a restriction on the identity.

Example   *Prove the identity $\dfrac{2 \cos^2 \theta - \cos \theta - 1}{\cos \theta - 1} = \dfrac{\sec \theta + 2}{\sec \theta}$. Note any restrictions.*

Since both sides of the equation are fairly complicated, it makes sense to simplify each side individually.

Left Side

$$\dfrac{2 \cos^2 \theta - \cos \theta - 1}{\cos \theta - 1}$$

$$= \dfrac{(2 \cos \theta + 1)(\cos \theta - 1)}{\cos \theta - 1}$$

$$= 2 \cos \theta + 1$$

Right Side

$$= \dfrac{\sec \theta + 2}{\sec \theta}$$

$$= \dfrac{\dfrac{1}{\cos \theta} + 2}{\dfrac{1}{\cos \theta}}$$

$$= \left(\dfrac{1}{\cos \theta} + 2\right) \cdot \cos \theta$$

$$= 1 + 2 \cos \theta$$

Note that the left side is undefined for $\cos \theta = 1$ and that because $\sec \theta = \frac{1}{\cos \theta}$, the right side is undefined for $\cos \theta = 0$. So the restrictions are $\cos \theta \neq 0$ and $\cos \theta \neq 1$.

We summarize the process of proving identities with some helpful hints.

A Strategy for Proving Identities

1. **Separate the equation into a left-side expression and a right-side expression and work with these separately.**

2. **Simplify the more complicated side of the equation first, looking for ways to use the basic trigonometric identities.**

3. **After simplifying one side as much as you can, work on the other side until both sides are the same.**

4. **If no other approach comes to mind, try expressing both sides in terms of sines and cosines.**

Part Two: Sample Problems

Problem 1   Prove that $(\cos \theta)(1 - \cos^2 \theta) = \cot \theta \cdot \sin^3 \theta$. Note any restrictions.

Solution

Left Side	**Right Side**
$(\cos \theta)(1 - \cos^2 \theta)$	$= \cot \theta \cdot \sin^3 \theta$
$= \cos \theta \cdot \sin^2 \theta$	$= \dfrac{\cos \theta}{\sin \theta} \cdot \sin^3 \theta$
	$= \cos \theta \cdot \sin^2 \theta$

The right side of the identity is undefined for $\sin \theta = 0$, so $\sin \theta \neq 0$ is a restriction.

Problem 2   Prove that $\dfrac{\sin \theta}{1 - \cos \theta} = \csc \theta + \cot \theta$. Note any restrictions.

Solution   Multiplying a fraction by a form of 1 is often a useful technique in proving identities.

Left Side

$$\dfrac{\sin \theta}{1 - \cos \theta}$$

Multiply by a form of 1
$$= \dfrac{\sin \theta}{1 - \cos \theta} \cdot \dfrac{1 + \cos \theta}{1 + \cos \theta}$$

$$= \dfrac{(\sin \theta)(1 + \cos \theta)}{1 - \cos^2 \theta}$$

Use a Pythagorean identity
$$= \dfrac{(\sin \theta)(1 + \cos \theta)}{\sin^2 \theta}$$

Simplify
$$= \dfrac{1 + \cos \theta}{\sin \theta}$$

Right Side

$$\csc \theta + \cot \theta$$

Use the definitions of $\csc \theta$ and $\cot \theta$
$$= \dfrac{1}{\sin \theta} + \dfrac{\cos \theta}{\sin \theta}$$

Add the fractions
$$= \dfrac{1 + \cos \theta}{\sin \theta}$$

The left side of the original identity is undefined for $\cos \theta = 1$. The right side is undefined for $\sin \theta = 0$. Therefore, the restrictions are $\cos \theta \neq 1$ and $\sin \theta \neq 0$.

Problem 3   Show that the equation $\dfrac{\sin \theta}{1 + \sin \theta} = \dfrac{1 - \sin \theta}{\sin \theta}$ is not an identity.

Solution   To show that an equation is not an identity, we need only find one value of θ for which the left side and the right side are not equal. Let's try $\theta = 30°$.

	Left Side	Right Side

$$\frac{\sin \theta}{1 + \sin \theta} \qquad = \frac{1 - \sin \theta}{\sin \theta}$$

$$= \frac{\sin 30°}{1 + \sin 30°} \qquad = \frac{1 - \sin 30°}{\sin 30°}$$

$$= \frac{\dfrac{1}{2}}{1 + \dfrac{1}{2}} \qquad = \frac{1 - \dfrac{1}{2}}{\dfrac{1}{2}}$$

$$= \frac{1}{3} \qquad = 1$$

Since the expressions are not equal for $\theta = 30°$, the equation is not an identity.

Part Three: Exercises and Problems

Warm-up Exercises

1 Prove that $\csc^4 \theta = (1 + \cot^2 \theta)^2$. State restrictions.

2 Prove that $(\cos^2 \theta)(\tan^2 \theta + 1) = 1$. State restrictions.

3 Determine whether each statement is True or False.
  a $\csc^2 \theta - \cot^2 \theta = 1$
  b $\tan^2 \theta = (\sec \theta + 1)(\sec \theta - 1)$
  c $\sin^2 \theta = \cos^2 \theta - 1$

4 Determine whether each statement is true for $\theta = \frac{\pi}{6}$.
  a $\tan \theta \cdot \cos \theta = \sin \theta$
  b $\csc^2 \theta - 1 = \cot^2 \theta$
  c $(\sin \theta + \cos \theta)^2 = 1 + \sin (2\theta)$
  d $\cos (2\theta) = \cos^2 \theta - \sin^2 \theta$

5 Determine whether each statement is true for $\theta = \frac{\pi}{2}$.
  a $\cos \theta \cdot \sec \theta = 1$
  b $\dfrac{\sin \theta}{\cos \theta} = \tan \theta$

6 Prove that $\frac{1}{\cos^2 \theta} - \frac{\sin^2 \theta}{\cos^2 \theta} = 1$. State restrictions.

7 Prove that $\frac{\cos^2 \theta - \sin^2 \theta}{\cos \theta - \sin \theta} = \cos \theta + \sin \theta$. State restrictions.

Problem Set

8 Determine whether each statement is True or False.
  a $\cos (30° + 60°) = \cos 30° + \cos 60°$
  b $\cos (30° + 60°) = \cos 30° \cos 60° - \sin 30° \sin 60°$

9 Use identities to evaluate each of the following.
 a $1 + \cot^2 30°$
 b $(\sec 10° - \tan 10°)(\sec 10° + \tan 10°)$
 c $\sin 15° \cdot \cot 15° \cdot \sec 15°$

10 Prove that $(\csc \theta + \cot \theta)^2(\csc \theta - \cot \theta)^2 = 1$. State restrictions.

11 Simplify each of the following to a single trigonometric function
 (sin x, cos x, tan x, sec x, csc x, or cot x).

 a $\dfrac{\cos x}{1 - \sin^2 x}$

 b $\sin x + \dfrac{\cos^2 x}{\sin x}$

 c $\dfrac{\cos x - \sin x}{\cot x - 1}$

 d $1 - \dfrac{\sin^2 x}{1 + \cos x}$

12 a Find the coordinates of P.
 b Find the coordinates of Q.
 c Find distance PQ to the nearest
   thousandth.

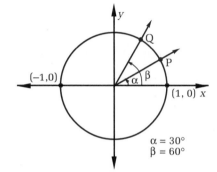

$\alpha = 30°$
$\beta = 60°$

13 Prove that $\dfrac{\cos^3 \theta - \sin^3 \theta}{\cos \theta - \sin \theta} = 1 + \cos \theta \sin \theta$. State restrictions.

14 Prove that $\dfrac{\sin \theta}{1 + \cos \theta} = \dfrac{\cos \theta}{1 + \sin \theta}$ is *not* an identity.

15 Use a calculator to evaluate the following.

 a $\sin^2 \dfrac{\pi}{10} + \cos^2 \dfrac{\pi}{10}$

 b $\sin \dfrac{\pi}{10} + \cos \dfrac{\pi}{10}$

16 Ida Entity supplied the following proof that $\sin \theta = \sqrt{1 - \cos^2 \theta}$:
 "If we square both sides, we get $\sin^2 \theta = 1 - \cos^2 \theta$, which is a
 valid identity. Therefore, $\sin \theta = \sqrt{1 - \cos^2 \theta}$ is an identity."
 a Show that $\sin \theta = \sqrt{1 - \cos^2 \theta}$ is not an identity by showing
   that it is false for $\theta = 210°$.
 b What did Ida do wrong?

17 Determine whether each statement is True or False.
 a $\cos 60° = 2 \cdot \cos 30°$
 b $\cos 60° = \cos^2 30° - \sin^2 30°$
 c $\sin 90° = 2 \cdot \sin 45°$
 d $\sin 90° = 2 \cdot \sin 45° \cos 45°$

18 Evaluate each of the following without using a calculator.

 a $\sin \left(\text{Arcsin } \dfrac{1}{3} \right)$

 b $\sin \left(\text{Arccos } \dfrac{1}{3} \right)$

 c $\sin \left(\text{Arccos } \dfrac{3}{5} \right)$

Problem Set, *continued*

19 The graph of $y = f(x)$ is shown. Draw the graph of $y = [f(x)]^2$.

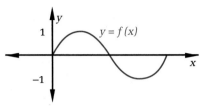

20 Determine whether each equation is True or False.

a $\tan (30° + 120°) = \tan 30° + \tan 120°$

b $\tan (30° + 120°) = \dfrac{\tan 30° + \tan 120°}{1 - \tan 30° \tan 120°}$

21 a Use the figure to show that
$\dfrac{\sin \theta}{1 - \cos \theta} = \csc \theta + \cot \theta$.

b Evaluate $(\sin \theta + \cos \theta)^2$.

c Evaluate $(\sin \theta)^2 + (\cos \theta)^2$.

22 Simplify to a single trigonometric function.

a $\dfrac{\tan^2 x + 1}{\tan x + \cot x}$

b $\dfrac{\sin \theta + \tan \theta}{1 + \sec \theta}$

c $\dfrac{\csc x}{\cot x + \tan x}$

d $\dfrac{\sin x}{(\sec x + 1)(1 - \cos x)}$

23 Prove each identity. State restrictions.

a $\dfrac{\tan x - 1}{\tan x + 1} = \dfrac{1 - \cot x}{1 + \cot x}$

b $\cot^2 x - \cos^2 x = \cot^2 x \cdot \cos^2 x$

c $(\tan x + \sec x)^2 = \dfrac{1 + \sin x}{1 - \sin x}$

24 Let $\sin x = a + 1$.

a Find $\sin x + \csc x$.

b Find the value of a for which $\sin x + \csc x = 3$.

25 Solve for x, where $0 \le x \le 2\pi$.

a $\dfrac{\tan^2 x + 1}{\tan x + \cot x} = 1$

b $\cos^2 x = \sin x + 1$

c $\tan x \sin x + \cos x = 2$

26 a Sketch $y = [f(x)]^2$ and $y = [g(x)]^2$.

b Sketch $y = [f(x)]^2 + [g(x)]^2$.

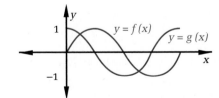

27 Prove that $\log_2 (\tan \theta) + \log_2 (\cos \theta) = \log_2 (\sin \theta)$. State restrictions.

28 Prove that $\dfrac{2 \sin^2 \theta + 5 \sin \theta \cos \theta + 2 \cos^2 \theta}{\sin \theta + 2 \cos \theta} = \dfrac{2 \sec \theta + \csc \theta}{\sec \theta \csc \theta}$. State restrictions.

29 Solve for $\{x : 0 \le x \le 2\pi\}$.

   a $\left(2 \cos x - \sqrt{2}\right)\left(\tan x - \sqrt{3}\right) = 0$

   b $\sin^2 (3x) = \dfrac{1}{2}$

   c $2 \cos^2 x + 7 \cos x + 3 = 0$
   d $\tan^2 x = 3(\sec x - 1)$
   e $\sin x + \cos x = 1$

HISTORICAL SNAPSHOT

THE ORIGIN OF TRIGONOMETRY
Astronomers develop a mathematical tool

Trigonometry was invented by astronomers as a means to an end. It grew out of their attempts to describe the paths of the sun, moon, planets, and stars.

Hipparchus of Nicaea (*c.* 180 B.C.–*c.* 125 B.C.) generally is credited with compiling the first trigonometric table, which gives corresponding arc and chord values for a series of angles. Hipparchus' other contributions to astronomy include a star catalog, improvements in astronomical constants, and the discovery of the *precession of the equinoxes*, a phenomenon caused by a wobbling of the earth on its axis.

Many of Hipparchus' achievements are presented in the works of Claudius Ptolemy (*c.* A.D. 150). Ptolemy also contributed to the

development of trigonometry. In his *Almagest,* he gives a formula for the sine and cosine of the sum and difference of two angles. The *Almagest* also contains a table of chords belonging to different angles, ascending by half angles. By applying his own half-angle formula, Ptolemy could approximate π as 3.1416.

Complete the trigonometric table below, using the sum and differences and the half-angle formulas.

Degree	Sin	Cos
0° 00'	0.0000	1.000
0° 30'		
1° 00'	0.0175	0.9998
33° 00'	0.5446	0.8387
33° 30'		

THE SUM AND DIFFERENCE IDENTITIES

Objectives

After studying this section, you will be able to
- Use the sum and difference identities
- Determine the angle between two graphed lines

Part One: Introduction

The Sum and Difference Identities

Does $\cos(60° + 90°) = \cos 60° + \cos 90°$? Let's check and see.

Left Side	Right Side
$\cos(60° + 90°)$	$= \cos 60° + \cos 90°$
$= \cos 150°$	$= \dfrac{1}{2} + 0$
$= \dfrac{-\sqrt{3}}{2}$	$= \dfrac{1}{2}$

The two expressions are not equal. We will develop a correct identity for $\cos(\alpha + \beta)$.

In the diagram, $\alpha > 0$ and $\beta > 0$. The coordinates of D are (1, 0). The coordinates of A and B are $(\cos \alpha, \sin \alpha)$ and $(\cos(\alpha + \beta), \sin(\alpha + \beta))$ respectively, from the definitions of the trigonometric functions. The coordinates of C are $(\cos \beta, -\sin \beta)$, since $\cos(-\beta) = \cos \beta$ and $\sin(-\beta) = -\sin \beta$. Using the distance formula, we have

$$(BD)^2 = [\cos(\alpha + \beta) - 1]^2 + \sin^2(\alpha + \beta)$$
$$= \cos^2(\alpha + \beta) - 2\cos(\alpha + \beta) + 1 + \sin^2(\alpha + \beta)$$
$$= 2 - 2\cos(\alpha + \beta)$$

$$(AC)^2 = (\cos \alpha - \cos \beta)^2 + (\sin \alpha + \sin \beta)^2$$
$$= \cos^2 \alpha - 2\cos \alpha \cdot \cos \beta + \cos^2 \beta + \sin^2 \alpha + 2\sin \alpha \cdot \sin \beta + \sin^2 \beta$$
$$= 2 - 2\cos \alpha \cdot \cos \beta + 2\sin \alpha \cdot \sin \beta$$

Since the central angles for chord BD and chord AC are equal, the chords must be the same length, so $(BD)^2 = (AC)^2$. Therefore,

$$2 - 2\cos(\alpha + \beta) = 2 - 2\cos \alpha \cdot \cos \beta + 2\sin \alpha \cdot \sin \beta$$
$$-2\cos(\alpha + \beta) = -2\cos \alpha \cdot \cos \beta + 2\sin \alpha \cdot \sin \beta$$
$$\cos(\alpha + \beta) = \cos \alpha \cdot \cos \beta - \sin \alpha \cdot \sin \beta$$

$$\boldsymbol{\cos(\alpha + \beta) = \cos \alpha \cos \beta - \sin \alpha \sin \beta}$$

Example   Verify that cos (60° + 90°) = cos 60° cos 90° − sin 60° sin 90°.

Left Side

cos (60° + 90°)

$= \cos 150°$

$= \dfrac{-\sqrt{3}}{2}$

Right Side

$= \cos 60° \cos 90° - \sin 60° \sin 90°$

$= \dfrac{1}{2} \cdot 0 - \dfrac{\sqrt{3}}{2} \cdot 1$

$= \dfrac{-\sqrt{3}}{2}$

We can replace β with $-\beta$ to get the identity for the cosine of a difference.

> ***cos (α − β) = cos α cos β + sin α sin β***

To develop the identity for the sine of a sum, we use the cofunction identity $\sin x = \cos \left(\frac{\pi}{2} - x\right)$.

$$\sin (\alpha + \beta) = \cos \left[\frac{\pi}{2} - (\alpha + \beta)\right]$$

$$= \cos \left[\left(\frac{\pi}{2} - \alpha\right) - \beta\right]$$

$$= \cos \left(\frac{\pi}{2} - \alpha\right) \cdot \cos \beta + \sin \left(\frac{\pi}{2} - \alpha\right) \cdot \sin \beta$$

$$= \sin \alpha \cdot \cos \beta + \cos \alpha \cdot \sin \beta$$

Similarly, we can show that $\sin (\alpha - \beta) = \sin \alpha \cdot \cos \beta - \cos \alpha \cdot \sin \beta$.

> ***sin (α + β) = sin α cos β + cos α sin β***

> ***sin (α − β) = sin α cos β − cos α sin β***

Example   Find the exact value of $\cos \left(\text{Arccos } \frac{3}{5} + \text{Arcsin } \frac{-5}{13}\right)$.

Let $\alpha = \text{Arccos } \frac{3}{5}$ and $\beta = \text{Arcsin } \frac{-5}{13}$.

$$\cos \left(\text{Arccos } \frac{3}{5} + \text{Arcsin } \frac{-5}{13}\right)$$

$$= \cos (\alpha + \beta)$$
$$= \cos \alpha \cdot \cos \beta - \sin \alpha \cdot \sin \beta$$

$$= \frac{3}{5} \cdot \frac{12}{13} - \frac{4}{5} \cdot \frac{-5}{13}$$

$$= \frac{56}{65}$$

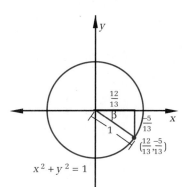

Example   *Find the exact value of sin 15°.*

$$\sin 15°$$
$$= \sin (45° - 30°)$$
$$= \sin 45° \cdot \cos 30° - \cos 45° \cdot \sin 30°$$

$$= \frac{\sqrt{2}}{2} \cdot \frac{\sqrt{3}}{2} - \frac{\sqrt{2}}{2} \cdot \frac{1}{2}$$

$$= \frac{\sqrt{6} - \sqrt{2}}{4}$$

The Angle Between Two Lines

We can derive an identity for the tangent of a sum as follows.

$$\tan (\alpha + \beta) = \frac{\sin (\alpha + \beta)}{\cos (\alpha + \beta)}$$

$$= \frac{\sin \alpha \cos \beta + \cos \alpha \sin \beta}{\cos \alpha \cos \beta - \sin \alpha \sin \beta}$$

$$= \frac{\sin \alpha \cos \beta + \cos \alpha \sin \beta}{\cos \alpha \cos \beta - \sin \alpha \sin \beta} \cdot \frac{\dfrac{1}{\cos \alpha \cos \beta}}{\dfrac{1}{\cos \alpha \cos \beta}}$$

$$= \frac{\tan \alpha + \tan \beta}{1 - \tan \alpha \tan \beta}$$

Similarly, we can obtain an identity for $\tan (\alpha - \beta)$.

➤ $$\boldsymbol{\tan (\alpha + \beta) = \frac{\tan \alpha + \tan \beta}{1 - \tan \alpha \tan \beta}}$$

➤ $$\boldsymbol{\tan (\alpha - \beta) = \frac{\tan \alpha - \tan \beta}{1 + \tan \alpha \tan \beta}}$$

A line whose equation is $y = mx + b$ has slope m. Let θ be the angle that the line forms with the x-axis. From Chapter 14 we know that $\tan \theta$ is equal to $\frac{\text{opposite side}}{\text{adjacent side}}$, which is also the slope of the line. Therefore, $\tan \theta = m$.

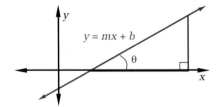

If two lines $y = m_1x + b_1$ and $y = m_2x + b_2$ form angles of θ_1 and θ_2 with the x-axis and if $\theta_2 - \theta_1 > 0$, then the angle between the lines is $\theta_2 - \theta_1$. We know that $\tan \theta_2 = m_2$ and $\tan \theta_1 = m_1$.

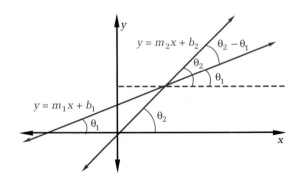

So tan $(\theta_2 - \theta_1) = \dfrac{\tan \theta_2 - \tan \theta_1}{1 + \tan \theta_2 \tan \theta_1}$

$$= \dfrac{m_2 - m_1}{1 + m_2 m_1}$$

 If θ is the angle measured counterclockwise from a line with slope m_1 to a line with slope m_2, then

$$\tan \theta = \dfrac{m_2 - m_1}{1 + m_1 m_2}$$

Example Find the acute angle formed by the lines whose equations are $y = 5x + 1$ and $y = 0.5x + 3$.

In this case, we let $m_2 = 5$ and $m_1 = 0.5$.

$$\tan \theta = \dfrac{5 - 0.5}{1 + 5(0.5)} \approx 1.2857$$

Using a trigonometric table or the $\boxed{\text{INV}}$ $\boxed{\text{tan}}$ keys on a calculator, we find that $\theta \approx 52.12°$.

Part Two: Sample Problems

Problem 1 Prove the identity $\tan\left(\theta + \frac{\pi}{4}\right) = \frac{\tan \theta + 1}{\tan \theta - 1}$.

Solution

Left Side

$$\tan\left(\theta + \frac{\pi}{4}\right)$$

$$= \dfrac{\tan \theta + \tan \dfrac{\pi}{4}}{1 - \tan \theta \tan \dfrac{\pi}{4}}$$

$$= \dfrac{\tan \theta + 1}{1 - \tan \theta}$$

Right Side

$$= \dfrac{\tan \theta + 1}{1 - \tan \theta}$$

Since the left side equals the right side, the equation is an identity.

Problem 2 A man is 150 feet from the base of a 90-foot-high cliff. The man's eyes are 5 feet 6 inches above the ground. On the top of the cliff is a 25-foot-high sign. From the man's viewpoint, what is the angle of elevation from the bottom of the sign to the top of the sign?

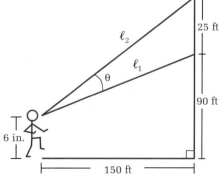

Solution The slope of line ℓ_1 is $\frac{90 - 5.5}{150}$, or ≈ 0.563.

The slope of line ℓ_2 is $\frac{115 - 5.5}{150}$, or 0.73.

Therefore, $\tan \theta \approx \frac{0.73 - 0.563}{1 + 0.563(0.73)} \approx 0.118$, and $\theta \approx 6.75°$.

Part Three: Exercises and Problems

Warm-up Exercises

1 Find each of the following.

a $\sin \alpha$
b $\sin \beta$
c $\sin (\alpha + \beta)$

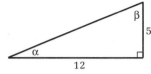

2 Determine whether each of the following statements is True or False.

a $\sin 70° = \sin 30° \cos 40° + \cos 30° \sin 40°$
b $\sin 70° = \sin 10° \cos 60° + \cos 10° \sin 60°$
c $\sin 70° = \sin 30° + \sin 40°$

3 Find each of the following.

a $\tan \angle POR$
b $\tan \angle QOR$
c $\tan \angle POQ$

Problem Set

4 Simplify.

a $\cos 40° \cos 30° + \sin 40° \sin 30°$
b $\sin 20° \cos 30° + \cos 20° \sin 30°$
c $\sin 50° \cos 40° + \cos 40° \sin 50°$

5 Prove that $\sin (\theta + \phi) + \sin (\theta - \phi) = 2 \sin \theta \cos \phi$.

6 Line L_1 has a slope of $\frac{2}{3}$, and line L_2 has a slope of $\frac{3}{2}$.

a Find $\tan \theta$.
b Approximate θ to the nearest degree.

7 a Compute the exact value of $\cos \left(\text{Arcsin } \frac{4}{5} \right)$.

b Use a calculator to evaluate $\cos \left(\text{Arcsin } \frac{4}{5} \right)$.

c Are your answers to parts **a** and **b** the same?

8 Use the sum and difference identities to simplify.

a $\sin (x + \pi)$ **b** $\cos (x + \pi)$
c $\sin (x + 90°)$ **d** $\sin (x + 60°)$

9 Determine whether each of the following statements is True or False.

    a $\sin 20° = 2 \sin 10° \cos 10°$ **b** $\sin 20° = 2 \sin 10°$

    c $\tan 20° = \cot 70°$

10 **a** Use a calculator to compute Arcsin (sin 30°).

    b Use a calculator to evaluate Arcsin (sin 150°).

    c Explain the relationship between your answers to parts **a** and **b.**

11 Suppose that $\sin \alpha = \frac{3}{5}$ and $\cos \beta = \frac{1}{4}$ for acute angles α and β. Find the following.

    a $\sin (\alpha + \beta)$ **b** $\cos (\alpha + \beta)$ **c** $\tan (\alpha + \beta)$

12 Find each of the following.

    a $\sin \angle AOC$

    b $\cos \angle AOC$

    c $\sin \angle BOC$

    d $\cos \angle BOC$

    e $\sin \angle AOB$

    f $\cos \angle AOB$

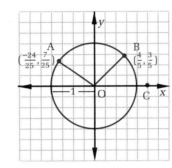

13 Prove that $\cot (\alpha + \beta) = \frac{\cot \alpha \cot \beta - 1}{\cot \alpha + \cot \beta}$.

14 Find the exact value of $\sin \left[\arcsin \left(\frac{5}{13} \right) - \arccos \left(\frac{-4}{5} \right) \right]$.

15 Find the acute angle formed by the lines with equations $y = \frac{5}{8}x + 2$ and $y = -\frac{1}{4}x - 5$.

16 A lighthouse keeper is 50 meters above sea level and sights a ship that is 200 meters from the base of the lighthouse. The ship moves away from the lighthouse at 3 meters per second. After 1 minute, by how many degrees (to the nearest hundredth) has the angle of depression changed?

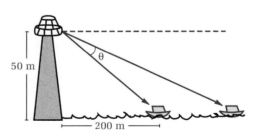

17 **a** Solve $\sin x = \frac{1}{2}$ for x.   **b** Solve $\sin y = 2$ for y.

18 Evaluate the following, using the sum and difference identities.

    a $\sin 75°$ (Hint: 75° = 45° + 30°)   **b** $\cos 75°$

    c $\cos 15°$ **d** $\sin 105°$

19 Prove that $\frac{\sin (x + y)}{\sin x \sin y} = \cot y + \cot x$.

Problem Set, *continued*

20 Evaluate each expression.

a $\log_2 \left(\sin \dfrac{\pi}{6} \right)$ **b** $\log_2 \left(\sin \dfrac{\pi}{2} \right)$

21 Find each of the following.

a $\tan \dfrac{\pi}{8}$ **b** $\tan 75°$

c $\dfrac{\tan \dfrac{5\pi}{8} + \tan \dfrac{\pi}{8}}{1 - \tan \dfrac{5\pi}{8} \tan \dfrac{\pi}{8}}$ **d** $\dfrac{\tan 70° - \tan 25°}{1 + \tan 70° \tan 25°}$

e $\dfrac{1 - \tan 20° \tan 10°}{\tan 20° + \tan 10°}$

22 Recall that $\cos (\theta + \phi) = \cos \theta \cos \phi - \sin \theta \sin \phi$ and $\cos (\theta - \phi) = \cos \theta \cos \phi + \sin \theta \sin \phi$.

  a Simplify $\cos (\theta + \phi) + \cos (\theta - \phi)$
  b Simplify $\cos (\theta + \phi) - \cos (\theta - \phi)$
  c Simplify $\cos (\theta + 60°) + \cos (\theta - 60°)$
  d If $2 \cos 110° \cos 70° = \cos \alpha + \cos \beta$, what is (α, β)?

23 Find the exact value of each of the following.

  a $\sin 75°$ **b** $\sin 105°$ **c** $\sin (-75°)$

24 Evaluate each of the following.

  a $\cos \left(\text{Arcsin} \dfrac{3}{5} - \text{Arccos} \dfrac{12}{13} \right)$ **b** $\tan \left(\text{Arcsin} \dfrac{3}{5} + \text{Arctan} \dfrac{1}{2} \right)$

  c $\sin (\text{Arcsin } 2 + \text{Arccos } 2)$

25 Prove that $\sin 3\theta = 3 \sin \theta - 4 \sin^3 \theta$.

26 Solve for y.

27 Use a calculator to compute the following for $\alpha = \dfrac{\pi}{6}$ (radian mode).

  a $\sin \alpha$ **b** $\alpha - \dfrac{\alpha^3}{3!} + \dfrac{\alpha^5}{5!}$

  c $\alpha - \dfrac{\alpha^3}{3!} + \dfrac{\alpha^5}{5!} - \dfrac{\alpha^7}{7!}$ **d** $\alpha - \dfrac{\alpha^3}{3!} + \dfrac{\alpha^5}{5!} - \dfrac{\alpha^7}{7!} + \dfrac{\alpha^9}{9!}$

15.3 THE DOUBLE- AND HALF-ANGLE IDENTITIES

Objectives

After studying this section, you will be able to
- Apply the double-angle identities
- Apply the half-angle identities

Part One: Introduction

The Double-Angle Identities

How does sin 60° compare with sin 30°? Since $\sin 60° = \frac{\sqrt{3}}{2}$ and $\sin 30° = \frac{1}{2}$, we see that $\sin 60° \neq 2 \cdot \sin 30°$. We will now develop the formulas for $\sin 2\theta$, $\cos 2\theta$, and $\tan 2\theta$, using the sum identities we derived in the last section.

$$\sin 2\theta = \sin (\theta + \theta)$$
$$= \sin \theta \cdot \cos \theta + \cos \theta \cdot \sin \theta$$
$$= 2(\sin \theta \cdot \cos \theta)$$

> $sin\ 2\theta = 2\ sin\ \theta\ cos\ \theta$

$$\cos 2\theta = \cos (\theta + \theta)$$
$$= \cos \theta \cdot \cos \theta - \sin \theta \cdot \sin \theta$$
$$= \cos^2 \theta - \sin^2 \theta$$

> $cos\ 2\theta = cos^2\ \theta - sin^2\ \theta$

We can obtain two other forms of the preceding identity by remembering that $\sin^2 \theta + \cos^2 \theta = 1$ and substituting for either $\cos^2 \theta$ or $\sin^2 \theta$ in the identity.

> $cos\ 2\theta = 1 - 2\ sin^2\ \theta$

> $cos\ 2\theta = 2\ cos^2\ \theta - 1$

The double-angle identity for the tangent function is derived by using $\tan 2\theta = \tan (\theta + \theta)$. You are asked to prove this identity in Warm-up Exercise 6.

> $tan\ 2\theta = \dfrac{2\ tan\ \theta}{1 - tan^2\ \theta}$

Example   *Find all possible values of θ between 0 and 2π for which*
sin 2θ + sin θ = 0.

$$\sin 2\theta + \sin \theta = 0$$

Use the identity for sin 2θ $$2 \sin \theta \cdot \cos \theta + \sin \theta = 0$$

$$\sin \theta \, (2 \cos \theta + 1) = 0$$

Use the Zero Product Property $$\sin \theta = 0 \text{ or } 2 \cos \theta + 1 = 0$$

$$\cos \theta = -\frac{1}{2}$$

Since $\sin \theta = 0$ when $\theta = 0$, $\theta = \pi$, or $\theta = 2\pi$ and since $\cos \theta = -\frac{1}{2}$
when $\theta = \frac{2\pi}{3}$ or $\theta = \frac{4\pi}{3}$, the solutions are $\left\{0, \frac{2\pi}{3}, \pi, \frac{4\pi}{3}, 2\pi\right\}$.

The Half-Angle Identities

The identities for $\sin \frac{\theta}{2}$, $\cos \frac{\theta}{2}$, and $\tan \frac{\theta}{2}$ are derived by solving a
cos 2θ identity for the appropriate function and then substituting
$\frac{\theta}{2}$ for θ.

We first derive the identity for $\sin \frac{\theta}{2}$.

$$\cos 2\theta = 1 - 2 \sin^2 \theta$$
$$2 \sin^2 \theta = 1 - \cos 2\theta$$

$$\sin^2 \theta = \frac{1 - \cos 2\theta}{2}$$

$$|\sin \theta| = \sqrt{\frac{1 - \cos 2\theta}{2}}$$

By substituting $\frac{\theta}{2}$ for θ in the preceding equation, we obtain the
following identity.

⯈ $$\boldsymbol{\sin \frac{\theta}{2} = \pm \sqrt{\frac{1 - \cos \theta}{2}}}$$

When you use this identity with a given angle you will have to
determine the appropriate sign to use.

The identity for $\cos \frac{\theta}{2}$ can be derived in the same manner by
beginning with $\cos 2\theta = 2 \cos^2 \theta - 1$. The derivation is asked for in
Warm-up Exercise 4.

⯈ $$\boldsymbol{\cos \frac{\theta}{2} = \pm \sqrt{\frac{1 + \cos \theta}{2}}}$$

Example   *Find the exact value of cos 195°.*

Since 195° is a third-quadrant angle, cos 195° will be negative.

$$\cos 195° = -\sqrt{\frac{1 + \cos 390°}{2}}$$

$$= -\sqrt{\frac{1 + \cos 30°}{2}}$$

$$= -\sqrt{\dfrac{1 + \dfrac{\sqrt{3}}{2}}{2}}$$

$$= -\dfrac{\sqrt{2 + \sqrt{3}}}{2}$$

Finally, we derive an identity for $\tan \frac{\theta}{2}$.

$$\tan \frac{\theta}{2} = \dfrac{\sin \dfrac{\theta}{2}}{\cos \dfrac{\theta}{2}} = \pm \dfrac{\sqrt{\dfrac{1 - \cos \theta}{2}}}{\sqrt{\dfrac{1 + \cos \theta}{2}}} = \pm \sqrt{\dfrac{1 - \cos \theta}{1 + \cos \theta}}$$

By multiplying both the numerator and the denominator by $\sqrt{1 + \cos \theta}$, we can obtain another form of this identity, $\tan \frac{\theta}{2} = \frac{\sin \theta}{1 + \cos \theta}$. (The derivation is asked for in problem **19**.) Notice that no $\pm$ appears in this identity because $1 + \cos \theta$ is never negative and $\sin \theta$ and $\tan \frac{\theta}{2}$ always have the same sign.

A third form of the $\tan \frac{\theta}{2}$ identity can be obtained by multiplying the numerator and the denominator of the preceding form by $1 - \cos \theta$.

$$\tan \frac{\theta}{2} = \dfrac{\sin \theta}{1 + \cos \theta} \cdot \dfrac{1 - \cos \theta}{1 - \cos \theta} = \dfrac{1 - \cos \theta}{\sin \theta}$$

➤ $$\boldsymbol{\tan \dfrac{\theta}{2} = \pm \sqrt{\dfrac{1 - \cos \theta}{1 + \cos \theta}}}$$

$$\boldsymbol{\tan \dfrac{\theta}{2} = \dfrac{\sin \theta}{1 + \cos \theta}}$$

$$\boldsymbol{\tan \dfrac{\theta}{2} = \dfrac{1 - \cos \theta}{\sin \theta}}$$

Part Two: Sample Problems

Problem 1   *Find the exact value of $\tan \left(2 \text{ Arcsin } \frac{8}{17} \right)$.*

Solution   Let $\alpha = \text{Arcsin } \frac{8}{17}$.

$$\tan \left(2 \text{ Arcsin } \frac{8}{17} \right) = \tan 2\alpha$$

$$= \dfrac{2 \tan \alpha}{1 - \tan^2 \alpha}$$

$$= \dfrac{2 \left(\dfrac{8}{15} \right)}{1 - \left(\dfrac{8}{15} \right)^2} = \dfrac{240}{161}$$

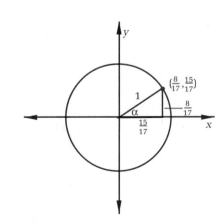

Problem 2   *Find the value of x and the value of angle θ in degrees.*

Solution   From the diagram, $\frac{x}{18} = \cos 2\theta$ and $\frac{x}{12} = \cos \theta$. Using the identity $\cos 2\theta = 2 \cos^2 \theta - 1$, we have

$$\frac{x}{18} = 2\left(\frac{x}{12}\right)^2 - 1$$

$$\frac{x}{18} = \frac{x^2}{72} - 1$$

$$4x = x^2 - 72$$

$$0 = x^2 - 4x - 72$$

Using the quadratic formula, we find that $x \approx 10.72$ or $x \approx -6.72$. Since the value of x must be positive, the value of x is approximately 10.72. Since $\cos \theta = \frac{x}{12}$, we have $\cos \theta \approx \frac{10.72}{12}$. Therefore, $\theta \approx 26.7°$.

Problem 3   *Prove the identity $\tan \frac{\theta}{2} \cdot (\sec \theta + 1) = \tan \theta$. Note any restrictions.*

Solution

Left Side	**Right Side**
$\tan \dfrac{\theta}{2} \cdot (\sec \theta + 1)$	$= \tan \theta$

$$= \frac{\sin \theta}{1 + \cos \theta} \cdot \left(\frac{1}{\cos \theta} + 1\right)$$

$$= \frac{\sin \theta}{1 + \cos \theta} \cdot \frac{1 + \cos \theta}{\cos \theta}$$

$$= \frac{\sin \theta}{\cos \theta}$$

$$= \tan \theta$$

The left side of the identity is undefined for $\cos \theta = -1$ and $\cos \theta = 0$. The right side is also undefined for $\cos \theta = 0$. So the restrictions are $\cos \theta \neq -1$ and $\cos \theta \neq 0$.

Problem 4   *Solve $\cos 2\theta = \cos \theta$ for all values of θ such that $0 \leq \theta \leq 360°$.*

Solution   We have three choices for an identity for $\cos 2\theta$. Let's choose $\cos 2\theta = 2 \cos^2 \theta - 1$ so that the resulting equation will be entirely in terms of $\cos \theta$.

$$\cos 2\theta = \cos \theta$$
$$2 \cos^2 \theta - 1 = \cos \theta$$
$$2 \cos^2 \theta - \cos \theta - 1 = 0$$
$$(2 \cos \theta + 1)(\cos \theta - 1) = 0$$
$$2 \cos \theta + 1 = 0 \text{ or } \cos \theta - 1 = 0$$

$$\cos \theta = \frac{-1}{2} \qquad \cos \theta = 1$$

The solutions are $\{0°, 120°, 240°, 360°\}$.

Part Three: Exercises and Problems

Warm-up Exercises

1 Determine whether each statement is True or False.

a $\cos^2 \theta = \dfrac{1 + \cos 2\theta}{2}$　　　**b** $\sin^2 \theta = \dfrac{1 - \cos 2\theta}{2}$　　　**c** $\sin^2 \theta = \dfrac{1 + \sin 2\theta}{2}$

2 Prove that $(\sin \theta + \cos \theta)^2 = 1 + \sin 2\theta$.

3 Find $\tan \angle ABC$.

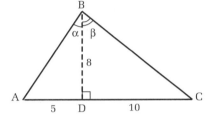

4 Prove that $\cos \dfrac{\theta}{2} = \pm\sqrt{\dfrac{1 + \cos \theta}{2}}$.

5 Determine whether each statement is True or False.

a $\sin\left(\dfrac{\alpha}{8}\right) = 2 \sin\left(\dfrac{\alpha}{4}\right) \cos\left(\dfrac{\alpha}{4}\right)$　　　　**b** $\cos\left(\dfrac{\alpha}{10}\right) = \cos^2\left(\dfrac{\alpha}{20}\right) - \sin^2\left(\dfrac{\alpha}{20}\right)$

6 Prove that $\tan 2\theta = \dfrac{2 \tan \theta}{1 - \tan^2 \theta}$.

7 Determine whether each statement is True or False.

a $\cos 8\theta = \cos^2 4\theta - \sin^2 4\theta$

b $\sin\left(\dfrac{1}{2}\alpha\right) = 2 \sin\left(\dfrac{\alpha}{4}\right) \cos\left(\dfrac{\alpha}{4}\right)$

c $\tan 3\theta = \dfrac{2 \tan\left(\dfrac{3\theta}{2}\right)}{1 - \tan^2\left(\dfrac{3\theta}{2}\right)}$

Problem Set

8 If $\cos 6\theta = 0.5400$, what is $\cos 3\theta$?

9 Prove that $(\sin \theta + \cos \theta)^{\csc^2 \theta - \cot^2 \theta + 1} = 1 + \sin 2\theta$.

10 Find the exact value of each of the following.

a $\tan 22.5°$　　　　　　　　　　　　　　**b** $\tan 75°$

11 Determine whether each statement is True or False.

a $\cos 105° = \sqrt{\dfrac{1 + \cos 210°}{2}}$　　　　**b** $\sin 105° = \sqrt{\dfrac{1 - \cos 210°}{2}}$

Problem Set, *continued*

12 Find the exact value of sin 75°.

13 The slope of line $\mathcal{M}$ is $\frac{2}{3}$. Find the exact value of the slope of line ℓ. Check your result by estimating α and doubling it, then finding the slope of ℓ.

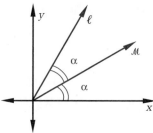

14 Solve for x, where $0 \le x \le 2\pi$.
 a $(2 \sin x + 1)(\sin x - 1) = 0$
 c $(2 \sin x - 1)(2 \cos x + 1) = 0$
 b $\left(2 \cos x + \sqrt{3}\right)(\cos x + 1) = 0$

15 Angles α and β are as shown. Find the following.
 a sin α and cos α
 b sin β and cos β
 c sin $(\alpha + \beta)$ and cos $(\alpha + \beta)$

16 Let $\cos x = \frac{4}{5}$. Find each of the following.

 a $\sin \dfrac{x}{2}$ **b** $\cos \dfrac{x}{2}$ **c** $\tan \dfrac{x}{2}$

17 If $\tan \gamma = \frac{1}{2}$ and $\tan \beta = \frac{1}{3}$, what is $\tan \alpha$?

18 Solve for x, where $0 \le x \le 2\pi$.
 a $\sin 2x = 2 \sin x$
 b $\cos 2x + \cos x = 0$

 c $\tan 2x = \dfrac{3}{4}$

19 Prove that $\tan \dfrac{\theta}{2} = \dfrac{\sin \theta}{1 + \cos \theta}$.

20 Simplify $\cos 5\theta \cos 3\theta + \sin 5\theta \sin 3\theta$ in terms of functions of θ.

21 Find all values of x for which $\cos 2x = 2 \cos x$.

22 Prove the following identities.
 a $\sin 4\theta = 4 \sin \theta \cos^3 \theta - 4 \sin^3 \theta \cos \theta$
 b $\cos 4\theta = 8 \cos^4 \theta - 8 \cos^2 \theta + 1$

23 Find $\cos(\theta + \phi)$ and $\sin(\theta + \phi)$.

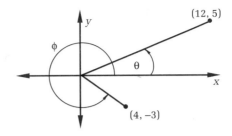

24 Solve for θ, where $0 \le \theta < 2\pi$.

   a $2\cos^2\theta - 3\cos x - 2 = 0$ **b** $\sin^2\theta + 2\cos\theta = 0$

   c $\cos 2\theta = 1 - 2\sin^2\theta$

25 **a** Use a half-angle identity to find an expression for $\sin 15°$.

    b Use a difference identity to find $\sin 15°$.

    c Show that your answers to parts **a** and **b** are equal.

26 Prove the identity $\sin 3\theta = (\sin\theta)(2\cos\theta - 1)(2\cos\theta + 1)$.

TRIGONOMETRY IN WINDSURFING

Pat LeMehaute designs from physics

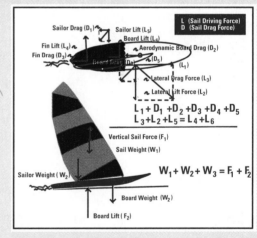

Pat LeMehaute is a writer, product tester, and windsurfing enthusiast who designs windsurfing boards. When he found little topical material on windsurfing, Mr. LeMehaute did his own experimentation and mathematical analysis to provide the basis for his designs. Windsurfing is governed by physical laws, so Mr. LeMehaute "used trigonometry and calculus and worked from physical theory," he says.

Mr. LeMehaute's first concern in constructing his board was to itemize all the forces on the board, such as the amount of board in the water, the lift and drag on the sail and fin, and the drag on the board and sailor. One method he uses is a "free-body diagram," applied so that "sailing along in a straight line and in a constant wind speed, all the forces acting on you and the sail board add up to zero," he says. "I analyze sines, tangents, and vectors. In the free-body diagram, the forces are represented by arrows and their magnitudes by the arrows' lengths. The lift on the sail is roughly one-hundred pounds, and the drag is about

twenty pounds, so the lift arrow is five times as long as the drag arrow."

Applying mathematical concepts to board sailing helps Mr. LeMehaute "obtain high speeds, be more scientific, and better understand the concepts of board sailing." Mr. LeMehaute holds a bachelor's degree in engineering science from the University of Florida. His high-tech background has more than scientific or mathematical benefits, flowing into personal satisfaction and aesthetic expression.

15.4 FINAL IDENTITIES AND TRIGONOMETRIC EQUATIONS

Objectives

After studying this section, you will be able to
- Use the product-to-sum and sum-to-product identities
- Solve trigonometric equations

Part One: Introduction

Product-to-Sum and Sum-to-Product Identities

There are times when it is necessary to convert a product of trigonometric functions to a sum of trigonometric functions or vice versa. The following identities, however, are not used as often as the others presented in this chapter.

To convert a product to a sum, we can use the identities expressed in the following theorems.

$$\sin \alpha \cos \beta = \frac{1}{2}[\sin (\alpha + \beta) + \sin (\alpha - \beta)]$$

We can prove this theorem by showing that the right side of the equation is equal to the left side.

Left Side

$\sin \alpha \cos \beta$

Right Side

$$= \frac{1}{2}[\sin (\alpha + \beta) + \sin (\alpha - \beta)]$$

$$= \frac{1}{2}(\sin \alpha \cos \beta + \cos \alpha \sin \beta + \sin \alpha \cos \beta - \cos \alpha \sin \beta)$$

$$= \frac{1}{2}(2 \sin \alpha \cos \beta)$$

$$= \sin \alpha \cos \beta$$

We have proved the theorem by verifying the identity. The following theorems can be proved in a similar manner.

$$\sin \alpha \sin \beta = \frac{1}{2}[\cos (\alpha - \beta) - \cos (\alpha + \beta)]$$

$$\blacktriangleright \quad \cos \alpha \, \cos \beta = \frac{1}{2}[\cos(\alpha - \beta) + \cos(\alpha + \beta)]$$

Example   *Find the exact value of cos 75° cos 15°.*

$$\cos 75° \, \cos 15° = \frac{1}{2}[\cos(75° - 15°) + \cos(75° + 15°)]$$

$$= \frac{1}{2}(\cos 60° + \cos 90°)$$

$$= \frac{1}{2}\left(\frac{1}{2} + 0\right)$$

$$= \frac{1}{4}$$

To convert a sum of trigonometric functions to a product, we can use the identities expressed in the following theorems.

$$\blacktriangleright \quad \sin \alpha + \sin \beta = 2 \sin \frac{\alpha + \beta}{2} \cos \frac{\alpha - \beta}{2}$$

$$\blacktriangleright \quad \cos \alpha + \cos \beta = 2 \cos \frac{\alpha + \beta}{2} \cos \frac{\alpha - \beta}{2}$$

Example   *Prove the identity $\frac{\cos 6\theta + \cos 2\theta}{\sin 6\theta + \sin 2\theta} = \cot 4\theta$.*

Left Side   **Right Side**

$$\frac{\cos 6\theta + \cos 2\theta}{\sin 6\theta + \sin 2\theta} \qquad\qquad = \cot 4\theta$$

$$= \frac{2 \cos \left(\dfrac{6\theta + 2\theta}{2}\right) \cos \left(\dfrac{6\theta - 2\theta}{2}\right)}{2 \sin \left(\dfrac{6\theta + 2\theta}{2}\right) \cos \left(\dfrac{6\theta - 2\theta}{2}\right)}$$

$$= \frac{2 \cos 4\theta \, \cos 2\theta}{2 \sin 4\theta \, \cos 2\theta}$$

$$= \cot 4\theta$$

Trigonometric Equations

We show several examples of solving trigonometric equations that are not identities.

Example   *Solve $-4 \cos^2 \theta - 8 \sin \theta + 7 = 0$ for θ.*

We first convert the equation to an equation in terms of only $\sin \theta$ by substituting $1 - \sin^2 \theta$ for $\cos^2 \theta$.

$$-4 \cos^2 \theta - 8 \sin \theta + 7 = 0$$
$$-4(1 - \sin^2 \theta) - 8 \sin \theta + 7 = 0$$
$$-4 + 4 \sin^2 \theta - 8 \sin \theta + 7 = 0$$
$$4 \sin^2 \theta - 8 \sin \theta + 3 = 0$$

Now we factor the quadratic.

$$(2 \sin \theta - 3)(2 \sin \theta - 1) = 0$$
$$2 \sin \theta - 3 = 0 \text{ or } 2 \sin \theta - 1 = 0$$

$$\sin \theta = \frac{3}{2} \qquad \sin \theta = \frac{1}{2}$$

The equation $\sin \theta = \frac{3}{2}$ has no solution, since for any value of θ, $-1 \le \sin \theta \le 1$. The equation $\sin \theta = \frac{1}{2}$ has the solutions $\left\{ \dots, -\frac{11\pi}{6}, -\frac{7\pi}{6}, \frac{\pi}{6}, \frac{5\pi}{6}, \frac{13\pi}{6}, \dots \right\}$. These solutions can be written as $\left\{ 2n\pi + \frac{\pi}{6}, 2n\pi + \frac{5\pi}{6} \right\}$, where n is any integer.

Example   If $\sin \theta - \cos \theta = 1$ and $0 \le \theta < 2\pi$, what is θ?

We begin by squaring both sides. In doing this, we may introduce extraneous solutions, so we will need to check our answers.

$$\sin \theta - \cos \theta = 1$$
$$(\sin \theta - \cos \theta)^2 = 1^2$$
$$\sin^2 \theta - 2 \sin \theta \cdot \cos \theta + \cos^2 \theta = 1$$
$$1 - 2 \sin \theta \cdot \cos \theta = 1$$
$$-2 \sin \theta \cdot \cos \theta = 0$$
$$\sin \theta \cdot \cos \theta = 0$$
$$\sin \theta = 0 \text{ or } \cos \theta = 0$$

We know that $\sin \theta = 0$ when $\theta = 0$ or $\theta = \pi$ and that $\cos \theta = 0$ when $\theta = \frac{\pi}{2}$ or $\theta = \frac{3\pi}{2}$. Let's check these apparent solutions.

Check

θ	$\sin \theta - \cos \theta$	$= 1?$
0	$\sin 0 - \cos 0 = 0 - 1 = -1$	No
π	$\sin \pi - \cos \pi = 0 - (-1) = 1$	Yes
$\frac{\pi}{2}$	$\sin \frac{\pi}{2} - \cos \frac{\pi}{2} = 1 - 0 = 1$	Yes
$\frac{3\pi}{2}$	$\sin \frac{3\pi}{2} - \cos \frac{3\pi}{2} = -1 - 0 = -1$	No

The only solutions of the equation $\sin \theta - \cos \theta = 1$ are $\theta = \pi$ and $\theta = \frac{\pi}{2}$.

Part Two: Sample Problems

Problem 1   Solve $\cos 6x \cos 2x - \sin 6x \sin 2x = 0.25$ for x, where $0° \le x \le 90°$.

Solution   This looks like the identity for $\cos (\alpha + \beta)$, with $\alpha = 6x$ and $\beta = 2x$.

$$\cos 6x \cos 2x - \sin 6x \sin 2x = 0.25$$
$$\cos (6x + 2x) = 0.25$$
$$\cos 8x = 0.25$$

Using the ⟨INV⟩ ⟨cos⟩ keys on a calculator, we find that the principal value of $(8x)°$ is $\approx 75.52°$. Since $0° \le x° \le 90°$, we know that $0° \le (8x)° \le 720°$. The terminal side of this angle can be in Quadrant I or IV.

Possible values of 8x	Values of x
$8x \approx 75.52°$	$x \approx 9.44°$
$8x \approx 360° - 75.52°$	$x \approx 35.56°$
$8x \approx 360° + 75.52°$	$x \approx 54.44°$
$8x \approx 720° - 75.52°$	$x \approx 80.56°$

The approximate solutions are $9.44°$, $35.56°$, $54.44°$, and $80.56°$.

Problem 2 *Solve $\sin 2x = \sin x$ for x.*

Solution
$$\sin 2x = \sin x$$
$$2 \sin x \cos x = \sin x$$
$$2 \sin x \cos x - \sin x = 0$$
$$\sin x(2 \cos x - 1) = 0$$

$$\sin x = 0 \text{ or } \cos x = \frac{1}{2}$$

The possible values of x are $\{ \ldots, -2\pi, -\pi, 0, \pi, 2\pi, \ldots \}$ or $\left\{ \ldots, -\frac{7\pi}{3}, -\frac{5\pi}{3}, -\frac{\pi}{3}, \frac{\pi}{3}, \frac{5\pi}{3}, \frac{7\pi}{3}, \ldots \right\}$—that is, $\left\{ n\pi, 2n\pi + \frac{\pi}{3}, 2n\pi - \frac{\pi}{3} \right\}$, where n is any integer.

It is important that in line 2 of our solution we did not divide both sides of the equation by $\sin x$. If we had, we would have lost the solutions of the form $n\pi$. Do not divide by quantities that could equal 0.

Problem 3 *If $AD = 25$ and $\sin \theta + \cos 2\theta = \frac{3}{4}$, what is the length of altitude $\overline{BD}$ in triangle ABC?*

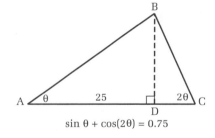

sin θ + cos(2θ) = 0.75

Solution
$$\sin \theta + \cos 2\theta = \frac{3}{4}$$

$$\sin \theta + 1 - 2 \sin^2 \theta = \frac{3}{4}$$

$$8 \sin^2 \theta - 4 \sin \theta - 1 = 0$$

This is a quadratic equation in $\sin \theta$. We use the quadratic formula, with $a = 8$, $b = -4$, and $c = -1$, to find that $\sin \theta \approx 0.683$ or $\sin \theta \approx -0.183$. Since θ is certainly between $0°$ and $180°$, we must use $\sin \theta \approx 0.683$. Using the ⟨INV⟩ ⟨sin⟩ keys on a calculator, we find that $\theta \approx 43.1°$. Since $\frac{BD}{AD} = \tan \theta$,

$$\frac{BD}{25} \approx \tan 43.1°$$

$$BD \approx 25 \cdot \tan 43.1°$$
$$BD \approx 23.4$$

Problem 4 Find the values of θ for which $\frac{1}{\sec 2\theta} + 1 = 2 - 2\sin^2\theta$.

Solution

$$\frac{1}{\sec 2\theta} + 1 = 2 - 2\sin^2\theta$$

$$\cos 2\theta + 1 = 2 - 2\sin^2\theta$$
$$2\cos^2\theta - 1 + 1 = 2 - 2\sin^2\theta$$
$$2\cos^2\theta + 2\sin^2\theta = 2$$
$$2 = 2$$

The original equation must be an identity. Therefore, the equation is true for all possible values of θ. Since there are no restrictions on the values of θ, the solution is $\{\theta : \theta \in \mathcal{R}\}$.

Part Three: Exercises and Problems

Warm-up Exercises

1 Determine whether each of the following is True or False.

a $\sin 50° \cos 20° = \frac{1}{2}(\sin 70° + \sin 30°)$

b $\sin 50° \sin 20° = \frac{1}{2}(\sin 70° + \sin 30°)$

c $\cos 50° \cos 20° = \frac{1}{2}(\sin 70° + \sin 30°)$

2 Write each sum as a product.
    a $\sin 3\theta + \sin 5\theta$ **b** $\cos 2\theta + \cos \theta$

3 Refer to the inequality $\sin \theta + \cos \theta > 1$.
    a Is $\theta = 70°$ a solution?   **b** Is $\theta = 50°$ a solution?
    c Is $\theta = 90°$ a solution?

Problem Set

4 Find (x, y) if $\sin \theta = \frac{3}{5}$.

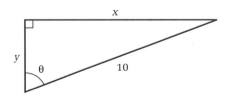

5 Simplify each expression.

  a $\dfrac{\cos 3x \cos 2x - \sin 3x \sin 2x}{\sin 5x}$ **b** $\dfrac{\sin 3x \cos x + \cos 3x \sin x}{\cos^2 2x - \sin^2 2x}$

6 Solve for θ, where $0 \le \theta < 2\pi$.

    a $\sin \theta = \cos \theta$ **b** $\sin \theta \cdot \cos \theta = 0$

7 Write each sum as a product.

    a $\sin 17° + \sin 3°$ **b** $\cos 50° + \cos 14°$

8 Refer to the equation $2 \cos^2 \theta + \cos \theta - 1 = 0$.

    a Solve for $\cos \theta$.

    b Solve for θ if $0 \le \theta < 2\pi$.

9 Prove the identity $\dfrac{\sin 4\theta + \sin 3\theta}{\cos 4\theta + \cos 3\theta} = \tan \dfrac{7\theta}{2}$.

10 Write each product as a sum.

    a $2 \cdot \cos 10° \cdot \cos 4°$ **b** $2 \cdot \sin 70° \cos 66°$

    c $2 \cdot \sin 13° \cdot \sin 9°$

11 Find the exact value of each of the following.

    a $\sin 165° \cdot \sin 15°$ **b** $\sin 255° \cos 15°$

    c $\cos 105° \cos (-15°)$

12 Simplify each expression.

    a $\dfrac{\sin 6\theta + \sin 2\theta}{\cos 6\theta + \cos 2\theta}$ **b** $\dfrac{\cos 10\theta + \cos 2\theta}{\sin 10\theta - \sin 2\theta}$

13 Write each expression as a product.

    a $\cos x + \cos y$ **b** $\cos 6\theta + \cos 2\theta$

    c $\cos 12\theta + \cos 8\theta$ **d** $\cos x - \cos y$

14 Solve each equation for θ, where $0 \le \theta < 2\pi$.

    a $2 \sin^2 \theta + 3 \sin \theta + 1 = 0$ **b** $2 \cos^2 \theta + 3 \sin \theta - 3 = 0$

 15 Find the measure of angle θ if $0° \le \theta < 90°$.

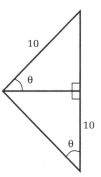

16 Solve for x.

    a $\dfrac{\cos x - \sin x}{\cos x + \sin x} = 1$ **b** $\dfrac{\cos x - \sin x}{\cos x + \sin x} = \dfrac{1 - \tan x}{1 + \tan x}$

Problem Set, *continued*

17 Find the exact value of tan 75° tan 75°. Show your method.

18 Solve for θ, where $0 \le \theta < 2\pi$.
a $2 \sin^2 \theta + \sin \theta - 1 = 0$
b $\sin^2 \theta - \sin \theta - 2 = 0$
c $4 \sin^2 \theta - 3 = 0$

19 Prove the following identities.
a $\tan \alpha = \dfrac{\sin (\alpha + \beta) + \sin (\alpha - \beta)}{\cos (\alpha - \beta) + \cos (\alpha + \beta)}$

b $\cos \theta \cos (\theta - 90°) = \dfrac{1}{2} \cos (2\theta - 90°)$

20 Prove the following identities.
a $\dfrac{\cos 5\theta + \cos \theta}{\sin 5\theta + \sin \theta} = \cot 3\theta$

b $\dfrac{\sin 10\theta + \sin 6\theta}{\cos^2 \theta - \sin^2 \theta} = 2 \sin 8\theta$

21 Solve for $\{x : 0° \le x \le 360°\}$.
a $\sin^2 x - 4 \cos^2 x = 0$
b $12 \cos^2 x = 15 - 20 \sin x$

22 Find all values of θ for which $\sin 4\theta = 2 \sin 2\theta - 8 \sin^3 \theta \cos \theta$.

23 In the diagram, $0° < \theta < 45°$.
a Find θ.
b Find x.

24 Prove that $\cos 20° = \dfrac{\sqrt{3}}{4} \sec 10° + \dfrac{1}{2}$. (Hint: Write an expression for $\cos 20° \cos 10°$.)

25 a Using a graphing program, determine the number of solutions the equation $\log x = \cos x$ has.
b Find the greatest value of x satisfying this equation.

26 Refer to the equation $\sin x = \dfrac{1}{4}x$.
a Find an upper bound and a lower bound of the solutions of this trigonometric equation.
b Using a graphing calculator or computer program, find the approximate solutions.

CHAPTER SUMMARY

CONCEPTS AND PROCEDURES

After studying this chapter, you should be able to
- Prove trigonometric identities (15.1)
- Use the sum and difference identities (15.2)
- Determine the angle between two graphed lines (15.2)
- Apply the double-angle identities (15.3)
- Apply the half-angle identities (15.3)
- Use the product-to-sum and sum-to-product identities (15.4)
- Solve trigonometric equations (15.4)

VOCABULARY

double-angle identities (15.3)
half-angle identities (15.3)
product-to-sum identities (15.4)

sum and difference identities (15.2)
sum-to-product identities (15.4)

THEOREMS AND IDENTITIES

$\sin 2\theta = 2 \sin \theta \cos \theta$

$\cos 2\theta = \cos^2 \theta - \sin^2 \theta$

$\cos 2\theta = 1 - 2 \sin^2 \theta$

$\cos 2\theta = 2 \cos^2 \theta - 1$

$\tan 2\theta = \dfrac{2 \tan \theta}{1 - \tan^2 \theta}$

$\sin \dfrac{\theta}{2} = \pm \sqrt{\dfrac{1 - \cos \theta}{2}}$

$\cos \dfrac{\theta}{2} = \pm \sqrt{\dfrac{1 + \cos \theta}{2}}$

$\tan \dfrac{\theta}{2} = \pm \sqrt{\dfrac{1 - \cos \theta}{1 + \cos \theta}}$

$\tan \dfrac{\theta}{2} = \dfrac{1 - \cos \theta}{\sin \theta}$

$\tan \dfrac{\theta}{2} = \dfrac{\sin \theta}{1 + \cos \theta}$

$\sin (\alpha + \beta) = \sin \alpha \cos \beta + \cos \alpha \sin \beta$

$\sin (\alpha - \beta) = \sin \alpha \cos \beta - \cos \alpha \sin \beta$

$\cos (\alpha + \beta) = \cos \alpha \cos \beta - \sin \alpha \sin \beta$

$\cos (\alpha - \beta) = \cos \alpha \cos \beta + \sin \alpha \sin \beta$

$\tan (\alpha + \beta) = \dfrac{\tan \alpha + \tan \beta}{1 - \tan \alpha \tan \beta}$

$\tan (\alpha - \beta) = \dfrac{\tan \alpha - \tan \beta}{1 + \tan \alpha \tan \beta}$

$\sin \alpha \cos \beta = \dfrac{1}{2}[\sin (\alpha + \beta) + \sin (\alpha - \beta)]$

$\sin \alpha \sin \beta = \dfrac{1}{2}[\cos (\alpha - \beta) - \cos (\alpha + \beta)]$

$\cos \alpha \cos \beta = \dfrac{1}{2}[\cos (\alpha - \beta) + \cos (\alpha + \beta)]$

$\sin \alpha + \sin \beta = 2 \sin \dfrac{\alpha + \beta}{2} \cos \dfrac{\alpha - \beta}{2}$

$\cos \alpha + \cos \beta = 2 \cos \dfrac{\alpha + \beta}{2} \cos \dfrac{\alpha - \beta}{2}$

REVIEW PROBLEMS

1 Determine whether each statement is True or False.

    a $\cos 30° = \sin 60°$ **b** $1 + (\cot 30°)^2 = (\sec 60°)^2$

    c $\cos^2 40° - 1 = \csc^2 40°$

2 Find each of the following.

    a $\sin \alpha$

    b $\sin \beta$

    c $\sin (\alpha + \beta)$

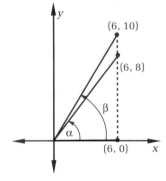

3 Evaluate.

    a $\sin \left(2 \text{ Arcsin } \dfrac{4}{5}\right)$ **b** $\cos \left(2 \text{ Arcsin } \dfrac{4}{5}\right)$

4 Write each product as a sum.

    a $\sin 4\theta \cos 3\theta$ **b** $\cos 4\theta \cos 6\theta$ **c** $\sin 2\theta \cos 8\theta$

5 Prove that $\dfrac{\cos \theta}{1 - \sin \theta} = \sec \theta + \tan \theta$. State restrictions.

6 Determine whether each equation is True or False.

    a $\sin (40° + 50°) = \sin 90°$ **b** $\sin 40° + \sin 50° = \sin 90°$

    c $\sin 40° \cos 50° + \cos 40° \sin 50° = \sin 90°$

7 a Express the volume of each figure as a function of θ.

    b If both figures have the same volume, what is θ?

8 Verify each identity.

   a $\tan \theta + \cot \theta = \sec \theta \cdot \csc \theta$ **b** $\sec^2 \theta + \csc^2 \theta = \sec^2 \theta \cdot \csc^2 \theta$

   c $\dfrac{\cos \theta}{1 + \sin \theta} = \dfrac{1 - \sin \theta}{\cos \theta}$

9 Determine whether each of the following is True or False.

   a $\cos 90° = 2 \cos 45°$ **b** $\cos 90° = \cos 30° + \cos 60°$

   c $\cos 90° = \cos^2 45° - \sin^2 45°$

10 Solve $\cos 2x + \sin^2 x = 1$ for x, where $0 \le x \le 2\pi$.

11 Prove each identity.

   a $\cos \left(\theta - \dfrac{\pi}{2} \right) = \sin \theta$ **b** $\sin \left(\theta - \dfrac{\pi}{2} \right) = -\cos \theta$

   c $\sin \left(\theta + \dfrac{\pi}{2} \right) = \cos \theta$ **d** $\cos \left(\theta + \dfrac{\pi}{2} \right) = -\sin \theta$

12 Determine whether the following statement is True or False.

$$\sin 15° = \sqrt{\dfrac{1 - \cos 30°}{2}}$$

13 Use identities to express each of the following in terms of functions of x.

   a $\sin 3x$ **b** $\cos 3x$

14 Determine whether each of the following is True or False.

   a $\tan \alpha = \dfrac{\sin \alpha}{\cos \alpha}$ **b** $\cot \alpha = \dfrac{\cos \alpha}{\sin \alpha}$

   c $\sin \alpha = \dfrac{1}{\csc \alpha}$

15 Prove that $\cos^4 \theta - \sin^4 \theta = \cos^2 \theta - \sin^2 \theta$.

16 If $\tan \beta = \frac{3}{4}$ and $\tan \alpha = -\frac{4}{3}$, what is $\tan (\alpha - \beta)$? Explain your answer.

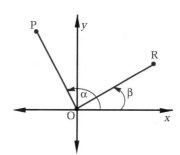

17 Change each sum to a product.

   a $\sin x + \sin y$ **b** $\sin 3\theta + \sin \theta$ **c** $\sin 10\theta - \sin 4\theta$

18 Determine whether each of the following is True or False.
  a $2 \sin 30° \cos 60° = \sin 90° - \sin 30°$
  b $\sin 90° + \sin 30° = 2 \sin 60° \cos 30°$

19 Use the diagram to find each of the
 following.

  a $\dfrac{\sin \theta}{1 + \sin \theta}$

  b $\dfrac{1 - \sin \theta}{\sin \theta}$

20 Solve $\tan 2x = \tan x$ for x.

21 Evaluate without using a calculator.
  a $\sin 40° \cos 5° + \cos 40° \sin 5°$
  b $\cos 18° \cos 12° - \sin 18° \sin 12°$

  c $\cos \dfrac{5\pi}{8} \cdot \cos \dfrac{3\pi}{8} + \sin \dfrac{5\pi}{8} \cdot \sin \dfrac{3\pi}{8}$

22 Prove the following identities.

  a $\dfrac{\cos x - \sin x}{\cos x + \sin x} = \dfrac{\cos 2x}{1 + \sin 2x}$

  b $1 + \tan x \tan 2x = \sec 2x$
  c $\sin (x + y) \sin (x - y) = \sin^2 x - \sin^2 y$

23 The segment OA is rotated $\frac{\pi}{2}$, π, and $\frac{3\pi}{2}$
 radians to form segments OA′, OA″,
 and OA‴.
  a Determine (x_1, y_1), (x_2, y_2), and (x_3, y_3).
  b Find the sine, the cosine, and the
   tangent of θ, $\theta + \frac{\pi}{2}$, $\theta + \pi$, and $\theta + \frac{3\pi}{2}$.

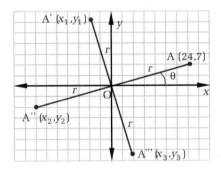

24 Evaluate the following expression.
$$\frac{\sin 10° \cdot \sin 20° \cdot \sin 30° \cdot \sin 40° \cdot \sin 50° \cdot \sin 60° \cdot \sin 70° \cdot \sin 80°}{\cos 10° \cdot \cos 20° \cdot \cos 30° \cdot \cos 40° \cdot \cos 50° \cdot \cos 60° \cdot \cos 70° \cdot \cos 80°}$$

25 The graph of $y = f(x)$ is shown. Draw the
 graph of $y = [f(x)]^2$.

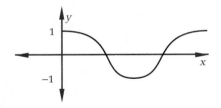

CHAPTER TEST

In problems 1–3, simplify each expression in terms of a single trigonometric function.

1 $\dfrac{\sin\theta + \cos\theta}{1 + \tan\theta}$

2 $(1 + \cos\theta)(\csc\theta - \cot\theta)$

3 $\dfrac{\sin\beta + \tan\beta}{\cos\beta + 1}$

4 If $\sin\theta = \dfrac{-8}{17}$ and θ is in the third quadrant, what is $\cot\theta$?

5 Find, to the nearest degree, the acute angle formed by the graphs of $y = \dfrac{-1}{2}x + 4$ and $y = \dfrac{4}{3}x - 2$.

In problems 6–8, solve each equation.

6 $3\tan^2\theta = 1$, where $-2\pi \le \theta \le \pi$
7 $4\sin\theta \cdot \cos\theta = 1$, where $0 \le \theta \le 2\pi$
8 $\cos 2\theta = \cos^2\theta$

9 If $\cos\theta = \dfrac{3}{5}$, what is $\cos 2\theta$?

10 Find $\cos(\beta - \alpha)$ if β is in Quadrant II and $\sin\beta = \dfrac{2}{3}$ and if α is in Quadrant I and $\cos\alpha = \dfrac{3}{4}$.

11 If $\sec\alpha = \dfrac{3}{2}$ and $\dfrac{3\pi}{2} < \alpha < 2\pi$, what is $\sin 2\alpha$?

12 Prove that $\dfrac{\cos\theta}{1 + \sin\theta} + \dfrac{1 + \sin\theta}{\cos\theta} = 2\sec\theta$.

13 Use the diagram to find $\sin\theta$.

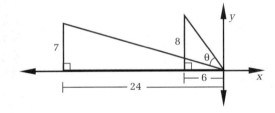

14 If $\tan 2\alpha = \dfrac{-24}{7}$, what is $\tan\alpha$?

15 Prove that $\sin 2\alpha = \dfrac{2\tan\alpha}{1 + \tan^2\alpha}$.

16 Suppose that $\sin\alpha = -\dfrac{3}{5}$, where $\pi < \alpha < \dfrac{3\pi}{2}$, and that $\cos\beta = \dfrac{24}{25}$, where $\dfrac{3\pi}{2} < \beta < 2\pi$. Find the following.
   a $\cos(\beta - \alpha)$ **b** $\sin(\alpha + \beta)$ **c** $\tan(\alpha + \beta)$

17 Prove that $\dfrac{\cos(\alpha + \beta) + \cos(\alpha - \beta)}{\sin(\alpha + \beta) + \sin(\alpha - \beta)} = \cot\alpha$.

TRIGONOMETRIC GRAPHS AND APPLICATIONS

Relationships among the sides and angles of a triangle, the basis of trigonometry, are illustrated in this painting by Kandinsky.

THE LAW OF SINES

Objective

After studying this section, you will be able to
- Apply the Law of Sines

Part One: Introduction

Solving Oblique Triangles

You have seen how to solve right triangles using the trigonometric functions. Now we will discuss solving triangles that are not right triangles.

In triangle ABC, we are given two angles and a side. By the AAS theorem, which you may remember from geometry, the two angles and the side determine a unique triangle.

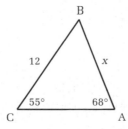

We drop a perpendicular (altitude) from B to side $\overline{CA}$. Now we can set up two equations involving sine.

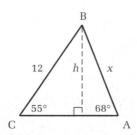

$$\sin 68° = \frac{h}{x} \qquad \sin 55° = \frac{h}{12}$$

$$x \sin 68° = h \qquad 12 \sin 55° = h$$

Thus, $x \sin 68° = 12 \sin 55°$.

$$x = \frac{12 \sin 55°}{\sin 68°} \approx \frac{12(0.8192)}{(0.9272)} \approx 10.6$$

In future problems, we can avoid the extra steps of putting in h and then removing it. Let's analyze the equation

$$x \sin 68° = 12 \sin 55°$$

This equation can be written as a proportion.

$$\frac{\sin 68°}{12} = \frac{\sin 55°}{x}$$

Notice that 12 is the measure of the side opposite the 68° angle and that x is the measure of the side opposite the 55° angle. The general form of this equation is called the *Law of Sines*.

If a, b, and c are the lengths of the sides opposite angles A, B, and C respectively in triangle ABC, then

$$\frac{\sin\angle A}{a} = \frac{\sin\angle B}{b} = \frac{\sin\angle C}{c} \qquad \text{or} \qquad \frac{a}{\sin\angle A} = \frac{b}{\sin\angle B} = \frac{c}{\sin\angle C}$$

Example *Use the information in the figure to find lengths p and q.*

Notice that the pattern of given information is ASA (angle-side-angle), so our answers will be unique. Notice also that $\angle R$ is 30°.

By the Law of Sines, $\frac{p}{\sin\angle P} = \frac{q}{\sin\angle Q} = \frac{r}{\sin\angle R}$, so $\frac{p}{\sin 40°} = \frac{14}{\sin 30°}$ and $\frac{q}{\sin 110°} = \frac{14}{\sin 30°}$. Therefore, $p = \frac{14\sin 40°}{\sin 30°} \approx 18.0$ and $q = \frac{14\sin 110°}{\sin 30°} \approx 26.3$.

Note The Law of Sines can also be used to determine the measure of an angle.

The Law of Sines gives unique answers when the given information follows an ASA or AAS pattern. (For SAS and SSS, you need a method presented in the next section.) When the pattern of information is SSA, however, there may be one solution, two solutions, or no solution at all. This is because either one triangle, two triangles, or no triangle may be constructed using the given information.

Part Two: Sample Problems

Problem 1 *Let $a = 20$, $b = 25$, and $\angle A = 50°$. Using the Law of Sines, find $\angle B$. How many triangles can be constructed on the basis of the given information?*

Solution According to the Law of Sines, $\dfrac{20}{\sin 50°} = \dfrac{25}{\sin\angle B}$

$$\sin\angle B = \frac{25\sin 50°}{20} \approx 0.9576$$

Arcsin 0.9576 ≈ 73°, so one solution is $\angle B \approx 73°$. However, the equation $\sin\angle B \approx 0.9576$ has two solutions. The other solution is $\angle B \approx (180 - 73)°$, or $\angle B \approx 107°$. Therefore, two triangles can be constructed on the basis of the given information.

Problem 2   Let $a = 20$, $b = 25$, and $\angle A = 72°$. Using the *Law of Sines*, find $\angle B$. How many triangles can be constructed on the basis of the given information?

Solution   According to the Law of Sines,

$$\frac{20}{\sin 72°} = \frac{25}{\sin \angle B}$$

$$\sin \angle B = \frac{25 \sin 72°}{20} \approx 1.1888$$

Pressing $\boxed{\text{INV}}$ $\boxed{\text{sin}}$ 1.1888 results in an error message on a calculator. (Why? What is the largest value $\sin \angle B$ can have?) This is therefore an impossible case. There is no solution. No triangle corresponds to the given information.

Part Three: Exercises and Problems

Warm-up Exercises

In problems 1 and 2, evaluate to the nearest thousandth.

1 $\dfrac{16.4 \sin 69.8°}{22.7}$

2 $\dfrac{15.9 \sin 47.6°}{\sin 67.5°}$

3 Determine $\angle A$ to the nearest degree.

4 Find lengths x and y, rounded to the nearest hundredth.

In problems 5–7, find each angle or side.

  5 $\angle P$

  6 r

  7 q

8 Find the area of equilateral $\triangle ABC$ shown.

Problem Set

9 a Find x and y to the nearest integer.

b Using (x, y) from part **a**, find the length of $\overline{PD}$ to the nearest integer.

In problems 10 and 11, evaluate.

10 $3^2 + 5^2 - 2 \cdot 3 \cdot 5 \cdot \dfrac{1}{2}$

11 $3^2 + 5^2 - 2 \cdot 3 \cdot 5 \cdot \cos 10°$

12 Evaluate.

a $\sin \dfrac{\pi}{2}$

b $\sin \left(\dfrac{\pi}{2} + 2\pi \right)$

c $\sin \left(\dfrac{\pi}{2} + 4\pi \right)$

d $\sin \left(\dfrac{\pi}{2} + 6\pi \right)$

13 a Copy and complete the table for y = sin x, rounding to the nearest thousandth.

x	0	$\frac{\pi}{6}$	$\frac{\pi}{4}$	$\frac{\pi}{3}$	$\frac{\pi}{2}$	$\frac{2\pi}{3}$	$\frac{3\pi}{4}$	π	$\frac{3\pi}{2}$	2π
y										

b Sketch the graph of y = sin x.

14 Use sin (α − β) to find sin 15°, where α = 45° and β = 30°.

15 Determine the exact value of x.

16 Two ranger stations are 100 miles apart. A forest fire is spotted. The angle measured at station 1 between station 2 and the fire is 61°. The angle measured at station 2 between station 1 and the fire is 48°. How far is it from station 1 to the fire?

17 What is the ratio of PQ to QR in △PQR?

696 Chapter 16 Trigonometric Graphs and Applications

In problems 18–21, find all possible values of θ to the nearest degree.

18

19

20

21

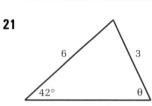

In problems 22–25, find the largest and smallest possible values of each expression.

22 $\sin \theta$ **23** $4 \sin \theta$

24 $\sin 5\theta$ **25** $4 \sin 5\theta$

26 Assume that $0° < \theta < 90°$. Explain each statement.

   a If $b = a \sin \theta$, then exactly one triangle is determined.

   b If $a \sin \theta < b < a$, then two triangles are determined.

   c If $b \geq a$, then exactly one triangle is determined.

   d If $b < a \sin \theta$, no triangle is determined.

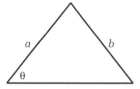

27 From a certain point, the angle of elevation to the top of a radio tower is 48°. From a point 100 feet closer to the tower, the angle of elevation is 72°. Find the height of the tower.

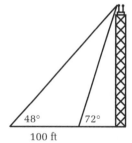

28 For the triangles in the diagram, $\sin \alpha = 0.5876$.

   a Find all possible values of α to the nearest degree.

   b Let $\theta = 32°$. Find all possible values of β.

   c If $\theta = 60°$, what happens to the possible values of β?

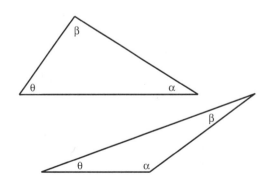

Problem Set, *continued*

29 Jenny and Jill are 2000 feet apart. Jenny spots José at a 40° angle, and Jill spots him at a 65° angle. How much farther from José is Jenny than Jill?

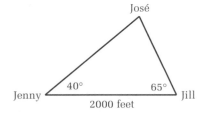

30 Philly can reach his second-floor window with an 18-foot ladder at a 75° angle to the ground. Willy claims that Philly could reach the window with a 16-foot ladder. Justify or disprove Willy's claim.

31 A pendulum swings between $\overline{AP}$ and $\overline{AQ}$. If AP = AQ = 18 cm, what are the measures of angles α_1 and α_2?

32 If $\overline{BD}$ bisects $\angle ABC$, what is the length of $\overline{BD}$?

33 Prove that the area *k* of △ABC is given by $k = \frac{1}{2}ab \sin \angle C$.

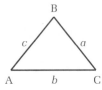

34 Find the radius *R* of the circle.

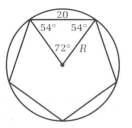

35 Prove that for any △ABC, $\frac{a}{\sin \angle A}$ is the diameter of the circle circumscribed about the triangle.

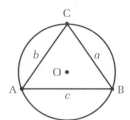

16.2 | THE LAW OF COSINES

Objective

After studying this section, you will be able to
- Apply the Law of Cosines

Part One: Introduction

Solving SAS and SSS Triangles

When we cannot use the Law of Sines to find the dimensions of a triangle, we can draw an altitude and use right-triangle methods.

Example   *Find the length of the third side in the triangle.*

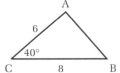

We are given SAS information, so the triangle is uniquely determined. However, the Law of Sines does not help. If we draw an altitude h, then by the Pythagorean Theorem, $6^2 = x^2 + h^2$ and $c^2 = (8 - x)^2 + h^2$.

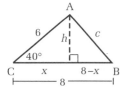

If $c^2 = (8 - x)^2 + h^2$, then
$$c^2 = 8^2 - 16x + x^2 + h^2$$
We substitute 6^2 for $x^2 + h^2$.
$$c^2 = 8^2 - 16x + 6^2$$
$$= 8^2 + 6^2 - 16x$$

By the definition of trigonometric functions in right triangles, $\cos 40° = \frac{x}{6}$, so $x = 6 \cos 40°$. Therefore,
$$c^2 = 8^2 + 6^2 - 16 \cdot 6 \cos 40°$$
$$\approx 26.46$$
$$c \approx 5.1$$

To get a general formula, we substitute a for 8, b for 6, and $\angle C$ for the 40° angle. The result is the *Law of Cosines.*

The Law of Cosines

If *a*, *b*, and *c* are the lengths of the sides opposite angles A, B, and C in a triangle, then
$$c^2 = a^2 + b^2 - 2ab \cos \angle C$$

The following alternative forms of the Law of Cosines may be used.

$$a^2 = b^2 + c^2 - 2bc \cos \angle A \qquad\qquad b^2 = a^2 + c^2 - 2ac \cos \angle B$$

We use the Law of Cosines when we are given the lengths of all three sides of a triangle (SSS) and must find the measure of an angle, or when we are given the lengths of two sides and the measure of the included angle of a triangle (SAS) and want to find the length of the third side.

Part Two: Sample Problems

Problem 1

The sides of a triangle are 8, 10, and 12. Find the measure of the largest angle.

Solution

Since we are given the lengths of three sides of a triangle (SSS), we can use the Law of Cosines. The largest angle is opposite the longest side. Let's label the largest angle C and the longest side c. The other two sides are a and b.

$$c^2 = a^2 + b^2 - 2ab \cos \angle C$$

$$\cos \angle C = \frac{a^2 + b^2 - c^2}{2ab}$$

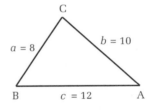

$$= \frac{64 + 100 - 144}{160}$$

$$= 0.125$$

Since $\cos \angle C = 0.125$, $\angle C \approx 82.8°$.

Problem 2

ABCD is a parallelogram. AD = 40, CD = 200, and $\angle D = 115°$. Find the length of $\overline{BD}$ and the measure of $\angle BDC$.

Solution

Since opposite sides of a parallelogram are equal in length, BC = 40. Since consecutive angles of a parallelogram are supplementary, $\text{m}\angle C = 65$. We can apply the Law of Cosines because $\triangle CBD$ has the SAS pattern.

$$(BD)^2 = 40^2 + 200^2 - 2(40)(200)(\cos 65°)$$
$$\approx 1600 + 40{,}000 - 16{,}000(0.4226)$$
$$\approx 34{,}838$$
$$BD \approx 187$$

We can use the Law of Sines to determine the measure of $\angle BDC$.

$$\frac{\sin \angle BDC}{40} \approx \frac{\sin 65°}{187}$$

$$\sin \angle BDC \approx \frac{40 \sin 65°}{187}$$

$$\approx 0.1939$$

Since $\sin \angle BDC \approx 0.1939$, $\angle BDC \approx 11.18°$.

Part Three: Exercises and Problems

Warm-up Exercises

1 Solve for a, b, and c to the nearest tenth.

$a^2 = 3^2 + 9^2 - 2 \cdot 3 \cdot 9 \cos 47°$
$b^2 = 5^2 + 6^2 - 2 \cdot 5 \cdot 6 \cos 120°$
$c^2 = 4^2 + 3^2 - 2 \cdot 4 \cdot 3 \cos 60°$

In problems 2–4, find angles α, β, and γ to the nearest degree.

2

3

4

In problems 5–7, find lengths x, y, and z to the nearest tenth.

5

6

7

Problem Set

8 Find the length of $\overline{AC}$ and the measures of $\angle A$ and $\angle C$.

9 Sketch the graph of each equation.

   a $y = x^2$ **b** $y = x^2 + 4$ **c** $y = (x + 4)^2$

In problems 10 and 11, evaluate.

10 $\sin\left(\text{Arccos}\,\dfrac{3}{5}\right)$ **11** $\sin\left(\text{Arcsin}\,\dfrac{4}{5} + \text{Arccos}\,\dfrac{5}{13}\right)$

12 The lines shown are parallel. Write an equation of ℓ.

Problem Set, *continued*

13 Let y = sin x. Copy and complete the table, then graph the equation.

x	0	$\frac{\pi}{4}$	$\frac{\pi}{2}$	$\frac{3\pi}{4}$	π	$\frac{5\pi}{4}$	$\frac{3\pi}{2}$	$\frac{7\pi}{4}$	2π	$\frac{9\pi}{4}$	$\frac{5\pi}{2}$
y											

14 Find the measure of ∠B to the nearest degree.

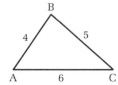

15 At noon, two cars leave the junction of two straight roads. One car travels at 50 miles per hour along one road; the other car travels at 41 miles per hour along the other road. If the cars' paths form an angle of 72°, how far apart (in a straight line) are the cars at 3 P.M.?

16 The distance from point A to point B cannot be measured directly. Use the information given in the diagram to find AB.

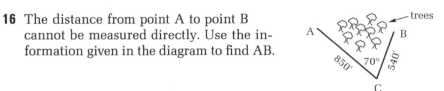

17 Find all possible values of x.

    a sin x = 1   **b** sin x = 0   **c** sin x = −1

18 Find the perimeter of regular pentagon ABCDE.

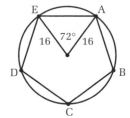

19 a Find the lengths of $\overline{AB}$, $\overline{BC}$, and $\overline{AC}$.
    b Find θ to the nearest degree.

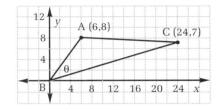

In problems 20–22, refer to the graph of y = f(x).

20 Sketch y = f(x − 2).
21 Sketch y = −f(x).
22 Sketch y = f(x + 2).

23 A 30-foot ladder and a 26-foot ladder both reach the top of a wall. The 30-foot ladder makes a 50° angle with the ground. Find angle θ to the nearest degree. (Remember to consider both cases.)

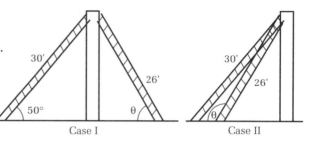

Case I   Case II

24 Find a so that m∠A = 60.

25 Find the length of a chord of a circle whose radius is 20 if the central angle of the chord is 18°.

26 Refer to the diagram.

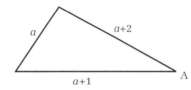

 a Find OB.
 b Find OA.
 c Find AB.
 d Find m∠A.

27 The lengths of the boundaries of a triangular plot of land are 80 feet, 100 feet, and 120 feet. Find the measure of the largest angle formed by the boundaries.

28 Two sides and a diagonal of a rhombus form a triangle whose perimeter is 50 centimeters. Find the measure of the angle between the sides of the rhombus if the perimeter of the rhombus is 72 centimeters.

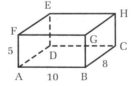

29 The dimensions of the rectangular box shown are 10 inches by 8 inches by 5 inches.

 a Find m∠FBH.
 b Find m∠CHA.

30 The area k of a triangle is given by the formula $k = \frac{1}{2}ab \sin \angle C$. The lengths of two sides of the triangle are 8 and 15.

 a Find the angle between the two given sides.
 b Find the length of the third side of the triangle.

31 The lengths of the sides of a triangle are 8, 10, and 14. Find the length of the median drawn to the longest side of the triangle.

32 Find the largest and smallest values of each expression.

   a $\sin \theta$ **b** $\sin \theta + 5$

   c $\sin (\theta - 4)$ **d** $\sin (\theta - 4) + 5$

33 Suppose that k is the area of $\triangle ABC$ and $s = \frac{a + b + c}{2}$. Prove that $k = \sqrt{s(s - a)(s - b)(s - c)}$.

MATHEMATICS IN MEDICINE

Dr. Sharon Unti uses mathematics on the spot

Sharon Unti, associate director of pediatric education at Children's Memorial Hospital in Chicago, wears two buttons on her gray doctor's jacket. One reads, "I love kids." The other displays her name in a colorful simulation of a child's printing. Besides her love of children, Dr. Unti's qualifications include her medical education and three years in a pediatric residency. Her college coursework—like most premedical programs—included calculus and advanced algebra. Now Dr. Unti instructs residents at the hospital—doctors receiving advanced training in pediatric medicine.

"The way I use mathematics directly," Dr. Unti says, "is in calculating dosages of medicine and amounts of fluids to give to children, such as children who have lost fluids due to a trauma or who are dehydrated. Such calculations are based on formulas. Most have been done for all realistic values of a child's height and weight and are available in reference tables. The calculations themselves often involve exponentials, logarithms, or ratios.

"One use of logarithms occurs when a child has an infection and we don't know exactly what bacteria may be present," Dr. Unti explains. "We coat a plate with five different antibiotics and grow five cultures from the infection site. Since the uninhibited growth of the culture is exponential, the resistance of the bacteria to each of the five antibiotics is reported as the log of the area of the plate covered by the bacteria after 48 or 72 hours. So if the culture has not grown at all at the end of the time period, its resistance to the antibiotic is 0, and we would use it on the child's infection."

Dr. Unti earned her bachelor's and medical degrees from Northwestern University in Evanston, Illinois, and Chicago.

GRAPHING SINE FUNCTIONS

Objectives

After studying this section, you will be able to
- Graph the sine function
- Translate the sine graph vertically and horizontally
- Change the amplitude of the sine graph

Part One: Introduction

The Graph of the Sine Function

The graph of $y = \sin x$ is illustrated below for $-\pi \leq x \leq 4\pi$. In this equation, x is the size of the angle in radians.

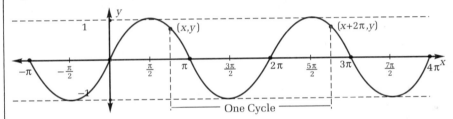

Notice some important features of the graph of the sine function.

1 The x-intercepts occur at integer multiples of π.
2 The range is $\{y: -1 \leq y \leq 1\}$.
3 The graph is **periodic.** That is, the graph repeats the same pattern over and over. The pattern is called a **cycle.** For the sine function, each cycle has the same length, called a **period.**
4 The maximum (highest) points occur when x is $\frac{\pi}{2}$, $\frac{5\pi}{2}$, $\frac{9\pi}{2}$, ..., $\frac{\pi}{2} + 2k\pi$, where k is an integer.
5 The minimum (lowest) points occur when x is $\frac{-\pi}{2}$, $\frac{3\pi}{2}$, $\frac{7\pi}{2}$, ... (again, in jumps of 2π).

   If you start at any point (x, y) on the sine graph and move left or right a distance of 2π, you will arrive at a point that is on the graph and has the same height, y. Thus, since $y = \sin x = \sin (x \pm 2\pi) = \sin (x \pm 4\pi) = \ldots$, the period of $y = \sin x$ is 2π.

Translating the Sine Graph

Once you have memorized the basic graph for $y = \sin x$, you are ready to apply your earlier work on horizontal and vertical shifts.

Just as the graph of $y = (x - 2)^2$ is nothing more than the graph of $y = x^2$ shifted two units to the right, the graph of $y = \sin(x - 2)$ is the standard sine graph shifted two units to the right. In physics, this shift is called a **phase shift**.

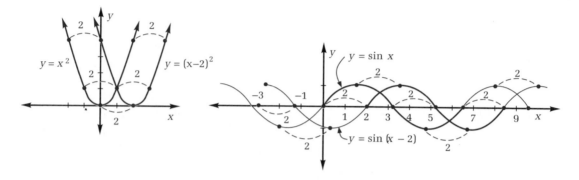

The graph of $y = \sin x - 3$ is the standard sine graph shifted down three units. *Each point* of the graph has been shifted down three units. Thus, the maximum value of this function is -2 and the minimum is -4.

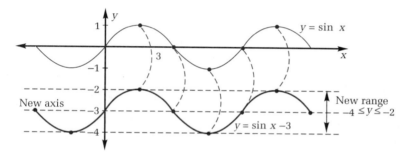

Amplitude Changes

The **amplitude** of a sine wave is its amount of deviation above and below the axis line.

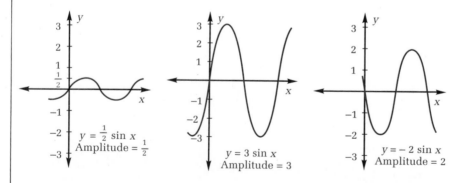

The amplitude of a sine graph is determined by the coefficient of the function. The amplitude of $y = a \sin x$ is $|a|$.

Part Two: *Sample Problems*

Problem 1   *Refer to the graph.*

    a What are the maximum and minimum values of the function?
    b What is the amplitude?
    c What is the period?
    d What is an equation of this sine graph?

Solution

    a The maximum and minimum values are 6 and −2 respectively.
    b The graph oscillates between $y = -2$ and $y = 6$. The axis line must be at $y = 2$, halfway between −2 and 6. Since 6 is four units above the axis, the amplitude is 4. In general, if the maximum value of y is a and the minimum value is b, then the amplitude is $\frac{1}{2}(a - b)$.
    c The graph repeats itself every 2π units, so the period is 2π.
    d The graph is not shifted horizontally, but it is shifted up two units. An equation is $y = 4 \sin x + 2$.

Problem 2   *Graph $y = \frac{3}{2} \sin \left(x - \frac{\pi}{6}\right) + 1$.*

Solution   The amplitude is $\frac{3}{2}$, the vertical shift is 1, and the phase shift is $\frac{\pi}{6}$ units to the right. We first locate the axis line and place the shifted zeros at $\frac{\pi}{6}, \frac{7\pi}{6}$, and $\frac{13\pi}{6}$. Halfway between these, we locate the maximum and minimum points 1.5 units above and 1.5 units below the axis line, $y = 1$. We connect the points with a smooth curve.

Part Three: *Exercises and Problems*

Warm-up Exercises

1 Refer to the graph of $y = f(x)$. What is the amplitude?

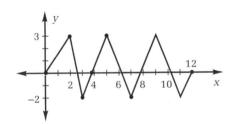

In problems 2–4, describe how each equation's graph is different from the graph of $y = \sin x$.

  2 $y = \sin \left(x - \frac{\pi}{6}\right)$ **3** $y = \sin x - 4$ **4** $y = 4.5 \sin x$

In problems 5–9, graph each equation.

5 $y = \sin x$ **6** $y = 3 \sin x$ **7** $y = -3 \sin x$

8 $y = 3 \sin x + 2$ **9** $y = 3 \sin \left(x + \dfrac{\pi}{6}\right)$

Problem Set

10 Copy and complete the table for $y = \cos x$, and sketch the equation's graph.

x	0	$\frac{\pi}{3}$	$\frac{\pi}{2}$	$\frac{2\pi}{3}$	π	$\frac{3\pi}{2}$	2π	$\frac{5\pi}{2}$	3π
y									

In problems 11 and 12, write an equation for each graph.

11

12

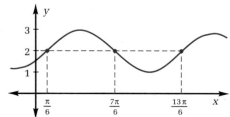

13 Find the smallest positive value of x satisfying each equation.

   a $\sin x = \dfrac{1}{2}$ **b** $\sin (2x) = \dfrac{1}{2}$

   c $\sin (3x) = \dfrac{1}{2}$ **d** $\sin \left(\dfrac{1}{2}x\right) = \dfrac{1}{2}$

In problems 14 and 15, write an equation for each graph.

14

15

16 Find lengths x and y.

17 **a** Find the coordinates of A, B, and C.
    b What is the period of the graph?

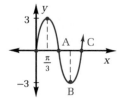

In problems 18–20, graph each equation.

18 $y = 3 \sin \left(x - \dfrac{\pi}{4}\right) + 2$

19 $y = -3 \sin \left(x - \dfrac{\pi}{4}\right) + 2$

20 $y = 3 \sin \left(x - \dfrac{\pi}{4}\right) - 2$

In problems 21 and 22, describe how the graph of each equation differs from the graph of $y = \sin x$.

21 $y = \sin x + 1$

22 $y = \sin (x + 1)$

23 Refer to the function $y = \pi \sin \pi x$.
   a Find the period of the function.
   b Find the amplitude of the function.

24 The amplitude of $y = A \sin x + 3$ is 4. Find the maximum value of y.

25 The diameter of the circle is 16.88, and $\overarc{CB} = 142.6°$. Find AC.

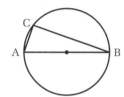

26 What is the equation of a sine curve with period 3π and amplitude 5?

27 Prove that $\dfrac{\cos 8x + \cos 2x}{\sin 8x - \sin 2x} = \cot 3x$.

28 Evaluate $\displaystyle\sum_{k=0}^{36} \sin (10k)°$.

29 Refer to the graph to find $x_1 + x_2 + x_3 + x_4$.

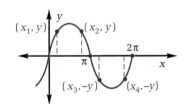

30 Find the period of the graph of $y = \dfrac{\tan (6x) + \tan (2x)}{1 - \tan (6x) \tan (2x)}$.

31 Prove that the area of quadrilateral PQRS is equal to $\frac{1}{2}$(PR)(QS)(sin θ).

CHANGING THE PERIOD

Objectives

After studying this section, you will be able to
- Graph the cosine function
- Stretch and shrink the sine and cosine graphs horizontally

Part One: Introduction

The Graph of the Cosine Function

The graph of $y = \cos x$ is shown at the right. Notice how much the cosine graph resembles the sine graph. In fact, the graph of $y = \cos x$ has exactly the same shape as the sine curve but is shifted $\frac{\pi}{2}$ units to the left. Can you prove that $\sin\left(x + \frac{\pi}{2}\right) = \cos x$?

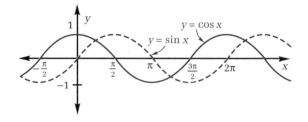

Learning to graph the cosine function is just as easy as learning to graph the sine function, but with a different set of basic points to memorize.

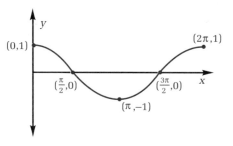

Period Changes

In the preceding section, you saw how sine graphs can be shifted upward, downward, to the left, and to the right. You also saw how the amplitude of a sine curve can be changed. We will now examine horizontal stretches and shrinks of the graphs of sine and cosine functions, which occur when the input value is multiplied by a constant.

With the help of a graphing calculator, we can graph the equation $y = \cos (2x)$.

Notice that two complete cycles fit between 0 and 2π, suggesting that the coefficient of the input variable tells us how many cycles will be compressed into the normal 2π period of the cosine curve.

The period of the graph of $y = \cos(2x)$ is thus equivalent to $2\pi \div 2$, or π. Similarly, the graph of $y = \cos(3x)$ will have a period of $2\pi \div 3$, with three cycles in the interval from 0 to 2π, and the graph of $y = \cos(6x)$ will have a period of $2\pi \div 6$, or $\frac{\pi}{3}$, with six cycles in the interval from 0 to 2π.

What will happen in the case of $y = \cos\left(\frac{1}{2}x\right)$? Since the coefficient of x is $\frac{1}{2}$, only half a cycle will fit into the interval from 0 to 2π. The period of the graph will therefore be 4π.

Such period changes are not found only in the graphs of cosine functions; they occur in the graphs of sine functions as well. The following table summarizes the graphs of these functions.

Summary of Sine and Cosine Graphs

In the graph of $y = a \sin[b(x - c)] + d$,

1. The amplitude is equal to $|a|$

2. The period is equal to $\dfrac{2\pi}{|b|}$

3. The phase shift, with respect to the graph of $y = \sin x$, is c units to the right (if $c > 0$) or c units to the left (if $c < 0$)

4. The vertical shift, with respect to the graph of $y = \sin x$, is d units upward (if $d > 0$) or d units downward (if $d < 0$)

Cosine graphs have the same properties, except that shifts are with respect to the graph of $y = \cos x$.

Part Two: Sample Problems

Problem 1 Graph $\sin\left(2x + \frac{\pi}{3}\right)$.

Solution We rewrite the equation in the form $y = a \sin[b(x - c)] + d$, as $y = \sin 2\left[x - \left(-\frac{\pi}{6}\right)\right]$, allowing us to see that the amplitude is 1; the period is $\frac{2\pi}{2}$, or π; and the phase shift is $\frac{\pi}{6}$ to the left.

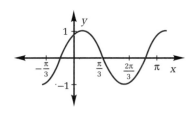

We could also have arrived at this graph by sketching the graph of $y = \sin(2x)$ and shifting it $\frac{\pi}{3} \div 2$, or $\frac{\pi}{6}$, units to the left.

Problem 2   Graph two cycles of $y = 3 \sin \left(\frac{1}{2}x\right)$.

Solution   In this case, the graph will have an amplitude of 3. The coefficient of x is $\frac{1}{2}$, so that only half a cycle will fit in the interval from 0 to 2π and the period will be $2\pi \div \frac{1}{2}$, or 4π. In order to show two cycles, therefore, we can use any interval of 8π units. We will use the interval from -4π to 4π.

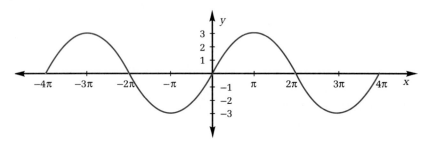

Problem 3   Write two equations, one in terms of the sine function and one in terms of the cosine function, for each graph.

a

b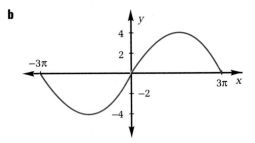

Solution   **a** We can begin by considering this as a cosine graph, with an equation of the form $y = a \cos [b(x - c)] + d$. Since the amplitude is 1, $a = 1$. There are two cycles between 0 and 2π, so $b = 2$. In comparison with the graph of $y = \cos x$, this graph shows no phase shift but is shifted one unit down, so $c = 0$ and $d = -1$. An equation that corresponds to the graph is therefore $y = \cos (2x) - 1$.

To represent the graph in terms of the sine function, we recall that $\cos x = \sin \left(x + \frac{\pi}{2}\right)$. Thus, the sine equation is the same as the cosine equation, but with $\frac{\pi}{2}$ added to the 2x—that is, $y = \sin \left(2x + \frac{\pi}{2}\right) - 1$, or $y = \sin \left[2\left(x + \frac{\pi}{4}\right)\right] - 1$.

b This graph differs from the graph of $y = \sin x$ in only two ways: Its amplitude is 4, and its period is 6π, so only one third of a cycle fits in the interval from 0 to 2π. It can therefore be represented by $y = 4 \sin \left(\frac{1}{3}x\right)$. For a corresponding cosine equation, we subtract $\frac{\pi}{2}$ from $\frac{1}{3}x$, obtaining $y = 4 \cos \left(\frac{1}{3}x - \frac{\pi}{2}\right)$, or $y = 4 \cos \left[\frac{1}{3}\left(x - \frac{3\pi}{2}\right)\right]$.

Problem 4   Graph each equation.

a $y = \sin (-2x)$ **b** $y = \cos (-2x)$

Solution

a Since the sine function is an odd function, $\sin(-\theta) = -\sin\theta$. The graph of $y = \sin(-2x)$ is therefore the same as that of $y = -\sin(2x)$, which is the reflection of the graph of $y = \sin(2x)$ over the x-axis.

b Since the cosine function is an even function, $\cos(-\theta) = \cos\theta$. The graph of $y = \cos(-2x)$ is therefore identical to the graph of $y = \cos(2x)$.

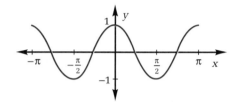

Part Three: Exercises and Problems

Warm-up Exercises

1 Graph each equation.

a $y = \cos x$ **b** $y = 2\cos x$ **c** $y = -2\cos x$
d $y = \cos(2x)$ **e** $y = \cos(-2x)$

2 One cycle of the graph of $y = 2\cos\left(x - \frac{\pi}{6}\right)$ is shown. Find the coordinates of points A, B, C, and D.

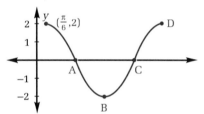

3 Find the period of the graph of the equation $y = \sin 8x \cos(-2x) + \sin(-2x)\cos 8x$.

Problem Set

4 Graph each equation.

a $y = \sin x$ **b** $y = \sin(2x)$

c $y = \sin(4x)$ **d** $y = \sin\left(\frac{1}{2}x\right)$

5 Find the amplitude and the period of each equation's graph.

a $y = 3\sin\left(2x - \frac{\pi}{4}\right) + 4$ **b** $y = -5\sin(3x) - 1$ **c** $y = 32\sin(\pi x)$

6 Write an equation involving the cosine function to describe the curve shown.

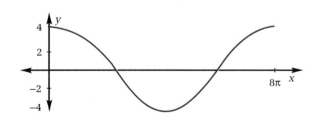

Problem Set, *continued*

7 Write an equation to represent the graph shown, using

   a The sine function
   b The cosine function

8 a Copy and complete the following table for $y = \tan x$.

x	0	$\frac{\pi}{6}$	$\frac{\pi}{4}$	$\frac{\pi}{3}$	$\frac{9\pi}{20}$	$\frac{\pi}{2}$	$\frac{11\pi}{20}$	$\frac{2\pi}{3}$	$\frac{3\pi}{4}$	π
y										

   b Sketch the graph of $y = \tan x$.

9 Use the diagram to find

   a $\cos \alpha$
   b $\sin \alpha$
   c $\cos \beta$
   d $\sin \beta$
   e $\cos (\beta - \alpha)$

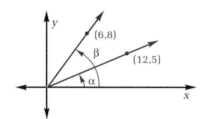

10 Let $f(8) = 7$.

   a Find $2[f(8)]$.   **b** Find $-2[f(8)]$.   **c** Find $\dfrac{1}{f(8)}$.
   d Find the value of x for which $f(2x) = 7$.
   e Find the value of x for which $f(x - 2) = 7$.

11 Graph each equation.

   a $y = 2 \sin \left(x - \dfrac{\pi}{4} \right)$ **b** $y = -3 \cos (2x)$ **c** $y = 4 \cos (3x) + 6$

12 a Write two equations involving the sine function to describe the curve shown.
   b Write two equations involving the cosine function to describe the curve shown.

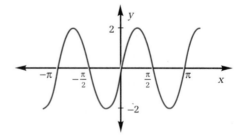

13 Find the period of the graph of each equation.

   a $y = \sin (7x) \cos (3x) + \sin (3x) \cos (7x)$
   b $y = \cos (9x) \cos (3x) - \sin (9x) \sin (3x)$

14 A certain triangle contains a 35° angle and a 97° angle. The length of the longest side of the triangle is 175 centimeters. Find the length of the shortest side.

15 Find the area of each triangle.

a

b

c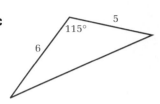

16 Find the domain and the range represented by four cycles (to the right of the y-axis) of each equation's graph.

    a $y = 2 \sin (3x) + 5$

    b $y = -2 \cos \left(\frac{1}{2}x\right) - 7$

17 Find the period of the graph of the equation $y = \sin (7x) \cos (-5x) + \cos (5x) \sin (-7x)$.

18 Graph each equation.

    a $y = \sin \left[2\left(x - \frac{\pi}{6}\right)\right]$

    b $y = \sin \left(2x - \frac{\pi}{3}\right)$

    c $y = \sin \left(2x - \frac{\pi}{3}\right) + 3$

    d $y = 2 \sin \left(2x - \frac{\pi}{3}\right) + 3$

19 Use a computer or a graphing calculator to graph each of the following equations.

    a $y = \sec x$ **b** $y = \csc x$ **c** $y = \tan x$ **d** $y = \cot x$

20 The graph of $y = \cos x$ is shown for the domain $\{x : 0 \le x \le 2\pi\}$. For what values in this domain is $\cos x \ge \frac{1}{2}$?

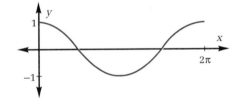

21 If the perimeter of $\triangle PQR$ is 60, what is the length of $\overline{QR}$?

22 Evaluate $\displaystyle\sum_{k=0}^{360} \cos k°$.

23 Use the diagram to prove that the product of the areas of $\triangle ABE$ and $\triangle CDE$ is equal to the product of the areas of $\triangle ADE$ and $\triangle BCE$.

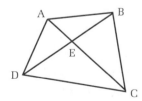

16.5 MORE TRIGONOMETRIC GRAPHS

Objectives

After studying this section, you will be able to
- Graph the tangent function
- Graph the secant function
- Graph the cosecant and cotangent functions

Part One: Introduction

The Tangent Function: $y = \tan x$

Since $\tan x = \frac{\sin x}{\cos x}$, the tangent function is
undefined whenever cos x is 0. Therefore,
the graph of $y = \tan x$ has vertical asymp-
totes at . . . , $-\frac{\pi}{2}, \frac{\pi}{2}, \frac{3\pi}{2}, \frac{5\pi}{2}$, . . .

The tangent function has zeros whenever
sin x is 0—that is, at . . . , $-\pi, 0, \pi, 2\pi$, . . .
A few convenient points occur whenever
tan x is 1 or −1—that is, at . . . , $\frac{-3\pi}{4}, -\frac{\pi}{4}, \frac{\pi}{4}$,
$\frac{3\pi}{4}, \frac{5\pi}{4}, \frac{7\pi}{4}, \frac{9\pi}{4}$, . . . Notice that the tangent
function is periodic and has a period of π.

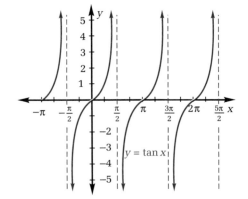

The Secant Function: $y = \sec x$

The values of the secant function are the
reciprocals of the values of the cosine function.

$$y = \sec x = \frac{1}{\cos x}$$

The secant function has no zeros; it does not
cross the x-axis. This function is undefined
whenever cos x = 0. Therefore, the graph of
the secant function has vertical asymptotes
at . . . , $\frac{-3\pi}{2}, -\frac{\pi}{2}, \frac{\pi}{2}, \frac{3\pi}{2}$, . . . If we compare
the graphs of the cosine and secant func-
tions, we see that the cosine of an angle
and the secant of the same angle are reciprocals. For example, cos $(-\pi) = -1$ and sec
$(-\pi) = -1$, and −1 and −1 are reciprocals;
cos 0 = 1 and sec 0 = 1, and 1 and 1 are
reciprocals; cos $\left(\frac{\pi}{3}\right) = \frac{1}{2}$ and sec $\left(\frac{\pi}{3}\right) = 2$, and
$\frac{1}{2}$ and 2 are reciprocals; and so forth.

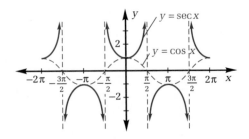

The Cosecant and Cotangent Functions:
$y = \csc x$ and $y = \cot x$

Here are the graphs of the cosecant and cotangent functions.
It is a good idea to memorize the critical features of the graphs of all
six trigonometric functions so that you can graph variations of them
quickly.

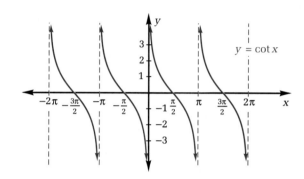

Part Two: Sample Problems

Problem 1   *Graph* $y = \sec\left(x - \frac{\pi}{6}\right)$.

Solution   Shift all points and the asymptotes of the graph of $y = \sec x$ to the
right $\frac{\pi}{6}$ units.

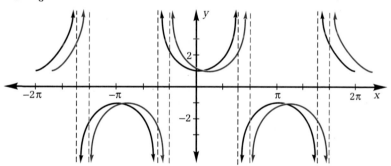

Problem 2   *Graph* $y = 0.25 \cot x$.

Solution   The only difference between this
graph and the graph of $y = \cot x$ is
the coefficient 0.25. This is not an
amplitude, since the graph does not
oscillate. The coefficient changes the
steepness of the graph. For example,
$\cot\left(\frac{\pi}{4}\right) = 1$, so $0.25 \cot\left(\frac{\pi}{4}\right) = 0.25$;
and $\cot\left(\frac{\pi}{3}\right) = \frac{1}{\sqrt{3}} \approx 0.5774$, so
$0.25 \cot\left(\frac{\pi}{3}\right) \approx 0.1443$.

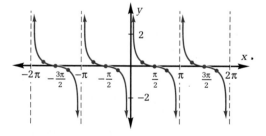

Problem 3   Graph $y = \tan\left(\frac{1}{2}x\right)$.

Solution   The normal period of $y = \tan x$ is π. In the graph of $\tan\left(\frac{1}{2}x\right)$, only half a cycle fits in the normal π interval. Therefore, the period of $y = \tan\left(\frac{1}{2}x\right)$ is stretched to $\frac{\pi}{0.5}$ or 2π. Notice that a zero remains at $(0, 0)$ and the asymptotes are twice as far from the y-axis as in the basic tangent graph.

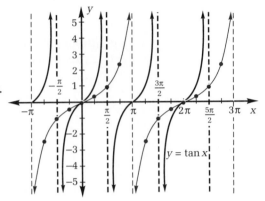

Problem 4   *The graph shown is based on the graph of $y = \csc x$. Find the equation of the graph.*

Solution   The vertex of each part of the graph is 0.5 or −0.5. Since the closest this graph gets to the x-axis is 0.5 unit, the coefficient of this cosecant function is 0.5. The length of one cycle of this graph is π. Notice that the period of $y = \csc x$ has changed so that two cycles fit into the normal 2π period. Therefore, the coefficient of x is 2. The equation of the graph is $y = 0.5 \csc (2x)$.

Part Three: Exercises and Problems

Warm-up Exercises

1 Graph each equation.

   a $y = \sec x$ **b** $y = 0.5 \sec x$ **c** $y = \sec (2x)$

2 Graph each equation.

   a $y = \csc x$ **b** $y = 2 \csc x$ **c** $y = 2 \csc \left(x + \frac{\pi}{2}\right)$

Problem Set

3 Graph each equation.

   a $y = \tan x$ **b** $y = \tan (3x)$ **c** $y = 2 \tan x$

4 Graph each equation.

   a $y = \csc x$ **b** $y = 2 \csc x$ **c** $y = \csc (2x)$
   d $y = -2 \csc x$ **e** $y = -2 \csc (2x)$

5 Graph each equation.

a $y = \sec\left(x - \dfrac{\pi}{6}\right) - 3$

b $y = \sec\left(x - \dfrac{\pi}{6}\right) + 3$

6 Write a tangent equation for the graph.

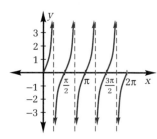

7 Find the smallest positive x value at which $y = 6 \sin(3x)$ intersects the line $y = 4$.

8 Patty was driving due west along a highway when she sighted a radio tower 25° to the north. Twenty minutes later, she was due south of the tower. If Patty was traveling 60 miles per hour, how far is the tower from the highway?

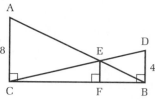

9 Graph each equation.

a $y = \sin x$

b $y = |\sin x|$

c $y = \sin^2 x$

10 An element is selected at random from
{tan 0°, tan 6°, tan 12°, . . . , tan (6k)°, . . . , tan 84°}.
Find the probability that the value is between $\frac{1}{2}$ and 2.

11 The lengths of two sides of a triangle are 186 centimeters and 305 centimeters. The measure of the angle between these two sides is 42.6. Find the area of the triangle.

12 a Find the length of $\overline{EF}$.
b Determine all possible measures of ∠ABC.

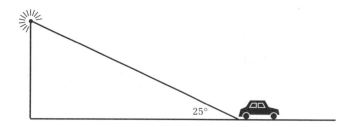

13 Let $\det\begin{bmatrix} a & b \\ c & d \end{bmatrix} = ad - bc$. Graph the following equation.

$$y = \det\begin{bmatrix} \cos(3x) & \sin x \\ \sin(3x) & \cos x \end{bmatrix}$$

14 Graph $y = \cos(3x)\cos x + \sin(3x)\sin x$.

Problem Set, *continued*

15 Find y.

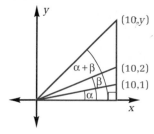

(10,y)

(10,2)

(10,1)

$\alpha + \beta$

β

α

16 Graph each equation, using a computer or a graphing calculator.

a $y = \tan x + \sec x$

b $y = \sec x + \csc x$

c $y = x \sin x$

d $y = x^2 + \sin (4x)$

SOOTHING SOUNDS
Sines and musical harmony

The graph of the sine function is commonly called a sine wave. One characteristic of a sine wave is that it is periodic: the peaks and valleys of the wave occur at consistent intervals. The interval between two peaks of a sine wave is called the *period.* The number of peaks that occur over a given range of x values is the wave's frequency.

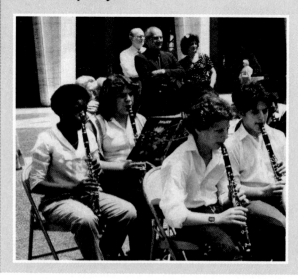

We are inclined to think of a sound as musical when it can be represented by a wave that is periodic and when it is associated with other periodic sounds. Variations in musical tones, such as pitch and loudness, can be represented by graphing variations of the sine function. For example, the period of a sine wave can be doubled by using the equation $y = \sin \left(\frac{x}{2}\right)$.

Sound waves whose periods are not multiples of each other produce sound patterns called beats, which we hear as dissonance. Two notes sounded together whose pitches are very close produce beats of a particular frequency. The beat frequency is the number of times the peaks of the waves correspond in a given time period. The effect can be produced by sounding the same note on two instruments that are not tuned to each other or by striking adjacent black and white piano keys.

CHAPTER SUMMARY

CONCEPTS AND PROCEDURES

After studying this chapter, you should be able to
- Apply the Law of Sines (16.1)
- Apply the Law of Cosines (16.2)
- Graph the sine function (16.3)
- Translate the sine graph vertically and horizontally (16.3)
- Change the amplitude of the sine graph (16.3)
- Graph the cosine function (16.4)
- Stretch and shrink the sine and cosine graphs horizontally (16.4)
- Graph the tangent function (16.5)
- Graph the secant function (16.5)
- Graph the cosecant and cotangent functions (16.5)

VOCABULARY

amplitude (16.3)
Law of Cosines (16.2)
Law of Sines (16.1)
period (16.3)
periodic (16.3)
phase shift (16.3)

REVIEW PROBLEMS

1 Graph each of the following equations.

   a $y = \cos x$ **b** $y = \cos (4x)$ **c** $y = \cos (\pi x)$

2 Find the measures of angles α, β, and γ.

3 Find x and y to the nearest hundredth.

4 Evaluate each expression.

   a $\sin \dfrac{\pi}{6}$ **b** $\sin \left(\dfrac{\pi}{6} + 2\pi \right)$ **c** $\sin \left(\dfrac{\pi}{6} - 2\pi \right)$

   d $\sin \left(\dfrac{\pi}{6} + 4\pi \right)$ **e** $\sin \left(\dfrac{\pi}{6} - 4\pi \right)$

5 Find length x.

6 A certain sound is represented by the periodic curve shown.

   a What is the curve's amplitude?

   b What is its period?

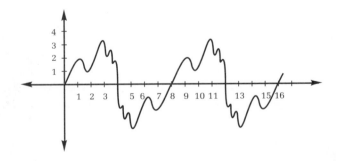

7 Copy and complete the following table.

Equation	Amplitude	Period	Range
$y = -2 \sin (3x)$			
$y = 4 \cos (2x)$			
$y = 3 \sin \left(\frac{1}{3}x\right) + 5$			

8 Graph each equation.

a $y = 2 \sin (3x)$ **b** $y = 2 \cos (3x)$

9 How many triangles are determined by each diagram?

a   **b**   **c**

10 Find the lengths of sides x, y, and z.

11 Find the measure of $\angle A$.

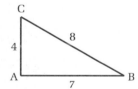

12 For which values of x in $\{x : 0 \le x \le 2\pi\}$ is $\sin x = \frac{1}{2}$?

13 Write an equation for the graph.

14 Using a computer or a graphing calculator, graph the following equations on the same coordinate system.

a $y = x$ **b** $y = \sin x$ **c** $y = x + \sin x$

Review Problems, *continued*

15 One cycle of the graph of y = 4 cos (3x) is shown.

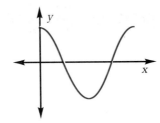

   a Find the domain and the range represented in the graph.

   b For which values of x in the domain is y = 2?

16 The period of y = 3 cos βx is 5. Find β.

17 Let A = $\begin{bmatrix} 3 & 2 & 1 \\ 4 & -1 & 2 \end{bmatrix}$ and B = $\begin{bmatrix} 1 & 0 \\ 3 & 2 \\ -5 & -1 \end{bmatrix}$.

An element is selected at random from the product A · B. Find the probability that the element is an odd number.

18 Find the relationship between x_1 and x_2.

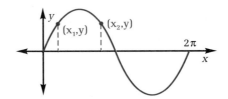

19 Graph each equation.

   a y = sin x   **b** y = sin (2x)   **c** y = sin $\left(2x + \dfrac{\pi}{4}\right)$

   d y = 5 sin $\left(2x + \dfrac{\pi}{4}\right)$ **e** y = 5 sin $\left(2x + \dfrac{\pi}{4}\right)$ − 3

20 What percentage of the total area under the normal curve shown is in the shaded region?

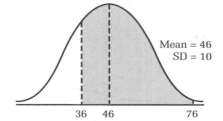

21 Given rhombus ABCD with perimeter 260 and m∠D = 70, find the lengths of the rhombus's diagonals.

22 A regular pentagon is inscribed in a circle with a 48-centimeter radius. Find the perimeter of the pentagon.

CHAPTER TEST

1 If $\theta = 62°$ and $\sin \alpha = 0.9272$, what are two possible values of α and the corresponding values of β?

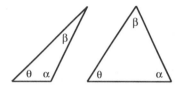

2 The measures of two angles of a triangle are 60 and 80. If the length of the longest side of the triangle is 12, what is the length of the shortest side?

3 Find the measure of acute $\angle B$.

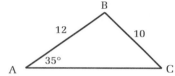

4 In $\triangle ABC$, $m\angle A = 45$ and $m\angle B = 75$. Find the ratio AB:BC.

5 The lengths of the sides of a parallelogram are 11 and 14. The measure of one of the parallelogram's angles is 150. Find the length of the parallelogram's shorter diagonal.

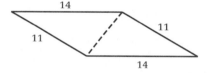

6 Find the area of the parallelogram in problem **5.**

7 Refer to the sine-curve graph.
a What is the amplitude?
b What is the period?
c What is the phase shift?
d What is the range?
e What is an equation for the sine-curve graph?

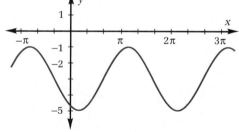

8 a Sketch the graph of $y = -3 \cos \left(x - \frac{\pi}{4}\right) + 2$.
b What is the amplitude?
c What is the phase shift?
d What is the range?

9 Sketch the graph of $y = 2 \sin \frac{1}{3}x$.

10 At what point does the graph of $y = 2 \sin \frac{1}{3}x$ reach its peak between 0 and 4π?

Handbook

THE REAL NUMBERS

Much of your work in algebra involves the set of **real numbers.** This is made up of all the numbers that can be assigned points on the real-number line.

When you first learned to count, you used the set of **natural numbers,** {1, 2, 3, 4, . . . }. The importance of the number zero led you to use the larger set of **whole numbers,** {0, 1, 2, 3, 4 . . . }. We form a still larger set by assigning **negative numbers** to points to the left of zero on the number line. The resulting set,

$$\{ \ldots, -3, -2, -1, 0, 1, 2, 3, \ldots \}$$

is called the set of **integers.**

The set of all integers and fractions composes the set of **rational numbers.** Every rational number can be written in the form $\frac{\text{an integer}}{\text{a natural number}}$. Every rational number can also be written as either a **terminating decimal** $\left(\text{for example, } \frac{3}{12} = 0.25\right)$ or a **repeating decimal** $\left(\text{for example, } \frac{2}{3} = 0.6666666...\right)$. Repeating decimals can be indicated by placing a bar over the repeating digit or digits. For example, $\frac{2}{3} = 0.\overline{6}$.

The remaining points on the number line correspond to the **irrational numbers.** When expressed as a decimal, an irrational number, such as $\sqrt{5}$ or π, neither terminates nor repeats. By combining the set of rationals and the set of irrationals, we form the set of real numbers.

PROPERTIES OF REAL NUMBERS

To use the real numbers accurately, we need to know their properties with respect to the operations of addition, subtraction, multiplication, and division. The following properties apply to all real numbers a, b, and c.

Name	Property	Example
Commutative Property of Addition	$a + b = b + a$	$4 + 7 = 7 + 4$
Commutative Property of Multiplication	$ab = ba$	$3 \cdot 6 = 6 \cdot 3$
Associative Property of Addition	$(a + b) + c = a + (b + c)$	$(5 + 8) + 9 = 5 + (8 + 9)$
Associative Property of Multiplication	$(ab)c = a(bc)$	$(3 \cdot 5)x = 3(5x)$
Difference Property	$a - b = a + (-b)$	$5 - 9 = 5 + (-9)$
Distributive Property of Multiplication over Addition or Subtraction	$a(b \pm c) = ab \pm ac$ $(a \pm b)c = ac \pm bc$	$2(x + 7) = 2x + 14$ $(x - y)z = xz - yz$
Quotient Property	$a \cdot \frac{1}{b} = \frac{a}{b}$	$3 \cdot \frac{1}{5} = \frac{3}{5}$
Additive Inverse Property	For every a, there is a number $-a$—called the *additive inverse*, or *opposite*, of a— such that $a + (-a) = 0$.	$8 + (-8) = 0$
Multiplicative Inverse Property	For every $a \neq 0$, there is a number $\frac{1}{a}$, called the *multiplicative inverse* of a, such that $a\left(\frac{1}{a}\right) = 1$.	$6 \cdot \frac{1}{6} = \frac{6}{6} = 1$
Property of the Opposite of a Quantity	$-(a + b) = -1(a + b)$ $\quad = -a - b$ $-(a - b) = -1(a - b)$ $\quad = -a + b$	$-(x + 2) = -x - 2$ $-(y - 4) = -y + 4$
Additive Identity Property	There is a number 0 such that $a + 0 = a$ and $0 + a = a$.	$3 + 0 = 0 + 3 = 3$
Multiplicative Identity Property	There is a number 1 such that $1 \cdot a = a \cdot 1 = a$.	$1 \cdot 7 = 7 \cdot 1 = 7$
Multiplication Property of Zero	$0(a) = a(0) = 0$	$4(0) = 0(4) = 0$

EQUATION SOLVING

A **variable** is a symbol used to represent a number. An **expression** is a mathematical phrase consisting of a number, a variable, or a group of numbers and variables connected by operations. The following are examples of expressions.

$$7 \qquad 5x \qquad 13y - 40 \qquad e^{-x} \qquad \frac{1}{x+1} \qquad |2z - 17|$$

An **equation** is a mathematical sentence stating that two expressions are equal for one or more values of the variable. Solving an equation means finding the value(s) of the variable that make the equation a true statement. The following is an example of an equation.

$$4(x + 12) = x^2 + x(7 - x)$$

An equation can be solved by applying a simple strategy. This consists of performing whatever operations are needed to isolate the variable on one side of the equation so that the result is in the form "variable = number."

Notice that we cannot carry this strategy out by means of the properties of real numbers alone. Using these properties with the sample equation yields $4x + 48 = 7x$. To proceed further, we need additional properties—the properties of equality.

Properties of Equality

Each of the following properties is true for all real numbers (represented by a, b, and c) unless otherwise noted.

Name	Property	Example
Reflexive Property	$a = a$	$21.4 = 21.4$
Symmetric Property	If $a = b$, then $b = a$.	If $y = 4$, then $4 = y$.
Transitive Property of Equality	If $a = b$ and $b = c$, then $a = c$.	If $x_1 = 9$ and $9 = x_2$, then $x_1 = x_2$.
Addition Property of Equality	If $a = b$ and $c = d$, then $a + c = b + d$.	If $x - 6 = 5$ and $6 = 6$, then $x = 11$.
Subtraction Property of Equality	If $a = b$ and $c = d$, then $a - c = b - d$.	If $x + 4 = 24$ and $4 = 4$, then $x = 20$.
Multiplication Property of Equality	If $a = b$ and $c = d$, then $ac = bd$.	If $\frac{x}{2} = 7$ and $2 = 2$, then $x = 14$.
Division Property of Equality	If $a = b$ and $c = d$, where c and d are not 0, then $\frac{a}{c} = \frac{b}{d}$.	If $3x = 15$ and $3 = 3$, then $x = 5$.
Zero Product Property	If $ab = 0$, then either $a = 0$ or $b = 0$.	If $x(x - 8) = 0$, then either $x = 0$ or $x - 8 = 0$.

We can now solve equations.

Example   Solve $4(x + 12) = x^2 + x(7 - x)$ for x.

$$4(x + 12) = x^2 + x(7 - x)$$

Distributive Property of Multiplication over Addition or Subtraction	$4x + 48 = x^2 + 7x - x^2$
Additive Inverse Property	$4x + 48 = 7x$
Subtraction Property of Equality	$48 = 3x$
Division Property of Equality	$16 = x$
Symmetric Property of Equality	$x = 16$

Solving Special Equations

Equations That Have No Solutions

It is possible to solve an equation accurately and yet obtain a false or meaningless result, such as $0 = 11$, $x = \sqrt{-3}$, or $|y| = -1$. Equations that lead to such results are said to have no real solutions.

Equations That Are Identities

Certain equations, such as $x + 3 = x + 3$, make true statements for all values of the variable. These equations are called **identities.** An identity expresses an equivalence that is always valid.

Absolute-Value Equations

An absolute-value equation is solved by isolating the absolute-value expression on one side and then applying the definition of *absolute value.*

Example   Solve $7 + |2x| = 21$ for x.

$$7 + |2x| = 21$$

Subtraction Property of Equality	$|2x| = 14$
By definition, $|a| = a$ or $|a| = -a$	$2x = 14$ or $-2x = 14$
Division Property of Equality	$x = 7 \qquad x = -7$

POLYNOMIAL EXPRESSIONS

A *monomial* is a real number, a variable, or a product of real numbers and variables. The expressions -15, $3z$, and $-7x^3y^5z$ are all monomials. The expressions $\frac{-15}{x + 8}$, $3\sqrt{z}$, $3|z|$, and $-7x^3y^5ze^w$ are not monomials.

The *coefficient* of a monomial is its numerical factor. For example, the coefficient in $-2.8x^7y^3z$ is -2.8.

The *degree of a monomial* is the sum of the exponents of the monomial's variables. The degree of $-2.8x^7y^3z$ is 11 because $7 + 3 + 1 = 11$.

A *polynomial* is an expression that is either a monomial or a sum or difference of monomials. Each monomial component of a polynomial is called a **term.** The terms of a polynomial are usually arranged in descending order of powers. The **leading coefficient** of a polynomial is the coefficient of the first term when the polynomial is written in descending order of powers. For example, the leading coefficient of $-x^3 + 5x + 2$ is -1.

The **degree of a polynomial** is equal to the greatest of the degrees of the polynomial's terms. Polynomials are classified by their degree and by their number of terms. The polynomial $-x^3 + 5x + 2$ is classified as a cubic (degree-three) trinomial. The polynomial $y^2 - 17$ is an example of a quadratic (degree-two) binomial.

SCIENTIFIC NOTATION

Scientific notation is an efficient way of expressing very large and very small numbers. To express a number in scientific notation, we rewrite it in the form $c \times 10^n$, where $0 < |c| < 10$ and n is an integer. Numbers written in scientific notation can be multiplied or divided exactly like other exponential expressions. They may be added or subtracted, however, only after being rewritten so that they contain the same power of 10.

Example   Write 186,000 in scientific notation.

$$186,000 = 1.86 \times 100,000$$
$$= 1.86 \times 10^5$$

Notice that we find the correct coefficient, 1.86, by moving the decimal point 5 places to the left and that 5 is also the correct power of 10.

Example   Write 0.0000051 in scientific notation.

$$0.0000051 = \frac{5.1}{1,000,000}$$
$$= 5.1 \times 10^{-6}$$

Notice that we find the correct coefficient, 5.1, by moving the decimal point 6 places to the right and that -6 is the correct power of 10.

In general, then, the power of 10 is numerically equal to the number of places the decimal point must be moved to give the correct coefficient. The exponent is positive if the decimal point is moved to the left; the exponent is negative if the decimal point is moved to the right.

All scientific calculators allow you to enter numbers in scientific notation. The key used to enter the power of 10 may be labeled EEX , EE , or EXP .

Example   Find the product $(-3.55 \times 10^{12})(6.00 \times 10^{-23})$.

Enter the following on a calculator.

3.55 $\boxed{\pm}$ $\boxed{\text{EE}}$ 12 $\boxed{\times}$ 6 $\boxed{\text{EE}}$ 23 $\boxed{\pm}$ $\boxed{=}$

The display should resemble $\boxed{-2.13 \qquad -10}$. The product is -2.13×10^{-10}.

SPECIAL FORMULAS FROM GEOMETRY

Perimeter Formulas

To find the perimeter of a polygon, we add the lengths of all its sides. The perimeter of a circle is called the circle's **circumference.** We calculate a circumference by using the formula $C = \pi d$ (where d is the diameter of the circle) or $C = 2\pi r$ (where r is the radius of the circle).

Area Formulas

The formulas for area that we will use in this book are summarized in the following diagrams. Areas are always expressed in square units.

Triangle

$A = \dfrac{bh}{2}$

Rectangle

$A = bh$ or $A = LW$

Parallelogram

$A = bh$

Square

$A = s^2$

Trapezoid

$A = \dfrac{h(b_1 + b_2)}{2}$

Circle

$A = \pi r^2$

Rectangular Box

Surface Area = $2lw + 2lh + 2wh$

Sphere

Surface Area = $4\pi r^2$

Volume Formulas

The formulas in the following diagrams are used to calculate volume, the space enclosed by a figure. Volume is always measured in cubic units.

Rectangular Prism

$V = lwh$

Pyramid

$V = \dfrac{Bh}{3}$, where B is the area of the base

Sphere

$V = \dfrac{4}{3}\pi r^3$

Right Circular Cylinder

$V = \pi r^2 h$

Right Circular Cone

$V = \dfrac{1}{3}\pi r^2 h$

NORMAL DISTRIBUTION TABLE

SD's from Mean	Cumulative Area	Percentile Rank	SD's from Mean	Cumulative Area	Percentile Rank
−3.4	0.0003	0	0.0	0.5000	50
−3.3	0.0005	0	0.1	0.5398	53
−3.2	0.0007	0	0.2	0.5793	57
−3.1	0.0010	0	0.3	0.6179	61
−3.0	0.0013	0	0.4	0.6554	65
−2.9	0.0019	0	0.5	0.6915	69
−2.8	0.0026	0	0.6	0.7257	72
−2.7	0.0035	0	0.7	0.7580	75
−2.6	0.0047	0	0.8	0.7881	78
−2.5	0.0062	0	0.9	0.8159	81
−2.4	0.0082	0	1.0	0.8413	84
−2.3	0.0107	1	1.1	0.8643	86
−2.2	0.0139	1	1.2	0.8849	88
−2.1	0.0179	1	1.3	0.9032	90
−2.0	0.0228	2	1.4	0.9192	91
−1.9	0.0287	2	1.5	0.9332	93
−1.8	0.0359	3	1.6	0.9452	94
−1.7	0.0446	4	1.7	0.9554	95
−1.6	0.0548	5	1.8	0.9641	96
−1.5	0.0668	6	1.9	0.9713	97
−1.4	0.0808	8	2.0	0.9772	97
−1.3	0.0968	9	2.1	0.9821	98
−1.2	0.1151	11	2.2	0.9861	98
−1.1	0.1357	13	2.3	0.9893	98
−1.0	0.1587	15	2.4	0.9918	99
−0.9	0.1841	18	2.5	0.9938	99
−0.8	0.2119	21	2.6	0.9953	99
−0.7	0.2420	24	2.7	0.9965	99
−0.6	0.2743	27	2.8	0.9974	99
−0.5	0.3085	30	2.9	0.9981	99
−0.4	0.3446	34	3.0	0.9987	99
−0.3	0.3821	38	3.1	0.9990	99
−0.2	0.4207	42	3.2	0.9993	99
−0.1	0.4602	46	3.3	0.9995	99
−0.0	0.5000	50	3.4	0.9997	99

TABLE OF SQUARES AND SQUARE ROOTS

n	n^2	$\sqrt{n}$	n	n^2	$\sqrt{n}$	n	n^2	$\sqrt{n}$
1	1	1.000	51	2,601	7.141	101	10,201	10.050
2	4	1.414	52	2,704	7.211	102	10,404	10.100
3	9	1.732	53	2,809	7.280	103	10,609	10.149
4	16	2.000	54	2,916	7.348	104	10,816	10.198
5	25	2.236	55	3,025	7.416	105	11,025	10.247
6	36	2.449	56	3,136	7.483	106	11,236	10.296
7	49	2.646	57	3,249	7.550	107	11,449	10.344
8	64	2.828	58	3,364	7.616	108	11,664	10.392
9	81	3.000	59	3,481	7.681	109	11,881	10.440
10	100	3.162	60	3,600	7.746	110	12,100	10.488
11	121	3.317	61	3,721	7.810	111	12,321	10.536
12	144	3.464	62	3,844	7.874	112	12,544	10.583
13	169	3.606	63	3,969	7.937	113	12,769	10.630
14	196	3.742	64	4,096	8.000	114	12,996	10.677
15	225	3.873	65	4,225	8.062	115	13,225	10.724
16	256	4.000	66	4,356	8.124	116	13,456	10.770
17	289	4.123	67	4,489	8.185	117	13,689	10.817
18	324	4.243	68	4,624	8.246	118	13,924	10.863
19	361	4.359	69	4,761	8.307	119	14,161	10.909
20	400	4.472	70	4,900	8.367	120	14,400	10.954
21	441	4.583	71	5,041	8.426	121	14,641	11.000
22	484	4.690	72	5,184	8.485	122	14,884	11.045
23	529	4.796	73	5,329	8.544	123	15,129	11.091
24	576	4.899	74	5,476	8.602	124	15,376	11.136
25	625	5.000	75	5,625	8.660	125	15,625	11.180
26	676	5.099	76	5,776	8.718	126	15,876	11.225
27	729	5.196	77	5,929	8.775	127	16,129	11.269
28	784	5.292	78	6,084	8.832	128	16,384	11.314
29	841	5.385	79	6,241	8.888	129	16,641	11.358
30	900	5.477	80	6,400	8.944	130	16,900	11.402
31	961	5.568	81	6,561	9.000	131	17,161	11.446
32	1,024	5.657	82	6,724	9.055	132	17,424	11.489
33	1,089	5.745	83	6,889	9.110	133	17,689	11.533
34	1,156	5.831	84	7,056	9.165	134	17,956	11.576
35	1,225	5.916	85	7,225	9.220	135	18,225	11.619
36	1,296	6.000	86	7,396	9.274	136	18,496	11.662
37	1,369	6.083	87	7,569	9.327	137	18,769	11.705
38	1,444	6.164	88	7,744	9.381	138	19,044	11.747
39	1,521	6.245	89	7,921	9.434	139	19,321	11.790
40	1,600	6.325	90	8,100	9.487	140	19,600	11.832
41	1,681	6.403	91	8,281	9.539	141	19,881	11.874
42	1,764	6.481	92	8,464	9.592	142	20,164	11.916
43	1,849	6.557	93	8,649	9.644	143	20,449	11.958
44	1,936	6.633	94	8,836	9.695	144	20,736	12.000
45	2,025	6.708	95	9,025	9.747	145	21,025	12.042
46	2,116	6.782	96	9,216	9.798	146	21,316	12.083
47	2,209	6.856	97	9,409	9.849	147	21,609	12.124
48	2,304	6.928	98	9,604	9.899	148	21,904	12.166
49	2,401	7.000	99	9,801	9.950	149	22,201	12.207
50	2,500	7.071	100	10,000	10.000	150	22,500	12.247

COMMON LOGARITHMS OF NUMBERS

x	0	1	2	3	4	5	6	7	8	9
1.0	.0000	.0043	.0086	.0128	.0170	.0212	.0253	.0294	.0334	.0374
1.1	.0414	.0453	.0492	.0531	.0569	.0607	.0645	.0682	.0719	.0755
1.2	.0792	.0828	.0864	.0899	.0934	.0969	.1004	.1038	.1072	.1106
1.3	.1139	.1173	.1206	.1239	.1271	.1303	.1335	.1367	.1399	.1430
1.4	.1461	.1492	.1523	.1553	.1584	.1614	.1644	.1673	.1703	.1732
1.5	.1761	.1790	.1818	.1847	.1875	.1903	.1931	.1959	.1987	.2014
1.6	.2041	.2068	.2095	.2122	.2148	.2175	.2201	.2227	.2253	.2279
1.7	.2304	.2330	.2355	.2380	.2405	.2430	.2455	.2480	.2504	.2529
1.8	.2553	.2577	.2601	.2625	.2648	.2672	.2695	.2718	.2742	.2765
1.9	.2788	.2810	.2833	.2856	.2878	.2900	.2923	.2945	.2967	.2989
2.0	.3010	.3032	.3054	.3075	.3096	.3118	.3139	.3160	.3181	.3201
2.1	.3222	.3243	.3263	.3284	.3304	.3324	.3345	.3365	.3385	.3404
2.2	.3424	.3444	.3464	.3483	.3502	.3522	.3541	.3560	.3579	.3598
2.3	.3617	.3636	.3655	.3674	.3692	.3711	.3729	.3747	.3766	.3784
2.4	.3802	.3820	.3838	.3856	.3874	.3892	.3909	.3927	.3945	.3962
2.5	.3979	.3997	.4014	.4031	.4048	.4065	.4082	.4099	.4116	.4133
2.6	.4150	.4166	.4183	.4200	.4216	.4232	.4249	.4265	.4281	.4298
2.7	.4314	.4330	.4346	.4362	.4378	.4393	.4409	.4425	.4440	.4456
2.8	.4472	.4487	.4502	.4518	.4533	.4548	.4564	.4579	.4594	.4609
2.9	.4624	.4639	.4654	.4669	.4683	.4698	.4713	.4728	.4742	.4757
3.0	.4771	.4786	.4800	.4814	.4829	.4843	.4857	.4871	.4886	.4900
3.1	.4914	.4928	.4942	.4955	.4969	.4983	.4997	.5011	.5024	.5038
3.2	.5051	.5065	.5079	.5092	.5105	.5119	.5132	.5145	.5159	.5172
3.3	.5185	.5198	.5211	.5224	.5237	.5250	.5263	.5276	.5289	.5302
3.4	.5315	.5328	.5340	.5353	.5366	.5378	.5391	.5403	.5416	.5428
3.5	.5441	.5453	.5465	.5478	.5490	.5502	.5514	.5527	.5539	.5551
3.6	.5563	.5575	.5587	.5599	.5611	.5623	.5635	.5647	.5658	.5670
3.7	.5682	.5694	.5705	.5717	.5729	.5740	.5752	.5763	.5775	.5786
3.8	.5798	.5809	.5821	.5832	.5843	.5855	.5866	.5877	.5888	.5899
3.9	.5911	.5922	.5933	.5944	.5955	.5966	.5977	.5988	.5999	.6010
4.0	.6021	.6031	.6042	.6053	.6064	.6075	.6085	.6096	.6107	.6117
4.1	.6128	.6138	.6149	.6160	.6170	.6180	.6191	.6201	.6212	.6222
4.2	.6232	.6243	.6253	.6263	.6274	.6284	.6294	.6304	.6314	.6325
4.3	.6335	.6345	.6355	.6365	.6375	.6385	.6395	.6405	.6415	.6425
4.4	.6435	.6444	.6454	.6464	.6474	.6484	.6493	.6503	.6513	.6522
4.5	.6532	.6542	.6551	.6561	.6571	.6580	.6590	.6599	.6609	.6618
4.6	.6628	.6637	.6646	.6656	.6665	.6675	.6684	.6693	.6702	.6712
4.7	.6721	.6730	.6739	.6749	.6758	.6767	.6776	.6785	.6794	.6803
4.8	.6812	.6821	.6830	.6839	.6848	.6857	.6866	.6875	.6884	.6893
4.9	.6902	.6911	.6920	.6928	.6937	.6946	.6955	.6964	.6972	.6981
5.0	.6990	.6998	.7007	.7016	.7024	.7033	.7042	.7050	.7059	.7067
5.1	.7076	.7084	.7093	.7101	.7110	.7118	.7126	.7135	.7143	.7152
5.2	.7160	.7168	.7177	.7185	.7193	.7202	.7210	.7218	.7226	.7235
5.3	.7243	.7251	.7259	.7267	.7275	.7284	.7292	.7300	.7308	.7316
5.4	.7324	.7332	.7340	.7348	.7356	.7364	.7372	.7380	.7388	.7396

x	0	1	2	3	4	5	6	7	8	9
5.5	.7404	.7412	.7419	.7427	.7435	.7443	.7451	.7459	.7466	.7474
5.6	.7482	.7490	.7497	.7505	.7513	.7520	.7528	.7536	.7543	.7551
5.7	.7559	.7566	.7574	.7582	.7589	.7597	.7604	.7612	.7619	.7627
5.8	.7634	.7642	.7649	.7657	.7664	.7672	.7679	.7686	.7694	.7701
5.9	.7709	.7716	.7723	.7731	.7738	.7745	.7752	.7760	.7767	.7774
6.0	.7782	.7789	.7796	.7803	.7810	.7818	.7825	.7832	.7839	.7846
6.1	.7853	.7860	.7868	.7875	.7882	.7889	.7896	.7903	.7910	.7917
6.2	.7924	.7931	.7938	.7945	.7952	.7959	.7966	.7973	.7980	.7987
6.3	.7993	.8000	.8007	.8014	.8021	.8028	.8035	.8041	.8048	.8055
6.4	.8062	.8069	.8075	.8082	.8089	.8096	.8102	.8109	.8116	.8122
6.5	.8129	.8136	.8142	.8149	.8156	.8162	.8169	.8176	.8182	.8189
6.6	.8195	.8202	.8209	.8215	.8222	.8228	.8235	.8241	.8248	.8254
6.7	.8261	.8267	.8274	.8280	.8287	.8293	.8299	.8306	.8312	.8319
6.8	.8325	.8331	.8338	.8344	.8351	.8357	.8363	.8370	.8376	.8382
6.9	.8388	.8395	.8401	.8407	.8414	.8420	.8426	.8432	.8439	.8445
7.0	.8451	.8457	.8463	.8470	.8476	.8482	.8488	.8494	.8500	.8506
7.1	.8513	.8519	.8525	.8531	.8537	.8543	.8549	.8555	.8561	.8567
7.2	.8573	.8579	.8585	.8591	.8597	.8603	.8609	.8615	.8621	.8627
7.3	.8633	.8639	.8645	.8651	.8657	.8663	.8669	.8675	.8681	.8686
7.4	.8692	.8698	.8704	.8710	.8716	.8722	.8727	.8733	.8739	.8745
7.5	.8751	.8756	.8762	.8768	.8774	.8779	.8785	.8791	.8797	.8802
7.6	.8808	.8814	.8820	.8825	.8831	.8837	.8842	.8848	.8854	.8859
7.7	.8865	.8871	.8876	.8882	.8887	.8893	.8899	.8904	.8910	.8915
7.8	.8921	.8927	.8932	.8938	.8943	.8949	.8954	.8960	.8965	.8971
7.9	.8976	.8982	.8987	.8993	.8998	.9004	.9009	.9015	.9020	.9025
8.0	.9031	.9036	.9042	.9047	.9053	.9058	.9063	.9069	.9074	.9079
8.1	.9085	.9090	.9096	.9101	.9106	.9112	.9117	.9122	.9128	.9133
8.2	.9138	.9143	.9149	.9154	.9159	.9165	.9170	.9175	.9180	.9186
8.3	.9191	.9196	.9201	.9206	.9212	.9217	.9222	.9227	.9232	.9238
8.4	.9243	.9248	.9253	.9258	.9263	.9269	.9274	.9279	.9284	.9289
8.5	.9294	.9299	.9304	.9309	.9315	.9320	.9325	.9330	.9335	.9340
8.6	.9345	.9350	.9355	.9360	.9365	.9370	.9375	.9380	.9385	.9390
8.7	.9395	.9400	.9405	.9410	.9415	.9420	.9425	.9430	.9435	.9440
8.8	.9445	.9450	.9455	.9460	.9465	.9469	.9474	.9479	.9484	.9489
8.9	.9494	.9499	.9504	.9509	.9513	.9518	.9523	.9528	.9533	.9538
9.0	.9542	.9547	.9552	.9557	.9562	.9566	.9571	.9576	.9581	.9586
9.1	.9590	.9595	.9600	.9605	.9609	.9614	.9619	.9624	.9628	.9633
9.2	.9638	.9643	.9647	.9652	.9657	.9661	.9666	.9671	.9675	.9680
9.3	.9685	.9689	.9694	.9699	.9703	.9708	.9713	.9717	.9722	.9727
9.4	.9731	.9736	.9741	.9745	.9750	.9754	.9759	.9763	.9768	.9773
9.5	.9777	.9782	.9786	.9791	.9795	.9800	.9805	.9809	.9814	.9818
9.6	.9823	.9827	.9832	.9836	.9841	.9845	.9850	.9854	.9859	.9863
9.7	.9868	.9872	.9877	.9881	.9886	.9890	.9894	.9899	.9903	.9908
9.8	.9912	.9917	.9921	.9926	.9930	.9934	.9939	.9943	.9948	.9952
9.9	.9956	.9961	.9965	.9969	.9974	.9978	.9983	.9987	.9991	.9996

Natural Logarithms of Numbers

x	0	1	2	3	4	5	6	7	8	9
1.0	0.0000	0.0100	0.0198	0.0296	0.0392	0.0488	0.0583	0.0677	0.0770	0.0862
1.1	0.0953	0.1044	0.1133	0.1222	0.1310	0.1398	0.1484	0.1570	0.1655	0.1740
1.2	0.1823	0.1906	0.1989	0.2070	0.2151	0.2231	0.2311	0.2390	0.2469	0.2546
1.3	0.2624	0.2700	0.2776	0.2852	0.2927	0.3001	0.3075	0.3148	0.3221	0.3293
1.4	0.3365	0.3436	0.3507	0.3577	0.3646	0.3716	0.3784	0.3853	0.3920	0.3988
1.5	0.4055	0.4121	0.4187	0.4253	0.4318	0.4383	0.4447	0.4511	0.4574	0.4637
1.6	0.4700	0.4762	0.4824	0.4886	0.4947	0.5008	0.5068	0.5128	0.5188	0.5247
1.7	0.5306	0.5365	0.5423	0.5481	0.5539	0.5596	0.5653	0.5710	0.5766	0.5822
1.8	0.5878	0.5933	0.5988	0.6043	0.6098	0.6152	0.6206	0.6259	0.6313	0.6366
1.9	0.6419	0.6471	0.6523	0.6575	0.6627	0.6678	0.6729	0.6780	0.6831	0.6881
2.0	0.6931	0.6981	0.7031	0.7080	0.7130	0.7178	0.7227	0.7275	0.7324	0.7372
2.1	0.7419	0.7467	0.7514	0.7561	0.7608	0.7655	0.7701	0.7747	0.7793	0.7839
2.2	0.7885	0.7930	0.7975	0.8020	0.8065	0.8109	0.8154	0.8198	0.8242	0.8286
2.3	0.8329	0.8372	0.8416	0.8459	0.8502	0.8544	0.8587	0.8629	0.8671	0.8713
2.4	0.8755	0.8796	0.8838	0.8879	0.8920	0.8961	0.9002	0.9042	0.9083	0.9123
2.5	0.9163	0.9203	0.9243	0.9282	0.9322	0.9361	0.9400	0.9439	0.9478	0.9517
2.6	0.9555	0.9594	0.9632	0.9670	0.9708	0.9746	0.9783	0.9821	0.9858	0.9895
2.7	0.9933	0.9969	1.0006	1.0043	1.0080	1.0116	1.0152	1.0188	1.0225	1.0260
2.8	1.0296	1.0332	1.0367	1.0403	1.0438	1.0473	1.0508	1.0543	1.0578	1.0613
2.9	1.0647	1.0682	1.0716	1.0750	1.0784	1.0818	1.0852	1.0886	1.0919	1.0953
3.0	1.0986	1.1019	1.1053	1.1086	1.1119	1.1151	1.1184	1.1217	1.1249	1.1282
3.1	1.1314	1.1346	1.1378	1.1410	1.1442	1.1474	1.1506	1.1537	1.1569	1.1600
3.2	1.1632	1.1663	1.1694	1.1725	1.1756	1.1787	1.1817	1.1848	1.1878	1.1909
3.3	1.1939	1.1970	1.2000	1.2030	1.2060	1.2090	1.2119	1.2149	1.2179	1.2208
3.4	1.2238	1.2267	1.2296	1.2326	1.2355	1.2384	1.2413	1.2442	1.2470	1.2499
3.5	1.2528	1.2556	1.2585	1.2613	1.2641	1.2669	1.2698	1.2726	1.2754	1.2782
3.6	1.2809	1.2837	1.2865	1.2892	1.2920	1.2947	1.2975	1.3002	1.3029	1.3056
3.7	1.3083	1.3110	1.3137	1.3164	1.3191	1.3218	1.3244	1.3271	1.3297	1.3324
3.8	1.3350	1.3376	1.3403	1.3429	1.3455	1.3481	1.3507	1.3533	1.3558	1.3584
3.9	1.3610	1.3635	1.3661	1.3686	1.3712	1.3737	1.3762	1.3788	1.3813	1.3838
4.0	1.3863	1.3888	1.3913	1.3938	1.3962	1.3987	1.4012	1.4036	1.4061	1.4085
4.1	1.4110	1.4134	1.4159	1.4183	1.4207	1.4231	1.4255	1.4279	1.4303	1.4327
4.2	1.4351	1.4375	1.4398	1.4422	1.4446	1.4469	1.4493	1.4516	1.4540	1.4563
4.3	1.4586	1.4609	1.4633	1.4656	1.4679	1.4702	1.4725	1.4748	1.4770	1.4793
4.4	1.4816	1.4839	1.4861	1.4884	1.4907	1.4929	1.4952	1.4974	1.4996	1.5019
4.5	1.5041	1.5063	1.5085	1.5107	1.5129	1.5151	1.5173	1.5195	1.5217	1.5239
4.6	1.5261	1.5282	1.5304	1.5326	1.5347	1.5369	1.5390	1.5412	1.5433	1.5454
4.7	1.5476	1.5497	1.5518	1.5539	1.5560	1.5581	1.5602	1.5623	1.5644	1.5665
4.8	1.5686	1.5707	1.5728	1.5748	1.5769	1.5790	1.5810	1.5831	1.5851	1.5872
4.9	1.5892	1.5913	1.5933	1.5953	1.5974	1.5994	1.6014	1.6034	1.6054	1.6074
5.0	1.6094	1.6114	1.6134	1.6154	1.6174	1.6194	1.6214	1.6233	1.6253	1.6273
5.1	1.6292	1.6312	1.6332	1.6351	1.6371	1.6390	1.6409	1.6429	1.6448	1.6467
5.2	1.6487	1.6506	1.6525	1.6544	1.6563	1.6582	1.6601	1.6620	1.6639	1.6658
5.3	1.6677	1.6696	1.6715	1.6734	1.6752	1.6771	1.6790	1.6808	1.6827	1.6845
5.4	1.6864	1.6882	1.6901	1.6919	1.6938	1.6956	1.6974	1.6993	1.7001	1.7029

x	0	1	2	3	4	5	6	7	8	9
5.5	1.7047	1.7066	1.7084	1.7102	1.7120	1.7138	1.7156	1.7174	1.7192	1.7210
5.6	1.7228	1.7246	1.7263	1.7281	1.7299	1.7317	1.7334	1.7352	1.7370	1.7387
5.7	1.7405	1.7422	1.7440	1.7457	1.7475	1.7492	1.7509	1.7527	1.7544	1.7561
5.8	1.7579	1.7596	1.7613	1.7630	1.7647	1.7664	1.7682	1.7699	1.7716	1.7733
5.9	1.7750	1.7766	1.7783	1.7800	1.7817	1.7834	1.7851	1.7867	1.7884	1.7901
6.0	1.7918	1.7934	1.7951	1.7967	1.7984	1.8001	1.8017	1.8034	1.8050	1.8066
6.1	1.8083	1.8099	1.8116	1.8132	1.8148	1.8165	1.8181	1.8197	1.8213	1.8229
6.2	1.8245	1.8262	1.8278	1.8294	1.8310	1.8326	1.8342	1.8358	1.8374	1.8390
6.3	1.8405	1.8421	1.8437	1.8453	1.8469	1.8485	1.8500	1.8516	1.8532	1.8547
6.4	1.8563	1.8579	1.8594	1.8610	1.8625	1.8641	1.8656	1.8672	1.8687	1.8703
6.5	1.8718	1.8733	1.8749	1.8764	1.8779	1.8795	1.8810	1.8825	1.8840	1.8856
6.6	1.8871	1.8886	1.8901	1.8916	1.8931	1.8946	1.8961	1.8976	1.8991	1.9006
6.7	1.9021	1.9036	1.9051	1.9066	1.9081	1.9095	1.9110	1.9125	1.9140	1.9155
6.8	1.9169	1.9184	1.9199	1.9213	1.9228	1.9242	1.9257	1.9272	1.9286	1.9301
6.9	1.9315	1.9330	1.9344	1.9359	1.9373	1.9387	1.9402	1.9416	1.9430	1.9445
7.0	1.9459	1.9473	1.9488	1.9502	1.9516	1.9530	1.9544	1.9559	1.9573	1.9587
7.1	1.9601	1.9615	1.9629	1.9643	1.9657	1.9671	1.9685	1.9699	1.9713	1.9727
7.2	1.9741	1.9755	1.9769	1.9782	1.9796	1.9810	1.9824	1.9838	1.9851	1.9865
7.3	1.9879	1.9892	1.9906	1.9920	1.9933	1.9947	1.9961	1.9974	1.9988	2.0001
7.4	2.0015	2.0028	2.0042	2.0055	2.0069	2.0082	2.0096	2.0109	2.0122	2.0136
7.5	2.0149	2.0162	2.0176	2.0189	2.0202	2.0215	2.0229	2.0242	2.0255	2.0268
7.6	2.0281	2.0295	2.0308	2.0321	2.0334	2.0347	2.0360	2.0373	2.0386	2.0399
7.7	2.0412	2.0425	2.0438	2.0451	2.0464	2.0477	2.0490	2.0503	2.0516	2.0528
7.8	2.0541	2.0554	2.0567	2.0580	2.0592	2.0605	2.0618	2.0631	2.0643	2.0656
7.9	2.0669	2.0681	2.0694	2.0707	2.0719	2.0732	2.0744	2.0757	2.0769	2.0782
8.0	2.0794	2.0807	2.0819	2.0832	2.0844	2.0857	2.0869	2.0882	2.0894	2.0906
8.1	2.0919	2.0931	2.0943	2.0956	2.0968	2.0980	2.0992	2.1005	2.1017	2.1029
8.2	2.1041	2.1054	2.1066	2.1078	2.1090	2.1102	2.1114	2.1126	2.1138	2.1150
8.3	2.1163	2.1175	2.1187	2.1199	2.1211	2.1223	2.1235	2.1247	2.1258	2.1270
8.4	2.1282	2.1294	2.1306	2.1318	2.1330	2.1342	2.1353	2.1365	2.1377	2.1389
8.5	2.1401	2.1412	2.1424	2.1436	2.1448	2.1459	2.1471	2.1483	2.1494	2.1506
8.6	2.1518	2.1529	2.1541	2.1552	2.1564	2.1576	2.1587	2.1599	2.1610	2.1622
8.7	2.1633	2.1645	2.1656	2.1668	2.1679	2.1691	2.1702	2.1713	2.1725	2.1736
8.8	2.1748	2.1759	2.1770	2.1782	2.1793	2.1804	2.1815	2.1827	2.1838	2.1849
8.9	2.1861	2.1872	2.1883	2.1894	2.1905	2.1917	2.1928	2.1939	2.1950	2.1961
9.0	2.1972	2.1983	2.1994	2.2006	2.2017	2.2028	2.2039	2.2050	2.2061	2.2072
9.1	2.2083	2.2094	2.2105	2.2116	2.2127	2.2138	2.2148	2.2159	2.2170	2.2181
9.2	2.2192	2.2203	2.2214	2.2225	2.2235	2.2246	2.2257	2.2268	2.2279	2.2289
9.3	2.2300	2.2311	2.2322	2.2332	2.2343	2.2354	2.2364	2.2375	2.2386	2.2396
9.4	2.2407	2.2418	2.2428	2.2439	2.2450	2.2460	2.2471	2.2481	2.2492	2.2502
9.5	2.2513	2.2523	2.2534	2.2544	2.2555	2.2565	2.2576	2.2586	2.2597	2.2607
9.6	2.2618	2.2628	2.2638	2.2649	2.2659	2.2670	2.2680	2.2690	2.2701	2.2711
9.7	2.2721	2.2732	2.2742	2.2752	2.2762	2.2773	2.2783	2.2793	2.2803	2.2814
9.8	2.2824	2.2834	2.2844	2.2854	2.2865	2.2875	2.2885	2.2895	2.2905	2.2915
9.9	2.2925	2.2935	2.2946	2.2956	2.2966	2.2976	2.2986	2.2996	2.3006	2.3016

TRIGONOMETRIC FUNCTIONS

deg.	rad.	sin	cos	tan	cot	sec	csc		
0°00'	.0000	.0000	1.0000	.0000	—	1.000	—	1.5708	90°00'
10'	.0029	.0029	1.0000	.0029	343.8	1.000	343.8	1.5679	50'
20'	.0058	.0058	1.0000	.0058	171.9	1.000	171.9	1.5650	40'
30'	.0087	.0087	1.0000	.0087	114.6	1.000	114.6	1.5621	30'
40'	.0116	.0116	.9999	.0116	85.94	1.000	85.95	1.5592	20'
50'	.0145	.0145	.9999	.0145	68.75	1.000	68.76	1.5563	10'
1°00'	.0175	.0175	.9998	.0175	57.29	1.000	57.30	1.5533	89°00'
10'	.0204	.0204	.9998	.0204	49.10	1.000	49.11	1.5504	50'
20'	.0233	.0233	.9997	.0233	42.96	1.000	42.98	1.5475	40'
30'	.0262	.0262	.9997	.0262	38.19	1.000	38.20	1.5446	30'
40'	.0291	.0291	.9996	.0291	34.37	1.000	34.38	1.5417	20'
50'	.0320	.0320	.9995	.0320	31.24	1.001	31.26	1.5388	10'
2°00'	.0349	.0349	.9994	.0349	28.64	1.001	28.65	1.5359	88°00'
10'	.0378	.0378	.9993	.0378	26.43	1.001	26.45	1.5330	50'
20'	.0407	.0407	.9992	.0407	24.54	1.001	24.56	1.5301	40'
30'	.0436	.0436	.9990	.0437	22.90	1.001	22.93	1.5272	30'
40'	.0465	.0465	.9989	.0466	21.47	1.001	21.49	1.5243	20'
50'	.0495	.0494	.9988	.0495	20.21	1.001	20.23	1.5213	10'
3°00'	.0524	.0523	.9986	.0524	19.08	1.001	19.11	1.5184	87°00'
10'	.0553	.0552	.9985	.0553	18.07	1.002	18.10	1.5155	50'
20'	.0582	.0581	.9983	.0582	17.17	1.002	17.20	1.5126	40'
30'	.0611	.0610	.9981	.0612	16.35	1.002	16.38	1.5097	30'
40'	.0640	.0640	.9980	.0641	15.60	1.002	15.64	1.5068	20'
50'	.0669	.0669	.9978	.0670	14.92	1.002	14.96	1.5039	10'
4°00'	.0698	.0698	.9976	.0699	14.30	1.002	14.34	1.5010	86°00'
10'	.0727	.0727	.9974	.0729	13.73	1.003	13.76	1.4981	50'
20'	.0756	.0756	.9971	.0758	13.20	1.003	13.23	1.4952	40'
30'	.0785	.0785	.9969	.0787	12.71	1.003	12.75	1.4923	30'
40'	.0814	.0814	.9967	.0816	12.25	1.003	12.29	1.4893	20'
50'	.0844	.0843	.9964	.0846	11.83	1.004	11.87	1.4864	10'
5°00'	.0873	.0872	.9962	.0875	11.43	1.004	11.47	1.4835	85°00'
10'	.0902	.0901	.9959	.0904	11.06	1.004	11.10	1.4806	50'
20'	.0931	.0929	.9957	.0934	10.71	1.004	10.76	1.4777	40'
30'	.0960	.0958	.9954	.0963	10.39	1.005	10.43	1.4748	30'
40'	.0989	.0987	.9951	.0992	10.08	1.005	10.13	1.4719	20'
50'	.1018	.1016	.9948	.1022	9.788	1.005	9.839	1.4690	10'
6°00'	.1047	.1045	.9945	.1051	9.514	1.006	9.567	1.4661	84°00'
10'	.1076	.1074	.9942	.1080	9.255	1.006	9.309	1.4632	50'
20'	.1105	.1103	.9939	.1110	9.010	1.006	9.065	1.4603	40'
30'	.1134	.1132	.9936	.1139	8.777	1.006	8.834	1.4573	30'
40'	.1164	.1161	.9932	.1169	8.556	1.007	8.614	1.4544	20'
50'	.1193	.1190	.9929	.1198	8.345	1.007	8.405	1.4515	10'
7°00'	.1222	.1219	.9925	.1228	8.144	1.008	8.206	1.4486	83°00'
10'	.1251	.1248	.9922	.1257	7.953	1.008	8.016	1.4457	50'
20'	.1280	.1276	.9918	.1287	7.770	1.008	7.834	1.4428	40'
30'	.1309	.1305	.9914	.1317	7.596	1.009	7.661	1.4399	82°30'
		cos	sin	cot	tan	csc	sec	rad.	deg.

deg.	rad.	sin	cos	tan	cot	sec	csc		
7°30′	.1309	.1305	.9914	.1317	7.596	1.009	7.661	1.4399	30′
40′	.1338	.1334	.9911	.1346	7.429	1.009	7.496	1.4370	20′
50′	.1367	.1363	.9907	.1376	7.269	1.009	7.337	1.4341	10′
8°00′	.1396	.1392	.9903	.1405	7.115	1.010	7.185	1.4312	82°00′
10′	.1425	.1421	.9899	.1435	6.968	1.010	7.040	1.4283	50′
20′	.1454	.1449	.9894	.1465	6.827	1.011	6.900	1.4254	40′
30′	.1484	.1478	.9890	.1495	6.691	1.011	6.765	1.4224	30′
40′	.1513	.1507	.9886	.1524	6.561	1.012	6.636	1.4195	20′
50′	.1542	.1536	.9881	.1554	6.435	1.012	6.512	1.4166	10′
9°00′	.1571	.1564	.9877	.1584	6.314	1.012	6.392	1.4137	81°00′
10′	.1600	.1593	.9872	.1614	6.197	1.013	6.277	1.4108	50′
20′	.1629	.1622	.9868	.1644	6.084	1.013	6.166	1.4079	40′
30′	.1658	.1650	.9863	.1673	5.976	1.014	6.059	1.4050	30′
40′	.1687	.1679	.9858	.1703	5.871	1.014	5.955	1.4021	20′
50′	.1716	.1708	.9853	.1733	5.769	1.015	5.855	1.3992	10′
10°00′	.1745	.1736	.9848	.1763	5.671	1.015	5.759	1.3963	80°00′
10′	.1774	.1765	.9843	.1793	5.576	1.016	5.665	1.3934	50′
20′	.1804	.1794	.9838	.1823	5.485	1.016	5.575	1.3904	40′
30′	.1833	.1822	.9833	.1853	5.396	1.017	5.487	1.3875	30′
40′	.1862	.1851	.9827	.1883	5.309	1.018	5.403	1.3846	20′
50′	.1891	.1880	.9822	.1914	5.226	1.018	5.320	1.3817	10′
11°00′	.1920	.1908	.9816	.1944	5.145	1.019	5.241	1.3788	79°00′
10′	.1949	.1937	.9811	.1974	5.066	1.019	5.164	1.3759	50′
20′	.1978	.1965	.9805	.2004	4.989	1.020	5.089	1.3730	40′
30′	.2007	.1994	.9799	.2035	4.915	1.020	5.016	1.3701	30′
40′	.2036	.2022	.9793	.2065	4.843	1.021	4.945	1.3672	20′
50′	.2065	.2051	.9787	.2095	4.773	1.022	4.876	1.3643	10′
12°00′	.2094	.2079	.9781	.2126	4.705	1.022	4.810	1.3614	78°00′
10′	.2123	.2108	.9775	.2156	4.638	1.023	4.745	1.3584	50′
20′	.2153	.2136	.9769	.2186	4.574	1.024	4.682	1.3555	40′
30′	.2182	.2164	.9763	.2217	4.511	1.024	4.620	1.3526	30′
40′	.2211	.2193	.9757	.2247	4.449	1.025	4.560	1.3497	20′
50′	.2240	.2221	.9750	.2278	4.390	1.026	4.502	1.3468	10′
13°00′	.2269	.2250	.9744	.2309	4.331	1.026	4.445	1.3439	77°00′
10′	.2298	.2278	.9737	.2339	4.275	1.027	4.390	1.3410	50′
20′	.2327	.2306	.9730	.2370	4.219	1.028	4.336	1.3381	40′
30′	.2356	.2334	.9724	.2401	4.165	1.028	4.284	1.3352	30′
40′	.2385	.2363	.9717	.2432	4.113	1.029	4.232	1.3323	20′
50′	.2414	.2391	.9710	.2462	4.061	1.030	4.182	1.3294	10′
14°00′	.2443	.2419	.9703	.2493	4.011	1.031	4.134	1.3265	76°00′
10′	.2473	.2447	.9696	.2524	3.962	1.031	4.086	1.3235	50′
20′	.2502	.2476	.9689	.2555	3.914	1.032	4.039	1.3206	40′
30′	.2531	.2504	.9681	.2586	3.867	1.033	3.994	1.3177	30′
40′	.2560	.2532	.9674	.2617	3.821	1.034	3.950	1.3148	20′
50′	.2589	.2560	.9667	.2648	3.776	1.034	3.906	1.3119	10′
15°00′	.2618	.2588	.9659	.2679	3.732	1.035	3.864	1.3090	75°00′
		cos	sin	cot	tan	csc	sec	rad.	deg.

TRIGONOMETRIC FUNCTIONS, *continued*

deg.	rad.	sin	cos	tan	cot	sec	csc		
15°00'	.2618	.2588	.9659	.2679	3.732	1.035	3.864	1.3090	75°00'
10'	.2647	.2616	.9652	.2711	3.689	1.036	3.822	1.3061	50'
20'	.2676	.2644	.9644	.2742	3.647	1.037	3.782	1.3032	40'
30'	.2705	.2672	.9636	.2773	3.606	1.038	3.742	1.3003	30'
40'	.2734	.2700	.9628	.2805	3.566	1.039	3.703	1.2974	20'
50'	.2763	.2728	.9621	.2836	3.526	1.039	3.665	1.2945	10'
16°00'	.2793	.2756	.9613	.2867	3.487	1.040	3.628	1.2915	74°00'
10'	.2822	.2784	.9605	.2899	3.450	1.041	3.592	1.2886	50'
20'	.2851	.2812	.9596	.2931	3.412	1.042	3.556	1.2857	40'
30'	.2880	.2840	.9588	.2962	3.376	1.043	3.521	1.2828	30'
40'	.2909	.2868	.9580	.2994	3.340	1.044	3.487	1.2799	20'
50'	.2938	.2896	.9572	.3026	3.305	1.045	3.453	1.2770	10'
17°00'	.2967	.2924	.9563	.3057	3.271	1.046	3.420	1.2741	73°00'
10'	.2996	.2952	.9555	.3089	3.237	1.047	3.388	1.2712	50'
20'	.3025	.2979	.9546	.3121	3.204	1.048	3.356	1.2683	40'
30'	.3054	.3007	.9537	.3153	3.172	1.049	3.326	1.2654	30'
40'	.3083	.3035	.9528	.3185	3.140	1.049	3.295	1.2625	20'
50'	.3113	.3062	.9520	.3217	3.108	1.050	3.265	1.2595	10'
18°00'	.3142	.3090	.9511	.3249	3.078	1.051	3.236	1.2566	72°00'
10'	.3171	.3118	.9502	.3281	3.047	1.052	3.207	1.2537	50'
20'	.3200	.3145	.9492	.3314	3.018	1.053	3.179	1.2508	40'
30'	.3229	.3173	.9483	.3346	2.989	1.054	3.152	1.2479	30'
40'	.3258	.3201	.9474	.3378	2.960	1.056	3.124	1.2450	20'
50'	.3287	.3228	.9465	.3411	2.932	1.057	3.098	1.2421	10'
19°00'	.3316	.3256	.9455	.3443	2.904	1.058	3.072	1.2392	71°00'
10'	.3345	.3283	.9446	.3476	2.877	1.059	3.046	1.2363	50'
20'	.3374	.3311	.9436	.3508	2.850	1.060	3.021	1.2334	40'
30'	.3403	.3338	.9426	.3541	2.824	1.061	2.996	1.2305	30'
40'	.3432	.3365	.9417	.3574	2.798	1.062	2.971	1.2275	20'
50'	.3462	.3393	.9407	.3607	2.773	1.063	2.947	1.2246	10'
20°00'	.3491	.3420	.9397	.3640	2.747	1.064	2.924	1.2217	70°00'
10'	.3520	.3448	.9387	.3673	2.723	1.065	2.901	1.2188	50'
20'	.3549	.3475	.9377	.3706	2.699	1.066	2.878	1.2159	40'
30'	.3578	.3502	.9367	.3739	2.675	1.068	2.855	1.2130	30'
40'	.3607	.3529	.9356	.3772	2.651	1.069	2.833	1.2101	20'
50'	.3636	.3557	.9346	.3805	2.628	1.070	2.812	1.2072	10'
21°00'	.3665	.3584	.9336	.3839	2.605	1.071	2.790	1.2043	69°00'
10'	.3694	.3611	.9325	.3872	2.583	1.072	2.769	1.2014	50'
20'	.3723	.3638	.9315	.3906	2.560	1.074	2.749	1.1985	40'
30'	.3752	.3665	.9304	.3939	2.539	1.075	2.729	1.1956	30'
40'	.3782	.3692	.9293	.3973	2.517	1.076	2.709	1.1926	20'
50'	.3811	.3719	.9283	.4006	2.496	1.077	2.689	1.1897	10'
22°00'	.3840	.3746	.9272	.4040	2.475	1.079	2.669	1.1868	68°00'
10'	.3869	.3773	.9261	.4074	2.455	1.080	2.650	1.1839	50'
20'	.3898	.3800	.9250	.4108	2.434	1.081	2.632	1.1810	40'
30'	.3927	.3827	.9239	.4142	2.414	1.082	2.613	1.1781	67°30'
		cos	sin	cot	tan	csc	sec	rad.	deg.

deg.	rad.	sin	cos	tan	cot	sec	csc		
22°30′	.3927	.3827	.9239	.4142	2.414	1.082	2.613	1.1781	30′
40′	.3956	.3854	.9228	.4176	2.394	1.084	2.595	1.1752	20′
50′	.3985	.3881	.9216	.4210	2.375	1.085	2.577	1.1723	10′
23°00′	.4014	.3907	.9205	.4245	2.356	1.086	2.559	1.1694	67°00′
10′	.4043	.3934	.9194	.4279	2.337	1.088	2.542	1.1665	50′
20′	.4072	.3961	.9182	.4314	2.318	1.089	2.525	1.1636	40′
30′	.4102	.3987	.9171	.4348	2.300	1.090	2.508	1.1606	30′
40′	.4131	.4014	.9159	.4383	2.282	1.092	2.491	1.1577	20′
50′	.4160	.4041	.9147	.4417	2.264	1.093	2.475	1.1548	10′
24°00′	.4189	.4067	.9135	.4452	2.246	1.095	2.459	1.1519	66°00′
10′	.4218	.4094	.9124	.4487	2.229	1.096	2.443	1.1490	50′
20′	.4247	.4120	.9112	.4522	2.211	1.097	2.427	1.1461	40′
30′	.4276	.4147	.9100	.4557	2.194	1.099	2.411	1.1432	30′
40′	.4305	.4173	.9088	.4592	2.177	1.100	2.396	1.1403	20′
50′	.4334	.4200	.9075	.4628	2.161	1.102	2.381	1.1374	10′
25°00′	.4363	.4226	.9063	.4663	2.145	1.103	2.366	1.1345	65°00′
10′	.4392	.4253	.9051	.4699	2.128	1.105	2.352	1.1316	50′
20′	.4422	.4279	.9038	.4734	2.112	1.106	2.337	1.1286	40′
30′	.4451	.4305	.9026	.4770	2.097	1.108	2.323	1.1257	30′
40′	.4480	.4331	.9013	.4806	2.081	1.109	2.309	1.1228	20′
50′	.4509	.4358	.9001	.4841	2.066	1.111	2.295	1.1199	10′
26°00′	.4538	.4384	.8988	.4877	2.050	1.113	2.281	1.1170	64°00′
10′	.4567	.4410	.8975	.4913	2.035	1.114	2.268	1.1141	50′
20′	.4596	.4436	.8962	.4950	2.020	1.116	2.254	1.1112	40′
30′	.4625	.4462	.8949	.4986	2.006	1.117	2.241	1.1083	30′
40′	.4654	.4488	.8936	.5022	1.991	1.119	2.228	1.1054	20′
50′	.4683	.4514	.8923	.5059	1.977	1.121	2.215	1.1025	10′
27°00′	.4712	.4540	.8910	.5095	1.963	1.122	2.203	1.0996	63°00′
10′	.4741	.4566	.8897	.5132	1.949	1.124	2.190	1.0966	50′
20′	.4771	.4592	.8884	.5169	1.935	1.126	2.178	1.0937	40′
30′	.4800	.4617	.8870	.5206	1.921	1.127	2.166	1.0908	30′
40′	.4829	.4643	.8857	.5243	1.907	1.129	2.154	1.0879	20′
50′	.4858	.4669	.8843	.5280	1.894	1.131	2.142	1.0850	10′
28°00′	.4887	.4695	.8829	.5317	1.881	1.133	2.130	1.0821	62°00′
10′	.4916	.4720	.8816	.5354	1.868	1.134	2.118	1.0792	50′
20′	.4945	.4746	.8802	.5392	1.855	1.136	2.107	1.0763	40′
30′	.4974	.4772	.8788	.5430	1.842	1.138	2.096	1.0734	30′
40′	.5003	.4797	.8774	.5467	1.829	1.140	2.085	1.0705	20′
50′	.5032	.4823	.8760	.5505	1.816	1.142	2.074	1.0676	10′
29°00′	.5061	.4848	.8746	.5543	1.804	1.143	2.063	1.0647	61°00′
10′	.5091	.4874	.8732	.5581	1.792	1.145	2.052	1.0617	50′
20′	.5120	.4899	.8718	.5619	1.780	1.147	2.041	1.0588	40′
30′	.5149	.4924	.8704	.5658	1.767	1.149	2.031	1.0559	30′
40′	.5178	.4950	.8689	.5696	1.756	1.151	2.020	1.0530	20′
50′	.5207	.4975	.8675	.5735	1.744	1.153	2.010	1.0501	10′
30°00′	.5236	.5000	.8660	.5774	1.732	1.155	2.000	1.0472	60°00′
		cos	sin	cot	tan	csc	sec	rad.	deg.

deg.	rad.	sin	cos	tan	cot	sec	csc		
30°00'	.5236	.5000	.8660	.5774	1.732	1.155	2.000	1.0472	60°00'
10'	.5265	.5025	.8646	.5812	1.720	1.157	1.990	1.0443	50'
20'	.5294	.5050	.8631	.5851	1.709	1.159	1.980	1.0414	40'
30'	.5323	.5075	.8616	.5890	1.698	1.161	1.970	1.0385	30'
40'	.5352	.5100	.8601	.5930	1.686	1.163	1.961	1.0356	20'
50'	.5381	.5125	.8587	.5969	1.675	1.165	1.951	1.0327	10'
31°00'	.5411	.5150	.8572	.6009	1.664	1.167	1.942	1.0297	59°00'
10'	.5440	.5175	.8557	.6048	1.653	1.169	1.932	1.0268	50'
20'	.5469	.5200	.8542	.6088	1.643	1.171	1.923	1.0239	40'
30'	.5498	.5225	.8526	.6128	1.632	1.173	1.914	1.0210	30'
40'	.5527	.5250	.8511	.6168	1.621	1.175	1.905	1.0181	20'
50'	.5556	.5275	,8496	.6208	1.611	1.177	1.896	1.0152	10'
32°00'	.5585	.5299	.8480	.6249	1.600	1.179	1.887	1.0123	58°00'
10'	.5614	.5324	.8465	.6289	1.590	1.181	1.878	1.0094	50'
20'	.5643	.5348	.8450	.6330	1.580	1.184	1.870	1.0065	40'
30'	.5672	.5373	.8434	.6371	1.570	1.186	1.861	1.0036	30'
40'	.5701	.5398	.8418	.6412	1.560	1.188	1.853	1.0007	20'
50'	.5730	.5422	.8403	.6453	1.550	1.190	1.844	.9977	10'
33°00'	.5760	.5446	.8387	.6494	1.540	1.192	1.836	.9948	57°00'
10'	.5789	.5471	.8371	.6536	1.530	1.195	1.828	.9919	50'
20'	.5818	.5495	.8355	.6577	1.520	1.197	1.820	.9890	40'
30'	.5847	.5519	.8339	.6619	1.511	1.199	1.812	.9861	30'
40'	.5876	.5544	.8323	.6661	1.501	1.202	1.804	.9832	20'
50'	.5905	.5568	.8307	.6703	1.492	1.204	1.796	.9803	10'
34°00'	.5934	.5592	.8290	.6745	1.483	1.206	1.788	.9774	56°00'
10'	.5963	.5616	.8274	.6787	1.473	1.209	1.781	.9745	50'
20'	.5992	.5640	.8258	.6830	1.464	1.211	1.773	.9716	40'
30'	.6021	.5664	.8241	.6873	1.455	1.213	1.766	.9687	30'
40'	.6050	.5688	.8225	.6916	1.446	1.216	1.758	.9657	20'
50'	.6080	.5712	.8208	.6959	1.437	1.218	1.751	.9628	10'
35°00'	.6109	.5736	.8192	.7002	1.428	1.221	1.743	.9599	55°00'
10'	.6138	.5760	.8175	.7046	1.419	1.223	1.736	.9570	50'
20'	.6167	.5783	.8158	.7089	1.411	1.226	1.729	.9541	40'
30'	.6196	.5807	.8141	.7133	1.402	1.228	1.722	.9512	30'
40'	.6225	.5831	.8124	.7177	1.393	1.231	1.715	.9483	20'
50'	.6254	.5854	.8107	.7221	1.385	1.233	1.708	.9454	10'
36°00'	.6283	.5878	.8090	.7265	1.376	1.236	1.701	.9425	54°00'
10'	.6312	.5901	.8073	.7310	1.368	1.239	1.695	.9396	50'
20'	.6341	.5925	.8056	.7355	1.360	1.241	1.688	.9367	40'
30'	.6370	.5948	.8039	.7400	1.351	1.244	1.681	.9338	30'
40'	.6400	.5972	.8021	.7445	1.343	1.247	1.675	.9308	20'
50'	.6429	.5995	.8004	.7490	1.335	1.249	1.668	.9279	10'
37°00'	.6458	.6018	.7986	.7536	1.327	1.252	1.662	.9250	53°00'
10'	.6487	.6041	.7969	.7581	1.319	1.255	1.655	.9221	50'
20'	.6516	.6065	.7951	.7627	1.311	1.258	1.649	.9192	40'
30'	.6545	.6088	.7934	.7673	1.303	1.260	1.643	.9163	52°30'
		cos	sin	cot	tan	csc	sec	rad.	deg.

deg.	rad.	sin	cos	tan	cot	sec	csc		
37°30′	.6545	.6088	.7934	.7673	1.303	1.260	1.643	.9163	30′
40′	.6574	.6111	.7916	.7720	1.295	1.263	1.636	.9134	20′
50′	.6603	.6134	.7898	.7766	1.288	1.266	1.630	.9105	10′
38°00′	.6632	.6157	.7880	.7813	1.280	1.269	1.624	.9076	52°00′
10′	.6661	.6180	.7862	.7860	1.272	1.272	1.618	.9047	50′
20′	.6690	.6202	.7844	.7907	1.265	1.275	1.612	.9018	40′
30′	.6720	.6225	.7826	.7954	1.257	1.278	1.606	.8988	30′
40′	.6749	.6248	.7808	.8002	1,250	1.281	1.601	.8959	20′
50′	.6778	.6271	.7790	.8050	1.242	1.284	1.595	.8930	10′
39°00′	.6807	.6293	.7771	.8098	1.235	1.287	1.589	.8901	51°00′
10′	.6836	.6316	.7753	.8146	1.228	1.290	1.583	.8872	50′
20′	.6865	.6338	.7735	.8195	1.220	1.293	1.578	.8843	40′
30′	.6894	.6361	.7716	.8243	1.213	1.296	1.572	.8814	30′
40′	.6923	.6383	.7698	.8292	1.206	1.299	1.567	.8785	20′
50′	.6952	.6406	.7679	.8342	1.199	1.302	1.561	.8756	10′
40°00′	.6981	.6428	.7660	.8391	1.192	1.305	1.556	.8727	50°00′
10′	.7010	.6450	.7642	.8441	1.185	1.309	1.550	.8698	50′
20′	.7039	.6472	.7623	.8491	1.178	1.312	1.545	.8668	40′
30′	.7069	.6494	.7604	.8541	1.171	1.315	1.540	.8639	30′
40′	.7098	.6517	.7585	.8591	1.164	1.318	1.535	.8610	20′
50′	.7127	.6539	.7566	.8642	1.157	1.322	1.529	.8581	10′
41°00′	.7156	.6561	.7547	.8693	1.150	1.325	1.524	.8552	49°00′
10′	.7185	.6583	.7528	.8744	1.144	1.328	1.519	.8523	50′
20′	.7214	.6604	.7509	.8796	1.137	1.332	1.514	.8494	40′
30′	.7243	.6626	.7490	.8847	1.130	1.335	1.509	.8465	30′
40′	.7272	.6648	.7470	.8899	1.124	1.339	1.504	.8436	20′
50′	.7301	.6670	.7451	.8952	1.117	1.342	1.499	.8407	10′
42°00′	.7330	.6691	.7431	.9004	1.111	1.346	1.494	.8378	48°00′
10′	.7359	.6713	.7412	.9057	1.104	1.349	1.490	.8348	50′
20′	.7389	.6734	.7392	.9110	1.098	1.353	1.485	.8319	40′
30′	.7418	.6756	.7373	.9163	1.091	1.356	1.480	.8290	30′
40′	.7447	.6777	.7353	.9217	1.085	1.360	1.476	.8261	20′
50′	.7476	.6799	.7333	.9271	1.079	1.364	1.471	.8232	10′
43°00′	.7505	.6820	.7314	.9325	1.072	1.367	1.466	.8203	47°00′
10′	.7534	.6841	.7294	.9380	1.066	1.371	1.462	.8174	50′
20′	.7563	.6862	.7274	.9435	1.060	1.375	1.457	.8145	40′
30′	.7592	.6884	.7254	.9490	1.054	1.379	1.453	.8116	30′
40′	.7621	.6905	.7234	.9545	1.048	1.382	1.448	.8087	20′
50′	.7650	.6926	.7214	.9601	1.042	1.386	1.444	.8058	10′
44°00′	.7679	.6947	.7193	.9657	1.036	1.390	1.440	.8029	46°00′
10′	.7709	.6967	.7173	.9713	1.030	1.394	1.435	.7999	50′
20′	.7738	.6988	.7153	.9770	1.024	1.398	1.431	.7970	40′
30′	.7767	.7009	.7133	.9827	1.018	1.402	1.427	.7941	30′
40′	.7796	.7030	.7112	.9884	1.012	1.406	1.423	.7912	20′
50′	.7825	.7050	.7092	.9942	1.006	1.410	1.418	.7883	10′
45°00′	.7854	.7071	.7071	1.000	1.000	1.414	1.414	.7854	45°00′
		cos	sin	cot	tan	csc	sec	rad.	deg.

SELECTED ANSWERS

1.1 Introduction to Problem Solving

Problem Set

1 Answers will vary. Possible answer: Draw a diagram.
2 Answers will vary. Possible answer: Build a model.
3 a 28 **b** 56 **c** 28n **4 a** 24 **b** 6 **5 a** *None*
b Possible answer:

R	W	B	G
G	B	W	R
W	R	G	B
B	G	R	W

6 a 100 **b** 90 **c** 45

1.2 Graphic Solutions

Problem Set

1 a

b Paul: $9; Quincy: $13; Ruth: $14; Sara: $5; Tom: $9
2 $\dfrac{n(n-1)}{2}$ **3 a** Via Lincoln, Wichita, and Albuquerque
b $41\frac{3}{4}$ hr **c** Via Lincoln, Denver, and Albuquerque
4 Many possible answers **5 a** $p_1p_2p_5p_4$ **b** Yes:
$p_1p_2p_5p_4p_3$ **c** No: a path cannot start at p_3, and once a
path reaches p_3, it cannot leave. **6** Job 1: Roel; job 2:
Noel; job 3: Joel; job 4: Zoel.

1.3 Geometric Modeling

Problem Set

1 275 **2** $\dfrac{n(n-1)}{2}$ **3 a** 15 **b** 12 **c** 9 **4** Any numbers
of the form a, $6 - a$, $10 - a$, $2 + a$ **5** Only **a, b** and **d**
can be drawn. If we call a vertex at which an even
number of segments meet an even vertex and one at
which an odd number of segments meet an odd vertex,
then only networks with all even vertices and those
with exactly two odd vertices can be traced. **6 a** 45
b 90 **7 a** 1 **b** 1 **c** 1 **d** 1 **e** 2 **f** 3 **g** 1 **h** 1 **i** 3 **j** 1
k 10 **8** Possible answers:

a

b

1.4 Finding a Pattern

Problem Set

1 a 13, 15; consecutive odd numbers **b** 19, 22; nth
term $= 3n - 2$ **c** 99, 120; nth term $= n^2 - 1$ **d** 29, 37;
nth term $= \frac{1}{2}(n^2 - n) + 1$ **e** 256, 512; nth term $= 2^{n-1}$
f 89, 144; each term (after first 2) is sum of 2
preceding terms. **2 a** 7, 11, 19, 35, 67 **b** 32, 64, 128,
256, 512
3 There are only 366 possible birthdays (including leap
year day), so at least 2 of the 367 people must share a
birthday. **4 a** 81 **b** 91 **5** 11 **6** 1, 6, 15, 20, 15, 6, 1; 1,
7, 21, 35, 35, 21, 7, 1 **7 a** 4; 9; 16; 25; the sums are
consecutive perfect squares **b** 1, 4, 9, 16, 25

8 It changes the value stored in the variable NS;
whereas the equation is a statement of equality, the
computer line is a command. **9 a** $3000 **b** 1200 or
1600 **c** $-$$2000; it means a loss of $2000, perhaps
because the income received from the sale of so few
sticks is less than production costs. **d** 700 or 2100
e Between 10,000 and $\approx$17,300 **f** Answers will vary.
Possible answer: because more workers and machinery
are needed to produce more sticks. **g** Answers will
vary. Possible answer: 1500, to generate the greatest
profit

1.5 A Recursive Solution

Problem Set

1 a $y = \sum\limits_{x=1}^{n} (2x - 1)$ **b** $y = x^2$ **c** $S_n = S_{n-1} + 2(n - 1)$
2 Answers will vary. Possible answer: Divide all
integers from 1 to $\sqrt{n}$ into n to see which leave no
remainder. **3** Answers will vary. Possible answer: Use
the process devised for problem 2 to create the set of
divisors, and then count the elements of the set.
4 $S_1 = 1$, $S_n = n \cdot S_{n-1}$ **5 a** 21 min **b** 22 min **c** At
least 24 min 38 sec, at most 24 min 40 sec **d** 36%

1.6 Demonstrations

Problem Set

1 a The set of all numbers of the form $2n$, where n is
an integer **b** Since the set of every other number is
the set of even numbers only if "number" is taken to
mean "integer" and if one element of the set is even
2 a -3, 3 **b** 4.5 **c** 0, 2 **3 a** Even **b** Odd **c** Odd
d Non-negative integer **4** "Opposite" means on the
other side of zero on the number line. Only positive
numbers are on the opposite side of zero from negative
numbers. **5** The number of chords between 7 points
on a circle is the same as the number of handshakes
between 7 people, $\dfrac{7(7 - 1)}{2} = 21$. **6** 512; 336

7 a $x = 4$ **b** $x = 243$ **c** $x = 27$ **d** $x = -9$ or $x = 9$
8 $(2m)(2n) = 4mn$ **9** 87.5% **10** 23; a possible
explanation is "by solving $77 - x = 31 + x$."
11 Explanations will vary, e.g., adding a negative
number moves left on the number line. Any number to
the left of a negative number is negative. **12** 4, 0, 6;
$(x, y) \to |x - y|$ **13** $6y - 18$ **14** $A = I - 1 + \frac{S}{2}$

2.1 The Language of Expressions

Warm-up Exercises

1 $2x + 8$ **2** -1 **3** $6x + 21$ **4** $a(x + y)$ **5 a** $5(3x + 8)$;
$15x + 40$ **b** $2x^2 + 4x$ **6** 31 **7** 80 **8** 5 **9** 11 **10** 8
11 26 **12** $32 - 12x$

Problem Set

13 $17x - 15$ **15** $(x + 3)(x + 2)$; $x^2 + 5x + 6$
16 a -17 **b** $9 + 3(-6) - 8 = -17$ **17 a** 21 **b** 17
c 21 **d** No **e** Yes **19** $7x + 6y$ **21 a** $27 - 2x$
b $2n - 5$ **c** $4(x + 7)$ **22 a** $5x$ **b** x^6 **23** -3 **25** 33
27 30 **28**

x	−4	−2	6	3	−6
y	31	21	−19	−4	41

29 a

b $x^2 + 21x + 90$ **30** $22r + 12s$ **31 a** ≈ 16.16
b ≈ 16.16 **33** 5 **35** $x^3 - 2x^2 + 6x - 12$ **37** $n(n + 1)$
is even since either n is even or $(n + 1)$ is even.
38 No; $n + (n + 1) = 2n + 1$, which is odd because $2n$
is always even. **39 a** 30 **b** 33 **c** 27 **d** No **e** Yes
f Yes **40** 86 **41 a** 169 **b** 97 **c** 169 **d** a and c **42** 42
43 $(x + 2)(x + 3)(x + 4)$; $x^3 + 9x^2 + 26x + 24$

2.2 Solving Equations

Warm-up Exercises

1 a or **b** **2** $z = 4$ or $z = 0$ **3 a** $P = 3x + 19$ **b** $x = 15$
4 Yes **5** Yes **6** $x = 7.5$

7

x	−4	−7	1	0	5
y	0	−3	5	4	9

8 a 4.9 lb **b** 0.7n **c** 36.2 lb **d** $W = 0.7n + 1.2$
9 a No **b** Yes **c** No **d** No **e** Yes **f** No

Problem Set

11 $x = 10$ **12 a** $x = -\frac{3}{8}$ **b** $x = -\frac{4}{3}$ **c** -4.5
13 a $-7, -2, 3, 4$ **b** $-4, -3, 2, 7$ **c** Reversed order
14 a $2.65 **b** $V = 0.05n + 0.1d + 0.25q$ **15 a** $4000
b 250 or any number between 400 and 600 inclusive
c Loss of $2000 **16 a** -2 **b** $\frac{3}{2}$ **17** $x = 4$; $y = -8$;
$z = 64$ **18 a** $\frac{-48}{5}$ **b** 16 **19** 150 cm^2 **21** 9

22 $5x + 15$ **23 a** 7 sec **b** 288 ft **25** $\frac{8x}{13}$ **27** Point E,
since to avoid retracing, a path must begin at a point

that is on the E-D loop and has 2 exit possibilities.
29 $y = -3$ or $y = 5$ **31 a** 9, 9 **b** 4, −4 **32 a** 13,
−13 **b** 10, −10 **c** 10, −16 **33** $a = 2x - 11$ **35** 31
37 $x = 2$ **38 a** 18 **b** 60 **c** −312 **d** −168 **39** $x = 6$
41 $4x^2 + 30x + 2$ **43** $x = \frac{a + 2b}{3}$
45 a

x	−6	−4	0	2	8	12
y	−6	−5	−3	−2	1	3

b A straight line **c** Yes **46 a** $36x + 144$ **b** $x = 3.25$
47 Let a and b be two odd numbers, i.e. $a = 2k + 1$
and $b = 2n + 1$. The product $(2k + 1)(2n + 1)$ is
equivalent to $4kn + 2k + 2n + 1$, which is odd, since
$4kn + 2k + 2n$ is even and adding 1 makes it odd.
48 a $(0, -2)$ **b** PR = 5; RQ = 12 **c** 30 **d** 13
49 a 16 sec **b** 32 sec **51** $-32x^2$ **53** $\frac{23}{3}$
54

x	−5	−4	−3	−2	−1	0	1	2	3	4	5
y	−5	−3	−1	1	3	5	7	9	11	13	15

55 $3x^2 - x + 11$ **56 a** 2 **b** −1; 5 **c** −2.5; 2; 6.5
57 $20,098p + 22,126w$

2.3 Solving Inequalities

Warm-up Exercises

1 c and **d**

2 ───○─────
       −5

3 ───○─────○──
       −1   6

4 $x > \frac{7}{2}$ ─────○────
                    $\frac{7}{2}$

5 a $y + 10 < 3y$ **b** $5n^2 \ne 20$
c $\sqrt{x} - \frac{1}{5} \ge \sqrt{3}$ **d** $6 < 2\pi r < 8$ **6 a** $-12 < -6$
b $12 > 6$ **7 a** $-5 \le -3$ **b** $10 \ge 4$ **8** $8(3x - 5) < 96$;
$x < \frac{17}{3}$ **9** $y > \frac{3}{5}$ **10** $3k \cdot 3k = 9k^2$, which contains a
factor of 9.

Problem Set

11 $x > -2$ ────○──────
                 −2

13 $z > -7$ ────○──────
                 −7

15 $x \le 7$ ──────●──
                   7

17 $x < -1$ **19** $x \ne -5$ **21** Answers will vary. One
possible answer is to think of and solve the problem as
an equation with x on the left side. Then consider the
inequality. **22 a** 1.2 hr **b** 8.4 mi **c** 2 hr 6 min
23 a $3x + 12 < 30$ **b** $x < 6$

24 a Possible table:

x	−3	−2	−1	0	1	2
y	−1	1	3	5	7	9

b Possible table:

x	−3	−2	−1	0	1	2
y	−2	−2	−2	−2	−2	−2

25 $14 < P < 28$ **26 a** Yes **b** No **c** Yes **27** $\left(-2, -\frac{1}{2}\right)$
29 $48x^3$ **31** $-12x^3 + 28x^2 + 20x$

33

	Small	Medium	Large
Thin crust	7.48	8.63	9.78
Thick crust	8.63	9.78	10.93

34 29 **35** $27x^2 + 6x$ **37** $3x^4y^2$ **39** 6 **40 a** $20 - x$
b $(0.9)x + 1.4(20 - x) = 22.00$ **c** 12 $0.90 stamps and 8
$1.40 stamps **41** 13 **43** $x = -3$ or $x = \frac{9}{2}$ **45** $x_3 = \frac{31}{5}$
47 $x \geq 29.6$ [number line: 29.6]

49 $n \neq 5$ [number line: 5]

51 $-1.4 < y < 1.4$ [number line: −1.4 1.4]

52 $A \geq 150$ cm² **53** $x < 2$ [number line: 2]

55 $x < 5$ [number line: 5]

56 $y = 2^x$ **57** .308, 12, 33
58 $a = 4, b = -11, c = -2$ **59** $z = 3$,
$z = -\frac{1}{3}$, or $z = \frac{8}{5}$ **61** $y = \frac{1}{9}$ **63** $\frac{-x^2}{2} - 128$ **64 a** No
real value **b** -3 **c** ≈ -0.293 **65 a** $y = -3x + 1$
b [graph] **66 a** $M\left(3, \frac{7}{2}\right)$, $N(5, 1)$
b $MN \approx 3.2$ **c** $AC \approx 6.4$ **67 a** $\frac{8}{27}$ **b** $\frac{2}{9}$ **c** 0 **d** $\frac{1}{27}$

2.4 Introduction to Graphing

Warm-up Exercises
1 a (11, 5) **b** 28 **2**

x	−2	−1	0	1	2
y	10	−7	−4	−1	2

3 −17 **4** 5 **5 a** D **b** E **c** A **d** C **e** B **6** 10

Problem Set
7 a −2 **b** 0 **c** −2.5 **d** 6 and 8 **8 a** 15 **b** (4, 3.5)
9 −2 **10** $\left\{x : \frac{7}{4} < x < 13\right\}$ **11** {−33, −6, 6, 39}
12 a No **b** No **c** Yes **d** Yes **13** $x = \frac{F - Q}{7}$
15 $x = \frac{c}{a + b}$ **16 a** $6x = 10x - 16$ **b** $x = 4$ **c** 4; 8
d 24 **17** $\frac{2}{5}$ **18 a** 60% **b** 80% **c** 79 **d** $\approx 58\%$ **19 a** 2
b 8 **20 a** $y = -x + 10$ **b** $y = \frac{1}{x}$ **21 a** (−1, 2) **b** 6, 8
c 10 **22** 62 **23** (14, 19) **24** $2 \leq x \leq 7$ and
$-6 \leq y \leq 4$; (2, 4), (7, 4), (7, −6), (2, −6) **25** $x = 10$
26 a 16 **b** 9.375 in. **c** 16:25 **27 a** 2 and 6
b {x : 2 < x < 6} **c** {h(x) : h(x) ≥ −3} **28** $4; Sam and
Bom each give Pim $2 **29** 75; (12.5, 7.5) **30 a** 6 **b** 4

2.5 Matrices

Warm-up Exercises
1 $\begin{bmatrix} -2 & 6 \\ 3 & -4 \\ -8 & 3 \end{bmatrix}$ **2** $\begin{bmatrix} 20 & -16 \\ -24 & 12 \\ 24 & -8 \end{bmatrix}$ **3** $\begin{bmatrix} 8 & -2 \\ -9 & 2 \\ 4 & -1 \end{bmatrix}$ **4** 11
5 [27] **6** $\begin{bmatrix} -13 \\ 29 \end{bmatrix}$ **7 a** 2×3 **b** B must have three rows
c C must have 2 columns **8** George: $326; Gracie:
$286

Problem Set
9 $\begin{bmatrix} 20 & -1 \\ -20 & 4 \\ 7 & 0 \end{bmatrix}$ **11** $\begin{bmatrix} 23 & -11 \\ -20 & 26 \\ 19 & -17 \end{bmatrix}$ **13** No, the number
of columns in P does not equal the number of rows in
Q. **15** $a = -14, b = \frac{22}{3}$ **16 a** Mother: $1500.48;
father: $2186.21; child 1: $660.64; child 2: $1095.65
b $5442.98 **c** $142.78 **17 a** $\begin{bmatrix} -71 & -52 \\ 36 & 62 \end{bmatrix}$

b $\begin{bmatrix} 59 & 13 \\ -4 & 42 \end{bmatrix}$ **c** $\begin{bmatrix} -52 & -71 \\ 62 & 36 \end{bmatrix}$ **19** 1.15
20 a $x^2 + 14x + 49$ **b** $(2x + 3)^2$

21 $16\pi < A < 100\pi$ **22** (5, 7) **23** $\frac{1}{2}$ **24 a** $x \approx 129.0$
b $x \approx 3.4$ or $x \approx -3.4$ **c** $x \approx 5.7$ **d** $x \approx 22.7$
25 a $2,390,000 **b**
$$\begin{bmatrix} 27{,}560 & 29{,}680 & 33{,}920 & 41{,}340 \\ 31{,}270 & 37{,}100 & 39{,}220 & 43{,}460 \\ 39{,}220 & 42{,}400 & 44{,}520 & 47{,}700 \\ 44{,}520 & 47{,}700 & 50{,}880 & 51{,}940 \end{bmatrix}$$
c $143,400 **26 a** $\frac{1}{4}$ **b** $\frac{1}{4}$ **27 a** 0 **b** Undefined
c Undefined **28** $\frac{5}{8}$ **29** $19 + \sqrt{41}$ **30 a** Yes **b** No
c No **d** Yes **31 a** $\begin{array}{l} \text{I} \\ \text{II} \\ \text{III} \end{array}\begin{bmatrix} 260 \\ 300 \\ 380 \end{bmatrix}$ **b** $940 **32** The number
you gave Igor **33** $\begin{bmatrix} 3 & 6 & 7 & x & x \\ 8 & 2 & 4 & 3x & x + 2 \\ 2 & 6 & 3 & 2x & 2x \\ 145 & 200 & 150 & 85x & 65x + 20 \end{bmatrix}$
34 b and e **35** (18, 14) **37** {x : x > 3.5} **39** {x : x ≤ 3}
40 $y = x - 7$
41 a [number line]

b [number line]

c [number line]

d [number line]

42 a 5 **b** 10 **c** 10 **d** 5 **e** 1

43 $\begin{bmatrix} -13 & 15 \\ 58 & 22 \end{bmatrix}$; $\begin{bmatrix} 45 & 29 \\ -16 & -36 \end{bmatrix}$; no

2.6 Probability

Warm-up Exercises

1 0 and 1, inclusive **2** Answers will vary. One possible answer is an election. **3 a** $\frac{1}{6}$; $\frac{7}{30}$; $\frac{1}{4}$; $\frac{7}{20}$ **b** 1 **4** 1

Problem Set

5 $\frac{5}{8}$ **6 a** $\frac{7}{12}$ **b** $\frac{5}{12}$ **7** 10 **8** $n(t) = 120t$ **9 a** No **b** Yes

c Yes **10** $\frac{5}{7}$ **11 a** -3 **b** -3 **c** -3 **12** 50 sec **13** No

14 $\left(-3, -\frac{22}{5}\right)$ **15** $(-3, 7)$

16 The lines all pass through $(0, -5)$ and the lines become more vertical as the coefficient of x increases.

17 $\begin{bmatrix} 2 & 3 & 5 \\ 7 & -2 & -9 \end{bmatrix}$ **18 a** -30 **b** 23 **c** 1 **19** $\frac{1}{2}$ **21** $\frac{1}{2}$

23 a 2×1 **b** $\begin{bmatrix} 4 \\ -3 \end{bmatrix}$

Review Problems

1 $8x^2 - 5xy - 2y^2$ **3** $x = 2.4$ **5 a** 10 **b** .6 **c** .4
7 $x < -6$ ⟵─────○──
$\qquad\qquad\qquad\quad -6$

9 $x = 8$, $y = 12$, $z = -52$
11 $x^2 + 5x + 6$ **13** $x^3 - 27$ **15** $A = w(w + 7)$
17 $\approx .40$ **18 a** $\frac{7}{12}$ **b** Undefined **19 a** 230 mi **b** 3:00
P.M. **c** 3:20 P.M. **20** $\begin{matrix} x \\ y \\ z \end{matrix}\begin{bmatrix} 3 & 5 & 0 & -1 \\ -3 & -4 & 2 & -3 \\ 1 & 1 & 15 & -7 \end{bmatrix}$

21 ≈ -74.52 **22** $-\frac{19}{3}$ **23** $\frac{8}{7}$ **24 a** 28 **b** 70 **c** 0
25 a -4 **b** $2x^2 + 48$
26 $\begin{matrix} \text{Hours of Overtime} \\ \text{Overtime Pay} \\ \text{Total Pay} \end{matrix}\begin{bmatrix} 6 & 8 & 4 & 10 \\ 90 & 120 & 60 & 150 \\ 430 & 460 & 400 & 490 \end{bmatrix}$
27 ●──────●────○──⟶
$\qquad\;\; -2 \qquad\qquad 6$

29 ⟵────○────────
$\qquad\qquad\; 4$

31 -152 **32** 0 **33 a** .05 **b** .2 **c** .7 **d** ≈ 45
e Answers will vary. **34 a** $B = 44 + 30h + p$ **b** $47
35 $w = 0$ **37** $y \approx 27.85$ **39** $x = 1$ **41 a** $45
b $267.50

Exponents and Radicals

Problem Set

1 $24b$ **3** True **5** False **6 a** 15,625 **b** 15,625 **c** 3125
d 3125 **7** $(x, y) = (5, 7)$ **9** False **11** $x^5 + 3x^2 - 2$

12 Possible table:

x	0	1	2	3	4
y	0	1	≈1.41	≈1.73	2

b Possible table:

x	-2	-1	0	1	2	3
y	$\frac{1}{4}$	$\frac{1}{2}$	1	2	4	8

13 $2x^6$ **14 a** $\frac{1}{36}$ **b** $\frac{9}{10}$ **c** $\frac{6}{5}$ **d** 6 **15** $\frac{x^{-15}}{w^{-20}y^{-10}}$ **17** $8x^6y^{14}$
18 2197; 793; no **19** $x^3 + 8y^3$ **20** 1: $x^9y^6z^{14}$ **21 a** 2
b 4 **c** 4 **d** 625 **22 a** 1 **b** -1 **c** 0
23 $s = 1 - 2x + 3x^2$ **24** $w = 125$; $x = 1$; $y = 3$; $z = 3$
25 $-\frac{1}{8}$ **26 a** i **b** iv **c** iii **d** ii **27** $\frac{y^{20}}{x^{30}}$ **29** $\frac{x^{15}}{y^{20}}$
30 $\frac{1}{\sqrt{5} + \sqrt{3}}$ **31** $-\frac{5yz}{6x^3}$ **33** x^8y^8 **34 a** $(x + 4)^2$
b $x^2 + 4^2$ **c** 0 **35** $\frac{1}{x + 1}$ **37** $\frac{3}{xy^{11}}$ **39** $(x, y) = (6, 9)$
41 True **43** False **44 a** $x = 49$ **b** No real solution
45 $2\sqrt{5}$ **47** $\frac{\sqrt{10}}{2}$ **49 a** $\sqrt{5}$ **b** $\sqrt{a + b}$ **51** $\frac{1}{2}$
53 $\frac{1 + \sqrt{5}}{4}$; $\frac{-1}{1 - \sqrt{5}}$ **54 a** iii **b** iv **c** ii **d** i **55** $15\sqrt[3]{2}$
56 $(x, y) = \left(\frac{9}{4}, \frac{1}{4}\right)$ **57 a** $2\sqrt{2}$ **b** $2\sqrt{3}$ **58** $n = 1$

3.1 Graphing Linear Equations

Warm-up Exercises

1 Answers will vary. Possible answers: $(0, 4)$, $(4, 6)$,
$(6, 7)$ **2** $\{k : k < 0\}$ **3** $-\frac{1}{2}$ **4** -2 **5** $a = 3$, $b = 9$, $c = 18$
7

9

11 $\frac{1}{5}$ **12 a** -2 **b** $\frac{1}{2}$

Problem Set

13 L_4, L_2, L_3, L_1
14 $(-4, -7)$ **15** Undefined
16 a False **b** True **c** False **d** False **e** True **17** $\frac{4}{3}$
18 a $R_b = 0.6(220 - A)$; $R_a = 0.7(220 - A)$;
$R_c = 0.8(220 - A)$ **b** ≈ 138 **c** $42\frac{1}{2}$ **19** $\frac{3}{5}$

20 a $y = -\frac{2}{3}x + 4$ **b** $y - 2 = \frac{3}{5}(x + 1)$

21 b **22 a** \$11.10 **b** 0.30x + 0.50(x + 3) **c** 63 boxes

23 a

	Sue	Sara	Kai
Le Chic	64.00	96.50	80.00
Le Pen	73.50	107.50	84.75
Bon Ton	75.25	107.25	77.75

b \$1.75 **c** Sara **24** $y - 1 = -\frac{2}{5}(x - 3)$ **25** $y = 0$

26 $k = \frac{23}{4}$ **27** 95 mi **28 a** $16B + 10G = 232,672$

b

c If $B = 5015$, $G = 15243.2$, and only whole numbers of tickets can be sold; answers will vary. **29 a** B **b** A, D, E **c** C, F **30 a** The decrease in value (in dollars) per year **b** Can't tell. Table predicts $-\$2400$, which is impossible. \$300 might be a reasonable guess. **31 a** 4 **b** 7 **32** $\frac{1}{4}$ **33** $\frac{13}{3}$

34 $\begin{bmatrix} -1 & 3 & -16 \\ 1 & 3 & 3 \end{bmatrix}$ **35 a** 1 **b** 2

3.2 Systems of Linear Equations

Warm-up Exercises

1 It satisfies both equations, so it is a solution.
2 $(x, y) = (12, 4)$ **3 a** Graphing **b** Substitution or guess and check **c** Multiplication-addition **d** Substitution
4 (4, 2) **5** (0, 5) **7 a** (1.5, −1.3) **b** (1.5, −1.25)

Problem Set

8 $x = 8$; $y = 4$ **9 a** $(x, y) = (7, 1)$ **b** $(x, y) = (5, 2)$
c $(x, y) = (0.5, 4.75)$ **d** $(x, y) = (4, -5)$ **10** 85¢

11 $x \approx 2.14$; $y \approx 2.57$ **12** $\frac{3}{5}$ **13** None **14** 2.75; 3.75; −7.25; 49.75 **15 a** $W = 4.75h + 0.01s$ **b** \$2200
16 −52 **17** $(x, y) = (2, 3)$ **19** x^7 **21** $25x^{10}$
23 $3x^7 - 2x^3$ **25** $(x, y) = (5, 9)$ **26** Yes—**b** or **c**

27 \$20.08 **28**

29 $\frac{5}{9}$ **30** 30

31 $w = 7$; $x = 8$; $y = 7$; $z = 0$ **32** 28 **33** 1

---

34 a $C_M = 12,895 + 1.16\left(\frac{x}{32}\right)$; $C_T = 10,550 + 1.16\left(\frac{x}{26}\right)$
b $\approx 280,322$ mi **c** $\approx 220,552$ mi and $\approx 340,092$ mi

3.3 Graphing Inequalities

Warm-up Exercises

1

2

3 **4** Yes

5 a {2, 4, 6, 7, 8, 9, 12, 13, 14, 15, 17} **b** {2, 6, 14, 15}
c {2, 4, 6, 8, 13, 14, 15} **d** {2, 4, 6, 8, 13, 14, 15}
6 a {multiples of 6} **b** {multiples of 15} **c** {multiples of 12} **7**

8 $6x + 5y \geq 30$

Problem Set

9

10

11 a

b $\left\{(x, y): y \leq \frac{2}{3}x + 3\right\}$

12 Any equations of the form $y - 7.5 = m(x - 0.5)$ and $y - 7.5 = -\frac{1}{m}(x - 0.5)$ where $m \neq 0$ **13** Answers will vary; $\left(\frac{11}{8}, \frac{51}{8}\right)$ **14 a** 176 **b** 14 **c** −6
d {x: x > −4} **15** $\frac{1}{8}$ **16 a** 1960–1969 **b** 1940–1949
c American **d** National **17** 75 lawns, 30 fences

18 a 20 **b** 100 **19**

20

21 $\{(x, y): y \geq -2x + 11\} \cap \{(x, y): y \geq \frac{1}{2}x - \frac{3}{2}\}$

22 a $\frac{87}{17}$, or ≈ 5.12 **b** $-\frac{95}{2}$, or -47.5

23 a $12.95c + 7.95t \leq 85$; $c + t \geq 4$
b

c The numbers of CD's and tapes represented by lattice points in the intersection of the inequalities' graphs **d** 1 CD, 9 tapes

25

27 $m = 4$; $b = -18$

28 $k_1 = -11$; $k_2 = -31$ **29** $\frac{1}{3}$ **30**

31 $x = 20$; $y = 4$ **32** $a = -\frac{1}{2}$, $b = -4$

33

34

x	-20	-10	-6	0	1	8	10	12	20	50
$f(x)$	40	20	20	20	20	20	20	24	40	100

35 a 31 **b** $2(n) + 5$ **36** $\frac{2}{9}$
37 a $x + y > 10$, $10 + x > y$, $10 + y > x$
b

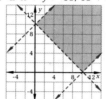

3.4 Functions and Direct Variation

Warm-up Exercises

1 $8.75 **2** Yes **3** Yes **4** $26 **5** Answers will vary. Possible answer: If the graph of the linear relationship passes through the origin, the data are directly proportional. **6** $x = \frac{30}{7}$ **7** $x = -\frac{16}{9}$ **8** 3

Problem Set

9 Yes **10** $17\frac{1}{2}$ **11** $(n, d) = (50, 7)$ **13** 51

15

	2^5	2^8	2^{11}
2^0	2^5	2^8	2^{11}
2^2	2^7	2^{10}	2^{13}

16 The slope of $\overleftrightarrow{PR}$ is -1, which is the opposite reciprocal of 1, the slope of $y = x$. **17** No; if x is negative, $-x$ is positive, and if $x = 0$, $-x = 0$.
19 $m = 3$, $b = 36$ **21** $-9, 4$

23 a $\frac{520}{18} \approx \frac{410.3}{14.2} \approx \frac{277.4}{9.6} \approx \frac{471}{16.3} \approx 28.9$ **b** ≈ 28.9 **c** Gas mileage in miles per gallon **24** 129; 53 **25** 13 quarters, 12 nickels **26** ≈ 2.569 **27** $(x, y) = (-12, 16)$
29

31

32 a

b 240 **33 a** 52 **b** 26 **c** He begins to repeat the numbers 1, 4, and 2. **34 a, c, e 35 a** 13.5
b 7.5 **36** 3 **37** 3.8; 4.4 **38** Colombian: ≈ 87.6 lb; Bolivian: ≈ 112.4 lb **39** 8 **40** Answers will vary. Possible answer: Animal II seems to be the predator, since its population is smaller and its numbers seem to increase only after the population of Animal I increases. **41 a** ≈ 1.05 **b** ≈ 90.53 **c** Yes

42 $h(x) = 4x - 3$ **43** $f(x) = x + 12$ **44** $\begin{cases} y \leq 3x \\ y \geq \frac{1}{4}x \end{cases}$

45 a $0.384 **b** $B = 7.5 + 0.384T$ **c** $330.96

3.5 Fitting a Line to Data

Warm-up Exercises

1 $y - 4 = -0.6(x - 9.9)$ **2 a** Answers will vary.
b ≈ -0.2 **c** $t = -0.2d + 16$ **3 a** 25 **b** ≈ 10.7 **c** 725
d 350 **4** $m \approx 1.7; b \approx -32.6$

Problem Set

5 a

b ≈ 12.7 cm **6 a** $e = 5.50h$ **b** Yes **c** Yes
7 $y = -1527.8x + 14,073.5$ **9 a** ≈ 5.49
b ≈ 120.7 **10** (5, 0) **11** $y = 3.23x + 17.8$
12

13 a Answers will vary. Possible answers:
Because when the refrigerator door is opened,
the temperature inside rises, and because the
refrigerator's thermostat keeps the temperature within
a certain range but not constant **b** ≈ 0
c $y = -0.05x + 37.8$ **d** The slope will decrease;
answers will vary. **14** 2; 5 **15** $\{x : x \geq 7\}$ **16 a, b**
17 a ≈ 43.56 km **b** ≈ 87.54 km **18 a** 12 **b** -1 **c** 1
19 \$6 (by buying 2 six-packs and discarding two

bottles) **20 a** 2 **b** $\frac{13}{3}$ **c** $\left(8, \frac{28}{3}\right)$ **d** $y = \frac{5}{6}x + \frac{8}{3}$

21

23

25

27 ± 4 **29** ≈ 1.1 **31 a** 10x

b $\frac{10x}{(x + 5)^2}$ **32 a** π **b** ≈ 150.8 in. **33** $h(x) = 4x - 3$

34 $\frac{1}{4}$ **35 a** $\begin{cases} y \leq \frac{3}{4}x + 6 \\ y > \frac{3}{4}x + 2 \end{cases}$ **b** $21\frac{1}{3}$

3.6 Compound Functions

Warm-up Exercises

1 14 **2** 3 **3** 2 **4** g(7.9) **5**

6

7 2 **8** 6 **9** 6

10 $w = -27$ or $w = 7$ **11** $w = -10$ or $w = 20$
12 $w = -10$ or $w = -20$ **13 a** $c(x) = \begin{cases} 2.75x \text{ if } x < 25 \\ 2.4x \text{ if } x \geq 25 \end{cases}$

b 27.5; 66; 60 **c** It's cheaper than buying 24.

Problem Set

15 Undefined **17** 20 **19** Undefined
20 a   **b**

21 a

b

c

22 a

b

c

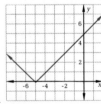

23 $x = -12$ or $x = 6$ **25** $x^2 - y^2$
26 a $c(x) = \begin{cases} 17.95x \text{ if } 1 \leq x \leq 10 \\ 15.95x \text{ if } 11 \leq x \leq 200 \\ 14.5x \text{ if } x > 200 \end{cases}$ **b** 125.65; 829.4;

5002.5 **c** 10 and 183–200 **27 a** Answers will vary.
$t = 0.05d + 0.50$ (where t is toll and d is distance
from eastern end) **b** $t = 0.0438d + 0.52$ **c** \$4.90

d ≈ 233.6 miles **28** $g(x) = 6x$ **29** $f(x) = -\frac{3}{2}x + 23$

30 $\frac{15}{2}$ **31 a** and **c; b** and **d a** 9 **b** 21 **c** 9 **d** 21
32 a $f(x) = x:(12 - x)$ **b** 4:8, or 1:2 **33 a** 3 **b** 0
c No real value **35** $p = \frac{4}{3}$ or $p = \frac{20}{3}$

37

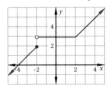

38 a $A(x) = 30(x + 1)$ **b** Yes **39** $\frac{5}{8}$

40 a

b

c

d

41 a 2 **b** 7 **42** $\begin{cases} y \le -\frac{4}{7}x + \frac{64}{7} \\ y \ge 4 \\ x \ge 2 \end{cases}$ **43 a, c 44 a, b, c, d**

45 $\{x : x \in \mathcal{R}\}$ **47** $\{x : x \in \mathcal{R}\}$ **49** $\{x : x \ge 0\}$
51 $\{(x, y) : 0 \le y \le x \text{ or } x \le y \le 0\}$ **53** $\{x : x \in \mathcal{R}\}$
55 $g(x) = \begin{cases} 2x - 8 \text{ if } x \ge 4 \\ 8 - 2x \text{ if } x < 4 \end{cases}$
57 $R(x) = \begin{cases} -x - 3 \text{ if } x \ge -3 \\ x + 3 \text{ if } x < -3 \end{cases}$ **59** $g(x) = |x - 2|$
61 $R(x) = -|x - 3|$ **62** By definition, $|a| = a$ if $a \ge 0$,
and $|a| = -a$ if $a < 0$. Therefore, $-|a| = a$ if $a \le 0$,
$-|a| < a$ if $a > 0$, $|a| = a$ if $a \ge 0$, and $|a| > a$ if
$a < 0$. Thus, $-|a| \le a \le |a|$.

Review Problems

1

x	-3	-2	-1	0	1	2	3	4
y	17	14	11	8	5	2	-1	-4

2 a Answers will vary. **b** Answers will vary.
c Answers will vary. **3** $x = 9.5$ or $x = -0.5$
5 $x = 11.3$ or $x = -22.7$ **7 a** $y = -0.773x + 63.2$

b

c Answers will vary. You may

remark that the data do not seem to be linearly
related. **8 a** $k = 2$ **b**

9 $(0, -3)$

10 Bolivian: 2500 lb;
Columbian: 1500 lb

11 a

b

c

12 a

b Yes **c** $\approx\$0.035$

d c = 0.035m **e** $\approx\$4.27$ **13 a** $200 + 6t$; $100 + 9t$
b 344 ft; 316 ft **c** In ≈ 33.3 sec **14 a** 3
b $3x + 4y = 12a$ **c** $\frac{4}{3}$ **15**

17   **19** 96 **20** x-intercept $= \frac{C}{A}$;

y-intercept $= \frac{C}{B}$ **21 a** $y = 43{,}652x + 38{,}345$

b $\approx 43{,}829$ **c** ≈ 23 mo **d** May **22** -1 **23** $(3, -8)$
24 No; one of the properties of absolute value is that
$|a + b| \le |a| + |b|$, so in some cases
$|x + y| \ne |x| + |y|$. **25** 38 **26**

27 a $y = 3554.3x - 7{,}025{,}000$ **b** $\approx \$48{,}057$

4.1 What Are Quadratics?

Warm-up Exercises
1 a ii **b** i **c** i **d** iii **e** ii **2 a** $4x^2 - 9$
b $6x^2 + 5x - 6$ **c** $9x^2 - 4$ **3 a** $9y^2 + 24y + 16$
b $16x_1^2 - 24x_1 + 9$ **4** $18x^2 + 49x + 10$; $\left\{x : x > -\frac{2}{9}\right\}$
5 $16x^2 + 56x + 49$ **6 a** $9x^2 + 6x + 1$ **b** 961 Because
we use a base-10 number system, the digits in part **b**
are the same as the coefficients and constant in part **a**.

Problem Set
7 a, b, e **8** $2x^2 + 11x + 15$ **9 a** 9 **b** 29 **c** 9 **d a** and
c **10 a** False **b** True **c** False **d** False **11** $y = -19$
13 Fred $= \frac{20}{9}$ **15 a** $25x^2 - 9$ **b** $36x^2 + 60x + 25$
c $16y^6 - 36x^2$ **d** $81a^2 - 18ab + b^2$ **e** $x^4 - 1$ **16 a** $\frac{1}{x^3}$
b $\frac{y^7 z}{x^7}$ **17** $x^2 + y^2 = 16$ **18** ≈ 29.09 **19 a** \$10.20
b \$4.88 **c** \$16.50 **d** 27.9 lb, 1–100 mi; 18.5 lb,
101–400 mi; 14.1 lb, 401–900 mi; 10.9 lb, 901–1500 mi;
8 lb, > 1500 mi **20 a** $(x, y) = \left(\frac{2}{11}, -\frac{16}{11}\right)$ **b** $(x, y) = \left(\frac{3}{7}, \frac{23}{7}\right)$

21 a $x = 3$ or $x = -4$ **b** $x = 0$ or $x = \frac{1}{3}$ **c** $x = 3$,
$x = -3$, or $x = -5$ **d** $x = 3$ **22** 1; 7; 10 **23** ≈ 1.414,
1.0, error, error; the calculator works only with real
numbers. **24** $d = 60t$; yes **25 a**

b

26 111 g **27** $(x + 2)^2 + (y - 5)^2 = 36$ **28** $x^2 + x$
29 3.5; 6.5 **30 a** $w_1 = 9$ or $w_1 = -1$ **b** $w_1 = 2$
31 a $\{(a, b) : ab < 0\}$ **b** $\{(a, b) : ab \ge 0\}$
32 a   **b**

c   **33**

34 a $10x^2 + 2x = 16x^2$ **b** $16x = 14x + 2$ **35 a** 100
b 4999 **36 a** $c = 19.2x + 690$ **b** \$16,050 **c** Answers
will vary. More machinery and workers might be
needed, so that the relationship would no longer be
linear. **37** 12 (for $y = 2$) or 204 (for $y = -14$)
38 ≈ 3.68 **39 a** $\sqrt{10x^2 + 18x + 9}$ **b** -0.9 **c** $\frac{3\sqrt{10}}{10}$
40

41 a $c(x) = \begin{cases} 95x & \text{if } x \le 10 \\ [95 - 0.50(x - 10)] & \text{if } x > 10 \end{cases}$

b

c 100 **d** 125 pieces of software

4.2 Factoring Quadratics

Warm-up Exercises
1 a i **b** i and iii **c** ii **d** iii **e** i and ii **f** iv
2 $(x + 3)(x + 4)$ **3** $(x + 7)^2$ **4** $(4x + 1)(2x - 3)$
5 $3x + 2$ **6** $5(x - 3)^2$ **7** $2(x + 3)(x - 1)$
8 $(x^2 + y^2)(x + y)(x - y)$ **9** $\pi(a + b)(a - b)$

Problem Set
11 $7(3y^2 + 4)$ **13 a**

	$3x$	4
$2x$	$6x^2$	$8x$
5	$15x$	20

b $(2x + 5)(3x + 4)$; $6x^2 + 23x + 20$ **14 a** False
b False **15** $0.78; $12.71 **16 a** $0.\overline{1}$, $0.\overline{2}$, $0.\overline{3}$, $0.\overline{4}$ **b** $0.\overline{7}$,
$0.\overline{8}$, and 1 **17** 144 **19** $16x^6$ **20** -9; 0; $4x^2$ **21** $6x^2$
23 $3x - 6$ **24 a** $ac + ad + bc + bd$ **b** $xy + 2y -$
$3x - 6$ **25 a** $P = 6x + 4y - 8$ **b** $P = 30$

26 a

x	-4	-3	-2	-1	0	1	2	3	4
y	89	48	19	2	-3	4	23	54	97

26 b

27 $w = \pm 3$; $x = 10$ or $x = -4$; $y = 2$ or $y = -12$;
$z = \frac{1}{6}$ **29** $49(4x^2 + w^2)$

31 a

b

c

d

32 a $a^3 - 3a^2b + 3ab^2 - b^3$ **b** $a^3 + a^2b - ab^2 - b^3$
c $a^3 - 3a^2b + 3ab^2 - b^3$ **d a** and **c**; **c** is a partially
expanded form of **a**.
33 a $-5, -1, 5$ **b** $x = -5$, $x = -1$, or $x = 0$
34 a $[f(x) + g(x)][f(x) - g(x)]$ **b** $(x + 7)(x - 1)$
c $(x + 7)(x - 1)$ **35 a** Evens are divisible by 2.
b $2a + 2b = 2(a + b)$ **36** $\frac{8}{9}$ **37 a** $x = 3$ or $x = -3$
b $y = 3$ or $y = -3$ **c** $x - 3 = 3$ or $x - 3 = -3$
d $x = 3$ or $x = -3$ **38** $f(67)$; since $(67, 0)$ is closer to
the axis of symmetry, $f(67)$ is closer to the vertex.
39 3.5 ft by 7 ft **40 a**

b

c

d

e

41 a $x^2(x + 1)(x - 1)$ **b** $(x^2 + y)(x^2 - y)$
c $y^4(x^2 + 1)(x + 1)(x - 1)$ **42** $f(x) = 2x + 1$
43 1040 mi **44 a** 2 **b** $\frac{13}{3}$ **c** $\left(8, \frac{28}{3}\right)$ **d** $y = \frac{5}{6}x + \frac{8}{3}$
45 $(x^2 + 3 - y)(x^2 + 3 + y)$ **46 a** $A(x) = 100 - x^2$
b $\{x : 0 < x < 10\}$ **c** $5\sqrt{2}$ **47** $x = 1$, $x = -\frac{1}{2}$, or $x = \frac{3}{4}$
48 $(x, y) = (1, 2)$ **49 a** $\frac{1}{2}$; 2.5; -2.5; undefined

b

50 $\frac{1}{2}$ **51**

4.3 Graphing Quadratic Functions

Warm-up Exercises

1 -6 or 6 **2** $y = 2(x - 4)^2 + 1$ **3** $y = -(x + 5)^2 + 9$

Problem Set

4 a

b

c

d

5 $a = 6$ and $b = 3$ or $a = -6$ and $b = -3$ **6 a iv**
b iii c ii d i 7 -7 **9** $x = -1$, $x = 2$, or $x = -2$
11

13 $x = 2$ **15** $10.5w - 12.5y$ **17** $x = -23.2$
19 a -1 and 5 **b** $\{x : -1 < x < 5\}$ **c** 2
20 $n \le 435$ **21 a** $\frac{3}{2}$ **b** -5 **c** Yes **22** $(x + 2)(x + 4)$;
$x^2 + 6x + 8$ **23**

24 −3, 2 **25** True **27** False
29 a x = 4 or x = −7 **b** x = 4 or x = −7
30 $\frac{3}{11}$ **31 a** $4(t − 3)^2$ **b** 36 ft **c** After 3 sec **d** After 6
sec **32 a** 2x − y **b** 2(x − y) **33 a**

b If the product of two numbers is zero, at least one of
the numbers must be zero, so the graph of xy = 0 is
the x- and y-axes. **34 a** $b = −\frac{8}{3}$ or b = 6 **b** {b:b ∈ ℛ}

c b = 0 **35** $\frac{1}{3}$ **36 a** $x^3 + a^3$ **b** $(x + 3)(x^2 − 3x + 9)$
37 (2x + 3)(x + 5) **39 a** $A = 6e^2$ **b** 3 **40** a − b = 0,
so division by a − b is undefined.

4.4 Solving Quadratic Equations

Warm-up Exercises

1 a $\frac{1}{3}$ **b** −2 **2 a** x = 0 or x = 3 **b** y = −2 or y = 2
c z = 0 or z = −4 **3 a** x = 4 or x = 5 **b** y = −8 or
y = 2 **c** $z = \frac{1}{2}$ or z = −3

Problem Set

5 x = 2 or $x = −\frac{3}{4}$ **7** −8 and 4 **8** −1 and 6
9

10 (3, 0) and (6, 0)

11 a $y = \frac{3}{2}$, y = −1, or y = 0 **b** y = 2, y = 1, or $y = \frac{2}{3}$

c $y = −\frac{1}{2}$, $y = \frac{1}{2}$, or y = 0 **13** $x = −\frac{1}{2}$ or x = 3

15 −1 or 4 **16** 0 or 7 **17** {x:3 < x < 18} **18 a** $\frac{1}{14}$

b $\frac{5}{28}$ **19 a** z = 7 or z = −2 **b** x = 0 or x = −9

21 $(x − 3y)^2$ **22** 15 **23** x = 0 or $x = −\frac{3}{2}$

24 4 hr 20 min **25** $2x^2 − 9x − 45 = 0$

26 $x \geq \frac{5}{2}$

27 Cashews: \$4.33; macadamias: \$9.46 **28** f(x) = −7
or f(x) = 2

29 a

b 200 ft **c** 264 ft

d After ≈ 6.06 sec **e** {t:0 ≤ t ≤ ≈6.06} **30 a** 20 **b** 192

31

x	−1	0	1	2	3	4	5
y	2	$\sqrt{3}$	$\sqrt{2}$	1	0	Undef.	Undef.

32 27 cm by 36 cm **33** No **34 a** Answers will vary.

b y = 946x − 1,879,685 **35** x = 8 or $x = \frac{5}{2}$

37 a x = −5, x = 0, or x = 5 **b** x = −8 or x = 8

38

39 9x(x − 3y) **41** (w + z)(x + y) **43** In ≈22.2 min
44 a x = −b or x = −a **b** x = −2c or x = −3d
c x = −3 or x = −a **45 a** y = 2x

b

46 a $d^2 = 3250t^2 − 700t + 100$ **b** ≈62.3 **c** After
≈0.108 hr, or ≈6.5 min **d** ≈7.89 miles **47 a** It
approaches zero. **b** It increases without limit. **48** 72
49 2x + h **50** 144.5

4.5 Completing the Square

Warm-up Exercises

1 a 16 **b** 9 **c** $\frac{81}{4}$ **d** 4 **e** $\frac{81}{16}$ **2 a** 6x **b** 16y **c** $8y^2x$

d 11x **3** 16 **4 a** (3, 4) **b** $\left(−\frac{1}{2}, 5\right)$ **c** (−3, 6)

d (5, −20) **5 a** x = 1 or x = −11 **b** x = 15 or
x = −1 **c** $x = −3 \pm \sqrt{14}$ **d** x = 25 **6 a** 14 **b** −6

Problem Set

7 $(x − 4)^2 + 29$ **9** $2(x + 25)^2 − 1200$
11 $(x + 25)^2 − 647$
13

15

16 a y = 2 **b** y = 12 or y = −3
17 x = 19; m∠1 = 91 **18** $x^2 + 3x − 10 = 0$

19 a $A(x) = 3x^2 + 6x$ **b** $B(x) = 2x + 4$ **c** $\frac{2}{3}$ **21** ± 10
22 $(x, y, z) = (6, 1, 161)$ **23 a** 12 **b** 7 **c** $a - 5$ **d** a
24 $x = 5$, $y = 5$ **25** $x = 5$ or $x = -2$
26 $y = x^2 - 2x - 3$ **27** ± 8 **28** Any equation of the
form $y = a(x - 4)^2 - 1$ **29 a** $z = 7$ or $z = -1$
b $x = \frac{7}{12}$ or $x = -\frac{1}{12}$ **30 a** $d(x) = 2x^2 - 4x + 4$ **b** 1
c 2 **31** $x = \frac{3 \pm \sqrt{5}}{2}$ **33 a** 140; 50 **b** 356.25 in.
c 50 in. **34 a** $x^2 - 2x - 35 = 0$ **b** $2x^2 - 9x + 4 = 0$
35 $(x, y) = (3, -1.5)$ **36 a** $y = 0$, $y = 3$, or $y = -3$
b $y = 1$ or $y = -3$ **c** $y = 4$ or $y = -4$ **37** Between
130 and 140 sheets **38** 4 **39** $x = 6$ or $x = -1$
41 $x \neq -1 \pm \sqrt{6}$ **42** $\frac{7}{2}; \frac{11}{4}$ **43 a** $\left(-\frac{17}{8}, -\frac{481}{16}\right)$
b $\left(-\frac{b}{2a}, -\frac{b^2 - 4ac}{4a}\right)$ **44** ± 10 **45** $f(x) = 2^x$ **46** 244

4.6 Applications of Quadratic Functions

Warm-up Exercises
1 $v_0 = 45$ ft/sec; $h_0 = 0$ ft **2** $v_0 = 32$ m/sec; $h_0 = 2$ m
3 $v_0 = 25$ m/sec; $h_0 = 0.5$ m
4 $v_0 = 31$ ft/sec; $h_0 = 0$ ft
5 a 164 ft **b** ≈ 23.6 m **6** $3.00 per cassette

Problem Set
7 $21,000 **8 a** $A(x) = x^2 + 6x - 16$ **b** $\{x : x > 2\}$
c 144 **d** $\{x : x > 7\}$ **9 a** In 2 sec **b** 16 ft **c** In ≈ 14.7
sec **10** $\{10, 11, 12, 20, 21, 30\}$ **11** $833.\overline{3}$ ft^2 **12 a** 2
and 5 **b** $\frac{7}{2}$ **13** $1.10 **14 a** $h(t) = -\frac{1}{2}(9.8)t^2 + 2.94t + 3$
b ≈ 3.44 m **c** ≈ 1.14 sec **15** $x \approx -46.23$
16 a $x = \pm 9$ **b** $x = \pm 9$ **17 a** $x = 6 + \sqrt{57}$ **b** $\sqrt{57}$ is
between 7 and 8. **c** Between 13 and 14 **19** $b = -\frac{5}{2}$ or
$b = 3$ **21** $x = 15$ or $x = -6$ **22 a** In ≈ 0.56 sec
b In ≈ 1.13 sec **c** In ≈ 1.39 sec **23** $\left\{n : n > 66\frac{2}{3}\right\}$
24 $-2, 8; -1, 4$
25 $x = \frac{-1 + \sqrt{5}}{2}$ **26 a** ≈ 5.03 sec and ≈ 19.12 sec after
launch **b** ≈ 743.16 m **c** ≈ 24.40 sec
27 a $A = (10 + x)\sqrt{36 - x^2}$ **b** ≈ 68.19

4.7 Data Displays

Problem Set
1 a

5	3	4										
4	0	1	1									
3	0	0	1	2	2	3	3	4	5	5	6	7	7	9
2	0	1	1	2	3	7	9	9	9			
1	8	9										

2 | 1 means 21 points scored during a game

b

2 a

b 17.4 **c** 1986 **d** 5.4 **3 a** True **b** False **c** True
d False **4 a** 37 **b** 8 **c** Cannot be determined **d** 8
5 1 **6 a** 88 and 16 **b** 72 **c** 62 and 81 **d** Those below
81 **e** Cannot be determined **7** $(x, y) = (2, 5)$
8 Answers will vary. **9 a** $\approx 62.5\%$ **b** $\approx 18.2\%$
c $\approx 5,400,00$ bu **10**

11 a $x^2 + 6x$ **b** 9 **c** $(x + 3)^2$; $x^2 + 6x + 9$
12 a 98 and 23 **b** 9 **c** 76 **d** 7 **e** 29
f Cannot be determined **13 a** $\frac{13}{90}$ **b** $\frac{1}{6}$
14 a In ≈ 0.66 min **b** ≈ 2752.5 ft^2

Review Problems
1 $6x^3 - 12x^2$ **3** $36y^2 - z^2$ **5** $9x^2 - 30x + 25$
7 $x = \pm 10$ **9** $z = 3$ or $z = -2$ **10** $y = \frac{1}{2}(x - 2)^2 - 5$
11 $\frac{5}{8}$ **13** $x = \pm 4$ **15 a** $A = 2x^2 - 6x$ **b** $\{x : x > 3\}$
c 216 **16** $16x^3 + 4x^2 + 7x + 5$ **17** $(3y - 1)(2y - 1)$
19 $(3x + 2)(2x + 3)$ **21** $(z - 9)(z - 8)$ **23 a** 47 **b** 56
c 77 **25** $x = 4 \pm \sqrt{21}$ **27** $x = \frac{-9 \pm \sqrt{87}}{3}$ **28 a** 40; 60;
84 **b** 42 **29 a** 36 ft **b** At $t = 3$ **c** At $t = -2$ and
$t = 8$ **d**

30 $\{x : x > 5\}$

31 $x^3 + 3x + \frac{3}{x} + \frac{1}{x^3}$ **32 a** 894,000 **b** $\approx 33.2\%$; $\approx 21\%$;
$\approx 8.9\%$ **33** $x = 5$ **35** $x = 3$ or $x = -1$
36 No such points.

37 a $V = 6x^2 + 11x + 6$ **b** $\{x : x > 0\}$
38 a $A(x) = -2x^2 + 12x + 144$ **b** 3 **c** 162
39 $(x + 1 + y)(x + 1 - y)$ **41** 96 trees per acre
42 $4x^3 + 3x^2 + 2x + 1$

5.1 Relations and Functions

Warm-up Exercises

1 a $\{(-2, 5), (-1, 2), (0, 5), (1,2), (2, 0)\}$

b

Input	−2	−1	0	1	2
Output	5	2	5	2	0

c **d**

2 b, c, d 3 Yes; no **4 a** 15 **b** $f(n) = \sum_{k=1}^{n} k$

5 a $\{-4, -2, 0, 2, 5\}$ **b** $\{-4, -2, 0, 5\}$ **c** $\{(-4, -2),$
$(-2, 0), (0, 5), (2, -4), (5, -4)\}$ **6 a** 16 **b** 4 **c** 3 **d** 9

Problem Set

7 Both **9 a** $\{(-2, 4), (0, 2), (2, 0), (4, 2), (6, 4)\}$

b

x	−2	0	2	4	6
f(x)	4	2	0	2	4

c **d**

e

10 a 0 **b** −1 **c** $x = 3$ **d** $x = -2$
or $x = 2$ **e** $\{-2, 0, 1, 2, 3\}$ **f** $\{-3, -1, 0, 1\}$ **11** No;
since each input can have only one output, no. of
outputs ≤ no. of inputs. **12 a** 60 **b** Impossible figure
c $\{x : x > 2\}$
13 $x < 2$ ⟵───○───⟶ **14** Answers
          2
will vary. For many scientific calculators, x must
be ≤ 69. **15 a** 9 **b** 2 **c** 31 **16 a** $C(q) = 80q$ **b** 280
17 a True **b** False **18** $\{F : F < 68\}$
19 **20 a** $A(x) = 5x + 36$

b $\{x : x > -3\}$ **21 a** $p(x)$ = year in which x was first
elected President of the U.S. **b** 1960; 1884 **23** No; yes

25 (6, 1) **27** $x = \frac{3 \pm \sqrt{105}}{4}$ **29** $x = 0$ or $x = 3$

30 a $M(x) = \frac{1}{5}(x + 120)$ **b**

c −120 **d** 30 **31 a** $d(x) = x^2 + 5$ **b** −5 and 5
32 a 1 **b** ≈3.73 **c** ≈63.43

5.2 More About Functions

Warm-up Exercises

1 a Domain: $\{x : x \geq 0\}$; range: $\{f(x) : f(x) \geq 3\}$
b Domain: $\{x : x \neq -5\}$; range is $\{g(x) : g(x) \neq 1\}$
c Domain: {integers greater than 2}; range: {positive
multiples of 180} **d** Domain: $\{y : y \neq -2$ and $y \neq -3\}$;
range: $\{h(y) : h(y) \geq 0$ or $h(y) \leq -48\}$ **2 a** 13
b $8x + 29$ **3 a** 50
b 196 **c** No **4 a** 7 **b** 7 **c** 9 **d** 9 **e** x
5 $g[f(x)] = f[g(x)] = x$ for all x **6 a** 7; 7 **b** 49; 49
c 15; 47 **d** Multiplication is commutative, but
composition of functions is not.

Problem Set

7 a None **b** $x \geq 4$ **c** x; $\{x : x \geq 4\}$ **d** $|x|$; $\{x : x \in \mathcal{R}\}$
e 5; 5 **f** Undefined; 4 **8 a** 11 **b** $\{3, 7\}$ **c** $\{11, 13\}$
9 $8 - 15y$; $-8 - 15y$ **10** $\{x : x < -5\}$ **11 a** 4; 4 **b** 9;
undefined **c** No (unless the domain of s is restricted)
12 1 or −6 **13** No; $f[g(x)] = 4x - 5$, and
$g[f(x)] = 4x + 5$, so $f[g(x)] \neq g[f(x)] \neq x$. **14** −1 and 6
15 a Yes **b** No **16** $\frac{3}{2}$ **17 a** 11 **b** 0 **c** −9 **d** −6 **e** 3
f −2 **g** 25 **h** 1 **18** −2 and 2 **19 a** $m(x) = 2x + 40$
b $-2 < x < 10$ **c** It increases from 44 to 50. **d** It
decreases from 24 to 15. **20** Same domain, same rule,
same range **21 a** 8 **b** 8 **c** No (unless the domain of f
is restricted) **22 a** 4; 4 **b** Yes **23 a** 5 **b** 5 **c** 5
24 a $\begin{bmatrix} 11 & 18 \\ 25 & 26 \end{bmatrix}$ **b** $\begin{bmatrix} 1 & 12 \\ 17 & -38 \end{bmatrix}$ **c** {(A, B): dimensions of
A = dimensions of B} **d** {(A, B): no. of columns in
A = no. of rows in B} **25 a** $h(x) = 0.0973x$ **b** The
sales tax charged on a purchase of x hamburgers.
26 a $\frac{x^2 - 9}{x}$; $\{x : x \neq 0, x \neq -3,$ and $x \neq 3\}$ **b** $\frac{x}{1 - 9x^2}$;
$\left\{x : x \neq 0, x \neq \frac{1}{3},$ and $x \neq -\frac{1}{3}\right\}$ **27 a** 2 **b** 3 **c** −5
d Undefined **e** INV$f(x) = f(x)$ for $\{x : x \neq 1\}$ **28 a** 16
b 20 **c** 24 **29** Domain: $\{x : 5 < x < 14\}$; range:
$\{P(x) : 27 < P(x) < 54\}$ **30** $\frac{4}{21}$ **31 a** $D(n) = \frac{n(n - 3)}{2}$
b {Integers ≥ 3} **c** $\{0, 2, 5, 9, 14, \ldots\}$
32 $T(p) = \left[\frac{p}{20}\right] + 1$ **33 a** 124,050 ft **b** 90.5 sec
c ≈178.55 sec

5.3 Inverse Functions

1 a (1, 0), (4, 2), (16, 4), (25, 5) **b**

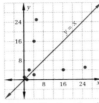

c They are reflections of each other over the graph of $y = x$. **2** INV$f(x) = \frac{x}{10}$ **3** INV$g(x) = x + 6$

4 INV$h(x) = \frac{x - 3}{6}$ **5** INV$p(x) = \sqrt{x + 1}$, where $x \geq -1$ **6** INV$g(x) = x^2 + 1$, where $x \geq 0$

7 INV$r(x) = \frac{1}{2x}$ **8 a** Domain is $\{-4, -1, 0, 6, 8\}$; range is $\{-2, -1, 1, 3, 4\}$. **b** $(-2, -4), (-1, -1), (3, 0), (1, 6), (4, 8)$ **c** Domain is $\{-2, -1, 1, 3, 4\}$; range is $\{-4, -1, 0, 6, 8\}$ **9 a**

b No **c** Yes, if the domain of g is suitably restricted—for instance to $\{x : x \geq 0\}$, in which case INV$g(x) = \sqrt{-x + 5}$.

Problem Set

10 a 6 **b** 64 **c** $\frac{n - 5}{2}$ **11** $\{(-2, 6), (0, 7), (1, 5), (4, 4), (7, 3)\}$ **12 a**

b 6; -10

c $f[g(x)] = -2\left(-\frac{1}{2}x + 4\right) + 8 = (x - 8) + 8 = x$ **d** Yes

13

x	0	1	2	3	4	5	8
f(x)	5	3	0	2	1	4	8
g(x)	2	4	3	1	5	0	8

14 $f(x) = 24 - 2x$ **15** $\frac{1}{10}$ **16** 42

17 a $\{f(x) : 1 < f(x) < 100\}$ **b** $g(x) = \sqrt{x}$ **c** Domain: $\{x : 1 < x < 100\}$; range: $\{g(x) : 1 < g(x) < 10\}$ **d** Yes; domain of INVf = range of f, and range of INVf = domain of f. **18 a** Output the number of sides of a polygon when the sum of its angles is input **b** $n = \frac{S}{180} + 2$ **c** $\{$positive multiples of $180\}$ **19** 6

20 INV$f(x) = -\sqrt{x}$ **21 a** Yes

b Yes

c Yes

d No

22 a

b No **c** Yes, if the domain of h is suitably restricted—for instance, to $\{x : x \geq 3\}$, in which case INV$h(x) = \sqrt{x - 4} + 3$

23 a INV$f(x) = \frac{x - 4}{3}$ **b** INV$f(x) = \frac{9}{x}$, where $x \neq 0$

c INV$f(x) = \frac{3}{2} - 2x$ **d** Answers will vary. Possible answer: If $x \geq -3$, INV$f(x) = \sqrt{x} - 3$. **24** ≈ 15.65 cm and ≈ 6.65 cm **25** INV$g(x) = -\frac{3}{2}x - 5$ **26 a** No

b Area of square with side length $2x$ **c** Total area of two squares with side length x **27 a** Yes **b** Yes **c** Answers will vary. **28 a** Yes

b No

c No

d Yes

29 $x = 0$ **31** $y = x$ **32** 10

33 They are inverses. **34 a** INV$T(x) = \frac{x}{0.07}$ **b** Purchase price on which a sales tax of x dollars is charged **35** $y = 1.18x + 4.69$ **36** $\frac{1}{5}$

37 INV$f(x) = \sqrt{\frac{x - k}{a}} + h$ **38 a** $\begin{bmatrix} 10 & 10 \\ 4 & 2 \end{bmatrix}$

b INV$f\left(\begin{bmatrix} a & b \\ c & d \end{bmatrix}\right) = \frac{1}{2}\begin{bmatrix} a - 4 & b \\ c & d - 4 \end{bmatrix}$

c $f \circ INVf\left(\begin{bmatrix} a & b \\ c & d \end{bmatrix}\right) = 2\left(\frac{1}{2}\begin{bmatrix} a-4 & b \\ c & d-4 \end{bmatrix}\right) + 4\begin{bmatrix} 1 & 0 \\ 0 & 1 \end{bmatrix}$

$= \begin{bmatrix} a-4 & b \\ c & d-4 \end{bmatrix} + \begin{bmatrix} 4 & 0 \\ 0 & 4 \end{bmatrix} = \begin{bmatrix} a & b \\ c & d \end{bmatrix}$

5.4 Operations on Functions

Warm-up Exercises

1 $f(x) = x - 2$ **2** $g(x) = \frac{2}{5}x$ **3 a** $-4 + \sqrt{3}$ **b** $-4\sqrt{3}$

c $-\frac{4}{\sqrt{3}}$ **d** $\sqrt{3} - 7$ **e** 5 **4 a** $A_r(x) = 2x^2 - 2x$

b $A_t(x) = \frac{x^2\sqrt{3}}{2}$ **c** It represents the total area of the
figure. **d** ≈ 1106.41 **5 a** $9x - 6$ **b** $9x^2 - 24x + 9$
c $27x^2 - 78x + 48$ **d** $9x - 16$ **e** $36x^2 - 126x + 104$
6 7 **7** **8** $h(3x)$ if $x \neq 0$

Problem Set

9 a $\sqrt{3x - 5}$ **b** $\sqrt[4]{x}$ **c** $\sqrt{x^2 - 5}$ **d** $\sqrt{2x - 6}$
e $\sqrt{\sqrt{x - 5} - 5}$ **10** $f(x) = -2x$
11 a   **b**   **c**

12 a

x	−4	−3	−2	−1	0	1	2	3	4
f(x)	9	4	1	0	1	4	9	16	25
f(x − 1)	16	9	4	1	0	1	4	9	16
f(x + 1)	4	1	0	1	4	9	16	25	36

b   **13** $g(x) = x^3$

14   **15** $\{x : x < -4 \text{ or } 4 < x < 8\}$

16 24 **17 a**   **b**

c   **d**

18   **19 c** **20**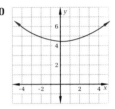

21 a $Q(x) = \frac{x^2 - x + 3}{3}$ **b** $R(x) = \frac{x^2 - 14x + 45}{x^2 - 4}$
c $x^2 - 14x + 45$ **d** $x^2 - 11$ **22 a** $g(x) = 2$
b   **c** $x^2 + 2$ **23 a**

b   **24 a** 15 **b** 27 **c** 42

25 $g(x) = x^2 - 4x$ **26** -122 **27 a** 0.7781 **b** 1.0791
c 0.9542 **d** 1.2552 **28** $g(2x)$ if $x > 0$, $2 \cdot g(x)$ if $x < 0$,
neither if $x = 0$ **30** No

31 a $h(x) = \frac{x}{2}$ **b**

32 a $f[g(x)] = \begin{cases} \sqrt{10} & \text{if } x < 4 \\ 0 & \text{if } x = 4 \\ 9 & \text{if } x > 4 \end{cases}$ **b**

c Domain: $\{x : x \in \mathscr{R}\}$; range: $\{0, \sqrt{10}, 9\}$

5.5 Discrete Functions

Warm-up Exercises

1 120 **2** 3,628,800 **3** $\approx 1.3 \times 10^{12}$ **4** $\approx 1.2 \times 10^{56}$
5 479,001,600 **6 a** 198,485 **b** 1,190,910 **7 a** 42 **b** 21
c 3,603,600 **d** 5005 **e** $P(a, b) \geq C(a, b)$ **8** 36^6, or
$\approx 2.18 \times 10^9$ **9** $26^2 \cdot 10^4$, or 6.76×10^6

Problem Set

10 a 9 **b** 97 **c** $n + 1$ **11 a** No **b** 330 days **12 a** 35
b 35 **13** 5 **15** 12 **17** $C(n, n - 1) = n$ **18** 4 **19** 8
20 $\frac{1}{6}$ **21** $\frac{1}{36}$ **22** 0 **23 a** 15; 15 **b** 6; 6 **c** 28; 28 **d** 56;
56 **e** $C(n, r) = C(n, n - r)$ **24 a** $\{-2, 1, 10\}$
b $\{y : -2 \leq y \leq 10\}$ **25** 35 **26 a** INV$f(x) = \frac{3}{2}(x + 6)$
b

c $(-18, -18)$ **27**

$1; \frac{1}{0}$, which is undefined

28 11 **29** Yes **30** $C(25, 2) = 300$; we need
to determine the number of sets of two people that can
be formed from a set of 25, and order does not matter.
31 8 **32** 6 **33** $k = 7$ **34** $f(x) = 8$ or $f(x) = 4$ **35 a** 50
b 1175 **c** $\frac{46}{587}$ **36 a** $0.75 **b** $0.25 **c** $\{w : 3 < w \leq 5\}$
d 25, 50, 75 **37 a** 2; 6; 24; 120 **b** $(x - 1)!$
38 a Answers will vary. **b** $y = 6.35x - 11,660$
39 a 10 **b** 40 **40 a** 1 **b** 0 **c** $\frac{1}{\sqrt{3}}$ or ≈ 0.5774 **d** 1
e 1
41
$$C(n - 1, k - 1) + C(n - 1, k)$$
$$= \frac{(n - 1)!}{[n - 1 - (k - 1)]!(k - 1)!} + \frac{(n - 1)!}{(n - 1 - k)!k!}$$
$$= \frac{(n - 1)!}{(n - k)!(k - 1)!} + \frac{(n - 1)!}{(n - k - 1)!k!}$$
$$= \frac{k \cdot (n - 1)!}{(n - k)!k!} + \frac{(n - k) \cdot (n - 1)!}{(n - k)!k!}$$
$$= \frac{[k + (n - k)] \cdot (n - 1)!}{(n - k)!k!}$$
$$= \frac{n \cdot (n - 1)!}{(n - k)!k!} = \frac{n!}{(n - k)!k!} = C(n, k)$$

5.6 Recursively Defined Functions

Warm-up Exercises

1 40; 160; 640

2

x	-3	-2	-1	0	1	2	3	4
$f(x)$	1	-1	-1	1	5	11	19	29

-2 0   2   4   6   8   10
2   2   2   2   2   2

3 Linear **4** 2; 6; 24; 120 **5** $f(x) = x!$, where x is a
positive integer

Problem Set

6 16; 22; 30; 120

7

x	-3	-2	-1	0	1	2	3	4
$f(x)$	-8	-12	-14	-14	-12	-8	-2	6

-4 -2 0   2   4   6   8
2   2   2   2   2   2

8 a 15 **b** 20 **9 a** 1; -1; 1 **b** -1 **c** 1 **d** $F(x) = (-1)^x$,
where x is a positive integer **10 a** $\{x : x \in \mathscr{R}\}$
b $\{f(x) : f(x) \geq -3\}$ **11** 35.71875 **12** 12 **13** $4x + 1$
14 $\begin{bmatrix} -1 & 0 \\ 0 & -1 \end{bmatrix}$; $\begin{bmatrix} -1 & 0 \\ 0 & 1 \end{bmatrix}$; $\begin{bmatrix} -1 & 0 \\ 0 & -1 \end{bmatrix}$; $\begin{bmatrix} -1 & 0 \\ 0 & 1 \end{bmatrix}$;
$\begin{bmatrix} -1 & 0 \\ 0 & -1 \end{bmatrix}$ **15 a** 41,664 **b** 249,984 **16 a** 8; 11;
15; 20 **b** Quadratic **17** $(x, y) = \left(-3, \frac{1}{2}\right)$
18 $(x, y) = \left(\frac{60}{17}, \frac{2}{17}\right)$ **19 a** $(\approx -0.5, \approx -1.5)$, $(\approx 2.5,$
$\approx 1.5)$ **b** $x \approx -0.41$ or $x \approx 2.41$ **20 a** Slope: 4;
y-intercept: -9 **b** $g(0) = 10$, $g(n) = g(n - 1) + 3$

21 a

n	0	1	2	3	4	5
$F(n)$	-4	2	8	14	20	26

b 6 **c** $F(x) = 6x - 4$, where x is a nonnegative integer
22 a 531,441 **b** 60,480

23

n	1	2	3	4	5	6
$F(n)$	4	6	22	94	492	3046

24 406 **25** $F(1) = 12$, $F(n + 1) = 3[F(n)] + 4$

26

n	1	2	3	4	5	6
$F(n)$	4	4	4	4	4	4
$g(n)$	0	0	0	0	0	0

27 a

n	1	2	3	4	5	6	7	8
$F(n)$	1	-1	2	-2	3	-3	4	-4

b 249 **c** -2617

28 a

Number of disks	1	2	3	4
Minimum number of moves needed to finish game	1	3	7	15

b $H(1) = 1$, $H(n) = 2[H(n - 1)] + 1$ **c** $H(1) = 1$;
$H(2) = 2(1) + 1 = 3$; $H(3) = 2(3) + 1 = 7$;
$H(4) = 2(7) + 1 = 15$ **29 a** 1; 1; 2; 3; 5; 8 **b** $F(1) = 1$;
$F(2) = 1$; $F(n + 1) = F(n) + F(n - 1)$, where $n \geq 2$

5.7 Measures of Central Tendency and Percentiles

Problem Set

1 75 **2** 260 **3**

8	0
7	0 0 1 1 2 2 2 2 3 3 6 9
6	1 3 3 4 5 5 5 6 6 7 8 9

7 | 2 indicates a height of 72 inches.

4 a Mean is ≈ 10.9;

mode is 0; median is 12. **b** Answers may vary. The median is probably best, since no student actually works the mean number of hours, and the mode doesn't indicate that a majority of students work more than 10 hours a week. **c** Mean increases to ≈ 11.3; mode is unchanged; median is unchanged. **5** A box-and-whisker plot does not show individual scores, as a stem-and-leaf plot does. **6** 6 **7** 123.2, 123.4, 123.6, 123.8, 124.0, 124.2, 124.4 **8** 9, 12, 15 **9** Answers will vary.

10 a

b

c

11 Mean is ≈ 8.1; mode is 8; median is 8. **14** (4, 0), (3, 0), (2, 0), (2, 1), (1, 1), (1, 0), (0, 2), (0, 1), (0, 0)

Review Problems

1 Yes **2 a** $18x - 5$ **b** $3x + 4$ **c** $12y + 4$
3 a Domain: $\{x : x \neq 0\}$; range: $\{f(x) : f(x) > 0\}$
b Domain: $\{x : x \in \mathcal{R}\}$; range: $\{g(x) : g(x) \in \mathcal{R}\}$
c Domain: $\{x : x \in \mathcal{R}\}$; range: $\{h(x) : h(x) \geq 0\}$ **4 a** -4
b 116 **5 a** and **c** **6** $\text{INV}g(x) = 3(x + 2)$ **7** 5 **8 a** x
b z **c** x, where $x \geq 0$ **d** y, where $y \neq 0$ **9 a** 3; 6; 18;
72 **b** $f(x) = 3x!$, where x is a nonnegative integer
10 a 38; 168 **b** ≈ 4.42; 8; 4 **11** $\{x : x \neq \pm 2\}$
13 {nonnegative integers} **15** {positive integers}
16 $\begin{bmatrix} -37 \\ -313 \end{bmatrix}$ **17 a** and **c**; **b** and **c** **18 a** 362,880
b 15,603,840 min, or ≈ 30 years, if played nonstop
19 336 **21**

$y = g(x)$

No

23

No

24 a $\left\{\frac{1}{3}, \frac{1}{4}, \frac{1}{5}, \frac{1}{6}, \frac{1}{7}, \frac{1}{8}\right\}$ **b** $\{0, 1, 2, 3, 4, 5\}$ **25** $\frac{1}{32}$ **27** If
$x \geq 0$, $\text{INV}r(x) = \sqrt{\frac{x + 3}{2}}$ **29** $\text{INV}t(x) = 2x - \frac{5}{4}$
30 $\frac{x - 5}{x}$; $\frac{1}{1 - 5x}$ **31 a** $P(x) = 6x + 8$ **b** $\{x : x > 0\}$;
$\{P(x) : P(x) > 8\}$ **c** $\text{INV}P(x) = \frac{1}{6}(x - 8)$ **d** The value of x
corresponding to a given perimeter **33** $g(n) = 4^{\frac{n + 1}{2}}$,
where $n \in$ {odd positive integers} **34 a** $x^2 - 2x - 2$
b $4 - x^2$ **c** $-x - 5$ **d** $x^2 + 12x + 33$ **e** $36x^2 - 3$
f $1 - 6x$ **35** $h(1) = 5$, $h(n + 1) = h(n) + 2(n + 2)$
36 $-5[p(x)]$ if $-\frac{\sqrt{3}}{3} < x < \frac{\sqrt{3}}{3}$; neither if $x = \pm \frac{\sqrt{3}}{3}$;
$p(-5x)$ if $x < -\frac{\sqrt{3}}{3}$ or $x > \frac{\sqrt{3}}{3}$

6.1 Beyond Plotting Points

Warm-up Exercises

1

2

3

4

5

x	-1	0	1	1.5
$f(2x)$	7	2	-15	-40

6

x	-1	0	1	2
$\frac{1}{2}[f(x)]$	$-\frac{1}{2}$	1	$-\frac{3}{2}$	$-\frac{15}{2}$

7

x	-2	-1	0	1	2
$f\left(\frac{1}{2}x\right)$	-1	1	2	$-\frac{1}{2}$	-3

8 a 1 **b** 3 **c** $\frac{1}{3}$ **9** Stretched horizontally by a factor of 2 **10** Shrunk vertically by a factor of $\frac{1}{2}$

Problem Set

11 2 **13** 4 **15** Stretched vertically by a factor of 2.5 and reflected over the x-axis **16 a** $(10, -2)$ **b** $\sqrt{89}$
17 Halfway between his face and the image **18 a** $\{0, 2, 4, 6\}$ **b**

19 $(2, 24)$ **21** $\left(2, \frac{12}{7}\right)$

22 a, b, c **23** -3 **24 a** 0 m **b** 8 sec **c** ≈ 1.6 sec and ≈ 6.4 sec **25** $\{(x, 4[f(x)]) : (x, 4[f(x)]) = (-2, 0), (3, 16), (7, 48), (9, -52)\}$ **26 a** 9 **b** $\frac{4}{9}$ **27** $f[g(1)] = 33$; $g[f(1)] = 117$ **28** 12 **29** $-2[f(b)], -f(b), f(b), 2[f(b)], f(2b), f(-3b)$ **30 a** $(-5, 25), (2, 4)$ **b** $\left(\frac{-5}{k}, 25\right), \left(\frac{2}{k}, 4\right)$
31 a

$y = f(x) + 2$

x	−3	−2	−1	0	1	2	3
f(x) + 2	5	4	3	2	3	4	5

b

x	−3	−2	−1	0	1	2	3
f(x) − 2	1	0	−1	−2	−1	0	1

c The graph of $y = f(x) + 2$ is moved up two units, and the graph of $y = f(x) − 2$ is moved down two units. **32** $x \approx -5.3$ or $x \approx 2.3$ **33** $x = 10$ or $x = -6$ **35** Adult: 18,458; Children's: 12,325 **36 a** $4ad - 4bc$ **b** $2ad - 2bc$ **c** Part **a** is double part **b**. **37** Over the entire year, he gains the most money with option **a**. **38 a** $\{x : x \neq 2\}$ **b** $\{x : x \in \mathcal{R}\}$ **39** $\approx 2.9 \times 10^{22}$ atoms

39   **41**

43 $(x, y) = (4, -2)$ **44** $f(x) = \frac{1}{2}(x - 2)^2 - 5$

45   **47**

48 35 days **49** $x^{6 - 3a}$ **51** **52 a** $(9, 15)$

b $(5, 15)$ **53** $a = -4; k = 10$ **54**

55 a

n	1	2	3	4	5	6	7	8
F(n)	1	2	4	8	16	32	64	128

b $F(n) = 2^{n-1}$

56 a $\frac{x + 1}{x} = \frac{x}{1}$ **b** $x = \frac{1 + \sqrt{5}}{2} \approx 1.62$ **57 a** 90 ft

b ≈ 320 ft **c** When $x \approx 53.1$ ft and $x \approx 266.9$ ft

6.3 Reflections and Symmetry

Warm-up Exercises

1 $(3, -7)$ **2** $(2, -4)$ **3** $(4, 2)$ **4** $(-3, -7)$ **5** No; neither point has a corresponding $(-x, -y)$ point. **6** $y = 0$ **7** $x = 0$ **8** $x = 3$ **9** $y = x$ or $y = -x$ **10** $y = -(x - 6)^2 - 4$ **11** $y = (x + 6)^2 + 4$

Problem Set

13 $(-2, -5)$ **15** $(2, 5)$ **17** $(5, -2)$ **19** $x = -2$ **21** None **22** $f(x) = 3x + 5$ **23**

25 **26 a** $(-2, -5), (3, -7), (6, -1)$

b $(2, -5), (-3, -7), (-6, -1)$ **27 a** -7 **b** 7 **c** 5 **d** -7 **28** 20% **29 a**

6.2 Translating Graphs

Warm-up Exercises

1 Right **2** Down **3** Up **4** Left **5** $(20, -7)$ **6** $(20, 6)$ **7** $(4, 5)$ **8** $(21, 5)$ **9** $y = (x - 3)^2$ **10** $y = (x + 5)^2$ **11** $y = x^2 + 4$ **12** $y = x^2 - 2$

Problem Set

13 $(4, 0)$; lowest **15** $(-2, 0)$; highest **17** $x = 0$ or $x = 6$ **19** $x = 2$ or $x = 8$ **21** $x = 1$ or $x = 5$ **23 a** 16; -16 **b** 4; -4 **24** $10\sqrt{2} + 5\sqrt{3}$

25 a **b** $y = x - 2$ **c** $y = x - b$

26 -3 **27**

29 -11 **31** -5 **32 a** 6 **b** 24 **c** 120

33 a **b**

34 $n = 5$ **35** $(-5, -3)$ **37** $k = \pm 10$ **38** $(-3, 3)$

b   **c**

c   **d**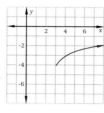

30 $(-2, 8)$
31 a $y = x^2$ **b** $y = (x - 2)^2$ **32 a** $C(h) = 20h + 55$
b At least 4.75 hr **33** Answers will vary. Possible
answer: A and A′ are reflections over $y = x$;
$AB = A′B$; $\overline{AA′}$ is perpendicular to $y = x$; M is the
midpoint of $\overline{AA′}$. **34**

35 $(4, 3)$ **36** $f(A) = \begin{bmatrix} 4.2 & -12 \\ 18 & 2 \end{bmatrix}$ **37** $x = 4 - \sqrt{3}$

39 $y = x$ or $y = -x$ **41** $y = -\frac{1}{2}x + k$, $k \in \mathcal{R}$ **42 a** 8
b 8 **c** Yes; both are the distance between x and y on a
number line. **43 a** 20 **b** 20 **c** 25 **44** 4

6.4 Graphing Other Functions

Warm-up Exercises

1 a   **b**

2 a i **b** ii **c** iii **3 a** $-3, -1, 1$ **b** $x = -3, x = -1$,
and $x = 1$ **c** $-5, -3, -1$

Problem Set

4 a ii **b** i **c** iii **d** iv **e** i **f** iv **g** i **h** iv **5 a** 2 **b** 3
c None **6 a** True; both equations are equivalent to
$xy = 1$. **b** True; 0 is in the domain of $y = x$ but not
$y = \frac{x^2}{x}$. **7 a** $(3, 7)$ **b** $(3, 10)$ **c** $\left(3, \frac{2}{5}\right)$ **8 a** $x = \frac{3 \pm \sqrt{41}}{4}$,
or $x \approx 2.35$ or $x \approx -0.85$ **b** $\frac{5}{2}$ **9 a** At $x = 3$ **b** At
$x = \frac{3}{2}$ **10** 20 mph; 10 mph **11 a** 4 **b** 3 **c** 4 **d** 2 **e** 0
f 2 **12 a**   **b**

13 40 **14 a** **15** $\{x : x \in \mathcal{R}\}$ **17** $\{x : x \neq 4\}$
19 a   **b** 1, ≈ 5.85, and ≈ -0.85

20 $x = 2$ or $x \approx 1.35$ **21** Successive differences
increase by a factor of 4.

x	-4	-3	-2	-1
$f(x)$	≈ 0.0039	≈ 0.0156	0.0625	0.25

0	1	2	3	4
1	4	16	64	256

22 a $-2, 0$, and 2 **b** 2, 4, and 6 **c** $-9, -7$, and -5
d $-1, 0$, and 1 **e** $-8, 0$, and 8 **23** $\sqrt{197}$, or ≈ 14.04
24 a $x = 3$ **b** $x = 4$ **c** $x = 1$
25 a

b   **c**

26 a None **b** None **c** $\frac{1}{2}$ and $-\frac{1}{2}$ **d** $\frac{1}{2}$ and $-\frac{1}{2}$ **27 a** $\frac{1}{x}$
b $\frac{1}{x}$ **c** g maps x to itself, so compound f, g functions
are preserved. **28 a** 0.48 lumen **b**

29 a $(0, 3)$, $(1, 4)$, and $(-1, 2)$ **b** $(4, 0)$, $(5, 1)$, and
$(3, -1)$ **c** $(-3, -2)$, $(-2, -1)$, and $(-4, -3)$

6.5 Asymptotes and Holes in Graphs

Warm-up Exercises

1 $x = -2$ and $x = 3$ **2 a** $x = -5$ **b** 0 and 3
3 a $y = 2$ and $y = -1$ **b** $x = -4$, $x = 0$, and $y = 0$
4 $y = 2$; $x = -1$ **5 a** ≈ 6.983 **b** ≈ 6.9983 **c** ≈ 6.99983
d ≈ 6.999983

Problem Set

6 $x = -7$ and $x = 3$ **7 a** $y = -1$; $x = 0$; and $x = 2$
b $y = 0$ and $x = 3$ **8**

9 **10 a**

b **11 a** $x = -1$ and $x = 2$

b $x = 4$ and $x = 10$ **12 a**

b $x = -4$, $x = 2$ **13** $x = 3$ **15** $x = \frac{1}{2}$ **16** Answers will vary. A possible response is shown.

17 $(x, y) = (-2, -3)$ **18** 362,880 **19 a** $\dfrac{4x(x - 2)}{(x + 5)(x - 2)}$

b $x = -5$ and $y = 4$ **c** 2 **20** $x = 6$ **21** $\dfrac{1}{\sqrt{5} + \sqrt{3}}$
22 a 7.5 mph **b** 2.5 mph **c** 15 mi downstream
23 $y = 2\dfrac{(x + 2)(x - 4)}{(x + 2)(x - 4)}$ **24** $x = 0$ and $y = 0$ **25 a** 18
b 9 **c** $f(x) = 3x$ **26** $(x, y) = (-2, 8)$ or $(x, y) = (2, 8)$

27 $x = 12$; $y = 12$ **28** A(3, 4, 0), B(0, 4, 5), C(3, 0, 5),
D(3, 4, 5) **29** $y = \dfrac{(x + 1)(x - 3)}{(x - 3)}$ **30 a** (0, 0); (0, 0) **b** (3, 0); (0, -27) **c** (-2, 0); (0, 8) **d** (-2, 0); (0, 8) **31** $x = 6$;
$x = -1$ **32** Slope of l:1; slope of m is undefined; slope of n:0

6.6 Measures of Dispersion

Problem Set

1 a 12 **b** 3 **c** Mean ≈ 1.71; mode = 1; median = 1
2 a 26 **b** 6 **3** Twosine

4 a

Scores	Deviation Score	Absolute Value of Deviation Score
23	-23	23
32	-14	14
50	4	4
54	8	8
71	25	25

b 14.8 **5** No **6** Mean deviation: ≈ 19.6; median deviation: $15.\overline{5}$ **7 a** 65 **b** Mean ≈ 70.5; median = 70; mode = 66 **c** ≈ 12.5

Review Problems

1 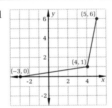 **2 a** 7 **b** 3.9 **3 a** 0; 80 **b** 0; 0

c Has hole at $x = 4$ and a vertical asymptote at
$x = -12$ **4** 58 **5** 1925 mi **6 a** $\left(3, \frac{1}{2}\right)$ **b** (3, 4) **7 a** v
b ii **c** iii **d** i **e** iv **8 a** -8; -4; -3; 4; 11 **b** 6
9 (2, 54) **10 a** $\{-14, -11, -8, -5, -2, 1, 4\}$ **b** $\{-56, -44, -32, -20, -8, 4, 16\}$ **c** $\{-4, -1, 2, 5, 8, 11, 14\}$
11 a 28.8 oz saline; 19.2 oz active ingredients
b $\approx 66.9\%$ **12** Answers will vary. Possible answer:
$f(x) = \dfrac{x + 2}{(x + 2)(x - 3)(x - 2)}$ **13 a**

b **c**

14 a (0, 9) **b** (10, 9) **c** (3, 13) **d** (3, 0) **e** (1.5, 9)
15 a 1; 3 **b** 4; 12 **c** $\frac{1}{3}$; 1 **16** $x = -\frac{1}{2}$ or $x = 2$

17 a $(3, 6)$ **b** $x = 3$ **c** $y = -2(x - 3)^2 - 6$
18 a $(-2, 0)$ **b** $(6, 0)$ **c** $(0, 5)$ **d** $(0, -7)$ **e** $(-2, -3)$
f $(7, 5)$ **19** $y = \pm\sqrt{x + 2}$ **20** $(-1, 1)$

Conics

1 Hyperbola; center $(0, 0)$; vertices $\left(0, \pm\frac{2\sqrt{2}}{3}\right)$;
asymptotes $y = \pm\sqrt{2}x$ **3** Ellipse; center $(0, 0)$; vertices
$(\pm 3, 0)$ and $(0, \pm 2\sqrt{2})$ **5** Circle; center $(0, 0)$; radius
$2\sqrt{2}$ **7 a** $\frac{x^2}{25} + \frac{y^2}{9} = 1$ **b** $x = y^2$ **c** $\frac{y^2}{4} - \frac{x^2}{4} = 1$
9 Hyperbola; center $(-2, -5)$; opens up and down;
asymptotes $y = \frac{7}{5}x - \frac{11}{5}$, $y = -\frac{7}{5}x - \frac{39}{5}$

11 Circle; center $(-5, 4)$; radius $\sqrt{41}$

13 Parabola; vertex $(4, -3)$; opens to right

14 Circle; center $(0, 0)$; radius 9

15 All except **e**. **a** Circle **b** Ellipse **c** Hyperbola
d Parabola **f** Parabola
17 **19**

20 $\frac{1}{3}$ **21** $\frac{x^2}{9} - \frac{y^2}{4} = 1$ **22** $(x - 6)^2 + (y - 1)^2 = 16$
23

24 $(x + 3)^2 + (y - 7)^2 = 25$

25 a ± 2 **b** $-1, -5$ **26 a–d**

27 x-intercepts: 1, 5; y-intercepts: $\pm\frac{3\sqrt{5}}{2}$
28 a $f(x) = \left(x + \frac{3}{2}\right)^2 - \frac{57}{4}$ **b** Parabola **c** $\left(-\frac{3}{2}, -\frac{57}{4}\right)$

7.1 Solving Problems with Systems of Equations

Warm-up Exercises
1 a Yes **2** Yes **3 a** 389 mph **b** 39 mph **4** $(r, c) =$
$(10, 6)$ **5** One solution **6** No solution **7** Many
solutions **8** Zelda is 31; Zuider is 14. **9** 13
Problem Set
11 Many solutions **13** $(x, y) = (6, 4)$ **15** No solution
17 Mary is 6; Sam is 18. **18** $(x, y, z) = \left(\frac{13}{2}, \frac{13}{4}, \frac{91}{4}\right)$
19 a $C_d = 22.5 + 0.18m$ **b** $C_s = 28.95 + 0.15m$
c 215 mi **20** $x = 4; y = 2$ **21** -20 **22 a** 4.7 **b** 37
23 a ≈ 0.83 mph **b** ≈ 4.17 mph **24** $(x, y) = (-2, 5)$
25 a $3, -4$, and 9 **b** $\frac{3}{2}, -2$, and $\frac{9}{2}$ **26** $\approx \pm 1.87$
27 a 42.5% **b** ≈ 243.4 L **28** $(m, b) = \left(\frac{6}{5}, \frac{13}{5}\right)$ **29** No
solution **31** $(x, y) = (14, 6)$ **32** $\frac{4}{5}$ **33** $x = 24; y = 6$
34

a $C_c = 255 + 85h$; $C_h = 115h$ **b** Jobs of more than
8.5 hr **35** $q = 4$ **36 a** $x = \frac{1}{3}$ or $x = -2$ **b** $-\frac{5}{3}$ **c** $-\frac{2}{3}$
37 $(x, y) = (3, 4)$ **38 a** 120° **b** If the triangles are
isosceles, $x = 30°, y = 30°$. If the triangles are not
isosceles we know only that $x + y = 60°$. **39** ≈ 1.62 qt
41 No solution

7.2 Linear Systems with Three Variables

Warm-up Exercises
1 No **2** 23 **3** $(4, 0, 0)$; $(4, 5, 0)$; $(4, 5, -6)$ **4** $(x, y, z) =$
$(13, -5, 11)$ **5** $(x, y, z) = (5, 3, 7)$

6 $y = -\frac{5}{8}x^2 + \frac{5}{4}x + \frac{75}{8}$ **7** $(x, y, z) = (1, 2, 4)$

Problem Set

9 $(x, y, z) = \left(\frac{16}{3}, \frac{35}{3}, 16\right)$ **10** $(x, y, z) = \left(9\frac{1}{2}, 5\frac{1}{2}, 14\frac{1}{2}\right)$
11 a 6 **b** 4 **c** 12 **d**

12 Bill is 16; his father is 48. **13** $y = -6x^2 + 20x - 7$
15 $(x, y, z) = (-1, 3, 5)$
16 a   **b** They are parallel.

17 4 **18** $x = 3$, $y = -5$, $z = 6$ is the solution to
the system represented by the matrix.

19 $\begin{bmatrix} 3 & 4 & 1 \\ 2 & -1 & 5 \\ -4 & 7 & 2 \end{bmatrix}\begin{bmatrix} x \\ y \\ z \end{bmatrix} = \begin{bmatrix} 11 \\ 9 \\ -4 \end{bmatrix}$ **20** 2,598,960

21 $\{(x, y): x + y = 5\}$ **22 a** $S(x) = (x + 2)^2$
b $T(x) = 3(x + 2)$ **c** $x = 1$ **23 a** $(3, 6)$ **b** $\sqrt{29}$, or
≈ 5.39 **c** $\sqrt{29}$, or ≈ 5.39 **24** $4.50 tickets: 12,452; $7.00
tickets: 9270; $12.50 tickets: 2480 **25** 8 of A, 6 of B, 5
of C **26 a** Yes, $f(n + 1) - f(n)$ increases uniformly as
n increases. **b** $f(n) = \frac{1}{2}n^2 - \frac{3}{2}n$ **27** 2.8 qt **28** 49

29 $(a, b, c) = \left(\frac{1}{2}, -\frac{1}{2}, 0\right)$ **30** 514 **31 a** $(0, 3, 5)$;
$(4, 3, 0)$; $(4, 0, 5)$ **b** $15x + 20y + 12z = 120$
32 $(a, b, c, d, e) = (9, 2, 1, 5, 7)$

7.3 Systems of Inequalities

Warm-up Exercises

1

2 No solutions

3 $y \leq -\frac{3}{4}x + 6$ **4**

5 $(-9, -2)$, $(-9, 0)$, $(4, -2)$, $(4, 0)$

6 No **7** $55x + 87y \leq 80,000$

Problem Set

9

10 $(2, 1)$, $(6, 0)$, $(9, 6)$, $(2, 6)$

11

13 $(x, y, z) = (0, 7, 5)$

14 $3x + 7y \leq 200$ **15**

16 $y = \frac{1}{3}$ or $y = -1$ **17**

18 a $(0, 0, 3)$; $(0, 4, 3)$; $(5, 4, 3)$; $(5, 0, 3)$; $(5, 0, 0)$;
$(5, 4, 0)$; $(0, 4, 0)$; $(0, 0, 0)$ **b** ABCD: $z = 3$; EFGH:
$z = 0$; DCFE: $x = 5$; BCFG: $y = 4$ **19 a** $(0, 0)$, $(3, 0)$,
$\left(\frac{16}{3}, \frac{7}{3}\right)$, $(0, 5)$ **b** $f(0, 0) = 0$; $f(3, 0) = 6$; $f\left(\frac{16}{3}, \frac{7}{3}\right) = \frac{53}{3}$;
$f(0, 5) = 15$ **20**

21 $\begin{cases} 2y - x \geq 1 \\ y \leq -\frac{24}{25}x^2 + \frac{48}{5}x - 18 \end{cases}$ **22** 10% **23** $\frac{1}{2}$ **24** 60 mph

25 a $\frac{3}{5}$ **b** $y = \frac{3}{5}x$; $y = -\frac{3}{5}x$ **c** Since the slope of $\overleftrightarrow{BD}$ is $\frac{3}{5}$, the ratio of the change in y to the change in x between any two points on the line is $\frac{3}{5}$.

26 $\begin{cases} y \le x + 5 \\ y \le -x + 5 \\ y \ge -x - 5 \\ y \ge x - 5 \end{cases}$ **27** $x \ge 2$; $y \ge 3$; $x + y \le 10$;

$200x + 375y \ge 1525$ **28** $f(-3, 1) = -9$ **29** 30

30 $(x, y, z) = (-2, 6, -2)$ **31** A: 720 mph; B: 770 mph

32 78 **33** $\begin{cases} y < 8 \\ x < 0 \\ y > x - 5 \\ y > -3x - 7 \end{cases}$ **34** 90

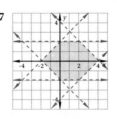

35 a $\begin{bmatrix} 1 & 0 & 1 & 1 \\ 1 & 0 & 1 & 1 \\ 1 & 1 & 0 & 0 \\ 2 & 1 & 3 & 0 \end{bmatrix}$ **b**

36 **37**

13

x	-2	-1	10	-5	$-\frac{1}{2}$
y	15	30	-3	6	60

14 12 **15** 733.$\overline{3}$ rpm **16 a** $x = 0$ and $y = 0$

b **17** Because $b \cdot h$ always

equals 48; yes **18** 1; 1; 1; 1; 1 **19**

21 $(x, y) = (7, -5)$ **22 a** \$2.00; \$0.50 **b** At least 134

23 6.25 **24**

25 **27** $(x - 10)(x + 1)$ **29** Cannot

be factored **30 and 31** **32** No; $\frac{y}{z}$,

not $y \cdot z$, equals a constant. **33 a**

b 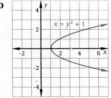 **c** No **34** $xy = 12$

7.4 Inverse Variation

Warm-up Exercises

1 **2** 216 **3** 216 **4** 216 **5** 24

6 a Yes **b** No **c** Yes **7** 0.05 **8** (6, 6) and $(-6, -6)$

Problem Set

9 **11**

35 a **b**

c $(1, 1), (-1, -1); (\sqrt{2}, \sqrt{2}), (-\sqrt{2}, -\sqrt{2})$

36 **37** $\left(-3, -\frac{1}{3}\right)$ **38 a** $1.03

b $0.82 **39 a**   **b** $x = 0$ and $y = 0$

c **d** $x = -2$ and $y = 3$

40 9 mph **41** 40 **42 a** 125 **b** 216 **c** 1000 **d** 8000
e 1,000,000 **43** ≈ 28 candles **45**

46 **47** $\dfrac{(x - 8)^2}{25} + \dfrac{(y - 10)^2}{4} = 1$

7.5 Nonlinear Systems

Warm-up Exercises

1 a $(0, 7.3), (0, 0.7)$ **b** No solution **c** $(2.4, 1.2)$,
$(2.4, -1.2)$ **2 a** $(20, -16)$ **b** No real solution **3** Yes
4 $(x, y) = (\sqrt{21}, 2)$ or $(x, y) = (-\sqrt{21}, 2)$ **5** $(x, y) =$
$(2, 3), (x, y) = (2, -3), (x, y) = (-2, 3)$, or $(x, y) =$
$(-2, -3)$ **6** $(3, 0), (-3, 0)$ **7** $(x, y) = \left(\frac{1}{3}, 0\right)$ or

$(x, y) = \left(-\frac{1}{3}, 0\right)$

Problem Set

9 $(x, y) = (4, 2\sqrt{5}), (x, y) = (4, -2\sqrt{5}), (x, y) =$
$(-4, 2\sqrt{5})$ or $(x, y) = (-4, -2\sqrt{5})$ **11** $(x, y) = (\sqrt{2}, 2)$
or $(x, y) = (-\sqrt{2}, 2)$ **12** $(\sqrt{2}, 2), (-\sqrt{2}, 2)$ **13 a** 375 m
b ≈ 267.9 m **c** 750 **14**

15 $(2 + x)(2 - x)$ **17** $5(5x - 1)(1 - x)$ **18** Possible
answer: $xy = -1$ **19** No real solution **21** No real
solution **23** 21 **24 a** 1; 8; 27; 64; 125 **b** n^3
25 a $xy = 24$ **b** **26 a** $a^3 - b^3$

b $a^3 + a^2b - ab^2 - b^3$ **27** 0 **28 a** $42.40 **b** $4.24
29 $-\frac{10}{3}$ **31** $x(x - 5)(x + 5)$ **33 a** $m = \frac{5}{9}; b = \frac{19}{3}$
b **c** **34** 2.5

35 a $12 sub.: 113; $19 sub.: 37 **b** 30% **36 a** $(6, -52)$
b $(-6, 20)$ **c** $(-3, 2)$ **d** $(3, -34)$ **37** $(15, 8)$ or $(8, 15)$
38 a 10 **b** $12.\overline{09}$ **c** 12

39 a

x	16	8	4	2
y	8	4	2	1

b

x	16	32	64	128
y	8	4	2	1

40 $\left(\frac{12}{5}, \frac{12}{5}\right), \left(\frac{12}{5}, -\frac{12}{5}\right), \left(-\frac{12}{5}, \frac{12}{5}\right), \left(-\frac{12}{5}, -\frac{12}{5}\right)$

41 a $-\frac{1}{16}$ **b** $\frac{1}{5}$ **42** No real solution **43** $(x, y) =$
$(2, -1)$ or $(x, y) = (-1, 2)$
44

7.6 Other Systems of Equations

Warm-up Exercises

1 $(x, y) = \left(\frac{1}{9}, -\frac{1}{3}\right)$ **2** $(x, y) = \left(4, -\frac{8}{3}\right)$ **3** 12 and $\frac{12}{5}$
4 $(x, y) = (3, 3)$

Problem Set

5 $(x, y) = \left(\frac{1}{3}, \frac{1}{2}\right)$ **6** $(x, y) = \left(\frac{9}{2}, -\frac{1}{2}\right)$ **7** $(x, y) = (0, 0)$ or

$(x, y) = (6, 3)$ **8** $\frac{15}{8}$ hr **9** $f(x) = \frac{5}{2}x^2 - \frac{1}{2}x + 4;$

$g(x) = \frac{1}{2}x^2 + \frac{5}{2}x + 3$ **10** ≈ 4.6 **11** 3.75 hr **12** $q = 0$ or

$q = -7731$ **13** $\frac{2}{3}$ **14** $w = 0, w = 1, w = -2,$ or $w = 3$

15 120 **16** 2 hr 24 min **17 a** $1; \frac{1}{10}; \frac{1}{100}; \frac{1}{1000}; \frac{1}{10,000}$

b 1.1111 **18** $(x, y) = \left(5, -\frac{1}{2}\right)$ **19** $(x, y) = (-12, -1)$

21 The opening had to be delayed. (It took 5 hr to fill
the pool.) **22 a** $\frac{V_1}{T_1} = \frac{V_2}{T_2}$ **b** 24 v **23** $(x, y) = (4, 2)$
24 $f(x) = 2x^2 + 17x - 43; g(x) = -x^2 - 12x + 31$
25 $(A, B, C, D) = (-4, 1, 12, 6)$ **26** Tom: $23\frac{1}{3}$ days;

Dick: 10 days; Harry: $17\frac{1}{2}$ days **27** $x \approx 4.01$ or

$x \approx -3.68$ **28** 4 km/hr; ≈ 9.8 km/hr; 16.5 km/hr

29 a $\text{INV}f(x) = \frac{1}{x} + 3$ **b** $f \circ \text{INV}f(x) = \frac{1}{\frac{1}{x} + 3 - 3} = x;$

$\text{INV}f \circ (fx) = \frac{1}{\frac{1}{x - 3}} + 3 = x$ **c**

30 a Yes; $xy = -4$ **b** No **c** No **d** Yes; $xy = 6$ **31** No
solution **33** $(x, y, z) = (4, -2, 5)$ **34 a** $(\sqrt{x}, \sqrt{y}) =$
$(3, 2)$ **b** $(x, y) = (9, 4)$ **35 a** 35 **b** 12 **36** $(x, y) =$
$\left(-\frac{3}{4}, \frac{3}{20}\right)$ **37 a** 52.75; 43 and 47; 51.5 **b** 22 **c** ≈ 7.08

Review Problems

1 a $h = 7; k = 4$ **b**

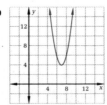

2 $(x, y) = (4, -1)$ **3** 480 rpm **4 a** 120 mph **b** 30 mph
5 7 and $\sqrt{39}$, 7 and $-\sqrt{39}$, -7 and $\sqrt{39}$, or -7 and
$-\sqrt{39}$ **6** $(x, y) = (5, 35)$ or $(x, y) = (-2, 0)$
7 a $(x + y)(x - y)$ **b** $(x^2 + y^2)(x + y)(x - y)$ **8** 15 min

9 $(x, y, z) = \left(-5, \frac{7}{2}, 4\right)$ **10** Run: ≈ 8.33 km/hr; swim:
≈ 1.18 km/hr **11 a** $x = 4$ **b** $x = -7$ **c** $x = 3$
12 79.8 or 7.2 **13 a** $(x, y) = (6, 6)$ or $(x, y) = (-6, -6)$

b The solutions represent the vertices of the
hyperbolic graph of the first equation in the system.

14 $\begin{cases} y \geq \frac{2}{5}(x - 8) \\ y \leq -\frac{2}{5}(x - 8) \\ x \geq -2 \end{cases}$ **15 a** ≈ 3.7 hr **b** 1.8 mph; 4.7 mph

16 $X = \begin{bmatrix} -1 \\ 3 \\ 5 \end{bmatrix}$ **17** $16.\overline{6}$ **18 a** $(x - 7)(x + 2)$

b $(3x - 7)(3x + 2)$ **c** $(x - 3)(x + 6)$

19

20 a 360 **b** $E = \frac{360}{n}$ **c** 30

21 $(x, y) = (-8, -4)$ **22**

23 $7.68 **24** $\frac{39}{34}$ **25** $y = 3x^2 + 12x + 6$

Factoring to Solve Equations and Inequalities

Problem Set

1 $-6, -2, 2$ **3** $-4, -2, \pm\sqrt{7}$ **5** $7, 6 \pm \sqrt{3}$
7 a **8** $y^2(y - 2)(y - 5)$ **9** $x = \pm 2$ or

b

c

$x = -4$ **11** $(x + 1)(x^2 - x + 1)$
13 $(2x - 5)(4x^2 + 10x + 25)$ **15** $x(x - 6)^2$
17 $(x^2 - 3x + 5)(x^2 + 3x + 5)$ **18 a** $(x^2 - 5)(x - 1)$
b $\{x : x < -\sqrt{5}$ or $1 < x < \sqrt{5}\}$ **c** The solutions of the
inequality are the values of x for which the graph of P
lies below the x-axis. **19**

21 a $a^3 + (a + 2)^3$ **b** $2(a + 1)(a^2 + 2a + 4)$
23 $(x^2 + 1)(x - 1)$ **24** $\{a : a \leq -2\sqrt{2}$ or $-2 \leq a \leq 2$ or
$a \geq 2\sqrt{2}\}$ **25** No real solutions **27** $z = \pm 2$ or $z = \pm 3$
29 $z \approx \pm 6.7$ or $z \approx \pm 0.3$ **31** $(b + 3)(b - 3)(b^2 + 3b + 9)$
32 a $\pi(x + y)^2 - 16\pi$ **b** $(x^2 + 2xy + y^2) - 16$ or
$(x + y)^2 - 16$ **c** $\frac{\pi[(x + y)^2 - 16]}{(x + y)^2 - 16} = \frac{\pi}{1}$
33 a $\{a : a = \pm(p + 1)\}$ **b** Yes; a can be 3 if $p = 2$.
34 a $y = x^3 - 2x^2 - 8x$ **b** $y = 3x^4 - 2x^2 - 1$
c $y = x^3 - 3x^2 - x + 3$ **d** $y = x^3 - 1$
35 $\{x : x > 2\}$

37 $\left\{x : x \leq -\frac{5}{2}$ or $-2 \leq x \leq 2\right\}$

39 a $y = 0$ or $y = \pm 1$

b $y = \pm 1$ or $y = \pm 4$

c $\{y : y \le -4 \text{ or } -1 \le y \le 1 \text{ or } y \ge 4\}$

8.1 Rational Exponents

Warm-up Exercises

1 a 6 **b** 4 **c** 16 **d** 8 **e** $\frac{1}{6}$ **f** 4 **2 a** $x^{\frac{3}{2}}$ **b** $x^{\frac{11}{12}}$ **3 a** 3
b 4 **c** -10 **4 a** ≈ -6.05 **b** ≈ 5598.82 **c** ≈ 0.03 **5 c**

Problem Set

6 $27^{\frac{5}{3}} = (3^3)^{\frac{5}{3}} = 3^5 = 243$ **7** x^2 **9 a** ii, iii, and iv **b** ii
and iv **c** iv and v **d** iv and v **e** ii and iv **10 a** 3
b 27 **c** $\frac{1}{27}$ **11** $2\sqrt{37}$, or ≈ 12.17 **12** 0; $\frac{3}{5}$ **13 a** $V = A^{\frac{3}{2}}$
b ≈ 58.1 cm³ **15** $n = -2$ **17** $n = \frac{10}{3}$ **19** 125 **20 a** 3
b 6 **c** 3 **d** $\frac{1}{2}$ **e** 0 **21** 2 **23 a** $(x - 15)(x + 2)$
b $(y + 17)(y - 17)$ **c** $3(a + 4)(a + 7)$
d $(5n + 4)(n - 4)$ **24 a** $x^{\frac{5}{3}}$ **b** x^4 **25** $4x^4y^6$ **27** $\frac{3y^2}{2x^2}$
29 a, b, c, and **f** **30 a** True **b** True **c** False **d** True
e False **31 a** $\approx 72°C$ **b** $\approx 45°C$ **c** ≈ 43 min **33** 1; x^2
34 Possible answers: $0.10110111011110\ldots$ and
$0.21221222122221\ldots$ **35** $x + y$ **37 a** ≈ 7.0711;
≈ 13.5721; ≈ 18.8030; ≈ 22.8653; ≈ 48.1004; ≈ 49.9804
b It approaches, but does not reach, 50.
38 a $\approx 2.26 \times 10^{-23}$ cm³ **b** $\approx 4.42 \times 10^{18}$
c $\approx 2.21 \times 10^{18}$

8.2 Solving Radical Equations

Warm-up Exercises

1 a $y = 81$ **b** $y = 8$ **c** $y = \frac{13}{4}$ **2 a** $k = 99$ **b** No real
solutions **3 a** No real solutions **b** $p = 125$
c $p = -125$ **4 a** $x = 8$ **b** $x = 5$ **c** $x = 1$ **d** $x = 341$
5 $10\sqrt{5}$ ft²

Problem Set

6 $a = \frac{7}{3}$ **7** $b = -\frac{4}{3}$ **8** $x = 10$ **9 a** -4 **b** 1
c 3 **d** $\frac{3}{2}$ **e** 3 **f** 5 **11** $x = 14$ **12 a** $r = 6$ **b** $r \approx 3.39$
13 ≈ 36.37 **15** $x = 256$ **17** $x \approx 101.59$ **19** $x = \frac{1}{16}$
21 $\frac{1}{5}\sqrt{15}$ **23** $5\sqrt{2}$ **25** $y = \frac{1}{3}$ **27** $y = \frac{3}{5}$ **28** 16 or -14
29 22 **31** $6\sqrt{2}$ **32** No solution **33** $3\sqrt{3}$ cm
34 $30\sqrt{2}$ in. **35** $n = 24$ or $n = 48$ **36** ≈ 10 cm²
37 ≈ 7 **38 a** $4x^8$ **b** $5x^{12}\sqrt{x}$ **c** $4x^6\sqrt{2}$ **d** $2|x^5y^3|\sqrt{6y}$
39 ≈ 6.18 **40** ± 7 **41** $(\sqrt[4]{x})^2 = x^{\frac{2}{4}} = x^{\frac{1}{2}} = \sqrt{x}$
42 $\sqrt{(-2 - 0)^2 + (3 - 6)^2} = \sqrt{13}$
$\sqrt{(0 - 3)^2 + (6 - 4)^2} = \sqrt{13}$
$\sqrt{(3 - (-2))^2 + (4 - 3)^2} = \sqrt{26}$
Since $(\sqrt{13})^2 + (\sqrt{13})^2 = (\sqrt{26})^2$, the triangle
determined by the three points is right. **43 a** 2 **b** 2

c 5 **d** 0.5 **e** The power of 10 that is equivalent to the
input value **44** $\approx 3.19\ \mu$ **by** $\approx 4.70\ \mu$ **45** $x = 25$
47 No real solution **49** 6 **50 a** $3S = 3 + 3^2 +$
$3^3 + 3^4 + \ldots + 3^{11}$ **b** $2S = -1 + 3^{11}$ **c** $S = 88,573$
51 a $x = -64$ or $x = 27$ **b** $x = -22$
52 $x(x^n + 4)(x^n + 1)$ **53** $x = -2$ or $x = 3$
55 $x = a + b - 1$ **56 a** 54 **b** 2

8.3 Introduction to Complex Numbers

Warm-up Exercises

1

Complex Number	Real Part	Imaginary Part	Conjugate
$2 + 5i$	2	$5i$	$2 - 5i$
$3 - 4i$	3	$-4i$	$3 + 4i$
$-2 + 7i$	-2	$7i$	$-2 - 7i$
$5 - 4i$	5	$-4i$	$5 + 4i$
$9i + 3$	3	$9i$	$3 - 9i$
$-6 - 5i$	-6	$-5i$	$-6 + 5i$
$-4i$	0	$-4i$	$4i$
16	16	$0i$	16

2 a $8i$ **b** $-5i$ **c** i **d** $\frac{3}{2}i$ **e** $2\sqrt{3}i$ **f** -3 **g** $\frac{1}{2}i$ **h** -15
i -49 **3** No **4 a** $-i$ **b** i **c** $-2i$ **d** $2i$ **5** $\begin{bmatrix} -1 & 0 \\ 0 & -1 \end{bmatrix}$

Problem Set

6 a -5 **b** $2\sqrt{5}i$ **c** $-2\sqrt{10}i$ **d** $12i$ **7 a** $-2i$ **b** $3i$
c $-\frac{5}{4}i$ **8** $4\sqrt{2}$ **9** $i^4 = (i^2)^2 = (-1)^2 = 1$ **10 a** $\frac{5}{4}i$ **b** $-\frac{5}{4}i$
c -4 **11 a** $-2 + 7i$ **b** $-4i + 3$ **c** 8 **12** $\frac{1}{3}$
13 a $x^2 + 9$ **b** $x^2 + 1$ **c** $x^2 + 2ix - 1$
14 a

b

c

d

15 a $(y + 2i)(y - 2i)$ **b** $(3i + 2x)(-3i + 2x)$
16 a $x = \pm 5$ **b** $x = \pm 6i$ **c** $x = \pm 7$ **d** $x = \pm 7i$
17 a -24 **b** $-3i$ **c** 3 **d** -8 **e** $-8 - 6\sqrt{2}$
f $(4 - 3\sqrt{6})i$ **18** Ezra was right, since the property
stating that $\frac{\sqrt{x}}{\sqrt{y}} = \sqrt{\frac{x}{y}}$ does not apply to roots with
negative radicands. The work should read
$\sqrt{-\frac{1}{9}} = \sqrt{\frac{1}{9}}\sqrt{-1} = \frac{1}{3}i$. **19** $\begin{bmatrix} -2 & -3 \\ 1 & -4 \end{bmatrix}$ **20** $\frac{5}{6}$
21 a ii **b** iv **c** i **d** iii **22 a** $(x + 5)(x - 5)$
b $(x + 5i)(x - 5i)$ **c** $(2x + 7)(2x - 7)$
d $(2x + 7i)(2x - 7i)$ **e** $4(x + 2)(x - 2)$

f $4(x + 2i)(x - 2i)$ **23** $\frac{1}{3}\pi a^7$ **24** $i^{-1} = \frac{1}{i} =$

$\frac{1}{i} \cdot \frac{i}{i} = \frac{i}{i^2} = \frac{i}{-1} = -i$ **25 a** $0.5i$ **b** $2.5i$ **c** 36

d $-6 + 2\sqrt{2}$ **27** $x = \pm 2\sqrt{3}i$ **29** $x = -4 \pm i$

31 $10 + 5i$ **32 a** $x = -1$ and $x = 4$ **b** 0 and 5

33 $x = -8i$ **35** $x = -12i$ **37** $x = -4i$

38 a $(x, y) = \left(2i, \frac{1}{2}i\right)$ **b** $(x, y) = (1, -2i)$

39 a $x^2 + 100 = 0$ **b** $x^3 + 25x = 0$ **40** $8; 9$

41 $16\pi; 20\pi$ **42** $x = 0$, $x = 10i$, or $x = -10i$

43 $x = 2i$ and $x = -2i$ **45** $x = 2$ or $x = 1$

8.4 Algebra of Complex Numbers

Warm-up Exercises

1

Complex Number	$a + bi$ Form	Real Part	Imaginary Part	Conjugate
$-5i - 7$	$-7 - 5i$	-7	$-5i$	$-7 + 5i$
$19i$	$0 + 19i$	0	$19i$	$-19i$
$2(5 + 3i)$	$10 + 6i$	10	$6i$	$10 - 6i$
27	$27 + 0i$	27	$0i$	27
$\sqrt{3} + \sqrt{-3}$	$\sqrt{3} + \sqrt{3}i$	$\sqrt{3}$	$\sqrt{3}i$	$\sqrt{3} - \sqrt{3}i$

2 a $(x + 11i)(x - 11i)$ **b** $(x + 11)(x - 11)$
c $(3x + 2i)(3x - 2i)$ **d** $9(x + 2i)(x - 2i)$ **3 a** $x = 3$
b $x = -3i$ **4 a** $(x, y) = (5, 7)$ **b** $(x, y) = (82, 39)$
c $(x, y) = (-6, 8)$ **d** $(x, y) = (5, 0)$
5 a $x^2 - 2x - 35 = 0$ **b** $x^2 + 25 = 0$

Problem Set

6 a $0 - \frac{5}{2}i$ **b** $\frac{3}{5} + \frac{1}{5}i$ **c** $-2 + 2i$ **d** $3 - 14i$ **e** $12 + 6i$
7 a 1 **b** 1 **c** i **d** $-i$ **8 a** $12 + 5i$ **b** $-5 - 4i$ **c** 25

d $\frac{12}{13} + \frac{5}{13}i$ **9 a** $-9i$ **b** $-13i$ **c** 0 **10 a** 58 **b** $\approx 62\%$

c $\approx 95\%$ **11 a** $\frac{4}{3}i$ **b** $\frac{4}{3}i$ **c** $\frac{4}{3}i$ **12 a** $x = \pm\frac{3}{2}i$

b $x = \pm 7i$ **13** $(x, y) = \left(2 + 3i, -\frac{2}{3} + i\right)$ **15** -13
17 a -16 **b** $x = 2 \pm 2i$ **18 a** $x = \pm 7i$ **b** $x = 1 \pm i$
c $x = 3 \pm 5i$ **19 a** $10 - 5i$ **b** $9 + 5i$ **c** $0 + 2i$
20 a $y = -(x + 5)^2 - 2$ **b** $y = (x - 5)^2 + 2$
c $y = -(x - 5)^2 - 2$ **d** $x = (y + 5)^2 + 2$ **21** 0
23 $-13 + 22i$ **25** $38i$ **27 a** $x = 16; y = -7$

b $x = \frac{13}{3}; y = \frac{10}{3}$ **c** $\{(x, y): x = 3y\}$ **28 a** 4 **b** $-8i$

c $6i$ **d** 25 **e** 5 **29 a** $3i$ **b** $2i$ **31** $x = -\frac{3}{4} \pm \frac{\sqrt{23}}{4}i$

33 $x = \frac{3}{2} \pm \frac{1}{2}i$ **35** $\pm 2\sqrt{5}i$ **36 a** 0 **b** $-1 + i$ **c** 0

d $-1 + i$ **37** $-10; 26$ **38** $\left(\frac{6}{7}, \frac{12}{5}\right)$ **39 a** $\frac{x^2}{4} + \frac{y^2}{9} = 1$

b $(x - 3)^2 + (y + 4)^2 = 9$ **c** $y = -\frac{1}{2}x^2 + 6$

d $\frac{(y - 2)^2}{16} - \frac{(x - 2)^2}{16} = 1$ **40 a** $x = 3; y = -9$ **b** $x = 7;$

$y = 10$ **41** $(x, y) = \left(3 - 2i, -1 + \frac{3}{2}i\right)$ **42** $-8 + 19i$
43 $-1 + i; -1; 0; i; -1 + i; -1; 0; i$ **44 a** $x = 8$
b $x = \pm 2\sqrt{2}$ **c** $x = 2$ or $x = -1 \pm \sqrt{3}i$ **d** $x = 9i$ or
$x = i$ **e** $x = 5i$ or $x = i$ **45** $\pm 2i$ **46 a** 82 **b** 85
47 $\{(a, b): 3b = 2a\}$

8.5 The Normal Curve

Problem Set

1 a 1000 square units **b** 25% **c** 25 **d** 85% **e** 85
2 $0.4; 8.8; 54.4; 136.4$ **3 a** 84.1% **b** 84

4

Data value	200	300	400	500	600	700	800
Percentile rank	1	2	15	50	84	97	99

5 65.9% **6 a** 81.8% **b** 84.1% **7 a** 2 **b** 15 **c** 84
d 97 **e** 99 **8** 84.1% **9** 99.9% **10** 97.7% **11** 95.4%

Review Problems

1 5 **3** 4 **5** $\frac{1}{27}$ **7** $(4 - \pi)\sqrt{3}$, or ≈ 1.49 **8** $x = -3$

9 a $0 + \frac{4}{3}i$ **b** $-2 + 6i$ **c** $\frac{30}{37} - \frac{5}{37}i$ **d** $144 + 0i$ **11** 64

13 a 405 and 555 **b** 360 and 600 **15** $-\frac{10}{7}i$ **17** $12i$

19 $-3 - 6\sqrt{7}$ **20 a** $2 + 9i$ **b** $\frac{1}{2} - \sqrt{3}i$ **c** $-15i$

d $-5 + 3i$ **e** $\sqrt{23}$ **f** $\frac{5}{7} + \frac{5}{7}i$ **21 a** $x^{\frac{17}{15}}$ **b** $y^{-1.5}$ **c** a^{19}

22 18.2% **23** $7 - 2i$ **25** $\frac{20}{29} + \frac{21}{29}i$ **27** $(x, y) = (7, -4)$
29 $(x, y) = (-70, -8)$ **31** $2, -2, 2i$, and $-2i$

32 $\begin{bmatrix} -1 + 3i & -14 + 8i \\ 4 - 8i & 6 + i \end{bmatrix}$ **33** $a = \frac{23}{3}$ **35** $a = \pm 5\sqrt{10}$

37 $a = \pm 6$ or $a = \pm 2\sqrt{41}$ **39 a** $x^2 + 121 = 0$
b $x^3 - 7x^2 + 20x - 24 = 0$ **41** $x = 3 \pm 3i$
43 $x = \pm\sqrt{7}i$ **44** 5

9.1 The Remainder and Factor Theorems

Warm-up Exercises

1 $((1)x - 3)x + 5$ **2** $((((3)x - 0)x - 2)x + 5)x - 9$
3 $4x^3 - 3x^2 + 2x - 7$ **4 a** Quotient: $2x^2 - 3x - 22$;
remainder: -106 **b** -106; the value of $P(x)$ when
$x = 5$ is equal to the remainder for $[P(x)] \div (x - 5)$.
5 $x^4 + x^3y + x^2y^2 + xy^3 + y^4$

Problem Set

6 0 **7** $(((5)x + 2)x + 6)x + 1$ **9** $3x^3 + 6x^2 - 7x + 9$
11 $2x^3 - 5x - 7$ **13** 39 **15 a** 4 **b** 5 **c** -6 **d** $-4x_1^2$
e $2x_1^3$ **f** 3 **17** $(x^2 - 3)^2$ **18**

19 $x^2 - 4x + 7$, remainder -1
21 $2(x - 4)(x^2 + 4x + 16)$ **23** $(2x - 3)(4x^2 + 6x + 9)$
24 a -7 **b** -13 **c** 71 **25 a** $x^2 + 5x + 6$;
$x^2 + 5x + 4$; I; 2 square units **b** $x + 4$, remainder 2
c Since $x^2 + 5x + 6 = (x + 1)(x + 4) + 2$, the area
of rectangle I is 2 square units greater. **26 a** 6 **b** 2
27 a $18x^3$; 20 **b** $18x^3$; 20 **c** x^3; 20
29 $3(3x - 5)(3x + 1)$

31 $x - 2$, remainder $-x - 9$ **32** $4, -\frac{3}{2}, \frac{5}{3}$

33 $-3 < z_1 < -2$; $0 < z_2 < 1$; $3 < z_3 < 4$
34 Quotient: $2x^3 - 4x^2 - x + 7$; remainder: -10
35 $x^2 + 8x + 6$ **36** 20,475 classes **37** $(x^2 + 5)(x^2 - 5)$
39 $(x^2 + 4)(x + 2)(x - 2)$ **40 a** $(((4)x - 3)x + 8)x + 42$
b $4x^3 - 3x^2 + 8x + 42$ **41 a** 0 **b** Yes; there is an
integer n such that $P(n) = 0$. **42 a** 60 **b** 12
43 $2x^2 - 14x + 48$, remainder -139 **44** $x = -4$ or
$x = \frac{2}{3}$ **45** $(x - 3)(x + 2)(x - 2)$ **46** Quotient:
$x^2 + 2x + 4$; remainder: 0 **47** $(6, -2, 4)$ **48** Quotient:
$ax^2 + (a + b)x + (a + 2b)$; remainder: $2a + 2b$ **49** For
any negative value of x, the powers x^5, x^3, and x^1 will
be negative. Since a, b, and c are also negative, each
term of $P(x)$ will represent a positive number when x is
negative. The sum of three positive numbers cannot be
0, so $P(x) \neq 0$ for any negative x. **50 a** $P(x) = \frac{1}{8}x^3 -$
$\frac{3}{8}x^2 - \frac{5}{4}x + 3$ **b** $g(x) = \frac{3}{5}x^2 - \frac{6}{5}x - \frac{9}{5}$ **c** $H(x) = \frac{1}{8}x^3 -$
$\frac{39}{40}x^2 - \frac{1}{20}x + \frac{24}{5}$ **d** $40[H(x)] = 5x^3 - 39x^2 - 2x + 192$;
$40[H(-2)] = 0$, so $H(-2) = 0$ **51** $2x + 1$

9.2 The Rational-Zeros Theorem

Warm-up Exercises

1 a $2x^3 + 3x^2 - 18x + 5$ **b** $x + 4$ **c** -3
d $2x^2 - 5x + 2$ **2** Quotient: $3x + 6$; remainder: 31
3 $2x - 1$, remainder 4 **4** $-1, \frac{1}{3}, 1, 2$ **5** $3x^4 - 26x^3 +$
$262x - 168$

Problem Set

6 $3x^2 - 2x$, remainder 6 **7** $\pm 1, \pm 5, \pm\frac{1}{2}, \pm\frac{5}{2}$
8 $x^3 - 6x^2 + 11x - 6$; $P(x) = x^3 - 6x^2 + 11x - 6$
9 $x = -3$, $x = -\frac{3}{2}$, or $x = \frac{3}{2}$ **10** $x^2 - 3x + 2$
11 $\approx -3.7, \approx 0.5, \approx 2.6$ **12** $\frac{2}{3}$ **13** $x^3 - 11x^2 + 10x +$
$72 = 0$ **14** 9 **15** $\pm 1, \pm 2, \pm 3, \pm 6, \pm\frac{1}{2}, \pm\frac{3}{2}, \pm\frac{1}{4}, \pm\frac{3}{4}$
16 The Rational-Zeros Theorem does not apply to
function P, Since $P(x)$ contains a nonintegral
coefficient. **17** $s = 4x^3 + 9x^2 - 23x + 16$ **18** -2 and
-1, 1 and 2, 2 and 3, and two between 5 and 6 **19** 1
21 $x = \frac{7}{a + b}$ **23** When $x = 2$, the value of the cubic
polynomial is 0, so by the Factor Theorem, $x - 2$ is a
factor of the polynomial. **25** $2x^2(3x - 5)(3x + 5)$
26 $f(x) = x^4 - 13x^2 + 36$ **27** $1, \frac{3 + 3\sqrt{5}}{2}, \frac{3 - 3\sqrt{5}}{2}$
28 $y = -3$, $y = -\frac{2}{3}$, $y = \frac{1}{2}$, or $y = 2$ **29** $2x^3 - 11x^2 +$
$22x - 21$ **30 a** $P(x) = x^3 + 4x^2 - 7x - 10$ **b** $P(x) =$
$9x^3 - 18x^2 + 11x - 2$ **31** 1, 8, 28, 56, 70, 56, 28, 8, 1
32 $-\sqrt{7}, -\sqrt{5}, \sqrt{5}, \sqrt{7}$ **33** $x^2 - 30x + 200 = 0$
34 a $-\sqrt{7}, \sqrt{7}, 4$ **b** $6 - \sqrt{7}, 6 + \sqrt{7}, 10$ **c** $-\frac{\sqrt{7}}{2}$,
$\frac{\sqrt{7}}{2}, 2$ **35** $x = -a$ or $x = -b$ **37** $\{x : x \neq -2, x \neq 2,$
$x \neq 3\}$ **38 a** $\pm 1, \pm 2, \pm\frac{1}{2}, \pm\frac{1}{3}, \pm\frac{2}{3}, \pm\frac{1}{6}$ **b** -13

9.3 Real Zeros of Polynomial Functions

Warm-up Exercises

1 When $P(x)$ is divided by $x + 2$, the terms of the
quotient and the remainder alternate in sign.
2 Answers will vary. Possible answer: 8; -4
3 ≈ -2.24

Problem Set

4 a Yes **b** No **c** No **d** No **5** Answers will vary.
Possible answer: 6; -3 **6** $\approx -1.414, \approx 1.414$ **7** ≈ 1.522
8 Answers will vary. Any 12 numbers greater than 5
are possible answers. **9** $3y^2(2 + y)(2 - y)$
11 $(2 - b)(4 + 2b + b^2)$ **12** Quotient: $x^2 - 2x - 1$;
remainder: 3 **13** $\approx -1.149, \approx 0.201$ **15** $x = -5$,
$x \approx -3.606$, or $x \approx 3.606$ **16** Possible answer: 6; 2
(since $x \not\geq 2$) **17** $(x, y) = (-2, 0)$ or $(x, y) = (2, 0)$
18 18 **19 a** 0 **b** -1 **c** -2 **d** -3 **20 a** 1 **b** $x + y$
c $x^2 + 2xy + y^2$ **d** $x^3 + 3x^2y + 3xy^2 + y^3$ **21 a** 4 **b** 3
c 0 **d** 4 **e** 3 **f** 0 **22 a** $((5)x - 7)x + 11$ **b** $20x^2 -$
$14x + 11$ **23** ≈ 1.72 **25** $\{x : x \leq 0 \text{ or } x \geq 6\}$
26

27 a $P(2)$ is negative, and $P(3)$ is
positive, so the graph of P must cross the x-axis (that
is, $P(x)$ must equal 0) somewhere between $x = 2$ and
$x = 3$. **b**

c No **28 a** 0 and 1,
2 and 3, 3 and 4 **b** $2 - \sqrt{3}, \frac{11}{5}, 2 + \sqrt{3}$ **29** $\{a : a \geq -1\}$
30 No; answers will vary—possible answer is that
$63 \cdot (-5) \neq 12$. **31 a** -16 **b** 11 **c** Since $P(2)$ is
negative and $P(3)$ is positive, $P(x)$ must equal 0 for
some value of x between 2 and 3. **32 a** 0 **b** -1
c Yes **d** No **33 a** 0 **b** $(0, -1)$ **c** 0 **d** 0 **34 a** $P(1) =$
$2 - 3 + 2 - 8 = -7$ and $P(2) = 32 - 12 + 4 - 8 = 16$;
since the value of $P(x)$ changes sign between $x = 1$ and
$x = 2$, there must be at least one zero between these
values. **b** ≈ 1.57

9.4 Four Useful Theorems

Warm-up Exercises

1 2 **2** -15; 50 **3** $\frac{2}{5}$ **4** No, since the equation contains
nonreal coefficients

Problem Set

5 7 7 $\frac{3}{2}$; −3 9 $x^2 - 25 = 0$ 11 $x^2 + 25 = 0$
13 a −6 b 36 14 a $1 + 0i$ b $1 + 0i$ c $1 + 0i$
15 $z = 5 + 15i$ 16 $x^2 - 4x + (1 - 4i) = 0$
17 a $\begin{bmatrix} 3+8i & -i \\ 15+2i & 1-7i \end{bmatrix}$ b $\begin{bmatrix} 3-4i & 8-i \\ -3+8i & 11-5i \end{bmatrix}$ 18 6
19 $x^4 - 6x^3 + 14x^2 - 24x + 40 = 0$ 21 5; 5; −2, 2
(multiplicity 2), −2i, 2i 22 $\{(x, y): x - iy = -i\}$
23 20 24 a 16; −6i b 8; $-\frac{5}{2}i$ c 3; −5i 25 $\frac{1}{5}$

26 $\begin{bmatrix} 1 & 0 \\ 0 & 1 \end{bmatrix}$ 27 a 20 b $\frac{1}{10}$ c $\frac{2}{5}$ 28 $\frac{1}{2}$ 29 a 8

b −3 (multiplicity 3), 3, −3i (multiplicity 2), 3i
(multiplicity 2) 30 $\begin{bmatrix} 0 \\ -7 \\ -7 \\ 25 \end{bmatrix}$ 31 a $z = -3i$ b $z = 16$

32 $x = -3i$ or $x = 8i$ 33 $\sqrt{3}$; $\sqrt{5}$ 34 a $w = -i$ or
$w = i$ b $w = -2i$ or $w = 2i$ 35 $x + yi = -\frac{\sqrt{2}}{2} - \frac{\sqrt{2}}{2}i$
or $x + yi = \frac{\sqrt{2}}{2} + \frac{\sqrt{2}}{2}i$ 36 a 1 b 3 c 3, −i, i
37 $x^4 + 45x^2 + 324 = 0$ 38 6; −8i

9.5 The Binomial Theorem

Warm-up Exercises

1 Row 8: 1, 8, 28, 56, 70, 56, 28, 8, 1; row 9: 1, 9, 36, 84, 126, 126, 84, 36, 9, 1; row 10: 1, 10, 45, 120, 210, 252, 210, 120, 45, 10, 1 2 $32x^5 + 400x^4y + 2000x^3y^2 + 5000x^2y^3 + 6250xy^4 + 3125y^5$ 3 −366,080x^4y^9

4 $C(n, r + 1) = \dfrac{n!}{[n - (r + 1)]!(r + 1)!} = \dfrac{n!}{\frac{(n-r)!}{n-r}r!(r + 1)}$
$= \dfrac{n!}{(n - r)!r!} \cdot \dfrac{n - r}{r + 1} = C(n, r) \cdot \dfrac{n - r}{r + 1}$

The relationship tells us that we can find the coefficient of each successive term by multiplying the coefficient of the preceding term by $\frac{n - r}{r + 1}$, where n is the power of the binomial and the preceding term is the $(r + 1)$th term of the expansion.

Problem Set

5 $p^3 + 3p^2q + 3pq^2 + q^3$ 7 First four: $x^{12} + 12x^{11}y + 66x^{10}y^2 + 220x^9y^3$; last four: $220x^3y^9 + 66x^2y^{10} + 12xy^{11} + y^{12}$ 8 −122,266y^6 9 Third term, 40x^6
10 a iii b ii c i d iv 11 a False b False c True
d False 12 ≈3.519 13 0, −5 15 $(x + y)^4$ 16 a 1, 2, 4, 8, 16, 32 b 4096 17 a $C(n, 0) = \frac{n!}{n!0!} = 1$

b $C(n, n) = \frac{n!}{0!n!} = 1$ 18 a 26,334x^5y^{17} b 26,334$x^{17}y^5$
19 59,049x^{10} − 984,150x^9y + 7,381,125x^8y^2 21 x^5 − 10x^4y + 40x^3y^2 − 80x^2y^3 + 80xy^4 − 32y^5 23 32x^5 − 80x^4y + 80x^3y^2 − 40x^2y^3 + 10xy^4 − y^5 24 $(x + 12)^2$
25 a x − 2, remainder 8 b $x^3 - 2x^2 + 4x - 8$, remainder 32 26 ≈−3.85, ≈1.33, ≈3.52 27 1
28 512w^9 + 6912w^8 + 41,472w^7 + 145,152w^6
29 a RRR, RRL, RLR, LRR, LLR, LRL, RLL, LLL
b RRRR, RRRL, RRLR, RLRR, LRRR, RRLL, RLRL,

RLLR, LLRR, LRLR, LRRL, LLLR, LLRL, LRLL, RLLL, LLLL c The numbers of ways in which he can reach the various junctions are the same as the numbers in Pascal's triangle, and the number of ways in which he can reach the nth level is the sum of the numbers in the (n − 1)th row of Pascal's triangle—that is, 2^{n-1}.
30 x = −2 or x = −1 31 a $V = x^3 + 9x^2 + 27x + 27$
b ≈1.64 32 5040 33 32x^5 + 40x^4y + 20x^3y^2 + 5x^2y^3 + $\frac{5}{8}xy^4$ + $\frac{1}{32}y^5$ 35 $(x + 2y)(x + 4)(x - 4)$
37 $(x - 2y)(x + 2y + 3)$ 39 $(x^2 - 6)(x + 2)$ 40 a 21
b 95 41 0 43 5^{20}
44 $0 = (1 - 1)^n$
$= [C(n, 0)](1^n) + [C(n, 1)](1^{n-1})(-1)$
$\quad + [C(n, 2)](1^{n-2})(-1)^2 + \ldots + [C(n, n)](-1)^n$
$= C(n, 0) - C(n, 1) + C(n, 2) + \ldots + (-1)^n[C(n, n)]$

45 $C(n, r) = \dfrac{n!}{(n - r)!r!} = \dfrac{n!}{r!(n - r)!} = \dfrac{n!}{[n - (n - r)]!(n - r)!}$
$= C(n, n - r)$

46 a The numbers in each row (after the first) describe the arrangement of numbers in the preceding row. For example, the third row is one 2 and one 1 so the fourth row is 1211. The next three rows are
1113213211
31131211131221
13211311123113112211 b 3 47 6x^5

9.6 Standard Deviation and Chebyshev's Theorem

Problem Set

1 41 2 a 0.75 SD b −2.5 SD 3 a 11.51% b 0.82%
4 a 25 b 5 5 ≈43.29; ≈16.92 6 43; 50; 57; 32.5
7 95 8 a ≈88.89% b Cannot be determined (To use Chebyshev's theorem, k must be greater than 1.)
9 ≈42% 10 $\frac{\sqrt{10}}{2}$, or ≈1.581 11 ≈77.45% 12 ≈0.03

Review Problems

1 Answers will vary. Possible answer: ≈−4.5, ≈2.3, ≈6.5 3 $(((-3)x - 4)x + 1)x + 7$ 4 16 5 Quotient: $4x^3 + 6x^2 + 19x + 49$; remainder: 132 7 ≈37.26 8 Yes
9 $f(x) = x^3 - 2x^2 - 11x + 12$ 11 $f(x) = x^2 - 6x + 2$
13 $f(x) = 12x^3 + 67x^2 - 32x - 12$ 15 Answers will vary. Possible answer: −3; 8 16 ±1, ±5, ±$\frac{1}{2}$, ±$\frac{5}{2}$; −5, $1 - \sqrt{2}$, $\frac{1}{2}$, $1 + \sqrt{2}$ 17 4 19 $x^4 - 4x^3y + 6x^2y^2 + 4xy^3 + y^4$ 20 ≈4.11 21 Since the coefficients and constant are positive, each term will be positive for any positive value of x. No set of positive numbers has a sum of 0, so there is no positive value of x for which P(x) = 0. 22 95 23 a 3 b 1 (multiplicity 3) 24 −4
25 20; 43.25; ≈6.58 26 a $x^4 - 2x^3 + 4x^2 - 8x + 16$
b Yes 27 19,683x^9 + 295,245x^8y + 1,968,300x^7y^2 + 7,654,500x^6y^3 28 −1, 1, −i, i 29 84% 30 4

10.1 Multiplying and Dividing Rational Expressions

Warm-up Exercises

1 Yes **2** No **3** Yes **4** No **5** Yes **6** Yes **7** Yes **8** Yes
9 $\frac{b}{a}$; $a \neq 0$, $b \neq 0$ **10** $x^2 - 12x + 35$; $x \neq -2$

Problem Set

11 $\frac{4}{5}$ **13** -1; $y \neq x$ **15** $(x + 5)^2$; $x \neq -5$ **16** $\{x : x \neq 0$,
$x \neq -2, x \neq -4\}$ **17** yz; $x \neq 0$, $y \neq 0$ **19** $\frac{x}{2y}$; $y \neq 0$

21

Expressions	GCF	LCM
4, 6, 8	2	24
9, 12, 6	3	36
$4x^2$, $6xy$, $2x^2y$	$2x$	$12x^2y$
$x(x - 2)$, $4(x - 2)$	$x - 2$	$4x(x - 2)$

23 $x^2 - 3x$; $x \neq 0$ **25** $\frac{2(x + 4)(x + 2)}{x^2 + 4}$; $x \neq 0$, $x \neq 2i$,
$x \neq -2i$ **26** 1; $x \neq 2$, $x \neq -5$, $x \neq -3$ **27** $\frac{x^2 - 25}{(x + 4)^2}$;
$x \neq 4$, $x \neq -4$, $x \neq 5$, $x \neq -5$ **28** $x + 5$
29 $\frac{(x^2 + 4)(x - 5)}{x + 2}$; $x \neq -5$, $x \neq -2$ **30 a** 0 **b** 0

c Undefined **d** Undefined **e** $\frac{-8}{5}$ **31 a** $\{x : x \neq -1$,
$x \neq -2\}$ **b** $\{x : x \neq -1, x \neq -2\}$ **32 a** 5 **b** 3 **c** ±2
33 a True **b** False **c** True **34** $\frac{18}{15}$ **35** $x = 4$ or
$x = -3$ **36** $x = 2$, $x = 4$ **37** Numerator is ten more
than denominator. **38** $8x^3 + 36x^2y + 54xy^2 + 27y^3$
39 $x = -4$ **40** $h = x - 2$ **41** $\frac{x + 4}{x - 5}$ **42** $\frac{x^2 - 4}{x^2 + 2x + 3}$;
$x \neq -1 + \sqrt{2}i$, $x \neq -1 - \sqrt{2}i$ **43** $8\frac{4}{7}$ min **44** g is
defined at $x = -2$, but f is not.
45 $x^6 + 6x^4 + 15x^2 + 20 + \frac{15}{x^2} + \frac{6}{x^4} + \frac{1}{x^6}$ **46** $x + 2$;
$x \neq -3y$ **47** $x \approx -2.81$, $x \approx 2.34$, $x \approx -0.75$ **49** 23

10.2 Rational Equations and Inequalities

Warm-up Exercises

1 42 **2** xy **3** xy **4** $x^2 - 1$ **5** $x = 2 \pm \sqrt{7}$ **6** $x = \frac{5}{4}$,
$x = -4$ **7** $-2, \frac{3}{2}, -\frac{1}{3}$ **8 a** 3 hr **b** 1 hr **c** 5 hr **d** $3\frac{3}{4}$
hr **e** $2\frac{1}{7}$ hr **9** $-\frac{5}{4} < x < -1$
10 ⟵————○——○————⟶
               3   5

Problem Set

11 $x = -4$ or $x = 3$ **13** $x = -3$ **15** $x = 6$ or $x = -4$
17 $x \neq 8$ **19** $x = 0$ **20** $a = \frac{3x}{4}$ **21** -2 **23** $\frac{-(x - 5)}{(9 - x^2)}$;
$x \neq \pm3$, $x \neq \pm2$ **25 a** $\frac{1}{10}$ **b** $\frac{1}{20}$ **c** $\frac{1}{x}$ **27** $x = \frac{7}{2}$ or
$x = -1$ **29** $x = 9$ **30** $-12, 3$ **31** $\frac{1}{3}$; $x \neq 0$, $x \neq 5$
33 $x > 12$ **35** $x \geq -3$; $x \neq 0$ **36 a** $\frac{7}{24}$ **b** $\frac{7}{12}$ **c** $\frac{7}{8}$

37 $\frac{2x^4}{x^2 + 3}$; $x \neq 0$, $x \neq \sqrt{3}i$, $x \neq -\sqrt{3}i$
39 ⟵——●————○——————●——⟶ $-4 \leq x < -1$ or $x \geq 3$
        -4 -1 3

41 ⟵——○————————○——⟶ $-5 < x < 0$
        -5 0

42 $x = 13$ **43** $1\frac{13}{47}$ hr **44** $p = \frac{A}{1 + rt}$ **45** -7 **46** 1,
$-2, \pm i\sqrt{3}$ **47** 6 or -2 **49** No real solution **50** $-2, 1,$
$-2 \pm i\sqrt{3}$ **51 a** 15 **b** 27 **52 a** $(1, 2)$ **b** $(a, a^2 + 1)$
c $m = a + 1$ **53** $x = a - 6$ **55** $x = a^2 + 3a + 9$
56 $\left\{a : a \neq 0, a \neq \frac{2}{3}\right\}$ **57 a** 100 min **b** Page 201
58 -4 and -5 **59 a** $\frac{x + 1}{x - 1}$; $x \neq 0$, $x \neq 1$ **b** $\frac{x - 1}{x - 3}$;
$x \neq 2$, $x \neq 3$ **c** $\frac{3x + 1}{3x - 1}$; $x \neq 0$, $x \neq \frac{1}{3}$ **60 a** $f(x) =$
$x - 3$ **b** [graph] **61** 14 (Technically this has

no solution, since by definition f is not a polynomial
function but a rational function.)

10.3 Adding and Subtracting Rational Expressions with Like Denominators

Warm-up Exercises

1 a ii **b** iv **c** i **d** iii **2** $\frac{6}{5}$ **3** 5 **4** $\frac{x - 1}{y}$; $y \neq 0$ **5** $5x$
6 $\frac{15}{x}$; $x \neq 0$ **7** x **8** $x = 8$ **9** -5; $x \neq 5$

Problem Set

10 $\frac{3}{5}$ **11** $x = 4$ **13** $\frac{4 + x}{3x}$; $x \neq 0$ **15** $y = 2$ **17** $x = -\frac{3}{a}$
19 a $\frac{x + 2}{x - 2}$ **b** 6 **21** -1; $x \neq \frac{3}{2}$ **23** $\frac{3}{2}$ **24 a** x^5 **b** x^5;
$x \neq 0$ **c** x^5; $x \neq 0$ **25 a** $x - 1$; $x \neq -3$ **b** $\frac{x^2 - 2x + 3}{x + 3}$;
$x \neq -3$ **26 a** 28 **b** $x(x^2 - 1)$ **c** $x^2 - 1$ **27 a** $\frac{x - 1}{x^2 + 1}$;
$x \neq i$, $x \neq -i$ **b** $x = -1$ **29** $x = -7$ **31** $\frac{4y}{x}$; $x \neq 0$
33 $x = 2$ **35** $\frac{9x + 1}{x^2}$; $x \neq 0$ **36** $x = -\frac{1}{8}$ or $x = -1$
37 $7, -1$ **39** 4 **41** $\frac{x + 3}{x^2 + 3x + 9}$; $x \neq 3$, $x \neq \frac{-3 + 3i\sqrt{3}}{2}$,
$x \neq \frac{-3 - 3i\sqrt{3}}{2}$ **42** $x = \frac{1}{4}$ **43 a** 3, 2
b **45** $(x - 1)(x - 2)$; $x \neq -2$

47 $\frac{x}{x + 7}$; $x \neq -7$ **48** $\approx 49\frac{3}{4}$ min

49 $x > 1$ or $x < -1$

50 $\dfrac{x^2 - 2x + 4}{x(x - 7)}$; $x \neq -2$, $x \neq 0$, $x \neq 7$ **51** $x = -\dfrac{1}{3}$ or

$x = 2$ **52 a** $\dfrac{x + 3}{x^2 + 3x + 9}$; $x \neq -3$, $x \neq \dfrac{-3 \pm 3i\sqrt{3}}{2}$

b $x = 3$ **53** $\dfrac{x - 1}{x + 2}$; $x \neq -1$, $x \neq -2$

59 $\{x : x \neq 0, x \neq -1\}$ **60** Machine A: 12 hr; machine B: 6 hr **61 a** $B(x) = x - 1$ **b** Restrictions are determined by the original expression. **62 a** $a = y$, $b = x$

b $h = \dfrac{h_1 h_2}{h_1 + h_2}$ **63** (3, 3), (3, 4), (3, 5), (4, 3), (5, 3)

10.4 Adding and Subtracting Rational Expressions with Unlike Denominators

Warm-up Exercises

1 48 **2** $x(x - 1)(x + 1)$ **3** 4 **4** x **5** Answers may vary. Possible answer: $x(x - 3)$ **6** Answers may vary. Possible answer: 27 **7** Answers may vary. Possible answer: $x(x - 2)(x - 3)$ **8** Answers may vary. Possible answer: $4(x - 2)(x + 2)$ **9** $\dfrac{x + 3}{x + 1}$; $x \neq -1$, $x \neq 3$

10 $\dfrac{x^2 - 5x + 25}{x(x - 5)}$; $x \neq -5$, $x \neq 0$, $x \neq 5$

Problem Set

11 $\dfrac{3y + 4x}{xy}$ **13** $\dfrac{3x^2 - 8y^2}{2xy}$ **14** A common denominator establishes a needed basis for comparison. **15** $x + 3$; $x \neq 3$ **17** $\dfrac{x^2 + 3x + 9}{x + 3}$; $x \neq 3$, $x \neq -3$ **18** $77\dfrac{1}{3}$

19 $x(x + 1)$ **21** $x^2 y^3$ **23** 12 ft **25** $\dfrac{5x + 2}{x(x - 3)}$; $x \neq 0$,

$x \neq 3$ **26** $\begin{bmatrix} x(x + 1) & x(x - 1) \\ 1 & \dfrac{x + 1}{x - 1} \end{bmatrix}$; $x \neq 0$, $x \neq 1$ **27** No

solution **28** $x^3 + 3x^2 y + 3xy^2 + y^3$ **29** $\dfrac{14x - 2}{(x + 3)(3x - 2)}$;

$x \neq -3$, $x \neq \dfrac{2}{3}$ **31** $\dfrac{10x - 14}{(x + 3)(3x - 2)}$; $x \neq -3$, $x \neq \dfrac{2}{3}$

32 $\dfrac{x^2(x - 1)^2}{(x - 3)(x + 2)^2}$ **33** $\dfrac{6}{5}$ **34** ≈ 8.90 **35** $\dfrac{xy}{x + y}$

37 $x = \pm\dfrac{3}{4}$ **38** $x = \dfrac{x_1 x_2}{x_1 + x_2}$ **39** $-1 < x \leq -\dfrac{1}{2}$ or

$x > 0$ ⟵———○——●——○——— **41** $x = 2a - 3$

42 a $\dfrac{x}{x + 7} = \dfrac{x + 2}{5x - 1}$ **b** $x = \dfrac{7}{2}$ **43** $\dfrac{3(x + 3)}{x(x - 2)}$; $x \neq 0$, $x \neq 2$

45 $\dfrac{7(2x + 1)}{x(x + 1)}$; $x \neq 0$, $x \neq -1$ **47** $x = 3$, $x = \sqrt{2}$

$x = -\sqrt{2}$ **48** $f(x) = 4x + 1$ **49** $3 < x \leq 5$ or

$-5 \leq x < -3$ **51** $x - 2$; $x \neq -5$ **52 a** A(a, a^3), B($-a$,

$-a^3$) **b** a^2 **c** $\{a : a > \sqrt{2}\}$ **53** $\dfrac{2(x^2 + 1)}{x^2 - 1}$; $x \neq 1$, $x \neq -1$

55 $\dfrac{x^2 + 1}{-2x}$; $x \neq 1$, $x \neq -1$

56

57 $\dfrac{-3}{x(x + 3)}$; $x \neq 0$, $x \neq -3$

10.5 Complex Fractions

Warm-up Exercises

1 $\dfrac{3}{2}$ **2** $\dfrac{b}{a}$ **3** $\dfrac{4}{15}$ **4** 3 **5** 2 **6** 3 **7** $\dfrac{3}{2}$ **8** $5x$

9 $(x - 2)(x + 2)$ **10** $x(x - 3)$

Problem Set

11 $\dfrac{x + 1}{x - 1}$; $x \neq 0$, $x \neq 1$ **13** $2x + 1$; $x \neq -1$ **15** $x \neq 0$,

$x \neq -2$, $x \neq -1$ **16 a** $\dfrac{6}{5}x$ **b** $x > 0$ **17** $-3x$; $x \neq 0$,

$x \neq 3$ **18** $\dfrac{3x - 5}{3x - 7}$; $x \neq 2$, $x \neq \dfrac{7}{3}$ **19** $\dfrac{-2x - 1}{4x}$; $x \neq 0$

21 a $\dfrac{24}{7}$ **b** $\dfrac{36}{13}$ **c** $\dfrac{240}{77}$ **23** $\dfrac{11}{2(x + 1)}$; $x \neq -1$ **24** $-\dfrac{1}{117}$

25 $\dfrac{y + x}{y - x}$; $x \neq 0$, $y \neq 0$, $x \neq y$ **27** $\dfrac{2x}{10 + x}$; $x \neq 0$,

$x \neq \pm 10$ **28 a** $f = \dfrac{d_o d_i}{d_o + d_i}$ **b** $d_i = \dfrac{f d_o}{d_o - f}$; $d_o \neq f$

29 $x \leq -3$, $0 < x \leq 3$, or $x > 6$ ⟵●——○——●——○⟶
$\qquad\qquad\qquad\qquad\qquad\quad$ −3 $\quad$ 0 $\quad$ 3 $\quad$ 6

31 $m = \dfrac{-1}{(x + 2)(x - 3)}$ **32** $\dfrac{(x + 3)^2}{(x + 2)(x + 4)}$; $x \neq 1$, $x \neq -2$,

$x \neq -3$, $x \neq -4$ **33** $x = -1$ **34** $\dfrac{11x + 6}{3x + 2}$; $x \neq 0$,

$x \neq \dfrac{-2}{3}$ **35** $\dfrac{3}{7}$ **36** $-\dfrac{1}{3}$; $x \neq -3$, $x \neq -\dfrac{3}{2}$ **37** $\dfrac{2x + 6}{3x}$;

$x \neq 0$, $x \neq -2$ **39** $\dfrac{4x}{x + 1}$; $x \neq \pm 1$, $x \neq 0$ **41** $\dfrac{2}{3}$

42 a $\dfrac{11}{30}$, $\dfrac{11}{15}$ **b** $2\dfrac{8}{11}$ hr **43** sc; $c \neq 0$ **44 a** $\dfrac{x}{2x + 1}$;

$x \neq -1$, $x \neq -\dfrac{1}{2}$ **b** $\begin{bmatrix} 1 & 0 \\ 2 & 1 \end{bmatrix}$ **c** $\dfrac{x}{3x + 1}$; $x \neq -\dfrac{1}{2}$, $x \neq -\dfrac{1}{3}$,

$x \neq -1$ **d** $\begin{bmatrix} 1 & 0 \\ 3 & 1 \end{bmatrix}$ **e** $\dfrac{x}{4x + 1}$; $x \neq -\dfrac{1}{3}$, $x \neq -\dfrac{1}{4}$, $x \neq -\dfrac{1}{2}$

$x \neq -1$ **f** $\begin{bmatrix} 1 & 0 \\ 4 & 1 \end{bmatrix}$ **45** $\dfrac{-10}{x(x + h)}$; $0 < x < h$, $h > 0$

46 a $A = 1$; $B = -2$; $C = 5$ **b** $A = 5$; $B = 1$ **c** $A = 2$;

$B = 1$ **47** $\dfrac{-4}{x(x + h)}$; $x \neq 0$, $h \neq 0$, $x \neq -h$ **48** 20 **49** 0

51

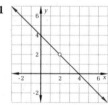

52 a $f(x)$ approaches $\dfrac{1}{2}$. **b** $f(x)$

approaches $\dfrac{5}{2}$. **53 a** $n = 3$; n must be positive. **b** 3

Review Problems

1 b, c, d, e, f 3 $5x - 7$; $x \neq -\frac{7}{5}$ **5** $\frac{1}{x-3}$; $x \neq -3$,

$x \neq 3$ **7** $\frac{13}{19}$ **9** $\frac{13}{19}$ **10 a** $\frac{x+2}{x}$ **b** 2 **11** Greatest
common factor: $3(x + 4)$; $x - 7$; $x + 3$ Least common
multiple: $6(x + 4)(x - 2)$; $3(x + 7)(x - 7)$; $x(x + 3)^2$
13 $y = 0$ or $y = 2$ **15** $y = 0$ **17** No solution
18 $(x + 2)^4$; $x \neq -3$, $x \neq 1$, $x \neq -1$, $x \neq 2$ **19** 4 and
-5 **21** $\frac{x^2 + 3}{x}$; $x \neq 0$ **23** $-\frac{4}{3}$ **25** 1; $x \neq \frac{2}{3}$ **27** $\frac{x+1}{x-1}$;
$x \neq 0$, $x \neq 1$, $x \neq -2$

29

30 $h = x - 2$ **31** $\frac{2x}{(x+y)(x-y)}$; $x \neq y$, $x \neq -y$

33 $\frac{x^2 - 2xy - y^2}{x^2 - y^2}$; $x \neq \pm y$ **34** $x = 5$ **35** $(x, y, z) =$
$(6, -4, 3)$ **36** $4, \frac{3 \pm i\sqrt{7}}{2}$ **37** $\frac{x-2}{x-1}$; $x \neq \pm 1$, $x \neq -4$

38 $\frac{-x}{x+3}$; $x \neq \frac{2}{3}$, $x \neq -3$ **39** $-1, \sqrt{2}$, or $-\sqrt{2}$

40 $-3 < x < 3$, $3 < x \leq 4$, **41** $x = -5$ or $x = 3$

43 $x = 4$ or $x = 7$ **45** $\frac{1}{y}$ **47** $\frac{x+7}{18x+5}$; $x \neq \frac{1}{3}$, $x \neq -\frac{5}{18}$

48 $\frac{1}{s^2c^2}$; $s \neq 0$, $c \neq 0$ **49** $b = 4$; $c = -6$ **50** $\frac{x+6}{x-6}$;
$x \neq 3$, $x \neq 6$ **51 a** $13,000 at 10%; $7,000 at 9%
b Answers will vary. Such considerations as maturity
time, bond security, and bond rating could guide Mr.
Vestor's decision. **52 a** 33 or more **b** No

Linear Programming

Problem Set

1

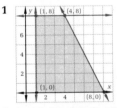

2 a $(0, 105)$; $(15, 105)$;

$(105, 15)$; $(30, 15)$; $(0, 75)$ **b** 345 **3** $(8, -10)$

4 $\frac{x}{12} + \frac{y}{10} \leq 55$, where x = the number of widgets
produced per week and y = the number of gimcracks
produced per week. **5 a** 60 **b** -20 **6** Maximum: 250;
minimum: -625

7 a $\begin{cases} x \geq 0 \\ y \geq 0 \\ 12x + 6y \leq 120 \\ 9x + 18y \leq 144 \end{cases}$ **b** $130x + 90y$ **c** $1400

---

d 8 bracelets, 4 necklaces

8

$(0, 0)$, $(0, 3)$, $(4, 11)$,
$(6, 11)$, $(6, 4)$

9 60 tape players, 140 CD players **10** 153; 52.5
11 $2700 **12** $41

11.1 Definitions and Graphs of the Exponential and Logarithmic Functions

Warm-up Exercises

1 Exponent **2** $\log_x z = y$ **3** $m^w = n$ **4 a** $w = 216$
b $w = 125$ **c** $w = \frac{1}{8}$ **5** $\frac{2}{5}$

6 a

x	0	1	2	3	4	-1	-2
10^x	1	10	100	1000	10,000	0.1	0.01

-3	-4
0.001	0.0001

b

x	1	10	100	1000	10,000	0.1	0.01
$\log_{10} x$	0	1	2	3	4	-1	-2

0.001	0.0001
-3	-4

Problem Set

7 a 16 **b** 4 **8 a** 1 **b** 0 **9 a** 8 **b** 1000 **c** 81 **10 a** 8
b 3 **c** -4 **11 a** 3 **b** $125^5 = 30,517,578,125$ **c** 5
12 a 5 **b** 2 **c** 16,777,216 **d** No real solution

13 a

x	0	1	2	3	-1	-2	-3	5	-4
2^x	1	2	4	8	$\frac{1}{2}$	$\frac{1}{4}$	$\frac{1}{8}$	32	$\frac{1}{16}$

b

x	1	2	4	8	$\frac{1}{2}$	$\frac{1}{4}$	$\frac{1}{8}$	32	$\frac{1}{16}$
$\log_2 x$	0	1	2	3	-1	-2	-3	5	-4

14 a 9^6 **b** 27^4 **c** 81^3 **15 a** $\frac{1}{3}$ **b** -3 **c** $-\frac{1}{3}$ **16** 2^{10n-1}

17 a

b $y = x$ **19** -1 **21** No real

value **23** $\log_3\left(\frac{1}{81}\right) = -4$ **25** $\log_2 363 = n$ **26** 10

27 $\frac{14 + 5\sqrt{3}}{11}$ **28** -4 is not a solution, since a base
cannot be negative. **29 a** 6 **b** 6 **c** 2 **d** 2 **30 a** iv
b i **c** iii **d** ii **31 a** 3 **b** 3 **c** $\sqrt{6} \approx 2.4495$

32 $\log_5 78,125 = 7$ **33** $x = \frac{-3 + 2\sqrt{3}}{3}$

34 a   **b**

35 a,b,c   **36** ≈ 0.861

37 a Domain: positive reals; Range: reals **b** Domain: reals; Range: positive reals **c** Domain: nonzero reals; Range: reals **38**   **39** c **40** $\frac{3}{2}$

41   **42 a**

b Because $g(x) = \text{INV}f(x)$ **43 a** No x-intercept; y-intercept: (0, 1); horizontal asymptote: $y = 0$ **b** No y-intercept; x-intercept: (1, 0); vertical asymptote: $x = 0$

44 a   **b**

c   **45** $x \approx 40.32$

11.2 Two Important Exponential and Logarithmic Functions

Warm-up Exercises

1 c, a, d, b **2 a** 3 **b** 3 **c** 3 **3 a** 0 **b** 0 **c** 0 **d** 0 **4** 4
5 -4 **6** $\frac{1}{2}$ **7** 5 **8** ≈ -3.8041 **9** ≈ 2.5478
10 ≈ -6.5023 **11** ≈ 3.9778 **12** 60 db

13 a ≈ 1.4314 **b** ≈ 0.4771 **c** ≈ -0.4771 **d** ≈ -1.4314
e ≈ 0.9542 **f** 0 **g** ≈ -0.9542 **14 a** $x \approx 3.9120$
b $x \approx 1.6990$ **c** $x \approx 403.4288$ **d** $x = 1,000,000$
15 a No solution **b** $y \approx 0.0024788$ **16 a** 5:1 **b** 25:1
c ≈ 1.8:1 **17** $x = 1$ **18** $b = \frac{1}{4}$ **19** 73 **20 a** ≈ 1.90849
b ≈ 1.90849 **c** ≈ 1.90849 **d** ≈ 1.90849 **21** ≈ 8.758
22 ≈ 63.9 yr **23** $\frac{2}{5}$ **24** 120 db **25 a** 2 **b** 3 **c** 4 **d** 5
26 a ≈ 1.3802 **b** ≈ 1.3802 **c** ≈ 1.3802 **d** ≈ 1.3802
27 a 4 **b** -4 **c** $\frac{1}{4}$ **28 a** 6 **b** e **c** 0 **29 a** 1
b ≈ 1.3010 **c** ≈ 1.6021 **d** ≈ 1.9031 **30 a** ≈ 10.874
b No real value **c** ≈ 7.051 **d** ≈ -16.811
31 \$16,974.07 **32** \$17,114.23; \$140.16 more
33 a $x \approx 1.8718$ **b** $x \approx 1.6990$ **c** $x = 3$
d $x \approx 3,467,368,505$ **e** $x \approx 14.9821$ **f** $x = 3$
34 a $x \approx 1.1297$ **b** $x = 566\frac{2}{3}$ **35 a** \$16,103.24
b \$16,141.43 **c** \$16,160.11 **d** \$16,160.74 **36** $x = 10^6$
or $x = 10^{-1}$ **37 a** Office: 35 db; street: 70 db
b ≈ 3162.6 times **38** -3 **39 a** $y \approx 1764.006$
b $y \approx 0.0001056$ **c** $y \approx 37.7839$ **d** $y \approx 0.001778$
40 $x = 387,420,489$ or $x \approx 0.00000000258117$
41 $x \approx 6.9078$ **42** $w = 1$ **43** $x \approx 1.386$ **45** $x \approx 3.255$
47 \$12,786.25

11.3 Properties of Logarithms

Warm-up Exercises

1 ≈ 0.7781 **2** ≈ 1.2552 **3** ≈ 1.2219 **4** ≈ 1.8060
5 ≈ 0.07525 **6** ≈ 0.4771 **7 a** iii **b** i **c** v **d** ii **e** iv

Problem Set

8 a 5 **b** 2 **c** 5 **9** (3, 2) **10 a** $\log_2\left(\frac{21}{2}\right)$ **b** $\log_4\left(\frac{125}{2\sqrt{3}}\right)$
c $\log_4\left(\frac{81}{4}\right)$ **d** $\log_2\left(\frac{243}{4}\right)$ **11** d, b, a = c **12** 1
13 $3\log_2 x + \frac{1}{2}\log_2(x - 3) - \log_2 y$ **15** $\ln\left(\sqrt{\frac{x^3}{z}}\right)$
16 $t \approx 39.9$ yr **17** 5 **19** 2 **21** 15 **23** 1 **24** 1
25 $\left[\frac{\log 108}{\log 200}\right]$ **26 a** -2 **b** $-x^{43}$ **c** x^{-8} **27 a** 6 **b** 3
c 2 **d** Yes **28** 16 **29 a** x **b** x **c** No. $g[f(x)]$ has as its domain positive reals. $f[g(x)]$ has all reals as its domain. **30 a** 10,000 **b** $\approx 16,487$ people **c** At
$t \approx 37.6$ **31** $y = \frac{\ln b}{\ln a}$ **32 a** $2c + d$ **b** $-3c$ **c** $4d$
d $2c - 3d$ **33** $\frac{1}{2}\ln(x - 1)$ **34 a** $a + b$ **b** $a + 1$
c $b - 1$ **35 a** ≈ 5.301 **b** ≈ 38.301 **c** ≈ 7.301
d ≈ 472.301 **36** ≈ 132.44 **37** $\ln\left(\frac{x + 1}{3(x - 1)}\right)$
38 $x \approx -1.456$ **39** ≈ 92.4 yr; ≈ 92.4 yr
40 a, b, c   **41** -1 **42** 8

43 a False **b** False **c** True **44** ≈ 73.3

11.4 Solving Exponential and Logarithmic Equations

Warm-up Exercises

1 $x = \frac{3}{2}$ **2** $x = 4$ **3** $x = 7$ **4** $x = 1$ or $x = e$ **5** $x = 2$
6 $\log_2 13 = \frac{\log_5 13}{\log_5 2}$ **7 a** 500 **b** ≈ 1660 **8** 20.25

Problem Set

9 a ≈ 4.8074 **b** ≈ −5.1699 **c** ≈ 3.0244
10 a b ≈ 2.6801 **b** b ≈ −0.2625 **c** b ≈ 2.5119
11 $x = 15$ **13** 6 **14** $\text{Log}_{a^n} x = \frac{\log_a x}{\log_a a^n} = \frac{\log_a x}{n}$ **15** $\frac{3}{4}$
16 a $x \approx 0.1099$ **b** $x \approx 59.1690$ **17** $x = 5$ **18** 10
b 7 **c** 2 **19 a** $x = 4.5$ **b** $x = \frac{a}{2}, a > 0$ **20** 1 **21 a** 2
b 3 **22** $\log_4 10 \approx 1.661$, $\log_5 15 \approx 1.682$, $\log_6 21 \approx 1.699$,
$\log_{10} 55 \approx 1.740$ **23** (≈ 1.54, 12) **24 a** $B_0 = \$1500$
b $B \approx \$4810.70$ **25 a** 10^{1000} **b** 1001 **26** $x = 2$ or
$x = -2$ **27** $x = 6$ or $x = 3$ **28 a** $2\ln x +$
$\ln y - \ln(x + 5)$ **b** $\ln|x| - \frac{1}{2}\ln y$ **29** $x = 2$
30 a ≈ 1.387 **b** ≈ 0.231 **c** ≈ ±0.977g **31 a** 5
b ≈ −0.3466 **c** ≈ 0.2210g **32** $x = 3$ **33 a** 9
b 9 **c** 27 **d** $\frac{1}{27}$ **e** 81 **f** Impossible. f is defined for
integers only. **34** $x = 64$ **35 a** $x = 256$ or
$x = 4^{-4} \approx 0.003906$ **b** $x = 4^{16} = 4{,}294{,}967{,}296$ or
$x = 0.25$ **36** $b = 2$ **37** $x = 10^4$ or $x = 1$ **38 a** $(0, e^3)$
b $(1, e^4)$

11.5 Applications of Exponential and Logarithmic Functions

Warm-up Exercises

1 7.1 **2 a** $k \approx 0.0000423$ **b** ≈ 5.8 lb/in.²
3 a $k \approx 0.0001238$ **b** ≈ 9727 yr old **4 a** Yes **b** ≈ 78°

Problem Set

5 ≈ 4.7 **6** About 4.3 lb/in.² **7** ≈ 3752
8 a $S \approx 10{,}000(10^{-0.1w})$ **b** ≈ 15,849 **9** $3\sqrt{2} + 3$
10 $k \approx 0.3143$ **11 a** Yes **b** \$266.77 **12 a** $x = \pm\sqrt{2}$
b $x = 0$ **c** $x = \pm 2$ **d** No real solutions **13** About
2.77 yr **14** $x^2 + 6x + 4$ **15** $x^2 + 2xy + y^2 - 9$ **16** 12
17 a $I_0 = 11{,}000$; $k \approx 0.09$ **b** ≈ 756,000 items
18 About 6 min 47 sec **19 a** ≈ 11.61 watts **b** ≈ 173.3
days **c** ≈ 402.4 days **20 a** 4.95 **b** 4.95 **c** 4.95

21 a

stop	1	2	3	4	5
n	1.4	2	2.8	4	5.6
$\log n$	≈ 0.146	≈ 0.301	≈ 0.447	≈ 0.602	≈ 0.748

6	7	8	9
8	11	16	22
≈ 0.903	≈ 1.041	≈ 1.204	≈ 1.342

b Yes **22** ≈ 0.9094 **23** $x = -1$ or
$x = -\log 2 \approx -0.3010$ **24** About 2,864,129 people
25 (≈ 0.5183, ≈ 0.0218)

11.6 Binomials and Binomial Distributions

Problem Set

1 a $0.2401W^4 + 0.4116W^3L^2 + 0.2646W^2L^2 +$
$0.0756WL^3 + 0.0081L^4$ **b** .2646 **2** ≈ .058 **3** 82 **4** $\frac{135}{4096}$
5 $\frac{20}{39}$, or ≈ .51 **6 a** $\frac{80}{243}$ **b** $\frac{112}{243}$ **7 a** .59049 **b** .32825
c .00856 **d** .99144 **8 a** ≈ .0112 **b** ≈ .0705 **9 a** 162
b ≈ 8.05 **10 a** ≈ 8.2718 × 10^{-25} **b** 40 **c** ≈ 4.47
d ≈ 86.43%

Review Problems

1 $3^4 = 81$ **3** $a^t = a^t$ **5** $x = -3$ **7 a** 8 **b** 6:1 **c** 36:1
d 2:1 **8 a** ≈ 1.135 **b** ≈ 1.135 **9** ≈ 5.792 **10 a** False
b True **c** False **d** True **e** False **11 a** $x = -6$ or
$x = 1$ **b** $x = 0$ **c** $x = e$ or $x \approx 0.0025$ **12** About
162.3 g **13** 4 **14** $\frac{112}{6561}$ **15 a** ≈ 2.698970 **b** ≈ 0.698970
c ≈ −1.301030 **d** ≈ 1.698970 **e** ≈ −0.301030
16 a ≈ 0.778 **b** ≈ 0.778 **c** ≈ 0.778 **d** ≈ 0.778
e ≈ 0.778 **17** \$19,863.49 **18** 20 mo

19 a

Number of heads	0	1	2	3	4	5
Probability	$\frac{32}{3125}$	$\frac{48}{625}$	$\frac{144}{625}$	$\frac{216}{625}$	$\frac{162}{625}$	$\frac{243}{3125}$

b

20 116 **21** ≈ 88.2°F

22 a

x	1	2	4	8	64	$\frac{1}{2}$	$\frac{1}{4}$	16	$\frac{1}{8}$
$\log_2 x$	0	1	2	3	6	−1	−2	4	−3

b

x	0	1	2	3	−2	−1	−3	4	−6
2^x	1	2	4	8	$\frac{1}{4}$	$\frac{1}{2}$	$\frac{1}{8}$	16	$\frac{1}{64}$

23 $x = 2$ **24** Between 4.137 lb/in.² and 3.349 lb/in.²
25 a 12 **b** ≈ .005 **26 a**

b

27 $w \approx -4.65988$ **28** ≈ 46.3

29 $x = 16$ or $x = \frac{1}{16}$ **30** ≈ 53.2 yr **31** $\frac{35}{128}$

32 About 22 wk **33 a** ≈ 3.57794 **34 a** $\ln\left(\frac{\pi x^3}{(x-2)^2}\right)$
b $\ln\left(\frac{\sqrt{xy}}{x-5}\right)$ **35 a** 2 **b** ≈ 3.419 **c** No solution
36 ≈ 126

12.1 Systematic Counting

Warm-up Exercises

1 Combinations **2** Permutations **3** Neither **4** 90
5 1365 **6** Answers will vary; yes **7** 180 **8** 5040

Problem Set

9 a 792 **b** 3,991,680 **10** 8 **11** 120 **12** 5040 **13** 1
14 a 120 **b** 120 **c** 105 **d** 105 **e** 3060 **f** 3060
15 362,880 **16** 6 **17 a** 5 **b** 2 **c** 1 **d** 3 **18** 3,628,800
19 Combinations **20** Permutations

21 a,b   **22** $\frac{1}{4}$

23 2738 **24** 1024 **25 a** 10,000,000 **b** No **26** 16
27 46 **28** 5148 **29 a** 5 **b** 7 **c** 0 **d** 12 **e** Yes,
because A ∩ B is empty **30** 6 **31** 1,693,440 **32** The
union of A and B includes one element for every
element in A and in B, counting the elements in the
intersection only once. If we then add the number of
elements in the intersection, we include the elements
that are counted twice. **33** 51 **34** Each of the n
elements are either in the subset or not. Therefore,
there are two choices for each element, or
$2 \cdot 2 \cdot 2 \cdot 2 \cdot \ldots \cdot 2 = 2^n$ possible subsets.

12.2 Sample Spaces, Events, and Probability

Warm-up Exercises

1 A is subset of the sample space S, so $0 \le \#(A) \le (S)$.
Therefore, $\frac{0}{\#(S)} \le \frac{\#(A)}{\#(S)} \le \frac{\#(S)}{\#(S)}$, and hence $0 \le P(A) \le 1$.

2 $P(\phi) = \frac{\#(A)}{\#(S)}$. Since $\#(A) = 0$, $\frac{\#(A)}{\#(S)} = \frac{0}{\#(S)} = 0$.
Therefore, $P(\phi) = 0$. **3** The probability of the union of
A and B includes the probability of the elements of A
and B, counting the probability of the elements in the
intersection only once. If we then add the probability
of the elements in the intersection, we include the
probability of the elements that are counted twice.

4 $\frac{33}{66,640}$, or ≈ .0005 **5** $\frac{1}{9}$

6 Answers will
vary. A tree diagram and
a lattice are shown.

7 a
Answers will vary.
A lattice is shown. **b** $\frac{3}{8}$

Problem Set

8 a 36 **b** 11 **9 a** $\frac{3}{7}$ **b** $\frac{6}{35}$ **10** 19 **11 a** 8 **b** 15 **c** 32
d 13 **e** C(n, 1) = n **12** ≈ .4 **13 a** $\frac{2}{\pi}$ **b** 1
14 a ≈ .8396 **b** ≈ .1541 **c** ≈ .0063 **d** 1; one of these
outcomes must occur. **15 a** {1, 2, 3, 4, 5, 7, 9, 16, 25}
b {1} **16 a** ≈ .196 **b** ≈ .035 **17** $\frac{1}{2}$ **18 a** ≈ .17 **b** ≈ .15
19 ≈ .007 **20 a** 25 **b** 15 **c** 14 **d** 26 **e** Yes **21** ≈ .17
22 $\frac{1}{7}$ **23** ≈ .003 **24** 62 **25** ≈ .007 **26 a** {(1, $\sqrt{2}$),
(1, $\sqrt{3}$), (1, 2), (1, $\sqrt{5}$), (1, $\sqrt{6}$) ($\sqrt{2}$, $\sqrt{3}$), ($\sqrt{2}$, 2),
($\sqrt{2}$, $\sqrt{5}$), ($\sqrt{2}$, $\sqrt{6}$), ($\sqrt{3}$, 2), ($\sqrt{3}$, $\sqrt{5}$), ($\sqrt{3}$, $\sqrt{6}$), (2, $\sqrt{5}$)
(2, $\sqrt{6}$), ($\sqrt{5}$, $\sqrt{6}$)} **b** $\frac{3}{5}$ **27** x = $\frac{5}{6}$ **28** .85 **29** $\frac{1}{10}$ **30** 81
31 a 3 **b** 32 **32** $\frac{1}{21}$ **33** ≈ .21

12.3 Probabilities of Unions

Warm-up Exercises

1 a No **b** Yes **2 a** Yes **b** No **c** Yes **3** $\frac{17}{100}$ **4** $\frac{6}{19}$

Problem Set

5 $\frac{3}{4}$ **6** $\frac{15}{51}$, or ≈ .294 **7 a** $\frac{1}{7}$ **b** $\frac{1}{21}$ **c** $\frac{1}{7}$ **d** $\frac{1}{21}$ **8** $\frac{6-\sqrt{3}}{6}$
9 1 **10** ≈ .00058 **11 a** {(1, 1), (1, 2), (1, 3), (1, 4), (1,5),
(1, 6), (2, 1), (2, 2), (2, 3), (2, 4), (2, 5), (2, 6), (3, 1), (3, 2),
(3, 3), (3, 4), (3, 5), (3, 6), (4, 1), (4, 2), (4, 3), (4, 4), (4, 5),
(4, 6), (5, 1), (5, 2), (5, 3), (5, 4), (5, 5), (5, 6), (6, 1), (6, 2),
(6, 3), (6, 4), (6, 5), (6, 6)} **b** {(2, 2), (2, 4), (2, 6), (4, 2),
(4, 4), (4, 6), (6, 2), (6, 4), (6, 6)} **c** $\frac{5}{9}$ **12 a** $\frac{11}{36}$ **b** $\frac{1}{36}$ **c** $\frac{1}{9}$
d 0 **13** No, unless A and B are mutually exclusive
14 ≈ .111 **15** 21 **16 a** $\frac{1}{6}$ **b** $\frac{1}{2}$ **c** $\frac{1}{2}$ **d** $\frac{1}{6}$ **17** ≈ .358
18 a 2 **b** 6 **c** 18 **d** 54 **19 a** −1 + i **b** −1
20 ≈ .1053 **21 a** $\frac{5}{8}$ **b** $\frac{3}{8}$ **22** 10 **23** 4 to 7 **24** ≈ .6
25 .125 **26 a** $\frac{3}{7}$ **b** $4.50 **27** Possible answer: 438,672
28 a $\frac{1}{13}$ **b** $\frac{1}{13}$
c $\frac{2}{13}$ **d** 0 **29 a** ⬭ ⬭ **b** ⬭⬭
30 ≈ .1545 **31 a** 33; 39 **b** 159; 319 **c** 55; 89 **32** $\frac{2}{15}$
33 a 0 **b** 1 **c** 0 **34 a** ≈ .45 **b** ≈ .49 **35** $\frac{1}{2}$ **36 a** 33
b 19 **c** 46 **37** 56

12.4 Probability of Intersections

Warm-up Exercises

1 No **2** Yes **3** No **4** Yes **5** .21 **6** $\frac{1}{52}$, or ≈.02 **7** $\frac{1}{4056}$

Problem Set

8 a Independent **b** Mutually exclusive **c** Dependent
d Mutually exclusive **9** ≈.0005 **10** $\frac{1}{2}$ **11 a** $\frac{1}{16}$ **b** $\frac{5}{32}$
c $\frac{27}{32}$ **d** $\frac{37}{96}$ **12 a** ≈.51 **b** ≈.09 **13** $\frac{1}{18}$ **14 a** 0 **b** 0
c $\frac{1}{6}$ **15** Cannot be determined **16 a** Independent
b Dependent **c** Dependent **17 a** Dependent
b Dependent **18** ≈.0088 **19 a** i or −1 **b** i − 1 or 0
20 a $\frac{1}{2}$ **b** $\frac{2}{3}$ **c** $\frac{3}{4}$ **d** $\frac{4}{5}$ **e** $\frac{5}{6}$ **f** $\frac{99}{100}$ **21 a** ≈.044
b ≈.042 **c** ≈.995 **22** Only if A and B are
independent **23** 60% **24 a** 3; $3\sqrt{3}$; 60 **b** $\frac{1}{2}$; $\frac{\sqrt{3}}{2}$; 60
25 .9775 **26** .5 **27** ≈.03 **28** ≈.17 **29** No; P(red) +
P(green) + P (blue) must be equal to 1. **30** 1 **31** ≈.39

12.5 Interpreting Probabilities

Warm-up Exercises

1 Answers will vary. Possible answer: Conduct the poll using students from different schools. **2** Answers will vary. Possible answer: Write a computer program that randomly generates the numbers from 1 through 6, inclusive. The program should be able to keep a running total of the numbers. If the total exceeds 30, the program should acknowledge a failure and try again. **3** Answers will vary. Possible answer: The poll could have been conducted from a very small sample of doctors.

Problem Set

4 Answers will vary. Possible answer: At least approximately half of the preceding year's graduating class was doing well in college. **5 a** $\frac{1}{5}$ **b** $\frac{1}{5}$ **c** 0
6 a Answers will vary. **b** 2 heads and 2 tails **c** No; probability indicates only the relative likelihood of an outcome. **7** Answers will vary. Possible answer: The time span over which the survey was conducted may have been too short to include enough students. **8** 70
9 Answers will vary. Possible answer: Gather inventory data from stores that distribute the product.
10 $\frac{3}{13}$ **11** Answers will vary. Possible answer: Distribute surveys to high school and college literature teachers who will distribute the surveys to their classes. **12 a** 0 **b** 3 **c** 15 **d** 24 **e** $k^2 - 1$ **f** $k^2 + 2k$
13 $\frac{2}{9}$ **14** 3 **15 a** ≈.007 **b** ≈.098 **c** ≈.39 **16** $\frac{4}{7}$
17 Possible answer: No, the margin of error was not significantly increased by retaking the test.
18 Possible answer: Based on similar previous conditions, it will probably rain over 30% of the listening area. **19** d **20** 5 **21** ≈.74 **22** ≈.18
23 Answers will vary.

Review Problems

1 a 120 **b** 24 **c** 6 **d** 2 **e** 1 **f** 1
2 a,b **c** 4 **3 a** {1, 2, 3, 4, 5, 6} **b** $\frac{1}{2}$
c $\frac{1}{3}$ **d** $\frac{2}{3}$ **e** $\frac{1}{6}$ **f** $\frac{5}{6}$ **g** $\frac{5}{6}$ **4 a**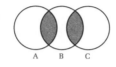
b **5** 27,600 **6 a** $\frac{1}{36}$ **b** $\frac{1}{6}$ **c** $\frac{1}{6}$ **d** 0
e 0 **f** $\frac{1}{36}$ **7 a** $\frac{1}{5}$ **b** $\frac{8}{15}$ **c** $\frac{2}{3}$ **d** $\frac{1}{15}$ **e** Yes **8** 2,118,760
9 $\frac{1}{2}$ **10** 1 **11** $\frac{7}{26}$ **12** .8 **13** Answers will vary. **14** $\frac{1}{4}$
15 a {3, 5, 6, 7, 9, 11, 12} **b** {3, 9} **c** 7 **d** 2 **e** 9
16 5,527,200 **17** 4 **18** $\frac{1}{2}$ **19 a** {($1, $1), ($1, $2),
($1, $3), ($2, $1), ($2, $2), ($2, $3), ($3, $1), ($3, $2), ($3, $3), ($4, $1), ($4, $2), ($4, $3)} **b** $2, $3, $4, $5, $6, $7
20 a $\frac{1}{4}$ **b** 1 **21** ≈.97 **22** 30 **23** $\frac{3}{55}$, or ≈.05
24 ≈.009 **25** 128 **26** $\frac{23}{45}$, or ≈.51

13.1 Sequences

Warm-up Exercises

1 −5, −3, −1, 1, 3, 5 **2** 0, 3, 8, 15, 24, 35 **3** 2, 3, 5, 7, 11, 13 **4** 2, 6, 14, 30, 62 **5** −4 **6** $\frac{1}{2}, \frac{1}{8}, \frac{1}{32}, \frac{1}{128}, \frac{1}{512}$
7 24, 48, 96, 192, 384 **8** 10, 15, 21, 28, 36 **9** 8, 15, 24, 35, 48

Problem Set

10 15, 21, 28, 36 **11** $4n$ **13** 40, 80, 160, 320, 640
14 ≈1.3333, ≈1.4762, ≈1.4975 **15** 55 **17** 85
18 a $24.99, $24.96, $24.91 **b** $74.86 **19** $\frac{1}{2}, \frac{2}{3}, \frac{3}{4}, \frac{4}{5}, \frac{5}{6}$
21 a 81 **b** 9th **22 a** 1, 6, 18, 40 **b** 1, 7, 25, 65 **23** 20
24 a $A(t) = 100 - t^2$ **b** 99, 96, 91, 84, 75, 64, 51, 36, 19
25 a $\sqrt{2}, \sqrt{5}, \sqrt{10}, \sqrt{17}$ **b** $\sqrt{26}, \sqrt{37}, \sqrt{50}$ **26** $j = 3$
27 $a_1 = 1, a_{n+1} = 3$ **28** $a_1 = 30\text{kg}; a_2 = 20\text{kg};$
$a_3 = 15\text{kg}; a_4 = 12\text{kg};$ **29 a** $A_1 = 64, A_n = \frac{A_{n-1}}{4}$

b $A_n = \frac{64}{4^{n-1}}$ **c** $A_{25} = \frac{64}{4^{24}} \approx 2.27 \times 10^{-13}\text{cm}^2$ **30** $1060, $1123.60, $1191.02, $1262.48, $1338.23

31

n	1	2	3	4	5
A	$262{,}144\sqrt{3}$	$65{,}536\sqrt{3}$	$16{,}384\sqrt{3}$	$4096\sqrt{3}$	$1024\sqrt{3}$

6	7	8
$256\sqrt{3}$	$64\sqrt{3}$	$16\sqrt{3}$

32 a $a_1 = 11$, $a_{n+1} = 10a_n - 9$ **b** $\{a_n\} = \{10^n + 1\}$

33 1, 3, 3, 1, $\frac{1}{3}$ **35** $5n(-1)^{n+1}$ **36** Answers will vary.

Possible answers: $\{a_n\} = \{2n + 2\}$: $a_1 = 4$, $a_{n+1} = a_n + 2$

37 a 0.3, 0.03, 0.003, 0.0003, 0.00003, 0.000003

b $s_1 = 0.3$; $s_2 = 0.33$; $s_3 = 0.333$; $s_4 = 0.3333$;

$s_5 = 0.33333$; $s_6 = 0.333333$ **c** $\frac{1}{3}$ **38** Answers will vary.

Possible answer: $a_1 = 1$, $a_{n+1} = a_n + 7$, 22 **39** $a_1 = 1$;

$a_2 = 3$; $a_3 = 7$; $a_4 = 15$; $a_5 = 31$; $a_n = 2^n - 1$, $n = 1, 2, 3, \ldots$

13.2 Series

Warm-up Exercises

1 $\sum_{n=1}^{4} n!$; 33 **2 a** 6, 12, 18, 24, 30 **b** 90 **3** 2, 7, 15, 26, 40 **4** 60 **5** 100 **6** $\{a_n\} = \{2n + 1\}$: 3, 5, 7, 9, 11

7 $2n - 1$

Problem Set

9 108 **11** log 120, or ≈ 2.08 **13** 1, -1, 1, -1, 1

14 a 385 **b** 505 **c** 649 **d** Added terms.

$\sum_{n=1}^{11}(n+1)^2 = \sum_{n=2}^{12} n^2 = 505 + 12^2 = 649$ **15** 34

16 Number of dots in the nth figure $= \frac{n(3n-1)}{2}$

17 110 **19** 6.6666 **21** $x = -3$ **22 a** $\frac{\sqrt{3}}{4}$, $\sqrt{3}$, $\frac{9\sqrt{3}}{4}$, $4\sqrt{3}$, **b** $\frac{15}{2}\sqrt{3}$ **23** $\approx 0.\overline{7}$ **24** 0, 2, 7, 26, 123 **25** 2.0

27 5, 3, -7 **28 a** $a_1 = 1$, $a_2 = \frac{1}{\sqrt{3}}$, $a_3 = \frac{1}{3}$, $a_4 = \frac{1}{3\sqrt{3}}$

b $\sum_{n=1}^{\infty} a_n = AB$ **29 a** $a_1 \approx 27.713$, $a_2 \approx 6.928$,

$a_3 \approx 1.732$, $a_4 \approx 0.433$, $a_5 \approx 0.108$ **b** $S_5 \approx 36.914$

31 log 604,800, or ≈ 5.78 **33** No sum **35** No sum

37 0 **38** Recursive: $a_1 = 5$, $a_n = a_{n-1} + 5$, $n = 2, 3, \ldots$; Closed: $a_n = 5n$, $n = 1, 2, \ldots$ **39** $a_n = 4n - 1$

40 44 **41** 1.25 **43** -1 **44** $\frac{4}{3}$

13.3 Arithmetic Sequences and Series

Warm-up Exercises

1 10, 13, 16, 19, 22 **2** 15, 12, 9, 6, 3 **3** 156 **4** $\frac{46}{3}$ and $\frac{56}{3}$ **5 a** 6 **a** 3 **b** $-4\sqrt{5}$ **7** $8 + 13\pi$ **8** 2

Problem Set

9 5, 10, 15, 20 **11** -6, -8, -10, -12 **13** 16.5, 16.75, 17.0, 17.25, 17.5 **15** 7, 11, 15 **17 a** 5 **b** 2 **c** 49

d 2,597 **18** 4, 11, 21, 34, 50 **19** 297 **21** $\frac{-23}{3}$ **22** 11

23 a 38, 64, 94, 128, 166 **b** $A_n = 2n^2 + 20n + 16$

24 3, 9, 18, 30 **25** 85 **26** 47.2 **27** 20, 24, 28

29 10,000 **31** 52; 700 **33** 19, 23, 27, 31, 35 **35** $\sum_{k=1}^{15} k^2$

37 \$82,050 **39** first = $7\sqrt{2}$, difference = $-5\sqrt{2}$,

sum = $-84\sqrt{2}$ **40** 3π, 5π, 7π, 9π, 11π, 13π **41** $d = \frac{1}{3}$

$\approx 24{,}163.7$ **42 a** 10π, 14π, 18π, 22π **b** $\pi(4n + 6)$

44 $\frac{12}{120}$ or $\frac{1}{10}$ **45 a** 31×10 **b** 460 **c** 1210

13.4 Geometric Sequences and Series

Warm-up Exercises

1 $8\sqrt{2}$; $14 + 15\sqrt{2}$ **2** 1.5; 190.5 **3** $-3i$; -3 **4 a** 4

b No sum **5** 3906.25 **6** $\approx \pm 9.80$ **7** 455 ft

Problem Set

9 5, 1.5, 0.45, 0.135, 0.0405, 0.01215 **11** $\frac{1}{2}$, $\frac{1}{4}$, $\frac{1}{8}$

13 Arith. series; first term: 8; comm. diff.: 5

15 Neither arith. nor geom.; first term: 1 **16 a** 1.024 in. **b** 0.5625 in.^{2} **17 a** $\sqrt{2}$, $2\sqrt{2}$, $3\sqrt{2}$, $4\sqrt{2}$, $5\sqrt{2}$ **b** 2,

$\frac{3}{2}$, $\frac{4}{3}$, $\frac{5}{4}$ **19** $\frac{1}{3}$ **21** -4, 1, -0.25, or 4, 1, 0.25 **23** Yes,

with comm. ratio 1 **24** 9, 12, 15 **25** $x = -15$

26 $\frac{\log 120}{4} \approx 0.52$ **27** 24.25 **28 a** ≈ 12.95 ft

b ≈ 180.79 ft **29** $\frac{10}{3}$ **31** $x = 12$ **32** 9, 16 **33** 6i, 18i, 54i; or $-6i$, 18i, $-54i$; or -6, $-18i$, 54; or 6, $-18i$, -54

34 $a_n = a_1 r^{n-1}$ If $a_n = 0$ and $a_1 \neq 0$, then $r^{n-1} = 0$. But this is true only if $r = 0$. Therefore, if $a_n = 0$ for one n value, then $a_n = 0$ for all $n > 1$. **35** 1,147.5 **36 a** If

$a = b$, then $x = r$. **b** $r = \frac{a+b}{2}$ **c** $x = \sqrt{ab}$

Review Problems

1 3, 6, 11, 18, 27 **3** 2, 3, 5, 7, 11 **5** 3, 9, 20, 38, 65

7 2, 5, 10, 17, 28 **9 a** -6 **b** 8.25 **11** ≈ 1.55 **13** 330

14 \$50 **15 a** ≈ 3.9 feet **b** ≈ 39.2 feet **16 a** 8, 11, 14, 17 **b** 32 **c** 180 **17** $1 - 2 + 3 - 4 + 5 - 6$ **18** 22, 27, 32, 37, 42 **19** 25, -100, 400, -1600, 6400 **20** 4, -8, 16, -32 **21** 14 **22** 4 **23** $a_n = 4n - 1$ **24** 0.9

25

n	1	2	3	4	5
s_n	0.5	0.75	0.875	0.9375	0.96875

26 a $\frac{2}{15}$ **b** $a_k = \frac{4}{(k+1)(k+2)}$

c $a_k = \frac{4}{(k+1)(k+2)} = \frac{4}{k+1} - \frac{4}{k+2}$

$\therefore \sum_{k=1}^{\infty} a_k = 4 \sum_{k=1}^{\infty} \frac{1}{k+1} - \frac{1}{k+2}$

$= 4\left(\frac{1}{2} - \frac{1}{3} + \frac{1}{3} - \frac{1}{4} + \frac{1}{4} - \frac{1}{5} + \ldots\right)$

$= 4\left(\frac{1}{2}\right)$

$= 2$

27 a $\frac{1}{32}$ **b** ≈ 5.91 **c** $\frac{\sqrt{3}}{3}$, or ≈ 0.57785 **29** 12,726

31 $\frac{n}{n+1}$ **33** $p = \frac{14}{15}$ **35** False **36** $\sum_{k=1}^{\infty} x^{k+1}$

37 $a_1 \approx 689.35; \frac{4}{7}$ **39** $a_1 = -531,441; -\frac{1}{3}$ **41** $a_n = \frac{x^n}{n}$
43 ≈ 7.97 **44** 3645 units **45** ≈ 4072 persons
46 a \$5,627,888.15 **b** Geometric sequence **47** $\frac{2s^2\sqrt{3}}{5}$
where s = length of side of original triangle **48** Since
$r > 1$, in fact $r = \frac{4}{3}$, the perimeter is infinite.

Mathematical Induction

Problem Set

1 $(1 + h)^1 \overset{?}{\geq} 1 + 1h$
  $1 + h \geq 1 + h$; True, since $1 + h = 1 + h$ for all h.
3 $1 \overset{?}{<} 2^1$
  $1 < 2$
5 i $(1 + h)^{n+1} \geq 1 + h(n + 1)$ **iii** $(n + 1) < 2^{n+1}$
6 For $n = 1$, $4(1) - 3 = 1[2(1) - 1]$
      $1 = 1$
For some n, $1 + 5 + 9 + \ldots + (4n - 3) = n(2n - 1)$
Add $4n + 1$ to each side.
  $1 + 5 + 9 + \ldots + (4n - 3) + (4n + 1)$
  $= n(2n - 1) + 4n + 1$
  $1 + 5 + 9 + \ldots + [4(n + 1) - 3]$
  $= 2n^2 - n + 4n + 1$
  $= 2n^2 + 3n + 1$
  $= (n + 1)(2n + 1)$
  $= (n + 1)[2(n + 1) - 1]$

7 i) For $n = 1$, $1^3 - 1 = 0$; 0 *is divisible by* 3.
  ii) Assume true for n:
    $n^3 - n$ *is divisible by* 3.
    $(n + 1)^3 - (n + 1) = n^3 + 3n^2 + 3n + 1 - n - 1$
    $\qquad = (n^3 - n) + (3n^2 + 3n)$
    $\qquad = (n^3 - n) + 3n(n + 1)$
According to the given statement,
$n^3 - n$ is divisible by 3.
$3n(n + 1)$ contains the factor 3, and is therefore
divisible by 3.
According to the distributive property, since each term
of the sum contains a factor of 3, the sum itself must
contain a factor of 3, so $(n + 1)^3 - (n + 1)$ is divisible
by 3.
8 i) $\frac{1(1 + 1)}{2} = 1$

  ii) Assume $1 + 2 + 3 + \ldots + n = \frac{n(n + 1)}{2}$ true for
    n. Add $n + 1$ to each side.
      $1 + 2 + 3 + \ldots + n + (n + 1) = \frac{n(n + 1)}{2} + n + 1$
      $= \frac{n(n + 1) + 2n + 2}{2}$
      $= \frac{n^2 + n + 2n + 2}{2}$
      $= \frac{n^2 + 3n + 2}{2}$
      $= \frac{(n + 1)(n + 2)}{2}$
      $= \frac{(n + 1)[(n + 1) + 1]}{2}$

9 i) $x^1 + y^1 = (xy)^1$
  ii) Assume $x^n + y^n = (xy)^n$ is true for n.
    $x^{n+1} \cdot y^{n+1} = x^n \cdot x^1 \cdot y^n \cdot y^1$
    $\qquad = x^n y^n \cdot x^1 y^1$
    $\qquad = (xy)^n \cdot (xy)^1$
    $\qquad = (xy)^{n+1}$

10 No; not true for $n \geq 6$.

11 i) $S_1 = \frac{a_1(r^1 - 1)}{r - 1} = a_1$
  ii) Assume $S_n = \frac{a_1(r^n - 1)}{r - 1}$ is true for n.
    Add $a_1 r^n$ to each side.
    $S_n + a_1 r^n = \frac{a_1(r^n - 1)}{r - 1} + a_1 r^n$
    $S_{n+1} = \frac{a_1(r^n - 1)}{r - 1} + \frac{a_1 r^n(r - 1)}{r - 1}$
    $\qquad = \frac{a_1 r^n - a_1 + a_1 r^{n+1} - a_1 r^n}{r - 1}$
    $\qquad = \frac{a_1(r^{n+1} - 1)}{r - 1}$

12 i) $\frac{3(3 - 3)}{2} = 0$. True; there are no diagonals for a
    triangle.

  ii) Assume the number of diagonals $\frac{n(n - 3)}{2}$ is true
    for n. For 1 more side, there are $n - 2$ more
    diagonals than before.
    $\frac{n(n - 3)}{2} + (n - 2) = \frac{n(n - 3)}{2} + \frac{2(n - 2)}{2}$
    $= \frac{n^2 - 3n + 2n - 4}{2}$
    $= \frac{n^2 - n - 4}{2}$
    $= \frac{n^2 + n - 2n - 4}{2}$
    $= \frac{n(n + 1) - 2(n + 1)}{2}$
    $= \frac{(n + 1)(n - 2)}{2}$
    $= \frac{(n + 1)[(n + 1) - 3]}{2}$

13 i) $a^1 - b^1 = a - b$; $a - b$ is a factor of $a - b$.
  ii) Assume $a^n - b^n$ contains a factor of $a - b$ for
    some n
    $a^{n+1} - b^{n+1} = a \cdot a^n - b \cdot b^n$
    $\qquad = a \cdot a^n - ba^n + ba^n - b \cdot b^n$
    $\qquad = a^n(a - b) + b(a^n - b^n)$
  Since $a^n(a - b)$ contains a factor of $a - b$ and since
  $b(a^n - b^n)$ contains a factor of $a - b$ (by
  assumption), $a^{n+1} - b^{n+1}$ contains a factor of
  $a - b$.

14 a Let m be any positive integer. When $n = 1$,
$a^m \cdot a^n = a^m \cdot a^1 = a^m \cdot a = a^{m+1}$.
Assuming that $a^m \cdot a^n = a^{m+n}$ for some n, we multiply
both sides by a.
$a^m \cdot a^n \cdot a = a^{m+n} \cdot a$
$a^m \cdot a^{n+1} = a^{(m+n)+1}$
$\qquad = a^{m+(n+1)}$

b Let m be any positive integer. When $n = 1$,
$(a^m)^n = (a^m)^1 = a^m = a^{m \cdot 1}$.
Assuming that $(a^m)^n = a^{mn}$ for some n, we multiply both sides by a^m.
$$(a^m)^n \cdot a^m = a^{mn} \cdot a^m$$
$$(a^m)^n \cdot (a^m)^1 = a^{mn + m}$$
$$(a^m)^{n+1} = a^{m(n+1)}$$

c Let m be any positive integer. When $n = 1$,
$\dfrac{a^m}{a^n} = \dfrac{a^m}{a^1} = a^m \cdot a^{-1} = a^{m + (-1)} = a^{m-1}$.

Assuming that $\dfrac{a^m}{a^n} = a^{m-n}$ for some n, we multiply both sides by a^{-1}.
$$\frac{a^m}{a^n} \cdot a^{-1} = a^{m-n} \cdot a^{-1}$$
$$\frac{a^m}{a^n} \cdot \frac{1}{a} = a^{(m-n)+(-1)}$$
$$\frac{a^m}{a^n \cdot a} = a^{m-n-1}$$
$$\frac{a^m}{a^{n+1}} = a^{m-(n+1)}$$

15 True; i) $2^1 \geq 1 + 1$
ii) Assume $2^n \geq n + 1$ true for n.
Then $2 \cdot 2^n \geq 2(n + 1)$
$$2^{n+1} \geq 2n + 2$$
$$\therefore \ 2^{n+1} \geq n + 2, \text{ since } n \text{ is a natural number.}$$
$$2^{n+1} \geq (n + 1) + 1$$

17 $1^3 = 1^2(1 + 1)^2 - 4$
$= 4 - 4$
$= 0$
False; $1 \neq 0$

19 When $n = 1$, $1^2 \geq \dfrac{1(1 + 1)}{2}$, or $1 \geq 1$.

We assume that $n^2 \geq \dfrac{n(n + 1)}{2}$ for some n. Since n is positive by definition, $2n > n$, so we can add $2n + 1$ to the left side and $n + 1$ to the right side without invalidating the inequality.
$$n^2 + 2n + 1 \geq \frac{n(n + 1)}{2} + n + 1$$
$$(n + 1)^2 \geq \frac{n^2 + n + 2n + 2}{2}$$
$$\geq \frac{n^2 + 3n + 2}{2}$$
$$\geq \frac{(n + 1)(n + 2)}{2}$$
$$\geq \frac{(n + 1)[(n + 1) + 1]}{2}$$

20 When $n = 1$, $n^2 + n = 1^2 + 1 = 2$, which contains a factor of 2.
Assuming that $n^2 + n$ contains a factor of 2 for some n,
$(n + 1)^2 + (n + 1) = n^2 + 2n + 1 + n + 1$
$= n^2 + n + 2n + 2$
$= (n^2 + n) + 2(n + 1)$
Since $n^2 + n$ contains a factor of 2 by our assumption and since $2(n + 1)$ also contains a factor of 2, $(n + 1)^2 + (n + 1)$ must contain a factor of 2.

21 When $n = 2$, $\log(a_1 \cdot a_2) = \log a_1 + \log a_2$ by Property 5 of Logarithms.
Assuming that $\log(a_1 \cdot a_2 \cdot \ldots \cdot a_n) = \log a_1 + \log a_2 + \ldots + \log a_n$ for some n, we add $\log a_{n+1}$ to each side.

$\log(a_1 \cdot a_2 \cdot \ldots \cdot a_n) + \log a_{n+1}$
$= \log a_1 + \log a_2 + \ldots + \log a_n + \log a_{n+1}$
$\quad \log[(a_1 \cdot a_2 \cdot \ldots \cdot a_n) \cdot a_{n+1}]$
$\quad = \log a_1 + \log a_2 + \ldots + \log a_n$
$\quad\quad \log(a_1 \cdot a_2 \cdot \ldots \cdot a_{n+1})$
$\quad\quad = \log a_1 + \log a_2 + \ldots + \log a_{n+1}$

22 When $n = 1$, $\overline{z^1} = \overline{z}^1$, or $\overline{z} = \overline{z}$, which is a true statement.
Assuming that $\overline{z^n} = \overline{z}^n$ for some n, we multiply both sides by $\overline{z}$.
$$\overline{z^n} \cdot \overline{z} = \overline{z}^n \cdot \overline{z}$$
$$\overline{z^n \cdot z} = \overline{z}^{n+1}$$
$$\overline{z^{n+1}} = \overline{z}^{n+1}$$

23 When $n = 1$, $5^n - 1 = 5^1 - 1 = 4$, which is divisible by 4.
Assuming that $5^n - 1$ is divisible by 4 for some n,
$5^{n+1} - 1 = 5 \cdot 5^n - 1$
$\qquad\quad = 5 \cdot 5^n - 5^n + 5^n - 1$
$\qquad\quad = 5^n(5 - 1) + (5^n - 1)$
$\qquad\quad = 4(5^n) + (5^n - 1)$
Since $4(5^n)$ is divisible by 4 and since $5^n - 1$ is also divisible by 4 (according to our assumption), $5^{n+1} - 1$ must be divisible by 4.

24 When $n = 1$, $180(n - 2) = 180 \cdot 1 = 180$, and we know from a theorem of geometry that the sum of the measures of a triangle's angles is 180.
Assuming that the sum of the interior angles of a polygon is $180(n - 2)$ for some n, we note that n is increased by 1, the sum of the angles is increased by 180. Therefore, the sum of the measures of the interior angles of a polygon with $n + 1$ sides is
$180(n - 2) + 180$
$= 180n - 360 + 180$
$= 180n - 180$
$= 180(n - 1)$
$= 180[(n + 1) - 2]$

25 When $n = 1$,
$$\sum_{k=1}^{n}\left(\frac{1}{(2k - 1)(2k + 1)}\right) = \frac{1}{(2 \cdot 1 - 1)(2 \cdot 1 + 1)} = \frac{1}{3} = \frac{1}{2(1) + 1}.$$

Assuming that $\displaystyle\sum_{k=1}^{n}\left(\frac{1}{(2k - 1)(2k + 1)}\right) = \frac{n}{2n + 1}$ for some n,

we add $\dfrac{1}{[2(n + 1) - 1][2(n + 1) + 1]}$ to each side.

$$\sum_{k=1}^{n}\left(\frac{1}{(2k - 1)(2k + 1)}\right) + \frac{1}{[2(n + 1) - 1][2(n + 1) + 1]}$$
$$= \frac{n}{2n + 1} + \frac{1}{[2(n + 1) - 1][2(n + 1) + 1]}$$
$$\sum_{k=1}^{n+1}\left(\frac{1}{(2k - 1)(2k + 1)}\right) = \frac{n}{2n + 1} + \frac{1}{(2n + 1)(2n + 3)}$$
$$= \frac{n(2n + 3) + 1}{(2n + 1)(2n + 3)}$$
$$= \frac{2n^2 + 3n + 1}{(2n + 1)(2n + 3)}$$
$$= \frac{(2n + 1)(n + 1)}{(2n + 1)(2n + 3)}$$

$$= \frac{n+1}{2n+3}$$
$$= \frac{n+1}{2(n+1)+1}$$

26 When $n = 1$, $2^1 - 1 = 1$, and it obviously only takes 1 move to transfer 1 disk.
Let $H(n)$ represent the number of moves needed to transfer an n-disk tower. In Section 5.6, problem 28, part b, it was established that $H(n) = 2[H(n-1)] + 1$. Assuming that $H(n) = 2^n - 1$ for some n,
$$H(n+1) = 2(H[(n+1)-1]) + 1$$
$$= 2[H(n)] + 1$$
$$= 2(2^n - 1) + 1$$
$$= 2 \cdot 2^n - 2 + 1$$
$$= 2^{n+1} - 1$$

27 When $n = 1$, $(x+y)^n = (x+y)^1 = x + y = 1x + 1y = [C(1,0)]x^1 + [C(1,1)]y^1$.
Assuming that $(x+y)^n = [C(n,0)]x^n + [C(n,1)]x^{n-1}y + [C(n,2)]x^{n-2}y^2 + \ldots + [C(n,n)]y^n$ for some value of n, we multiply both sides by $(x+y)$.
$(x+y)(x+y)^n = (x+y)([C(n,0)]x^n + [C(n,1)]x^{n-1}y + [C(n,2)]x^{n-2}y^2 + \ldots + [C(n,n)]y^n)$
$(x+y)^{n+1}$
$= (x[C(n,0)]x^n + x[C(n,1)]x^{n-1}y + x[C(n,2)]x^{n-2}y^2 + \ldots)$
$\quad + (y[C(n,0)]x^n + y[C(n,1)]x^{n-1}y + \ldots + y[C(n,n)]y^n$
$= [C(n,0)]x^{n+1} + [C(n,1)]x^n y + [C(n,2)]x^{n-1}y^2 + \ldots$
$\quad + [C(n,0)]x^n y + [C(n,1)]x^{n-1}y^2 + \ldots + [C(n,n)]y^{n+1}$
$= 1x^{n+1} + (n+1)x^n y + [C(n,2) + C(n,1)]x^{n-1}y^2$
$\quad + \ldots + 1y^{n+1}$
$= [C(n+1,0)]x^{n+1} + [C(n+1,1)]x^{(n+1)-1}y$
$\quad + [C(n+1,2)]x^{(n+1)-2}y^2 + \ldots + [C(n+1,n+1)]y^{n+1}$

14.1 The Unit Circle

Warm-up Exercises

1 24 **2** $\left(-\frac{\sqrt{3}}{2}, -\frac{1}{2}\right)$ **3** $\sqrt{7}$ **4** $\left(-\frac{15}{17}, -\frac{8}{17}\right)$
5 $\left(\frac{\sqrt{3}}{2}, \frac{1}{2}\right)$ **6** $\left(\frac{1}{\sqrt{2}}, \frac{1}{\sqrt{2}}\right)$ **7** $\left(\frac{1}{2}, \frac{\sqrt{3}}{2}\right)$ **8** $\left(\frac{\sqrt{3}}{2}, -\frac{1}{2}\right)$
9 $\left(\frac{1}{\sqrt{2}}, -\frac{1}{\sqrt{2}}\right)$ **10** $\left(\frac{1}{2}, -\frac{\sqrt{3}}{2}\right)$

Problem Set

11 $(0, 1)$ **13** $(0, -1)$ **15** $(1, 0)$ **17 a** $\frac{25}{36}\pi$, or ≈ 2.182
b $\frac{47}{36}\pi$, or ≈ 4.102 **18** $\left(-\frac{3}{5}, \frac{4}{5}\right)$ **19 a** $-120°$ **b** $\frac{2\pi}{3}$, or
≈ 2.094 **20** $\beta = 435°$; $\gamma = -2.85°$ **21** $\left(\frac{8}{17}, \frac{-15}{17}\right)$
22 $A = \left(-\frac{1}{2}, \frac{\sqrt{3}}{2}\right)$; $B = \left(-\frac{1}{2}, -\frac{\sqrt{3}}{2}\right)$; $C = \left(\frac{1}{2}, -\frac{\sqrt{3}}{2}\right)$
23 $\left(\frac{12}{13}, \frac{5}{13}\right)$ **24 a** $\frac{\pi}{3}$, or ≈ 1.047 **b** $\frac{\pi}{3}$, or ≈ 1.047 **c** $\frac{\pi}{3}$,
or ≈ 1.047 **25** $-310°$, $-50°$, $310°$ **26 a** $(-b, a)$
b $(-a, -b)$ **27** $\left(\frac{2}{\sqrt{5}}, \frac{1}{\sqrt{5}}\right)$ or $\left(\frac{-2}{\sqrt{5}}, \frac{-1}{\sqrt{5}}\right)$ **28** ≈ 218
revolutions **29 a** ≈ 1.3 **b** ≈ 7.9 **c** $6:1$ **d** $6:1$ **30** 30
31 $\left(\frac{5}{\sqrt{29}}, \frac{2}{\sqrt{29}}\right)$, $\left(\frac{-5}{\sqrt{29}}, \frac{-2}{\sqrt{29}}\right)$ **32** ≈ 13.37 in.

14.2 The Circular Functions

Warm-up Exercises

1 $\cos\theta \approx -0.82$; $\sin\theta \approx -0.57$; $\tan\theta \approx 0.70$; $\sec\theta \approx -1.22$; $\csc\theta \approx -1.75$; $\cot\theta \approx 1.44$
2 a $\left(\frac{1}{2}, \frac{\sqrt{3}}{2}\right)$ **b** $\left(-\frac{\sqrt{2}}{2}, \frac{\sqrt{2}}{2}\right)$ **c** $\left(\frac{\sqrt{3}}{2}, -\frac{1}{2}\right)$ **d** $(\approx -0.17,$
$\approx 0.98)$ **3 a** $(\approx -0.77, \approx 0.64)$ **b** ≈ -0.84 **4** $\pm\frac{\sqrt{15}}{4}$
5 ± 2 **6** $\pm\frac{4}{3}$ **7 a** iii **b** i **c** ii **d** iv **8** $\pm\frac{\sqrt{7}}{4}$

Problem Set

9 a $\approx 22.79°$ **b** $\approx 61.93°$ **c** $\approx 8.21°$ **d** $\approx 53.13°$
e $\approx 84.26°$ **f** Impossible **10 a** $\pm\frac{8}{\sqrt{353}}$ **b** $\pm\frac{\sqrt{3}}{2}$
c $\pm\frac{1}{2\sqrt{2}}$ **11 a** ≈ 0.951 **b** ≈ 0.951 **c** ≈ 3.078 **d** ≈ 3.078
12 $\sin\theta = -\frac{24}{25}$, $\cos\theta = \frac{7}{25}$; $\tan\theta = -\frac{24}{7}$; $\cot\theta = -\frac{7}{24}$;
$\sec\theta = \frac{25}{7}$; $\csc\theta = -\frac{25}{24}$ **13 a** $(1, 10)$ **b** $\sqrt{101}$
c $\left(\frac{1}{\sqrt{101}}, \frac{10}{\sqrt{101}}\right)$ **d** ≈ 84.29 **14** $\sin\theta = -\frac{15}{17}$,
$\cos\theta = -\frac{8}{17}$; $\tan\theta = \frac{15}{8}$; $\cot\theta = \frac{8}{15}$; $\sec\theta = -\frac{17}{8}$;
$\csc\theta = -\frac{17}{15}$ **15 a** $2\sqrt{21}$ **b** $\frac{2}{5}$ **c** $\frac{\sqrt{21}}{5}$ **d** ≈ 66.42
16 ≈ 0.98, ≈ 0.94, ≈ 0.87, ≈ 0.77, ≈ 0.64, 0.50, ≈ 0.34,
≈ 0.17, 0.00, ≈ -0.17 **17 a** $(\approx 0.342, \approx 0.940)$
b ≈ 0.470 **18** $152°$ **19 a** ≈ 208.00 **b** $(\approx -3.53,$
$\approx -1.88)$ **20 a** $90°$ **b** $270°$ **c** $0°$, $180°$, $360°$ **21 a** 270
b 225 **c** ≈ 323.13 **d** ≈ 35 **22** sine: ≈ 0.866; cosine:
-0.5; tangent: ≈ -1.732; cotangent: ≈ -0.577; secant:
≈ -2; cosecant: ≈ 1.155 **23 a** $\approx \pm 0.719$ **b** $\approx \pm 1.035$
c ≈ 1.439
24 a $\quad 1 + \tan^2\theta = \sec^2\theta$ **b** $\quad 1 + \cot^2\theta = \csc^2\theta$
$\quad\quad \frac{\cos^2\theta + \sin^2\theta}{\cos^2\theta} = \sec^2\theta \quad\quad \frac{\sin^2\theta + \cos^2\theta}{\sin^2\theta} = \csc^2\theta$
$\quad\quad\quad \frac{1}{\cos^2\theta} = \sec^2\theta \quad\quad\quad\quad \frac{1}{\sin^2\theta} = \csc^2\theta$
$\quad\quad\quad \sec^2\theta = \sec^2\theta \quad\quad\quad\quad \csc^2\theta = \csc^2\theta$
25 For any θ, $\sin^2\theta + \cos^2\theta = 1$, but $0.625^2 + 0.54^2 \approx 0.682$. **26 a** $\left(\frac{\sqrt{2}}{2}, \frac{\sqrt{2}}{2}\right)$ or $\left(-\frac{\sqrt{2}}{2}, -\frac{\sqrt{2}}{2}\right)$
b $\left(-\frac{\sqrt{2}}{2}, -\frac{\sqrt{2}}{2}\right)$ or $\left(\frac{\sqrt{2}}{2}, -\frac{\sqrt{2}}{2}\right)$ **c** $(-1, 0)$
d $\left(-\frac{1}{2}, \frac{\sqrt{3}}{2}\right)$ or $\left(-\frac{1}{2}, -\frac{\sqrt{3}}{2}\right)$ **27** $\approx 76.39°$ or $\approx 283.61°$
28 a II **b** III **29 a** $y = \frac{x}{\sqrt{3}}$ **b** $y = -\frac{x}{\sqrt{3}}$ **30 a** a **b** b
c $\frac{b}{a}$ **d** c **e** d **f** $\frac{d}{c}$ **31 a** $\cos^2\theta$ **b** $\sec^2\theta$ **c** $-\tan^2\theta$
32 a $135°$ **b** $60°$ or $-60°$ **c** $60°$ or $300°$ **d** $135°$ or $225°$
34 Depending on the value of θ, $\tan\theta = \frac{\sqrt{1-\cos^2\theta}}{\cos\theta}$ or
$\tan\theta = -\frac{\sqrt{1-\cos^2\theta}}{\cos\theta}$

14.3 Coordinate Defintions

Warm-up Exercises

1 a $65°$ **b** $40°$ **c** $20°$ **d** $38°$ **e** $57°$ **f** $88°$ **2 a** $-\frac{\sqrt{3}}{2}$
b $-\frac{\sqrt{3}}{2}$ **c** $-\frac{\sqrt{3}}{3}$ **d** 2 **e** Undefined **f** $-\frac{1}{2}$ **3** $\pm\frac{12}{13}$ **4** $\frac{8}{17}$

5 $\pm\frac{3}{4}$ **6** $\frac{1}{\sqrt{5}}$; $\frac{2}{\sqrt{5}}$; $\frac{1}{2}$ **7** $\approx26.57°$ **8 a** I **b** II **c** III **d** IV
9 $\sin\theta = \frac{24}{25}$; $\cos\theta = -\frac{7}{25}$; $\tan\theta = -\frac{24}{7}$; $\cot\theta = -\frac{7}{24}$; $\sec\theta = -\frac{25}{7}$; $\csc\theta = \frac{25}{24}$ **10 a** $-\frac{6}{\sqrt{85}}$; $\frac{7}{\sqrt{85}}$; $-\frac{7}{6}$
b ≈130.60

Problem Set

11 a $\frac{5}{2\sqrt{6}}$ **b** $\frac{3}{\sqrt{10}}$ **12** (≈-0.88, ≈-0.47) **13** Tangent and secant for {. . . , $-270°$, $-90°$, $90°$, $270°$, . . .}, cotangent and cosecant for {. . . , $-360°$, $-180°$, $0°$, $180°$, $360°$, . . .} **14** (≈2.91, ≈11.64) **15 a** $45°$, $135°$, $225°$, or $315°$ **b** $0°$, $180°$, or $360°$ **c** $45°$ or $225°$

16 a (≈8.19, ≈5.74) **b** ≈23.49 **17** $-\frac{3}{\sqrt{13}}$ **18 a** Equal **b** Equal in absolute value but different in sign

c Supplementary **d** $\propto$ or $180 - \beta$ **19 a** $\frac{b}{a}$ **b** b **c** a

d $\frac{b}{a}$ **e** $-a$ **f** $-b$ **20 a** $-225°$, -135, $135°$, $225°$
b $-225°$, $-45°$, $135°$, $315°$ **21** $(-4, 4\sqrt{3})$ **22 a** $60°$ or $300°$
b $45°$, $135°$, $225°$, or $315°$ **c** $0°$, $180°$, or $360°$ **d** $0°$, $90°$, $270°$, or $360°$ **23** The coordinates of the points in Quadrants II, III, and IV are identical in absolute value to those of the corresponding points in Quadrant I, and the signs of the coordinates can be determined by the point's directions from the x- and y-axis.

24 a $S = \frac{1}{2}$ or $S = -1$

b $\sin x = \frac{1}{2}$ or $\sin x = -1$ **c** $x = 30°$, $x = 150°$, or $x = 270°$ **25** $\frac{\sqrt{313}}{13}$ or $-\frac{\sqrt{313}}{13}$ **26** ≈0.32
27 a $\approx-331.6°$, $\approx-28.4°$, $\approx28.4°$, $\approx331.6°$
b $\approx-354.3°$, $\approx-185.7°$, $\approx5.74°$, $\approx174.26°$
28 a ≈386.37 ft **b** ≈373.21 ft **29** ≈0.18
30 a ≈67.66 **b** $\approx44°$ or $\approx136°$ **31** $9\sqrt{3}$ **32** ≈8.77 m; ≈8.24 m **33** $\sin x = \sin x$; $\cos x = \sqrt{1 - \sin^2 x}$;
$\tan x = \frac{\sin x}{\sqrt{1 - \sin^2 x}}$; $\cot x = \frac{\sqrt{1 - \sin^2 x}}{\sin x}$;
$\sec x = \frac{1}{\sqrt{1 - \sin^2 x}}$; $\csc x = \frac{1}{\sin x}$

14.4 Inverse Trigonometric Functions

Warm-up Exercises

1 a and **b** **2 a** $100° + 360° \cdot k$ **b** $140° + 180° \cdot k$
c $80° + 90° \cdot k$ **3 a** $60°$ **b** $120°$ **c** $135°$ **d** No; the Arccos function's range is restricted to angles from $0°$ to $180°$. **4 a** $45°$ **b** $45° + 360° \cdot n$ or $315° + 360° \cdot n$
c $60°$ **d** $60° + 360° \cdot n$ or $300° + 360° \cdot n$

Problem Set

5 a ≈0.7424 **b** ≈-1.6129 **6 a** $440°$, $800°$, $1160°$, $1520°$, $1880°$ **b** $-280°$, $-640°$, $-1000°$, $-1360°$
7 a $-45°$ **b** $135° + 180° \cdot n$ **8 a** $\frac{7}{2}$ **b** $\approx74.05°$ **9** $60°$, $300°$, $420°$, $660°$, $780°$ **10 a** $48.59°$ or $131.41°$ **b** $65.91°$ or $294.09°$ **c** $115.47°$ or $244.53°$ **d** $60°$ or $120°$
11 Arccos; Arcsin; Arctan **12** $\theta \approx 53.13° + n \cdot 360°$
13 $60°$, $120°$, $240°$, $300°$ **14 a** $\approx50.95°$ **b** ≈0.7766
c Arccos 0.63; sin (Arccos 0.63) **15 a** 3 **b** ≈3.2838
16 $180°$ **17** $\approx38°$ **18 a** $140°$ **b** $30°$ **c** $30°$ **d** $30°$
e $-30°$ **19 a** $\frac{1}{2}$ **b** $60°$ **20 a** 8π **b** 8π **c** 0 **21 a** 2
b ≈1.1254 **22** $\approx30°45'13''$ **23 a** ≈0.7599 **b** ≈0.2116
c ≈1.4372 **d** ≈-2.0996 **24 a** $\frac{\sqrt{3}}{2}$ **b** 0 **c** -1 **d** $\frac{2}{\sqrt{3}}$
e $\frac{1}{2}$ **25 a** $\approx(360° \cdot n + 48.19°)$ or $\approx(360° \cdot n + 311.81°)$
b $180° \cdot n + 135°$ **26** $\approx89°18'$ **27** $\approx143.14°$ **28** $50°$, $170°$, $410°$, $530°$ **29 a** -1 **b** -1 **c** The values are equal. **30 a** $\sin x = -\frac{3}{5}$ or $\sin x = \frac{1}{2}$ **b** $x = 30°$, $x = 150°$, $x \approx216.87°$ or $x \approx323.13°$ **31** $60° + n \cdot 360°$
32 $\pm\frac{\sqrt{2}}{2}$, or $\approx\pm0.7071$ **33** $\approx63.43°$ **34** $35° + 180° \cdot n$
35 $90°0'$ **36** $\sec x \geq 1$ for all values of x, and the domain of the arccos function is between -1 and 1 inclusive, so arccos (sec x) exists only for values of x for which $\sec x = \pm1$. **37** ≈230.62 **38** $\approx26.57°$ or $\approx206.57°$ **39 a** $\approx33.69°$ **b** ≈3.328

14.5 Right Triangles

Warm-up Exercises

1 45 **2 a** $\cot\theta$ **b** $\sin\theta$ **c** $\csc\theta$ **d** $\tan\theta$
3 a $x \approx 7.49$ **b** $x \approx 10.80$ **c** $\theta \approx 38.68°$ **4** $\theta \approx 48.59°$

Problem Set

5 a $-\frac{4}{5}$ **b** $-\frac{3}{4}$ **c** $\frac{3}{5}$ **d** $-\frac{3}{4}$ **e** $\frac{-4}{5}$ **6** $\approx38.66°$ **7 a** $\frac{3}{5}$
b $\frac{3}{5}$ **8** $\approx63.4° + 180° \cdot n$ **9** ≈85 ft **10** $\approx53.13°$
11 a ≈0.5736 **b** $\frac{5}{8}$ **12 a** ≈16.78 **b** ≈167.8 **13 a** 0.8
b The ratio BC:AC is equal to the ratio QR:PR.
14 ≈5.5 **15** ≈19.5 **16** $\overline{DC}$ **17** $\approx1.8°$ **18** $\approx2.20°$
19 ≈13.9 **20** ≈567.13 sq. units **21** ≈2.75 **22** ≈29.71
23 ≈1.42; ≈355 ft **24 a** ≈0.3511; 0.6 **b** ≈0.5852
c $\approx20.56°$; $\approx36.87°$ **d** ≈0.5575 **25** $\approx77.57°$; ≈33 paces **26** $\approx23.2°$ **27** ≈180.42 **28** ≈46.40 **29** ≈78.56
30 a $\approx45.10°$ **b** ≈72.25 **31** ≈19.47 **32** ≈0.9511
33 a $\approx118.07°$ **b** $\approx5.91°$ **34** $\approx107.95°$ and $\approx72.05°$

14.6 Radian Measure

Warm-up Exercises

1 a $\frac{\pi}{3}$ **b** $\frac{7\pi}{6}$ **c** $-\frac{5\pi}{12}$ **d** $\frac{5\pi}{2}$ **e** $-\frac{\pi}{6}$ **2 a** $45°$ **b** $-210°$
c $480°$ **d** $-60°$ **e** $-120°$ **3** ≈1.92

Problem Set

4 ≈1272.35 in. **5** $\left(\frac{\sqrt{3}}{2}, \frac{1}{2}\right)$; $\left(-\frac{1}{2}, \frac{\sqrt{3}}{2}\right)$ **6 a** ≈0.87

b ≈ -6.98 **c** ≈ 0.44 **d** ≈ 3.60 **e** ≈ -1.31 **7** ≈ 0.8192
8 a 2π **b** π **c** $\frac{2\pi}{3}$ **d** $\frac{4\pi}{5}$ **9** -1 **11** 1 **13** $\sqrt{3}$ **15** $-\frac{\sqrt{2}}{2}$
17 $-\frac{\sqrt{3}}{3}$ **19** $\frac{2\sqrt{3}}{3}$ **21** 2 **23** $-\frac{\sqrt{3}}{2}$ **24** $\approx 114.5916°$
25 ≈ 4.89 **26 a** $\frac{3}{10}; \frac{3}{5}$ **b** $\frac{1}{2}$ **c** $\approx 16.70°; \approx 30.96°$
d ≈ 0.5393 **27** 6π **28 a** $\frac{1}{2}$ **b** $\sqrt{3}$ **c** -1 **d** $\frac{2\sqrt{3}}{3}$ **e** 1
29 a ≈ 0.6442 **b** ≈ 0.3624 **c** ≈ 1.7778 **30 a** ≈ 0.1361
b ≈ -0.4532 **31** ≈ 57.98 **32 a** $x \approx 21.25$ **b** $x \approx 15.57$
c $x = 7.5$ **d** $x = 10\sqrt{2}$ **e** $x \approx 11.76$ **33** $x = 2$
34 ≈ 0.2618 and $15°$ **35** The sum of the squares of the
coordinates is 1. **37** $\frac{24}{7}$ **39** Neither; both areas are
≈ 38.30 sq. units. **40** 38.4 **41 a** $\frac{\pi}{3}, \frac{2\pi}{3}, \frac{4\pi}{3}, \frac{5\pi}{3}$ **b** $\frac{\pi}{3}, \frac{2\pi}{3}$,
$\frac{4\pi}{3}, \frac{3\pi}{2}$ **c** $\frac{\pi}{6}, \frac{7\pi}{6}$ **42** $\approx 146.31°$ **43** 1; $\frac{\sqrt{2}}{2}; \frac{1}{2}; -\frac{\sqrt{2}}{2}; -\frac{\sqrt{3}}{2}$;
-1 **44** ≈ 26.57 **45 a** $\frac{\sqrt{d^2-1}}{d}$ **b** 1 **46** ≈ 23.9 in.^{2}
47 ≈ 13.17 in.

14.7 Trigonometric Relationships

Warm-up Exercises

1 a True **b** True **c** True **d** True **e** True **2 a** a
b $-a$ **c** b **d** b **e** $-b$ **f** $-a$ **g** a **h** $-b$ **3** $\cos(-\theta)$
$= \cos\theta$ **a** $\frac{\sqrt{3}}{2}$ **b** $\frac{\sqrt{3}}{2}$ **c** $\frac{\sqrt{2}}{2}$ **d** $\frac{\sqrt{2}}{2}$ **e** $-\frac{1}{2}$ **f** $-\frac{1}{2}$
4 $\sin(-\theta) = -\sin\theta$ **a** $\frac{1}{2}$ **b** $-\frac{1}{2}$ **c** $\frac{\sqrt{2}}{2}$ **d** $-\frac{\sqrt{2}}{2}$ **e** $-\frac{\sqrt{3}}{2}$
f $\frac{\sqrt{3}}{2}$ **5 a** $-\frac{11}{5\sqrt{5}}$ **b** $-\frac{2}{5\sqrt{5}}$ **c** $\frac{11}{2}$ **6 a** True **b** True
c False **d** True

7

Problem Set

8 a $\cos\theta$ **b** $-\sin\theta$ **c** $\cos\theta$ **d** $-\sin\theta$ **e** $-\sin\theta$
9 a 0.2 **b** -0.2 **c** 0.2 **d** 0.2 **e** 0.2 **10 a** Even
b Odd **c** Odd **d** Odd **e** Even **f** Odd **11 a** $-\tan 35°$
b $-\tan 80°$ **12 a** $\frac{b}{c}$ **b** $\frac{b}{c}$ **c** $\frac{\pi}{2}$ radians, or $90°$

13

θ	2π	$\frac{13\pi}{6}$	$\frac{9\pi}{4}$	$\frac{7\pi}{3}$	$\frac{5\pi}{2}$
$\sin\theta$	0	$\frac{1}{2}$	$\frac{\sqrt{2}}{2}$	$\frac{\sqrt{3}}{2}$	1
$\cos\theta$	1	$\frac{\sqrt{3}}{2}$	$\frac{\sqrt{2}}{2}$	$\frac{1}{2}$	0
$\tan\theta$	0	$\frac{\sqrt{3}}{3}$	1	$\sqrt{3}$	Undef.
$\cot\theta$	Undef.	$\sqrt{3}$	1	$\frac{\sqrt{3}}{3}$	0

14 a $\alpha = \frac{\pi}{2} - \theta$, or $\alpha = 90° - \theta$ **b** $\frac{7}{\sqrt{53}}$ **c** $\frac{\pi}{2}$ radians,
or $90°$ **d** $\frac{7}{\sqrt{53}}$ **15 a** $\sqrt{61}$ **b** $\frac{6}{\sqrt{61}}$ **c** $\frac{6}{5}$ **d** $\frac{9}{\sqrt{142}}$

16 a $8\sin\theta$ **b** $6\sin\theta$
17 a $\sin(90° - \theta) = \cos\theta$
$\qquad = 1\cos\theta - 0\sin\theta$
$\qquad = \sin 90°\cos\theta - \cos 90°\sin\theta$
b $\cos(90° - \theta) = \sin\theta$
$\qquad = 0\cos\theta + 1\sin\theta$
$\qquad = \cos 90°\cos\theta + \sin 90°\sin\theta$
18 a $-\frac{5}{12}$ **b** $\frac{5}{12}$ **c** $\frac{5}{12}$ **d** $-\frac{5}{12}$ **19** $\overline{CD}$ **20 a** ≈ 1.0419
b ≈ 3.8302 **21** $\left(\theta + \frac{\pi}{3}\right) + \left(\frac{\pi}{6} - \theta\right) = \frac{\pi}{2}$, so $\theta + \frac{\pi}{3}$ and
$\frac{\pi}{6} - \theta$ are complementary angles. Therefore, since
$\sin\alpha = \cos\beta$ when α and β are complementary,
$\sin\left(\theta + \frac{\pi}{3}\right) = \cos\left(\frac{\pi}{6} - \theta\right)$. **22 a** $(-4, -3)$ **b** $-\frac{4}{5}; -\frac{3}{5}; \frac{3}{4}$
23 a $(5, -12)$ **b** $\frac{5}{13}; \frac{5}{13}$ **24 a** Even **b** Odd **c** Even
d Even **e** Even **f** Odd **25 a** $-\sin\left(\frac{\pi}{4}\right)$ **b** $-\cos\left(\frac{\pi}{6}\right)$
c $\tan\left(\frac{4\pi}{9}\right)$ **26** $-\sin x$ **27 a** $\frac{1}{2}$ **b** $\frac{\sqrt{3}}{2}$ **c** $\frac{\sqrt{3}}{2}$ **d** $\frac{1}{2}$ **e** $-\frac{1}{2}$
f $-\frac{\sqrt{3}}{2}$ **28** ≈ 1.71 ft
29 $f(-x) = \frac{-x}{1!} - \frac{(-x)^3}{3!} + \frac{(-x)^5}{5!} - \frac{(-x)^7}{7!} + \frac{(-x)^9}{9!}$
$\qquad = -\frac{x}{1!} + \frac{x^3}{3!} - \frac{x^5}{5!} + \frac{x^7}{7!} - \frac{x^9}{9!}$
$\qquad = -\left(\frac{x}{1!} - \frac{x^3}{3!} + \frac{x^5}{5!} - \frac{x^7}{7!} + \frac{x^9}{9!}\right)$
$\qquad = -f(x)$
30 $f(-x) = 1 - \frac{(-x)^2}{2!} + \frac{(-x)^4}{4!} - \frac{(-x)^6}{6!} + \frac{(-x)^8}{8!} - \frac{(-x)^{10}}{10!}$
$\qquad = 1 - \frac{x^2}{2!} + \frac{x^4}{4!} - \frac{x^6}{6!} + \frac{x^8}{8!} - \frac{x^{10}}{10!}$
$\qquad = f(x)$

Review Problems

1 Sine: $\frac{12}{13}$; cosine: $-\frac{5}{13}$; tangent: $-\frac{12}{5}$; cotangent: $-\frac{5}{12}$;
secant: $-\frac{13}{5}$; cosecant: $\frac{13}{12}$ **2** $-312°, -228°, -132°,$
$-48°, 48°, 132°, 228°, 312°$ **3 a** $\frac{1}{2}$ **b** $\frac{1}{2}$ **c** $\frac{\sqrt{3}}{2}$ **d** $\pm\frac{\sqrt{3}}{2}$
4 ≈ 1927 ft **5** 90; 180; 270; 360; 45; 300; 315; 150
6 a -1 **b** 1 **c** Undefined **d** Undefined **7** ≈ 3076.04
8 ≈ 140.19 **9 a** 1 **b** 0 **c** $\frac{\sqrt{2}}{2}$ **d** $-\frac{\sqrt{2}}{2}$ **e** -1 **f** $\frac{\sqrt{2}}{2}$
10 ≈ 0.9962 **11 a** -6 **b** 2 **12** 30 **13 a** ≈ 0.9352
b ≈ -0.9352 **14 a** Tangent **b** ≈ 286 ft
15 a $\approx 261.27°$ **b** $\approx -217.15°$ **c** $\approx 875.48°$
d $\approx -300.80°$ **e** $\approx -57.30°$ **16** ≈ 0.13 in. **17** $\left(-\frac{4}{5}, \frac{3}{5}\right)$
and $\left(\frac{4}{5}, -\frac{3}{5}\right)$ **18** $-\frac{2\sqrt{2}}{3}$ **19** $-\frac{3}{4}$ **20 a** $8\tan\theta$ **b** $9\sin\theta$
c $2\cos\theta$ **21 a** $\frac{\pi}{6}$ **b** $\frac{3\pi}{10}$ **c** $\frac{\pi}{4}$ **22** $(22.5 + 90n)°$, where
n is an integer **23 a** $\frac{\sqrt{2}}{2}$ **b** -1 **c** $-\frac{\sqrt{2}}{2}$ **d** $-\frac{\sqrt{2}}{2}$
e $-\frac{\sqrt{2}}{2}$ **f** 1 **24 a** $AC = \frac{1}{\sqrt{2}}$; $BC = \frac{1}{\sqrt{2}}$ **b** $AC = \frac{1}{2}$;
$BC = \frac{\sqrt{3}}{2}$ **c** $AC = \frac{\sqrt{3}}{2}$; $BC = \frac{1}{2}$ **25** ≈ 40.54

15.1 Basic Trigonometric Identities

Warm-up Exercises

1 $\csc^4 \theta = (\csc^2 \theta)^2 = (1 + \cot^2 \theta)^2$; $\sin \theta \neq 0$

2 $(\cos^2 \theta)(\tan^2 \theta + 1) = \cos^2 \theta \sec^2 \theta = \frac{\cos^2 \theta}{\cos^2 \theta} = 1$;
$\cos \theta \neq 0$ **3 a** True **b** True **c** False **4 a** Yes **b** Yes
c Yes **d** Yes **5 a** No **b** No

6 $\frac{1}{\cos^2 \theta} - \frac{\sin^2 \theta}{\cos^2 \theta} = \frac{1 - \sin^2 \theta}{\cos^2 \theta} = \frac{\cos^2 \theta}{\cos^2 \theta} = 1$; $\cos \theta \neq 0$

7 $\frac{\cos^2 \theta - \sin^2 \theta}{\cos \theta - \sin \theta} = \frac{(\cos \theta + \sin \theta)(\cos \theta - \sin \theta)}{\cos \theta - \sin \theta}$
$= \cos \theta + \sin \theta$; $\cos \theta \neq \sin \theta$

Problem Set

8 a False **b** True **9 a** 4 **b** 1 **c** 1
10 $(\csc \theta + \cot \theta)^2(\csc \theta - \cot \theta)^2 = (\csc^2 \theta - \cot^2 \theta)^2$
$= 1^2 = 1$; $\sin \theta \neq 0$

11 a $\sec x$ **b** $\csc x$ **c** $\sin x$ **d** $\cos x$ **12 a** $\left(\frac{\sqrt{3}}{2}, \frac{1}{2}\right)$

b $\left(\frac{1}{2}, \frac{\sqrt{3}}{2}\right)$ **c** ≈ 0.518

13 $\frac{\cos^3 \theta - \sin^3 \theta}{\cos \theta - \sin \theta}$
$= \frac{(\cos \theta - \sin \theta)(\cos^2 \theta + \cos \theta \sin \theta + \sin^2 \theta)}{\cos \theta - \sin \theta}$
$= \cos^2 \theta + \cos \theta \sin \theta + \sin^2 \theta$
$= (\sin^2 \theta + \cos^2 \theta) + \cos \theta \sin \theta$
$= 1 + \cos \theta \sin \theta$; $\cos \theta \neq \sin \theta$

14 Let $\theta = 0°$. $\frac{\sin 0}{1 + \cos 0} = 0$, but $\frac{\cos 0}{1 + \sin 0} = 1$
Therefore, the equation is not an identity. **15 a** 1
b ≈ 1.2601 **16 a** $\sin 210° = -0.5$ but
$\sqrt{1 - \cos^2 210°} = 0.5$
Therefore, equation is false for $\theta = 210°$. **b** Ida used
an algebraic property of equations instead of
simplifying each side separately. $\sqrt{1 - \cos^2 \theta} =$
$\sqrt{\sin^2 \theta} = |\sin \theta|$, and $\sin \theta = |\sin \theta|$ is not an
identity, since it is a true statement only for values of
θ with a positive sine. **17 a** False **b** True **c** False

d True **18 a** $\frac{1}{3}$ **b** $\frac{2\sqrt{2}}{3}$ **c** $\frac{4}{5}$ **19**

20 a False **b** True
21 a $\frac{\sin \theta}{1 - \cos \theta} = \frac{\sqrt{a^2 + b^2} + b}{a} = \csc \theta + \cot \theta$

b $\frac{(a + b)^2}{a^2 + b^2}$ **c** $\frac{a^2}{a^2 + b^2} + \frac{b^2}{a^2 + b^2} = \frac{a^2 + b^2}{a^2 + b^2} = 1$ **22 a** $\tan x$
b $\sin x$ **c** $\cos x$ **d** $\cot x$

23 a $\frac{\tan x - 1}{\tan x + 1} = \frac{\frac{\sin x}{\cos x} - 1}{\frac{\sin x}{\cos x} + 1} = \frac{\frac{\sin x - \cos x}{\cos x}}{\frac{\sin x + \cos x}{\cos x}} = \frac{\sin x - \cos x}{\sin x + \cos x}$

$= \frac{\frac{\sin x - \cos x}{\sin x}}{\frac{\sin x + \cos x}{\sin x}}$

$= \frac{1 - \frac{\cos x}{\sin x}}{1 + \frac{\cos x}{\sin x}} = \frac{1 - \cot x}{1 + \cot x}$; $\cos x \neq 0$, $\sin x \neq 0$,
$\sin x \neq -\cos x$

b $\cot^2 x - \cos^2 x = \frac{\cos^2 x}{\sin^2 x} - \cos^2 x = \left(\frac{1}{\sin^2 x} - 1\right) \cdot \cos^2 x$
$= (\csc^2 x - 1) \cdot \cos^2 x = \cot^2 x \cdot \cos^2 x$; $\sin x \neq 0$

c $(\tan x + \sec x)^2 = \left(\frac{\sin x}{\cos x} + \frac{1}{\cos x}\right)^2 = \left(\frac{\sin x + 1}{\cos x}\right)^2$

$= \frac{(\sin x + 1)^2}{1 - \sin^2 x} = \frac{(\sin x + 1)^2}{(1 + \sin x)(1 - \sin x)} = \frac{1 + \sin x}{1 - \sin x}$;
$\cos x \neq 0$, $\sin x \neq -1$, $\sin x \neq 1$

24 a $\frac{a^2 + 2a + 2}{a + 1}$ **b** ≈ -0.618 **25 a** $x = \frac{\pi}{4}$ or $x = \frac{5\pi}{4}$

b $x = 0$, $x = \pi$, $x = \frac{3\pi}{2}$, or $x = 2\pi$ **c** $x = \frac{\pi}{3}$ or $x = \frac{5\pi}{3}$

26 a [graph: $y = [g(x)]^2$, $y = [f(x)]^2$] **b** [graph]

27 $\log_2 (\tan \theta) + \log_2 (\cos \theta)$
$= \log_2 (\sin \theta) - \log_2 (\cos \theta) + \log_2 (\cos \theta)$
$= \log_2 (\sin \theta)$; $\sin \theta > 0$, $\cos \theta > 0$

28 $\frac{2 \sin^2 \theta + 5 \sin \theta \cos \theta + 2 \cos^2 \theta}{\sin \theta + 2 \cos \theta}$
$= \frac{2(\sin^2 \theta + \cos^2 \theta) + 5 \sin \theta \cos \theta}{\sin \theta + 2 \cos \theta}$
$= \frac{2 + 5 \sin \theta \cos \theta}{\sin \theta + 2 \cos \theta}$
$= \frac{2 + 5 \sin \theta \cos \theta}{\sin \theta + 2 \cos \theta} \cdot \frac{\sin \theta - 2 \cos \theta}{\sin \theta - 2 \cos \theta}$
$= \frac{2 \sin \theta - 4 \cos \theta + 5 \sin^2 \theta \cos \theta - 10 \sin \theta \cos^2 \theta}{\sin^2 \theta - 4 \cos^2 \theta}$
$= \frac{2 \sin \theta(1 - 5 \cos^2 \theta) + \cos \theta(-4 + 5 \sin^2 \theta)}{\sin^2 \theta - 4 \cos^2 \theta}$
$= \frac{2 \sin \theta(1 - 5 \cos^2 \theta) + \cos \theta(-4 + 5 - 5 \cos^2 \theta)}{1 - \cos^2 \theta - 4 \cos^2 \theta}$
$= \frac{2 \sin \theta(1 - 5 \cos^2 \theta) + \cos \theta(1 - 5 \cos^2 \theta)}{1 - 5 \cos^2 \theta}$
$= 2 \sin \theta + \cos \theta$
$= \frac{2}{\csc \theta} + \frac{1}{\sec \theta}$
$= \frac{2 \sec \theta + \csc \theta}{\sec \theta \csc \theta}$; $\sin \theta \neq 0$, $\cos \theta \neq 0$,
$\sin \theta \neq \pm 2 \cos \theta$, $\cos \theta \neq \pm \frac{\sqrt{5}}{5}$

29 a $\left\{\frac{\pi}{4}, \frac{7\pi}{4}, \frac{\pi}{3}, \frac{4\pi}{3}\right\}$ **b** $\left\{\frac{\pi}{12}, \frac{\pi}{4}, \frac{5\pi}{12}, \frac{7\pi}{12}, \frac{3\pi}{4}, \frac{11\pi}{12}, \frac{13\pi}{12}, \frac{5\pi}{4},\right.$
$\left.\frac{17\pi}{12}, \frac{19\pi}{12}, \frac{7\pi}{4}, \frac{23\pi}{12}\right\}$ **c** $\left\{\frac{2\pi}{3}, \frac{4\pi}{3}\right\}$ **d** $\left\{\frac{\pi}{3}, \frac{5\pi}{3}, 0, 2\pi\right\}$

e $\left\{0, \frac{\pi}{2}, 2\pi\right\}$

15.2 The Sum and Difference Identities

Warm-up Exercises

1 a $\frac{5}{13}$ **b** $\frac{12}{13}$ **c** 1 **2 a** True **b** True **c** False **3 a** -3
b 2 **c** 1

Problem Set

4 a $\cos 10°$ **b** $\sin 50°$ **c** $2 \sin 50° \cos 40°$
5 $\sin (\theta + \phi) + \sin (\theta - \phi)$
$= \sin \theta \ \cos \phi + \cos \theta \ \sin \phi + \sin \theta \ \cos \phi - \cos \theta \ \sin \phi$
$= \sin \theta \ \cos \phi + \sin \theta \ \cos \phi + \cos \theta \ \sin \phi - \cos \theta \sin \phi$
$= 2 \sin \theta \cos \phi$

6 a $\frac{5}{12}$ **b** $\approx 23°$ **7 a** $\frac{3}{5}$ **b** 0.6 **c** Yes **8 a** $-\sin x$

b $-\cos x$ **c** $\cos x$ **d** $\frac{1}{2} \sin x + \frac{\sqrt{3}}{2} \cos x$ **9 a** True
b False **c** True **10 a** 30° **b** 30° **c** The principal
value of $\arcsin \frac{1}{2}$ is 30°. **11 a** $\frac{3 + 4\sqrt{15}}{20}$ **b** $\frac{4 - 3\sqrt{15}}{20}$

c $\frac{3 + 4\sqrt{15}}{4 - 3\sqrt{15}}$ **12 a** $\frac{7}{25}$ **b** $-\frac{24}{25}$ **c** $\frac{3}{5}$ **d** $\frac{4}{5}$ **e** $\frac{4}{5}$ **f** $-\frac{3}{5}$

13 $\cot (\alpha + \beta) = \dfrac{\cos (\alpha + \beta)}{\sin (\alpha + \beta)}$

$= \dfrac{\cos \alpha \cdot \cos \beta - \sin \alpha \cdot \sin \beta}{\sin \alpha \cdot \cos \beta + \cos \alpha \sin \beta} \cdot \dfrac{\frac{1}{\sin \alpha \sin \beta}}{\frac{1}{\sin \alpha \sin \beta}}$

$= \dfrac{\frac{\cos \alpha \cos \beta}{\sin \alpha \sin \beta} - 1}{\frac{\sin \alpha \cos \beta}{\sin \alpha \sin \beta} + \frac{\cos \alpha \sin \beta}{\sin \alpha \sin \beta}}$

$= \dfrac{\cot \alpha \cot \beta - 1}{\cot \beta + \cot \alpha}$

14 $-\dfrac{56}{65}$ or $\dfrac{16}{65}$ **15** $\approx 46.04°$ **16** $\approx 6.54°$

17 a $x \in \left\{ \dfrac{\pi}{6} + n{\cdot}2\pi, \dfrac{5\pi}{6} + n{\cdot}2\pi \right\}$ **b** No solution

18 a $\dfrac{\sqrt{6} + \sqrt{2}}{4}$ **b** $\dfrac{\sqrt{6} - \sqrt{2}}{4}$ **c** $\dfrac{\sqrt{6} + \sqrt{2}}{4}$ **d** $\dfrac{\sqrt{6} + \sqrt{2}}{4}$

19 $\dfrac{\sin (x + y)}{\sin x \sin y} = \dfrac{\sin x \cos y + \cos x \sin y}{\sin x \sin y} \cdot \dfrac{\frac{1}{\sin x \sin y}}{\frac{1}{\sin x \cdot \sin y}}$

$= \dfrac{\cos y}{\sin y} + \dfrac{\cos x}{\sin x}$

$= \cot y + \cot x$

20 a -1 **b** 0 **21 a** $\sqrt{2} - 1$ **b** $2 + \sqrt{3}$ **c** -1 **d** 1
e $\sqrt{3}$ **22 a** $2 \cos \theta \cos \phi$ **b** $-2 \sin \theta \sin \phi$ **c** $\cos \theta$
d $(180°, 40°)$ **23 a** $\dfrac{\sqrt{2} + \sqrt{6}}{4}$ **b** $\dfrac{\sqrt{2} + \sqrt{6}}{4}$ **c** $\dfrac{-\sqrt{2} - \sqrt{6}}{4}$

24 a $\dfrac{63}{65}$ **b** 2 **c** No real value

25 $\sin 3\theta = \sin (\theta + 2\theta)$

$= \sin \theta \cdot \cos 2\theta + \cos \theta \sin 2\theta$
$= \sin \theta \cdot \cos (\theta + \theta) + \cos \theta \sin (\theta + \theta)$
$= \sin \theta \cdot (\cos \theta \cos \theta - \sin \theta \sin \theta) + \cos \theta$
$\quad (\sin \theta \cos \theta + \cos \theta \sin \theta)$
$= \sin \theta (\cos^2 \theta - \sin^2 \theta) + \cos \theta (2 \cos \theta \sin \theta)$
$= \cos^2 \theta \sin \theta - \sin^3 \theta + 2 \cos^2 \theta \sin \theta$
$= 3 \cos^2 \theta \sin \theta - \sin^3 \theta$
$= 3 \sin \theta \cdot (1 - \sin^2 \theta) - \sin^3 \theta$
$= 3 \sin \theta - 3 \sin^3 \theta - \sin^3 \theta$
$= 3 \sin \theta - 4 \sin^3 \theta$

26 $y \approx 4.12$ **27 a** 0.5 **b** ≈ 0.500002133
c ≈ 0.499999992 **d** ≈ 0.5

15.3 The Double- and Half-Angle Identities

Warm-up Exercises

1 a True **b** True **c** False
2 $(\sin \theta + \cos \theta)^2 = \sin^2\theta + 2 \sin \theta \cos \theta + \cos^2\theta$
$= 1 + 2 \sin \theta \cos \theta$
$= 1 + \sin 2\theta$

3 ≈ 8.57

4 $\cos 2\left(\dfrac{\theta}{2}\right) = 2 \cos^2 \dfrac{\theta}{2} - 1$

$2 \cos^2 \dfrac{\theta}{2} = 1 + \cos \theta$

$\cos^2 \dfrac{\theta}{2} = \dfrac{1 + \cos \theta}{2}$

$\cos \dfrac{\theta}{2} = \pm \sqrt{\dfrac{1 + \cos \theta}{2}}$

5 a False **b** True

6 $\tan 2\theta = \tan (\theta + \theta) = \dfrac{\tan \theta + \tan \theta}{1 - \tan \theta \tan \theta}$

$= \dfrac{2 \tan \theta}{1 - \tan^2 \theta}$

7 a True **b** True **c** True

Problem Set

8 ≈ 0.8775 **9** $(\sin \theta + \cos \theta)^{\csc^2\theta - \cot^2\theta + 1}$

$= (\sin \theta + \cos \theta)^2 = \sin^2 \theta + \cos^2 \theta + 2 \sin \theta \cos \theta = 1 + \sin 2\theta$ **10 a** $\sqrt{2} - 1$ **b** $2 + \sqrt{3}$ **11 a** False **b** True
12 $\sin 75° = \dfrac{\sqrt{2 + \sqrt{3}}}{2}$ **13** $m\ell = \dfrac{12}{5}$; $\alpha \approx 33.69°$; so

$\tan 2\alpha = \dfrac{12}{5}$ **14 a** $\left\{ \dfrac{\pi}{2}, \dfrac{7\pi}{6}, \dfrac{11\pi}{6} \right\}$ **b** $\left\{ \dfrac{5\pi}{6}, \pi, \dfrac{7\pi}{6} \right\}$

c $\left\{ \dfrac{\pi}{6}, \dfrac{2\pi}{3}, \dfrac{5\pi}{6}, \dfrac{4\pi}{3} \right\}$ **15 a** $\dfrac{3}{5}; \dfrac{4}{5}$ **b** $\dfrac{8}{17}; \dfrac{15}{17}$

c $\dfrac{77}{85}; \dfrac{36}{85}$ **16 a** $\approx \pm 0.3162278$ **b** ≈ 0.9486833 **c** $\pm\dfrac{1}{3}$

17 1 **18 a** $\{0, \pi, 2\pi\}$ **b** $\left\{ \dfrac{\pi}{3}, \pi, \dfrac{5\pi}{3} \right\}$ **c** $\{\approx 0.32, \approx 1.89,$
$\approx 3.46, \approx 5.03\}$

19 $\tan \dfrac{\theta}{2} = \pm \sqrt{\dfrac{1 - \cos \theta}{1 + \cos \theta}} \cdot \dfrac{\sqrt{1 + \cos \theta}}{\sqrt{1 + \cos \theta}}$

$= \pm \sqrt{\dfrac{1 - \cos^2 \theta}{(1 + \cos \theta)^2}} = \pm \sqrt{\left(\dfrac{\sin \theta}{1 + \cos \theta} \right)^2}$

$= \dfrac{\sin \theta}{1 + \cos \theta}$

20 $\cos^2\theta - \sin^2\theta$

21 $\{\ldots, \approx -248.5°, \approx -111.5°, \approx 111.5°, \approx 248.5°, \ldots\}$

22 a $\sin 4\theta = \sin 2(2\theta)$
$= 2 \sin 2\theta \cos 2\theta$
$= 2(2 \sin \theta \cos \theta)(\cos^2 \theta - \sin^2 \theta)$
$= 4 \sin \theta \cos^3 \theta - 4 \sin^3 \theta \cos \theta$

b $\cos 4\theta$
$= \cos 2(2\theta)$
$= \cos^2 2\theta - \sin^2 2\theta$
$= (\cos^2 \theta - \sin^2 \theta)^2 - 4 \sin^2 \theta \cos^2 \theta$
$= \cos^4 \theta - 2 \sin^2 \theta \cos^2 \theta + \sin^4 \theta - 4 \sin^2 \theta \cos^2 \theta$
$= \cos^4 \theta + \sin^4 \theta - 6 \sin^2 \theta \cos^2 \theta$
$= \cos^4 \theta + (1 - \cos^2 \theta)^2 - 6 \cos^2 \theta \cdot (1 - \cos^2 \theta)$
$= \cos^4 \theta + 1 - 2 \cos^2 \theta + \cos^4 \theta - 6 \cos^2 \theta + 6 \cos^4 \theta$
$= 8 \cos^4 \theta - 8 \cos^2 \theta + 1$

23 $\cos (\theta + \phi) = \dfrac{63}{65}$; $\sin (\theta + \phi) = -\dfrac{16}{65}$ **24 a** $\left\{ \dfrac{2\pi}{3}, \dfrac{4\pi}{3} \right\}$

b $\{\approx 2.00, \approx 4.29\}$ **c** $\{\theta : 0 \le \theta < 2\pi\}$ **25 a** $\dfrac{\sqrt{2 - \sqrt{3}}}{2}$

b $\dfrac{\sqrt{6} - \sqrt{2}}{4}$

c $\dfrac{\sqrt{6} - \sqrt{2}}{4} = \dfrac{\sqrt{(\sqrt{6} - \sqrt{2})^2}}{4}$

$= \dfrac{\sqrt{6 - 2\sqrt{12} + 2}}{4}$

$= \dfrac{2\sqrt{2 - \sqrt{3}}}{4} = \dfrac{\sqrt{2 - \sqrt{3}}}{2}$

26 $\sin 3\theta = \sin (2\theta + \theta)$
$= \sin 2\theta \cos \theta + \sin \theta \cos 2\theta$
$= 2 \sin \theta \cos^2 \theta + \sin \theta (2 \cos^2 \theta - 1)$
$= 2 \sin \theta \cos^2 \theta + 2 \sin \theta \cos^2 \theta - \sin \theta$
$= 4 \sin \theta \cos^2 \theta - \sin \theta$
$= \sin \theta (4 \cos^2 \theta - 1)$
$= \sin \theta (2 \cos \theta + 1)(2 \cos \theta - 1)$

15.4 Final Identities and Trigonometric Equations

Warm-up Exercises

1 a True **b** False **c** False **2 a** $2 \sin 4\theta \cos \theta$
b $2 \cos \dfrac{3\theta}{2} \cos \dfrac{\theta}{2}$ **3 a** Yes **b** Yes **c** No

Problem Set

4 $(6, 8)$ **5 a** $\cot 5x$ **b** $\tan 4x$ **6 a** $\left\{ \dfrac{\pi}{4}, \dfrac{5\pi}{4} \right\}$

b $\{0, \frac{\pi}{2}, \pi, \frac{3\pi}{2}\}$ **7 a** $2 \sin 10° \cos 7°$ **b** $2 \cos 32° \cos 18°$

8 a $\cos \theta = \frac{1}{2}$ or $\cos \theta = -1$ **b** $\{\frac{\pi}{3}, \pi, \frac{5\pi}{3}\}$

9
$$\frac{\sin 4\theta + \sin 3\theta}{\cos 4\theta + \cos 3\theta} = \tan \frac{7\theta}{2}$$

$$\frac{2 \sin \frac{4\theta + 3\theta}{2} \cdot \cos \frac{4\theta - 3\theta}{2}}{2 \cos \frac{4\theta + 3\theta}{2} \cdot \cos \frac{4\theta - 3\theta}{2}} = \tan \frac{7\theta}{2}$$

$$\frac{2 \sin \frac{7\theta}{2} \cdot \cos \frac{\theta}{2}}{2 \cos \frac{7\theta}{2} \cdot \cos \frac{\theta}{2}} = \tan \frac{7\theta}{2}$$

$$\frac{\sin \frac{7\theta}{2}}{\cos \frac{7\theta}{2}} = \tan \frac{7\theta}{2}$$

$$\tan \frac{7\theta}{2} = \tan \frac{7\theta}{2}$$

10 a $\cos 14° + \cos 6°$ **b** $\sin 136° + \sin 4°$

c $\cos 4° - \cos 22°$ **11 a** $\frac{2 - \sqrt{3}}{4}$ **b** $\frac{-2 - \sqrt{3}}{4}$ **c** $-\frac{1}{4}$

12 a $\tan 4\theta$ **b** $\cot 4\theta$ **13 a** $2 \cos \frac{x + y}{2} \cos \frac{x - y}{2}$

b $2 \cos 4\theta \cos 2\theta$ **c** $2 \cos 10\theta \cos 2\theta$ **d** $-2 \sin \frac{x + y}{2}$
$\sin \frac{x - y}{2}$ **14 a** $\{\frac{7\pi}{6}, \frac{3\pi}{2}, \frac{11\pi}{6}\}$ **b** $\{\frac{\pi}{6}, \frac{\pi}{2}, \frac{5\pi}{6}\}$ **15** ≈ 38.17
16 $\{n\pi\}$, where n is an integer **b** $\{x : x \in \Re\}$

17 $\frac{2 + \sqrt{3}}{2 - \sqrt{3}}$; $\tan 75 \cdot \tan 75$
$$= \tan (30 + 45) \cdot \tan (30 + 45)$$
$$= \frac{\tan 30 + \tan 45}{1 - \tan 30 \tan 45} \cdot \frac{\tan 30 + \tan 45}{1 - \tan 30 \tan 45}$$
$$= \frac{\frac{\sqrt{3}}{3} + 1}{1 - \frac{\sqrt{3}}{3}(1)} \cdot \frac{\frac{\sqrt{3}}{3} + 1}{1 - \frac{\sqrt{3}}{3}(1)}$$
$$= \frac{\frac{\sqrt{3} + 3}{3}}{\frac{3 - \sqrt{3}}{3}} \cdot \frac{\frac{\sqrt{3} + 3}{3}}{\frac{3 - \sqrt{3}}{3}}$$
$$= \frac{\sqrt{3} + 3}{3} \cdot \frac{3}{3 - \sqrt{3}} \cdot \frac{\sqrt{3} + 3}{3} \cdot \frac{3}{3 - \sqrt{3}}$$
$$\frac{(\sqrt{3} + 3)^2}{(3 - \sqrt{3})^2} = \frac{(\sqrt{3} + 3)(\sqrt{3} + 3)}{(3 - \sqrt{3})(3 - \sqrt{3})} = \frac{3 + 6\sqrt{3} + 9}{9 - 6\sqrt{3} + 3}$$
$$\frac{12 + 6\sqrt{3}}{12 - 6\sqrt{3}} = \frac{2 + \sqrt{3}}{2 - \sqrt{3}}$$

18 a $\{\frac{\pi}{6}, \frac{5\pi}{6}, \frac{3\pi}{2}\}$ **b** $\frac{3\pi}{2}$ **c** $\{\frac{\pi}{3}, \frac{2\pi}{3}, \frac{4\pi}{3}, \frac{5\pi}{3}\}$
19 a $\tan \alpha = \frac{\sin (\alpha + \beta) + \sin (\alpha - \beta)}{\cos (\alpha - \beta) + \cos (\alpha + \beta)}$
$$= \frac{\sin \alpha \cos \beta + \cos \alpha \sin \beta + \sin \alpha \cos \beta - \cos \alpha \sin \beta}{\cos \alpha \cos \beta + \sin \alpha \sin \beta + \cos \alpha \cos \beta - \sin \alpha \sin \beta}$$
$$= \frac{2 \sin \alpha \cos \beta}{2 \cos \alpha \cos \beta}$$
$$= \tan \alpha$$
b $\cos \theta \cos (\theta - 90°)$
$$= \frac{1}{2}(\cos [\theta - (\theta - 90°)] + \cos [\theta + (\theta - 90°)])$$
$$= \frac{1}{2}[\cos 90° + \cos (2\theta - 90°)]$$
$$= \frac{1}{2}[0 + \cos (2\theta - 90°)]$$
$$= \frac{1}{2} \cos (2\theta - 90°)$$

20 a $\cot 3\theta = \frac{\cos 5\theta + \cos \theta}{\sin 5\theta + \sin \theta}$
$$= \frac{2 \cos \frac{5\theta + \theta}{2} \cdot \cos \frac{5\theta - \theta}{2}}{2 \sin \frac{5\theta + \theta}{2} \cdot \cos \frac{5\theta - \theta}{2}}$$
$$= \frac{2 \cos 3\theta \cdot \cos 2\theta}{2 \sin 3\theta \cdot \cos 2\theta}$$
$$= \frac{\cos 3\theta}{\sin 3\theta}$$
$$= \cot 3\theta$$

b $2 \sin 8\theta = \frac{\sin 10\theta + \sin 6\theta}{\cos^2 \theta - \sin^2 \theta}$
$$= \frac{2 \sin \frac{10\theta + 6\theta}{2} \cdot \cos \frac{10\theta - 6\theta}{2}}{\cos^2 \theta - \sin^2 \theta}$$
$$= \frac{2 \sin 8\theta \cos 2\theta}{\cos 2\theta}$$
$$= 2 \sin 8\theta$$
21 a $\{\approx 63.43°, \approx 116.57°, \approx 243.43°, \approx 296.57°\}$
b $\{\approx 9.59°, \approx 170.41°\}$ **22** $\{\theta : \theta \in \Re\}$ **23 a** $\approx 41.41°$
b $x \approx 7.937$

24 $\cos 10° \cos 20° = \frac{1}{2}[\cos (20° - 10°) + \cos (10° + 20°)]$
$$= \frac{1}{2}(\cos 10° + \cos 30°)$$
$$= \frac{1}{2}\left(\cos 10° + \frac{\sqrt{3}}{2}\right)$$
$$\cos 20° = \frac{\frac{1}{2} \cos 10° + \frac{\sqrt{3}}{4}}{\cos 10°}$$
$$= \frac{1}{2} + \frac{\sqrt{3}}{4} \cdot \frac{1}{\cos 10°}$$
$$= \frac{1}{2} + \frac{\sqrt{3}}{4} \cdot \sec 10°$$
$$= \frac{\sqrt{3}}{4} \sec 10° + \frac{1}{2}$$

25 a 3 **b** ≈ 6.87 **26 a** 4; -4 **b** $x = -2.47$, $x = 0$, or
$x = 2.47$

Review Problems

1 a True **b** True **c** False **2 a** 0.8 **b** ≈ 0.857
c ≈ 0.926 **3 a** $\frac{24}{25}$ **b** $-\frac{7}{25}$ **4 a** $\frac{1}{2}(\sin 7\theta + \sin \theta)$

b $\frac{1}{2}(\cos 2\theta + \cos 10\theta)$ **c** $\frac{1}{2}(\sin 10\theta - \sin 6\theta)$
5 $\sec \theta + \tan \theta$
$$= \frac{1}{\cos \theta} + \frac{\sin \theta}{\cos \theta}$$
$$= \frac{1 + \sin \theta}{\cos \theta} \cdot \frac{1 - \sin \theta}{1 - \sin \theta}$$
$$= \frac{1 - \sin^2 \theta}{\cos \theta(1 - \sin \theta)} = \frac{\cos^2 \theta}{\cos \theta(1 - \sin \theta)} = \frac{\cos \theta}{1 - \sin \theta};$$
$\cos \theta \neq 0$, $\sin \theta \neq 1$
6 a True **b** False **c** True **7 a** $V_{cyl} = 36\pi \cos \theta$;
$V_{cone} = 72\pi \sin^2\theta \cos \theta$ **b** $\frac{\pi}{4}$

8 a $\tan \theta + \cot \theta = \frac{\sin \theta}{\cos \theta} + \frac{\cos \theta}{\sin \theta}$
$$= \frac{\sin^2\theta + \cos^2\theta}{\cos \theta \sin \theta}$$
$$= \frac{1}{\cos \theta \sin \theta}$$
$$= \sec \theta \csc \theta$$
b $\sec^2\theta + \csc^2\theta = \frac{1}{\cos^2\theta} + \frac{1}{\sin^2\theta}$
$$= \frac{1}{\cos^2\theta \sin^2\theta}$$
$$= \sec^2\theta \csc^2\theta; \sin \theta \neq 0, \cos \theta \neq 0$$
c $\frac{\cos \theta}{1 + \sin \theta} = \frac{\cos \theta}{1 + \sin \theta} \cdot \frac{1 - \sin \theta}{1 - \sin \theta}$
$$= \frac{1 - \sin \theta}{\cos \theta}; \sin \theta \neq 1, \sin \theta \neq -1$$
9 a False **b** False **c** True **10** $\{0, \pi, 2\pi\}$
11 a $\cos \left(\theta - \frac{\pi}{2}\right) = \cos \theta \cos \frac{\pi}{2} + \sin \theta \sin \frac{\pi}{2}$
$$= 0 \cos \theta + 1 \sin \theta$$
$$= \sin \theta$$

b $\sin\left(\theta - \frac{\pi}{2}\right) = \sin\theta\cos\frac{\pi}{2} - \cos\theta\sin\frac{\pi}{2}$
$$= 0\sin\theta - 1\cos\theta$$
$$= -\cos\theta$$

c $\sin\left(\theta + \frac{\pi}{2}\right) = \sin\theta\cos\frac{\pi}{2} + \cos\theta\sin\frac{\pi}{2}$
$$= 0\sin\theta + 1\cos\theta$$
$$= \cos\theta$$

d $\cos\left(\theta + \frac{\pi}{2}\right) = \cos\theta\cos\frac{\pi}{2} - \sin\theta\sin\frac{\pi}{2}$
$$= 0\cos\theta - 1\sin\theta$$
$$= -\sin\theta$$

12 True **13 a** $3\sin x - 4\sin^3 x$ **b** $4\cos^3 x - 3\cos x$

14 a True **b** True **c** True

15 $\cos^4\theta - \sin^4\theta = (\cos^2\theta + \sin^2\theta)(\cos^2\theta - \sin^2\theta)$
$$= \cos^2\theta - \sin^2\theta$$

16 $\tan(\alpha - \beta)$ is undefined. $\tan\alpha$ and $\tan\beta$ are the slopes of the lines QP and QR. Since these are negative reciprocals, the lines are perpendicular. So $\alpha - \beta = 90°$ **17 a** $2\sin\frac{x+y}{2}\cos\frac{x-y}{2}$

b $2\sin 2\theta\cos\theta$ **c** $2\sin 3\theta\cos 7\theta$ **18 a** True **b** True

19 a $\frac{a}{\sqrt{a^2+b^2}+a}$ **b** $\frac{\sqrt{a^2+b^2}-a}{a}$ **20** $\{n\pi\}$, where n is an integer **21 a** $\frac{\sqrt{2}}{2}$ **b** $\frac{\sqrt{3}}{2}$ **c** $\frac{\sqrt{2}}{2}$

22 a $\frac{\cos x - \sin x}{\cos x + \sin x} = \frac{(\cos x - \sin x)(\cos x + \sin x)}{(\cos x + \sin x)(\cos x + \sin x)}$
$$= \frac{\cos^2 x - \sin^2 x}{\cos^2 x + 2\cos x\sin x + \sin^2 x}$$
$$= \frac{\cos 2x}{1 + 2\sin x\cos x}$$
$$= \frac{\cos 2x}{1 + \sin 2x}$$

b $1 + \tan x\tan 2x = 1 + (\tan x)\left(\frac{2\tan x}{1 - \tan^2 x}\right)$
$$= 1 + \frac{2\tan^2 x}{1 - \tan^2 x}$$
$$= \frac{1 - \tan^2 x + 2\tan^2 x}{1 - \tan^2 x}$$
$$= \frac{1 + \tan^2 x}{1 - \tan^2 x}$$
$$= \frac{1 + \frac{\sin^2 x}{\cos^2 x}}{1 - \frac{\sin^2 x}{\cos^2 x}}$$
$$= \frac{\frac{\cos^2 x + \sin^2 x}{\cos^2 x}}{\frac{\cos^2 x - \sin^2 x}{\cos^2 x}} = \frac{1}{\cos 2x} = \sec 2x$$

c $\sin(x + y)\sin(x - y)$
$$= \frac{1}{2}(\cos[(x + y) - (x - y)] - \cos[(x + y) + (x - y)])$$
$$= \frac{1}{2}(\cos 2y - \cos 2x)$$
$$= \frac{1}{2}[1 - 2\sin^2 y - (1 - 2\sin^2 x)]$$
$$= \frac{1}{2}(2\sin^2 x - 2\sin^2 y)$$
$$= \sin^2 x - \sin^2 y$$

23 a $(-7, 24)$; $(-24, -7)$; $(7, -24)$ **b** $\sin\theta = \frac{7}{25}$;
$\cos\theta = \frac{24}{25}$; $\tan\theta = \frac{7}{24}$; $\sin\left(\theta + \frac{\pi}{2}\right) = \frac{24}{25}$; $\cos\left(\theta + \frac{\pi}{2}\right) =$
$-\frac{7}{25}$; $\tan\left(\theta + \frac{\pi}{2}\right) = -\frac{24}{7}$; $\sin(\theta + \pi) = -\frac{7}{25}$;
$\cos(\theta + \pi) = -\frac{24}{25}$; $\tan(\theta + \pi) = \frac{7}{24}$; $\sin\left(\theta + \frac{3\pi}{2}\right) =$

$-\frac{24}{25}$; $\cos\left(\theta + \frac{3\pi}{2}\right) = \frac{7}{25}$; $\tan\left(\theta + \frac{3\pi}{2}\right) = -\frac{24}{7}$ **24** 1

25

16.1 The Law of Sines

1 ≈ 0.678 **2** ≈ 12.709 **3** $17°$ **4** $x \approx 24.25$; $y \approx 27.58$
5 $64°$ **6** ≈ 7.09 **7** 18.87 **8** ≈ 1363.68

Problem Set
9 a $(283, \approx 490)$ **b** ≈ 868 **11** ≈ 4.46 **12 a** 1 **b** 1 **c** 1
d 1 **13 a** 0; 0.5; ≈ 0.707; ≈ 0.866; 1; ≈ 0.866; ≈ 0.707;
0; -1; 0 **b** **14** $\frac{\sqrt{6} - \sqrt{2}}{4}$

15 $5\sqrt{6} - 5\sqrt{2}$ **16** ≈ 78.6 mi **17** ≈ 0.88 **19** $\approx 63°$ or $\approx 117°$ **21** No solution **23** 4; -4 **25** 4; -4 **26 a** If $b = a\sin\theta$, the triangle is a right triangle (since $a\sin\theta$ is the length of the vertical altitude of the triangle shown). Therefore, since there is only one such altitude, only one triangle is determined. **b** If $a\sin\theta < b < a$, the side with length b can meet the base either to the left or to the right of the altitude, so two triangles are determined. **c** If $b \geq a$, the side with length b can only meet the base to the right of the altitude, so only one triangle is determined. **d** If $b < a\sin\theta$, the side with length b is shorter than the altitude—an impossibility, since the altitude is the shortest possible segment connecting the upper vertex and the base. Therefore, no triangle is determined.
27 ≈ 173.77 ft **28 a** $\approx 36°$ or $\approx 144°$ **b** If $\alpha \approx 36°$, $\beta \approx 112°$; if $\alpha \approx 144°$, $\beta \approx 4°$. **c** If $\alpha \approx 36°$, $\beta \approx 84°$; if $\alpha \approx 144°$, the sum of α and θ exceeds $180°$, so no such triangle exists. **29** ≈ 546 ft **30** Willy is wrong. The height of the window is $18\sin 75°$, or ≈ 17.39, feet. A 16-foot ladder is therefore too short to reach it.
31 $\alpha_1 \approx 58.34$; $\alpha_2 \approx 121.66$ **32** ≈ 6.44 **33** The length of the altitude from B to $\overline{AC}$ is $a\sin\angle C$. Since $k = \frac{1}{2}bh$, $k = \frac{1}{2}\cdot b\cdot a\sin\angle C = \frac{1}{2}ab\sin\angle C$.
34 $R \approx 17.01$ **35** Draw the diameter from C through O. Label its other endpoint A′, and draw $\overline{A'B}$. $\angle A' = \angle A$, since they are inscribed angles intercepting the same arc. $\angle A'BC = 90°$, since this is an angle inscribed in a semicircle. In right triangle A′BC, $\sin\angle A' = \frac{a}{CA'}$, so $\sin\angle A$ is also equal to $\frac{a}{CA'}$. Therefore, CA' (the diameter) is equal to $\frac{a}{\sin\angle A}$.

16.2 The Law of Cosines

1 $a \approx 7.3$; $b \approx 9.5$; $c \approx 3.6$ **2** $\approx 72°$ **3** $\approx 59°$ **4** $\approx 18°$
5 ≈ 11.6 **6** ≈ 8.1 **7** ≈ 47.3

Problem Set

8 AC $\approx$ 3.5; m$\angle$A $\approx$ 48; m$\angle$C $\approx$ 117

9 a

b

c

11 $\frac{56}{65}$ **12** $y = 2(x - 3)$

13

x	0	$\frac{\pi}{4}$	$\frac{\pi}{2}$	$\frac{3\pi}{4}$	π	$\frac{5\pi}{4}$	$\frac{3\pi}{2}$	$\frac{7\pi}{4}$	2π	$\frac{9\pi}{4}$	$\frac{5\pi}{2}$
y	0	$\frac{\sqrt{2}}{2}$	1	$\frac{\sqrt{2}}{2}$	0	$\frac{-\sqrt{2}}{2}$	-1	$\frac{-\sqrt{2}}{2}$	0	$\frac{\sqrt{2}}{2}$	1

14 $\approx$ 83 **15** $\approx$ 162 mi **16** $\approx$ 836.74 ft **17 a** $x = \frac{\pi}{2} +$ $n \cdot 2\pi$ **b** $x = 0 + n \cdot \pi$ **c** $x = \frac{3\pi}{2} + n \cdot 2\pi$ **18** $\approx$ 94.05

19 a 10; 25; $\approx$ 18.03 **b** $\approx$ 37° **21**

23 $\approx$ 62° or $\approx$ 118° **24** Impossible **25** $\approx$ 6.3

26 a $\approx$ 20.62 **b** $\approx$ 26.93 **c** $\approx$ 22.36 **d** $\approx$ 48.37

27 $\approx$ 82.8 **28** $\approx$ 45.77 **29 a** $\approx$ 76.29 **b** $\approx$ 68.67

30 a 30° or 150° **b** $\approx$ 9 or $\approx$ 22.3 **31** $\approx$ 5.74 **32 a** 1; -1 **b** 6; 4 **c** 1; -1 **d** 6; 4 **33** By the Pythagorean Theorem,

$h^2 = c^2 - x^2$

$h^2 = b^2 - (a - x)^2$

Therefore,

$c^2 - x^2 = b^2 - (a - x)^2$

$c^2 - x^2 = b^2 - a^2 + 2ax - x^2$

$2ax = a^2 - b^2 + c^2$

$x = \frac{a^2 + c^2 - b^2}{2a}$

But $h^2 = c^2 - x^2 = (c + x)(c - x)$

Therefore, $h^2 = \left(c + \frac{a^2 + c^2 - b^2}{2a}\right)\left(c - \frac{a^2 + c^2 - b^2}{2a}\right)$

$h^2 = \left(\frac{2ac + a^2 + c^2 - b^2}{2a}\right)\left(\frac{2ac - a^2 - c^2 + b^2}{2a}\right)$

$h^2 = \left(\frac{(a + c)^2 - b^2}{2a}\right)\left(\frac{b^2 - (a - c)^2}{2a}\right)$

$4a^2h^2 = (a + c - b)(a + c + b)(b - a + c)(b + a - c)$

Since $s = \frac{a + b + c}{2}$,

$b - a + c = 2s - 2a$

$b + a - c = 2s - 2c$

$a + c - b = 2s - 2b$

$a + c + b = 2s$

$4a^2h^2 = (2s - 2a)(2s - 2c)(2s - 2b)(2s)$

$= 16s(s - a)(s - c)(s - b)$

$\frac{a^2h^2}{4} = s(s - a)(s - c)(s - b)$

$\frac{ah}{2} = \sqrt{s(s - a)(s - c)(s - b)}$

16.3 Graphing Sine Functions

Warm-up Exercises

1 2.5 **2** Shifted $\frac{\pi}{6}$ units to the right **3** Shifted 4 units down **4** Amplitude is 4.5. **5**

6

7

8

9

Problem Set

10

x	0	$\frac{\pi}{3}$	$\frac{\pi}{2}$	$\frac{2\pi}{3}$	π	$\frac{3\pi}{2}$	2π	$\frac{5\pi}{2}$	3π
y	1	0.5	0	-0.5	-1	0	1	0	-1

11 $y = 2 \sin x - 2$ **13 a** $\frac{\pi}{6}$ **b** $\frac{\pi}{12}$ **c** $\frac{\pi}{18}$ **d** $\frac{\pi}{3}$ **15** $y = 2 \sin x$ **16** $x \approx 25.7$; $y \approx 37.6$ **17 a** A$\left(\frac{2\pi}{3}, 0\right)$, B$(\pi, -3)$, C$\left(\frac{4\pi}{3}, 0\right)$ **b** $\frac{4\pi}{3}$ **19**

21 Shifted 1 unit up **23 a** 2 **b** π **25** $\approx$ 5.41

26 $y = 5 \sin \frac{2}{3}x$

27 $\frac{\cos 8x + \cos 2x}{\sin 8x - \sin 2x} = \frac{2 \cos 5x \cos 3x}{2 \sin 3x \cos 5x}$

$= \frac{\cos 3x}{\sin 3x} = \cot 3x$

28 0 **29** 4π **30** $\frac{\pi}{8}$

16.4 Changing the Period

Warm-up Exercises

1 a   **b**

c   **d**

e   **2** $\left(\frac{2\pi}{3}, 0\right)$; $\left(\frac{7\pi}{6}, -2\right)$; $\left(\frac{5\pi}{3}, 0\right)$;

$\left(\frac{13\pi}{6}, 2\right)$ **3** $\frac{\pi}{3}$

Problem Set

4 a   **b**

c   **d**

5 a 3; π **b** 5; $\frac{2\pi}{3}$ **c** 32; 2 **6** $y = 4\cos\left(\frac{1}{4}x\right)$

7 a $y = 3\sin\left(x + \frac{\pi}{4}\right)$ **b** $y = 3\cos\left(x - \frac{\pi}{4}\right)$

8

x	0	$\frac{\pi}{6}$	$\frac{\pi}{4}$	$\frac{\pi}{3}$	$\frac{9\pi}{20}$	$\frac{\pi}{2}$	$\frac{11\pi}{20}$
y	0	$\frac{\sqrt{3}}{3}$	1	$\sqrt{3}$	≈ 6.3	Und.	≈ -6.3

$\frac{2\pi}{3}$	$\frac{3\pi}{4}$	π
$-\sqrt{3}$	-1	0

b   **9 a** $\frac{12}{13}$ **b** $\frac{5}{13}$ **c** $\frac{3}{5}$ **d** $\frac{4}{5}$ **e** $\frac{56}{65}$

10 a 14 **b** -14 **c** $\frac{1}{7}$ **d** 4 **e** 10 **11 a**

b   **c**

12 a $y = 2\sin(2x)$; $y = -2\sin(-2x)$ **b** $y = 2\cos\left[2\left(x - \frac{\pi}{4}\right)\right]$; $y = 2\cos\left[2\left(x + \frac{3\pi}{4}\right)\right]$ **13 a** $\frac{\pi}{5}$ **b** $\frac{\pi}{6}$

14 ≈ 101.13 cm **15 a** 84 **b** ≈ 13.6 **c** ≈ 13.6

16 a Domain: $\left\{x : 0 \le x \le \frac{8\pi}{3}\right\}$; range: $\{y : 3 \le y \le 7\}$
b Domain: $\{x : 0 \le x \le 16\pi\}$; range: $\{y : -9 \le y \le -5\}$

17 No period **18 a**

b   **c**

d [graph] **19 a** [graphs]

b [graphs] **c** [graphs]

d [graphs] **20** $\left\{x : 0 \le x \le \frac{\pi}{3} \text{ or } \frac{5\pi}{3} \le x \le 2\pi\right\}$

21 ≈ 21.96 **22** 1

23

Area of $\triangle ABE$
$= \frac{1}{2}(AE)(BE)(\sin \angle AEB)$

Area of $\triangle ADE$
$= \frac{1}{2}(AE)(DE)(\sin \angle AED)$
$= \frac{1}{2}(AE)(DE)(\sin \angle AEB)$

Area of $\triangle BCE$
$= \frac{1}{2}(CE)(BE)(\sin \angle BEC)$
$= \frac{1}{2}(CE)(BE)(\sin \angle AEB)$

Area of $\triangle CDE$
$= \frac{1}{2}(CE)(DE)(\sin \angle DEC)$
$= \frac{1}{2}(CE)(DE)(\sin \angle AEB)$

$A_{\triangle ABE} \cdot A_{\triangle CDE}$
$= \frac{1}{2}(AE)(BE)(\sin \angle AEB) \cdot \frac{1}{2}(CE)(DE)(\sin \angle AEB)$
$= \frac{1}{2}(AE)(DE)(\sin \angle AEB) \cdot \frac{1}{2}(CE)(BE)(\sin \angle AEB)$
$= A_{\triangle ADE} \cdot A_{\triangle BCE}$

16.5 More Trigonometric Graphs

Warm-up Exercises

1 a **b**

c **2 a**

b **c**

Problem Set

3 a **b**

c **4 a**

b **c**

d **e**

5 a **b**

6 $y = \tan (2x)$ **7** ≈ 0.243 **8** ≈ 9.33 mi

9 a **b**

c

---

10 $\frac{2}{5}$ **11** $\approx 19{,}199.59$ cm^2 **12 a** $\frac{8}{3}$

b $0 < m\angle ABC < 90$ **13**

14 **15** ≈ 3.06

16 a **b**

c **d**

Review Problems

1 a **b**

c

2 $\alpha \approx 71.8$; $\beta \approx 58.8$; $\gamma \approx 18.2$

3 $x \approx 32.71$; $y \approx 20.10$ **4 a** $\frac{1}{2}$ **b** $\frac{1}{2}$ **c** $\frac{1}{2}$ **d** $\frac{1}{2}$ **e** $\frac{1}{2}$

5 ≈ 15.665 **6 a** 3.5 **b** 8

7

Equation	Amplitude	Period	Range
$y = -2 \sin (3x)$	2	$\frac{2\pi}{3}$	$\{y: -2 \leq y \leq 2\}$
$y = 4 \cos (2x)$	4	π	$\{y: -4 \leq y \leq 4\}$
$y = 3 \sin \left(\frac{1}{3}x\right) + 5$	3	6π	$\{y: 2 \leq y \leq 8\}$

8 a **b**

9 a 1 **b** 2 **c** 0 **10** $x \approx 11.6$; $y \approx 8.1$; $z \approx 47.3$

11 ≈ 89 **12** $\frac{\pi}{6}, \frac{5\pi}{6}$ **13** $y = 4 \sin x$

14 a,b,c

15 a Domain: $\left\{x : 0 \le x \le \frac{2\pi}{3}\right\}$; range: $\{y : -4 \le y \le 4\}$

b $\frac{\pi}{9}, \frac{5\pi}{9}$ **16** $\frac{2\pi}{5}$ or $\frac{-2\pi}{5}$ **17** $\frac{1}{2}$

18 $x_1 + x_2 = \pi$ **19 a**

b **c**

d **e** **20** $\approx 84.1\%$

21 ≈ 106.49; ≈ 74.56 **22** ≈ 282.14 cm

GLOSSARY

abscissa The first of an ordered pair of coordinates; an x-coordinate. (p. 45)

absolute value The numerical value of an expression considered without regard to its sign. The absolute value of a number a, symbolized $|a|$, is equal to a if a is positive or zero or to $-a$ if a is negative. (p. 24)

algorithm A step-by-step procedure for solving a problem in a finite number of steps. (p. 13)

amplitude The maximum distance of a sine or cosine graph from its axis. (p. 706)

antilogarithm The number corresponding to a base raised to a logarithmic power. For example, since log 100 = 2, the base-10 antilogarithm of 2 is 100. (p. 481)

arithmetic mean **1** One of the terms between two designated terms of an arithmetic sequence. (p. 577) **2** See **mean.**

arithmetic sequence A sequence in which the difference of any two successive terms is constant. (p. 576)

arithmetic series A representation of the sum of a specified number of terms of an arithmetic sequence. (p. 577)

array A finite number of successive terms of a sequence. (p. 564)

asymptote A line that is approached but never reached by a curved graph. (p. 269)

axis of symmetry A line that divides a graph into two parts that are mirror images of each other. (p. 142)

base In an exponential expression, the quantity that is raised to a power. (p. 70)

bimodal Having two modes. (p. 229)

binomial probability experiment Any probability experiment that can be modeled by a binomial expansion. Such an experiment consists of a finite number of independent trials, with each trial resulting in one of two possible outcomes and with the probabilities of these outcomes being the same for each trial. (p. 570)

binomial theorem A formula for the expansion of expressions of the form $(x + y)^n$, where n is a positive integer. (p. 412)

bisection A method of approximating a real zero of a function by repeated averaging of values on either side of the zero. (p. 398)

boundary-value algorithm A procedure for determining the solutions of inequalities by locating the specific regions of the real-number line or the coordinate plane that represent the solutions. (p. 94)

box-and-whisker plot A statistical diagram showing the outliers and the quartiles of a set of data values. (p. 173)

central angle An angle whose vertex is the center of a circle. (p. 603)

circumference The perimeter of a circle. (p. 731)

closed-form formula A formula that shows the relationship between any input of a function and its corresponding output. (p. 221)

coefficient The numerical factor in a monomial. (p. 729)

cofunctions A pair of trigonometric functions that output equal values when their inputs are angles complementary to each other. Sine and cosine, tangent and cotangent, and secant and cosecant are cofunctions. (p. 633)

combination function A function that for a pair of inputs (n, r) outputs the number of groups of r elements that can be selected from a set of n elements. (p. 214)

common difference The difference between any two successive terms of an arithmetic sequence. (p. 576)

common factor A factor shared by all the terms of a polynomial. (p. 135)

common logarithm A base-10 logarithm. (p. 480)

common ratio The ratio between any two successive terms of a geometric sequence. (p. 583)

completing the square Rewriting a quadratic polynomial so that it contains a perfect-square trinomial. (p. 157)

complex fraction A rational expression containing a fraction in the numerator, the denominator, or both. (p. 454)

complex number Any number that can be expressed in the form $a + bi$, where $i = \sqrt{-1}$ and a and b are real numbers. The term a is known as the number's real part, and the term bi is known as its imaginary part. (p. 359)

composite function A function made up of two other functions, with the outputs of one being used as the inputs of the other. (p. 190)

compound function A function in which different rules are applied to different inputs. (p. 114)

conditional probability The probability that a certain event will occur, given that another event has previously occurred. (p. 543)

conjugates **1** A pair of expressions of the form $a + b\sqrt{c}$ and $a - b\sqrt{c}$, whose product will always be rational if a, b, and c are rational. (p. 73) **2** A pair of complex numbers of the form $a + bi$ and $a - bi$, whose product will always be a real number. (p. 359)

conjunction A statement in which two possible outcomes are connected by *and*, representing the intersection of two events. (p. 542)

constant of variation The value of the quotient of two quantities that vary directly or of the product of two quantities that vary inversely. Also called *constant of proportionality*. (p. 101)

constraint One of the restrictions that defines the domain in a linear-programming problem, represented by a linear inequality. (p. 467)

cosecant A trigonometric function equivalent to the reciprocal of an angle's sine. (p. 611)

cosine A trigonometric function equivalent to the x-coordinate of the point where the terminal ray of an angle in standard position intersects a unit circle. (p. 610)

cotangent A trigonometric function equivalent to the reciprocal of an angle's tangent. (p. 611)

coterminal angles Any angles that have the same terminal ray when in standard position. (p. 604)

degree (*of a monomial*) The sum of the powers to which the variables in a monomial are raised. (p. 729)

degree (*of a polynomial*) The greatest of the degrees of a polynomial's terms. (p. 730)

dependent events Two events such that the occurrence of one affects the probability of the occurrence of the other. (p. 543)

deviation score The difference between a particular value in a set of data and the set's mean. (p. 276)

directed graph A network whose segments indicate direction. Also called *digraph*. (p. 7)

direct variation A relationship between two variable quantities in which the quantities' quotient is constant. (p. 101)

discrete function A function whose domain is a set of numbers that can be listed. (p. 213)

discriminant The expression $b^2 - 4ac$ associated with a quadratic equation in the form $ax^2 + bx + c = 0$. (p. 150)

disjunction A statement in which two possible outcomes are connected by *or*, representing the union of two events. (p. 535)

domain The set of all inputs for which a function produces meaningful outputs. (p. 184)

ellipse A conic section that is the graph of an equation of the form
$$\frac{(x - h)^2}{a^2} + \frac{(y - k)^2}{b^2} = 1$$
where a, b, h, and k are real. (p. 284)

equation A mathematical sentence stating that two expressions have the same value. (p. 30)

even function Any function f for which $f(-x) = f(x)$ for all values of x. (p. 646)

event The element or elements in a sample space that satisfy specified conditions. (p. 529)

expand To rewrite a factored expression as a single polynomial. (p. 127)

exponent In an exponential expression, the number indicating how many times the base is used as a factor. (p. 70)

exponential equation An equation containing a variable in an exponent. (p. 495)

expression A mathematical phrase consisting of a number, a variable, or a group of numbers and variables connected by operations. (p. 23)

extraneous root A value of the variable that is obtained by solving an equation but which is not in fact a solution of the equation. (p. 350)

factor To rewrite an expression as the product of its factors. (p. 127)

factorial function A function that for a nonnegative integral input n outputs the number of ways in which n items can be arranged. (p. 213)

Fibonacci numbers The elements of the infinite sequence 1, 1, 2, 3, 5, 8, 13, . . . , in which the first two elements are 1's and each succeeding element is the sum of its two predecessors. (p. 223)

first differences The differences between successive outputs of a recursively defined function. (p. 223)

fitted line A line whose equation approximately represents a linear relationship between data values. (p. 107)

function A relation in which each input is paired with exactly one output. (p. 184)

geometric mean One of the terms between two specified terms of a geometric sequence. (p. 584)

geometric sequence A sequence in which the quotient of any two successive terms is constant. (p. 583)

geometric series A representation of the sum of a specified number of terms of a geometric sequence. (p. 585)

hyperbola A conic section that is the graph of an equation of the form
$$\frac{(x - h)^2}{a^2} - \frac{(y - k)^2}{b^2} = 1 \text{ or}$$
$$\frac{(y - k)^2}{b^2} - \frac{(x - h)^2}{a^2} = 1$$
where a, b, h, and k are real. (p. 284)

identity An equation that makes a true statement for all possible values of the variable(s). (p. 729)

imaginary number See *pure imaginary number.*

independent events Two events such that the occurrence of one does not affect the probability of the occurrence of the other. (p. 542)

inequality A mathematical sentence stating that two expressions are not equal. (p. 38)

initial ray The ray at which the rotation of an angle begins. (p. 603)

intercept A point at which a graph crosses one of the coordinate axes. (p. 46)

intersection The set of all elements common to two sets. (p. 95)

inverse functions Any pair of functions f and g such that $f[g(x)] = g[f(x)] = x$ for all values of x in the domains of f and g. (p. 191)

inverse variation A relationship between two variable quantities in which the quantities' product is constant. (p. 313)

lattice point A point having integral coordinates. (p. 21)

leading coefficient The coefficient of the first term of a polynomial written in descending order of powers. (p. 730)

like terms Terms containing the same variables raised to the same powers. (p. 23)

linear Having a degree of one. (p. 30)

linear programming A method of finding the maximum or minimum output of a function whose domain can be represented by a polygonal region of the coordinate plane. (p. 467)

line of best fit A line whose equation, determined by the method of least squares, represents a linear relationship between data values. Also called *regression line*. (p. 108)

logarithm The power to which a given base must be raised to equal a given number. (p. 475)

lower bound of zeros A value that is less than any of the real zeros of a given polynomial function. (p. 396)

mathematical induction A method of proving a statement true for all natural numbers by showing that it is true for the first natural number and that if it is true for a number n, it is also true for $n + 1$. (p. 597)

matrix A rectangular arrangement of data. (p. 52)

mean A measure of central tendency equal to the sum of a set of data values divided by the number of values. (p. 228)

mean deviation A measure of variation equal to the sum of the absolute values of the deviation scores of a set of data values divided by the number of values. (p. 276)

median A measure of central tendency equal to the middle value (or the mean of the two middle values) in an ordered set of data values. (p. 173)

mode A measure of central tendency equal to the value that occurs the greatest number of times in a set of data values. (p. 228)

model A mathematical or diagrammatic representation of a situation. (p. 4)

monomial A real number, a variable, or a product of real numbers and variables. (p. 729)

multiplication-addition method An algebraic method of solving a system of equations. (p. 88)

multiplicity The number of times a particular value is a zero of a polynomial function. (p. 404)

mutually exclusive Having no outcome in common. (p. 536)

natural logarithm A base-e logarithm. (p. 481)

nested form A form of polynomial expression used to simplify calculator and computer calculations. (p. 381)

network A geometric model consisting of points joined by segments. (p. 10)

normal curve The graph of a normal distribution. (p. 372)

normal distribution A set of data values whose frequencies decrease symmetrically about a single value that corresponds to the data's mean, mode, and median. (p. 372)

odd function Any function f for which $f(-x) = -f(x)$ for all values of x. (p. 646)

opposite A number equal in absolute value but opposite in sign to a given number. (p. 24)

ordered pair A pair of numbers in the form (x, y), used to represent a solution of an equation in two variables or an input and corresponding output of a relation. (p. 31)

ordinate The second of an ordered pair of coordinates; a y-coordinate. (p. 45)

origin The intersection of the axes of a coordinate plane. Its coordinates are $(0, 0)$. (p. 45)

outlier scores The greatest and the least value in a set of data values. (p. 173)

parabola A conic section that is the graph of an equation of the form
$$y = a(x - h)^2 + k$$
where a, h, and k are real. (p. 142)

partial sum of a sequence The sum of a specified number of terms (beginning with the first) of a sequence. (p. 564)

Pascal's triangle A triangular arrangement of numbers in which each row begins and ends with a 1 and each interior element is the sum of two adjacent elements in the preceding row. (p. 410)

percentile rank A number representing the percentage of the data values in a set that are less than a given value. (p. 229)

periodic Repeating the same pattern over and over. The repeated pattern in a periodic graph is called a cycle, and its length is called the period of the graph. (p. 705)

permutation function A function that for a pair of inputs (n, r) outputs the number of arrangements of r elements that can be selected from a set of n elements. (p. 214)

phase shift A leftward or rightward shift of the graph of a periodic function. (p. 706)

polynomial An expression consisting of a monomial or a sum or difference of monomials. (p. 729)

probability The ratio of the number of elements in a specified event to the number of elements in the sample space of which it is a part. (pp. 60, 529)

proportion An equation of the form $\frac{a}{b} = \frac{c}{d}$, where a, b, c, and d are real numbers, $b \neq 0$, and $d \neq 0$. (p. 102).

pure imaginary number A number of the form ki, where k is real and nonzero and $i = \sqrt{-1}$. (p. 358)

quadrant One of the four regions into which the axes divide the coordinate plane. (p. 45)

quadratic Having a degree of two (p. 127)

quartile A value corresponding to the 25th, the 50th, or the 75th percentile of a set of data. (p. 173)

radian A unit of angular measurement equivalent to the measure of a central angle that intercepts a 1-unit-long arc of a unit circle. (p. 640)

radicand The expression under a radical sign. (p. 344)

range 1 The set of all meaningful outputs of a function. (p. 184) **2** A measure of dispersion equal to the difference between the greatest value and the least value in a set of data. (p. 275)

rational equation An equation that contains at least one rational expression. (p. 435)

rational expression Any expression that can be written as a ratio of polynomials. (p. 427)

recursive Involving a specified beginning value and a formula for obtaining each succeeding value from its predecessor(s). (p. 16)

reference angle For an angle in standard position, the first-quadrant angle whose terminal ray forms the same acute angle with the x-axis. (p. 619)

reflection The mirror image of a graph with respect to a specified line. (p. 200)

relation A set of ordered pairs. (p. 183)

restricted value Any value of a variable for which the denominator of a rational expression is equal to zero. (p. 427)

root A solution of an equation. (p. 144)

root index In a radical expression, the number that indicates the number of times the expression must be used as a factor to produce the radicand. (p. 344)

scalar A quantity by which a matrix is multiplied. (p. 52)

sample A group selected to be representative of an entire population. (p. 552)

sample space The set of all possible outcomes of an experiment. (p. 528)

scientific notation The expression of a number in the form
$$c \times 10^n$$
where $0 < |c| < 10$ and n is an integer. (p. 730)

secant A trigonometric function equivalent to the reciprocal of an angle's cosine. (p. 611)

second differences The differences between the first differences of the outputs of a recursively defined function. (p. 223)

sequence The ordered outputs of a function whose domain is the set of natural numbers. Also called *progression*. (p. 563)

series A representation of a partial or total sum of the terms of a sequence. (p. 570)

sigma notation A method of expressing the sum of a specified number of terms of a sequence. (p. 12)

sine A trigonometric function equivalent to the y-coordinate of the point where the terminal ray of an angle in standard position intersects a unit circle. (p. 610)

slope The ratio of the change in x values to the change in x values between any two points on a line in the coordinate plane. (p. 79)

standard deviation A measure of dispersion equal to the square root of the variance of a set of data. (p. 417)

standard position The position of an angle whose initial ray coincides with the positive x-axis. (p. 603)

standard radical form The form $a\sqrt{b}$, where a is a rational number and b is an integer having no perfect-square factors. (p. 73)

stem-and-leaf plot A form of organized representation of a set of data. (p. 172)

substitution An algebraic method of solving a system of equations. (p. 88)

synthetic division An algorithm for determining the quotient and the remainder when a polynomial $P(x)$ is divided by a binomial of the form $(x - a)$. (p. 389)

system of equations A group of two or more equations, the solutions of which consist of the values that simultaneously make all of the equations true statements. Also called *simultaneous equations*. (p. 87)

tangent A trigonometric ratio equivalent to the quotient of an angle's sine and cosine. (p. 611)

term **1** One of the elements of a sequence. (p. 563) **2** One of the monomials of which a polynomial consists. (p. 729)

terminal ray The ray at which the rotation of an angle ends. (p. 603)

tree diagram A diagram consisting of branches, each of which represents a possible outcome or choice. (p. 7)

union The set of elements in one or both of two sets. (p. 95)

unit circle A circle with its center at the origin of a coordinate system and a radius of one unit; the graph of $x^2 + y^2 = 1$. (p. 604)

upper bound of zeros A value that is greater than any of the real zeros of a given polynomial function. (p. 396)

variable A symbol used to represent a number. (p. 728)

variance A measure of dispersion equal to the average of the squares of the deviation scores of a set of data values. (p. 417)

Venn diagram A diagram used to represent the relationships among sets. (p. 522)

x-axis The horizontal axis of a coordinate system. (p. 45)

x-coordinate A value representing the distance of a point from the y-axis on a coordinate plane. (p. 45)

y-axis The vertical axis of a coordinate system. (p. 45)

y-coordinate A value representing the distance of a point from the x-axis on a coordinate plane. (p. 45)

zero (of a polynomial function) An input value for which a polynomial function outputs a value of zero. The real zeros of a polynomial function correspond to the x-intercepts of the function's graph. (p. 144)

INDEX

from origin to point, 618
with sine and cosine, 666
in three-dimensional space, 266
between two points, 47, 128
Distributive property
of exponentiation
over division, 71
over multiplication, 71
of multiplication
over addition, 24, 33, 135, 336, 727, 729
over subtraction, 336, 727, 729
Division property
of equality, 31, 728, 729
of inequality, 38
Domain
and asymptotes, 269
discrete, 221
in functions
exponential, 262, 473
factorial, 213
linear, 101, 184, 190
in logarithmic, 474
in permutation, 214
in reciprocal, 261
in sequences, 563, 564
restrictions on, 190, 199
in trigonometric identities, 660, 676
split, 114
Double-angle identities
cosine, 673
sine, 673
tangent, 673

E

Ellipse
area of, 363
as conic section, 284, 285, 287
major axis of, 285
minor axis of, 285
origin, 285
Ellipsis, 563
use of in sequences, 213, 220, 564, 565, 570, 571, 576, 583, 585, 586
Empty set, 300
Equal elemental
probability(ies), 528. See also Probability.
Equality, properties of.
Equations, 30, 728. See also Systems of equations.
absolute-value, 729
cubic, 336
equivalent, 30
exponential, 495–96
identities, 729
linear
analyzing data, 502
general form, 81

graphing, 79–83, 84. See also Graph(s).
identity, 292
slope. See Slope.
solving, 31–32, 87–89, 728
systems of, 87–89
logarithmic, 496
and properties of equality
addition, 30, 728
division, 31, 728, 729
multiplication, 31, 728
reflexive, 728
subtraction, 30, 728, 729
transitive, 728
zero product, 31, 33, 145, 149, 336, 350, 728
quadratic, 336, 676, 682. See also Quadratics.
quartic, 336–37
radical, 349–51
rational, 435–36
solving, 30–32, 390, 435, 495–96, 728. See also Factoring, completing the square; Quadratics, formula.
trigonometric, 681–82
identities. See Trigonometry(ic) identities.
with no solutions, 729
Event(s), 529. See also Probability.
dependent, 543
independent, 542
mutually exclusive, 536, 543
Expected value (number), 511
Exponential change, 345
Exponential curve, 502
Exponential equation, 495–96
Exponential function, 262, 473–74, 501
applications of, 483, 485, 486, 502
Exponent(s), 70, 730. See also Functions, exponential.
negative, 70
power rule, 70, 71, 343, 489
product rule, 70, 71, 343, 350, 489
quotient rule, 70, 71, 489
rational, 343, 350
scientific notation, 730
Expressions. See also Equations.
cubic, 127
equivalent, 23, 25
expanded form, 127, 128. See also Quadratics.
language of, 23–25, 728
like terms, 23
linear, 127, 128, 135
order of operations, 25
polynomial, 127, 729–30

quadratic, 127–28
radical, 71–72
rational. See Rational expressions.
Extraneous root, 350
Extraneous solutions, 682. See also Root(s).

F

Factor(s). See also Factoring.
common, 135, 427
difference of two cubes, 337
sum of two cubes, 337
Theorem, 384
Factoring, 336–38, 350, 404
completing the square, 157, 158, 164, 166, 247, 337, 357
difference of two squares, 136, 337
discriminant, 150, 151, 337. See also Quadratics, formula.
perfect-square trinomials, 128, 136, 143, 151, 157, 337
quadratics, 135–36, 149–50. See also Quadratics, formula.
rational
equations/inequalities, 435–36
expressions, 427–28
functions, 434–35
Factor Theorem, 384. See also Factoring; Polynomials.
Fibonacci sequence, 17, 222–23
Finite, 564, 570. See also Finite geometric series.
Finite geometric series, 585
Finite series, 570
First differences, 223
45°-45°-90° triangle, 612, 619
Functions. See also Relation(s).
absolute value, 239
closed form, 221
relationship with recursive, 221
cofunctions, 633
combination, 214–15, 411–12, 522
composite, 190, 191
compound, 114, 115
cubic, 260, 262, 404, 405
degree of, 223
directly proportional, 101
discrete, 213
domain. See Domain.
exponential, 262, 473–74, 501
applications, 483, 485, 486, 502
factorial, 213

Credits

Cover

1 Titan, Saturn's largest satellite. JPL, NASA's Regional Planetary Image Facilities; **2** Warbler bird egg. © 1988 Chip Clark, Arlington, Virginia; **3** Saturn's ring system. JPL, NASA's Regional Planetary Image Facilities; **4** Egyptian papyrus *Book of the Dead* (detail). Courtesy of the Trustees of the British Museum, London; **5** Fossil ammonite. © 1988 Chip Clark, Arlington, Virginia; **6** Mesa Verde, Colorado pueblo. Galen Rowell/Mountain Light, Albany, California; **7** Galena crystals. © 1986 Chip Clark, Arlington, Virginia; **8, 12, 15, 16** *Engram* (detail) from a painting by Cathy Halstead. Acrylic on canvas 24″ × 36″, Goldman-Kraft Gallery, Ltd., Chicago; **9** *Dancers*, 1990, Carol Tornatore; **10** Test tube re-creation of Earth's primeval chemistry. B. B. Armstrong and D. W. Deamer, Department of Zoology, University of California, Davis; **11** Chicken egg. © 1988 Chip Clark, Arlington, Virginia; **13, 18** Based on medieval drawings by Villard de Honnecourt: **14** Voyager spacecraft. JPL, NASA's Regional Planetary Image Facilities; **17** Ocean tide whirlpool. Ardea, London.

Fine Art and Photographs

v Milton and Joan Mann, Cameramann International, Park Ridge, Illinois; **vi** (above) Historical Pictures Service, Chicago; (below) JPL, NASA's Regional Planetary Image Facilities; **vii** Based on medieval drawings by Villard de Honnecourt; **viii** (above) United States Postal Service, Washington, D.C.; (below, left) © 1985 Southern Illinois University/Peter Arnold, Inc., New York; (below, right) © Manfred Kage, Peter Arnold, Inc., New York; **x, xiii** © 1988 Chip Clark, Arlington, Virginia; **xi** The Bettmann Archive, New York; **2** The Metropolitan Museum of Art, Michael C. Rockefeller Memorial Collection, Bequest of Nelson A. Rockefeller, 1979 (1979.206.394); **22** (detail) Courtesy the Trustees of the British Museum, London; **29** (left) Carmine Fantasia; (above, right) The Bettmann Archive, New York; (below, right) The Granger Collection, New York; **78** The British Library, London; **93** Amy Iezzoni; **120** Illinois Bell Telephone Company/Milton and Joan Mann/Cameramann International, Park Ridge, Illinois; **126** *Bush Tucker Dreaming at Wingellina*, 1988, William Sandy (Pitjantjatjarra tribe), Courtesy John Weber Gallery, New York; **156** (left) © 1977 Sidney Harris, New Haven, Connecticut: (above, right) Michael Marsland/Yale University, New Haven, Connecticut; (below, right) Figure from *The Physics of Baseball* by Robert K. Adair, © 1990 by Robert K. Adair, Reprinted by permission of Harper & Row, Publishers, Inc., New York; **182** Algimantas Kezys, Stickney, Illinois; **232** Corporate Photographers, Inc., New York; **238** Paul A. Otto, Lake St. Louis, Missouri; **239** (detail) Paul A. Otto, Lake St. Louis, Missouri; **259** Carmine Fantasia; **290** © Georg Gerster/Comstock, New York; **297** (above) U.S. Postal Service, Washington, D.C.; (below) Library of Congress, Washington, D.C.; **305** (left) Ken Kohl; (right) © Camerique/H. Armstrong Roberts, Chicago; **342** *Ghost Chamber with the Tall Door*, 1925, Paul Klée. The Metropolitan Museum of Art, Berggruen

Klée Collection, 1987 (1987.455.16);   **356** © Camerique/H. Armstrong Roberts, Chicago;   **357** *Prayer Wheel*, 1954, Jean Tinguely. The Museum of Fine Arts, Houston. Museum purchase with funds provided by D. and J. de Menil;   **371** Richard Dicker;   **380** © Georg Gerster/Comstock, New York;   **395** (left) Leonard Ramist; (right) © Henley and Savage/TSW/Click Chicago;   **409** Reprinted by permission of the University of Minnesota Press, ©1957, 1974 The University of Minnesota, Renewed 1985 by The Estate of Oystein Ore;   **426** *Untitled*, 1960, Lee Bontecou, The National Trust for Historic Preservation, Nelson A. Rockefeller Collection;   **433** Rob Mustard Photography, Redondo Beach, California;   **441** (detail) (below) Courtesy the Trustees of the British Museum, London;   **472** Dennis Murphy, Dallas;   **508** (left) UPI/Bettmann Newsphotos, New York; (right) © Keven Schafer/Peter Arnold, Inc., New York;   **518** Stan Barough;   **520** *Japanese Rain on Canvas*, 1972, David Hockney, acrylic on canvas, 48″ × 48″, © 1972 David Hockney;   **549** (both) The Bettmann Archive, New York;   **560** (left) Pat Linnell, Washington, D.C.; (right) © 1990 The Time, Inc. Magazine Company, New York, Reprinted by permission;   **562** Weese Hickey Weese Architects, Ltd., Chicago;   **582** (above) David Williams; (below) The Stock Shop, New York;   **590** © 1977 Sidney Harris, New Haven, Connecticut: **602** *Construction in Space with Balance on Two Points*, 1925, Naum Gabo, Yale University Art Gallery, Gift of H. Wade White;   **618** Milton and Joan Mann/Cameramann International, Park Ridge, Illinois;   **652** (above) Instock/Don Rogers, Fort Lauderdale, Florida;   **658** © Richard Hamilton Smith, St. Paul;   **659** Hugh Sitton/TSW/Click Chicago;   **665** Historical Pictures Service, Chicago;   **692** *Variegation in the Triangle*, 1927, Wassily Kandinsky, Galerie Adrien Maeght, Paris;   **704** (above) Carmine Fantasia; (below, left) © 1985 SIU/Peter Arnold, Inc., New York; (below, right) © Manfred Kage/Peter Arnold, Inc., New York;   **720** (above) © Richard Megna/Fundamental Photographs, New York; (below) © Cecile Brunswick/Peter Arnold, Inc., New York.

Illustrations

Pawel Bodytko   v, 30, 35, 45, 52, 60.

Kathleen Mattingly   295, 303, 315, 327.

Carol Tornatore   xii, 12, 19, 364, 442, 680.

Robert Voigts   102, 110, 112, 113, 120, 135, 154, 162, 164, 165, 197, 198, 214, 228, 243, 250, 293, 301, 308, 336, 381, 416, 418, 432, 437 (both), 471, 516, 538, 545, 552, 553, 563, 581, 625, 710.

Staff Credits

Executive Editor	Geraldine Macsai
Editor	Kathryn D. Wroblewski
Associate Editor	Robert Newman
Production Manager	Susan W. Nisson
Production Editors	Zana Courser
	Roslyn Weinstein
Copyeditor	Sandra Linabury
Senior Designer	Adrienne McGrath
Photo Research	Carmine Fantasia
Cover Design	Carol Tornatore

Teacher's Edition developed and produced by
A.W. Kingston • Publishing   Nashua, N.H.